The Chemical Biology
of Fishes

The Chemical Biology of Fishes

Volume 2: Advances 1968-1977

With a Supplementary Key to the Chemical Literature

R. MALCOLM LOVE
Torry Research Station, Aberdeen
Scotland

1980

ACADEMIC PRESS
A Subsidiary of Harcourt Brace Jovanovich, Publishers
LONDON   NEW YORK   TORONTO   SYDNEY   SAN FRANCISCO

Academic Press Inc. (London) Ltd
24–28 Oval Road
London NW1

US edition published by
Academic Press Inc.
111 Fifth Avenue,
New York, New York 10003

British Library Cataloguing in Publication Data

Love, Robert Malcolm
The chemical biology of fishes.
Vol. 2: Advances, 1968–1977
1. Fishes – Physiology   2. Biological chemistry
I. Title
597' .01'92   QL639.1   72–92397

ISBN 0–12–455852–6

Printed in Great Britain by
Lonsdale Universal Printing Ltd,
Salisbury Road, Larkhall, Bath BA1 6QY

Ce livre est dédié au
PROFESSEUR ALBERT SERFATY
et à la brillante équipe
qu'il a rassemblé autour de lui

Preface

This book continues the survey begun in "The Chemical Biology of Fishes" (1970), now referred to as Volume I. It presents aspects of world literature published since 1968, together with a few papers missed earlier. It is in effect a supplement, so its bibliographical references start to number where those of Volume I left off. Work already described in Volume I is briefly summarised in small print at the beginning of many of the sections as a background to the material which follows. As before, I have made each section complete in itself, occasionally using the same research results in more than one context.

Since the book is meant for a wide readership, I have tended to spell out in simple terms biochemical or biological concepts which are part of the normal grammar of either field, at the risk of irritating both groups of specialists. It is hoped that this will help the general reader as well as the specialist in the other discipline.

A considerable proportion of the first volume was devoted to discussing methods of sampling, and to pointing out pitfalls that could be encountered in trying to obtain authentic resting or "normal" values in fish tissues. Here it will be assumed that improved sampling techniques have passed into general use. We shall envisage all resting values as lying within a range, sometimes extensive, and see how far environmental and other factors can push individual values towards the extremes, or even extend the range itself as a result of what Somero and Hochachka (1971) term "biochemical restructuring".

Some readers of Volume I were disappointed that it was not a textbook of fish biochemistry, but the general aim was for it to be a biology of fish as seen through chemical analysis. This remains the objective in the present compilation, although as biologists are tending to use a more biochemical approach and biochemists are becoming more interested in fish, the overall view is now more biochemical and indeed more sophisticated than before.

However, we need to be aware that some standard biochemical techniques may be too drastic for the examination of the delicate materials of which a fish is composed. In a provocative book, Hillman (1972) says: "Biochemistry, which originally studied living tissues, has been carried away by an enthusiasm for physical techniques which may change the nature of the study so that what we discover is more a function of the method we use than the properties we seek to elucidate . . . the result of the application of high energy to unstable materials." He was referring to mammalian biochemistry, but his remarks apply with even more force to studies on fish tissues. In constructing model systems, we must realize that 37°C is *not* the physiological temperature for many fish enzymes as distinct from those of mammals, and both the contractile proteins and the collagens from some fish species denature rapidly even at room temperature, and must be maintained near 0°C for study.

Isolated analyses of single substances in tissues are never likely, on their own, to set the scientific world alight. It is only when we follow the delicate balance maintained between many constituents, and their subtle shifts under the influence of outside phenomena or spontaneous alterations in behaviour, that there opens for us an enthralling field of study. This very subtlety sometimes makes the effects difficult to measure or even to identify, so it is here that the experimentalist comes into his own, enhancing the stresses that occur naturally to the point where the responses of the fish can be detected and measured— by using exercise channels, thermostatically controlled aquaria and other artificial environments such as abnormal salinities, and feeding special diets or submitting the fish to starvation for longer periods than would be customary in the wild. My favourite experiment from the more recent literature involved attaching small metal weights to swimming sharks (Malins and Barone, 1970), whereupon the fish increased the proportion of the more buoyant substances in their livers; very neat.

What sort of long-term benefit should one expect from such work? I believe that it could be no less than a revolution in fish biology, enabling one not only to measure the biological condition of a specimen caught in the wild, but also to be able to state whether it is currently improving or deteriorating; which stock it has come from; its customary swimming activity; the average temperature of the water it has been living in; how recently its last meal was eaten and of what it consisted; its diet during the preceding month; its exact position on the maturity scale; the number of eggs it is likely to produce at the next spawning and the hatching rate of those eggs. Some of these objectives lie in the sphere of hope rather than achievement, but work completed has shown that even now this approach can point to the potential characteristics of fish from different grounds during their subsequent freezing for use as food for mankind, indicating which ones have the texture enabling them to be cold-stored satisfactorily, which will develop an unpleasant flavour and which will disintegrate (Love, 1975). Chapter 5 represents an attempt to review the progress made so far and the future potential in this field. An extension of these objectives must then be the adaptation of all sorts of chemical techniques to the conditions encountered on a fishing vessel at sea.

When Volume I was completed, it was suspected that some of the fish listed alphabetically in Part 3 had appeared more than once under different names. Further reading during the intervening years has confirmed this suspicion, identifying several aliases unwittingly used, so that it is now possible to put together some of the groups of chemical data formerly separated under different synonyms. The table at the beginning of Part 3 of this volume lists the duplicated entries so that pairs of sets of data can be combined by those possessing a copy of the earlier work.

With regret I note the recent appearance of a new class, the finfish, which is supposed to be a general name for fish as distinct from shellfish. "Lateral eyes" have also arrived, being the eyes which we all know but now specifically distinguished from the pineal body which is sometimes light-sensitive. Perhaps it is naïve to regret even more the establishment of new Latin names for fish which are already well known under other names. For example, the logical and convenient grouping of gadoid fishes, *Gadus morhua*, *G. aeglefinus*, *G. merlangus*, *G. virens* and *G. poutassou*, has been destroyed and replaced by *Gadus morhua*, *Melanogrammus aeglefinus*, *Merlangius merlangus*, *Pollachius virens* and *Micromesistius poutassou*, thus to confuse future generations of students. Some effort has been made to bring the nomenclature in the present index of fish names up to date, but one cannot avoid the feeling that the time taken could have been better employed. These remarks do not apply to common names, which tend to be more stable than their scientific counterparts. In the very readable introduction to their list of common and scientific fish names, Bailey, Fitch *et al.* (1970) make the point that any new common name should not be intimately tied to the scientific name so that "the vagaries of scientific nomenclature do not entail constant changing of common names."

The scheme for indexing chemical values is exactly as before. The reader may discover whether the concentration of a certain substance has been determined in a certain species by consulting Part 3 where the fish are listed under their scientific (Latin) names. The Appendix (p. 683) enables him to find these from their common names. Alternatively, he can refer to the name of the substance (Part 2) and see which organs have been analysed. By using Parts 2 and 3 together it is in many cases possible to see whether the "resting" concentration of a certain substance has been measured in a certain organ of a certain species before seeking out the original paper. Work embodying obviously unsatisfactory sampling procedures, such as measuring glycogen in muscle which has been frozen and thawed, or the composition of fish maintained on highly unnatural diets, have not been included in the indexes; neither have references to values of mixtures of substances such as "creatin + creatinine". Data derived from the extraction of entire fish (apart from larvae) have likewise been omitted, since their physiological significance is often doubtful. If information on any substance or species has already been tabulated in Volume I, the fact is noted.

The main purpose of the text of the present volume is to review work which represents new concepts or extends earlier ones, and not to restate conclusions already reached in Volume I. There are, however, three sections which include both earlier and recent information.

Firstly, the short passages in Part 2 which describe the particular role of many of the chemical substances in fish have been re-written and expanded in the light of new knowledge.

Secondly, the short descriptions of each fish species (Part 3) have been extended through reading many more biological reference books. It is often quite difficult for a biochemist (or a biologist for that matter) to lay his hands readily on the sort of information likely to help him choose the species most appropriate to his experiments—the habitual activity of the fish, the tolerated salinity range, the most favoured diet, depth and temperature and any unusual features such as the ability to breathe air. Though these notes are short, they are the distillate of a considerable amount of descriptive literature.

Finally the index of common names has been extended by the same further reading and now comprises all discoverable names of the species described in both volumes.

A proportion of the chemical data and, indeed, of the chemical–physiological conclusions in the earlier book arose as a sort of bonus or "spin-off" from work planned for entirely different reasons, usually technological. This is now less true: most of the work to be described in the present volume was done as a main objective, and a glance through recent issues of, for example, *Comparative Biochemistry and Physiology*, shows that more people are using fish in the sort of work which used to be confined to small mammals. Malins and Sargent (1974) remark: "We sense the presence of greater numbers of bio-chemists and biophysicists showing an interest in marine organisms than ever before." One effect of this has been the appearance of several excellent reviews of topics that I might have covered in more detail in the present volume. Rather than cover the ground again I will simply refer to them and digest the relevant parts briefly for the benefit of the general reader.

There has also been a shift in emphasis away from "hunted" food fish to cultured fish. By far the greatest amount of chemical data in Part 3 of the earlier book was listed under the important commercial species, the Atlantic cod (*Gadus morhua*), while in the present list it is the rainbow trout (*Salmo gairdneri*) from culture ponds, followed by carp (*Cyprinus carpio*), which have been the most investigated. It has also been noticeable that of the fish described in this volume which did not appear in Volume I, an important proportion are the sort of small, freshwater tropical species that are often tended in aquaria. In Volume I there were almost none.

There no longer seems to be a universal experimental fish for laboratory work. I thought in Volume I that the goldfish would acquire this title, and these fish are indeed used in experiments involving wide ranges of temperature acclimation, but many experiments on general fish metabolism and nutrition are being done on rainbow trout, osmoregulation is almost invariably studied with eels, salmonids and the occasional hagfish, while starvation and anaerobiosis seem best investigated with carp. Killifish and various antarctic species are favoured for studies on the prevention of freezing at low temperatures and, in short, the wonderful diversity of fish types is now being exploited as a short cut to solving problems in specific areas.

It has to be said that the book reviews the fisheries chemical and physiological literature as it is, and not as one might have liked it to be had it been possible to direct and coordinate the work of the world's fisheries laboratories. This means that the overall picture is unbalanced, with certain areas of investigation receiving a disproportionate amount of attention. To be more specific, the topic which has attracted the greatest effort, judging by the number of cards in my filing system, is that of acclimating fish to different temperatures, a field, one would have thought, of rather limited interest.

The new science of pollution research will soon give added stimulus to physiological–chemical research in fish; no doubt we shall learn more about the ways in which fish tissues function as a direct result of studying their reactions to foreign materials. Indeed, the extraordinary discrimination shown by cod liver tissue, which preferentially stores hydrocarbons with odd-numbered carbon chains from a mixture containing all chain-lengths of *n*-alkanes (Hardy, Mackie *et al.*, 1974) gives a hint of the sort of information to be revealed.

Part of the intended purpose of this book is as an aid to investigators active in their laboratory, fish farm, research boat or aquarium. Anyone starting in this field soon discovers that the hardest part of the work is often just keeping the experimental animals alive. I should like to end by quoting from a paper by Harden Jones and Scholes (1974), not to discourage would-be fisheries scientists, but to engender a realistic approach and help anyone new to the field at least to enter it with his eyes open.

Aeration failure led to the death of one fish in experiment 3 and three fish in experiment 5. There was no explanation for the death of a fourth fish in experiment 5 (at 16°C). The loss of five fish held at −1.5°C in experiment 7 was caused by a single overnight failure in the cooling system when the temperature fell to −2°C and ice formed on the water surface in several tanks. There were three other deaths in this experiment, one fish dying from infection, a second with an over-inflated swimbladder, and a third for whose death there was no apparent explanation.

Reproduced by courtesy of Dr Harden Jones

I am grateful to Dr John Roberts (1971) for pointing out the most serious error in Volume I. On p. 209, the counterflow heat exchanger, which enables certain tunas to maintain their body temperature above that of the surroundings, is stated as being located in the gills, but is in fact located in the red lateral muscle. For readers wishing to know more about this interesting system there is now a detailed description (Stevens, Lam and Kendall, 1974) accompanied by photographs. An important feature is the reduced speed of blood flow in the network of blood vessels, allowing increased time for the heat to be exchanged.

April 1980   MALCOLM LOVE
East Silverburn,
Kingswells AB1 8QL,
Scotland.

Acknowledgements

I gratefully acknowledge the help of the following friends who have read sections of the manuscript and given constructive criticism.

John Blaxter, Tony Burd, Colin Cowey, Forbes Robertson, Derek Ross, John Sargent, Peter Tytler, Clement Wardle, Carol Wittenberger, Françoise Vellas, and not least my wife Muriel.

Contents

Chapter 5   Seasonal Variation and Some Alternative Approaches
               to Fish Biology   350

PART 2

PART 3

1 The Nature of Fishes

A. Comparison with warm-blooded animals

1. GENERAL

The chemistry of fish tissues inevitably resembles that of the tissues of warm-blooded animals through the biochemical ground-plan common to all living creatures. It now seems clear, for example, that at least the majority of the major metabolic pathways, so well characterised in mammals, are present in fish. Tarr (1973) has reviewed the subject, presenting as in standard biochemical text-books the schemes of the Embden–Meyerhof, tricarboxylic and hexose monophosphate pathways, but giving bibliographical references to all enzymes which have been positively identified in fish tissues. Enzymes of the hexose monophosphate pathway have also been identified by Shimeno and Takeda (1972) in three fish species.

On the other hand, the very different way of life of aquatic organisms compared with land animals has caused fish to evolve a number of structures and systems unique to themselves.

We saw in Volume 1 that, because fish do not have to support their own weight, it is not inconvenient for them to carry around a large mass of white muscle which is used only in moments of emergency or stress, operating anaerobically. Normal cruising is effected by a relatively small strip of aerobically powered dark muscle which is often clearly demarcated from the white (in land animals the two types are usually mixed). The support obtained from the medium also allows the fish to subsist on very little energy and so to endure astonishing periods of total deprivation from food, several instances being known of starvation lasting for more than a year. The non-essential nature of white muscle means that it can be broken down for energy purposes to a far greater extent than would be tolerated by land animals, and, as we shall see later (p. 176), many of the myofilaments can be reduced to a state of complete disorganisation without actually engendering the death of the fish. A less

1

energetic existence means in most cases a far lower consumption of oxygen, so that under arctic conditions where the solubility of oxygen in the serum alone is quite high, some fish lead normal active lives with reduced amounts of haemoglobin in their blood or even with none at all.

So great is the diversity among fish species themselves that generalised comparisons between fish and land animals are risky—often the most marked differences can be seen in comparison with only a few fish species and not with fish as a whole. Nevertheless, a few generalisations are possible.

2. OXYGEN CAPACITY

Again, presumably because fish use much less energy in supporting themselves, their blood volume forms a smaller proportion of their body than does that of other vertebrate groups—Conte, Wagner and Harris (1963) give values for the proportion of teleost blood as 1·8 to 3·8% of their body weight compared with 5·5 to 9·5% in mammals and up to 13% in birds. On the other hand, Wardle (1971), who worked with *Pleuronectes platessa*, concluded that the relatively abundant lymph makes a substantial contribution to the circulation of metabolites, and that in muscle and skin its abundance compensates for a sparse vascular system. Be that as it may, mammals and birds weighing 3 to 30 grams are able to expend energy at a sustainable rate which is 10 to 100 times more than that of active fish like salmon (Brett, 1972). The salmon is unusually active among fish, though, and an anaerobic burst of energy from a 100-gram salmon can use up as much oxygen as the aerobic demand of a 100-gram mammal.

Some of this book is concerned with the way in which fish can adapt to their environment, and in this connection fish haemoglobins are more polymorphic than those of mammals (Iuchi, 1973). This means that they exist in different forms, variations in the proportions of which enable the fish to deal successfully with a greater range of environmental conditions than would otherwise be possible. Eels (*Anguilla anguilla*) kept in water deficient in oxygen increase the proportion of that haemoglobin which has a higher oxygen affinity. Mammals cannot do this (Wood and Johansen, 1973), but the amino acid compositions of their haemoglobins are on the whole similar to those of fish (Geraskin, Logunov and Luk'yanenko, 1972: *Acipenser* spp.).

3. ENERGY SOURCES

The three primary constituents which furnish a fish with energy for swimming (carbohydrates, proteins and lipids) all differ to some extent from those of warm-blooded animals, either in their composition or the way in which they are stored or used.

a. Carbohydrates

Carbohydrates seem to play a less important role in fish than in mammals. Indications are seen from the observations that diets containing the most carbohydrate cause the highest mortality when fed to starving *Cyprinus carpio* (Créac'h and Murat, 1974) and give rise to the lowest rate of growth in *Salmo gairdneri* (Luquet, Léger and Bergot, 1975). The diets of many fish consist almost exclusively of protein, differing from those of man and domesticated mammals which often consume a large proportion of carbohydrates. Much of the energy expended by fish in swimming therefore comes from the oxidation of lipids or from glucose derived from amino acids (gluconeogenesis). Adrenocortical steroids appear to accelerate gluconeogenesis (Butler, 1968: *Anguilla rostrata*), and it is possible that the high steroid levels found in the blood of starving salmon near the end of their spawning runs provide energy for the fish from gluconeogenesis after the exhaustion of most of their lipid reserves.

Murat (1976a) could find no glycogen phosphorylase in *Cyprinus carpio* liver, and regarded proteins as the main fuel for this species. The same view was held by Nagai and Ikeda (1972, 1973), who concluded that most of the depot lipids are synthesised from amino acids as well. These workers regarded carp as existing in a perpetual state of diabetes because of the impaired glucose utilisation, but it happens to be one of a number of species that can live anaerobically for long periods, and its unusually large stores of glycogen in the liver and heart probably reflect the facility (Murat, 1976a), although glycolysis is not the only anaerobic pathway operating (Johnston, 1975a).

Nagayama, Ohshima and Umezawa (1972) observed that the hexokinase activity in the livers of carp and of three other species of freshwater fish is only $\frac{1}{3}$ to $\frac{1}{7}$ of the values found in rat livers, this enzyme being taken as an indicator of the uptake of glucose into the appropriate metabolic pathway, while Patent (1970) found that the hormones which affect the concentrations of glucose and glycogen in different tissues of land animals have very little effect on the concentrations in the elasmobranch *Squalus acanthias* and the related *Hydrolagus colliei*. He suggested that such hormones might be more important in the control of lipid metabolism in elasmobranchs, but clearly much extra work would be needed to establish this.

Mammals and fish differ in their response to starvation, for while rat livers are rapidly depleted of glycogen, those of at least some species of fish maintain their glycogen levels for long periods (various authors quoted by Dave, Johansson–Sjöbeck *et al.*, 1975: eels; Murat, 1976b: carp). The former authors suggested that the difference stems from the more highly developed nervous sytem possessed by mammals, which requires glucose in order to function properly.

Another important way in which the carbohydrate metabolism of fish differs from that of mammals concerns the behaviour of lactate in the muscle after exercise. In man during and following exercise, lactate accumulates rapidly in the blood, being derived from the anaerobic catabolism of muscle glycogen. Exercise also increases the circulation of blood through the muscles. In fish muscle on the other hand the vascular flushing appears to decrease as effort or distress intensify, and there is a marked delay before any lactate is transferred to the blood (various authors reviewed by Mearns, 1971; Piiper, Meyer and Drees, 1972). Under most experimental conditions the lactate is in fact retained in the muscle (Dando, 1969a; C. S. Wardle, personal communication) and reconverted to glycogen there, rather than being transported to the liver for reconversion (R. Batty and C. S. Wardle, unpublished). The fall in muscle lactate to resting levels after exercise is very much slower in fish than in mammals, taking time of the order of 24 hours instead of about 20 minutes (C. S. Wardle, personal communication: *Gadus morhua*; Piiper, Meyer and Drees, 1972: *Scyliorhinus stellaris*). The extent of retention within the muscle seems to vary according to the amount of stress undergone by the fish, and a cod (*Gadus morhua*) which swims of its own desire probably releases lactate into the blood more readily than one forced to swim in an experimental apparatus (C. S. Wardle, unpublished).

b.   *Proteins and their excretion*

Not only are many mammals adapted to accept a considerable proportion of carbohydrate in their diet: they may actually suffer a slight retardation in growth when restricted to a high protein diet because of the energy needed to eliminate the excess nitrogen. Fish by contrast can take a high protein diet in their stride, as it were, because they have the added ability to get rid of waste nitrogen through their gills (Ashley, 1972). In general they are able to excrete most of it as ammonia because it can be eliminated continuously and rapidly. In contrast, the spasmodic mode of excretion of terrestrial vertebrates would lead to the build-up of toxic concentrations, so that they must convert nearly all of their nitrogen to less harmful compounds (urea or uric acid). It should be noted, however, that aquatic organisms do not have pathways to turn all of their waste nitrogen into ammonia: there is always a variable proportion of urea excreted as well (Watts and Watts, 1974). The pathways of ammonia and urea formation are described in detail on pp. 159 and 161.

Mammals can convert arginine and glycine to non-essential amino acids (DeLong, Halver and Mertz, 1959, quoted by Mertz, 1972) and so can *Oncorhynchus tschawytscha*, but in contrast the fish cannot convert urea or diammonium citrate into amino acids for growth purposes.

c. *Lipids*

Differences between the lipids of warm-blooded animals and of fish seem to stem largely from the lower temperatures at which most fish live, and the consequent need for "softer" lipids to maintain the plasticity of cell membranes, which are rich in phospholipids, at lower temperatures. There is in fact some evidence that at least some species of fish have different essential fatty acid requirements from mammals (Lee and Sinnhuber, 1973). A much bigger proportion of unsaturated fatty acids are found in fish lipids than in mammalian lipids, typically 18:1 and 22:6[1]. Such fatty acids are usually already present in the food, and they subsequently influence the pattern of the fish lipids. The lipids of marine and freshwater fish are not the same because of differences in the diet, but each species can to some extent impose a pattern of its own on the dietary lipid.

4. HORMONES

Differences between fish and mammals are also found among the hormones—in the quantities present, the identities of hormones fulfilling specific functions and in the response of the fish to hormone injections. In connection with the latter, it is worth pointing out that in some of the earlier work the hormones injected had not been prepared from the same species as the experimental animal (were not the "homologous" hormones). For example, it was often more convenient to use mammalian insulin for injection into fish, assuming that its action would be similar to the corresponding fish insulin, since a certain amount of amino acid substitution does not seem to affect insulin activity. It is now realised that such an assumption is not always justified (P. T. Grant, personal communication). Still on the subject of insulin, it seems that only in anurans, reptiles and mammals is pancreatectomy invariably followed by diabetes mellitus: in fish and birds removal of

---

[1]This is the conventional way of writing fatty acids with 18 carbon atoms and one double bond, and 22 carbon atoms and 6 double bonds, respectively.

the pancreas has very variable results, depending on the species (Hardisty, Zelnik and Moore, 1975). Further, treatment with strep-tozotocin, a drug which inhibits insulin release by the pancreas, causes marked hyperglycaemia in mammals but only slight hyperglycaemia in *Gadus morhua*. At the same time, it causes a 50% increase in blood fatty acids, suggesting that insulin in fish may be more important in lipid metabolism than in carbohydrate metabolism (Thomas, 1971).

Fish have no parathyroids, but calcium and phosphorus seem to be regulated by the Corpuscles of Stannius and the ultimobranchial body, the latter organ secreting calcitonin, which is said to govern bone deposition and mobilisation, counterbalancing the effects of various other hormones (Lopez and Deville-Peignoux, 1974). Calcitonin differs in its action, not only between fish and mammals, but also among different fish species (Hayslett, Epstein *et al.*, 1972). In mammals it reduces the reabsorption of mono- and divalent ions by the kidney tubules, but is found by these authors to have no influence on the renal function of *Squalus acanthias*. In mammals it also inhibits bone re-absorption, and the calcium levels in the serum may be reduced follow-ing an injection of this hormone, especially in pathological conditions where bone turnover is high. Other authors quoted by Hayslett, Epstein *et al.*, (1972) have shown that serum calcium is in fact reduced in *Ictalurus melas* and *Anguilla anguilla* following calcitonin injection, but not in *Fundulus heteroclitus*, the inconsistency being ascribed to inter-species differences in bone structure.

Idler, Truscott and Stewart (1969) have reviewed the field of steroids in fish, and have noted several outstanding quantitative differences between the concentrations of the hormones in fish and in mammals. High concentrations of cortisol frequently occur in the plasma of certain fish, and unusually high concentrations of cortisone and testosterone have also been reported.

At least one pituitary hormone differs from its mammalian counter-part. While chimaeriform fish possess, like the mammals, oxytocin in the neurohypophysis, the corresponding hormones in other orders of fish are not quite the same, and have been given other names: glumito-cin in the Batoidea, valitocin in the Selachii and isotocin in the super-order Teleostei (Acher, Chauvet and Chauvet, 1972). An appendix to Volume 1 shows the family relationships of the different fish genera.

In mammals, the catecholamines, especially noradrenaline, have a lipolytic action, causing an elevation of free fatty acids in the blood. In teleosts, however, the action is not well defined, and the hormone sometimes inhibits and sometimes promotes lipolysis, according to species (Mazeaud, 1973, and other authors quoted by him).

Injections of thyroxine increase the free fatty acid concentration in the blood of *Cyprinus carpio*, agreeing with observations on mammals (Murat and Serfaty, 1970), but, in contrast to the mammalian response, cause a reduction in blood sugar (hypoglycaemia) and an increase in the glycogen of heart and muscle. Murat and Serfaty (1971) found that the hypoglycaemia occurred only at certain times of the year.

Seasonal variation is so much a part of fish physiology compared with that of non-hibernating warm-blooded animals that it will be given a chapter to itself (p. 350), even though the phrase "seasonal variation" has often been used loosely just to describe phenomena of unknown origin (Volume 1, p. 169).

5. VITAMINS

Finally, vitamins differ in their mode of action as fish differ from mammals in their requirements.

In its visual function, vitamin A_1 (retinol) is the prosthetic group of different proteins, forming light-sensitive pigments for the retina with different spectral sensitivities according to the luminous environment usually experienced by the fish. The proportions of visual pigments can change seasonally with the change in the angle of the sun above the horizon, and fish alone can form a separate series of visual pigments from vitamin A_2 (dehydroretinol) to gain extra sensitivity at the red end of the spectrum when they live in fresh water.

The proportion of pigment based on dehydroretinol is increased by both thyroxine (Beatty, 1969b: *Oncorhynchus nerka*; Jacquest and Beatty, 1972; Cristy, 1974: *Salmo gairdneri*) and prolactin (Cristy, 1974).

The concentration of vitamin C (ascorbic acid) varies seasonally, as probably do all the vitamins more than in mammals, and deficiency results in certain symptoms, such as lordosis, peculiar to fish. Lordosis (illustrated in Fig. 15(b), p. 59) appears to result from a breakdown of vertebral collagen (M. Sato, personal communication, 1977).

Deficiency in other vitamins can also give rise to symptoms found only in fish, for example "clubbed" gills resulting from deficiency of tocopherol or pantothenic acid. For a recent list of symptoms arising from vitamin deficiencies, the reader is referred to the review by Ashley (1972), who also compares them with the corresponding symptoms shown by other vertebrates.

Vitamin D (ergocalciferol) probably differs in its synthesis, metabolism and physiological function in fish as compared with mammals (Oizumi and Monder, 1972). Fish rarely or never exposed to sunlight accumulate the vitamin and are thought by these authors to be able to synthesise it. Conversely, goldfish extensively exposed to sunlight possess little or none of the vitamin. Oizumi and Monder (1972) have also concluded that the presence of vitamin D in fish need not be correlated with the formation or maintenance of bone, since many fish without bony skeletons do store vitamin D to some extent.

6. CONCLUSIONS

This brief introduction is enough to indicate that, while fish perforce resemble mammals in some respects in order to function at all, they exhibit fundamental differences extending, as we have seen, even to the way in which they generate energy for swimming and dispose of the waste products.

The fact is that fish, with a very long evolutionary history, are specialists superbly adapted to their environment, and while a few features may be considered "primitive" compared with those of mammals, it is more usual for specific features to be adaptations to the aquatic life. One can therefore never take a conclusion reached with the aid of experimental mammals and assume that it applies to fish as well. The point has been made before, but is worth repeating.

B. Growth and development

1. DEVELOPMENT OF THE EGG

We have seen in Volume 1 how the growth of female gonads is accompanied by increases in serum calcium and magnesium and, up to a certain stage, in liver weight. Serum cholesterol is minimal just before spawning and rises later (both sexes), while serum phospholipid falls. Maturing ovaries become yellow in some species as yolk is laid down, and the deposition of protein in the gonad is marked by an increased concentration of *free* amino acids and in the quantity of DNA.

The composition of the eggs influences their hatching rate, both riboflavin and iron having been shown to promote hatching.

Eggs respire and steadily use up some of their protein and lipid, particularly the former, for energy purposes during development. The respiration accelerates after hatching.

Studies with the ultracentrifuge have revealed the genesis of an extra protein some 18 days after fertilisation, which seems to mark the beginning of development of the blood system. Similarly a sudden increase in the amount of acetylcholinesterase seems to indicate a definite stage in the development of the nervous system. Changes in the amino acid composition, fatty acid distribution and mineral balance have all been investigated to some extent and are tabulated in Volume 1. The levels of certain substances could indicate the "quality" of eggs and the exact stage of maturation of the fish, so there appears to be potential in continued effort in this field.

a. Condition of the parent fish

In an investigation on the growth and survival of plaice (*Pleuronectes platessa*) reared from eggs in a hatchery, Shelbourne (1974, 1975) found that many young fish develop irregular colourless patches on the skin, rendering them easily visible to predators on release into the wild. Fast-growing larvae tend to be more normally pigmented, while overcrowding increases the numbers of piebald or completely albino fish.

Of great interest in the present context is his discovery that the extent of the abnormality is also influenced by the condition of the parents at the time of spawning, eggs from acclimated fish which have enjoyed plenty of space giving rise to a high proportion of normally pigmented young. More abnormalities develop among the progeny of unacclimated, overcrowded, injured or starving females, suggesting that the trouble is transmitted to the eggs while they are still in the ovary.

In a similar way, Baltic cod (*Gadus callarias*) females with large livers, that is, with livers rich in lipid, spawn eggs containing more lipid than usual (Grauman, 1972). The reverse is also true. We have seen in Volume 1 (pp. 90–91) how cod generate a greater proportion of eggs as they grow older, and hence deplete their own bodies more extensively with each year of spawning. Kuznetsov (1973) has shown a similar increase in the fecundity of *Abramis brama*, and established that as more eggs are produced their lipid contents decrease. Thus the female fish distributes its available lipid among the existing eggs, rather than producing fewer eggs of constant composition. We might therefore have expected to see better survival in the fewer eggs of younger fish because of their greater share in maternal resources, but the resources often in fact increase as the fish grow older. According to Bagenal (1971), older *Pleuronectes platessa*, and presumably other species, produce larger eggs, and as the older fish spawn earlier in the season, the mean egg size steadily decreases as the season progresses and younger fish begin to shed their eggs.

Shreni and Jafri (1974) have suggested that egg cholesterol reflects parental intake, noticing that the eggs of carnivores contain more cholesterol than those of herbivorous fish. Conclusions based on differences between species are dangerous because species differ for so many reasons, but this may perhaps be another instance of egg composition being influenced by the parent.

Sabodash (1970) made the curious observation that the eggs from certain female carp aged 3, 6 and 11–14 years contained respectively 47·5, 29 and 16·5 milligrams of zinc per 100 grams dry matter. This might have suggested a more rapid synthesis of certain enzymes and insulin in the larvae born of younger fish, but by the end of gastrulation the zinc content of all the eggs had stabilised at $21 \cdot 5$ milligrams, so the significance of the initial observation is not clear.

Since newly spawned eggs can absorb little nutriment directly from the water (see p. 146 for a discussion of direct absorption), it follows that they must contain adequate quantities of essential substances if they are to grow. In the maturing ovaries the essential *free* amino acids therefore predominate over those that can be synthesised from others (Maksimov, 1969: *Cyprinus carpio*). The total amino acid content of the eggs is influenced by the protein content of the diet of the parent fish (Kim, 1974a: *Cyprinus carpio*).

The role of carotenoids, so often found in ovarian tissue, is not completely established but Georgiev (1971: *Salmo gairdneri*) noted that eggs with a low carotenoid content show the highest mortality[1]. The vitamin A and carotenoid content is highest in the last eggs to mature, suggesting that the steady passage of vitamin and pigment to the ovary concentrates them in fewer and fewer eggs as those maturing earlier are shed. Where the *Salmo gairdneri* parent fish receive supplements of vitamin A and vitamin E, higher concentrations show up later in the eggs, but the vitamin D level does not reflect the level in the parental diet (Kinumaki, Sugii *et al.*, 1972), supporting the idea of independent synthesis of this vitamin by the young fish.

Aside from constituents which are known to be transferred from parent fish to egg, certain constituents of the ovarian free fluid have also been shown to correlate with the hatchability of the eggs, glucose and bilirubin positively and lactic dehydrogenase negatively (Satia, Donaldson *et al.*, 1974: *Salmo gairdneri*). The results of the complete analysis are given in Table 1. The survival of larvae after hatching has been shown to correlate positively with the content of cysteine plus cystine in the egg (Vladimirov, 1974: *Cyprinus carpio*). Zhukinskii and Gosh (1973: *Abramis brama, Misgurnus fossilis*) suggested that the intensity of oxidative phosphorylation or of ATPase activity might be used for the measurement of spawn quality. Perhaps the activity of any enzyme in the major metabolic cycles would indicate an intrinsic vigour; it is an idea which deserves to be followed up.

The old Yorkshire farmer's advice to the young man seeking a wife[2] was "Have a good look at the mother first, lad" to get an idea of how the daughter would develop. A "courting" fish would need more

---

[1]M. Hata, on the other hand, has found that such eggs develop and hatch normally (personal communication, 1977).

[2]Reference: Herriott, J. (1974) "Vet in Harness", p. 159. Michael Joseph, London.

information than this: he would also need to know the mother's nutritional state at the time of spawning.

TABLE 1

Chemical composition of the ovarian fluid of *Salmo gairdneri*. (After Satia, Donaldson *et al.*, 1974. Reproduced with permission of Dr Benedict Satia)

Albumin	$0.06 \pm 0.02\%$
Alkaline phosphatase	7.00 ± 3.89 IU
Bilirubin	0.05 ± 0.05 mg%
Calcium	8.00 ± 1.04 mg%
Chloride	8.00 ± 0.16 Meq/l
Cholesterol	2.00 ± 0.19 mg%
Glucose	5.25 ± 3.30 mg%
Lactic dehydrogenase	5.50 ± 2.05 IU
Magnesium	1.48 ± 1.05 Meq/l
Phosphate (inorganic)	11.49 ± 4.41 mg%
Potassium	1.25 ± 0.19 Meq/l
Protein (total)	$0.04 \pm 0.05\%$
Sodium	5.50 ± 3.11 Meq/l
Uric acid	0.18 ± 0.07 mg%

There are two reports of parental condition influencing the sperm as distinct from the eggs. Nedovesova and Zhukinskii (1975: "sea roach") found that the RNA content of each sperm increases steadily as the parent males grow older, while the phospholipid content decreases (Kim, 1974b: *Cyprinus carpio*).

b.   *Changes in eggs and larvae during development*

i.   *Carbohydrates, proteins and lipids*

Gluconeogenesis occurs during early development. An increase in glycogen was observed by Jirge (1970) in the livers of *Tilapia mossambica* larvae during growth, and it has been found to accumulate in the spawn of *Carassius auratus* at the time of fertilisation up to the formation of the morula. A further increase in glycogen occurs at gastrulation (Danilenko, 1970). The larvae of *Gambusia affinis* when 2 millimetres long appear to lack glycogen completely in the central nervous system. When they reach 2·5 millimetres, it can be detected in certain definite areas of the brain, and during further development it appears in other areas of the central nervous system. In contrast, it disappears from the cytoplasm of the Mauthner cells soon after birth (Benedetti, 1974).

Tables 12 and 13 of Volume 1 showed the changes in combined amino acids during development and revealed that the biggest all-round change occurred during the transition from egg to larva, especially in the concentration of proline.

Here in Table 2 we see that the concentrations of many of the *free* amino acids increase steadily from egg through larva to fry, presumably reflecting protein synthetic activity. Immature young (post-fry) show further increases in aspartic acid, serine, proline, glycine and alanine. This is an interesting combination, because all of these amino acids, apart from aspartic acid which is present in only small amounts, occur in connective tissue (reviewed by Yamaguchi, Lavéty and Love, 1976.)

TABLE 2

Change in the composition of free amino acids (mg%) in carp muscle with the growth of the fish. (After Sakaguchi and Kawai, 1970a. Reproduced with permission of Dr M. Sakaguchi)

Amino acid	Fertilised egg	Larva	Fry	Immature	Mature (male)
Alanine	0·3	4·5	17·0	37·8	21·5
Arginine	33·0	16·2	13·6	6·7	17·3
Aspartic acid	tr.	0·1	1·3	1·9	1·7
Cysteine	0	tr.	4·0	2·5	2·2
Glutamic acid	0·7	2·4	11·4	10·9	4·5
Glycine	0·2	4·8	60·1	96·9	62·9
Histidine	tr.	23·0	318·4	165·5	126·6
Isoleucine	0·1	1·7	3·4	2·1	2·0
Leucine	0·3	2·7	5·8	4·6	3·7
Lysine	9·2	21·9	43·3	35·8	75·7
Methionine	0·1	0·9	2·5	2·3	2·2
Phenylalanine	0·8	2·0	3·7	2·7	0·3
Proline	0·1	2·3	15·6	26·1	22·0
Serine	1·4	5·4	6·8	16·6	6·4
Threonine	0·1	tr.	23·1	15·1	16·3
Tyrosine	0·1	1·4	3·4	2·1	13·1
Valine	0·3	2·1	4·5	3·0	2·6

tr. = trace.   Only trace amounts of tryptophan were found throughout.

Perhaps these figures in Table 2 show the thickening of myocommata, the connective tissue sheets which transmit the energy of muscular contraction to the spinal column, in response to the greater forces involved in the swimming of bigger fish.

Soluble proteins of various stages from egg to larva have been separated by electrophoresis (Jurcă, Cazacu and Cazacu, 1973: *Cyprinus carpio, Hypophthalmichthys molitrix* and *Ctenopharyngodon idella*) and found to vary in quantity and to some extent in electrophoretic mobility according to species and developmental stage. Quantitative changes have also been seen in two out of five soluble proteins separated by electrophoresis from the eggs and larvae of *Oryzias latipes* by Hori (1973). Such observations will be of much more interest when the identities and functions of the proteins have been identified by, for example, immunological techniques. At least some of them are enzymes. Proteolytic enzymes have in fact been identified among the bands separated by electrophoresis from the soluble proteins of *Salmo gairdneri* eggs just before hatching. They are thought to function by dissolving the egg envelope, enabling the larva to escape (Hagenmaier, 1972).

Larval haemoglobins have been found to be as polymorphic as adult haemoglobins (Iuchi and Yamagami, 1969: *Salmo gairdneri*), that is, they separate into several components during electrophoresis. They differ in some respects from the adult pattern, however, and the shift from larval to adult types occurs after hatching, being completed at the time of complete absorption of the yolk.

Small changes in the proportions of fatty acids during the development of *Salmo gairdneri* eggs have been reported (Volume 1, Table 14); all fatty acids decrease to some extent, but C_{20} unsaturated fatty acids are burned up to a greater extent than the others.

Watanabe and Ando (1972: *Salmo gairdneri*) showed that if unfertilised eggs are kept alive they split some of the long-chain fatty acids, so that fragments containing less than 12 carbon atoms appear in quantity. In the fertilised eggs, there is a tendency for *free* cholesterol to become esterified, while the total cholesterol declines slightly. After hatching, according to Chepurnov and Tkachenko (1973: *Gobius melanostomus*), cholesterol tends to remain while phospholipids and triglycerides are used up[1]. Unfortunately the whole cycle from egg to fish was not followed in one species by these authors, but Takama, Zama and Igarashi (1969) have analysed eggs of *Oncorhynchus keta* right from fertilisation to the larval stage 139 days later. Here the total sterol shows no obvious trend throughout development, but most of the sterol is present in the yolk and very little in the body of the larva. A similar distribution is found in the glycerides and lecithin, but more cephalin occurs in the larva than in the yolk.

The fatty acids most characteristic of the fry are 16:0 and 22:6 (Hayes, Tinsley and Lowry, 1973: *Salmo gairdneri*; Atchison, 1975: *Salvelinus fontinalis*), and in the later part of development these acids are seen to be withdrawn preferentially from the yolk, while acids 18:1 and 18:2 are retained and accumulate (same authors). It should be remembered that, while these changes reflect the need of the larva, they

---

[1]The opposite appears to be the case in *Pollachius virens*, in which sterol esters have been reported by Nechaev, Eremenko *et al.* (1975) to constitute the basis of reserve lipid of the eggs at spawning, and afterwards of the developing embryos and larvae.

are relative: absolute amounts of each fatty acid decline in line with the steady loss of total lipid from the system which, incidentally, probably accounts for the increase in the *concentration* of carotenoids from the third to the thirtieth day after fertilisation in the eggs of *Salmo gairdneri* (Jitariu, Chera *et al.*, 1975).

The use of yolk lipid for energy is illustrated in Fig. 1, which shows how most of the lipid lost by the yolk is retained by the fry up to day 54,

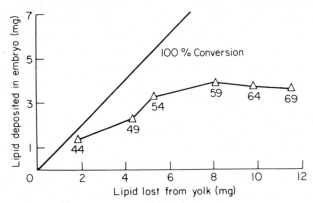

FIG. 1. Deposition of lipid in the embryo as it is lost from the yolk. Figures by experimental points show the number of days after fertilisation (*Salmo gairdneri*) After Hayes, Tinsley and Lowry (1973). Reproduced with permission of Professor I. J. Tinsley.

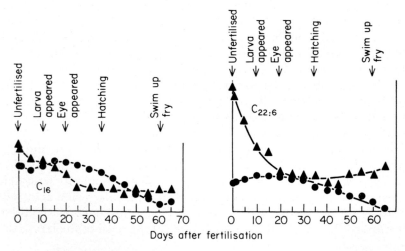

FIG. 2. Changes in the proportions of fatty acids $C_{16:0}$ and $C_{22:6}$ in the eggs and larvae of *Salmo gairdneri* during development. ●, in triglyceride fraction; ▲, in phospholipid fraction. After Ando (1968). Reproduced with permission of the author.

after which there is less gain, changing to a loss after day 59, although it is still being withdrawn from the yolk. Ando (1968) studied the complex changes in the individual fatty acids during the development of *Salmo gairdneri* eggs. In Fig. 2 the behaviour of the most important acids, 16:0 and 22:6, have been selected for illustration. They can be seen to decline steeply in the phospholipid fraction until the "eye" stage is reached, but to increase slightly in the triglycerides to form a

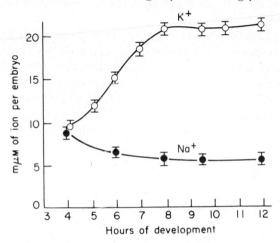

Fig. 3. Sodium and potassium contents of eggs of *Misgurnus fossilis* during the first few hours of development. After Beritashvili *et al.* (1969). Reproduced with permission of Dr D. R. Beritashvili.

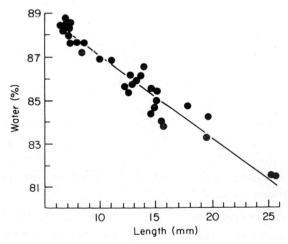

Fig. 4. The decline in water content of larvae of *Pleuronectes platessa* as they grow. After Ehrlich (1974). Reproduced with permission of the author.

broad peak. Other fatty acids behave more or less irregularly, but most of them show a decline in the phospholipid fraction.

ii. *Inorganic constituents*

Fig. 3 shows the behaviour of potassium and sodium during the early development of the eggs of *Misgurnus fossilis*. The increase in potassium suggests the formation of proteinaceous tissues at the expense of yolk, but it is unwise to read too much into these results because of the short period covered.

We should probably expect a decline in sodium in the later stages of development because of the decrease in extracellular fluid revealed as an overall loss of water. Fig. 4 shows this loss very convincingly in the larvae of *Pleuronectes platessa*. It is interesting to note how it stops declining immediately after the yolk is finished if no extraneous food is offered (Fig. 5), and then increases again as the symptoms of starvation supervene, after the manner of adult fish, with increase in extracellular

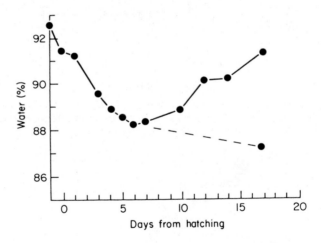

FIG. 5. Water content of the larvae of *Pleuronectes platessa* when no food is offered at the end of the yolk-sac stage. The broken line shows the continuing decline in water content when the larvae are fed. After Ehrlich (1974). Reproduced with permission of the author.

space. Further details of the effects of starvation on fish are given in the section beginning on p. 166.

iii. *Enzymes and hormones*

The development of a functional digestive system can be observed in fish embryos by following the first appearance of digestive enzymes and their subsequent increase. The activities of a trypsin, a pepsin, amylase and maltase are almost undetectable in the eggs of *Salmo gairdneri* after hatching, but all increased linearly thereafter for the 50 or 60 days during which they were studied by Kawai and Ikeda (1973a).

In *Cyprinus carpio*, maltase and amylase activities have been found to develop as the larva develops, starting at a point 7 to 10 days after hatching. *Acanthopagrus schlegeli*, a carnivorous fish, clearly shows some amylase activity 11 days after hatching, and greater activity later. Kawai and Ikeda (1973b), who made these observations, found that the appearance of peptic activity in this species could be aligned with the differentiation of the gastric gland.

Enzymes which exist as a changeable proportion of isozymes according to the metabolic needs of a tissue are potentially a rich source of interest in the field of larval development. Shaklee, Champion and Whitt (1974) submitted several enzymes to electrophoretic analysis, extracting them from *Erimyzon sucetta* which were developing from eggs to 3 weeks post-hatching. Many of the enzymes exhibited rich patterns of ontogenetic change, while a few remained relatively unmodified throughout the experimental period. Several enzymes from particular metabolic pathways exhibited coincident changes suggestive of co-ordinate control. The appearance of rather tissue-specific isozymes was closely correlated with the morphological and functional differentiation of the particular tissues. For further details the reader is referred to the original paper, but the isozyme patterns of lactic dehydrogenase are of such wide interest in studies on fish that their development is illustrated in Fig. 6.

A diagrammatic illustration of changes in the electrophoretic pattern of lactic dehydrogenase in embryos of *Salmo gairdneri* is given by Boulekbache, Rosenberg and Joly (1970), who noted that in the unfertilised egg and blastula stages the enzyme was of type "M" (characteristic of anaerobic glycolysis), while later, at gastrulation, some of type "H" (aerobic metabolism) appeared also. They suggested that the regulation of aerobic and anaerobic metabolism might play a part in embryonic differentiation.

The energy requirements of fish embryos are met partly by glycolysis and respiration, so the eggs have been found to contain most of the essential enzymes of glycolysis, the tricarboxylic acid cycle and the respiration chain (authors quoted by Neyfakh and Abramova, 1974). The latter writers point out that the enzymic profile may be misleading if the yolk has been removed from the embryo before assay, because considerable quantities of enzymes are to be found there.

In a series of publications, Yurowitzky and Milman have reported studies on the metabolic pathways favoured by oocytes (egg cells developing within the parent fish), mature eggs and embryos of the loach (*Misgurnus fossilis*). All of the enzymes shown in Table 3 increased during oogenesis in the ovary, but there was no difference between the concentrations in the mature oocyte and fertilised egg stages (Yurowitzky and Milman, 1971). The activities of enzymes of the phosphotriose glycerate group maintained constant proportions throughout development, apart perhaps from enolase, despite great increases in activity. It was therefore concluded that "biosynthesis of this group of enzymes occurs in a co-operative manner". In contrast, the ratios of phosphofructokinase:pyruvate kinase activities were not constant.

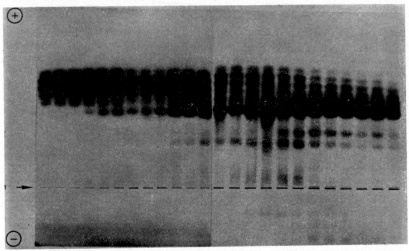

Fig. 6. Patterns of isozymes of lactic dehydrogenase as *Erimyzon sucetta* develop from eggs (left side of the picture) to 3 weeks post-hatching (right side). After Shaklee, Champion and Whitt (1974). Reproduced with permission of Dr J. B. Shaklee.

The carbohydrate metabolism undergoes a fundamental change when the egg is spawned (Yurowitzky and Milman, 1972). Although the pattern of enzymes involved in gluconeogenesis does not change, maturation of the oocyte is followed by a complete loss of hexokinase activity and a decrease in glycogen synthetase, while the glycogen phosphorylase activity increases ten-fold. Thus the oocyte converts maternal glucose into glycogen, but the embryo later uses this glycogen as fuel. Danilenko (1971: *Carassius auratus, Cyprinus carpio*) has also noted a build-up of glycogen in oocytes during maturation.

Yurowitzky and Milman (1973b) then confirmed that the increased glycogenolysis in the embryos is accompanied by an increase in the amount of hexose monophosphates, and in the rates of respiration and of lactate formation. It is now thought (Yurowitzky and Milman, 1975a) that glycogen breakdown in the egg after spawning is not accelerated by the reported increased glycogen phosphorylase activity, but by means of the enzyme which cuts the glucose branches off the

TABLE 3

Enzyme activities at different stages of oogenesis in *Misgurnus fossilis*. (After Yurowitzky and Milman, 1971. Reproduced with permission of Drs Yu. G. Yurowitzky and L. S. Milman)

Enzyme	Stages of oogenesis			
	Vacuolisation. Diameter of oocyte 200 μm	Vitellogenesis. Diameter of oocyte 400 μm	Mature oocyte diameter 800 μm	Egg after fertilisation
1. *Enzymes of phosphotriose glycerate group*				
Aldolase	2·4±0·2 (0·40)	16·0±1·3 (0·66)	260±2·4 (0·65)	260±2·4 (0·65)
Triose phosphate dehydrogenase	6·0±0·3 (1)	24·0±1·0 (1)	400±2·8 (1)	400±2·8 (1)
Triose phosphate isomerase	3·0±0·1 (0·50)	16·0±0·9 (0·66)	240±2·0 (0·60)	240±1·5 (0·60)
Phosphoglycerate kinase	1·8±0·1 (0·30)	7·0±0·3 (0·29)	80±1·8 (0·25)	80±2·0 (0·25)
Enolase	2·0±0·1 (0·33)	9·6±0·5 (0·40)	70±2·5 (0·18)	70±3·0 (0·18)
2. *Enzymes of gluconeogenesis*				
Fructose diphosphatase	0·75±0·04 (1)	4·0±0·3 (1)	24±0·8 (1)	24±0·8 (1)
PEP-carboxykinase	0·2±0·02 (0·27)	0·8±0·04 (0·20)	3·2±0·2 (0·13)	3·2±0·2 (0·13)
3. *Enzymes of hexose monophosphate shunt*				
Glucose-6-P- dehydrogenase	1·2±0·1 (30)	3·6±0·2 (18)	10·8±0·6 (7)	11·0±0·7 (7)
6-phosphogluconate dehydrogenase	0·08±0·01 (2)	0·4±0·02 (2)	3·4±0·2 (2·4)	3·4±0·2 (2·4)
Transketolase	0·04±0·005 (1)	0·2±0·02 (1)	1·4±0·15 (1)	1·4±0·15 (1)
Transaldolase	0·2±0·02 (5)	1·2±0·1 (6)	2·4±0·15 (1·7)	2·4±0·15 (1·7)

Figures are units per 10^4 cells. The *relative* activities with triose phosphate dehydrogenase, fructose diphosphatase or transketolase as reference enzymes are given in parenthesis. Each mean represents 7–8 determinations and the standard deviation is given.

glycogen molecule (amylo-1,6-glucosidase). The "debranching" activity increases during early embryogenesis at the point when glycogen synthetase activity begins to decline (Yurowitzky and Milman, 1975b) and it may be the controlling factor in glycogenolysis.

Yermolaeva and Milman (1974) have shown that the changeover from gluconeogenesis to glycogenolysis can be followed by measuring changes in the ATP:ADP-phosphate ratio or the NAD:NADH ratio; both ratios are roughly halved at the changeover.

Just one report of a change in hormone concentration during larval development has come to the attention of the writer. The concentration of adrenaline in the larvae of *Salmo gairdneri* increases suddenly at the point of hatching, perhaps to promote the physical effort required to break out of the egg shells (Meyer and Sauerbier, 1977).

2. STUDIES ON FOETUSES

Some fish, particularly members of the shark family, give birth to live young, when they are said to be viviparous. In the period under review, scientific interest has centred on the osmoregulatory ability of the foetuses and on the extent of their protection by the mother fish from environmental salinity. Thorson and Gerst (1972) studied the viviparous shark *Carcharhinus leucas*, and found that although osmoregulatory mechanisms may be present in foetuses, independent osmoregulation does not in fact seem to occur before birth. This is because the uterine fluid is similar to maternal serum in all respects apart from having a very low protein content. Sea water does not enter the uterus.

A different situation is found in *Squalus acanthias*, another viviparous species, which does open the uterus to the surrounding medium in late pregnancy so that the foetus is bathed in sea water (Gitlin, Perricelli and Gitlin, 1973). Table 4 shows that the uterine fluid in early pregnancy differs markedly from sea water in having more potassium and much more urea, and less sodium, chloride and calcium, but that in late pregnancy it is almost indistinguishable from the surrounding water apart from having rather more urea. There are therefore species differences which preclude generalisation.

Foetuses of the guppy (*Poecilia reticulata*), a viviparous teleost, were thought by Dépêche and Schoffeniels (1975) never to achieve complete independence from maternal osmoregulatory control, but to become more autonomous towards mid-gestation. Urea seems important in the osmoregulation of early foetuses, but as gestation advances, concentrations decline almost to the low levels of the parent fish. Thus when the parent is placed in hypertonic saline, the young foetus responds with a higher urea concentration, while the older foetus increases its pool of *free* amino acids.

The adaptation of adult fish to changes in salinity is considered more fully on p. 283. The object of the present short section has been to draw attention to changes in adaptation as foetuses develop.

TABLE 4

Composition of the uterine fluid of *Squalus acanthias* compared with that of sea water. (After Gitlin, Perricelli and Gitlin, 1973. Reproduced with permission of Dr David Gitlin)

Substance	Uterine fluid		Sea Water
	1st trimester	3rd trimester	
Urea mM/l	254	2·5	0·03
Sodium mEq/l	344	432	445
Chloride	378	524	510
Potassium	18	9·6	9·5
Calcium mg%	20	36	36

3. METAMORPHOSIS

We have seen (Volume 1, p. 80) that metamorphosis of parr to smolt in salmon is accompanied by an increase in guanine and hypoxanthine in the skin as the fish become silvery. New bands appear in the electrophoresis of the haemoglobin, perhaps representing haemoglobins with higher affinity for oxygen, and the fish acquire the ability to osmoregulate in salt water —they die if they are transferred to the sea too soon.

The metamorphosis of eels and lampreys is accompanied by consistent changes in plasma proteins and haemoglobins which appear on electrophoresis. The patterns of muscle extracts do not appear to change. There are also small changes in the ionic constituents.

There is interplay between water temperature and photoperiod in the induction of metamorphosis, but the relationships are not yet properly established and there appear to be differences according to species. *Salmo gairdneri* seem to require not only a low temperature, but also an advanced photoperiod for early parr-smolt transformation (Zaugg and McLain, 1976) but in *Salmo salar* the water temperature is the main controller of silvering, photoperiod having a negligible influence (Johnston and Eales, 1970). According to Zaugg and McLain (1976), the latter situation applies also to *Oncorhynchus kisutch*, which are induced to metamorphose by a warm (15°C) environment only, but Vanstone and Markert (1968) had observed that the guanine level in the belly skin was influenced by the lighting conditions, so it is too soon to reach a firm conclusion. These authors observed in addition that metamorphosis is accompanied by a streamlining of the body shape, so that the weight:length ratio changes; the effect has also been noted by Pinder and Eales (1969: *Salmo salar*) and Fessler and Wagner (1969: *Salmo gairdneri*). If the young smolts are prevented from migrating to the sea, some die and a few may revert to the parr form, but, contrary to popular belief, the remainder can grow as well as or even better than the sea-run form if given suitable food (Saunders and Henderson, 1969b: *Salmo salar*). The salinity corresponding with optimal growth changes seasonally, the physiology of the fish favouring life in the sea in spring and summer, and life in fresh water during autumn and winter, but the migration is not obligatory (same authors).

The concentrations of *free* amino acids, especially of glycine and taurine, are reduced in the muscle during the metamorphosis of *Salmo salar* (Fontaine and Marchelidon, 1971a, 1971b). This may relate to the synthesis of guanine, which is deposited in the skin at the same time, since glycine is necessary for the synthesis of the purine nucleus (Fontaine and Marchelidon, 1971a).

The level of guanine in the skin does not seem to correspond with the intensity of silvering in all species, however. Hayashi (1971) observed that the degree of silveriness can alter independently of the amount of guanine in the bellies of *Oncorhynchus masou*, while the guanine and hypoxanthine in *Salmo gairdneri* and *Salmo trutta* has been observed to decline steadily as the fish grow from parr onwards (Fujii, Yamada and Onishi, 1971), rather than increase as one might have expected.

Several workers have suggested that thyroid activity promotes smoltification and migration to the sea (reviewed by Godin, Dill and Drury, 1974). Fontaine, Mazeaud and Mazeaud (1963: *Salmo salar*) noted that, of all stages in the life cycle, smolts have the highest concentration of adrenaline, noradrenaline and 17-hydroxysteroids in the blood, and considered that these hormones enable the smolt to swim continuously on its way to the sea. A further adaptation for long swimming is seen in *Anguilla anguilla* at the silvery stage (Lewander, Dave *et al.*, 1974) in the form of an increase in the quantity of dark muscle (see p. 100 for a review of the use of dark muscle in continuous swimming).

Continuous activity requires an increased supply of oxygen to the muscles, and Johansson, Dave *et al.* (1974) have shown that at metamorphosis the haemoglobin concentration of the blood of *Anguilla anguilla* increases. A more intense activity probably accounts for the increase in the amount of compact muscle in the ventricle of smoltifying *Salmo salar* reported by Poupa, Gesser *et al.* (1974).

The evidence on the nature of the haemoglobins developed after metamorphosis is at present confusing. Iuchi (1973) described the adult haemoglobin of *Salmo gairdneri* as having a greater Bohr effect than that of the juvenile fish. This means that a lowered pH, for example in vigorously working muscle which produces lactic acid, tends to cause the haemoglobin to give up its oxygen, to the benefit of the contractile tissue. However, Hashimoto (1972) found that the metamorphosis of *Salmo salar* results in a *reduction* in the proportion of haemoglobin which possesses a Bohr effect and an increase in the fraction which does not. The final conclusion must await the investigation of other species.

The glycolipids of the erythrocytes of *Salmo gairdneri* have been reported to change with metamorphosis from globosides to sialoglycolipids (Nambu, Yamagami and Terayama, 1975). The physiology of the change is not known.

Studies on enzymes seem to show that metamorphosis of *Anguilla anguilla* results in more vascularisation of the muscles, or that they function more aerobically than in fish at the "yellow" or larval stage. This means that they become better adapted for continuous swimming. Boström and Johansson (1972) showed that the activity of the enzymes of the hexose monophosphate shunt and of the citric acid cycle increase in both dark and white muscles after metamorphosis, as does the activity of cytochrome oxidase, another aerobic enzyme. In contrast, the enzymes of anaerobic glycolysis, pyruvate kinase and lactic dehydrogenase, which are equally active in the red and white muscles of larval eels, decline in activity in the dark muscle after metamorphosis, probably reflecting a decline in anaerobic bursts of activity and a changeover to steady aerobic contractions in this muscle.

One of the most important manifestations of metamorphosis in salmonids is the development of the ability to osmoregulate in sea water. This ability appears at smoltification and precedes actual entry into the sea. The change in osmoregulation can be seen as a change in salinity preference. Young *Oncorhynchus kisutch* in an experimental salinity gradient have been shown by Otto and McInerney (1970) to choose 7% in June and gradually increase the preferred concentration to 13% by February. With the approach of smolt transformation, the occasions when the fish are found in fresh water are greatly reduced.

Fish in salt water guard against osmotic dehydration by drinking sea water and then excreting salt through the "chloride cells" (see p. 293) of the gills. The energy required comes from the breakdown of adenosine triphosphate (ATP) and as gills are required to excrete more salt they incorporate greater concentrations of an ATPase which is activated by sodium and potassium ions (Na-K-ATPase) and inhibited by the drug ouabain—the topic is covered in more detail on p. 289. There are now several reports which show that the activity of this enzyme increases at metamorphosis. Species studied were *Salmo gairdneri* (Zaugg and McLain, 1972; Adams, Zaugg and McLain, 1973; Zaugg and Wagner, 1973), *Oncorhynchus kisutch* (Giles and Vanstone, 1976a) and *Salmo salar* (McCartney, 1976). Increases in enzyme activity in the gill are matched by decreases in the kidney (McCartney, 1976), where it assists in the resorption of sodium from the glomerular filtrate—an important conservation measure for freshwater fish which would be disastrous in the sea. When *Salmo gairdneri* smolts are held in fresh water over the period when they should have entered the sea, they lose their silvery colour and resume the appearance of parr. At the same time, the ATPase activity of the gills declines to near the pre-smolt levels (Zaugg and McLain, 1972).

Metamorphosis and the increase in gill ATPase are inhibited in *Salmo gairdneri* by water temperatures in excess of about 13°C (Zaugg and Wagner, 1973), though their rate of growth is greater at higher temperatures (Adams, Zaugg and McLain, 1973). The latter authors propose that ATPase activity be used as an index of metamorphosis.

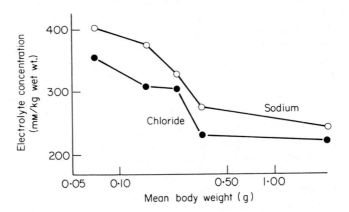

Fɪɢ. 7. Change in sodium and chloride concentration from whole body analysis of eel leptocephalus larvae, showing the genesis of osmoregulation with growth. After Hulet, Fischer and Reitberg (1972). Reproduced with permission from the University of Miami.

In a way, eels undergo two metamorphoses. As minute larvae they are known as leptocephali, and are semi-transparent and leaf-like. At this stage their ionic composition closely approximates to that of sea water; they are unable to create a special environment for their tissues which differs from the surrounding medium, and in this they resemble hagfish (*Myxine glutinosa*: Volume 1, p. 137). Fig. 7 shows that, as the leptocephali grow, their osmoregulatory ability increases and they can reduce the sodium and chloride concentrations down to levels more usual for vertebrate tissues, at which concentrations they presumably function better. On the other hand, the metamorphosis from yellow eel to silver eel brings about no striking changes in any constituents, at least of the blood (Table 5). Similarly, the mineral constituents of the serum of lampreys (*Petromyzon marinus*) show virtually no changes between larva, metamorphosed downstream lamprey, parasitic adults or migrating–spawning adults, apart from a smallish increase in sodium and chloride at metamorphosis (Urist and van de Putte, 1967).

TABLE 5

The constituents of the blood of *Anguilla anguilla* before ("yellow") and after ("silver") metamorphosis. (After Larsson and Fange, 1969. Reproduced with permission of Dr Ragnar Fange)

Constituent	Yellow eel	Silver eel
Calcium (mEq/l)	7.4 ± 0.3	6.2 ± 0.5
Chloride (mEq/l)	143.9 ± 2.2	147.7 ± 2.9
Cholesterol (ester) (mg%)	352 ± 19	317 ± 23
Cholesterol (free) (mg%)	159 ± 17	218 ± 20
Free fatty acids (µmol/l)	422 ± 18	346 ± 55
Glucose (mg%)	53.1 ± 9.2	51.3 ± 6.5
Haematocrit (%)	38.2 ± 0.7	43.0 ± 1.8
Haemoglobin (%)	11.3 ± 0.5	12.6 ± 0.4
Lactate (mg%)	12.9 ± 1.8	14.1 ± 1.9
Phosphorus (inorganic) (mg%)	5.2 ± 0.4	3.8 ± 0.3
Potassium (mEq/l)	4.5 ± 0.2	3.5 ± 0.2
Sodium (mEq/l)	165.1 ± 1.3	164.9 ± 1.8
Triglycerides (mmol/l)	6.1 ± 0.6	5.9 ± 0.6
Urea (mg-N%)	7.4 ± 0.1	6.7 ± 1.0

Metamorphosis and the reshaping of the body seem to consume a considerable proportion of the energy resources of the fish. Increased breakdown of lipid has been noted in *Salmo gairdneri* (Fessler and Wagner 1969), *Salmo salar* (Pinder and Eales, 1969) and *Anguilla anguilla* (Lewander, Dave *et al.*, 1974). In addition, Ota and Yamada (1971), who also noted increased lipid utilisation, this time in *Oncorhynchus masou*, found fatty acids 16:0 and 18:1 to be the main source of energy during the parr–smolt transformation. *Anguilla anguilla* changing from the yellow to the silver form appear to consume 18:0 and 20:4 acids, since the concentrations decline in the liver, but the story is complicated in this report by an increase of 14:0 and 16:0 in the gonads during the metamorphosis (Dave, Johansson *et al.*, 1974).

Metamorphosis of *Plecoglossus altivelis* seems to involve an immediate change of diet, since the quantities of gastric amylase and pepsin increase (Tanaka, Kawai and Yamamoto, 1972).

The exact contributions of temperature, photoperiod and any other factors to the triggering of metamorphosis are still not certain, though they clearly vary between species. The subject is important to fish farmers, because young salmon grow more quickly as smolts than as parr, but it does not yet seem possible to ensure 100% metamorphosis at one time in a batch of fish, and parrs which remain "lose" a whole year, during which time they grow very little. The discovery by Kato (1972) that parr placed on a blue background rapidly take on the appearance of smolts offers promise in fish cultivation.

4. FURTHER GROWTH

It was shown in Volume 1 that, quite apart from the fact that bigger fish become sexually mature and must drain nutriments from their body tissues to meet the needs of spawning, the mere fact that length has increased brings about a number of changes. Several tissues change in proportion to the total body weight—myocommata, swim bladders and muscle cells all become thicker and the liver is disproportionately bigger, containing a higher concentration of vitamin A.

The diet will change as carnivorous fish grow larger simply because they can now tackle bigger and often different prey, and so they may require a modification in the proportions of their digestive enzymes.

Sodium in the muscle of replete cod decreases as the fish lengthen, but in those species which are increasingly depleted by spawning as they grow older the muscle sodium becomes greater in bigger fish during the spawning period, corresponding with an increase in extracellular space.

The cartilage of elasmobranchs deposits more minerals as the fish grow, while the muscle of cod may contain more glycogen.

The blood of larger fish acquires an increased capacity for carrying oxygen, and the proportions of different haemoglobins as revealed by electrophoresis may change markedly.

Other constituents which increase or decrease according to the size of the fish were listed in Table 18 of Volume 1, but it must be borne in mind that the reasons for the correlations between body size and the concentration of a constituent are often uncertain, so that there may be no means of predicting the behaviour in species other than the few studied. The same criticism applies to some of the more recent findings.

a. *Changes in diet*

Actual evidence for a change in body chemistry resulting from a change in diet is still scant, although there are well-known instances of a variety of prey organisms being eaten in sequence by fish as they grow (for example, Bass and Avault, 1975: *Sciaenops ocellata*). Siddiqui (1975a) noted that the glucose, cholesterol, iron and non-protein nitrogen in the blood of *Clarias batrachus* increased with increasing size, and suggested that the adults of this species ate "more nutritive food" in the form of insects, shrimps and worms. However, systematic studies do not appear to have been done, and some of the changes have already been recorded in other species not known for consuming a more nutritious diet as they grow. Blood glucose in *Catla catla* (Table 18, Volume 1), and the carbohydrate contents of the muscle of *Gadus morhua* (Love, Robertson *et al.*, 1974a) and *Carassius carassius* (Mar'yanovskaya, 1972) are known to rise with age, but it seems unlikely that these species gradually become better fed. Bigger fish may perhaps lay down greater energy reserves as a protection against excessive depletion at the spawning period: several species are known to become more fecund as they grow larger. They were listed in Volume 1, and the same behaviour has since been noted in *Reinhardtius hippoglossoides* (Lear, 1970).

The increased level of iron in the blood of larger *Clarias batrachus* (Siddiqui, 1975a) presumably reflects an increased haemoglobin content, which has already been reported in several species in Volume 1 (Tables 17 and 18) and more recently in *Heteropneustes fossilis* (Pandey, Pandey *et al.*, 1976) and *Hippoglossoides platessoides* (Smith, 1977). Lientz and Smith (1974), reporting that the haematocrit and haemoglobin content of *Salmo clarkii* increased with size, suggested, as did Siddiqui (1975b), that it could be due to a change in nutritional status. However, they also considered the possible role of environmental oxygen.

The concept of the changed diet of a larger fish affecting its composition is attractive and deserves study, but the effects are likely to be more subtle than those mentioned so far.

b. *Metabolic rate and activity*

The increased haemoglobin concentrations in the blood of larger fish, mentioned above, probably reflect the inverse relationship between the gill area per unit body weight and the body weight, which is typical of teleosts (Muir and Hughes, 1969, quoted by Murphy and Houston, 1974), and also perhaps the longer time needed to transport the oxygen from the gills to various parts of the body. The oxygen consumption of larger fish has indeed been shown to be less than that of smaller fish per unit weight (Saunders, 1963: *Gadus morhua;* Muravskaya, 1972: *Trachurus mediterraneus ponticus, Spicara smaris* and *Scorpaena porcus*), but if the physical difficulties of transport are removed by using a model system with minced white muscle supplied with metabolites, then the oxygen consumption is the same for tissues from differently sized fish (Gordon, 1972a: various species).

Physical differences are manifested in other ways also: smaller fish have disproportionately large stomachs (Ishiwata, 1968: *Trachurus japonicus*) hence perhaps in part their more rapid growth. Against this, the growth rate depends, at least in captive fish, on rank in the social hierarchy, the largest fish being dominant and laying claim to most of the food. Thus larger fish tend to grow more quickly, and any disparity in sizes becomes more pronounced with time (Symons, 1970: *Salmo salar*). Fish farmers guard against this by separating their stock into groups of similar sizes at regular intervals.

Body dimensions in relation to the resistance of the water enables smaller fish to swim a greater number of lengths per second than larger ones can, and the muscle from smaller fish can contract more quickly (C. S. Wardle, 1976, unpublished: *Gadus morhua*).

The metabolic rates of *Pseudolabrus celidotus* and *Clarias batrachus* were shown by Morris (1965) and Jordan (1976), respectively, to vary inversely with the size, in some seasons at least, and this phenomenon is reflected in the excretion of nitrogenous compounds, which is not directly proportional to the body size but decreases as the fish grow (Gerking, 1955b: *Lepomis macrochirus*; Muravskaya, 1972: three species).

This reduced activity in older fish seems to be simply a function of body length and need not be regarded as aging.

c.   *Influence on offspring*

It was noted earlier (p. 9) that the female *Gadus callarias* with the most lipid in their livers spawned eggs richer than usual in lipid. Grauman (1972) showed that the size of the females of this species was also strongly correlated with the lipid content of their eggs. The same effect was found in Volga sturgeon (*Acipenser* sp.: Fig. 8) by Krivobok

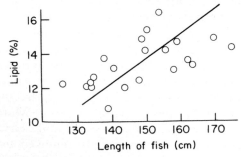

FIG. 8. Lipid content of eggs (wet weight) in relation to the size of the parent fish (*Acipenser* sp.). After Krivobok and Storozhuk (1970). Reproduced with permission of Dr A. Ya. Storozhuk.

and Storozhuk (1970), who observed that the eggs of young, small females had the least weight[1] and the smallest content of dry matter, lipid and total nitrogen. These three parameters rise consistently as sturgeon grow, but the weight of the eggs reaches a maximum when the parent fish is 26 to 30 years old, after which it begins to decrease.

The same sort of relationship applies to viviparous species. Wilson and Milleman (1969) found that the largest female *Cymatogaster aggregata* give birth to the largest offspring and also to the greatest number so that, as in fish which lay eggs, fecundity is related to parent size.

d. *Temperature compensation*

A full discussion of the adaptation of fish to changes in temperature will be presented later (p. 318). The purpose of this section is to show the influence of growth on temperature adaptation.

Small fish seem to adapt better than those which have passed their rapid growth phase; like some of us, the latter have become more set in their ways. Adult *Gadus morhua*, for example, cannot adapt to temperatures greater than 15°C or 16°C, but at 2 years old or less they can adapt and live for prolonged periods at as much as 18°C (P. Dando, personal communication). One can think of a number of reasons why this should be so. Collagen, for example, is more thermally unstable in cod than in many other species, and Andrejeva (1971) has demonstrated small differences in the shrinkage temperatures of collagens from cod living in different localities which depend, presumably, on the ambient temperature. If the temperature were raised, a young cod could begin to lay down a more thermally stable collagen as it grew, while an older fish would have almost completed a matrix of less stable collagen and would perish at the higher temperature. It seems likely that a similar situation could apply to the myofibrillar proteins, which are notoriously unstable in cod, but there is as yet no experimental evidence for differences between the proteins of cod from cold and from less cold water. Again, it is possible that older fish have more difficulty in modifying the lipids of their central nervous system to a pattern suited to higher temperatures (Driedzic, Selivonchick and Roots, 1976).

Cytochrome oxidase and succinic dehydrogenase change their activity as the ambient temperature changes, so that the metabolism of the fish is not seriously affected by the water temperature. However, small *Carassius auratus* take less time to reach a new steady state after a

---

[1]Dr T. Kato (private communication, 1977) has observed that the eggs of *Salmo gairdneri* also vary in size in proportion to the size of the parent.

temperature shift than do larger fish (Sidell, Wilson *et al.*, 1973), presumably because the rate of synthesis of modified enzymes is quicker in
younger animals. The brain, liver and muscle of young *Etroplus
maculatus* have also been found to compensate for changes in temperature (as measured by oxygen consumption) more effectively than those
of older fish (Parvatheswararao, 1972), and similarly the metabolic rates
of *Forsterygion varium* and *F. robustum* were found by Morris (1965) to
adapt more fully to cold when the fish are small.

Reduced ability to thermocompensate in bigger fish can probably
be regarded as a slowing down in the synthesis of stable molecules by
less actively proliferating tissue—an aspect of aging, in fact.

e. *Nucleic acids*

Deoxyribose nucleic acid (DNA) carries the genetic material of each
cell and is present in the nucleus in fixed quantity. Ribose nucleic acid
(RNA) is present in variable quantity in the nucleus and cytoplasm,
and is concerned with the transfer of the genetic code of the nuclear
DNA into the body of the cell and the creation of actual sequences of
amino acids in the synthesis of new protein. While these facts have been
known for some time, it is only recently that RNA:DNA ratios have
been utilised in the study of the vigour of protein synthesis, and hence
of growth, in fish.

Schattenberg (1973: *Macropodus opercularis*) has shown that when
young skeletal muscle cells grow in length, the elongation occurs at
their ends, and that the concentration of ribosomes (bodies containing
RNA) is highest in the "youngest" region where the terminal myofibrils
are being formed, beyond the last completed sarcomere[1]. As soon as the
terminal myofibril region has expanded to nearly the full length of a
new sarcomere, the concentration of ribosomes falls, to rise again
further on in the next terminal region to be formed beyond the new
Z-disc.

The concept of RNA being the most concentrated in the most
actively growing material can be extended to whole fish. The RNA:DNA
ratio is therefore higher in a 1-year-old fish than in a 2-year-old at a
comparable growth stage (Haines, 1973: *Cyprinus carpio, Micropterus
dolomieui*) because of the higher growth rate of the younger fish. Those

---

[1]"Sarcomeres" are the segments into which muscle cells are divided and give muscle its
characteristic striped appearance. The Z-disc is the name given to the boundary between
sarcomeres. Greer-Walker (1970) has shown that the sarcomeres of *Gadus morhua* increase in
length with increase in body length up to about 10 cm, but that in all bigger fish the sarcomere
size does not increase further.

accustomed to measuring the age of fish will know how the accretions round the otoliths and scales (Volume 1, p. 162) become narrower with each successive year, corresponding with a successive decline in the rate of growth. The main point to remember is that if the growth rate of a fish is to be measured by the RNA:DNA ratio, for example through several seasons or on different diets, then only fish of the same age ("year group") can be compared. The same restriction applies to RNA:DNA determinations on liver tissue (Malikova and Loyanich, 1974: *Salmo gairdneri*).

Measurement of DNA alone gives information on the number of cells present, but again values need to be interpreted with care. If a sharply delineated organ, such as the liver, can be analysed in its entirety so much the better, but if only in part then the expression of DNA in a unit weight of tissue may be misleading. For example, an increase in the volume of each cell will lead to an apparent fall in the concentration of DNA (as has been observed in the liver of male *Limanda aspera* by Pirskii, Morozova and Berdyshev (1969), though the absolute amount in the whole organ should not be affected. Further problems arise if the number of nuclei in each cell changes, as has been found in the muscle of mice by Williams and Goldspink (1971), where the number increases even after the cells have ceased to grow in length. Some confirmation by histology of changes in cell number or dimensions will do much to allay doubts here and keep results on a sound footing.

Greer-Walker (1970: *Gadus morhua*) has in fact shown histologically that during growth both the dark and the white muscle fibres increase in number throughout life. DNA determinations would probably have been misleading because of the simultaneous inrcease found in the diameters of both sorts of fibre. Greer-Walker's results are reproduced in Fig. 9. It extends the information presented in Fig. 40 of Volume 1 by describing the situation in red muscle for the first time and by showing a decline in the cross-sectional area of the white cells of the biggest fish—perhaps another manifestation of aging. There seems to be an exact parallel in the aging of the muscle cells of rats. Tauchi, Yoshioka and Kobayashi (1971) showed that in senility the volume (so, presumably, the diameter) of white muscle fibres decreases, but that of dark fibres does not. The number of cells diminishes in both types of muscle.

Luquet and his collaborators have studied cell numbers and growth using DNA determinations. With this technique they have found, like Greer-Walker (1970), that the number of muscle cells, this time of *Salmo gairdneri*, increases continuously throughout life (Luquet and Durand, 1970). Since the cell number is insufficient to account for the increase in the weight of muscle, it was concluded that the cells also enlarge, the enlargement accounting for 70–90% of the weight increase.

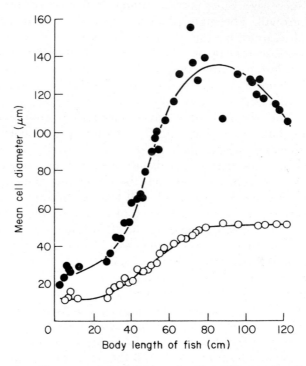

FIG. 9. The mean diameters of dark (○) and white (●) muscle cells from *Gadus morhua* of different body lengths. Each point is the mean of 100 cells. After Greer-Walker (1970). Reproduced with permission of the author.

Liver seems also to grow predominantly by an increase in cell numbers (Luquet and Hannequart, 1971); the sizes of the cells increase by only 28%. The brain, on the other hand, was found to grow essentially by multiplication of cells rather than by an increase in their size (Luquet and Hannequart, 1974: *Cyprinus carpio*). This mechanism probably differs from that found in mammals, in the brains of which the total quantity of DNA is fixed soon after birth (same authors).

f.   *Lipid and protein*

It will have been noticed by now that the distinction between mere increase in body size and aging is not always sharp. In the same way, alterations in the pattern of lipid and protein rarely seem to relate to simple physical growth, but much more clearly to sexual maturation. These constituents will therefore be looked at more appropriately on pp. 39 and 42.

g. *Other substances*

A list of tissue constituents reported to change as the fish increase in size has already been given as Table 18 in Volume 1. Here in Table 6 are further findings, offered as before with little comment. When the reasons for all the changes eventually become known, the naiveté of the list will be obvious, and it will also perhaps be clear which of the relationships arc peculiar to one species only, and which of general applicability. The sort of information I had in mind is the "amino acids" which increase, with size, in herring muscle according to Plorina (1970). Now the actual amino acids involved were given as proline, alanine, glycine and tyrosine, all of which, with the possible exception of tyrosine, are integral parts of the collagen molecule. Fish appear to lay down new collagen in the muscle during starvation (Volume 1, p. 102; Lavéty and Love, 1972; Love, Yamaguchi et al., 1976) as discussed fully later (p. 198), and only the bigger fish are depleted by spawning--so here again we probably have a manifestation of maturation rather than a simple size increase.

Not all changes are caused by maturation. The increase in blood haemoglobin has already (p. 27) been discussed in relation to a reduced gill area (relative) found in bigger fish, and the increased whole-body calcium presumably relates to the increased calcification of scales and other hard tissues in older fish. Strontium concentrations usually change hand-in-hand with calcium in vertebrate tissue (Eisler and LaRoche, 1972), so would be expected to increase in older fish. Mercury concentrations are of particular interest to students of pollution, but most of the increases reported here seem to be natural acquisitions, relating as they do to fish from large masses of ocean water. An increase in the mercury content of fish muscle with body size has in fact been discovered in preserved fish caught 90 years ago, long before mercury pollution was known (Barber, Vijayakumar and Cross, 1972). This still tells us nothing about the steady accumulation of mercury in fish tissues, of course, but at least it might stop us from worrying about it.

TABLE 6

Substances investigated in relation to the size of the fish

Substance	Tissue	Species	Change as fish grow[a]	Reference
ATPase	Gill	*Carassius auratus*	Decrease[a]	Murphy and Houston (1974)
Amino acids[b]	Muscle	*Clupea harengus*	Increase	Plorina (1970)
free Amino acids	Muscle	*Labeo rohita, Cirrhina mrigala Catla catla*	Increase[c]	Siddiqui, Siddiqui and Ahmad (1973)
Bile acids	Bile	*Salmo gairdneri*	Increase	Denton, Yousef et al. (1974)
Calcium	Blood	*Clarias batrachus*	Decrease	Siddiqui (1975a)
	Whole fish	*Fundulus heteroclitus*	Increase	Eisler and LaRoche (1972)
Cholesterol	Blood	*Clarias batrachus*	Increase	Siddiqui (1975a)
Chromium	Whole muscle	*Salvelinus namaycush*	Increase	Tong, Youngs et al. (1974)
Copper		*Pomatomus saltatrix Antimora rostrata*	No change	Cross, Hardy et al. (1973)
	Most organs	*Salmo gairdneri, Salvelinus fontinalis*	Increase	Berman and Vitin' (1968)
Cortisol	Blood	*Carassius auratus*	Increase	Singley and Chavin (1975a)
Ergocalciferol	Various organs	Many species	Either direction	Yamakawa, Kinumaki et al. (1965)
Ergosterol	Blood, Spleen, Kidney	*Cyprinus carpio*	Decrease	Chernyshov, Yakubov et al. (1972)
Glucose	Blood	*Carassius auratus*	Decrease over part of size range	Chavin and Young (1970)
Glucose-6-phosphatase		*Clarias batrachus*	Increase	Siddiqui (1975a)
	Liver	*Hippoglossoides platessoides*	Increase	Smith (1976)
Haematocrit	Blood	*Salmo clarkii*	Increase	Lientz and Smith (1974)
Haemoglobin				
Hypoxanthine	Muscle	*Thunnus albacares*	Increase	Aldrin and Grandgirard (1971)
Iron	Most organs	*Salmo gairdneri Salvelinus fontinalis*	Increase	Berman and Vitin' (1968)

Manganese	Muscle	*Pomatomus saltatrix* *Antimora rostrata*	No change	Cross, Hardy *et al.* (1973)
	Blood	*Clarias batrachus*	Increase	Siddiqui (1975a)
	Most organs	*Salmo gairdneri* *Salvelinus fontinalis*	Increase	Berman and Vitin' (1968)
Mercury	Whole body	*Salmo gairdneri*	Increase	Kondratovics (1969)
	Muscle	*Pomatomus saltatrix* *Antimora rostrata*	No change	Cross, Hardy *et al.* (1973)
	Muscle	Various deep-sea fish	Increase	Barber, Vijayakumar and Cross (1972)
		Freshwater fish	Increase	Bligh (1972)
		Oregon marine fish	No change	Childs and Gaffke (1973)
		Antimora rostrata *Pomatomus saltatrix*	Increase	Cross, Hardy *et al.* (1973)
Molybdenum	Whole	*Salvelinus namaycush*	Decrease	Tong, Youngs *et al.* (1974)
Non-protein nitrogen	Blood	*Clarias batrachus*	Increase	Siddiqui (1975a)
Protein	Blood	*Salmo gairdneri*	Increase[c]	Galasun and Shemchuk (1971)
Pyruvate kinase	Liver	*Hippoglossoides platessoides*	Increase	Smith (1976)
Sodium	Blood	*Carassius auratus*	Increase	Murphy and Houston (1974)
Spermatocrit	Semen	*Stizostedion vitreum*	No change	Gregory (1969)
Strontium	Whole	*Fundulus heteroclitus*	Increase	Eisler and LaRoche (1972)
Tin	Whole	*Salvelinus namaycush*	Decrease	Tong, Youngs *et al.* (1974)
Trace metals			No change	
Zinc	Most organs	*Salmo gairdneri* *Salvelinus fontinalis*	Increase	Berman and Vitin' (1968)
	Muscle Pancreas	*Torpedo marmorata*	Decrease	Fischer and Güthert (1968)
	Muscle	*Antimora rostrata* *Pomatomus saltatrix*	No change	Cross, Hardy *et al.* (1973)

[a]Not often significant.

[b]Certain amino acids probably associated with connective tissue.

[c]Other work suggests that this relationship may change according to the stage of maturity of the fish.

5. MATURATION

a. *Introduction*

In earlier work (Volume 1, p. 98), glycogen and *free* amino acids were shown to be transferred from the body of the female fish to the maturing ovary. Most of the individual combined amino acids in the gonads change up or down in an apparently aimless way, but proline and glycine decline steadily, probably reflecting the "dilution" of existing ovarian or testicular connective tissue with swelling eggs or sperm. Muscle shows a small increase in proline and glycine as it becomes depleted of non-collagenous proteins, but the picture here is complicated by the apparent synthesis of collagen during any kind of depletion, associated with maturation or simply with a shortage of food.

Maturation of salmonid species has been found to be accompanied by a decrease in lipid reserves, but the energy expended in the spawning migration probably accounts for much of this.

Sex hormones show steady increases during maturation, declining abruptly after spawning.

Female fish have often been observed to be larger than males, which mature the earlier of the two sexes. The female gonad is bigger than that of the male, so maturation often results in greater depletion of the female body reserves. The levels of protein and calcium in the blood of females also become greater than those of the males as they mature.

It was shown in Volume 1, p. 97, that fish tend to become mature at a particular length rather than at a particular age. The finding has been confirmed by work on *Glossogobius giuris* (Marquez, 1960), *Gadus callarias* (Thurow, 1970) and *Coregonus clupeaformis* (Reshetnikov, Paranyushkina *et al.*, 1970). The smaller size of the males of many species at maturity compared with the females is probably explained by the relatively smaller male gonad requiring a smaller "transporter".

Maturation in *Coregonus clupeaformis* depends not only on achieving specific size, but also on attaining a definite level of lipid reserves, the actual value being specific to each population (Reshetnikov, Paranyushkina *et al.*, 1970). This sort of precondition might explain why *Stizostedion vitreum* mature at a shorter length in one part of Lake Erie than another, males from the two localities relating to each other in the opposite way from the relationship between the two groups of females (Wolfert, 1969).

In *Tilapia*, a raised temperature is also needed before the oocytes will develop. Katz and Eckstein (1974) showed that the surrounding temperature has to be at least 22°C before the reproductive processes can begin. *Salmo gairdneri* seem to require a progressively diminishing photoperiod to induce spermatogenesis (Breton and Billard, 1977).

b. *Hormones*

The initiation of reproduction by temperature in female *Tilapia aurea* (same authors) results in large increases in testosterone, 11-ketotesto-sterone, 11-β-hydroxytestosterone and deoxycorticosterone in the blood, the latter increasing 38-fold. Such increases appear to be a general phenomenon which has been noted in other species; testosterone has also been observed to rise in the blood of males as maturation develops (Sangalang, Weisbart and Idler, 1971: *Acipenser oxyrhynchus;* Campbell, Walsh and Idler, 1976: *Pseudopleuronectes americanus*), and high androgen levels have been found in the blood of both sexes of *Carassius auratus* in the spawning season (Schreck and Hopwood, 1974). The latter authors found that at spawning the plasma oestrogens rise parallel to the androgens in the females, but that in males the oestrogen level remains the same throughout the year. In *Pseudopleuronectes americanus*, the testosterone rises more in the females than the males as spawning approaches (Campbell, Walsh and Idler, 1976), the principal rise in males being in 11-ketotestosterone. The rate of secretion of cortisol increases in both sexes of *Oncorhynchus nerka* during maturation (Donaldson and Fagerlund, 1970). Not surprisingly, gonadotropin, the pituitary hormone which stimulates production of the other hormones by the interstitial cells of the gonads, has also been shown to increase in the plasma as maturity develops (Crim, Watts and Evans, 1975: 4 salmonid species).

Various effects have been attributed to the rise in sex hormones in the blood of maturing fish. In Volume 1 it was shown (pp. 61–62) that oestradiol, rising during the spawning season or injected at other times, causes the level of calcium in the blood to rise, and Mugiya and Watabe (1977) have now discovered that, at least in *Carassius auratus* and *Fundulus heteroclitus*, the rise following oestradiol injection is supplied by the withdrawal of calcium from the scales. No calcium appears to be withdrawn from the vertebrae, jaw or otoliths. Butler (1968) suggested that the corticosteroids might serve the energy requirements of spawning (and starving) salmon by stimulating gluconeogenesis, but Dockray and Pickering (1972) have reviewed papers showing that the alimentary canal is at the same time caused to atrophy by these hormones, reducing the possible intake of nourishment to zero. The alimentary canal of lampreys also atrophies during spawning migration, and Pickering (1976: *Lampetra fluviatilis*) has shown that gonadectomy at the start of the migration prevents the change, or reverses it if it has already progressed to some extent. Both oestradiol and testosterone were shown to stimulate the degeneration of the alimentary canal, which can be regarded as the utilisation of non-essential tissues for the development of the gonads in starving fish.

The skin of *Oncorhynchus nerka* has been observed to thicken in response to an injection of 11-ketotestosterone, which also makes the flesh redden (Idler, Bitners and Schmidt, 1961), but curiously enough it was androgens which were found to cause a *loss* of flesh colour in the same species by Donaldson and Fagerlund (1969), who noted that injections of cortisol do not affect the colour. Clearly much work still remains to be done on the action of hormones in maturing fish, but some observations on carotenoids shed at least some light, as we shall see in a moment.

c.   *Carotenoids*

While the actual function of carotenoids in maturation is only just beginning to come to light, it seems clear that they accumulate in the liver and flesh during the feeding season and then pass from these tissues into the gonads as they ripen (Loginova, 1969: *Salmo gairdneri*). The flesh of spawning *Oncorhynchus nerka* has been noted as containing much less carotenoid than that of prespawning fish taken from the sea (Crozier, 1970), but there is some evidence that carotenoids do not enter the flesh until maturation has at least started (N. Lewtas, personal communication: *Salmo salar*). In contrast to the carotenoids from the flesh, those from the skin and fins do not decrease during maturation, presumably because their function in camouflaging the fish has priority. The redistribution from liver and flesh to gonad has also been seen in *Salmo trutta*, *Perca fluviatilis*, *Leuciscus cephalus* and *Barbus barbus* by Shnarevich and Sakhnenko (1971), who suggested that the amount of pigment in the eggs could serve as a measure of the stage of maturity. Donaldson and Fagerlund (1970) themselves (see previous section) found that the loss of carotenoid pigment from *Oncorhynchus nerka* flesh could be halted if the fish were gonadectomised, but one wonders how the loss of flesh pigment could then be induced by androgen injections (Donaldson and Fagerlund, 1969) *into gonadectomised salmon*. The loss from the flesh must surely be governed by the hormones from the gonads and not simply through the gonads requiring to be dosed with carotenoids as they enlarge. Unfortunately it was not shown where the carotenoid went when caused to leave the flesh of the gonadectomised fish. The reddening of the flesh resulting from injections of 11-ketotestosterone, reported by Idler, Bitners and Schmidt (1961), is at present unexplained, but perhaps more than one hormone is needed to deplete it of pigment and the stage of maturity could also be important.

Deufel (1975) has presented evidence to show that carotenoids fulfil an important function in reproduction and are not "just a playful diversion of Nature, as is often assumed". He quoted trout farmers as saying that red-coloured trout eggs were better than pale yellow ones, and showed that canthaxanthin and astaxanthin are sperm activators, beta-carotene being less effective. Of three-year-old *Salmo gairdneri*, 65% spawned if fed canthaxanthin compared with 25% of unfed controls. The location and function of this effect are still unknown, as are the requirements for optimal reproduction— from a few trials they seemed to be in the region of 40 mg canthaxanthin per kg of feed. Carotenoids are especially important in salmonids. Deufel (1975) regards them as hormones influencing growth, fertilisation, maturation and embryonic development. On the other hand, M. Hata (personal communication, 1977) suggests that they may be more important for protecting the eggs from sunlight after spawning.

d. *Lipids*

As a general statement it appears to be true that maturation involves the transfer of lipid from the liver, muscle or gut to the gonad, though much more is used to supply energy than to make yolk (Shatunovskii, Bogoyavlenskaya *et al.*, 1975: *Gadus callarias*). While the developing gonads are still small, the feeding of the fish can more than keep pace with their lipid requirements so that, for example in *Gadus callarias* where most of the lipid is stored in the liver, the initial period of maturation is accompanied by an increase in both body and liver weights. As the gonad grows, however, its lipid requirements outstrip the now restricted intake, and the body and liver suffer a sharp loss (Krivobock and Tokareva, 1972). An increase in liver lipid during the early ripening of the gonads, followed by a decrease, has also been noted in *Gadus morhua* (Turuk, 1972) and in an unnamed flounder from the White Sea (Shatunovskii, 1967), while a decrease of lipid from muscles and "viscera" occurs in *Coregonus clupeaformis* as spawning approaches (Potapova and Titova, 1969). Perhaps it was the variations in the availability of food at a particular stage of gonad development that gave rise to Mazeaud's (1973) observation that an increase in ovarian function results in an increase in the liver lipids of some species of teleosts and elasmobranchs, while in other teleosts it is castration which causes the increase.

A different situation seems to apply in *Salmo gairdneri* in which the lipid, especially triglycerides and *free* fatty acids, actually increases in the liver during later maturation of the females (Takashima, Hibiya *et al.*, 1971), being transported there from the visceral adipose tissue, and presumably thence to the oocytes. A concomitant increase in blood lipid marks the activity of transport. Further work has shown that the liver of this species can be made to hypertrophy and to contain more protein, lipid and nucleic acids if the fish are injected with oestrogen (Takashima, Hibiya *et al.*, 1972). These authors concluded that, in natural maturation, lipoprotein is synthesised in the liver and then released into the blood under the influence of ovarian steroid hormones. They emphasized, however, that non-ovarian hormones might be important in maturation because the secretory activity of the thyroid and adrenals varies throughout the year. In addition, they demonstrated by experiment that the administration of thyroid extract to the fish depresses the levels of serum lipid and lipoprotein, while Woodhead (1969: *Gadus morhua*) showed that thyroxine also inhibits the hypercalcaemia which occurs in response to oestradiol injection or to natural maturation. The protein synthetic activity of the liver as measured by the RNA content has been shown (Takashima, Hibiya *et al.*, 1972) to increase under the influence of oestrogen (diethylstilboestrol), and to decline with androgen (methyltestosterone). It is presumably egg protein which is being synthesised.

Regarding the relative utilisation of the different lipid classes, no very clear picture has so far emerged, being partly obscured by species differences. The lipids and proteins in the blood serum of maturing female *Salmo trutta* have been shown to fall (Felinska, 1972), but in contrast the free cholesterol increases by 140%, because, it is thought, of its role as a precursor of hormones. Shatunovskii and Novikov (1971) noted that there is little change in the relative proportion of phospholipids in the muscle as lipid is transferred to the ovary (same species). The content of triglycerides in the oocytes almost doubles up to the beginning of vitellogenesis, after which both this fraction and the sterol esters are reduced.

In the males on the other hand it appears that phospholipids are selectively removed from the muscle during maturation and, towards the final ripening, the cholesterol falls as well. The selection of phospholipids from the muscle is marked by a rise of this fraction in the blood.

In the antarctic fish *Notothenia rossii*, cholesterol and *free* fatty acids have been noted to drain from the muscles of the females during maturation, and to accumulate in the ovaries (Shatunovskii and Kozlov, 1973). The phospholipids and triglycerides of the ovaries, on the other hand, are more concentrated in immature fish and decline during maturation. Sterol esters are mobilised in the muscle of maturing males, but the authors considered that they are used to supply energy for swimming and for the synthesis of cholesterol in the liver.

Haddock (*Melanogrammus aeglefinus*) seem to exhibit a more fundamental distinction between the sexes, according to Shevchenko (1972). The females concentrate on the accumulation of protein, rather than lipid, as they prepare for maturation, while the males accumulate more lipid because their gonads need less protein, and they expend more energy in moving about the spawning grounds. They are also said to use more energy than the females during spawning, as are male *Gadus callarias* (Shatunovskii, Bogoyavlenskaya *et al.*, 1975) and, by inference, male *Pollachius virens* (Storozhuk, 1975). Like cod, the haddock accumulates most of its reserve lipids in the liver, and Shatunovsky and Shevchenko (1973) observed that triglycerides especially and phospholipids to a lesser extent are deposited during the period of heavy feeding. As in the earlier paper (Shevchenko, 1972), it was reported that the males accumulate more lipid than the females, and also that the phospholipid and sterol ester contents increase significantly along with triglycerides. During the fattening period, the relative proportions of triglycerides (both sexes) and sterol esters (males) also increase in muscle lipids. In mature haddock ovary, the main lipid is phospholipid and in the testis it is phospholipid and triglyceride. During the maturation of females, the reserves of triglyceride largely disappear, while males expend mostly phospholipid.

The last part of this somewhat complex account serves to show that the male and female fish really have to be considered separately in any discussion of maturation because of their differing requirements. Sex differences are considered more fully on p. 46.

The amounts of total lipid, neutral lipid and *free* fatty acids being actively transported by the blood to the foetus in the viviparous species *Zoarces viviparus* increase steadily throughout pregnancy, decreasing just before parturition (Pekkarinen and Kristoffersson, 1975).

As fish mature repeatedly in successive years, they appear to accumulate bigger and bigger stores of lipid, presumably to supply gonads which, at least in some species, increase in size with the years disproportionately to the body size of the fish (Volume 1, p. 90). Thus as fish grow older, they acquire a progressively greater mass of lipid in the muscle (Khawaja and Jafri, 1968: *Wallago attu, Mystus seenghala;* Piatek, 1970: *Anguilla anguilla;* Groves, 1970: *Oncorhynchus nerka*) or the liver (Turuk, 1972; Berger and Panasenko, 1974; Ross and Love, unpublished: *Gadus morhua*). Minick and Chavin (1972a: *Carassius auratus*) showed that the concentration of *free* fatty acids in the serum increases progressively each year after first maturation. The connection with maturation was very marked in this instance because all age-groups of fish had been fed an identical diet. Presumably none of these relationships would apply to fish at an advanced stage of maturation, but during or just after the periods of heavy feeding.

The nature of the lipid as well as its quantity changes with increasing age. Stepanova (1971) found that the level of unsaturated fatty acids in the lipids of *Pleuronectes herzensteini* increases in older fish irrespective of sex. The very unsaturated acid 22:6, which is of major importance in fish lipids, has also been noted to increase in *Oncorhynchus kisutch* with age without regard to its availability in the diet (Tinsley, Krueger and Saddler, 1973).

e.   *Amino acids and proteins*

In growing tissues the concentrations of *free* amino acids are higher than in quiescent tissues (various authors quoted by Sorvachev and Shatunovskii, 1968), and various reports in the period under review have described such increases in the gonads of maturing fish (Sorvachev and Shatunovskii, 1968: "flounder"; Nasedkina and Puskareva, 1969: *Oncorhynchus gorbuscha*; Maslennikova, 1970: *Gadus callarias*). Studies on individual amino acids, whether free or combined, are somewhat difficult to interpret (as they were in work reviewed in Volume i), since the concentrations of some of them rise during only a part of the maturation process and then fall, or vice versa. It appears that definite trends are rare, though Maslennikova (1970) has noted consistent changes in amino acids grouped together as acid, neutral or basic: neutral amino acids (alanine, leucine, isoleucine and valine) are found (free) in the highest concentration in the mature ovaries of *Gadus callarias*, while most of the *free* amino acids of the liver have acid properties (aspartic and glutamic acids). As testes ripen, their proteins are found to contain more of the "alkaline" amino acids lysine and arginine (Maslennikova and Korzhenko, 1972), alkaline proteins being characteristic of tissue with multinuclear cells. In the course of spermatogenesis, the number of nuclei in testicular tissue rises because of the nearly two-fold rise in the number of cells per unit volume.

Sorvachev and Shatunovskii (1968) noted that as the concentrations of *free* amino acids rise in the developing gonads, there is a fall in the corresponding amino acids of the liver. The concentration of *free* amino acids in the muscles of sexually mature individuals is lower than in those of young immature fish (same authors), but it is not known whether the lower concentration results from transfer to the gonads or simply from the fact that the muscle at that time is not actively growing; body growth occurs outside the spawning season.

The concentration of a phosvitin-like protein as been observed to rise steadily in the eggs of *Salmo gairdneri* as they mature (M. Suyama, personal communication, 1977). This observation seems to be the only one holding promise for measuring the exact stage of maturation of a fish through protein analysis.

Maturation causes complex changes in the blood proteins, some of which have been characterised. The total proteins of the plasma of *Anguilla japonica* have been reported to decrease by Ochiai, Ogawa *et al.* (1975), but such findings are less informative than the results of more detailed studies. Cellulose acetate electrophoresis has revealed pattern differences associated with maturation (Pesch, 1970: *Pseudopleuronectes americanus*), while a specific antigen has been found in the maturing females of all salmonid species submitted to immunoelectrophoresis by Utter, Hodgins and Allendorf (1974). This was probably an egg protein (ovovitellin), which has also been observed in the serum or plasma of maturing females (or males treated with oestrogen) by Plack and Fraser (1970: *Gadus morhua*), Aida, Ngan and Hibiya (1973: *Plecoglossus altivelis*) and Kirsipuu (1975: *Esox lucius*). The latter author also observed that some glycoprotein fractions do not vary with the sex of the fish or the season. Goedmakers and Verboom (1974: *Esox lucius*) found, like the other authors, a relationship between the stage of maturation and the ovovitellin content of the blood, but concluded that it could be used to assess the degree of maturity only in the early stages of maturation. In the later stages there was too much variation between individuals for the ovovitellin index to be useful.

The circulating egg protein appears to be synthesised in the liver under the control of female hormones, since oestrogen injection causes the protein to appear in the liver (Plack and Fraser, 1970: *Gadus morhua*) and induces hypertrophy of the nuclei, nucleoli, endoplasmic reticulum and RNA in the liver of immature or male fish (Aida, Hirose *et al.*, 1973: *Plecoglossus altivelis*). As already noted on p. 30, the quantity of RNA can be taken as a measure of protein synthetic activity, and Imura and Saito (1968) showed that there is three times as much of it in the livers of *Oncorhynchus keta* with mature ovaries as there is in those males.

Shatunovskii and Novikov (1971: *Salmo trutta*) noted that the albumin of blood decreases during the maturation of females, unlike the males, so that there is a marked relative increase in α-globulin. In contrast, Girzadaite and Lesauskiene (1972: *Vimba vimba*) found a high level of albumins in fish at the spawning grounds and a low level of $\alpha 1$ and $\alpha 2$

globulins, which, they concluded, had been utilised in the construction of the gonads. This appears to be another example of species differences destroying an otherwise clear picture, but the latter authors do point out a "complex recasting of protein metabolism" during the later stages of maturation.

f. *Other blood constituents*

The levels of constituents in the blood do not necessarily reflect changes occurring in other tissues. Further, concentrations can alter through increases or decreases in the plasma volume rather than in the actual amount of circulating substances, so changes must be interpreted with care. Pickford, Grant and Umminger (1969; *Fundulus heteroclitus*) could indeed find little in the way of changes in the blood serum that could be related to maturation, though there was a trend towards lower osmolality. The increases in blood calcium as female fish mature (Volume 1, pp. 61–62) seems to be in no doubt, however, and has more recently been observed in *Gadus morhua* (Woodhead, 1969), *Gadus callarias* (Ipatov and Shaldaeva, 1974) and *Zoarces viviparus* (Kristoffersson, Broberg and Oikari, 1974). It is interesting to note that injections of oestradiol, which normally induce the same effect, fail to raise the blood calcium if the fish were recently spawned. Presumably they are now drained of resources for synthesising the ovovitellin–calcium complex.

Stress appears to reduce plasma volume (Volume 1, p. 47), so that the concentration of haemoglobin increases. Perhaps therefore it is variations in the amount of asphyxial stress on sampling that account for certain contradictory results. Gelineo (1969) reported that maturation in more than 50 fish species was associated with an increase in the concentration of haemoglobin in the blood, confirmed by Fourie and Hattingh (1976) in *Cyprinus carpio*. Kristoffersson, Broberg and Oikari (1974) found a steady *decrease* in that of *Zoarces viviparus* almost up to the point of parturition, while Hutton (1968) found no significant change during the spawning migration of *Oncorhynchus gorbuscha*[1]. The same author could find no trend in the urea or creatinine concentrations in the blood[2], but a decline in glucose and *free* fatty acids under the

---

[1]Haematological measurements likewise do not relate to maturation in *Barbus holubi* (van Vuren and Hattingh, 1976).

[2]These two constituents in *muscle*, along with ammonia, creatine, trimethylamine oxide and certain *free* amino acids, were also reported by Vyncke (1970: *Squalus acanthias*) to have no relationship with maturity.

influence of oestrone was reported by Mazeaud (1973: *Carassius auratus*).

The increase in circulating retinal (vitamin A₁ aldehyde) with maturation of the female and not of the male is strikingly shown in Fig. 10.

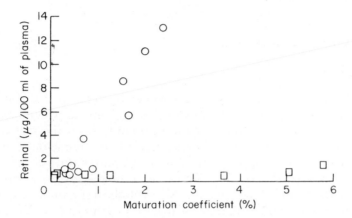

FIG. 10. Concentrations of retinal (vitamin A₁ aldehyde) in the blood of female (○) and male (□) *Gadus morhua* during the progress of maturation. After Plack and Pritchard (1968). Reproduced with permission of Dr P. A. Plack.

The egg requires vitamin A so that the future larva will be able to see: the sperm does not. Plack and Pritchard (1968), who made this observation, also found that the rise in retinal could be induced by injecting oestradiol, and suggested that the vitamin might be transported by the egg phosphoprotein complex described above (p. 43).

g. *Inorganic constituents*

The roles of trace elements in fish are in many cases completely unknown, but it is not unlikely that much of their physiological effect is through the biocatalyst system (Berman and Vitin', 1968). These authors noted that the requirements of trace elements within any species differ at different stages of maturation. Ilzina (1968: *Rutilus rutilus*) noted a somewhat variable accumulation of manganese, iron, copper and zinc in various tissues, particularly the ovaries, with the development of maturation. After spawning, the concentrations in the ovaries were seen to drop, especially copper which decreased from 514 to 8·8 mg per 100 g of ash, but curiously the levels of all the elements decreased in other tissues as well, muscle, liver, bone and scales being mentioned.

Julshamn and Braekkan (1976) studied a number of elements in the ovaries of *Gadus morhua* during maturation, and discovered several clear trends. In this species the copper increases with progress of maturation, as do sodium and manganese. The potassium, calcium, magnesium, iron, zinc and cobalt all decline.

6. SEX DIFFERENCES

a. *General*

It will have become clear during the foregoing account that differences between the sexes appear in many of the phenomena which have been observed during maturation, stemming mainly from the fact that the male gonad is often relatively smaller than that of the female, so drains the body less of its resources[1]. Also, males tend to mature earlier and be smaller than females of the same age, probably because growth is retarded by sexual development. Most of the remaining differences, apart from hormonal, originate in the list of materials which must be transferred from other tissues into the developing eggs, rather than sperm, to give the young larvae a start in life.

Female fish of the same age as males have been found to be the larger by Barroso (1967: *Hirundichthys affinis*), Pinhorn (1969: *Gadus morhua*), Thurow (1970: *Gadus callarias*), Planquette (1975: *Lates niloticus*) and various workers of the fisheries laboratory, Lowestoft (personal communication: *Pleuronectes platessa, Solea solea*). However, of the marine wolf-fishes, only *Anarhichas latifrons* (= *Lycichthys denticulatus*) has the larger females: in *Anarhichas lupus* and *A. minor* it is the males which grow faster and mature later (Beese and Kändler, 1969).

Since the male gonad is relatively smaller, it is not surprising that male fish can restore their expended resources after spawning more quickly than can the females (Krivobok and Tokareva, 1972: *Gadus callarias*).

Shevchenko's conclusion (1972) that male haddock expend more energy on the spawning ground and so require more lipid is confirmed for *Platichthys flesus* by Lapin (1973), who described their "prolonged participation in the spawning process". J. A. Lovern (personal communication) observed that male *Salmo salar* fought each other all the way to the spawning ground, and Wohlschlag (1964) reported that

_____

[1]Thus when female pickerels (probably *Lucioperca lucioperca*) change from females to males in their 4th year of life, they are able to lay down more protein in their bodies, being now less depleted by spawning (Shul'man, 1972, p. 179).

male *Trematomus bernacchi* and *T. borchgrevinki* had in general higher respiratory rates than the females anyway.

If it is true that males are more active than females—and further evidence is really needed to state this categorically—there are also signs that males die earlier (see also Volume 1, p. 117). When female *Gadus*

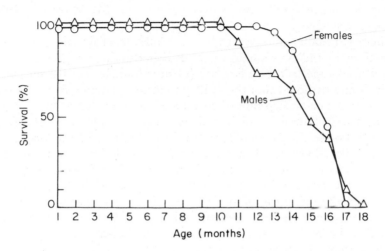

Fig. 11. Survival of 10 male and 25 female *Cynolebias bellotti* maintained at 22°C. After Liu and Walford (1969). Reproduced with permission of Dr R. K. Liu.

callarias reach 6 years of age and males 5 years, the rate at which lipids and carbohydrates accumulate in the liver slows down, so what can be taken as a sign of aging occurs sooner in the males (Bogoyavlenskaya and Vel'tishcheva, 1972). In a population of *Pleuronectes herzensteini* from Russia it was noted by Stepanova (1971) that there were more females present than males, and hence, probably, a higher male mortality. The most convincing evidence, however, arises from work by Liu and Walford (1969) on *Cynolebias bellotti*, the males of which clearly have the shorter life-span (Fig. 11).

b. *Hormones*

It was stated in Volume 1 (p. 120) that both male and female hormones are usually found together in both sexes of fish, and in the occasional case there is, for example, a higher concentration of blood testosterone in the *female* at all stages of maturity. This does not mean hirsute females and "sissy" males—merely that the male and female hormones have a common origin in cholesterol, and do not necessarily act in opposition to one another.

It has since been reported that in *Salmo gairdneri* there is no significant difference between the androgen contents of the blood of the two sexes (Schreck, Lackey and Hopwood, 1972) or oestrogen contents (Schreck, Lackey and Hopwood, 1973) although, at least in *Oncorhynchus gorbuscha*, there is much more gonadotropin in the plasma of females (Crim, Meyer and Donaldson, 1973). Blood adrenaline has also been reported as not significantly different between the sexes (M. Mazeaud, 1969a: *Petromyzon marinus*).

There is usually more cortisol in the plasma of female *Oncorhynchus nerka* than in males (Donaldson and Fagerlund, 1970) and more in male *Polyodon spathula* than females (Grant, Mehrle and Russell, 1970), but it should be noted that the ability to clear hormones from the blood can vary: the clearance rate of cortisone has been shown to be greater in males than females, which at least partly accounts for the higher concentration in the blood of females (Fagerlund and Donaldson, 1970, same species). Plasma cortisol also varies at different times during the day. Garcia and Meier (1973: *Fundulus grandis*) found two peaks, 1 hour and 9 hours after sunrise, in the male while that of the female exhibits but one peak during the night. The physiological basis of these observations remains to be established, as it obviously does with respect to the other hormones, especially whenever contradictory species differences occur (Volume 1, p. 121).

c.   *Carbohydrates*

While much of the energy of fish comes from gluconeogenesis (p. 3), it would be interesting to see whether the alleged greater vigour of the males was accommodated by a difference in carbohydrate reserves. In the case of liver glycogen, there really does seem to be more glycogen set aside for male activity, though in *Oncorhynchus tschawytscha* and *O. nerka* where this was observed by Connor, Elling *et al.* (1964), no difference in swimming performance was noted. In the early stages of maturation of *Gadus callarias*, the glycogen content of males is 50 to 100% greater than it is for the females, but the picture is reversed immediately before spawning (Bogoyavlenskaya and Vel'tishcheva, 1972). This is difficult to square with the fact that females transfer glycogen from liver to gonad during development (Volume 1, p. 119), but perhaps it is near the terminal stages of maturation that the females have completed their glycogen transfer while the males are burning theirs most intensively. Anyway, these authors do state that the onset of spawning causes expenditure of lipid from the bodies of the females and glycogen from the males.

The concentration of liver glycogen has been found to be the greater in male *Coregonus nasus* by Valtonen (1974) in line with the other observations. It was pointed out that the size of the male liver is in fact smaller, probably because of the copious materials needed for yolk production in the females.

Finally, the concentration of liver glycogen has been found to be the higher in male *Gadus morhua* and *G. navaga* (Shatunovskii and Denisova, 1968), so the glycogen relationship is almost completely consistent.

Blood glucose is not informative: we have seen before that it does not necessarily reflect the level of liver glycogen (Volume 1, pp. 202 and 274) but tends to remain steady. Hence Shatunovskii and Denisova 1968) found that male and female *Gadus navaga* do not differ with respect to blood glucose, while *G. morhua* females have a higher concentration than males, the reverse of the liver glycogen picture. Blood glucose has been found to be relatively lower in male *Clarias batrachus* (Siddiqui, 1975a) and in male *Catostomus commersonii* and *Esox lucius* at certain times of the year (Mackay and Beatty, 1968b). *Catostomus commersonii* also exhibit a seasonal variation in blood glucose in the males but not in the females (same authors). Blood glucose which is higher in migrating male fish than in females has been reported by Hutton (1968: *Oncorhynchus gorbuscha*).

d.   *Plasma proteins and liver RNA*

There are a few observations on the total protein or the albumin: globulin ratios in relation to the sex of the individual. The amount of the total protein seems not to characterise a particular sex (authors quoted by Palacios, Rubió and Planas, 1972: several species), and although female *Lophius piscatorius* tend to have the higher plasma protein of the two sexes, it may not be significant (Palacios, Rubió and Planas, 1972). No difference has been found in the concentrations of plasma proteins of *Sebastiscus marmoratus* (Yamashita, 1968b) or of *Polyodon spathula* (Grant, Mehrle and Russell, 1970), while Jackim and LaRoche (1973) noted that the rate of take-up of ^{14}C-leucine, used as a measure of general protein synthesis, does not vary between male and female *Fundulus heteroclitus*.

Turning to the classical categories of proteins, we see more serum albumin and globulin in male *Salmo gairdneri* (Galasun and Shemchuk, 1971) and more albumin in the serum of male *Salmo trutta* during the ripening of the gonads, while in the females the albumin fraction decreases (Shatunovskii and Novikov, 1971).

The plasma proteins of certain fish will bind iodine, and among these there is more bound iodine in the plasma of males (Huang and Hickman, 1968).

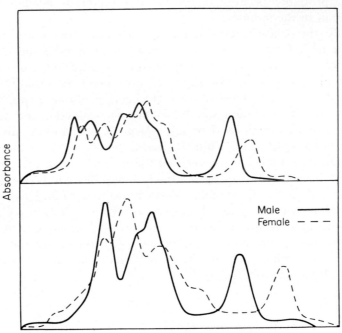

Fig. 12. Densitometer traces of electrophoretic patterns of plasma proteins of *Pseudopleuronectes americanus* caught in December. Upper diagram: immature. Lower diagram: mature. Migration from left to right. After Pesch (1970). Reproduced with permission of the author.

While Grant, Mehrle and Russell (1970) found no differences in the electrophoretic patterns of the serum proteins of *Polyodon spathula* according to sex, other papers do report variations in the electropherograms (Yamashita, 1968a: four species of *Fugu*; Yamashita, 1969: *Sebastiscus marmoratus*; Pesch, 1970: *Pseudopleuronectes americanus*). The results of the latter author are reproduced in Fig. 12, which shows that the main differences appear only when the fish are sexually mature.

If we survey all these papers on protein in relation to the sex of the individual, it seems that the most distinctive difference is still the appearance of protein associated with calcium in the developing female (ovovitellin), absent in the male. Since the genesis of the protein seems to be linked to an increase in liver RNA, it is presumably hepatic in origin (Aida, Ngan and Hibiya, 1973; Aida, Hirose *et al.*, 1973:

Plecoglossus altivelis). A higher level of RNA in the liver of female fish compared with males has also been observed by Imura and Saito (1968: *Oncorhynchus keta*), Imura and Saito (1969: *O. nerka kennerlyi*) and Popov and Georgiov (1971: *Salmo gairdneri*). One must of course beware of concentration effects: the RNA could appear to increase because of a reduction in the amount of liver oil, but such effects probably do not apply here, since Imura and Saito (1969) stated specifically that it was the absolute amount of liver RNA which increased. Using the ratio of RNA:DNA rather than RNA alone eliminates this source of error. Imura and Saito (1968: *Cyprinus carpio*) noted a much higher concentration of RNA in the female gonad than the male. Taken at the right stage of maturation this would indicate the more rapid rate of growth.

Within the nucleic acids, adenine and uracil nucleotides have been found to be more concentrated in relation to guanine and cytosine in females (Seki, 1968: *Oncorhynchus keta;* Pirskii, Morozova and Berdyshev, 1969: *Limanda aspera*).

e. *Lipids*

Present information on sex differences in lipid distribution represents an advance on that reported in Volume 1 (pp. 118–120), and in spite of the usual interspecies contradictions it is possible to get a rather clearer picture of the situation.

The difference in gonad size between sexes, resulting in a difference of lipid needs, can be illustrated by values given by Ziecik and Nodzynski (1964) for *Pleuronectes flesus*, the gonads of which attain 18% of the body weight in females and only 4·2% in males. At the end of spawning, the female gonads form 5% of the body weight while those of the male form 2·5%, a smaller relative decrease which leaves less to be made up the following year. Chepurnov and Tkachenko (1973) calculated that the overall total of lipids in the gonads of male *Gobius melanostomus* are almost ten times less than that of the females, so little is required to be taken from the depots during maturation.

Since the difference in lipid requirements is so great, it is surprising that female fish have sometimes, and only sometimes, been shown to carry the greater reserve in their livers. The reason may be that liver lipid is sometimes assayed when maturation is advanced, when of course the females will already have transferred much of their store. Also many species carry large reserves of lipid in their muscles. On the other hand, the observation by Shevchenko (1972) that the liver lipid of male *Melanogrammus aeglefinus* increases four-fold during the feeding period, while that of the females increases only 1·5 times, cannot be explained in this way.

Valtonen (1974) quoted other authors who showed that in "many teleosts" the liver is smaller in males preparing to spawn than in females which must produce yolk. Campbell and Love (1978) found the same difference in *Melanogrammus aeglefinus*, and Valtonen's own results (Fig. 13) show very clearly that female *Coregonus nasus* have larger livers than either males or immatures for the greater part of the year. The

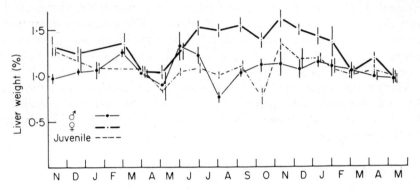

FIG. 13. Weight of liver (percent of body weight) of mature female *Coregonus nasus* during the year, compared with males or immatures. After Valtonen (1974). Reproduced with permission of the author.

reserve lipids have been shown to increase after spawning more in female *Pleuronectes flesus* than in males (Ziecik and Nodzynski, 1964), and female *Mallotus villosus* have been shown usually to contain more lipid than males by Ackman, Ke *et al.* (1969). Turuk (1972) showed that mature *Gadus morhua* females accumulate slightly more lipid than the males, but the difference is barely detectable. In the case of *Petromyzon marinus*, Kott (1970) found that female livers were the larger when the lampreys had been caught in Lakes Ontario or Huron, but were smaller than those of the males if both sexes had come from Lake Erie. This could be due to a discrepancy in the spawning times, but in any case the male livers were observed to have the higher lipid content. Kott (1971) reaffirmed that male lampreys have more liver lipid than females, and Shatunovsky and Shevchenko (1973) showed that male *Melanogrammus aeglefinus* also accumulate more liver lipid than females between spawning seasons. This study needs to be completed by research embracing other species.

If we turn from the accumulation of reserves to their withdrawal during maturation, the picture is less confusing. Shatunovskii and Novikov (1971) found that more lipid is removed from the muscle of female *Salmo trutta* than males as maturation advances, while Shchepkin (1971) demonstrated a somewhat greater reduction in the liver lipid of female *Scorpaena porcus*. Bogoyavlenskaya and Vel'tishcheva (1972: *Gadus callarias*) concluded that females withdraw mostly lipid from their bodies while males withdraw glycogen, and in the spring, presumably after spawning, female *Scomber scombrus* are left with less residual muscle lipid than the males (Ackman and Eaton, 1971). Not that females tolerate a more extreme depletion of lipid than males, incidentally: *Perca flavescens*, either males or females, have been shown to die when their total body lipid has dropped to about 2% of the total dry weight of the fish (Newsome and Leduc, 1975). These authors believed that the rise in average lipid content in the spring is only apparent, resulting from the death of numerous other fish of the same species that had mobilised too much of their lipid during the winter.

The lipid classes predominating in the gonads differ in the final stages of maturation, testis having more sterol esters, phospholipids and *free* fatty acids, and ovaries having more cholesterol and triglycerides (Shatunovskii and Novikov, 1971: *Salmo trutta*). In *Melanogrammus aeglefinus*, the most important lipids of the testis are phospholipids and triglycerides while that of the ovaries is phospholipid (Shatunovskii and Shevchenko, 1973). During maturation, male haddock tend to accumulate sterol esters, phospholipids and triglycerides, while females for the most part accumulate triglycerides only. Triglycerides predominate in the ovaries of *Gobius melanostomus* (Chepurnov and Tkachenko, 1973) while, in the muscle, triglycerides are the most important lipid class in the males, phospholipids in the females.

The liver and muscle of male *Notothenia rossii* contain more sterol esters than those of the females, which contain more *free* fatty acids and phospholipids (Shatunovskii and Kozlov, 1973).

Wax esters are important in certain species, usually deep-water teleosts or fish fromcold surface waters (Kayama and Nevenzel, 1974). In the gouramy (*Trichogaster cosby*) they are important in the ovary but are replaced by triglycerides as the newly hatched fry use up the egg sac and take external food. They form a very minor component in mature males (Sand, Hehl and Schlenk, 1971a).

Blood cholesterol is much more concentrated in male *Clarias batrachus* (Siddiqui, 1975a) and *Polyodon spathula* (Grant, Mehrle and Russell, 1970). On the other hand, maturation of male *Salmo trutta* results in a reduction in blood cholesterol, the phospholipids increasing at the same time (Shatunovskii and Novikov, 1971).

The pattern of utilisation of lipids also differs between the sexes. Ackman, Ke *et al.* (1969: *Mallotus villosus*) observed that the lipids from frozen male capelin underwent more hydrolysis during cold storage than those from females, and believed that it related to differing catabolic requirements: males require rapid breakdown of depot lipid, and hence non-specific hydrolysis of fatty acids, whereas the less active females show some selectivity and tend to break down the longer-chain mono-unsaturated fatty acids. Sterol esters build up in the livers of female *Melanogrammus aeglefinus* and *Gadus morhua* in the early stages of vitellogenesis but fall sharply later, presumably being incorporated into the gonad (Shatunovskii and Shevchenko, 1973). At this time the main fraction of lipid reserve—the triglycerides—breaks up, but the males seem to use mostly phospholipids largely, one assumes, for energy purposes.

Explanations of these various observations, based on biochemistry at the level of the cell or on cell physiology, are notably few, authors for the most part being lucky even to establish clear relationships between the concentrations of various lipid classes and certain stages of maturation. Traditionally, lipid stored as a source of energy was considered to be triglycerides, phospholipids being inviolate as essential constituents of certain tissue fractions. Even this classification of uses is not certain in fish, however, following observations (Volume 1, p. 242) of phospholipid depletion during starvation.

The stage of food balance is obviously critical, that is, in order to understand an increase or a decrease in a lipid fraction in the gonad or other tissue, we need to know whether the intake of dietary lipid is sufficient to supply the needs of the gonad *and* to allow some to be deposited in the reserves, or if the reserves are in fact being broken down. Since authors are not always aware of the situation in their fish brought in for analysis, the results can contradict one another at different stages of maturation, and one frequently reads of a fraction which increases during maturation and then suddenly falls as spawning approaches. The observation of Krivobok on the increase and then decrease in liver weight during maturation (Volume 1, p. 63) has done much to help in the understanding of anomalies and indeed of interspecies contradictions as well.

Broadly speaking, females lay in stores of lipids to be transferred to the ovary for use by the developing embryo before it can feed[1], while males use glycogen and lipid stores as fuel, putting only a relatively small quantity into the testis. Surveying the observations made so far, however, so as to include all investigated species, one has the impression

---

[1]This also is a composite situation: presumably the embryos store only a proportion for tissue synthesis, burning the remainder.

that various lipid fractions can be used interchangeably for deposit in the eggs or for energy. The deposition of cholesterol in the ovary probably reflects the increase in the quantity of cell wall material as the oocytes grow, while an increase in blood cholesterol may reflect general lipid transport.

f. *Miscellaneous substances*

Hormone activity of some sort has been thought to induce a higher haematocrit value in male fish of various species (Volume 1, p. 121), but since fish with greater habitual activity also have higher haematocrits (Volume 1, p. 148), we may be observing further evidence for greater activity among male fish. Recent papers have confirmed that male fish have a higher haematocrit or a higher haemoglobin concentration than females, species showing the effect being *Esox lucius* (Mulcahy, 1970), 53 species of fish (Gelineo, 1969), *Cyprinus carpio* (Svoboda, 1973) and *Salmo gairdneri* (Georgiev, 1972b). The latter author noted that in

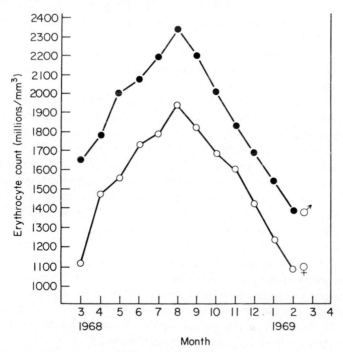

FIG. 14. Erythrocyte count in male and female *Tilapia zillii* throughout the year. After Ezzat, Shabana and Farghaly (1974). Reproduced with permission of Dr A. A. Ezzat.

sterile females the erythrocyte count and haemoglobin concentration in the erythrocytes is greater than in spawning females, suggesting that maturity bring less physical activity in its train. *Tilapia zillii* has been shown to have more erythrocytes in the male than the female throughout the year, values for both sexes rising to a maximum at the spawning season (Ezzat, Shabana and Farghaly, 1974). The results are shown in Fig. 14.

In male *Thymallus thymallus* the haemoglobin content of the erythrocytes is higher than in the females, but only in spring and winter: in summer and autumn the positions are reversed (Pavlović, Mladenović-Gvozdenović and Kekić, 1972). On the other hand (same authors) the haemoglobin content of the erythrocytes of *Salmo trutta* is higher in the females at all seasons.

Inorganic substances continue to fascinate several groups of workers, but usually only vague explanations for trends are possible, such as the ions forming part of hormones or enzymes, or activating them.

If maturity engenders different degrees of depletion between the two sexes, then we might expect differences in the blood sodium or potassium, both of which decrease during starvation (Volume 1, p. 247). However, perhaps because the many species of fish examined were never seriously depleted, Natochin and Lavrova (1974) could find no significant differences between males and females in the contents of sodium, potassium, calcium[1] or magnesium in their blood sera. The possibility still remains.

The collagens of both skin and muscle have been reported to be more acetic-acid-soluble in females than in males (Gantayat and Patnaik, 1975: *Ophicephalus punctatus*). This indicates less cross-linking in females and could correspond with greater depletion-linked collagen turnover (see the account of depletion leading to apparent collagen synthesis on p. 198); that is, another manifestation of more depletion in females.

Zinc, along with magnesium, has been noted as more concentrated in the livers of female *Coregonus nasus sensu* (Hyvärinen and Valtonen, 1973), and in female *Salmo gairdneri* there is more of it in the gonad, along with iron and cobalt (Kondratovics, 1969). The testis of this species accumulates more manganese and copper, according to the same author, but Berman and Vitin' (1968) found the ovary to be six times richer in manganese and twice as rich in copper. They also reported that the ovary contains more iron than the testis, presumably because of the need of the young larvae to make haemoglobin before an external supply of iron has been established.

---

[1]Siddiqui (1975a) has reported more calcium in the plasma of male *Clarias batrachus*, also more iron and cholesterol, than in females.

The above report of zinc being more concentrated in the female gonad (Kondratovics, 1969: *Salmo gairdneri*) agrees with the findings of Berman and Vitin' (1968: same species), but the latter authors found more zinc in the *male* muscle, gill and bones. Copper, iron and manganese also tended to be more concentrated in male tissues, apart from the gonad.

Retinol (vitamin A_1) has been reported to be more concentrated in the livers of maturing males compared with females (Georgiev, 1972a: *Salmo gairdneri*). This could reflect the transfer of retinol by females to the developing ova for the future synthesis of visual pigments, but it could also indicate a greater mobilisation of liver lipid by the males, which leaves the retinol untouched and so increases its concentration (Volume 1, p. 291).

Carotenoids are extensively deposited in the ova of maturing females, and Crozier (1970: *Oncorhynchus nerka*) has reported that by the time spawning occurs, 85% of the astaxanthin present in the females is in the eggs, while the males still retain 95% of it in their skin.

The dorsal hump of *Oncorhynchus gorbuscha* is present only in migrating males. Robinson and Mead (1970) regarded it as an energy source, but the reason for lipid being accumulated in this particular location is obscure; there seems to be no corresponding reserve in the females.

The hepatic arginase activity has been reported by Onishi and Murayama (1969; 1970: various salmonids) to increase in males and decrease in females during maturation. As we shall see (p. 116), extra physical activity leads to increased nitrogen excretion, so perhaps the purpose of male arginase activity is to deal with the excretion of extra endogenous arginine, apart from any variations in dietary arginine that there may be.

In Volume 1 (p. 122) were tabulated a number of substances reported not to differ according to the sex of the fish. To these we may now add brain cholinesterase (Edwards, 1971: *Roccus americanus*), various nitrogenous extractives from muscle—*free* amino acids and dipeptides, urea, ammonia and trimethylamine oxide (Vyncke, 1970: *Squalus acanthias*), the guanine and cytosine content of liver DNA (Booke, 1968: several species) and the haematocrit, protein and urea of the blood (Yamashita, 1968b: *Sebastiscus marmoratus*). It is better to think of "differences not detected" rather than "no differences".

As we conclude this section on sex differences, we might do worse than spare a sympathetic thought for the choirmasters of boys' choirs. They must continually recruit new boys to replace the older ones whose voices have deepened during maturation, because of the sudden growth of the vocal chords in males which does not occur in females. Oddly

enough, a similar phenomenon occurs in *Opsanus tau*, in which the
swim bladders, after a period of equal growth between males and
females, grow more quickly in the males to produce a deeper sound
when vibrated by the drumming muscles (Fine, 1975). No doubt the
female toadfish, like female man, finds the sound attractive.

7.   AGING

There are few studies on the effects of aging on fish; those reported in Volume 1 are
largely anatomical, rather than chemical, showing the degeneration of various
tissues and sometimes their substitution by connective tissue. There is loss of skeletal
muscle and a degeneration of the thyroid, perhaps originating in loss of function by
the pituitary. The melting point of fish lipids tends to rise with age, and the serum
globulin increases.
    Well-known changes occur in mammalian collagen as a result of aging, but until
recently nothing has been reported on the connective tissues of fish.

Small fish species tend to live for a shorter time than large, but the
relationship is not a strict one. The two smallest species of fish in the
world are also the smallest known vertebrates, *Pandaka pygmaea*, which
reaches 11 mm in length, and *Mistichthys luzonensis* (up to 14 mm).
These have been reported by Liu and Walford (1970) to live for two
years in the laboratory, longer than, for example, any of the South
American "annual fishes" (*Cynolebias* spp.) which are considerably larger.

Cynolebias bellotti have been used for the general study of aging by Liu
and Walford (1969), who found emaciation, disturbance of equilibrium
and spinal curvature to be the most characteristic symptoms (Fig. 15).
Changes also appear in the gill filaments (Fig. 16) and the thyroid.

The reproductive systems of some species have been shown to degenerate in old age, though Gregory (1969) found no correlation between
the age of *Stizostedion vitreum* and the sperm count.

Woodhead studied changes in the testis (1974a) and ovary (1974b)
of Siamese fighting fish, *Betta splendens*. At the onset of aging, testicular
cells in all stages of development, including mature sperms, are still
present, but there is a marked reduction in their numbers. They still
resemble the cells of younger mature fish but are now clearly inter-
spersed with more connective tissue. In more aged fish these features
are more pronounced, the testis being atrophic and reduced in size,
and containing germ cells which can no longer be classified as belonging
to a particular stage. In extreme cases the testes consist only of isolated
atrophied cysts of spermatogonia lying within a network of connective
tissue. These changes resemble those occurring in the testis of hypophysectomised fish, so Woodhead (1974a) suggested that they result from a
decline in pituitary gonadotropins.

Both sexes of *Betta splendens* can live for a considerable period after the cessation of their reproductive lives, as in many other animals including man. The aged Socrates was once asked if he were still capable of intercourse, and is reputed to have replied "No, thank God." Evidently there are compensations.

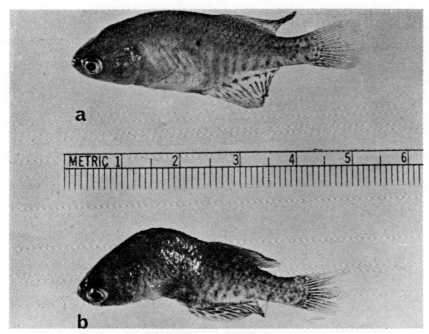

Fig. 15. (a) Normal female *Cynolebias bellotti*. (b) Aged female showing advanced lordosis, emaciation and exophthalmia. After Liu and Walford (1969). Reproduced with permission of Dr R. K. Liu.

The first degenerative change in the reproductive organs of female *Betta splendens* (Woodhead, 1974b) is a failure of vitellogenesis, together with atrophy of any yolky eggs already present, but with no obvious impairment of the growth and development of earlier stage oocytes. After this, oil deposition becomes irregular and finally ceases.

The first change to appear in the primary oocytes is pycnosis of the nucleus, then the cell becomes irregular in shape and stains in a non-uniform manner.

Finally the ovaries become shrunken, with thickened walls and much connective tissue within, amongst which can be seen a few degenerated eggs. Woodhead (1974b) concluded that in this species there is only partial failure of the pituitary, involving just the gonadotropic hormones.

Guppies (*Poecilia reticulata*) appear to age differently in that, although the ovaries become infiltrated with connective tissue, the oocytes in early stages of development show no signs of degeneration, and appear capable of subsequent ripening and fertilisation.

FIG. 16. (a) Normal gill epithelium × 100 (*Cynolebias bellotti*). (b) Degenerate gill epithelium from aged individual. After Liu and Walford (1969). Reproduced with permission of Dr R. K. Liu.

The quantity of connective tissue in and around the heart also increases as a manifestation of aging, the process being continuous from an early age (Santer, 1976: *Pleuronectes platessa*)

Previous studies on older *Gadus morhua* have indicated that death follows the excessive depletion associated with a sequence of annual spawnings (Volume 1, pp. 91–92), but some very old (16 to 19 years) specimens have since been found by Wiles (1969) to exhibit shrunken and withered ovaries. He regarded the condition as abnormal, noting that fibrous repair tissue is usually present in the spent ovaries of cod of like age but not to the same extent as in these fish. It seems likely that hormonal imbalance or insufficiency is occurring from time to time, and microscopic sections reveal clear areas, nodules or cysts in the ovarian walls, necrosis of the reproductive tissue and absence of germinal cells.

Greer-Walker's finding (1970) of a decline in the diameters of the muscle cells of the largest size of cod has already been illustrated (Fig. 9, p. 32). The comparable decline in the muscle fibres of rats has been assumed without question to be the result of senility (Tauchi, Yoshioka and Kobayashi, 1971), but Greer-Walker considered the possibility that in fish it might be a device to overcome internal friction which would have hindered the flexure of such a thick tail—much as a rope gains in flexibility if it is composed of finer strands.

As we have seen (p. 41), cod become more fecund as they grow older, and compensate by laying down increasing energy stores in the feeding season. However, it is possible that death eventually supervenes through the breakdown in the compensation mechanism with aging: Bogoyavlenskaya and Vel'tishcheva (1972) observed that Baltic cod reduce the intensity of lipid and glycogen deposition when they are more than 5 (male) or 6 (female) years old. This they regarded as a true manifestation of aging. I am beginning to wonder whether a progressive increase in the fecundity of cod (Volume 1, p. 90) resulting in their eventual death is in fact the whole story. The finding by Wiles (1969) of a *few* obviously senile ovaries seems to fit rather well with the Russian finding of a reduction in lipid and glycogen reserves. There is no more information available on cod at present, but some neat work by Jafri and Shreni (1975) on *Ophicephalus punctatus* is so similar as to strengthen doubts of "over-reproduction" and engender a more cautious attitude. In this species, like cod, fecundity increases with age so that larger fish tend to be more depleted by spawning, but there comes a time when it decreases again as the result of the aging. Liver cholesterol (Fig. 17) rises each year up to 4 years of age, and then drops sharply. Jafri and Shreni (1975) concluded that this is a manifestation of aging related to sexual activity and the demand for sex hormones which are derived from cholesterol. Changes in the cholesterol content may not follow the level of total lipid reserves, but the pattern does resemble that observed by Bogoyavlenskaya and Vel'tishcheva (1972).

Fish synthesise proteins at reduced rates as they grow older. Tano and Shirahata (1975) demonstrated a steady decline in the incorporation of radioactive uridine into the brain RNA of *Oncorhynchus nerka* with the passage of time, and Mataix, Gómez-Jarabo *et al.* (1976) found that the ingestion of food decreases with age, an effect independent of its protein content (*Salmo gairdneri*). This group also found a decrease in the protein conversion index and protein efficiency ratio with increased age (Gómez-Jarabo, Mataix *et al.*, 1976: same species). Sorvachev and Shatunovskii (1968: "flounder") found that the sum of *free* amino acids in the muscle is lower in older individuals and concluded that the rate of protein synthesis has fallen. The amount of blood albumin has also been shown to decrease (Adamova and Novikov, 1973: 3 species of herbivorous fish). These three findings all point in the same direction, so it is difficult to align the finding by Somkina and Krichevskaya (1968) that the *free* amino acids in the brains of several species actually increase with age.

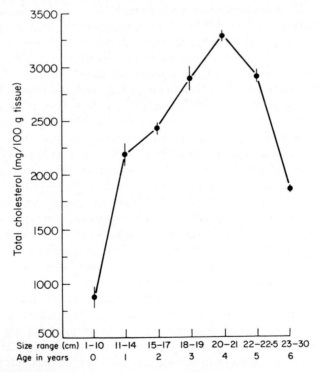

FIG. 17. Cholesterol in the livers of *Ophicephalus punctatus* of increasing age. After Jafri and Shreni (1975). Reproduced with permission of Dr A. K. Jafri.

It is to be expected that the requirements for different enzymes and other small-weight soluble proteins will change as the fish grow older, and alterations in the electrophoretic patterns of soluble proteins of the eye lens have been reported by Haen and O'Rourke (1969a: *Salmo*

gairdneri), of the muscle by Haen and O'Rourke (1969b: *Salmo trutta,
S. gairdneri*) and of the plasma by Pesch (1970: *Pseudopleuronectes
americanus*).

Most animals become less adaptable as they grow older. *Scardinius
erythrophthalmus* changes the proportions of the visual pigments rhodopsin
and porphyropsin in its retina in a regular annual cycle as light conditions change, but seems to lose much of its ability to do this after
about 5 years of age (Bridges and Yoshikami, 1970a). The authors
stressed that the change is not caused by older fish preferring to live
continuously in darker parts of the pond.

Sabodash (1969) has noticed that the zinc content of the eggs and
sperm of *Cyprinus carpio* declines as the fish grow older, particularly in
the second and third year of spawning. In eggs from carp aged 3, 6
and 11–14 years, the concentrations of zinc were found to be, respectively, 47·5, 29 and 16·5 mg per 100 g dry matter (Sabodash, 1970).
The reason is unknown, but at least the trend is progressive. The fall in
egg cholesterol, followed by a rise, as carp grow older, and the rise in
phospholipid, followed by a fall (Kim, 1974b) seem unlikely to be
simple consequences of aging.

It was remarked in Volume 1 (p. 128) that aging has been well
characterised in mammals through a study of their collagens, so that
the tissue could shed light on aging in fish. Nothing was then known
about fish connective tissues in this context, though it was realised that
one did not see obviously lined or wrinkled fish.

Some progress has now been made: fish collagen has turned out to
be of unusual interest and seems to be unique among vertebrates in
that, at least in *Gadus morhua*, a considerable proportion of it is renewed
annually, and so retains most of the characteristics of "young" collagen
from year to year (Love, Yamaguchi *et al.*, 1976). As we shall see more
fully later (p. 199), the annual cycle of depletion causes a marked
thickening of cod connective tissue, followed later in the year by its
being whittled down to its original thinness. The result is that the
collagen of myocommata of cod more than 100 cm long becomes just
fractionally less soluble in acid buffer compared with that of cod about
45 cm long, but mammalian collagen becomes many times less soluble
with aging (various authors quoted by Love, Yamaguchi *et al.*, 1976).

8. SPAWNING DEATH

The state of knowledge up to 1968 on spawning death was reviewed in Volume 1,
p. 112. Fish which spawn once and then die are the five species of *Oncorhynchus*, eels

(*Anguilla*) and lampreys (*Lampetra*). While starvation, as shown by a drop in glycogen levels at the time of spawning, may contribute to the death of the fish, life can be prolonged for only a limited period by giving food to the spawned fish. Widespread degeneration of internal organs and also of the pituitary occurs, and an inability to clear excess cortisol from the body after spawning seems to characterise fish in this state. Immature *Salmo gairdneri* implanted with pellets which slowly release cortisol into the blood stream develop all the symptoms of post-spawning degeneration seen in Pacific salmon, so this hormone seems to be central to the phenomenon. Further evidence that hormones are important in causing the death of the fish comes from the fact that castration prolongs life by several years.

More recent work confirms that hormones play an important part in the death of the fish, but Woodhead (1975) concludes that we still cannot ascribe death with any certainty to a particular hormone.

The activity of the fish during spawning is reflected in the levels of adrenaline and noradrenaline in the blood, which are higher than in fish newly entering the river (Fontaine, Mazeaud and Mazeaud, 1963: *Salmo salar*). These hormones are unlikely to be lethal, however, since the levels are higher still at metamorphosis (smoltification), and are higher after spawning in fish of good condition than in sick fish.

The thymus gland of *Leucopsarion petersi* atrophies remarkably during lethal spawning (Tamura and Honma, 1970). The spleen degenerates and becomes infiltrated with connective tissue, while the haematopoietic centre of the kidney also decreases. Thus a significant role is postulated for the loss of haemopoiesis, loss of immunity and endocrine imbalance in the spawning death of this species.

Triplett and Calaprice (1974) attempted to prolong the post-spawning life of *Oncorhynchus gorbuscha* and *O. nerka* by the administration of various hormones, but without success. Ascorbic acid was also administered, and, while it did not prolong life, at least it prevented the necrosis of the skin usually seen at this time. In the final stages, these authors noted a big increase in blood potassium, which could signify release by the disintegrating muscle cells. On the other hand, Natochin and Lavrova (1974) reported a *reduction* in blood potassium in spawning salmonids. Probably large fluctuations are common anyway.

Unlike *Oncorhynchus* species, many *Salmo salar* survive to spawn again. However, fewer males than females return (MacDonald, 1970, who reports only a single instance of male predominance in repeat spawners of this species), but it is not known whether male hormones are more toxic than those of females or that the savage fighting among males migrating upstream takes its toll. There may be a nutritional cause: male *Salmo salar*, at least in captivity, stop feeding some 8 weeks before spawning and several weeks after, while females continue to feed throughout the spawning period. Consequently among farmed salmon the sleekest, plumpest fish are found to be nearly all females (I. Mac-Farlane, personal communication, 1977).

A decline in cellular proliferation appears to precede the ultimate disfunction of most of the internal organs. Imura and Saito (1969) found that the absolute amounts of RNA[1] decreased in the liver, pyloric caecae, kidney, spleen, heart and muscle of *Oncorhynchus nerka kennerlyi* during spawning migration. Enzyme studies also seem to presage disaster. Márquez (1976: *Oncorhynchus gorbuscha*) found that GOT[2], LDH[3], α-hydroxybutyrate dehydrogenase and creatine phosphokinase all increase in the serum as spawning approaches, and noted that these enzymes rise also in the blood of man following cardiac infarction, damage to or degeneration of the liver, or kidney failure. It is not known why the enzymes rise in this way, but by analogy Márquez suggested that the rises indicate accelerated aging in the fish.

As spawning approaches, a decreasing ability of the liver to function properly further characterises these unfortunate fish. The decline in liver lipid is not just a measure of energy expended; the liver also loses its ability to synthesise triglycerides or cholesterol, as measured by failure to incorporate radioactive precursors (Phleger, 1971: *Oncorhynchus gorbuscha*). Trams (1969a) found that the livers of the same species have very low levels of microsomal azo-reductase activity when the fish have been caught on the spawning grounds, indicating a partial breakdown of the hepatic detoxication function. The liver also fails progressively in its ability to oxidise labelled palmitic acid to labelled CO_2.

Loss of liver function would obviously cause death. Trams (1969b: *Oncorhynchus gorbuscha*) postulated a degeneration just as fundamental in his suggestion that the central nervous system gradually ceases to control the pituitary, resulting in the functioning of several organs beginning to proceed autonomously instead of in a coordinated manner. Autonomy would clearly be incompatible with life. His suggestion was based on a decline in the cholinesterase activity of the pituitary.

Oncorhynchus gorbuscha and *O. nerka* were shown by Patton and Trams (1973) to suffer a striking reduction in the triglycerides of heart lipids after spawning. Authors quoted by Patton, Zulak and Trams (1975) have shown that fatty acids are of fundamental importance in the respiration of heart muscle, and are necessary to sustain the beating mechanism; contractions in heart tissue cultures cease with the loss of

---

[1]RNA, ribose nucleic acid, increases in concentration whenever cells are actively proliferating and can be used under certain conditions as a measure of the activity of growth (see p. 30).

[2]Glutamate-oxaloacetate transaminase.

[3]Lactic dehydrogenase.

lipase activity. Patton, Zulak and Trams (1975) suggested that the triglycerides of salmon heart serve to supply these necessary fatty acids. The desperate need of the fish for triglycerides is emphasised by their observation that, even after the fish has spawned, injected radioactive fatty acids are still actively incorporated into the triglycerides of the heart although the fish may be just a few hours from death. The big loss of heart triglycerides from whatever cause seems to be yet another reason why Pacific salmon cannot survive spawning.

In these days of advanced medicine it is rare to examine superficially healthy old people and find that they have something wrong with them; usually they have up to twenty malfunctions or diseases in evidence at the same time. Using a phrase like "programmed death" would be psychologically unacceptable in human medicine: here in considering salmon and the other genera it is almost inescapable, and it is remarkable how catastrophic decay seems to hit almost every aspect of the life machine.

2 Anatomical Diversity, Musculature and Swimming

A. Anatomical diversity

In Volume 1 the heterogeneous nature of fish muscle, formerly re-garded as a uniform material, was demonstrated and discussed at length, so as to codify a more meaningful procedure for sampling. In addition, a survey of the differences between white and dark muscle led to conclusions about their differing functions.

We shall now take the improved sampling as normal procedure, and see if subsequent studies tell us any more about the way in which the various tissues function, and in particular about how fish swim.

The varying nature of organs other than muscle can be dismissed in a few words. That the left ovary of *Mallotus villosus* is about 9 times more fecund than the right (Winters, 1971) is of little interest here, but it is within our remit to note that blood vessels change their nature according to their distance from the heart. Lander (1964) found that the content of arterial elastin in four species of elasmobranch declines from the proximal end of the ventral aorta through the afferent and efferent arteries up to the dorsal aorta. Presumably the arterial walls lose their need to stretch as the surges of pressure from the heart become smoothed out after passing through increasing lengths of pipe.

It was shown earlier that the concentration of vitamin A varies in different lobes of the liver (Volume 1, p. 38), and now we learn that glycogen also occurs in a non-uniform way, being most concentrated near the periphery of the liver lobe (Falkina and Davydova, 1970: *Cyprinus carpio*). These authors noted it as being common to find cells completely devoid of glycogen in the midst of glycogen-rich hepatic tissue.

A similar distribution of liver glycogen has been found by Khalilov and Inyushin (1966: quoted by Plisetskaya and Kus'mina, 1972: *Tinca tinca, Cyprinus carpio*), but Svoboda, Baranyiova and Vavruska (1972) found no significant differences between the glycogen concentrations of eight different parts of the hepatopancreas of a carp, though there was much variation between one fish and another. These anomalies perhaps relate to different degrees of satiation with glycogen in the fish used by the different workers.

Turning now to the bulk of white muscle, we find that no clear differences have ever been reported between the protein concentrations of the left and the right fillets[1] (Volume 1, pp. 35–36). More recently it has been shown that there is also no difference measurable between the concentrations of trimethylamine oxide (Yamagata, Horimoto and Nagaoka, 1969: *Thunnus albacares*). On the other hand, differences do appear in different areas within the one side, certain physical properties of the muscle (Bykov, 1969: *Cyprinus carpio*) and electropherograms of muscle extracts (Haen and O'Rourke, 1969b) being reported to change as one moves about the fillet.

In comparison with the dorsal region of the fish, the underside contains less volatile basic nitrogen (Aldrin and Grandgirard, 1971: *Thunnus albacares*) and more lipid (Alexander, 1970: *Arius dussumieri, Ophicephalus striatus*; Ackman and Eaton, 1971: *Scomber scombrus*). Such lipid distribution has already been discussed in Volume 1, pp. 36–37, and these reports only confirm previous findings.

Most of the investigations have centred on differences between the head and tail ends of the lateral muscle. Always one looks closely, hoping to find clues as to which part is the more active in swimming, but unfortunately there is little to help from published material.

The protein content of *Parastromateus niger* musculature does not vary appreciably between head and tail (Venkataraman, Solanki and Kandoran, 1968), nor does the protein, lipid or water of three *Caranx* spp. (Frontier-Abou, 1969), but most reports seem to show that the lipid content increases steadily towards the tail region (Volume 1, pp. 36–37; Venkataraman, Solanki and Kandoran, 1968: *Parastromateus niger*; Alexander, 1970: *Arius dussumieri, Ophicephalus striatus*; Wills and Hopkirk, 1976: *Anguilla australis*). Unfortunately these authors do not state definitely that the white muscle was freed from dark muscle before

---

[1]This and the following remarks apply only to "round" fish which are bilaterally symmetrical. The upper and lower fillets of flat fish do show some chemical differences.

analysis, and the lipid-rich dark muscle forms a steadily increasing proportion of the musculature towards the tail (Volume 1, p. 7). The fact could explain the presence of more lipid overall in the tail region, and also of more glycogen, which is richer in dark muscle than in white[1] (Volume 1, p. 20), and has been reported as more concentrated in the tail than the head region by various authors quoted by Manohar (1970), by Manohar (1970: *Esox lucius*) and by Morozova (1973: *Scorpaena porcus*). Glycogen has been shown not to vary in different parts of the musculature by Svobodova, Baranyiova and Vavruska (1972: *Cyprinus carpio*) and Morozova (1973: *Trachurus mediterraneus ponticus*), and actually to decrease towards the tail by Manohar (1970: *Catostomus commersonii*).

The most revealing papers relate to enzyme activities. Morishita and Takahashi (1969: *Seriola quinqueradiata, Salmo gairdneri, Scomber japonicus* and *Kareius bicoloratus*) observed a sharp increase in the activities of esterase and lipase in the musculature of the tail region, and point out that these two enzymes are more abundant in dark than in white muscle. Jankowsky (1968a: *Anguilla anguilla*) found that the respiratory activity of muscle increases towards the tail, and that the difference along the body cannot be explained by changes in water, protein or lipid content. He also found that the activity of cytochrome oxidase does not vary along the body provided that one is careful to sample only deep white muscle near the vertebral column: if one takes peripheral muscle near the tail the enzymic activity is much greater. Thus he concluded that the difference in oxygen uptake in muscle taken from various parts of the body originates in the different proportions of dark muscle in the samples.

Jankowsky's report undoubtedly contains the key to much of the work reported in this section, accounting for example for the apparent increase in lipid towards the tail. The greater concentrations of DNA in the tail region (Volume 1, p. 3) are explained by the smaller cell sizes and hence the greater number of cell nuclei in unit weight. The greater concentration of sodium (Volume 1, pp. 3 and 7) is probably explained by the greater proportion of extracellular space surrounding the narrower cells, and of caudal connective tissue which, unlike muscle, is rich in sodium and poor in potassium (Volume 1, reference 765).

Perhaps the conclusion to be deduced from this section is disappointingly simple considering the number of workers who have taken

---

[1]C. S. Wardle (personal communication) points out that this difference can be enhanced during capture stress, because white muscle glycogen is then largely converted to lactate whereas dark muscle glycogen does not seem to decrease. Much skill is required to obtain authentic glycogen values from white muscle without some loss.

the trouble to sample different parts of one fillet. The work tells us nothing about muscle function. We may sum the conclusions of both volumes by saying that several major constituents vary between the head and tail parts of the fillet. Lipid may vary through differences in the number of lipid storage cells, themselves distributed to achieve buoyancy and the correct orientation, and also through variations in the proportion of dark muscle in different parts of the (whole) musculature. The variations in other constituents probably originate in the unequal sizes of the muscle cells, the diameters of which are smaller towards the tail, and in the proportion of connective tissue, which increases.

B. Dark muscle

1. INTRODUCTION

The cells of the dark muscle which lies just under the skin of most species of fish are thinner than those of the white muscle, and contain much more haem pigment and cytochrome c. Many other chemical differences have been demonstrated, the most noteworthy being that dark muscle contains in most cases more glycogen and lipid and less protein and water than does white muscle. The more time a fish habitually spends in swimming, the more dark muscle it possesses, and certain very active species contain additional dark muscle deep within the musculature. It has up to now been generally agreed that white muscle is used sporadically and that it uses mainly carbohydrate as fuel, operating anaerobically, while dark muscle operates aerobically and continuously, using lipid. A persistent controversy has centred on the possible function of dark muscle as a supplementary liver, taking catabolites from white muscle and exchanging them for fuel. While most workers prefer the theory that dark muscle is in fact an active contractile organ in its own right, there is still some evidence on the other side, and controversy still enlivens the field.

Analytical differences between dark and white muscle were summed up in a large Table in Volume 1 (pp. 20–25). Reports of this kind published in the period under review will be disposed of in a similar way (Table 7). Some "new" compounds are described as more concentrated, or less concentrated, in dark muscle as compared with white, and on the whole there is good agreement with the observations listed in Volume 1. The most notable difference is over the concentration of trimethylamine oxide, which has now been shown by Tokunaga (1970a) to be consistently more concentrated in dark muscle only when the fish are migratory. Non-migratory fish have consistently less trimethylamine oxide in the dark muscle than the white. The true function of this compound is still incompletely worked out, although it was reported in Volume 1 (p. 288) to be more concentrated in the blood of more active fish.

The position of ATPase is equivocal, but rather more species show more activity of this enzyme in white muscle than dark, and Johnston, Frearson and Goldspink (1972) cite other authors supporting the correlation between the speed of contraction of a muscle and its ATPase[1] activity. White muscle is usually reckoned to be equivalent to the fast muscle of other animals. The striking contrast in the activities of this enzyme in at least one species is shown histochemically in Fig. 21 (p. 82).

Reports of higher lipid values in dark muscle are amply confirmed in Table 7, but, more interestingly, it obviously contains more glycogen as well. Any view of dark muscle as an aerobic and lipolytic tissue must therefore not exclude its additional ability to use carbohydrates for energy purposes. More will be said of this later. In the meantime let us see what advances have been made in the study of dark muscle since Volume 1 was completed.

2.   DARK MUSCLE IN GENERAL

In the first place, there are similarities linking the dark muscle of all vertebrates. Thus, rabbit dark muscle has less ATPase activity than white muscle (Syrovy, Gaspar-Godfroid and Hamoir, 1970), while higher vascularisation, number of mitochondria and activities of cytochrome oxidase and succinic dehydrogenase have been noted in the dark muscle of the domestic hen (Krompecher, Laczko et al., 1970) though these attributes were all lower than in heart muscle. Lipids were noted to be taken up preferentially by the dark fibres, rather than the "glycogen-utilising white fibres" of pigeon (Vallyathan, Grinyer and George, 1970), while exercising rats to exhaustion was found by Reitman, Baldwin and Holloszy (1973) to deplete the lipids from the dark, not the white fibres. Hess (1970, quoted by Gordon, 1972b) also noted the physiological similarities between the dark muscle fibres of fish and the slow fibres of other vertebrates, but warned that there are structural differences. Gordon (1972b) concluded that the white and dark fibres of fish should not be considered as completely equivalent to the fibres named similarly in the muscles of other vertebrates.

---

[1]ATPase (adenosine triphosphatase), which has an additional important role in salt excretion (p. 289), occurs in muscle where it splits adenosine triphosphate and in so doing releases energy for contraction.

TABLE 7

Chemical differences between dark and white muscle

a. *Constituent is more concentrated in the dark muscle*

Constituent	Species	Reference
Acid phosphatase	*Clarias magur*	Jafri and Mustafa (1976b)
	Heteropneustes fossilis	
	Scomber colias	Myzliwski, Zawistowski and Dabrowski (1969)
Adenosine triphosphatase	*Cyprinus carpio*	Syrovy, Gaspar-Godfroid and Hamoir (1970)
	Myxine glutinosa	Dahl and Nicolaysen (1971)
Alkaline phosphatase	*Clarias magur*	Jafri and Mustafa (1976b)
	Heteropneustes fossilis	
Aspartate aminotransferase	*Cyprinus carpio*	Masic and Hamm (1971a)
Bismuth	*Thunnus albacares*	Golovkin, Krainova *et al.* (1973)
Cathepsin B	*Cyprinus carpio*	Créac'h (1972)
Chromium	*Thunnus albacares*	Golovkin, Krainova *et al.* (1973)
Cobalt		
Copper		
Cytochrome oxidase	*Anguilla anguilla*	Malessa (1969)
		Boström and Johansson (1972)
Dehydroascorbic acid	*Catla catla*	Krishnamoorthy and Narasimhan (1972)
Diketogulonic acid		
Dimethylamine	*Anoplopoma fimbria*	Tokunaga (1970a)
	Chelidonichthys kumu	
	Cololabis saira	
	Cypselurus sp.	
	Katsuwonus pelamis	
	Konosirus punctatus	
	Parapristipoma trilineatum	
	Sardinops melanosticta	
	Scomber japonicus	
	Sebastes inermis	
	Seriola quinqueradiata	
	Theragra chalcogramma	
	Thunnus albacares	
	Thunnus obesus	
	Trachurus japonicus	
Esterase[b]	*Seriola quinqueradiata*	Morishita and Takahashi (1969)
Fumarase	*Anguilla anguilla*	Boström and Johansson (1972)
Glucose	*Cyprinus carpio*	Wittenberger, Coprean and Morar (1975)

Constituent	Species	Reference
Glucose-6-phosphate dehydrogenase	*Anguilla anguilla*	Boström and Johansson (1972)
Glycogen[ab]	*Cirrhina mrigala*	Bokdawala and George (1967a)
	Cyprinus carpio	Wittenberger, Coprean and Morar (1975)
	Harengula humeralis	Wittenberger, Coro *et al.* (1969)
	Katsuwonus pelamis	George (1975)
	Labeo fimbriatus	Bokdawala and George (1967b)
	Labeo rohita	
	Pollachius virens	Johnston and Goldspink (1973a)
	Salmo gairdneri	Dean (1969); Johnston (1975a); Nag (1972)
	Scomber colias	Myzliwski, Zawistowski and Dabrowski (1969)
	Scomber scombrus	
Glycogen phosphorylase	*Cyprinus carpio*	Murat, Parent and Balas (1972)
Glycolytic enzymes	*Cirrhina mrigala*	Bokdawala and George (1967a)
Haemoglobin[a]	*Cyprinus carpio*	Hamoir, Focant and Distèche (1972)
Hypoxanthine[a]	*Xiphias gladius*	Dyer and Hiltz (1969)
Iron	*Thunnus albacares*	Golovkin, Krainova *et al.* (1973)
Lead		
Lipase[a]	*Cirrhina mrigala*	Bokdawala and George (1967a)
	Kareius bicoloratus	Morishita and Takahashi (1969)
	Labeo fimbriatus	Bokdawala and George (1967b)
	Labeo rohita	
	Scomber japonicus	Morishita and Takahashi (1969)
	Seriola quinqueradiata	
Lipid[a]	*Alosa kessleri pontica*	Lisovskaya and Petkevich (1968)
	Brachydanio rerio	Waterman (1969)
	Cirrhina mrigala	Bokdawala and George (1967a)

continued overleaf

Table 7 (*continued*)

Constituent	Species	Reference
	Engraulis encrasicholus ponticus	Lisovskaya (1973)
		Lisovskaya and Petkevich (1968)
	Gadus morhua	Love, Hardy and Nishimoto (1975)
	Harengula humeralis	Wittenberger, Coro *et al.* (1969)
	Labeo fimbriatus	Bokdawala and George (1967b)
	Labeo rohita	
	Notothenia spp.	Lin, Dobbs and DeVries (1974)
	Salmo gairdneri	Dean (1969)
		Nag (1972)
	Scomber colias	Mysliwski, Zawistowski and Dabrowski (1969)
	Scomber scombrus	
	Trachurus mediterraneus ponticus	Lisovskaya (1973)
Malate dehydrogenase	*Anguilla anguilla*	Boström and Johansson (1972)
Mitochondria[a]		Jankowsky (1968a)
	Cyprinus carpio	Hamoir, Marechal and Bassleer (1973)
	Pollachius virens	Patterson and Goldspink (1972)
	Salmo gairdneri	Dean (1969)
		Nag (1972)
Myoglobin[a]	*Cyprinus carpio*	Hamoir, Focant and Distèche (1972)
Oxidative enzymes	*Cirrhina mrigala*	Bokdawala and George (1967a)
6-Phosphogluconate dehydrogenase	*Anguilla anguilla*	Boström and Johansson (1972)
Phospholipids[a]	*Engraulis encrasicholus ponticus*	Lisovskaya (1973)
	Scomber scombrus	Ackman and Eaton (1971)
	Trachurus mediterraneus Ponticus	Lisovskaya (1973)
Reducing sugars	*Cyprinus carpio*	Wittenberger, Coprean and Morar (1975)
Squalene	7 species of marine fish	Lewis (1971)
Succinic dehydrogenase	*Anguilla anguilla*	Malessa (1969)
	Brachydanio rerio	Waterman (1969)

Constituent	Species	Reference
	Cyprinus carpio	Brotchi (1968)
	Many species	Fukuda (1958b)
	Myxine glutinosa	Dahl and Nicolaysen (1971)
Taurine[a]	*Cyprinus carpio*	Partmann and Schlaszus (1973)
Triglycerides	*Engraulis encrasicholus ponticus*	Lisovskaya (1973)
	Trachurus mediterraneus ponticus	
Trimethylamine	*Anoplopoma fimbria*	Tokunaga (1970a)
	Chelidonichthys kumu	
	Cololabis saira	
	Cypselurus sp.	
	Katsuwonus pelamis	
	Konosirus punctatus	
	Parapristipoma trilineatum	
	Sardinops melanosticta	
	Scomber japonicus	
	Sebastes inermis	
	Seriola quinqueradiata	
	Theragra chalcogramma	
	Thunnus albacares	
	Thunnus obesus	
	Trachurus japonicus	
Trimethylamine oxide[a]	*Alosa kessleri pontica*	Lisovskaya and Petkevich (1968)
	Cololabis saira	Tokunaga (1970a)
	Engraulis encrasicholus ponticus	Lisovskaya and Petkevich (1968)
	Konosirus punctatus	Tokunaga (1970a)
	Sardinops melanosticta	
	Scomber japonicus	
	Seriola quinqueradiata	
	Thunnus albacares	Yamagata, Horimoto and Nagaoka (1969)
	Thunnus obesus	Tokunaga (1970a)
Ubiquinone	11 species	Higashi, Terada and Nakahira (1972)

b. *Constituent is less concentrated in the dark muscle*

ATPase	*Cyprinus carpio*	Syrovy, Gaspar-Godfroid and Hamoir (1970)
	Gadus morhua	Johnston, Frearson and Goldspink (1972)

continued overleaf

Table 7 (*continued*)

Constituent	Species	Reference
	Pleuronectes platessa	
	Pollachius virens	
	Salmo gairdneri	Nag (1972)
	Trigla lucerna	Johnston and Tota (1974)
Aluminium	*Thunnus albacares*	Golovkin, Krainova *et al.* (1973)
Amino acids, *free*, especially glycine and histidine	*Cyprinus carpio*	Partmann and Schlaszus (1973)
Ascorbic acid	*Catla catla*	Krishnamoorthy and Narasimhan (1972)
Calcium	*Thunnus albacares*	Golovkin, Krainova *et al.* (1973)
Cholesterol[ab]	*Trachurus mediterraneus ponticus*	Lisovskaya (1973)
Creatin[a]	*Salmo gairdneri*	Johnston (1975a)
Free fatty acids	*Engraulis encrasicholus ponticus*	Lisovskaya (1973)
	Trachurus mediterraneus ponticus	
Glycolytic enzymes	*Cyprinus carpio*	Hamoir, Focant and Distèche (1972)
Magnesium	*Thunnus albacares*	Golovkin, Krainova *et al.* (1973)
5'-Nucleotidase	*Clarias magur*	Jafri and Mustafa (1976b)
Potassium[a]	*Thunnus albacares*	Golovkin, Krainova *et al.* (1973)
Trimethylamine oxide[b]	*Anoplopoma fimbria*	Tokunaga (1970a)
	Chelidonichthys kumu	
	Cypselurus sp.	
	Lateolabrax japonicus	
	Parapristipoma trilineatum	
	Sebastes inermis	
	Theragra chalcogramma	
	Trachurus japonicus	Okaichi, Manabe and Hashimoto (1959)
		Tokunaga (1970a)
Vanadium	*Thunnus albacares*	Golovkin, Krainova *et al.* (1973)
Zinc[b]		

c. *No consistent difference between dark and white muscle*

Vitamin E	*Clupea harengus*	Engelhardt, Geraci and Walker (1975)

[a]Agreeing with observations on this constituent in Table 3, Volume 1.
[b]Disagreeing.

3.   ANATOMICAL FEATURES

a.   *Vascularity*

Dark muscle is well supplied with blood vessels in order to maintain its continuous function. We can see these (Fig. 18) in the section of dark muscle of *Brachydanio rerio* prepared by Waterman (1969), who also demonstrated histologically the high level of glycogen (Fig. 19) reported in the chemical literature. Cameron (1975) used radioactive microspheres to follow the distribution of blood flow to the tissues from the dorsal aorta of *Thymallus arcticus*. He found that the white muscle of the

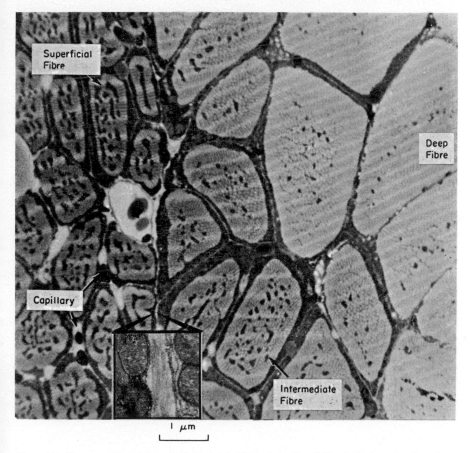

Fig. 18. Cross-section through dark and white muscle of *Brachydanio rerio*, showing blood capillaries in the dark muscle. Reproduced with permission of Professor R. E. Waterman, who kindly supplied the picture.

whole fish accounts for about 50% of the blood flow, but only because
of its greater mass: on the basis of unit weight, the dark muscle receives
about ten times as much blood as the white. The superiority of blood flow
probably explains the fact that the temperature of dark muscle is higher
than that of the white (Lindsey, 1968, deduced from data in reference
203, Volume 1; Carey and Teal, 1969a; *Isurus oxyrhynchus, Lamna nasus*).

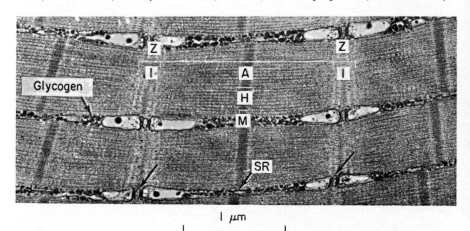

I μm

FIG. 19. Longitudinal section through dark muscle of *Brachydanio rerio*, showing
glycogen granules. SR, sarcoplasmic reticulum. Reproduced with permission of
Professor R. E. Waterman, who kindly supplied the picture.

Johnston and Goldspink (1973b) noticed how the lactate levels in
the white muscle of *Carassius carassius* take up to 8 hours to fall to the
resting level after strenuous exercise, in contrast to that of the dark
muscle which has dropped within 30 minutes. This difference they
attributed to the difference in circulation.

Lactic dehydrogenase (LDH) exists in two forms known as H (found
in heart muscle) and M (found in ordinary white muscle), which can
be separated electrophoretically (Volume 1, Fig. 17). Gesser and
Poupa (1973) concluded that the relative distribution of the two forms
is governed by the oxygen availability in the tissue, the heart being
very vascular and white muscle having little blood supply. Dark muscle
has an LDH almost exclusively of the "heart" type, again suggesting
good vascularity.

b.   *Quantity*

The proportion of dark muscle to white in a section across the musculature changes as one moves along the fish. Malessa (1969: *Anguilla*

anguilla) found it comprising 11 to 14·5% of the total musculature about 10 cm posterior to the anus. Greer-Walker and Pull (1975) measured the proportion in many species from histological cross-sections at a place one third of the fish length from the tail. The highest value given was for *Scomber colias*, an active fish, at 29·8%. *Melanogrammus aeglefinus* has 12·5% at the sample site, *Pollachius virens* has 10·8% and *Merlangius merlangus* 11·7%. *Gadus morhua* has 17% of dark muscle at a site one third of the fish length from the tail, as distinct from immediately anterior to the last dorsal fin (20·5%: Greer-Walker, 1970), or posterior to the last dorsal fin (31 to 36%: Love, Robertson *et al.*, 1974a, calculated from the quantity of haem pigments present). Nag (1972), who found 15% of dark muscle in the tail region of *Salmo gairdneri* by weight, considered the increase in dark muscle towards the tail end to be of importance in the mechanics of swimming, having regard to the concept that the caudal peduncle[1] together with the caudal fin acts as a "main locomotory organ". Gatz (1973) also cut sections in the middle of the caudal peduncle to obtain a value of 12·5% in the same species. Over the whole musculature, the *average* amount of dark muscle has been calculated to be 7·4% of the myotomal mass in *Carassius carassius* (Johnston and Goldspink, 1973d).

Having quoted all these figures, we must now add a warning that the actual amount of dark muscle present increases somewhat when fish are acclimated to lower temperatures (Malessa, 1969: *Anguilla anguilla;* Wodtke, 1974: *Anguilla anguilla;* I. Johnston, personal communication, 1976: *Carassius auratus*) and this factor was not taken into account by the various workers who measured them.

c. *Non-uniformity of dark muscle*

Small differences have been detected in dark muscle from different sites. Greer-Walker (1970: *Gadus morhua*) observed a slight increase in the diameters of the individual cells taken from places increasingly near the tail, and Frontier-Abou (1969: *Caranx ignobilis, C. Sexfasciatus* and *C. Stellatus*) found that while the "proximate"[2] composition of white muscle is essentially the same from one end of the animal to the other, the dark muscle contains more lipid in the anterior part of the fish and conversely more water and protein in the posterior part. During the fattening period, it is the anterior dark muscle which accumulates most of the lipids.

---

[1]The most posterior bit of real body flesh just before the tail fin.
[2]Protein, lipid, water and ash.

d.   *Dark muscle at other sites*

Webb (1970, quoted by Webb, 1971) gave a figure of 4% for the proportion of clearly demarcated dark muscle in *Salmo gairdneri*, but found that
there was in addition about three times this quantity present as single
dark fibres scattered amongst the white muscle, making an overall
figure in excess of 16%. The high figure in the caudal peduncle of cod
obtained by Love, Robertson *et al.* (1974a), being calculated from the
concentrations of haem pigments in white and dark muscle, presumably includes such individual isolated dark muscle cells as well, although
their contribution to the total figure is not known. The interpenetration
of white muscle with dark is enhanced in salmonids, so much so that
the white muscle is designated "mosaic" muscle, meaning a mosaic of
white and dark cells. These small-diameter fibres occurring in the bulk
of the myotome differ from those in "pure" dark muscle under the skin
in the amount of ATPase present, which resembles that of the surrounding white muscle (Johnston, Ward and Goldspink, 1975).

As already stated, the rays and puffer fish have dark muscle supplying
power to their propellant fins, and in the same way the dark muscle of
antarctic nototheniid fish is restricted to the pectoral girdle: it is the
pectoral fins which propel the fish during sustained low-speed cruising
(Lin, Dobbs and DeVries, 1974). A mixture of dark and white fibres
has also been reported in the jaw muscle of *Salmo gairdneri*, the dark
presumably for the continuous jaw movements associated with respiration and the white for suddenly siezing prey (P. Tytler, private
communication). Figure 20 shows typical dark muscle taken from the
jaw muscle (*adductor mandibularis*): the large lipid globules are noteworthy and confirm the many chemical studies. The numerous mitochondria (m) tend to be globular in shape. Munshi, Ojha and Mittal
(1975) have reported mixtures of fibres in the jaw and opercular
muscles of *Bagarius bagarius* as well, but the phenomenon is not universal
and the *adductor mandibularis* muscles of *Channa punctatus* (Ojha and Munshi
1975) and *Macrognathus aculeatum* (Ojha, 1975) contain only white
fibres.

The extra deep-seated dark muscle, occurring in tunas in addition to
the ordinary (superficial) dark muscle, has always been a puzzling
feature. Certainly tunas are very active fish, but then it would be
expected that they would simply have a larger proportion of dark
muscle rather than a different distribution. Ameyaw-Akumfi (1975:
Katsuwonus pelamis) has now put forward an interesting explanation,
based on a study of the tendon system and the organisation of the
myotomes. It is that virtually the whole of the tuna body muscle acts

on the caudal peduncle and the tail fin, so as to produce extensive movement of the tail with negligible undulations of the body, this type of movement being generally recognised as characteristic of swiftly swimming fish. Norman (1963, quoted by Ameyaw-Akumfi, 1975) proposes that the powerful forward thrust of tunas originates in the crescent shape of the caudal fin. Ameyaw-Akumfi (1975) concludes that the shape of the myotomes makes undulatory swimming almost impossible, so that even at slow speeds the tuna derives most of its propulsion from movement of the tail fin and caudal peduncle.

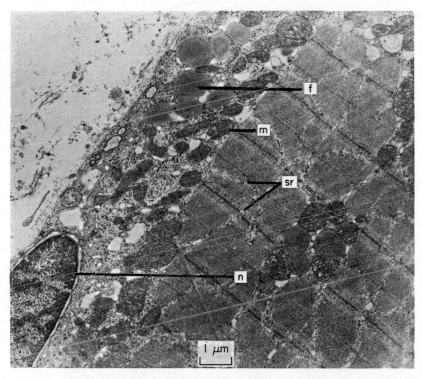

FIG. 20. Longitudinal section through the dark muscle of the *adductor mandibularis* (jaw muscle) of *Salmo gairdneri*. f, Lipid droplets; m, mitochondrion; sr, sarcoplasmic reticulum; n, nucleus. Reproduced with permission of Dr P. Tytler, who kindly supplied the photograph.

Still on the subject of active swimming in tunas, Johnston and Tota (1974) have pointed out that while the ATPase activity of the dark muscle of the gurnard *Trigla lucerna* is only 23% of that of its white muscle (it contracts more slowly), the ATPase activity of tuna (*Thunnus thynnus*) dark muscle is as much as 50% of that of its white muscle, suggesting that although the dark muscle is used in continuous swimming, it has a relatively high rate of contraction in these active fish. These authors also showed that the ATPase activities of the superficial and deep-seated dark muscles are about the same.

While the ATPase activity of tuna dark muscle is about twice that of the gurnard and other investigated species, the enzymic activity of white muscle is similar in all species.

The contrast in ATPase activities between white and dark muscle in *Salmo gairdneri* is illustrated histochemically in Fig. 21.

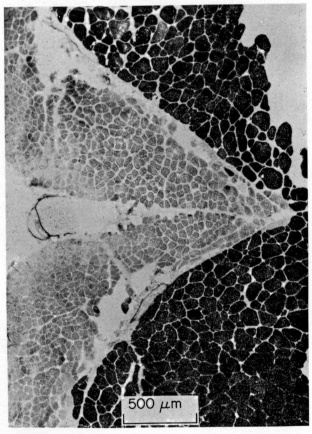

FIG. 21. Section of *Salmo gairdneri* myotome cut in the region of the lateral line and stained for ATPase activity. The pale triangle in the middle is dark muscle (little enzyme activity) and the two intensely stained parts are white muscle (strong activity). After Johnston, Ward and Goldspink (1975). Reproduced with permission of Dr I. Johnston, who kindly supplied the photograph.

e. *Intermediate pink fibres*

As stated in section (d) above, isolated dark fibres can occur scattered through the main bulk of white muscle, especially in salmonids. However, situated between the lateral dark muscle and the adjacent white or mixed muscle there is a group of "pink" fibres, which appear to be intermediate in function between the other two. They have been extensively studied by members and ex-members of Goldspink's group, and a few examples are shown diagrammatically in Fig. 22. A section from *Carassius carassius* musculature is shown in Fig. 23.

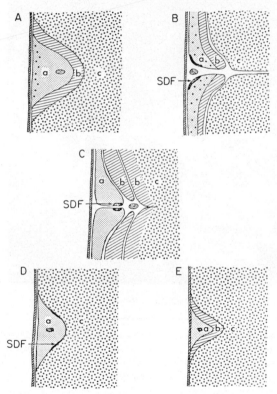

Fig. 22. Histological distribution of different muscle types in the mytomal muscle under the skin. A, *Mugil cephalus;* B, *Pollachius virens;* C, *Carassius carassius;* D, *Chanda ranga;* E, *Mollienesia* sp.; a, dark muscle; b, intermediate pink fibres; c, white muscle; SDF, very small diameter fibres. After Johnston, Patterson *et al.*, (1974). Reproduced with permission of Dr I. Johnston.

These fibres have an intermediate level of staining for oxidative enzymes and lipids (George and Bokdawala, 1964, quoted by Johnston,

Ward and Goldspink, 1975, who obtained similar results for succinic dehydrogenase). The ATPase intensity on the other hand is high, resembling that of the white muscle (Johnston, Patterson *et al.*, 1974: several species).

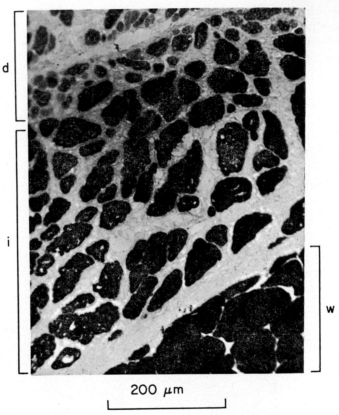

200 μm

FIG. 23. Section through the lateral musculature of *Carassius carassius*. d, dark muscle; i, intermediate pink fibres; w, white muscle. After Johnston, Patterson *et al.* (1974). Reproduced with permission of Dr I. Johnston, who kindly supplied the photograph.

Patterson, Johnston and Goldspink (1975) pointed out that a description of the division of labour between dark and white muscle fibres would be incomplete without a knowledge of the metabolism and function of these intermediate fibres. They suggested that their occurrence might be associated with a particular type of locomotory activity, since in some species the quantity present is comparable with that of the dark fibres.

f. *Fine structure*

As we have seen (Volume 1, Fig. 14; this volume, Fig. 23), the diameters of dark muscle cells are smaller than those of white. There are
also differences in the dimensions of the myofilaments and in the
volumes and surface areas of the T-system[1] and sarcoplasmic reticulum.
In *Salmo gairdneri* (Nag, 1972), the white muscle contains nearly three
times as much sarcoplasmic reticulum as does the dark, and it is not
unusual to find in the fast muscle of other animals a sarcoplasmic
reticulum with a very large surface area which can be related to the
increased calcium uptake during the contraction of the myofilaments.
Nag considers that the rate of contraction is limited by specific calcium
binding and the transporting activity of the membranes of the sarcoplasmic reticulum, also the surface area of the reticulum relative to the
sarcoplasmic volume. The transverse tubules are wider in white muscle,
and so are the terminal cisternae (illustrated in Fig. 57a). These structural
differences between dark and white muscle do not appear to be universal. In *Pollachius virens* no significant difference has been found
between the proportions of sarcoplasmic reticulum or T-system in the
two types of fibre (Patterson and Goldspink, 1972). The disparity
between *Salmo gairdneri* and *Pollachius virens* is unexplained, but could
perhaps relate to the capacity for relatively fast habitual swimming
exhibited by the latter species. Patterson and Goldspink (1972) consider that *Pollachius virens* is the exception, and that other vertebrates
do show variations in the proportion of sarcoplasmic reticulum and
T-system according to fibre type.

The ratio of the numbers of mitochondria in dark and white muscle
is 7:3 in *Salmo gairdneri* (Nag, 1972), but it can be more than this: the
proportion of total fibre area in *Anguilla anguilla* occupied by mitochondria is 15% in dark muscle but less than 1% in white (Jankowsky,
1968a). There are even more mitochondria in the dark muscle of
Pollachius virens: 25·4% as against 1·2% in white (Patterson and
Goldspink, 1972).

Mitochondria in dark muscle have been observed to be globular in
shape (Fig. 20, p. 81), those in white being more elongated (Fig. 24).
Many of those from dark muscle appear to contain a larger number of
cristae (Nag, 1972: *Salmo gairdneri;* see also Volume 1, reference 194).
The mitochondria from dark muscle have also been reported to be
more metabolically active, those from deep-seated dark muscle consuming three times as much oxygen as those from white muscle when

---

[1]A system of tubules which penetrate the cells, illustrated in Volume 1, Fig. 12.

the complete electron transport chain is operative (Modigh and Tota, 1975: *Thunnus thynnus*).

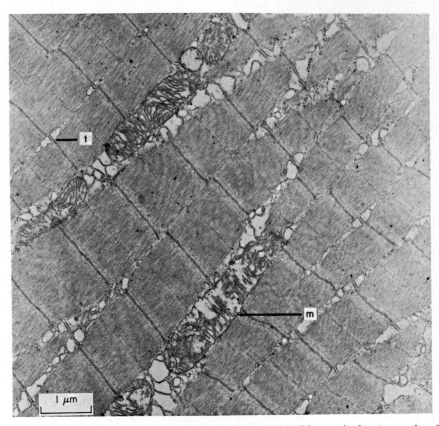

FIG. 24. Longitudinal section through the "mosaic" (white-equivalent) muscle of *Salmo gairdneri* showing the elongated shape of white muscle mitochondria in contrast to those from dark muscle (see Fig. 20). t, triad of the "T" system; m, mitochondrion. Reproduced with permission of Dr P. Tytler, who kindly supplied the photograph.

4.   SOME THOUGHTS ON WHITE MUSCLE

Up to now we have concentrated almost exclusively on dark muscle and its adaptation for slow continuous contraction, the white muscle being dismissed as everything which dark muscle is not, or as a mass of inactive and largely unused tissue which is called upon just occasionally, like an army in peace-time. It is probably a good idea, therefore, to pause for a moment to realise that white muscle is also well designed in its role as a "coiled spring", and a coiled spring which is in fact

frequently used and rewound. Larval fish appear to possess only white
muscle for a while (Greer-Walker, 1968: *Gadus morhua*) and their movement is characterised by a series of quick darts. Fish in an exercise
channel can be seen to undulate steadily and unremarkably at low
speeds, but when the water flow is increased beyond a certain speed
they drift backwards, unable to keep up, until with a sudden violent
kick of the tail they are back in the desired place, having used white
muscle.

The white muscle of fish at the microscopic level has been described
by Best and Bone (1973), who suggest that it has been so constructed as
to afford the largest number of contractile units within a given space.
Thus there are few blood capillaries (in this case, paucity of blood
supply can actually be considered as a possible advantage) and the
nerve fibres do not pass along between the muscle fibres. The larger
diameter of the muscle fibres means a smaller proportion of sarcolemma
and extracellular space, and the greatly reduced number of mitochondria again leaves more space for myofilaments. Like Jankowski
(1968a), these authors quote a figure of 15% as the proportion of cross-
sectional area of slow muscle occupied by mitochondria. Patterson and
Goldspink (1973a) give actual figures for the proportion of contractile
material in *Carassius carassius*: 89·6% of the total fibre volume in white
muscle, compared with only 72·2% in dark.

Best and Bone (1973) reason that the power required for fast swimming must be greatly in excess of that needed for slow cruising, even a
modest increase in speed needing a great deal of additional power. The
penalty of having such a concentrated mass of power units is that it
can operate only anaerobically and for short periods. However, as we
shall see on p. 105, the anaerobic muscle will hypertrophy if the fish is
forced to swim quickly over a prolonged period, and so presumably
it can increase its effectiveness.

There is a limit to the speed at which even the white muscle can
contract, and this curtails the maximum speed of the fish ("stride rate"),
despite any hypertrophy that may have occurred. The maximum speed
of contraction varies with the size of the fish, becoming progressively
slower as the fish grow, which is the reason for the extremely rapid
darts that tiny fish can make (Wardle, 1975, 1977). A cod 10 cm long
is capable of swimming in bursts of 25 body-lengths per second, while
a mere 6 per second is the limit for a fish 1 m long (same references).

The size of the units which we are talking about is illustrated in an
example by Wardle (1975), who showed that the shortest time in which
a cod 73·4 cm long could contract one lateral muscle completely was
40 ms.

5. COMPARISON BETWEEN DARK MUSCLE AND OTHER TISSUES

a. *Heart muscle*

If we accept that the strip of lateral dark muscle operates more or less continuously, noting that fish which swim without pause for all of their lives possess more of it, then it is not difficult to see similarities between dark muscle and heart tissue. A few parallels have been drawn in Volume 1, p. 30, and the red colour, vascularity, large number of mitochondria and continuous activity in the heart make it an obvious choice for comparison. The morphological similarity of the two tissues was also pointed out by Dean (1969). In Volume 1, Fig. 17, it was shown that dark muscle contains the isozyme of lactic dehydrogenase found in heart muscle rather than in white muscle, and this observation has since been confirmed by other writers (Lush, 1970: *Pollachius virens, Gadus morhua*; Wilson, Whitt and Prosser, 1973: *Carassius auratus*). The "heart" isozyme is thought to be associated with a more aerobic metabolism, in which lactate is metabolised into the Krebs cycle.

On the whole, dark muscle seems to be somewhat less metabolically active than heart muscle, containing, for example, a smaller proportion of the "heart" isozyme of lactic dehydrogenase than does heart muscle itself (Jeng and Chiang, 1974: *Scomber australasicus*). Hamoir, Focant and Distèche (1972: *Cyprinus carpio*) showed that dark muscle possesses less myoglobin and haemoglobin than are found in heart muscle, but that each of these tissues possesses more than occur in white muscle. Modigh and Tota (1975: *Thunnus thynnus*) compared enzyme activities and found that the highest values of succinic dehydrogenase and succinate cytochrome C reductase activities are to be found in the mitochondria of the outer myocardial layer, then in those of the deep-seated dark muscle, the inner myocardial layer and the white muscle, in that order.

b. *Liver*

To point out similarities between dark muscle and liver at this late stage is not to reopen the whole controversy of active contractile tissue *versus* metabolic tissue as the role of dark muscle. We have seen enough evidence in both volumes by now to realise that dark muscle is normally a contractile organ liberally supplied with the means of continuous aerobic metabolism and able to perform physical work indefinitely within a limited range of output. Even the innervation and the mechanism of membrane excitation are thought to be similar to those of the white muscle (Yamamoto, 1972: *Carassius auratus*). Braekkan's original thesis (Volume 1, p. 27 onwards) was based largely on similarities in the vitamin composition of dark muscle and liver, and these are now insufficient as they stand to identify dark muscle as a provincial branch of the hepatic system. We know that dark muscle is metabolically active: the issue now is whether it carries out metabolic services on behalf of the white muscle or not. Let us examine the evidence.

Most of the thoughts on dark muscle function in this context are based on studies of its carbohydrate metabolism during exercise. The breakdown of lipid is slow and does not seem to correlate with fatigue in forced swimming (Pritchard, Hunter and Lasker, 1971: *Trachurus symmetricus*). These writers were able to measure a decline in dark muscle lipid concentration only after a swimming period of 6 hours at fairly low speeds. On the other hand, failure to swim after exercise is linked to almost complete depletion of glycogen *in white muscle only*. The manner of glycogen use in the dark muscle mirrors that in the liver, declining only slightly over a prolonged period and not correlating with failure to swim. This finding is not surprising in the light of Wittenberger's calculation (1972: *Scomber scombrus*) that the glycogen turnover in dark muscle is 40 times that in white, which would indicate that it is replaced as used.

We are therefore left with a situation in which the white muscle after exercise contains almost no glycogen and much lactate, while in close proximity there is dark muscle with its source of energy apparently hardly touched. Patterson and Goldspink (1972: *Pollachius virens*) noted the very small numbers of mitochondria present in white muscle, less than one twentieth of the number in dark, and concluded that if white muscle were used at intermediate speeds there simply was not the oxidative machinery present to deal with such a build-up of lactic acid[1], conceding therefore a possible element of truth in the idea of dark muscle assisting as a metabolic organ. Against this idea is the very great difference in time needed for recovery in the two tissues: Johnston and Goldspink (1973b) noted that the lactate levels of *Carassius carassius* white muscle have still not returned to the unexercised state 5 hours after strenuous exercise, while in dark muscle less than 30 minutes suffices. Similarly, glycogen is replaced rapidly in dark muscle, slowly in white, so if the difference in energy reserves after exercise is in fact caused by differences in the rates of diffusion, then the concept of dark muscle

---

[1]Basile, Goldspink *et al.* (1976) have suggested that some of it might be metabolised by the very active mitochondria of spongy heart muscle—yet another line of thought.

supplying materials to the white receives a setback—how would the metabolites get into the white muscle?

Only one worker seems to have demonstrated actual transfer of metabolites between the tissues: Dr Carol Wittenberger has tackled the problem with great persistence, and appears in the end to have forged the framework of a convincing case.

Earlier papers were equivocal. He noted that *Cyprinus carpio* struggling in air or swimming moderately exhibit a build-up of lactate in the dark muscle and liver only, but not in the white muscle. This was interpreted (reference 1353, Volume 1) by assuming that lactate was formed in *white* muscle, but then diffused into the dark muscle. It is difficult to be enthusiastic about this interpretation, bearing in mind the slow diffusion possible throughout the white muscle. Extirpation of dark muscle in *Trachurus mediterraneus ponticus* "provoked strong disturbances of muscle performance" (Wittenberger, 1968b), but such an operation would be bound to interfere with performance in ways other than metabolic—notably nervous. Forced contractions of isolated muscle (dark and white together) were found to cause decreases in the glycogen of the dark muscle only, but here again the effect could have been caused by the highly artificial conditions; perhaps the contractions were carried largely by the dark muscle, and the determination of glycogen in white muscle is difficult anyway because of its low concentration and rapid decline after death. One could go on. However, recent work has yielded results of a much more stimulating character.

Isolated pieces of dark and white muscle from *Cyprinus carpio* were incubated, either separately or still joined as whole musculature. It was found (Wittenberger, 1973) that, as one would expect, the glycogen content of both tissues decreased during the incubation, but then there was a surprise: where the dark and white muscle were still joined as in life, the decrease was proportionately the same in both tissues, but when they were separated and incubated under identical conditions, the glycogen in the white muscle decreased far more than that of the dark, suggesting that in the intact whole musculature there was transfer of glucose from dark muscle to white. The circulatory system had of course been destroyed in isolating the tissue, but nevertheless this was a remarkable finding. Similarly, the lactate content of dark muscle was shown to increase more during incubation if white muscle was still attached to it.

Wittenberger, Coprean and Morar (1975) then added various substances to the incubation medium. Phloridzin reduces membrane transport of glucose, and so was considered likely to influence its transfer between the two tissues. Such proved to be the case. Combined pieces of muscle (white attached to dark) were incubated in a glucose-free medium, when it was found that the glycogen decreased in both tissues. If phloridzin was also present, the glycogen diminished much more in the white muscle, whereas it decreased less in the dark muscle, the implication being that in the absence of the drug the glycogen is being transferred as glucose from the dark muscle to the white, helping to keep up the level in the latter tissue, whereas phloridzin interfered with this transfer. There was also less free glucose in white muscle and more of it in dark muscle after incubation with phloridzin.

It seems to be impossible to load dark muscle with labelled glycogen so as to observe its appearance later in the white: injected glucose would distribute itself between the two tissues, and it could still be argued that the injected carbohydrate might behave differently from the natural carbohydrate resource of the fish. However, by following carbohydrate decay, Wittenberger and his colleagues have gone a long way towards providing evidence that stands up well to criticism.

When dark muscle by itself was incubated in a glucose solution, no glycogen loss occurred, and whenever insulin was present as well the glycogen even increased. However, when the dark muscle was attached to white, the glycogen in it decreased in the presence of glucose, the decrease not being diminished in the additional presence of insulin. As a corollary, insulin reduced the loss of glycogen seen when white muscle was incubated by itself in glucose solution, but reduced it more when the white muscle was joined to dark. These findings suggested to the group that the insulin had enhanced the transfer of glucose from dark muscle to white.

The only doubt which still gently nags concerns the transfer of so much material between the two tissues in the absence of circulation. Wittenberger envisages direct transfer of substances from cell to cell, bearing in mind evidence from other workers. A comparatively rapid diffusion through the extracellular space is also not unreasonable.

The remaining information associating dark muscle with liver can be disposed of briefly, as it comprises similarities in composition or behaviour which may or may not be coincidental. Thus, slices of carp liver and dark muscle oxidise glucose at the same rate (Wittenberger and Deaciuc, 1970), and injection of ^{14}C glucose into dark muscle results in strong labelling of both this tissue and liver (Wittenberger, 1972: *Scomber scombrus*). Annual variations in the level of glycogen in dark muscle show, as in liver, a minimum in July and higher values in winter (Murat, 1976a: *Cyprinus carpio*), while cold acclimation of *Anguilla anguilla* results in a comparable increase in the proportion of mitochondrial protein in both tissues (Wodtke, 1974). Finally, dark muscle resembles liver in the quantities of lipid (Wittenberger, Coro *et al.*, 1969) and squalene (Lewis, 1971) present.

Apart from the last two observations, this list of similarities at least shows us that dark muscle and liver are both active in metabolism. On the other hand they differ in that liver is much more important in the synthesis of urea than is dark muscle (Vellas and Serfaty, 1974) and some other liver functions, such as the formation of bile, seem unlikely to be delegated to the dark muscle.

Verbal discussions with workers actively studying dark muscle at the present time lead one away from the earlier concept that dark muscle is aerobic and powered by lipid, as distinct from white muscle (anaerobic and powered by carbohydrate). By general consent, dark muscle, while more aerobic than white, can use any form of energy source and operate continuously.

It was always difficult in any case to regard lipid as the sole or even the principal fuel when the glycogen concentration of dark muscle is so much higher than that of the white—indeed, Shul'man, Sigaeva and Shchepkin (1973) have shown that over a long period of forced exercise it is the white muscle which consumes the more lipid, at least in *Trachurus mediterraneus ponticus*. In addition, Crabtree and Newsholme (1972) have found that hexokinase has greater activity in dark muscle than in white, emphasising the importance of glucose as a source of energy in dark muscle. As long ago as 1967, Bokdawala and George (1967a: *Cirrhina mrigala*) showed that dark muscle fibres are loaded with lipid, lipase and the oxidative enzymes, and hence are well adapted for aerobic metabolism using lipid for energy—but that they also contain high concentrations of glycogen and the glycolytic enzymes indicating that they are well adapted both for synthesising and using glycogen. The only other point to be made is that in spite of its incessant use, or perhaps because of it, the speed of contraction of dark muscle is slower than that of white, as shown by its lower ATPase activity (Johnston, Frearson and Goldspink, 1972; various authors quoted by Bilinski, 1974).

After pointing out that dark muscle is better adapted than white to synthesise both glycogen and triglycerides, Bilinski (1974) says:

> The possibility that, compared with mammals, the red and white muscles of fish represent two separate locomotor systems which utilise different metabolites seems unlikely from a biochemical point of view. Although pronounced quantitative differences in enzyme activities exist in fish between the red and white skeletal muscle, there is no evidence for a strict compartmentation between the two types with respect to the aerobic and anaerobic pathways or with respect to the utilisation of fatty acids and carbohydrates.

This more or less expresses the present view of the fish muscular system, but there clearly is compartmentation between aerobism and anaerobism.

6. DARK AND WHITE MUSCLE IN STARVATION

The ways in which fish adapt to starvation are considered in detail later (p. 166). Here we note the relative priorities given by the starving fish to the two muscle types during their mobilisation to maintain life.

It is impressive to see how extremely starved fish still cruise apparently effortlessly, even when they are known to have extensive disorganisation of the white muscle and a water content of over 90%. The reason is that although the activity of the catheptic enzymes has been seen to be greater in dark muscle than in white (Y. Makinodan, personal communication, 1977), dark muscle is in fact less changed by starvation, and is able to continue functioning oblivious of the destruction all around it (see Fig. 59b). Patterson and Goldspink (1973a: *Carassius carassius*) found that starvation leads to no significant loss of contractile material in the dark muscle, the most significant changes being a decrease in mitochondria from 16·2 to 5·9% of the fibre volume and an increase in the volumes of sarcoplasmic reticulum and T-system. Munro and Love (unpublished: *Gadus morhua*) have demonstrated a loss in the activity of succinic dehydrogenase in dark muscle during starvation, and, since it is a mitochondrial enzyme, the loss presumably also reflects mitochondrial destruction, which is illustrated in Fig. 25.

Water and protein determinations confirm the differing responses of dark and white muscle. Probably because of the greater concentration of contractile units, white muscle in nourished fish contains less water than dark[1]—81·7% as against 82·4% (Patterson, Johnston and Goldspink, 1974: *Pleuronectes platessa*). However, after 30 weeks without food, the water content has risen to 95·1% in the white muscle, but to only 85·6% in the dark, which is therefore the less depleted. Dark muscle is also less affected than white by the starvation of *Pollachius virens* (Bratland, Krishnan and Sundnes, 1976). The progress of starvation in the same species is illustrated in Fig. 26 (Johnston and Goldspink, 1973c). The lag period before proteins are mobilised, during which lipid and carbohydrate reserves are drawn upon,[2] is shown very

---

[1]This relationship does not apply in fish containing appreciable proportions of muscle lipid.

[2]Stirling (1976: *Dicentrarchus labrax*) has shown that these reserves are used at different rates, lipid declining steadily and carbohydrate dropping rapidly in the initial stages of starvation.

clearly in the white muscle curve. This lag has also been illustrated in
the muscle of *Gadus morhua* (Love, 1969), Fig. 68 of this volume, page 186.

Patterson, Johnston and Goldspink (1974) showed in addition that
30 weeks of starvation reduced the "insoluble" (presumably structural)

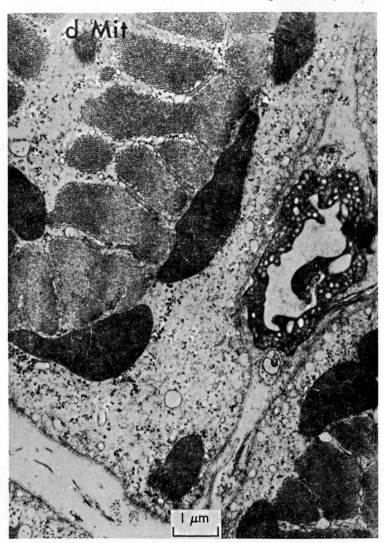

FIG. 25. Cross-section through dark muscle of a starving *Carassius carassius* showing
degenerating mitochondrion (d Mit) and the empty space which would be occupied
by the whole mitochondrion in the nourished cell. After Patterson and Goldspink
(1973a). Reproduced with permission of Dr S. Patterson, who kindly supplied the
photograph.

protein of dark muscle to 54% of its initial value, but that the white muscle had only 15% of it left—a remarkable degree of self-dismantling.

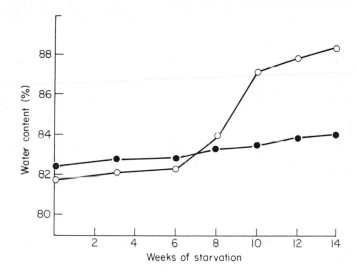

FIG. 26. The changes in water content of white (○) and dark (●) muscle of *Pleuronectes platessa* during starvation. After Johnston and Goldspink (1973c). Reproduced with permission of Dr I. Johnston.

A study of *Gadus morhua* which had been submitted to starvation (Love and Lavéty, unpublished) again demonstrated that, as in plaice, the water content of dark muscle is always greater than that of white in nourished fish. At the outset of starvation, dark and white muscle tissues gain water hand-in-hand, with dark muscle samples sometimes more hydrated than the corresponding white. The two types of tissue are obviously mobilising their expendable protein, which in dark muscle is largely "soluble" or non-structural, according to Patterson, Johnston and Goldspink (1974). However, after the water content of white muscle has exceeded about 87% it appears as though the dark muscle has little more to give without serious interference with its function, and further hydration of the white leads to little further hydration in the dark (Fig. 27).

The ribose nucleic acid (RNA) and deoxyribose nucleic acid (DNA) decrease by comparable amounts in both tissues (Patterson, Johnston and Goldspink, 1974), probably corresponding with the loss from the nuclei of euchromatin material observed by Patterson and Goldspink (1973a) in starving *Carassius carassius*.

Glycogen in the dark muscle of *Pleuronectes platessa* starved for 30 weeks has been observed to drop to 52%, and in white muscle to 23%, of their respective control values (Patterson, Johnston and Goldspink, 1974), but the control levels were so very different in the two tissues (635 and 182 mg%, respectively) that it is difficult to comment.

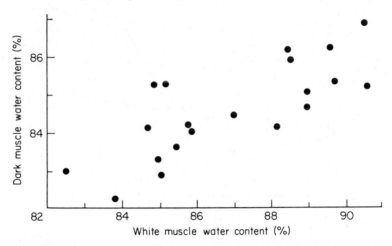

FIG. 27. The water contents of white and dark muscle of *Gadus morhua* during starvation in an aquarium. Each point represents values from a single fish. After Love and Lavéty, unpublished.

Twelve weeks of starvation reduced the dark muscle lipid of *Pleuronectes platessa* by half and perhaps by the same proportion in white, but the reduction in the latter was not statistically significant (Johnston and Goldspink, 1973c). The curve is shown in Fig. 28, but it really needs supplementing by information on the lipid fractions, since the mobilisation of lipids involved in cellular structure (cholesterol, phospholipids) obviously tells us more than that of lipids used just as energy stores (triglycerides).

Figure 29 shows that a species which carries some lipid reserves in the flesh (*Salmo gairdneri*) mobilises all of the four major fractions to some extent in both types of muscle after 5 weeks without food, but that triglyceride is utilised more than the other fractions. Triglyceride is also preferentially restored to dark muscle on refeeding the starving fish with palmitic acid (Fig. 30), while of the small amount of lipid channelled into the white muscle, most is incorporated into phospholipid, presumably to make good some structural deterioration. The flesh of these specimens of *Salmo gairdneri* contained more lipids than, for example, the Gadoids—5·1% in the dark muscle and 2·2% in the white—and starvation for 5 weeks appeared not to deplete the liver. Similar observations have been made on starving pike (*Esox lucius*), which mobilises lipid deposits in the intestinal region before making any inroads into the liver lipid (Ince and Thorpe, 1976).

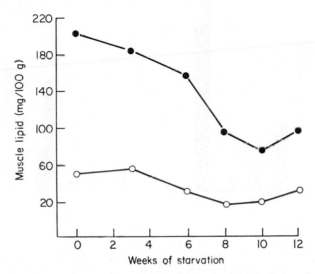

FIG. 28. Changes in the total lipid of dark (●) and white (○) muscle during the starvation of *Pleuronectes platessa*. After Johnston and Goldspink (1973c). Reproduced with permission of Dr I. Johnston.

A different situation arises in *Gadus morhua*, where the content of lipid is usually less than 2% in the dark muscle (Love, Hardy and Nishimoto, 1975) and 1% or considerably less in the white (Volume 1, reference 268; Castell and Bishop, 1973; Love, Hardy and Nishimoto, 1975). In such fish, triglycerides form a relatively minor proportion of even the neutral lipids, and seasonal changes in the nutritional state of the fish are reflected by an increase or decrease in the phospholipid of the white muscle (Love, Hardy and Nishimoto, 1975). Ross (1978) has shown that artificial starvation results in a steady decrease in the phospholipid as a proportion of the total lipid in both tissues, on the basis of muscle water content. For want of further evidence we may guess that this represents a loss of contractile material and cell walls in white muscle (Fig. 31) and of mitochondrial membranes in dark (Fig. 32), assuming that the mitochondria decrease as in *Pleuronectes platessa*. It also means that the lipids of dark muscle, at least in this species, are still structural and not an energy store. Any lipids used to supply energy

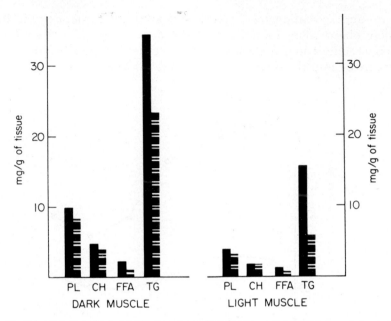

FIG. 29. Lipid fractions in dark muscle and white muscle of *Salmo gairdneri*. Solid columns represent fed fish, broken columns fish after starvation for 5 weeks. PL, phospholipids; CH, free cholesterol; FFA, free fatty acids; TG, triglycerides. After Robinson and Mead (1973). Reproduced with permission of Dr J. S. Robinson and Dr J. F. Mead.

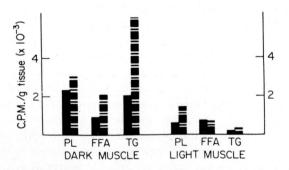

FIG. 30. Incorporation of radioactivity into dark and light muscle phospholipid, free fatty acid and triglyceride fractions of fed and starved trout 8 hours after force-feeding radioactive palmitic acid. Broken columns represent the starved fish, solid columns the fed controls. After Robinson and Mead (1973). Reproduced with permission of Dr J. S. Robinson and Dr J. F. Mead.

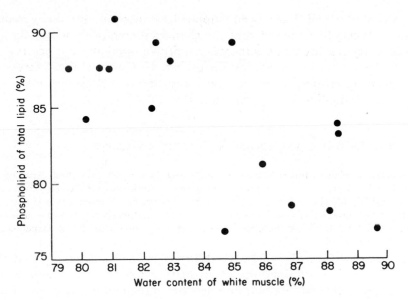

FIG. 31. The concentration of phospholipid in total white muscle lipid during the prolonged starvation of *Gadus morhua*. After Ross (1978). Reproduced with permission of the author.

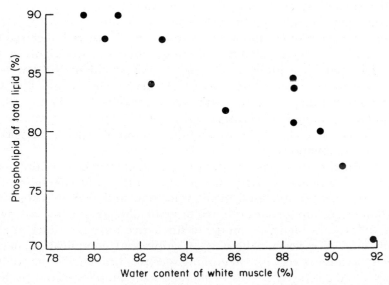

FIG. 32. The concentration of phospholipid in the total dark muscle lipid of *Gadus morhua* during starvation, the extent of which is indicated by the water content of the white muscle. After Ross (1978). Reproduced with permission of the author.

for swimming will have been supplied, as needed, by the vascular system. It should be noted that the changes shown in these two figures occur as the resources of the muscle are drawn upon and not necessarily at the beginning of the starvation period. In contrast, the reserves of the liver are reduced from the start, and here the depletion takes the form of a reduction in triglycerides (Ross, 1978).

7. USE OF DARK AND LIGHT MUSCLE IN SWIMMING

When the division in function between light and dark muscle was first explored, it was found (Volume 1, p. 34) that, during slow swimming, electric currents were generated by only the dark muscle fibres, while in more rapid activity they originated in the white muscle. It could not be ascertained whether currents were then still proceeding from the dark muscle, because they were swamped by the larger white muscle output.

It has now been shown by Hudson (1973: *Salmo gairdneri*) that the electrical activity of dark muscle is neither inhibited nor augmented when the underlying mosaic muscle (the equivalent of white muscle in non-salmonids) becomes functional, so we now know that dark muscle is active at all swimming speeds. The maximum cruising (sustainable) speed was shown to lie somewhere in excess of 3·75 tail-beats per second, but the mosaic muscle begins to play its part at between 3·05 and 3·6 tail-beats per second, that is, below the maximum cruising speed. A bigger proportion of the mosaic muscle becomes involved once the fish has started true high-velocity swimming—one or two vigorous tail beats followed by a glide, a sequence which, incidentally, has been calculated to result in a large saving of energy when compared with continuous swimming at the same average velocity (Weihs, 1974). Webb (1970, quoted by Hudson, 1973) found that mosaic muscle becomes active at 80% of the maximum sustainable speed, supporting Hudson's observations.

Smit, Amelink-Koutstaal *et al.* (1971) used oxygen consumption as a measure of muscular activity in *Carassius auratus*, and concluded that both types of fibre are used at all velocities, and that it is merely a question of the proportions of dark to white changing as the fish swim more quickly—a high percentage of the active fibres are dark at slow speeds, and vice versa. There is an additional complication in this species, because at very low swimming speeds ("browsing") the goldfish propels itself solely by means of the adductor muscles of the pectoral fins. The fibres of these muscles, needless to say, are dark. Fin movement also propels *Cyprinus carpio* during swimming at 0·3 to 0·5 lengths per second. Intermediate pink fibres are recruited at 1·1 to 1·5 lengths per second and the whole musculature is in action at speeds above about 2 lengths per second (Johnston, Davison and Goldspink, 1977, using electromyography).

There is a possibility that the dark muscle will select glycogen or lipid to supply its energy depending on the swimming activity at the time. Bokdawala and George (1967b: *Labeo* spp.) considered that the glycogen might be used during periods of low activity, but Patterson and Goldspink (1973b: *Carassius carassius*) showed that octanoate (lipid-type) was oxidised more slowly than pyruvate (carbohydrate intermediate) in a model system, and concluded that ATP synthesis in the living fish would therefore be slower when lipid is the substrate. It seems doubtful, therefore, that lipid catabolism can play a major role during intensive activity in white muscle nor, presumably, in dark muscle at high swimming velocities, bearing in mind that there is plenty of glycogen available in this tissue.

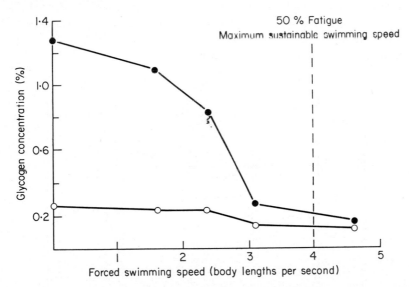

FIG. 33. Changes in the concentration of glycogen in the dark muscle (●) and white muscle (○) of *Pollachius virens* after forced swimming at various speeds. After Johnston and Goldspink (1973a). Reproduced with permission of Dr I. Johnston.

The glycogen of both types of muscle certainly does decrease during swimming, and by studying glycogen levels after forced swimming for 6 hours at various speeds, Johnston and Goldspink (1973a: *Pollachius virens*) obtained valuable confirmation of the individual roles of dark and white muscles. Their results are shown in Fig. 33, where it can be seen that the glycogen level in the dark muscle is decreased by any swimming activity, and decreases further with every increase in velocity until at 3·1 lengths per second there is little of it left. The lower initial level in the white muscle, on the other hand, does not fall until the fish are swimming at more than 2·3 lengths per second (3 lengths per second in *Carassius auratus:* Johnston and Goldspink, 1973d). At 4 lengths per second in *Pollachius virens* it was found that 50% of the fish were fatigued and could not maintain their speed, so it appears that in this species the white muscle starts to be used at a velocity below, but not far below, the maximum cruising speed, agreeing with the conclusions of Hudson.

Success in demonstrating the swimming velocities at which dark and white muscles operate was also achieved by Matyukhin, Neshumova and Dement'yev (1975: *Thymallus arcticus baicalensis*), this time through a study of the rise in temperature which accompanies activity. The results (Fig. 34) show clearly that the temperature increment increases uniformly from +0·01 to +0·08°C in the dark muscle as the fish swim faster, but that in white muscle it is increased only at speeds above 87 centimetres per second. In the recovery period after swimming the temperature increment declines rapidly.

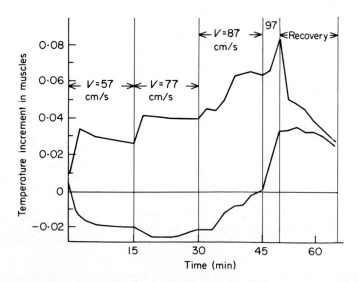

FIG. 34. Temperature change in dark (upper curve) and white (lower curve) muscle of the Baikal grayling after swimming at increasing speeds and during recovery (water temperature=12°C). After Matyukhin, Neshumova and Dement'yev (1975). Reproduced with permission of all the authors *per* A. N. Lyubansky, Copyright Agency of the USSR.

Johnston and Goldspink (1973a) also measured lactate levels, and while the lactate in dark muscle showed no clear trend with swimming activity, presumably because of its rapid removal by the vascular system, that of the white muscle increased at greater swimming velocities (Fig. 35). There was, however, an anomaly, since the lactate values rose at swimming velocities above 1·6 lengths per second, while more than 2·3 lengths per second were needed to deplete the glycogen. Bearing Wittenberger's observations in mind (p. 90) we may accept that the white muscle glycogen, at swimming speeds between 1·6 and 2·3 lengths per second, was being renewed from the dark muscle stores.

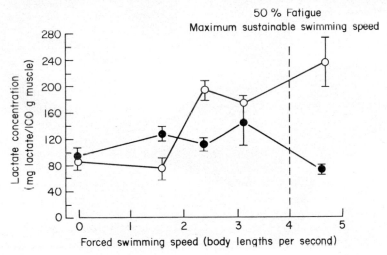

FIG. 35. Changes in the concentration of lactate in the dark muscle (●) and white muscle (○) of *Pollachius virens* after forced swimming at various speeds. After Johnston and Goldspink (1973a). Reproduced with permission of Dr I. Johnston.

8. DYNAMICS OF DARK MUSCLE

a. *Quantity*

Up to now it has been implied, if not actually stated, that any one species of fish has a certain proportion of dark fibres of a particular composition within its musculature, either as a discrete mass or as single cells interleaving the white fibres to enable it to cruise. In fact, though, recent work has shown that both the proportion and the composition may change to meet special requirements. Some larval fish do not at first possess functional dark muscle (Greer-Walker, 1968: *Gadus morhua*) so the tissue presumably develops as the growing fish acquire a different style of swimming, ceasing to move in a series of quick darts. Lewander, Dave *et al.* (1974) have also shown that metamorphosis in *Anguilla anguilla* is accompanied by a pronounced development of the amount of dark muscle, which they interpret as an adaptation for spawning migration.

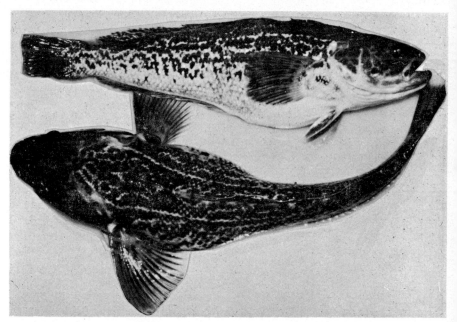

FIG. 36. *Notothenia rossii*, an antarctic fish which in adult life swims only with its pectoral fins: note their large size. Photograph kindly supplied by Mr J. G. M. Smith.

The reverse occurs in the antarctic fish *Notothenia rossii*, which is pelagic in its early life and shows a well-marked streak of dark muscle, but then changes to a demersal way of life at one or two years of age and lives in among the weeds. It now uses only its pectoral fins for locomotion, and powerful bands of dark muscle develop at their base. At the same time, the lateral dark muscle fades until it can no longer be distinguished from white muscle (Johnston and Walesby, personal communication, 1976). The photograph (Fig. 36) shows the very large pectoral fins of the adult form, eminently suited for propelling the fish along.

A fall in temperature results in a slowing down of most chemical and biochemical reactions (unless ice forms in the tissue, when certain

reactions may speed up: Love and Elerian, 1964), and it is a characteristic readily observable that, because of an elaborate system of adaptation (p. 325), the swimming activity of fish tends not to slow down at
lower temperatures. Part of this can be seen in the dynamics of dark
muscle, which actually increases in the quantity present (references
quoted on p. 79), in the amount of cytochrome oxidase present
(Malessa, 1969) and the proportion of mitochondria, which is doubled
(Wodtke, 1974). The latter author also noted that low temperature
adaptation (7 or 11°C as compared with 25 or 29°C) resulted in the
respiratory rate increasing in the dark muscle to 240% of that at the
higher temperature. Any reduction in enzymic activity is evidently com-
pensated at least in part by an increase in the quantity of enzyme present.

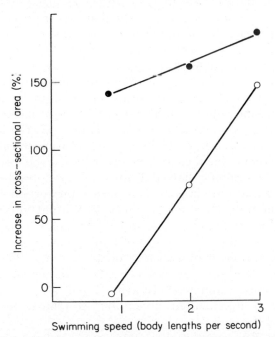

Fig. 37. Increase in cross-sectional area of dark (●) and white (○) muscle of
Pollachius virens as a result of training for 42 days at different velocities. After Greer-
Walker and Pull (1973). Reproduced with permission of Dr M. Greer-Walker.

Exercise also changes the quantity of muscle present, as devotees of
the Body Beautiful have long known (*H. sapiens*), but Greer-Walker
and Pull (1973: *Pollachius virens*) have demonstrated that different
swimming velocities effect different changes in the cross-sectional areas
of dark and white muscle after 42 days (Fig. 37). The graph shows that

at less than 1 length per second the dark muscle increases enormously in area with no change in the white muscle, but that at 2 and 3 lengths per second there is a steep rise in the absolute quantity of white muscle also. The rise in the amount of dark muscle is quite gentle at higher velocities after its initial surge. All of this fits in perfectly with what we know already—that at low swimming velocities the white muscle is not used, but that dark muscle is used at all velocities.

b. *Composition*

Trimethylamine oxide appears to play a complex role in fish muscle (Volume 1, pp. 288–289), and as mentioned earlier (p. 70) it is more concentrated in dark muscle than in white (Yamagata, Horimoto and Nagaoka, 1969: *Thunnus albacares*), provided that the fish are migratory (Tokunaga, 1970a). In non-migratory fish the reverse relationship holds. The physiological background to this observation is unknown.

A relatively high content of myoglobin is the most obvious characteristic of dark muscle, although it is apparently not present in the mitochondria-rich parts of the musculature of those antarctic fish which exist without haemoglobin (I. Johnston, 1976, personal communication: *Champsocephalus gunnari*; see also Volume 1, pp. 177–179 for a description of haemoglobinless fish). If the myoglobin is chemically treated to make it non-functional, then the steady-state oxygen consumption of the dark muscle is roughly halved at lower oxygen pressures, and it has been suggested that the pigment transports a proportion of the oxygen required by the mitochondria (Wittenberg, Wittenberg and Caldwell, 1975: pigeon breast muscle). The myoglobin content has been found to be directly related to the amount of habitual exercise undertaken by the muscles of various mammals and birds (Lawrie, 1950: horse, hen, pigeon and pig), and the pigment is clearly fundamental to the aerobic part of dark muscle function. Lawrie (1953) also showed that the concentration of mammalian myoglobin is related to the aerobic synthesis of ATP.

When Love, Robertson *et al.* (1974a) extracted the dark muscle of *Gadus morhua* for total haem pigments after draining off the blood, they found that the coloration varied according to the ground where the fish had been caught (Table 8), those from the two Spitzbergen grounds being significantly darker than the rest. Little difference in pigmentation could be seen between the other groups, apart from those from the Faroe Bank, which were appreciably paler. Love, Robertson *et al.* (1974a) concluded tentatively that the differences might relate to swimming activity, since the Spitzbergen cod migrate long distances

each year to spawn off the coast of Norway, and while such cod are
also to be found off Bear Island, the situation there is complicated by
the presence of other populations (Volume 1, reference 1287). Be that
as it may, the dark muscle of the Bear Island cod was also somewhat
darker than that from the other grounds. Later, Love, Munro and
Robertson (1977) examined fish from the same Spitzbergen stock in
February at the southernmost extent of their migration off the Lofoten
Islands, and obtained values of $0\cdot416\pm0\cdot116$ and $0\cdot403\pm0\cdot085$ in two
batches of 9 fish, which results are comparable with those of the cod
caught in the autumn at the other end of the run (Spitzbergen, Table 8).
The figures were higher than those obtained from a few of the local
Lofoten cod population.

TABLE 8

Intensity of haem pigmentation (mostly myoglobin) in the dark muscle of *Gadus
morhua* caught on different grounds. (After Love, Robertson *et al.*, 1974a)

Fishing ground	Map reference	Mean optical density of about 50 fish
South Spitzbergen	76–18N 16–15E	$0\cdot428\pm0\cdot112$
Isfjorden (W. Spitzbergen)	77–58N 12–04E	$0\cdot400\pm0\cdot102$
Bear Island	74–18N 20–13E	$0\cdot334\pm0\cdot080$
E. Iceland	{ 65 27N 13–08W { 64–20N 12–30W	$0\cdot323\pm0\cdot083$
N. Cape, Norway	72–25N 26–30E	$0\cdot305\pm0\cdot068$
Tana Fjord	71–04N 28–40E	$0\cdot298\pm0\cdot050$
Faroe Plateau	62–34N 06–24W	$0\cdot297\pm0\cdot073$
Scots Klondyke	58–35N 03–33E	$0\cdot294\pm0\cdot086$
Aberdeen Bank	57–05N 01–15W	$0\cdot273\pm0\ 051$
Faroe Bank	60–53N 08–20W	$0\cdot219\pm0\cdot056$

The units are optical density of an acid-acetone extract at 512 nm. Samples are listed in
descending order.

Faroe Bank cod are a known stationary stock (Volume 1, reference 613; Jamieson and Jones, 1967), and this information seems to
fit with the results in Table 8, where their dark muscle is seen to be
pale. Cod from Loch Torridon (W. Scotland) are known from tagging
experiments (A. D. Hawkins, personal communication, 1976) to move
hardly at all from their point of release, and the dark muscle colour
from such cod is lower still: $0\cdot2$ extinction units (Love, Munro and
Robertson, 1977).

Finally, the latter workers forced cod to swim in a channel for 4 weeks
and showed that the pigmentation had become significantly deeper than
in unexercised controls, so that the differences seen in Table 8 were at
least not entirely genetic.

The unexercised control fish in this experiment were interesting in their own right, because the pigmentation was paler (0.17 ± 0.04) than that of any stock of fish killed or captured, and indicated that the muscle had faded in the short period that the fish had been kept undisturbed. There was therefore scope for seasonal variation in the natural pigment- ation should fish of a particular stock in the wild vary their degree of swimming activity. Such proved to be the case (Fig. 38), the smoothness of the curve suggesting that the phenomenon is real. We shall have more to say on the subject of seasonal variation later (Chapter 5). Perhaps the maximum of the curve in Fig. 38 relates to the activity used in following prey. There is little real evidence yet for this attractive idea, but Hettler (1976) noted that the metabolic rate (oxygen con- sumption) of *Brevoortia tyrannus* more than doubled at feeding time, attributing it initially to the "result of increased muscular activity associated with rapid swimming during the feeding process".

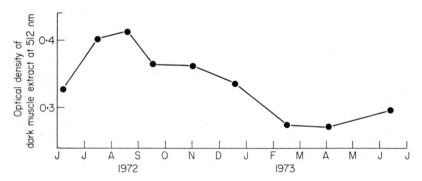

FIG. 38. Seasonal variation in the intensity of dark muscle colour in *Gadus morhua* caught off the east coast of Scotland. Values are thought to relate to the swimming activity of the fish. After Love, Munro and Robertson (1977).

Up to now in this volume we have tended to look at chemical and other properties of fish from a descriptive point of view. Here now is the first glimmering of a theme which I hope to develop in Chapter 5: the use of chemical information to enable one to characterise fish from the wild. Perhaps the recent swimming activity of a batch can be quanti- fied without one's having to go into the water oneself to watch them.

If we look further into the results quoted in Table 8 and study the distribution of colour between the individual fish, we find that it differs between migratory and non-migratory fish in an interesting way. Figure 39(a) shows the distribution in Faroe Bank fish, and is typical of the non-migratory stocks in the survey, showing a normal distribution tailing off evenly on either side. Figure 39(b) on the other hand shows a wide horizontal spread with no clear peak: only the Spitzbergen batches showed patterns like this. The Faroe Bank pattern is consistent with a group of fish which vary somewhat among themselves but are individually consistent in their swimming activity, while the Spitzbergen cod appear to show different degrees of fading according to the time spent resting on their feeding ground after the long migration from the spawning ground: perhaps those with the deepest pigmentation were newly arrived.

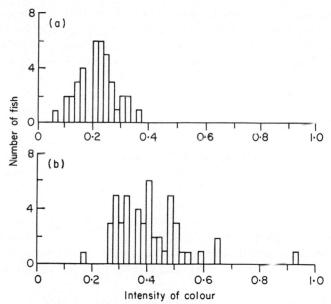

FIG. 39. The distribution of dark muscle pigmentation between cod of a batch caught in September 1968 (a) on the Faroe Bank (b) off Spitzbergen. Faroe Bank cod are a stationary stock and show "normal distribution" of pigmentation, while Spitzbergen cod are strongly migratory, showing a more even spread of results and darker colour. After Love, Munro and Robertson (1977).

C. Swimming activity

1. INTRINSIC ACTIVITY

Species which are intrinsically active seem to show distinctive features which distinguish them from more sedentary species (Volume 1, p. 147 onwards). Facilities for the rapid exchange of oxygen are markedly better, both by way of larger gill areas and higher concentrations of blood haemoglobin. So persistent is their need for oxygen, however, that unlike sluggish species they die rapidly in water of low oxygen content.

They possess a greater proportion of dark muscle, and their blood sugar content is higher than that of relatively inactive fish, perhaps, though not necessarily, reflecting the rapid mobilisation and transport of carbohydrate. They eat more, and secrete more digestive enzymes into the gut. More thyroxine circulates in the blood of active fish, and their muscle ATPase activity is greater, allowing more rapid release of chemical energy to be used in contraction. Several compounds involved in metabolism, including most of the vitamins, are generally more concentrated in the tissues of active fish.

Some of these observations have been confirmed in recent papers. That the blood of active fish contains more haemoglobin has been restated by Swarts (1969), Gelineo (1969) and Cameron (1970a), and likewise the oxygen consumption of the white muscle of very active fish has been shown by Gordon (1972a) to be greater than that of less active fish when minced and supplied with metabolites. This suggests a greater content of mitochondria, and probably indicates the interpenetration of individual dark muscle cells into the white.

A proportion of the haemoglobin of at least one active species of fish has no Bohr effect (defined on p. 123), so it can still absorb oxygen at low pH. The advantage to the fish is that after emergency exertion, when much lactate is produced, there is still some haemoglobin capable of absorbing oxygen at the gills so that swimming can be maintained (Powers, 1972: *Catostomus clarkii*). Perhaps to protect the tissues against the effects of a sudden flooding with lactic acid, carnosine, anserine and histidine are more plentiful in the white muscle of active species, where they probably act as buffers (M. Sakaguchi, personal communication, 1977).

Blood thyroxine has been shown to be high in migratory marine species such as mackerel and mullet, but is higher still in those that migrate from the sea to rivers, for example salmon, trout, and shad (Leloup and Fontaine, 1960).

Intrinsic activity in fish makes them vulnerable to low oxygen concentrations in the surrounding water. They are also vulnerable to starvation, and Patent (1970) and authors quoted by him have shown that less active fish can conserve their liver glycogen for considerable periods, while active fish cannot, noticeable decreases occurring after even a few days. The need of active fish for a supply of carbohydrate is shown vividly by Leibson and Plisetskaya (1968), who injected fish of varying degrees of intrinsic activity with insulin (Fig. 40). The level of blood sugar quickly dropped, but recovered the most quickly in the most active fish (*Spicara smaris*) and the most slowly in the most sluggish (*Lampetra fluviatilis*, which took 11 days compared with 1 day).

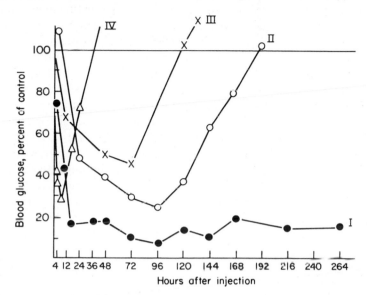

FIG. 40. The effect of injections of insulin (30–60 IU/kg) on the blood sugars of (I) *Lampetra fluviatilis* (very sluggish); (II) *Raja* sp.; (III) *Scorpaena* sp.; (IV) *Spicara smaris* (most active). After Leibson and Plisetskaya (1968). Reproduced with permission of Drs L. Leibson and E. Plisetskaya.

The activity of carbohydrate metabolism is suggested by the level of lactic dehydrogenase (LDH) activity, which is highest in the muscle of migratory or very active species (Kurogi, 1969; Marquez, 1976). This enzyme, as already mentioned, can occur as an aerobic (H) form, which usually predominates in the heart and dark muscle, and an anaerobic form (M) found in white muscle. Many flat fish, however, appear to have only a single (M-type) isozyme of LDH, the same in the heart as in the skeletal muscle. Since the usual H isozyme in other species is geared to prolonged activity in the heart, it appears that the sedentary habits of flat fish result in a relatively feeble heart action showing little difference from white muscle in its turnover and metabolic activity (Cowey, Lush and Knox, 1969: *Pleuronectes platessa*; Gesser and Poupa, 1973: many species).

Succinic dehydrogenase activity is greater in the muscle of pelagic than in non-pelagic species (Fukuda, 1958b), reflecting the increased numbers of mitochondria in the more active fish. It is also greater in the brain of more energetic species (Mengebier, 1976).

The levels of corticosterone and cortisol are usually higher in the blood of active species (Chuiko, 1968; Leibson, 1972; Idler, 1973).

Active swimming may perhaps engender a greater turnover of muscle proteins than is found in more slowly-moving forms; Sorvachev and Novikov (1968) have observed increased concentrations of certain *free* amino acids in the muscle of migrating *Salmo trutta* as compared with a local population. Excretion of the nitrogen of degraded proteins is also enhanced by active swimming (Muravskaya and Belokopytin, 1975).

Active species tend to have less connective tissue in their musculature (Tsuchiya and Takahashi, 1950). At first sight this is surprising, since one might have expected a greater need for tendon material to transmit the greater contractile power to the skeleton and for more binding material to prevent the strongly contracting elements from coming apart. However, perhaps this shows again that stronger muscle needs to contain as many contractile units in a given volume as possible (see p. 87), which means eliminating most other structures. Besides, Yamaguchi, Lavéty and Love (1976) have shown that the myocommata[1] of *Anarhichas lupus*, an active swimmer, are considerably stronger than those of either *Gadus morhua* or *Merluccius merluccius* without being any thicker. Extra strength in connective tissue can be achieved by forming a greater number of inter-molecular cross-links, so there does not have to be more of it.

Bone and Roberts (1969) considered that bottom-dwelling elasmobranchs from deeper water are more active than bottom dwellers from shallow water because of a relatively scarcity of food in the former habitat and a consequent need for continuous hunting. Elasmobranchs from deeper water contain more lipid of low specific gravity, and are near to neutral buoyancy (they have no swim bladders), while the shallow water group are found to be denser. These authors considered that the lower density suits the more active life; certainly the fish would consume less energy in rising from the bottom.

It has been established that the addition of small quantities of mucous material to the outer surface of a fish brings about a considerable reduction in resistance to turbulent currents. Such properties are displayed by fast-swimming fish in contrast to slow species (Chaikovskaya, 1974). As an example, the concentration of protein with high molecular weight and reactive side chains on the surface of *Correina umbra* (fast-swimming) is greater than that on *Scophthalmus maeoticus* (slow), though no correlation has been found between the glycoprotein content of the mucus and the swimming velocity (Uskova, Chaikovskaya *et al.*, 1970).

---

[1]The thin connective tissue membranes which bind together the muscle blocks in fish.

Active fish may possess a different kind of mucus, in addition to possessing more of it. Døving, Nordeng and Oakley (1974) found that the olfactory bulb cells of *Salvelinus alpinus* responded differently to the odours from migratory or non-migratory stocks of the same species. They suggested that the mucus was the principal source of the odour, which could conceivably act as a pheromone to assist in guiding the fish home after their migration.

So much for intrinsic activity. There are just two final points to be made. Different species of fish often differ widely from one another in their chemistry and physiology; the fact that one species just happens to be more active than another may not be the direct cause of a particular difference, and it is always as well to contrast another pair of species of differing activity to see whether the same chemical or other difference appears, and if not to treat the whole matter with reserve. The observations are always presumed to be beyond question, but interpretations of anything at all based on differences between two or more species can be based on shifting sand.

The second caution applies to the sampling of local and migrating stocks of fish, certain differences in which could reflect relative differences in activity. It might be assumed that the migratory stocks are the more active, but in fact fish *can* use tidal motion to migrate long distances, rising off the bottom during tidal flow in one direction and lying immobile during reverse flow. In contrast the local stock could be actively hunting for food. Increased activity can cause an increase in the numbers of dark muscle mitochondria, but if the fish should starve during migration they would tend to decrease. It is the interaction of factors like these that brings interest if also exasperation to this kind of study.

2.   EXERCISE AND TRAINING

a.   *Exercise*

Table 6 of Volume 1 is a list of tissue components which change in concentration as a result of exercise in experimental channels ("flumes"). Blood catecholamines and lactate increase, while glycogen and glucose in the muscle decrease as do compounds supplying energy, especially ATP. Liver glycogen on the other hand shows little change or even an increase, since the period of 15 minutes or so used by most investigators is insufficient to deplete liver glycogen appreciably—times of the order of a day are needed.

The effects of various kinds of stress, such as anoxia or trawling, were then discussed together with those of forced exercise. Here I shall attempt to keep the effects of stress and exercise separate as far as possible.

Placing the fish into a highly artificial environment with flowing water obviously does involve some stress, but workers interested in stress as such have in recent years tended to go beyond this with severe—sometimes gruesome—conditions so that they might study the reactions of the fish, and those results are reviewed in a section on the general stress reaction, p. 232.

Effects of exercise which differ between dark and white muscle have been discussed already (pp. 101–103); the present section covers general observations on exercise.

Wardle (1972b) showed that if *Pleuronectes platessa* were *forced* to swim, they retained the resulting lactate within the muscle, rather than sending it via the blood stream to the liver, unless the metabolic processes responsible for lactate retention were damaged in some way. Similarly, Börjeson and Höglund (1975) noted that the rise in muscle lactate in *Salmo salar*, resulting from violent threshing about, had to be considerable before significant transfer to the blood could be detected, either immediately or later. Retention of lactate in the muscle may well be universal, but other investigators who exercised their fish, often stressfully, reported slow rises in blood lactate (Wendt, 1965: *Salmo salar*; Beamish, Volume 1, reference 85: *Gadus morhua*; Dando, 1969a: *Gadus morhua, Pleuronectes platessa, Scophthalmus rhombus*). Others again have noted delayed transfer. Beamish (Volume 1, reference 85), Dando (1969a) and also Piiper and Baumgarten (1969), who stimulated *Scyliorhinus stellaris* electrically to exhaustion, noted that the highest blood lactate levels were not reached until after the termination of the exercise, during the recovery period, agreeing with observations reported in Volume 1, p. 44.

Depletion of carbohydrates in relation to exercise is not always as logical as might be expected. Pritchard, Hunter and Lasker (1971: *Trachurus symmetricus*) reported that failure to swim was associated with almost complete depletion of glycogen in the white muscle. Hoffman, Disney *et al.* (1970: *Tilapia nilotica*) on the other hand could find no clear difference between the muscle glucose levels of rested fish and those exercised to exhaustion.

Only the carbohydrates of muscle would be expected to be affected by physical exertion, and in fact Astakhova (1976: *Trachurus mediterraneus ponticus*) has shown that brain glycogen does not decrease during exercise. Similarly, one would not expect changes in, for example, ovarian glycogen, which can reach relatively high levels.

Changes in carbohydrates and their end-products depend to some extent on the reserves in the fish, and hence are subject to seasonal variations. Wendt (1965: *Salmo salar*) showed that exercise to the point of exhaustion caused the blood lactate to rise to 76·3 mg% in summer but to only 38·8 mg% in winter. Wendt and Ericson (1972: *Salmo salar*) demonstrated a striking difference in the change in blood glucose following exercise (or the stresses associated with it). Only in the summer did it rise sharply; in winter little change was seen (Fig. 41).

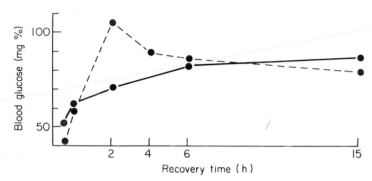

FIG. 41. Blood glucose levels after exercise and during post-exercise recovery in hatchery-reared *Salmo salar* at different seasons. Upper curve: August 1967. Lower curve: Feb-Mar 1968. After Wendt and Ericson (1972). Reproduced with permission of Dr C. Wendt.

The severity of swimming activity appears to govern the type of fuel used. From the value of the aerobic respiratory quotient (RQ)[1], Kutty (1968: *Carassius auratus, Salmo gairdneri*, quoted by Kutty, 1972) concluded that during spontaneous activity the fish depends on carbohydrates as the source of energy, but that in *Carassius auratus* forced to swim for prolonged periods, there appears to be a changeover to lipid or protein. Kutty (1972) showed from RQ measurements that *Tilapia mossambica* utilises more protein for energy as the exercise period becomes prolonged.

Trachurus mediterraneus ponticus has been observed to use lipid from both dark and white muscle when exercised to exhaustion (Shul'man, Sigaeva and Shchepkin, 1973). According to Krueger, Saddler *et al.* (1968: *Oncorhynchus kisutch*), the actual fatty acids used depend on the swimming speed, acids 18:1, 16:0 and 16:1 being preferentially used after swimming at 52 cm/s and 22:6, 18:2 and 20:4 at 59 cm/s. The relationships between these speeds and the maximum sustainable speed were not given, but the fish were only 8 cm long, so from what

---

[1] RQ is the volume of carbon dioxide produced divided by the volume of oxygen used. The value depends upon the fuel being used, and is unity for carbohydrates and less than this for lipids or proteins.

we have already seen (p. 102) it is likely that more mosaic muscle was being used at the higher speed.

Authors quoted by Watts and Watts (1974) showed that increasing fatigue gives rise to greater quantities of ammonia in the blood and muscle. More recent work confirms that nitrogen metabolism is more intensive during forced activity. The total protein in the serum increases (Kondrat'eva, 1975: *Trachurus trachurus*), while *free* amino acids (apart from arginine and alanine) are consumed and decrease significantly (Mehrle, Stalling and Bloomfield, 1971: *Salmo gairdneri*). Greater excretion of nitrogen follows, and in *Spicara smaris* 86% of it is in the form of ammonia, the remainder as urea (Muravskaya, 1972; Muravskaya and Belokopytin, 1975). An increased concentration of ammonia in the muscle of exercised fish has also been reported by Driedzic and Hochachka (1976: *Cyprinus carpio*). *Free* aspartic acid decreases and *free* alanine increases in the muscle, analogous to the findings in the serum of *Salmo gairdneri* mentioned above (Mehrle, Stalling and Bloomfield, 1971).

Extreme fatigue may result in a partial breakdown of muscle membranes and leakage of cellular components into the blood stream (Watts and Watts, 1974). Perhaps for this reason, the osmotic concentrations of the plasma of exercised *Salmo gairdneri* are always higher than those of rested fish (Rao, 1969).

Exercise, or the stresses accompanying it, brings about increases in the levels of cortisol and the catecholamine hormones in the blood (Volume 1, Table 6). Higgs and Eales (1971: *Salvelinus fontinalis*) found evidence of a slight increase in thyroid activity. This is the only report relating to forced swimming, but Leloup and Fontaine (1960: *Salmo gairdneri*) pointed out that fish struggling upstream during the spawning migration would have an increased need for thyroid hormone. In addition, several authors quoted by Stevens (1973) have shown that thyroxine, either injected or introduced into the water of the aquarium, increases the spontaneous activity of the fish.

Forced swimming for 24 hours has been shown to cause a rise in plasma growth hormone and prolactin concentrations (McKeown, Leatherland and John, 1975: *Oncorhynchus nerka*).

For a general account of the roles of the different endocrine glands and hormones in migration, the reader is referred to the review by Woodhead (1975).

b.   *Training*

In Volume 1, p. 48, it was reported that *Salmo gairdneri* could be habituated to exercise, and while they showed higher lactate concentrations in muscle and plasma when fatigued, it was more rapidly removed during the rest period.

All that we have seen so far on the modifications to white and in particular to dark muscle in response to prolonged swimming (p. 105 onward) —an increase in actual muscle volume, mitochondria, cytochrome oxidase and myoglobin—can be considered as results of "training". The single report of myoglobin fading in fish rested for several weeks can be taken as a sign of loss of physical, as distinct from biological condition.

Certain intangible benefits seem to accrue from training as well: fish taken from the exercise channel look more lively, shiny and firm than their lounging counterparts (L. J. Munro, author's laboratory), and grow more quickly as well as being healthier (G. Goldspink in conversation). During the voyage in which *Gadus morhua* were caught on different grounds (reported in Table 8, p. 107) it became obvious that trawled Spitzbergen fish, newly arrived from their long migration, were far more vigorous than their counterparts from other grounds. They flipped about furiously on the deck when released from the net and, placed in a tank on the ship, swam positively and continuously for 3 hours when encouraged with a broom handle[1]. Attempted repeats on cod from any other ground became mere essays in corpse stirring.

TABLE 9

Glycogen and lactate levels (mg%) in trained and untrained *Salvelinus fontinalis* exercised to exhaustion. (After Poston, McCartney and Pyle, 1969. Reproduced with permission of Dr G. L. Rumsey, Director, Tunison Laboratory)

	Trained			Untrained		
	Resting	Exhausted	24-hour Recovery	Resting	Exhausted	24-hour recovery
Muscle glycogen	67	19	44	85	5	23
Muscle lactate	54	334	41	45	455	43
Blood lactate	11	192	41	11	309	21

Poston, McCartney and Pyle (1969) exercised *Salvelinus fontinalis* for 20 weeks in a channel and found that, although the growth rate and body composition were not affected, the stamina of the fish improved. Vigorous exercise was reported to reduce the muscle glycogen less[2] and to give rise to less lactate in the blood and muscle of the trained fish, though the values after a subsequent rest of 24 hours were not greatly different between the two batches (Table 9). Wendt and Saunders

---

[1]Potentially longer: the unfortunate man detailed off to exercise them to exhaustion (M. Muslemuddin) was himself exhausted first.

[2]A given weight of glycogen would of course be needed for the same energy output, trained fish or untrained, but this observation suggests greater efficiency of swimming with habituation, or increasing use of lipid.

(1973) found that trained *Salmo salar* also tended to exhibit less blood lactate after exercise, though the effect was not always seen. They pointed out that while physical training might result in enhanced circulation to the muscles, such enhancement had not in fact been shown in fish, in contrast to mammals. They therefore preferred to think of the training improving the cardiovascular and respiratory performance, so that more oxygen is available to metabolise the lactate. Higher levels of lactate have been found (Volume 1, p. 48; Hochachka, 1961) in fatigued *Salmo gairdneri* which have been trained than in fatigued controls (untrained). Hochachka (1961) suggested that their tolerance might stem from a greater supply of tissue buffers which prevent the lactate from damaging the fish. He expressed the difference in stamina between trained and untrained fish as a difference in the amounts of fuel that they are able to burn in a given time.

Assuming that there are no startling revelations still to come from future work, we may conclude that training improves the oxygen supply and also the tolerance of the tissue to lactate. The speed with which the fish are sampled after exercise probably decides whether one finds higher or lower lactate levels in the trained fish than in the controls, and it is not unreasonable to conclude that the greater vigour of trained fish leads to momentary high levels of lactate which do not damage the tissue and are swiftly eliminated anyway. Low levels of lactate seen in trained human athletes (Robinson and Harmon, 1941, quoted by Poston, McCartney and Pyle, 1969), probably reflect improved circulation and suggest that even a short delay in biopsy leads to a rapid fall in lactate.

Table 9 shows that after rest for 24 hours, the trained fish replace more glycogen in their muscle than do the untrained. Figure 42 (Hochachka, 1961) shows that the replacement begins almost from the moment of rest in trained fish, but has shown no signs of starting even after 10 hours in the controls. The same author noted that trained fish possess higher levels of blood haemoglobin and larger hearts.

Changes in the activity of muscle enzymes have been studied in mammals by several authors, but little is known as yet of their behaviour in fish.

The duration of the exercise was found to be more important than its intensity in producing hypertrophy of the muscle cells in mice (Greer-Walker, 1966). The type of exercise has also been shown to be important in determining the lactic dehydrogenase (LDH) pattern of muscle in man (Karlsson, Sjödin *et al.*, 1975). Athletes trained in endurance show an increase in the heart-type, that is, the aerobic isozyme of LDH, while strength-trained athletes show an increase in muscle-type (anaerobic) LDH in their legs. The total concentration of LDH is also greater than in the muscle of endurance-trained athletes.

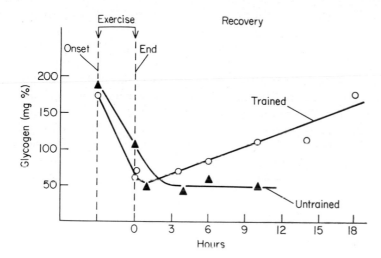

FIG. 42. The decrease and recovery of glycogen in the muscle with exercise and rest in trained and untrained *Salmo gairdneri*. The time scales of the exercise and recovery periods are not the same. After Hochachka (1961). Reproduced with permission of the author.

The dark muscle of the legs of rats was found by Booth and Kelso (1973) to show losses in the activity of cytochrome oxidase after immobilisation in plaster. Conversely, cytochrome-c increased in the legs of rats subjected to a programme of prolonged exercise (Terjung, Winder *et al.*, 1973). In various papers, Holoszy (quoted by Terjung, Winder *et al.*, 1973) has shown that regular exercise brings about an increase in the size and the number of mitochondria of (mammalian) skeletal muscle, resulting in increases in some mitochondrial enzymes if not in others. Succinic dehydrogenase (SDH) is a mitochondrial enzyme, and a programme of regular exercise has been shown to increase the SDH activity in hamsters (Howells and Goldspink, 1974) and man (Gollnick, Armstrong *et al.*, 1973), the latter authors demonstrating a concomitant rise in phosphofructokinase activity. While the relative abundance of mitochondria can therefore be monitored by measuring, for example, SDH activity, it is not safe to attempt to follow the "exercise history" of fish in this way, because of the possibility of starvation occurring at the same time, reducing mitochondrial numbers (Fig. 25, p. 94). In preliminary trials with a Beamish-type exercise tube, Munro and Love (unpublished, *Gadus morhua*) found that continuous swimming resulted in a *decrease* in dark muscle SDH activity because the fish could not be induced to eat enough food to cover their energy requirements, and after 2 months were in an advanced state of starvation. Similarly, the Spitzbergen cod at the southernmost extremity of their migration, while showing a deepening of haem pigmentation in their dark muscle (Love, Munro and Robertson, 1977) actually had less SDH activity than was found in the local, non-migratory stock, and were seen to be starving by their engorged, dark-blue gall bladders. Gentle exercise with adequate feeding, however, promoted increased SDH activity (Munro and Love, unpublished).

Training in a steady flow of water has also been observed to raise the levels of plasma cortisol (Forster, 1970: *Anguilla anguilla*) and serum LDH, the latter returning to the control level by the 10th day of exercise (Klar, 1973: *Salmo gairdneri*).

D. Buoyancy

An account of swimming mechanisms would be incomplete without a consideration of buoyancy, manipulation of which enables the swimming fish to save energy.

In Volume 1, p. 36, it was suggested that the uneven distribution of lipid in the musculature helps to keep the fish on an even keel. Certain deep-sea fish lay down stores of wax esters to maintain buoyancy (Volume 1, p. 142) and elasmobranchs, which have no swim bladder, possess large quantities of the hydrocarbon squalene, which has a specific gravity of only 0·86.

1.   INTRODUCTION

Fish achieve suitable buoyancy in relation to their surroundings by means of a gas-filled "swim bladder" in which the volume of gas can be varied, by storing substances of low density or by a combination of the two. There is also some evidence that the skeletons of certain species consist of poorly calcified or oil-filled bones, while the muscle of others is very watery, all in the cause of neutral buoyancy. Again, the swim bladders of some species are filled with lipid.

A change from one system to another as the fish grow older was noted by Butler and Pearcy (1972: *Stenobrachius leucopsarus, Diaphus theta*), who found that the relative volume of the swim bladder decreases with age, lipids gradually taking over the primary function of buoyancy. It was concluded that the older fish would find it easier to migrate up or down, since a gas-filled swim bladder would impose some restraints. Two out of three species of *Myctophidae* were found by Nevenzel, Rodegker *et al.* (1969) to have gas-filled swim bladders as juveniles, but to collapse them and fill them with wax esters as they grow. They concluded that a high wax ester content correlates with a pattern of daily vertical migration.

As already noted, elasmobranchs have large, oil-filled livers to fulfil the function of swim bladders, and three marine species of bony fish with oil-filled bones also lack swim bladders (Lee, Phleger and Horn, 1975: *Schedophilus medusophagus, Peprilus simillimus, Anoplopoma fimbria*). Where fish have fat-filled swim bladders, they do not have additional oil in the bones. However, this picture is not universal. Phleger and Grimes (1976) have now concluded that the presence or absence of a swim bladder does not invariably mean the absence or presence of oil-filled bones, taking as examples *Sebastes ruberrimus*, which has 24% to 32% of oil (dry matter basis) in its bones *and* a swim bladder, and several other species with swim bladders and somewhat less oil.

Fish may utilise the flow of the water to buoy themselves up, presumably by holding their pectoral fins at a suitable angle. They do not then need other aids to the same extent, and with only one exception fish have been found to be less buoyant if they have been living in flowing, as distinct from still, water (Machniak and Gee, 1975: *Noturus gyrinus, Ictalurus melas;* Pinder and Eales, 1969: *Salmo salar* parr; Gee, Machniak and Chalanchuk, 1974: 19 freshwater species; Gee, 1977: *Pimephales promelas*). Only *Esox lucius* becomes significantly more buoyant in a current (Gee, Machniak and Chalanchuk, 1974). A negative buoyancy is thought by these authors to assist in maintaining position in fast-flowing and turbulent waters of rivers and wave-washed beaches, whereas near-neutral buoyancy assists ease of movement in still water. Where rivers are fast flowing for only short periods because of periodical rainstorms (for example many rivers of South America), the local fish are not able to adjust their buoyancy when placed in a current, because it is not important for them to maintain their positions for such a short time. Where rivers flow powerfully for long periods, however, the fish usually possess adaptive mechanisms (Gee and Gee, 1976), buoyancy adjustment proceeding more quickly at higher temperatures (Gee, 1977: *Pimephales promelas*).

2. THE SWIM BLADDER AND GAS SECRETION

The swim bladder is a remarkable organ. Although the walls are thick and made largely of collagen, suggesting an organ capable of withstanding great pressures, the collagen is in fact less cross-linked than t' of skin or myocommata (Mohr, 1971: *Gadus morhua*) and so ruptures easily—indeed, the swim bladders of gadoids have been shown to burst when the pressure is quickly reduced to about 70% of the adapted level (Tytler and Blaxter, 1973). Cod caught by trawling and then kept in aquaria at the laboratory are found subsequently to exhibit scars where the swim bladder had burst and then healed up. It therefore acts as a safety valve and the fish is not killed by the release of external pressure. Not all species are as fortunate: the stomachs of *Sebastes marinus*, for example, are always everted by the expansion of the swim bladder on capture, and such fish can be obtained alive only by first removing the swim bladder gas with a syringe (G. Rollefsen, personal communication).

Although it is mechanically weak, the swim bladder must obviously be capable of preventing the enclosed gases from diffusing into the body cavity, and this it does by means of a silvery layer which contains overlapping crystals of guanine (Denton, Liddicoat and Taylor, 1972: *Conger conger, Anguilla anguilla;* Lapennas and Schmidt-Nielsen, 1977: seven species). Removal of this layer increases the permeability about 100 times and leaves a material only a little less permeable than ordinary connective tissue. The wall of the pneumatic duct of the swim bladder of *Conger conger* is not silvered, and thus has permeability properties similar to those of connective tissue (same authors). Other species also have a duct which connects the swim bladder with the exterior, and they can therefore expel excess gas without damage[1], increasing the amount of gas enclosed by gulping it in at the surface of the water (Machniak and Gee, 1975: *Noturus gyrinus*). Usually, however, the amount of gas is increased by being secreted by the "rete mirabile", a richly vascular gland which exposes a large area of capillaries to the interior of the swim bladder. The fastest known rate of bladder inflation by this means is that of *Pomatomus saltatrix*, which can refill its empty bladder in about 4 hours (Wittenberg, Schwend and Wittenberg, 1964, quoted by Ross, 1976).

The means whereby gas is secreted has interested a number of workers—after all, a deep-water fish requiring extra swim bladder volume must pump in gas against a pressure of many hundreds of atmospheres, so a remarkable mechanism must be present. Brunori (1975) considers that no single mechanism can operate under all conditions, and that the full story has not yet been told.

Since the main conclusions have been stated by several writers with some overlap, I felt it better to summarise the subject without individual

---

[1] In other species again the excess gas escapes by diffusion across the "oval", a modified on of the posterior part of the bladder wall (Harden Jones and Marshall, 1953).

attribution: the papers drawn upon are by Phleger and Benson (1971): Phleger, Benson and Yayanos (1973); Phleger and Holtz (1973); Bilinski (1974: a review); Brunori (1975); Noble, Pennelly and Riggs (1975); Baines (1975) and Hayden, Cech and Bridges (1975).

The swim bladders of surface fish are filled largely with nitrogen, but those in fish living at more than 30 metres of depth contain 90% or more of their gas as oxygen, together with small quantities of nitrogen, carbon dioxide and argon. Deep-sea fish have an unusually large rete mirabile, and the mechanism of oxygen release centres on two properties, possessed by some haemoglobins, which seem to be more marked in fish than in mammals.

In the Bohr effect, the *affinity* of haemoglobin for oxygen decreases as the pH falls, so that active tissues such as muscle, which generate much carbon dioxide and lactate, encourage the blood to unload its oxygen at the site of activity. A lowered pH in the rete could therefore cause oxygen to be given up into the swim bladder by this mechanism, but the Bohr effect may be of minor importance because it is still possible for the blood to remain saturated with oxygen at higher pressures. More important is probably the Root effect, in which a drop in pH reduces the actual *capacity* of the blood for oxygen, so that the haemoglobin can remain unsaturated even in the presence of high concentrations of oxygen. The effect is measured in the laboratory by determining the degree of oxygen saturation of the blood at different pH values. However, at the highest oxygen pressures even the Root effect is said to be inoperative, so is not considered as the sole mechanism at the greatest depths. No auxiliary mechanisms have been suggested so far, but it is clear that the Root effect is important in gas release, since the extent to which it operates varies according to the depth at which the fish live: the pH has a smaller effect on the blood of sedentary, shallow-water fish than on that of active deep-water species. The Root effect is said to be absent from elasmobranchs which have no swim bladder at all, but the logical story is spoiled by *Pseudopleuronectes americanus*, which lacks a swim bladder but still shows a Root effect. Explanations are pure conjecture at present.

The lowered pH required for oxygen release is provided by lactic acid. Now in most tissues, the anaerobic production of lactic acid from glucose is inhibited by the presence of oxygen (the Pasteur effect), but this effect is absent from the gas gland and lactic acid can be generated even under the huge partial pressures of oxygen encountered in the swim bladder at depth.

Thus when a fish dives, a mechanism controlled by the brain causes a rapid conversion of glucose to lactic acid in the rete mirabile. The drop in the pH of the blood leaving this organ is transmitted through a countercurrent diffusion system to the blood arriving. The pH fall affects the component of the haemoglobin possessing the Root effect, and oxygen liberation follows.

Three of the papers listed above (Phleger and colleagues) describe the presence of heavy deposits of lipid in the swim bladders of deep-sea fish. It consists mostly of cholesterol with some phospholipid, and it is strange that the constituent fatty acids are largely unsaturated in spite of the presence of so much oxygen under pressure[1]. Shallow-water fish have been observed to have a thin fatty lining within the swim bladder lumen, while the fatty lining almost fills the lumen of deep-sea forms. Apart from any buoyancy that these lipids may have in their own right, they may provide a clue to the mechanism of oxygen secretion at high pressures, the authors suggesting that they might dissolve the gas and facilitate its secretion in some way. More information is needed. Alternatively, the cholesterol might not be connected with buoyancy at all, but result from a synthesis favoured by high pressures—preliminary work has shown that synthesis of cholesterol from acetate is enhanced in this manner.

3.   LIPIDS AND SQUALENE

It was suggested in the previous section that a gas-filled swim bladder imposes restraints on the ability of the fish to change depth quickly. The lipid distribution about the bodies of *Clupea harengus* and *Clupea pallasii* varies greatly in quantity according to season, and the discovery that the swimbladder volume varies inversely with lipid content, within certain limits, suggests that the body lipid is important in the buoyancy of these species (Brawn, 1969a) and is not just an energy store. Freedom of vertical movement is assured by the herrings having relatively small swimbladder volumes, and by the presence of a duct leading directly from the bladder to the exterior, so that gas can be discharged rapidly during ascent (same author). The parr of *Salmo salar* also vary both the quantity of their body lipid and the swimbladder volume during the annual cycle, but the situation is different here because the parr, dwelling in rivers, are not subject to great changes in depth, and so the seasonal change in swimbladder volume does not

---

[1]Double bonds $-C=C-$ are especially reactive and more susceptible to oxidation than single bonds $-C-C-$. Fatty acids possessing one or more double bonds in the chain are said to be unsaturated.

correlate with tissue density, that is, with the density of a gas-free fish (Pinder and Eales, 1969).

Herrings may need a swim bladder because their body lipids, needed as energy reserves, consist almost entirely of triglycerides (up to 95% of the lipid present: R. Hardy, personal communication, 1977), which seem to be some of the least buoyant lipids, being surpassed by diacyl glyceryl ethers (Malins and Barone, 1970; Lewis, 1970a), wax esters, squalene and pristane (Lewis, 1970a). The latter, with a density of only 0·78, is probably the most effective of the naturally occurring buoyant substances but for some reason it rarely occurs in fish in significant amounts (Lewis, 1970a).

As recalled in the introduction (p. 121), elasmobranchs maintain a buoyancy near to neutral by means of their large livers which contain squalene. When Corner, Denton and Forster (1969) captured five elasmobranch species and a holocephalan from deep waters and placed them in surface waters or laboratory sea water, they observed that the fish all floated —that is, they had to use energy to maintain a particular depth. However, when the salinity, temperature and pressure of the shallow water, as compared with the deep water, were taken into account, it appeared that all of the fish must have been very close to neutral buoyancy in their natural surroundings on the sea bed. All of the fish had enormous oily livers rich in squalene.

A dynamic situation appears to occur in the fatty livers of *Squalus acanthias*, another elasmobranch. Diacyl glyceryl ethers and tri-glycerides are the main lipids present, and since the former compounds show an especially active turnover, and have a lower specific gravity (0·908) than triglycerides (0·922), Malins and Barone (1970) postulated that the fish might be able to adjust their buoyancy by regulating the proportions of the two. As an experimental check, they attached lead weights to half of their captured dogfish and kept them for 50 hours along with unweighted fish, and found that the proportion of diacyl glyceryl ethers, which give 14% more lift in sea water than triglycerides do, was significantly higher in the weighted group. In this way the fish in the wild are probably able to maintain neutral buoyancy as required.

A high wax ester content has been claimed by Nevenzel, Rodegker *et al.* (1969) to correlate with a deep-water habitat and a pattern of daily vertical migration. Two out of three species of *Myctophidae* (lantern fish) from deep water were found to have gas-filled swim bladders as juveniles, but these were collapsed and filled with wax esters in older fish. The wax esters were largely monoenes and dienes[1], and occurred

---

[1]With one or two double bonds present, respectively.

in the muscle and adipose tissue as well, serving primarily as buoyancy agents in this group of fish. However, in mullets and gouramis, which inhabit shallower waters, the wax esters are laid down only in the roe, not in other tissues, and in such cases are thought by these authors to serve simply as an energy reserve.

The wax esters of cetyl and oleyl alcohols are found all over the body of *Ruvettus pretiosus*, the castor oil fish, not just in the swim bladder or liver. The tissues richest in this low-density lipid are the dermis and the bones of the head, so that the living fish at rest probably hovers in the water with the head elevated (Bone, 1972).

Lee, Phleger and Horn (1975) found large quantities of lipid in the bones (including skulls) of *Schedophilus medusophagus*, *Peprilus simillimus* and *Anoplopoma fimbria*. These fish all lack swim bladders, but the authors warned that the presence of oil-filled bones does not necessarily mean neutral buoyancy, and their finding that triglyceride (the least buoyant lipid we have considered) ranged from 64 to 97% of the bone oil adds strength to their point.

4.   WATERY MUSCLE AND POORLY CALCIFIED BONE

Deep-water fish without swim bladders may also achieve a buoyancy close to that of the surrounding water by attenuating the solid structures of their bodies to the absolute minimum. The pioneer work in this interesting field was carried out by Denton and Marshall (1958), who observed that *Gonostoma elongatum* and *Xenodermichthys copei*, fairly common deep-water fish, solved their buoyancy problems by reducing the quantity of their main swimming muscles. The contractile tissue which remains is very watery and the skeletons are poorly ossified, so that although neither possesses a swim bladder, the former fish is often within 0·5% and the latter within 1·2% of neutral buoyancy. The dry weights were found to be about 12·6 and 10·0% of the wet weights, respectively, compared with about 28% for a typical coastal marine fish, *Ctenolabrus rupestris*. Lipid is clearly not a factor in the buoyancy regulation of these fish, since it averages only about 3% of the total wet weight, but the protein content at 4 to 7% of the wet weight is very low indeed compared with the 16% or so normally found in marine fish.

A related species, *Gonostoma denudatum*, also occurs in deep water, and in contrast to *G. elongatum* described above, it is much better ossified— but it also possesses a swim bladder.

The reduced ossification is reflected in the ash content: 1·5% of the wet body weight in *Xenodermichthys copei* compared with *Ctenolabrus rupestris* (the "normal" fish) which has 4·5%. The muscular system is particularly reduced along the trunk and tail, but the parts of the skeleton concerned with holding and swallowing prey, that is, the jaw complex, are better ossified. These fish are not by any means tireless hunters, however, and Denton and Marshall (1958) describe them rather uncharitably as mere floating traps.

There is some indication that the tendency to wateriness in fish without swim bladders progresses according to the depth of the habitat (Childress and Nygaard, 1973: Fig. 43), and Bone and Roberts (1969) had already noted a reduced density in deep-water bottom-dwelling forms compared with shallow-water bottom dwellers, though as they were studying elasmobranchs the difference in density presumably reflects differences in lipid, particularly from the liver, rather than wateriness.

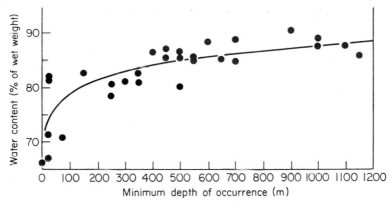

FIG. 43. The relationship between the water content of the tissues and the minimum depth of occurrence in a group of midwater fish. Each point represents a different species. The points on the original Figure relating to fish possessing swim bladders have been removed. The regression line relates only to fish without swim bladders. After Childress and Nygaard (1973). Reproduced with permission of Dr J. J. Childress.

Fish without swim bladders, found in depths from 100 to 1000 metres, have been characterised by Blaxter, Wardle and Roberts (1971) as having soft bodies with water contents of 88 to 95%, large lymph ducts, low haematocrits (5 to 9%), small hearts and a low proportion of dark muscle. The last three characteristics seem to reflect a low level of activity in these fish. Species possessing swim bladders have characteristics opposite to all of those listed above, water contents ranging from 70 to 83% and haematocrits from 14 to 35%, large hearts and so on. Some active surface species have less water still (64 to 74%)—presumably because of a greater lipid content—and haematocrits of up to 57%.

These authors found that the usual ionic concentrations are maintained in watery fish. Protein systems are stable over a rather narrow range of ionic concentrations, and the fact that there is much less protein present does not change the requirements of the remainder.

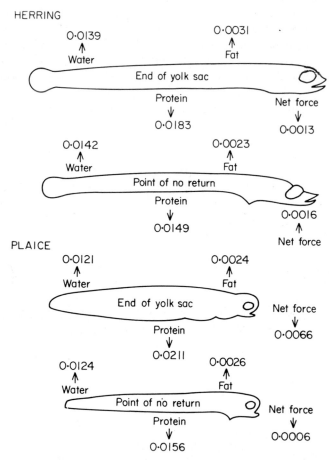

FIG. 44. Buoyancy forces on the larvae of *Clupea harengus* and *Pleuronectes platessa* at the end of the yolk-sac stage and at the "point of no return", a fatal degree of starvation. Note the emaciation and slight decrease in length in the starving larvae. Forces are shown as dynes per mg wet weight. Arrows show the direction of the force. After Blaxter and Ehrlich (1973). Reproduced with permission of Dr J. H. S. Blaxter and of Springer-Verlag.

As we have seen in Volume 1 (p. 225 onwards), starvation also causes the muscle water to rise and the protein to fall. Such changes, along

with a decrease in the lipid concentration, have been shown as changes
in buoyancy forces, up or down, by Blaxter and Ehrlich (1973). Their
studies on the larvae of *Clupea harengus* and *Pleuronectes platessa* are shown
in Fig. 44, the "point of no return" being that at which the larvae have
become so emaciated that they can no longer eat even when food is
proffered. The results demonstrate a progressive decrease in sinking
rate because of water being taken up by the body and protein lost.
This observation is useful confirmation of the effect of wateriness on
the buoyancy of adult fish. Lipid was also lost from these herring larvae.
With the approach of death, the larvae became denser again as their
osmoregulation failed, the salts in the sea water dehydrating them and
causing shrinkage.

FIG. 45. A jelly cat (*Anarhichas latifrons=Lycichthys denticulatus*) from near Bear Island.
The tail of this specimen could not be fitted into the field of view of the (fixed) camera
on the ship. The water content of the muscle of these fish can be more than 95% in
the natural state. Author's photograph. Crown Copyright reserved.

It is possible that the wateriness developed during starvation differs
from that designed to keep the fish neutrally buoyant, though as always
comparisons between species are risky.

A soft watery species without a swim bladder, well known to trawl
fishermen in northern waters, is the "jelly cat", *Anarhichas latifrons=
Lycichthys denticulatus* (Fig. 45), which is always thrown overboard as
useless. The water content of a specimen caught by the writer off Bear
Island in September 1974 (Love and Lavéty, 1977) was 95·4%, and is
compared with naturally starving gray sole (*Glyptocephalus cynoglossus*)

and artificially starved cod in Figs. 46, 47 and 48. All three specimens had similar water contents, but since there is more tissue in evidence in

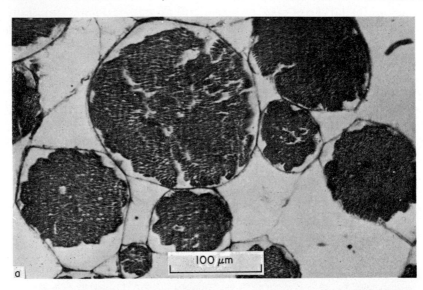

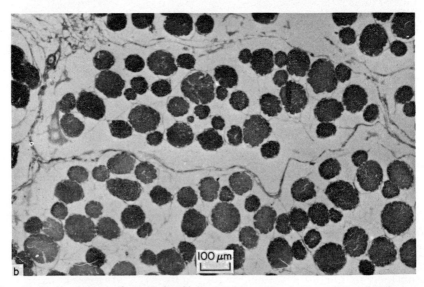

FIG. 46. Sections across the muscle of jelly cat (*Anarhichas latifrons*). The muscle water content of this specimen was 95·3%. Observe the remarkably normal appearance of the widely spaced cells, which are rounded and only slightly shrunken inside their collagen frames. The picture at lower magnification shows how bundles of cells are separated by even bigger spaces. After Love and Lavéty (1977).

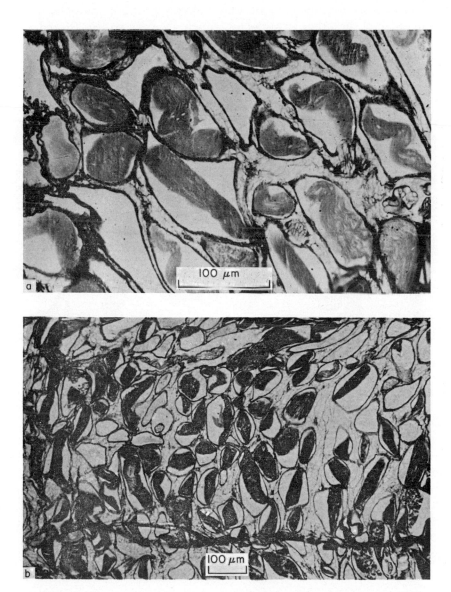

FIG. 47. Sections across the muscle of a cod (*Gadus morhua*) artificially starved in an aquarium until the muscle water content was 93·4%. Notice how the collagen outlines the original shapes of the cells, but the contractile material has shrunk to a small proportion of its original volume. The picture at lower magnification in particular shows a number of collagen outlines where the cellular material has disappeared altogether. After Love and Lavéty (1977).

the jelly cat section, the contents of its cells are probably more hydrated than those of the other two species, which are very widely spaced and irregularly shaped. The most interesting feature, however, is the shape of the cells. Those of the cod and gray sole are polygonal[1], and in the well-nourished state they approximate to hexagons so as to pack as

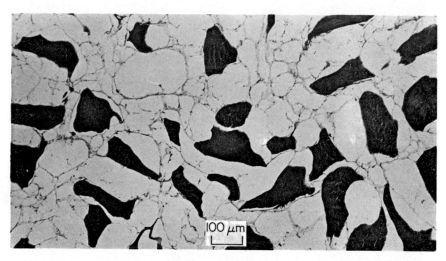

FIG. 48. Section across the muscle of naturally starving gray sole (*Glyptocephalus cynoglossus*) with water content of 96% in the muscle. As in cod (Fig. 47) the original outlines of the cells can be seen as collagen frames. Histological section kindly supplied by Dr D. H. Shaw, St John's, Newfoundland.

much contractile material as possible into a given volume of muscle (see p. 87) with minimal extracellular fluid. The cells of the jelly cat in contrast are rounded in cross-section, suggesting that the extracellular space is always considerable and there would be no question of cells fitting together in geometrical patterns. Body fluids are less dense than sea water in all but the most primitive vertebrates, so the jelly cats will have a buoyancy advantage.

[1]Sections of the white muscle of starving *Cyprinus carpio* also closely resemble those of cod and gray sole and are illustrated in Fig. 56, p. 173.

3 Feeding and Starving

A. Feeding

1. INTRODUCTION

The effect of ingesting different substances on the composition of fish tissues was reviewed in Volume 1 (p. 198) in the hopes of identifying the nature of the diets consumed by specimens captured from the wild. Results were not encouraging because fish can modify ingested lipids to some extent and they degrade all dietary proteins to individual amino acids before resynthesising them into characteristic fish tissue proteins. Thus seasonal variations in the diet, for instance, would be difficult or impossible to follow. However, dimethyl sulphide, certain toxins, zinc, trimethylamine oxide and the vitamins were observed to be stored unchanged, so could give an idea of the sort of concentrations habitually taken. Lipids and carotenoids might perhaps perform this function to some extent, but being modified by the fish they are indicators only. Another possible method of studying dietary habits is by studying the proportions of enzymes in the gut, which have been reported to change according to the type of food passing through. Studies of this kind up to 1968 were promising, but too few in number to allow any general conclusions to be made.

Certain inorganic nutrients were observed to be absorbed directly from the water (Ca, Cl, Co, I, Sr and SO_4) and glucose in solution supported the life of the fish for a period before giving rise to liver damage and diabetes.

The section concluded with a short account of the substances essential to the survival of the fish, and a list of symptoms of vitamin deficiencies. Halver's book, "in press" when my Volume 1 was being written, is now in print, and is recommended as a source of information on all aspects of nutritional requirements and deficiencies (Halver, 1972).

> It's a very odd thing—
> As odd as can be—
> That whatever Miss T. eats
> Turns into Miss T.

At first sight it looks as though Walter de la Mare, who wrote those lines, thought of Miss T. as being composed of cream buns, sandwiches and other materials far removed from mammalian body constituents, but it is more likely that he realised that she would select the calcium from the cream and put it into her bones, and burn up as much of the buns as she required for energy, laying down the remainder as lipid under her skin.

Fish also select materials as required, and vary little in their own *principal* body constituents as long as all the essential ingredients are provided. We have already noted (p. 26) that a change of diet as fish grow bigger has not so far been shown to lead to fundamental changes in body composition, and diets as disparate as trout pellets, crab (*Carcinus maenas*) and fillets of saithe (*Pollachius virens*), all of which are more than 94% absorbed, have been shown to produce the same body composition in *Dicentrarchus labrax* (Stirling, 1976), at least as regards "proximate" constituents (see footnote to page 79).

Were it not for this ability of fish to compensate for some of the differences in their diet in this way, there would be much more variation in their own tissues than there is, since the diet varies from numerous causes. For example, the distribution of types of prey eaten by *Salvelinus fontinalis*, *Salmo clarkii* and *Salmo gairdneri* are seldom random, but are eaten in proportions which repeatedly characterise individual fish. Preferences for particular kinds of prey tend to occur, even where both absolute and relative abundance of potential prey are constant (Bryan and Larkin, 1972).

Groups of cod can feed more effectively than single fish (Brawn, 1969b), since they cooperate in digging for deeply buried food and assist each other to consume pieces of food too large to be swallowed by pulling them apart.

Other qualitative variations in the food arise in different seasons, at different depths, and, as we have already noted, with increase in the size of the captor fish (Kohler and Fitzgerald, 1969; Daan, 1973).

On the other hand, minor constituents may vary widely according to the nature of the diet. The most striking example seems to be thiaminase, which varies in the liver and intestine of *Hypophthalmichthys molitrix* according to the type of diet (Arsan and Malyarevskaya, 1969). The amount of thiamine (aneurin, vitamin B_1) in the tissues varies inversely as the thiaminase, and shows steadily increasing concentrations as the fish are fed on blue-green algae, green algae, "mixed food", protococcoid algae or *Daphnia*. Starving fish contain the most thiamine, presumably through consuming no thiaminase. The results are illustrated in Fig. 49.

Later we shall see other examples of minor constituents which cannot be synthesised by the fish varying in concentration with the diet.

Carotenoids are an obvious example and an irritating one at that, as aquarium owners know: gorgeously coloured pet fish often fade when given artificial diets, and as fish culturists are aware, the public is not keen to buy salmon with a flesh the colour of cod muscle. Each species has its own carotenoid requirements, however, so that they respond differently to a fixed level of dietary carotenoid: Czeczuga (1973) showed that closely related species differ markedly in carotenoid content after being reared on almost identical diets.

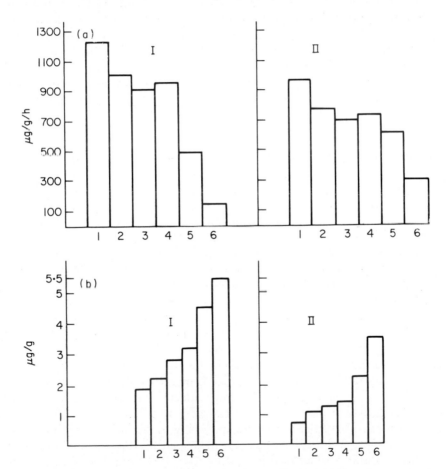

Fig. 49. Variation in the thiaminase activity (upper diagrams (a)) and concentration of thiamine (lower diagrams (b)) in the liver (I) and intestine (II) of *Hypophthalmichthys molitrix*, in relation to diet. 1, Blue-green algae. 2, Green algae. 3, Mixed food. 4, Protococcoid algae. 5, *Daphnia*. 6, No food. After Arsan and Malyarevskaya (1969). Reproduced with permission of Dr A. Ya. Malyarevskaya.

There may also be variations in the rate of deposition of ingested substances into different organs. Cserr, Fenstermacher and Rall (1972) showed that many compounds introduced via the blood stream enter the brain and cerebrospinal fluid far more slowly than into the extra-cellular fluids in general. Here is a ray of hope for those interested in what a fish *was* eating, not yesterday but a fortnight ago. No experiments have so far been carried out.

The main point of this introduction is to show that qualitative differences in the diet are likely to influence the composition of the fish only if they affect the proportions of constituents which the fish cannot synthesise from other food materials or reserves. Major body constituents can be remarkably similar in fish on different diets, or differ remarkably among different species on the same diet. Only when the quantity of the feedstuff is insufficient for the needs of the fish are far-reaching changes in the main constituents brought about. These are described later (p. 182).

2. PROTEINS AND GENERAL FEEDING LEVEL

Measurement of blood constituents tends to be uninformative. It has been shown that blood glucose rises little after feeding (Volume 1, p. 202), although it is in any case difficult to find a "natural" diet with much carbohydrate in it. Similarly, during starvation, blood glucose tends to remain at a constant level until a very late stage is reached (Volume 1, p. 251) although liver glycogen declines steadily.

We now learn that the level of serum protein is unaffected by the protein composition of the diet, even where it ranges from 30 to 60% of the ingested material (Zeitoun, Ullrey and Tack, 1974: *Salmo gairdneri*), though the growth of the fish is abnormal on a low protein intake.

Differences in the levels of food provided by different natural habitats have been held responsible for differences in growth rate, longevity, fecundity and time of spawning (Leggett and Power, 1969: *Salmo salar*). It is interesting to note in passing that the poorer diet in this study gave rise not only to low fecundity but also to increased mortality, unlike the situation in mammals where chronic underfeeding appears to prolong life (Deyl, 1972).[1] *Salmo salar* are however peculiar among salmon in that a proportion of them survives spawning to reproduce the following year and after, and it would seem from this paper that survival depends on the availability of a nourishing diet after spawning. We have seen in Volume 1 (p. 114) that, in contrast, no amount of feeding will enable

---

[1]According to Szepesi (1976), a restricted diet may modify the lifespan of warm-blooded animals by altering the appearance, rate of development or severity of some diseases. This does not *necessarily* mean an increased longevity, however.

Oncorhynchus species to survive, although their lives can be prolonged for several weeks after spawning by giving them food.

The RNA:DNA ratio (see p. 30) indicates the activity of protein synthesis and is a powerful tool for investigating the effectiveness of different diets in promoting growth. Satomi and Nose (1971: *Salmo gairdneri*) showed that an increase in the protein level of the diet results in an almost exactly proportional increase in the nucleic acid ratios in the white muscle and digestive tract tissue of the fish. Dark muscle and liver also show an approximately proportional relationship at lower levels of dietary protein, but it is difficult to observe at higher levels.

The RNA has in addition been shown to increase in the livers of *Pleuronectes platessa* with a higher intake of dietary protein (Cowey, Brown *et al.*, 1974).

Although enhanced growth has been shown in this way to follow the consumption of a diet enriched in protein, there are limits to the amount of protein that a fish can convert to body material. One might imagine that overfeeding a fish would simply result in excess material passing through the gut unchanged and being voided in the faeces, but this does not in fact happen, at least in *Lepomis macrochirus* (Gerking, 1955a). Here it was found that increasing the rate of feeding (meal worms) did not affect the efficiency of protein *absorption*, which remained at 96% or more of the dietary protein, but when it was pushed towards the maximum that the fish would accept, the efficiency of protein *utilisation* for growth began to decrease. The results are shown strikingly in Fig. 50. Excessive feeding evidently gives rise to greater excretion of nitrogen. In a survey of *Gadus morhua* from different fishing grounds, Love, Robertson *et al.* (1974a) found indications that the best-nourished fish had the highest concentrations of urine nitrogen, lending support to the observations of Fig. 50.

An increase in the intake of food has been shown to raise the levels of body lipids in fatty species such as *Engraulis encrasicholus* (Shulman, 1972, p. 161, English edition) and *Ammodytes personatus* (Sekiguchi, Nagoshi *et al.*, 1976) and also of species not so obviously fatty. Satomi and Nose (1971) showed that at higher rates of protein feeding the white muscle (though not the dark muscle) of *Salmo gairdneri* acquires higher concentrations of phospholipids. This seems to indicate an increase in membranous structures as more protein is deposited. *Lepomis macrochirus* also shows an increase in lipid (total lipid in this case) as the level of feeding of meal worms increases (Gerking, 1955a), and *Blennius pholis* acquires more liver lipid at higher food levels (Wallace, 1973). However, this sequence of events is not universal. Jones and Hislop (1972) demonstrated that the percentages of lipid and protein in the bodies of *Melanogrammus aeglefinus* and *Merlangius merlangus* are independent of the level of feeding (squid muscle). At higher levels the girths of the fish increase noticeably, although their composition has not changed. The increases in body lengths, on the other hand, are hardly affected by variations in the rate of feeding, and Davis (1934, quoted by Jones and Hislop, 1972) suggested that the maximum growth rate of

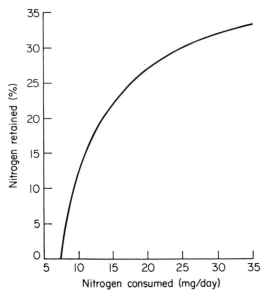

Fig. 50. Efficiency of protein utilisation for growth in relation to protein consumption (*Lepomis macrochirus*). Note how the amount retained decreases proportionately as more is fed. The amount retained is also steadily reduced for a given intake as progressively larger fish are used (Gerking, 1971). After Gerking (1955a). Reproduced with permission of the author.

a fish is determined genetically. Provided that *Gadus morhua* are not actually starving, the relative proportions of protein and lipid in their bodies also seem to be independent of the feeding level. Edwards, Finlayson and Steele (1972), who fed various levels of plaice fillets to this species, found that the fish did increase in length at a greater rate as the feeding level increased, but that at higher feeding rates the advantage was slight. Girth, as in *Merlangius merlangus* and *Melanogrammus aeglefinus*, was influenced much more, and, when the dietary intake exceeded three times the standard metabolic requirements, the lateral musculature thickened so much as to interfere with the action of swimming. The marked corpulence of Faroe Bank cod reported in

Volume 1, p. 158, appears therefore to be a manifestation of a luxuriant food supply. Edwards, Finlayson and Steele (1972) concluded that energy is not stored as lipid in *Gadus morhua*[1]; food consumed in excess of maintenance is laid down partly as liver growth but most of it goes to augment the size of the lateral and tail muscles.

Nothing has been said here about the nutritional requirements for different amino acids. The reader is referred to the detailed review by Mertz (1972), which also describes deficiency symptoms.

3. CARBOHYDRATES

Diets rich in carbohydrates are unnatural to fish (Volume 1, p. 202), but that is not to say that fish do not consume any at all—carnivorous fish consume appreciable quantities, especially from the livers of their prey.

While, as we shall see later, the prime source of energy in *Cyprinus carpio* is protein and not carbohydrate (Nagai and Ikeda, 1972), a proportion of starch added to their diet causes less nitrogen to be excreted, indicating a "nitrogen-saving" effect, that is, the use of some carbohydrate for energy purposes in place of the usual protein (Erman, 1969: same species). A nitrogen saving has also been noted in *Pleuronectes platessa* and *Scophthalmus maximus* fed with carbohydrate in their diet (Adron, Blair *et al.*, 1976), while relatively high levels of digestible carbohydrates can be added to the diet of *Ictalurus punctatus* in place of lipid without affecting growth rates or feed conversions (Garling and Wilson, 1977). On the other hand, *Salmo gairdneri* gain weight more rapidly if sucrose is eliminated from their diet (Léger, Luquet and Boudon, 1976).

Feeding by force results in a high hyperglycaemia if *Cyprinus carpio* have not been fed for some time, but daily force-feeding produces a smaller effect (Santa and Motelica-Heino, 1972). The daily feeding perhaps stimulates the production of insulin and so quicker utilisation of ingested carbohydrates, but stress alone causes a rise in blood glucose (Volume 1, p. 46), and the fish might just be adapting to the handling.[2] Insulin probably does contribute to the situation, however, since repetition of the glucose injection not only results in reduced

---

[1]This is probably an over-simplification: the livers of well-fed cod enlarge because of their increased lipid content.

[2]"Overshoot", the overcompensation of a depleted level on refeeding to concentrations higher than in the controls fed continuously, will be referred to more than once in this narrative—for example in Fig. 86. Its application in "Chemical Biology" is discussed in Chapter 5.

maximum values in the blood, but also an increased rate of removal after the peak (Fig. 7 of Wardle, 1972a: *Pleuronectes platessa*, and C. S. Wardle, personal communication, 1976). Palmer and Ryman (1972) fed glucose to *Salmo gairdneri* and observed a pronounced and persistent hyperglycaemia which they attributed to an insufficiency of circulating insulin. While this suggests that glucose is not a major constituent of the natural diet, a much stronger indication comes from observations on *Carassius auratus* fed on a high carbohydrate diet for long periods (same authors). The livers increase grossly in size because of glycogen accumulation, protein metabolism is impaired, and there are signs of change in the lipids. Palmer and Ryan (1972) suggested that the upset is the response of a metabolic system normally adapted to diets low in available carbohydrate. Similar troubles afflict these fish when kept in a glucose solution without other sources of food: the engorgement of the liver, hyperglycaemia and increased glucose content of the muscle are not changed by insulin, but restoration of a normal diet in clean water brings all the values back to normal (Sterne, Hirsch and Pele, 1968b).

Hayama and Ikeda (1972: *Cyprinus carpio*) observed that it takes more than 10 days for a high carbohydrate diet to work its way through to the blood stream and show as hyperglycaemia, and Nagai and Ikeda (1973) concluded that carp are in a permanent state resembling diabetes, having a depressed utilisation of glucose. In the situation arising from the administration of diets rich in carbohydrate, it seems likely that, after absorption through the gut wall, much of the glucose either remains unused for a long period within the body or is excreted unchanged. Although the activities of digestive enzymes can adapt to the composition of the diet to a considerable degree, it appears that in fish generally the digestibility of carbohydrate is much lower than that of protein. The proportion of carbohydrate consumed which is actually assimilated also declines as its proportion in the diet increases (Cowey and Adron, unpublished, quoted by Cowey and Sargent, 1972). Some adaptation to 10–20% of starch in the diet of the carnivorous *Seriola quinqueradiata* has been noted by Shimeno and Hosokawa (1975). Their fish were seen to increase the activity of the enzymes of the pentose phosphate pathway, and so were probably converting some carbohydrate into lipid, and also to increase the enzymes of glycolysis. On the other hand, the enzymes of gluconeogenesis decreased.

In order to check the idea that amino acids, rather than glucose, are the primary source of energy for carp, Nagai and Ikeda (1972) compared the effects of administering radioactive glutamic acid, as a representative amino acid, with those of administering radioactive glucose. The radioactivity of the products formed showed that much more "expired" carbon dioxide originated in glutamate than in glucose. Very little glucose was converted into hepatopancreatic[1] lipid, but some was converted into glycogen. A great deal of glutamate became incorporated into lipid, little into glycogen. The authors concluded that in this species the oxidation of amino acids is more important than glucose oxidation, and that lipid for storage is synthesised principally from amino acids; only a little glucose seems to be converted into glycogen. The importance of amino acids was thus established, and the authors repeated their thesis that the energy utilisation of the carp resembles that of diabetic mammals.

A diet especially enriched in carbohydrates has been found to result in improved performance (shortened work time) in human athletes (Karlsson and Bengt, 1971), but nothing comparable seems to occur in fish. On the contrary, Poston (1975) found that *Salmo trutta* fed the diet with the highest protein content had the highest stamina (swimming velocity × time) in an exercise channel: diets with a high glucose content did not give rise to good stamina.

The growth of *Salmo gairdneri* on a high protein diet is appreciably suppressed if the diet is supplemented with sucrose, even where both groups of fish ingest the same quantity of protein (Luquet, Léger and Bergot, 1975).

A final pointer to the unnaturalness of carbohydrate intake is the observation by Créac'h and Murat (1974) that the diets richest in carbohydrate cause the highest mortality during the refeeding of severely starved carp.

4. LIPIDS

In Volume 1 (p. 201) it was shown that some species of fish could synthesise polyunsaturated fatty acids from non-fatty precursors, but that the general pattern of the lipids of a fish was strongly influenced by the lipids of the diet.

Similar conclusions arise from more recent work, so no fundamental change in outlook is called for. It is clear, however, that the ability to increase the chain length of ingested fatty acids or to desaturate them varies considerably between species.

Feeding a high-fat diet has been shown to reduce ammonia excretion in *Salmo gairdneri* (Atherton and Aitken, 1970) and, as in diets enriched with carbohydrate (p. 139), to result in an increased proportion of ingested nitrogen being retained for growth (Atherton and Aitken,

---

[1]The pancreas and liver of carp are combined in a single organ called the hepatopancreas

1970; Austreng, 1976; de la Higuera, Murillo *et al.*, 1977), especially at higher ambient temperatures. The nitrogen-sparing action of lipid was found by Adron, Blair *et al.* (1976) to be more effective than that of carbohydrate in *Scophthalmus maximus* and *Pleuronectes platessa*.

The strong influence of the pattern of dietary lipids on those of the fish has been noted by several recent authors, being measurable in *Salmo gairdneri* within a week of a change in diet (de la Higuera, Murillo *et al.*, 1976). It was reported by Castell, Lee and Sinnhuber (1972) to affect the fatty acid composition of the phospholipids to a greater degree than that of the neutral lipids of *Salmo gairdneri*, but one would like to know how true this is in other species having different ratios of neutral lipids (stored for later mobilisation) to phospholipids (incorporated as essential constituents of cell membranes and other structures). Feeding after severe starvation is followed by the restitution of many degraded structures, so that it would also be interesting to know if the latter then differ in composition according to the diet: the field is unexplored at present. It is on the other hand the depot (storage) lipids of the body of *Allothunnus fallai* which are influenced by the dietary lipids (Bishop, James and Olley, 1976). They become like those of the zooplankton on which the fish feed, but the liver lipids pursue an independent course and are typical of the liver lipids of fish generally. A similar observation was made by Stickney and Andrews (1972), who found that the fatty acids laid down in the whole carcasses of *Ictalurus punctatus* followed the proportions in the diet very closely, whereas the liver lipids did not. It is as though the liver lipids are needed for specific purposes, so need to be of a controlled composition, while the reserve lipids of the body are burned for energy, where a wide range of different fatty acids would be effective. Worthington and Lovell (1973) calculated that genetic and other factors account for about 5% of the variance in the fatty acid composition of the body lipids of this species, while diet accounts for 93%. A similar study on liver lipids might well have led to contrary conclusions. It is, however, not advisable to read too much into the effects of different diets on liver and muscle lipids, since Pokrovskii, Levachev and Gapparov (1973) found that the composition of lipids in the mitochondrial membranes—surely "structural"—of rat livers also change with changes in the lipids of the diet.

In contrast to the situation in *Allothunnus fallai* or *Ictalurus punctatus*, the fatty acid composition of the liver lipids of *Salmo gairdneri* is influenced by the diet more than that of the muscle (Varesmaa, Laine and Niinivaara, 1968). Once again one has the uncomfortable feeling of having in the end revealed nothing useful; it just has to be remembered that energy stores differ among different species in location and importance, and such differences probably go hand-in-hand with variations in the composition of the lipids found there.

The requirements for specific fatty acids probably also vary among species. *Ictalurus punctatus* has been found to gain less weight when fed fatty acids of short or medium chain length as compared with mixtures containing all the fatty acids. The fish also do not thrive on a fat-free diet, or on diets rich in 18:2 or 18:3 fatty acids (Stickney and Andrews, 1972). In contrast, *Oncorhynchus tschawytscha*, which also grows very slowly on a fat-free diet, recovers its growth rate completely when 18:2 (linoleic) acid is given and shows some improvement after consuming 18:3 (linolenic) acid (Lee and Sinnhuber, 1973). The latter authors pointed out that no definite figure could be given for the optimum level of lipids in fish diets without considering factors like the type of lipid and the amount of protein being consumed at the same time. Highly unsaturated fatty acids, and 18:2 and 18:3 acids, in that order of effectiveness, have also been shown to cure the deficiency symptoms[1] of *Salmo gairdneri* reared on a fat-free diet (Higashi, Kaneko *et al.*, 1966).

Excess lipid in the diet can give rise to undesirable symptoms. Roberts (1970) reported lateral swellings on the musculature of large numbers of *Pleuronectes platessa* reared in the warm effluent waters of a power station. On histological examination they proved to be abnormal deposits of areolar lipid tissue, which appeared to arise from the abnormal environment which encouraged continuous, as distinct from regular, high-level feeding on the lipid-rich diet. A diet rich in lipids also depresses the activities of enzymes which promote lipid synthesis within the fish (Lin, Romsos *et al.*, 1977: *Oncorhynchus kisutch*).

In some species the polyunsaturated long-chain fatty acids peculiar to fish can be synthesised from shorter carbon chains. Much attention centres on the acid 22:6 which tends to occur in large quantities in fish. In *Oncorhynchus kisutch* it is laid down in amounts relating primarily to the size of the fish rather than its availability in the diet (Tinsley, Krueger and Saddler, 1973). *Salmo gairdneri* fed on 18:2 and 18:3 acids can produce 20:3, 22:5 and 22:6 acids in substantial quantities (Owen, Adron *et al.*, 1975), but marine flatfish seem to have a more limited capacity to elongate the chain length or to desaturate them (create more double bonds). These workers found that 70% of the radioactivity of administered radioactive 18:3 acid appears later in the 22:6 acid of the fish, but that turbot (*Scophthalmus maximus*) converts only 3 to 15% of labelled precursors into fatty acids of longer chain length, and does not

[1]The posterior part of the body is discoloured, hard and rough, and becomes constricted in shape. The caudal (tail) fin becomes worn away, sometimes leaving the end of the spinal column exposed. No internal disease has been observed.

increase the number of double bonds. They suggested that turbot in the wild probably receive adequate polyunsaturated acids in the diet, which they therefore have no need to modify. Ross (1978) has shown that chain elongation and desaturation of 18:3 acid administered to another marine teleost (*Gadus morhua*) are also small, perhaps for the same reason.

Wax esters are the principal type of lipid present in most pelagic marine invertebrates and in teleost fish from deep waters or from cold waters near the surface. It was suggested earlier that only a few organisms were in fact capable of synthesising these compounds, but that the wax esters, once synthesised, were transferred along the food chain to the fish. Recently, though, Kayama and Nevenzel (1974) have demonstrated synthesis in a number of fish species starting from acetate, long-chain alcohols or fatty acids. Muscle was shown to be a major site of biosynthesis, and the hepatopancreas to be even more active. Thus both invertebrates and fish can make their own wax esters from dietary lipids.

The serum of *Anguilla japonica* is blue-green in colour because of the presence of a complex chromoprotein containing small quantities of biliverdin and sugar and a considerable proportion of lipid (Yamaguchi, Hashimoto and Matsuura, 1968). The intensity of serum colour varies with the season and seems to vary with the amount of food eaten. These authors suggest that the role of this complex is the transport of lipid, so that the remarkable rise in pigmentation in summer follows that in the intake of lipid which has to be transported by the blood. A difference in pigment concentration between cultured and wild eels is explained on the basis of a difference in food supply, and the disappearance of pigment in the serum of migrating eels is probably related to the reduced eating which occurs when the gonads are close to maturity.

This alone of recent observations seems to hold promise as a method for studying feeding patterns, though unfortunately it is confined to eels. As already noted, it is unusual for the measurement of a blood constituent to be informative because of frequent homeostases.

5. CAROTENOIDS

As a general statement, the fate of carotenoids ingested by fish resembles that of fatty acids, in that some are deposited unchanged while some are converted into other carotenoids before being deposited, interspecies differences in the fish exerting an overriding influence.

As an example of the latter, dietary β-carotene is metabolised to astaxanthin in *Carassius auratus* (Hata and Hata, 1972a; Hsu, Rodriguez and Chichester, 1972) but not in *Cyprinus carpio* (Katayama, Miyahara *et al.*, 1972) or *Chrysophrys major* (Katayama, Shintani *et al.*, 1972). Similarly, lutein is converted to astaxanthin in *Cyprinus carpio* (Katayama, Tsuchiya and Chichester, 1971) but not in *Carassius auratus* (Hata and Hata, 1972a).

Zeaxanthin also is converted to astaxanthin in *Carassius auratus*, through the intermediate 4-keto-zeaxanthin, the conversion apparently taking place in the skin rather than the intestine (Hata and Hata, 1972b).

Other precursors of astaxanthin are lutein ester and canthaxanthin, both found in pond algae. The pathway of the former is from lutein ester to α-doradexanthin, β-doradexanthin and astaxanthin (Katayama, Tsuchiya and Chichester, 1971: *Cyprinus carpio*). More intermediates appear to be involved in the formation of astaxanthin from β-carotene (Hsu, Rodriguez and Chichester, 1972), and this conversion takes place to a comparatively small extent (Hata and Hata, 1972a: *Carassius auratus*).

Dietary astaxanthin has been shown to be deposited as such in the body of *Chrysophrys major* (Katayama, Shintani *et al.*, 1972) and *Cyprinus carpio* (Katayama, Miyahara *et al.*, 1972).

Lutein, β-carotene and to some extent canthaxanthin can all be synthesised from precursors provided by non-specific carotenoids such as torularhodin and torulene, but α-carotene is found in fish only when it occurs in the diet (Savolainen and Gyllenberg, 1970: *Salmo gairdneri*).

Commercial interest in carotenoid deposition centres on the creation of an acceptable colour in the flesh of salmonids for eating or on the retention of brilliant colours in the skins of fish for show.

As regards *Salmo gairdneri*, a satisfactory flesh colour can readily be obtained by feeding diets containing shrimp waste or synthetic canthaxanthin, but the situation in *Salmo salar* is more complex, and appears to be tied to the reproductive cycle. Experience at a culture unit (P. N. Lewtas, personal communication, 1976) seems to show that carotenoids enter the flesh in quantity only as the gonads begin to mature, and then leave again just as rapidly as the gonads grow bigger. There is logic in this, but it means careful timing on the part of the culturist if a red-coloured flesh is to be obtained.

6. VITAMINS

Some species of fish can convert dietary carotene or astaxanthene into retinol (vitamin A_1) or dehydroretinol (vitamin A_2). Most of their vitamins appear to be derived from the diet (Volume 1, p. 200), because, unlike mammals, fish seem to lack the kind of resident intestinal microflora which synthesise vitamins.

The latter conclusion has been confirmed by Malikova (1957: quoted by Arsan and Malyarevskaya, 1974), who showed that the consumption of food with a low content of vitamins, especially riboflavin (vitamin B_2) leads to reduced vitamin concentrations in fish organs and tissues. On the other hand, the intestines of *Cyprinus carpio* seem to be able to synthesise cyanocobalamin (vitamin B_{12}) when the fish are restricted to a B_{12}-free diet (Kashiwada, Teshima and Kanazawa, 1970).

The quantities of vitamins required for growth by different species of fish are listed by Halver (1972: Table III, p. 39). Requirements differ little among salmonids, but by comparison *Cyprinus carpio* seem to need less of the B vitamins. Symptoms characteristic of deficiency of the different vitamins are listed in Volume 1, p. 208, in Halver (1972: Table II, p. 36), Snieszko (1972), Cowey and Sargent (1972) and Ashley (1972: Table I, p. 442), the last-mentioned review distinguishing between symptoms exhibited by different species. The deficiency symptoms exhibited by *Anguilla japonica* are given by Arai, Nose and Hashimoto (1972).

Other species differences can be seen. *Salvelinus fontinalis* and *Gadus morhua* cannot convert β-carotene to vitamin A, and so differ from *Perca fluviatilis* and *Leuciscus leuciscus*, which can (Poston, 1969b). In addition, tocopherol (vitamin E) deficiency leads to ceroid deposits in the spleen of *Oncorhynchus tschawytscha* but not, apparently, in *Cyprinus carpio* (Watanabe, Takashima *et al.*, 1970).

Although the proportions of vitamins A_1/A_2 in a fish generally relate to the illumination of the habitat (see Volume 1, p. 181), they can be upset by an abnormal preponderance of one vitamin in the diet. Thus the addition of cod liver oil (rich in vitamin A_1) to the diet of *Salmo gairdneri* increases the proportion of A_1 at the expense of A_2 in the fish (Georgiev, 1972a). Consumption of this vitamin in excess, likewise excesses of vitamins D (Poston, 1969c: *Salvelinus fontinalis*) and E, induce changes in the body weight and haematocrit in *Salmo trutta* as they do in mammals (Poston and Livingston, 1971a). Niacin (nicotinic acid) fed to excess causes an increase in liver lipids and a concomitant decrease in body lipids (Poston, 1969a: *Salvelinus fontinalis*). On the other hand, "additional" riboflavin, niacin, pantothenic acid, choline and cyanocobalamin in the diet seem to have no effect beyond inducing a slight weight gain when administered to *Ictalurus punctatus* (Deyoe, Tiemeier and Suppes, 1968).

7.   DIRECT ABSORPTION OF SUBSTANCES FROM THE ENVIRONMENT

A few examples of direct absorption were given in Volume 1, pp. 205–207.

Although Kondratovics (1969: *Salmo gairdneri*) stated that the concentrations of trace elements in the body, especially zinc and cobalt, depend on those in the food, this is by no means their only source, and most workers regard the environment as supplying a significant proportion of inorganic constituents. Anonymous work (1969) carried out on fish from different Russian lakes, for example, showed that the quantities of manganese, iron, copper and zinc in the muscle and liver reflect the geochemical characteristics of the earth surrounding the lakes. As we have now come to expect, the responses to varying amounts of trace elements in the environment differ according to species.

Ogino and Kamizono (1975), who studied the actual requirements of *Salmo gairdneri* and *Cyprinus carpio* for minerals found the studies complicated by the fish taking part from the food, part from the water. Diets deficient in copper give rise to anaemia, lack of cobalt or manganese causes malformation of bones, while zinc is essential for a normal rate of growth (C. Ogino and T. Watanabe, personal communication, 1977). Magnesium deficiency results in loss of appetite, poor growth, some mortality, sluggishness and convulsions (Ogino and Chiou, 1976: *Cyprinus carpio*).

Incorporation of inorganic substances into the fish is often highly selective. Manganese and zinc are readily absorbed, and their tissue concentrations are tens of thousands of times greater than those in the water (Berman, 1969: *Abramis brama, Esox lucius*), although in fact the food is the main source of these elements: along with silicon, iron and copper they are less concentrated in the fish than in their food, so the fish eliminate some microelements. Barium in *Esox lucius* and strontium in both species are selectively retained, and are more concentrated than in either the food or the environment. Berman (1969) has also shown that fish utilise both sources for most of their microelements. The concentration of cobalt in the flesh of many fish from the Caspian Sea is higher than that of nickel, although the relative concentrations are reversed in the sea water itself (Magomaev, 1972). The contribution of the diet to the intake of these elements was not stated. The concentration of calcium in the bony structures (scales and bones) of freshwater fish is regulated by the fish and is independent of the composition of the lake from which they were taken. In contrast, the strontium concentration in the same structures exhibits great variations according to the habitat (Berg, 1972). The scales of *Salmo trutta* from fresh water contain less than 200 μg of strontium per gram, while those from the same species living in the sea contain more than 300 μg/g, so the marine and freshwater forms of the fish can be distinguished. Bagenal, Mackereth and Heron (1973), who made this observation, also found that the centre portions of the scales of *Salmo salar*, representing freshwater life, contained 110 and 179 µg/g (two specimens), while the outer parts, representing marine life, contained 308 and 348 µg/g, illustrating the sequence of habitats of the fish.

The eggs of fish also can absorb considerable quantities of trace elements from the water. Radioactive studies showed that "trout" eggs absorb phosphorus, carbon (from HCO_3) and calcium (Shekhanova, 1966, quoted by Berman and Vitin', 1968), and copper, manganese, strontium and barium have all been observed to enter the eggs of *Salmo gairdneri* during incubation (Todorov, Naplatorova and Suikova, 1971). On the other hand, Zeitoun, Ullrey *et al.* (1976) concluded that all of the phosphorus and copper found in the larvae of this species on hatching could have come from the unfertilised oocyte. The environment contributed 26% of the sodium, 30% of the iron and 13% of the zinc found at hatching, and in addition to these ions, calcium and potassium were enriched in the larva, at the post yolk-absorption stage, from the surrounding water (same authors). A remarkable increase in the content of manganese after the fertilisation of the eggs of *Oryzias latipes* was reported by Hori and Iwasaki (1976), a total content of 0·51 mµg per unfertilised egg preceding a content of 2·61 mµg per embryo after gastrulation. The extra material had been actively absorbed from the medium.

This account has so far been concerned exclusively with the absorption of inorganic substances. It is, however, more than likely that they tell only part of the story. The epithelium of the kidney duct of *Petromyzon marinus*, for example, has the ability to absorb small quantities of exogenous protein (Youson, 1975) and the question immediately arises as to what normal body constituents are to be found in natural waters which could be utilised by the fish. *Free* amino acids were detected in the north Atlantic by Pocklington (1971), while Riley and Segar (1970) found both free and combined amino acids in the waters of the Irish Sea, principally alanine, serine, glycine, threonine and valine. Astonishingly, dissolved ATP has also been found in sea water in significant concentrations (0·1 to 0·6 µg/l), and appears to be utilised by marine bacteria (Azam and Hodson, 1977).

The particulate matter from the surface waters of the north Atlantic was found by Schultz and Quinn (1972) to contain the long-chain polyunsaturated fatty acids typical of marine fish, but material of this nature may not be of immediate use. More likely to be utilised are the free fatty acids found in the coastal waters of west Brittany in concentrations of 10–40 µg/l by Treguer, le Corre and Courtot (1972), which represented about 1% of the dissolved organic matter. Volatile acids (acetic, propionic, isobutyric, n-butyric, isovaleric and n-valeric) have been found, both in the water and the bottom mud of the Nagara River, where fish with an offensive odour had been caught (Ose, Funasaka and Sato, 1975). These compounds were also found in high concentrations in the muscle and digestive organs of the fish, but not in the livers.

A single report of the presence of cyanocobalamin in the Atlantic was mentioned in Volume 1 (p. 74), and two further papers have appeared since. Seasonal cycles were found in the concentration of cyanocobalamin in the waters of the Strait of Georgia, British Columbia (Cattell, 1973), and in the surface waters of Lake Tsuki (Ohwada, Otsuhata and Taga, 1972), where thiamine and biotin were also found, both dissolved and in the particulate matter of the lake.

Hydrogen ions appear to be absorbed from the environment, judging by the close correlation between the pH of the water and that of the blood of the fish (Labat, Kugler-Laffont *et al.*, 1969: *Cyprinus carpio*, *Tinca tinca*, *Perca flavescens*). The blood pH of carp was shown to be about 6·3 at an ambient pH of 4, rising to about 7·3 at 8·5. Ammonium and nitrate ions have also been observed to be taken up from the environment, this time by the fry of *Cyprinus carpio*, *Carassius carassius* and *Misgurnus anguillicaudatus* (Ito, 1976).

8. MISCELLANEOUS SUBSTANCES

Evidence that the trimethylamine found in the muscle of fish originated in the diet was presented in Volume 1, p. 202. The flesh of young trout accumulates it if present in the diet but not otherwise, and eels taken from the sea contain a little in their bodies while those from fresh water have none. Marine zooplankton is rich in this compound, while freshwater zooplankton contains only traces.

Trimethylamine oxide has now been shown as exogenous to *Anguilla japonica* (Hashimoto and Okaichi, 1958b), falling rapidly to zero when the fish are maintained on a diet free of it. The muscle of *Carassius auratus* remains free of trimethylamine oxide as long as there is none in the diet, but it can be measured in the muscle 2 hours after the fish has ingested some (Hashimoto and Okaichi, 1958a). These workers found that continued feeding of the compound maintained the level in the muscle, but that in subsequent fasting it dropped to zero in 2 days—see Fig. 51.

This is not the whole story, however, because starvation of marine fish for 25 days does not cause a similar fall in trimethylamine oxide concentration (Okaichi, Manabe and Hashimoto, 1959: *Fugu niphobles*, *Monacanthus cirrhifer*, *Trachurus japonicus*), suggesting that it performs

some function in fish in the marine environment. The last word on the
origins and roles of the compound has not yet been said, but it has been
regarded as a non-toxic end-product of ammonia excretion and may
have osmoregulatory functions (reviewed briefly in Volume 1, p. 288).

Various dietary organisms can impart unpleasant odours or flavours
to the flesh of fish. In Volume 1, p. 199, it was stated that consumption
of a marine invertebrate ("blackberry") results in an unpleasant smell
in *Gadus morhua*, identified as dimethyl sulphide. Similarly, *Mytilus* (a
shellfish) larvae can cause the flesh of *Clupea harengus* to taste bitter.

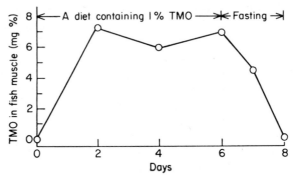

FIG. 51. Trimethylamine oxide in the muscle of *Carassius auratus* fed a diet containing
1% of the same compound. Note how the concentration falls rapidly when the fish
are starved beyond day 6. After Hashimoto and Okaichi (1958a). Reproduced with
permission of Professor K. Hashimoto on behalf of the late Professor Y. Hashimoto.

Dimethyl sulphide has again been identified in fish, this time in
Scomber scombrus (Ackman, Hingley and MacKay, 1972), originating in
the pteropod *Spiratella retroversa*. Its precursor, β-dimethylpropiothetin,
also probably occurs in certain algae from brackish water, which evolve
dimethyl sulphide when treated with alkali (Granroth and Hattula,
1976). Geosmin was discovered by Yurkowsky and Tabachek (1974) in
fish from various saline lakes of west Canada. The source was thought to
be the metabolites of the bacterium *Streptomyces*, and the compound
imparted a "muddy" flavour to the flesh. Similar findings are reported
by Persson (1977b: *Abramis brama*). Off-flavours found in fish which
have consumed certain algae (such as *Oscillatoria* spp.: Persson, 1977a)
are also produced if phenolic substances and oil are present in the
water (Mann, 1969). Such materials are taken up through the gills and
skin and are deposited in the fatty parts of the fish. Other compounds
proved to cause unpleasant tastes are *p*-toluidine, pyridine, resorcinol
and phloroglucinol, especially in the presence of detergents. The

frequency of occurrence of these compounds in the natural environment was not, however, stated.

9. INFLUENCE OF DIET ON ENZYMIC ACTIVITY

The shape and structure of the intestines of fish may be modified by the nature of the diet. The proportions of enzymes produced relate to the habitual diets of individual species and the quantities can vary seasonally. A single report (Volume 1, pp. 204–205) showed that the activity of amylase in various parts of the alimentary canal of *Tilapia* becomes modified according to the diet. There is need for further research, because the only other report showed *no* variation of this kind in the amylolytic or proteolytic activity in the gut of *Cyprinus carpio*.

a. *Digestive secretions*

Reichenbach-Klinke (1972) makes the point that natural food such as zooplankton participates significantly in the digestion of the consuming fish by supplying digestive enzymes. Some of the seasonal variation in enzyme activity may therefore be caused by differences in the number of organisms consumed. All other reports describe variations originating in the fish themselves.

The seasonal variation in stomach protease activity described by Onishi and Murayama (1970) related only to cultivated salmonids living on a commercial diet, so the consumption of living organisms was presumably minimal. Likewise the increase in amylase in all parts of the intestine from spring to autumn reported by Stroganov and Buzinova (1969) relates to a purely vegetarian fish, the grass carp (*Ctenopharyngodon idella*). These reports do however add to the pre-liminary findings reported in Volume 1 that the digestive secretions are modified by the quantity or nature of the food consumed. There are further reports along the same lines.

The intestinal protease of *Cyprinus carpio* increases or decreases according to the protein (fish meal) content of a diet with constant starch content (Kawai and Ikeda, 1972). The activities of pepsin, trypsin, amylase and maltase all increase in the intestine of *Salmo gairdneri* with increase in the protein content of the diet (Kawai and Ikeda, 1973a), although the latter two enzymes digest carbohydrate. A general increase in the activity of the secretory cells seems to be in-dicated. The addition of various proportions of phosphatide to the diet was reported by Shterman (1969: *Salmo gairdneri*, *S. salar*) to increase the alkaline phosphatase activity of the intestine, while Brizinova and Strel'tsova (1969: *Salmo gairdneri*) found that dietary phosphatide aided the digestion of protein. The latter authors also demonstrated improved protein digestion following an increase in the protein content of the diet.

There is a marked lag between the filling of the digestive tract with food and the maximum rate of enzyme secretion, at least in *Cyprinus carpio* (Onishi, Murayama and Takeuchi, 1976). In this species, the activities of protease and amylase reach their peaks when the absorption of the degraded food materials has already set in.

The remaining reports relate enzyme activities to dietary differences between different species rather than to modifications within a species. Yoshida and Sera (1970) found that fish which feed on organisms such as shrimps and zooplankton, which have chitinous shells, have high chitinolytic activity in part of the stomach, while that in the stomach of *Konosirus punctatus* or *Mugil cephalus*, which feed on phytoplankton, detritus or microbenthos, is low or negligible. *Scorpaena porcus* and *Conger conger* consume a relatively large proportion of chitin and generate much chitinolytic activity in the intestine (Colin, 1972), whereas the herbivore *Boops salpa* shows weak activity and *Crenilabrus pavo*, which eats mostly echinoderms (rich in calcium carbonate) has only traces.

Large quantities of calcium carbonate are eaten by some of the fish living on coral reefs, and this results in a high level of carbonic anhydrase being present in the gut. Smith and Paulson (1975) found that the intestinal mucosa of *Acanthurus triostegus* and *Scarus jonesi*, which eat coral, had twelve times the carbonic anhydrase activity of that of *Holocentrus spinifer*, which is a predator and does not ingest calcium carbonate, although it lives around the reef.

Cellulase in the alimentary tract seems to be anomalous in that its activity does not relate to the food habits of a large number of species as reported in the literature (Stickney and Shumway, 1974). The activity also bears no relation to the phylogeny of the fish, nor to the presence or absence of a morphologically recognisable stomach. Fish within a family sometimes show cellulase activity even where other members of the same family, on almost identical diets, have none. Stickney and Shumway (1974) concluded that the enzyme activity was probably more closely related to the microflora of the alimentary tract than to the presence or absence of cellulose within the food consumed.

Finally, Vegas-Velez (1973) noted that the intestines of *Boops boops*, *Diplodus annularis* and *Pagellus acarne*, which are all ominorous fish, had less lipolytic and proteolytic activity than those of carnivores.

b.   *Other enzymes*

Turning now to enzymes in other tissues, we find that histidine deaminase and urocanase in muscle increase in activity if *Cyprinus carpio* are fed a high protein diet, or a low protein diet which is supplemented by histidine (Sakaguchi and Kawai, 1970b). These enzymes are thought to regulate the level of free histidine in muscle by breaking it down as required. A feed rich in lactose raises the lactase activity in the intestines of calves, while in *Salmo gairdneri* it increases lactase activity nearly three-fold in the intestine and eight-fold in the liver (Nagayama and Saito, 1969).

Salvelinus fontinalis maintained in a hatchery have considerably higher glucose-6-phosphate dehydrogenase activity in their livers than have their wild counterparts from ponds or streams. Yamauchi, Stegeman and Goldberg (1975), who observed this, attributed the difference to a higher content of carbohydrate in hatchery diet.

Teleosts can be divided into two broad groups according to the activity of arginase in the liver (Cvancara, 1969b). Those with a high level of activity are largely carnivorous, while omnivorous or herbivorous fish exhibit low activity. As usual[1], one species has been found not to fit into the scheme; *Coregonus artedi* has the highest level of arginase activity of all the fish investigated, but is not a carnivore. This species apart, the general conclusion of the report is that dietary arginine, as distinct from arginine from the body proteins, probably contributes substantially to urea production in teleosts. The underlying bio-chemistry may be unfamiliar to some readers, but we will consider excretion of urea and other substances in more detail in the section immediately following.

B. Excretion

1. INTRODUCTION

The Classical Greek writer who rather unkindly described womankind as "a goddess built on a sewer" was only drawing attention to the limited life of proteins. Even where animals starve, the nitrogenous end-products of protein breakdown are constantly being produced and excreted, though in *Anguilla japonica* and probably other species there is a sharp decline in output during the first few days after the cessation of feeding (Volume 1, p. 257).

Since land animals retain their excretory products for varying periods between urinary bladder discharges, it is essential that toxic substances

---

[1]See Preface to Volume 1, p. ix.

are not produced in appreciable quantities. Ammonia is therefore an unsuitable vehicle for the elimination of nitrogen from the body, and most mammalian nitrogenous excretion takes the form of urea, a relatively inert and non-toxic material. It is the un-ionised form of ammonia (NH_3) which is toxic, rather than the ionised form (NH_4^+)—authors quoted by Sousa and Meade (1977)—since it passes the more readily through cell membranes. The toxicity of excreted ammonia therefore depends very much on the pH, temperature and salinity of the water, which affect the equilibrium between the two forms. An increase of one pH unit leads to a ten-fold increase in the toxic form, and, conversely, at a low pH most of the ammonia in a fish culture tank will not harm the fish (Hampson, 1976). Ammonia poisoning causes hyperplasia, proliferation, "clubbing" and eventual fusion and consolidation of the gill lamellae, causing the fish to die from asphyxiation (same author).

Birds excrete nitrogen as the solid, insoluble uric acid, which has the additional advantage of enabling them to conserve water. Only fish are able to tolerate a high proportion of their waste nitrogen as ammonia, because it can be eliminated rapidly and continuously through the gills. As an extra safeguard, their tissues also appear to be more tolerant towards ammonia than are those of animals which excrete urea ("ureotelic species") or uric acid ("uricotelic species")—Wilson, Anderson and Bloomfield (1969). An interesting link between fish and ureotelic species can be seen in *Periophthalmus sobrinus*, an amphibious fish which always excretes both urea and ammonia[1], but shifts the ratio of the two in the direction of urea when it is out of water, reducing the toxic build-up (Gordon, Boëtius et al., 1969). Gordon, Fischer and Tarifeño (1970) observed the same effect in the Chilean clingfish, *Sicyases sanguineus*. Similarly when lung-fish aestivate and seal themselves up in coccoons during the dry season, it is urea and not ammonia which accumulates, although they excrete ammonia when swimming freely (Smith, 1930; DeLaney, Lahiri et al., 1977: *Protopterus;* Carlisky and Barrio, 1972: *Lepidosiren*). The Australian lungfish, *Neoceratodus forsteri*, remains completely aquatic throughout the year, and its capacity for synthesising urea is correspondingly reduced (Funkhouser, Goldstein and Forster, 1972). *Dicentrarchus labrax* reduces the rate of ammonia excretion and increases the proportion of urea if the level of ammonia in the aquarium water increases or the volume of water is reduced (Guerin-Ancey, 1976b).

---

[1]Uric acid has not been detected in the excretory products of the related *Periophthalmus expeditionium* or of *P. gracilis* (Gregory, 1977).

Aquatic organisms do not have pathways to turn all of their waste nitrogen into ammonia: there is always a variable amount of urea present as well (Watts and Watts, 1974). Table 10 lists the proportions of urea excreted in relation to the total nitrogen in some freshwater teleosts. Vellas-Clos (1973) points out that her results are higher than those of other authors because of the difference in water volume in which the experimental fish were maintained—nitrogenous outflow is suppressed if they are confined in too small a volume.

TABLE 10

Urea nitrogen excreted as a percentage of total excreted nitrogen, in a group of freshwater fish. (After Vellas-Clos, 1973. Reproduced with permission of the author)

Species	Dietary habit	Time of capture	Urea nitrogen as percent of excreted nitrogen
Cyprinus carpio	Omnivorous	November	25
Esox lucius	Carnivorous	December	19
Perca fluviatilis	Carnivorous	November	17
Sander lucioperca	Carnivorous	April	26
Tinca tinca	Omnivorous	February	21

These fish were starved for 8 days before being sampled, so the results are for endogenous nitrogen. *Engraulis mordax*, a marine species, excretes 13% of its total nitrogen as urea, about 1% as creatin, 68% as ammonia and 18% in other forms (McCarthy and Whitledge, 1972).

As discussed in Volume 1 (p. 139), elasmobranchs retain urea to help prevent their bodies from being dried out by the strong salt solutions in which they swim. Osmoregulation seems to be its sole function, and the concentration is reduced when euryhaline elasmobranchs enter fresh water (Thorson, Cowan and Watson, 1973). Urea passes readily through most internal membranes, so is distributed throughout the body, though the liver tends to contain less of it. Outside the elasmobranchs only *Latimeria*, the coelacanth, possesses comparable concentrations (Lutz and Robertson, 1971; Watts and Watts, 1974). Elasmobranchs do in fact excrete urea through the kidneys in the usual way, but some of it is then reabsorbed by the kidney tubules rather than being allowed to pass out into the bladder, the reabsorption being in some way linked with a simultaneous reabsorption of sodium (Schmidt-Nielsen, 1973: *Squalus acanthias*). Elasmobranch tissues tolerate urea, but the fish appear not to be completely adapted to it since it has been shown to inhibit enzymes both of oxidative processes and of glycolysis (Mályusz and Thiemann, 1976: *Scyliorhinus canicula*). None of the elasmobranch enzymes have been found to work better in the presence of urea, contrary to what one might have expected.

Un-ionised ammonia is not tolerated well by any group of fish, and the levels in the blood of elasmobranchs are no higher than those in teleosts (Watts and Watts, 1974). The concentrations in the tissues of most fish are lower than the corresponding concentrations of tissue urea, in spite of ammonia being produced in the greater quantity (Pandian, 1975).

2.   GILL VERSUS KIDNEY

We have already begun to answer the question as to why fish need a kidney at all when the gills serve so effectively as a route for excretion: in the kidneys it is possible for certain necessary substances to be re-absorbed as they travel down the tubule, so that only unwanted sub-stances are voided. The presence of ATPase[1] in the kidney indicates reabsorption of sodium from the glomerular filtrate, and it seems to be particularly significant that the activity of this enzyme declines when *Salmo salar* prepare to migrate from fresh water to the sea (McCartney, 1976): no obvious purpose would be served by retaining body sodium in a marine environment, although there does seem to be some re-absorption as we shall see in a moment.

Recent evidence shows that the reabsorptive process continues after the urine has left the kidney and has entered the bladder. There is much less sodium in bladder urine than in urine still in the ureter (Forster and Danforth, 1972: *Lophius americanus*; Foster, 1976: *Platichthys stellatus*), the sodium transport being mediated by ATPase here also (Renfro, Miller *et al.*, 1976: *Pseudopleuronectes americanus*). There is an inverse relationship between sodium and magnesium in the bladder (Natochin and Gusev, 1970: *Scorpaena porcus*; Beyenbach and Kirschner, 1975: *Salmo gairdneri*; Foster, 1976: *Platichthys stellatus*; Griffith, Umminger *et al.*, 1976: *Latimeria chalumnae*), an example of which is illustrated in Fig. 52.

Beyenbach and Kirschner (1975) pointed out that the two ions are excreted together by the kidney, a fact inconsistent with an exchange system. It is only when the urine has lain in the bladder for some time that the inverse relationship develops. Presumably the bladder re-absorbs sodium and water, thereby concentrating the magnesium, a view likewise held by Foster (1976). Natochin and Gusev (1970), who favoured the idea of an exchange between the two ions in the bladder,

---

[1]ATPase, adenosine triphosphatase, breaks down adenosine triphosphate, liberating energy. The enzyme is very important at the gill surfaces, where it provides energy for the extrusion of ions against a concentration gradient.

found that inhibition of sodium reabsorption prevented the concentration of magnesium from rising, but presumably water absorption had been inhibited also. Water reabsorption would be the important aspect of this process in marine fish, and sodium reabsorption important in freshwater fish.

These studies show why fish really do need a bladder. It always used to puzzle me why they did not just allow the urine to dribble out continuously—after all, they have no underclothing or carpets to ruin.

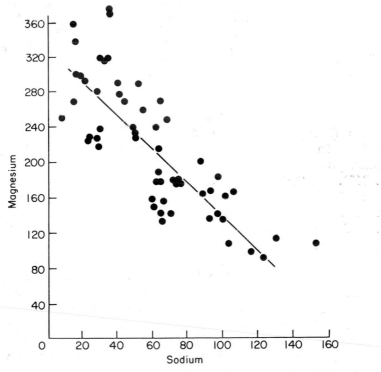

Fig. 52. Relationship between sodium and magnesium in the urine of *Scorpaena porcus* (mEq/l). After Natochin and Gusev (1970). Reproduced with permission of Professor Yu. V. Natochin.

As well as reabsorbing essential materials, kidneys are also needed for the excretion of less diffusible nitrogenous end-products such as creatin, creatinine and uric acid; much of the ammonia, urea and amine- or amine oxide derivatives diffuse through the gills (Smith, 1929b). From the same reference it is known that in *Carassius auratus* and *Cyprinus carpio* the gills excrete six to ten times the quantity of waste nitrogen that appears in the urine. More recent work by Vellas-Clos (1973) shows an even smaller relative contribution by the kidneys of three freshwater species (Table 11), and Fromm (1963) calculated that only about 3% of the total waste nitrogen is excreted by the kidneys of *Salmo gairdneri.*

TABLE 11

The division of excretion between gills and kidneys in some freshwater fish. (After Vellas-Clos, 1973. Reproduced with permission of the author)

Species	Urea nitrogen		Total excreted nitrogen	
	Excreted via gills	Excreted via kidneys	Excreted via gills	Excreted via kidneys
Cyprinus carpio	91·3	8·7	93·9	6·1
Sander lucioperca	94·5	5·0	93·8	6·2
Tinca tinca	72·3	27·7	92·2	7·8

The kidneys of many species of antarctic fish do not possess glomeruli. Dobbs (1974) considered that this modification ("aglomerulism") might be important in preventing the loss of those special glycoproteins which protect polar fish from freezing at sub-zero temperatures (see p. 345). On the other hand, the tubular epithelium of such kidneys successfully secretes magnesium and calcium against a concentration gradient, while little potassium or sodium are found in the urine, the latter fact probably being linked to the high concentration of urinary magnesium.

There is a possible third route for excretion apart from the gills or kidneys. This is the slime of hagfish, in which the calcium and magnesium concentrations have been noted by Munz and McFarland (1964: *Eptatretus stoutii*) to be more concentrated than in liver or muscle. However, since undisturbed animals may spend weeks or even months without noticeable secretion of slime, its contribution to ionic regulation is unknown. Stressed *Eptatretus* pour out enormous quantities, so the idea is attractive.

3. SOURCES OF NITROGENOUS WASTE-PRODUCTS

a. *Ammonia*

The prime source of ammonia is the deamination of amino acids (Vellas and Serfaty, 1974; Pandian, 1975) and the breakdown of purines and pyrimidines (Vellas and Serfaty, 1974). Tolerance towards ammonia varies among animals, but the upper critical concentration is always low: Pandian (1975) quotes values of 0·3 to 5·5 mg ammonia nitrogen per 100 ml as having been measured in the blood of teleosts. For this reason a "buffering" or protective mechanism is necessary, and the role appears to be filled, at least in part, by glutamic acid, which can detoxify (absorb) or liberate the ammonia for excretion as the occasion demands. Vellas and Serfaty (1974) summarise the effect in the following scheme:

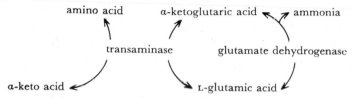

Glutamate dehydrogenase has indeed been found in several organs, including liver, of *Anguilla rostrata* (Volume 1, reference 790), but injection of sodium glutamate into a hepatic vein of *Cyprinus carpio* (Volume 1, reference 985) failed to increase the ammonia output from the liver. While, therefore, the degradation of glutamic acid may well be the main source of ammonia in some species of teleost (Goldstein and Forster 1970), its role in *Cyprinus carpio* is in some doubt, and Vellas and Serfaty (1974) assign to it an intermediate, rather than a principal role in nitrogen metabolism. These workers did in fact find glutamate dehydrogenase activity in isolated liver and other tissues of *Cyprinus carpio*, and concluded that glutamic acid was contributing in some fashion to ammonia regulation.

The participation of glutamine in the liberation and fixation of ammonia, on the other hand, seems to be clear. This compound is respectively broken down or synthesised by glutaminase or glutamine synthetase, and both of these enzymes have been found in fish by workers quoted by Vellas and Serfaty (1974). Injection of glutamine results in a great increase in ammonia excretion (Pequin, 1967), and a surge in the glutamic acid concentration of the blood. There are also increases, presumably by transamination, in other amino acids (Vellas and Serfaty, 1974), but if the liver is ligatured before the injection there is no increase in ammonia output (Dargent, 1966, quoted by Vellas and Serfaty, 1974). Unlike ammonia or glutamate, glutamine is not excreted by the gills, at least in *Salmo gairdneri* (Walton and Cowey, 1977).

Vellas and Serfaty (1974) also perfused other substances into a liver–intestine model, studying the ammonia concentration of the emergent fluid. Amino acids caused no change in the ammonia, apart from L-leucine which doubled the concentration—a somewhat puzzling finding. Urea and its precursors (ornithine, citrulline, arginine) likewise caused no increase in ammonia, but big increases resulted from the perfusion of asparagine and, as already noted, glutamine. Purine derivatives—adenosine, ATP, guanylate and guanosine—were actively deaminated during perfusion and caused ammonia to flow from the model.

Much information on nitrogen excretion is given in this fascinating paper, to which the reader is referred for further details.

Unlike Vellas and Serfaty (1974), Janicki and Lingis (1970) found that L-aspartate was also an important precursor of ammonia, being converted by liver homogenates from 4 species of teleost, though not by liver homogenates from two species of elasmobranch. It appears that in this case a transamination is involved in the liberation of ammonia, since none was formed in the presence of transaminase inhibitors.

Ammonia appears to be eliminated at the gills in two ways. It can diffuse out passively and there also appears to be an exchange system, at least in *Carassius auratus*, whereby a molecule of sodium enters the gills for every ammonia molecule extruded (Maetz and Garcia-Romeu, 1964, quoted by Pandian, 1975). The system would clearly assist a freshwater fish to maintain its ionic balance against the concentration gradient.

b. *Urea and uric acid*

As with ammonia, urea is produced principally by the liver. This is particularly so in carnivorous fish; in omnivorous species the kidneys contribute an appreciable proportion (Vellas-Clos, 1973). There is more than twice as much urea present at any one time in the liver as in the muscle tissue (Vellas and Serfaty, 1974: *Cyprinus carpio*), and it is interesting to those seeking similarities between liver and dark muscle (see p. 88) to note that the quantity of urea in dark muscle is the same as in white muscle and not as in liver.

Mammals produce urea as a non-toxic end-product from ammonia, which has been produced as in fish by the deamination of amino acids. The non-biochemist reader desiring further information should consult a standard text-book for details of the ornithine–urea (Krebs-Henseleit) cycle. Briefly, the ammonia to be detoxified is combined with carbon dioxide, and under the action of carbamoyl phosphate synthetase, with ATP to supply the energy, it forms carbamoyl phosphate. Ornithine transcarbamoylase converts this to citrulline, which in turn is combined with aspartic acid to form argino-succinic acid. This is split to fumaric acid and to arginine and the arginine is finally converted to ornithine and urea, at each stage with the help of the appropriate enzymes. The point is that the two enzymes named above, the first two in the cycle,

do not occur in most bony fish, or as Brown and Cohen (1960), who
discovered the fact, better expressed it, "are below the present limits
of detection". They investigated *Lepisosteus osseus*, *Amia calva*, *Cyprinus
carpio*, *Perca flavescens* and *Salmo trutta*.

The only fish which seem to possess the complete mechanism for
making urea from ammonia are the elasmobranchs, which need large
quantities of urea for osmoregulatory purposes (Volume 1, p. 139), the
coelacanth (*Latimeria*) which also maintains high concentrations of urea
in its tissues, and lungfish (*Protopterus*) which must, as already noted
(p. 154), detoxify the ammonia excreted during aestivation (Volume 1,
reference 177). The latter two fish are more closely related to terrestrial
vertebrates than are the teleosts.

We are thus left with the problem of the origin of urea in all of the
other species of fish—a problem unexpected in view of the invariable
occurrence of this compound.

All authors agree that it cannot be derived from ammonia via the
Krebs–Henseleit cycle, but since the final enzyme of the cycle, arginase,
is present in teleost livers it is likely that arginine consumed with the
food can give rise to some urea (Vellas and Créac'h, 1972; McCarthy
and Whitledge, 1972; Vellas-Clos, 1973) and Vellas and Serfaty (1974)
suggested that arginine from catabolised tissue of the fish itself could
also contribute.

The main source of urea, however, appears to be uric acid (Vellas
and Serfaty, 1974), which in turn is produced from purine nucleotides,
according to the following scheme quoted from Vellas and Serfaty
(1974):

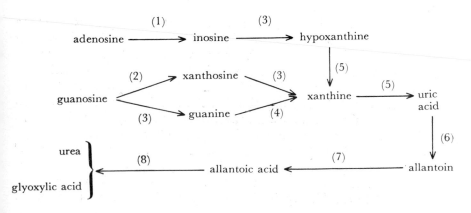

(1) Adenosine deaminase; (2) guanosine deaminase; (3) nucleoside phosphorylase; (4)
guanase; (5) xanthine oxidase; (6) uricase; (7) allantoinase; (8) allantoicase.

Goldstein and Forster (Volume 1, reference 408) had earlier proposed uric acid as a precursor of urea, demonstrating uricase, allantoinase and allantoicase activity in the livers of 18 teleost species.

That amino acids which are precursors of purines (glutamine, serine and glycine) also contribute to the urea output was demonstrated by Vellas-Clos (1973), who injected both these compounds and purine nucleotides into carp and observed an increase in the quantity of urea excreted. The pyrimidine nucleosides cytosine and thymine cause no increase, but contribute to the output of ammonia. Because of the lack in teleosts of enzymes needed for the ornithine-urea cycle, the injection of ornithine likewise caused no increase in urea excretion.

4. VARIATIONS IN NITROGENOUS EXCRETION

Fish kept at higher temperatures eat more food (Wallace, 1973: *Blennius pholis*) and empty their stomachs more frequently (Tyler, 1970: *Gadus morhua*). It is therefore not surprising to note that the quantity of urea synthesised and excreted by *Cyprinus carpio* follows the seasonal variation in intensity of metabolism (Vellas-Clos, 1973; Vellas and Serfaty, 1974). This is a temperature effect, and a rise in temperature also increases the ammonia excretion of the same species (Lachner, 1972) and the urea and ammonia excretion of *Ophicephalus punctatus* (Ray and Medda, 1976).

The endogenous nitrogen excretion[1] of carp also increases steadily with a rise in temperature (Ogino, Kakino and Chen, 1973), which presumably relates to the observation (Volume 1, p. 222) that starving fish die sooner at higher temperatures through having burned up their reserves more rapidly.

As a corollary, Savitz (1969) showed that endogenous nitrogen excretion decreases steadily in *Lepomis macrochirus* with decreasing temperatures down to 15·6°C. Below this the excretion rate does not change, indicating some sort of adaptation, a subject reviewed at length on p. 325. In the meantime it should be noted that adaptation to temperature change can destroy any simple relationships such as are seen in ordinary chemical reactions. In the present context, the gill proteins are indeed degraded more rapidly in *Gillichthys mirabilis* adapted to 26°C than to 8°C, but muscle proteins turn over more rapidly at 8°C (Somero and Doyle, 1973). Changes in the rate of tissue degradation in response to short-term changes in temperature were found by these workers not to exhibit "typical" Q_{10} responses[2], and it was concluded

---

[1]Nitrogen excretion during maintenance on a nitrogen-free diet.

[2]The change in the rate of a reaction resulting from a 10-degree change in temperature.

that the situation was highly complex, depending on, among other factors, the rates at which the proteins were rendered susceptible to the action of the proteolytic enzymes.

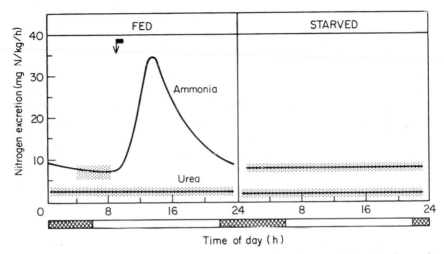

FIG. 53. Daily pattern of nitrogen excretion in fed and starved *Oncorhynchus nerka*, showing how feeding affects the excretion of ammonia but not of urea. Time of feeding is indicated by an arrow. After Brett and Zala (1975). Reproduced with permission of Dr J. R. Brett.

Forced swimming was shown by Muravskaya and Belokopytin (1975) to increase the nitrogen excretion of *Spicara smaris* over the "resting" level, so presumably the contractile proteins have a shorter life in active use. Probably because they stimulate activity, thyroid hormones and their analogues can also under certain conditions increase the output of both urea and ammonia (Ray and Medda, 1976: *Ophicephalus punctatus*).

Finally, Brett and Zala (1975: *Oncorhynchus nerka*) showed in a striking way that ammonia excretion increases sharply about 4 hours after feeding, while urea is not affected (Fig. 53). Starving fish exhibit steady levels for both compounds. Ammonia is therefore the chief excretory product of exogenous nitrogen.

There is a possibility that the output of less diffusible nitrogenous end-products also increases during feeding. Love, Robertson *et al.* (1974a) found that the total urine nitrogen was highest in the group of wild *Gadus morhua* which had the highest liver lipid content of all the groups in the survey and, apart from the unusual Faroe Bank cod, the highest muscle protein and lowest muscle water contents. They were presumably therefore the best fed (again apart from those from the Faroe Bank), and the results may show an increased output of creatin, which as we have seen forms more than half of the urinary nitrogen. On the other hand, the results may simply confirm an increased output of urinary ammonia—or even that these fish were just hunting vigorously for food and increasing their rate of muscle catabolism (see p. 163).

5. BILE

Since it contains broken-down blood pigments, bile must be considered a true route for excretion, although the interest is wider than might be expected. This is because the gall bladder, like the urinary bladder, also has the ability to concentrate its contents, and, as we shall see in Chapter 5, the time lapse involved may show us something of the feeding behaviour of fish from the wild (p. 377).

Diamond (1962a, 1962b: *Rutilus rutilus*) showed that the gall bladder concentrates bile by absorbing sodium, chloride and water in isotonic proportions, and pointed out that many organs share with the gall bladder the ability to transport water and salt together. He deduced that the volume of the gall bladder could be only 1/30th of the volume of the daily bile output, but because of the concentrating ability of the membrane the bladder could hold up to half of the daily output. During its stay in the bladder, the bile may decrease in volume by about 90%, but the pigments, bile acids and cholesterol are not absorbed, so increase in concentration by up to ten times. Absorption stops when the bile has been reduced to 8 to 10% of its original volume, but as it remains isotonic with plasma, some of the constituents must have been osmotically inactive.

Diamond (1962a, 1962b) used a gall-bladder model in the laboratory. A more recent approach has been through comparing the composition of bile as it forms in the liver ("hepatic bile") with that in the gall-bladder. Boyer (1971) and Boyer, Schwartz and Smith (1976) collected bile in cannulas from the liver ducts before it had had contact with the gall-bladder epithelium, and found big differences between it and bile from the gall bladder, though, like Diamond, they found that the osmolality was little different—slightly less if anything. Their results with two species of elasmobranch are shown in Table 12. In *Squalus acanthias*, the bile acids and calcium are greatly concentrated, the sodium potassium and magnesium slightly so and the chloride and bicarbonate less concentrated. In *Raja erinacea* only the bile acids are more concentrated, the ionic constituents being diluted by contact with the gall bladder.

TABLE 12

A Comparison between Bile from the Liver and Bile from the Gall Bladder. (After Boyer, Schwartz and Smith, 1976. Reproduced with permission of Dr James L. Boyer)

	Bile acids mM	Sodium mM	Potassium mM	Chloride mM	Bicarbonate mM	Magnesium mg%	Calcium mg%
1. *Squalus acanthias*							
Hepatic bile	21±12	271±14	5·0±0·9	224±21	5·8±3·5	9·0±2·0	18±0
Gall-bladder bile	353±77	366±40	6·5±0·7	79±49	0·8±0·3	10·5±1·5	58·7±9·6
2. *Raja erinacea*							
Hepatic bile	7·96±5·2	295±12	13·0±2·1	280±25	6·2±2·0	6·2±1·7	32·8±4
Gall-bladder bile	35·2±10	267±31	4·6±0·8	221·5±25	5·1±1·7	2·7±0·3	20·7±3·1

The gall-bladder bile of *Myxine glutinosa* was shown by Robertson (1976) to have much higher concentrations of sodium, calcium and magnesium, and less chloride, than blood plasma.

Although the gall bladder has this ability to concentrate materials, it must be remembered that when the fish has taken food, the bladder discharges at least some of its contents into the intestine (well known in mammals, demonstrated in fish by Eales and Sinclair, 1974: *Salvelinus fontinalis*), the bile salts aiding digestion by emulsifying dietary lipids. The concentrating activity then has to start again.

The ability of the gall-bladder membrane to concentrate bile seems to vary in warm- and cold-blooded vertebrates according to the mode of feeding, being greater in animals with intermittent gastric emptying time and less in those with continuous digestive activity (Esteller, de la Higuera *et al.*, 1975).

The rate of water and salt absorption of isolated gall bladders increases with rise in temperature (Mackay, 1975: *Carassius auratus, Salvelinus fontinalis*), but the compositions of bile samples from *Carassius auratus* which had been held by the same writer in aquaria at 10 or 30°C for 1 month were the same. Mackay suggested that although the concentrating activity of the gall bladder must have slowed down at 10°C, the feeding and digestion would also proceed at a slower rate.

The discharge of bile is a means whereby cholesterol, bile acids, broken-down blood pigments and salts are excreted. The behaviour of bile during starvation is considered in the next section (p. 224) and its study in relation to food intake is described in Chapter 5, p. 377.

C. Starvation

In Volume 1 it was shown that *Anguilla anguilla* can live without food for over 4 years, and that other species can starve for many months and still make a complete recovery on refeeding. The protein of white muscle is extensively drawn upon during starvation, and while liver lipid is almost all consumed, the lipids of brain, heart and gill are not touched. Depletion of body lipid in fatty species results in an increase in the water content of the muscle, giving rise to a "fat–water line", that is, an inverse dynamic relationship between the two constituents in the muscle, while non-fatty species have a "protein–water line" of similar nature. Although fatty and non-fatty fish have different distributions of reserve lipid, both respond to starvation in a similar way in that much of the lipid, whether in liver or muscle, is drawn upon before the protein is utilised. Any reserves of carbohydrate are used first of all[1].

---

[1]This does not now seem to be true for all species, for example *Cyprinus carpio* which maintains its carbohydrates during long periods of starvation.

Protein fractions of the blood all decrease during starvation with the exception of γ-globulin, which rises relative to the others. The relative amounts of connective tissues also rise in the muscle, since they are not utilised as much as are the contractile proteins. Some *free* amino acids of the blood decrease, others increase. In the muscle the total *free* amino acids decrease to about $\frac{1}{6}$ of their normal values, and most of the individual *free* amino acids decrease also.

Severe starvation causes an increase in extracellular space because of shrinkage of the muscle cells. There is therefore an increase in muscle sodium, a largely extracellular ion, and a corresponding decrease in total potassium, which is intracellular. Blood glucose tends to remain stable for a large part of the starvation period, merely marking the transport of energy from liver to muscle, so that it cannot be used as an indicator of starvation. On the other hand, the steady decline in the count of erythrocytes seems to mark the progress of depletion quite clearly.

1. INTRODUCTION

A great deal of work on the starvation of fish has been published since Volume 1 was completed, and it has not been easy to disentangle the various viewpoints to present a logical story. Some workers have realised that materials are mobilised in a certain sequence, but many others have considered the changes in individual constituents in isolation. As usual, a number of findings are appropriate to only one or two species, and cannot be extrapolated to others.

Different organs are depleted to differing extents during starvation. In particular, the fish mobilises more protein from white muscle than from dark: this aspect of starvation has already been considered in detail in the section on dark muscle (p. 93), and is mentioned here only in passing. As regards other organs, the intensity of proteolysis at the beginning of starvation increases in the order muscle, spleen, liver, kidney and, most of all, intestine, while after prolonged starvation the order is intestine, liver, kidney, spleen and white muscle (Créac'h, 1972: *Cyprinus carpio*). The gonads are little affected in this species.

a. *Maturation*

Natural starvation is not always just a matter of shortage of food. Several species seem to reduce their food intake during the final stages of maturation, perhaps because of the sheer bulk of gonad within their body cavity (Thomson, 1926, quoted by Shevchenko, 1972: *Melanogrammus aeglefinus*; Stanek, 1973; Berger and Panasenko, 1974: *Gadus morhua*; Hashimoto, 1974: *Gadus macrocephalus*), quite apart from those species in which the alimentary canal degenerates at this time.

Maturation tends to be inhibited during unnatural starvation, though the stage of maturation reached before feeding ceases is important. Female *Gadus morhua* starved from the month of September have been seen in this laboratory to develop quite large gonads and even to spawn (February–March), while *Cyprinus carpio* starved from November

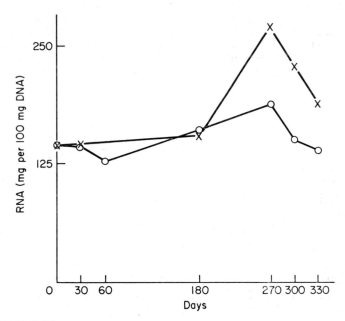

FIG. 54. RNA:DNA ratio in the muscle of *Cyprinus carpio*. The upper curve shows the fed controls, lower, starved. Peaks indicate an increase in protein synthetic activity. After Bouche, Vellas and Serfaty (1973). Reproduced with permission of Dr G. Bouche.

show increases in ovary weight for several months (Créac'h, 1972). The start of maturation in *Salmo gairdneri* is likewise not affected by starvation (Shimma, Ichimura and Shibata, 1976: starvation for 55 days). On the other hand, Wilkins (Volume 1, reference 1345) found no sexual development at all in starving *Clupea harengus*, and de Vlaming (1971) noted that the gonads of starving *Gillichthys mirabilis* begin development, but quickly regress if starvation begins at a time of active gametogenesis. Hypertrophy of the testes has been seen in the early stages of starvation by Sasayama and Takahashi (1972: *Carassius auratus*), but lengthy abstention from food causes progressive loss of accumulated spermatozoa and testicular shrinkage.

b. *Continuing processes*

The regeneration of damaged limbs continues during starvation (Conant, 1973: *Protopterus*). Even the protein synthesis which increases for a time each year when fish grow is not altogether suppressed during a prolonged period of starvation (Bouche, Vellas and Serfaty, 1973: *Cyprinus carpio*). Figure 54 shows the RNA:DNA ratio in the muscle of carp, which gives a measure of protein synthetic activity. The upper (control) curve shows a big surge at the beginning of summer as the fish increase in length, but the really interesting feature of this figure is the similar if smaller peak in the starving fish at the same time. The biological clock will not be completely denied even under these conditions; perhaps it is triggered by the pituitary in response to increased photoperiod.

Since the dark muscle with which fish cruise is less affected by starvation than is white, the starving fish usually show a normal demeanour and style of cruising (this laboratory: *Gadus morhua*; Volume 1 reference 1345: *Clupea harengus*), but the latter species has been observed to become less timid as a result of starvation, and all species become less active probably, at least in part, through a decrease in the output of thyroid hormones (Leatherland, Cho and Slinger, 1977: *Salmo gairdneri*). Activity can be artificially stimulated by the administration of this hormone, and the energy reserves then decrease more quickly (Narayansingh and Eales, 1975: *Salvelinus fontinalis*).

c. *Metabolic rate*

The reduction in activity is mirrored in a steady decrease in oxygen consumption, but Beamish (1964) has pointed out that part of the reduced demand comprises oxygen not now required for the assimilation of the food. Saunders (1963) did the complementary experiment, showing that feeding cod which had previously starved increased the oxygen consumption by 40 to 90% for a few days, after which it subsided.

Fish starve more slowly at lower temperatures (Volume 1, p. 222), and probably for this reason Marinescu (1975) could not detect any change in oxygen consumption as a result of starving *Idus idus* maintained at 5°C, though a decrease was measurable at 25°C.

Adaptation to lower temperatures as shown by increased enzymatic activity and higher oxygen consumption is eventually inhibited by starvation. Campbell and Davies (1975) found that after starvation for 60 days, *Blennius pholis* adapted at 10°C could not maintain the higher level of metabolism which distinguished them from those adapted to 20°C, both groups now consuming oxygen at the same rate when the readings were taken at 15°C.

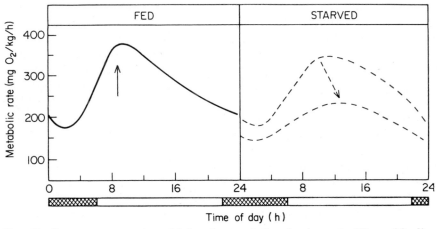

FIG. 55. Oxygen consumption of fed and starved *Oncorhynchus nerka*. Time of feeding indicated by arrow. After Brett and Zala (1975). Reproduced with permission of Dr J. R. Brett.

The oxygen consumption of *Protopterus aethiopicus* was reported to rise after a 5-month fast by Smith (1930), who regarded it as evidence for an increase in protein catabolism. Such an increase has long been regarded as a terminal feature of starvation in mammals, marking the end of lipid and carbohydrate reserves, but we should not expect to see it in fish which subsist largely on energy provided by amino acids. Presumably *Protopterus* begins its aestivation with a supply of carbohydrates and lipids as energy reserves.

Brett and Zala (1975) showed that the oxygen consumption of non-starving *Oncorhynchus nerka* rose sharply each day, the peak corresponding with the feeding time. Presumably the rise leading to the peak reflected anticipatory swimming activity. During subsequent starvation for 22 days, the peak appeared daily but progressively decreased in amplitude. At least some of this peak (illustrated in Fig. 55) is therefore a reflection of physical movement rather than energy needed for digesting food.

d. *Adaptation to starvation with age*

Many fish at the spawning season become more depleted each year as they grow older (Volume 1, p. 91). There now seems little doubt that older fish are able to undergo a degree of starvation which would kill younger specimens, that is, they develop compensatory mechanisms as they grow.

In this laboratory it has been found that only bigger (more than 75 cm) *Gadus morhua* can attain water contents in the muscle of over 90%, smaller cod dying when the value has reached about 86%. The same applies to *Cyprinus carpio* (Murat, 1976a), which have been submitted to starvation for over a year by Serfaty's group, but which survive only as large specimens. Ikeda, Ozaki and Yasuda (1974) starved *Carassius auratus*, and found that all the 1-year fish died during the experiment but that those of 2 years survived. No mechanisms for this survival have so far been postulated. Since greater muscle hydration is possible in larger fish, their survival is something more than just the acquisition of greater energy reserves, although the fact that small fish lose more weight in a given period of starvation (Créac'h, 1972: *Cyprinus carpio;* Higashi, Terada *et al.*, 1976: *Anguilla japonica*) shows that they use up their reserves more quickly anyway, presumably by being more active.

Older fish larvae also live longer than younger larvae without food (Satomi, 1969: *Cyprinus carpio;* Blaxter and Ehrlich, 1973: *Pleuronectes platessa*), but this is probably just a measure of their increased reserves.

e. *Miscellaneous observations*

Although the edges of the scales of *Carassius auratus* are resorbed on starvation and regenerated on refeeding (Ikeda, Ozaki and Yasuda, 1974), this is not the case in *Oncorhynchus nerka*, which leave no record in their scales of a 20-week (Bilton and Robins, 1971a) or 30·5-week (Bilton and Robins, 1971b) period of starvation. No new circuli are formed during starvation in this species, but other authors quoted by Bilton and Robins (1971a) showed that narrow circuli do form. These phenomena probably depend ultimately on the concentration of protein in the blood and so may vary according to the season.

The rings within the otoliths (see Volume 1, pp. 159 and 162) of fish are light or dark according to the amount of protein in the endolymph (Volume 1, references 881 and 882), and as we shall see in Chapter 5 (p. 374), this protein is greatly reduced during starvation (Robertson and Love, unpublished), so a period of depletion would show as a permanent record in the otolith pattern.

Some vitamins are required in amounts proportional to the amount of food eaten, so animals on a vitamin-deficient diet develop deficiency symptoms more quickly than those abstaining from food altogether. On the other hand, vitamin B_{12} (cyanocobalamin) is synthesised by the microflora of the gut (Volume 1, reference 1382), and starvation can cause changes in the microflora or even its complete disappearance (Margolis, 1958, quoted by Karamucheva, Georgiev et al., 1972: several species; Piavaux, 1973: *Tilapia macrochir;* Yoshimizu, Kimura and Sakai, 1976b: *Oncorhynchus masou*), so that, in this instance, the shortage of a vitamin could conceivably be more acute during starvation than during incomplete nourishment.

Symons (1968) found that starvation of the parr of *Salmo salar* resulted in an increase in aggressive behaviour, the fish charging and nipping each other and establishing stronger social hierarchies than usual, dominant fish nipping their subordinates more frequently. It was suggested that under natural conditions such behaviour could cause the fish to disperse further in search of food.

In Volume 1, p. 246, it was shown that starvation of *Gadus morhua* causes an increase in the water and sodium and a decrease in the potassium of muscle, changes which are reversed on refeeding. Créac'h, Murat and Bouche (1970: *Cyprinus carpio*) have now found the same changes in liver, kidney and spleen (and intestine: Noaillac-Depeyre, 1974) and have confirmed those in muscle. They also showed that the daily excretion of ions was greater from starving carp (300 days) than from controls, 2·3 times as much potassium and 1·4 times as much sodium leaving the body in 24 hours. The excretion of potassium is logical enough, since the steady erosion of protein structures liberates intracellular potassium, and Créac'h (1972) has found that the loss of protein and of potassium are essentially parallel, but the increase in sodium excretion is unexpected in view of its increase in starving tissue. Perhaps the fact that the fish had been placed in deionised water for the purpose of measuring efflux had exaggerated the outflow of sodium.

These authors also noted small increases in both the sodium and the potassium of the blood, the opposite effect to that found in *Gadus morhua* (Volume 1, reference 765). However, in the present case, starvation had lasted for only 64 days, when few other symptoms had yet become manifest.

Danilov and Shevchenko (1973) found that *Cyprinus carpio*, *Silurus glanis* and *Tinca tinca* lost iron, copper, manganese and zinc from the lateral muscle when starved for several months in ponds, but that from February onwards the constituents increased again, eventually exceeding the initial values. These changes may not have been caused by the starvation at all; further knowledge of their roles in the muscle would make interpretation easier.

2. HISTOLOGICAL STUDIES

a. *Muscle*

The most thorough histological study of starving white muscle is that on *Cyprinus carpio* by Gas (1972), and several of her outstanding pictures are now presented.

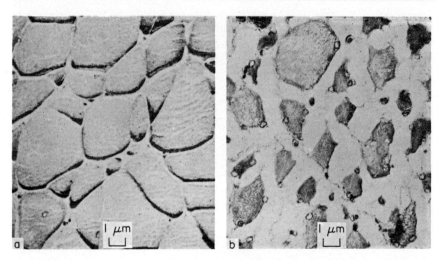

FIG. 56. (a) Cross-section through the muscle of *Cyprinus carpio* starved for 6 months (light microscope). The appearance is very similar to that of unstarved fish. (b) Starved for 11 months, showing shrinkage of contractile material. Both pictures kindly supplied by Mme N. Gas.

Figure 56(a) shows a cross-section after 6 months of starvation (optical microscope). The section has essentially the same appearance as that of unstarved fish, with little, if any, increase in the extracellular space and indications from the stain that glycogen is still present. In Fig. 56(b) at the same magnification the fish has starved for 11 months, and now shows the extensive cellular shrinkage and increase in extracellular fluid seen in cod and gray sole (Figs 47 and 48). Figure 57 shows (a) longitudinal and (b) cross sections of normally fed carp under high magnification, as a yardstick of subsequent change. The nine wide strips (Fig. 57(a)) are myofibrils and the fine hair-like parallel lines the myofilaments which are the actual molecular units of contraction. The irregularly shaped bodies between the myofibrils are parts of the sarcoplasmic reticulum, much of which is in the form of "triads"—

two irregular triangles with apexes turned outwards, with a small oval
hole, part of the "T" system (see Volume 1, Fig. 12), between them.
The dark serrated line in the myofibril which appears to run through
the middle of each triad, with the small hole, is the Z line, composed

FIG. 57. (a) Longitudinal section of well-nourished muscle from *Cyprinus carpio*
(electron microscope). (b) Cross-section. A description of the structures that can be
seen is given in the text. Z, Z line; T, triad. Pictures kindly supplied by Mme N. Gas.

largely of actin. These structures can all be identified again in the starved specimens, so the picture establishes our points of reference. In cross-section (Fig. 57(b)) the filaments can be seen partly as thicker dots, which are myosin molecules, and as much smaller dots which surround the myosin: these are sections through strands of actin. The extensive pervasion by the sarcoplasmic reticulum also shows well in this photograph.

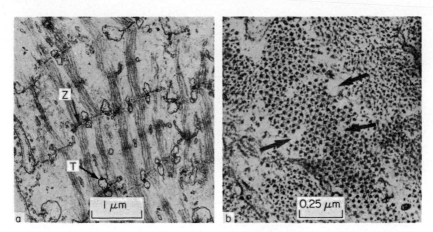

FIG. 58. (a) Longitudinal section of muscle of *Cyprinus carpio* starved for 12 months, showing disappearance of many of the contractile filaments. (b) Cross-section of muscle of *Cyprinus carpio* starved for 8 months, showing a few gaps (arrowed). T, triad; Z, Z line. Both pictures kindly supplied by Mme N. Gas. Picture (b) appeared in a paper by Gas (1972).

The astonishing effect of starvation for 12 months is shown in Fig. 58(a), where whole groups of contractile filaments have disappeared. Two clear rows of triads are still visible, running roughly from left to right in the photograph. The start of this process is shown in Fig. 58(b) (starvation for 8 months only), when gaps in the groups of filaments begin to appear. Some of these are indicated by arrows.

The fish shown in Fig. 59(a) was starved for 14 months. The parallel orientation in the myofilaments (Fig. 57(a)) has been largely destroyed, but the larger units, the myofibrils, are still recognisable, the four vertical serrated Z lines being very clear and more or less parallel, and the triads along each Z line well defined, though now swollen. The tissue appears to have been completely drained of myosin: only actin filaments are left, judging by their connections with the Z lines. The final disorganisation is shown in Fig. 59(b) (15 months of starvation). Several Z lines can still be seen, but all orientation has been lost.

Grossly swollen vesicles of the sarcoplasmic reticulum are much in evidence, distributed at random, and the actin filaments run in all directions. It is unbelievable that fish in such a state were still alive and

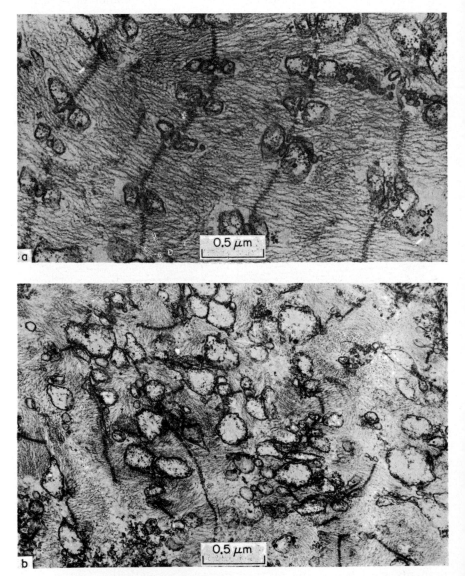

FIG. 59. (a) "Longitudinal" section through the white muscle of *Cyprinus carpio* starved for 14 months. (b) Starved for 15 months. Disorganisation is now complete. After Gas (1972). Photograph kindly supplied by Mme N. Gas.

swimming, though presumably only the dark muscle was operative for this purpose.

b. *Liver*

The liver cells diminish in size during starvation, so that the nuclei crowd together and the *concentration* of DNA, though not the absolute amount per liver, increases. The perils of estimating constituents as

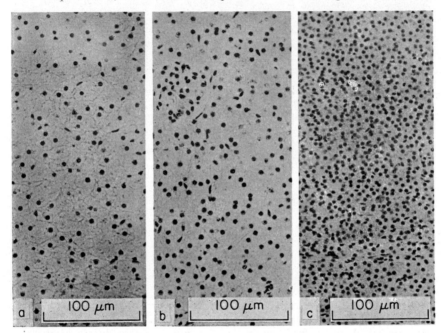

Fig. 60. Shrinkage of the cytoplasm of liver cells (*Cyprinus carpio*) during starvation resulting in the nuclei crowding together. Stain: Methanol-Feulgen. (a) Nourished. (b) Starved for 4 months. (c) Starved for 12 months. Photograph kindly supplied by Mme N. Gas.

grams per gram of liver, rather than, say, grams per whole liver of a 100 centimetre fish, are admirably illustrated in Fig. 60, where the cell nuclei have been emphasised by suitable staining (Feulgen). Figure 61 shows the eventual disappearance of glycogen from a carp liver cell. The process is slow, and after 6 months there is still plenty of glycogen left *in this species*.

Illustrations such as these bring life to tables of analytical figures.

Gas (1973) lists the most important changes seen in the liver as the progressive diminution of glycogen and its disappearance after about 8 months[1], the appearance of a network of collagen fibres, reduction of cellular volume, the intracellular accumulation of particles containing iron and finally the disappearance of cellular organisation. Figure 62 is an electron photomicrograph of a nourished liver cell (*Cyprinus carpio*).

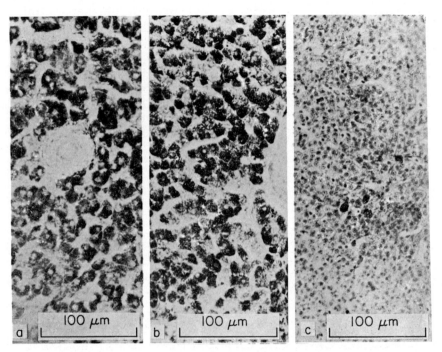

FIG. 61. Section of liver (*Cyprinus carpio*) stained for glycogen, showing its disappearance only after prolonged starvation. Stain: Gendre, P.A.S. (a) Nourished. (b) Starved for 6 months. (c) Starved for 13 months. Photograph kindly supplied by Mme N. Gas.

Little can be seen of the fine structure because of the myriad glycogen particles, but the large nucleus (N) is clearly demarcated. Figure 63 shows the complex situation at same magnification after starvation for 14 months. The nuclei, smaller in size, are surrounded by numerous "residual bodies" (CR), and lipid droplets (L), derived together from the "autophagic vacuoles" (Gas, 1976, p. 105) which may themselves have originated in the endoplasmic reticulum (Gas and Serfaty, 1972). Some collagen fibrils are marked with an asterisk.

---

[1]Disappearance is preceded by the glycogen's being localised in pockets ("glycogenosomes") limited by 1 or 2 smooth membranes. This stage is seen after 5 or 6 months of starvation (Gas and Serfaty, 1972).

There is a wealth of information in the many pictures published by
Gas and Pequignot (1972), Gas and Serfaty (1972), Gas (1973) and
Gas (1976) to which the reader is referred for further information. I
have selected only some of the most prominent features for re-publica-
tion here.

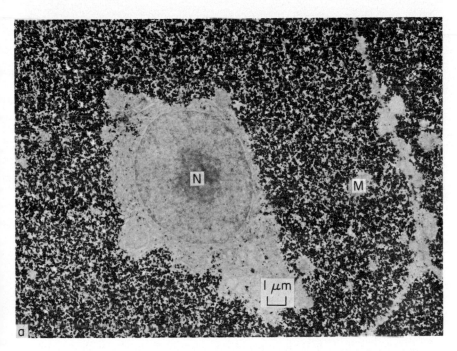

FIG. 62. Liver cell of nourished *Cyprinus carpio*. Fixed: glutaraldehyde-osmium
tetroxide. Shadowed: P.A.T. Ag. N, nucleus. Photograph kindly supplied by Mme
N. Gas.

c. *Intestine*

The stomach, intestine and pyloric caecae all degenerate after migrating
salmon have ceased feeding (Volume 1, p. 114). Noaillac-Depeyre
(1974), Gas (1976) and Gas and Noaillac-Depeyre (1976) have made
some interesting observations on the intestines of starving *Cyprinus
carpio*. The internal absorptive surfaces of intestines are not smooth,
but their surface areas are enormously increased by minute finger-like
processes (micro-villi), which project from them into the lumen (Fig.
64(a)). After starvation for 6 months, these are shortened and reduced
in number (Fig. 64(b)). A 13-month period sees their persistence in the

proximal section of the intestine (Fig. 64(c)) but their complete disappearance in the middle section (Fig. 64(d)), having evidently been
used by the fish to enable it to survive.

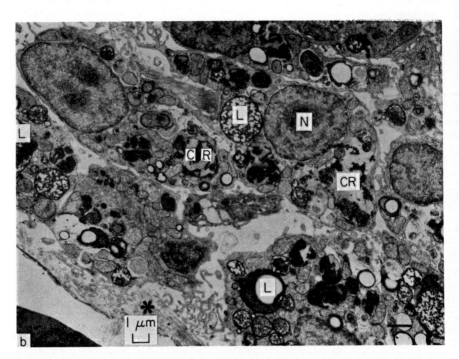

Fig. 63. Liver cell of *Cyprinus carpio* starved for 14 months. Glutaraldehyde-osmium
tetroxide; P.A.T. Ag. CR, residual bodies; N, nucleus; L, lipid globules; *, collagen.
Photograph kindly supplied by Mme N. Gas.

Noaillac-Depeyre (1974) has calculated the time of cell renewal by
the classical technique using colchicine, which arrests cell division at
metaphase. An expression connecting the number of mitoses stopped in
metaphase with the total number of nuclei at a given time after
administration of colchicine showed that the cells of the anterior
intestinal mucous layer were renewed much more quickly in June
(186 hours), when the fish were eating, than in December (1309 hours)
when food was not being taken. The renewal of the anterior part of the
intestine was quicker than that of the posterior part. Severe experimental
starvation is accompanied, as in muscle and liver, by a bloating of the
sarcoplasmic reticulum of the intestine and increasing fragility of the
membranes.

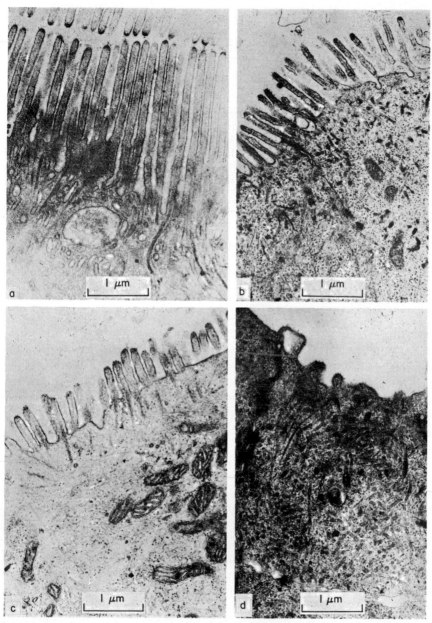

Fig. 64. Inner surface of the intestine of *Cyprinus carpio* after various periods of starvation. Glutaraldehyde-osmium tetroxide. (a) Nourished. "Villi" of normal length.
(b) Starved for 6 months. (c) Starved for 13 months, proximal section of the intestine.
(d) Starved for 13 months, middle section of the intestine. After Gas and Noaillac-
Depeyre (1976). Reproduced with permission of Mme N. Gas, who kindly supplied
the photograph.

The length of the intestine decreases during starvation (same author) by 18% (7 or 13 months). The loss in weight is more dramatic: by 45% of the initial weight after 7 months and by 65% after 13 months. The diameter of the anterior intestine decreases from 4·9 to 3·3 mm after 13 months.

d. *Skeleton*

A study of the fine structure of the skeleton of the starving fish larva would be interesting, since the whole bodies have been shown to decrease in length (Blaxter and Ehrlich, 1973, illustrated in Figure 43 of this volume: *Pleuronectes platessa, Clupea harengus*; Bilton and Robins, 1973: *Oncorhynchus nerka*) but they have not been examined histologically.

3. PRINCIPAL CONSTITUENTS

a. *Interrelationships and conversions*

In Volume 1 (p. 225 onwards) it was shown that changes in the nutritional condition of fish resulted in changes in the lipid : water ratio in the muscle of fatty fish or the protein : water ratio in that of non-fatty fish. Here we shall consider rather the sequence in which substances are mobilised, bearing in mind one of the purposes of Chapter 5, this volume, which is to select combinations of methods of analysis to reveal the stage of depletion reached by a fish and the direction in which the nutrients are flowing.

The water content of non-fatty muscle rises in starvation when protein is mobilised, but not until "energy" substances other than protein have been largely used up. Many authors are now convinced that, apart from any changes in the carbohydrate, which we shall consider in a moment, the first effect of starvation is the mobilisation of lipids (Nagai and Ikeda, 1971: *Cyprinus carpio*; Niimi, 1972a: *Micropterus salmoides*; Larsson and Lewander, 1973: *Anguilla anguilla*; Créac'h and Murat, 1974: *Cyprinus carpio*; Dave, Johansson-Sjöbeck *et al.*, 1975: *Anguilla anguilla*; Stirling, 1976: *Dicentrarchus labrax*; Ince and Thorpe, 1976: *Esox lucius*; Lyzlova and Verzhbinskaya, 1976: *Lampetra fluviatilis*). The same effect has been noted by Speck and Urich (1969) in the crayfish, *Orconectes limosus*. Species differences occur, and although *Micropterus salmoides* shows an initial preference for lipid breakdown, it does mobilise some protein at the same time, an activity attributed by Niimi

(1972a) to the relatively low lipid reserves in this species. *Esox lucius* is interesting in that lipid deposits outside the liver (in the intestinal region) are used first before any change can be seen in the liver lipid (Ince and Thorpe, 1976).

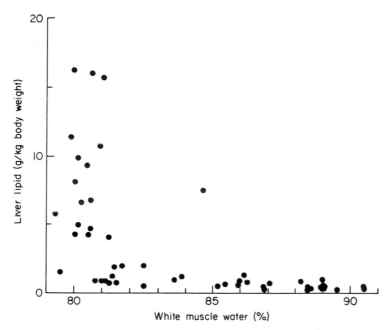

FIG. 65. The relationship between liver lipid and the water content of the white muscle of *Gadus morhua*. A wide range of liver lipid contents is seen when the muscle shows no depletion (79–81% water). The water rises in the muscle only when most of the liver lipid has been used up. This Figure illustrates the *sequence* in which energy reserves are utilised in this species: firstly lipid, then protein. After Ross (1978). Reproduced with permission of the author.

A convincing picture of sequential mobilisation is shown in Fig. 65. *Gadus morhua* seem to be starving whenever the water content of the muscle rises above 81% (Volume 1, reference 757). We see now that above this value only low levels of liver lipid are found, while below 81% of water in the muscle a range of lipid levels can be found, some of them quite high. The values show that liver lipid content is no guide to the state of the muscle, but presumably does indicate the level of energy reserves in this species.

Studies on changes in carbohydrate reserves are complicated by the synthesis of carbohydrates from proteins (gluconeogenesis), by species

differences and by the fact that blood glucose and muscle glycogen tend
to maintain their levels for a considerable time by drawing on glycogen
from the liver.

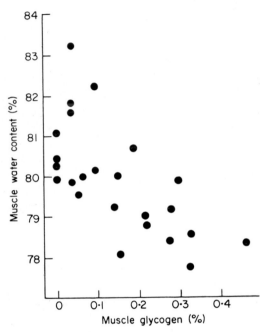

FIG. 66. The relationship between water content and glycogen in the muscle of
Cyprinus carpio subjected to different degrees of starvation. Correlation coefficient:
−0·67. After Tanaka (1969a). Reproduced with permission of the author.

The sequence of mobilisation, in some species at least, appears to be
clear: in *Dicentrarchus labrax* the carbohydrates begin to decline at the
outset of starvation and outstrip the mobilisation of lipids—as Stirling
(1976) puts it: "Starvation caused a *rapid* initial decrease in carbohydrate
and a *progressive* decline in lipid in all tissues" (my italics). This author
also notes that both lipid and protein are inversely related to the
moisture content of the whole fish. A similar situation arises in *Seriola
quinqueradiata* during starvation for 21 days: Shimeno and Hosokawa
(1975) found that the amount of lipid and protein in the liver gradually
decreases, but that the amount of glycogen "falls sharply at the very
beginning".

The reverse occurs in *Cyprinus carpio*. After 22 days without food, there
is appreciable depletion of liver lipids, while the glycogen is untouched;

after 100 days the lipid is exhausted but 1·6% of the glycogen remains
(Nagai and Ikeda, 1973). On the other hand, muscle glycogen does
decline when the fish has reached the stage of mobilising its muscle
proteins (when the water content rises) and Tanaka (1969a) has
demonstrated a clear relationship between the rise in muscle water
with starvation and a fall in muscle glycogen (Fig. 66), supporting the

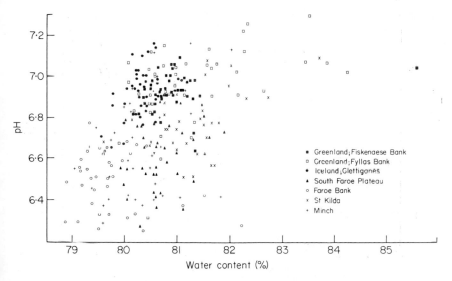

FIG. 67. The relationship between water content and post-mortem pH in the muscle
of *Gadus morhua* from various fishing grounds. After Love (1969). Reproduced with
permission of D. J. Grossman on behalf of FAO.

concept that protein is mobilised only when the more readily available
energy reserves have been used. Low muscle glycogen has been seen to
characterise *Gadus morhua* from the wild with raised muscle water
contents also (Fig. 67). In this Figure, the post-mortem pH is taken as
a measure of muscle glycogen before death. Stress in the trawl would
make nonsense of actual glycogen determinations, but much of the
lactic acid formed during the stress is probably retained in the muscle,
and augmented by that formed after death, causing the pH of the
muscle to fall—a relatively low pH therefore indicates a previous high
glycogen content. Love (1969) showed that when cod are starved in an
aquarium, there is a delay of about 9 weeks during which the lipid and
carbohydrate of the liver are assumed to be mobilised, and then the pH
and water in the muscle rise together (Fig. 68).

Gluconeogenesis, the synthesis of carbohydrates from amino acids, seems to be a central feature of the starvation of eels and salmonids, so that "loss of carbohydrates" cannot really be measured meaningfully. The phenomenon has been shown to occur in starving rats (Tepperman, Fabry and Tepperman, 1970) and starving man (Pozefsky, Tancredi *et al.*, 1976), and in the latter case an accelerated release of amino acids from skeletal muscle was demonstrated also.

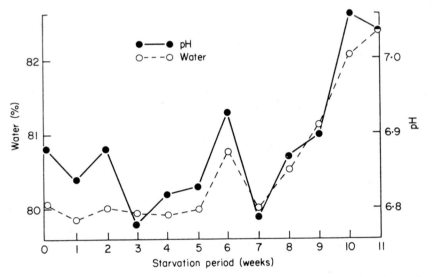

F<small>IG</small>. 68. The water content and pH of the muscle of *Gadus morhua* starved for increasing periods in an aquarium at 9°C. After Love (1969). Reproduced with permission of D. J. Grossman on behalf of FAO.

Triglycerides have been shown by Larsson and Lewander (1973) to be the main source of energy for the European eel *Anguilla anguilla* during the first 95 days without food, but an increase in the glutamate-oxaloacetate transaminase in the liver and the maintenance of glycogen levels suggest that gluconeogenesis was occurring at the same time. Only in the later stages of starvation (145 days) was a decrease in liver glycogen detected. The glycogen content of the muscle was maintained throughout the experiment, and in fact Dave, Johansson-Sjöbeck *et al.* (1975) observed a slight increase in muscle glycogen and blood glucose up to day 96 of the starvation period in the same species[1]. The most striking demonstration of gluconeogenesis in eels has come from a study

---

[1]Slight increases in blood glucose also appear to occur in starving *Raja erinacea* (Grant, Hendler and Banks, 1969).

of *Anguilla japonica* by Inui and Yokote (1974), in which liver glycogen decreased in the early stages of fasting, but then steadily increased thereafter (Fig. 69). The activities of both glutamate-oxaloacetate transaminase and glutamate-pyruvate transaminase were enhanced in the liver.

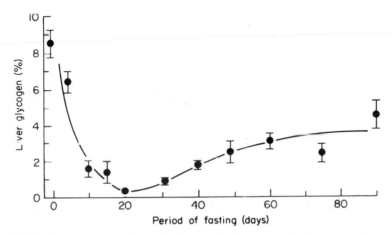

FIG. 69. The liver glycogen of *Anguilla japonica* during a period of fasting in the summer time, showing an initial fall followed by a rise due to gluconeogenesis. After Inui and Yokote (1974). Reproduced with permission of Dr M. Yokote.

As regards salmonids, the liver glycogen of *Oncorhynchus nerka* has been shown to double, approximately, between the time when the fish have arrived at the mouth of the river and when they eventually reach the spawning ground in starving condition (Volume 1, reference 215), though artificial starvation of this species for 30 days causes some loss (McKeown, Leatherland and John, 1975) comparable with the initial stages in *Anguilla japonica* shown in Fig. 69. In contrast, the glycogen content of the liver of male *Petromyzon marinus*, 14 to 15% of the liver weight at the start of the spawning run, is completely used when the spawning ground has been reached (Kott, 1971). Amino transferase activity has been shown to increase in the liver of *Salmo gairdneri* after 9 weeks of starvation (Jürss and Nicolai, 1976), again indicating gluconeogenesis in a salmonid.

The long period for which *Cyprinus carpio* retain high levels of liver glycogen immediately suggests gluconeogenetic activity in this species also, and evidence by Wittenberger and Giurgea (1973) strengthens the idea, although the findings are not quite straightforward. These writers found that starvation for 12 months increases five-fold the activity of glutamate-oxaloacetate transaminase (GOT) in the liver but that glutamate-pyruvate transaminase (GPT) activity decreases. GOT is therefore probably the transaminase involved in the gluconeogenesis, but in higher vertebrates it is GPT, and a curious additional outcome of these experiments is the finding of an enormous increase (almost 20-fold) in the latter enzyme in the dark muscle. Perhaps gluconeogenesis is not confined to the liver in this species, whose need for carbohydrate on the site of energy-use, as protection against anoxic conditions, puts some sort of logic into the findings.

Gluconeogenesis is promoted by circulating corticosteroids (reviewed by Chester Jones, Ball *et al.*, 1974) of which a six-fold increase is associated with the spawning migrations of Pacific salmon. These hormones are secreted by the adrenal cortex when prompted to do so by "ACTH" (adrenocorticotropic hormone) which comes from the pituitary. Thus hypophysectomy results in a reduced liver glycogen, while subsequent daily injections of hydrocortisone increase it (Butler, 1968: *Anguilla rostrata*). Swallow and Fleming (1969) found that starving *Tilapia mossambica* injected with ACTH had heavier livers than the uninjected (starving) controls and concluded that the liver glycogen level had been maintained. Plasma cortisol has been observed to increase during the starvation of *Anguilla anguilla* also (Dave, Johansson-Sjöbeck *et al.*, 1975).

It appears that the corticosteroids act in mammals by stimulating GPT activity in the liver (Rosen, Roberts *et al.*, 1958), so perhaps, from the observations of Wittenberger and Giurgea (1973) noted two paragraphs previously, they also stimulate GOT activity in fish. Inui and Yokote (1974) noted that both GPT *and* GOT activity increased when *Anguilla japonica* starved.

The scheme proposed by Rosen, Roberts *et al.* (1958) is as follows:

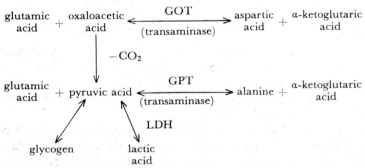

Cahill, Owen *et al.* (1969) posed the question: How does muscle tissue match the release of amino acids with the requirements of gluconeogenesis, and how does it *know* the quantity needed by the liver? When animals are fed, insulin seems to serve as the body's signal to the peripheral tissues to extract fuel from the circulating fluid, and so it was suggested that insulin might play a central role in starvation also, at least in mammals and birds. Fasting has certainly been shown to reduce circulating insulin and increase the amount of glucagon (Cuendet, Loten *et al.*, 1975: mice), concurrently with the release of "glycogenic" amino acids, particularly alanine (Pozefsky, Tancredi *et al.*, 1976: man). Insulin has been seen as the leading hormone in this context in fish by Inui and Yokote (1974), who observed that the "beta" (insulin-secreting) cells of the islet tissue of fasting *Anguilla japonica* showed a reduction in their cell size and condensation of the granules, signs of hypofunction. Presumably this aspect of gluconeogenesis is also ultimately under the control of the pituitary.

b. *Individual behaviour*

i. *Water*

When starvation of *Gadus morhua* was seen in histological sections to result in an increase in the extracellular fluid (Volume 1, reference 765), it was assumed that the morphological change corresponded with the increased water content of the whole muscle. However, it has since been pointed out that extracellular water is insufficient on its own to account for all of the increased tissue water (Créac'h, Murat and Bouche, 1970; Créac'h and Serfaty, 1974), and that hydration of the cells themselves must be included in the reckoning. The remarkable Figs 58 and 59 (pp. 175 and 176) of the present volume now leave no doubt of the hydration in progress within the cell walls—the gross bloating of the sarcoplasmic reticulum, the disappearance of groups of myofilaments and finally a wider spacing of the residual actin myofilaments overall as the myosin is removed. Créac'h and Gas (1971) sum up the changes, concluding that the shrinking diameters of each cell reflect the reduced numbers of constituent myofibrils. Some of them disappear completely.

It is likely that the watery spaces within the cells interconnect. Evidence for this, which incidentally confirms the hydration of the cell contents as a whole, comes from an unusual direction.

Love and Haraldsson (1958: *Gadus morhua*) and Piskarev, Krylov and Luk'yanitsa (1958: *Esox lucius*) found that the size of the ice crystals in frozen muscle increased as fish were kept for longer periods after death before freezing. Now it is one of the characteristics of muscle in rigor mortis to be wetter to the touch than the surface of living muscle, and there is clearly more free water about. Love and Haraldsson (1961) further showed that if the ("dry") stimulable muscle was frozen quite slowly, the film of extracellular fluid froze, after which an ice crystal was seeded within the cell and grew to a considerable size as the temperature fell. However, when the "wet" dead muscle was frozen, the extracellular fluid froze as before, but then, by concentrating its minerals to hyperosmotic levels, it sucked free fluid out of the cell by

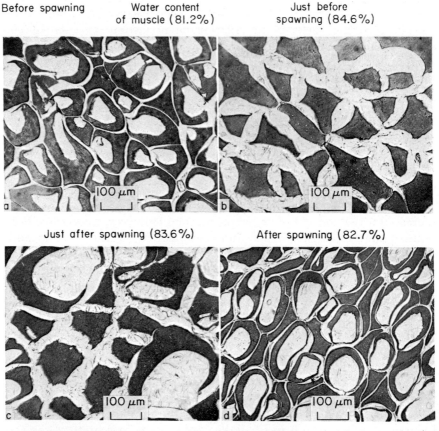

FIG. 70. The appearance of muscle from *Theragra chalcogramma* while frozen, showing how the ice crystals (white spaces) change in muscle of differing water contents. The cells are in cross-section, and in (a) and (d) each cell, surrounded by a thin film of extracellular fluid (now frozen) contains one big intracellular ice column. In (b), all the ice has formed outside the cells, which have shrunk and become dehydrated. In (c), both intracellular and extracellular freezing are seen together. See text for discussion. After Tanaka (1969b). Reproduced with permission of the author, who kindly supplied the photographs.

exosmosis and augmented itself. Eventually the cell became too de-hydrated to freeze, and the final picture at equilibrium was of a shrunken dehydrated cell surrounded by a relatively large body of ice. This is a large field of research that will not be described in detail here, being reviewed in Volume 1, reference 760. The point to be made is that a cell containing free fluid can dehydrate and freeze externally, while a cell with most or all of the water engaged with the protein structures will not shrink by dehydration through the cell wall following external freezing. Some ice will form within it once the temperature is low enough, but many water molecules are not free to move towards the nearest ice crystal and perforce freeze where they are (present writer, unpublished).

Tanaka (1969b: *Theragra chalcogramma*) has elegantly applied a knowledge of these phenomena to studying free water in muscle during starvation, by imposing slow freezing well before spawning, just before spawning, just after, and well after spawning when the fish has almost recovered. Figure 70(a) shows that where the gross water content is only 81·2%, the intracellular water is not free to diffuse from the cell—one could almost say that its interior is "dry"—and very little water freezes outside the cell. Note the single big ice crystal within each cell. When the total muscle water has risen to 84·6% (Fig. 70(b)), much of the freezable water has diffused through the cell wall and frozen exterior to the cell. It must have been "free" water and not bound to protein structures. When the water content has started to decline after spawning to 83·6% (Fig. 70(c)), some cells have formed ice interiorly, some exteriorly, while near-complete recovery (Fig. 70(d)): water content= 82·7%) has again shown "dry" cell interiors and little or no diffusion of water through to the extracellular space. I apologise for giving a sketchy background and assuming some detailed knowledge of a highly specialised field on the part of the general reader, but these pictures are a definitive demonstration of hydration within a cell, as well as without, during starvation.

Tanaka (1969b) also counted the percentage of muscle cells with intracellular ice at this rate of freezing in fish with differing water contents. His diagram (Fig. 71) may make the foregoing account easier to understand.

ii. *Carbohydrates*

Little remains to be added to what we have said already. The carbo-hydrates of blood and muscle are remarkably stable in some species during starvation (*Cyprinus carpio*: Murat, 1976a; *Carassius auratus*: Chavin and Young, 1970) but decline in others (muscle of *Notopterus*

notopterus: Narasimhan and Sundararaj, 1971b; blood: Joshi, 1974, and liver: Ahsan and Ahsan, 1975, of *Clarias batrachus*). Joshi (1974) reviewed numerous earlier papers on the subject and found the overall picture contradictory. Species differences are marked and may relate to habitual activity: sluggish species seem to maintain glucose levels for

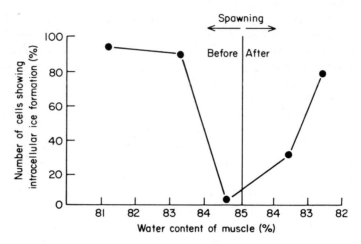

FIG. 71. The proportion of frozen muscle cells (*Theragra chalcogramma*) which contain intracellular ice, in relation to the biological condition of the fish as measured by water content in the muscle. After Tanaka (1969b). Reproduced with permission of the author.

the longest period. Since the materials first to be used for energy in starving *Cyprinus carpio* are proteins or lipids, an actual increase in blood glucose is sometimes seen in the early stages of starvation (Nagai and Ikeda, 1971). The glycogen content of the saccus vasculosus has also been seen to increase (Narasimhan and Sundararaj, 1971b: *Notopterus notopterus*), perhaps a device to safeguard the brain against excessive glucose deficiency during starvation. In the brain itself, the concentration of glycogen does decline somewhat in this species, but in *Clarias batrachus* it is rigorously maintained over a 90-day starvation period, while the glycogen concentrations in blood, liver and muscle all decline (Khanna and Bhatt, 1972).

iii.   *Proteins (apart from collagen) and amino acids*

Volume 1, Table 35, showed that in starving carp the concentrations of some *free* amino acids in the blood increase, while others decrease. A somewhat clearer picture now emerges from the work of Timoshina and Shabalina (1972: *Salmo gairdneri*) shown in Table 13. It looks as though the *free* amino acids of the blood are drawn upon and decrease for the first few weeks, after which the fish start to mobilise their protein reserves and eventually restore the circulating level.

TABLE 13

Free amino acids in the blood of *Salmo gairdneri* during the course of starvation. (After Timoshina and Shabalina, 1972. Reproduced with permission of the authors)

Duration of starvation (days)	0	14	26	66	97	126
AMINO ACID[a]						
Alanine	10·0	5·0	tr.	4·5	5·5	8·2
Arginine	3·8	tr.	tr.	3·2	4·0	3·8
Aspartic acid	13·5	8·0	8·0	10·0	9·5	10·0
Cystine	18·0	15·0	tr.	20·0	18·5	17·7
Glutamic acid	9·0	6·5	3·5	5·0	6·5	8·0
Glutamine	5·0	3·8	tr.	4·0	5·0	4·5
Glycine	10·0	6·5	6·5	9·0	9·0	11·2
Histidine	13·5	7·5	7·5	8·0	13·5	15·0
Leucine+isoleucine	6·0	4·5	2·5	4·0	5·5	5·6
Lysine	10·0	7·5	tr.	7·5	10·0	22·0
Methionine	8·0	8·0	tr.	7·4	6·5	6·0
Phenylalanine	10·0	8·0	tr.	8·0	8·5	9·0
Serine	7·5	7·5	2·5	6·5	7·5	7·0
Threonine	6·5	5·0	tr.	4·5	5·0	5·0
Tyrosine	9·0	tr.	tr.	8·5	9·0	8·7
Valine	20·0	13·5	tr.	15·0	13·5	16·5

[a]mg% dry weight.   tr.=trace.

The rate at which fish can utilise circulating amino acids does not seem to be altered by starvation. Ince and Thorpe (1976) injected amino acids into the blood system of *Esox lucius* and found that the rise in blood amino acids (half an hour) and subsequent fall to previous levels (3 hours) were almost identical in freshly-caught fish and those starved for 3 months. It would be interesting to observe the reaction after other periods of starvation.

The classical fractions of blood protein, albumins and globulins, decrease in the blood of *Cyprinus carpio*, with the exception of γ-globulin which shows a relative increase (Volume 1, p. 232), and more recently Carbery (1970: *Salmo trutta*) has shown that as the total serum protein declines during starvation, the albumin:globulin ratio declines as well. Snieszko (1972) suggested using the albumin:globulin ratio as a nutritional indicator because of the near-disappearance of blood albumin during starvation.

Timoshina (1970) reported that the proportions of *combined* amino acids in the muscle proteins did not change during the starvation of

Cyprinus carpio, Silurus glanis, Tinca tinca or *Esox lucius*. Timoshina and Shabalina (1972) reached a similar conclusion with *Salmo gairdneri*. While the myofilaments of a cell would not change in their amino acid composition just because some of their companions had been broken down and removed during starvation, these reports do not tell quite the whole story. The proportion of connective tissue in muscle increases during starvation, as we shall see in the next section, and it is therefore to be expected that the proportions of glycine, proline and hydroxy-proline will increase as starvation progresses. In Volume 1, p. 101, small increases in proline and glycine were in fact shown in the muscle of starving *Salmo salar*, and Créac'h (1972) has shown that in *Cyprinus carpio* starved for 8 months the (combined) glycine content of the muscle nearly doubles, while only small changes occur in the other amino acids.[1]

There are no reports of collagen synthesis in starving mammals. In any case, it is difficult to make comparisons with fish because of the relatively short period for which they can subsist without food. However, Adibi (1971) submitted rats to starvation and concluded, like Timoshina (1970), that the proportions of bound amino acids showed no difference whether or not the animal was starving. On the other hand, the composition of the *free* amino acid pool[2] changed markedly and was potentially informative. This has also been shown in fish. Table 36 of Volume 1 showed that the concentration of total *free* amino acids declines very much in muscle and slightly in the intestine, increasing in liver, kidney and spleen (*Cyprinus carpio* starved for 8 months). Winter starvation has since been shown to cause reductions in almost all of the *free* amino acids of the muscle of the four freshwater species studied by Timoshina (1970). Fontaine and Marchelidon (1971a) demonstrated similar falls in the *free* amino acids of the muscle and some increases in the brain of migrating smolts of *Salmo salar*, concluding that the swimming activity as they head towards the sea is greater than that of the parr and temporarily outstrips the food supply.

In Volume 1, p. 240, it was concluded that little could be learned in physiological terms from the changes in the *free* amino acid contents of various organs during starvation. The trouble with the more recent work is that fish are usually starved for just one period of time to be compared with unstarved controls, whereas several periods are really needed. The one instance where several periods have been used (Table 13, p. 193) seems to show the fish drawing on its *free* amino acid pool

---

[1]Neither proline nor hydroxyproline were determined here.

[2]"Pool"—a term which implies that *free* amino acids are not tied to a particular organ, but are relatively at liberty to circulate around the body.

at the outset of starvation and then restoring it by breaking down other protein reserves. It would not be surprising if this pattern were to be followed in other tissues in addition to blood.

Degradative proteolytic activity in the form of various dipeptidases was studied in various organs of *Cyprinus carpio* by Créac'h, Serfaty and Vellas (1969), but seemed not to change after a 6-month fast. After 8

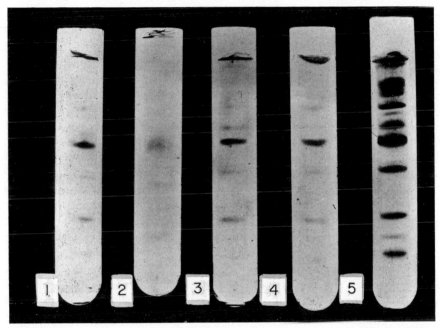

FIG. 72. Electropherograms (polyacrilamide gel) of water extracts of muscle from starving *Gadus morhua*. Nos 1–4, Starving to varying extents; 5, fed control. The most severely starved fish, with muscle water content over 90%, is no. 2. After Love and Robertson (unpublished). Crown Copyright.

to 9 months (Créac'h, Nopoly and Serfaty, 1969) the proteolytic activities of kidney, spleen and white and dark muscle did increase, but there was little change in the liver, and the increases were not striking anyway.

Certain amino acids ("essential") cannot be synthesised from others and so must be supplied by the diet. The non-essential amino acids can be synthesised by the fish, which suffers no deficiency symptoms in a diet freed from them. Measuring the proportions of different amino acids in the bodies (whole animals minus internal organs) of *Cyprinus carpio*, Maslova (1973) observed that it is the non-essential amino acids that tend to be used up during starvation and which tend to be laid down more plentifully during summer feeding. Thus for example the lysine:arginine ratio is increased in times of dearth and decreased in times of plenty. The observations would be easier to interpret if free and combined amino acids had been separated, but nevertheless new indicators of biological condition are always interesting. Similar trends in non-essential *free* amino acids were reported in blood, liver, kidney and spleen by Créac'h (1972: same species).

Proteins of small molecular weight, extractable from muscle with water and separable by electrophoresis, are largely enzymes, though not all have been identified. Classically they were called muscle "myogens", and the patterns obtained by electrophoresis are characteristic of each species and have been used to identify them (Volume 1, Figs 54 and 55). It might be expected, therefore, that marked increases in any proteolytic enzymes in the muscle of starving fish would be seen either as new electrophoretic bands or as increases in existing ones. Nothing of this kind has so far been observed. In Fig. 72, the electropherograms of white muscle extracts of *Gadus morhua* are displayed for comparison. Sample 5 is that of a normally-fed fish, and numbers 1 to 4 are from fish of varying degrees of starvation, number 2 being the most severely starved fish with a muscle water content of over 90%. It is clear that no new bands are shown by this method, and all existing bands become fainter, several invisible. It is a striking demonstration of the decrease in general metabolic activity of muscle during starvation. A similar attenuation or disappearance of protein bands in the haemolymph of shrimps starved for 4 weeks was reported by Cuzon and Ceccaldi (1972).

The decline in all types of protein in solution can be followed in the refractive index of the fluid obtained when dead, that is, "wet" (see p. 189) muscle is submitted to pressure. Declerk and Vyncke (1973: *Reinhardtius hippoglossoides*) showed that the refractive index ranges from 1·3454 in fish with 70·2% of water in the muscle to 1·3400 in very soft fish with a water content of 83·8%. The measurement of nutritional condition by this means is extremely rapid, though it is not as precise as is the measurement of water content.

The ability of starving *Cyprinus carpio* to synthesise proteins differs between liver and muscle. Bouche and Vellas (1975) injected radioactive lysine and followed the synthesis and decay of radioactive protein in the fish, corresponding with protein built with the aid of the injected material and its subsequent breakdown. They found (Fig. 73) that in nourished fish the radioactivity increases over a period of 3 days in the liver and then declines slowly. In starving fish it reaches the same level in only 1 day, and then decreases almost as rapidly. During starvation, therefore, the liver rapidly siezes any circulating amino acids and synthesises protein with them, but the product has only a short life before being broken down again.

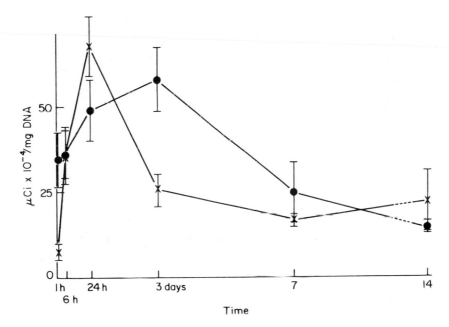

FIG 73. The effect of starvation on the incorporation of radioactivity into liver proteins, following injection of radioactive lysine. ●, Fed controls; ×, starving. After Bouche and Vellas (1975) and Bouche (1975). Reproduced with permission of Dr G. Bouche.

Proteins in the *muscle* of nourished carp also increase over a 3-day period and then slowly decline (Fig. 74) because of the limited life of muscle tissue, which as we have seen (p. 163) breaks down more rapidly if the fish are actively swimming. In starvation, however, there is no protein synthesis at all. The path of amino acids in the muscle of this species is strictly in one direction even if some are circulating. In starving *Fundulus heteroclitus* the incorporation of radioactive lysine does continue but on a reduced scale (Jackim and LaRoche, 1973).

To follow the rate of degradation of protein by measuring the entry of a radioactively labelled amino acid, which was previously incorporated into the protein, into the *free* amino acid pool could give a false impression if the animal is actively synthesising at the same time—the liberated

radioactive amino acid could be re-incorporated into a protein structure, so a simultaneous measure of incorporation or re-incorporation
would be useful. Little, Atkinson and Frieden (1973), who studied
starving frogs (*Rana catesbiana*), used an ingenious method involving
leucine radioactively labelled in two ways. The protein of the frog was

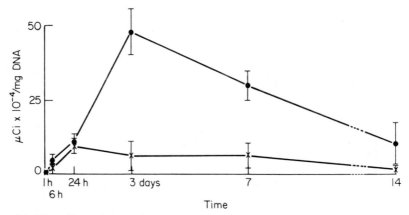

FIG. 74. The effect of starvation on the incorporation of radioactivity into muscle
proteins, following injection of radioactive lysine. Other details as in Fig. 73.

first labelled by injecting H^2-leucine (leucine labelled with tritium) for
each of 5 days before determinations were done. The animals were then
injected once with ^{14}C-leucine (leucine labelled with radioactive carbon). Decrease of the latter from the *free* amino acid pool reflected the
rate of synthesis of protein, so the rate of increase of the $^2H:^{14}C$ ratio in
the pool gave a measure of protein degradation, corrected for simultaneous synthesis. The double labelling technique has not been used to
study starving fish so far, but seems worth considering.

Free histidine, which is plentiful in the muscle of dark-fleshed fish, is
thought to be regulated by histidine deaminase and urocanase, which
mediate the first two steps of the degradative process. Sakaguchi and
Kawai (1970b) measured the activities of the enzymes in the livers of
Cyprinus carpio (the enzymes are not found in muscle) fasted for 2 weeks
and found no change in activity, perhaps even an increase, but feeding
the fish on a low-protein diet caused a marked fall. The period of
starvation may have been too short to bring about a change.

iv. *Collagen*

When musculature is degraded for use during starvation, it is the
contractile proteins (myofilaments, Fig. 57) and soluble proteins

(myogens, Fig. 72) which are removed, while connective tissues, according to earlier reports, are used either to a lesser extent or not at all.

In Volume 1, p. 233, it was shown that aspartic acid and valine in *Pomolobus pseudoharengus* varied seasonally, with a minimum at the spawning time, marking the breakdown of contractile proteins, while hydroxyproline and hydroxylysine showed maxima, probably relative increases representing untouched collagen. The collagen content of *Clupea harengus* also has been shown to increase at the spawning time (Volume 1, pp. 102 and 103) but in this case histological sections showed that the skin actually becomes thicker.

While collagen may show a relative increase due to the mobilisation of other substances, it can show a real increase under the action of hormones. Idler, Bitners and Schmidt (1961) showed that injecting 11-ketotestosterone thickened the skins of *Oncorhynchus nerka*. McBride and van Overbeeke (1971) gonadectomised male *Oncorhynchus nerka* and then injected them with various hormones, finding that 11-ketotestosterone increased the thickness of the skin more than three-fold and that 17 α-methyl testosterone was even more effective. Gonadectomised females injected with oestradiol also increased their skin thickness, but to a lesser extent—not quite twice the resting level. Such differences between the actions of male and female hormones show also in salmonids maturing naturally—male epidermis becomes thicker than that of females; hypophysectomy prevents either change from taking place (various authors quoted by Hay, Hodgins and Roberts, 1976). Thiourea has been found to inhibit the skin thickening to some extent in naturally mature *Oncorhynchus nerka*, but it does not affect the skin thickness of gonadectomised fish (McBride and van Overbeeke, 1975).

It seems almost certain that maturation, either by its hormonal action or by the starvation associated with it, brings about an increase in the proportion of collagen in *Clupea harengus*. Apart from the various reports reviewed in Volume 1, Plorina (1970) has now shown that the muscle protein decreases in its tryptophan content and increases in, among other amino acids, glycine and proline when herring become larger. He is probably again reporting the effects of maturation. The only contrary evidence up to now relates to herring larvae, in which starvation reduces the amount of collagen surrounding the intestine (Ehrlich, Blaxter and Pemberton, 1976: Fig. 75).

In the musculature of *Cyprinus carpio* starved for a long period, Créac'h and Gas (1971) noted an increase in glycine and hydroxyproline and a reduction in the number of sulphydryl groups, in which contractile tissue is rich. They observed that the connective tissue within the muscle seemed little altered by the starvation, so the change in amino acids was again presumably relative. Gas (1972) reported that the collagen of the septa, that is, the myocommata, was also little altered.

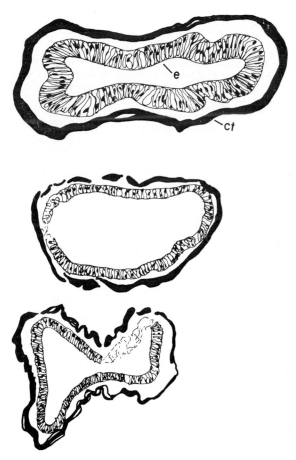

Fig. 75. The effect of starvation on the intestine of *Clupea harengus* larvae. Top: 21 mm, 79-day-old larva, feeding. e, Epithelial cells; ct, connective tissue. Middle picture: 20 mm 85-day-old larva starved for 6 days. Bottom picture: 23 mm 91-day-old larva starved for 12 days. All pictures traced from actual photographs. Note emaciation of both epithelial cells and the connective tissue. After Ehrlich, Blaxter and Pemberton (1976). Reproduced with permission of Dr K. F. Ehrlich.

Créac'h (1972) starved carp for 8 months, during which time they lost 42% of their weight. The striking relative increase in collagen in different parts of the musculature is shown in Fig. 76. It is much more striking than the increase in white muscle glycine (4·95 rising to 8·63 grams per 16 grams of protein nitrogen) because glycine is found also in contractile tissue and some of it therefore drains away during starvation.

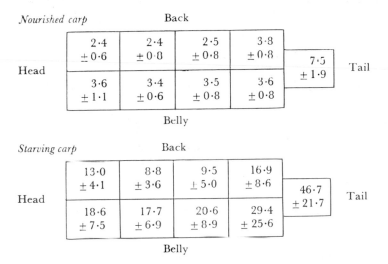

Nourished carp — Back

| 2·4 ±0·6 | 2·4 ±0·0 | 2·5 ±0·8 | 3·8 ±0·8 | 7·5 ±1·9 |
| 3·6 ±1·1 | 3·4 ±0·6 | 3·5 ±0·8 | 3·6 ±0·8 | |

Head ... Tail — Belly

Starving carp — Back

| 13·0 ±4·1 | 8·8 ±3·6 | 9·5 ±5·0 | 16·9 ±8·6 | 46·7 ±21·7 |
| 18·6 ±7·5 | 17·7 ±6·9 | 20·6 ±8·9 | 29·4 ±25·6 | |

Head ... Tail — Belly

FIG. 76. Collagen content of different parts of the white skeletal muscle of nourished and starved *Cyprinus carpio*. After Créac'h (1972). Reproduced with permission of the author.

While reports in the literature, apart from those relating to the skin of herrings, seem to describe apparent increases in collagen caused by the removal of other substances, there is a growing body of evidence to show that collagen is actually synthesised during starvation. Gas (1973) mentioned the deposition of collagen in the liver as a special feature of the starvation of *Cyprinus carpio*. In the writer's laboratory it seemed strange that the myocommata from starving *Gadus morhua* were always so very easy to dissect and scrape free from muscle cells: after a while it dawned that they were in fact much tougher than those from fed fish, and hence were easier to handle. Lavéty and Love (1972) showed that their tensile strength increased proportionately as the water content of the muscle increased (Fig. 77). The increase in strength partly reflects thickening, but Love, Yamaguchi *et al.* (1976) showed that during starvation the myocommata are in fact thickened with a stronger collagen (with more *inter*-molecular cross-links) than is present in non-starved fish. The skin is also thickened, but with collagen of similar strength. Detailed studies showed that the extra collagen is in other respects similar to the collagen already there—in molecular shape, *intra*-molecular cross linking, imino acid[1] and amino acid composition and in the temperature at which it is converted to gelatin. Myocomma thickness increases also according to the length of the fish (Volume 1, p. 6) so Fig. 78 allows for this and relates myocomma thickness to both the water content of the musculature and the body length.

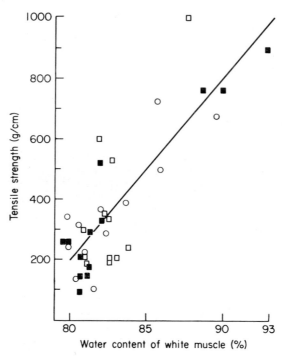

FIG. 77. Weight in grams needed to break strips of myocomma 1 cm wide, dissected from the musculature of *Gadus morhua*. The different levels of starvation are indicated by the water contents of the muscle. Each value is the mean of 6–10 measurements. Body lengths: ○, 60–69·9 cm; ■, 70–79·9 cm; □, 80–89·9 cm. After Lavéty and Love (1972).

The collagen of the myocommata of older fish is weaker (less cross-linked between the molecules) than that of younger fish, but in life the older fish make up for this by disproportionate increases in the thickness (same authors). Thus doubling the length of a cod results in an average loss of 50% in myocomma strength per unit thickness, but a 170% increase in the thickness.

---

[1]Proline and hydroxyproline, substances found only in collagen.

It follows that the myocommata of cod and perhaps those of other species thicken annually, following the pattern of winter starvation. The return to summer feeding must result in the myocommata being then whittled down to their "normal" thickness, and there is presumably a period during which active degradation takes place. In June

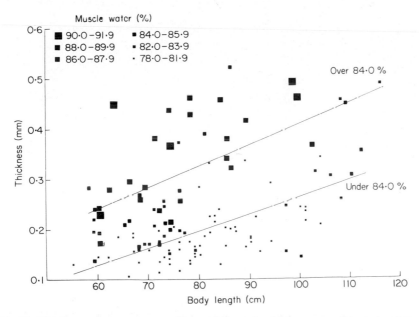

FIG. 78. Thickness of myocommata dissected from the thickest part of the musculature of *Gadus morhua* of different body lengths, and undergoing different degrees of starvation. Each point is the mean of 5 determinations and the size of the symbol used indicates the severity of starvation as measured by the muscle water content—the bigger the symbol, the more severely starved. After Love, Yamaguchi *et al.* (1976).

1966 the writer's group landed a haul of Faroe Bank cod from which it was impossible to dissect the myocommata because of their extremely soft nature. It was astonishing that the musculature had held together at all. This single observation is the only known example which could be interpreted as "normalisation".

The thickening of skin during starvation is not universal. Inui and Yokote (1974) found a striking *reduction* in the thickness of the skin when *Anguilla japonica* were fasted (Fig. 79) for 60 days. Their illustrations are at the same magnification, and show that skin after starvation is not only about a quarter of the thickness of that of the fed controls, but contains fewer goblet and clavate cells.

In mammals, collagen alters profoundly with age. It becomes less digestible with collagenase (Goll, Hoekstra and Bray, 1964: cattle) and

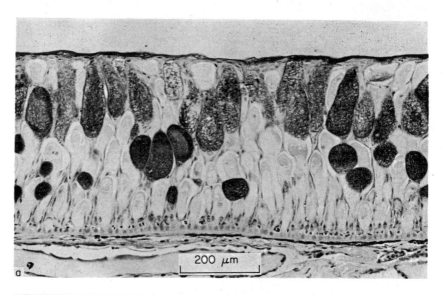

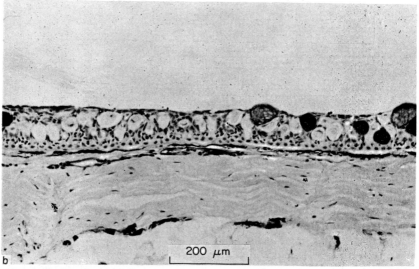

FIG. 79. Sections through the skin of *Anguilla japonica*. Fixed with Zenker-formol. Stain: PAS. The dark cells are goblet cells, unstained are clavate cells. (a) Fed control. (b) After starvation for 60 days, when both types of cell are reduced in size and number. After Inui and Yokote (1974). Reproduced with permission of Dr M. Yokote, who kindly supplied the photographs.

much less soluble in salt solution or dilute acid (Carmichael and Lawrie, 1967: cattle; Szeredy, 1970: cattle and pigs; Nageotte and Guyon, 1934, quoted by Harkness, Marko *et al.*, 1954: rats; Eichhorn and Butzow, 1966: rats; Bakerman, 1962: man). In contrast, J. Lavéty (unpublished) found that the proportions of salt- and acid-insoluble

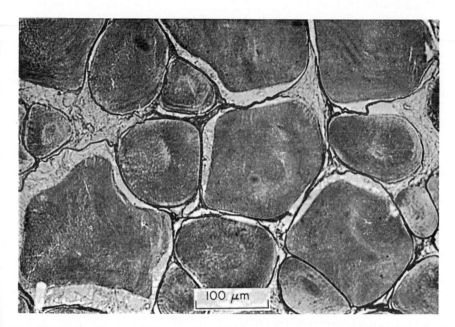

FIG. 80. Section through white muscle of *Gadus morhua*, water content 82·9%, stained with trichrome to show the connective tissue which appears black in this picture. The cell contents have just begun to shrink away from the collagen framework. After Love (unpublished). Crown copyright.

collagens of cod increase only slightly with age, compared with many-fold in mammals, and the salt-soluble fraction, the least cross-linked material, also increases: an unheard-of accompaniment of aging. In contrast to aged man, one does not see older cod with wrinkled skins, and the annual renewal of much of the collagen probably means that much of it remains "young".

Chemical determinations of the collagen surrounding each cell, as distinct from that in cleaned myocommata, tend to be inaccurate because of the preponderance of other amino acids. However, I have the impression that this also increases during starvation. Staining for connective tissue, one seems to see a clear ring of collagen colour round each cell only when the fish have starved for a while, even where little increase in extracellular space has yet occurred. Figure 80 shows cod muscle with 82·9% of water, where the cell contents have only just started to shrink. The use of coloured filters brings up the collagen in black in this picture, and an extensive network of it can be seen. Unstarved fish seem to have less. Unfortunately, these observations are not yet quantifiable.

v.   *Lipids*

We have seen (p. 41) how under natural conditions starvation is often linked to the reproductive cycle, so that there are differences in its effect on the two sexes. Females tend to lay down the greater reserves in the feeding season and to become the more depleted at spawning. Thus, starvation of *Salmo gairdneri* causes reduction in the lipids of liver, "viscera" and plasma, but the depletion is more severe in mature females than in immatures because of the additional transfer of lipids to the gonad (Takashima, Hibiya *et al.*, 1971) which would be much less in the case of males.

Figures 31 and 32 (p. 99) showed that lipids are mobilised from both dark and white muscle in a similar way in *Gadus morhua*, both tissues losing "structural" phospholipids.

Figure 81 (Ross, 1978) shows that myocommata also apparently yield lipids for metabolism in times of need, though at least part of this fall in lipids could be the consequence of the thickening of the myocommata with lipid-reduced material. When we realise that myocommata comprise about 2% of the weight of the musculature and dark muscle 10% or less (Love, Hardy and Nishimoto, 1975), then the contributions of the different tissues are seen in perspective; white muscle is the major source, even though the concentration is greater in dark muscle. Robinson and Mead (1973) starved the more fatty *Salmo gairdneri* for 5 weeks and found that mosaic muscle (see p. 80) lost 49% of its lipids while dark muscle lost only 31%. However, dark muscle is richer in lipids and in absolute terms lost 15·6 mg/g of tissue, while mosaic muscle lost only 10·8 mg/g. They considered dark muscle as constituting less than 5% of the total musculature, so again it was the equivalent of white muscle in this species which yielded the more lipids.

It is probably worth labouring the point that the importance of an organ as a lipid store determines the proportion of triglycerides to phospholipids in it. Thus the white muscle of *Gadus morhua* contains no fatty globules, and the lipid consists largely of phospholipids which decrease only when tissue structures are broken down, while the liver, the primary storehouse of this species, contains lipids which are largely triglycerides. The lipid reserves of both *Gadus callarias* and *Macrurus rupestris* can indeed be assessed with reasonable accuracy by simply weighing the livers (Podrazhanskaya and Iarzhombek, 1970), a procedure which would not be useful in fatty fish such as *Clupea harengus*.

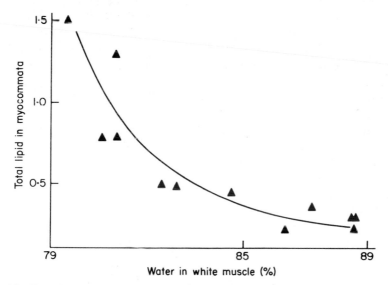

FIG. 81. The lipid content of white muscle myocommata from *Gadus morhua* of different nutritional states. The degree of starvation is measured by the white muscle water content. At least some of the fall in lipid concentration is probably a reflection of the thickening of myocommata already illustrated in Fig. 78. After Ross (1978). Reproduced with permission of the author.

Where appreciable lipid reserves occur in the muscle, the distinction between muscle lipids and liver lipids becomes blurred. Lambertsen (1972), for example, found little difference between the fatty acid compositions of muscle- and liver-lipids in *Anarhichas lupus*, *Pleuronectes platessa*, *Sebastes marinus* or *Labrus berggylta*, all of which have more than 1·5% of lipid in the muscle as compared with about 0·6% in *Gadus morhua*. The muscle of elasmobranchs tends to be more fatty still, and *Deania* sp., *Centroscymnus* sp., *Squalus acanthias* and *Prionace glauca* show similar distributions of the major classes of lipid in both liver and muscle (Sargent, Gatten and McIntosh, 1973). Their serum contains cholesterol esters and wax esters in addition to the other material. The latter authors concluded that different neutral lipids are relatively uniformly distributed in the bodies of sharks, with no one lipid class being confined to a specific tissue. This is in marked contrast to non-fatty species such as *Gadus morhua*.

We saw in Fig. 74 (p. 198) how synthesis of proteins from injected precursors ceased in the muscle of carp during starvation, but continued in the liver. Kluytmans and Zandee (1974) showed that radioactive acetate became incorporated into the lipids of both the liver and the remainder of the body of *Esox lucius* starved for 2 months. They concluded that the activity of the system for synthesising lipids is fairly independent of the level of starvation, but that there is a shift in acetate incorporation from structural lipids in starving fish to storage lipids after refeeding.

A certain basic minimum of structural lipids must clearly be maintained if the fish are to stay alive. Newsome and Leduc (1975) found that if the overall lipid content of *Perca flavescens* drops below 2·2% of the total dry weight, death ensues whether the fish are male or female, mature or immature.

Where fish keep stores of reserve lipid in the muscle, these probably start to be mobilised as soon as food intake ceases, but, when the muscle lipid is structural only, we may guess that it retains its original level until the protein structures begin to be broken down. Figures 31 and 32 (p. 99) showed that the phospholipid content declines steadily as the water content rises, but the water content does not change for some 9 weeks in this species at 9°C (Fig. 68, p. 186).

Initial breakdown of the most readily accessible lipid store invariably seems to mean breakdown of triglycerides, and relative increases in other classes which have been utilised less or not at all. Thus seasonal variation in the total muscle lipids of clupeiforms (*Sardina pilchardus*, *Clupea sprattus* and *Engraulis encrasicholus*), which are all fatty fish, is in essence a variation in the neutral lipids such as triglycerides, the absolute values of phospholipids remaining about the same (Viviani, Cortesi *et al.*, 1968). Migration of the parr form of *Oncorhynchus masou* also results in a loss of flesh lipids, the remainder being poorer in triglycerides and relatively richer in phospholipids and sterols (Ota and Yamada, 1974). A similar change is seen in the liver lipids of *Scorpaena porcus* during the synthesis of sex products (Shchepkin, 1971), and the lipids of the hump of male *Oncorhynchus gorbuscha* in the later stages of migration (Robinson and Mead, 1970). It is not confined to fish: the proportion of cholesterol increases also in the liver and adipose tissues of rabbits during starvation (Swaner and Connor, 1975), while a decrease of phospholipids in the livers of mice occurs only when the liver cells are breaking down (Coleman, 1973).

Changes in the proportions of the different fatty acids will result from these shifts in the ratios of different lipid classes. The proportions of 14:0, 16:1 and 18:1 (see p. 5 for definition) acids decline almost continuously in the liver lipids of *Anguilla anguilla* during starvation, and have been proposed by Dave, Johansson-Sjöbeck *et al.* (1976) as possible indicators of nutritional condition. Similarly, Ota and Yamada (1974: *Oncorhynchus masou*) noted that it is chiefly the acids with one double bond (monoenoic) which are used during migration, though polyenoic acids (with several double bonds) decrease during the later

TABLE 14

The fatty acid composition (as percent of lipids) of organs of starving and well-fed *Merluccius capensis*. (After Wessels and Spark, 1973. Reproduced with permission of Dr J. P. H. Wessels)

Fatty acid	White muscle		Dark muscle		Skin		Liver	
	Fat	Lean	Fat	Lean	Fat	Lean	Fat	Lean
14:0	1·73	1·02	2·99	2·31	3·28	2·73	3·97	6·11
16:0	23·57	20·70	18·51	17·73	21·36	19·96	20·27	25·23
16:1	4·95	3·02	6·75	6·00	7·05	6·45	8·10	10·02
17:0	0·68	0·45	0·72	0·82	0·42	1·05	1·14	1·47
18:0	4·36	4·95	2·28	2·80	2·87	3·44	2·52	2·83
18:1	20·46	15·12	23·76	19·56	26·02	22·40	23·17	20·58
20:1	4·36	2·89	6·74	5·97	6·80	6·46	6·65	5·39
20:5	6·58	7·81	7·01	7·17	6·68	6·32	8·51	7·07
22:5	1·65	2·14	2·15	2·72	1·65	2·18	1·73	1·40
22:6	24·01	36·94	19·25	26·11	17·19	20·21	13·37	11·79

Fatty acids occurring in very small amounts have been omitted.

stages. Ackman (private communication quoted by Iverson, 1972) also suggested that spawning depletion of *Oncorhynchus* species would result in the utilisation of long-chain monounsaturated acids such as 20:1 and 22:1 before that of the shorter-chain and polyunsaturated acids. The levels of polyenoic acids such as 20:5 and 22:6 were found by Hayashi and Yamada (1975c) to be maintained or proportionally increased at the commencement of starvation of *Fugu vermicularis porphyreus*, decreasing only when starvation was prolonged. The net effect is that the degree of unsaturation of the lipids increases as depletion develops; Shul'man (1972, p. 225, English edition) noted that the unsaturation reaches its maximum in wintering fatty fish from the Azov and Black Seas, ascribing to this effect a compensatory reaction to the low water temperature. The cause is more likely to be the selective mobilisation of triglycerides, though an increase in unsaturation would certainly keep the lipids more plastic (see p. 339 and Volume 1, pp. 216–217). The situation is different in the flesh of non-fatty species because of their low triglyceride content, and Ross and Love (1979) have demonstrated a progressive decline in the unsaturation of the flesh lipids of starving *Gadus morhua*.

Wessels and Spark (1973: *Merluccius capensis, M. paradoxus*) classified their fish from the wild as well fed if they had creamy-coloured livers or starving if the livers were red.[1] Creamy livers usually contained proportionately less 22:6 acid and more of the saturated 16:0. The results of one of their trials are shown in Table 14. As it happens, the liver lipids of these particular *Merluccius capensis* do not show the reduction in 22:6 when well fed, but in all other organs this fatty acid decreases in nourished specimens, increasing during starvation. The iodine values,[2] again with the one exception, show pronounced increases as a result of starvation, indicating an increase in the overall unsaturation (number of double bonds). The unsaturated acids 20:5 and 22:5 display the same trend but less consistently than 22:6. The relative increases in highly unsaturated fatty acids are largely the result of the fish using up their 18:1 acid during starvation, and the important 16:0 is also drawn upon in several instances, along with minor components such as 16:1.

These hake species are "non-fatty" like the gadoids. Phospholipids from a given tissue are richer in 22:6 than are triglycerides from the same source; 22:5 or 20:5 acids do not show the same difference. Hence (Table 14) there is more 22:6 acid in white muscle, the lipids of which are largely phospholipids, than in dark muscle or liver in which the phospholipids are "diluted" by neutral lipids. The contrast with the work of Ross and Love (1979) on *Gadus morhua*, which does utilise 22:6 acid from the muscle during starvation, probably means that the hake break down muscle structures less readily than cod during starvation.

Recently a completely new series of fatty acids has been discovered by Glass, Krick and Eckhardt (1974) in *Esox lucius*. Altogether 8 different acids have been detected (Glass, Krick *et al.*, 1975), and their common distinguishing feature is a furan ring.[3] They are found primarily in liver and testis lipids and have been reported as comprising as much

---

[1]The idea is not new. The Reverend Samuel Ward, writing before 1776, said: "The liver of a ling is extremely white, so long as the fish continues in season, and abounds with a fine flavoured oil; but as soon as it goes out of season, the liver becomes very red and affords no oil. This is, in some degree, the case with cod and other fish, but the difference is not so very remarkable."

[2]Iodine in solution is reduced by these double bonds, so the quantity of standard iodine decolorised gives a measure of the total unsaturation.

[3]A five-membered ring with oxygen as one of the members. The general formula of these acids is:

$$\text{Me } [CH_2]_m \overset{R_1 \quad\quad R_2}{\diagdown\!\!\diagup_{O}\diagup} [CH_2]_n \, COOH$$

where R_1 and R_2 are either H or Me.

as 92% of the cholesterol ester fraction of male pike liver. Wide seasonal variations have been reported by the same authors. Work in this laboratory (Gunstone, Wijesundera *et al.*, 1976: *Gadus morhua*) seems to show that the degree of starvation is the main factor governing the concentration in the liver; the latter rises during initial starvation and falls again in the final stages as cholesterol esters, presumably from cell membranes, are utilised (Fig. 82). The function of these compounds is as yet unknown. In a range of fish species, Gunstone, Wijesundera *et al.* (1976) found that the predominant furan acid was that with 22 carbon atoms.

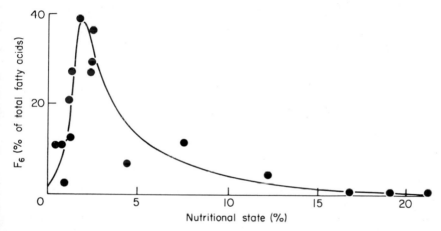

FIG. 82. The F_6 furan fatty acid as a percentage of the total fatty acids of *Gadus morhua* liver lipids. The "nutritional state" is the total liver lipid as a percentage of the total liver lipid of Faroe Bank cod, of the same body length, caught in September, such fish being assumed to be fully fed. After Ross (1978). Reproduced with permission of the author.

As regards circulating lipids, starvation in mammals leads to a rapid and marked increase in serum free fatty acids (FFA), but changes of comparable magnitude have not been observed in fish (Bilinski, 1974). However, if one surveys the literature as a whole, it appears that the length of time the fish were starved is critical, and there may be species differences as well. It must also be remembered that reactions in fish usually take longer to start than in mammals. Thus *Opsanus tau* starved for 30 to 90 days (Volume 1, reference 1250) and *Oncorhynchus nerka* starved for 30 days (McKeown, Leatherland and John, 1975) show decreases in the FFA of the plasma; *Salmo gairdneri* starved for moderate periods show either a steady increase in FFA (Shibata, Kinumaki and

Ichimura, 1974a), a modest increase (Volume 1, reference 105) or no change (Mazeaud, 1973; Robinson and Mead, 1973); *Anguilla anguilla* show no rise for the first 95 days, but a marked rise follows this period (Larsson and Lewander, 1973) or, rather, followed on this particular occasion. Mazeaud (1973) reported no change in the FFA of *Tinca tinca*

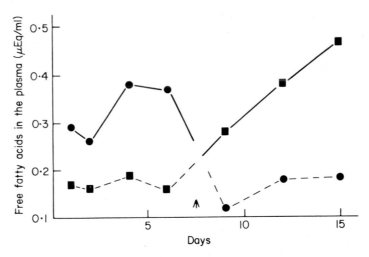

Fig. 83. The effect of alternate feeding and starvation on the free fatty acid level of *Cyprinus carpio* plasma. ●, Starting with starvation, then feeding; ■, starting fed, then submitting to starvation. (Changeover indicated by arrow.) —, Alimentary canal is empty; _ _ _, alimentary canal is full. Starvation raises blood FFA, feeding lowers it. After Mazeaud (1973). Reproduced with permission of the author.

starved for 124 days, but confirmed that it rose in *Anguilla anguilla* after long starvation. In *Cyprinus carpio* he showed convincingly that the FFA content rises at the beginning of starvation, falling again if the fish are fed after 7 days[1] (Fig. 83), but that only a small increase over the normal resting level could be seen after starving for 127 days. What is clearly needed is sampling over a long period at frequent intervals; this would show the rises and falls in the intensity of mobilisation of tissue lipids.

vi. *Blood constituents*

We have just seen how mobilisation of tissue lipids can result in an increase in the circulating free fatty acids, which does not correlate simply with the severity of starvation.

---

[1]A decrease in FFA has also been observed to follow the feeding of starving *Anguilla rostrata* (Mayerle and Butler, 1971).

Several authors have plotted the changes in various other constituents of the blood at fairly frequent intervals, again without revealing any clear general trends apart from a tendency for proteins to diminish. Most of the substances studied by Siddiqui (1975b: *Clarias batrachus*) showed "increases" up to the second day of starvation, presumably resulting from haemoconcentration, before declining for the remaining 108 days. It is not uncommon to find irregular changes, such as fall–rise–fall (Créac'h and Bouche, 1969: sodium in *Cyprinus carpio;* Dave, Johansson-Sjöbeck *et al.*, 1975: glucose in *Anguilla anguilla*) or rise–fall–rise (Créac'h and Bouche, 1969: potassium in *Cyprinus carpio*) which require more detailed physiological knowledge before they can be interpreted.

Counts of the various cells suspended in the blood also vary during starvation. In Volume 1, p. 255, it was shown that red and white cell populations decrease in *Salmo gairdneri* and *Lota lota*, but in the latter species the decrease in red cells is preceded by an increase, again the probable result of haemoconcentration.

Some recent papers have shown that starvation causes a reduction in the numbers of red cells of *Cyprinus carpio* (Créac'h and Bouche, 1969), *Tinca tinca* (Bange-Barnoud, Bange *et al.*, 1971: haematocrits as low as 4% were recorded) and *Salmo gairdneri* (Kawatsu, 1974) and in the numbers of white cells of *Salmo gairdneri* (Haider, 1972) and *Anguilla anguilla* (Johansson-Sjöbeck, Dave *et al.*, 1975). However, the fall in the numbers of red cells reported by Kawatsu (1974) was preceded by a rise, and in *Anguilla anguilla* the fall was less than the initial rise, so that all starving fish had higher haematocrits than the controls (Johansson-Sjöbeck, Dave *et al.*, 1975). In this experiment, starvation had been carried out for "only" 164 days, and the shape of the curve suggests that the haematocrit would in the end have fallen below that of unstarved eels, confirming the observations of other writers.

The dissenting voice among these authors is that of Smirnova (1967), who found no decrease in the red cell count during the starvation of *Lota lota* or *Abramis brama*, but a reduction in the volume of plasma leading to haemoconcentration—a fairly general phenomenon as we have now seen. However, Smirnova's contribution is to show that the numbers of red cells are maintained in these species in the almost complete absence of haematopoiesis (blood cell manufacture) by an increase in their life span. In warm-blooded animals the life span can also be extended, for example from 91 days in active dormice to 270 days during hibernation, and from 15 days in active hamsters to 160 days during hibernation. In her own work she showed that the mean life span of blood cells in satiated *Lota lota* is 104 days, increasing to a maximum of 490 days after starvation for 7 months, with intermediate values in less starved fish. By analogy with the figures quoted for mammals, it almost looks as though starvation prolongs the life span in consequence of the reduced swimming activity of starving fish, though there is no way of proving this.

Blood cell counts during starvation seem therefore to be governed by three variables, not all necessarily acting together at a given time. These are a decrease in the generation of new cells (Volume 1, Fig. 102 bottom curve), variation in the volume of the plasma and an increase in the life span of the cells. A possible fourth is the withdrawal of restoration of cells by the spleen, but no information has been published.

In pursuance of our aim of characterising the physiological state of captured fish, we now give the limits of usefulness of haematocrit determinations: "normal" figures tell us nothing, but a fish with low values is probably starving. Remember, though, that a starving fish may have normal or even elevated haematocrit values.

Marine elasmobranchs guard against the dehydrating effects of the sea salt by retaining urea in their blood (and other tissues). The urea content of the serum responds to a change in the external salinity to keep the animal in osmotic balance, but Haywood (1973a, b) has now shown that starvation interferes with this process. Since starving fish are catabolising less protein, less urea is formed, and the elasmobranch studied, *Poroderma africanum*, has been found when starving to have lower urea levels in its blood over the whole range of external salinities than the levels achieved by well-fed fish. The results are illustrated in Fig. 84.

vii. *Nucleic acids*

We have already seen (p. 30) that the deoxyribose nucleic acid (DNA) is a constant quantity in the cell nucleus, while the amount of ribose nucleic acid (RNA) varies directly with the activity of protein synthesis, and hence can be used as a measure of growth rate.

By the same token, a study of the nucleic acids can be used to follow the course of starvation. Onishi (1970) showed that the nuclear-, ribosomal- and soluble RNA in the livers of rats all decrease exponentially during starvation in parallel with the loss of body weight. Bulow (1969, 1970) showed that the response in *Notemigonus crysoleucas* is very rapid when the starved fish are refed. His results on the nucleic acids of whole fish (Fig. 85) illustrate the constancy of DNA while the RNA mirrors the nutritional changes. It is usual to express such results as RNA:DNA ratios, showing the change in synthetic activity in relation to the number of nuclei and eliminating the effect of volume changes in the tissue, but Bouche (1975: *Cyprinus carpio*) has discovered that while muscle DNA can be reckoned a "tissue constant" for most of the starvation period, it does diminish after 11 months, indicating lysis of the nuclei. Similarly in the liver it diminished between the 8th and 10th months of starvation (Bouche, Gas and Créac'h, 1969). The *content* of

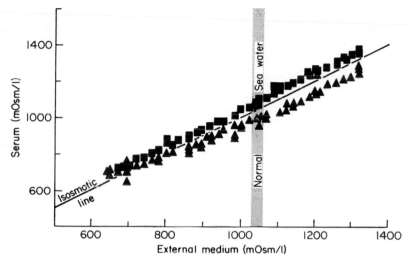

FIG. 84. The effect of food intake on the serum osmolality of *Poroderma africanum* placed in solutions of different salinity. ■, Fed twice per week; ▲, fed once per month. The lower osmolality of the fish with the lower food intake probably reflects a reduced synthesis of urea. After Haywood (1973a). Reproduced with permission of the author.

DNA in the liver does not change in the first months of starvation, but after the 4th month the *concentration* increases continuously because of the loss of liver cytoplasm and increased packing of nuclei (see Fig. 60, p. 177). The diminution in the volume of the liver of starving carp is much greater than that of mammals which have died from starvation (Bouche, 1975).

The response to refeeding is slower following severe starvation than following a starvation as slight as that illustrated in Fig. 85. Bouche, Créac'h *et al.* (1973), who refed severely starved *Cyprinus carpio*, found that when a rise in the *free* amino acid concentration in the liver could first be measured, the ribosomal RNA had not changed, showing the "ineptitude" of the liver cells at incorporating the amino acids into proteins. It took 15 days before a diminution in the level of *free* amino acids was detected, accompanied by an increase in RNA.

RNA is found in small cellular bodies, the ribosomes. When these associate into larger units they are known as polysomes, the functional units of protein synthesis. Bouche, Narbonne and Créac'h (1972) separated them from a liver homogenate on a centrifuge density gradient and found that their quantity and their degree of polymerisation

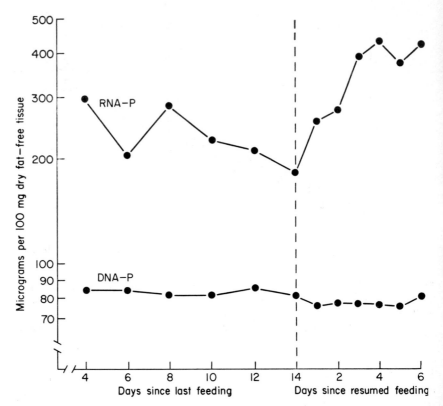

FIG. 85. The response of RNA and DNA (expressed as phosphorus) in whole *Note-migonus crysoleucas* to refeeding after starvation. Note the rapid response of RNA, no response in DNA. After Bulow (1969). Reproduced with permission of the author.

decreases progressively with starvation, running parallel with the decrease of protein synthesis. Ribosomal (and polysomal) RNA decreases at the same time, an effect illustrated in the lower curve of Fig. 86.

When the fish were refed, an enormous increase in ribosomal RNA, also shown in Fig. 86, occurred, as the fish phrenetically replaced their lost protein while the food lasted. A similar effect was seen in the soluble RNA (not illustrated). Thus refed starving fish can temporarily exhibit a concentration of RNA even higher than that in fish fed continuously throughout the experimental period. This "overshoot" will be referred to again in Chapter 5: a fish with abnormally high RNA must be synthesising protein *after a setback*. There is just one warning: fish of increasing age synthesise proteins at progressively lower rates, so environmental studies using RNA:DNA determinations must always be carried out on a single age-group (Haines, 1973).

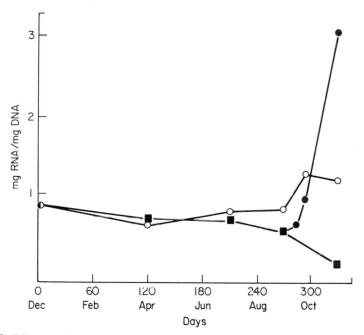

Fig. 86. Ribosomal and polysomal RNA (in relation to DNA) from the liver of *Cyprinus carpio* in relation to starvation and refeeding. ■, Starving; ●, starving-refed; ○, continuously fed controls. After Bouche, Narbonne and Serfaty (1972). Reproduced with permission of Dr G. Bouche.

viii. *Excretion*

The excretion of nitrogen declines rapidly at the beginning of starvation, when the stomach empties, and then either declines very slowly over a long period or may even increase when the fish come to the end of their lipid and carbohydrate reserves and start to mobilise muscle proteins (Volume 1, pp. 256–257).

The initial decrease in excreted nitrogen has been shown also in *Salmo gairdneri* (Fromm, 1963). The subsequent increase has been confirmed by Vella-Clos (1973), who found a fall in the total nitrogen excreted by *Cyprinus carpio* after two months of starvation but a rise from the low value after 5 months. Urea nitrogen was being excreted at the rate of 28 mg per kg per 24 hours at the start of starvation, falling to 12 mg after 2 months, but rising again to 40 after 5 months. A great deal of extra work would be needed to establish the level which would characterise starvation, however. There is a great deal of scatter among the results from individual carp, and the time of year probably super-imposes its own pattern: Créac'h, Vellas *et al.* (1971) found no significant difference between the nitrogen excretion rates of January carp starved either for 8 days or for 6 months.

Vellas and Créac'h (1971) observed an increase in the concentration of urea, uric acid and arginase in the livers of *Cyprinus carpio* starved for 12 months (dry weight basis), and Marinescu (1973) found a continuous increase in the liver arginase activity during the starvation of *Idus idus* between 0 and 21 days. Perhaps therefore the phenomenon is not confined to *Cyprinus carpio*. The concentration of free ammonia has been found to increase in the dark and white muscle, liver, kidney and spleen of the latter species after 6 months without food (Pequin, Parent and Vellas, 1970), but the proportion of ammonia nitrogen in the total excreted nitrogen did not change during the two weeks for which Fromm (1963) starved *Salmo gairdneri*.

Starvation for 14 days has been shown to reduce the total level of non-protein nitrogen in *Micropterus salmoides* (Niimi, 1972b), and when *Lepomis macrochirus* starved from 7 to 28 days, the total nitrogenous excretion was found to be less than in the controls. In this case the controls were fed on glucose only, so their greater excretory rate may have related to greater swimming activity. Much of the advantage of these studies has been lost through sampling only one or two batches of fish for, usually, only a short period of starvation. Detailed surveys might well reveal the point at which lipid catabolism ceases and cell breakdown (protein catabolism) begins.

ix. *Hormones*

Higgs and Eales (1973) reported that starvation for 1 to 2 weeks at 12 to 13°C reduces the concentration of thyroxine circulating in the blood of *Salvelinus fontinalis* and *Ictalurus punctatus* to less than half of its former value. Presumably in this way the swimming activity of the fish is "curtailed" and energy conserved.

The growth ("somatotropic") hormone, as in mammals, appears to play an important role in survival during starvation. Olivereau (1970) found that the cells in the hypophysis which secrete this hormone become very active after *Cyprinus carpio* have starved for 8 months. The cells hypertrophy and lose their cytoplasmic granules, developing a conspicuous endoplasmic reticulum. The nuclei increase in size and there is an increase in RNA, again indicating a higher level of protein synthesis. This activity following starvation has also been seen in *Anguilla anguilla* and, less markedly, in spawning *Salmo salar* and

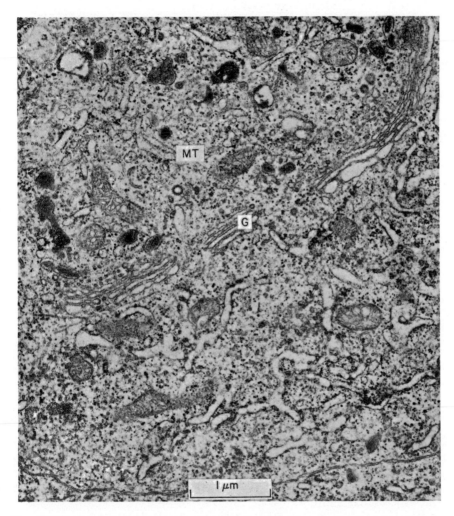

FIG. 87. Somatotropic tissue in the hypophysis of *Cyprinus carpio* after starvation for 12 months. The Golgi apparatus (G) is very active, and secretory granules are being formed at the extremities of the saccules. Large granules are, however, virtually absent from the tissue. MT, microtubule. Fixed in glutaraldehyde-sodium cacodylate buffer, stained with uranyl acetate–lead citrate. After Gas (1975). Photograph kindly supplied by the author.

Oncorhynchus sp. No increase in the growth hormone (or of prolactin) circulating in the plasma of *Oncorhynchus nerka* was reported by McKeown Leatherland and John (1975), but their fish had starved for only 30 days.

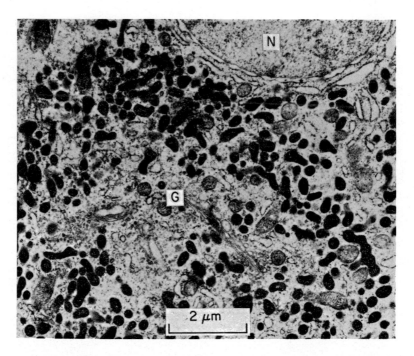

FIG. 88. Somatotropic tissue in the hypophysis of *Cyprinus carpio* starved for 9 months and then refed for 15 days. Secretory granules are being retained, and occupy much of the cytoplasm. The Golgi apparatus (G) is reduced compared with the previous picture. N, nucleus. After Gas (1975). Photograph kindly supplied by the author.

For elegant histological demonstration of the phenomenon we turn again to Serfaty's group. The secretory granules, probably the hormone itself, disappear from the stimulated somatotrophic cells of the hypophysis during starvation, reappearing (that is, not being secreted) when the fish are fed again (Figs. 87 and 88).

We have seen (p. 37) that plasma cortisol increases markedly in migrating salmon, and may promote gluconeogenesis, the conversion of protein reserves into carbohydrate to supply energy for the journey upstream. Wingfield and Grimm (1977) have now shown that plasma cortisol also rises during the season of poor feeding in *Pleuronectes platessa*, even in immature fish, presumably again to assist in the mobilisation of reserves.

x. *Enzymes*

Studies on rats have shown that the concentrations of the enzymes involved in urea synthesis increase during starvation, while those promoting the synthesis of lipids decrease (Volume 1, p. 253).

Zakhar'in (1969) has confirmed that the activities of glucose-6-phosphate dehydrogenase and 6-phosphogluconate dehydrogenase, both indirectly involved in lipid synthesis, decrease in the livers (and other organs: Pokrovskii and Koronikov, 1970) of starving rats, increasing sharply on refeeding. Interestingly, the activities in the brain do not change during starvation. The synthesis of carbohydrate from amino acids is enhanced in rat livers during starvation (Pokrovskii and Pyatnitskaya, 1969), judging by the increase in transaminase activity, and the increasing mobilisation of rat tissues has been marked by the enhanced activity of 5 lysosomal enzymes during a fast of up to 120 hours (Desai, 1969).

Turning now to fish, we find that two of the enzymes of the pentose phosphate pathway, glucose-6-phosphate dehydrogenase and 6-phosphogluconate dehydrogenase, decrease during the starvation of *Salvelinus fontinalis*, marking, as in rats, a reduction in the formation of lipid (Yamauchi, Stegeman and Goldberg, 1975). The level is slowly restored on refeeding without, apparently, showing the "overshoot" in activity seen in mammals, so enzyme assays could not be used to identify refeeding after fasting, in contrast to RNA (Fig. 86).

Shimeno and Hosokawa (1975) found that the enzymes of the pentose phosphate pathway in *Seriola quinqueradiata* also were markedly reduced during starvation for 21 days, and so were the enzymes of glycolysis. As in rats, glucose-6-phosphatase activity was increased during the fast.

Ornithine aminotransferase in various organs of *Squalus acanthias* and *Parophrys vetulus* has been shown to decrease during 4 or 6 weeks of starvation (Wekell and Brown, 1973). These authors also reported a marked reduction in spawning (starving) *Oncorhynchus tschawytscha* as compared with the parr stage. This enzyme catalyses a reversible step in the pathway interconverting arginine, proline and glutamate, and in mammals has been thought to be closely associated with the ornithine –urea cycle. In teleosts it may be a link in glutamate synthesis and ammonia production. One might therefore expect its activity to increase in the later stages of starvation.

It is also known in mammals to be closely associated with proline formation, so again one might expect it to increase in activity during advanced depletion in the light of what seems to be collagen synthesis in starving *Gadus morhua* (Fig. 78, p. 203).

Créac'h (1972) carried out extensive studies on the enzymes which break down the tissues of *Cyprinus carpio*. It has already been noted in several reports by Siebert's group (listed in Volume 1, p. 525) that fish muscle is unusually rich in proteolytic eyzynes, probably in readiness for the repeated spells of starvation which are natural to fish, but Créac'h found that such enzyme activity is not much changed when starvation actually occurs. Proteolytic activity in liver, kidney, spleen and red and white muscle was found not to be modified to any great extent by prolonged starvation, and the activity of cathepsin B was in fact reduced. The physiological role of this enzyme is not well established (same author) and it is difficult to understand the significance of the reduced activity. Dipeptidases varied in activity from organ to organ. Summing up, Créac'h (1972) concluded that during starvation the stock of proteases and peptidases present in the tissues, apart from cathepsin B, remains high, but shows no evidence of extra synthesis.

xi. *Endolymph*

The calcareous bodies lying within the ear cavities of fish ("otoliths") grow continuously by accretion, but the nature of the material laid down varies, appearing darker in summer than in winter, so that a cross-section from the otolith of a fish several years old resembles the section through a tree trunk, with concentric rings corresponding with the years of age (Volume 1, pp. 159–161). The fluid surrounding the otolith is known as endolymph, and it, too, changes seasonally in its composition, containing more of a certain albumin in summer than in winter (Volume 1, reference 881).

Figure 89 shows how *Gadus morhua* from the wild with muscle water contents below 81%, that is, well-nourished fish, can have endolymph protein contents anywhere within a wide range (low values were largely from fish caught in March and April). Cod artificially starved in an aquarium with muscle water contents over 84% have consistently low values, so it might be thought that the protein value in nourished fish would fluctuate rapidly according to the time lapsed since the last meal. Further experiments (Fig. 90) have so far failed to support this idea. When fish are starved and then refed, the protein content of the otolith fluid more or less follows the muscle water content, and does not jump immediately after refeeding. Besides showing more random fluctuations, therefore, these determinations seem to be less useful than determinations of water content as a measure of nutritional condition.

Otolith fluid is not simply an ultrafiltrate of the blood, and radio-calcium injected into the peritoneum is always more concentrated in serum than in otolith fluid (Mugiya, 1974: *Salmo gairdneri*). On the other hand, the calcium isotope reaches its maximum concentration in both fluids at about the same time (about 3 hours) after injection. Mugiya considers the composition of this fluid to be controlled by the secretory action of cells at certain sites on the membranous labyrinth.

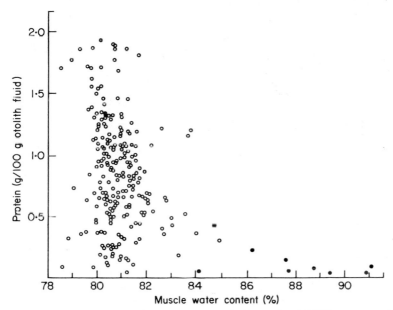

FIG. 89. Protein content of the endolymph of *Gadus morhua* of different nutritional states as indicated by the water content of the white muscle. ○, Cod from the wild; ●, after various periods of artificial starvation in an aquarium. Muscle with more than 81% of water indicates some depletion, so the fall in endolymph protein is tardy. After Robertson and Love (unpublished).

Fish flesh containing radioactive calcium was fed to *Cyprinus carpio* (reference 587, Volume 1), and it was shown that the calcium is increasingly deposited on the otolith for the first 6 days after a 4-day feed and then stops increasing. In other words, calcium from the food is deposited on the otolith within 10 days from the beginning of feeding. However, it is clear from the somewhat sketchy experiment illustrated in Fig. 90 that the protein content of the endolymph probably does not build up until the levels in previously starving fish as a whole have been restored. Other tissues seem to have priority.

Watanabe and Miyamoto (1973) quote other authors as showing that protein levels in endolymph are markedly lower than those in serum and conclude, like Mugiya (1974), that endolymph is not just a trans-udate of serum but is autonomously secreted. I suspect that the relation-ship between serum protein and endolymph is rather subtle, depending on, among other things, the overall protein balance of the fish and the feeding level. Other profound differences between serum and endolymph have been shown by Watanabe and Miyamoto (1973) as follows:

	Sodium (mEq/l)	Potassium (mEq/l)
Endolymph	83	112
Serum	124	2

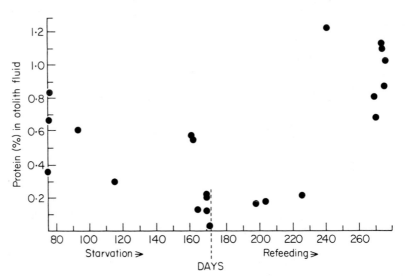

FIG. 90. Protein content of the endolymph of *Gadus morhua* during starvation and refeeding. After Robertson and Love (unpublished).

Clearly the secretion of endolymph is highly selective. Similar results have been reported previously (Volume 1, reference 321), when it was also noted that plasma did *not* differ appreciably from cranial fluid as regards ionic composition.

xii. *Bile*

We have seen (p. 164) how bile acids, bile pigments, cholesterol and calcium are markedly concentrated by the gall bladder, since water and some ions are filtered out of the bile while these substances are not, or diffuse to a lesser extent. The phenomenon is clearly relevant to the study of starvation, since bile is often a pale, amber fluid in fed fish, and dark blue during starvation (Volume 1, references 253 and 756).

The transport of ions across the bladder membrane is independent of the salinity of the environment, several teleost species giving similar results when taken from fresh or from salt water (Hirano and Bern, 1972).

Sodium, bicarbonate and chloride, but not potassium or bile salts, have all been found to diffuse out of the bile during its stay in the gall bladder of guinea pigs (Shaw and Heath, 1974).

Hepatic bile, before entering the gall bladder, has been described by Hunn (1972b: freshwater species) as a protein-free filtrate of plasma with bile salts, pigments and lipids added by the liver cells. He found that sodium, potassium and bicarbonate diffuse out of the gall bladder. Boyer (1971: *Squalus acanthias*) found big reductions in bicarbonate and chloride concentrations after hepatic bile had entered the gall bladders but increases in sodium, potassium and calcium. Calcium showed the biggest increase of the inorganic substances, from 18 to 59 mg%, but this was overshadowed by the enormous increase in bile acid concentration from 21 to 353 mg%.

Starvation of *Salmo gairdneri* was shown by Denton, Yousef *et al.* (1974) to result in an increase in cholic acid and a decrease in chenodesoxycholic acid, so the retention is a selective process. Bile salts are complex mixtures of substances which differ according to fish species (Volume 1, p. 140). The main bile acid of gall bladder bile of *Gadus morhua* is cholic acid (Kallner, 1968); about 20% of the bile acids are dihydroxy-cholanoic acids, of which the main constituent is deoxycholic acid. Chenodeoxycholic acid and ursodeoxycholic acids occur in almost equal amounts as minor constituents.

Apart from the paper by Denton, Yousef *et al.* (1974), all this work relates to differences brought about in bile as it enters the gall bladder. The potential of the various changes for yielding information on the starvation of fish in the wild was noted by Love (1975), who found that the pale straw colour of the bile of actively feeding fish would begin to turn green in as few as 9 hours after the commencement of starvation, that of others taking up to about 30 hours depending, presumably, on the fullness of the stomach at capture and the speed of digestion. This means that a fish with blue bile has not fed for at least 9 hours, and observations on bile colour are not vitiated by the fish vomiting at capture and voiding their stomach contents. A *flaccid* blue gall bladder probably means the beginning of feeding after starvation; the time taken to empty all of the blue bile depends on the temperature.

Up to now we have been taking the water content of the muscle as a measure of depletion. However, it takes some 9 weeks of starvation before the muscle water of a replete fish begins to rise (Fig. 68, p. 186), so that a whole span of the depletion process can go un-noticed. Also, fish can apparently feed continuously throughout the year and still show a rise in the muscle water at around the spawning time. *Gadus morhua* off the coast of Scotland have been observed to eat fairly consistently (Volume 1, p. 98), and those in the Norwegian fjords seem to have food in their stomachs at all times (Ola Vahl, personal communication, 1977). The rise in their muscle water contents must therefore reflect a rate of food *absorption* inadequate for the demands of

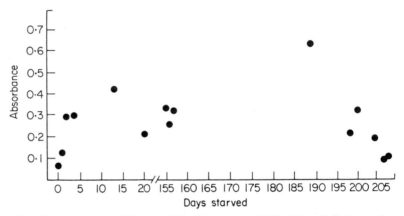

FIG. 91. Absorbance at 400 nm of bile from the gall bladder of *Gadus morhua* after increasing periods of starvation. After Love, Kim and Gomez (unpublished).

reproduction, rather than actual starvation as carried out in the laboratory, that is, a complete abstention from food. It is not unreasonable to suppose that a blue bile colour on the other hand indicates actual starvation, even if it does not show for how long it has been going on.

Figure 91 shows that the intensity of bile colouration rises rapidly to a maximum in about 2 days when starvation is initiated, and after this period it remains high until the fish have starved completely for a very long time, presumably reflecting an eventual reduced destruction of red blood cells, coupled with leakage of bile into the intestine.

Inorganic substances behave similarly, showing a big change at the outset and little change thereafter, although calcium eventually falls again. Calcium and sodium rise during the starvation of this species, while potassium falls (Fig. 92). Magnesium seems to exhibit no clear trend.

We shall record the behaviour of these substances in bile again in Chapter 5 when we consider seasonal variations. Their behaviour is completely consistent with the picture drawn here, seasonal rises in pigmentation or calcium concentration coinciding with falls in potassium.

4. REFEEDING

Commercial diets are satisfactory for refeeding fish starved for relatively short periods, and the restoration to normal levels of various substances, such as liver glycogen, which rises, and soluble protein concentration and transaminase (for gluconeogenesis) activity in the liver, which fall

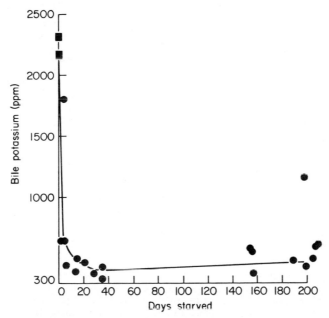

FIG. 92. The potassium concentration of bile from the gall bladder of *Gadus morhua* after increasing periods of starvation. After Love, Kim and Gomez (unpublished).

(Jürss and Nicolai, 1976: *Salmo gairdneri*) follows as a matter of course. However, severely starved fish pose extra problems because of their slim hold on life, and refeeding with a complete diet was shown by Créac'h (1972: *Cyprinus carpio*) to kill the whole batch. A preliminary injection with glucose, amino acids and vitamins into the body cavity reduced mortality to 20%, but the shock of injection was clearly causing some deaths. A satisfactory diet was finally devised which virtually eliminated mortality when fed for three weeks prior to administering a normal synthetic diet (Bouche, Murat and Parent, 1971). It consists of a mixture of casein and vitamins set in gelatin, and experience in the writer's laboratory has shown that severely starved *Gadus morhua* also recover well with its aid. A high-protein diet following this causes the carbohydrates in the blood to fall, suggesting that they are necessary for metabolising the protein (Murat, Parent and Serfaty, 1972: *Cyprinus carpio*). Such a diet gives rise to only feeble activity in the pentose phosphate pathway, suggesting immediate use of the amino acids for tissue repair and energy purposes rather than the formation of lipids (Créac'h and Murat, 1974: *Cyprinus carpio*).

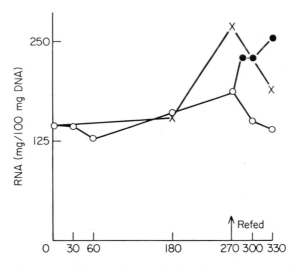

FIG. 93. The effect of refeeding on muscle RNA (*Cyprinus carpio*). The rise in both groups of fish at 270 days is the seasonal surge in growth, illustrated already in Fig. 54. ○, Starving; ●, refed; ×, continuously fed controls. After Bouche, Vellas and Serfaty (1973). Reproduced with permission of Dr G. Bouche.

Murat (1976a: *Cyprinus carpio*) found that the special diet following severe starvation caused no increase in blood glucose or tissue glycogen and just 5% mortality after 15 days. In contrast, when the carp were given the complete commercial diet from the outset, the blood glucose rose to normal in 8 days, liver glycogen doubled, reaching half the normal value, and the mortality was 87%.

An important aspect of refeeding in relation to the study of fish from the wild (Chapter 5) is the occurrence of "overshoot" phenomena, the temporary rise in levels above those of continuously fed controls. We have already seen in Fig. 86 (p. 217) how the ribose nucleic acid (RNA) levels in carp liver rise far above the control levels on refeeding starving carp. Figure 93 shows a similar effect in muscle. The issue here was complicated by seasonal variation which accounts for the peak in both groups at 270 days, but after this the refed group reached higher values than in the fish fed continuously.

Créac'h (1972) noted that the level of glucose in the blood of starving *Cyprinus carpio* rose to over 100 mg% on refeeding, and that after 2 months it had dropped to normal levels of about 50 mg%. The physiological condition as judged from behaviour appeared to be restored to normal after refeeding for 2 months, and the fish could be distinguished from fed controls only by their lower haemoglobin concentrations and by their more voluminous livers which were very rich in glycogen and potassium.

Ince and Thorpe (1976) force-fed *Esox lucius* which had been starved for 3 months, and found the liver lipid and muscle glycogen levels to be higher than in freshly captured fish. This important finding undoubtedly holds the key to the sudden drop in the pH of the muscle after death seen by us at the beginning of summer feeding in *Gadus morhua* (Love, 1975), and ties in with the very low pH values which we have seen on refeeding starving cod, the (presumed) high carbohydrate values giving rise to more lactic acid than usual after death. This will be discussed in more detail in Chapter 5.

In Ince and Thorpe's experiments, the glycogen levels of refed *Esox lucius* rose only a little, and the plasma free fatty acid and protein concentrations changed hardly at all. Blood glucose, plasma cholesterol and haematocrit values returned to the levels found in freshly-captured fish, and those of amino acid nitrogen showed some overshoot. In work of this kind, the length of the preliminary period of starvation, and the time after the beginning of refeeding at which the animals are killed for analysis are critical, and a variety of results can be obtained. Sampling at several points over an extended period clearly would give more information than is possible from a single batch.

4   Reactions and Adaptations to the Environment

A.   General reactions to stress

1.   INTRODUCTION

Stress takes people in odd ways. As Shakespeare puts it:

> And others, when the bagpipe sings i' the nose
> Cannot contain their urine. . .
> *Merchant of Venice*, IV, 1

Indeed, the stress of capture may well account for the high proportion of empty urinary bladders seen in fish taken off the deck.

Swimming may or may not be stressful according to the conditions under which it takes place, but some authors seem to assume that it always is so when the fish are in an experimental apparatus.

The most characteristic general response to stress, from whatever source, is a pronounced rise in blood sugar (Volume 1, pp. 45–46), which seems to occur whenever the physical activity exceeds what is normal for the fish. A number of blood constituents increase in concentration during suffocation, probably as a result of loss of plasma by the blood into other tissues and perhaps the release of blood cells by the spleen, leading to an increased capacity for taking up oxygen. Stress can cause the death of the fish, sometimes hours later, by, it is thought, a lethal flooding of the tissues with lactic acid. This effect has been noted especially in salmonids. A more recent view is that in these cases the lactate is released by the muscle *because* the fish are dying (C. S. Wardle, personal communication).

Capture stress often causes fish to stop eating for several days, so that it is not possible to compare fish in the early stages of starvation with fed fish if both groups were caught together (for example, Volume 1, Figure 92).

2. BLOOD GLUCOSE

The rise in blood glucose resulting from stress has now been very thoroughly documented. The results recorded in a number of publications are summarised in Table 15, which shows not only the large number of species investigated but also the wide range of conditions which cause the stress response. The plasma glucose has even been shown to rise when *Oncorhynchus kisutch* come into contact with the effluents of pulp mills (McLeay, 1977; not included in the Table). Figure 94

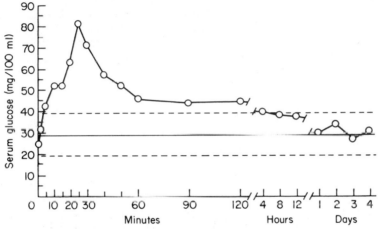

FIG. 94. The response of the serum glucose level of *Carassius auratus* to stress (a saline injection at zero time). The horizontal line represents the mean resting level ± standard deviation. After Chavin (1973). Reproduced with permission of the author.

illustrates the typical response to a stress, induced in this case by a saline injection. The base line was established by analysing the blood of 300 fish under standard conditions, and Chavin (1973), from whose work the illustration is taken, suggests the determination of serum glucose as a means of assessing environmental changes, since it is rapid, practicable and quantitative.

Once the raised glucose has declined again to resting levels, it cannot easily be raised a second time by stresses such as simulated catching procedures in the tank (Wardle, 1972a: *Pleuronectes platessa;* Fletcher, 1975: *Pseudopleuronectes americanus*). For some reason, the blood glucose of tank-adapted freshwater fish seems to respond to stress stimuli much more readily than that of captive marine fish (several authors, reviewed by Wardle, 1972a), though both respond in the same way when taken for the first time from the wild.

TABLE 15

Reports of a rise in blood glucose as a response to various stresses

Stress	Species	Reference
Aquarium transfer	*Carassius auratus*	Chavin (1964); Chavin and Young (1970)
Asphyxiation		Chavin and Young (1970)
	Cyprinus carpio	F. Mazeaud (1969; 1973)
	Heteropneustes fossilis	Tandon and Joshi (1973)
Capture	*Heteropneustes fossilis*	Tandon and Joshi (1973)
	Melanogrammus aeglefinus	Wardle (1972a)
	Pleuronectes americanus	Fletcher (1975)
	Pleuronectes platessa	Wardle (1972a)
Handling	*Carassius auratus*	Umminger and Gist (1973)
	Oncorhynchus kisutch	Wedemeyer (1972)
	Salmo gairdneri	
	Salvelinus fontinalis	Houston, Madden *et al.* (1971a)
Injection		
Sham	*Carassius auratus*	Umminger and Gist (1971; 1973)
With adrenaline	*Cyprinus carpio*	Mazeaud (1973)
	Lampetra fluviatilis	Leibson and Plisetskaya (1969)
	Squalus acanthias	Patent (1970)
With noradrenaline	*Cyprinus carpio*	Mazeaud (1965)
		Murat (1976a)
With prolactin	*Carassius auratus*	Umminger (1973a)
With saline	*Carassius auratus*	Chavin (1964; 1973)
		Umminger (1973a)
Thermal Shock		
Slowly 15→32°C	*Cyprinus carpio*	Grigo (1975)
Abruptly 30→10°C	*Ictalurus punctatus*	Block (1974)
Abruptly 10→20°C	*Oncorhynchus kisutch*	Wedemeyer (1973)
	Salmo gairdneri	
Transport	*Heteropneustes fossilis*	Tandon and Joshi (1973)
	Lampetra fluviatilis	Leibson and Plisetskaya (1969)
Miscellaneous		
Anaesthesia	*Salvelinus fontinalis*	Houston, Madden *et al.* (1971b)
Recovery from anaesthesia in new surroundings	*Idus idus* (muscle glucose)	Gronow (1974b)
Sham operation	*Anguilla japonica*	Inui (1969)
Forced swimming	*Trachurus mediterraneus ponticus*	Morozova and Trusevich (1971)
Held by tail	*Salmo gairdneri*	Terrier and Perrier (1975)
Putting in small cage and shaking cage	*Seriola quinqueradiata*	Ikeda, Ozaki and Uemitsu (1975)

Regardless of what is injected, the act of the injection itself is clearly stressful. This was underlined by Leibson and Plisetskaya (1969), who showed that insulin injected into *Lampetra fluviatilis* reduced the blood glucose as in mammals, but not before there had been a rise caused by the stress of the injection itself.

The blood glucose rises through the mobilisation of tissue glycogens, particularly that of the liver. Umminger and Gist (1971) showed that sham injections into *Carassius auratus* resulted in an increased serum glucose and a decline in the glycogens of liver and muscle at 20°C. The decline did not appear at other temperatures. As we shall see in a moment, adrenaline is closely concerned with the stress effect in blood glucose, and Hayashi and Ooshiro (1975b) showed that its injection into *Anguilla japonica* stimulates glycogenolysis in the liver. Thorpe and Ince (1974), who observed the same effect in *Esox lucius*, pointed out that the response would provide for increased glucose supplies needed during predatory activity. This concept of extra energy being available to the stressed fish is probably the correct view of the phenomenon. It would assist the fish to escape from a stressful situation where it was able to do so.

The most convincing demonstration of the role of the liver in raising blood glucose in response to stress comes from the work of Inui (1969: *Anguilla japonica*). He showed that sham operation (opening the body of the fish without removing anything) caused the usual rise in blood glucose, but that if the liver were removed as well, the rise did not take place (Fig. 95).

3. ADRENOCORTICAL RESPONSE

a. *Catecholamines*

The rises in blood glucose which follow the administration of adrenaline or noradrenaline (reported in Table 15) are more than just the physical effects of the injection. The glucose level was noted by F. Mazeaud (1965: *Cyprinus carpio*) to be proportional to the amount of noradrenaline injected, and adrenaline added to liver slices of *Anguilla japonica* was shown by Hayashi and Ooshiro (1975b) to increase the output of glucose.

The effects of injecting either adrenaline or noradrenaline into the body cavity of *Cyprinus carpio* are illustrated in Fig. 96 (Murat, 1976a), the control fish having been sham-injected. A similar illustration is to be found in the paper by Thorpe and Ince (1974: *Esox lucius*), the glucose maximum appearing some 30 minutes after injection, but unlike the results shown in Fig. 96 these authors found that six and more hours after injection the blood glucose levels of the adrenaline-injected fish

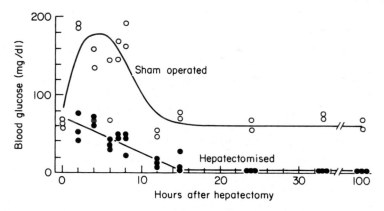

FIG. 95. Changes in the blood glucose of hepatectomised and sham operated *Anguilla japonica*, showing how the liver must be present if the glucose is to rise in response to the stress of surgery. After Inui (1969). Reproduced with permission of the author.

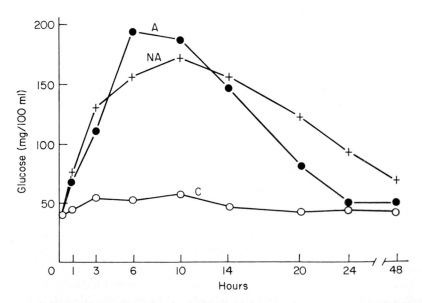

FIG. 96. Effects of injecting 100 µg per 100 g body weight of (A) adrenaline and (NA) noradrenaline on the blood glucose level of *Cyprinus carpio*, compared with sham-injected controls (C). After Murat (1976a). Reproduced with permission of the author.

had become significantly *lower* than those of the controls. This eventual hypoglycaemia occurred after the injection of adrenaline at several different concentrations.

Patent (1970) observed that injected adrenaline raises the blood glucose of *Squalus acanthias* but not of *Hydrolagus colliei*, attributing the fact to the greater natural activity of the latter species.

Adrenaline added to liver tissue in the laboratory has been shown by Umminger and Benziger (1975: *Ictalurus nebulosus*) to stimulate glycogen phosphorylase activity, that is, to promote the liberation of energy through the breakdown of stored glycogen. On the other hand, Umminger, Benziger and Levy (1975: *Fundulus heteroclitus*) found that stressing the intact fish does not produce any measurable change in the activity of this enzyme.

Stresses resulting in increased catecholamine levels in the blood include, among others that one can imagine, "muscular agitation", asphyxia, haemorrhage and wounding (Mazeaud, 1964: *Cyprinus carpio*; M. Mazeaud, 1969a: *Petromyzon marinus*). A Nembutal injection (anaesthetic) renders *Scyliorhinus canicula* immobile in about 15 minutes, at which time the adrenaline and noradrenaline concentrations of the blood have become much lower than those in the controls (M. Mazeaud, 1969c). The levels still rise, however, during asphyxia while under the anaesthetic.

Incidentally, it is the adrenaline which is responsible for the "blanching" of skin colour shown by certain species (for example *Pterophyllum scalare*: Adler, 1975) when they are frightened, causing the dark particles of melanin in the pigment cells to contract. It also raises the level of cyclic 3'5'-adenosine monophosphate in the blood, a compound which could be a "second messenger" in the hyperglycaemic response to stress (Terrier and Perrier, 1975).

b.   *Adrenocortical hormones*

While the response of blood glucose to adrenaline is rapid, the hormones of the pituitary–adrenocortical axis cause a rise in glucose which develops more slowly and is of longer duration (deRoos and deRoos, 1972: elasmobranchs). The hormones themselves take an appreciable time to increase. Stressed *Carassius auratus* do not show a rise in serum cortisol until 10 to 22 minutes after capture (Spieler, 1974). Singley and Chavin (1975a) showed that when *Carassius auratus* are acclimated to their environment, no method of capture will affect the serum cortisol levels provided that the time from capture to death is less than 3 minutes. Similarly, neither immobilisation in ice, anaesthesia in MS

222 (tricaine methane sulphonate) nor electrical immobilisation affect the level.

Histochemical changes have been found in the adrenocortical cells of this species a few minutes after the fish had received an injection of saline (Chavin, 1964).

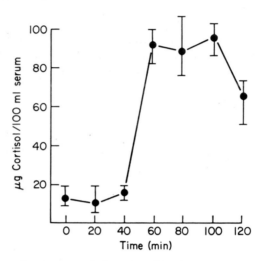

FIG. 97. An increase in serum cortisol produced in *Oncorhynchus kisutch* by stress. The aquarium water was stirred with a hand net for 30 seconds every 5 minutes. After Wedemeyer (1969). Reproduced with permission of the author.

Plasma cortisol levels have also been noted to rise as a response to stress by Donaldson and McBride (1967: *Salmo gairdneri*, draining most of the water from the aquarium), Wedemeyer (1969: *Oncorhynchus kisutch, Salmo gairdneri*, temperature shock, agitation or reducing the water level), Fagerlund and Donaldson (1970: *Oncorhynchus nerka*, sampling stress), Porthé-Nibelle and Lahlou (1974: *Carassius auratus*, stirring), Fryer (1975: *Carrassius auratus*, sampling) and Singley and Chavin (1975b: *Carassius auratus*, dilute salt immersion).

Figure 97 shows the typical rise in serum cortisol induced by stress, with a delay period of over 40 minutes. However, in Singley and Chavin's work (1975b: *Carassius auratus*), a very rapid response was obtained, cortisol and adrenocorticotropic hormone (ACTH) rising within 15 seconds of salt immersion. The authors attributed the speed of this response to the release of stored pre-existing cortisol, and pointed out that the storage of corticoids in the adrenal cortex is well documented. They suggested adopting the estimation of ACTH and corticoid hormones as criteria of stress in teleosts. Fagerlund and Donaldson

(1970: *Oncorhynchus nerka*) showed that the secretion rates of cortisol and cortisone are similar in rested fish, but that during stress the cortisol is secreted at many times the rate of the cortisone.

Finally, Wedemeyer (1969: *Oncorhynchus kisutch, Salmo gairdneri*) showed that the ascorbic acid (vitamin C) content of the adrenals decreases during stress, and recalled that stress decreases an animal's resistence to infection.

4. LACTATE

We have seen (p. 114) how the lactate produced by fish is largely retained by the muscles (Wardle, 1972b: *Pleuronectes platessa*) and perhaps metabolised there rather than transported to the liver by the blood. Stress usually involves varying amounts of muscular threshing about, so it is obvious that lactate will be found in the muscle and usually also in the blood. There is nothing new in this: the present paragraph is just a reminder. *Heteropneustes fossilis* recovering after netting and transport showed a blood glucose maximum 2 hours after the end of the stress and a lactate peak after 4 hours (Tandon and Joshi, 1973). Rises in blood lactate or muscle lactate accompaning anoxic stress have been mentioned by Gronow (1974b: *Idus idus*) and Hemmingsen and Douglas (1970: *Chaenocephalus aceratus*), temperature stress by Braune and Gronow (1975: *Idus idus*) and following adrenaline or noradrenaline injection (Murat, 1976a: *Cyprinus caprio*). In the case of prolonged swimming stress (several hours), Morozova and Trusevich (1971: *Trachurus mediterraneus ponticus*) noted that the levels of both the glucose and lactate gradually decreased again, though values were always above the resting level. In this species the lactate always rises more in the blood than in the muscles, even at the beginning of the stress period, in contrast to *Pleuronectes platessa* as reported by Wardle (1972b).

5. LIPIDS

Mazeaud (1973) showed that stresses which raise the level of blood glucose in *Cyprinus carpio*—feeding, injecting with glucose or adrenaline, asphyxia—automatically reduce the free fatty acids (FFA) in the blood, and concluded that the glucose was inhibiting lipolysis. However, in *Salmo gairdneri*, he found that the blood glucose and FFA rose together as a stress response. Mazeaud concluded that "apparently there exists in teleosts a certain heterogeneity in the mechanisms governing lipolysis during the syndrome of adaptation to stress." The synchrony of changes in glucose and FFA in the blood under asphyxial stress in *Cyprinus carpio* is illustrated in Fig. 98 (F. Mazeaud, 1969).

Chavin (1973) showed that sham injection, or the injection of saline or casein, all resulted in decreases in the serum FFA of *Carassius auratus*. The reduction was first measurable $2\frac{1}{2}$ minutes after injection, and

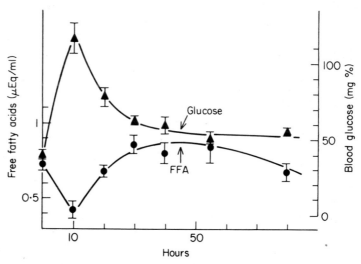

Fɪɢ. 98. Changes in the glucose and free fatty acids of the blood of *Cyprinus carpio* after asphyxia for 2 hours. After F. Mazeaud (1969). Reproduced with permission of the author.

became statistically significant after 15 minutes. Twelve hours after injection it began to rise again. Thyroxine reduces the level of blood glucose in *Cyprinus carpio* (Murat and Serfaty, 1970), an effect opposite to that seen in mammals. At the same time, the FFA level of the plasma rises, again showing the reverse effect.

A different phenomenon appears to be involved in *Oncorhynchus gorbuscha* which were stressed by tagging and being confined. In this case there was extensive mobilisation of specific fatty acids in the muscle followed by their transfer to the liver. Liver lipid increased from 5·9% in the controls to 10·4% in the tagged specimens, accompanied by a diminution in total muscle weight and an increase in liver weight (Saddler and Cardwell, 1971). Salmon are accustomed to mobilising much of their lipid during migration, and its transfer to the liver preparatory to use seems logical. It is however not clear why they should transfer lipid in response to stress, but Saddler and Cardwell pointed out that the fish were also starving under the conditions of the experiment, so this might account for the effect. The starvation, rather

than the capture, handling, anaesthesia and confinement again probably explains the substantial loss of polyunsaturated fatty acids undergone by *Oncorhynchus keta* artificially introduced into sea water by
Saddler, Koski and Cardwell (1972).

6. HAEMATOLOGICAL RESPONSES

Asphyxia differs from other forms of stress in the context of blood
cell counts. The fish tries to compensate for the lack of oxygen by
increasing the concentration of red blood cells. Khan and Siddiqui
(1970) found that the packed cell volume increased from 31% to 65%
of the whole blood when *Ophicephalus punctatus* were kept in sealed jars
of water until they died. The thrombocytes also increased in like manner,
so the blood clotted more quickly during the progress of asphyxiation.
This "haemoconcentration" also appears as a response to anaesthetic
by tricaine methane sulphonate, an effect noted by Houston, Madden
et al. (1971a: *Salvelinus fontinalis*).

However, other forms of stress have the opposite effect. Capture
stress in *Labeo umbratus* results in a *decrease* in the concentration of
haemoglobin, in the red and white cell counts and in the osmolarity and
specific gravity of the blood (Hattingh and van Pletzen, 1974). Suturing
a catheter into a blood vessel was found to have a similar effect in
Salvelinus fontinalis (Houston, DeWilde and Madden, 1969). Capture of
Seriola quinqueradiata by angling was found by Ikeda, Ozaki and Uemitsu
(1975) to reduce the level of blood constituents and to result in enlarged
spleens, where presumably the various blood cells are temporarily
stored. Using the fall in white blood cell numbers as an indication of
stress, Slicher, Pickford and Pang (1966) found that *Fundulus heteroclitus*
could become habituated to being handled each day. They then gave
a much smaller response to the stress of capture and being held in small
jars. Cold shock was found by Agrawal and Srivastava (1976) to cause
an increase in the numbers of circulating leucocytes and thrombocytes,
but not of erythrocytes, in *Colisa fasciata*.

Stress imposed by leading *Sebastiscus marmoratus* on a hook was found
by Yamashita (1968b) not to change the electrophoretic pattern of the
blood proteins, although the concentration of total serum proteins
increased.

7. INORGANIC SUBSTANCES AND OSMOREGULATION

We have seen in Volume 1 (pp. 138 and 143) that because of the difference in osmotic concentrations between the body fluids of fish and

the water in which they swim, freshwater fish tend to become water-logged and marine fish to be sucked dry. Mechanisms which compensate for this are known as osmoregulatory mechanisms, which have a separate section in this chapter (p. 283). The point here is that these mechanisms consume energy, and a stressed fish may use so much energy in other ways that the osmoregulation is made temporarily ineffective. Thus, Stevens (1972) noted that handling or exercise causes an increase in the body weight of *Tilapia mossambica* living in fresh water and a decrease in those living in salt water, the water movements presumably diluting or concentrating the blood, respectively. It is therefore important to note whether freshwater or saltwater species were being described when one reads reports of changes in the blood ions in response to stress. Stanley and Colby (1971) showed that the survival of *Alosa pseudoharengus* stressed by capture and handling is assisted by adding a little salt to the (fresh) water, thus bringing the surroundings nearer to the concentrations found within the fish. Kirk (1973) found that this technique does not speed the recovery of *Ictalurus punctatus* from the effects of anoxia.

Although Norton (1975) found that handling does not affect the plasma sodium concentration of *Ictalurus punctatus*, other publications tell of apparent failure to osmoregulate during stress, which incidentally accounts at least in part for the changes in the blood cell counts reported in the previous section. Thus Wedemeyer (1972) found a fall in plasma chloride and calcium in *Oncorhynchus kisutch* and *Salmo gairdneri* handled in fresh water, the effect being partially or even completely alleviated by adding sodium chloride to the water. Concentrations of both sodium and chloride in the serum decline in *Carassius auratus* stressed by saline injection (Umminger, 1973a), and the same effect occurs when fish of the same species are sham injected (Umminger and Gist, 1973). As a corollary, the serum osmolarity of *Pseudopleuronectes americanus*, a salt-water fish, *increase* during the first 5 to 6 hours after capture (Umminger, 1970d).

A simple mechanism therefore seems to underlie the effects of stress on the concentrations of blood ions. However, it is not impossible for other factors to operate at the same time. Pickering (1973: *Lampetra fluviatilis*), for example, pointed out that stress increases the ventilation rate, and that this must promote ion exchange across the gills. Several stresses acting on *Cyprinus carpio* were found by Szakolczai (1969) always to elicit the detachment of the mucous epithelium from the intestine, with consequent leakage of serum into the lumen. This would also presumably alter the concentrations of substances in the blood remaining in the circulatory system. Singley and Chavin (1975b) suggested that alterations in such blood constituents as sodium, potassium and chloride could be mediated by the increased flow of adrenocortical hormones.

It may be unwise, therefore, to take too uncomplicated a view of changes in blood constituents as a response to stress.

8.   MISCELLANEOUS OBSERVATIONS ON STRESS

a.   *Temperature shock*

Wedemeyer (1973) transferred *Salmo gairdneri* and *Oncorhynchus kisutch* suddenly from water at 10 to a 20°C environment (non-lethal). Blood glucose and haemoglobin values rose, while cholesterol levels fell. Results were somewhat irregular at the beginning of this experiment. No change in the osmolarity of the serum of *Cyprinus carpio* was seen by Grigo (1975) on gradual non-lethal transfer to higher temperatures, but in a sudden lethal transfer from 15 to 32°C the osmotic values increased just before death. Fatal stress seems to cause a different response, therefore: most other stresses we have described so far *dilute* the blood of freshwater fish.

Ictalurus punctatus acclimated to 30°C were cold shocked by being exposed suddenly to an environment at 10°C. Here the effects were more in line with what we have seen already, with a drop in plasma osmolarity, chloride and haematocrit[1] and the usual rise in glucose (Block, 1974). Reaves, Houston and Madden (1968) investigated the effects of both cold shock and heat shock on *Salmo gairdneri*, and found decreased sodium and chloride levels in the plasma in each case, also an increase in the volume of the extracellular fluid. The response seemed at least in part to be independent of both the direction and magnitude of the change.

b.   *Bradycardia*

Roberts (1973) reviewed the work of several authors which showed that almost any disturbance or rapid environmental change will slow or inhibit the heartbeat, a phenomenon known as bradycardia. Its advantage to the fish is not certain, although in the case of oxygen deprivation a reduced cardiac activity would reduce the need for

---

[1]Small changes the reverse of these were seen during the first 10 minutes. These bigger trends covered 48 hours after the stress.

oxygen: the heart rate of *Cyprinus carpio* slows down under anoxic conditions (Pequin and Serfaty, 1962). The effect is illustrated in Fig. 99, which shows a missed heartbeat caused by the appearance of the experimenter's hand over the tank.

If some small change in the environment is repeatedly linked to, say, a mild electric shock which causes bradycardia, the fish soon associates the change with the shock, and will show bradycardia even where the shock is omitted (Otis, Cerf and Thomas, 1957: *Carassius auratus*). When the fish has been thus conditioned, the way is open to the experimenter

FIG. 99. Electrocardiogram of *Gadus morhua* showing increased TP period due to the appearance of the experimenter's hand (arrow) over the tank. T, recovery wave; P, initial wave (auricle); QRS, ventricular contraction. After Wardle and Kanwisher (1974). Reproduced with permission of Dr C. S. Wardle.

to measure the minimum change or the quality of stimulus that the fish can detect. Chapman and Hawkins (1973: *Gadus morhua*) have revealed the range of sounds that fish can hear, using this technique, and Blaxter and Tytler (1972: several gadoids) have measured the minimum pressure change that fish can detect. In some experiments the latter authors found that the bradycardia occurred *in anticipation* of the intended stimulus. Presumably the fish recognised other indications unwittingly given by the experimenter.

c.   *Effect of stress on the slime*

Smith and Ramos (1976) noted that dying fish often show red blotches on their surface originating in free haemoglobin, and reasoned that smaller stresses might release smaller but still measurable quantities. Such proved to be the case. Unstressed *Mugil cephalus*, *Chanos chanos*, *Caranx ignobilis*, *Albula vulpes* and *Chaetodon miliaris* were found to have no detectable haemoglobin in their slime, but within 2 to 4 minutes of holding the fish in air it gave a positive reaction to a haemoglobin test strip. The simple application of the strip was suggested as a means of detecting incipient stress or the presence of factors which in time would debilitate a culture stock.

B. General geographical influences

1. INTRODUCTION

In Volume 1, p. 169, the point was made that the phrase "seasonal variation" can often be used blindly to label phenomena which we do not understand, mostly changes in certain constituents which follow a rhythmic pattern from year to year.

The same criticism applies to the phrase "ground-to-ground variation"—often we just do not know the characteristic of a fishing ground which influences a particular characteristic of the fish. Nevertheless there is a considerable literature on the subject, and I shall try to point out possible mechanisms whenever these suggest themselves. The main environmental factors will be considered one by one in isolation later on in the chapter.

Meristic characters (Volume 1, p. 152) such as numbers of vertebrae or fin rays seem to correlate with the temperature of the ground, or rather the temperature at the time that the fish had reached a certain developmental stage. However, the influence of temperature varies according to the locality from which the larvae are taken (Volume 1, p. 157), indicating the presence of a genetic factor as well. Variations in the date of spawning also seem to relate to the mean water temperature, and variations in the characteristics of the otoliths to the temperature and food supply. Differences in the colours of the fish seem to reflect the colour of the sea bottom, black volcanic (Icelandic) grounds yielding a dark fish and white crushed shells on the Faroe Bank a very pale-coloured fish. Here too a genetic factor has been indicated by the absence of certain chromatophores in fish from certain localities. Differences in shape probably reflect, at least to some extent, the food supply as we have seen in the present volume (p. 138), although freshwater fish sometimes appear as slim-bodied river forms or deeper-bodied lake forms, so water flow may also be involved.

The electrophoresis of water-extracts of muscle yields a number of bands, most of which appear to be enzymes. It is not clear whether real differences exist between fish of different populations, but the patterns of blood serum and particularly of haemoglobins, which exist in several different forms, show more promise. Various other proteins show polymorphism and have been studied in the same context.

2. PHYSICAL CHARACTERS

Meristic differences have again been reported in the period under review. In *Salmo gairdneri* the numbers of vertebrae, gill rakers and fin rays were found by Kwain (1975) to correlate with the rate of growth at the embryonic stage. Longer incubation periods were usually associated with more meristic elements. In the wild, this largely means that lower temperatures result in a bigger number of units such as vertebrae, in line with earlier work illustrated in Volume 1, Fig. 58. However, other factors may be involved: MacCrimmon and Kwain

(1969) found that the dorsal and anal fin rays of the same species were also affected by the light intensity during the post-eyed incubation period, the greatest number of fin rays being found in fish incubated at an intensity of 10 lux.

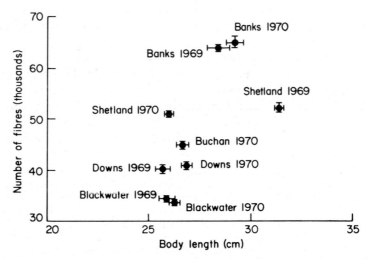

FIG. 100. The identification of different stocks of *Clupea harengus* by counting the total number of muscle cells in a section through the body of the fish. 2×standard error for length and number is drawn through each point. After Greer-Walker, Burd and Pull (1972). Reproduced with permission of Dr M. Greer-Walker.

There are differences in the numbers of white skeletal muscle fibres in a specified part of the musculature of *Clupea harengus* from different parts of the North Sea. Greer-Walker, Burd and Pull (1972), who discovered this, showed that these differences persisted in specimens taken in two successive years. They did not postulate a mechanism for the phenomenon originating in the ground, and saw no evidence of genetic control. Their results are shown in Fig. 100.

Transitory exposure to a change in background colour causes a change in the colour of the skin of many species of fish. A light background causes the clumps of melanin[1] in the pigment cells to contract, in a dark background they spread to colour a bigger proportion of the skin, and Scotsmen say that on a tartan[2] background the fish will explode in the attempt to make their skin colour match! The short-term change is complete in *Ictalurus melas*, for example, in 6 to 8 hours

[1]A black pigment derived from tyrosine.
[2]A chequered colour pattern characteristic of the national costume.

(Khokhar, 1971), but many workers believe that prolonged exposure causes an actual loss or a synthesis of pigment (Odiorne, 1957; Ahmad, 1972).

FIG. 101. Specimens of *Gadus morhua* from the Faroe Bank (upper) and Aberdeen Bank (lower) after being kept together in an aquarium for 4½ months. Although the colour differences are not as marked as in the newly-caught fish, they do persist and the fish can be readily distinguished from one another. After Love (1974).

The upbringing of the fish affects the change. Sumner and Wells (1933) showed that while the longer-term pigmentation or depigmentation (according to background) of *Poecilia reticulata* was usually complete within two or three weeks, dark-reared adult fish put on to a white background *never* became as thoroughly depigmented as those born and reared on white. This observation suggests again a critical stage in development during which the fish become permanently predisposed towards a dark or a light pigmentation; from the design of the experiment, any genetic differences are clearly ruled out. This being so, Love's observation (1974: *Gadus morhua*) that the very light-coloured Faroe Bank cod do not attain the same darker colour of fish from another ground, even after several months, probably does not have a genetic basis. Figure 101, which illustrates fish from the two grounds after living in the same aquarium for $4\frac{1}{2}$ months, shows that some modification has occurred. Faroe Bank fish are considerably paler than this in the wild—see the illustration in Volume 1, Fig. 62—but the two fish can still easily be distinguished. The distinction in this experiment was maintained for at least a further 4 months (Love, 1974), after which the experiment was terminated.

The synthesis of melanin is controlled by the melanophore-stimulating hormone (MSH) from the pituitary, and long-term administration of this hormone causes an increase both in the number of melanophores and their melanin content (Wilson and Dodd, 1973: *Scyliorhinus canicula*). The skin melanophores require the presence of MSH for their maintenance or they degenerate, leaving only some static epidermal pigment. The melanin content of the skin falls, over a six-month period, to some 50% of the control value when the pituitary is removed (same authors). Conversely a high level of circulating MSH more than doubles the melanin content. Presumably the hormone is released in response to visual stimuli: not only do fish respond to the colour of the background as described, but the skin of blind fish darkens in response to what seems to them to be a pitch-black habitat; the occasional dark fish that shows up in a shoal is almost invariably blind. Conversely, "evolutionarily" blind fish which live in the permanent darkness of caves (for example, *Anoptichthys jordani*) have lost almost all their pigment because, presumably, it no longer affords protection from predators.

3. FEEDING

Differences between grounds in the weight of fish at a given age probably result from different combinations of food supply and temperature. In colder arctic waters there may be less food available because of the reduced amount of sunshine, but laboratory experience has also shown that food is absorbed much more slowly at lower temperatures.

Figure 102 is an effective description of the "quality" of a number of atlantic fishing grounds. Note again the position of the corpulent Faroe cod (illustrated in Volume 1, Fig. 62), which obviously enjoy a very favourable environment.

Studying *Platichthys flesus* from the White and Black Seas, Lapin (1973) found that the fish living at the lower temperatures contain the higher lipid reserves, and Shul'man (1972: several species) found that the lipid reserves of Black Sea and Azov Sea fish are in turn higher than those in fish from the Mediterranean. High lipid contents were noted in Mediterranean fish living near the outflows of the rivers Po and Rhône. Marked differences in the nutritional state (liver lipid, liver glycogen, urine nitrogen, muscle protein) of *Gadus morhua* from ten fishing grounds were reported by Love, Robertson *et al.* (1974a) and in the muscle pH (a reflection of carbohydrate reserves) of the same species from some other grounds by Love, Robertson *et al.* (1974b). It is hard to comment in more than general terms on these papers at present, especially as fish with the highest liver glycogen had the lowest liver lipid—which criterion should be taken as reflecting the nutritional conditions on the ground? We shall have more to say on this subject in Chapter 5.

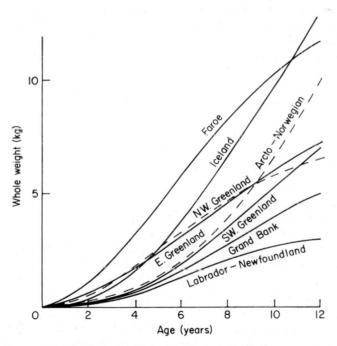

Fig. 102. Curves relating body weight to age in 10 north Atlantic stocks of *Gadus morhua*. After Clayden (1972). Reproduced with permission from the Ministry of Agriculture, Fisheries and Food (Crown Copyright).

Traces of certain strong-flavoured substances such as dimethyl sulphide enter the flesh of fish which have eaten certain invertebrates (Volume 1, p. 199). An "earthy" taint in the flesh of *Mugil cephalus* has been ascribed to the consumption of an odoriferous species of *Actinomyces* which causes a similar taint in salmon (G. L. Kesteven, 1942, quoted by Connell, 1974). *Salmo gairdneri* cultured in ponds have been known to acquire a muddy-earthy flavour presumably derived from the earth of the ponds (Iredale and York, 1976). Differences such as these can, sometimes just seasonally, characterise certain fishing grounds. Mr Alf Preston, a fish-processing factory manager, told me that cod from Bear Island acquire a distinctive "weedy" smell which pervades the factory at certain seasons. Cod from Spitzbergen likewise give off an odour resembling iodine. This observation seems similar to that of Lunde (1930, quoted by Skramstad, 1969), who found that the actual iodine content of *Melanogrammus aeglefinus* from the Norway coast was higher than that of haddock from California. Lunde suggested that the iodine content of the plankton in the two localities might differ.

A number of organs of *Misgurnus fossilis* and *Abramis brama* from Lake Burtnieku (Russia) are richer in trace elements than are the same organs of these fish from Lake Rushonu. For example, roach livers from the first lake contain 24% more manganese, 13% more copper, 29% more zinc and 6% more iron (Berman and Ilzin', 1968). The authors attributed this distinction to differences in the food in the two lakes. On the other hand, Klokov and Frolenko (1970) could find no consistent differences in the concentrations of 18 elements in *Oncorhynchus gorbuscha* from different areas. Bakhteyeva (1975) found differences in the sodium, potassium, calcium and magnesium in the blood serum of salmonid species from different local populations, the reasons being unknown except that some fish were spawned out. This observation seems more likely to reflect differences in the degree of depletion than geographical factors, and is probably irrelevant to the present section.

So far, there seem to be no clear chemical differences originating in the quality of the water, or the food supply, which characterise one particular ground exclusively. Trends do seem to be present, but they are tantalisingly indefinite. The best achievement so far seems to be that of Lapi and Mulligan (1976), who managed to assign 63% of sea-caught *Oncorhynchus nerka* to their correct lake of origin (from three possible lakes) by analysing the centres of the scales, the part laid down when the fish lived in fresh water, for seven trace elements and carrying out multivariate analyses on the results.

4.   MATURATION AND FECUNDITY

Fish spawn at different times, depending on their geographical location (Volume 1, p. 159). This means that the water content of the muscle rises to different maxima according to the stock: in *Gadus morhua* it peaks in March in the North Sea and in May off the coast of Canada (Volume 1, Fig. 63, also Pinhorn, 1969). An even bigger disparity has been reported in this species by Serebryakov (1967), who found cod spawning in February–April on George's Bank (Canada) and May–July in Newfoundland coastal areas. I used to assume that these differences reflect only the differences in the temperature of the water, but the amount of light may also be important. Poston and Livingston (1971b) found that, under hatchery conditions, continuous light accelerates maturity in male *Salmo trutta* by 14 weeks, while continuous darkness retards it by 6 weeks. The maturation of females was seen to be retarded both by continuous light (1 month) and continuous darkness (2 months), showing that the natural daily rhythm of light and darkness is also important. *Salmo gairdneri*, on the other hand, give the best spermatogenic response in the testes when the daily photoperiod is progressively reduced (Breton and Billard, 1977).

Merlangius merlangus, the whiting, also spawns progressively later as one moves North, and Hislop and Hall (1974) found that the fecundity decreases in the same geographical direction. At a given length the fecundity is highest in the southern North Sea, intermediate in the Minch (NW Scotland) and northern North Sea and lowest at Iceland.

5. POLYMORPHISM

The fact that a number of proteins exist in more than one form (polymorphism), which can be separated by electrophoresis or identified immunologically, has clear potential for identifying different stocks of fish and may eventually yield information on the physical nature of the grounds from which they come. Earlier work is reviewed in Volume 1, pp. 163 to 167. Polymorphic differences are almost always genetic, but the sort of ground which predisposes a stock of fish to synthesise a particular form of protein is not usually obvious. The ideal situation would be that in which the tissues are extracted in some way and the components of the resulting fluid or the blood are separated to reveal the stock from which the fish has come, but unfortunately it is not as easy as that. Usually one has to take a considerable number of fish from any one ground and note the frequency with which one form of protein occurs.

The many techniques available, and the results obtained, have been reviewed in detail by de Ligny (1969), referred to "in press" in Volume 1, but now with the correct reference available.

Fry and Hochachka (1970) have reviewed work on the generation of different isoenzymes by fish living at different temperatures, and studies on the polymorphism of numerous proteins and their application in identifying sub-populations of tuna species have been described by Fujino (1970).

The most recent review to come to the writer's attention is that of Utter, Hodgins and Allendorf (1974), who themselves found starch gel electrophoresis to be more effective for studying genetic differences in fish populations than serological methods. A feature of their review is the tabulation of different gel and buffer systems, and the enzymes which each will separate when a current is applied. They noted that *Clupea pallasii* and *Cololabis saira* fail to reveal significant variations among populations, perhaps because both species live in large breeding groups. They do exhibit polymorphism, but the proportions of the different forms do not vary in fish from different fishing localities. On the other hand, *Salmo gairdneri* show much more diversity and so more potential for population studies.

The separation of different forms of a protein by electrophoresis depends on each form having a different charge. This is not always so. Utter, Hodgins and Allendorf (1974) reported that forms of lactic dehydrogenase found in *Oncorhynchus nerka* vary in their Michaelis constant (degree of dissociation with the substrate) but that the enzymes so distinguished from one another cannot be separated electrophoretically. Different forms of the same protein would have had some of their amino acids substituted by others, but in this case the charges on the substitute amino acids must have been the same. Nei (1971, quoted by Utter, Hodgins and Allendorf, 1974) estimated that only 40% of the amino acid substitutions in polymorphism would be detectable by electrophoresis. The reviewers pinpointed the major future direction of work as "gaining a better understanding of the relationship between biochemical genetic variation and environmental factors", so the relationships in which we are primarily interested here have still, apparently, to be established.

The Hardy–Weinberg relationship is a central point of reference in this field. It states that in a randomly mating population in the absence of disturbing forces like selection or mutation the expected distribution of genotypes (inheritable characteristics) is determined by the random combination of alleles (variants of a characteristic gene). Different combinations of alleles give the "phenotypes", which in the present context can often be separated electrophoretically, and if the proportions of these deviate from those expected by random combination, then it is likely that differences in survival or departures from random mating are involved.

Recent studies in which the polymorphism of various proteins has been used to decide if fish from two or more grounds differ genetically are now summed in Table 16 without further comment. Observed differences may result from long isolation of populations, leading to the

TABLE 16

The use of polymorphic proteins for studying different stocks of fish

Species	Populations studied	Findings	Reference
a. *Esterase*			
Abramis blicca	One population examined	Serum esterase potentially useful for population analysis	Nyman (1969)
Acerina cernua			
Anguilla anguilla	East and West Atlantic	Liver esterase showed large variations, so not able to conclude whether the two populations are produced from one or two gene pools	Pantelouris, Arnason and Bumpus (1976)
Clupea harengus	Ballantrae, Blackwater and Dunmore (Scotland, Ireland and England, respectively)	Muscle esterase showed marked difference between Dunmore and Blackwater stocks, Ballantrae being intermediate	
Merluccius productus	Puget Sound and Pacific Ocean	Vitreous humour esterase showed highly significant frequency difference between grounds	Simonarson and Watts (1969)
Pollachius virens	Norway, Iceland	Serum esterase showed a distribution of phenotypes which was almost the same in fish from both grounds	Utter (1969)
Salmo salar	N. America, Europe	Consistent differences found (liver)	Moller and Naevdal (1973)
Salvelinus alpinus	7 isolated populations	Differences found in liver esterase	Nyman and Pippy (1972) Saunders and McKenzie (1971)
b. *Eye Lens Protein*			
Decapterus pinnulatus	Hawaii, Kauai (islands 300 miles apart)	Two electrophoretic patterns common to both grounds, two exclusive to Kauai, suggesting separate breeding populations	
Salvelinus alpinus	7 isolated populations	Differences found	Smith (1969) Saunders and McKenzie (1971)

TABLE 16 *continued*

Species	Populations studied	Findings	Reference
c. *Haemoglobins (H) and Transferrins (T)*			
Anguilla spp. (H)	E and W Atlantic	Identical patterns given	Poluhowich (1970)
Anguilla anguilla (T)	Atlantic, Mediterranean	Some combinations of bands found only in Atlantic stocks, some only in Mediterranean	Drilhon, Fine *et al.* (1966)
Gadus morhua (T)	Faroe Plateau, Faroe Bank	Some genetic isolation indicated between these two stocks	Jamieson and Jones (1967)
(H, T)	Various stocks in North Sea	Concluded that most cod in N. Sea belong to one race	Jamieson and Thompson (1972)
(H, T)	Norwegian coastal type, migratory Arctic type	Genetically separate. Not known why no interbreeding occurs	Møller (1968)
Hippoglossus stenolepis (T)	East Bering Sea, north-east Pacific south to British Columbia	Four molecular species found in different combinations. Gene frequency analysis used to study 10 geographic areas. Haemoglobin not thought useful in population analysis	Tsuyuki, Roberts and Best (1969)
Merluccius productus (T)	Puget Sound, Pacific Ocean	Significant difference between grounds	Utter (1969)
Pollachius virens (H, T)	Norway, Iceland	Distribution of types similar	Møller and Naevdal (1973)
d. *Lactic Dehydrogenase*			
Fundulus heteroclitus	One stock studied	Polymorphism shown to disappear if the fish were kept in the dark for a long time	Massaro and Booke (1971)
Gadus morhua	E. Scotland, E. Canada	The proportion of one form of heart LDH varied slightly but significantly between populations	Lush and Cowey (1968)

Oncorhynchus nerka	Asia, Bristol Bay, Gulf of Alaska	Three phenotypes of serum LDH found. Their proportions varied sufficiently among different populations to suggest that certain populations could be identified	Hodgins, Ames and Utter (1969)
Pollachius virens	W. Scotland, Faroe, Iceland	Polymorphism shown, but gene frequencies did not vary between populations	Lush (1970);
Salvelinus alpinus	7 isolated populations	Liver LDH varied among populations	Saunders and McKenzie (1971)
e. *Malate Dehydrogenase*			
Platichthys stellatus	Asia, Oregon	Differences found	Johnson and Beardsley (1975)
f. *Myogen (from muscle)*			
Anoplopoma fimbria	Alaska to Oregon	Two polymorphic proteins appeared singly or in pairs, giving three possible combinations. Frequencies observed gave no evidence of separate populations.	Tsuyuki and Roberts (1969)
g. *Phosphoglucomutase*			
Clupea harengus	Norway, Faroe, Clyde, Shetland, Dogger Bank	Gene frequencies differed between the first three and the last two groups	Lush (1969)
Oncorhynchus nerka	Alaska, Bristol Bay, Washington State	Promising for identifying area of origin of salmon caught on high seas	Utter and Hodgins (1970)

TABLE 16 *continued*

Species	Populations studied	Findings	Reference
h. *Serum Protein*			
Gadus morhua	Labrador, Greenland	Seven bands given from each ground (5 globulin +2 albumin) but the patterns differed clearly between the grounds (gene frequencies differed)	Ullrich (1968)
Salmo salar	N. America, Europe	Consistent differences in electrophoretic behaviour supports suggestion that there are two sub-species of *Salmo salar*	Nyman and Pippy (1972)
		Indications that populations of different river systems are genetically distinct. They cannot be identified by electrophoresis in high-seas fishery, but European or American salmon can sometimes be distinguished	Wilkins (1972)—a review
i. *Tetrazolium Oxidase*			
Oncorhynchus tschawytscha	N. Pacific, Seattle	Difference in gene frequencies found	Utter (1971)

propagation of diverse chance mutations. On the other hand, the observation by Massaro and Booke (1971: *Fundulus heteroclitus*) that LDH polymorphism disappears if the fish are kept in the dark gives hope that features of the ground may eventually show through as well, although the latter is an unusual phenomenon.

C.   Cultured fish

To compare fish raised in a hatchery with their natural counterparts is to study a more specialised "geographical influence", with diet playing an important role.

In Volume 1 (p. 51 onwards) it was shown that cultured fish tend to be deficient in carotenoids, body protein and ash, and that they almost always contain more lipid than do wild fish, such lipid being the more saturated. Abnormal fatty degeneration of the liver may be the result of feeding partially oxidised lipids to cultured fish. "Hard" or saturated lipids in the diet are also unnatural to fish and cause, among other symptoms, anaemia resulting from degeneration of the haematopoietic tissue.

Eggs laid by cultured fish tend not to thrive as well as eggs from a natural fish population, and, as we have seen in the present account (p. 9), overcrowding of parent fish in a tank gives rise to unnaturally pigmented offspring.

Differences in behaviour between the two types of fish probably have repercussions in other attributes. Close confinement makes cultured fish unusually aggressive, and when released into a stream they probably lose feeding time and use up excessive amounts of energy, contributing to their relatively high mortality.

Apart from being made deficient in certain constituents, or metabolically damaged by artificial diets, cultured fish can be regarded as having to some extent adapted to a special environment, a situation not necessarily bad. This was shown by Reisenbichler and McIntyre (1977), who crossed hatchery-reared (H) *Salmo gairdneri* with wild (W) specimens, comparing the "hybrid" HW with HH and WW. In streams, the wild fish WW showed the highest survival rate, while HW had the highest growth rate wherever there were differences. In the hatchery pond, HH had the highest survival and growth rates, showing that they were best adapted to the pond environment. The selection procedure of hatcheries may cause an eventual genetic difference from the wild fish, as suggested by the fact that if they are crossed with wild fish, a reduced number of smolts is produced.

If wild and hatchery-reared parr of *Salmo salar* are placed together in unfamiliar streams containing resident parr, the hatchery-reared parr are found in the area in greater numbers one and two weeks later, the

wild parr having fled (Symons, 1969). The greater aggression of
hatchery fish (Volume 1, reference 337) perhaps enables them to stand
up better to the residents.

The swimming activity of *Katsuwonus pelamis* kept captive appears to
be less than that of the wild fish. Stevens and Fry (1971) found that
where the wild fish could maintain a temperature in their dark muscle

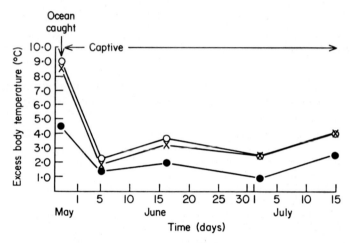

FIG. 103. The decrease in excess body temperature which occurs when *Katsuwonus
pelamis* are kept in captivity. It may be reduced because of a decline in swimming
activity. ○, Dark muscle; ×, white muscle; ●, brain. After Stevens and Fry (1971).
Reproduced with permission of Dr E. D. Stevens.

which was 9·1°C above that of the ambient water (25·6°C), those in
tanks could maintain only a 2 to 4 degree differential (Fig. 103), which
suggests suppressed swimming. This agrees with Webb (1971), who
remarked that a decline in swimming performance during captivity is
well known. Hochachka (1961) found that the swimming capacity of
wild *Salmo gairdneri* is superior to that of hatchery fish, and quoted
Vincent (1960) as showing that they have more stamina. Michael
Greer-Walker (in conversation, 1974) concludes from his experience
that it is *never* possible to make fish from an aquarium swim as fast as
wild ones unless they have been in captivity for only a short time. The
hearts of cultured *Salmo salar* kept in cages in the sea are smaller than
those of their wild counterparts (Max Keith, in conversation, 1974),
again suggesting reduced activity. The calmer demeanour of hatchery
fish is an advantage to the culturists, however, because it results in a
reduced consumption of expensive food.

A group of fish in a hatchery differ little among themselves in the stimuli received from their environment and in their responses to them. It seems likely that wild fish will be stimulated in a greater variety of ways. Perhaps for this reason, the pH of the blood of *Ictalurus punctatus*, while similar on average between captive and wild fish, shows a greater standard deviation among wild fish (LeTendre, 1968), presumably reflecting greater variations in lactate output from different causes. On the other hand, the mean diameters of the cell nuclei of the adrenal cortex of wild and hatchery-reared *Salmo salar* are similar, suggesting at least to Davis and Fenderson (1971) that the two groups respond similarly to environmental stresses. Both of these results should perhaps be interpreted with some reserve.

The high protein content of artificial diets has been suggested as a reason for the increase in alanine aminotransferase activity in the liver and gut of *Ictalurus punctatus* (Wilson, 1973a). High protein diets have shown to increase the activity of this enzyme in rats (Szepesi and Freedland, quoted by Wilson, 1973a). The finding is not surprising, as the enzyme functions to convert excess alanine to glucose (gluconeogenesis) for use as an energy source. The muscle glucose of well-fed *Tilapia nilotica* from an aquarium has been shown by Hoffman, Disney *et al.* (1970) to exceed that of fish from ponds, possibly through the same mechanism. A high protein diet also causes greater liver growth in cultured *Pleuronectes platessa* than in wild (Cowey, Brown *et al.*, 1974), as judged by the greater amount of ribose nucleic acid present (see p. 30).

Captive fry of *Oncorhynchus gorbuscha* on a hatchery diet have been shown to embody $1\frac{1}{2}$ to 2 times as much lipid as fry of the same size hatched on a natural spawning ground (Kamyshnaya and Shatunovsky, 1969). The extra lipid is probably triglyceride; these authors reported a lower proportion of phospholipids and cholesterol esters in the hatchery fry. Roberts (1974) in fact reported much higher levels of triglycerides in teleosts raised in a hatchery than in the wild, and the same applies to fatty fish: *Clupea harengus* reared at a laboratory contain more triglycerides than their native counterparts (Balbontin, de Silva and Ehrlich, 1973). The total lipid of this species is also higher when the fish are artificially reared (same authors), as it is in *Pleuronectes platessa* (Ehrlich, 1975). One of the enzymes of the pentose phosphate pathway which can be instrumental in lipid synthesis (glucose-6-phosphate dehydrogenase) has been noted as much more active in *Salvelinus fontinalis* from a hatchery than in those from ponds or streams (Yamauchi, Stegeman and Goldberg, 1975). This again could be significant in the present context.

Feeding pattern rather than the actual composition of the diet may be responsible for the excess lipid in artificially reared fish. Simply restricting the food intake has been shown by Cho, Slinger and Bayley (1976: *Salmo gairdneri*) to produce carcasses with relatively more protein and less lipid.

Fig. 104. Colour differences between trawled and farmed *Solea solea*. Only the skin has been removed. Reproduced with permission of Mr A. Hume, who kindly supplied the picture (Crown Copyright).

The main pitfall for the unwary is that if lipids in an artificial diet are oxidised, or partially so, a number of pathological symptoms soon develop in the fish (Volume 1, p. 54). In addition, poor appetite and muscular dystrophy have been reported by Sakaguchi and Hamaguchi (1969) to occur in *Seriola quinqueradiata* fed with deliberately oxidised oil.

Diet is presumably responsible for differences in carotenoid pigmentation. In the eggs of *Salmo gairdneri* developing naturally, the main pigment is astaxanthin, while in those bred artificially it is largely or even entirely lutein (Georgiev, 1971).

If fish in an aquarium are overcrowded, the ammonia content of the water will tend to rise. As we have seen (p. 159), fish detoxicate ammonia by converting it to glutamine, and Levi, Morisi *et al.* (1974) have shown that the concentration of glutamine in the brain of *Carassius auratus* from aquarium water containing unusually high levels of ammonia reaches as much as ten times the usual. Crowding also reduces the oxygen

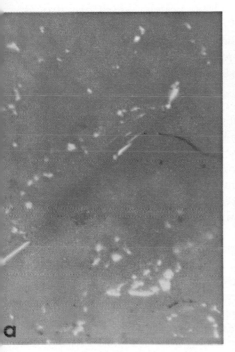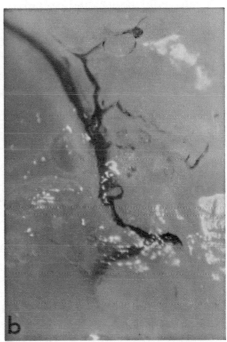

Fig. 105. Part of the flesh of (a) wild and (b) farmed *Pleuronectes platessa,* showing the deposit of melanin around a blood vessel in the farmed specimen. Reproduced with permission of Mr A. Hume, who kindly supplied the picture (Crown Copyright).

content of the water, and Cameron (1971) has shown that the proportion of haemoglobin carried in the blood as the oxidised form (met-haemoglobin) can be 17% of the total where *Salmo gairdneri* have come from a hatchery compared with 2·9% in a wild stock. The process is self-regulating to some extent. The rate of oxygen consumption of over-crowded *Gadus morhua* declines because the reduced space for swimming restricts activity (Saunders, 1963). Reduced activity makes smaller demands on energy resources, and so the liver glycogen content of over-crowded *Cyprinus carpio* increases as well (Falkina and Davydova, 1970).

A variety of differences in minor components probably accounts for the fact that, after cooking, the muscle of trawled *Pleuronectes platessa* differs in flavour from cultured fish of the same species (Hume, Farmer and Burt, 1972), though not necessarily in an adverse way. A number of cultured teleost species have been shown to have a darker skin than those from the wild, perhaps because the bottoms of the ponds are dark coloured, and in addition the flesh tends to be darker (Fig. 104). This is especially noticeable around the blood vessels, which are strongly blackened by deposits of melanin (Love and Hume, 1975). The direct cause is unknown. Figure 105(a) shows the darkest discoverable part of the muscle of a wild *Pleuronectes platessa*, and Fig. 105(b) part of a farmed fish of the same species, showing a heavy melanin deposit around a blood vessel.

Actual values of "proximate" constituents (footnote, p. 79) of various species of reared and wild fish are tabulated in the review by Blaxter (1975), to which the reader is referred for further information. He points out that wild salmonid fry swim better but are less aggressive than those from a hatchery, and that some species of hatchery fish will not take normal food after a long time on artificial diets. These characteristics mean that hatchery fish are unlikely to thrive when released into the wild, especially as, for example, reared *Pleuronectes platessa* also lack normal avoidance responses.

Scophthalmus maximus reared in captivity show damage in their kidneys which, on histological examination, appears to involve calcification of the tubules. However, chemical analysis by Cowey, Coombs and Adron (1976) failed to show any difference between the total calcium, magnesium or phosphorus contents of the kidneys of reared and wild fish, so the observation remains a mystery at present.

D.   Individual environmental factors

1.   DEPTH

a.   *Pressure*

i.   *Introduction*

We have seen (p. 122) that because fish from very deep water may live at as much as 1000 atmospheres of pressure, there are sure to be difficulties in attempting to secrete gas into the swim bladder, and decompression problems whenever the fish rise towards the surface.

Deep water fish therefore often exist without a swim bladder altogether, and adjust their specific gravity to values close to that of seawater by reducing the quantity of skeletal muscle and increasing its water content. Figure 43 (p. 127) showed that as fish live at progressively greater depths, they tend to become more watery, and the bones become less dense for the same reason.

Where fish do possess swim bladders, the proportion of argon to nitrogen decreases with increasing depth, argon being the more soluble of the two gases (Buell, 1973: *Salmo gairdneri*).

ii. *Lipids*

Phleger, Benson and Yayanos (1973) attributed the presence of large quantities of cholesterol in the swim bladders of deep-sea fish to the effects of pressure. The synthesis of cholesterol from radioactive acetate was shown to be enhanced by pressure in the deep-water fish *Orthopristis forbesi*. The hydrocarbon squalene, the more immediate precursor of cholesterol, has a very low density, so again pressure would tend to favour the formation of the denser cholesterol; during cyclisation, a significant decrease in volume occurs. These authors found experimentally that pressure does increase the rate of conversion of squalene to cholesterol in the gas gland of the shallow water grunt *Anisotremus davidsoni*, though not in one of the deep ocean fish *Coryphaenoides acrolepis*.

A number of deep-water species possess high proportions of wax esters in their bodies. Nevenzel, Rodegker *et al.* (1969) concluded that the compounds serve as buoyancy agents and enable the fish to undertake daily vertical migrations which would be much more difficult if they had continually to adjust the pressures within their swim bladders.

Phleger and Benson (1971: *Coryphaenoides acrolepis, C. abyssorum, Antimora rostrata*) found that the proportion of unsaturated fatty acids in the fatty lining to the swim bladder increase as fish live at greater depths, but also pointed out that the temperature decreases from 6·3°C at 730 metres to less than 2°C at 3800 metres, so that the change may be a temperature phenomenon (see p. 339). The fatty acids of phospholipids show no change in unsaturation with depth. In contrast, the liver lipids of 6 gadiform species were shown by Hayashi and Hamada (1975a) to contain fewer polyunsaturated acids with increasing depth of habitat, while the monoenoic (one double bound only) acid content tended to increase.

Pomazhanskaya, Pravdina and Chirkovskaya (1975) noted that the unsaturation of brain phospholipids increases with increasing depth, but considered that low temperature does not in itself explain all the features of fatty acid composition observed nor the extremely low phospholipid content of the brains of abyssal (about 6000 metres deep) fish. The relative contents of different lipid classes within the phospholipids appeared to these workers not to differ between shallow- and deep-water fish. The single ultra-abyssal fish which they investigated (*Leucicorus* sp.) had the highest polyunsaturated fatty acid content in the brain phospholipids.

Apart from the lower temperatures requiring a more fluid lipid (unsaturation gives rise to a softer consistency) in, for example, membrane structures to preserve normal function, no explanations have been offered for the effects of depth as such on the fatty acid composition. Pomazhanskaya, Pravdina and Chirkovskaya (1975) have said that the answer probably lies in "the effect of other factors of the deep sea environment" and we must leave the subject at that.

iii. *Blood constituents*

After studying 53 species of fish, Gelineo (1969) concluded that there is no definite relationship between the depth of the habitat and the haemoglobin concentration of the blood, so the processes of gas exchange evidently proceed normally. However, the decline in oxygen binding capacity with lowered blood pH (the Root effect) is more pronounced in deep-water fish than shallow-water fish where both possess swim bladders (Baines, 1975). This assists the deep-water fish to inflate their swim bladders with oxygen from the blood despite high ambient pressures (see p. 123).

In the Antarctic, shallow-water fish maintain relatively high concentrations of certain solutes in their blood serum to prevent freezing should they come into contact with ice. The danger is reduced for the same species living in deeper water, in which DeVries and Wohlschlag (1969) have found lower concentrations of, for example, non-protein nitrogen.

Apart from the latter observation, studies on the effects of depth compare deep-water species with shallow-water species, a procedure beset with the usual disadvantages of interspecies comparisons. However, in this case it is almost unavoidable. As Gordon (1972a) points out, there are practically no families of fish which include both deep- and shallow-water forms, so the two groups have probably been evolutionarily separate from each other for a long time. Deep-sea forms are generally smaller and probably less active than shallow-water fish.

iv. *Enzymes*

Studies on the effects of pressure on enzyme systems have been carried out by Hochachka and his colleagues. They are full of interest, because whereas temperature affects all chemical reactions in the same way by altering the kinetic energy of the reactants, pressure varies in its effect, activating, for example, fructose diphosphatase, inhibiting pyruvate kinase and having no effect on lactic dehydrogenase. Moreover, pressure can act in any of these three ways on a given enzyme-catalysed reaction according to the temperature. Where two or more enzymes compete for a common metabolite, differential effects of pressure can alter profoundly the direction in which material flows at critical junctions in a metabolic pathway. These conclusions were formulated by Hochachka, Moon and Mustafa (1972), who review the effects of pressure on specific reactions in particular species of fish. In another review, Hochachka (1972) states that the pH dependencies of enzymes also are affected by the hydrostatic pressure, and that at alkaline pH the maximum velocity characteristics of certain fish enzymes are strongly accelerated by increased pressures. While pointing out that there are still many unanswered questions about adaptation to depth, he regards it as adaptation to temperature, pressure and an uncertain supply of oxygen.

Hochachka's group have made some detailed studies on *Antimora rostrata*, a fish from very deep water. Hochachka (1975a) found that citrate synthase from the gills of this fish depolymerises at higher pressures to form subunits of greater activity. The lactic dehydrogenase differs in its characteristics from those of warm-blooded animals, and its Michaelis constant, a measure of the affinity of the enzyme for its substrate, is unaffected by pressure at low temperatures—a favourable situation for a fish living on the abyssal floor (Baldwin, Storey and Hochachka, 1975). The binding of acetylcholinesterase to its substrate tends to be disrupted by low temperatures and high pressures, but the enzyme in this species is, to quote Hochachka, Storey and Baldwin (1975), "designed" to minimise the effect, allowing binding to the substrate with high efficiency despite the extreme physical conditions of its environment. There is much more of interest in the work of this energetic group than is shown in the present short account, and the reader is recommended to browse through the originals, especially the review by Hochachka (1972).

b.   *Illumination*

The effect of the nature of the environmental illumination on the type of photo-sensitive pigments in the retinas of fish was considered in some detail in Volume 1, pp. 179–187. A number of pigments are present, consisting of retinal (vitamin A_1 aldehyde) or dehydroretinal (vitamin A_2 aldehyde) in combination with different proteins. Fish usually maintain one or more pigments such that their sensitivity is maximal at the light wavelength which predominates in the environment. The maximum sensitivity of freshwater fish eyes is often at about 540 nm (540 mμ in the older notation of Volume 1), the pigments being based on dehydroretinal, while the eyes of marine fish, like mammals, are maximally sensitive to about 500 nm, with pigments based on retinal. Deep-water fish often possess pigments most easily decomposed at about 480 nm, since the light penetrating is increasingly blue at increasing depths. Muddy coastal waters induce a maximum sensitivity at around 510 nm, higher than the norm for shallow marine fish.

In multipigment species, the presence of the various pigments is an inherited character, but the proportions of each can change according to the ambient illumination. They can therefore alter in some species as the daylight period changes seasonally or as the angle of the sun on the water rises and falls during the year. Migration from river to ocean can also bring about a change in the proportions of the pigments. The ability to vary the maximum visual sensitivity is most pronounced in fish which migrate or occupy habitats of variable illumination.

i. *Physiological phenomena*

Changes in the amount of sunlight received by the fish probably trigger physiological processes, particularly maturation. Concurrent temperature effects, which could be confused with the effects of illumination, are virtually eliminated in the Antarctic, where seasonal temperature changes are only of the order of $\pm 0.05°C$, but where there is still a rise in the respiratory activity of fish in the summer season (Wohlschlag, 1964: *Trematomus bernacchi*). Maintenance in complete darkness for $6\frac{1}{2}$ months was found by Pang (1971: *Fundulus heteroclitus*) to delay testicular maturation in both adults and juveniles, and to cause hypocalcaemia and scoliosis in juveniles. Unlike mammals, fish seem to be able to synthesise vitamin D in the absence of sunlight (Oizumi and Monder, 1972), and *Carassius auratus*, which may be extensively exposed to light, seem in contrast to possess little or none of this vitamin (Bills, 1954, quoted by Oizumi and Monder, 1972).

The pineal body, purely an endocrine gland in the brain of mammals, appears to be sensitive to light in some fish, particularly lampreys (Young, 1935) and functions as a third "eye" in the reptile *Sphenodon*. In the eyeless cave fish *Anoptichthys jordani*, the outer segment organisation of the pineal gradually degenerates as the fish grow older, eliminating even this potential light sensor. However, if the fish are reared in a brightly illuminated aquarium, degeneration is delayed (Herwig, 1976), so that at least some parts of these curious fish may respond to light. Phenomena like this should be interpreted sparingly at the present state of our knowledge. The pineal of *Jenkinsia stolifera* also responds to light in a way, in that it is covered by fewer melanophores when the fish is in the open sea than when it has entered a dark cave (Breder and Bird, 1975).

The activity of hydroxyindole-0-methyltransferase in the pineal increases sharply with the onset of darkness in *Salmo gairdneri*, but Smith and Weber (1976), who made the observation, found that the effect could be abolished by blinding both eyes of the fish and not by covering the pineal with opaque material. Also, surgical exposure of the pineal region to the light did not restore the enzymic response to changes in lighting.

No change in the activity of acetylserotonin methyltransferase has been found in the pineals of *Salmo gairdneri* or *Hesperoleucus symmetricus* kept in constant light, constant darkness or a daily cycle (Hafeez and Quay, 1970).

ii. *Carotenoids*

Carotenoids have been identified in the corneas of *Perca fluviatilis*, *Amia calva* and *Esox lucius* by Bridges (1969), who pointed out that all of these fish prefer shallow water and bask in the sun. *Lepisosteus platyrhynchus*, another basking species, also has a yellow cornea which is often more heavily pigmented towards its dorsal edge. The retina is thus shielded from intense blue radiation. The carotenoid pigmentation of the cornea of *Hexagrammos octogrammus*, a shallow-water fish, can change rapidly from negligible in the dark to deep red in bright light. The pigmentation was considered by Orlov and Gamburtzeva (1976) to improve the resolution of the eye by eliminating loss of contrast due to a blue veil of light scattered within the eye and to chromatic aberration, which can be quite important in the fish eye. The deep colour produced in bright light is tolerable because the fish can "remove its sunglasses" after dark.

iii. *Visual pigments*

Recent reports on the proportions of different visual pigments have extended the work reported in Volume 1, but bring few surprises. Relationships are usually not completely straightforward and anomalies abound, awaiting further fundamental study. The pigments found in the rod or cone outer segments are as follows:

1. Porphyropsins: pigments based on dehydroretinal (vitamin A_2) plus protein. The wavelength of light to which they are most sensitive (λ_{max}) is about 530 nm, varying according to the protein involved. These pigments are mostly characteristic of fish in a freshwater environment.

2. Rhodopsins: pigments based on retinal (vitamin A_1) plus protein, with λ_{max} at about 500 nm. They are found chiefly in mammals and marine fish living in shallow or moderate depths.

3. Chrysopsins: these are simply rhodopsins but with λ_{max} at about 480 nm. They are found exclusively in the retinas of deep-water fish.

Light entering the eye bleaches these pigments, and the reaction stimulates the optic nerve so that the fish sees. Many fish possess more than one pigment in their retina, thus increasing the range of spectral sensitivity.

The position of λ_{max} can vary considerably according to the protein which forms part of the pigment. It is in fact possible for a rhodopsin and a porphyropsin almost to coincide in spectral sensitivity, though this is unusual, rhodopsins usually being more sensitive to light at shorter wavelengths. An example of close correspondence is found in the paper by Bridges (1967b), who describes a rhodopsin from *Coregonus* sp. with λ_{max} at 520 nm and a porphyropsin from *Carassius carassius* with λ_{max} at 521·2 nm.

Dartnall (1972) studied the chrysopsins of several deep-water species. The one with the lowest wavelength for its maximum sensitivity appears to be that found in the elasmobranch *Centroscymnus coelolepis*, with λ_{max} at 472 nm. The castor oil fish, *Ruvettus pretiosus*, lives at the same depth as the coelacanth (*Latimeria chalumnae*), and the λ_{max} for the chrysopsins of these species are respectively 474 nm and 473 nm—all three probably respectively minor variations of the same pigment. Dartnall noted that these were remarkably precise adaptations to sunlight filtered through a considerable depth of oceanic water. Below 100 m such light is generally most intense at wavelengths between 470 and 476 nm, and the best visual performance is obtained where the wavelengths of the absorption maximum of the visual pigment (greatest sensitivity) matches that of most of the incident light. *Hydrolagus colliei* is often found below 80 m depth, and the λ_{max} of its chrysopsin is 484 nm (Beatty, 1969a; Crescitelli, 1969). It can also be found in shallow water, but such temporary migration does not alter the sensitivity of the pigment. On the other hand, *Anguilla rostrata* starts to produce a chrysopsin in its retina just as it is about to enter deep water, so as to improve its future perceptivity. In the young, freshwater ("yellow") stage this eel possesses two pigments, a rhodopsin with λ_{max} at 501 nm and a porphyropsin with λ_{max} at 523 nm, giving a wide range of sensitivity in relatively shallow habitats. When metamorphosis takes place to the "silver" form, which migrates downstream, a third pigment appears with λ_{max} at 482 nm (Beatty, 1975). A similar adaptation occurs in *Anguilla anguilla*.

Munz and McFarland (1973) measured the spectral distribution of light in the air and under the clear waters off the Marshall Islands. They found that at twilight the underwater spectrum narrows and shifts to shorter wavelengths as a result of increased absorption of yellow-orange light by the atmosphere. At the twilight period the diurnal fish seek cover and then, after a "quiet period", the nocturnal species, with different spectral sensitivities, emerge. The quiet period is the most critical time and is visually difficult because the light intensity falls between the thresholds of photopic and scotopic vision.[1] Predators take advantage of this and tend to increase their activity. The λ_{max} of the rhodopsins of the fish which are in evidence before, during and after the quiet period tend to match that of the background light, maximising their ability to see.

A number of fish which are the prey of others disguise their body shapes when at rest at night; the bold skin patterns seen during the daytime fade and the fish merge with the background. This phenomenon is seen in both fresh- and salt-water species (Emery, 1973), and presumably compensates to some extent for the visual acuity of the predators.

Salvelinus willughbii exists as two distinct populations in Lake Windermere (England), one spawning in the autumn in shallow water (1 to 3 m) and one in spring in 17 to 20 m. This difference in depth may characterise the two groups only at spawning time, but in any case it is not great enough to alter the visual pigments, the λ_{max} of which is 510 to 511 nm in both populations, a combined result from a rhodopsin of λ_{max} 508 nm mixed with about 12% of porphyropsin (Bridges, 1967a). On the other hand, cichlid fishes from the surface waters of Lake Malawi possess visual pigments with λ_{max} just above 500 nm, contrasting with species living deeper than 100 m, where the pigments absorb maximally at about 492 nm (Muntz, 1976).

We have seen in Volume 1 (p. 183) that while the presence of both kinds of pigment (based on both vitamins A_1 and A_2) is an inherited character of some species, their proportion may change during the life of the fish according to the light conditions encountered. Regular seasonal variation is therefore possible (Volume 1, Fig. 72). The visual pigments of *Scardinius erythrophthalmus* kept in continuous light were found by Bridges and Yoshikami (1970a) to comprise 0 to 20% of porphyropsin, the remainder being rhodopsin. After covering the eyes to simulate darkness, they found that the proportion of porphyropsin had increased to 60 to 100% after 12 days, 80 to 100% after 40 days. Clear differences were found in the pigmentation of each eye where one eye only was covered with a black cap, so the mechanism controlling the

---

[1]Daylight and night vision, in which cones and rods, respectively, are the functional light-sensitive cells.

proportion of pigments is localised within the eye rather than, for example, in centrally controlled endocrine mechanisms. About half of the freshwater species examined have both rhodopsin and porphyropsin (various authors quoted by Bridges and Yoshikami, 1970a). Work by Bridges and Yoshikami (1970b: *Scardinius erythrophthalmus*) demonstrated a continuous interchange of vitamins A_1 and A_2 between their binding sites on the proteins of the visual pigments and other sites in the body. It is therefore possible for the proportions of rhodopsin to porphyropsin to change even without bleaching (exposure to light) as an intermediate step. Although the proportions of visual pigments change with a change in illumination, the proportions of the two vitamins A in the liver (the main storage organ) remain constant.

Using radioactive tracers, Hata, Hata and Onishi (1973: *Carassius auratus, Channa argus*) showed that vitamins A_1 and A_2 were also interconvertible in the fish, and that β-carotene could be a precursor for either.

It must again be stressed, however, that the response of a fish to a change in the light conditions varies very much with the species. For example, Allen, McFarland *et al.* (1973) found that darker conditions increase the proportion of rhodopsin in the eyes of *Salvelinus fontinalis* and *Salmo gairdneri*—the opposite to the effect found in *Scardinius erythrophthalmus*—while *Salmo trutta* maintains a high proportion regardless of light intensity. Further, low temperatures favour a higher proportion of porphyropsin whatever the light conditions are, at least in *Salmo gairdneri* (Cristy, 1976; Tsin and Beatty, 1977) and *Notemigonus crysoleucas* (Allen and McFarland, 1973). Interpretation of seasonal changes may therefore be difficult.

Some *Osmerus mordax* have been landlocked in fresh water in Quebec and New Brunswick since the ice age 9,000 to 11,000 years ago. They show remarkable genetic differences, some populations having pure porphyropsin retinas, others pure rhodopsin (Bridges and Delisle, 1974). The finding calls into question the selective advantage of a porphyropsin system in fresh water, although non-landlocked groups progressively increase the proportion of porphyropsin as they migrate from sea to river for spawning. The same authors point out that the loss or partial loss of porphyropsin and its replacement by rhodopsin is not caused by any lack of vitamin A_2 in the body; sometimes it accounts for more than half of the liver retinols (vitamins A).

Thyroxine injected into *Oncorhynchus nerka* has been shown by Beatty (1969b) to cause a marked increase in the proportion of porphyropsin in the retina, when compared with sham-injected controls which have mostly rhodopsin. Jacquest and Beatty (1972) found that the proportion of porphyropsin in *Salmo gairdneri* retinas could be increased by either feeding a diet rich in vitamin A_2 (an unexpected finding in the light of work described above), injecting thyroxine or injecting thyroid-stimulating hormone. In line with the conclusion of Bridges and Yoshikami (1970a), they concluded that in fish possessing more than one pigment the site for vitamin interconversion is probably the eye, though the proportions of the two vitamins in the liver may sometimes change as well. Cristy (1974) showed that thyroxine dissolved in the aquarium water would increase the proportion of porphyropsin in *Salmo gairdneri*, and that injected prolactin acted in the same way. Allen (1977) also found that thyroxine in the water increased the proportion of porphyropsin in *Salmo gairdneri* eyes, but that if he changed the conditions of light or temperature the influence ceased.

In view of the influence of diet on the proportion of visual pigments, Beatty (1969c) called into question the whole idea of the pigments being controlled by the light of the habitat. However, he noted that the burbot *Lota lota*, the only freshwater gadoid, was also the only gadoid with two visual pigments. We have seen much evidence in the foregoing account to show that the light condition is at any rate a factor of overwhelming importance in the control of the proportions of visual pigments. The evidence is supplemented by the interesting observation of Denton, Muntz and Northmore (1971) that the proportions of rhodopsin to porphyropsin show a progressive change dorso-ventrally in the retina of *Scardinius erythrophthalmus*. This could well be an adaptation to the different spectral qualities of the up-welling and down-welling light, though as the authors point out the situation is complicated by the difference in the quality of the light illuminating the fish near the surface or on the bottom.

2. pH

A low pH is often found in the water of small streams which are surrounded by peat or bog. The main effect on the fish seems to be an inhibition of oxygen uptake at the gills, presumably by the operations of the Bohr and Root effects (see p. 123). Packer and Dunson (1972) found that *Salvelinus fontinalis* are killed at an ambient pH of 2 to 3·5, oxygen uptake being strongly inhibited and much sodium being lost. The rate of sodium loss, rather than the absolute quantity, seems important in determining the survival time, but it may be a manifestation of impending death expressed as a breakdown of osmoregulation, rather than a cause of death. The Bohr and Root effects vary widely between species, and while acid waters inhibit oxygen consumption in *Lepomis macrochirus* and *Ictalurus nebulosus*, they appear to enhance it in *Lepomis gibbosus* (Pegg, Kellar and Harner, 1976).

3. OXYGEN CONCENTRATION

In Volume 1, pp. 176–179, it was shown that sudden asphyxia produces the usual stress reaction, a rise in blood glucose. Swimming speed is affected below a certain concentration of ambient oxygen, but above it the speed is independent of concentration. The number of red blood cells in circulation increases when the oxygen supply is reduced. Temperature fluctuations are important, because less oxygen will dissolve in the environmental water at higher temperatures, and vice versa. It is not just coincidence that fish which live satisfactorily without any haemoglobin at all come from the Antarctic where at constant low temperatures the sea dissolves a relatively large volume of oxygen.

a. *Introduction*

Figure 106 shows that water dissolves only about half as much oxygen at 30°C as at 0°C. Some of the physiological distress associated with higher temperatures may therefore reflect a lack of oxygen rather than too high a temperature as such.

A rise in temperature usually induces a faster metabolic rate and hence a greater demand for oxygen, which in fish would tend to be unfulfilled by the warmer water, so the relatively slow rate of oxygen consumption of many tropical species confers an adaptive advantage (Coulter, 1967). The rotting of vegetation by microorganisms in shallow pools or on the bottoms of lakes in the summer time can reduce the oxygen concentration almost to zero, and fish from such an environment generally possess accessory breathing organs, enabling them to use atmospheric air which they gulp at the surface. *Clarias batrachus* possesses a dual system of this kind, and Jordan (1976) showed that its oxygen intake is reduced if it is kept forcibly submerged, although it still relies on aerobic metabolism. Anaerobism is possible in some species and will be considered in a moment.

The oxygen content of water is also reduced by an increase in salinity (Holliday, 1969). It is perhaps for this reason that young salmonids entering the sea from the river synthesise a haemoglobin with a higher affinity for oxygen than that used during their river existence (Volume 1, p. 176).

Some fish live in ponds the surfaces of which freeze over in the winter time, cutting off virtually all fresh supplies of oxygen for months on end, while any organic decay on the bottom completes the removal of existing sources. Incredibly, certain fish survive a winter under such conditions. Blažka (1958) found that *Carassius carassius* need oxygen at a concentration of 1·7 ml/l when their metabolism is aerobic, but that they show no signs of asphyxiation under oxygen-free conditions at low temperatures. Anoxia is not tolerated at higher temperatures, presumably because of the increase in metabolic rate. Blažka found that

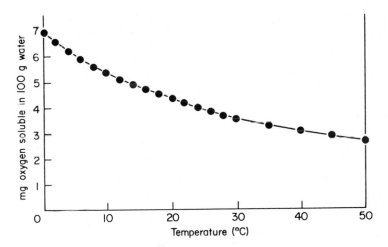

FIG. 106. The solubility of oxygen in water at different temperatures. One atmosphere pressure of pure oxygen was used to obtain these figures (air comprises only 21% of oxygen, so the corresponding figures would be lower). After Powers (1974). Reproduced with permission of the author.

this species tolerates anoxia for at least 2 months at 5°C, and during the time it does not accumulate lactic acid, excreting only carbon dioxide. It tends to lay down lipid during a winter spent under anoxic conditions. At oxygen concentrations below 2 parts per million, the respiratory quotient (see footnote on p. 115) and ammonia quotient (volume of ammonia/volume of oxygen) increase sharply in *Tilapia mossambica*, indicating increased breakdown of protein at inadequate oxygen levels (Kutty, 1972), but the high carbohydrate levels in the liver and heart of *Cyprinus carpio* are considered by Murat (1976a) and others to indicate the source of energy of this species in anoxia. In the absence of oxygen the Krebs cycle is blocked, and the final product is lactic acid or, in effective adaptation to anoxia, succinate, propionate and lipids are produced. L-alanine has also been observed, along with succinate, in the dark muscle of *Carassius carassius* at very low tensions of oxygen (Johnston, 1975c). It is probably because *Cyprinus carpio* are often presented with conditions of low available oxygen in the natural state that they retain their carbohydrate reserves tenaciously, preferring during periods of starvation to mobilise protein and leave the carbohydrate virtually intact. The role of carbohydrates in anoxia will be considered more fully later. Here we simply point out that life without oxygen is possible in certain species of fish.

Another tolerant species is *Rasbora daniconius*, which was put into a sealed jar by Mathur (1967) in the expectation that it would die. Instead it lived for 81 days at 29 to 31°C, another specimen surviving for 102 days. The oxygen concentration in the water in which the fish had just died was found to be nil, while there was 39 mg/l of carbon dioxide, the pH being 9·9, perhaps from the excretion of ammonia.

It is surprising to learn that excessive aeration of the water can kill fish. Salmonids begin to die when the water is 114% saturated with air (Nebeker and Brett, 1976), a situation which can arise in rivers under conditions of severe turbulence or (Wedemeyer, Meyer and Smith, 1976) when saturated ice-cold water warms up, for example at a hatchery. The observable symptom seen at saturation levels of 115 to 120% is severe emphysema (gas bubbles in the tissues) under the skin of the fins, in the mouth and on the head and operculum. The emphysema is worse at higher oxygen:nitrogen ratios, but the total gas saturation level must always exceed 100% before any symptoms develop (Nebeker, Bouck and Stevens, 1976). Supersaturation of the water can also result in gas bubbles forming inside the sensing chambers of the lateral line organ. The fish becomes insensitive to pressure waves and shows symptoms of disorientation (Wedemeyer, Meyer and Smith, 1976). While premature human infants are blinded by elevated tensions of oxygen, a condition known as retrolental fibroplasia, fish seem to be immune to this kind of oxygen toxicity, and their retinas function normally (Ubels, Hoffert and Fromm, 1977: *Salmo gairdneri, Carassius auratus*). Hyperoxia increases the chloride influx at the gills of *Anguilla anguilla* maintained in fresh water (Bornancin, de Renzis and Maetz, 1977).

Swimming speed has again been shown to be affected by oxygen concentration at low levels. Kutty (1968) showed that *Carassius auratus* accustomed to air-saturated water would swim at 3 lengths per second at a level of 2 parts per million of ambient oxygen, but only 1 length per second at 1 part per million. The swimming speed of *Salmo gairdneri* declined from 4 lengths per second at about 2·5 parts per million to 1 length per second at about 2 parts per million. At the same time, the concentration of blood lactate increased (Mearns, 1971: same species, also some other salmonids).

b. *Adaptation to hypoxia*

The muscle tissue of *Carassius auratus gibelio* uses less oxygen when the fish has become accustomed to reduced concentrations in the water, presumably by undertaking less physical activity, but the oxygen consumption of the gill tissue itself simultaneously increases (Krebs, 1975). The underlying mechanism has not so far been demonstrated.

The first response of fish to hypoxia is to increase their respiration rate (movements of opercula) and ventilatory stroke volume (Cech and Wohlschlag, 1973: *Mugil cephalus*). The heart rate also increases (Bamford, 1974: *Salmo gairdneri;* Cech, Rowell and Glasgow, 1977: *Pseudopleuronectes americanus*) and all of the effects follow hypoxic conditions after a delay of about 5 seconds, suggesting that the receptors respond to oxygen changes in the blood rather than directly to changes in the surrounding water (Bamford, 1974). The latter author concluded that while the existence of oxygen receptors in the pharynx has not been disproved, most of the oxygen monitoring is carried out in the brain.

Wood and Johansen (1973) noted three stages in the adaptation of *Anguilla anguilla* to conditions of low oxygen. During the first day, they increase their breathing rate[1] as already noted for other species. During the second and third days they seem unable to maintain this activity, their tolerance to hypoxia is reduced and an oxygen debt, as shown by large concentrations of lactic acid, prevails. By the seventh day the blood has acquired an increased oxygen affinity and oxygen capacity, more oxygen is delivered to the tissues and the normal acid-base status is restored.

The Root effect, in which carbon dioxide reduces the oxygen capacity of the haemoglobin, would be a disadvantage to fish kept in a confined space where the carbon dioxide content of the water builds up. Börjeson and Höglund (1976) found that there is a decline in the Root effect of the haemoglobin of *Salmo salar* adapted to raised levels of carbon dioxide.

Changes in the Bohr or Root effects of the haemoblogins seem however to be secondary factors in the adaptation of fish to low levels of oxygen. When the red blood cells of *Anguilla* species adapted to high or low oxygen concentrations are burst, the freed haemoglobins seem not to differ in oxygen affinity between the two groups. Adaptation to different oxygen concentrations does in fact occur, but it can be observed only in the intact red cells. It depends on the concentrations of nucleoside triphosphates, which strongly depress the affinity of haemoglobin

---

[1]In a complementary study, Dejours, Toulmond and Truchot (1977) have shown that hyperoxia *decreases* the speed of ventilation of a number of species.

for oxygen. Adaptation to low oxygen levels results in a marked fall in the concentrations of these compounds, allowing greater oxygen takeup by the red cells. Adenosine triphosphate behaves in this way, and its concentration within the cells directly reflects the oxygen concentration to which the fish has become habituated. Guanosine triphosphate is even more important, affecting oxygen affinity more, and having a bigger range of possible concentrations within the cell (Weber, Lykkeboe and Johansen, 1975, 1976: *Anguilla anguilla;* Torracca, Raschetti *et al.,* 1977: *Carassius auratus*). A similar effect was observed by Wood, Johansen and Weber (1975) in *Pleuronectes platessa* in which the level of red cell adenosine triphosphate increased, lowering the oxygen affinity, when the ambient oxygen was increased from low to normal. However, the level surprisingly decreased again when the oxygen concentration was increased further to abnormally high concentrations, so the relationship between adenosine triphosphate and ambient oxygen is not completely straightforward. Kaloustian and Poluhowich (1976: *Anguilla rostrata*) also found that guanosine triphosphate was more effective than adenosine triphosphate, but that the combination of the two in the presence of sodium chloride was more effective than either in isolation at the same concentration.

The way in which these phosphates operate to lower the affinity of the haemoglobin for oxygen is uncertain, but the latter authors seem to be thinking in terms of conformational change in the haemoglobin, complicated in *Anguilla rostrata* by a multiple haemoglobin system.

As already noted, the isolated haemoglobin probably shows few modifications according to the ambient oxygen concentrations, although species differences in oxygen binding capacity may mirror the oxygen levels of the habitat (Weber and de Wilde, 1975: *Pleuronectes platessa* compared with *Platichthys flesus*). Attempts to modify the proportions of different haemoglobins present in *Oncorhynchus kisutch* by exposing the fry to extreme variations in dissolved oxygen have, however, been unsuccessful (Giles and Vanstone, 1976b).

Houston (1973) concluded that the capacity of the blood for carrying oxygen is one of the less important factors which help to compensate for hypoxic conditions, ventilation and heart output playing more central roles. The conclusion is based on the finding that while some species, such as *Salvelinus fontinalis*, *Salmo gairdneri* and *Carassius auratus*, do show increases in the abundance of red blood cells, haematocrit and haemoglobin concentrations (various authors), other species show little or no change in these characteristics following acclimation to lower concentrations of oxygen. Moreover, any changes which do occur are insufficient to account for all of the variations in oxygen uptake.

Nevertheless, a number of striking changes in haematocrit have been recorded, and the phenomenon is clearly important in many fish if not in others. The similarity between the annual variation in water temperature and the haematocrit of *Catostomus* spp. was noted by Powers (1974), who concluded that the effect related to oxygen shortage

FIG. 107. The correspondence between the seasonal cycle of water temperature (●) and that of the haematocrit (○) of *Catostomus* species. After Powers (1974), who believes that the phenomenon relates to oxygen shortage at the higher temperatures. Reproduced with permission of the author.

only (see Fig. 106, p. 271) and not to temperature as such. His results are illustrated in Fig. 107, and in Fig. 108 he showed that not only did the haematocrit increase steadily with higher temperatures of acclimation, but also that the concentration of adenosine triphosphate declined, increasing further the affinity of the red cells for oxygen (p. 273).

An increased haematocrit does not necessarily mean an increased concentration of haemoglobin. Soivo, Westman and Nyholm (1974a, b) showed that asphyxia of salmonid species causes the red cells to swell (a reversible effect) and so increase the haematocrit value. In addition, however, Swift and Lloyd (1974) showed that an initial response of *Salmo gairdneri* to anoxia is to concentrate the blood. The increased haematocrit here correlates with an increased output of urine, presumably as water is removed from the plasma. Returning the fish to well-oxygenated water lowers the rate of urine output. Longer exposure to hypoxia seemed to show that the volume of blood increased again, but the higher haematocrit was maintained, suggesting to Swift and Lloyd (1974) that extra red cells had been brought into circulation from storage (probably the spleen).

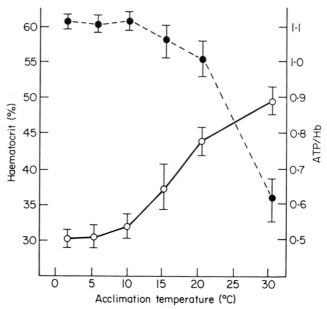

FIG. 108. The increase in haematocrit (○) and decrease in the amount of ATP in the blood cells (●) with increased temperature. After Powers (1974). Reproduced with permission of the author.

A field population of *Lagodon rhomboides* was shown by Cameron (1970b) to decrease the volume of their red cells at higher temperatures. The haematocrit therefore decreased although the blood cell count and haemoglobin concentration had increased. All three parameters increased in *Mugil cephalus* under the same conditions.

Georgiev (1972b) studied *Salmo gairdneri* kept at a trout farm at high altitude where the oxygen content of the water was only 6·6 mg/l. The effect on the fish was to raise the red cell count and also their haemoglobin concentration. Air-breathing fish behave in the same way. The air-breathing eel, *Amphipnous cuchia*, which must have periodic access to air, increases the number of red cells and the concentration of haemoglobin if it is asphyxiated by being kept submerged. The fish responds similarly if it is made to rely exclusively on its accessory breathing organ in the air (Singh, Thakur and Yadav, 1976). The African lungfish (*Protopterus* sp.) also takes steps to improve its exchange of gases during aestivation by increasing the haematocrit and the haemoglobin concentration of the blood (DeLaney, Shub and Fishman, 1976; Johansen, Lykkeboe et al., 1976). The affinity of the haemoglobin for oxygen is also increased by markedly reducing the concentration of guanosine triphosphate (Johansen, Lykkeboe et al., 1976).

In spite of some exceptional behaviour patterns, the overall response of fish to oxygen-lack is reasonably consistent.

c. Fish without haemoglobin

An antarctic "ice fish" with colourless blood containing no haemoglobin is illustrated in Volume 1, p. 178. It is possible for these remarkable fish to obtain enough oxygen for living because of the greater solubility of oxygen in the very cold water. Even so, the plasma of this particular species (*Chaenocephalus aceratus*) holds only 0·7% of oxygen by volume compared with about 6% in red-blooded species from the same locality. Erythrocytes are in fact present, but they do not contain haemoglobin (Holeton, 1975). Since the fish clearly thrive, it is of obvious interest to examine their mode of operation and response to lowered oxygen concentrations.

Holeton (1970) concluded that the irrigation of the gills of *Chaeno-cephalus aceratus* requires very little energy, being similar to that in many haemoglobinful benthic species. The fish has a low blood pressure and high cardiac output, the latter being regulated by changes in stroke volume, not heart rate (Hemmingsen, Douglas et al., 1972), in contrast to mammals. Enlarged capillaries assist blood flow and presumably facilitate gas exchange, as does the low viscosity of *Chaenocephalus* blood. The oxygen consumption of this species is low, but comparable with that of red-blooded antarctic species (Holeton, 1970). The scaleless skin does not appear to be a vital factor in compensating for the lack of haemoglobin[1], and the gill area is similar to that of other species, increasing in almost direct proportion to the body weight as the fish grows (Holeton, 1975). The heart, however, is two to three times larger than that of red-blooded fish of the same weight (Everson and Ralph, 1970; Holeton, 1976), and maintains about ten times the resting pumping rate of *Gadus morhua* (Everson and Ralph, 1970). The spleen and "many other parts of its body" are comparatively large, and it is suggested that this may be a consequence of the greatly reduced swimming musculature

---

[1]Skin does respire. Kirsche and Nonotte (1977) found that it consumes 4·5 nanomoles of oxygen per minute per square centimetre in *Anguilla anguilla*, *Salmo gairdneri* and *Tinca tinca*, but that such consumption only approximates to its own needs. It does not supply other organs.

(see Volume 1, Fig. 68), which accounts for only 9 to 15% of the body weight, compared with, for example, some 65% in salmonids (same author), 36% in *Gadus morhua* or 53% in *Clupea harengus* (Waterman, 1964). The resting oxygen uptake, given as 0·02 ml/g/h by Hemmingsen and Douglas (1970), is comparable with that of several species of red-blooded fish, but the maximum uptake possible is not known. No actual advantages of being without haemoglobin have so far come to light.

The consumption of oxygen by *Pagetopsis macropterus*, another haemoglobinless species, was found by Hemmingsen, Douglas and Grigg (1969) to range at 0°C from 0·012 to 0·022 ml/g/h, a rate which was only a quarter to a half that of *Notothenia* species which possess haemoglobin. *Pagetopsis* seems to have an efficient and well-regulated system for oxygen uptake, and it was noticed by these authors that the dorsal fin was raised and stretched (see Fig. 109) whenever the oxygen content of the water dropped markedly, suggesting function as an additional gas exchanger. The rate of oxygen consumption was little affected if the oxygen in the water was lowered from 160 to 30 mmHg. This species also seems to have a high cardiac output, and the skin appears to participate in respiration, judging by its high vascularity.

Lactic acid levels in the blood of resting *Chaenocephalus aceratus* are low (2 to 6 mg%) and are still not unduly high after anoxic stress, when they reach 24 to 36 mg%, compared with values reported in the literature for other species under stress (up to 130 mg%). The ability to tolerate high lactate concentrations would have indicated enhanced reliance on anaerobic metabolism in emergencies, but this is not indicated by these results—the fish are largely aerobic (Hemmingsen and Douglas, 1970). These authors regard the main compensation for lack of haemoglobin as a high blood volume (6·1 to 9·3%, w/w) compared with species possessing normal blood. Unlike Holeton (1976), they regard cutaneous respiration as important. Hypoxia results in increased opercular movement.

These fish do not exist "marginally" as sedentary and sluggish animals but are probably capable of an existence similar to that of other antarctic species (Hemmingsen and Douglas, 1972).

d.   *Carbohydrate metabolism*

When oxygen supplies are limited, glycogen serves as a primary energy source. Mobilisation is initiated by glycogen phosphorylase which comes between the fuel depot and the enzyme machinery required for its degradation (Hochachka, 1972). Probably because of its strategic position, the activity of glycogen phosphorylase is under tight control by hormones, ions and metabolites. It can be triggered by adrenaline, noradrenaline and glucagon, and a central role is also played by calcium (same author).

FIG. 109. *Pagetopsis macropterus*, a haemoglobinless fish from the Antarctic. Photograph kindly supplied by Dr A. L. DeVries.

Hypoxia has been found by Wittenberger (Volume 1, reference 1352) to increase the glycogen content of muscle, especially of the dark muscle, of *Salmo trutta*, presumably by promoting transport from the liver.

In *Tinca tinca* starved of oxygen, the hepatopancreas releases insulin, which favours the uptake of amino acids and glucose by the muscle (Demael-Suard, Garin *et al.*, 1974). A sharp fall in blood insulin seen after the longest period of asphyxia probably presages death. Damael-Suard (1972: *Tinca tinca*) considered the adrenaline to be an immediate but short-term response to anoxia, increasing the gluconeogenesis in the liver, but thought of the insulin, released more slowly, as the longer-lasting influence which ensures the supply of energy essential to the tissues.

Murat (1976a: *Cyprinus carpio*) concluded that it is the reduced oxygen tension resulting from higher water temperatures which causes an increase in the concentration of heart glycogen, which would therefore be available as an energy source in the event of a further reduction in oxygen.

Many invertebrate facultative anaerobes are thought to utilise simultaneously both carbohydrates and amino acids, with the production of a variety of end-products. From studies on respiratory quotient (see footnote to p. 115), Kutty (1972) concluded that two species of fish, *Carassius auratus* and *Salmo gairdneri*, also increase their protein catabolism at low oxygen concentrations. With observations such as these in mind, Driedzic and Hochachka (1975) investigated the utilisation of amino acids in the muscle of *Cyprinus carpio*, but found none of the end-products known to build up in invertebrate tissues and no mobilisation of the *free* amino acid pool. Thus, at least in this fish species, the white muscle seems to depend solely on glycogenolysis during anoxia. The same probably applies to *Salmo gairdneri, Salmo trutta, Lepomis macrochirus* and *Ictalurus nebulosus*, which have been found to produce only lactic acid during hypoxia: the report by Blažka (1958) of free fatty acid production by anoxic *Salmo trutta* may have been based on faulty interpretation of the experimental results (Burton and Spehar, 1971).

The concentration of blood glucose in *Labeo capensis* was noted by Hattingh (1976a) to rise not only in anoxia, but also when the ambient carbon dioxide concentration was increased, perhaps giving a hint of the trigger mechanism.

A reduced oxygen supply reduces the rate of feeding and slows the passage of food through the gut. The digestibility of the principal constituents of the diet is not affected but, ironically, it is the hydrolysable carbohydrates which become less easily digested under these conditions in spite of their importance in anaerobic metabolism (Shcherbina and Kazlauskene, 1974: *Cyprinus carpio*).

It is clearly important that the enzymes of the glycolytic cycle should be able to function actively under anoxic conditions, and should not be inactivated by the lactate produced. Johnston (1975b) found that the pH optimum of pyruvate kinase from *Carassius carassius* dark muscle was broad and low, and so was well adapted to perform during sustained anaerobiosis. Gesser and Poupa (1974) found that there was a strong positive correlation between the ratio of pyruvate kinase: cytochrome oxidase in the hearts of different species and the ability of this tissue to function under acute anoxia, PK/CO being a convenient estimate of the anaerobic: aerobic glycolytic capacity.

e. *Pathways other than glycolysis*

Despite the evidence of the previous section that glycolysis provides much of the anaerobic energy, there is evidence that additional pathways sometimes operate. Johnston (1975a: *Salmo gairdneri*) found hints of non-glycolytic mechanisms during anoxia, especially in the dark muscle: L-alanine and succinate were observed to accumulate as anaerobic end-products, the mechanism of their production being as yet unclear. Glycolysis did increase significantly during hypoxia, but only in the white muscle. Stores of glycogen decreased by 70 to 85% in both dark and white muscle, while the glucose concentration increased in dark muscle only. Van den Thillart, Kesbeke and van Waarde (1976) found that lactate production did not cover all of the energy needs of *Carassius auratus* completely deprived of oxygen. They found increases in the concentrations of alanine, creatin, carbon dioxide and ADP. The concentrations of ATP and creatin triphosphate decreased in anoxia, while AMP, glutamate and volatile fatty acids did not change significantly.

For a more detailed appraisal of anaerobic metabolism in the animal kingdom, the reader is referred to the review by Hochachka (1975b), who describes several possible biochemical pathways. A number of cycles operate at once, and numerous end-products (succinate, isobutyrate, isovalerate, acetate, propionate) form, succinate and propionate accumulating in the largest quantities. Proline also is an important end-product of energy metabolism under anaerobic conditions, and various transaminases convert glutamate and α-ketoglutarate to propionate and other end-products such as alanine. Facultative anaerobes usually have very low glutamate dehydrogenase activity—ammonia is undesirable as an end-product because of its toxicity (see p. 154). Hochachka (1975b) calculated that as many as 13 moles of ATP could be produced by one mole of glucose-6-phosphate when metabolism was proceeding along these various pathways. This is more than is produced by straightforward aerobic glycolysis, and shows how some organisms successfully exploit the environments in which oxygen is scarce or absent.

f. *Miscellaneous*

Lack of oxygen causes a decrease in protein synthesis as measured by the incorporation of radioactive leucine. The effect becomes measurable when the level of dissolved oxygen falls below 2·5 mg/l (Jackim and LaRoche, 1973: *Fundulus heteroclitus*).

A high level of carbon dioxide in the surrounding water leads in *Salmo gairdneri* to an increase in the concentration of blood bicarbonate and a compensatory fall in blood chloride, though curiously not in blood sodium (Lloyd and White, 1967: Fig. 110). It is probably a

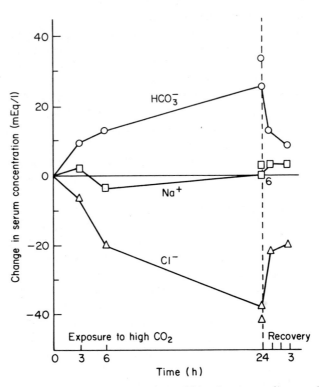

Fig. 110. The changes in the concentrations of bicarbonate, sodium and chloride in the serum of *Salmo gairdneri* exposed to high levels of dissolved carbon dioxide. After Lloyd and White (1967). Reproduced with permission of Dr R. Lloyd.

compensation of this sort which accounts for the abnormally high excretion of several ions by the same species kept in water in which the concentration of oxygen is gradually reduced (Hunn, 1969a), though unlike the pattern observed in Fig. 110, this author noted an abnormally high excretion of sodium in addition to chloride.

Figure 111 shows that a reduction in the oxygen concentration of the water in which *Mugil cephalus* swim reduces its proportion in the gas of the swim bladder.

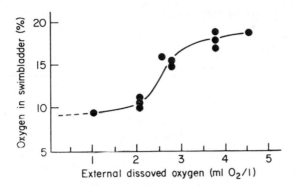

Fig. 111. Correlation of swimbladder oxygen content with the level of oxygen dissolved in the water (*Mugil cephalus*). After Moore (1970). Reproduced with permission of the author.

4. SALINITY

Both seawater and freshwater fish usually maintain their body fluids at ionic concentrations different from that of the environment, seawater fish opposing the tendency to be dehydrated by the relatively strong salt solution, and freshwater fish managing not to become waterlogged, producing some ten times the volume of urine of marine fish. The total inorganic material in the solid tissues does not differ greatly in the two types, but that in the blood is less in freshwater fish,

Marine elasmobranchs resist dehydration by carrying high concentrations of urea in their blood and other tissues. Freshwater elasmobranchs also possess higher concentrations of urea than freshwater teleosts, but less than marine elasmobranchs. Trimethylamine oxide may also serve to reduce the osmotic strain suffered in salt water, being more concentrated in marine teleosts than in those from fresh water, and most concentrated in marine elasmobranchs (Volume 1, Table 28).

Some differences are found between the lipid compositions of marine and freshwater fish, apparently resulting from differences in the diet.

Certain species survive transfer from fresh water to salt or vice versa ("euryhaline" species). There have been indications that the concentrations of *free* amino acids in the tissues follow that of the environmental salt, so may assist in preserving osmotic equilibrium. However, broadly speaking, the main way in which marine fish guard against dehydration is to drink sea water and then excrete the excess of salt afterwards. This point was made in Volume 1, and in the present volume we examine the mechanisms whereby the salts are excreted: it is a complex story.

Young salmon parr in the rivers die if they are abruptly transferred to the sea, but if they metamorphose to "smolts", they survive transfer, so metamorphosis must involve a change in the osmoregulatory mechanisms as well as a change in shape and the acquisition of a silvery colour.

A large Table in Volume 1 (Table 30) showed the ionic composition of various tissues of fish acclimated to fresh or salt water. The Table showed that sodium, potassium, magnesium, calcium and chloride tended to be more concentrated in most of the tissues when the fish were in salt water.

a. *Changes in tissue inorganic substances according to the salinity of the medium*

As regards the gross changes in the ionic composition of the serum which occur when fish which tolerate changes in salinity are transferred from fresh water to diluted or full-strength sea water, little can be added to the information surveyed in Volume 1, Table 30. The concentration of at least one ion increases in *Petromyzon* sp. (Urist and van de Putte, 1967), *Fundulus heteroclitus* (Pickford, Grant and Umminger, 1969), *Salmo gairdneri* (Rao, 1969), *Oncorhynchus tschawytscha* (Urist and van de Putte, 1967; Snodgrass and Halver, 1971), *Salvelinus alpinus* (Roberts, 1971), *Anguilla rostrata* (Poluhowich and Parks, 1972), *Anguilla anguilla* (Kirsch, 1972a), *Aphanius dispar* (Lotan, 1973) and probably many others. Thus a part of the way in which fish adapt to increased salinity is by allowing their internal salinity to rise.

This remark applies to tolerant (euryhaline) species. In fish which do not tolerate large changes in external salt concentration (stenohaline species) the internal salinity changes in an uncontrolled way on transfer and may exceed the range within which the tissues can function. For example, the fry of *Oncorhynchus kisutch* die within 36 hours after a 60% rise in body chloride (Black, 1951). *Carassius auratus* die in 30 minutes if suddenly transferred to sea water or in 2 to 3 hours in half-strength sea water, but this species can be induced to survive indefinitely in half-strength sea water if the salt concentration of the medium is raised gradually. It still does not excrete the excess salt—the plasma sodium rises to the same level as that of the environment—but its tissues have now adapted to the higher salt concentrations; in the words of Lahlou, Henderson and Sawyer (1969), who made the observation, these fish are osmoconformers rather than osmoregulators.

Fundulus parvipinnis uses a combination of adaptive procedures in order to survive in a wide range of salinities. From fresh water, through full-strength sea water—34 parts of salt per thousand (34‰)—up to 60‰ it osmoregulates, that is, it maintains its internal ionic concentrations constant by drinking salt water and excreting the excess salt. Beyond this, up to the astonishing level of 128‰ of environmental salt, the tissues become dehydrated and the plasma salt concentration rises while the fish continues to live normally (Feldmeth and Waggoner, 1972).

The mode of excretion of the salts which have diffused into the fish and been taken in with the water drunk has attracted the attention of many workers, and occupies much of this present section. Even now, a number of questions remain unresolved and the field is in a state of change.

To begin with, the fish does not simply excrete little parcels of concentrated sea-salt, but treats the different ions independently. Whether
the external ions become more concentrated or more dilute, therefore,
the change within the fish is not uniform. When *Anguilla anguilla* are
placed in a more dilute environment, the chloride concentration in
the plasma falls considerably, but the sodium, magnesium and bicarbonate remain reasonably constant (Farrell and Lutz, 1975). During
adaptation of this species to more salty water, the sodium and chloride
show an initial parallel increase, but at equilibrium the fish retains
more chloride than sodium and increases its excretion of bicarbonate
(Kirsch, 1972a). If the sea water in which *Eptatretus stoutii* are swimming
is diluted, the sodium and chloride of the blood decline in proportion to
their decrease in the medium, but the magnesium and calcium remain
at their initial concentration (McFarland and Munz, 1965). *Carassius
auratus*, a freshwater fish, will, as stated earlier, adapt to diluted sea
water, and the plasma sodium increases more than plasma chloride,
while the increase in potassium is not significant (Zadunaisky, 1972).
The same occurs in the *muscle* of freshwater *Salvelinus alpinus* put into sea
water: there is a large increase in sodium but the potassium remains
near its previous level (Roberts, 1971).

We may conclude, then, that while the total ionic content of fish
tissues tends to rise or fall in parallel with that of the environment, the
fish is selective and allows only certain of the ions to change, so that in
many species there is in fact no direct relation between the potassium,
calcium and magnesium concentrations in the blood serum and their
concentrations in the environment (Natochin and Lavrova, 1974).

The selectivity is best illustrated from the work of Pickford, Grant
and Umminger (1969), who showed that when *Fundulus heteroclitus* are
transferred from sea water to fresh water, each serum ion changes in
different proportion (Table 17). Note that in this species it is the
potassium which changes most.

As far as can be seen, the ionic composition of the serum changes more
than that of other tissues when the external ions change. Indeed,
Snodgrass and Halver (1971), who measured variations in the potassium, sodium, magnesium and calcium in *Oncorhynchus tschawytscha*,
reported a "remarkable constancy" in the composition of various
organs although the plasma cation concentration changed with each
alteration in the ionic environment. The ovary fluid of gestating *Zoarces
viviparus* also maintains a constant osmotic pressure in a variable
environment, although that of the plasma follows the external changes
(Raschack, 1969). It should however always be remembered that
behaviour tends to vary between species so that, for example, there is no

correlation between the osmotic pressure of the blood of *Sebastiscus marmoratus* and that of the (variable) surrounding salines (Yamashita, 1970a), while that of the blood of *Seriola quinqueradiata* follows that of its environment (Yamashita, 1970b).

TABLE 17

Changes in the concentrations of ions in the blood serum of *Fundulus heteroclitus* transferred from sea water to fresh water. (After Pickford, Grant and Umminger, 1969. Reproduced with permission of Professor Grace Pickford)

Ion (mM/l)	Seawater group	Freshwater group	Percent change in fresh water
Bicarbonate	13·32	11·82	—4·06
Calcium	2·29	2·04	—10·92
Chloride	145·8	126·4	—13·31
Magnesium	2·07	1·69	—18·36
Phosphate	5·34	5·14	—3·75
Potassium	4·76	3·04	—36·13
Sodium	183·0	172·3	—5·85

Some fish seem to possess ionic reserves which can be drawn upon in water low in minerals. Couillault (1967) reported a reserve of chloride in *Phoxinus phoxinus* which could be used in case of need to maintain the level in the blood. When *Fundulus kansae* are kept in water deficient in calcium, this ion is mobilised from bones and scales (Fleming, Brehe and Hanson, 1973), thus maintaining the internal environment, at any rate for a limited period. The mobilisation is inhibited by the hormone calcitonin, which may therefore prolong the life of the fish in a medium deficient in calcium (Copp, 1976).

b. *Exchange mechanisms across the gill*

The salt balance within a fish is maintained almost entirely by the gills and the kidneys. The general pattern is by now clear. In fresh water the fish loses precious minerals through the urine, since the kidney is not completely efficient (Fleming, 1974), and it must therefore replace them by taking them in through the gills (and through the intestines from foodstuffs). Since gills expose a large area to the surroundings, they passively take in surplus water which must be removed by the kidneys if the fish is not to swell up and die. In sea water, the fish loses precious tissue water passively through the gills, and makes up for it by drinking sea water, absorbing it through the intestine and then getting rid of the surplus salts through the gills and kidneys.

The gill, then, is a multipurpose organ, supplying not only the means for gas exchange, but also for the clearance of nitrogenous waste and the maintenance of acid-base and mineral balance (Maetz, 1971), the latter involving both the excretion of unwanted salts while the fish is in the sea and their acquisition while in fresh water. It is the method by which the gill excretes and absorbs ions that has attracted so much attention, but as late as 1975, Girard and Istin could still say that the mechanisms of the exchange of ions at external membranes are still poorly understood, and Maetz and Bornancin that "the biochemical characterisation of the gill is most unsatisfactory."

There has been an unusually large number of reviews of the subject within a short space of time, and the reader is recommended to consult them for a full presentation of the evidence, which is often puzzling. These are by Conte (1969: quoted as "in press" in Volume 1, and with incorrect title), Maetz (1971), Maetz (1973), Fleming (1974), Maetz (1974), Evans (1975) and Maetz and Bornancin (1975), and, together with evidence from individual recent research papers, they have all been drawn upon to make the following short account.

In the marine environment, fish drink 0·2 to 1·5% of their body weight per hour, and 70 to 80% of this water is absorbed, along with monovalent ions, the divalent ions being largely unabsorbed and passing out with the faeces. At the gill, there are large exchange fluxes for both sodium and chloride, and, according to Maetz (1971), the exchange of internal sodium with external sodium and chloride with chloride involves 25 to 75% of the internal sodium chloride per hour. However, sodium is also actively extruded by a mechanism which uses energy and which appears to involve the simultaneous absorption of an equivalent amount of potassium from the medium. The way in which the potassium in the environment stimulates sodium outflow is illustrated in Fig. 112.

Further evidence for sodium–potassium exchange comes from the work of Maetz (1973), who found that flounders kept in sea water which has been freed from potassium show a progressive increase of internal sodium. After return to normal sea water, the internal sodium declines.

The drug ouabain is a specific inhibitor of Na-K-ATPase ("transport ATPase"). Eels in sea water which contains ouabain acquire increased levels of internal sodium. There are, however, still some unsettled features of this mechanism, and Maetz and Bornancin (1975) state that definitive proof of the involvement of membrane-bound ATPase in the Na/K exchange is still lacking.

The procedure used to remove excess ingested chloride is not so clear, but Maetz and Bornancin (1975) speak of "active extrusion" linked to the Na/K exchange mechanism. Addition of potassium to the external

medium stimulates the extrusion of sodium and chloride together
(Maetz, 1973: seawater adapted *Anguilla anguilla* transferred to fresh
water).

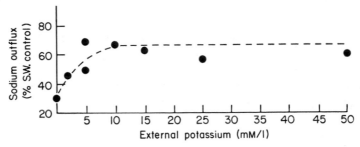

FIG. 112. The effect of external potassium ions on the relative outflow of sodium from
Dormitator maculatus. After Evans, Mallery and Kravitz (1973). Reproduced with
permission of Dr David Evans.

The excretion of sodium across the gills of seawater teleosts represents
20 to 50% of all the internal sodium per hour. This is at least ten times
the amount introduced by drinking and intestinal absorption, and presumably gives a measure of the massive inward diffusion at the gill
(Maetz, 1973).

In fresh water, this high turnover of sodium drops from 45% to only
0·2% (Motais, 1967, quoted by Maetz, 1974: *Pleuronectes flesus*). The
fish appear to acquire sodium and chloride from very dilute solutions
by exchanging them for hydrogen, ammonium and bicarbonate ions
(Maetz, 1971), that is, by linking acquisition to metabolic excretory
processes. It was Krogh (1938, quoted by Fleming, 1974) who suggested
that sodium could be exchanged for ammonium and chloride for bicarbonate, and Maetz and various colleagues (quoted by Fleming,
1974) showed that ammonium salts added to the environmental water
depress sodium uptake, and stimulate it if injected into the fish. Ker-
stetter, Kirschner and Rafuse (1970, quoted by Fleming, 1974) obtained evidence that sodium exchanges also with hydrogen ions, and
current opinion seems content to implicate both ammonium and
hydrogen ion excretion in the acquisition of sodium (Fleming, 1974).

Carbonic anhydrase is thought by Maetz (1971) to supply the
hydrogen ions, and its inhibitor, diamox, suppresses a proportion of the
sodium uptake. Adaptation of *Anguilla anguilla* to fresh- or salt water is
accompanied by changes in the distribution of isoenzymes of carbonic
anhydrase in the gills, probably reflecting changes in osmoregulatory
needs (Girard and Istin, 1975), but Mashiter and Morgan (1975)
found no difference in the total activity of the enzyme in the gills of

Platichthys flesus (=*Pleuronectes flesus*) adapted to fresh- or salt water, and so cast some doubts on the whole model.

Species differences are a constant feature of studies on fish, and Gerard and Istin (1975) concluded that the chloride/bicarbonate exchange could not occur in *Anguilla anguilla* adapted to fresh water because in this species the gills are impermeable to chloride (Motais, 1967, quoted by the same authors).

The permeability of the membranes separating the internal and external environments may also change with external salinity. Acclimation of teleosts to fresh water involves a sharp reduction in the movement of both sodium and chloride, and in *Fundulus heteroclitus*, *Tilapia* spp. and other species, a part of the reduction in sodium flow results from a change in the permeability of the fish to this ion (Evans, 1969). All freshwater species appear to be more permeable to *water* than are marine species, but the permeability of euryhaline fish varies according to species, some being more permeable in fresh water than in sea water, some less (same author). The calcium concentration of the (fresh) water exerts a powerful influence on water diffusion at the gill surface (Oduleye, 1975: *Salmo trutta*) and this ion also seems to be essential to the sodium/potassium exchange in salt water (Maetz, 1973: *Anguilla anguilla*). It appears to inhibit loss of sodium from the gill at low external salinities, so that the marine teleost *Lagodon rhomboides* can tolerate fresh water provided that calcium is present (Carrier and Evans, 1976).

Maetz (1974) warns in his review that extreme caution is necessary when evaluating the active and passive components of ion transfer and water permeability across even simple isolated epithelial membranes. The system is much more complicated when whole animals are studied, in part because stress from handling upsets water and mineral balance. He also points out that while a sodium/ammonium exchange is certainly possible in fresh water, it does not occur automatically: seawater fish excrete ammonia and sodium together, and fish in sodium-free water still excrete ammonia. Evans (1975) considers the uptake of sodium and chloride from fresh water to be secondary to the excretion of bicarbonate, hydrogen ions and ammonia, and that exchange for sodium and chloride may well occur in sea water even though sodium chloride uptake is then unwanted.

c.   *Energy and ATPase*

The excretion or acquisition of salts across a membrane against a concentration gradient requires energy. Where the ambient salinity is the same as that of the body fluids of the fish ("isotonic saline", which has been calculated as $7 \cdot 5\%_0$ in *Salmo gairdneri*—Rao, 1969—and $11 \cdot 6\%_0$ in *Tilapia nilotica*—Farmer and Beamish, 1969), the energy required is minimal, increasing both in more dilute and in more concentrated media. At a salinity of $30\%_0$, it was calculated in the latter two papers

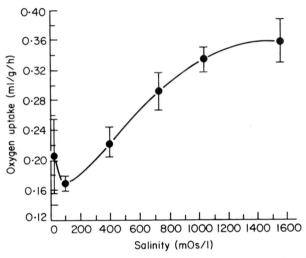

F IG. 113. The effect of salinity on the metabolic rate of *Mugil cephalus*. After Nordlie and Leffler (1975). Reproduced with permission of Dr Frank Nordlie.

that just under a third of the total energy consumed by the fish is needed for osmoregulation, perhaps an unreasonably high assessment. When the salinity of the water in which *Tilapia mossambica* were swimming was raised, it was found by Bashamohideen and Parvatheswararao (1972) that cytochrome oxidase activity and oxygen consumption both increased. The oxygen requirements at different salinities are admirably illustrated in Fig. 113, the minimum of the curve presumably marking the spot where internal and external salinities coincide.

The greater oxygen needs at higher salinities appear to be reflected in the faster heartbeat reported by various workers (reviewed by Holliday, 1969), but this is not an invariable sequel to stronger salt solutions, Helle and Holliday (unpublished, quoted by Holliday, 1969), for example, finding that the heartbeat is slowed in *Salmo salar* larvae. However, there seems no doubt that more oxygen is consumed, and Pora and Precup (1971: *Gobius melanostomus*) found that an increased salinity slowly accelerates the excretion of nitrogen, presumably another manifestation of faster metabolic rate.

Since the maintenance of a constant internal salt balance requires positive effort, severe additional stress may impair its effectiveness. Thus the concentrations of sodium and calcium in the plasma tend towards those of the environment, fresh or salt, when the fish is subjected to cold shock (Stanley and Colby, 1971: *Alosa pseudoharengus*) or physical disturbance (Lahlou, Crenesse *et al.*, 1975: *Salmo gairdneri*) and, as a corollary, *Salmo gairdneri* and *Oncorhynchus kisutch* placed in isotonic saline suffer less stress, as manifested by raised blood glucose (see p. 231), when handled by the experimenter (Wedemeyer, 1972). Anaesthesia by tricaine methane sulphonate also changes a number of aspects of the water/electrolyte balance (Madden and Houston, 1976).

TABLE 18

Reports of an increase in the Na-K-ATPase activity of the gills
of fish transferred from fresh water to salt water

Species	Reference
Anguilla anguilla	Sargent and Thomson (1974)
	Scheer and Langford (1976)
Anguilla japonica	Kamiya and Utida (1968)
Anguilla rostrata	Butler and Carmichael (1972)
	Forrest, Cohen *et al.* (1973)
Fundulus heteroclitus	Epstein, Katz and Pickford (1967)
Oncorhynchus kisutch	Zaugg and McLain (1970)
Salmo gairdneri	Pfeiler and Kirschner (1972)

Since ATP appears to be the source of energy for eliminating sodium at the gill surface, it follows that ATPase activity increases when euryhaline fish are transferred from fresh water to salt, and any time spent in adjusting at intermediate salinities (in the estuary) allows for the development of ATPase activity. The phenomenon has been observed in several species (Table 18). Its development, and its decline when saltwater fish are returned to fresh water, are shown in Fig. 114.

Some ATPase activity is stimulated by magnesium ions, and is written "Mg-ATPase". Kamiya and Utida (1968) showed that transfer of *Anguilla japonica* from fresh water to salt results in almost no change in the Mg-ATPase activity over a 30-day period, although the Na-K-ATPase activity increases more than four-fold. Sargent and Thomson (1974) have concluded that the Na-K-ATPases in the gills of freshwater- and seawater eels are indistinguishable.

In the metamorphosis of salmonid parrs to smolts, the young fish are preparing themselves physiologically for migration from the river to

the sea, and although there is no premigratory change in body electrolyte composition (Miles and Smith, 1968: *Oncorhynchus kisutch*), an
increase in gill Na-K-ATPase activity can be observed. Young *Oncorhynchus kisutch* show the increase in late March as seaward migration

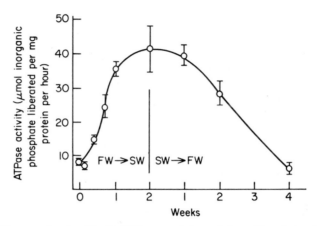

Fig. 114. Changes in the Na-K-ATPase activity of the gills of *Anguilla japonica*
following transfer from fresh water to sea water and then from sea water to freshwater.
After Utida, Kamiya and Shirai (1971). Reproduced with permission of Dr S. Utida.

begins, but the activity of the enzyme declines again if they are forced
to remain in fresh water until midsummer (Zaugg and McLain, 1970).
The effect has also been seen in smolts of *Oncorhynchus tschawytscha* and
Salmo gairdneri (Zaugg and McLain, 1972) and Zaugg and Wagner
(1973) noted that enzyme activity becomes especially marked when the
smolts of *Salmo gairdneri* begin to exhibit migratory behaviour. It has
indeed been experimentally observed that salmonids are better able to
tolerate salts after smoltification (various authors reviewed by Saunders
and Henderson, 1969a: *Salmo salar*), and several authors reviewed by
Wagner (1974) have shown that the adaptation occurs *before* the more
obvious signs of metamorphosis can be seen.

When yellow (pre-metamorphosed) *Anguilla anguilla* are transferred
from fresh water to salt, they increase both the number of chloride cells
in the gills and also the amount of Na-K-ATPase per chloride cell.
When, however, they metamorphose to the silver form, they acquire
the greater number of chloride cells while still in fresh water, though
subsequent transfer to salt water does increase the Na-K-ATPase concentration to some extent (Thomson and Sargent, 1977).

As occurs so often in fish physiology, the results of some investigations
have pointed to conclusions opposite to the foregoing—or, in the

despairing words of W. Hodgkiss, "People have been doing too many experiments!" Scheer and Langford (1976: *Anguilla anguilla*) conclude that a "substantial proportion" of total sodium extrusion does not depend on Na-K-ATPase. Kirschner (1969: *Anguilla anguilla, Platichthys flesus*) found no essential difference between the ATPase activities of fish adapted to salt or to fresh water (a finding also demonstrated in *Liza ramada* by Gallis and Bourdichon, 1976), and concluded that while an increase in enzyme activity might be concomitant with adaptation to sea water, it is not in fact essential. ATPase has been found to be more active in the gills of *Oncorhynchus nerka* migrating *up*stream by Natochin, Krayushkina *et al.* (1975), and Lasserre (1971) has found greater enzyme activity when saltwater *Crenimugil labrosus* and *Dicentrarchus labrax* are transferred to fresh water, associating the rise with increased activity in acquiring sodium and potassium from the dilute medium. Gallis and Bourdichon (1976) confirmed Lasserre's results with *Crenimugil labrosus*(=*Chelon labrosus*), the change in activity, incidentally, being seen only in the Na-K-ATPase, not in the Mg-ATPase.

It is difficult to comment yet on these findings. ATPase may well be involved in the acquisition of sodium from fresh water, thus being responsible, as pointed out by Whitelaw (1973), for the movement of sodium in both directions, and its activity may vary according to the ion level in the particular river or source of laboratory fresh water, but we must agree with Gallis and Bourdichon that the function of the enzyme in this instance is at present speculative. However, it should be borne in mind that plasma sodium rises in fish placed in salt water to a degree which varies between species (see Volume 1, p. 193), so that the activity of extrusion presumably varies inversely as the salt tolerance of their tissues.

d. *Chloride cells*

The electrolyte transfer discussed in the preceding sections takes place largely through the medium of special, characteristically shaped cells, which are abundant in the gill epithelium of marine teleosts.

They were first described by Keys and Willmer (1932, quoted by Maetz, 1974), and called chloride cells because they stain heavily with silver ions and because of their morphological similarity to the cells of the stomach which secrete hydrochloric acid (Maetz, 1974). A further reason for them to be known as chloride cells is because sodium estimations were difficult before the introduction of flame photometry, and investigators limited their studies to chloride (Potts, 1976). Chloride has indeed been shown by histochemical techniques to be present in the "pits" of chloride cells of fish adapted to sea water (Maetz, 1974), but sodium is transported as well.

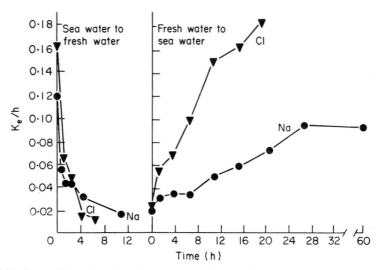

FIG. 115. Rate of loss of sodium ions from smolts of *Salmo salar* after transfer from sea water to fresh water, and from fresh water to sea water, in early May at 10°C. After Potts, Foster and Stather (1970). Reproduced with permission of Dr W. T. W. Potts.

Maetz (1971) pointed out that the switch in gill function from freshwater to seawater types on transfer to more concentrated salt solutions is far from instantaneous, because synthesis of functional sites and specialised cells is involved. Thus the rate of excretion of sodium and chloride rises slowly and steadily when *Salmo salar* smolts are transferred from fresh water to salt, but falls almost at once when they are transferred to fresh water (Potts, Foster and Stather, 1970: Fig. 115).

Figure 116 shows the actual numbers of chloride cells found in the gills of *Anguilla japonica* while adapting to salt water and then readapting to fresh water. The similarity to Fig. 114, which showed the increase and decline in ATPase activity under the same circumstances suggests a close connection between these cells and the transport enzyme. The same authors also showed that four freshwater species possess few chloride cells and little Na-K-ATPase activity, nine marine species possess both in abundance, and that transfer of *Anguilla japonica, Salmo gairdneri* and *Acanthogobius flavimanus* from fresh water to sea water causes an increase in each.

In two euryhaline teleosts, *Anguilla anguilla* and *Cichlosoma biocellatum*, adaptation to distilled water is accompanied by an *increase* in the number of chloride cells (Maetz, 1974), analogous to the increase in ATPase described in the previous section. This indicates a desperate attempt by the fish to acquire minerals, and perhaps supports such an explanation for the increase in ATPase.

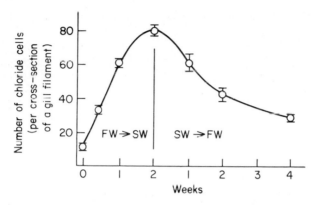

Fɪɢ. 116. Changes in the number of chloride cells in a section of gill filament when *Anguilla japonica* are transferred from fresh water to sea water and vice versa. After Utida and Hirano (1973). Reproduced with permission of the Editor of "Responses of Fish to Environmental Changes" (Dr Walter Chavin).

Chloride cells have a highly developed plasma membrane, and the dense population of mitochondria reflects their high energy turnover (Maetz and Bornancin, 1975).

Figure 117(a), (b) and (c) illustrate some of the features characteristic of these cells. The low-power views of the gills of seawater-adapted eels show the enormous numbers of chloride cells, which make up a substantial proportion of the primary filament. The electron photomicrograph shows the apical pit, large numbers of mitochondria and an extensive "smooth tubular system".

Karnaky, Ernst and Philpott (1976) studied the changes in structure brought about by increasing the salinity of the medium. Taking the Na-K-ATPase of the gills of *Cyprinodon variegatus* in 50% sea water as unity, they found it to be 1·6 in full-strength sea water and 3·9 in 200% sea water. The chloride cells in 200% sea water showed a marked hypertrophy and an increase in the already extensive system of branching tubules. This is illustrated in Fig. 118. Modifications in the ultrastructure have also been noted by Olivereau (1971). When eels are transferred from fresh water to salt, the apical pit appears in the chloride

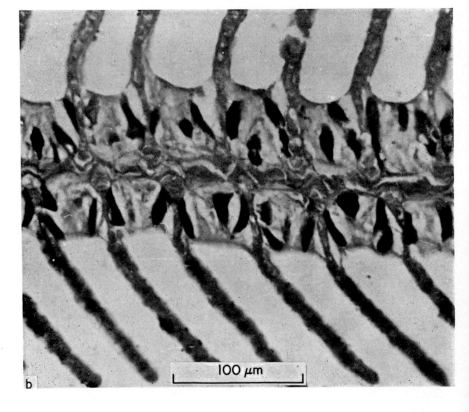

200 μm

100 μm

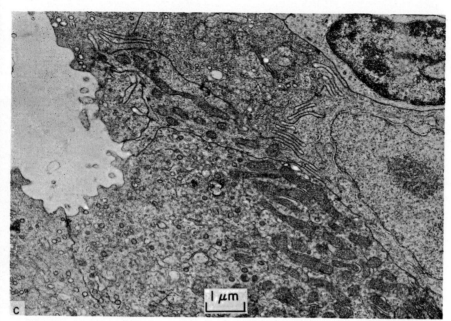

Fig. 117. (a) A low-power view of two gill filaments from seawater-adapted *Anguilla anguilla*. Stained with zinc iodide-osmium tetroxide. The chloride cells show up as black dots. This picture shows their large number and uniform distribution. (b) A portion of 117(a) at higher magnification. (c) Electron photomicrograph of one chloride cell (same species). The concave area of the outer surface is the characteristic "apical pit". Numerous mitochondria and an extensive "smooth tubular system" can be seen. The latter is also characteristic of chloride cells. Reproduced with permission of Drs S. G. George and B. J. S. Pirie. Photographs kindly supplied by Dr J. R. Sargent.

cells (Utida and Hirano, 1973: *Anguilla japonica*) and their succinic dehydrogenase activity increases 2·5 times (Sargent, Thomson and Bornancin, 1975: *Anguilla anguilla*). *Fundulus heteroclitus* and *Hemitripterus americanus* possess chloride cells not only along the gill filaments but also in the epithelium on the inside surface of the operculum. Such epithelium is exposed to rapid water flow similar to that bathing the gills, and its chloride cells possess all the features we have seen so far (Degnan, Karnaky and Zadunaisky, 1977; Karnaky, Degnan and Zadunaisky, 1977; Karnaky and Kinter, 1977).

e. *Evidence of nervous and hormonal control at the gills*

We have seen that transfer of fish to a medium of different salinity often results in a change in the number of chloride cells, but the agents

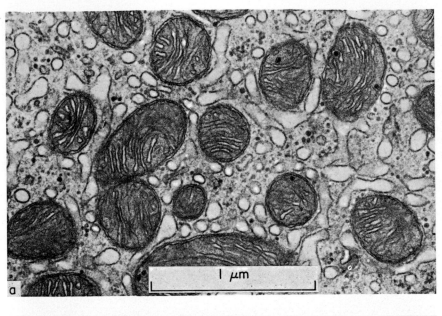

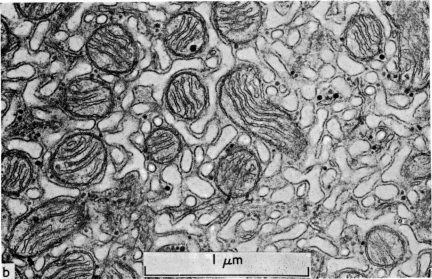

FIG. 118. Fine structure of part of a gill chloride cell from *Cyprinodon variegatus* which had become acclimated to (a) full-strength sea water, (b) double-strength sea water. The increase in salinity proliferates the tubular system. The small dense granules in both pictures are thought to be glycogen. The large "striped" bodies are mitochondria. After Karnaky, Ernst and Philpott (1976). Reproduced with permission of Dr Karl Karnaky (who kindly supplied the photographs) and the Rockefeller University Press.

effecting the change have not been mentioned. Only one report implicates direct nervous control: Pequignot and Gas (1971: *Tinca tinca*) showed that cutting the vagus nerve causes a reduction in the number of chloride cells, whether the fish have been in fresh or salted water. Otherwise the agents promoting synthesis or destruction appear to be hormones, perhaps secreted in response to a change in the mineral concentrations of the blood.

i. *Prolactin*

Numerous investigators have shown that removal of the pituitary (hypophysectomy) causes euryhaline fish to die when they are placed in fresh water, but that life can be prolonged by injecting prolactin, a pituitary hormone. In sea water the hypophysectomised fish are able to survive, but may acquire increased levels of blood sodium (Mac-Farlane and Maetz, 1974). Many papers on the subject have been reviewed by Dharmamba and Maetz (1972) and MacFarlane and Maetz (1974). The hormone is clearly important, though, according to Chidambaram, Meyer and Hasler (1972), its site and mode of action are still not fully understood. Fish which spend all of their lives in fresh water survive hypophysectomy for much longer periods (Griffith, 1974: 14 freshwater species of *Fundulus*).

Fish placed in fresh water after removal of the pituitary show extreme pallor (perhaps through loss of melanophore-stimulating hormone), sluggishness and loss of balance. Moribund fish always have very low levels of sodium and chloride in their blood, and Maetz (1974) identifies the main role of prolactin as the control of sodium leakage from the gills. During the adaptation of euryhaline fish to fresh water, the leakage may be a remnant of the active sodium extrusion characterising saltwater existence, and the role of prolactin may be related to the reduction of Na-K-ATPase activity which follows entry into low ambient salinity. Prolactin appears to be critical in the shut-down of active extrusion, either by hastening the destruction of chloride cells or the synthesis of an inhibitor of the sodium carrier, or more simply by inducing the secretion of mucus (Dharmamba and Maetz, 1972). This latter is not as unlikely as it might seem. Olivereau and Lemoine (1972) have found that hypophysectomy reduces the secretion of mucus by the *skin* of *Anguilla anguilla* and that injections of prolactin restore it, though they do not alter the secretion from the skin of intact eels (Lemoine and Olivereau, 1973). The mucus was assayed by measuring the content of N-acetyl neuraminic acid. Unfortunately, similar work on gill mucus seems to show that the pituitary is less important here than in mucus secretion by the skin (Lemoine, 1974).

The cells of the pituitary which secrete prolactin have been identified, and Nagahama, Nishioka and Bern (1973) studied them by light- and electron microscopy in *Gillichthys mirabilis* and *Platichthys stellatus*, euryhaline teleosts, after transfer from salt water to fresh. In the sea, the secretory granules are smaller and the cellular organelles are poorly developed, but within 3 hours of transfer to fresh water the prolactin cells show definite signs of activation: exocytosis of the granules and the development of rough endoplasmic reticulum.

The prolactin content of the pituitary parallels the amount of granulation in, and size of, the prolactin cells. When the euryhaline *Poecilia latipinna* is completely adapted to a given salinity, the rate of prolactin secretion, inversely proportional to the salinity, is directly proportional to the prolactin content of the pituitary. During adaptation to new salinities, however, the prolactin content and rate of secretion are temporarily independent of one another (Ball and Ingleton, 1973). This probably explains the observation that in *Mugil cephalus* adapting to fresh water there is a negative correlation between the pituitary prolactin content and the blood serum level (Sage, 1973), which seems to contradict the previous findings. One should probably distinguish between a quick loss of prolactin from the pituitary to meet an urgent osmoregulatory need and a continuing situation where synthesis keeps pace with secretion. Thus *Anguilla anguilla* at the beginning of adaptation (3 days in fresh water) contain less prolactin in the pituitary than salt-water adapted specimens (Aler, 1971), and *Oncorhynchus nerka* entering the river to spawn lose prolactin from the pituitary, but during migration the concentration in both pituitary and serum increases considerably (McKeown and van Overbeeke, 1972).

The release of prolactin from the prolactin cells may occur in response to a change in the osmotic concentration of the blood, and could also be under the control of the nervous portion of the pituitary, the hypothalamus (Ensor and Ball, 1972). These reviewers consider that prolactin affects sodium flow not only at the gill but also the kidney, the urinary bladder and possibly the skin. Not only does it prevent excessive sodium outflow in fresh water, but in some species it also appears to stimulate the active uptake of sodium.

In addition to these effects, prolactin appears to control water movement at membrane surfaces, increasing water flow through the body (same authors), although Maetz (1974) warns that the mode of action in this context needs further investigation. Ogawa (1974) quoted various authors showing that prolactin promotes water permeability at the gill, but his own results on *Anguilla japonica* and *Salmo gairdneri* showed the opposite effect, as did those of other workers on *Gasterosteus aculeatus* and

Carassius auratus. He suggested that the contradictory results might reflect differences in measuring technique. Urinary bladders in euryhaline fish of seawater origin are permeable to water while the fish are in the sea, but become much less permeable in fresh water so that large volumes of urine are voided. Prolactin appears to be involved in the change (Hirano, Johnson *et al.*, 1973). Bladders from euryhaline fish of fresh-water origin are relatively impermeable irrespective of the environmental salinity.

Calcium ions act in a similar way to prolactin, decreasing the permeability of gills to water (Ogawa, 1974: *Anguilla japonica*, *Salmo gairdneri;* Ogawa, 1975: *Anguilla japonica;* Oduleye, 1975: *Salmo trutta*). Certain concentrations of calcium in the fresh water in which hypophysectomised *Salmo trutta* are placed also prolong life (Oduleye, 1976).

Although sea-adapted *Oncorhynchus nerka* appear to maintain some prolactin in their blood (Leatherland, McKeown and John, 1974), the prolactin of the marine form of *Gasterosteus aculeatus*, if it exists, is insufficient to prevent the fish from dying when they are transferred to fresh water (Leatherland and Lam, 1969), a mortality which is reduced by prolactin injections. These fish live in the sea in late autumn and early winter, and at such time appear to be "physiologically hypophysectomised" (Lam and Leatherland, 1970) as regards prolactin secretion The effect could simply be a response to the higher sea temperatures found in the autumn: Umminger and Kenkel (1976) have shown that, at least in *Fundulus heteroclitus*, a *low* temperature stimulates prolactin release when the fish are in salt water.

In mammals, prolactin influences milk production (hence its name), regulating the transport of water, ions and other osmoactive molecules across the mammary epithelium (Bern, 1975: a review).

ii. *Cortisol and ACTH*

The other important hormone which influences the water and ion balance in fish is cortisol, which is secreted by the cortex of the adrenal body when stimulated by the pituitary hormone ACTH (adrenocorticotropic hormone). Thus destruction of the pituitary produces the symptoms of cortisol insufficiency, which can be cured either by ACTH or cortisol injections (Müller, Böke *et al.*, 1974, among others).

Johnson (1973) wrote a large review of the hormonal control of mineral balance in teleosts, and discussed the difficulties of trying to derive functional generalities. As examples, the stimulation of both inflow *and* outflow of sodium by cortisol, the ingestion of equal amounts of water by some fish whether in fresh or salt water, and the equal rates of kidney (glomerular) filtration for other fish in either medium confound attempts to generalise. However, he was prepared to admit a fairly consistent antagonism between prolactin and cortisol in sodium movement and water permeability. Prolactin is the important hormone after transfer of fish from sea water to fresh, while cortisol is more important in the salt environment. Prolactin may act primarily at the level of osmotic permeability, cortisol being most important in the "sodium pump", a term used to denote active transport as distinct from diffusion. More specifically, gill ATPase activity decreases after hypophysectomy and is restored after cortisol injections (Butler and Carmichael, 1972: *Anguilla rostrata*). Robertson (1974) has also concluded that generalisations about hormonal control are impossible if all species are to be included, pointing out that cortisol does not in fact occur in *Myxine glutinosa* or *Petromyzon marinus*.

Forrest, Cohen *et al.* (1973) found that treatment with cortisol before transfer of *Anguilla rostrata* from fresh water to salt accelerates adaptation, the maximum rate of sodium excretion being obtained in 3 to 4 days instead of 9 to 14 days. ATPase activity in the gills was found to increase in proportion to the sodium output in these experiments, and Scheer and Langford (1976) found that removal of the anterior hypophysis prevents the increased enzyme activity when *Anguilla anguilla* are transferred to salt water, a fraction of ATPase activity being stimulated by cortisol injections. They considered, however, that a substantial proportion of sodium outflow does not depend on ATPase, and found no convincing evidence that the rate of secretion of cortisol changes with acclimation to a saline medium.

The reason for the latter conclusion may have been that the rise in cortisol is in fact transitory. Hirano and Utida (1971) had already noted that when *Anguilla japonica* are transferred to sea water, the highest level of circulating cortisol is reached 2 hours after transfer, but it has returned to the level found in the freshwater eel after a further 22 hours. A considerable rise in serum cortisol has also been seen in *Carassius auratus* transferred to dilute salt solution from fresh water. A response was observed by Chavin (1973) in as little as 15 seconds after transfer, and the cortisol reached a maximum in about an hour before declining. Porthé-Nibelle and Lahlou (1974) also noticed a transitory rise in circulating cortisol in this species, noting that after 3 days the level has returned to that of control fish kept in fresh water.

A clear demonstration of the sequence of events in *Anguilla rostrata* has been given by Forrest, Mackay *et al.* (1973), and is illustrated in Fig. 119. When the freshwater specimens are transferred to the sea, plasma cortisol rises, reaches a peak on the second day and remains high for 5 to 7 days, during which time adaptive changes in sodium transport by gill (and gut) epithelium are thought to permit the elevated serum sodium level gradually to return to normal. When *Anguilla anguilla* have adapted fully to either fresh or salt water, the cortisol levels in the blood are the same, but according to Henderson, Sa'di and Hargreaves (1974) there is a higher rate of production in sea water, matched by a higher clearance rate so that the concentration is not higher.

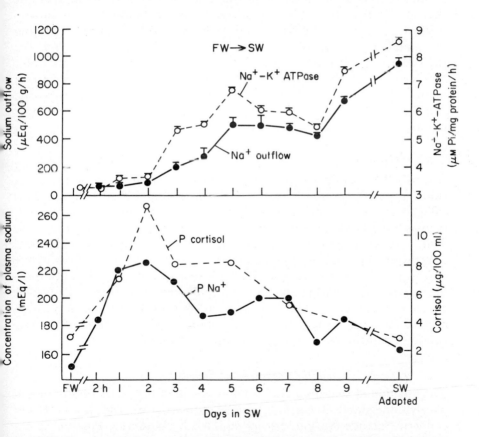

FIG. 119. Changes which occur when *Anguilla rostrata* are transferred from fresh water to sea water. The upper diagram shows a progressive increase in ATPase activity and an increase in the excretion of sodium with time spent in sea water. The lower diagram shows that plasma sodium rises initially but then falls steadily as the fish adapts. Cortisol similarly rises to a maximum 2 days after transfer and then gradually declines to its initial value. After Forrest, Mackay, Gallagher and Epstein (1973). Reproduced with permission of the authors.

In addition to accelerating sodium excretion, cortisol also increases the inflow of water across gill membranes, according to the work of Ogawa (1975), who used isolated gills of *Anguilla japonica*.

iii. *Thyroxine*

The activity of the thyroid gland usually relates to the overall metabolic activity of the fish. It is often assessed by measuring the height of the "colloid" cells which produce thyroxine.

Studies in relation to salt adjustment are not convincing as yet. The thyroid activity of *Fundulus heteroclitus* has been found greater in seawater than in fresh (McNabb and Pickford, 1970), perhaps reflecting the metabolic energy needed to secrete salt. On the other hand, the thyroid cell heights decrease in *Petromyzon marinus* placed in salt water (McKeown and Hazlett, 1975). Henderson and Chester Jones (1974) in their review conclude that the precise relation between thyroxine and osmoregulation is unclear, but they suggest that the hormone may influence the salinity preferred by the fish.

iv. *Adrenaline*

Girard (1976), using isolated heads of *Salmo gairdneri*, found sodium and chloride excretion in sea water to be inhibited by adrenaline. This catecholamine is a "stress" hormone which constricts the blood vessels, increases the blood pressure and the heart rate to enable an animal to deal with an emergency. It has already been noted (p. 291) that osmoregulation tends to break down during severe stress, and the above observation seems to indicate that it is deliberately held in abeyance, the adrenaline ensuring that all available energy is directed towards escape from the crisis. This is a different concept from the usual, which regards the outside stress as a wrecker of the normal functions of the fish, causing death in extreme cases (Volume 1, pp. 46 to 48).

v. *Hormone(s) from the Corpuscles of Stannius*

The function of the small bodies known as the Corpuscles of Stannius is poorly understood. According to their ultrastructure, they are probably endocrine glands (various authors quoted by Unsicker, Polonius *et al.*, 1977). Surgical removal is followed by an increase in calcium inflow, which causes an increase in the calcium content of the serum and of most of the internal organs (Fontaine, Delerue *et al.*, 1972: *Anguilla anguilla*). The rise in blood calcium seen in several other species after operation was reported by the same workers to be halted by injections of extracts of Corpuscles of Stannius.

Changes in the appearance of these bodies have been seen to occur in *Mugil cephalus* in response to an increased salinity of the medium. The vascularisation and the size of the nuclei increase, and the position of the nucleus within the cell is altered (Johnson, 1972, quoted by Holloway, 1974), perhaps indicating increased secretory activity in the salt water. Wendelaar Bonga, Greven and Veenhuis (1976: *Gasterosteus aculeatus*) distinguished two types of cell in the Corpuscles of Stannius. The activity of type 1 increases on transfer to salt water, being activated by calcium ions, while activity in type-2 cells is promoted in fresh water. The authors suggested that type 2 cells might produce a hormone involved in sodium or potassium control.

Variations in the histological appearance of the Corpuscles from *Morone americana* indicate a cycle of secretory activity in an anadromous coastal population. On the other hand, the structure in a land-locked population of the same species does not vary, so Holloway (1974) concludes that the activity of the Corpuscles of Stannius is probably determined by the environmental salinity rather than, for example, the sexual cycle.

Little else is known about these bodies, but they appear to have some part in regulating calcium and perhaps other ions.

The hormonal control of osmoregulation is a complex system which, because of our imperfect understanding of it and especially of the nature of species differences, appears to be full of contradictions. It is not impossible that the wide seasonal variations in, for example, the sex hormones will influence the type of result obtained with other hormones at different times of the year and will further hinder a straightforward interpretation of the results. Readers seeking fuller presentations of the evidence are referred to the large review by Henderson and Chester Jones (1972, with 1268 references) and also the reviews by Henderson and Chester Jones (1974) and Bern (1975).

f. *Excretion in the urine*

In his review, Maetz (1974) concluded that, except in mammals and some insect larvae, the kidney is unsuitable for the excretion of salt. The sodium which is excreted by the urine forms a variable fraction of the total excreted sodium, but is a negligible component at high external salinities, which is to say that the gills are the most important route for salt from the body. The volume of urine in marine teleosts is low anyway, and while it is the channel for excreting nitrogenous compounds of relatively high molecular weight, such as creatinine (p. 157), it contains little sodium or chloride (Potts, 1976).

Some salts *are* lost through the kidneys, though, and Miles (1971) showed that when *Oncorhynchus kisutch* are transferred from sea water to fresh, the proportion of salts excreted is dramatically reduced. His diagram for sodium excretion is reproduced in Fig. 120.

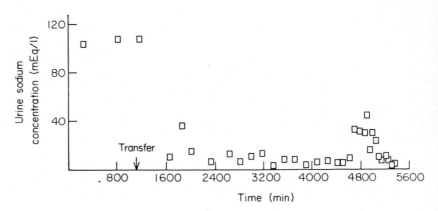

FIG. 120. The reduction in sodium excretion through the kidneys when *Oncorhynchus kisutch* are transferred from salt water to fresh at the point indicated by the arrow. After Miles (1971). Reproduced with permission of the author.

A kidney is essentially an ultrafilter, which allows water and substances of small molecular weight to ooze out of the blood but retains proteins (except in pathological conditions) and all of the blood cells. The reduced loss of ions such as sodium which is seen when a fish enters fresh water is essential for survival, and appears to be achieved by their reabsorption from the ultrafiltrate as it trickles down the kidney tubules on its way to the bladder. About half of the filtered water is reabsorbed, as is almost all of the filtered sodium (Jampol and Epstein, 1970). Active transport of this kind requires energy, and sure enough the ATPase activity in the kidneys rises when fish are transferred from salt water to fresh (Lasserre, 1971: *Crenimugil labrosus, Dicentrarchus labrax;* Gallis and Bourdichon, 1976: *Chelon=Crenimugil labrosus*). The rise is not universal: it does not occur, for example, in *Liza ramada* adapted to fresh water for 3 months (Gallis and Bourdichon, 1976), but these authors state that other euryhaline teleosts such as eels and salmon do show the change in ATPase activity on transfer, so the phenomenon is evidently widespread.

There are some indications that the hormone renin exercises influence on ion excretion. Plasma renin activity increases in response to sodium depletion in man and other mammals (Laragh and Sealey, 1973, quoted by Nishimura, Sawyer and Nigrelli, 1976), but although freshwater teleosts usually have a higher renin activity in the kidney than do marine teleosts (Mizogami *et al.*, 1968, quoted by Sokabe, Oide *et al.*, 1973), clear evidence of a relationship between sodium balance and renin activity is lacking (Nishimura, Sawyer and Nigrelli, 1976). Variations of unknown origin in both plasma and kidney renin activities, and among different teleost species, are relatively large and it is difficult to compare results from different laboratories. Sokabe, Oide *et al.* (1973) proposed that renin may regulate the glomerular filtration rate by constricting the efferent arterioles of the kidney, but their paper does not really confirm this, and they conclude that further study is needed to elucidate the role of the hormone.

The process of ion reclamation when fish are in fresh water continues in the urinary bladder. Agarwal and John (1975) presented histological evidence from several freshwater teleost species to show that the bladder is not a mere passive storage organ, but increases its surface area by extensions into the lumen which are potential sites for ingress or egress of material. The work of various authors quoted by Foster (1976) has shown that sodium uptake by the bladder wall increases during acclimation to fresh water, and Utida, Kamiya *et al.* (1974) have actually found an increase in Na-K-ATPase activity when marine *Platichthys stellatus* are transferred to fresh water, the increase also occurring when the marine fish are injected with prolactin, simulating the results of freshwater transfer. In *Kareius bicoloratus*, which does not survive transfer to fresh water, prolactin does not increase ATPase activity, and its seems likely that the differing responses of these two species reflects their respective tolerances to change.

g.   *Absorption of water by the intestine*

i.   *Introduction*

In Volume 1, p. 187, it was stated that marine teleosts maintain their water balance by drinking sea water and then excreting the ions afterwards. Maetz and Skadhauge (1968) have shown, using a radioactive tracer in the water, that the drinking rate of *Anguilla anguilla* rises proportionately to the rise in the external sodium concentration. Dall and Milward (1969) lowered the external salinity and found that the drinking rate of the marine fish *Pelates quadrilineatus* decreased but that of the amphibious *Periophthalmus vulgaris* increased, while the rates of three other species were not related to the external salinity. From the fact that the salinity of the fluid in the lumen of the gut is highly variable they concluded that water absorption is probably regulated at the gut wall rather than by the drinking rate, and that water drinking also serves to carry excretory products along the gut to the exterior.

The oesophagus and stomach both absorb water in quantities which increase after adaptation to salt conditions (Hirano and Mayer-Gostan, 1976: *Anguilla japonica*). Absorption is less than that occurring in the intestine, but these other sections of the alimentary tract clearly contribute to the water balance.

ii.   *The influence of cortisol*

Studies on *Anguilla japonica* have shown that the flow of water across the wall of the isolated intestine is greater when the eels were previously adapted to sea water than to fresh water (Hirano, Kamiya *et al.*, 1967). The effect is not seen if the pituitary has been removed, and Hirano and Utida (1968, 1971) showed that in fact the increased rate of water absorption by the gut of the seawater eel is induced by the short-term increase in cortisol, which circulates after transfer of the fish to salt water. Intestinal absorption of water can be increased in freshwater eels by injections of either ACTH or cortisol. The maximum cortisol level was attained in these experiments 1 to 2 hours after injection, and the intestinal water absorption was maximal after 24 hours; the delay suggests that cortisol acts indirectly. Pituitary hormones other than ACTH are without effect.

iii.   *Alkaline phosphatase*

Utida and Isono (1967) showed that when *Anguilla japonica* are adapted to sea water, the activity of the alkaline phosphatase of the intestine increases. The same effect has been seen in *Salmo gairdneri* (Utida, 1967, quoted by Utida and Isono, 1967). Sodium chloride at concentrations like those in the sea enhances the activity of alkaline phosphatase in model systems, but it enhances the enzyme isolated from seawater species more than that from freshwater species (same authors). In the intestine of salt-adapted *Anguilla japonica* it can be three times as active as in the freshwater fish, but there do not appear to be differences in the properties of the purified enzymes prepared from the two groups of eels (Oide, 1970). Water movement is reduced if inhibitors of alkaline phosphatase (EDTA, borate or cysteine) are added to the mucosal surface (Oide, 1973a), and the increase in alkaline phosphatase seen on seawater adaptation does not occur after hypophysectomy (Oide, 1973b).

The exact physiological role of this enzyme has not so far been explained, but its activity in gill tissue also increases when fish are adapted to sea water (Cvancara and Conte, 1970: *Oncorhynchus nerka*), so it is clearly an important mediator of salt and water transport. The delay in intestinal water absorption after cortisol injections may be the time needed for alkaline phosphatase synthesis, but direct evidence is lacking on this point.

h.   *Osmoregulation in elasmobranchs*

i.   *The rectal gland*

Salt excretion at the gills has been discussed up to now in bony fish (teleosts). In elasmobranchs, the ancient class of fish with cartilagenous skeletons, the ATPase activity at the gills is low, but is high in a structure peculiar to them, the rectal gland. Sodium enters the bodies of marine elasmobranchs via the gills and the food, being excreted through the rectal gland and to a lesser extent through the kidney, there being little or no active transport at the gills. Fänge and Fugelli (1963) considered that the rectal gland of the shark *Selache maxima* secretes sodium and chloride, but since that of *Chimaera monstrosa* has a less developed structure, its secretory capacity is probably limited. The tissues of this species seem to have a high tolerance to salt to compensate for the lack of osmoregulation: the concentration in the plasma is unusually high. The volume of sodium chloride solution secreted by the rectal gland of *Squalus acanthias* is enough to account for most of its salt-excretory requirements, the concentration of salt in the excretory fluid being about twice that of the plasma and greater, in fact, than that of sea water (Burger and Hess, 1960). The output of fluid appears to be controlled by a steroid, 1α-hydroxycorticosterone, from the adrenals (Holt and Idler, 1975). Ligation of the rectal gland results in an increase of blood sodium and chloride (Haywood, 1975: *Poroderma africanum*).

The only comparable organ found in a bony fish appears to be the "dendritic organ", a small external organ posterior to the anus of certain catfish. Ligation in *Cnidoglanis macrocephalus* has been shown to cause an increase in plasma sodium when the fish are in salt water (Kowarsky, 1973). Catfish of the genus *Plotosus* also possess this organ, and Umminger, Pucke and Levy (1976: *Plotosus lineatus*) found in it numerous chloride cells, while none appeared to be present in the gills.

ii.   *Retention of nitrogenous compounds*

The chief means whereby marine elasmobranchs guard against being dehydrated by the sea water is the retention of relatively high concentrations of nitrogenous compounds in their blood. In Volume 1,

p. 144, are quoted a few values of blood urea, the highest concentration being 1326 mg% of urea nitrogen, while over 1% of trimethylamine oxide is also found (Volume 1, Table 28).

In teleosts, urea is filtered out of the blood by the kidneys and voided but in elasmobranchs it is reabsorbed later by the kidney tubules, the reabsorption being linked in some way to the reabsorption of an equivalent amount of sodium (Schmidt-Nielsen, 1973: *Squalus acanthias*). Urea and trimethylamine oxide in the plasma of elasmobranchs diminish if the environmental salinity decreases[1] (Goldstein, Oppelt and Maren, 1968: *Negaprion brevirostris*, this species clearing the compounds from its body at a greater rate rather than synthesising less of them). On the other hand, *Raja erinacea* transferred from full-strength to diluted sea water decrease their rate of synthesis of urea as well as increasing the clearance at the kidneys (Goldstein and Forster, 1971b), and *Scyliorhinus canicula* and *S. stellaris* in diluted sea water appear actually to synthesise *more* urea (Watts and Watts, 1966, quoted by Watts and Watts, 1974), so that as usual one is limited to speaking of the behaviour of individual species only. De Vlaming and Sage (1973: *Dasyatis sabina*) found that variations in the environmental salinity induce greater changes in plasma "sodium chloride" than in plasma urea, unless the environment has become very dilute.

The rate of excretion of urea at the gills of *Raja erinacea* and *Raja radiata* mirrors exactly the concentration in the plasma, so changes in the external salinity do not alter the urea permeability. Again, some other elasmobranch species do show differences in permeability to urea (Payan, Goldstein and Forster, 1973).

To provide urea in elasmobranchs for osmoregulatory purposes requires continuous catabolism of proteins. Thus if the fish are starved they may be unable to maintain the optimal level of blood urea (Haywood, 1973b: *Poroderma africanum*).

We have seen how the study of urea production and retention is assisted by experiments in which the environmental water is diluted to varying extents. Unusual interest attaches to the behaviour of the few species of completely freshwater elasmobranchs. *Potamotrygon motoro* and *P. circularis* are elasmobranchs from the Amazon river system which never enter salt water, and they are found to have only 2 to 3 mg of urea nitrogen per ml of serum, perivisceral fluid, cranial fluid and pericardial fluid, and never more than 5 mg (Thorson, Cowan and Watson, 1967). It was shown by Thorson (1970) that these two species

---

[1]Curiously, urea excretion at the gills of *Anguilla anguilla* is also increased when the fish are in fresh water as distinct from the sea (Masoni and Payan, 1974). This seems to indicate osmotic assistance from urea in at least one teleost.

fail to increase their urea concentration appreciably even when exposed to a saline environment which is gradually strengthened to a concentration approaching that of sea water (the upper saline limit for *P. motoro* is 20·6‰: Griffith, Pang *et al.*, 1973). In such hypertonic external media, the osmolarity of the body fluids does rise to some extent, but it is largely as a result of an increase in sodium chloride (also calcium and magnesium—Griffith, Pang *et al.* 1973) rather than by urea accumulation. The activities of the enzymes of the ornithine–urea cycle in the liver are one half to one twentieth of those found in marine rays, and the rate of incorporation of radioactive bicarbonate into urea by liver slices is also markedly reduced (Goldstein and Forster, 1971a). In addition to their low level of urea synthesis, these fish have a relatively poor ability to reabsorb the urea through their kidney tubules. Their levels of urea are far lower than those of the marine elasmobranchs *Pristis* sp. and *Carcharinus leucas* which are able to live in fresh water for long periods (same authors).

When *Carcharinus leucas* enter rivers, the concentrations of potassium, calcium, bicarbonate, phosphate and protein in the serum change little from when the fish were in the sea, but the magnesium drops to only 37%, sodium and chloride to 80% and urea to about 47% of their previous levels. The mean haematocrit values are much the same in both environments, indicating that the blood is not being diluted on entry of the fish into fresh water (Thorson, Cowan and Watson, 1973).

j. *Nitrogenous compounds in teleosts*

In Volume 1 (pp. 187–188) it was shown that the specific gravity of the blood correlates with the salinity of the environment, the amount of circulating protein being an important factor. The quantities of *free* amino acids seem to assist the osmoregulation of invertebrates, but the small number of studies on fish were equivocal, since the quantity in salmon was greater when the fish were in fresh water, not salt water as expected. It was commented that work on additional species was urgently required, and as we shall see in a moment, this has now been done.

Recent studies on total circulating protein are not very clear. *Tilapia zillii*, a euryhaline species, shows an increase in the level of total serum protein with increases in external salinity, though alpha and beta globulins decrease (Farghaly, Ezzat and Shabana, 1973). However, *Tinca tinca* and *Scorpaena porcus* show decreased protein concentrations (Cordier and Barnoud, quoted by Farghaly, Ezzat and Shabana, 1973). The important point may be that *Tilapia zillii* can adjust to different salinities while the latter two species cannot. In any case "protein" is too miscellaneous a collection of substances to study in this context, because the osmotic pressures of the different components vary.

The osmotic pressure of the serum of *Seriola quinqueradiata* changes according to that of the environment, and Yamashita (1970b) found that the proportions of certain components (separated by electrophoresis) also change with the salinity.

The hagfish (*Myxine glutinosa*) appears not to osmoregulate, and Table 26 in Volume 1 shows that the concentrations of the different ions in the serum resemble those in the sea water in most respects. Cholette, Gagnon and Germain (1970) adapted *Myxine* to various concentrations of sea water, and found that the serum is always in osmotic equilibrium. As the concentration of the environment increases, the water content of the tissues decreases and these authors concluded that, while the content of *free* amino acids in the blood is low under all conditions studied, they play an active role in intracellular osmotic regulation.

It looks now as though the behaviour of *free* amino acids in *Salmo salar* (Volume 1, reference 249) is atypical. Their increase when the fish enter fresh water probably just reflects the fact that the gonads are growing and, together with starvation, causing the body proteins to be broken down. Any osmotic consequences of the increased presence of the *free* amino acids are probably coincidental. This conclusion is based on the considerable number of more recent reports which relate an increase in *free* amino acids in other species to an increase in external salinity (and vice versa: Boyd, Cha *et al.*, 1977: *Raja erinacea, Dasyatis sabina*), and so suggest that they play a role in preserving the osmotic balance of the fish. With only one exception, the reports speak with one voice, and are most conveniently summed up in a table (Table 19).

Some of the authors noted the individual amino acids concerned, a proportion of which vary in response to external salinity, while others do not. Alanine, glutamic acid, glycine and proline are almost always reported to change, but taurine changes with salinity in some species only (*Agonus cataphractus, Pleuronectes flesus, Crenimugil labrosus*) and not in others (*Anguilla anguilla, Fundulus diaphanus*)—see Table 19 for references.

It seems reasonably certain that *free* amino acids really are a factor in the osmoregulation of teleosts. There is only one dissenting voice— Pickford, Grant and Umminger (1969) reported a *decrease* in the total amino acid content of the serum of *Fundulus heteroclitus* when the fish were transferred to sea water from fresh. In Table 19 there is only one reference showing an increase in the *free* amino acids of serum, and that is in the non-osmoregulating *Myxine glutinosa*, so we must suspend judgement until further species have been examined.

Hashimoto and Okaichi (1958b) showed that the trimethylamine oxide (TMAO) in *Anguilla japonica* was exogenous in origin and dropped to zero if the fish were fed a diet freed from it. In the context of the present section, they observed that the concentrations within the fish were not affected by the salinity of the water. In elasmobranchs, however, this compound does seem to have an osmoregulatory role, its concentration being much higher than in marine teleosts (Volume 1, Table 28). Forster and Goldstein (1976) have now shown that in *Raja erinacea* transferred from full-strength to 50% sea water the concentration is almost halved.

TABLE 19

Reports linking the concentrations of *free* amino acids in tissues to the external concentration of salt

Species	Tissue	Reference
Acipenser güldenstadti	Brain	Somkina (1975)
Agonus cataphractus	Muscle	Colley, Fox and Huggins (1974)
Anguilla anguilla		Colley and Huggins (1970)
		Huggins and Colley (1971)
Crenimugil labrosus		Lasserre and Gilles (1971)
Dasyatis americana	Erythrocytes, Muscle	Forster and Goldstein (1976)
Fundulus diaphanus	Tissues in general	Ahokas and Sorg (1977)
Myxine glutinosa	Serum	Cholette and Gagnon (1973)
Paralichthys lethostigmus	Muscle	Lasserre and Gilles (1971)
Platichthys flesus	Erythrocytes	Fugelli and Zachariassen (1976)
		Zachariassen (1972)
Raja erinacea	Erythrocytes, Muscle	Forster and Goldstein (1976)
Saltwater fish in general	Brain	Somkina and Krichevskaya (1968)
	Muscle	Cuong and Vinogradova (1968)
Tilapia mossambica	Muscle, gill, liver, Heart, kidney	Venkatachari (1974)

k.   *Extracellular space and tissue hydration*

While the water contents of the muscle of *Fundulus heteroclitus* adapted to fresh and salt water are virtually identical (78% and 78·7%), published data by a number of workers suggest that there is an appreciable degree of tissue dehydration when *Anguilla anguilla* adapt to salt water (Pickford, Grant and Umminger, 1969). Changes in overall hydration of a tissue seem to represent, at least partly, changes in the volume of extracellular fluid.

"Extracellular space" is a quantity that can be measured in a number of ways, each of which gives a different answer, so the investigator has to decide for himself which method most nearly represents his own concept. Substances possessing relatively large molecules can be

injected, and are assumed not to penetrate into the cells. Their subsequent dilution within the body gives a measure of the free inter-
connecting fluid, but does not include fluids separated from the blood or
lymph systems such as cerebro-spinal fluid or endolymph (otolith fluid).
Inulin is a substance favoured for this purpose. Again, one may assume
that all of the chloride or the sodium is external to the cells, and measure
their concentration in, say, muscle and compare it with the concentration in the blood plasma. One's answer includes fluid circulating in the
T-system (illustrated in Volume 1, Fig. 12) as well as the spaces between
muscle cells.

Unfortunately a fraction of both sodium and chloride does seem to
exist within the cells (Lutz, 1972a), so the figures for "sodium space"
and "chloride space" are numbers only, without very much physiological significance. However, there is no reason why one should not
study them for purposes of comparison, in this case during transfer of
fish to waters of different salinities.

A table quoting results from different authors is presented by Lutz
(1972a). This gives values for chloride space of different fish species
ranging from 6·4 in *Salmo trutta* to 20·2 in *Carassius auratus* (grams of
extracellular fluid per 100 grams tissue water)—a considerable spread.
This author also showed that the extracellular space of *Perca fluviatilis*
muscle was 7·79 from inulin injections, 7·82 from chloride determinations and 11·78 from sodium determinations. The spread of answers
between methods applied to other organs was greater and ranged in the
gut, for example, from 30·6 by inulin injection to 62·2 from sodium
values. Gras, Perrier *et al.* (1969: *Salmo gairdneri*) found that the value
obtained by inulin increased significantly under the influence of
adrenaline, so stress also may vitiate the results.

When *Raja erinacea* and *Dasyatis americana* were transferred by Forster
and Goldstein (1976) from full-strength sea water to 50% sea water,
there was a 70% increase in the chloride space of the muscle tissue,
which presumably means a swelling in the diluted medium. The
complementary result has been reported by Kirsch (1972a), who found
that the transfer of *Anguilla anguilla* from fresh water to salt results in a
10% decrease in the chloride space. However, the sodium space *increases*
in the same species transferred in the same way (Mayer and Nibelle,
1969). One might guess that the penetration of tissues with sodium ions
on transfer of a euryhaline species into salt water might well interfere
with determinations of extracellular space based on sodium. Plasma
sodium would be significantly higher than when the fish were in fresh
water, and Meyer and Nibelle (1969) suggested that adaptation of the
eel to sea water may well be accompanied by increases in salt within the

cells. Kirsch (1972a) stated that sodium space and chloride space are not the same. Lutz's values (1972a) bear this out, and we must leave the subject there. If the assessment of the situation appears to be superficial, it is probably one result of using an indirect method of measurement.

l. *Blood*

Hydration or concentration of the plasma can be monitored by measuring the volume of blood cells on centrifuging whole blood ("haematocrit"). The haematocrit values for young (18-month-old) *Oncorhynchus keta* are 36·7% to 47·1% respectively in fresh and salt water, that is, the fish adapt to salt water with difficulty and the blood becomes concentrated through loss of water. Older fish (25 months) adapt readily and the haematocrit does not change between the two media (Kashiwagi and Sato, 1968).

The ionic composition of the red blood cells alters with the ambient salinity, particularly chloride, which is in passive equilibrium between plasma and cells (Munroe and Poluhowich, 1974: *Anguilla rostrata*). Poluhowich (1972) showed that the haemoglobin of *Anguilla rostrata* is polymorphic, consisting of two major and perhaps one or more minor components. The major components exhibit opposing oxygenation behaviour in response to changes in the ionic environment in such a way that the combination maintains a constant overall oxygen affinity. The requisite amount of oxygen is therefore delivered to the tissues in the face of changing ambient salinities—at least in this species. Kaloustian and Poluhowich (1976: same species) believe that differences in the ionic concentrations within the red cells stimulate the synthesis or destruction of ATP and GTP, thus further adjusting the oxygen affinity of the blood (see pp. 273–274).

m.   *Osmoregulation during development*

The gradual achievement of osmotic independence by the foetuses of viviparous species as they develop has already been discussed on p. 20, and the acquisition of euryhalinity as salmonids metamorphose from parrs to smolts on p. 23. The fact that these fish need to metamorphose at all is a curious one, especially as their eggs and larvae are purely freshwater forms. Indeed, the rate of hatching of *Oncorhynchus nerka* eggs decreases if the water becomes more saline, and almost all of the early fry ("alevins") die in any salinity more concentrated than that of river water (Kashiwagi and Sato, 1969).

n. *Miscellaneous differences between marine and freshwater fish*

Up to now, virtually all of this description of the responses of fish to changes in salinity has, by definition, related to fish which can move between the two media without harm. However, stenohaline fish from salt water differ in some general respects from stenohaline, purely freshwater species, not usually as a result of varying salinity as such, but through differences in the diets in the two environments and a few exotic causes such as differences in the gut microflora. These are now collected in a fairly random way, along with some additional miscellaneous differences between single species which migrate between the two media.

i. *Lipids*

We have seen from Volume 1 (pp. 145–146) that while the two groups of fish probably do not differ in their mechanisms for the deposition, synthesis and interconversion of fatty acids, there are more C18 unsaturated fatty acids in freshwater fish and less C20 and C22 groups. Otherwise the average unsaturation (number of double bonds) is of the same order and the general proportions of fatty acid mixtures are the same. Both groups seem able to synthesise polyunsaturated fatty acids from non-fatty precursors. In general, the fatty acid composition of the fish reflects the marine or freshwater habitat, but individual species can modify the pattern of ingested lipids to some extent.

Similar findings apply to the fatty acids of the phospholipids. The phosphatidyl choline, phosphatidyl ethanolamine and phosphatidyl serine of *Oncorhynchus nerka* muscle and liver contain more 18:2 and 18:3 fatty acids when the fish are in fresh water than in the sea. 18:2 (linoleic acid) is more abundant in relation to 18:3 (linolenic acid) in the freshwater stage of the fish compared with the marine form. On the other hand, the fatty acid composition of the phospholipids of the brain remains "fairly" constant and does not follow a transfer of habitat. Probably the membrane phospholipids of the brain cells are required to be of constant composition in order to function properly (Akulin, 1969; Akulin, Chebotareva and Kreps, 1969; Kreps, Chebotarёva and Akulin, 1969).

The phosphatidyl choline and phosphatidyl ethanolamine of the gill are enriched in fatty acid 22:6 when *Anguilla anguilla* enter the sea, a fact associated by Meister, Zwinglestein and Jouanneteau (1973) with the increase in ATPase activity of the gill membrane.

The average unsaturation of the lipids of wild *Oncorhynchus keta* appears not to differ between the two environments, but if the freshwater form is artificially introduced into salt water there are decreases in polyunsaturated fatty acids (Saddler, Koski and Cardwell, 1972).

ii. *Carotenoids*

In general, tunaxanthin is characteristic of marine fish and lutein of fish from fresh water (Matsuno, Higashi and Akita, 1973). Matsuno, Nagata and Chiba (1975) reared *Mugil cephalus* in each of the two environments and found the major carotenoids of the skin of the marine group to be zeaxanthin and diatoxanthin, while those of the freshwater group were lutein and zeaxanthin. The departure of the experimental conditions from the natural, especially as regards diet, is not clear but zeaxanthin, not lutein, has also been shown as the characteristic carotenoid of *Hypomesus transpacificus* (=*H. olidus*) from fresh water (Matsuno, Katsuyama *et al.*, 1974), so the general relationship is not universal. Probably the dietary preferences of different species play an important part in their colouration.

iii. *Enzymes*

Acclimation of a freshwater fish, *Heteropneustes fossilis*, to dilute saline solutions has been shown by Subramanyam (1974) to cause an increase in succinic dehydrogenase activity in the liver, an increase possibly related to a general increase in metabolic rate caused by the osmotic stress. Bailey, Fishman and Mulhern (1969) found a six-fold increase in the mutarotase activity of freshwater fish kidney compared with that of saltwater fish, and concluded that the enzyme has some relation to ion reclamation in fresh water. Lactic dehydrogenase also differs in the distribution of its activity among tissues of freshwater- and saltwater species (Kurogi, 1969).

The enzyme activity of glucuronide conjugation is weak in fish, but Smith (1964, quoted by Nagayama, Yamada and Tauti, 1968) noticed that it is stronger in marine than in freshwater forms. Nagayama, Yamada and Tauti (1968: *Salmo gairdneri*, also two species of *Tilapia*) investigated two enzymes responsible for glucuronide conjugation, uridine diphosphate glucose dehydrogenase and UDP glucuronyl transferase, and found no evidence for induction when the fish are adapted to salt water—in fact the activity of the former enzyme (in the liver) decreases.

iv. *Other phenomena*

Chernyshov, Yakubov *et al.* (1972) observed that euryhaline fish tend to have greater reserves of antioxidant in the lipids of the liver than are possessed by freshwater, stenohaline fish. According to these authors, the euryhaline fish also possess a mechanism for transferring these substances from the liver to the gill when the external salinity changes.[1] The physiological significance of this is not clear, but it could be related to the observation of Shenoy and James (1972) that, after death, the carcases of *Tilapia mossambica* have a shorter "life" on cold storage at −18°C if the fish had been caught in brackish water than in fresh water—lipid oxidation plays, as we shall see on p. 368, a considerable part in the flavour deterioration of frozen fish. On the other hand, spoilage in melting ice, which is also more rapid in *Tilapia* from brackish water (same authors), relates mostly to bacterial multiplication after the death of the fish, and it has been shown by Yoshimizu, Kimura and Sakai (1976a: *Oncorhynchus masou*) that the intestinal microflora are quite different if the salmon have been reared in fresh water as distinct from salt. It is not impossible that the bacterial species responsible for spoilage also differ.

In Volume 1 (p. 154) it was shown that the average number of vertebrae in the backbone of a fish varies according to the temperature of the environment which was current at a certain developmental stage of the larva. Salinity on the other hand does not influence the number of vertebrae (Fahy and O'Hara, 1977). Little seems to be known of the effects of temperature on ionic regulation itself, but according to Houston (1973), who has reviewed the subject, recent studies display an increasing awareness of the potential importance of this factor.

We have seen (p. 311) that elasmobranchs which live permanently in fresh water do not increase the concentration of urea in their tissues if the external salinity is increased, that is, by inhabiting fresh water for a long time they have lost the power to osmoregulate. In contrast, *Petromyzon marinus* which have been landlocked in the Great Lakes ever since the Wisconsin glacial ice receded do still retain some osmoregulatory ability, although they have not needed it for some thousands of years (Mathers and Beamish, 1974). Maybe the freshwater elasmobranchs have always lived in fresh water: the issue is not yet settled.

Euryhaline fish can survive transfer to salt water after an adaptation period in which the external salinity is raised gradually. Basulto (1976) has shown that tolerance to sea water is also increased when the parr of *Salmo salar* are fed on a diet enriched with salts, the ambient salinity remaining the same.

5. TEMPERATURE

In Volume 1 (p. 209 onwards) the range of temperatures over which fish survive was shown to be large, though no single species survives over the whole range. A rise in

---

[1]Ubiquinone has also been observed to be transferred to the gill on change of salinity (Sato, Sato and Koizumi, 1972: *Oncorhynchus keta*).

temperature causes increased rates of growth, both in eggs and fish, and of digestion of food. Depletion in the absence of food is enhanced at higher temperatures because of the increased metabolic rate, and blood lactate is cleared more quickly after exercise.

On the other hand, compensatory mechanisms appear to exist so that the metabolic rates of fish from warm water and from cold water are often not greatly different. Muscle from fish adapted to lower temperatures contains more mitochondria, and a number of enzymes have been shown to become more active at lower temperatures. In some but not all species the increased metabolic rate at lower temperatures seems to be influenced by greater activity in the thyroid gland.

The contractile proteins actin and myosin and the connective tissue protein collagen are more thermally stable in warm-water fish, and the lipids found in tissue membranes become more unsaturated at lower temperatures, perhaps to maintain their flexibility.

Considerable interest attaches to the way in which fish from very cold habitats avoid being frozen. Work reviewed in Volume 1 showed some rather irregular fluctuations in the inorganic ions of the plasma which occur as a response to lowered temperatures, especially a rise in chloride, which could reduce the susceptibility of the fish to freeze. Also the blood glucose can rise dramatically in *Fundulus* sp., with a presumed similar effect. It is only in the present volume that a clearer picture emerges and other compounds which really seem to be specific "anti-freezes" are revealed. Fish which live on the bottoms of cold fjords, out of contact with ice, are often merely supercooled and go rigid and die if they are touched with ice. Shallow-water fish from the same region however possess plasma with a lower freezing point, so the fish are protected in the case of accidental contact.

The present account reviews many new papers but introduces no radical rethinking of the subject. The field is not fundamentally different from that outlined in small print above, although the new interest by students of the environment in "heat pollution", the effect of wasted heat from power stations and factories on animal and plant populations, has meant almost a plethora of support for research projects.

a. *Physiological phenomena directly related to temperature*

A number of characteristics of fish are influenced by temperature in the same way as are simple chemical reactions. The rate at which the stomach empties increases with increased temperature (Shrable, Tiemeier and Deyoe, 1969: *Ictalurus punctatus*), but in the case of cod (*Gadus morhua*) there is a fairly low upper limit: the rate of emptying is not increased above about 15°C, and at 21°C the fish will not feed anyway (Tyler, 1970). The response of blood sugar concentration to the influence of adrenaline, glucagon and insulin occurs more rapidly at higher temperatures and returns to normal sooner (Murat and Parent, 1975: *Cyprinus carpio*).

In the case of basal respiration (at rest), the rate varies in the classical manner with the temperature of the environment, but when the fish are active the rates do not run parallel to the basal rates, depending to some extent on the range of temperature tolerated by the species involved (degree of eurythermy). The oxygen concentration of the environment is also important, since up to a point the level of respiration follows it (Charlon, 1969: fish in general).

At 34°C, the rate of incorporation of radioactive tyrosine into brain protein, a measure of protein synthesis, has been shown by Lajtha and Sershen (1975: *Carassius auratus*) to be 20 times that at 10°C. Urine flow increases steadily with temperature from 2 to 18°C, with a 2·2-fold increase for every 10°C rise (Mackay and Beatty, 1968a: *Catostomus commersonii*) and endogenous nitrogen excretion increases over the temperature range of 15·6 to 32·2°C (Savitz, 1969: *Lepomis macrochirus*), though in this species there is no change between 7·2 and 15·6°C, perhaps indicating some adaptation at the lowest temperatures. In *Dicentrarchus labrax*, the rates of excretion of ammonia and urea rise steadily with increase in temperature within the investigated range of 12 to 24°C (Guerin-Ancey, 1976a). Water and electrolytes are excreted at greater rates at 26 than at 4°C (Malvin, Carlson *et al.*, 1970: *Petromyzon marinus*).

The rate of secretion of mixed gases into the swim bladder of *Lepomis macrochirus* appears to be independent of temperature, but the proportion of oxygen increases at higher temperatures (McNabb and Mecham, 1971). In *Pimephales promelas*, on the other hand, the rate of change of volume is greater at higher temperatures (Gee, 1977).

Greater activity and more rapid metabolism at higher temperatures seems to be indicated by the greater concentrations of glycolytic intermediates (glucose and fructose phosphates) found in the muscle of *Carassius auratus* within 3 hours of exposure to higher temperatures (Freed, 1971).

Increased metabolic rates can lead to increased rates of growth and a shorter life. *Gadus morhua* from the North Sea mature in about 3 years, grow relatively rapidly and have died off at about 8 years of age, while cod from cold arctic waters mature at about 11 years and many live for more than 20 years. However, if fish adaptively modify their metabolism to temperature instead of merely following it, the reverse can happen, and Liu and Walford (1970) found not only increased longevity at lower temperatures but also increased growth (*Cynolebias* spp.). Accelerated mortality at higher temperatures probably therefore occurs only in those fish which do not adapt. We shall have much more to say about adaptation later.

Higher temperatures can lead not only to more rapid body growth, but also to the rate at which the diameters of the scales increase. The number of days required to form a ridge on the scale of *Carassius auratus* has been found to be only 5 days at 27·5°C compared with 20 days at 12·5°C (Ouchi, 1969).

b. *Raised body temperature*

Since raising the body temperature can evidently increase the inter-change of metabolites, certain very active fish would benefit by main-taining their body temperature above that of their surroundings, and several species achieve a considerable measure of temperature contol. The fact was mentioned briefly in Volume 1, p. 209, as was the heat exchanger used for the purpose. This takes the form of a network of fine blood vessels in the surface musculature (not the gills as stated in Volume 1) and has been described in detail by Stevens, Lam and Kendall (1974). The major fraction of metabolic heat (70 to 90%) is lost through the fins and body wall of fish not possessing this system, the remainder being lost through the gills, where 80 to 90% of the heat of the circulating blood is lost. Any heat not lost at the gills owes its retention to the transfer between afferent and efferent arteries within the gill bar (Stevens and Sutterlin, 1976: *Hemitripterus americanus*). It is possible that some fish attempt to reduce heat loss at the gills in an emergency; below —1·85°C the gills of several species of *Trematomus* become progressively paler as circulation is reduced and blood is withdrawn from the periphery. This could be in order to reduce heat loss from the visceral core, and enhanced activity of the pectoral fins at the same time may generate some heat (Morris, 1970), though Smith (1970) states that the death-throes and convulsion of *Notothenia neglecta* do not raise the body temperature.

Hartree and Hill (1921, quoted by Carey and Teal, 1969a) found that the power available from vertebrate muscle increases about 3-fold with each ten-degree rise in temperature, and C. S. Wardle (in press) has shown that in *Gadus morhua* an increase in temperature raises the possible "burst speed" (maximum acceleration), while a decrease lowers it. A raised temperature would therefore benefit this species, and work by Greer-Walker (1968) has indicated that cod do indeed maintain a temperature above that of their surroundings, which rises markedly during activity. The temperature of *Makaira mitsukurii* was thought by Morrow and Mauro (1950) usually to be close to that of the environ-ment, but like that of cod to rise above it during violent activity. In the light of these observations it is perhaps surprising that some very active fish do not in fact retain heat. For example, the body temperatures of

Salmo salar and *Salmo trutta* after violent exercise are never more than
1·3°C above the temperature of the surrounding water in spite of their
vigour (Lyman, 1968). Perhaps their metabolism adapts to lower
temperatures so that they have no need to keep warm.

Apart from the isolated observation on *Gadus morhua* reported above,
fish which maintain a raised body temperature are either sharks (*Isurus
oxyrhynchus, Lamna nasus*: Carey and Teal, 1969a; *Carcharhinus limbatus*:
Carey, Teal and Kleijn, 1972) or tunas (*Thunnus thynnus*: Carey and
Teal, 1969b; Carey, Teal *et al.*, 1971). The latter authors reported that
while *Thunnus albacares* and *Katsuwonus pelamis* keep at a fixed temperature difference above the environment, *Thunnus thynnus* can thermoregulate, keeping a constant deep body temperature during marked
changes in the temperature of the surroundings. The "constant temperature" may vary by as much as 5°C between different fish from the same
school (Carey and Lawson, 1973). The countercurrent heat exchanger
in the blood supply also keeps the temperature of the eye and the brain
of *Thunnus thynnus* above that of the surroundings (Linthicum and
Carey, 1972).

The tuna *Thunnus obesus* and the shark *Carcharhinus obscurus* on the
other hand appear not to control their body temperatures (Carey and
Lawson, 1973).

c.　*Temperature preferences, optima and lethal extremes*

While some fish thermoregulate, most exercise some degree of selection
and if possible swim away from water of unfavourable temperature.
The preferred temperatures of a large number of species, with their
upper and lower avoidance temperatures, have been tabulated by
Coutant (1977). The highest temperature selected by any fish appears to
be 40°C, preferred by *Cyprinodon macularius*, while antarctic species
prefer very low temperatures: authors quoted by Andriashev (1970)
found, from swimming activity, that the optimal temperature for
Trematomus borchgrevinki is —1·9 to —1·7°C. Activity declines at —0·8°C
and ceases at +2°C, while the fish die at about +5°C.

The preferred temperature is presumably that at which the fish
functions best physiologically (Umminger and Gist, 1973), so it is
perhaps not surprising that *Carassius auratus* are less stressed by handling
when they are at 32°C, which is near their preferred temperature range
of 24 to 30°C (review: Coutant, 1977). Their serum electrolytes are
least affected by mechanical stress when they are maintained at about
20°C (Umminger and Gist, 1971).

The upper limit at which a fish will survive indefinitely can be extended upwards by acclimation[1], and the lethal temperature is related to the acclimation just before the test rather than to the temperature of the long-term prior habitat (Horoszewics, 1973: 14 species of freshwater fish). Acclimation has its limits, and for each species there is a temperature above which no possibility of survival exists—for example 27°C for *Salmo gairdneri* (Charlon, Barbier and Bonnet, 1970). The preferred temperature, as distinct from the lethal temperature, also varies according to acclimation, and therefore varies seasonally with that of the environment (Cherry, Dickson and Cairns, 1975: many species).

We have seen how fish are less stressed by extraneous factors if they are at their temperature optima. As a corollary, the upper lethal temperature can be extended upwards by minimising effort or stress from other sources. Thus, *Fundulus* species tolerate higher temperatures in an isosmotic medium[2] (Garside and Jordan, 1968) and *Carassius auratus* have been induced to tolerate higher temperatures by rich oxygenation of the water (Weatherley, 1970, 1973), in the latter case to a temperature fractionally above 40°C. For some reason, the upper lethal temperature is also raised by long prior exposure to daylight (Weatherley, 1973: *Carassius auratus;* Terpin, Spotila and Koons, 1976: *Rhinichthys atratulus*).

Returning to voluntary preference in fish, it is interesting to note that the power of the fish to detect a lethal high temperature becomes dulled after prior acclimation to low temperatures (several authors reviewed by Beitinger and Magnuson, 1976). Fish acclimated in this way and then placed in a temperature gradient may foolishly explore water hotter than their critical thermal maximum and die. Beitinger and Magnuson (1976) themselves found the same phenomenon in *Lepomis macrochirus*.

It is probably some part of the brain which detects (or should detect) the high temperature, and which governs subsequent temperature selection whether or not the fish has become acclimated. Crawshaw and Hammel (1974) found that *Ictalurus nebulosus* selected a temperature of 26°C when given a free choice, but that if the rostal brain stem alone were warmed by implanting thermodes regulated by circulating water, the fish chose cooler and cooler environments as its brain was progressively warmed. Müller (1977) exposed the heads and the tails of

---

[1]Once a resistance to higher temperatures has been acquired, it is lost relatively slowly after the fish are transferred to a cooler environment (Allen and Strawn, 1971).

[2]The upper lethal temperature is lowered in this species by as much as 6°C if the fish are in completely fresh water or in full sea water, as distinct from the optimum diluted sea water (Garside and Jordon, 1968), presumably through the extra effort required for osmoregulating.

Carassius auratus and *Salvelinus fontinalis* simultaneously to different temperatures until they were acclimated, finding that the subsequent temperature selection corresponded with the acclimation of the head.

Salvelinus alpinus, the arctic char, leaves the ocean in the autumn and chooses to spend the winter in fresh water (Andrews and Lear, 1956, quoted by DeVries, 1974). This choice avoids any chance of the fish becoming frozen—the temperature of liquid fresh water can never fall below the freezing point of the fish, while that of sea water can. We shall see in a later section (p. 346) that some fish avoid freezing by synthesising certain "antifreeze" compounds which circulate in their blood. Here we see the avoidance response apparently being used for the same purpose.

A fascinating development in the study of temperature preference has been the discovery that fish may be able to cure themselves of disease by seeking a higher environmental temperature. Covert and Reynolds (1977) found that their *Carassius auratus* specimens preferred a temperature of 27·9°C when given a choice, but when injected with live bacteria (*Aeromonas hydrophila*) they preferred 32·7°C. None of the fish which had found the higher temperature and stayed there died, but there was considerable mortality among those forcibly kept at lower temperatures.

Little is really known of the "weakest link in the chain", the vital process which first breaks down at high temperatures, causing the death of the fish, although some workers believe that the central nervous system is the first to be seriously affected. Roberts (1973) pointed out that the death of a fish occurs at temperatures lower than are lethal to any individual constituent cell, but the coordinating part of the fish which is apparently so vulnerable is unknown.

Protein synthesis has been found to be destroyed or damaged by high temperatures. Jackim and LaRoche (1973) found that as *Fundulus heteroclitus* were gradually warmed, the incorporation of radioactive leucine into muscle protein increased up to a critical point around 26°C, beyond which it decreased sharply.

A sex difference has been observed. Female *Gambusia affinis* are more heat tolerant than males, but no difference between gravid and non-gravid females is apparent (Johnson, 1976).

There is a temperature at which fish grow maximally, which probably differs from that optimal in other ways. It strikes a balance between efficient absorption of food in the gut and higher energy consumption at higher temperatures, as compared with inefficient absorption and lower energy demands at lower temperatures (Atherton and Aitkin, 1970: *Salmo gairdneri*). The optimum growth temperature also depends on the dietary intake, being for example 15°C in *Oncorhynchus nerka* on a high ration but shifting to progressively lower temperatures as the intake is more restricted (Brett, Shelbourne and Shoop, 1969).

Since temperature optima for one species depend on the physiological facet being considered, they vary also according to the stage of the life cycle. McCormick, Jones and Hokanson (1977) found that the maximum percentage of hatching of *Catostomus commersonii* occurred at a temperature of 15°C, but the young fish put on maximum weight at 27°C. This species spawns in the spring time in shallow water where temperatures are rather low, but grows most rapidly later in the summer, so the feeling of these authors is that the fish do best at the prevailing seasonal temperature. *Catostomus commersonii* move into warmer waters as they grow, but avoid 31°C or above.

d.   *Metabolic adjustments*

   i.   *Oxygen uptake at different temperatures*

Sudden transfer of fish to water at higher temperatures constitutes exposure to shock, and the oxygen consumption rises. Gradual increase of temperature may encourage more vigorous swimming and so greater oxygen consumption, but the fish may alter the activity of its enzymes or the pathways of metabolism so that its respiration is almost the same at the different temperatures. Similarly, a temperature decrease may reduce the oxygen consumption or have little effect. Trusevich (1974) noted a sharp reduction in the swimming activity when *Trachurus mediterraneus ponticus* were cooled by only 4 degrees, and Muravskaya and Belokopytin (1975) found that the oxygen consumption of *Spicara smaris* was lower at 13°C than at 20°C, with the difference more marked in the resting than the swimming fish.

Adaptive changes can be seen from the work of Peterson and Anderson (1969), who found that the spontaneous activity of *Salmo salar* can be separated into two phases. A transient phase occurs during the actual period of temperature change, and is characterised by a peak of activity which correlates with the rate, rather than the amount, of temperature change. This is followed by a stable phase, which, measured either by oxygen consumption or activity, starts after about 2 weeks regardless of the direction of the temperature change. These fish adjust their metabolism to minimise the influence of whatever final temperature is attained: at the same test temperatures, the oxygen consumpton of fish previously acclimated to 6°C is always *higher* than that of those acclimated at 18°C. Fish acclimated at 6°C are also the more active at an intermediate test temperature. The enhanced physical activity may have been stimulated by an increased output of thyroid hormone observed at low temperatures by workers reviewed by McNabb and Pickford (1970) and later by Leatherland, Cho and Slinger (1977: *Salmo gairdneri*). Meuwis and Heuts (1957, quoted by Crawshaw, 1977) found that the respiratory frequency of *Cyprinus carpio* doubled when the temperature increased from 32 to 36°C, but that after 48 hours it was only 15% above the original level.

The oxygen consumption of the gills of *Carassius auratus* was found by Ekberg (1958) to be higher at a given temperature in 10°C-acclimated fish than in those adapted to 30°C, but brain or liver homogenates showed no statistical difference. Increased oxygen consumption has also been noted in cold-adapted *Opsanus tau* (Haschemeyer, 1973). *Blennius pholis* seem to show a partial adaptation, since their resting oxygen consumption at 25°C is only 1·4 times higher than in fish kept at 10°C (Wallace, 1973).

So far, the story has appeared reasonably clear. However, Wilson, Somero and Prosser (1974) point out that metabolic compensation is highly complex and cannot be understood adequately or strictly quantified by observing the changes in oxygen consumption. Complete adaptation involves both changes in pathways which modify the oxygen requirements and changes in the organism in response to differences in ambient oxygen supply (often more plentiful at lower temperatures), as well as any direct responses that there may be to the temperature as such.

We are on even more uncertain ground when we attempt to compare different species which happen to live at widely differing temperatures. Wohlschlag (1964) studied five stenothermal species which normally live at a constant —1·9°C, and concluded that the log of the oxygen consumption per log of the body weight tends to be higher than in more temperate species. Similarly, Gordon (1972a) found that shallow-water fish from cool average temperatures possess muscle which, when minced and supplied with metabolites, consumes more oxygen than that from fish from warmer waters. However, Holeton (1974) has called the concept into question. Almost all of the arctic marine fish which he examined showed rates of oxygen uptake which were well below levels considered to be "cold-adapted". Also, for some 48 hours after capture and handling, there was a steady decline in oxygen uptake before fairly consistent values were attained. The decline was attributed primarily to recovery from fright and oxygen debt and to the emptying of the gut. Holeton pointed out that the concept of cold adaptation of arctic fish, widely accepted at that time, was based on data from just two studies, suggesting that artefacts could arise from the methods which had been used, and that a much more critical approach would be necessary in future.

Thus the natural sequel to a raised temperature is greater activity and oxygen consumption, a lowered temperature depressing both, but internal adjustments may occur in the fish to minimise the changes. Fish species living permanently in very cold waters may or may not adapt to maintain an active metabolism—further studies are needed.

Even if a fish requires more oxygen at higher temperatures, there is no guarantee that it will get it: oxygen is less soluble in warmer water so the ambient concentration tends to fall (Fig. 106, p. 271). Several species of fish have been shown to adapt to the situation by increasing the number of red cells in circulation, and so the concentration of haemoglobin in their blood, when the water temperature rises (*Salvelinus fontinalis*: Houston and DeWilde, 1969; *Mugil cephalus, Lagodon rhomboides*: Cameron, 1970b; *Tilapia zillii*: Farghaly, Ezzat and Shabana, 1973; *Salmo gairdneri, Carassius auratus*: Houston and Cyr, 1974; *Cyprinus carpio*: Grigo, 1975; *Heterodontus francisci*: Neale, Honn and Chavin, 1977). The oxygen affinity of the blood has been shown to vary directly with the water temperature, and indeed to vary seasonally (Grigg, 1969: *Ictalurus nebulosus*, though not in *Salmo gairdneri*: Weber, Wood and Lomholt, 1976). The affinity of haemolysates has also been shown to increase in fish kept at higher temperatures (Vaccaro, Raschetti *et al.,* 1975: *Carassius auratus*), the increase being ascribed to a cofactor which acts allosterically on the haemoglobin molecule. The nature of the cofactor is not known, but seems unlikely to have been GTP or ATP (p. 274) because of the dilution caused during haemolysis. It is thought to alter the Bohr effect (p. 123) in an adaptive way.

As noted above, *Carassius auratus* increase their haemoglobin concentration and haematocrit at higher temperatures, but they (and *Salmo gairdneri*: Weber, Wood and Lomholt, 1976) also synthesise an additional form of haemoglobin which perhaps enhances the oxygen-carrying capacity of the blood. Houston and Cyr (1974) found that two haemoglobin components can be detected by electrophoresis in the blood of *Carassius auratus* held at 2°C, but that those acclimated at 20 or 35°C exhibit three. Multiple haemoglobins do not, however, necessarily indicate the ability of one species to live at widely differing temperatures. Grigg (1974) points out that *Trematomus bernacchi* and *T. borchgrevinki*, which live under very stable thermal conditions in the Antarctic, have more than one component of haemoglobin present. Rigorous analysis of the heterogeneity of haemoglobin in species from warm and cold waters also show no significant difference (same author).

TABLE 20

Enzymes shown to be more active when assayed in tissues of cold-adapted fish than from warm-adapted fish of the same species

Enzyme	Temperatures studied (°C)	Species	Tissue	Reference
Acetyl cholinesterase	10, 29	Rhodeus amarus	Brain	Hauss (1975)
ATP-ase (Mg-activated)	1, 26	Carassius auratus	Muscle	Johnston, Davison and Goldspink (1975)
Aldolase	5, 25	Cyprinus carpio	Gill	Haschemeyer (1973)
	14, 22	Idus idus	Gill, Liver, muscle	Jankowsky (1968b)
Cytochrome oxidase	seasonal	Anguilla anguilla	Dark muscle	Malessa (1969)
	10, 30	Carassius auratus	Brain, gill, Muscle, liver	Caldwell (1969)
	—	Idus idus	Muscle	F. R. Wilson (1973)
	14, 22			Jankowsky (1968b)
	5, 12, 18	Salmo gairdneri		Milanesi and Bird (1972)
Glucose-6-phosphatase	−1·5, 4, 11	Fundulus grandis	Liver	Benziger and Umminger (1971)
Glucose-6-phosphate dehydrogenase	—	Limanda aspera	Muscle	Behrisch (1972)
		Mugil cephalus	Liver	Hochachka and Clayton-Hochachka (1973)
	5, 10, 15	Salvelinus fontinalis		Yamauchi, Stegeman and Goldberg (1975)

Enzyme	Temperatures	Species	Tissue	Reference
Hexose-6-phosphate dehydrogenase	5, 10, 15			
Isocitrate dehydrogenase	10, 20	*Idus idus*	Muscle	Passia (1973)
Lactic dehydrogenase	15, 38	*Cyprinus carpio*	Serum	Grigo (1975)
	10, 29	*Rhodeus amarus*	Bain	Hauss (1975)
Malic dehydrogenase	14, 22	*Idus idus*	Gill, liver, muscle	Janowsky (1968b)
NADH-cytochrome-C reductase	10, 30	*Carassius auratus*	Gill	Caldwell (1969)
	7, 27	*Salmo gairdneri*	Gill, liver	Hazel and Schuster (1976)
(Oxidation of acetate and palmitate)	5, 18		Muscle	Dean (1969)
Pepsin	5, 12	*Salvelinus fontinalis*	Gastric mucosa	Owen and Wiggs (1971)
6-phosphogluconate dehydrogenase	5, 25	*Cyprinus carpio*	Gill	Haschemeyer (1973)
	—	*Limanda aspera*	Muscle	Behrisch (1972)
	5, 10, 15	*Salvelinus fontinalis*	Liver	Yamauchi, Stegeman and Goldberg (1975)
Pyrophosphatase	0, 22	*Misgurnus fossilis*	Liver	Mester, Scripcariu and Niculescu (1973)
Succinate-cytochrome-C reductase	10, 30	*Carassius auratus*	Gill	Caldwell (1969)
	7, 27	*Salmo gairdneri*	Gill, liver	Hazel and Schuster (1976)
Succinic dehydrogenase	5, 25	*Carassius auratus*	Muscle	Hazel (1972)
Tryptophan pyrrolase	—	*Salmo gairdneri*		Dean (1973)

ii. *Enzymes and metabolic pathways*

When we examine metabolic adaptation to temperature in more detail, it becomes clear that the activity of many enzymes increases when the fish have adapted to lower temperatures, allowing normal or almost normal metabolism to continue.

Not every enzyme becomes more active at low temperatures. The specific activity of glucose-6-phosphatase in the livers of *Carassius auratus* and *Ictalurus nebulosus* does not change with adaptation to different temperatures, though it does in *Fundulus grandis* as we shall see in Table 20 (Benziger and Umminger, 1971). Choline acetyl transferase, the enzyme which synthesises acetyl choline, is more active in the brain of *Carassius auratus* acclimated to higher temperatures, according to the work of Hebb, Morris and Smith (1969), the reverse of previous findings, and brain cholinesterase increases with elevated summer temperatures, declining in winter, in *Roccus americanus* (Edwards, 1971). Mester, Scripcariu and Niculescu (1973), who studied the isozyme patterns of malate dehydrogenase and succinic dehydrogenase of *Misgurnus fossilis* concluded that there was no thermal compensation, at least as regards glycolysis. In the muscle of *Cyprinus carpio*, lactic dehydrogenase and glutamate-oxaloacetate transaminase activities are lower after adaptation to 15°C, compared with 38°C (Grigo, 1975).

However, a considerable number of enzymes are on record as more active at *lower* temperatures, that is, the fish compensate. These are listed in Table 20. Interspecies comparisons, for example that glyceraldehyde-3-phosphate dehydrogenase from the muscle of the antarctic fish *Dissostichus mawsoni* shows greater activity at 0°C than the same enzyme from the rabbit (Greene and Feeney, 1970), are as usual of lesser value in the present context.

The large numbers of enzymes, species and organs shown in Table 20 testify to the widespread nature of enzymic adaptation to low temperatures. When we come to the actual mechanism of adaptation, however, we find that there are several alternatives, depending on the enzyme or the species in question; readers wishing to go into more detailed aspects of the subject are referred to the excellent reviews by Fry and Hochachka (1970) and Hazel and Prosser (1974) and the paper by Smith (1973).

One possibility is simply to increase the concentration of the enzyme present. Evidence for this seems to be negative from the work of Feeney and Osuga (1971), and Fry and Hochachka (1970) considered that "from a functional point of view the selective or functional advantage of producing increased amounts of inefficient or inactive enzymes is not entirely evident". Nevertheless it remains a possibility. Wodtke (1974: *Anguilla anguilla*) found that acclimation to cold increases the quantity of mitochondria in the liver and dark muscle, and so presumably that of the mitochondrial enzymes. The ultrastructure of the mitochondria was also observed by Jankowsky (1968a: same species) to change, the cristae being more tightly packed, resulting, it was concluded, in increased oxidative capacity. Jankowsky also found that the mitochondrial count increased in the muscle of *Idus idus* adapted to cold.

Umminger (1974) suggested that an increase in the concentration of the substrate might also be a mechanism operative under cold conditions, pointing to the high levels of sugar found in the blood of polar fish.

However, the principal way in which fish adapt their metabolism to low temperatures is by modifying the enzymes themselves. Temperature has been demonstrated to influence the interactions of enzymes with substrates, inhibitors and allosteric effectors, as well as promoting conformational changes and altering the effectiveness of alternative metabolic pathways when they compete for a common substrate (Hazel and Prosser, 1974). These reviewers also state that physiological acclimation probably involves feedback to the genetic material of the fish and subsequently to the protein synthetic system, producing for example at low temperatures those isozymes which were virtually absent from the warm-acclimated fish. Many enzymes from cold-blooded animals are also characterised by a direct relationship between the assay temperature and their Michaelis constant (Km), such that, as the temperature is reduced, less substrate is required to saturate the enzyme.

The modification of enzymic activity under a new temperature regime can take up to 4 weeks. The transition is not always a smooth progression, but may show several short-term oscillations (Sidell, Wilson *et al.*, 1973). The curious fluctuations in cytochrome oxidase activity as *Carassius auratus* are adapted to a colder temperature are shown in Fig. 121(a) and to a warmer temperature in Fig. 121(b) (same authors); it is almost as though the fish "resist" metabolic change. Sidell (1977: *Lepomis cyanellus*) has shown that cytochrome-c also increases in the muscle at lower temperatures of acclimation.

The penalty paid for the change in the enzyme conformation which ensures the maintenance of catalytic activity at lower temperatures is a greater instability of the enzyme molecule (Smith, 1973). An example is myosin in its function as ATPase. There is a clear direct relationship between its stability, as measured by the rate of decline in its ATPase activity at a fixed temperature, and the environmental temperature at which the fish species usually lives (Johnston and Goldspink, 1975), the fish from the coldest water having the most unstable myosin. Species adapted to tropical environments seem to require enzymes with a more rigid molecular structure to confer thermal stability. The correlations between thermal stability and the environmental temperature of teleosts

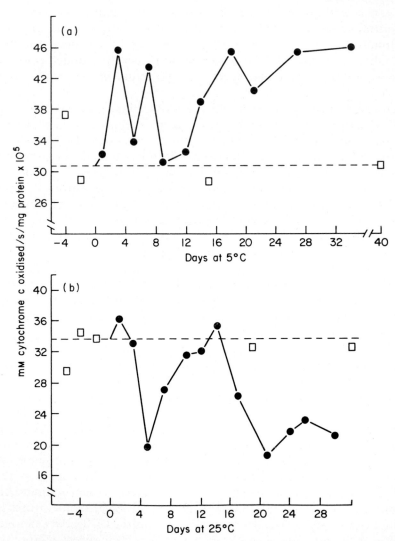

FIG. 121. (a) Cytochrome oxidase activity of homogenised muscle from *Carassius auratus* transferred from 15 to 5°C (●). Controls remaining at 15°C are shown by the broken line and square symbol in both diagrams. (b) *Carassius auratus* transferred from 15 to 25°C (●). After Sidell, Wilson *et al.* (1973). Reproduced with permission of Dr C. Ladd Prosser and Springer-Verlag.

are somewhat less marked in some of the mitochondrial enzymes (same authors). The structural rigidity of the pyruvate kinase of the muscle of low-temperature fish, again as measured by heat inactivation, has also been shown to correlate positively with the adaptation temperature (Low and Somero, 1976).

A low activation energy implies that a larger proportion of the enzyme molecules would be in an activated state at a given temperature than that of molecules with high activation energy. Greene and Feeney (1970) observed that glyceraldehyde-3-phosphate dehydrogenase from the muscle of the antarctic fish *Dissostichus mawsoni* has low activation energy, as has the glucose-6-phosphate dehydrogenase and 6-phospho-gluconate dehydrogenase from the muscle of *Limanda aspera* under winter conditions (Behrisch, 1972), the succinic dehydrogenase of the muscle of antarctic fish *Trematomus bernacchii* (Somero, Giese and Wohlschlag, 1968), the Mg-ATPase of the muscle of *Carassius auratus* at 1°C compared with 26°C (Johnston, Davison and Goldspink, 1975) and the pyruvate kinase of low-temperature fish (Low and Somero, 1976).

An increased affinity of enzymes for their substrates, as expressed by a low Michaelis constant, has been observed in some enzymes of fish at low temperatures: lactic dehydrogenase and pyruvate kinase (Hochachka and Somero, 1968; Somero and Hochachka, 1968, both quoted by Feeney and Osuga, 1971), lactic dehydrogenase (Behrisch, 1972), and glucose-6-phosphate dehydrogenase (Hochachka and Clayton-Hochachka, 1973). The behaviour of NADP-isocitrate dehydrogenase from liver appears to be somewhat complex, its affinity for the substrate being maximal at the temperature at which the fish (*Salmo gairdneri*) was previously acclimated (Moon and Hochachka, 1971b).

Isoenzyme ("isozyme") formation at different temperatures has been studied by a number of workers who have separated them by electro-phoresis, the interest lying in the fact that some isozymes function better than others at low temperatures. Thus the maintenance of enzyme heterogeneity might increase the adaptability of fish, such as salmonids, which are customarily exposed to fluctuating thermal regimes (Moon and Hochachka, 1971a; Moon, 1975). The idea is that the presence of more than one variant broadens the tolerance limits or optimal func-tioning range of a biochemical reaction, but Somero and Soulé (1974) do not agree. They studied enzymes in fish from habitats which vary in temperature by as much as 20°C during the year, or as little as a few tenths of one degree (Antarctica), and found that by no criteria did the enzymes of the fish from thermally variable habitats display higher levels of polymorphism than those from stable environmental tempera-tures. Rather, the results tended to suggest that populations which have existed for the longest time, in evolutionary terms, in stable environments may possess greater numbers of isozymes, which are advantageous to the fish although allelic diversity accumulates very slowly in natural populations.

On the other hand, there is plenty of evidence that where "warm" and "cold" variants of an enzyme exist together, their proportions can change according to the current environmental temperature. Diversity in a number of enzymes of *Salmo gairdneri* was observed by Somero and Hochachka (1971), who found that the isozymes from fish acclimated at 18°C function well only at temperatures above 10 to 12°C, while fish maintained at 4°C possess isozymes which work best at 2 to 5°C. The phenomenon was aptly described as "biochemical restructuring" in response to seasonal temperature changes.

The proportion of different isozymes of lactic dehydrogenase from the liver differs according to the acclimation temperature of *Carassius auratus* (Hochachka, 1965). The isozyme pattern does not however vary in tissues other than liver, a restriction which applies also to lactic dehydrogenase and glucose-6-phosphate dehydrogenase in acclimated *Semotilus atromaculatus*. Kent and Hart (1976) who made this observation concluded that synthesis of special isozymes as a mechanism of thermal compensation may be limited to specific enzymes in specific tissues. Muscle from *Fundulus heteroclitus* also yields isozymes of lactic dehydrogenase which vary in proportion according to the temperature (Bolaffi and Booke, 1974).

In the liver of *Mugil cephalus* two isozymes of glucose-6-phosphate dehydrogenase are present at all temperatures, but form 2 increases in activity during warm acclimation. Kinetic studies of form 1 indicate that enzyme-substrate and enzyme-NADP (nicotinamide adenine dinucleotide phosphate) affinities increase at low temperatures, while inhibition by NADPH decreases (Hochachka and Clayton-Hochachka, 1973). Various authors quoted by Fry and Hochachka (1970) have reported changes with temperature in the isozyme pattern of lactic dehydrogenase in liver, muscle pyruvate kinase and acetyl cholinesterase in the brain.

A different aspect of the dynamics of isozyme formation emerges from the work of Tsukuda and Ohsawa (1974) and Tsukuda (1975). These workers found that the lactic dehydrogenase from the liver of *Carassius auratus* adapted to 8 or 18°C consisted of 5 isozymes, while those adapted to 28°C possessed only 3. However, the reduction in number at the highest temperature was only temporary, and on prolonged acclimation the missing isoenzymes eventually reappeared, the process being speeded in well-aerated water. The interpretation of this observation is not easy, but it clearly calls into question some of the early work, suggesting that a longer acclimation might have covered up the finding of different proportions of isozymes in those cases also.

Indeed, a number of authors have found no changes in isozyme patterns with acclimation to different temperatures. F. R. Wilson (1973) and Wilson, Whitt and Prosser (1973), who found no change in the lactic dehydrogenase pattern of *Carassius auratus*, warned that the white muscle *could* show different patterns, but only if it were contaminated with variable proportions of dark muscle. The 5 isozymes of lactic dehydrogenase found in the brain of *Rhodeus amarus* by Hauss (1975) did not change in number or electrophoretic mobility with acclimation temperature. Reviewing his own work, Somero (1975b, c) recalled that he has not found changes in the isozyme patterns during seasonal or artificial acclimation to different temperatures except in *Salmo gairdneri*, which differs from most other species in having an additional set of genes added to the established family of isozyme loci. The advantage of variable isozymes is that, since they can be selectively synthesised, the organism need not maintain poorly functioning proteins within its cells, but Somero concludes that most eurythermal fish simply possess enzymes capable of functioning over very broad ranges of temperature, compared with the same enzymes from stenothermal fish.

To sum up, it is reasonably certain that the proportions of isozymes can change in a manner which enables fish to adapt to different temperatures and maintain a fairly constant rate of metabolism, but the effect is limited to certain enzymes in specific organs of a few species, and alternative mechanisms exist by which the metabolism is adjusted to long-term changes in temperature.

A metabolic pathway which appears to be affected by temperature is the pentose shunt, which absorbs a bigger proportion of metabolities at lower temperatures. For example, the livers of *Salvelinus fontinalis* show greater activities of glucose-6-phosphate dehydrogenase and 6-phosphogluconate dehydrogenase after acclimation at 5°C compared with 10 or 15°C. The phenomenon is probably associated with increased lipogenesis under cold conditions (Yamauchi, Stegeman and Goldberg, 1975). Earlier, Hochachka and Hayes (1962) had observed that the respiration of muscle homogenates from *Salvelinus fontinalis* acclimated to 15°C was almost completely inhibited by iodoacetate, a compound which inhibits glyceraldehyde-3-phosphate dehydrogenase. After acclimation to 4°C, the rate of respiration was higher and less sensitive to the inhibitor, and more radioactive acetate was incorporated into the lipid. Taken together with other evidence of incorporation of radioactive CO_2 into glycogen, this indicated that the Embden–

Meyerhof pathway predominated at the higher temperature, while the pentose phosphate pathway became more active under colder conditions.

Several references have been made to changes in the isozyme pattern of lactic dehydrogenase at different temperatures. The proportion of these isozymes determines the direction taken by pyruvate, according to the work of Somero (1973) and Wilson, Somero and Prosser (1974). At low temperatures, but not at higher temperatures, pyruvate strongly inhibits lactic dehydrogenase in *Gillichthys mirabilis*. Lactic dehydrogenase can therefore act as a "valve" to direct pyruvate towards the Krebs cycle under aerobic (low-temperature) conditions, whereas it can be converted anaerobically to lactate at higher temperatures. Fish living at high temperatures probably tend to rely more on glycolytic means for ATP generation than those at low temperatures, where more oxygen is available and the fish can operate the tricarboxylic cycle in conjunction with the Embden-Meyerhof pathway. This change of pathway is probably therefore not the consequence of temperature change as such, but of its effect on oxygen solubility.

e.   *Proteins and amino acids*

It has been suggested (Volume 1, reference 954) that the properties of fish tissue proteins are affected by the environmental temperature at which they were synthesised.

In the present account, we have seen already (p. 331) that the stability of muscle myosin, usually assessed from the rate of decline in its ATPase activity, is greater in fish from warmer waters. Similar papers on this theme have been published by Shkorbatov, Gurevich *et al.* (1970: *Poecilia reticulata*), Johnston, Frearson and Goldspink (1973: 19 species), Arai, Kawamura and Hayashi (1973: 10 species) and Johnston, Walesby *et al.* (1975: *Notothenia rossii*, *Amphiprion sebae*). The effect can be very striking. Johnston, Davison and Goldspink (1975) adapted *Carassius auratus* to widely differing temperatures and measured the ATPase activity of the myosin after incubation for various times at 37°C, a temperature which usually damages fish proteins. Their results (Fig. 122) show that the enzyme activity has virtually disappeared after incubation for half an hour when the living fish had been accustomed to a temperature of 1°C, but has only just started to decline in myosin from fish previously held at 26°C. The stability of the proteins of the muscle, serum and eye lens, as measured by the proportion made insoluble by heat, has also been shown to be greater in this species acclimated to 28°C compared with 18°C (Tsukuda and Ohsawa, 1971).

Studies on growth rate and protein synthesis at different temperatures can be complicated when the fish will accept food only within a limited temperature range. Thus *Cyprinus carpio* steadily lose weight from December to April despite daily feeding because of the lower temperatures. They eat at a reduced rate below 10°C and cease altogether

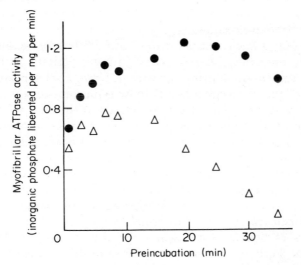

Fig. 122. Myofibrillar ATPase activity in the muscle of *Carassius auratus* which had been pre-incubated for various times at 37°C. △, Living fish previously acclimated to 1°C; ●, living fish previously acclimated to 26°C. After Johnston, Davison and Goldspink (1975). Reproduced with permission of Dr I. Johnston.

below 4°C (Bouche, 1975). Cultured *Salmo salar* also seem to consume a negligible quantity of food throughout the winter (I. McFarlan, 1977: personal communication). However, there is evidence that if they can eat, then protein synthesis is enhanced at lower temperatures. *Carassius auratus* acclimated at 5°C incorporate radioactive leucine (at 5°C) at a much higher rate than those acclimited at 25°C (Das and Krishnamoorthy, 1969). A higher content of ribose nucleic acid in the muscle and liver of *Ophicephalus punctatus* acclimated at 15°C compared with 25°C, also indicates a more rapid rate of tissue growth (Ray and Medda, 1975). On the other hand, deoxyribose nucleic acid shows little change in turnover over a range of 30 centigrade degrees (Nieto and Johnson, 1972: *Carassius auratus*). Ponomarenko (1971) noted that over the previous 15 years, low temperatures had predominated in the Barents Sea, which should have led to a reduction in the growth rate of *Gadus morhua*. In actual fact the rate had increased, particularly in younger fish. From 1950 to 1965, *Melanogrammus aeglefinus* had also grown better than in the period of higher temperatures in the 1930s. Ponomarenko linked the increased growth to subsistence on more calorific food—capelin and euphausids—for which the above two species compete. This is potentially a fairly complex relationship, and not all of the factors have been studied together. While it is possible that, for example, the digestive enzymes compensate for the low temperatures and become more active, it is well known (p. 319) that food moves more slowly through the gut at lower temperatures, so the fish may be able to grow more rapidly only through reduced swimming activity or by greater efficiency of absorption. During the winter, *Gadus morhua* residing in the cold waters of the Norwegian fjords show symptoms of starvation—for example the water content of the muscle rises—but the fish appear to feed continuously throughout the period, so that despite the full stomachs the rate at which the food is actually absorbed appears not to match the metabolic requirements, especially in relation to gonad building (O. Vahl, 1976: personal communication). Further work is needed to clarify the relationship between growth and temperature: possibly the growth of the fish is enhanced over a restricted range of low temperatures only.

We have seen (p. 79) that the proportion of dark muscle of at least three species of fish increases when the fish are acclimated to low temperatures. Perhaps it is naive to attribute this change to the fish's taking advantage of the more aerobic conditions found at low temperatures to lay down more aerobic muscle.

Umminger (1970b: *Fundulus heteroclitus*) found a decrease at low temperatures in those serum proteins which correspond with human gamma globulin. Noting that disease breaks out more readily in fish in warmer water, he suggested that since pathogens grow more slowly at low temperatures there is less need for an immune response. This effect is not found in *Salmo trutta*, in which the proportion of serum globulin does not change at different temperatures (Volume 1, reference 1033).

The temperature of denaturation of fish skin collagen is related to the temperature at which the fish species usually lives (Volume 1, p. 215). *Theragra chalcogramma* is a cold-water species possessing skin collagen which shrinks below 40°C, while that of the eurythermal *Cyprinus carpio* is stable even above 50°C. The air-breathing asian fish *Ophicephalus striatus* can spend part of its time on land and is therefore accustomed to relatively high temperatures. The thermal shrinkage temperature of the skin collagen is 57°C (Gowri and Joseph, 1968), almost as high as that of calf skin (60°C).

It now seems clear that even within one species the properties of the collagen may vary with the temperature of the habitat. Gantayat and

Patnaik (1975) showed that the skin collagen of *Ophicephalus punctatus* from cooler waters is more soluble, that is, less cross-linked, than that from warmer waters. The shrinkage temperatures of the collagens of *Merlangius merlangus* and *Gadus morhua* have been shown by Andrejeva (1971) to vary with the place of capture, warmer habitats leading to higher shrinkage temperatures. There is room for more work here, especially on the effect of the aging of the fish on the change in the properties of its collagen after transfer to a different temperature.

f. *Lipids*

While the composition of lipids in a fish depends to a considerable extent on the diet, some modification is possible, and acclimation to different temperatures results in changes in the saturation of the structural lipids, as distinct from the storage depots. Membranes—cell walls, mitochondrial membranes and others—become more rigid as the temperature falls, and fish adapt by substituting more of the soft unsaturated fatty acids for the harder saturated acids, thus retaining flexibility. The physical texture of the membranes seems to be an essential condition for their correct functioning (Volume 1, pp. 216–217).

It is likely that any changes in the gross quantity of total lipid at different temperatures merely reflect changes in the rate of absorption of food in relation to energy output. For example, Stickney and Andrews (1971) and Andrews and Stickney (1972) reported an almost linear increase in the total carcass lipid of *Ictalurus punctatus* with increase in environmental temperature, rising from 24% at 18°C to 44% at 34°C. Further, seasonal changes in the saturation of neutral (storage) lipids of *Clupea harengus membranus* (Shatunovskii, 1970) are more likely to reflect changes in the diet than deliberate modifications in response to temperature.

The total body lipids of eight species of Indian fish were shown by Gopakumar and Nair (1972) to be more saturated than those of fish from cooler waters, confirming earlier observations, and Irving and Watson (1976) showed that the lipids from the mitochondrial membranes of tropical fish (*Plectropoma maculatum*, *Lethrinus chrysostomus*, *Acanthurus xanthopterus* and *Mugil cephalus*) are more saturated than those from cold-water fish. Such lipids are structural (mostly phospholipids) rather than energy reserves such as triglycerides, and indeed Patton (1975) has shown directly that it is the phospholipids of tropical fish which contain more saturated fatty acids when compared with those of antarctic fish: 35% of saturated acids compared with 17%.

Thomson, Sargent and Owen (1975, 1977) observed an increase in the saturation of the lipids from the gills when *Anguilla anguilla* were held at relatively high temperatures. The lipids of the intestinal mucosa were studied by Kemp and Smith (1970: *Carassius auratus*), who found that raising the environmental temperature by 20°C halved the quantity of 20:4 and 22:6 fatty acids and doubled the quantity of 18:0. Smith and Kemp (1971) showed that the changes were complete in 3 or 4 days.

De Torrengo and Brenner (1976) fed specific fatty acids to *Pimelodus maculatus*, observing that their desaturation by the fish was greater at 15°C than at 30°C. The effect can be reproduced in model systems in the laboratory: Leslie and Buckley (1976: *Carassius auratus*) have shown that the phosphatidyl choline produced from precursors by choline phosphotransferase contained in liver microsomes becomes more saturated as the incubation temperature is raised from 10°C to 30°C. Farkas and Csengeri (1976) fed radioactive sodium acetate to *Cyprinus carpio* and found that the livers incorporated more radioactivity into long-chain polyunsaturated fatty acids at 5°C than at 22°C. The most interesting point is that the distribution of radioactivity among different fatty acids depends on the temperature at the time of the experiment and not on the temperature regime immediately beforehand, suggesting that fish can adjust the pattern of biosynthesis of fatty acids very rapidly to the prevailing temperature, ensuring that their membranes possess the correct physicochemical properties. These authors believe that temperature influences the lipid metabolism directly and that endocrines are not involved, although the exact mechanism remains to be elucidated.

The lipids of the central nervous system also adapt to changes in temperature. At low temperatures the fatty acids of the glycerophosphatides become more unsaturated (Volume 1, reference 607), and while the amounts of the major individual glycerophosphatides of the brain remain relatively constant over a large temperature range, a rise in temperature is characterised, at least in *Carassius auratus*, by an increase in the proportion of plasmalogen (Driedzic and Roots, 1975: *Salvelinus fontinalis;* Driedzic, Selivonchick and Roots, 1976; Selivonchick and Roots, 1976: *Carassius auratus*). The content of total lipid does not change (Driedzic and Roots, 1975).

Synaptic functions are extremely sensitive to temperature changes, and the synapse may well be the primary site of any adaptation (Hazel and Prosser, 1974). Synaptic membranes are rich in gangliosides, which may be involved in synaptic transmission. Breer and his colleagues have shown that as the temperature is lowered, the proportion of poly-sialogangliosides in the brain increases, whether one considers related species living at widely differing temperatures (Breer, 1974, 1975) or changes in the environmental temperature of a eurythermal species (Breer and Rahmann, 1976: *Carassius auratus*).

g. *Inorganic substances*

Apart from the hagfish (Volume 1, p. 137), fish maintain levels of inorganic substances in their body fluids which differ from those of the surroundings. When the water temperature changes, there is often a readjustment of the internal ionic levels, but it is often not clear why a given change has occurred. An alteration in the temperature may affect the metabolic rate in such a way that the osmoregulation becomes more efficient. Too rapid a change causes thermal shock and a breakdown in osmoregulation, so that the internal milieu becomes more salty when the fish is in salt water or more dilute when in fresh water. At the point of thermal death, either from shock or from exposure to temperatures outside the tolerated range, the plasma ionic concentration is usually near that of the surroundings. Finally, certain polar species appear to increase the concentration of certain substances in their blood as the temperature approaches their freezing point to protect themselves from fatal ice formation in their tissues. This aspect will be considered in more detail later (p. 345).

There may therefore be some sense in the apparently random findings of different authors which will be presented briefly below, but the mechanism operating in a particular instance is not obvious.

In a review of the subject, Houston (1973) stated that, at the time of writing, surprisingly little had been published on the effects of temperature on water and salt balance, but that interest was growing. He pointed out that even sublethal temperature shifts provoke "substantial alterations in body fluid status", and that the ionoregulatory systems of the teleost are highly sensitive to temperature change. He also observed, as have we throughout this book, that different species respond differently. Ions are lost more rapidly into the urine at higher temperatures (apart from potassium), and since nitrogen metabolism increases at higher temperatures (various authors, same review), the higher nitrogen excretion could increase ion absorption by exchange (see p. 288). Houston (1973) finally suggests that some thermocompensatory mechanisms, for example increases in enzyme activity at lower temperatures, could be aided by the changes in the mineral concentration, a point made also by Houston, Madden and DeWilde (1970).

Umminger (1969e) adapted *Fundulus heteroclitus* to temperatures near zero, and found that the sodium, chloride and overall osmolarity of the serum increase when the fish are living in salt water, and decrease when they are in fresh water. The increase in osmolarity in salt water is not, however, a manifestation of osmotic failure, since in a salt environment the increase in organic constituents of the serum ($\pm 95\%$) is greater than that of the inorganic substances ($\pm 13\%$), and also the new levels are now maintained for as long as the fish is alive (Umminger, 1969a, d). It was concluded that osmotic and ionic regulation are less effective in the cold, but no so poor as to cause the death of the fish. Again there are species differences, and the related fish *Fundulus grandis* does die within seven days of being cooled to $\pm 1 \cdot 5°C$, through, it is thought, osmotic imbalance (Umminger, 1971a). Both the overall osmolarity and the chloride concentration of *Salmo gairdneri* plasma increase when the saline solution in which the fish have been placed is cooled from 15 to 5°C (Rao, 1969), and osmolarity, sodium, chloride and magnesium all increase when *Esox lucius*, *Myoxocephalus scorpius* and *Myoxocephalus quadricornis* are acclimated to $\pm 0 \cdot 1°C$ in the brackish water of the Baltic, about 6‰ (Oikari, 1975a). A seasonal variation caused by temperature change has been noted in the sodium and potassium of *Cyprinus carpio* plasma, but not in the chloride, calcium or magnesium (Houston, Madden and DeWilde, 1970).

When the sodium and chloride rise in the blood of *Fundulus heteroclitus* placed in salt water and cooled, histological studies of the gills show that at subzero temperatures the chloride cells become inactive and mucus cells are stimulated, so that the gills become covered with a thick mucous coating. At the same time, the prolactin cells of the pituitary become more active, showing large, round nuclei and prominent nucleoli. Hypophysectomy abolishes the rise in sodium induced by low temperatures. These observations were made by Umminger and Kenkel (1975), who concluded that prolactin release at subzero temperatures inactivates the chloride cells, leading to the rise in the level of serum electrolytes. The mucus may protect the supercooled blood from being seeded by ice crystals through the gills (same authors).

Another way of looking at these results is to consider that marine fish allow the concentrations of internal inorganic ions to rise under cold conditions in order to reduce the concentration difference between them and the environment, and thus reduce the osmotic work load (Prosser, Mackay and Kato, 1970). The concept receives support from the work of Allanson, Bok and van Wyk (1971) on the freshwater fish *Tilapia mossambica*. This fish goes into a coma when the temperature is reduced to 11°C, suffering reduction in the osmolarity, sodium and chloride of the plasma, but showing no signs of coma nor of changes in osmolarity if it is placed in 5 parts per thousand of NaCl before the temperature is reduced: the "osmotic gap" has been reduced and the fish is therefore stressed to a smaller degree.

A fall in internal ionic concentrations when freshwater, as distinct from marine, fish are chilled, has also been observed by Prosser, Mackay and Kato (1970: *Carassius auratus*, 15 or 25→5°C), Umminger (1970a: *Fundulus heteroclitus*; 1971b: *Ictalurus nebulosus*, *Fundulus heteroclitus*, *Cyprinus carpio*→temperatures near freezing), Stanley and Colby (1971: *Alosa pseudoharengus*: acute exposure to cold. This species normally osmoregulates equally well in fresh or salt water) and Catlett and Millich (1976: *Carassius auratus*, 21·5→1°C). DeVries (1974), who reviewed the subject, suggested that the loss of electrolytes might be the effect of the low temperatures on the transport enzymes.

h. *Carbohydrates*

Umminger (1969b) tabulated the work of other writers to show that when a considerable number of fish species are acclimated to low temperatures, the glucose concentration of the blood increases by up to 455%. The species showing most change are *Opsanus tau*, *Fundulus heteroclitus* and *Cyprinus carpio*, in decreasing order of magnitude. No change was shown by *Micropterus salmoides*, *Tinca tinca* or *Salvelinus fontinalis*. Acclimation to 2°C brings about a 73% increase in serum glucose in *Fundulus heteroclitus*, but further change to −1°C causes the glucose to have increased by 440% (Umminger, 1967). In further extensive work (Umminger, 1971e), it was shown that a concentraton of as much as 1066 mg% was possible in the blood of *Fundulus heteroclitus*, the highest blood glucose level ever reported in fish.

Both hypophysectomised and control fish develop hyperglycaemia at −1·5°C, so the process is not controlled by the pituitary (Umminger, 1970c, 1972a). Umminger (1971c) suggested that the effect might be brought about by a decrease in insulin production, and subsequently (Umminger and Bair, 1972, 1973) it was shown that at low temperatures the beta cells of the pancreas, which produce insulin, do indeed atrophy, while the alpha cells, which produce glucagon, hypertrophy and degranulate. The agent controlling these phenomena is not known.

The serum glucose levels are raised by depleting the liver glycogen. Since the fish do not eat at low temperatures, the liver glycogen is eventually exhausted, and when the serum glucose values fall to normal the fish die, though their life can be prolonged by adding glucose to the water (Umminger, 1969c, f; 1972b). It has been concluded (Umminger, 1969b) that the purpose of elevating serum glucose is to permit survival in the supercooled state by retarding the onset of lethal ice crystal growth. However, the fact that the fish tend to die when the serum glucose falls even though they do not actually freeze suggests that the glucose benefits them in some other way, perhaps not connected with freezing. In any case, the greater increase in serum glucose when the

fish are in cold fresh water as compared with cold salt water does not
point to protection from freezing, since it is not possible for the body
fluids of fish to freeze while they are in fresh water. Umminger (1969e)
could offer no explanation for this difference. The increased breakdown
of liver glycogen is accomplished by increasing the activity of glycogen
phosphorylase (Umminger and Bair, 1972; Umminger, 1973b), presumably mediated by glucagon (Benziger and Umminger, 1974). No
change is seen in the activity of glucose-6-phosphatase (Benziger and
Umminger, 1973).

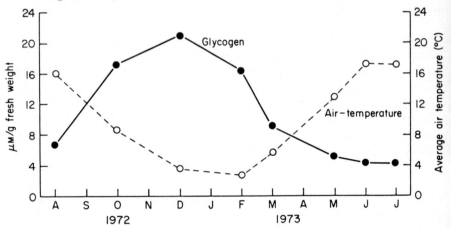

Fig. 123. Seasonal changes in the glycogen content of the brain of *Scardinius erythrophthalmus* in relation to the monthly average air temperature. After Breer and
Rahmann (1974). Reproduced with permission of Professor H. Rahmann.

A possible mechanism for the decline in insulin activity at low
temperatures emerges from the work of Moule and Yip (1973: *Ictalurus
nebulosus*), who found that at 12°C radioactive leucine was no longer
incorporated into the insulin but only into the pro-insulin. When the
temperature was raised to 22°C, the conversion of pro-insulin to insulin
was observed. Thus the enzyme responsible for converting pro-insulin
to insulin may be the controlling step, showing little activity at 12°C.

   Figure 123 shows that the glycogen of brain tissue also rises with
falling temperature (Breer and Rahmann, 1974: *Scardinius erythrophthalmus*). It is one of the clearest correlations published, and yet this
curious behaviour of carbohydrate is really not simple, and at the
present stage of our knowledge seems to contain anomalies. Thus, the
concentrations of glucose in the blood of *Thymallus thymallus* and *Salmo
trutta* are higher in winter *even where the temperature is kept constant* (Pavlovic
1968). Also, while we have seen that a rise in blood sugar induced by

low temperatures brings about a fall in liver glycogen, Dean (1969: *Salmo gairdneri*) observed a rise in liver glycogen when the temperature was lowered from 18 to 5°C, and the liver glycogen concentrations in *Thymallus thymallus* and *Salmo trutta* were observed by Pavlovic (1968) to be higher in winter. When Murat (1976a) maintained *Cyprinus carpio* at temperatures below 5°C, he found a wide range of blood glucose values (from 30 to as much as 250 mg%), which he interpreted as an absence of regulation and very slow turnover. Further information on the total nutritional reserves, state of sexual maturity, and the extent of the independent influence of circadian rhythms would probably clear away some of the doubtful features of this field.

j. *Resistance to freezing*

Earlier work described in Volume 1, pp. 218–220, showed that, as we have also seen in the present section, the mineral concentration of the body fluids of marine fish cooled to low temperatures tends to rise. While this would presumably lower the freezing point of the fish to some extent, it may just represent a chance modification in, or a breakdown of, the osmoregulation. Umminger's finding of a large rise in blood glucose could also presage self-protection by the fish, but even here, in the light of recent work, the glucose may rise for reasons other than the prevention of freezing, especially as it rises more in *Fundulus heteroclitus* in fresh water, where the fish is in no danger from freezing, than in sea water, where it is at risk (see below). In Volume 1, p. 219, it was said that "adaptive resistance to freezing obviously occurs in this species", but such confidence now seems unjustified.

More recently, Umminger has told DeVries (DeVries, 1974) that the high levels of blood glucose attained in *Fundulus heteroclitus* do not protect the fish from freezing at subzero temperatures if it be touched by ice. However, there have been advances in the field since Volume 1 was written, with the discovery of a series of substances which really do prevent fish from freezing.

According to Scholander and Maggert (1971), fish can adapt to subzero environments in either of two ways. Those that live on the bottom of, for example, the fjords of Labrador where the temperature is about −1°C, possess a plasma which freezes at −0·9°C, and so exist in a supercooled state for long periods. They freeze and die if they accidentally touch a piece of ice: it is the absence of ice on the sea bottom which enables them to survive, but they have in fact no defence against it. Fish from shallow water, which encounter floating ice, possess plasma with a lowered freezing point. They do appear to supercool slightly, but possess materials in the blood which inhibit ice growth even when the supercooled plasma is seeded. The defence is linked to the colloidal fraction of the plasma, which ceases to be protected if the protein is removed.

Extensive studies by DeVries and his colleagues have done much to elucidate the identities and structures of the compounds responsible. DeVries and Wohlschlag (1969) found that the plasma freezing points of *Trematomus bernacchii* and *T. Hansoni* from shallow waters of the Antarctic ranged from −1·87 to −2·07°C, the water temperature being −1·87°C. Sodium chloride, urea and free amino acids in the serum accounted for only 39 to 46% of the depression of the freezing point below 0°C, much of the remaining depression being caused by hitherto undiscovered glycoproteins. When these fish were caught in deeper waters, the freezing point of the serum was slightly higher and the content of glycoproteins correspondingly reduced. The lowest temperatures in the fluid Antarctic Ocean are found just below the ice (DeVries, 1970), where these species appear to thrive. Figure 124 shows a specimen of *Trematomus borchgrevinki* actually resting on the ice without harm.

The glycoproteins are soluble in trichloroacetic acid, appearing in the "non-protein nitrogen" fraction which is five times as concentrated in the plasma of *T. borchgrevinki* as in that of temperate marine fish (DeVries, 1970). They lower only the freezing point of the serum, not the remelting point which is near to zero, perhaps because they are adsorbed on to the surfaces of the ice crystal nuclei, preventing them from propagating (DeVries, 1971). If the glycoprotein molecules are degraded at all, the "antifreeze" properties are destroyed. Complexing their hydroxyl groups with sodium borate also destroys the ability to prevent crystal growth, but it is restored if the borate is removed by dialysis (DeVries, 1971). Curiously, they are not appreciably concentrated in the liquid phase when freezing actually takes place, a further indication that they function by binding on the surface of "seed" ice crystals (Duman and DeVries, 1972). In freezing aqueous solutions, Raymond and DeVries (1972) found that the glycoproteins are incorporated into the ice at a concentration identical to that in the liquid. They concluded that the glycoproteins probably have a highly ordered structure which permits them to fit into the ice lattice.

A total of 8 distinct glycoproteins has been isolated, ranging in molecular weight from 2 600 to 33 700. They are now known to consist entirely of repeating units of alanine-threonine-alanine, in which the threonine bears a disaccharide identified by Shier, Lin and DeVries (1972: *Trematomus borchgrevinki*) as beta-D-galactopyranosyl-(1→4)-2-acetamido-2-deoxy-alpha-D-galactopyranose.

Using radioactively labelled glycoproteins, DeVries, DeVries *et al.* (1974: *Dissostichus mawsoni*) showed that they are distributed between the coelomic fluid, pericardial fluid and intracellular fluid. They account for 4% of the constituents of the blood (Dobbs, Lin and

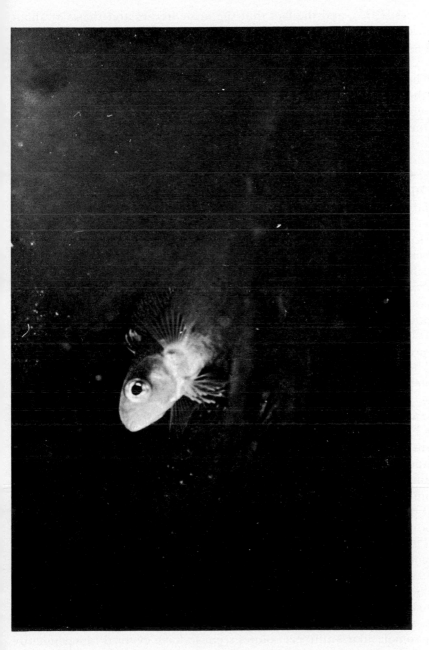

FIG. 124. *Trematomus borchgrevinki* resting on an ice crystal of sub-ice platelet layer, McMurdo Sound, Antarctica. The fish is unharmed at sub-zero temperatures in contact with ice, because of the development of "antifreeze" glyco-proteins within its body. Photograph kindly supplied by Dr A. L. DeVries.

DeVries, 1974), and the fact that the urine freezes and thaws at about the same temperature shows that they are not excreted. They are also not found in bile (DeVries, DeVries *et al.*, 1974) or the vitreous humour (DeVries, 1974).

These "antifreeze" compounds appear to be absent from the blood of the antarctic species *Notothenia neglecta, N. rossii* and *Trematomus newnesi*, according to Smith (1970). Here the small increase in osmolarity of the serum seen in winter is caused by an increase in sodium and chloride, but the fish survive subzero temperatures largely by super-cooling. In some way, these fish can resist death by freezing for periods of several hours even when in contact with subzero ice, and Smith (1970) found that seeding is not transmitted through the skin, though it is liable to occur through the gills.

The compounds are not limited to antarctic fish. Duman and DeVries (1975) found similar substances in the blood of fish from Nova Scotia. According to these writers, there are now eleven families of teleost fish which contain species known to produce an antifreeze in response to subzero temperatures, ranging from the Osmeridae, Clupeidae and cod families to more advanced spiny-rayed fish like the Cottidae, Stichaeidae Nototheniidae and Chaenichthyidae. Raymond, Lin and DeVries (1975) isolated antifreeze compounds from *Eleginus gracilis* and *Myoxocephalus verrucosus*.

The true antarctic fish do not alter their circulating levels of glyco-proteins, but others do and indeed exhibit a seasonal variation in their concentration. Exposure to 10 to 12°C for 3 weeks, for example, causes *Pseudopleuronectes americanus* to lose all of its antifreeze (DeVries, 1974), but Duman and DeVries (1974) have shown that, for the compounds to disappear, a long photoperiod is necessary in addition to the higher temperature, just to ensure that the fish do not shed their protection during a chance short-term rise in temperature. In contrast, when summer fish are acclimated to various combinations of low temperature and photoperiod, it is found that low temperatures always promote the production of antifreeze regardless of photoperiod.

The same writers found what seems to be a genetic difference between populations of *Anoplarchus purpurascens*. Those from Alaska produce anti-freeze compounds in their blood at low temperatures, while those from California cannot do so, even when acclimated to cold. Life in a cold climate for thousands of years seems therefore gradually to engender the ability to make these interesting compounds. The point is that macromolecular antifreeze solutes seem to have evolved independently in more than one group of fish—those present in the winter flounder, *Pseudopleuronectes americanus*, for example, having a different composition from those found in the Nototheniids (Duman and DeVries, 1976), and also a different molecular structure, that is, helical conformation and degree of asymmetry (Ananthanarayanan and Hew, 1977).

Although Smith (1972) concluded that increases in inorganic constituents are unlikely to contribute significantly to the freezing resistance of polar fish, he nevertheless recorded increases in the sodium, potassium and chloride of the serum of *Notothenia neglecta* and *N. rossii*. The freezing points of both serum and urine of *Trematomus bernacchii* have been shown to fall at subzero temperatures by Potts and Morris (1968), who attributed it mostly to increases in the chloride concentration, and the winter depression of the freezing point of *Taurulus bubalis* plasma was ascribed to "electrolytes" by Raschack (1969). Both urine and serum osmoconcentrations of eleven species of antarctic teleosts were shown to be conspicuously greater than those of temperate species, elevated serum osmolarity being largely the result of increased sodium and chloride, and urine having increased magnesium and chloride (Dobbs and DeVries, 1975). Evidence touched on in Volume 1 (pp. 219–220) seemed to indicate that low temperatures are lethal to *Gadus morhua* even where they do not actually freeze. More recent work by Harden Jones and Scholes (1974) suggests that this is not so, since cod can live for at least 80 days at 0°C; the deaths reported in the earlier work must have been due to some other cause. These authors also quote Leivestad (1965) as keeping cod alive for 60 days at −1·4°C. The relevance to the present context is that blood chloride, which increases from about 150 to about 190 mEq/l as the fish are cooled from 10°C to below zero, can no longer be considered to represent a simple breakdown in osmoregulation. While, as we have seen, thermal shock causes a rise in the body electrolytes of saltwater fish and a fall in freshwater fish, the increases described here do seem to be "intentional". According to Feeney (1974), they do lower the freezing point a little, but weight for weight they are less effective than the glycoproteins. The reason why antarctic fish possess raised salt concentrations in addition to glycoproteins is not at present clear.

5 Seasonal Variation and Some Alternative Approaches to Fish Biology

A. Introduction: the objectives

Every fisherman knows that as the seasons change, so does the nature of the fish that he catches. Sometimes they are bright-eyed and lively and flip furiously about on the deck, while at other times they just lie down and die. Their flesh may feel firm and springy or soft and flabby, their shape and colour may vary, and sometimes they make a more appetising food for man than they did even a few weeks previously. There are also numerous changes in the chemical constituents. Everyone involved in fishing, marketing fish or scientific research is aware of "seasonal variation" as a fact of life, and yet, as I pointed out in Volume 1 (pp. 169–171), the underlying mechanisms of the changes are often unknown and we sometimes use the phrase "seasonal variation" as a cloak for our ignorance. Indeed, the subject was dismissed briefly in Volume 1 because it seemed more appropriate to discuss known mechanisms under their own headings such as maturation or starvation.

However, there have been advances in the field during the last eight years, and the topic is now to receive a chapter to itself, because it is becoming apparent that measurable phenomena which change during the year can form the basis of an extended fish biology. The state of any living system can be expressed by the set of numerical values of its variables at that moment; the difficulty lies in pinpointing those parameters which are useful and which ones may be disregarded.

Shul'man (1972, p. 3) who made these remarks, has also given much thought to the formulation of a new biology, regarding all the parameters together as expressing the "syndrome" of the state of the fish. A summary of our present aims has already been given in the preface to the present volume. Let us look briefly at the methods already available for routine use by a semi-skilled technician.

1.   EXISTING TECHNIQUES

As fish become better nourished, they become more corpulent and so heavier without necessarily changing in length. The weight of the fish in relation to the cube of the length, expressed by the formula: $W/L^3 \times 100$ (many authors, for example Hoar, 1939: *Salmo salar*) is known as the condition factor and is widely used as a rough guide. The length in relation to the age shows how rapidly a fish is growing, so the age in years is needed and is usually measured by counting the rings on the otoliths or scales.

The state of maturity is measured either on a subjective scale, the "Hjort Scale" (I =immature; II to V =maturing; VI =spawning; VII =spent) after looking at the gonad, or by weighing the gonad and expressing it as a fraction of the total body weight, the "gonadosomatic index". For fish which store much of their lipid reserves in the liver it is sometimes profitable to express the weight of the liver as a fraction of the body weight, the "hepatosomatic index". Where the lipid reserves are held in the flesh, the total lipid content measured by weight after, say, ether extraction is used to indicate the nutritional condition. Examination of the stomach contents indicates the nature of the food.

These techniques comprise just about all of the armoury at the disposal of technicians wishing to obtain rapid information about captured fish. They answer a number of questions but are somewhat limited in scope. The "condition factor" is particularly vulnerable to criticism. Figure 47 shows that as non-fatty fish starve and mobilise their muscle proteins, the contractile tissue diminishes, and at least a part of the space which it formerly occupied becomes filled with fluid. The total volume of the musculature therefore does not shrink in proportion to the degree of mobilisation of the protein, and while the bodies of starving *Gadus morhua*, for example, do definitely look thinner (Volume 1, reference 756), they would become much more emaciated if the shrinking muscle cells retained their normal form and their normal proportion of extracellular fluid, when the condition factor would be more realistic. A reduced condition factor could be caused by starvation, but not necessarily so, and it is not quantitative in terms of energy reserves, underestimating for example the amount of protein mobilisation in a starved fish as mentioned above. The Hjort scale suffers from being subjective, and there are difficulties in distinguishing the different stages of ripening, so that different workers may give different assessments, although an expert can identify accurately the degree of maturity from histological sections.

While an examination of the degree of fullness of fish stomachs can be made quantitative, simply noting the number of empty stomachs may not take account of fish that vomit during capture or those which are eating regularly but happen just to have transferred the stomach contents into the intestine. As Shul'man (1972: p. 12) points out, the indexes of stomach and intestine filling by no means always correlate with the rate of food consumption, because the rates of assimilation and passage through the digestive tract differ markedly under different conditions. As we saw in Fig. 65, the lipid content of the liver of *Gadus morhua* does fall in the early stages of starvation, but having reached a low value it remains there while depletion continues and mobilisation of the muscle proteins begins, so that a source of energy is still available to the fish. The hepatosomatic index therefore gives information on just a part of the depletion sequence, and the same low values could be found in fish showing a wide range of actual depletion. It therefore needs supplementing with information on protein mobilisation. The gonadosomatic index certainly shows the increase in the size of the gonads, but it must be remembered that more than one species of fish produce a disproportionately larger number of eggs (relative to body weight) in each successive year of their lives (for example, Volume 1, Fig. 44), and this change reflects a bigger gonad mass. The musculature accordingly becomes more severely depleted in older fish (Volume 1, Fig. 45), resulting in a bigger loss in weight.

Virtually none of the important theoretical aspects of ecology and fisheries can be solved to the full without resorting to physiological–biochemical indicators. Such indicators must not, of course, be used in isolation, but in close conjunction with other indexes characterising the state of the fish (Shul'man, 1972: p. 233).

2.   INDICATIONS SO FAR

Before broaching the subject of new approaches, I should like to gather together the suggestions submitted by various writers up to now, drawing on both Volume 1 and the present work. Authors have proposed determinations of this compound or that enzyme as objective measurements of a nutritional or developmental status in the fish, or a response to some stimulus from the environment. These suggestions are listed in Table 21 as a source of ideas for those wishing to follow them up. I shall not say much more about them here, since a number of them are tentative, derived from work on a single species and not backed up by further extensive trials. They are usually the speciality of the workers who first investigated them and have rarely been brought into general use as aids to fish biology. However, looking at the table one cannot but feel a sense of excitement at the potential, not only for learning about the state of the fish, but also about the environment from which it came.

B.   Fish muscle considered as a foodstuff

1.   INTRODUCTION

Investigators all over the world study the degree of success attainable with different techniques for preserving fish muscle as an acceptable food for mankind. Drying, salting, pickling, smoking and, particularly nowadays, freezing are all used in the industry, some special techniques being traditional and peculiar to one country or even just one locality. Research is directed towards finding out the effect of the process on the raw material with the object of defining optimum conditions. In the writer's laboratory we were particularly concerned with the effects of low temperature on fish muscle (reviewed in Volume 1, reference 760), but it soon became apparent that the variations in the raw material could actually be greater than the changes produced by freezing, and that no systematic studies had been done to explain the variability on a rational basis.

The attributes which govern the desirability of fish muscle as food are flavour, odour, texture (in the eater's mouth), colour and surface appearance, and, quite astonishingly, all five attributes can now be said to vary according to the season. They also vary with the catching locality but as "ground effects" really relate to such factors as differences in the date at which spawning occurs (because of disparities in the water temperature and the photoperiod), currents and local variations in the food supply, they are not really factors in their own right. Genetic factors seem rarely to be involved, except possibly in local variations in the skin colour (Love, 1974) and the ability of some stocks of fish to manufacture "antifreeze" in their blood at low temperature (p. 348).

TABLE 21

Tentative means for studying attributes of fish, summarised from the texts of Volume 1
and the present Volume (most are suggestions with little experimental backing)

a. Information about the fish itself

Attribute	Substance to be measured (I=increase; D=decrease)	Organ	Reference (Volume 1 or 2 and number of text page)
Maturation in females	Alanine (I)	Ovary	*1*, 66
	Free amino acids (I)		*1*, 99
	Calcium (I)	Blood	*1*, 61, 62, 125
	Calcium (D)	Ovary	*2*, 46
	Carotenoids (I)		*1*, 67; *2*, 27
	Cobalt (D)		*2*, 46
	Copper (I)		
	Enzymes (various) (I)	Oocyte	*2*, 18
	Fatty acids C_{18} (I)	Ovary	*1*, 65
	Fatty acids C_{16} (D)		
	Glycine (D)		*1*, 66
	Glycine:alanine ratio (D)		*1*, 101, 125
	Glycogen (I)		*2*, 18
	Iron (D)		*2*, 46
	Leucine (I)		*1*, 66
	Lipoprotein (I)	Blood	*2*, 40
	Magnesium (D)	Ovary	*2*, 46
	Manganese (I)		
	Pantothenic acid (D)		*1*, 68
	Potassium (D)		*2*, 46
	Proline (D)		*1*, 66
	Retinal (I)	Blood	*2*, 45
	Sex hormones (I)		*1*, 111; *2*, 37
	Sodium (I)	Ovary	*2*, 46
	Zinc (D)		
Maturation in males	Glycine:alanine ratio (D)	Testis	*1*, 101, 125
	Sex hormones (I)	Blood	*1*, 111
Quality of eggs	ATPase activity (I)	Egg	*2*, 10
	Carotenoids (I)		*2*, 38

	Iron (I)		*1*, 70
	Oxidative phosphorylation (I)		*2*, 10
	Riboflavin (I)		*1*, 69
Metamorphosis (parr to smolt)	ATPase (I)	Gill	*2*, 23
	Catecholamines (I)	Blood	*2*, 22
	Glycine (D)	Muscle	
	Guanine (I)	Skin	*1*, 80; *2*, 22
	17-Hydroxysteroids (I)	Blood	*2*, 22
	Hypoxanthine (I)	Skin	*1*, 80; *2*, 22
	Taurine (D)	Muscle	*2*, 22
Tendency to migrate	Thyroid activity (I)	—	*1*, 110
	Trimethylamine oxide more concd in dark muscle than in white		*2*, 70
Habitual activity (high compared with low)	Anserine (I)	Muscle	*1*, 151
	Carnosine (I)		
	Glucose (resting) (I)	Blood	*1*, 150
	Haematocrit (I)		*1*, 149
	Iodine (I)		*1*, 150
	Vitamins, various (I)	Muscle	
Activity over last week or so	Myoglobin (I)	Dark muscle	*2*, 106
	Succinic dehydrogenase (I)	Muscle	*2*, 111
	Thyroxine (I)	Blood	*2*, 110
Stress	*cyclic* 3'5'-adenosine monophosphate (I)	Blood	*2*, 235
	Adrenaline (I)		*1*, 40, 43
	Adrenocorticotropic hormone (I)		*2*, 236
	Cortisol (I)		*2*, 235
	Glucose (I)		*1*, 46; *2*, 231
	Haemoglobin (I)	Slime	*2*, 242
Present rate of growth	*Free* amino acids (I)	Any tissue	*2*, 42
	RNA:DNA ratio (I)	Muscle	*2*, 30
Level of feeding	Nitrogen (I)	Urine	*2*, 137
	RNA:DNA ratio (I)	Muscle	*2*, 137
Approximate nature of food	Proportions of protease, amylase, lipase	Intestine	*2*, 151

continued overleaf

Table 21 continued

Starvation	Albumin:globulin ratio (D)	Blood	2, 193
	Free amino acids (D)	Muscle	1, 241; 2, 194
	Arginase (I)	Liver	2, 218
	Bile acids, pigment (I)	Bile	2, 225
	Cortisol (I)	Blood	2, 220
	Enzymes of pentose phosphate pathway (D)	Liver	2, 221
	Gamma globulin (I)	Blood	1, 232
	Growth hormone (I)		2, 218
	Haematocrit (D)	Blood	1, 225; 2, 213, 214
	Lipid (D)	Muscle, liver	1, 224
	Lipid saturation (I)	Muscle	2, 209
	Lysine:arginine ratio (I)	Muscle	2, 196
	Opacity (I)	Muscle	1, 224
	Potassium (D)	Muscle and other organs	1, 246; 2, 172
	Reddening (I)	Liver	2, 210
	Refractive index (D)	Muscle press juice	2, 196
	RNA (D)	Liver, muscle	2, 214
	Sodium (I)	Muscle	1, 246
	Succinic dehydrogenase (D)	Dark muscle	2, 93
	Thyroxine (D)	Blood	2, 218
	Water (I)	Muscle	1, 228
Refeeding after starvation	Glucose "overshoot" (I)	Blood	2, 229
	Post-mortem pH (D)	Muscle	
	Ribosomal RNA (I)	Liver, muscle	2, 216, 228
Ability of tissue to function in anoxic conditions	Pyruvate kinase:cytochrome oxidase ratio (I)	Heart	2, 280

b.   Information about the habitat from which fish taken

Illumination	Analysis of the spectral sensitivity of the visual pigments in mixed-pigment species	Retina	1, 183

Colour of ground	Intensity of pigmentation	Skin	*1*, 158
Temperature (habitual)	Thermal denaturation temperature or hydroxyproline content of collagen (I)	Skin etc.	*1*, 215; *2*, 29
Temperature (recent)	Degree of unsaturation of lipids (D)	Muscle, liver	*1*, 216; *2*, 339 onwards
	Haematocrit (I)	Blood	*2*, 327
	Formation of glycoprotein "antifreeze" at sub-zero temperatures, or its disappearance at higher temperatures (few species only)	Blood	*2*, 345 onwards
Temperature during earlier larval stage	Meristic characters, such as more vertebrae at lower temperatures		*2*, 243
Oxygenation	Haematocrit (D)	Blood	*2*, 239
Identification of fresh water body in which fish originated	Pattern of trace elements	Middle of scales	*2*, 248

---

c. Chemical "markers" used to measure the quantity or proportion of a tissue fraction (no references to text)

For estimating in a mixture the amount of	*Actually measure*
Cell wall	Cholesterol
Connective tissue	Hydroxyproline
Dark muscle in the fillet of a non-fatty species	Myoglobin
Extracellular fluid in muscle	Sodium
Mitochondria	SDH or other mitochondrial enzyme
Mitochondrial membrane	Cardiolipid
Number of cells or nuclei	DNA
Slime (mucus)	n-acetyl neuraminic acid

---

2. GAPING AND pH

The muscle cells of fish are bound together by sheets of connective tissue, which sometimes become weakened, allowing the flesh to fall to pieces ("gaping"). In the present account we are not concerned with causes of gaping such as rough handling or leaving on the deck to lie in the sun (briefly listed by Love, 1973, 1975), but with the fact that the phenomenon tends to vary seasonally.

We have seen in Volume 1, Fig. 7, how muscle cells are connected to myocommata by thin tubular processes which are extensions of the

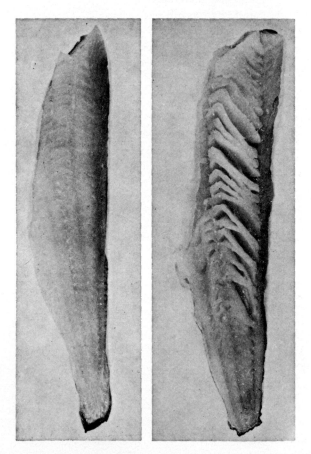

FIG. 125. The phenomenon of gaping seen in a fillet of *Gadus morhua*, compared with a normal fillet. From the Annual Report of Torry Research Station (1969), Crown Copyright, 1970. Reproduced with permission of the Director.

myocommata themselves. They are in fact the collagen framework illustrated in cross-section in Fig. 80 (p. 205). It is when these tubules break at the junction with the myocommata that the fish gape, as shown in severe form in Fig. 125. The seasonal variation is illustrated in Fig. 126, the worst incidence being in June–July, with a smaller peak, which is not seen every year, in November–December.

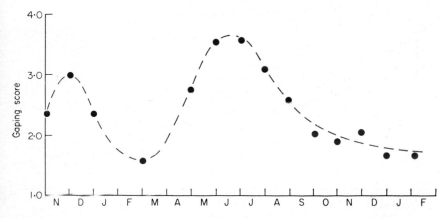

FIG. 126. Seasonal variation in the gaping of cod muscle after death (1969–1970), estimated by comparing the fillets with a series of photographs of gaping of increasing severity. The main peak appears every year, but the subsidiary in November–December is seen only in years when the post-mortem pH falls at that time. After Love (unpublished).

The mechanical strength of myocommata is influenced to an extraordinary degree by small changes in the pH (Love and Haq, 1970a: *Gadus morhua;* Love and Haq, 1970b: *Merlangius merlangus, Melanogrammus aeglefinus*). Studies on isolated myocommata from *Gadus morhua* have shown that they are more than four times as strong at pH 7·1 as at pH 6·2 (Love, Lavéty and Garcia, 1972). Figure 126 relates to the years 1969–1970, when the average pH was low in the summer months and exhibited a secondary fall in December–January (Love, Haq and Smith, 1972), corresponding with the two periods of extensive gaping. It seems likely, therefore, that the post-mortem pH[1] can in many instances be the most important factor influencing the gaping of fish.

---

[1]The pH of muscle is usually close to neutrality during life. It is the pH which has become lower after death, because of the anaerobic accumulation of lactic acid, which affects the strength of the connective tissues. It reaches its minimum value in *Gadus morhua* in 15 hours after death, or less (MacCallum, Jaffray *et al.*, 1967).

At the same time, gaping becomes a serious problem for the fishing industry only when the fish have been frozen: there is an additional disruptive effect caused by small crystals of ice which form within the connective tissue if freezing is done more than a day after death (Love and Lavéty, 1972). Thus fish which were stale before being frozen gape badly. A study of the seasonal variation in gaping is however largely a study of post-mortem pH. This will be considered in section 4, below.

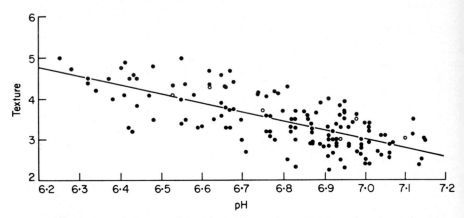

Fig. 127. The influence of post-mortem pH on the texture of cooked cod muscle as eaten. The water contents of all these samples lay within the narrow range of 80·0 to 80·9%. Texture scores above 3 represent firm or tough samples, below 3 soft or sloppy. Hollow symbols represent two points in the same position. After Love, Robertson *et al.* (1974b).

3. TEXTURE AND pH

A close association between the texture of cooked fish and the post-mortem pH has been established for some time (Kelly, Jones *et al.*, 1966; Cowie and Little, 1966: *Gadus morhua*). Mammalian muscle differs in that its texture for eating purposes is influenced by several independent factors, none of which really predominates (Kruggel, Field and Miller, 1970). Love, Robertson *et al.* (1974b: *Gadus morhua*) found that the texture showed a high (negative) correlation with pH, and poorer correlations with muscle water (negative) and body length (positive). The steady toughening of texture with fall in pH is shown in Fig. 127, an effect so pronounced that fish to be used for freezing and cold storage, which toughens them further, should not have a post-mortem pH of less than 6·6 (T. R. Kelly, 1969) or even 6·7 (K. O. Kelly, 1969). It is obvious, therefore, that any systematic studies on seasonal variation in the pH of fish would be of great importance to the food industry, since low-pH fish should not usually be frozen.

4. SEASONAL VARIATION IN THE POST-MORTEM pH

Since a fall in the pH of fish muscle after death invariably means an increase in the amount of lactic acid formed (MacCallum, Jaffray et al., 1968; Kida and Tamoto, 1969), it would appear at first sight to give a measure of the carbohydrate reserves of the muscle at the point of death, but the situation is not straightforward. Figure 128 shows that the amount of glycogen in the muscle at the moment of death does correlate with the fall in pH after death—but only sometimes. A similar variable correlation was observed by Takeuchi and Ishii (1969).

If the vigour of struggling immediately before death were to vary seasonally, this would vary the quantity of muscle glycogen already decomposed at the point of death and the quantity of lactic acid formed subsequently from residual glycogen. However, since the lactic acid formed during capture struggle appears to be retained in the muscle (Dando, 1969a; R. Batty and C. S. Wardle, unpublished), the amount of struggling should not alter the final value of the post-mortem pH, since such lactic acid is simply added to that formed passively after death. Experience in the writer's laboratory amply confirms this: the muscle of *Gadus morhua* forced to swim or struggle before death, either in a tank on the trawler or in an aquarium at the laboratory, reaches the same post-mortem pH as that of fish killed at once on capture or removal from an aquarium (Love and Muslemuddin, 1972).

The amount of lactic acid formed in the muscle after death is much less than equivalent to the amount of glycogen previously present. This is because much of the glycogen is split hydrolytically to glucose after death (Tarr, 1973). Such glucose would not alter the post-mortem pH of the muscle, so any variation in the proportions of glycogen converted to glucose or lactic acid might account for the unsatisfactory relationship between glycogen content and subsequent post-mortem pH (Fig. 128).

Since there is a correlation between *liver* glycogen and post-mortem muscle pH (Love, Robertson et al., 1974a: *Gadus morhua*), and an inverse correlation between the water content of muscle and its post-mortem pH (Tanaka, 1969a: *Cyprinus carpio*) it seemed likely that the pH would be high all winter and low all summer, reflecting food intake, but such proved to be too simple a view. A survey (Fig. 129) showed that the muscle pH of almost all the cod after death lies above 6·6, but that for a short period in the summer some lower values appear,

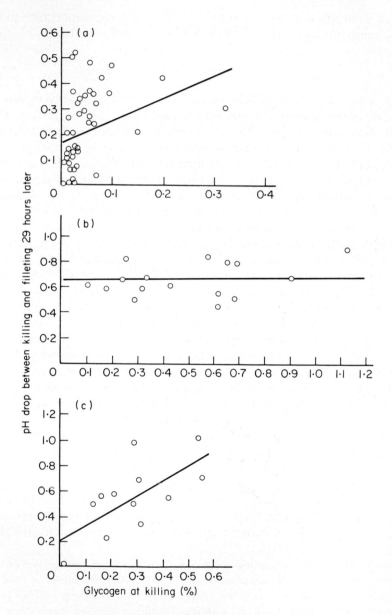

FIG. 128. Graphs showing the variable correlation between the glycogen content of *Gadus morhua* muscle at killing and the subsequent post-mortem fall in pH 29 hours later. (a) Fish caught in traps on June 21st; (b) July 19th; and (c) August 2nd, 1965. After MacCallum, Jaffray *et al.* (1967). Reproduced with permission of the Fisheries Research Board of Canada (per Mr E. J. Sandeman).

followed by a return to the previous level[1]. Continuation of the survey for several years has shown that while the dates of the "undesirable" period of low pH can vary somewhat from year to year (Fig. 130) between May and August, it is usually brief in any one year. Sometimes there appears to be more than one minimum, perhaps the effect of

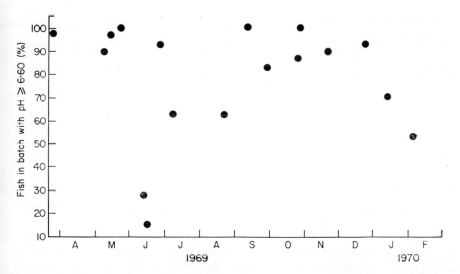

FIG. 129. The proportion of a batch of 20 *Gadus morhua* having a post-mortem pH of 6·6 or greater. The sudden drop in June is thought to be the result of feeding following a period of starvation. After Love (1979).

sampling different local groups of fish. Similar results were obtained in the same species from a wide variety of fishing grounds (Love, 1979), so the phenomenon is not confined to one area. The small peak in the gaping curve seen in November–December (Fig. 126) corresponds with a lesser and intermittent trend for the pH to be lower also. This may correspond with increased feeding resulting from the oceans being stirred up by the November storms, which gives a temporary increase in the food supply. Refeeding *Gadus morhua* starved for 185 days at 9°C in an aquarium was shown by Love (1979) to result in very low muscle pH values if the fish were refed for about 105 days, in one case a value

---

[1] These graphs (Figs 129 and 130) are drawn as "% of fish with pH higher than 6·6" since this value is a proposed limit if the fish is to be frozen as food. However, it is also worth reminding the reader that, since pH is a logarithmic function, values should not, strictly speaking, be averaged in the ordinary way, but converted to their arithmetic equivalents, averaged, and then reconverted to logs (Hofman, 1973).

of 5·87 being obtained. This is lower than anything previously observed in cod from the wild. Starving this species but not refeeding produces pH values in the muscle (after death) which are always greater than 6·8.

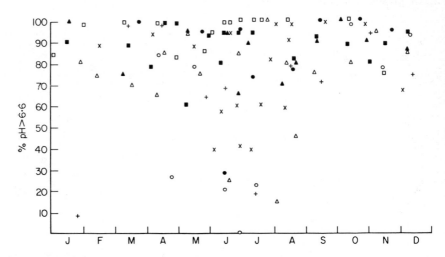

FIG. 130. As in Fig. 129: the variation in post-mortem pH of *Gadus morhua* muscle as studied over a number of years. The period of low pH is usually short, though in 1971 and 1973 there were several minima. ●, 1969; ○, 1971; +, 1972; ×, 1973; □, 1974; ■, 1975; △, 1976; ▲, 1977. After Love (1979).

Despite the variability shown in Fig. 130, the phenomenon appears to be one of "overshoot", an overcompensation for starvation, followed by a readjustment to normal values. Créac'h (1972) observed that the level of blood glucose in starving *Cyprinus carpio* rises to unusually high levels on refeeding, subsiding to normal levels after 2 months. The fish are then indistinguishable from the controls fed continuously except for one feature—an unusually high level of glycogen in the liver. Since Love, Robertson *et al.* (1974a) found a good correlation between high liver glycogen values and low muscle pH, it appears likely that the muscle pH of these starving and refed carp would also be low. Ince and Thorpe (1976) refed starving *Esox lucius* and found that the muscle glycogen became more concentrated than in the muscle of freshly captured fish. Shul'man (1972: p. 50) also quotes several workers as demonstrating that when carp are given the customary quantity of feed after starvation, the intensity of synthetic processes is higher than in control fish fed continuously ("regenerative synthesis").

Thus as regards the purpose of this present chapter, to indicate techniques which give new information about captured fish, an unusually low pH in the muscle indicates refeeding *following starvation*. From what we have seen already (p. 217), an unusually high RNA level gives the same indication.

Seaburg and Moyle (1964) studied the summer food intake of a number of freshwater fish species and concluded that the greatest volumes of food were found in the stomachs in early summer and least in late summer. The phenomenon is probably fairly general (Keast, 1970). If such a situation occurred in *Gadus morhua*, it would still probably not account for the rise in post-mortem muscle pH after the summer fall, since the rate of absorption of food, which depends on the temperature, is more important than the relative volume of food in the stomach, provided that the fish is not actually starving. "Overshoot" still seems to be the best explanation for the observed phenomenon.

The action of insulin in fish is more complex than in mammals, and varies with the species of fish, the season and the physiological state (Leibson, Plisetskaya and Leibush, 1976). Therefore the mechanism of the refeeding phenomenon can only be guessed at, though insulin is almost certainly involved at some stage. The hormone has a variable effect on liver glycogen, but is known to increase muscle glycogen sometimes (Fingerman, 1974; Lewander, 1976). Its secretion is triggered by a rise in blood glucose, and the release of insulin is proportional to the glucose concentration (Maske and Munke, 1956: Pleuronectidae; Khanna and Gill, 1973: *Channa punctatus*; Bhatt, 1974: *Clarias batrachus*; Ince and Thorpe, 1977: *Anguilla anguilla*). However, the foods given in refeeding experiments have usually been low in carbohydrate (fish muscle or squid muscle), and so on their own are unlikely to raise the blood glucose so very much.

On the other hand, a high-protein diet has also been observed to promote insulin release from the pancreas (Ahmad and Matty, 1975: *Salmo gairdneri*) and Ince and Thorpe (1977) found that arginine and lysine injected into *Anguilla anguilla* both stimulate insulin release.

In the absence of any further evidence, we may therefore conclude that while refeeding may also initiate gluconeogenesis in the liver, it probably stimulates the pancreas to secrete insulin and thus to promote glycogen synthesis in the muscle.

There is in addition a relationship between the post-mortem pH of the muscle of *Gadus morhua* and their body lengths. The first survey done by Love, Robertson *et al.* (1974b), which covered fish from several grounds, seemed to show no relationship whatsoever (Fig. 131), but it is quite obvious after a moment's thought that these fish were in variable stages of starvation so that, at any body length, one could find any pH value. However, it can be seen that only the small fish from the Faroe Bank exhibit high pH values, those of all the larger fish being low. A return visit to this ground, where, as we saw earlier, the fish are very well nourished, confirmed the effect (Fig. 132).

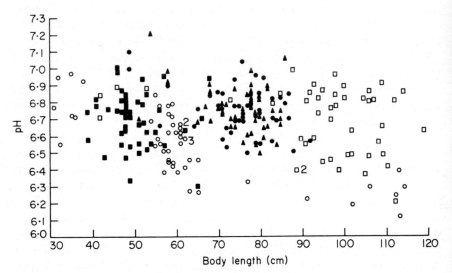

FIG. 131. Individual post-mortem pH values of the muscle of *Gadus morhua* caught on different grounds in September 1971: the relationship with body-length. ○, Faroe Bank; ●, North Cape Bank (N. Norway); ■, Aberdeen Bank; △, Scolpen Bank (White Sea); □, Bear Island. After Love, Robertson *et al.* (1974b).

It seems clear that bigger fish when well nourished either have greater glycogen reserves in their muscle, perhaps part of a general nutritional safeguard against their greater depletion at the time of spawning, or convert more glycogen into lactate after death. It is not possible to carry out meaningful glycogen determinations on cod caught by trawling because of the long stress time.

The horizontal phase of pH at body lengths above 80 cm (Fig. 132) is curious. At first it was thought that the glycolytic enzymes were not functioning below about pH 6·2, but a return visit to the Faroe Bank (September 1974: Love, unpublished) gave results with a horizontal phase at pH 6·6. In any case, our experiments with starving-refed fish have shown (Love, 1979) that a pH as low as 5·8 is possible in this species. The shape of the curve in Fig. 132 remains unexplained at present.

From what we have learned again and again about species differences, it is not surprising to learn at this point that the striking seasonal
variation in post-mortem muscle pH of *Gadus morhua* (Fig. 130) does not
occur in *Melanogrammus aeglefinus*. The small undulation (Fig. 133) seen
by Connell and Howgate (1969) lies within narrow limits, and was not

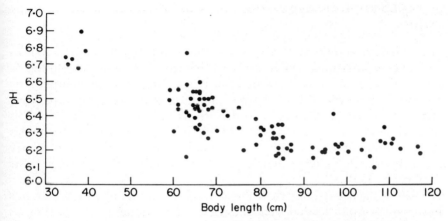

FIG. 132. The relationship between the post-mortem pH of the muscle and body-
length, in well-nourished *Gadus morhua* from the Faroe Bank (caught September,
1972). After Love, Robertson *et al.* (1974b).

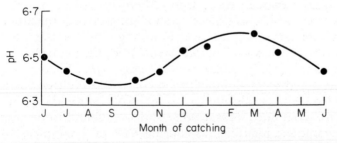

FIG. 133. Seasonal variation in the post-mortem pH of the muscle of *Melanogrammus
aeglefinus*. After Connell and Howgate (1969). Reproduced with permission of Dr
J. J. Connell.

in fact observed by Love (1979) in haddock taken from different
grounds. The consistently low pH of this species after death is however a
constant feature, which causes extensive gaping on almost every occasion
that they are frozen whole, thawed and filleted. Haddock are rarely
suitable, therefore, for this type of presentation. More interesting would

be the physiological reason for the lower pH, at present unknown. One would have imagined that greater carbohydrate reserves would signify a more active species, but haddock in fact live in a more leisurely way than cod, grazing the bottom where the cod actively pursue prey (R. Jones, personal communication).

5.   COLD-STORE FLAVOUR/ODOUR, AND SEASONAL VARIATION IN LIPIDS

When fish are kept in the frozen state, they gradually develop a characteristic taste and smell which has been likened to cardboard, cold tea or fish meal. It becomes very strong in fatty fish such as pelagic clupeids or salmonids, but even if there is almost no lipid in the fish, the off-flavour (and odour) can still develop quite strongly. The reason is that it is derived largely from the oxidation of the unsaturated fatty acid moieties of phospholipids (A. S. McGill, personal communication) and nearly all of the muscle lipids of "non-fatty" fish such as *Gadus morhua* consists of phospholipids.

Tasting the cooked muscle of *Gadus morhua* caught on various grounds in the north Atlantic after a short period of frozen storage, K. J. Whittle (unpublished, quoted by Love, 1975) found that the samples from the Faroe Bank had a far stronger off-flavour and odour than those from other grounds. Love, Hardy and Nishimoto (1975) showed that both in June and September the lipid content of cod from this ground is always slightly higher than in those from Aberdeen Bank, one of the other grounds from which fish were examined. Further, the lipid fraction which varies according to season and ground is the phospholipid fraction (the precursor of the off-flavour) not the neutral lipid. Finally, Ross and Love (1979) starved some *Gadus morhua* for two months and then cold stored them along with fed controls. After thawing and cooking, the fed controls exhibited a strong off-flavour and odour, while the starved fish contained almost none and were found to be good to eat.

The compound identified as causing most of the unpleasant changes detected by the eater is *cis*-4-heptenal (McGill, 1974; McGill, Hardy *et al.*, 1974: *Gadus morhua*), and Ross and Love (1979) reported 23 nmol of this compound per kilogram of fed control muscle after cold storage (10 weeks at $-10°C$), compared with only 3·5 nmol in the starved fish Thus the flavour (and odour) of cooked non-fatty fish which has been cold stored will be subject to seasonal variation according to the degree of starvation undergone.

The effect of varying degrees of starvation on the proportion of unsaturated fatty acids in flesh lipid has also been studied. C22:6 is the most important fatty acid and also the most unsaturated, and its steady decline during starvation (Fig. 134) fits in with the reduced formation of *cis*-4-heptenal in starved cold-stored fish.

Any other seasonal or ground-to-ground variations in the flavour probably relate to the diet, certain unpleasant flavours, for example, being associated with a certain type of alga in the food chain.

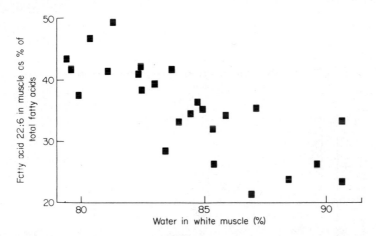

FIG. 134. The decline in the proportion of fatty acid 22:6 in the muscle of *Gadus morhua* during starvation. The progress of starvation is shown from the water content (80–81% is the normal, replete level). After Ross (1978). Reproduced with permission of the author.

6.   SEASONAL VARIATION IN THE COLOUR OF THE DARK MUSCLE

This topic has already been covered in the section on dark muscle (p. 108). Briefly, people eating fish grow to expect a certain product to have a certain colour, and wide departures from what is regarded as normal are looked on with disfavour (Love, 1978). The colour of the dark muscle intensifies when the fish become more active, so migratory stocks of fish have the darkest dark muscle (Love, Munro and Robertson, 1977: *Gadus morhua*), and there is a well-marked seasonal cycle. Figure 38, repeated here in miniature as a reminder, seems to show evidence of increased swimming activity as prey become more plentiful. If a  really white food product is required from cod flesh, therefore, one should use winter-caught fish, avoiding the migratory Spitzbergen–Bear Island–Norway stock (Love, 1978).

7. TRANSLUCENCY

Another aspect of the appearance of fish muscle is its translucency. We have seen (Volume 1, p. 224) how the muscle of starving non-fatty fish becomes more hydrated. Perhaps because of a shift in the water–ion–protein balance during depletion, the gel-like appearance of the flesh gives place to a white opacity which can be measured. Its intensity is proportional to the degree of protein depletion, and, like the water content, it fluctuates regularly on a seasonal basis (Fig. 135). The dead-white appearance is generally considered to be less attractive than the normal bluish translucence, but it can be avoided by taking non-fatty fish for use as food only outside their spawning season.

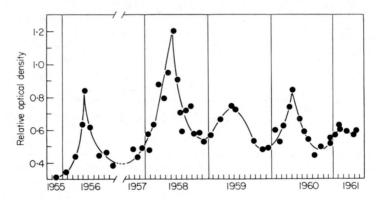

FIG. 135. Seasonal variation in the opacity of whole muscle tissue (freed from myo-commata) from *Gadus morhua*. An increase in opacity seems to follow the hydration which is seen at around the spawning season. After Love (1962: Volume 1, reference 759).

C.   Biological condition. The "syndrome" of the fish

1.   INTRODUCTION

It was Shul'man (1972), or rather his translator, who identified the aim of future studies of condition as the close specification of the "syndrome" of the fish. In practical terms this means identifying the parameters which give new insights into the state of a fish captured at a particular moment. Where more than one parameter measures the same phenomenon, for example water content and opacity measurements (Fig. 135 above), which give measures of protein depletion, then one uses only the most convenient or the most accurate (in this case water content), and discards the others. In studying the seasonal variations in different parameters, one notes the cases in which the peak or peaks formed each year coincide, and selects in future only one of them for measurement. Surprisingly, most of the parameters to be described below possess seasonal maxima which in fact do *not* coincide, so that new insights are possible. Regrettably, all of the work to be described in the remainder of this section relates solely to *Gadus morhua*, but this is the only species to have been studied in the present context and, while the phenomena remain to be confirmed in other species, there is no reason why they should not be of wide occurrence, perhaps in modified forms. In addition, to be honest, they also suffer from the drawbacks of suggestions made by other writers summed up in Table 21 (p. 354), in that they are the "speciality of the worker(s) who first investigated them, are tentative, derived from work on a single species and not backed up by further extensive trials ...". Taking that as read, however, let us see what possibilities for studying the "syndrome" of the fish emerge.

2. EARLIER WORK ON *Gadus morhua*

In Volume 1, Fig. 45, we saw that starvation results in a rise in the water content of the white muscle, the annual maximum coinciding with the time of spawning or slightly after it. A miniature reproduction of the Figure is given here as a reminder. However, artificial starvation in an aquarium showed that there is a considerable lag period while other energy sources are being used, before the water content starts to rise (Volume 1, Fig. 84; miniature reproduced here). If we consider that a muscle water content of 81% or above represents starvation, then the Figure shows that a fish could have starved totally for as much as 8 weeks at 9°C without the fact being detected by the measurement of muscle water. At lower temperatures the time would be more than 8 weeks.

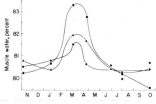

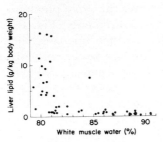

Turning now to Fig. 65 of the present volume (see miniature), we see that the level of lipid reserves in *Gadus morhua* varies within wide limits where the water content of the muscle is below about 81%, but is always low when the water content is higher than this. It shows clearly that in this species the liver lipid is used before the muscle protein during starvation. However, it is possible, from our own limited information, that the sequence may change somewhat if spawning, rather than just shortage of food, is involved. In that case, protein can be removed from the muscle while considerable reserves of lipid remain in the liver.

We may consider that the muscle water content gives information on the later stages of simple starvation and, at least in theory, the liver lipid indicates the progress of the earlier stages. This is true only in a general way, however, because cod from different grounds accumulate different maximum quantities of liver lipid, and variation between individuals makes it impossible to decide for how long the fish has starved. The most we can say is that a large creamy liver indicates a good state of nutrition, while a small reddish or brownish one shows depletion. Neither muscle water nor liver lipid determinations *on their own* give any idea of the dynamics of the situation: we do not learn that a starving fish is at the moment recovering or still getting worse. What are needed are phenomena which are observed only at a particular, narrowly defined stage of starvation, and for the rest of this chapter we shall consider some tentative approaches and their limitations.

3.   PROPOSALS

a.   *Protein insolubility*

When the muscle of well-fed cod is homogenised with neutral 5% sodium chloride, about 95% of it dissolves. However, we saw in Volume

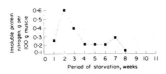

1, Fig. 92 (see miniature for reminder) that the insoluble fraction rises to a peak about two weeks after the beginning of artificial starvation. The mechanism is unknown, but the phenomenon at least marks a definite stage of depletion, and when seasonal data from early work were re-examined, a well-marked cycle became apparent (Fig. 136). The stock of fish examined spawn at the beginning of March, but the

Figure shows that there are clear signs of preparation for gonad building as early as November. The fish are almost certainly not starving at that time in the sense of being actually deprived of food (Volume 1, reference 1049), but the peak in Fig. 136 probably shows the point at which the absorption of protein from the gut is failing to match the requirements of the gonads, so the muscle must be preparing in some way for mobilisation. This seems to be the most likely interpretation of the phenomenon, since the *total* protein nitrogen in the muscle has not diminished at this stage (see the first two entries in Table 34 of Volume 1).

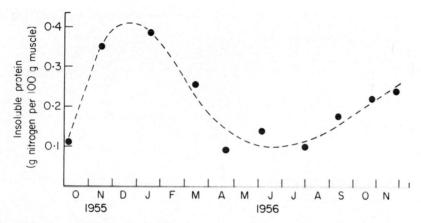

FIG. 136. Seasonal variation in the amount of white muscle protein which will *not* dissolve in chilled neutral 5% NaCl on homogenisation (*Gadus morhua*). Some points are drawn from unpublished work, others from Volume 1, Table 34.

b.   *Endolymph protein*

Otoliths, the calcareous bodies in the heads of many species of fish, grow by accretion from the fluid which bathes them ("endolymph"). In the winter the accreted layers are largely calcium carbonate, but in the summer there is also a considerable proportion of protein mingled with it (Volume 1, p. 160). If the otolith is broken across the middle, the winter and summer accretions appear respectively as white and dark rings when viewed with transmitted light (Volume 1, Fig. 64 and 65), and afford a way of measuring the age of the fish. More recently it has been shown that, at least in larval fish, minute light and dark rings on the otoliths alternate even on a daily basis (Brothers, Mathews and Lasker, 1976), so that up to nearly 2 months after hatching the larva can be aged in days (Fig. 137), presumably reflecting daily feeding.

Daily rings have been observed also on the otoliths of *Lepomis gibbosus*, *L. cyanellus* and *Tilapia mossambica* (Taubert and Coble, 1977) and some cold-temperate species (Pannella, 1971). Little is really known of the physiology of deposition of material on to the otoliths, but, once formed, the otolith material appears not to be resorbed at any time later (Simkiss, 1974).

Fɪɢ. 137. Daily growth rings on the otolith of a larval *Engraulis mordax*. The fish was caught in June 1975 off the Baja California peninsula, and was 20·4 mm long. There are about 45 rings, which shows the fish to be about 50 days old. There is a 5-day period between hatching and yolk absorption when no rings are formed. Photograph kindly supplied by Dr E. B. Brothers.

Since the formation of a ring which contains protein coincides with an increase in the protein content of the endolymph (Volume 1, reference 881), it seems possible that the endo-lymph composition might reflect an aspect of fish nutrition.

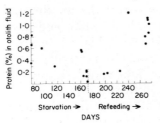

Figure 90 showed (see miniature) that total starvation brings the endolymph pro-tein content down to very low values and that refeeding raises it again, but that there is a great deal of variation between individual fish. The rise after refeeding is not instantaneous, but seems to be rapid after a certain point. Values in fish from the wild (Fig. 138) are never as low as in those kept completely without food in an aquarium, and with summer feeding they rise steadily and continuously throughout the season. The positions of the maxima, in September of one year and

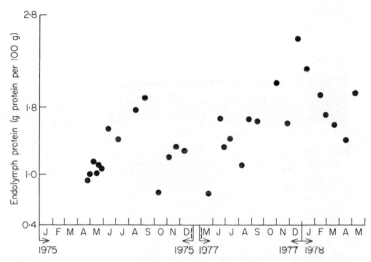

FIG. 138. Seasonal variation in the protein of the endolymph of *Gadus morhua*. Each point is the mean value from a batch of 20 fish. After Love (unpublished). Crown Copyright.

December of the other, seem to suggest that the protein concentration of endolymph continues to rise for as long as the fish is in positive protein balance. It is most unlikely to reflect feeding level. Otherwise, it appears that with high muscle water contents the endolymph protein is always low, but with water contents approaching normal, any value within the range can be obtained (Fig. 89—see minia- ture for reminder). The analogy with liver lipid (Fig. 65) is obvious, but really low en- dolymph protein values are seen consistently only in fish with muscle water contents above about 84%, as compared with about 81% for liver lipid.

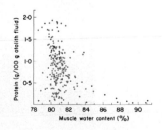

This parameter is probably of less practical application than some others because of the wide variation, but at least we can say that a high

FIG. 139. A graded selection of bile samples from a single haul of *Gadus morhua* caught near Aberdeen in September 1977. A large volume of dark blue or green bile indicates starvation, and a small volume of pale fluid is found in actively feeding fish. Author's photograph. Crown Copyright.

endolymph protein concentration shows a satisfactory food intake *which has been in progress for some time*. An advantage of the technique is that it is quite rapid and could be carried out at sea.

c. *Bile*

We have seen already that the colour absorbence of bile rises rapidly during starvation (Fig. 91—see miniature) and that changes take place in certain ions. An illustration of the range of colours obtainable in a single haul of *Gadus morhua* is shown in Fig. 139. It will be noticed that as the colour darkens, the volume of the bile increases. There is, however, no (negative) correlation between bile volume and the volume of the stomach contents.

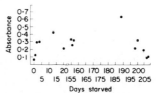

Taking *Gadus morhua* from the sea, the writer's group became aware that all of the fish from some grounds had pale yellow bile, while all of those from other grounds had blue or green bile. By placing in an aquarium some live fish from a batch with pale yellow bile, Love (1975) found that it took a minimum of 9 hours without food before the first pale tinge of green appeared in the bile—perhaps a result of the oxidation of bilirubin glucuronide to biliverdin glucuronide, the former compound being readily oxidisable at low pH values (K. Yamaguchi, personal communication). After 30 hours all of the remaining fish were found to possess a recognisably green bile. We have seen from Fig. 91 that the colour intensifies for three days or so and then remains dark for a long subsequent period of starvation. The decline in colour after very long starvation is puzzling at first, but observations show that, during starvation, bile tends to leak into the intestine. Presumably after a long period without food the bile pigments are produced in diminishing quantities.

Turning now to seasonal variation in *Gadus morhua* from the vicinity of Aberdeen, we find indications that the fish are actually starving, as distinct from requiring more nourishment than is supplied by the feed, in the month of May (Fig. 140). If these indications are right and the food supply really does become worse for a short time at the end of the winter, it would reinforce the idea of "overshoot" as an explanation for the abnormally low pH which is usually seen in June or July; the fish seem to overcompensate for their depleted carbohydrate reserves once food again becomes available. If a stomach is empty because the food has just passed into the intestine, then either the bile is small in volume and straw-coloured or the (blue) gall bladder is virtually empty or at least flaccid. Truly starving fish have firmly swollen gall bladders. An examination of the gall bladder may therefore give a more realistic picture than counting the number of empty stomachs, which may in any case have been emptied by vomiting during capture.

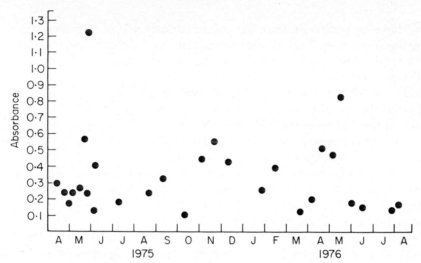

FIG. 140. Seasonal variation in the absorbance at 400 nm of bile from *Gadus morhua* caught near Aberdeen. Each point is the mean of 20 samples. There are indications from this diagram that cod starve in May. After Love, Kim and Gomez (unpublished).

To sum up: pale straw-coloured bile indicates continuous feeding over a period. A large, firm deep-blue gall bladder with a tight, thin skin means starvation in progress. A blue gall bladder with wrinkled skin of uneven appearance seems always to indicate the resumption of feeding after starvation.

d.   *The production of insulin*

Since the release of insulin by the pancreas is triggered by an increase in the circulating glucose or amino acids (p. 365), it is reasonable to expect that circulating insulin will reflect the feeding level. Limited studies seem to show that the nutritional state in the early stages of starvation or of refeeding after starvation are indeed faithfully reflected in the blood insulin concentration, although the present slow and sophisticated method needed to measure insulin detracts from its usefulness as a quick "marker". Thorpe and Ince (1976) found that the level in *Salmo gairdneri* after feeding for 7 days was 4·2 ng/ml, increasing to 5·7 after a further 7 days, and declining to 2·2 ng/ml after a subsequent 7-day starvation period. Ross (1978) in this laboratory has shown a similar effect in *Gadus morhua*, the insulin concentration in the blood being 2·1 ng/ml after starvation and 5 ng/ml after refeeding. More points on the time scale are needed, and so far no one has delineated the pattern of any seasonal variation.

The pancreas ("Brockman Body" in cod) shows somewhat inconsistent variations in its size, probably related to its secretory activity (Lavéty and Love, unpublished observations over a 3-year period). However, the scatter of individual results here almost certainly precludes its use for determining the feeding level of individual fish.

Measurements of the great variations in the vascularity of the Brockman Body have so far produced no conclusive results.

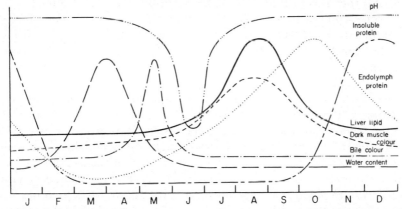

Fig. 141. Diagrammatic representation of the manner in which various parameters change throughout the year in *Gadus morhua*. It is hoped that, by measuring more than one at a given time, new insights on the biological condition of cod, especially the dynamics of nutrition, may be obtained.

4. CONCLUSIONS

The seasonal variations of the different parameters discussed in this chapter, together with water content and pH, are summarised schematically in Fig. 141. The most encouraging feature is that their peaks are well spaced from one another, so that a composite picture emerges and we are nearer to being able to describe the "syndrome" of the fish rather than different aspects of the same attribute.

It will be realised that some of these studies are as yet in an early stage and that Fig. 141 gives expression to a number of speculative approaches. However, let us take some actual instances and see where we stand by comparison with the use of earlier skills.

1. Norwegian arctic cod—caught off Tromsø in February 1974—were observed by the writer to possess dark muscle of a deep chocolate-brown colour, the characteristic of migratory fish. The large creamy-coloured livers showed that they had fed well during the journey, but a rise in the muscle water content (the highest value was 82·7%) suggested that the protein intake had been barely sufficient for the requirements of the gonads. All of the gall bladders were very large, turgid and blue, so the fish had abstained from food for at least a few days: perhaps they did not eat while spawning. However, the rich state of the livers showed that they had only recently stopped feeding. The pH values of the muscle after death were uniformly high (over 6·8), so that recent feeding had been continuous and regular.

2. Some observations on *Gadus morhua* taken in early summer and autumn from different grounds are listed in Table 22. Not all of the parameters illustrated in Fig. 141 were measured on these voyages.

If we look at the "classical" parameters first, we find differences according to the fishing ground only, not according to the season. The most corpulent fish, those with the highest condition factor, are those from Faroe Bank and the leanest were caught off Bear Island—but this we know already from direct observation and measurements of the caudal peduncle (Volume 1, p. 158). Further, in these fishing grounds there is almost no difference between fish caught in September and those caught in June, although the former are satiated after the summer and the latter have not long started their heavy feeding. The "condition factor" therefore seems to yield minimal information here. Again, the information to be gained from the weights of the livers is curious. The cod caught in September may be in their best nutritional condition, but those from Aberdeen Bank have less than half of the liver, that is, less than half of the liver *oil*, of the Bear Island/Spitzbergen migratory fish. The relative proportion of liver in the Faroe Bank fish will seem less because of the greater plumpness of these fish. The most likely explanation for the differences between livers is that the stocks which will later swim many hundreds of miles lay down the most lipid for fuel, so that liver size is not automatically high and uniform in satiated fish. In June, near the start of refeeding, the liver size differs little from September levels in Aberdeen Bank and Bear Island fish, and is actually greater in Faroe Bank fish, perhaps again because it is expressed as a

TABLE 22

Some characteristics of *Gadus morhua* caught on several grounds at different seasons

Ground	Colour of Bile (number of pale yellow/total)	Weight of heart (percent of body weight)	Water content (muscle) %	Brockman body (percent of fish weight $\times 10^3$)	Condition factor $\dfrac{W \times 100}{L^3}$	pH of muscle (post-mortem)	Liver weight (percent of fish weight)
a. September 1974							
Aberdeen Bank	46/48	0·17±0·04	80·9±0·59	1·19±0·99	1·03±0·08	6·93±0·13	1·91±1·09
Bear Island	Not recorded	0·12±0·03	80·8±0·55	2·53±1·15	0·92±0·08	6·94±0·11	5·10±1·67
Spitzbergen	36/50	0·13±0·02	81·0±0·64	1·85±0·88	0·95±0·07	6·96±0·09	4·27±0·84
Faroe Bank	47/50	0·11±0·02	80·1±0·71	1·48±0·54	1·20±0·11	6·80±0·18	3·88±2·05
b. June 1975							
Aberdeen Bank	17/35	0·12±0·02	81·5±1·34	0·93±0·48	1·03±0·09	6·74±0·12	2·15±0·80
Bear Island	0/35	0·13±0·03	81·2±0·64	1·94±1·06	0·86±0·10	6·77±0·14	4·20±1·64
Faroe Bank	34/35	0·12±0·02	79·9±0·41	1·47±0·56	1·27±0·10	6·48±0·10	4·76±1·18

Numbers given are means ± standard deviations.

proportion of the total body weight, which in the latter is leaner at the end of the winter.

We learn rather more about the state of the fish from some of the "newer" parameters. The September-caught fish are all fully nourished (from the low water contents in the muscle), are nearly all actually feeding (from the colour of the bile) and have been feeding for some time (from the post-mortem pH which is not unduly low). *Some of* the Bear Island fish may recently have been feeding more heavily than those from any of the other grounds (high average Brockman Body weight, but high standard deviation[1]). In June, the musculature of the Faroe Bank fish has already recovered from the winter starvation (water content) and the fish are feeding heavily, being in the middle of the "overshoot" period for post-mortem pH. The pH of the June fish from the other two grounds has dropped a little, at least indicating *some* feeding after starvation, and if our interpretation of the changes in the Brockman Body weight is correct, then the fish from Bear Island again appear to be feeding the most heavily at that time. Both Aberdeen Bank and Bear Island fish are still showing signs of winter starvation (a muscle water content of $81 \cdot 1\%$ or more) and the blue biles suggest that the Bear Island fish were not actually feeding at the time of capture. A final point is that the fish known to remain in a small area throughout their lives, the Faroe Bank stock (Jones, 1966; Jamieson and Jones, 1967), have the smallest hearts, and the migratory Spitzbergen/Bear Island fish have the largest.

Time will tell whether we have learned anything really new. In the meantime, at least some potential exists, and the idea of examining a combination of phenomena which illustrate a *sequence* of events seems sound.

D.   Miscellaneous observations on variable constituents

1.   DIURNAL VARIATIONS

Fish have been shown to alter their swimming activity in a definite pattern according to the time of day. The changes probably relate to feeding, and seem to be intimately linked to the photoperiod. Loco-motor activity increases at dawn and decreases after dusk in *Lepomis*

---

[1]Recent results in the writer's laboratory (October, 1978) have shown that the Brockman Body increases steadily in size when cod are refed after starving in an aquarium. Much more work is needed to put the idea on a sound basis.

macrochirus (Beitinger, 1975), but tends not to follow unnatural photo-periods imposed by the experimenter. High metabolic rates as measured by oxygen consumption have been reported at both dawn and dusk in *Oncorhynchus nerka* (Brett, 1972). Mršulja and Rakić (1974) found that the evening hours represent the most active time for *Serranus scriba*, and also the optimal time for learning in behaviour experiments. At the same time, the glycogen content of various parts of the brain falls. Serum glucose has been reported to rise during the hours of darkness in *Carassius auratus* (Shapiro and Hoffman, 1975), perhaps through reduced locomotor activity and hence reduced demand. The explanation given by these writers, that darkness acts as a kind of stress, is not on the face of it very convincing.

The serotonin (5-hydroxytryptamine) content of the brains of *Fundulus grandis* has been shown by Fingerman (1976) to be higher during the day than the night, and to correlate to some extent with swimming activity. Adrenocorticotropic hormone shows peaks in *Carassius auratus* blood, occurring 4 and 7–9 hours after the onset of light, though it is not clear whether it is in fact the daylight which triggers the secretion (Singley and Chavin, 1976). The cortisol in the blood follows the same pattern (Chavin, 1973; Singley and Chavin, 1975a). Plasma cortisol shows a maximum at dawn in *Fundulus grandis*, plus another maximum which differs according to the sex of the individual (Garcia and Meier, 1973). Srivastava and Meier (1972) concluded that the daily variation in cortisol does not depend automatically on that of the adreno-corticotropic hormone from the pituitary.

Serum prolactin also exhibits diurnal variations linked to the photo-period (McKeown and Peter, 1976: *Carassius auratus;* Spieler, Meier and Loesch, 1976: *Mugil cephalus;* Leatherland, McKeown and John, 1974: *Oncorhynchus nerka*). The latter authors also showed a daily rhythm in circulating growth hormone (same species).

De Vlaming and Sage (1972: *Cyprinodon variegatus, Fundulus similis*) made the curious observation that the *response* to an injection of prolactin also varies diurnally. Eight hours after the beginning of the light period, the hormone causes the fish to lay down lipid, while two hours after the beginning the injection results in lipid catabolism. These differences occur regardless of whether the control fish are increasing or decreasing their lipid stores. The authors warned experimenters to pay attention to "physiological time" when conducting endocrine experiments.

The gonadotropic hormone present in the pituitary glands of *Salmo gairdneri* and *Salvelinus fontinalis* has been found to be fairly constant for most of the day by O'Connor (1972), but to exhibit a sudden fall in the early morning, probably corresponding with its release into the body of the fish. The daily release occurs at a specific time within the photoperiod. On the other hand, Schreck, Lackey and Hopwood (1972) could find no diurnal variation in the blood androgen levels of *Salmo gairdneri*.

The concentration of chloride in the plasma of *Fundulus chrysotus* and *F. grandis* has been found to vary markedly during the day by Meier, Lynch and Garcia (1973), but the times of high and low concentrations during the day may vary seasonally, so these authors concluded that it is not possible to describe a single daily rhythm to characterise the species. On the other hand, Davis and Simco (1976a: *Ictalurus punctatus*) concluded that there is no diurnal variation in plasma chloride, nor in any season nor under any variations in the environment which were studied. Here again the picture would be much clearer if the underlying physiology were known.

2. SEASONAL VARIATIONS

At the present state of knowledge there are still numerous cycles of function or chemistry which are unexplained. Some are bizarre—the maximum seaward movement of *Oncorhynchus kisutch* fry was shown by Mason (1975) to coincide with the time of the new moon in successive lunar cycles, and showed no obvious relationships with river flow or temperature. However, a large proportion of the observations can now be linked directly or indirectly with the increased temperature found in summer, and its accompaniments, an increased food supply and, sometimes, sexual activity.

The body weight of *Cyprinus carpio*, for example, decreases from December to April in the northern hemisphere even though the fish are fed daily (Bouche, 1975). The water temperature is below 10°C at this time, and growth is resumed only when it exceeds this value. The RNA level of the liver rises with the temperature even where the fish are starving, so the fish almost appear to anticipate the restoration of feeding. In many fish species, the annual growth cycle is irregular, the greatest growth usually occurring outside the spawning cycle and at the beginning of the warm season (Volume 1, reference 1286: *Gadus morhua;* Lockwood, 1974: *Salmo trutta*).

Phenomena associated with the seasons sometimes shown the age of the fish. Circuli form not only on otoliths and scales, but also on parts of the skeleton such as the opercular bones. In *Tilapia melanotheron* such rings were considered by Fagade (1974) to reflect changes in salinity rather than food intake.

The enhanced physical activity in the spring associated with higher temperatures is also related to an increased synthesis of adrenaline and noradrenaline, and of their direct precursors DOPA (3,4-dihydroxy-phenylalanine) and dopamine (3,4-dihydroxyphenylethylamine). Pustovoitova-Vosilene (1972: *Cyprinus carpio*), who made the observations, said that in the spring the fish have to lead a "more intense form of life", and that the "entire endocrine system, as well as the nervous system" change accordingly. Seasonal variations in the oxygen consumption of *Heteropneustes fossilis* correlate with the activity of the thyroid gland (Pandey and Munshi, 1976), while other reports link thyroid activity to the spawning cycle, itself often triggered by a particular combination of temperature and photoperiod (Nishikawa, 1975: *Oryzias latipes*; White and Henderson, 1977: *Salvelinus fontinalis*). It was noticed by Twelves, Everson and Leith (1975) that the maximum thyroid activity in *Notothenia coriiceps neglecta* occurred about a month before spawning, so they preferred to consider the correlation as between thyroid activity and sea temperature rather than with reproduction as such. Wiggs (1974) reviewed papers purporting to correlate thyroid activity with locomotor activity, reproduction or osmoregulation, and concluded that there was still no general understanding of the role of the thyroid in fish.

The concentration of haemoglobin in the blood is lower in winter and increases in the spring time (Umminger and Mahoney, 1972: *Pseudopleuronectes americanus*; Kristoffersson, Broberg and Oikari, 1974: *Zoarces viviparus*). This is almost certainly a response to increased physical activity rather than any reduction in the oxygen concentration caused by the higher temperature: Denton and Yousef (1975: *Salmo gairdneri*) found that it changed seasonally even though the water temperature was kept constant. Berman and Vitin' (1968) observed an increase in the iron contents of the bodies of young *Salmo gairdneri* as springtime approached (doubtless the same effect), which he attributed to heightened metabolic activity.

Seasonal changes in other elements are not so easy to interpret. Zinc is lost during the winter and gained from the environment in the spring (Berman and Vitin', 1968: *Salmo gairdneri*). Chloride, calcium and magnesium are relatively stable throughout the year, but sodium and potassium vary seasonally (Houston, Madden and DeWilde, 1970: *Cyprinus carpio*). The most likely reason for changes in sodium and potassium is the alteration in the proportions of cells (rich in potassium) to extracellular fluid (rich in sodium), that is, starvation effects in winter (Volume 1, p. 246). Hyvärinen and Valtonen (1973: *Coregonus nasus sensu*) reported a rise in the copper content of liver to a maximum in March and April, followed by a steady decline. The magnesium content of the liver dropped to a minimum in May. These authors suggested that the changes reflected changes in the enzymic composition of the fish, because both elements activate a number of enzymes.

The increased metabolic activity of fish in the summer time is reflected in the greater excretion of nitrogen (Vellas and Serfaty, 1974; Infante, 1974: *Cyprinus carpio*) and enhanced activity of enzymes such as xanthine oxidase, protease (Uchiyama, Ehira *et al.*, 1969: *Cyprinus carpio*) and probably very many others.

The levels of carbohydrate are strongly influenced by the season, but in a complex way which depends very much on the species. In *Cyprinus carpio*, the seasonal variations of glucose or glycogen in the blood, liver, heart and perhaps white muscle continue even when the temperature is kept constant (Murat and Parent, 1975). Liver glycogen is maximal in January, but in heart and white muscle it reaches a peak in July, and in dark muscle in November (Murat, 1976a). Morozova and Trusevich (1971: *Trachurus mediterraneus ponticus*) concluded that it was impossible to obtain a figure which could be said to represent the resting level of blood glucose even in a single species. According to their results, the level in the year 1968 was almost ten times higher than in 1967. Year-to-year variations certainly appear in the present writer's studies on seasonal changes in the nutritional state of *Gadus morhua*: Faroe Bank cod in September 1974 had lower levels of muscle glycogen than in September 1972 or 1971, as judged by the post-mortem pH.

The glycogen content of the muscle of *Cyprinus carpio* falls to a minimum in April, according to Takeuchi and Ishii (1969), while in *Thymallus thymallus* and *Salmo trutta*, both blood glucose and liver glycogen fall in the summer (Pavlovi , 1968). Blood glucose reaches a maximum in February in *Fundulus heteroclitus*, corresponding with the minimum temperature (Leach and Taylor, 1977) and perhaps protection from freezing (see p. 343). In this species there appears also to be a "metabolic" factor in blood glucose levels, and a second, smaller, maximum appears in July (same authors). Injections of thyroxine into mammals causes hyperglycaemia, but in *Cyprinus carpio* the blood sugar is reduced. Further, it is reduced only during the winter period; in the summer, thyroxine does not affect the level of blood sugar (Murat and Serfaty, 1971).

This list of changes in the levels of carbohydrates is unsatisfactory in that no clear picture emerges. Obviously several factors influence the level revealed by analysis. We have, however, learned enough in this volume (especially pp. 361–368) to have some idea of the reasons for the appearance of very high or very low levels. We have seen how refeeding after starvation results in very high levels of carbohydrate, which then fall to more normal levels. The "overshoot" in *Gadus morhua* usually occurs in June or July, while (Fig. 141) the liver lipid does not rise to a maximum until August. It is likely, therefore, although experimental evidence is sparse, that liver glycogen rises quickly on refeeding, and liver lipid follows later after continued feeding. This seems the most likely explanation of the otherwise curious observation of Laugaste (1969: *Abramis brama*) that seasonal differences in lipid levels are negatively correlated with those of glycogen.

PART 2　Index of Chemical Substances

*It is cheating to copy the work of another man; you should
copy the work of TWO other men—they call that research.*
SOURCE UNKNOWN

The Introduction to Part 2 of Volume 1 (pp. 259 to 262) should be read also as an
introduction to the present section.

The short notes on many of the substances are taken from the texts of Volume 1 and
the present work, or from papers already quoted in the text in other connections, or
from papers supplying chemical data for Parts 2 or 3. They are intended as condensed
sources of outline information, not found elsewhere, about the specific roles of substances in fish tissues. For their roles in mammals the reader should consult a standard
biochemical textbook.

Since information from very many papers is contained in these accounts, they are
presented in note form, as briefly as possible and *without attribution* to source, simply
in order to conserve space. Where a reference is quoted, it has not appeared anywhere
else in this or the previous book, and was abstracted solely for that piece of information. Most of the vitamin deficiency symptoms have been quoted from Ashley
(1972).

Information for Parts 2 and 3 of this volume is drawn from 1328 references,
compared with about 740 in Volume 1.

References to concentrations of chemical substances in fish which were reared on
artificial diets are not included.

*Numbers in italics refer to pages in the text; those not italic are references in the Bibliography.
The symbol ‡ in front of a substance shows that further information on that substance can be
found in Volume 1.*

‡ACETATE *149, 281*
　Muscle 3419

ACETOACETATE
　Liver 3572

ACETOACETYL CoA DEACYLASE
　Liver 3026

‡ACETYL CHOLINE *330*
Brain 2957; Cholinergic vesicles from the electric organ 2957; Duodenum 2957; Electric organ 1556, 1862, 1863, 2303; Heart 2957; Ileum 2957; Kidney 2957; Liver 2957; Oesophagus 2957; Rectum 2957; Spleen 2957; Stomach 2957

‡ACETYL CHOLINESTERASE *8, 263, 328, 334*
Blood 1989; Brain 2222, 3362

N-ACETYL GALACTOSAMINE
Sialic acid glycoprotein in slime 1467, 3652

N-ACETYL GLUCOSAMINE
Sialic acid glycoprotein in slime 3652

‡*N*-ACETYL HISTIDINE
The role of this compound in fish is uncertain, but it may function as a donor of acetyl groups in acetylation. The hearts of freshwater teleosts contain about 50 mg%, but it is virtually absent from marine teleosts.
Brain 1504; Heart 1504; Lens 1504, 2181

N-ACETYL NEURAMINIC ACID (a type of sialic acid) *299, 357*
Quantity reflects quantitative variations in mucus in the gill, and has been used as a measure of the amount of mucus in the skin. The amount present correlates with the intensity of prolactin secretion in eels in fresh water.
Gangliosides 2472; Gill 2548; Sialic acid glycoprotein in slime 1467; Skin 2932, 2933

ACETYL SEROTONIN METHYLTRANSFERASE *265*
Pineal 2095

ACID GLUCOSIDASE
Muscle 2757

ACID PHOSPHATASE *72*
Blood 3525, 3526; Brain 2317, 3010; Dark Muscle 2316; Egg (unfertilised) 2874, 3227; Embryo 2874; Heart 2317; Intestinal mucus 3010; Intestine (small) 3226, 3230; Kidney 2317; Liver 2317, 3010; Mesentery 2958; Muscle 2316, 2317, 2757; Oesophagus 3226, 3230; Ovary 2317; Pituitary 2532; Pyloric caecae 2958, 3230; Rectum 3226, 3230; Spleen 2317; Stomach 3226, 3230

ACID RIBONUCLEASE
Egg 2486; Embryo 2486; Muscle 2757

"ACTOMYOSIN"
Dark Muscle 2830; Muscle 2830

ADENOSINE DEAMINASE *161*
Brain 2873; Liver 2873

‡ADENOSINE DIPHOSPHATE (ADP) *20, 281*
The level in muscle is reduced during exercise.
Dark muscle 3458; Erythrocytes 2550; Heart 3196; Liver 1584, 3196, 3219, 3220,

3721; Muscle 1852, 1871, 1951, 2428, 2456, 2918, 3196, 3367, 3419, 3457; Oocytes 3704

ADP-Ribose—*see* NADH

‡Adenosine monophosphate (AMP) *281*
  The level in muscle is reduced during exercise.
  Dark muscle 3458; Erythrocytes 2550; Heart 3196; Liver 1584, 3196, 3219, 3220, 3721; Muscle 1852, 1871, 1951, 2428, 2456, 2918, 3196, 3366, 3367, 3419, 3457, 3482; Oocytes 3704

AMP Deaminase
  Erythrocytes 2480; Gill 3572; Muscle 3572

cyclic 3'5'-Adenosine monophosphate (cAMP) *235, 355*
  Level in blood rises greatly in response to fright, stress or adrenaline injection. It could be a "second messenger" in the hyperglycaemic response to stress.
  Blood 3417; Gill 1771

2'3' *cyclic* Adenosine monophosphate-3'-phosphoester hydrolase
  Adrenal 3450; Brain 3450; Kidney 3450; Liver 3450

Adenosine triphosphatase (ATPase) *10, 23, 24, 34, 71, 72, 75, 80–82, 84, 92, 110, 156, 287, 291–295, 302, 303, 306, 307, 309, 316, 328, 331, 336, 337, 354, 355*
  Releases the energy from ATP for muscular contraction and tends to be more active in white muscle than in dark. Present in gills to provide energy for ion transport, increasing in concentration when euryhaline fish are transferred from fresh water to salt, also when salmon parr in rivers metamorphose to smolts. Its activity has therefore been proposed as an index of metamorphosis. In the gill the enzyme is activated by sodium and potassium ions, and so often called Na-K-ATPase. What appears to be another form, Mg-ATPase, may be identical with Na-K-ATPase. In kidneys, ATPase engenders resorption of sodium from the glomerular ultrafiltrate, and in the bladder, resorption of sodium from the urine. Its concentration increases in the kidneys when fish are transferred from salt water to fresh, to conserve sodium. ATPase activity is also high in the rectal gland of elasmobranchs.

. Na-K-ATPase
  Bladder 1947, 3532; Brain 1772; Chloride cells from gill 2369; Dark muscle 2344, 2345, 2830; Gill 1575, 1642, 1974, 2075, 2321, 2378, 2379, 2638, 2640, 2821, 2863, 3022, 3023, 3024, 3182, 3202, 3424, 3714, 3716; Intestine 2321; Kidney 1772, 2075, 2321, 2638, 2640, 2863; Liver 1772, 2075, 2621; Liver plasma membrane 2621; Muscle 1642, 1772, 2075, 2344, 2345, 2414, 2830; Ovary 1772; Pink (intermediate) muscle 2344; Rectal gland 2075, 2224, 2272, 2321; Rostral organ 2075; Testis 1772; Ventricle 1503

. Ca-ATPase
  Heart 1505

. Mg-ATPase
  Bladder 1947, 3532; Dark muscle 2353; Gill 1575, 1974, 2075, 2321, 2378, 2821, 3023, 3182; Intestine 2321; Kidney 1974, 2075, 2321; Liver 2075, 2621; Liver

4. HCO_3-ATPase
The means whereby animals store energy for almost instantaneous release: it breaks down during muscular activity. It is also present in red blood cells, along with guanosine triphosphate, where it reduces the capacity of the haemoglobin for oxygen by influencing the Root effect towards higher pH values. Its concentration may therefore fall under conditions of low ambient oxygen unfavourable to the fish, so that the blood is enabled to take up more of whatever oxygen is available.
(Some of these remarks apply equally to noradrenaline).
Increases in the blood during exercise or stress, and during the spawning of salmonids, where it may reflect extra physical activity. It also rises on smoltification, perhaps as an accompaniment of seaward swimming. In embryos of *Salmo gairdneri* at hatching the increased concentration may result from the effort used to free themselves from the egg. Concentrations in the blood have not been shown to be significantly different between the sexes. Injection of adrenaline (and noradrenaline) causes a rise in blood glucose, and glycogen phosphorylase and glucose-6-phosphatase activities in the liver are stimulated. The two compounds sometimes inhibit lipolysis, sometimes promote it, according to species, though a reduced free fatty acid (FFA) concentration in the blood (reduced lipolysis) is the most usual effect. In some species the catecholamines (adrenaline and noradrenaline) can cause a rise or a fall in blood FFA according to experimental conditions. Injection also causes a sharp temporary increase in the number of leucocytes of the blood (*Colisa fasciatus*) almost identical to the rise seen after cold shock. Erythrocytes and thrombocytes are not affected. Considerable amounts of adrenaline are found in the Corpuscles of Stannius (*Salmo gairdneri*) and the spleen (*Gadus morhua*), but the content in the latter organ decreases on severing the sympathetic nerve.
Increases in blood in response to stress. Exhibits a diurnal rhythm like that of mammals. Secretion often maximal at dawn, the peak preceding that of cortisol.

‡ADRENOSTERONE—Volume 1 only

AGRANULOCYTES
Blood 1898

‡ALANINE *188, 189, 257, 271, 281, 312, 346, 354*
Dark muscle 2340; 2342; Liver 2704; Muscle 2340, 2342, 3419

ALANINE AMINOTRANSFERASE—*see* Glutamate-pyruvate transaminase (GOT) *257*

ALBUMIN *11, 43, 49, 62, 193, 222, 356*
Blood 1717, 1911, 2023, 2077, 2267, 3063, 3154, 3242, 3523, 3524, 3525, 3526;
Ovarian fluid 3187

ALDEHYDE OXIDASE
Intestine, Kidney, Liver: 2468

ALDOLASE *19, 328*
Egg 3703; Erythrocytes 1475; Liver 2366; Muscle 1789, 2366, 2880; Oocytes 3703

‡ALDOSTERONE
Blood 1688, 1969, 2274

ALK-1-ENYLACYLGLYCEROPHOSPHATIDYL CHOLINE
Brain 1849, 1850

ALK-1-ENYLACYLGLYCEROPHOSPHATIDYL ETHANOLAMINE
Brain 1849, 1850

ALK-1-ENYL DIGLYCERIDE
Egg, Liver, Muscle: 2118

ALK-1-ENYL ETHERS
Brain 1850

ALKALINE PHOSPHATASE *11, 72, 151, 308, 309*
Does not seem to change its properties in the intestine of fish transferred from fresh
water to salt, but it can then be three times as active. The exact physiological role
has not so far been explained, but the activity is also increased in the gill when fish
are adapted to sea water. The enzyme is inhibited by EDTA, borate and cysteine.
Blood 1989, 2464, 2773, 2858, 3093, 3404, 3523, 3525, 3526; Brain 2317, 3373;
Dark muscle 2316; Egg (unfertilised) 2874, 3227; Embryo 2874; Gill 3373; Heart
1989, 2317, 3373; Hepatopancreas 3373; Intestine 2923, 3226, 3230, 3378; Kidney
1989, 2317, 3373; Liver 1989, 2317; Mesentery 2958; Muscle 1989, 2316, 2317,
3373; Oesophagus 3226, 3230; Ovarian fluid 3187; Ovary 2317, 3228; Pyloric
caecae 2958, 3230; Rectum 3226, 3230; Spleen 2317, 3373; Stomach 3226, 3230

ALKALINE RIBONUCLEASE
Egg 2486; Embryo 2486

N-ALKANES (series)
Liver 2119; Muscle 2119

ALKYL DIACYL GLYCEROLS
Associated mainly with sharks, especially the squaloid sharks. There may be a tendency to find these compounds in fish which are rich in wax esters.
Blood, Liver, Muscle: 3180

ALKYL DIGLYCERIDE
Egg, Liver, Muscle: 2118

ALLANTOICASE *161, 162*
Liver 1775, 2071, 3547

ALLANTOINASE *161, 162*
Liver 1775, 2071, 3547

‡ALUMINIUM *76*
Dark muscle 2571; Gill 3017, 3563; Kidney 2040, 3563; Liver 2040, 3018, 3563; Muscle 2040, 2571, 2677, 3017, 3019, 3467, 3563; Ovary 2040; Scales 2440, 3017, 3563; Skeleton 3017; Spleen 3563; Swim bladder 3563

AMINE OXIDASE (mixed function)
Liver 2030

D-AMINO ACID OXIDASE
Kidney, Liver, Pyloric caecae: 1923

‡AMINO ACIDS (combined) *2, 10, 11, 33, 34, 36, 42, 133, 139–141, 148, 158, 159, 162, 170, 186, 188, 193–196, 202, 279, 280*
The pattern in proteins changes little between species, even when sharks are included. Fish in general tend to possess greater proportions of leucine, isoleucine and lysine than other animals. White muscle differs little from superficial dark muscle in its amino acid composition, but deep-seated dark muscle shows some small differences. The amino acids essential to the diet of fish are arginine, histidine, isoleucine, leucine, lysine, methionine, phenylalanine, threonine, tryptophan and valine. Non-essential acids tend to be used from the body during starvation and laid down more plentifully during summer feeding. Fish muscle contains on average 407 mg% of tryptophan, compared with 282 mg% in warm-blooded animals.
"Antifreeze" glycoprotein 1861, 1917, 3109; Apomyoglobin 1685; Biliverdin protein 3669; Blood 2946, 3433; Brain 1938; Collagen (from myocomma) 2609, 2772, 3672; Collagen (from skin) 2051, 2609, 2772, 3672; Collagen (from swim bladder) 2772, 3092; Cytochrome c 2965; Desamidoglucagon 3447; Dinogunellin (a toxic phospholipid from roe) 2138; Egg 2848; 3187; Egg shell 3152; Elastoidin fibres from pectoral fin 2426; Electric organ 2946; Fructose diphosphate aldolase 2448; α-globulin 2859; Glucagon 3447; Glyceraldehyde-3-phosphate dehydrogenase 2064; Growth hormone 1914; Haemoglobin 1567, 1703, 2002, 2019, 2305, 2561, 2860, 2964, 3472, 3594; Haptoglobin 2444; Isotocin 1412; Kidney 1749; Larva 3393; Lens (from eye) 2050; Liver 1749, 2705; Lysozymes (from plasma) 1935; Muscle 1410, 1485, 1655, 1749, 1786, 1938, 2013, 2118, 2235, 2406, 2422, 2456, 2663, 2854, 2946, 3019, 3057, 3082, 3101, 3124, 3276, 3433, 3468, 3561, 3690; Muscle cell walls 1577; Myocomma 2484; Myoglobin 1495, 1946, 3441; Nerve 2946; Otolith protein 1812; Ovary 1749; Oviduct 2118; Proglucagon 3447;

Prolactin 1914; Rhodopsin 3271; Scales 3117; Sialic acid glycoproteins 3652; Skin 1655, 2484; Slime 2447, 3527; Spleen 1749; Superoxide dismutase 1494; Testis 1749, 2118, 2705; Thyroglobulin 1620; Vasotocin 1412; Yolk 3393

‡AMINO ACIDS (free) *8, 10, 12, 21, 22, 34, 36, 42, 44, 57, 62, 76, 112, 116, 148, 167, 192–194, 196–198, 215, 227, 280, 283, 311–313, 346, 354–356, 378*
Increase in tissues undergoing active protein synthesis, so increase in the gonads during maturation but not in muscle. Free amino acids may assist osmoregulation in a hypertonic environment. As yet there is only limited evidence that amino acids in solution are chemical signals for olfactory communication in fish. Many of the amino acids found to be effective olfactory stimuli also stimulate taste receptors (*Ictalurus punctatus*).
Alimentary tract 1749, 3637; Bile 1749; Blood 1594, 1749, 2290, 2553, 2744, 2898, 3140, 3433, 3434, 3637, 3691; Brain 1594, 1938, 1939, 2553, 3326, 3565, 3637; Dark muscle 2977; Egg 2848, 3719; Electric organ 3565; Embryo 1824, 3719; Erythrocytes 1594, 1965; Fry 2857; Gill 3637; Heart 1594, 3637; Kidney 1749, 2553, 2857, 3637; Larva 3719; Liver 1749, 2553, 2679, 2704, 2857, 3329, 3637; Muscle 1410, 1430, 1507, 1720, 1749, 1851, 1852, 1882, 1938, 1939, 2013, 2105, 2118, 2422, 2455, 2456, 2625, 2679, 2687, 2704, 2854, 2977, 3019, 3057, 3164, 3166, 3200, 3250, 3277, 3331, 3366, 3367, 3369, 3433, 3567, 3637; Parietal muscle 2255; Wing muscle 1594; Oocytes 1824; Ovary 1749, 2679, 2704, 2857; Oviduct 2118; Spleen 1749, 3637; Testis 1749, 2118; Ventricle 3552

‡AMINO ACIDS (free: a single figure for all of them collectively)
Blood 1945, 2078, 2079, 2476, 3232; Embryotrophe (environment for the embryo) 2476; Erythrocytes 1945; Gill 3548; Heart 3548; Kidney 3548; Lens 2101; Liver 3548; Muscle 1945, 3482, 3548; Urine 2078

x-AMINO ADIPATE
Blood, Brain, Erythrocytes, Heart, Wing muscle: 1594

α-AMINO BUTYRATE
Blood 1594; Erythrocytes 1594; Heart 1594; Muscle 2455, 2456, 3200, 3366; Wing muscle 1594

β-AMINO BUTYRATE
Blood, Erythrocytes, Heart, Wing muscle: 1594

‡γ-AMINO BUTYRATE (GABA)
An unusual amino acid of which the physiological role is not well known (Friedman and Shibko, 1973).
Alimentary tract 3637; Blood 1594, 2946, 3637; Brain 1594, 2553, 3217, 3326, 3637; Cerebellum 2943; Electric organ 2946; Erythrocytes 1594, 1965, 3710; Gill 3637; Heart 1594, 3637; Kidney 3637; Liver 3637; Muscle 1410, 2946, 3366, 3637; Wing muscle 1594; Nerve 2946; Spleen 3637

AMINO GALACTOSE
Antifreeze glycoprotein of blood 3109

δ-Amino laevulinic dehydratase
Blood 1907; Epigonal organ 1907; Erythrocytes 2216; Kidney 1907; Leydig's organ 1907; Spleen 1907

Amino sugars
Muscle cell wall 1577

Amino tripeptidase
Hepatopancreas, Intestine, Pancreas, Pyloric caecae: 3186

‡Ammonia or ammonium ions *4, 5, 44, 57, 116, 141, 149, 150, 154–164, 218, 221, 258, 259, 271, 272, 281, 288, 289, 320*
The main excretory product of fish, derived from the deamination of amino acids and the breakdown of purines and pyrimidines. It is the chief compound deriving from exogenous nitrogen (apart from exogenous arginine) and the rate of its excretion increases after feeding, while that of urea does not. Excretion of ammonia increases during periods of physical activity. Some urea is always produced by fish, and excretion tends to be in the form of urea and not ammonia whenever nitrogen cannot be easily and continuously excreted by the gills, as in amphibious fish during a spell on land and lungfish which aestivate. This is because ammonia is extremely toxic, and fish blood has been found to contain concentrations of the order of only 1 to 5 mg ammonia nitrogen per 100 ml, elasmobranchs being no more tolerant to it than are teleosts. It is the un-ionised form, NH_3, which is toxic, not the ionised (NH_4^+) which does not readily pass through cell membranes. Thus in an aquarium, if the pH of the water is low, the ammonia in the water can be largely in the "safe" ionised form. Symptoms of ammonia poisoning comprise hyperplasia of gill lamellae, followed by "clubbing" and eventual fusion so that the fish dies through asphyxiation. Ammonia is voided through the gills by simple diffusion and also, apparently, by an exchange mechanism involving sodium uptake from the environmental water.
Alimentary tract 3637; Bile 3135; Blood 1594, 2008, 2049, 2476, 2553, 2686, 2898, 3009, 3134, 3135, 3431, 3637; Body fluids 3304; Brain 1594, 2553, 3007, 3637; Dark muscle 3007; Embryotrophe (the environment of the embryo in viviparous species) 2476; Erythrocytes 1594; Gill 3007, 3637; Heart 1594, 3007, 3637; Intestine 3007; Kidney 2553, 3007, 3637; Liver 2553, 3007, 3572, 3637; Muscle 1410, 1430, 1851, 1852, 2455, 2456, 3007, 3134, 3135, 3304, 3331, 3366, 3367, 3567, 3637; Spleen 3007, 3637; Superoxide dismutase 1494; Urine 2083, 2686, 3303; Uterine fluid 3431; Wing muscle 1594

Amylase *16, 17, 26, 151, 152, 355*
Alimentary tract 2940; Blood 2150; Dark muscle 2810; Gall bladder 2939; Heart 2480, 2810; Hepatopancreas 2393, 2820, 2939, 2940, 3260; Intestinal contents 2939; Intestine 1425, 2480, 2800, 3256; Kidney 2480; Larval digestive organs 2395; Liver 1425, 2480, 2810; Mesentery 2958; Muscle 2810; Pancreas 1425; Pyloric caecae 2393, 2480, 2936, 2937, 2938, 2958; Spleen 2480; Stomach 1425, 2480

α-Amylase
Embryo 3708, 3709; Oocyte 3709

γ-Amylase
Embryo 3708, 3709; Liver 2811; Oocytes 3709

AMYLO-1,6-GLUCOSIDASE
Embryo 3708, 3709; Oocyte 3709

ANDROGEN *37, 38, 48, 384*
Blood 3207, 3208, 3209

‡ANDROSTENE DIONE—Volume 1 only

‡ANDROSTERONE—Volume 1 only

ANEURIN—*see* thiamine

ANGIOTENSINOGEN
Blood 2890, 2891

‡ANSERINE (β Alanyl-L-1-methylhistidine) *110, 355*
Found in the muscle of teleosts, not elasmobranchs. Increases in the muscle of *Salmo salar* on smoltification and further when the fish enters the sea. It may therefore act as an osmoregulator, but it is also thought to be a tissue buffer, especially as it is more plentiful in the white muscle of active fish than in sluggish fish. It may protect the tissues against the effects of sudden formation of lactic acid.
Dark muscle 2977; Muscle 1766, 2455, 2977, 3366, 3367, 3368, 3369

ANTIMONY
Heart, Liver, Muscle: 2534

ARGINASE *57, 153, 161, 218, 356*
Converts arginine to urea in the liver. Teleosts with a high enzyme activity are largely carnivorous, while omnivorous or herbivorous fish exhibit low activity. The exception is *Coregonus artedi*, which is not carnivorous but has a high arginase activity in the liver. The enzyme has been observed to increase in concentration during starvation.
Brain 1776; Gill 1653, 1776; Heart 1653, 1776; Kidney 1653, 1776, 3544, 3547, 3634; Liver 1653, 1776, 2035, 2071, 2256, 2694, 2936, 2937, 3112, 3113, 3544, 3547, 3634; Muscle 1653, 1776; Ovary 1653, 1776; Oviduct 1653; Pancreas 1653; Rectal gland 1653; Shell gland 1653; Spiral valve 1653; Spleen 1653, 1776; Testis 1653, 1776; Uterine gland 1653

‡ARGININE *153, 159–161, 196, 221, 356, 365*
Increases to high concentrations in the gonad during maturation.
Blood 1653; Kidney 3544, 3547; Liver 3544, 3547

ARGININOSUCCINATE LYASE
Liver 2256, 3112

ARGININOSUCCINATE SYNTHETASE
Liver 2035, 2256, 3112

‡ARSENIC
Fish contain arsenic in the form of both lipid-soluble and water-soluble arseno-organic compounds (Lunde, 1972). In *Boreogadus saida* the arsenic concentration

has been shown to correlate positively with body length.
Brain 3638; Dark muscle 2613; Embryo 3638; Heart 2534; Liver 1560; 1561, 2534, 2611, 3638; Muscle 1560, 1561, 1631, 2534, 2613, 2886, 3638; Ovary 3638; Spiral valve 3638; Spleen 3638; Stomach 3638; Uterus 3638; Yolk sac 3638

ARYL SULPHATASE
Muscle 2757

ASCORBIC ACID (*see* Vitamin C)

ASCORBIC ACID OXIDASE
Dark muscle 2475; Muscle 2475

ASPARTATE AMINOTRANSFERASE (*see* Glutamate oxaloacetate transaminase) *72*

‡ASPARTIC ACID *160, 188, 199*
Liver 2704

‡ASTAXANTHIN (whether or not measured as astacene) *39, 57, 144, 145, 258*
Widely distributed in the skin of fish, but usually found in the flesh of salmonids only. It is more effective as a colour in the skin of fancy carp than is lutein. In the skin of several Japanese red fish species it has been found as a diester, with oleic and palmitic acids in the 3 and 3' positions. Dietary astaxanthin can be deposited unchanged, but the pigment can also be formed from other carotenoids in the diet, depending on the fish species. For example, *Salmo gairdneri* cannot convert β-carotene, lutein or zeaxanthin into astaxanthin, but *Carassius auratus* can oxidise all three to the pigment (Hata and Hata, 1973). Neither *Chrysophrys major* nor *Evynnis japonica* can convert dietary β-carotene to astaxanthene, but can use dietary astaxanthin directly (Katayama, Miyahara et al., 1973). The pigment can itself act as a precursor of vitamin A in certain species. It has been thought to act as a fertilisation hormone, activating sperm and, in eggs, producing positive chemotaxis. However, *Salmo gairdneri* eggs completely free from carotenoid can be fertilised and then develop normally.
Egg 1998, 2132; Fin 1783; Gill 1783; Intestine 1779, 1782, 1783; Liver 1779, 1782, 1783; Muscle 1779, 1783, 2136, 2507; Ovary 2507; Skin 1783, 2136; Skin + fins 2715, 2716, 2717, 2719, 2723, 2724, 2725; Sperm 1782; Testis 1781

ASTAXANTHIN DIESTER
Skin 3466

AZO-REDUCTASE *65*

BALENINE
Muscle 3367, 3368

‡BARIUM *147, 148*
In *Thunnus alalunga*, 70% of the whole-body barium is to be found in the skeleton.
Bone 2981; Caecum 2981; Egg 3438; Epidermis 2981; Gill 2981; Kidney 2981; Liver 2981, 3018; Muscle 2981, 3017, 3019; Scales 2440, 3017; Slime 2981; Spleen 2981; Teeth + jawbone 2981

‡*n*-BUTYRIC ACID—Volume 1 only for bibliography. This volume page reference *149*

CADMIUM
The concentration in whole fish is not related to the body weight (*Boreogadus saida*). Fish flesh usually contains a negligible quantity. More is found in the internal organs.
Blood 2390; Bone 2786; Brain 3638; Dark muscle 2390, 2613; Egg 2390; Embryo 3638; Fin 2786; Gill 1622, 2390, 2786, 3638; "Gonad" 1622, 3638; Heart 1622, 2390, 2534; Intestine 3638; Kidney 1622, 2390, 3638; Liver 1561, 1622, 2390, 2534, 2611, 3638; Muscle 1561, 1622, 1631, 1707, 1709, 1884, 1893, 1972, 2148, 2390, 2534, 2613, 2786, 2886, 2901, 3638; Ovary 2364, 3638; Pyloric caecae 2390; Scales 1716, 2786; Skin 2786; Spermatic sac 2390; Spiral valve 3638; Spleen 1622, 2390, 3638; Stomach 3638; Uterus 3638; Yolk sac 3638

‡CAESIUM
Distributed uniformly throughout all the organs (*Thunnus alalunga*).
Bone 2269, 2981; Caecum 2981; Epidermis 2981; Gill 2981; Kidney 2981; Liver 2269, 2981; Muscle 2269, 2981; Ovary 2269; Skin 2269; Slime 2981; Spleen 2981; Teeth + jawbone 2981

CALCITONIN *6*
A hormone produced by the epithelium of the ultimobranchial gland (on the pericardium). Its role in fish is still not completely clear; it reduces serum calcium levels in some species but not in others, and governs bone deposition and mobilisation. The ultimobranchial gland hypertrophies during the migration and spawning of *Salmo salar*, when plasma calcium is low. In this species it is thought to cause a fall in plasma calcium and a rise in plasma phosphate. From experiments with *Salmo gairdneri* it seems that the hormone protects the skeleton from mineral loss during calcium deprivation. It has no effect on blood calcium in *Squalus acanthias*, which, being an elasmobranch, has no bony skeleton. Hypercalcaemia causes hyperplasia in the ultimobranchial gland. The response of *Fundulus kansae* to calcitonin varies seasonally: most prominent in July (increased rate of calcium uptake) and undetectable in February. In *Oncorhynchus nerka*, plasma calcitonin has been found to be higher in females than in males during all stages of migration. The level falls sharply after spawning.
Blood 3588; Stomach 2668; Transverse septum 2668; Ultimobranchial gland 1729, 2668

‡CALCIUM *6, 8, 11, 20, 21, 25, 33, 34, 36, 37, 44, 46, .50, 56, 76, 85, 133, 134, 147, 148, 1.58, 164–166, 222–226, 240, 248, 260, 279, 283, 285, 286, 289, 291, 301, 304, 305, 311, 342, 354, 385*
Values ranging from 9 to 198 mg% have been measured in the muscle of different species, where it is largely bound to protein. In *Thunnus alalunga*, 95% of the calcium of the fish is found in the skeleton, compared with 79% in the skeleton of *Fundulus kansae*. In the latter species, 18% is found in the skin and scales, and 2 to 3% in the soft tissues. The concentration in the ovaries (*Gadus morhua*) declines during maturation, probably a "dilution" effect from lipid entering the oocytes. Blood calcium levels seem to be independent of the concentration in the environment, but in the females of many egg-laying species it rises as maturation progresses

(no change in males). This calcium is probably part of a protein, ovovitellin, which is synthesised in the liver under hormonal stimulus and is presumably used in the developing eggs. Calcium can be absorbed directly from the surrounding water, especially in the presence of phosphate, and indeed direct absorption is said to meet a large part of the requirements of teleosts (Simmons, 1971). The major sites of influx and efflux are the gills, fins and oral epithelium, all of which are effective in marine fish, but of which the gills are the most important in fresh water (same author). Regulation is carried out by hypercalcaemic hormones of the pituitary and by hypocalcaemic hormones of the Corpuscles of Stannius (Pang, Pang and Sawyer, 1974) and the ultimobranchial body. In environments low in calcium, the ion can be mobilised from bones and scales (*Fundulus kansae*). The concentration of calcium in the medium affects the flux of other ions also. No definite trend is seen in the level of muscle calcium during starvation. Circulating calcium acts in a similar way to prolactin, decreasing the permeability of the gills to water. Otoliths consist largely of calcium carbonate; their rate of uptake of calcium varies seasonally (*Cyprinus carpio*), and calcium taken by *Cyprinus carpio* with the food continues to be deposited on the otolith for several days after the end of feeding, even when the fish are put into clean, fresh water.

Abdominal muscle 3386; Alkaline gland 2692; Aqueous humour 1717, 2692; Bile (from gall bladder) 1595, 1596, 2261, 2263, 2264, 2265, 2625, 2656, 2692, 3135; Bile (from liver) 1596; Blastula 3718; Blood 1484, 1595, 1596, 1636, 1637, 1641, 1714, 1717, 1734, 1740, 1813, 1840, 1908, 1909, 1921, 1948, 2024, 2054, 2055, 2056, 2057, 2076–2080, 2082, 2108, 2161, 2176, 2244, 2261, 2262, 2265, 2278, 2288, 2294, 2464, 2465, 2476, 2499, 2503, 2514, 2540, 2583, 2622, 2624, 2625, 2649, 2650, 2686, 2692, 2808, 2858, 2862, 2864, 2865, 2866, 2922, 2924, 2933, 2934, 2971, 3015, 3037, 3038, 3039, 3063, 3090, 3111, 3134, 3135, 3205, 3278, 3279, 3292, 3339, 3342, 3343, 3353, 3406, 3427–3431, 3455, 3492, 3503, 3523–3526, 3558, 3559, 3588, 3606, 3717; Body fluids 2625, 2922, 3304; Bone 1528, 2623, 2981; Brain 3313; Caecum 2981; Cerebral fluid 1908, 2692, 3111, 3427, 3429, 3430; Cupula 1908; Dark muscle 3386; Egg 2236, 3718; Embryo 2236; Embryotrophe 2476; Endolymph 1908; Epidermis 2981; Erythrocytes 2080, 2636, 3360; Fin 3176; Fry 3718; Gill 2981, 3313; Gut fluid 2649, 3038; Gut (intracellular) 2623; Gut lumen 1788; Gut wall 2622, 2892; Heart 3313, 3386; Intestinal fluids 2922; Kidney 1740, 2040, 2981, 3313, 3386; Larva 3718; Liver 2040, 2268, 2622, 2625, 2981, 3313, 3386; Liver (intracellular) 2623; Lorenzinian jelly 1908; Muscle 1681, 1786, 2040, 2244, 2313, 2622, 2624, 2625, 2677, 2923, 2981, 3021, 3057, 3090, 3134, 3135, 3294, 3313, 3343, 3386, 3467, 3690; Muscle cells 3135; Muscle (intracellular) 1681, 2623, 3134; Notochordal fluid 2076; Oocytes 3718; Ovarian fluid 3187; Ovary 2040, 2364; Pericardial fluid 2692, 3427, 3429, 3430; Perivisceral fluid 1636, 2692, 3427, 3429, 3430; Rectal gland 1637, 2692, 3654; Rete mirabile 3360; Scales 1528, 1716; Semen 2057, 3292; Seminal plasma 1765, 2072, 2073; Slime 2808, 2981; Sperm 2072, 2698; Sperm cytoplasm 2073; Spleen 2981; Teeth + jawbone 2981; Urine (from bladder) 1636, 1637, 1641, 1840, 1948, 1960, 2078, 2240, 2260, 2650, 2686, 2808, 2862, 2866, 3038, 3079, 3111, 3205, 3654; Urine (from kidney) 1948; Uterine fluid 2024, 3431; Vertebrae 2464; Vitreous humour 1717, 2288

‡CANTHAXANTHIN *39, 145*
The most useful dietary carotenoid for imparting a red colour to the flesh of cultured salmonids.

Egg 2132; Fin 1782, 1783; Gill 1983; Intestine 1779, 1783; Liver 1779, 1783; Muscle 1779, 1783, 2136; Skin 1783; Sperm 1782; Testis 1781

CARBAMOYL PHOSPHATE SYNTHETASE *160*
An enzyme of the Krebs-Henseleit cycle which does *not* occur in most teleosts. Kidney 3634; Liver 1443, 1777, 2035, 2256, 3112, 3587, 3634

CARBOHYDRASE
Hepatopancreas, Intestine, Pyloric caecae, Stomach: 2393

CARBOHYDRATE (as glucose) *47, 48*
Blood 1827, 1831, 2076, 2078, 2079, 3310, 3311; Dark muscle 3357; Larvae (whole) 1874, 1875; Liver 3357; Muscle 1486, 3357; Notochordal fluid 2076; Ovary 3357; Skin 3686; Testis 3357; Urine 2078

‡CARBON DIOXIDE *123, 272, 280–282*
Blood 1576, 2078; Swimbladder gas 1794, 2142, 2144; Urine 2078

CARBONIC ANHYDRASE *152, 288*
Bile 3309; Blood 1794, 2131, 2700, 3309; Erythrocytes 1668; Gas gland + rete bundle + epithelium 1794; Gill 2700, 2764, 3309; Intestinal mucosa 3309; Intestine 2700; Intestine (large) 3309; Intestine (small) 3309

CARBOXYPEPTIDASE A
Mesentery 2958; Pyloric caecae 2958

CARBOXYPEPTIDASE B
Mesentery 2958; Pyloric caecae 2958

‡CARDIOLIPID (diphosphatidyl glycerol) *357*
Rich in mitochondrial membranes, so determinations of cardiolipid can give an indication of mitochondrial count.
Bone 3233; Brain 2469; Cartilage 3233; Dark muscle 1581; Gill filaments 2746, 3420, 3726, 3727; Intestinal mucosa 2746, 3726; Kidney 2746, 3726; Liver 2746, 3726, 3727; Muscle 1581, 2746, 2987, 3726; Nerve tissue 1680, 2457; Phospholipid 2407; Salt (rectal) gland 1530, 2377

‡CARNOSINE *110, 355*
Freshwater fish contain a higher proportion, in relation to anserine, than marine fish. Synthesis in fish has still to be demonstrated, so the compound may originate in the diet. The carnosine levels in teleosts are very variable, so the importance of suggested roles is still not established, but, along with anserine and histidine, it occurs in greater concentration in the white muscle of active than in sluggish species. While physiological roles for these compounds have not definitely been established, it seems likely that they act as buffers to protect the tissues from sudden accumulations of lactic acid. They must presumably contribute to the intracellular osmotic pressure, but the quantity of carnosine present, though variable, does not appear to correlate with changes in the external salinity.
Muscle 2689, 2977, 3366–3369; Parietal muscle 2255

CATHEPSIN B *222*
Dark muscle, Kidney, Liver, White muscle, Spleen: 1749

CELLULASE *152*
Intestine 2800

‡CEPHALIN (*see* Phosphatidyl ethanolamine)

‡CEREBROSIDE
More concentrated in dark muscle than in ordinary muscle.
Brain 2469–2471, 3222; Brain myelin 3222; Egg 1454; Electric lobes 2472; Electric organ 2472; Muscle 2472; Nerve 2233; Pacemaker nucleus 2472; Rectal gland 2376; Tectum opticum 2472; Telencephalon 2472

CHENODESOXYCHOLIC ACID *225*
Bile 1823; Bile salts 2408

CHITINASE
Blood 1910; Brain 1910; Caecal mucosa 1719; Cardiac stomach 1910; Erythrocytes 1910; Gastric mucosa 1719; Gill 1910; Intestinal mucosa 1719; Lymph 1910; Lymphomyeloid tissue 1910; Pancreas 1910; Pronephros 1910; Pseudobranch 1910; Pyloric caecae 1910; Pyloric stomach 1910; Rectal gland 1910; Spleen 1910; Thymus 1910

‡CHLORIDE *11, 20, 21, 24, 25, 133, 164–166, 225, 240, 241, 272, 274, 282–289, 294, 299, 304, 305, 309–311, 314, 315, 319, 341, 342, 346, 348, 349, 384, 385*
Mostly extracellular in muscle tissue. Concentration therefore increases during starvation, when extracellular space increases. Chloride also increases in various tissues when euryhaline fish enter the sea, and when the ambient temperature falls, so values are higher in winter in at least some species. Relatively large diurnal variations have been noted in *Fundulus chrysotus* and *F. grandis*, but since the times of high and low concentration may vary seasonally, it is not possible to describe a single daily rhythm characteristic of the species.
Alkaline gland 2692; Aqueous humour 1717, 2217, 2692, 2693, 3711; Bile (from gall bladder) 1595, 1596, 1636, 1836, 2261, 2264, 2265, 2625, 2656, 2692, 3135; Bile (from liver ducts) 1596; Blood 1428, 1438, 1444, 1575, 1576, 1595, 1633, 1636, 1637, 1641, 1666, 1674, 1702, 1714, 1717, 1794, 1800, 1805, 1806, 1813, 1827, 1831, 1840, 1860, 1905, 1906, 1908, 1909, 1916, 1932, 1948, 1965, 2006, 2008, 2024, 2047, 2054, 2055, 2056, 2057, 2076, 2077, 2079, 2082, 2113, 2114, 2164, 2165, 2182, 2201, 2217, 2244, 2261, 2265, 2278, 2288, 2429, 2432, 2476, 2499, 2514, 2517, 2518, 2520, 2540, 2555, 2556, 2579, 2622, 2625, 2639, 2640, 2649, 2650, 2664, 2678, 2686, 2692, 2693, 2711, 2745, 2764, 2805, 2808, 2862, 2864, 2894, 2895, 2896, 2897, 2920, 2924, 2925, 2933, 2934, 2963, 2971, 2972, 2997, 3037, 3038, 3039, 3041, 3063, 3090, 3111, 3130, 3134, 3135, 3205, 3275, 3292, 3310, 3311, 3339, 3418, 3427, 3428, 3429, 3430, 3431, 3492, 3497, 3501, 3502, 3503, 3505, 3506, 3509, 3517, 3520, 3521, 3523, 3524, 3525, 3526, 3558, 3559, 3603, 3604; Body fluids 2625, 3304, 3430; Bone 2623; Brain 1957; Cerebrospinal fluid 2692; Cranial fluid 1908, 2280, 2692, 3111, 3427, 3429, 3430; Cupula 1908; Egg 2115; Embryo 1824, 2115; Embryo blood 2359; Embryotrophe (fluid bathing embryo) 2476; Endolymph (from canal) 1908, 2692; Endolymph (from labyrinth) 1908; Erythrocytes 1674, 3418, 3710; Erythrocytes

(intracellular) 2805; Gut fluid 2649, 3038; Gut (intracellular) 2623; Gut wall 2622; Liver 2622, 2625; Liver (intracellular) 2623; Lorenzinian jelly 1908, 2280, 2692; Muscle 1430, 1582, 1633, 1641, 1681, 2006, 2244, 2489, 2622, 2625, 2639, 3090, 3130, 3134, 3135, 3294; Muscle cells 2006, 3135; Muscle (extracellular) 1633; Muscle (intracellular) 1429, 1681, 2623, 3134; Notochordal fluid 2076; Oocytes 1824; Ovarian fluid 3187; Pericardial fluid 2077, 2692, 3427, 3429, 3430; Perilymph 2692; Perivisceral fluid 1636, 2077, 2692, 3427, 3429; Rectal gland 1637, 2692, 3654; Rectal gland fluid 2232; Semen 2057, 3292; Seminal plasma 1765, 2072, 2073; Sperm 2072; Urine (from bladder) 1636, 1637, 1641, 1840, 1944, 1948, 1960, 2078, 2083, 2182, 2240, 2260, 2431, 2650, 2686, 2808, 2862, 2896, 2897, 2997, 3038, 3079, 3111, 3205, 3654; Urine (from kidney) 1948; Urine (from ureter) 1944; Uterine fluid 2024, 3431; Vitreous humour 1717, 2288

‡CHOLESTEROL. *8, 9, 11, 13, 25, 26, 34, 40, 41, 53, 55, 61–63, 65, 76, 96, 98, 124, 164, 166, 207, 208, 211, 224, 229, 241, 257, 261, 357*
An important constituent of cell walls, to the extent of about half the lipid. Cholesterol determinations can therefore give a measure of the biomembrane content of a system. Also is a direct precursor of bile salts and bile acids. An important precursor of steroid hormones, including androgens, oestrogens and corticosteroids. In fish serum it is minimal at the times of greatest sexual activity, presumably because of its conversion to these sex hormones. It has been reported to decrease in the livers of old *Ophicephalus punctatus*, perhaps because of a reduced demand for sex hormones (fecundity decreases with age in this species). Cholesterol is more concentrated in the blood of active than of sluggish species. Carnivores appear to possess more cholesterol in their nervous system and their eggs than do herbivores. The lipid deposited in the swim bladders of deep-sea fish is largely cholesterol, synthesis of which appears to be enhanced at high pressures.
Adipose fin 2578, 3283; Adrenal 1712; Bile 2988; Blood 1437, 1441, 1734, 1802, 1886, 1920, 1954, 2055, 2056, 2076–2079, 2265, 2267, 2284, 2495, 2514, 2515, 2518, 2555, 2556, 2761, 2762, 2765, 2858, 3011, 3039, 3063, 3138, 3162, 3179, 3180, 3237, 3242, 3253, 3278, 3279, 3339, 3403, 3426, 3492, 3525, 3603, 3604; Brain 1479, 1954, 3222, 3268, 3269; Cerebrum 2578, 3283; Corpuscles of Stannius 1712; Dark muscle 1581, 2445, 2555, 3138, 3246; Egg 1479, 1691, 1987, 2001, 2330, 2425, 2445, 3267; Embryo 2330; Erythrocytes 1419, 1954, 2637; Gastric muscle 3246; Gill 2578, 3283, 3727; "Gonad" 1691, 2555, 2578, 3283; Heart 2578, 2992, 3269, 3283; Heart muscle 1954, 3246; Hump (*Oncorhynchus gorbuscha*) 3137; Kidney 2578, 3269, 3283; Liver 1690, 1691, 1785, 1802, 1954, 2117, 2318, 2445, 2495, 2555, 2572, 2578, 2768, 3020, 3138, 3179, 3180, 3239, 3241, 3245, 3253, 3269, 3283, 3727; Muscle 1581, 1690, 1691, 1785, 1802, 1954, 2117, 2445, 2495, 2555, 2578, 2779, 3019, 3056, 3138, 3180, 3239, 3241, 3242, 3245, 3246, 3269, 3283; Myelin (from brain) 3222; Nerve 2233; Nerve (olfactory) 2407; Notochordal fluid 2076; Ovarian fluid 3187; Ovary 1690, 1785, 2117, 2310, 3239, 3241, 3242, 3269, Salt (rectal) gland 1530, 2377; Scales 2578, 3283; Skin 2445, 2578, 3283; Skull 2538, 3028; Slime 2559; Sperm 2425; Spinal cord 2538, 2578, 3268, 3269, 3283; Spine 3028; Spleen 1954, 2578, 3269, 3283; Swim bladder 2578, 2990, 3283; Swim bladder foam 3032; Testis 1690, 2117, 2445, 3239, 3241, 3242; Urine 2078; Vein (posterior cardinal) 1712; Yolk 2847

CHOLIC ACID *225*
Bile 1823; Bile salts 2408

‡Choline *146*
Occurs both free and as a component of lecithin (phosphatidyl choline). Richer in dark muscle than in white, and in deep-seated dark muscle than in superficial dark muscle. Most of the choline in fish is obtained from the diet.
Egg 1454; Kidney 2910; Muscle 3125, 3567

Choline acetyl transferase *330*
Electric organ 2302

Choline phosphotransferase *340*
Brain microsomes, Liver microsomes: 2551

Choline plasmalogens
Brain, Myelin from brain, Myelin from spinal cord: 3222

Cholinesterase *57, 65, 330*
Brain 1869; Electric lobes 3474; Electric organ 1556, 2302, 2474; Forebrain 3474; Medulla 3474; Muscle 3474; Pacemaker 3474; Tectum opticum 3474

Chondroitin sulphate
Aorta 3344

‡Chromium *34, 72*
Ranges from 0·12 to 5 mg% dry matter in the muscle of various species. The concentration in muscle + bone has been reported to increase with age (*Salvelinus namaycush*). It tends to accumulate in the kidney and liver (*Cyprinus carpio*). When the surrounding water contains high levels of chromium, it becomes concentrated especially in the cytosol of liver and gill, and on returning the fish (*Salmo gairdneri*) to clean water it is rapidly depleted from tissues apart from kidney, liver, gill, gall bladder and bile.
Bile 1632; Blood 1632, 2390; Bone 2786, 3115; Bone (opercular) 1632; Bone (vertebral) 1632; Brain 1632; Colon 1632; Dark muscle 2390, 2571; Egg 2390; Erythrocytes 1632; Fin 2786; Gall bladder 1632; Gill 1632, 2390, 2786, 3315; Heart 1632, 2390; Intestine (small) 1632; Kidney 1632, 2040, 2390, 3115; Kidney (posterior) 1632; Liver 1632, 2040, 2390, 3018, 3115; Mesenteric lipid 1632; Muscle 2015, 2040, 2390, 2571, 2786, 2886, 3115; Ovary 2040; Pyloric caecae 1632, 2390; Scales 2440, 2786; Skin 1632, 2786; Spermatic sac 2390; Spleen 1632, 2390; Stomach 1632

Chymotrypsin
Mesentery, Pyloric caecae: 2958

Citrate
Blood 3525, 3526; Muscle 1852, 1951; Oocytes 3704

Citrate synthase *263*
Embryo 3688; Heart 1505; Oocyte 3688

Citrulline *159, 160*
Blood 1594; Erythrocytes 1594; Heart 1594; Muscle 2455; "Wing" muscle 1594

‡COBALT *46, 56, 72, 133, 147, 354*

Ranges from 0·053 to 0·231 mg% dry matter in the muscle of 30 species. Deficiency results in bone malformation (*Salmo gairdneri*). The concentration of cobalt in muscle is higher than that of nickel (several species), despite the fact that in sea water there is more nickel than cobalt. In *Salmo gairdneri* it is most concentrated in the kidney, least in muscle, and has been noted to accumulate in the kidney and liver of *Cyprinus carpio* also. The concentration in the ovaries of *Gadus morhua* declines during maturation, presumably because of the accumulation of lipid. It constitutes a part of the vitamin B_{12} molecule.

Blood 2124, 2390; Bone 2124, 2269, 2786, 2850, 3002, 3115; Dark muscle 2390; 2571; Egg 2390; Fin 2786; Gill 1540, 2390, 2786, 2850, 3002, 3115; "Gonad" 3002; Gut 3002; Heart 2390; Kidney 2040, 2124, 2390, 3115; Liver 1540, 1904, 2040, 2124, 2269, 2390, 2611, 2850, 3002, 3018, 3115; Muscle 1540, 2040, 2124, 2269, 2390, 2491, 2677, 2786, 2850, 3002, 3019, 3115; Ovary 2040, 2269, 2363, 2364; Pancreas 1904; Pyloric caecae 2390; Scales 2786; Skin 2269, 2786, 3002; Spermatic sac 2390; Spleen 2124, 2390, 3002

‡COENZYME A—Volume 1 only

‡COLLAGEN *29, 33, 56, 58, 63, 130–132, 178, 194, 198–202, 204–206, 222, 319, 338, 339, 357, 359*

The amino acids of fish collagen resemble those of mammalian collagen, but contain less proline and hydroxyproline, more serine and threonine. Fish collagen is less stable and more easily dissolved than is mammalian collagen. The thermal denaturation temperature rises, as does the hydroxyproline content, according to the normal environmental temperature of the living fish, and there are indications that the denaturation temperature can vary within a single species according to habitat temperature (K. Kelly, personal communication, 1978). The skin and myocommata of *Gadus morhua* thicken markedly during starvation, the myocommata being thickened by a more cross-linked collagen than usual. These tissues are presumed to return to normal thickness on refeeding. On the other hand, the skin of *Anguilla japonica* becomes much thinner during starvation, and the goblet and clavate cells are much reduced. The skin of *Clupea harengus* has been reported to thicken during maturation, probably because of the associated starvation. Injection of 11-ketotestosterone causes the skin of *Oncorhynchus nerka* to thicken, so hormones may be involved in the phenomenon seen in herring also. The mechanical properties and the degree of covalent cross-linking between collagen molecules vary between the collagens of skin, swim bladder and myocomma, presumably according to the mechanical strength required in each location.

Arterial tissue 2508; Muscle 3462; Muscle cell walls 1577

CONNECTIVE TISSUE (total) *36, 58–60, 63, 69, 70, 112, 122, 167, 194, 199, 358, 360*
Muscle 3462

‡COPPER *34, 45, 46, 56, 57, 72, 147, 148, 172, 248, 354, 385*

An important activator of many enzymes such as cytochrome oxidase, and connected with porphyrin metabolism. Lack of copper causes anaemia in *Salmo gairdneri*. Its concentration ranges from 0·02 to 7·78 mg% dry matter in the muscle of different species. It is essential to fish, but little is known of their requirements for copper or of their regulatory mechanisms. Some regulation does appear to be involved, because the concentration in the tissues of *Morone saxatilis* does not change with diets containing different quantities of copper. The concentration in the blood has been shown to correlate with changes in both proteins and calcium, and in the ovaries of *Gadus morhua* it increases during maturation, so is evidently necessary for the larva. It is more concentrated in the blood of active than of sluggish fish. In *Coregonus nasus sensu*, there is a smooth seasonal curve for hepatic copper, with a maximum in March. In the liver it does not seem to be linked to the sex of the fish, but in *Salmo gairdneri* muscle there is more in males than in females, while the ovary is twice as rich in copper as the testis. In general, muscle copper does not correlate with the length of the fish, but there are reports of a slight decrease as the fish grow.

The content of copper in the liver of freshwater fish ranges from 2·33 to 4·04 mg% fresh weight, some tens of times the concentration in the muscle, bone, scales and skin. The kidney contains 6·9 to 16·3 mg% of ash, probably on account of the haematopoietic function of this organ.

Bile 1533; Bile + gall bladder 2941; Blastula 3718; Blood 1933, 2390, 2963, 3015, 3677, 3717; Bone 1533, 1534, 2281, 2786, 2850, 3017; Brain 3638; Dark muscle 2390, 2571, 2613; Egg 2001, 2390, 2941, 3438, 3718; Embryo 3638, 3718; Erythrocytes 2636; Fin 2786; Fry 2941, 3718; Fry + yolk 3718; Gill 1533, 1622, 1627, 2281, 2390, 2786, 2850, 2941, 3017, 3563, 3564, 3638, 3677; "Gonad" 1622, 3638; Heart 1622, 1890, 2390, 3564; Hepatopancreas 3677; Intestine 1890, 3677; Kidney 1533, 1622, 1627, 1890, 2040, 2390, 2941, 3563, 3564, 3638, 3677; Larva 3718; Liver 1533, 1534, 1561, 1622, 1627, 1769, 1890, 2040, 2268, 2281, 2390, 2611, 2850, 2941, 3018, 3563, 3564, 3638; Lung 1890; Muscle 1561, 1622, 1707, 1708, 1709, 1763, 1793, 1884, 1893, 2040, 2390, 2491, 2571, 2613, 2677, 2786, 2828, 2829, 2850, 2886, 2901, 2941, 3017, 3019, 3294, 3402, 3467, 3563, 3564, 3638; Oocytes 3718; Ovary 1533, 2040, 2281, 2364, 3638; Pancreas 1890; Pyloric caecae 2390; Scales 1533, 1534, 2281, 2440, 2786, 3017, 3563; Skin 2786, 2941; Spermatic sac 2390; Spiral valve 3638; Spleen 1534, 1622, 1890, 2390, 3563, 3564, 3638; Stomach 1890, 3638; Swim bladder 3563; Superoxide dismutase 1494; Testis 1534, 2941; Uterus 3638; Vertebrae 3677; Yolk sac 3638

CORTICOSTEROIDS (total) *37, 188*
Blood 1844, 1963, 3460

‡CORTICOSTERONE *112*
The level in the blood is usually higher in more active species.
Blood 1688, 1704, 1969, 2274, 2275, 2576, 3172, 3456, 3608

‡CORTISOL *6, 34, 37, 48, 64, 112, 116, 120, 188, 220, 235–237, 301–304, 308, 309, 355, 356, 383*
Considered a typical plasma steroid in bony fish where aldosterone is typical of amphibians and reptiles. Lungfish, which are phylogenetically close to terrestrial animals, possess similar quantities of each hormone. In man, cortisol and cortisone are both secreted and are interconvertible. In *Oncorhynchus* sp., cortisone is converted to cortisol, but the reverse reaction is the more important. Cortisone is thought to be biologically inactive in mammals except where it is converted to cortisol. Its function in fish is not known. Cortisol is usually the major adrenal steroid in teleosts, but occasionally cortisone assumes this role. Cyclostomes have very low levels of plasma corticosteroids, probably because of their relatively small amounts of adrenal tissue.

The steroid hormones become bound to plasma proteins, perhaps as a protection against too-rapid catabolism or a protection for the fish against too high a concentration (Moon and Idler, 1974). Both progesterone and pregnenolone are converted to cortisol and cortisone in the adrenocortical tissue (Sandor, Vinson *et al.*, 1966: *Anguilla anguilla*).

The concentration of cortisol in the blood increases during exercise, and the usual level tends to be higher in active species. Stress raises the concentration in the blood, sometimes quite slowly (several minutes), but rapidly if there is a store of preformed cortisol present in the adrenal cortex. Perhaps because of its link with physical activity, cortisol shows a marked variation throughout the day (*Fundulus grandis*), which differs between the sexes. The daily rhythm seems not to depend on the rhythm in pituitary adrenocorticotropic hormone. The serum cortisol levels of *Fundulus heteroclitus* have been reported to show no definite seasonal trend and no consistent difference between the sexes.

Circulating cortisol increases when euryhaline fish are transferred from fresh water to salt water (the opposite to prolactin). It is thought to increase the absorption of water by the intestine, and to stimulate the active extrusion of sodium. Only cortisol was found to promote water- and sodium transport across the isolated intestine of *Anguilla japonica*, and in *Anguilla rostrata* it has been found to induce increased activity of Na-K-ATPase in the gill. Authors quoted by Doneen and Bern (1974) have proposed that prolactin reduces and cortisol increases the osmotic permeability of the urinary bladder in sea water.

Cortisol is also thought to promote gluconeogenesis. The high levels found in spawning salmon may therefore supply energy at a time when lipid reserves have been exhausted. The disadvantage is that the same hormone seems to cause much or all of the post-spawning decay in these fish, which seem unable to clear it from their bodies as they become moribund.

Cortisol has not been found in *Myxine glutinosa* or *Petromyzon marinus*.
Blood 1578, 1688, 1704, 1802, 1844, 1846, 1847, 1856, 1921, 1942, 1969, 1970, 1976, 2055, 2056, 2122, 2176, 2196, 2203, 2274, 2275, 2527, 2547, 2555, 2556, 2576, 2742, 2891, 2961, 3068, 3172, 3289, 3290, 3334, 3600, 3603, 3608, 3609, 3639

‡Cortisone *6, 48, 237*
A higher concentration of this hormone is found in the blood of fish than of mammals. The clearance rate from the blood is higher in males than females, hence there is a higher concentration in females. *See also under cortisol.*
Blood 1688, 1844, 1900, 2275, 2555, 2961, 3172, 3609

‡Creatin *44, 76, 157, 164, 281*
As creatin phosphate, this compound supplies energy for muscular contraction. The quantity of creatin in the testis has been found to increase markedly during the maturation of *Oncorhynchus nerka*, indicating the build-up of an energy store in the sperms to enable them to swim. *Myxine* appears to acquire creatin from the sea water, but other fish probably synthesise it. Creatin is excreted through the kidneys, not the gills, and forms more than half of the urinary nitrogen. Excreted creatin in *Cyprinus carpio* predominates over creatinine, a situation different from that in mammals.
Blood 2078, 3134; Body fluids 3304; Dark muscle 2340, 2348; Liver 2625; Muscle 1882, 2340, 2348, 2455, 2456, 2625, 3134, 3135, 3304, 3367, 3369, 3419, 3567; Notochordal fluid 2076; Urine 2078, 2083, 3303

CREATIN PHOSPHATE *281*
(*see* under creatin)
Dark muscle 3458; Larval brain 3149; Larval spinal cord 3149; Muscle 2690, 2899, 3134, 3419, 3457

CREATIN PHOSPHOKINASE *65*
Blood 1989; Dark muscle 2344; Heart 1989; Kidney 1989; Liver 1989; Muscle 1989, 2344; Pink (intermediate) muscle 2344

‡CREATININE *44, 157, 305*
Formed by the spontaneous (non-enzymic) cyclisation of creatin. The levels in muscle do not appear to correlate with the levels of creatin. Once formed, creatinine is not metabolised further, and is excreted unchanged. The levels of these compounds in the blood are usually of the order of 0·5 to 2 mg%. *See also under creatin.*
Blood 1594, 1813, 1911, 2078, 2267, 3134, 3154; Body fluids 3304; Brain 1594; Erythrocytes 1594; Heart 1594; Liver 2625; Muscle 2455, 2456, 2625, 3134, 3135, 3367, 3369, 3567; Muscle ("wing") 1594; Notochordal fluid 2076; Seminal plasma 1765; Urine 2078, 2083, 3303

α-CRYPTOXANTHIN
Skin + fins 2716–2718, 2725

"CRYPTOXANTHIN"
Skin 2726; Skin + fins 2715, 2719–2725, 2727

‡CYANOCOBALAMIN (Vitamin B_{12}) *146, 149, 172*
The heart is often richest in this vitamin: 425 μg% has been found in *Gadus pollachius*. Liver contains more than does flesh, and dark muscle more than white. Fatty fish of the herring type contain more in their flesh than non-fatty teleosts or elasmobranchs, and in general the muscle of active fish contains more than that of sluggish fish. Appreciable quantities are found in sea water, where they may form a source for fish. Cyanocobalamin appears to be synergistic in its action with folic acid. Deficiency in salmonids results in poor appetite, reduced haemoglobin, erratic erythrocyte counts and fragmentation of erythrocytes. It can be synthesised in the intestine (*Cyprinus carpio*).
Blood 2868; "Digestive organs" 1522; "Gonad" 1522; Liver 1522; Muscle 3125, 3295

CYNTHIAXANTHIN
Muscle 2136; Skin 2136, 2726; Skin + fins 2715–2725, 2727

CYSTATHIONINE
Parietal muscle 2255

CYSTINE—Volume 1 only

CYTIDINE DIPHOSPHATE
Liver 1584

‡CYTIDINE MONOPHOSPHATE
Liver 1584, 3219

  Occurs in constant amount in each cell nucleus: in fishes in general and teleosts in
  particular, about 2 pg per nucleus; in diploid poeciliid fish, ranges from 1·3 to
  1·92 pg, while a value as low as 0·8 pg has been reported in one teleost. The
  concentration in muscle therefore depends on the sizes of the cells, in *Gadus morhua*,
  for example, being high at the head and tail ends of the musculature and lower in
  the middle where the cells are longest and broadest. Similarly, as fish grow, the
  DNA concentration in the muscle tends to fall. Myocommata are packed with
  nuclei and correspondingly rich in DNA. As eggs develop, the DNA increases at
  the expense of ribose nucleic acid, the sum of the two nucleic acids remaining
  roughly constant.

Blood 2282; Brain 1527, 1915, 2616, 3217; Cell (individual) 3203; Dark muscle 2282, 2315, 2824, 2985; Egg 2001, 2856, 3676, 3719; Embryo 3676, 3719; Erythrocytes 1706, 2194, 3136, 3425; Erythrocyte "ghosts" 2849; Fry 3223; Gill 2282; "Gonad" 2025, 2282; Heart 2282, 2283; Hepatopancreas 3481; Intestine 1527; Kidney 1527, 2282, 2283, 2856; Larva 3223, 3719; Liver 1527, 1584, 1589, 1739, 1881, 2125, 2282, 2283, 2373, 2621, 2681, 2856, 3105, 3391; Liver plasma membrane 2621; Muscle 1527, 1584, 1589, 2059, 2085, 2098, 2282, 2283, 2315, 2614, 2824, 2856, 2985, 3105; Nuclei 1705, 2195, 2998; Ovary 1527; Pancreas 1527; Pituitary 1527, 2025; Pyloric caecae 2282, 2283; Slime 2447; Sperm 2872, 3676; Spleen 1527, 2282, 2283; Testis 1527

DESOXYCHOLIC ACID
Bile salts 2408

DIACYL GLYCEROPHOSPHATIDYL CHOLINE
Brain 1849, 1850

DIACYL GLYCEROPHOSPHATIDYL ETHANOLAMINE
Brain 1849, 1850

DIACYL GLYCERYL ETHERS *125*
Give buoyancy to certain elasmobranchs which have no swim bladders. They give 14% more lift in sea water than do triglycerides. Buoyancy in *Squalus acanthias* appears to be regulated by changing the proportions of diacyl glyceryl ethers and triglycerides in the liver: artificially weighting the fish results in an increase in the former compounds.
Blood 3179; Heart 2399; Intestine 2399; Kidney 2399; Lipid depot 2399; Liver 2399, 3179; Muscle 2398, 2399, 2400; Ovary 2399; Spleen 2399; Stomach 2399

DIATOXANTHIN *317*
Skin + fins 2715–2721, 2723–2725, 2727

DIGLYCERIDES
Blood 3242; Egg 2118; Heart 2992; Liver 2117, 2118, 2439; Mesentery 2439; Muscle 2117, 2118, 2439, 2948, 3242; Olfactory nerve 2407; Ovary 2117, 2439, 3242; Slime 2559; Testis 2117, 2439, 3242; Yolk 2847

DIGLYCOSYLCERAMIDE
Rectal gland 2376

‡20β-DIHYDROCORTISONE—Volume 1 only

‡20β-DIHYDRO-17αHYDROXYPROGESTERONE
Blood 1652

‡DIHYDROXYACETONE PHOSPHATE
Embryo 3689; Erythrocytes 2550; Liver 1572; Muscle 1572; Oocytes 3689

DIHYDROXY-α CAROTENE
Skin 1516

DIHYDROXYPHENYLALANINE (*see* DOPA)

‡17α 20β-Dihydroxy-pregn-4-ene-3-one—Volume 1 only

9'10'-Dihydro-β-zeacarotene-3, 17'-diol
Skin + fins 2727

Diketogulonic acid 72
Dark muscle, Muscle: 2475

‡Dimethylamine 72
More concentrated in dark muscle than in white.
Dark muscle 3439; Eye 3665; Gall bladder 3665; "Gonad" 3665; Intestine 3665;
Liver 2110, 3665; Muscle 2110, 3439, 3665; Pyloric caecae 3665; Skin 3665;
Spleen 3665

Diphosphatidyl glycerol (see Cardiolipid)

Diphosphoinositide
Cerebellum, Electric lobes, Electric organ, Forebrain, Muscle, Pacemaker nucleus
(in medulla), Tectum opticum: 2474

‡Diphosphopyridine nucleotide (see Nicotinamide adenine dinucleotide)

DOPA (3,4-Dihydroxyphenylalanine) 385
Heart, Intestine, Kidney: 3091

Dopamine (3,4 dihydroxyphenylethylamine) 385
Heart, Intestine, Kidney: 3091

α-Doradecin
Skin + fins 2715–2717, 2719, 2725

‡Elastin 67
Arterial tissue 2508; Muscle 3462

Enolase 18, 19
Egg, Oocyte: 3703

Eosinophils
Blood 1814, 1898, 2868, 2969

Epimerase
Muscle 3398

Ergosterol (see Vitamin D)

EPIoestriol—Volume 1 only

‡Erythrocytes (red blood cells) 55, 56, 167, 213, 214, 239, 274–277
Decrease in number during starvation. Their ionic composition alters with ambient
salinity, particularly chloride which is in passive equilibrium between plasma and

cells. Erythrocytes contain ATP and GTP, which strongly depress the affinity of haemoglobin for oxygen. The concentrations of the compounds fall when environmental oxygen becomes unfavourably low, enabling the fish the better to utilise what is left.

Blood (count) 1424, 1476, 1550, 1647, 1669, 1698, 1749, 1814, 1822, 1898, 1911, 1932, 1949, 2052, 2077, 2140, 2141, 2146, 2218, 2326, 2333, 2362, 2373, 2626, 2633, 2634, 2801, 2868, 2905, 2967, 2969, 3154, 3288, 3371, 3408, 3520, 3566

Esterase *69, 72, 251*

More abundant in dark than in light muscle. Polymorphism of this enzyme in various organs has been investigated in relation to race and stock separation, with some success.

Blood 2221; Cholinergic vesicles from electric organ 3725; Dark muscle 2843; Liver 2843; Muscle 2843

Estrogen (*see* Oestrogen)

Ethanolamine

Blood 1594, 2946; Brain 1594; Electric organ 2946; Erythrocytes 1594; Heart 1594; Kidney 2910; Muscle 2455, 2946, 3366; Parietal muscle 2255; Wing muscle 1594; Nerve 2946

Ethanolamine plasmalogen

Brain, Brain myelin, Spinal cord myelin: 3222

‡Fatty acids (combined, individual) *5, 13–16, 25, 54, 65, 115, 124, 142, 143, 207–210, 316, 354*

Fatty acid	Marine fish (%)	Freshwater fish (%)
14:0	5·0	6·4
16:0	16·1	17·0
18:0	3·0	3·2
14:1	0·6	1·4
16:1	9·4	15·5
18:1	21·0	19·6
20:1	7·0	1·3
22:1	5·5	1·9
18:2	1·3	3·0
18:3	0·7	4·2
18:4	1·6	1·5
20:4	2·0	3·1
20:5	1·9	1·5
22:5	1·9	1·5
22:6	8·5	3·9

18:1 is the most abundant fatty acid.

The fatty acids in fish lipids are a much more complex mixture than those of land animals, which embody fewer and more saturated acids. Fish contain many unsaturated acids, and the most unsaturated one, 22:6, is present in considerable quantity. In *Oncorhynchus kisutch* the proportion of 22:6 laid down depends on the size of the fish rather than its availability in the diet. In *Gadus morhua* the unsaturated fatty acids of the flesh tend to be used preferentially during starvation, so a seasonal cycle in saturation occurs. Seasonal changes can also be caused by changes in the diet, since dietary lipids influence the composition of the fish lipids, but the influence is not over-riding, since fish impose their own pattern to some extent. The fatty acid pattern of freshwater fish differs from that of marine fish, probably because of dietary differences. There have been reported to be more C_{18} unsaturated fatty acids in freshwater fish and less C_{20} and C_{22} acids. On the other hand, the fatty acid composition of the phospholipids of brain remains fairly constant and does not follow transfer of habitat. The Table on p. 414 gives the *average* composition of the principal fatty acids in a number of Japanese marine and freshwater fish (after Yamada and Hayashi, 1975. Reproduced by courtesy of Dr. M. Yamada)

Unlike starving *Gadus morhua*, which steadily utilise 22:6, *Oncorhynchus kisutch* conserves this acid during an extended period of exercise or during dietary restriction. The difference is probably because 22:6 is preferentially incorporated into phospholipids (*Salmo gairdneri*); *Gadus morhua* utilise phospholipids during starvation, while salmonids utilise triglycerides.

The proportion of unsaturated fatty acids present in the phospholipids of fish tissues increases at lower temperatures. This is thought to relate to the fluidity and flexibility of membranes, so that tissues can remain mobile and membranes can function properly when the temperature falls.

Alk-1-enyl diglyceride 2118; Alkyl diacyl glycerols 3180; Alkyl diglyceride 2118; Biliverdin protein from blood 3671; Brain 2469, 3008, 3118; Cholesterol esters 1712, 2026, 2538, 2762, 3180, 3581; Corpuscles of Stannius 1712; Dark muscle 1413, 1546, 1801, 3117, 3118, 3616; Diacyl glyceryl ethers 2399; Diglycerides 2118, 2663, 2948; Dinogunellin (a toxic phospholipid from roe) 2138; Egg 1454, 1471, 1657, 2118; Embryo 2160; Epididymis 3118; Erythrocytes 1419, 1565; Fry 1471; Galactosyl ceramide 3488; Gangliosides 2469, 2472, 2904, 3488; Gills 2441, 3424; Glucosyl ceramide 3488; Glycerides 2780, 2781, 3394; Glycerophosphoryl choline 1849; Glycerophosphoryl ethanolamine 1849; Glyceryl ethers 2118, 2779; "Gonad" 1801; Heart 3118; Heart mitochondria 2296, 3197; Hump (from *Oncorhynchus gorbuscha*) 3137; Intestine 2441; Kidney 2910, 3118; Liver 1413, 1449, 1546, 1801, 1803, 1912, 2007, 2014, 2026, 2118, 2152–2155, 2234, 2441, 2504, 2663, 3118, 3153, 3158, 3224, 3616, 3666, 3667; Liver mitochondria 2296, 3197; Lysophosphatidyl choline 1565, 3568; Mesentery 3118; Monoglycerides 2118, 2663; Monophosphoinositide 2474; Muscle 1413, 1414, 1466, 1546, 1597, 1712, 1801, 1803, 1817, 2118, 2151–2155, 2406, 2441, 2449–2451, 2492, 2504, 2505, 2663, 2748, 2779, 2948, 2951, 3117, 3118, 3158, 3224, 3265, 3446, 3469, 3483–3485, 3568, 3616, 3627, 3666, 3667; Muscle mitochondria 3197; Muscle + skin 3568; Nerve tissue 1680; Neutral lipids 1731, 2117, 2151–2153, 3389, 3446; Oocytes 1832; Ovary 2153, 2154, 2399, 2441, 3170, 3238, 3333, 3616, 3666, 3667; Phosphatidyl choline 1419, 1530, 1565, 1603, 1680, 2469, 2473, 2474, 2663, 2747, 2910, 3088, 3387, 3388, 3568; Phosphatidyl ethanolamine 1419, 1530, 1565, 1603, 1680, 2469, 2473, 2474, 2663, 2747, 2910, 3088, 3568; Phosphatidyl inositol 1565, 1680, 2469; Phosphatidyl serine 1419, 1565, 1680, 2469, 2473, 2474, 3088; Phospholipids 1416, 1731, 1912, 2026, 2117, 2118, 2151, 2234, 2538, 2663, 2747, 2762, 2847, 2948, 2987, 3028, 3029, 3031, 3265, 3389, 3394, 3446, 3568; Retina 2882; Skin 1546, 3568, 3616; Slime 1546; Sphingomyelin 1565, 2469, 2474, 2663, 2910; Spleen 1832, 3118; Sterol esters 2118, 2663, 2948; Sulphatide 3488; Swim bladder 3029; Swim bladder fatty foam 3032; Tapetum lucidum 2882; Testis 1657, 2026, 2153, 2441, 3118, 3666, 3667; Triglycerides 1416, 1546, 1832, 2026, 2118, 2151, 2155, 2234, 2235, 2310, 2399,

2538, 2663, 2747, 2762, 2847, 2948, 2987, 3028, 3031, 3180, 3387, 3568, 3616, 3627; Trunk 3365; Wax esters 2155, 2310, 2399, 2780, 2781, 3170, 3180; "White collagenous subdermal material" 2234; Yolk 1471, 2847

‡*FREE* FATTY ACIDS (FFA) *6, 7, 25, 39–41, 44, 53, 66, 76, 98, 148, 211, 212, 229, 237, 238, 280*

In the blood, FFA sometimes fall when glucose rises as a response to stress, but in some species FFA and glucose rise together. In several species, including cyclostomes, FFA have been shown to have the same order of magnitude as those in mammals, between 0·2 and 0·7 μEq/ml. They appear to be absent from the serum of *Scyliorhinus canicula*. The species investigated with the highest levels appear to be *Gardonus rutilus* and *Anguilla anguilla*. FFA in circulation are associated with protein, which may or may not be albumin. Their speed of renewal shows that they serve as intermediates between lipid reserves and various organs. The regulation of FFA level in the blood seems to be comparable with that of blood glucose.

Blood 1437, 1802, 1816, 1954, 2278, 2284, 2495, 2514, 2515, 2517, 2518, 2533, 2555, 2660, 2734, 2765–2767, 2816, 3000, 3011, 3138, 3242, 3253, 3434; Brain 1954; Dark muscle 1581, 3138, 3237, 3246; Depot fat 2399; Egg 1691, 1987, 2118, 2330; Embryo 2330; Erythrocytes 1419, 1954, 2637; Gastric muscle 3246; "Gonad" 1691, 2398, 2400; Heart 2399, 2992; Heart muscle 1954, 3246; Hump (*Oncorhynchus gorbuscha*) 3137; Intestine 2399; Kidney 2399; Liver 1691, 1954, 2117, 2118, 2155, 2399, 2439, 2495, 2557, 2572, 2663, 2948, 3138, 3239, 3241, 3243; Mesentery 2439; Muscle 1581, 1691, 1731, 1954, 2117, 2118, 2398, 2399, 2400, 2439, 2495, 2660, 2663, 3056, 3138, 3239, 3241–3243, 3246, 3387, 3389, 3434, 3446, 3568; Olfactory nerve 2407; Ovary 2117, 2310, 2399, 2439, 3239, 3241–3243; Slime 2559; Spleen 1954, 2399; Stomach 2399; Swim bladder 2400, 2990, 3029; Swim bladder (fat-filled) 2398; Testis 2117, 2439, 2441–2443; Yolk 2847

FURAN FATTY ACIDS *210, 211*

A series of fatty acids, recently discovered as constituents of lipids in, so far, 20 species of male fish (Glass, Krick *et al.*, 1977). They incorporate a furan ring in their structure and are found primarily in liver and testis lipids, mostly as esters of cholesterol in the liver and in triglycerides of testis. Wide seasonal variations have been found, and the concentration in the liver rises during starvation (*Gadus morhua*), decreasing again only in the final stages of depletion. Eight members of the new series have been detected so far. Their metabolism and function are as yet unknown. Glass, Krick *et al.* (1977) reported their occasional presence in the livers of female fish also.

Liver 2026, 2092; Phospholipid 2026; Testis 2026; Triglyceride 2026

SATURATED FATTY ACIDS *339*

Muscle 3389

UNSATURATED FATTY ACIDS *42, 141, 143, 144, 148, 209, 210, 239, 261, 262, 316, 339, 340, 368*

Blood 1954; Brain 1954; Erythrocytes 1954; Heart muscle 1954; Liver 1954; Muscle 1954, 3057; Spleen 1954

FATTY ALCOHOLS

Blood 2845; Muscle glycerides 2781; "Gonad" 2398; Muscle 2398; Swim bladder (fat-filled) 2398; Wax (from muscle) 2780, 2781; Wax esters (from ovary) 3170

FUMARASE *72*
Cholinergic vesicles of electric organ 3725; Dark muscle 1580; Gas gland 1579; Muscle 1579, 1580

‡GADOLINEUM
Dark muscle, Muscle: 2571

‡GALACTOSAMINE
"Antifreeze" glycoprotein 1917; Cornea 2770, 3087; Skin mucopolysaccharide 3098

‡GALACTOSE
"Antifreeze" glycoprotein 1917, 3109; Cornea 2770; Egg 1454; Haptoglobin 2444; Ichthyocol 3337; Muscle 3685; Skin collagen 3141

β-GALACTOSIDASE
Heart, Intestine, Kidney, Liver, Pyloric caecae, Spleen, Stomach: 2840

GALACTOSYL CERAMIDES
Salt (rectal) gland 1530, 2377; Testis 3488

GANGLIOSIDES *340*
Are glycosphingolipids which contain sialic acids, principally N-acetyl neuraminic acid. They are mainly localised in the membranes of the central nervous system. They may be involved in synaptic transmission, participate in the regulation of cell permeability, act as receptors for a number of toxins and have antigenic properties.
Brain 2469; Cerebellum 2472; Electric lobes 2472; Salt (rectal) gland 1530, 2377; Tectum opticum 2472; Telencephalon 2472

GLOBULIN *43, 49, 58, 167, 193, 311, 338, 356*
One of the "classical" fractions of blood proteins, as distinct from albumins. They tend to increase in relative concentration during starvation.
Blood 2023, 2267, 3154, 3242, 3523–3526

GLUCAGON *189, 279, 319, 343, 344*
A hormone produced by the alpha cells of the pancreas, which acts in opposition to insulin. Its physiological role is well established in mammals but not very clear in fish. In mammals it raises the level of blood glucose, but in fish it produces decreases, increases or no effect at all (Fingerman, 1974). It may be involved in lipid metabolism in fish. Injection of mammalian glucagon into *Channa punctatus* has been shown to cause degeneration of the alpha cells of the pancreas, and, later, degeneration of the beta cells (Gill and Kanna, 1976). Lampreys are insensitive to glucagon. The hormone increases in the blood during starvation (insulin decreases).

‡GLUCOSAMINE
Cornea 2770, 3087; Haptoglobin 2444; Slime 3476

‡GLUCOSE *3, 4, 10, 11, 18, 25–27, 34, 44, 49, 72, 91, 92, 113–115, 123, 133, 136, 139–141, 167, 184, 186, 192, 213, 218, 227–229, 231–235, 237, 238, 241, 257, 270, 279–281, 291, 319, 343–345, 355, 364, 365, 378, 383, 386*
Glycogen in the process of being transported from liver or intestine to other

organs circulates in the blood as glucose, and although the level may rise after feeding, it usually maintains remarkably constant levels during starvation until the liver glycogen has been exhausted. Muscle glucose decreases during exercise.

Insulin and glucagon control the circulating level of glucose in the blood, but the catecholamines, adrenaline and noradrenaline, can effect a rapid glycogenolysis in the liver, causing raised blood glucose as a source of energy for pursuit or escape. Exercise, stress, spawning or increased metabolism from other causes all produce increases in blood glucose. The highest value ever reported is 1066 mg% in the blood of *Fundulus heteroclitus* cooled to 0·1°C. It is not certain that glucose levels in this species at low temperatures act specifically as "anti-freezes", but glucose undoubtedly rises as the temperature falls, especially as the freezing point is approached.

High-carbohydrate diets are not natural to fish, and some species seem permanently deficient in insulin, resulting in poor tolerance to administered glucose, which would have been rapidly metabolised by mammals. Continued administration of glucose, either by feeding, injection or absorption from the aquarium water, eventually results in pathological symptoms developing in the liver.

In *Cyprinus carpio*, a high blood glucose increases the synthesis of triglycerides in adipose tissue and reduces lipolysis (directly or indirectly), thus lowering the level of free fatty acids circulating in the plasma (the "Randle Cycle"). Lowering the blood glucose permits the liberation of FFA from adipose tissue. The FFA enter musculature where they are oxidised, reducing the peripheral utilisation of glucose and contributing to the maintenance of glycaemia. However, there is a lack of correlation between FFA and glucose in *Salmo gairdneri*.

Not surprisingly, seasonal variations have been reported by several authors. However, because of the multiplicity of factors involved, such effects can be difficult to interpret. It has been concluded that glycaemia levels are impossible to specify, even in one species in a state of rest. *Trachurus mediterraneus ponticus*, for example, has shown a blood glucose level in 1968 which was almost ten times higher than in 1967.

Glucose accumulates in the ovary during maturation.

Alkaline gland 2692; Aqueous humour 2692; Blood 1428, 1523, 1525, 1539, 1584, 1640, 1669, 1687, 1689, 1702, 1734, 1794, 1802, 1813, 1815, 1816, 1886, 1908, 1055, 1056, 1058, 2076–2079, 2113, 2116, 2143, 2262, 2267, 2278, 2284, 2288, 2291–2293, 2361, 2416–2419, 2513, 2514, 2516–2518, 2527, 2533, 2540, 2544, 2555, 2560, 2633, 2634, 2660, 2665, 2667, 2692, 2699, 2734, 2742, 2766, 2785, 2802, 2804, 2808, 2810, 2812, 2816, 2851, 2852, 2924, 2994, 3039, 3063, 3111, 3234, 3278, 3279, 3284, 3288, 3339, 3405–3407, 3417, 3426, 3455, 3492, 3499, 3501–3507, 3509, 3517, 3576, 3603, 3614, 3615, 3664, 3686, 3696; Brain 1607, 2250; Cerebrospinal fluid 2692; Collagen (from skin) 3141; Cornea 2270; Cranial fluid 1908; 2692, 3111; Dark muscle 2340, 2342, 3645; Endolymph 1908; Erythrocytes 2550; Ichthyocol 3337; Larval brain 3149; Larval spinal cord 3149; Liver 1607, 2342, 2783; Muscle 1745, 1951, 2085, 2086, 2219, 2340, 2342, 2783, 3025, 3645, 3685; Notochordal fluid 2076; Oocytes 3704, 3707; Ovarian fluid 3187; Pericardial fluid 2692; Slime 3652; Urine 2078, 2808, 3111; Vitreous humour 2288

GLUCOSE DEHYDROGENASE
Liver 2836, 2837, 3235

GLUCOSE KINASE
Muscle, Nerve: 3551

‡GLUCOSE-1-PHOSPHATE
Level reduced in muscle by exertion.
Muscle 1638

‡GLUCOSE-6-PHOSPHATASE *34, 221, 328, 330, 344*
Blood 2839; Brain 3010; Dark muscle 2810; Embryo 3701; Gill 2838; Heart 2810, 2838; Hepatopancreas 2834; Intestinal mucus 3010; Intestine 2838; Kidney 2838; Liver 1523, 1525, 1739, 2621, 2810, 2838, 2839, 2880, 3010, 3256, 3305, 3540; Liver plasma membrane 2621; Muscle 2810, 2838; Spleen 2838

‡GLUCOSE-6-PHOSPHATE *281*
Level rises in muscle during exertion.
Erythrocytes 2550; Larval brain 3149; Larval spinal cord 3149; Muscle 1638, 1852, 1951, 2085, 2086; Oocytes 3707

GLUCOSE-6-PHOSPHATE DEHYDROGENASE *19, 73, 153, 221, 257, 328, 333–335*
Blood 2839, 3258; Brain 1915; Dark muscle 1580, 3258; Egg 3703; Embryo 1889; Erythrocytes 1475; Gas gland 1579; Gill 2838; Heart 2838, 3258, 3684; Hepato-pancreas 3258; Intestine 2838, 3258; Kidney 3258; Liver 1488, 1955, 1956, 2837–2839, 2880, 3256, 3258, 3684; Muscle 1579, 1580, 2838, 3258, 3551; Nerve 3551; Oocytes 1889, 3703; Pyloric caecae 3258; Spleen 2838

GLUCOSE PHOSPHATE ISOMERASE (*see* Phosphoglucomutase)

α-GLUCOSIDASE
Dark muscle 2843; Heart 2840; Intestine 2840; Kidney 2840; Liver 2840, 2843; Muscle 2843; Spleen 2840; Stomach 2840

β-GLUCOSIDASE
Heart, Intestine, Kidney, Liver, Pyloric caecae, Spleen, Stomach: 2840

GLUCOSYL CERAMIDES
Salt (rectal) gland 1530, 2377; Testis 3488

GLUCURONATE
Blood, Urine: 2078

β-GLUCURONIDASE
Liver 2621; Liver plasma membrane 2621; Muscle 2757

‡GLUTAMATE *140, 141, 159, 188, 221, 281, 312*
Brain (medulla) 2910; Liver 2704, 3572; Muscle 3419

GLUTAMATE DECARBOXYLASE
Blood, Brain, Erythrocytes, Kidney, Liver: 1964

‡GLUTAMATE DEHYDROGENASE *159, 281*
Alimentary tract 3633; Blood 1989; Brain 3007, 3010, 3633; Dark muscle 3007; Embryo 3688; Gill 3007, 3572, 3633; Heart 1989, 3007, 3633; Intestine 3007, 3010; Kidney 1989, 3007, 3572, 3633; Liver 1739, 1989, 2938, 3007, 3010, 3572, 3633; Muscle 1989, 3007; Oocytes 3688; Spleen 3007, 3633

‡Glutamate oxaloacetate transaminase (GOT) = Aspartate amino transferase *65, 72, 186–188, 257, 330*
Alimentary tract 3633; Blood 1702, 1989, 2664, 2773, 3162; Brain 3373, 3633; Dark muscle 3648; Egg 2793; Gill 2685, 3373, 3633; Heart 1989, 3373, 3633; Hepatopancreas 2834, 3373; Internal adductor muscle of pectoral fin 3648; Intestine 3373; Kidney 1989, 2685, 3373, 3633; Liver 1736, 1989, 2291–2293, 2366, 2518, 2936–2938, 3633, 3648; Muscle 1989, 2366, 3373, 3648; Sperm 2793; Spleen 3373, 3633

Glutamate pyruvate transaminase (GPT) = Alanine aminotransferase *187, 188*
Alimentary tract 3633; Blood 1989, 2773, 3162; Brain 3373, 3633; Dark muscle 3648; Egg 2793; Gill 3373, 3633; Heart 1989, 3373, 3633; Hepatopancreas 2820, 2834, 3373; Internal adductor muscle of pectoral fin 3648; Intestine 3373; Kidney 1989, 3373, 3633; Liver 1739, 1989, 2291–2293, 2366, 2936–2938, 3633, 3648; Muscle 1989, 2366, 2702, 3373, 3648; Sperm 2793; Spleen 3373, 3633

Glutamic acid (*see* Glutamate) *140, 159, 188*

‡Glutaminase *159*
Gill, Kidney, Liver: 3572

‡Glutamine *159, 160, 162, 259*
An important intermediate in ammonia excretion, rendering it non-toxic to the fish. The ammonia can later be liberated from the glutamine, as expedient, by the breakdown of the latter by glutaminase. Injection of glutamine results in a great increase in ammonia excretion.
Blood 1594; Brain 1594, 3007; Dark muscle 3007; Erythrocytes 1594; Gill 3007; Heart 1594, 3007; Intestine 3007; Kidney 3007; Liver 3007, 3572; Muscle 3007; "Wing" muscle 1594; Spleen 3007

Glutamine synthetase *159*
Serves to provide the glutamine for the various metabolic pathways, and hence plays a part in ammonia detoxication in fish (*see* under glutamine). The activity of the enzyme is higher in brain than in other organs (*Ictalurus punctatus*), perhaps to keep ammonia concentrations especially low here.
Brain 3010, 3546, 3592, 3636; Gill 3636; Intestinal mucus 3010, 3546; Kidney 3010, 3546, 3636; Liver 3010, 3546, 3592, 3636; Spleen 3010, 3546

γ-Glutamyl transferase
Brain, Intestinal mucus, Kidney, Liver, Spleen: 3010

‡Glutathione
More concentrated in dark than in ordinary muscle.
Kidney, Liver, Ovary, Testis: 1748

Glutathione reductase
Embryo 1889; Erythrocytes 1485; Oocytes 1889

Glyceraldehyde-3-phosphate
Embryo, Oocytes: 3689

GLYCERALDEHYDE-3-PHOSPHATE DEHYDROGENASE *330, 333, 335*
Erythrocytes 1475; Liver 2880; Muscle 1789

GLYCERIDES
Adipose fin 2578, 3283; Adrenal 1712; Cerebrum 2578, 3283; Corpuscles of
Stannius 1712; Egg 3388; Gill 2578, 3283; "Gonad" 2578, 3283; Heart 2578, 3283;
Kidney 2578, 3283; Liver 2578, 3283; Muscle 2578, 3056, 3283; Posterior cardinal
vein 1712; Scales 2578, 3283; Skin 2578, 3283; Spinal cord 2578, 3283; Spleen
2578, 3283; Swim bladder 2578, 3283

‡GLYCEROL
Egg 1454

GLYCEROL KINASE
Heart 3196; Liver 2536, 3196; Muscle 3196

GLYCEROL PHOSPHATE DEHYDROGENASE
Dark muscle 1580; Gas gland 1579; Heart 1505, 3196; Liver 3196; Muscle 1579,
1580, 1744, 3196

‡α-GLYCEROPHOSPHATE
Liver 1572; Muscle 1572, 1852

α-GLYCEROPHOSPHATE DEHYDROGENASE
Embryo 3702; Liver 1956, 2880; Muscle 1956

GLYCERYL ETHERS
Muscle 2779

‡GLYCERYLPHOSPHORYL CHOLINE—Volume 1 only

‡GLYCINE *162, 194, 199–201, 312, 354, 355*
One third of the amino acids of collagen are glycine molecules. The concentration
of glycine in the gonads therefore declines progressively during maturation as the
sex products accumulate and "dilute" the connective tissue.
Brain (medulla) 2944; Corium, Elastoidin, Ovokeratin, Scales, Swim bladder
collagen, Swim bladder elastin, Swim bladder tunic: 2087

‡GLYCOGEN *3, 4, 7, 11, 18–20, 26, 36, 48, 49, 53, 54, 61, 64, 67–71, 73, 77, 89–92, 96,
101–103, 110, 113, 114, 117–119, 136, 140, 141, 173, 177, 178, 184, 185, 187, 188,
192, 227–229, 233, 235, 246, 247, 259, 278–281, 335, 343–345, 354, 361, 362, 364–366,
383, 386, 387*
The biochemical pathways of synthesis and breakdown are close to those found in
mammals. Fish have low glycogen reserves in the liver and muscle compared with
mammals, but that in the brain is higher and tends to be rigorously maintained
there during starvation. Brain glycogen levels are also maintained at their "resting"
values during physical exercise. It is more concentrated in the livers of male fish
than of females, perhaps because males of some species tend to swim more actively
on the spawning ground than females, and so presumably need a greater reserve.
Glycogen accumulates in the ovaries during maturation.

It is more concentrated in dark muscle than in white, and differs in concentration in different parts of the musculature. It is the chief fuel for muscle contraction and can be very rapidly mobilised—during "burst" activity, half of the reserves of the white muscle can be depleted in 15 seconds, with equivalent lactate production. The ratio of liver glycogen to muscle glycogen has been quoted as 30:1 to 50:1 compared with 10:1 in mammals. The ratio 7:1 has been quoted for *Salmo salar* at certain seasons. There is a clear positive correlation between the glycogen concentration in the liver (hepatopancreas in *Cyprinus carpio*) and that in the muscle, so there are seasonal variations in both tissues, depending to some extent on the nutritional state. A circadian rhythm has been described in the brain of *Serranus scriba*, with a minimum at about 8 p.m., when the fish are most active and have the greatest ability to learn. The glycogen then rises to a maximum at about midnight. Adaptation to cold often results in greater glycogen reserves being laid down in the liver.

In many species, starvation causes reduction in the liver glycogen from the outset, and glycogen tends to be utilised before protein or lipid. There are species differences, however, and *Cyprinus carpio* tends to preserve the glycogen in its hepatopancreas during starvation. The liver glycogen of salmon migrating upstream in a starving state can actually increase, presumably by gluconeogenesis from the breakdown of amino acids. Liver glycogenolysis is stimulated by adrenaline and suppressed by insulin (*Anguilla japonica*). See also glycogen phosphorylase.
Blastula 3705; Brain 1470, 1607, 1958, 2250, 2416, 2851, 2852, 3049, 3052, 3686; Cerebellum 2797; Dark muscle 1563, 1808, 1996, 2340, 2342, 2344, 2347–2349, 2555, 2810, 2985, 3089, 3374, 3643–3646, 3648; Egg 2001, 3705; Electric organ 2121; Embryo 3705, 3706; Embryo liver 3550; Gas gland 1794; Gastrula 3705; Heart 1808, 1815, 2206, 2810, 2812, 2816, 3052, 3196, 3686; Hepatopancreas 2832, 3162, 3372; Kidney 3686; Larval brain 3149; Larval liver 3550; Larval spinal cord 3149; Liver 1431, 1523, 1559, 1589, 1607, 1640, 1725, 1749, 1752, 1753, 1794, 1802, 1808, 1815, 1816, 1886, 2052, 2116, 2157, 2206, 2284, 2291–2293, 2342, 2347, 2348, 2366, 2416, 2419, 2518, 2523, 2543, 2555, 2560, 2607, 2660, 2665, 2667, 2699, 2783, 2785, 2802, 2804, 2810, 2811, 2812, 2851, 2852, 2966, 2980, 2994, 3025, 3039, 3052, 3089, 3196, 3499, 3507, 3540, 3550, 3576, 3613, 3615, 3643, 3646, 3648, 3686; Lung 3686; Medulla oblongata 1958, 2797; Muscle 1510, 1559, 1563, 1589, 1640, 1725, 1749, 1794, 1802, 1808, 1886, 1996, 1052, 2206, 2219, 2284, 2292, 2340, 2342, 2344, 2347–2349, 2416, 2518, 2523, 2543, 2555, 2660, 2667, 2690, 2691, 2699, 2783–2785, 2802, 2810, 2812, 2816, 2851, 2852, 2899, 2980, 2985, 3039, 3052, 3076, 3089, 3196, 3304, 3372, 3374, 3507, 3613, 3615, 3643–3646, 3648; Myocardium 3049; Oocytes 1792, 3705; Ovary 1559, 3686; Pink (intermediate) muscle 1563, 2344; Retina 1855; Rhombencephalon 2797; Saccus vasculosus 2851; Spleen 3686; Tectum opticum 2797; Telencephalon 2797; Testis 3686

GLYCOGEN PHOSPHORYLASE *3, 18, 19, 73, 235, 278, 279, 344*
Completely absent from the liver of *Cyprinus carpio*, which uses an amylase to mobilise liver glycogen, but all other investigated species seem to use glycogen phosphorylase for this purpose. The enzyme catalyses the first step in the degradation of glycogen for energy production. Probably because of its strategic position, its activity is under tight control by hormones, ions and metabolites. It can be activated by adrenaline, noradrenaline and glucagon, and a central role is played by calcium.
Dark muscle 2810, 2815; Embryo 3701; Heart 2810, 2815; Liver 1523, 1525, 2810, 2815, 3514, 3515, 3540; Muscle 2810, 2815; Oocytes 3704

GLYCOGEN SYNTHETASE = Uridine diphosphate glucose-glycogen glucosyl transferase
18, 20
Blastula 3705; Dark muscle 2287; Egg 3705; Embryo 3705, 3706, 3708, 3709;
Gastrula 3705; Liver 2287; Muscle 2287; Oocytes 3704, 3705, 3709

GLYCOLIPID
Brain 1479; Egg 1479; Swim bladder 2990

GLYCOPROTEIN *43, 112, 346, 349, 357*
Blood 2079

GLYCYL-L-LEUCINE DIPEPTIDASE
Dark muscle, Kidney, Liver, Muscle, Spleen: 1749, 1756

‡GOLD—Volume 1 only

GONADOTROPIN (gonadotrophin) *37, 48, 58, 60, 383*
Released into the blood by the pituitary each day at a time linked to the photo-
period. The function of this hormone is to promote the development of the gonads.
Blood 1542, 1610, 1759, 1760, 2020; Pituitary 1610, 2020, 2906, 3639

GRANULOCYTES (count)
Blood 1907, 2633, 2634, 3154

GROWTH HORMONE (Somatotropic hormone) *116, 218, 220, 383*
Originates in the pituitary: the concentration in the blood increases during
prolonged exercise and during starvation.
Blood 2660

‡GUANINE *21, 22, 57, 122, 355*
Forms the basis of the silvery substance in the scales of many fish species, but the
level in the skin does not always correspond with the intensity of silvering. Increases
in the skin of salmon parr when they metamorphose to smolts. A silvery layer
containing overlapping crystals of guanine prevents gases from diffusing through
the walls of the swim bladder.
Eye 1867; Liver 3066; Scales 1966; Skin 1867, 1966, 2156; Swim bladder 1867,
3148

GUANOSINE DEAMINASE *161*
Liver 2873

‡GUANOSINE DIPHOSPHATE
Liver 1584, 3721

‡GUANOSINE MONOPHOSPHATE
Liver 1584, 3219, 3220, 3721

‡GUANOSINE TRIPHOSPHATE *274, 277, 315, 327*
Present in the erythrocytes of some species of fish, where it influences the Root
Effect towards higher pH values, reducing their capacity for oxygen. It is 2 to 6

times more effective in the role than is ATP. Release of oxygen at tissue sites is therefore expedited under certain conditions, and by reducing the quantity of GTP present in the blood cells, the fish can adapt to lower ambient oxygen concentrations. The level of GTP in muscle tissue falls during exertion.
Erythrocytes 1995, 2331, 3597; Liver 1584, 3219, 3721

L-GULONOLACTONE OXIDASE
Catalyses the conversion of L-gulono-γ-lactone to vitamin C, so fish without the enzyme require the vitamin in the diet. Yamamoto, Sato and Ikeda (1978) have shown it to be present in the livers of *Cyprinus carpio*, *Carassius carassius cuvieri*, *Tribolodon hakonensis* and *Parasilurus asotus*, so these species are independent of dietary vitamin C. The enzyme was not detected in 8 other species examined, including *Salmo gairdneri* which is known to exhibit vitamin deficiency symptoms.
Hepatopancreas 3677

‡HAEMATOCRIT *25, 27, 34, 55, 57, 127, 146, 213, 214, 229, 241, 274–277, 311, 315* (definition), *327, 355–357*
Subject to so many influences that haematocrit determinations on their own may not give reliable information. Most fish have a lower haematocrit than most mammals, and the value in fish is much more variable. Capture stress causes a rise in haematocrit, perhaps through loss of plasma. The haematocrit has been shown to decrease when serial samples are taken because, it is thought, interstitial fluids pass into the blood stream of haemorrhaging fish and constitute a source of variation (Jones and Pearson, 1976: *Lepomis macrochirus*). A persistently low ambient oxygen concentration causes an increase in the haematocrit, which enables the fish the better to extract the remaining gas. Probably for this reason, acclimation to higher temperatures also results in an increase in haematocrit—oxygen is less soluble in warm water. However, sudden asphyxia causes the red blood cells to swell, giving erroneously high haematocrit readings. In severe cases they will not shrink to their normal size afterwards, even when sampled with a syringe filled with oxygen. Anaesthesia gives rise to higher haematocrit values (using tricaine methane sulphonate), though sometimes it can reduce them. Starvation causes a fall to, eventually, very low values. This is because after a while no new blood cells are produced, but the effect is modified because the life of existing blood cells is greatly prolonged, perhaps because of the reduced swimming activity of starving fish.
Any change in osmoregulation alters the haematocrit, even where the number of blood cells in the circulation has not changed, because of changes in the plasma volume. Thus, transfer of a fish to a different salinity will often change the haematocrit, especially at first.
Active pelagic fish have much higher haematocrit values (up to 57%) than sluggish, and the values are low in deep-water fish without swim bladders (5–9%). Values increase steadily as fish grow bigger.
The haematocrit rises in males and falls in females at around the spawning time, perhaps through a difference in physical activity, so could be used temporarily for sexing fish. It also changes markedly when *Anguilla japonica* have become mature in response to hormone injections.
Red blood cells are produced by and stored in the spleen, so splenectomy causes an immediate decrease in haematocrit (*Scyliorhinus canicula*). However, the values recover after 3 weeks, perhaps because of the activity of other sites of red blood cell production.

Blood 1505, 1550, 1633, 1647, 1669, 1698, 1702, 1735, 1749, 1794, 1822, 1886, 1907, 1911, 1916, 1936, 1949, 2008, 2052, 2057, 2139–2141, 2146, 2217, 2218, 2241, 2257, 2262, 2284, 2300, 2331–2334, 2362, 2429, 2476, 2514, 2516–2518, 2533, 2660, 2664, 2665, 2678, 2801, 2846, 2868, 2891, 2896, 2905, 2924, 2961, 2967, 2969, 3015, 3063, 3108, 3142, 3154, 3288, 3293, 3314–3316, 3339, 3343, 3371, 3377, 3430, 3455, 3507, 3520, 3559, 3566, 3570, 3598, 3604, 3606, 3656

‡HAEMOGLOBIN *2, 13, 21–23, 25–27, 33, 34, 44, 55, 56, 73, 88, 106, 110, 118, 123, 124, 229, 239, 241–243, 252, 259, 262, 270, 273–278, 315, 327, 355, 385*
See under haematocrit for factors causing changes in the concentration. For example, the concentration of haemoglobin is directly correlated with the body weight (*Hippoglossoides platessoides*), so small fish have a low blood oxygen solubility, despite a high weight-specific oxygen consumption.

Unlike that of mammals, the haemoglobin of fish contains some isoleucine. It also contains less histidine than mammalian haemoglobin and more tryptophan.

Unlike the "higher" fish, lampreys and hagfish have monomeric myoglobin-like haemoglobin which consists of single haem-polypeptide molecules.

Many different forms of haemoglobin, some of which can be separated by electrophoresis, are found in fish as distinct from mammals and birds. Sometimes the electrophoretic patterns differ between fish of different populations, and sometimes change during growth, metamorphosis or maturation. This multiplicity may be considered a mechanism of adaptation to variable physiological requirements and widespread differences in the oxygen concentrations of the habitat. The cold waters of the Antarctic are so rich in oxygen that some species of fish possess greatly reduced concentrations of haemoglobin, while others have none at all, relying solely on the solubility of oxygen in the plasma, which seems sufficient for them to lead full and active lives.

At least some of the haemoglobin of most fish shows pronounced Bohr and Root Effects, a reduced affinity and capacity (respectively) for oxygen at lowered pH values. The production of lactic acid in contractile tissue therefore encourages the circulating haemoglobin to give up its oxygen at sites where it is most needed. Local production of lactic acid is also thought to be the mechanism causing fish blood to give up its oxygen in the gas gland of the swim bladder, even where oxygen at high pressure is already present. Control over the absorption of oxygen at the gills is also exercised by ATP and GTP, both of which are present in the red cells and reduce oxygen uptake. These compounds diminish under conditions of low ambient oxygen, allowing the fish to make better use of whatever oxygen is available.

Elasmobranchs have evolved a special haemoglobin which is stable in high concentrations of urea. The oxygen affinity of haemoglobin in man is greatly altered by urea, but that of elasmobranchs is unaffected.
Blood 1476, 1505, 1550, 1584, 1647, 1698, 1702, 1734, 1735, 1749, 1814, 1822, 1907, 1911, 1932, 1936, 1949, 2052, 2082, 2139–2141, 2146, 2206, 2217, 2218, 2241, 2247, 2300, 2326, 2331–2334, 2362, 2373, 2514, 2516–2518, 2626, 2633, 2634, 2664, 2678, 2801, 2868, 2905, 2924, 2967, 2969, 3063, 3142, 3154, 3288, 3293, 3316, 3371, 3377, 3437, 3520, 3566, 3570, 3604, 3606, 3656, 3657; Erythrocytes 1647, 1698, 1907, 1911, 2326, 2332, 2334, 2634, 2969, 2995, 3154, 3288, 3315, 3371

‡HEPARIN—Volume 1 only

HEPARITIN SULPHATE
Aorta 3344

HETEROPHILS
Blood 2868

HEXOKINASE *3, 18, 92*
Blood 2839; Brain 1915; Dark muscle 1580, 2344; Erythrocytes 1475; Gas gland 1579; Gill 2838; Heart 1505, 2838; Intestine 2838; Kidney 2838; Liver 2836, 2838, 2839, 2880, 2938; Muscle 1579, 1580, 1744, 2344, 2842· Oocytes 3704; Pink (intermediate) muscle 2344; Spleen 2838

‡HEXOSAMINES
Blood 3094, 3095; Corium 2087; Cornea 1678, 2770; Egg yolk protein 2844; Elastoidin 2087; Ichthyocol 3337; Mucopolysaccharide from skin 1434; Ovokeratin 2087; Swim bladder 2087

‡"HEXOSE"
Blood 3094, 3095; Corium 2087; Cornea 2770; Egg yolk protein 2844; Elastoidin 2087; Ovokeratin 2087; Scales 2087; Swim bladder 2087

‡HEXOSE DIPHOSPHATE—Volume 1 only

HEXOSE MONOPHOSPHATES
Embryo 3706, 3708; Oocytes 3704

HEXOSE-6-PHOSPHATE DEHYDROGENASE *329*
Liver 3345, 3684

‡HEXURONIC ACID
Blood 3094; Ichthyocol 3337; Mucopolysaccharide from skin 3098

HISTAMINE
Alimentary tract 2956; Brain 3662; Duodenum 2955; Eye 3662; Heart 3662; Ileum 2955; Liver 3662; Muscle 2120; Stomach 2955

‡HISTIDINE *110, 153, 198*
The muscle of fatty, dark-fleshed, active and migratory species contains much more free histidine than that of white-fleshed sluggish species, which may still contain combined histidine as a major component of the muscle proteins. In the active fish, the free amino acid may act as a buffer, protecting the tissues from the effects of sudden increases in lactic acid. The level is regulated by histidine deaminase and urocanase, which mediate the first two steps of the degradative process. For some reason, the muscle of freshwater fish contains more than that of marine fish.
Blood 3166; Dark muscle 3166; Kidney 3166; Lens 2181; Liver 3166; Muscle 1766, 1882, 3166

HYALURONIC ACID
Aorta 3344

HYALURONIDASE
Intestine, Pyloric caecae, Stomach, Stomach mucous membrane: 2436

HYDROCARBONS
Occur in all marine organisms, but generally account for 1% or less of the total lipid-soluble material.
Adipose fin 2578; Blood 1437, 3180; Cerebrum 2578; Egg 1987, 2118; Erythrocytes 1419; Gill 2578; "Gonad" 2578; Heart 2578; Kidney 2578; Liver 2118, 2578, 3180; Muscle 2118, 2568, 2578, 2779, 2948, 3180; Scales 2578; Skin 2578; Slime 2559; Spinal cord 2578; Spleen 2578; Swim bladder 2578

α-HYDROXYBUTYRATE DEHYDROGENASE 65

4-HYDROXY α-CAROTENE
Muscle 1782

‡17-HYDROXYCORTICOSTEROID
Blood 3150

1α-HYDROXYCORTICOSTERONE 309
An adrenal hormone which appears to control the output of salt from the rectal gland of elasmobranchs.
Blood 2276, 3456, 3608

18-HYDROXYDEOXYCORTICOSTERONE
Blood 1969

4-HYDROXY-4-KETO-β-CAROTENE
Sperm 1782; Testis 1781

HYDROXYMETHYLGLUTARYL COA SYNTHASE
Liver 3026

‡17α-HYDROXYPROGESTERONE
Blood 1652, 1688

‡HYDROXYPROLINE 194, 199, 202, 357
Present in fish collagens in smaller concentrations than in mammalian collagens. It is the imino acid which stabilises the collagen molecule, and collagens with less hydroxyproline denature at lower temperatures. Different species of fish seem to possess collagens with hydroxyproline contents/denaturation temperatures appropriate to the temperature of their usual habitat. Within one species, Gadus morhua, however, it has now been shown that the skin of those from the cold Labrador ground always denatures at a temperature below that which denatures the skin of North Sea cod (K. Kelly, personal communication, 1978).
Blood 1594, 2898; Bone 2484; Corium 2087; Egg shell 3152; Elastoidin 2087; Erythrocytes 1594; Eye lens 2050; Heart 1594; Hepatopancreas 2484; Intestine 2484; Kidney 2484; Muscle 1749, 2455, 2456, 2484; Muscle cell walls 1577; Myocomma collagen 2484, 2772, 3672; Ovokeratin 2087; Scales 2087, 2484; Skin 2484; Skin collagen 2051, 2772, 3672, 3695; Spleen 2484; Swim bladder collagen 2087, 2772; Swim bladder elastin 2087; Swim bladder tunic 2087, 2484; Wing muscle 1594

17-HYDROXYSTEROIDS—Volume 1 only for bibliography. This volume page reference 22

11-β-Hydroxytestosterone *37*
  Blood 2273, 2391

5-Hydroxytryptamine *see* Serotonin

‡Hypoxanthine *21, 22, 34, 73, 161, 355*
  Present in skin, where it increases during the metamorphosis of salmon parr. It is more concentrated in dark than in mosaic muscle (*Salmo gairdneri*). It is virtually absent from the white muscle of some common food-fish. but since its concentration rises progressively after death, its analysis in fish flesh has been made the basis of a test of freshness of fish for human consumption.
  Blood 2873; Cerebrospinal fluid 2873; Dark muscle 1865; Extradural fluid 2873; Eye 1867; Muscle 1583, 1865, 1872, 2406, 2490, 3482; Scales 1966; Skin 1867, 1966, 2156; Swim bladder 1867

Hypoxanthine-guanine phosphoribosyl transferase
  Brain, Liver: 2873

‡Ichthylepidin—Volume 1 only

‡Inosine *161*
  Muscle 2455, 2490, 2846, 3482; Skin 1966, 2156

‡Inosine monophosphate
  Shows a large increase in the muscle during exertion.
  Liver 2490, 3219, 3220; Muscle 1583, 1582, 1871, 1873, 2455, 2456, 2918, 3366, 3367, 3419, 3482; Skin 2156

‡Inosinic acid
  Skin 1966

‡Inositol
  A vitamin of the B group, deficiency in which results, in fish, in anaemia, anorexia, bloated stomach, poor growth and lesions in the skin. It used to be considered an important carbohydrate reserve in elasmobranchs, but this may not be true. The absolute amount increases in the gonad of *Oncorhynchus nerka* during maturation.
  Alimentary tract 3453; Gut wall 3453; Liver 3453; Muscle 3295, 3453

‡Insulin *5, 6, 91, 110, 111, 139, 140, 189, 233, 279, 319, 343, 344, 365, 378, 379*
  In higher vertebrates, this pancreatic hormone is primarily concerned with carbohydrate metabolism, but it seems to have a wider role in fish, where its effects are complex and vary with the season and the fish species and their physiological state.
    There is considerable scope for amino acid substitution without loss of function in the insulin molecule. Some fish insulins are very different from others—for example, *Myxine* insulin appears not to incorporate zinc in the molecule. However, structural or immunological differences do not correspond with differences in biological activity, and sometimes a mammalian insulin can be more effective than the insulin of another fish.

Removal of the pancreas has very variable results, depending on the species of fish: diabetes does not always occur—for example in the yellow form of *Anguilla rostrata*.

The administration of insulin can cause hypoglycaemia, sometimes with convulsions, and sometimes accompanied by the depletion of hepatic glycogen. However, some investigators have obtained slight hyperglycaemia, and others, increased liver glycogen levels after administration. Insulin has been found to promote glycogen deposition in the livers (*in vitro*) of *Notemigonus crysoleucas* acclimated to 12°C, but to deplete it in those acclimated to 25°C (de Vlaming and Pardo, 1975). Muscle glycogen may be strongly increased or unaffected by insulin. Where it is increased, there appear to be two independent effects operating: an increased permeability of the muscle membrane to glucose, and the activation of some enzymes, especially glycogen synthetase, which result in the augmented accumulation of glycogen in the muscle.

The speed with which injected insulin acts depends on the temperature. In *Cyprinus carpio*, for example, the blood sugar rises first of all due to the handling and injection; it then falls after 8 hours at 30°C, after 14 hours at 20°C and has been shown to change little after 24 hours at 6°C.

Insulin appears to favour the uptake of amino acids, as well as glucose, by the muscle and, according to Castilla and Murat (1975), insulin significantly reduces protein turn-over. The half-life of labelled proteins was found to double under the action of insulin.

The hormone also appears to play a part in the lipid metabolism of fish, and faulty lipid metabolism may result from pancreatectomy in teleosts and elasmobranchs. Thomas (1971) found that insulin injected into *Gadus morhua* caused a 50% rise in the fatty acids of the blood, but other authors have noted decreases. Perhaps these changes are simply caused by the alterations in the level of blood glucose, which stimulates or inhibits lipid release from adipose tissue when it falls or rises, respectively.

Injections of glucose into fish stimulate insulin release by the beta cells of the pancreas. It now seems clear that proteins act in a similar way, and leucine has been found to stimulate insulin release to an extent comparable with that of glucose (*Opsanus tau*). Arginine and lysine stimulate insulin release to a greater extent than glucose in *Anguilla anguilla*.

The drug streptozotocin inhibits insulin release, and treated *Gadus morhua* exhibited a slight hyperglycaemia (Thomas, 1971). At the same time, the number of secretory granules "imprisoned" in the pancreas could be seen by electron microscopy to increase under the action of the drug.
Blood 1426, 1815, 1816, 3051, 3052; Islet tissue 2703

IODIDE
Muscle 3294

‡IODINE (protein-bound) *50, 133, 355*
Protein-bound iodine in the plasma is lowest in freshwater fish, higher in marine species and very high in euryhaline species, especially during migration where it presumably reflects thyroid activity. Similarly, active fish have more circulating in their blood than have more sluggish species. The ovary contains more than the testis, and relatively high levels are also found in the spleen and bile, while appreciable amounts are found in the stomach and liver. Iodine is essential to the fish,

but the content in the muscle may vary according to the catching locality, perhaps because of differences in the iodine content of plankton.
Blood 2178

‡Iron *8, 26, 27, 34, 45, 46, 56, 57, 73, 147, 148, 172, 248, 354, 355, 385*
In general, the higher the organism is up the evolutionary scale, the more iron is present in the blood. Fish sperm contain the smallest amount of any tissue. The iron content of eggs relates directly to their hatching rate. The concentration in the ovary of the parent female declines during the progress of maturation. Dark muscle contains more haem pigmentation than white muscle and this is reflected in the iron content. The bile of freshwater fish contains 1.7% of iron in the ash (up to 283 mg per kg dry matter). In the liver, the element occurs mainly as ferritin, a protein which contains about 23% of iron on a dry weight basis. The concentration of iron in the livers of Black Sea fish is as high as 5% of the ash, which is ten times higher than the content of this element in the livers of freshwater fish. Gills have an apparently high concentration of iron, but contamination with blood is probably the reason. Kidneys contain a considerable amount (380–610 mg% ash), probably because of their haematopoietic function.
Bile 1533, 1838; Blastula 3718; Blood 1838, 1858, 2963, 3002, 3003, 3278, 3279, 3717; Bone 1533, 1534, 1838, 2281, 2786, 2850, 3002, 3004, 3017, 3115; Brain and nerve cord 3003; Cartilage 3003; Dark muscle 2571, 2613; Egg 3718; Erythrocytes 3002; Fin 2786; Fry 3718; Fry + yolk 3718; Gill 1533, 1622, 2281, 2786, 2850, 3002, 3003, 3017, 3115, 3563, 3564; "Gonad" 1622, 3002, 3003; Heart 1622, 1890, 3002, 3003, 3564; Intestine 1838, 1890, 3002, 3003, 3570; Kidney 1533, 1622, 1838, 1890, 2040, 3002, 3003, 3115, 3563, 3564, 3570; Larva 3718; Liver 1533, 1534, 1561, 1622, 1838, 1890, 2040, 2281, 2850, 3002–3004, 3115, 3563, 3564, 3570; Lung 1890; Muscle 1561, 1622, 1763, 1786, 1793, 1838, 2040, 2313, 2491, 2571, 2613, 2677, 2786, 2850, 2901, 3002–3004, 3017, 3019, 3057, 3115, 3294, 3467, 3563, 3564, 3690; Myoglobin 3441; Oocytes 3718; Ovary 1533, 2040, 2281, 2364; Pancreas 1890; Pyloric caecae 3570; Rectal gland 3003; Scales 1533, 1534, 2281, 2786, 3017, 3563; Skin 3002, 3003, 2786; Spleen 1534, 1622, 1838, 1890, 3002, 3003, 3563, 3564, 3570; Stomach 1890; Swim bladder 3563; Testis 1534

Isocitrate
Oocytes 3704

Isocitrate dehydrogenase *329*
Brain 2776; Gill 2685, 2776; Heart 2776; Kidney 2685; Liver 2776; Muscle 2776, 2979, 3551; Nerve 3551

Isocryptoxanthin
Skin + fins 2724

Isomerase
Muscle 3398

Isozeaxanthin
Fin 1783; Gill 1783; Intestine 1779, 1782, 1783; Liver 1779, 1782, 1783; Muscle 1779, 1783; Skin 1783; Sperm 1782; Testis 1781

α-Ketoglutarate *159, 188, 281*
Liver 3572

The more aerobic nature of the dark muscle is reflected in the relatively large proportion of aerobic LDH (H-form) found there. Thus in *Scomber australasicus* as much as 73% of the LDH from dark muscle has been found to be of the H type, while the white muscle contains none of it, only the M type. The heart itself contains 90% of its LDH in the H form. Only the M form exists in the electric organ of *Electrophorus electricus* (Matta, Hassón-Volloch and Hargreaves, 1975), showing that the organ is largely anaerobic in function.

The isozymes can vary in proportion according to the temperature of acclimation; at least some of this variation could reflect differences in the solubility of oxygen in the water at different temperatures.

The activity of LDH has been found to be greater in both the serum and the blood of more active, as distinct from less active, species.
Blood 1702, 1789, 1989, 2012, 2438, 3162; Brain 3010, 3373; Cholinergic vesicles of the electric organ 3725; Dark muscle 1580, 2344; Electric organ 2302; Embryo 3702; Erythrocytes 1475; Fin 3213; Gas gland 1579; Gill 2685, 3373; Heart 1505, 1989, 2012, 3373; Hepatopancreas 3373; Intestinal mucus 3010; Intestine 3373; Kidney 1989, 2685, 3373; Liver 1789, 1955, 1989, 2012, 2621, 2880, 3010, 3305; Liver plasma membrane 2621; Muscle 1487, 1579, 1580, 1744, 1789, 1956, 1989, 2012, 2344, 3305, 3373, 3551, 3630; Nerve 3551; Ovarian fluid 3187; Pink (intermediate) muscle 2344; Spleen 3373; Ventricle 3083, 3305.

LAMINARINASE
Intestinal mucus 3034

LANTHANUM
Tends to accumulate in the bone tissue (Rehwoldt, Karimian-Teherani and Altman, 1974: *Cyprinus carpio*).
Bone, Gill, Kidney, Liver, Muscle, Scales: 2440

LEAD *73*
70% of the total lead in *Thunnus alalunga* has been found in the bones.
Blood 2390; Bone 2786, 2981; Caecum 2981; Dark muscle 2390, 2613; Dermis 2981; Eggs 2390; Epidermis 2981; Fin 2786; Gill 2390, 2786, 2981; Heart 2390; Kidney 2390, 2981; Liver 2390, 2981; Muscle 1631, 1707–1709, 2015, 2390, 2613, 2786, 2886, 2901, 2981, 3018, 3019, 3402; Ovary 2364; Pyloric caecae 2390; Scales 2440, 2786, 2981; Skin 2786; Slime 2981; Spermatic sac 2390; Spleen 2390, 2981; Teeth + jawbone 2981

‡LECITHIN (*see* Phosphatidyl choline)

‡LECITHINASE—Volume 1 only

‡LEUCINE—Volume 1 only for bibliography. This volume page references *281, 324, 337, 344, 354*

LEUCINE AMINO PEPTIDASE
Dark muscle 1749, 1756; Kidney 1749, 1756; Liver 1749, 1756; Mesentery 2958; Muscle 1749, 1756; Pyloric caecae 1958; Spleen 1749, 1756

LEUCOCYTES (white blood cells) *213, 239*
Blood 1424, 1476, 1550, 1698, 1814, 1898, 1907, 1911, 1949, 2077, 2309, 2326, 2333, 2373, 2633, 2634, 2801, 2868, 2967, 2969, 3154, 3408, 3566

‡LIPASE *66, 69, 73, 92, 355*
    More abundant in dark than in light muscle.
    Dark muscle 1563; Intestine 1425, 2800; Liver 1425; Muscle 1563; Pancreas 1425

β-LIPOPROTEIN *354*
    Blood 3162

‡LITHIUM
    Liver 3018

LUTEIN *145, 258, 317*
    The most characteristic and predominant carotenoid of freshwater fish, but not
    universally: for example it does not predominate in *Coreoperca kawamebari*, and
    zeaxanthin predominates in the skin of *Hypomesus transpacificus* (= *H.olidus*).
    Lutein in the diet is converted to astaxanthin by *Cyprinus carpio* but not by *Carassius
    auratus*.
    Egg 1998, 2132; Fin 1782, 1783; Gill 1783; Intestine 1779, 1783; Liver 1779, 1783,
    2132; Muscle 1779, 1782, 1783, 2136; Skin 1783, 2136, 2726; Skin + fins 2715–
    2725, 2727

LUTEIN MONOEPOXIDE
    Fin 1782; Muscle 1782; Testis 1781

‡LYMPHOCYTES
    Blood 1550, 1669, 1814, 1898, 1907, 1911, 2326, 2333, 2633, 2634, 2801, 2868, 2969

LYSOLECITHIN (*see* Lysophosphatidyl choline)

‡LYSOLECITHINASE—Volume 1 only

‡LYSOPHOSPHATIDYL CHOLINE
    Blood 2845; Brain 3436; Bone 3233; Cartilage 3233; Electric organ 1556; Erythro-
    cytes 1565; Gall bladder + bile 3436; Gill 3420; "Gonad" 3436; Intestine 3436;
    Kidney 3436; Liver 3727; Muscle 2042, 2987, 3056, 3265; Swim bladder 2990;
    Swim bladder fatty foam 3032; Yolk 2847

LYSOPHOSPHATIDYL ETHANOLAMINE
    Bone 3233; Electric organ 1556

LYSOZYME
    Blood 1910, 1934; Brain 1910; Erythrocytes 1910; Gill 1910, 3173; Kidney 1934;
    Liver 3173; Lymph 1910, 1934; Lymphomyeloid tissue 1910; Mucus 1934;
    Pancreas 1910; Peritoneal exudate cells 1934; Pronephros 1910; Pseudobranch
    1910; Rectal gland 1910; Spleen 1910, 1934; Stomach 1934; Thymus 1910

‡MAGNESIUM *8, 11, 46, 56, 76, 147, 156–158, 164–166, 226, 248, 260, 283, 285, 286,
    291, 311, 342, 349, 354, 385*
    An important activator of enzymes such as peptidases, carboxylases and phos-
    phatases. It is required for oxidative phosphorylation, and is an activator of
    pyruvate kinase, sodium being an inhibitor. Intestinal ATPase is in part activated

by magnesium and inhibited by sodium (*Carassius auratus*). Perhaps because of its importance in so many metabolic processes, its concentration changes little in plasma (any changes go hand-in-hand with changes in sodium) or in the intracellular parts of tissues. In liver, the concentration falls to a minimum in May (*Coregonus nasus sensu*), perhaps because the food intake and metabolic rate are low at this time; it rises again when feeding increases. The concentration in the livers of females is higher than in males (same species).

It occurs in muscle mostly in the bound form, and ranges in different species from 17 to 147 mg%, decreasing in starvation because of a decrease in the intracellular phase.

The concentration in the ovaries of *Gadus morhua* declines during maturation.

There seems to be no relationship between the concentration in the blood serum of many species and the concentration in the environment, but cold shock and anoxia increase the serum level, as does the seaward migration of euryhaline species. It has also been reported to rise during sexual activity.

There is an inverse relationship between sodium and magnesium in the urine, but this is usually seen only when the bladder has been full for some time; probably magnesium and sodium are excreted together, but the bladder then reabsorbs some water *and sodium*. In *Salmo gairdneri* the effect is seen only when the fish are in fresh water, and some uncertainty about the mechanism still exists.

Some magnesium is stored in the bones, whence it can be withdrawn if a diet deficient in magnesium is fed. Deficiency results in loss of apetite, poor growth, some mortality, sluggishness and convulsions.

Abdominal muscle 3386; Alkaline gland 2692; Aqueous humour 1717, 2692; Bile (from bladder) 1595, 1636, 2261, 2263–2265, 2625, 2692; 3102, 3135; Bile (from liver tubules) 1596; Blastula 2237, 3718; Blood 1537, 1595, 1636, 1637, 1641, 1714, 1717, 1740, 1813, 1840, 1908, 1909, 1916, 1948, 1965, 2054–2057, 2076–2079, 2082, 2176, 2244, 2261, 2265, 2278, 2465, 2476, 2503, 2540, 2622, 2624, 2625, 2649, 2650, 2686, 2692, 2808, 2862–2866, 2924, 2925, 3037–3039, 3090, 3102, 3111, 3134, 3135, 3205, 3292, 3313, 3314, 3339, 3353, 3427–3431, 3492, 3503, 3523–3526, 3606, 3717; Body fluids 2625, 3304, 3430; Bone 2623; Brain 3313; Cranial fluid 1908, 2692, 3111, 3427, 3429, 3430; Cupula (after digestion) 1908; Dark muscle 3386; Egg 2237, 3718; Embryotrophe (fluid surrounding embryo) 2476; Endolymph 1908; Erythrocytes 2636, 3360; Fin 3176; Gill 3313; Gut fluid 2649, 3038; Gut (intracellular) 2623; Gut lumen (perhaps same as gut fluid) 1788; Gut wall 2622; Heart 3313, 3386; Kidney 1740, 2040, 3313, 3386; Larva 3718; Liver 2268, 2622, 2625, 3313, 3386; Liver (intracellular) 2623; Lorenzinian jelly 1908; Muscle 1681, 1951, 2040, 2244, 2462, 2463, 2489, 2622, 2624, 2625, 2677, 2924, 3021, 3090, 3134, 3135, 3294, 3313, 3386, 3467; Muscle cells 3135; Muscle (intracellular) 1681, 2623, 3134; Notochordal fluid 2076; Oocytes 3718; Ovarian fluid 3187; Ovary 2040, 2364; Pericardial fluid 2692, 3427, 3429, 3430; Perivisceral fluid 1636, 2692, 3427, 3429; Rectal gland 1637, 2692, 3654; Rete mirabile 3360; Scales 1716, 2440; Semen 2057, 3292; Seminal plasma 1765, 2072, 2073; Slime 2808; Sperm 2072, 2698; Sperm cell cytoplasm 2073; Urine (from bladder) 1537, 1538, 1636, 1637, 1641, 1840, 1948, 2078, 2083, 2240, 2260, 2650, 2686, 2808, 2861–2863, 2866, 3038, 3079, 3102, 3111, 3205, 3654; Urine (from kidney) 1948; Urine (from ureter) 1538; Uterine fluid 3431; Vitreous humour 1717

MALATE
Liver 1572; Muscle 1572, 1852

‡MALATE DEHYDROGENASE *74, 253, 329, 330*
  Blood 1920; Dark muscle 1580, 2344; Embryo 3688; Gas gland 1579; Gill 2685; Heart 1505, 3196; Kidney 2685; Liver 3196; Muscle 1579, 1580, 2344, 3196; Oocytes 3688; Pink (intermediate) muscle 2344

MALIC ENZYME
  Egg 2796; Embryo 1889; Oocytes 1889; Testis 2794, 2795

MALTASE *17, 151*
  Hepatopancreas 2393; Intestine 2393; Larval digestive organs 2395; Pyloric caecae 2393; Stomach 2393

‡MANGANESE *35, 45, 46, 56, 57, 147, 148, 172, 248, 354*
  An activator of alkaline phosphatase.
  The highest concentrations are found in the bones, for example 44–54 mg per kg dry matter in *Rutilus rutilus* and 60–67 mg in *Abramis brama*. Gill tissue is quite rich in maganese (9–16 mg). The element was the only one of all the trace elements investigated by Berman and Vitin' (1968) in which the concentration increased uninterruptedly in the bodies of young *Salmo gairdneri* irrespective of seasons, though the rate of accumulation was very slow in winter. They suggested that the latter result may have been only apparent, caused by depletion of body substances during the winter which would have made the bones a bigger proportion of the whole body weight. There is more manganese in male muscle and gill than in the corresponding organs of the female, but ovaries contain higher concentrations than do testes. The concentration in the ovary of *Gadus morhua* declines during maturation.
  In *Salmo gairdneri* the liver contains about 3 times as much manganese as the muscle. The range in the muscle of various species has been reported as 0.02–5.46 mg%.
  Food constitutes the major pathway for accumulation; little is absorbed from the water (*Pleuronectes platessa*). There is no evidence for a change in concentration with age in the latter species.
  Manganese deficiency results in malformation of the bones.
  Bile 1533; Blood 2390, 3003; Bone 1533, 1534, 2281, 2786, 2850, 3001, 3004, 3017; Brain and nerve cord 3003; Cartilage 3003; Dark muscle 2390, 2571; Egg 2001, 2238, 2390, 3438; Embryo 2238; Erythrocytes 2636; Fin 2786; Gill 1533, 1622, 2281, 2390, 2786, 2850, 3001, 3003, 3017; "Gonad" 1622, 3003; Gut 3001, 3003; Heart 1622, 1890, 2390, 3001, 3003; Intestine 1890; Islet tissue 1904; Kidney 1533, 1622, 1890, 2040, 2390, 3001, 3003; Liver 1533, 1534, 1622, 1890, 1904, 2040, 2281, 2390, 2850, 3001, 3003, 3004, 3018; Lung 1890; Muscle 1622, 1763, 1793, 1884, 1893, 1904, 2040, 2390, 2491, 2571, 2677, 2786, 2850, 3001, 3003, 3017, 3019, 3294, 3402, 3467; Ovary 1533, 2040, 2281, 2364; Pancreas 1890, 1904; Pyloric caecae 2390; Rectal gland 3003; Scales 1533, 1534, 2281, 2440, 2786, 3017; Skin 2786, 3001, 3003; Spermatic sac 2390; Spleen 1534, 1622, 1890, 2390, 3003; Stomach 1890; Testis 1534, 3001

‡MANNOSE
  Cornea 2770; Haptoglobin 2444; Ichthyocol 3337; Skin collagen 3141; Slime 3652

‡MERCURY (in fish from waters not known to be contaminated) *33, 35*
  Of all animals, fish especially tend to concentrate mercury in their tissues. The concentrations in the tissues are much higher than in either the surrounding fresh-

or salt water. Recent disquiet over the possible poisoning of fish for human con-sumption by industrial wastes has been soothed by the finding that specimens of tunas and swordfish caught between the years 1878 and 1909 and now preserved in museums contain just as much mercury as present-day fish (Miller, Grant et al., 1972). There is evidence that man-made pollution of fresh waters has increased the mercury concentration within the fish, but the levels in seawater fish are mostly, probably, "natural". Fish absorb mercury from the sea in increasing amounts as the pH falls, and not according to the concentration present (Tsai, Boush and Matsumura, 1975). Where the mercury level of *Perca flavescens* and *Ambloplites rupestris* rose through living in contaminated waters, it was found by Laarman, Willford and Olson (1976) not to fall when the fish were transferred to a clean environment. The only reduction in concentration in the muscle was the dilution caused by the fish growing and not by release of mercury.

90-year-old preserved specimens of *Antimora rostrata* also possess similar mercury concentrations to "modern" specimens, and also show the same relationship between fish size and mercury concentration. This element seems to accumulate steadily in fish, unlike other elements, and since the rate of accumulation exceeds the elimination rate, the life expectancy of a fish is important in determining the levels achieved (*Pomatomus saltatrix* and *Antimora rostrata*). Significant regressions between body length and mercury content have been found in *Gadus morhua* (males only) and *Merlangius merlangus* by de Clerk, Vanderstappen and Vyncke (1974), *Carassius carassius*, which showed a curvilinear relationship (Matsunaga, 1975) and *Osmerus mordax* (Knight and Olson, 1974, who could not decide from the evidence whether the relationship was linear or exponential). Older females of the latter species contained significantly more than males of the same age. The positive correlation between body size and mercury concentration seems to be confined to some species only, and is not seen in others, in some cases heavier specimens containing lower concentrations of mercury.

Mercury tends to go into the myofibrillar- rather than the sarcoplasmic proteins (*Thunnus obesus*, *T. thynnus*, *Xiphias gladius*) and is present mostly in the form of methyl mercury rather than the free element. Kidney, liver and gill tissues contain the highest concentrations, while muscle, bone, skin and blood contain least.
Abdominal muscle 3487; Blood 2390, 3274, 3397; Brain 1715, 3397, 3638; Dark muscle 2390, 2613, 3397, 3487; Egg 2390; Embryo 3638; Gall bladder 1715, 3397; Gill 1622, 2390, 3274, 3397, 3638; "Gonad" 1622, 1715, 3638; Heart 1622, 1715, 2390, 2534, 3397; Intestine 1715, 3397; Kidney 1622, 1953, 2390, 3397, 3487, 3638; Liver 1622, 1953, 2390, 3397, 3487, 3638; Muscle 1463, 1496, 1557, 1622, 1631, 1697, 1707–1709, 1763, 1928, 1952, 1953, 2015, 2148, 2371, 2390, 2482, 2534, 2613, 2751, 2828, 2829, 2887, 2888, 3127, 3214, 3274, 3397, 3402, 3487, 3529, 3626, 3638, 3649; Ovary 2364, 3274, 3638; Pyloric caecae 1715, 2390, 3397; Skin and scales 3397; Spermatic sac 2390; Spiral valve 3638; Spleen 1622, 1715, 2390, 3274, 3397, 3487, 3638; Stomach 1715, 3274, 3397, 3638; Testis 3274, 3397; Trunk 2099, 2100; Uterus 3638; Yolk sac 3638

1-METHYL HISTIDINE—Volume 1 only.
Found only in teleosts, not elasmobranchs.

17α-METHYL TESTOSTERONE *40, 199*

METHYL TRANSFERASE
Adrenal, Kidney: 1625

‡MOLYBDENUM *35*
The concentration in muscle and bone is said to decrease as *Salvelinus namaycush* grow older.
Bone 3573; Brain 3573; Gill 3573; "Gonad" 3573; Intestine + contents 3573; Kidney 3573; Liver 3018, 3573; Muscle 3573; Skin 3573; Spleen 3573; Stomach + contents 3573

MONOAMINE OXIDASE
Brain, Retina: 1631

MONOCYTES
Blood 1898, 2077, 2326, 2969, 3154

MONOENOIC ACIDS *209*
Muscle 3389

MONOGLYCERIDES
Egg 2118; Liver 2117, 2118, 2439; Mesentery 2439; Muscle 2117, 2118, 2439; Ovary 2117, 2439; Slime 2559; Testis 2117, 2439; Yolk 2847

MONOPHOSPHOINOSITIDE
Cerebellum, Electric lobes, Electric organ, Forebrain, Muscle, Pacemaker nucleus (in medulla), Tectum opticum: 2474

‡MUCOPOLYSACCHARIDES
Aorta 3344; Skin 1434

MUTAROTASE *317*
The enzyme which catalyses the interconversion of anomeric forms of aldoses. The kidneys of freshwater fish contain about 6 times the amount found in saltwater fish, so the enzyme may be related to the function of ion reclamation in fresh water, where fish must filter off excess water but retain salts, sugars and amino acids.

‡MYOGLOBIN *74, 88, 106, 107, 117, 355, 357*
Unlike haemoglobin, does not possess a Bohr effect. It is said to be especially a carrier of oxygen to the mitochondria. Much more concentrated in dark muscle than in white, and the concentration changes according to the habitual swimming of the fish, increasing in migratory fish during migration and in fish forced to swim in an exercise channel, decreasing in fish which rest more than usual. There are indications that the concentration in the dark muscle of migratory fish falls once the fish have reached their destination.
Dark muscle, Pink muscle, White muscle: 2344

NEURAMINIC ACID
Egg, Oocytes: 3099

NEUTRAL LIPIDS *41, 97, 142, 207, 208, 210, 368*
Blood 3000, 3180; Brain 1479; Egg 1479; Liver 2117, 2152, 2153, 2155, 3180; Muscle 2117, 2152, 2153, 2155, 3180, 3389, 3446; Ovary 2117, 2153; Swim bladder 2990; Testis 2117, 2153

NITRITE
Muscle 1864

NITROGEN GAS *123, 261, 272*
Swimbladder gas 1794

NEUTRAL Mg *P*-NITROPHENYLPHOSPHATASE
Liver, Liver plasma membrane: 2621

K-*P*-NITROPHENYLPHOSPHATASE
Liver, Liver plasma membrane: 2621

NON-ESTERIFIED FATTY ACIDS (*see* Free fatty acids)

NON-PROTEIN NITROGEN *26, 35, 346*
Bile 3135; Blood 1827, 1831, 2056, 2078, 2079, 2361, 3039, 3135, 3278, 3279, 3492; Dark muscle 1996, 3357; Liver 3357; Muscle 1996, 3135, 3357; Ovary 3357; Parietal muscle 2255; Testis 3357; Urine 2078

‡NORADRENALINE *6, 22, 64, 232–235, 237, 279, 385*
Sometimes promotes and sometimes inhibits lipolysis of lipid reserves, resulting in changes in the FFA content of the blood. Acts as neurotransmitter in circulatory regulation and probably modulates behaviour patterns. An increase in the levels of noradrenaline in the brain may therefore be associated with increased motor activity. Marked rises have been noted in the anterior parts of the alevin at the start of free larval swimming. Considerable amounts are found in the Corpuscles of Stannius (Unsicker, Polonius *et al.*, 1977: *Salmo gairdneri*).
Atrium 2738; Blood 1940, 2736, 2737, 2739; Embryo 2754; Heart 2738, 2740, 3091; Intestine 3091; Kidney 2088, 2740, 3091, 3340; Larva 2754; Pronephros (primitive kidney) 2088; Spleen 1409; Ventricle 2738

NUCLEOSIDASE
Dark muscle, Heart muscle, Kidney, Liver, Muscle: 1408

NUCLEOSIDE DIPHOSPHATASE
Liver, Liver plasma membrane: 2621

5'-NUCLEOTIDASE (5'-Ribonucleotide phosphohydrolase) *76*
Brain 1468, 2314, 3229; Dark muscle 2316; Electric organ 2302; Heart 1468, 2314, 3229; Intestine 1468, 2314; Kidney 1468, 2314, 3229; Liver 1468, 2314, 2621, 3229; Liver plasma membrane 2621; Muscle 1468, 2314, 2316, 3229; Ovary 1468, 2314; Pyloric caecae 2314; Spinal cord 1468, 2314; Spleen 1468, 2314, 3229; Stomach 1468, 2314

CYCLIC-3'5'-NUCLEOTIDE PHOSPHODIESTERASE
Brain, Cerebellum, Heart, Liver, Medulla oblongata + spinalis, Muscle, Olfactory bulb, Optic tectum, Spleen: 3674

‡OESTRADIOL *37, 40, 44, 45, 199*
A female sex hormone which causes blood calcium to rise in the maturing female fish. The extra calcium is obtained from the diet and by withdrawal from the

scales (not bones or otoliths) in at least two species.
Blood 3639

‡Oestriol—Volume 1 only

Oestrogen *37, 43, 48*
Blood 3208, 3210

‡Oestrone— Volume 1 only for bibliography. This volume page reference *45*

Oligo-1,4→1,4 glucantransferase
Embryo 3708, 3709; Oocytes 3709

‡Ophidin—Volume 1 only

‡Ornithine *159, 160, 162, 311*
Alimentary tract 3637; Blood 1594, 2553, 2898, 2946, 3637; Brain 1594, 2553,
3217, 3637; Electric organ 2946; Embryo 1824; Erythrocytes 1594; Gill 3637;
Heart 1594, 3637; Kidney 2553, 3637; Liver 2553, 3637; Muscle 1410, 2105, 2455,
2946, 2977, 3200, 3366, 3637; Nerve 2946; Oocytes 1824; Parietal muscle 2255;
Spleen 3637; Wing muscle 1594

Ornithine aminotransferase *221*
Heart, Liver, Rectal gland, Spleen: 3611

‡Ornithine transcarbamoylase (Carbamoyl transferase) *160*
An enzyme of the Krebs-Henscleit cycle which does not occur in most teleosts.
Kidney 3634; Liver 2035, 2071, 2256, 3112, 3634

3-Oxoacid CoA transferase
Liver 3026

‡Oxygen gas *2, 123, 270–283, 290, 315, 320, 325–327, 336, 385*
Swimbladder gas 1794, 2142, 2144

‡Oxytocin—Volume 1 only for bibliography. This volume page reference *6*

‡Pantothenic acid *7, 146, 354*
A vitamin of the B group of little-known function. Acts as a coenzyme. The ovary
contains the highest concentration, which declines during maturation. Next in
order are dark muscle and liver. Ordinary muscle is poor in pantothenic acid, but
active fish possess more than inactive. More has been found in the eggs of hatchery
fish than in "wild" eggs. The best-known symptom of deficiency is "clubbing" of
the gills, but anorexia, necrosis of the jaw and fins and poor weight gain have also
been observed.
Alimentary tract 3453, 3454; Gut wall 3453, 3454; Liver 3453, 3454; Muscle 3211,
3295, 3453, 3454; Ovary 3211

‡*PARA*-amino benzoic acid (PABA)
Muscle 3295

PARTIAL GLYCERIDES
Blood 2845; Depot fat 2399; "Gonad" 2398, 2400; Heart 2399; Intestine 2399; Kidney 2399; Liver 2399; Muscle 2399; Ovary 2399; Spleen 2399; Stomach 2399; Swim bladder 2400

‡"PENTOSE"
Corium 2087; Egg yolk protein 2844; Elastoidin 2087; Ovokeratin 2087; Scales 2087; Swim bladder 2087

‡PEPSIN *16, 17, 26, 151, 329*
Intestine 3256; Larval digestive organs 2395

PHENYLALANINE
Blood 2743

PHENYLETHANOLAMINE-*N*-METHYL TRANSFERASE
Heart, Kidney, Muscle: 2740

PHOSPHATASE
Dark muscle 1408, 2843; Heart muscle 1408; Kidney 1408; Liver 1408, 2843; Muscle 1408, 2843

PHOSPHATIDIC ACID
Bone 3233; Brain 2551, 3222, 3436; Cartilage 3233; Gill 3420; "Gonad" 3436; Liver 2551; Muscle 2042, 2987; Myelin (from brain) 3222; Nerve 1680, 2457; Swim bladder 3436

‡PHOSPHATIDYL CHOLINE (Lecithin) *13, 316, 340*
A constituent of phospholipids which is more concentrated in dark muscle than in white in *Sardinops melanosticta* but more concentrated in white muscle than in dark in *Gadus morhua*. It comprises as much as 30% of the dissolved solids of mammalian bile, but has been found only in trace amounts in fish bile.
Blood 2845; Bone 3233; Brain 1479, 2469, 2551, 3064, 3222; Cartilage 3233; Cerebellum 2474; Cerebrum 2755; Dark muscle 1581; Egg 1454, 2001, 3388; Electric lobes 2474; Electric organ 1556, 2474, 3451; Erythrocytes 1419, 1565; Forebrain 2474; Gill 2746, 3420, 3726, 3727; Intestinal mucosa 2746, 3726; Kidney 2746, 3726; Liver 2454, 2551, 2663, 2746, 2755, 3726, 3727; Muscle 1581, 2042, 2454, 2474, 2663, 2746, 2755, 2987, 3056, 3265, 3387, 3451, 3726; Myelin (from brain) 3222; Myelin (from spinal cord) 3222; Nerve 1680, 2233, 2457; Ovary 2755, 3169; Pacemaker nucleus (in medulla) 2474; Phospholipid (from nerve) 2407; Rectal gland 1530, 2377; Swim bladder 2990; Swim bladder fatty foam 3032; Tectum opticum 2474; Testis 2755; Yolk 2847

‡PHOSPHATIDYL ETHANOLAMINE (Cephalin) *13, 316*
Much richer in the phospholipids of dark muscle than of white (*Gadus morhua*). This is the only major difference in the lipid composition of the two tissues of this species.
Blood 2845; Bone 3233; Brain 1479, 2469, 2551, 3064, 3222, 3436; Cartilage 3233; Cerebellum 2474; Cerebrum 2755; Egg 1454, 3388; Electric lobes 2474; Electric organ 1556, 2474; Erythrocytes 1565; Forebrain 2474; Gall bladder + bile 3436; Gill 2746, 3420, 3436, 3726, 3727; "Gonad" 3436; Heart 3436; Intestinal mucosa

1955, 2838, 2938, 3256, 3684; Muscle 1579, 1580, 2838; Oocytes 1889, 3703; Spleen 2838

‡PHOSPHOGLUCOSE ISOMERASE
Blood 2839; Gill 2838; Heart 2838; Intestine 2838; Kidney 2838; Liver 2838, 2839, 3256; Muscle 2838; Spleen 2838

2-PHOSPHOGLYCERATE
Erythrocytes 2550

‡3-PHOSPHOGLYCERATE (given in Volume 1 as 3-phosphoglyceric acid)
Embryo 3689; Erythrocytes 2550; Oocytes 3689

‡PHOSPHOGLYCERIC ACID
Erythrocytes 2550

‡PHOSPHOGLYCEROKINASE *19*
Egg 3703; Embryo 3702; Erythrocytes 1475; Muscle 1789; Oocytes 3703

PHOSPHOHEXOSEISOMERASE
Embryo 3701

‡PHOSPHOLIPASE—Volume 1 only

PHOSPHOLIPIDS = Phosphatides *5, 11, 13, 40, 41, 53, 54, 63, 74, 96–99, 124, 137, 142, 206, 208, 210, 257, 261, 262, 316, 339, 368*
Fish lipids can be divided into two main types: firstly "neutral" lipids, mostly glycerides and cholesterol, and secondly phospholipids which as the name suggests contain phosphorus. The phospholipids comprise phosphatidyl-choline, -inositol, -serine and -ethanolamine, cardiolipid, phosphatidic acid, sphingomyelin, lysophosphatidyl choline and some smaller fractions. When fish lay down lipid as stored energy, to be used as required, it is mostly triglycerides which are stored. The flesh of fatty species such as *Clupea harengus* and *Scomber scombrus* contains large quantities, which rise and fall with the seasons. Non-fatty species such as *Gadus morhua* show similar fluctuations in the triglycerides of the liver. Phospholipids on the other hand are thought to be essential parts of the structure of tissues, particularly membranes, and so are less liable to be mobilised on starvation. The phospholipids of *Gadus morhua* liver, for example, increase relative to triglycerides when the fish starve, since triglycerides are being used up. However, fish are unusual among vertebrates in that contractile proteins are readily mobilised in times of need. Thus, when the triglycerides in the liver of *Gadus morhua* have been reduced to a low level, the muscle begins to be broken down, and at the same time the content of phospholipids decreases; there are almost no triglycerides in the flesh of this species.
Cardiolipid is thought to be an important constituent of mitochondrial membranes, so is richer in dark muscle than in white.
The very unsaturated fatty acid 22:6 is more plentiful in phospholipids than in triglycerides (*Gadus morhua*), and indeed forms more than half of the fatty acids of phosphatidyl ethanolamine.
Adipose fin 2577, 2578, 3283; Adrenal 1712; Blood 1437, 1802, 1954, 2079, 2267, 2495, 2556, 2761, 2762, 2765, 2845, 3047, 3138, 3237, 3242, 3339; Brain 1479,

1954, 3064, 3222; Brain stem 2474; Cerebellum 2457, 2474; Corpuscles of Stannius 1712; Dark muscle 2234, 2555, 2599, 3138, 3246; Depot fat 2399; Egg 1479, 1691, 2118, 2223, 2330, 2425; Electric lobes 2457, 2474; Electric nerve 2457; Electric organ 2457, 2474; Embryo 2223, 2330; Erythrocytes 1419, 1954; Erythrocyte ghosts 2849; Forebrain 2457, 2474, 2577, 2578, 3283; Gastric muscle 3246; Gill 2577, 2578, 3283, 3726, 3727; "Gonad" 1691, 2398, 2400, 2555, 2577, 2578, 3283; Heart 2399, 2577, 2578, 2992, 3283; Heart muscle 1954, 3246; Intestine 2399; Intestinal mucosa 3726; Kidney 2399, 2577, 2578, 3283, 3726; Liver 1690, 1691, 1802, 1954, 2117, 2118, 2234, 2399, 2439, 2454, 2495, 2555, 2572, 2577, 2578, 2871, 3138, 3239, 3241, 3243, 3245, 3283, 3726, 3727; Mesentery 2439; Muscle 1690, 1691, 1802, 1954, 2042, 2117, 2118, 2234, 2398, 2399, 2400, 2439, 2454, 2474, 2495, 2555, 2577, 2578, 2599, 2871, 2948, 3056, 3138, 3239, 3241–3243, 3245, 3246, 3265, 3283, 3389, 3446, 3726; Muscle cell walls 1577; Myelin (from brain) 3222; Myocomma 2599; Ovary 1416, 1690, 2117, 2399, 2439, 3239, 3241–3243; Pacemaker nucleus 2474; Posterior cardinal vein 1712; Rhombencephalon 2457; Scales 2577, 2578, 3283; Skin 2577, 2578, 3283; Skull 2538, 3028, 3031; Slime 2559; Sperm 2425; Spinal cord 2457, 2538, 2577, 2578, 3029, 3031, 3283; Spleen 1954, 2399, 2577, 2578, 3283; Stomach 2399; Swim bladder 2400, 2577, 2578, 2990, 3283; Swim bladder (fat-filled) 2398; Swim bladder fatty foam 3032; Tectum opticum 2457, 2474; Testis 1690, 2117, 2439, 3239, 3241–3243; White collagenous subdermal material 2234; Yolk 2847

‡Phosphopyruvate—Volume 1 only

Phosphopyruvate hydratase
    Muscle 1789

‡Phosphorylase
    Dark muscle 2344; Dark muscle (from new-born fish) 3054; Embryo 2763, 3705, 3706, 3708, 3709; Heart muscle (from new-born fish) 3054; Liver 1524, 1815; Muscle 1744, 1815, 2344, 2691, 3551; Muscle (from new-born fish) 3054; Nerve 3551; Oocytes 3709; Pink (intermediate) muscle 2344; Retina 1631

Phosphorylase kinase
    Dark muscle, heart muscle, white muscle (all from new-born fish): 3054

Plasmalogen 340
    Glycerides with ether-linked alkyl groups. Appear to be important in membrane function. The quantity in brain lipids increases at higher acclimation temperatures. Egg 1454

Polyenoic acids 209
    Muscle 3389

Polyglycerophosphatides
    Brain 3064; Cerebellum, Electric lobes, Electric organ, Forebrain, Muscle, Pacemaker nucleus (in medulla), Tectum opticum: 2474

Polyoxyxanthophyll
    Intestine, Liver, Muscle: 1779

POLYSACCHARIDES
Slime 2447

‡POTASSIUM *11, 15, 16, 20, 21, 25, 46, 56, 64, 69, 76, 148, 158, 164, 165, 167, 172, 213, 224–226, 229, 241, 248, 283, 285–289, 293, 305, 311, 341, 342, 349, 354, 356, 385*
The main intracellular ion. It varies both in plasma and muscle independently of other ions, so probably plays an independent physiological role. No relationship has been detected between the concentration of potassium in the blood and that in the environment (many species). It rises in the blood at the spawning death of salmonids, perhaps by release from disintegrating tissues. Variations in the plasma concentration would have widespread effects on general body metabolism, altering the resting (electrical) potential of most cells and regulating their basal metabolism and glycolytic processes. They also regulate the production of the mineralocorticoid hormones by the adrenal cortex.

The concentration in the muscle of fish varies from 112 to 1000 mg%, according to species. In the ovaries of *Gadus morhua*, the concentration declines with maturation, probably because of the diluting effect of lipid being laid down in the eggs. Plasma potassium concentration increases with increasing temperature in some freshwater species and varies in inverse relation to the temperature in some marine species. These relationships are not universal and their mechanisms are not known.

The intracellular phase of fish muscle decreases in severe starvation, so there is a corresponding decline in the overall potassium concentration.

Connective tissue is poor in potassium, so the tail ends of the musculature of fish, which embody much connective tissue, contain lower concentrations of potassium than the middle part which contains a bigger proportion of contractile tissue.

Alkaline gland 2692; Aqueous humour 1717, 2692, 3711; Bile (from gall bladder) 1595, 1836, 2261, 2263–2265, 2625, 2692, 3135; Bile (from liver) 1596; Blastula 3718; Blood 1428, 1484, 1584, 1595, 1596, 1633, 1636, 1637, 1641, 1642, 1674, 1700, 1714, 1717, 1734, 1735, 1749, 1750, 1767, 1794, 1802, 1813, 1840, 1905, 1906, 1908, 1909, 1932, 1945, 1948, 1958, 1965, 2024, 2054–2057, 2076–2080, 2082, 2108, 2176, 2182, 2201, 2244, 2261, 2262, 2265, 2278, 2288, 2429, 2465, 2476, 2503, 2514, 2519, 2520, 2530, 2540, 2555, 2556, 2562, 2622, 2624, 2625, 2639, 2640, 2649, 2650, 2686, 2692, 2805, 2808, 2862–2866, 2894–2897, 2922, 2924, 2933, 2934, 2963, 2972, 3037–3039, 3090, 3111, 3121, 3130, 3134, 3135, 3160, 3205, 3275, 3292, 3310, 3311, 3313, 3314, 3339, 3342, 3343, 3353, 3418, 3427–3431, 3492, 3501–3503, 3505, 3506, 3520, 3521, 3523–3526, 3558, 3559, 3584, 3717; Bone 2623, 2981; Brain 1957, 1958, 3313; Caecum 2981; Cerebellum 2392; Cerebrospinal fluid 1767, 1908, 1958, 2692; Cranial fluid 2280, 2692, 3111, 3427, 3429, 3430; Cupula (after digestion) 1908; Egg 1531, 3718; Embryo 1824, 3718; Embryotrophe 2476; Endolymph (from canal) 1908, 2692, 3584; Endolymph (from labyrinth) 1908; Epidermis 2981; Erythrocytes 1674, 1945, 2080, 2550, 2636, 2805, 3360, 3418, 3710; Fry 3718; Gill 1642, 2981, 3313; Gut fluid 2649; Gut (intracellular) 2623; Gut lumen 1788; Gut wall 2622, 2892; Heart 2875, 3313; Intestinal fluid 2922, 3038; Kidney 1749, 1753, 2040, 2981, 3313; Larva 3718; Lateral line canal fluid 2562; Liver 1749, 1753, 2040, 2622, 2625, 2981, 3313; Liver (intracellular) 2623; Lorenzinian jelly 1908, 2280, 2692; Medulla + cerebellum 2392; Microsomes (from muscle) 2253; Mitochondria (from muscle) 2253; Muscle 1430, 1582, 1633, 1641, 1681, 1700, 1720, 1749, 1945, 2040, 2244, 2253, 2429, 2489, 2622, 2624, 2625, 2639, 2677, 2875, 2924, 2981, 3021, 3057, 3090, 3121, 3130, 3134, 3135, 3294, 3304, 3313, 3331, 3343, 3455, 3467; Muscle cells 3135; Muscle (extracellular) 1633; Muscle (intracellular)

1429, 1633, 1681, 2623, 3090, 3134; Myofibrils 2253; Notochordal fluid 2076; Oocytes 1824, 3718; Optic lobe (in brain) 2392; Ovarian fluid 3187; Ovary 2040, 2364; Parietal muscle 2255; Pectoral fin muscle 2875; Pericardial fluid 2077, 2692, 3427, 3429, 3430; Perilymph 2692; Perivisceral fluid 1636, 2077, 2692, 2922, 3427, 3429, 3430; Rectal gland 1637, 2692, 3654; Rectal gland fluid 2232; Rete mirabile 3360; Scales 1716; Semen 2057, 3292; Seminal plasma 1765, 2072, 2073; Slime 2808, 2981; Sperm 2072; Sperm cell cytoplasm 2073; Spinal cord 2392; Spleen 1749, 1753, 2981; Stomach wall muscle 2875; Teeth + jawbone 2981; Testis 2057; Tongue retractor muscle 2875; Urine (from bladder) 1636, 1637, 1641, 1840, 1948, 1960, 2078, 2182, 2240, 2260, 2650, 2686, 2808, 2862, 2863, 2866, 3038, 3079, 3111, 3205, 3654; Urine (from kidney) 1948; Uterine fluid 2024, 3431; Ventricle (intracellular) 3552; Vitreous humour 1717, 2288

‡Pregnenolone—Volume 1 only

‡Pristane *125*
A hydrocarbon with a density of only 0·78. However, it rarely occurs in significant amounts in fish, so it is probably not used as a buoyancy agent.
Liver 2007, 2403, 2557; Muscle 2568

‡Progesterone
Blood 1688

Prolactin *7, 116, 220, 232, 269, 299–302, 307, 342, 383*
A pituitary hormone with a broad spectrum of physiological activities. The concentration in the serum changes by a circadian rhythm which depends on the length of the photoperiod: longer photoperiods and higher temperatures stimulate its release from the pituitary (*Carassius auratus*). In teleosts, the pineal may respond to changes in day length and modify prolactin release (Sage and de Vlaming, 1975). Prolactin secretion is also regulated by the osmolality of the environmental water and the blood, and the circulating prolactin level controls secretion by a direct feedback. No change resulting from capture stress has been found in the prolactin secretion of *Carassius auratus*, in contrast to rats (Spieler and Meier, 1976). On the other hand the concentration in the plasma does increase during prolonged exercise.

An injection of prolactin can cause fish to lay down body lipid *or* to hydrolyse and release body lipid according to the stage in the photoperiod when it was carried out (Sage and de Vlaming, 1975; de Vlaming, Sage and Tiegs, 1975; Pardo and de Vlaming, 1976; Spieler, Meier and Loesch, 1976). The liver may be one of the target organs for prolactin action. The time-dependent effects of injected prolactin may result from rhythms in plasma adrenocorticoids, which could influence tissue sensitivity to the hormone, an effect termed "temporal hormonal synergism" (Spieler, Meier and Loesch, 1976).

Osmoregulatory activity by prolactin has been reported by various authors, since it appears to affect the permeability of the membranes of the gill, intestine, kidney and bladder. It also affects the movement of electrolytes across the skin by increasing the production of slime. The amount of *N*-acetyl neuraminic acid in skin has in fact been shown to correlate with the amount of prolactin secreted in fresh water (*Anguilla anguilla*). Hypophysectomy is followed by a fall in the amount of skin mucus.

Essentially, prolactin enables euryhaline fish to survive transfer from salt water to fresh. The mode of action is still not fully understood, but it probably inhibits the outward leakage of sodium. In this it is antagonised by cortisol, so the optimum ion balance is probably achieved by a balance between the two hormones. Doneen and Bern (1974) point out that, because these hormones act in opposite fashion, the interpretation of experiments in which prolactin is injected may be complicated by the effects of endogenous cortisol. Although prolactin is implicated in the regulation of electrolytes in teleosts, it does not appear to occur in cyclostomes.

In *Salmo gairdneri*, which has a mixture of visual pigments in its retinas, an increased secretion of prolactin appears to increase the proportion of porphyropsin (based on vitamin A_2).
Blood 2532, 2660; Pituitary 3160

‡PROLINE *194, 199, 202, 221, 281, 312, 354*
An imino acid which is also an important end product of energy metabolism, especially under anaerobic conditions. Occurs in high concentration in connective tissue, so its concentration in the gonads declines during maturation as sex products accumulate.
Collagen (from myocommata) 2772; Collagen (from skin) 2772; Collagen (from swim bladder) 2087, 2772; Corium 2087; Elastin (from swim bladder) 2087; Elastoidin 2087; Ovokeratin 2087; Scales 2087; Swim bladder tunic 2087

‡PROPIONATE *149, 271, 281*
Muscle 3419

PROPIONYL CoA
Egg 2796

‡PROTEASE *151, 152, 222, 355, 386*
Alimentary tract 2940; Blood 2150; Dark muscle 2843; Hepatopancreas 2325, 2940, 3481; Intestinal contents 2939; Intestine 2325, 2393, 2800; Mesentery 2958; Muscle 2843; Oesophagus 2393; Pharynx 2393; Pyloric caecae 2936–2938, 2958; Rectum 2325; Stomach 2936, 2937

PROVITAMIN D
Liver 3020; Muscle 3019

PURINE NUCLEOSIDASE
Dark muscle, Heart muscle, Kidney, Liver, Muscle: 1408

PURINE NUCLEOSIDE ORTHOPHOSPHATE RIBOSYL TRANSFERASE
Brain 2873

PUTRESCINE
Brain 3217

PYRIDINE NUCLEOTIDE TRANSHYDROGENASE
Dark muscle, Kidney, Liver, Mitochondria (from muscle), Nuclei (from muscle): 3167

‡PYRIDOXINE (Vitamin B$_6$)

A vitamin of the B group, deficiency of which generates a number of symptoms in fish, such as anorexia, ataxia, convulsions, hyperirritability, anaemia, a gasping respiration, weight loss and increased mortality. There is also evidence of brain or nerve damage. It performs an enzymic function and is constantly consumed during metabolism. Marine fish possess higher concentrations than freshwater fish, and active species more than sluggish. The concentration increases in the ovary during maturation.

Alimentary tract 3453, 3454; Gut wall 3453, 3454; Liver 3453, 3454; Muscle 3211, 3295, 3453, 3454; Ovary 3211

PYROPHOSPHATASE *329*

Dark muscle, Heart muscle, Kidney, Liver, Muscle: 1408

‡PYRUVATE *101, 188, 336*

Blood 1749, 1753, 1789, 2298; Dark muscle 2340, 2342, 2344; Embryo 3689; Erythrocytes 2550; Liver 1572, 1639, 1749, 1753, 1789, 2342, 3572; Muscle 1572, 1639, 1745, 1789, 1951, 2085, 2086, 2340, 2342, 2344; Oocytes 3689, 3707; Pink (intermediate) muscle 2344

PYRUVATE CARBOXYLASE

Embryo 3688; Liver 3025; Mitochondria (from liver) 3196; Oocytes 3688

PYRUVATE DEHYDROGENASE

Embryo, Oocytes: 3688

‡PYRUVATE KINASE *18, 23, 35, 263, 280, 331, 333, 334, 356*

That in the dark muscle of *Carassius carassius* differs markedly from the mammalian enzyme by being under close regulation by metabolites. It is subject to allosteric regulation, inhibited by ATP and certain amino acids, and activated by fructose-1, 6-diphosphate, which overrides all the inhibitory effects. The low broad pH optimum (6·8) in this species may relate to function under anaerobic conditions. Brain 1915; Dark muscle 1580, 2344; Erythrocytes 1475; Gas gland 1579; Liver 2880, 2938, 3305; Muscle 1579, 1580, 1789, 2344, 3551, 3630; Nerve 3551; Pink (intermediate) muscle 2344

RED BLOOD CELLS (*see* Erythrocytes)

‡RENIN *306, 307*

A hormone from the kidney which is said to regulate glomerular filtration rate by constricting the efferent glomerular arterioles. Freshwater teleosts usually have higher renin activity than do marine teleosts, but the hormone is not found in more primitive vertebrates, cyclostomes and elasmobranchs. Plasma renin level increases in man and other mammals in response to sodium depletion, but this relationship has not so far been demonstrated in fish. It is also not known whether the renin-angiotensin system stimulates the release of mineralocorticoids in fish— there is no clear correlation between plasma renin levels and those of plasma sodium or cortisol.

Blood 2891, 3317; Kidney 2890, 2891

the contractile cells decrease in diameter towards the tail (hence there is a greater proportion of extracellular fluid) and because the tail end contains a bigger proportion of connective tissue (*Gadus morhua*). Sodium rises in muscle during severe starvation because of an increase in extracellular space, but falls in the blood plasma. It rises in the muscle of eels on metamorphosis. Decreases in the muscle of *Gadus morhua* with increased body length *provided* that the fish are not depleted. Thermal shock (sudden cooling) causes the muscle to gain sodium, perhaps by depressing the active extrusion. Acclimation to lower temperatures results in higher sodium concentrations in the plasma. Dark muscle is richer in sodium than white muscle, perhaps again because of the smaller diameters of the cells. The concentration in fish larvae declines as they develop, because of the decrease in extracellular fluid. It increases in the ovaries of *Gadus morhua* during maturation.

The internal concentrations in the fish are maintained at levels different from those of the surroundings (except in fish larvae and hagfish) by extrusion or acquisition at the gills and kidneys, the energy being supplied by ATP. The urinary bladder may also reabsorb sodium from the urine. The homeostasis is usually not perfect, and the concentration in tissues, particularly the blood, increases when euryhaline fish enter salt water and declines when they enter fresh water.

Alkaline gland 2692; Aqueous humour 1717, 2692, 2693, 3711; Bile (from gall bladder) 1595, 1596, 1636, 1836, 2261, 2263–2265, 2625, 2656, 2692, 3135; Bile (from liver) 1596; Blastula 3718; Blood 1428, 1444, 1484, 1490, 1537, 1575, 1576, 1584, 1595, 1596, 1633, 1636, 1637, 1641, 1642, 1666, 1674, 1714, 1717, 1734, 1735, 1749, 1750, 1794, 1800, 1802, 1806, 1813, 1840, 1856, 1857, 1860, 1905, 1906, 1908, 1909, 1916, 1921, 1932, 1942, 1944, 1945, 1948, 1958, 1965, 2008, 2024, 2047, 2054–2057, 2076–2080, 2082, 2108, 2164, 2176, 2182, 2201, 2244, 2261, 2262, 2265, 2278, 2288, 2429, 2432, 2461, 2465, 2466, 2476, 2499, 2500, 2503, 2514, 2519, 2520, 2530, 2540, 2555, 2556, 2562, 2622, 2624, 2625, 2639, 2640, 2649, 2650, 2655, 2686, 2692, 2693, 2711, 2731, 2802, 2804, 2805, 2808, 2831, 2862–2866, 2891, 2894–2897, 2920, 2922, 2924, 2925, 2932–2934, 2963, 2972, 2997, 3037–3039, 3041, 3090, 3111, 3121, 3130, 3134, 3135, 3160, 3202, 3205, 3275, 3292, 3310, 3311, 3313, 3314, 3339, 3342, 3343, 3353, 3418, 3427, 3429, 3430, 3431, 3455, 3492, 3494, 3497, 3501–3503, 3505, 3506, 3509, 3517, 3520, 3521, 3523–3526, 3558, 3559, 3584, 3711, 3717; Body fluids 1636, 2625, 3430; Bone 2623; Brain 1957, 1958, 3313; Cerebellum 2392; Cerebrospinal fluid 1908, 1958, 2692; Cranial fluid 2280, 2692, 3111, 3427, 3429, 3430; Cupula (after digestion) 1908; Egg 1531, 3718; Embryo 1824, 3718; Embryotrophe (fluid surrounding embryo) 2476; Endolymph (from canal) 1908, 2692, 3584; Endolymph (from labyrinth) 1908; Erythrocytes 1674, 1945, 2080, 2550, 2636, 2805, 3360, 3418, 3710; Fin 3176; Fry 3718; Gill 1642, 2199, 3313; "Gonad" 2033; Gut fluid 2649, 3038; Gut (intracellular) 2623; Gut lumen 1788; Gut wall 2622, 2892; Heart 2875, 3313; Intestinal fluid 2922; Kidney 1749, 1753, 3313; Larva 3718; Lateral line canal fluid 2562; Liver 1749, 1753, 2023, 2622, 2625, 3313; Liver (intracellular) 2623; Lorenzinian jelly 1908, 2280, 2692; Medulla + cerebellum 2392; Microsomes (from muscle) 2253; Mitochondria (from muscle) 2253; Muscle 1430, 1582, 1633, 1641, 1681, 1720, 1749, 1786, 1945, 2023, 2244, 2253, 2429, 2489, 2622–2625, 2639, 2875, 2924, 3021, 3090, 3121, 3130, 3134, 3135, 3294, 3313, 3331, 3343, 3467; Muscle cells 3135; Muscle (extracellular) 1633; Muscle (intracellular) 1429, 1633, 1681, 2623, 3090, 3134; Myofibrils 2253; Notochordal fluid 2076; Oocytes 1824, 3718; Optic lobe 2392; Ovarian fluid 3187; Ovary 2364, 3342; Parietal muscle 2255; Pectoral fin muscle 2875; Pericardial fluid 2077, 2692,

3427, 3429, 3430; Perilymph 2692; Perivisceral fluid 2077, 2692, 2922, 3427, 3429; Rectal gland 1637, 2692, 3654; Rectal gland fluid 2232; Rete mirabile 3360; Scales 1716, 2440, 3342; Semen 2057, 3292; Seminal plasma 1765, 2073; Slime 2808; Spinal cord 2392; Spleen 1749, 1753; Stomach wall muscle 2875; Testis 2057, 3342; Tongue retractor muscle 2875; Urine (from bladder) 1537, 1538, 1636, 1637, 1641, 1840, 1944, 1948, 1960, 2078, 2182, 2240, 2260, 2431, 2461, 2500, 2650, 2655, 2686, 2808, 2861–2863, 2866, 2896, 2897, 2997, 3038, 3079, 3111, 3205, 3654; Urine (from kidney) 1948; Urine (from ureter) 1538, 1944; Uterine fluid 2024, 3431; Ventricle (intracellular) 3552; Vitreous humour 1717, 2288

SOMATOTROPIC HORMONE (*see* growth hormone)

SPERM (count) *35*
Semen 2057

SPERMIDINE
Brain 3217

SPERMINE
The lower content of spermine in fish brain compared with mouse brain may perhaps reflect the thin neuronal layers in comparison with the extensive fibrous zones in fish brain, since relatively high spermine concentrations are characteristic of brain areas rich in nerve cells (Seiler and Lamberty, 1973; *Salmo gairdneri*, *Scardinius erythrophthalmus*).
Brain 3217

‡SPHINGOMYELIN
Richer in dark muscle than in white muscle.
Blood 2845; Bone 3233; Brain 2469, 2551, 3064, 3436; Cartilage 3233; Cerebellum 2474; Cerebrum 2755; Egg 1454; Electric lobes 2474; Electric organ 1556, 2474, 3451; Erythrocytes 1419, 1565; Forebrain 2474; Gall bladder + bile 3436; Gill 2746, 3420, 3436, 3726, 3727; "Gonad" 3436; Intestine 3436; Intestinal mucosa 2746, 3726; Kidney 2746, 3436, 3726; Liver 2454, 2551, 2663, 2746, 2755, 3726, 3727; Muscle 2042, 2454, 2474, 2663, 2746, 2755, 2987, 3056, 3265, 3451, 3726; Nerve 1680, 2233, 2457; Ovary 2755; Pacemaker nucleus (in medulla) 2474; Phospholipid 2407; Rectal gland 1530, 2376, 2377; Swim bladder 2990, 3436; Swim bladder fatty foam 3032; Tectum opticum 2474; Testis 2755; Yolk 2847

SPHINGOSINE
Egg 1454

SPINDLE CELLS
Blood 2969

‡SQUALENE *74, 92, 120, 125, 261*
A hydrocarbon intermediate in cholesterol synthesis. Its only important route is to bile salts and cholesterol. On the other hand, in deep-sea sharks where the liver contains much squalene, there is only a slight elevation of the cholesterol content (Kayama and Shimada, 1972). Its synthesis has been shown to proceed via mevalonic acid as in mammals (Sargent, Williamson and Towse, 1970: *Squalus acanthias*).

The main function of squalene in fish is as a buoyancy agent in sharks which have no swim bladder. Some shark livers can be as much as 90% of squalene (wet weight), and as their livers tend to be large, as much as 25% of the wet weight of the fish can be squalene. Since its specific gravity is only 0·86, it gives an upthrust of about 0·19 g per gram in sea water. It is 80% more effective as a buoyancy agent than cod liver oil. It cannot be rapidly eliminated, nor turned over metabolically; it also cannot be further oxidised to provide metabolic energy.

Apart from sharks, only the eulachon (*Thaleichthys pacificus*) possesses squalene as a major component (10% of the lipid). In other teleosts, the highest concentrations are found in the liver, skin and dark muscle (68, 64 and 60 parts per million, respectively, averaged by Lewis, 1971, from 7 species). It is thought to be excreted through the skin.

There is no consistent relationship between the squalene content of an organ and its lipid content.
Liver 2007, 2403, 2557; Muscle 2568; Slime 2559

STEROL ESTERS *40,41, 53, 54*
Blood 2845, 3242; Egg 1691, 2118; Electric organ 3451; Erythrocytes 1419; Gill 3727; "Gonad" 1691; Liver 1691, 2118, 2439, 2557, 2572, 2871, 3239, 3241, 3243*, 3727; Mesentery 2439; Muscle 1691, 2118, 2439, 2871, 2948, 3239, 3241, 3242, 3243*, 3451; Ovary 2399, 2439, 3239, 3241, 3242, 3243*; Slime 2559; Testis 2439, 3239, 3241, 3242, 3243*; Yolk 2847
*Given by the translator as "steryl ethers" which could be glyceryl ethers.

STEROLS
Blood 2845; Depot lipid 2399; Egg 2118, 3388; "Gonad" 2398, 2400; Heart 2399; Intestine 2399; Kidney 2399; Liver 2119, 2399, 2871; Muscle 2118, 2398, 2399, 2400, 2871, 2948, 3387; Ovary 2399; Skull 3031; Spine 3031; Spleen 2399; Stomach 2399; Swim bladder 2400; Swim bladder (fat-filled) 2398

STRONTIUM *33, 35, 133, 147, 148*
95% of the strontium of *Thunnus alalunga* is contained in the skeleton, and the increase in total body strontium with increased length (*Fundulus heteroclitus*) is consistent with the steady increase in calcium content: the Ca/Sr levels appear relatively constant in ashed samples of vertebrate tissues. This relationship is not, however, universal, and from the bony structures of freshwater fish it may vary according to species, season and locality. It is absorbed primarily through the gills, to a small extent through the skin, and not at all through the digestive tract (Tomiyama, Kobayashi and Ishio—no date given). The scales accumulate more strontium when the fish are in the sea than in fresh water; in *Salmo salar*, the centre portions of the scales (laid down in fresh water) have been found to contain 110–179 µg/g, while the peripheral part representing the marine phase contained 308–348 µg/g. Similarly, in *Salmo trutta*, the freshwater form (brown trout) contained less than 200 µg Sr/g in the scales, while the marine form (sea trout) showed more than 300 µg/g in the scales.
Bone 1528, 2786, 2981; Caecum 2981; Egg 3438; Epidermis 2981; Fin 2786; Gill 2786, 2981; Kidney 2981; Liver 2981, 3018; Muscle 2786, 2981, 3019; Scales 1478, 1528, 2440, 2786; Skin 2786; Slime 2981; Spleen 2981; Teeth + jawbone 2981

SUCCINATE *271, 281*
Dark muscle 2340, 2342; Muscle 2340, 2342

SUCCINIC DEHYDROGENASE *29, 71, 74, 84, 88, 93, 111, 119, 120, 297, 317, 329, 330, 333, 355–357*
A mitochondrial enzyme. Its activity is greater in the muscle and brain of pelagic species than in more sluggish ones, reflecting the increased numbers of mitochondria in active fish (that is, greater turnover of metabolites). The activity in dark muscle can be made to increase (*Gadus morhua*) if the fish are forced to swim in an exercise channel, but only if their food intake is adequate for their metabolic needs.
Brain 2750; Dark muscle 1563, 1580, 2344; Gill 1727, 2863; Islet tissue 3018; Kidney 2863, 3363; Liver 3363; Mitochondria (from heart) 2296; Mitochondria (from liver) 2296; Muscle 1563, 1580, 2166, 2344; Pink (intermediate) muscle 2344

SUCCINATE-INT-DEHYDROGENASE
Liver, Liver plasma membrane: 2621

SUCRASE
Intestine, Liver, Pancreas, Stomach: 1425

"SUGAR" (mostly glucose) *7, 111, 230*
Blood 1451, 1455, 1492, 1547, 1548, 1592, 1686, 1749, 1798, 1818, 1903, 1911, 2062, 2063, 2082, 2139, 2150, 2503, 2509, 2643, 2649, 2790, 2791, 2823, 2832, 2916, 2993, 3154, 3216, 3310, 3411, 3562, 3619; Muscle 1745; Muscle cell wall 1577; Slime 2447

‡SULPHATE *133*
Mostly combined in tissues as part of the methionine and cysteine molecules.
Alkaline gland 2692; Aqueous humour 2692; Bile 2692; Blood 1813, 2076, 2078, 2079, 2692, 2808, 2862, 3038, 3111, 3134, 3135, 3523–3526; Body fluids 3304; Cranial fluid 2692, 3111; Gut fluid 3038; Muscle 3134, 3304; Muscle (intracellular) 3134; Notochordal fluid 2076; Perivisceral fluid 2692; Skin mucopolysaccharide 1434, 3098; Urine 2078, 2808, 2862, 3028, 3111

SULPHATIDES
Brain 2469–2471, 3222; Electric lobes 2472; Electric organ 2472; Muscle 2472; Myelin (from brain) 3222; Nerve 2233; Pacemaker nucleus 2472; Rectal gland 1530, 2376, 2377; Tectum opticum 2472; Telencephalon 2472; Testis 3488

TARAXANTHIN
Intestine, Liver, Muscle: 1779

‡TAURINE *75, 312, 355*
Richer in dark muscle than in white. Occurs in large quantities in fish hearts, as in vertebrate heart musculature in general. It is thought more likely to be an energy store than an osmoregulator because of its considerable seasonal variation. Much taurine probably comes to fish in their food: there are high levels in marine invertebrates.
Alimentary tract 3637; Blood 1594, 2553, 2946, 3637; Brain 1594, 2553, 3637; Cerebellum 2943; Dark muscle 2977; Electric organ 2946; Embryo 1824; Erythrocytes 1594, 1965, 3710; Gill 3637; Heart 1594, 3637; Kidney 2553, 3637; Liver

2553, 3637; Muscle 1410, 1430, 1720, 1882, 2105, 2455, 2456, 2946, 2977, 3166, 3200, 3331, 3366, 3369, 3567, 3637; Nerve 2946; Oocytes 1824; Parietal muscle 2255; Spleen 3637; Ventricle 3552; Ventricle (intracellular) 3552; Wing muscle 1594

‡TESTOSTERONE *6, 37*

A male steroid hormone which *can* occur in the higher concentration in the female of a species. Unusually high concentrations can be found in fish as distinct from mammals. In *Carassius auratus* the level in the blood is high at the spawning time and low in winter in both males and females.
Blood 1652, 1795, 2275, 2391, 2868, 3172, 3639

‡THALLIUM—Volume 1 only

THIAMINASE *134, 135*

Dark muscle 2297, 2299; Gill 2299; "Gonad" 2297; Intestine 1464, 2297, 2299; Kidney 2297, 2299; Liver 1464, 2297, 2299; Muscle 2297, 2299, 3473; Pyloric caecae 2297, 2299; Spleen 2297; Stomach 2299

‡THIAMINE (Aneurin, Vitamin B_1) *134, 135, 149*

The quantity found in a fish depends on the level in the diet. Excess quantities are not stored. Starving fish may possess larger quantities than fed fish, perhaps because they are consuming no thiaminase which degrades the vitamin. The highest concentration has been found in the retina (27·7 mg% dry matter). Dark muscle is richer than white muscle. Deficiency symptoms include, among others, anorexia, anaemia, corneal opacity, fatty liver, haemorrhage in the brain and vascular degeneration, degeneration of muscle tissue. Moribund fish lose control of the dorsal and pectoral fins, and there is a loss of equilibrium leading to a slow, rolling movement.
Alimentary tract 3453, 3454; Gut wall 3454; Intestine 1464, 3453; Liver 1464, 2298, 3453, 3454; Muscle 1786, 2298, 2313, 3295, 3453, 3454, 3690

THORIUM
Liver 2611

THREONINE ALDOLASE
Dark muscle, Liver, Muscle: 2835

‡THREONINE ETHANOLAMINE PHOSPHATE
Lens 2181

THROMBOCYTES (count) *239*

Comparable to the platelets of mammals. Not usually seen in blood smears of circulation blood except from fish under stress or which have been injured. Thus the blood clotting time of a stressed fish is less than that of a resting fish (Wedemeyer, Meyer and Smith, 1976).
Blood 1424, 1669, 1814, 1907, 2077, 2333, 2633, 2868

THYMIDINE PHOSPHORYLASE
Brain, Liver: 2873

‡THYMINE—Volume 1 only for bibliography. This volume page reference *162*

THYROXINE *7, 40, 110, 116, 163, 169, 218, 238, 268, 269, 304, 326, 355, 356, 386*
The hormone which contains iodine and is secreted by the thyroid gland. It appears to have very many effects on fish. Its physiological role has not yet been clearly defined, although its influence on the physical activity and migration seem to be of most importance.
The concentration is greater in the blood of active rather than inactive fish, and injections of thyroxine increase spontaneous activity and oxygen consumption. Circulating thyroxine declines during starvation. On the other hand, there is said to be a reduction in the swimming activity and aggressive behaviour in *Salmo salar* treated with thyroxine. In *Cyprinus carpio* it has been found to activate hepatic glycogenolysis and increase the catabolism of circulating glucose, also to stimulate the secretion of insulin and favour gluconeogenesis. The glycogen concentrations in heart and muscle are increased. Serum lipid and lipoprotein are depressed, while free fatty acids in the blood are increased, by thyroxine injections. In general, the hormone engenders the mobilisation rather than the deposition of lipid.
The levels of thyroxine in the blood vary seasonally in many species. It promotes smoltification in salmonids and encourages their migration to the sea. A clear relationship with osmoregulation has not been established, but thyroxine may control the salinity preference of the fish. It is said to influence the sodium balance.
Where fish possess paired visual pigments based on both vitamins A_1 and A_2, an increase in thyroxine leads to an increase in the porphyropsin-type pigments (based on A_2).
Treatment with thyroxine often leads to silvering of the skin (many teleosts), so there appears also to be an influence on guanine metabolism.
Blood 1445, 1854, 2177, 2178, 2190, 2266, 2529, 2945, 3477, 3618

‡TIN *35*
Values in the muscle of different species range from 0·017–3·06 mg%. In *Salvelinus namaycush* it has been observed that the concentration of the tin in muscle and bone decreases as the fish grow older.
Kidney 2040; Liver 2040, 3018; Muscle 2040, 2677, 3019; Ovary 2040; Scales 2440

‡TITANIUM
Dark muscle 2571; Liver 3018, Muscle 2571, 3019; Scales 2440

TOCOPHEROL (*see* Vitamin E)

TRANSALDOLASE *19*
Egg 3703; Muscle 3398; Oocytes 3703

‡TRANSAMINASE—Volume 1 only for bibliography. This volume page references *159, 221, 227*

TRANSFERRIN *252*

TRANSKETOLASE *19*
Egg 3703; Erythrocytes 1738; Muscle 3398; Oocytes 3703

‡TRIGLYCERIDES *13, 25, 39–41, 53, 54, 65, 66, 75, 92, 96–98, 100, 125, 126, 186, 206, 208, 209, 257, 339*
The attachment of a fatty acid to each of the three hydroxyl groups of glycerol results in a compound known as a triglyceride. Any fatty acid can be found in any of the three positions, but it is possible for all three to be the same. The main or even the sole function of triglycerides is as an energy store, so the adipose tissue of any fish, whether it be in the liver, flesh or body cavity, is always rich in triglycerides. For example, the liver lipid of well-fed *Gadus morhua* can be more than 90% triglyceride and only about 5% of the "structural" phospholipid, while after severe starvation it is possible for the liver lipid to be only 5% triglyceride and 70% phospholipid, since most of the triglyceride has been utilised (the remaining lipid is largely cholesterol). Triglycerides are also the chief fraction of the reserve lipids of the oocytes.
They are one of the least buoyant lipids, so are not stored to any great extent by fish without swim bladders. Other lipids such as wax esters give much more upthrust. Adipose fin 2577; Blood 1437, 1954, 2495, 2514, 2518, 2555, 2556, 2761, 2762, 2845, 3138, 3162, 3179, 3180, 3237, 3242, 3253; Brain 1479, 1954; Cerebrum 2577; Dark muscle 1581, 2234, 2555, 3138, 3246; Depot lipid 2399; Egg 1454, 1479, 1691, 1987, 2118; Erythrocytes 1419, 1954; Gastric muscle 3246; Gill 2577, 3727; "Gonad" 1691, 2398, 2400, 2577; Heart 2399, 2577, 2992; Heart muscle 1954, 3246; Hump (*Oncorhynchus gorbuscha*) 3137; Intestine 2399; Kidney 2399, 2577; Larva 1874, 1875; Liver 1546, 1690, 1691, 1802, 1954, 2117, 2118, 2234, 2399, 2439, 2495, 2518, 2555–2557, 2572, 2577, 2871, 3138, 3179, 3180, 3239, 3241, 3243, 3245, 3253, 3727; Mesentery 2439; Muscle 1486, 1546, 1581, 1690, 1691, 1802, 1954, 2117, 2118, 2234, 2398, 2399, 2400, 2439, 2495, 2518, 2555, 2556, 2577, 2871, 2948, 3138, 3180, 3239, 3241–3243, 3245, 3246, 3387; Nerve (olfactory) 2407; Ovary 1416, 1690, 2117, 2310, 2399, 2439, 3169, 3239, 3241–3243; Rectal gland 2377; Scales 2577; Skin 1546, 2577; Skull 2538, 3028, 3031; Slime 1546, 2559; Spinal cord 2577; Spleen 1954, 2399, 2577; Stomach 2399; Swim bladder 2400, 2577; Swim bladder (fat-filled) 2398; Testis 1690, 2117, 2439, 3239, 3241–3243; Vertebral column 2538, 3028, 3031; White collagenous subdermal material 2234; Yolk 2847

TRI-IODOTHYRONINE
Blood 2945

TRI-ISOPHOSPHATE DEHYDROGENASE
Muscle, Nerve: 3551

‡TRIMETHYLAMINE *75, 149*
Richer in dark muscle than in white muscle, regardless of whether the fish are migratory or not (see under TMAO).
Dark muscle 3439; Muscle 1583, 1871, 1873, 2380, 2388, 2456, 3367, 3439, 3482

TRIMETHYLAMINE OXIDASE
Liver 2030, 2035

TRIMETHYLAMINE OXIDE (TMAO) *44, 57, 68, 70, 75, 76, 106, 133, 149, 150, 283, 310, 312, 355*
A nitrogenous compound found in the tissues of marine but not of freshwater fish. As an excretory product it resembles urea in its non-poisonous nature, small

molecular weight and almost neutral reaction, and it may be a means of detoxifying ammonia. Some marine teleosts such as *Lophius piscatorius* have been thought to excrete up to 50% of their waste nitrogen as TMAO (note: this conclusion comes from a very old paper—Grollman, 1929—and I have not seen such a large figure quoted more recently). Concentrations in different species have been tabulated by Groninger (1959), who concluded that the primary origin of TMAO in marine animals remains to be explained.

It is solely exogenous in origin in at least some freshwater species. The muscle of *Carassius auratus* remains free of it while the fish is fed a TMAO-free diet, but, two hours after ingestion, TMAO can be measured in the muscle and a level of 6 mg% can be maintained. However, it falls to zero again two days after the end of feeding it to the fish. TMAO is also exogenous to *Anguilla japonica*, and the salinity of the medium has no connection with the retention of the compound, which drops to zero in a few days on a TMAO-free diet both in fresh water and in 25‰ salt water. However, *Fugu niphobles*, *Monacanthus cirrhifer* and *Trachurus japonicus* have been shown to retain their previous level of muscle TMAO when fed a TMAO-free diet, or starved, for 25 days, so it seems likely that the compound fulfils a function in marine teleosts. In marine elasmobranchs the concentration is higher than in any teleosts, and here the compound is thought to serve an osmoregulatory function, like urea. All elasmobranchs maintain relatively high concentrations, but differ in their ability to synthesise it from precursors. The nurse shark, *Ginglymostoma cirrhatum*, can convert choline to TMAO (Goldstein and Funkhouser, 1972) and the same has been observed in the lemon shark (*Negaprion brevirostris*). Both species also appear able to convert trimethylamine to TMAO. However, *Squalus acanthias* and *Raja erinacea* cannot use precursors in this way, and all their TMAO may have originated in their diet.

In the dark-fleshed migratory fish such as *Scomber japonicus* and *Sardinops melanosticta*, *Katsuwonus pelamis*, etc. the strip of lateral dark muscle is much richer in TMAO than is the whiter muscle. The reverse is true in non-migratory white-fleshed fish such as *Sciaenops ocellata*, *Trigla* sp., *Lateolabrax japonicus*, *Theragra chalcogramma*, etc., where the white muscle is richer than the dark. The reason is unknown.

The blood of active species contains more than that of sluggish species, and there is more in the muscle of fish caught in arctic waters than in more temperate waters. Well-marked seasonal changes have been seen in the TMAO of muscle of *Clupea harengus* and juvenile *Seriola quinqueradiata*, but the mechanism is again obscure.

Food technologists have long been interested in this compound, because it is reduced to trimethylamine (TMA) by "spoilage" bacteria after the death of the fish, giving it its characteristic "fishy" taste. More recently it has been discovered that when fish carcasses are frozen, the TMAO is gradually converted to dimethylamine and formaldehyde during cold storage (Tokunaga, 1970b). The latter compound could be the cause of the characteristic toughening of the texture found on long cold storage, but it cannot account for the changes occurring in all species, since the conversion of TMAO to DMA and formaldehyde occurs only in gadoid species.

Bile 2625; Blood 1636, 1945, 2076, 2078, 2079, 2625, 3111, 3134, 3428-3430; Body fluids 2625; Cranial fluid 3430; Dark muscle 2929, 3439, 3668; Embryo + yolk 3110; Erythrocytes 1945; Liver 2625; Muscle 1700, 1882, 1945, 2111, 2129, 2380, 2455, 2456, 2625, 2929, 3134, 3135, 3151, 3367, 3439, 3567, 3668; Noto-chordal fluid 2076; Urine 1636, 2078

‡Triose phosphate
   Muscle 1951

‡Triose phosphate dehydrogenase *19*
   Egg 3703; Embryo 3702; Heart 1505; Oocytes 3703

Triose phosphate isomerase
   Egg 3703; Erythrocytes 1475; Muscle 1789; Oocytes 3703

Triphosphoinositide
   Cerebellum, Electric lobes, Electric organ, Forebrain, Muscle, Pacemaker nucleus,
   Tectum opticum: 2474

Triphosphopyridine nucleotide (*see* Nicotinamide adenine dinucleotide phosphate)

‡Trypsin *16, 151*
   Hepatopancreas 2325; Intestine 1425, 2325, 3256; Larval digestive organs 2395;
   Liver 1425; Mesentery 2958; Pancreas 1425; Pyloric caecae 2958; Rectum 2325

‡Tunaxanthin *317*
   In general, this carotenoid characterises marine as distinct from freshwater fish,
   but it predominates in the skin and fins of at least one freshwater species, *Coreoperca
   kawamebari*.
   Fin 1782, 1783; Gill 1783; Intestine 1783; Liver 1783; Muscle 1783; Skin 1783,
   2726; Skin + fins 2715–2718, 2720, 2723–2725

‡Tungsten—Volume 1 only

‡Tyrosine *320*
   Collagen (from swim bladder), Corium, Elastin (from swim bladder), Elastoidin,
   Ovokeratin, Scales, Swim bladder tunic: 2087

‡Ubiquinone *75*
   A natural benzoquinone which is now recognised as an essential component in the
   electron transfer chain of mitochondria for many forms of life. It increases in
   concentration in the gills of *Oncorhynchus keta* when they enter rivers to spawn. An
   increase in ubiquinone in *Cyprinus carpio* which had been fed tocopherol suggests
   conversion of the one to the other.
      Ascent of the evolutionary tree corresponds in many cases with an increase of
   ubiquinone in the heart, so cyclostomes contain less than elasmobranchs, which in
   turn contain less than teleosts.
   Bone 2186; Dark muscle 2186; Gill 2186, 3188; Heart 2186, 3188; Kidney 2186,
   3188; Liver 2186, 3188; Muscle 2186; Ovary 2186; Skin 2186; Spleen 2186;
   Stomach + intestine 2186; Testis 2186

‡Uracil
   Liver RNA 3066

‡Uranium
   The average figure for fish muscle has been given as 2.1×10^{-5} mg/g.
   Liver 2611

Urate oxidase
Liver 1711, 2071, 2873

‡Urea *4, 5, 20, 21, 25, 44, 57, 92, 116, 153–156, 158–163, 214, 218, 221, 283, 310, 311, 318, 320, 346*
A medium for the excretion of nitrogen which, unlike ammonia, is of low toxicity. No fish excrete all of their nitrogen as urea, but where excretion becomes inhibited, or intermittent, as in amphibious fish on land or in aestivating lungfish sealed up in cocoons, much more urea and less ammonia are produced.

In teleosts in general, urea is excreted in small quantity in relation to the total nitrogen. It cannot be derived from the Krebs-Henseleit cycle, since two of the enzymes are missing in teleosts, but is thought to be derived from arginine, both exogenous and endogenous, purine nucleotides and those amino acids which are precursors of purines (glutamine, serine, glycine). Most of it is produced by the liver.

Urea passes rapidly through most internal membranes, so it is found in all tissues. The quantity present in dark muscle is similar to that in white muscle but differs from that in the liver.

Elasmobranchs contain much higher concentrations than teleosts. They use it to maintain osmotic balance with salt water, so the concentration is diminished in euryhaline elasmobranchs living in fresh water. Starving elasmobranchs may be unable to maintain an optimum level of urea, since their rate of nitrogen catabolism is insufficient and retention is not complete. The concentration of urea in the urine of elasmobranchs is lower than that in the serum, so although some is continually lost there is some reabsorption by the kidney tubules from the urine, by, it is thought, a mechanism involving the simultaneous reabsorption of sodium. The only other fish having urea concentrations comparable with that of the elasmobranchs is the coelacanth (*Latimeria chalumnae*).

Although elasmobranchs maintain high urea concentrations for osmotic purposes, they are not more tolerant to it in other ways. None of their enzymes is enhanced by urea and indeed the enzymes of both oxidative processes and glycolysis are inhibited by it. They do not use the control of urea concentration in their bodies to extend the range of tolerated external salinities. *Scyliorhinus canicula*, for example, is stenohaline and swells up and dies if placed in diluted sea water, rather than increasing the elimination of urea.

Alimentary tract 3546, 3547, 3637; Alkaline gland 2692; Aqueous humour 1717, 2692; Bile 2625, 2692; Blood 1594, 1636, 1637, 1666, 1717, 1811, 1813, 1827, 1831, 1886, 1905, 1906, 1945, 2008, 2024, 2049, 2076–2079, 2165, 2267, 2288, 2466, 2514, 2625, 2686, 2692, 2996, 2997, 3039, 3111, 3134, 3135, 3187, 3310, 3339, 3428–3431, 3492, 3524–3526, 3546, 3547, 3558, 3559, 3603, 3604, 3637; Blood (from embryo) 2359; Body fluids 2625, 3304, 3430; Brain 1594, 3637; Cerebrospinal fluid 2692; Cranial fluid 2692, 3111, 3429, 3430; Dark muscle 3546; Embryo + yolk 1824, 3110; Endolymph 2692; Erythrocytes 1594, 1945; Gill 3637; Heart 1594, 3637; Kidney 3544, 3546, 3547, 3637; Liver 2625, 3544, 3546, 3547, 3587, 3637; Lorenzinian jelly 2692; Muscle 1410, 1681, 1945, 2105, 2118, 2625, 3134, 3135, 3166, 3304, 3367, 3546, 3547, 3567, 3637; Muscle (intracellular) 1681; Notochordal fluid 2076; Oocytes 1824; Pericardial fluid 2692, 3429, 3430; Perilymph 2692; Perivisceral fluid 1636, 2692, 3429; Rectal gland 1637, 2692, 3654; Seminal plasma 1765, 2072, 2073; Sperm 2072; Sperm cell cytoplasm 2073; Spleen 3546, 3547, 3637; Urine 1636, 1811, 2078, 2083, 2686, 2997, 3111, 3303, 3654; Uterine fluid 2024, 3431; Vitreous humour 1717, 2288; Wing muscle 1594

‡Uric acid *4, 11, 154, 157, 161, 162, 218*
Formed from exogenous and endogenous purine nucleotides and also by the catabolism of proteins *via* purines. It is converted to urea for excretion. There is more uric acid in dark muscle than white muscle.
Blood 1734, 2267; Body fluids 3304; Kidney 3544, 3547; Liver 3544, 3547; Muscle 3304; Ovarian fluid 3187; Seminal plasma 2073, 2998; Sperm 2998; Sperm cell cytoplasm 2073; Urine 2083, 3303

‡Uricase *161, 162*
Kidney 3544; Liver 2621, 3544, 3547; Liver plasma membrane 2621

‡Uridine diphosphate
Liver 3219, 3220, 3721

UDP-Glucose
Liver 3722

UDP-Glucose pyrophosphorylase
Embryo 3706, 3709; Ooctes 3709

UDP-Glucuronic acid
Liver 3722

UDP-Hexoses
Liver 3219, 3220, 3721; Oocytes 3704

UDP-*N*-Acetyl galactosamine
Liver 3219, 3722

UDP-*N*-Acetyl glucosamine
Liver 3219, 3721

UDP-*N*-Acetyl hexosamine
Liver 3220

UDP-Uronic acids
Liver 3219, 3220

Uridine monophosphate
Liver 1584, 3219, 3220, 3721

‡Uridine triphosphate
Liver 1584, 3721

‡Uronic acid
Cornea 1678, 2770; Mucopolysaccharide (from skin) 1434

‡Vanadium *76*
The concentration in the muscle has been found to range from 0·059–0·722 mg% in 34 species of fish.
Kidney 2040; Liver 2040; Muscle 2040; 2677; Ovary 2040

‡VITAMIN A₁ (retinol, axerophthol) *7, 10, 26, 45, 57, 67, 145, 146, 263, 265, 267, 268*
Many fish obtain this vitamin from their food. Some species but not all can synthesise it from carotenoid precursors. There are great variations according to the age of the fish (a tendency to increase with age), the geographical locality, the sex and the season. The liver is the main storage organ, and the concentration can vary in different parts of it. Values ranging from 70 to 119 400 units per 100 g have been quoted for body lipid (Kizevetter, 1968) and from 179 to 9 819 000 units per 100 g liver. In flat fish there is more in the flesh and skin of the upper fillet than the lower. The halibut (*Hippoglossus hippoglossus*) is well known as a rich source (liver), and the species with the highest concentration in the muscle is the Japanese lamprey (*Entosphenus japonicus*). The concentration of the aldehyde of the vitamin ("retinal") in the blood of female *Gadus morhua* (not males) increases steadily during maturation, and during the same period it accumulates in the ovary.

Deficiency results in oedema and the formation of ascites fluid, exophthalmus, and haemorrhage in the kidneys. Probably the main function of the vitamin is in the formation of the visual pigment rhodopsin, a combination of protein and vitamin A₁, which occurs exclusively in the retinas of most marine fish and, in an admixture with porphyropsin (see under vitamin A₂), in the retinas of freshwater fish. While the possession of either pigment is determined genetically, their proportion in mixed-pigment species is governed by the illumination of the habitat and by certain hormones.

Alimentary tract 3237; Blood 3237; Egg 1998; Eye 3237; "Gonad" 3237; Heart 3237; Hepatopancreas 2137, 3395; Kidney 3237; Liver 1500, 2137; Mesentery 2439; Muscle 2137, 2439, 3395, 3690; Ovary 2439; Spleen 3237; Stomach 3237; Testis 2439

VITAMIN A₁ ALDEHYDE (Retinal) *45, 354*
Blood 3047

‡VITAMIN A₂ (Dehydroretinal) *7, 145, 146, 263–265, 267–269*
Occurs in the retinas of some freshwater species and occasional marine species as the basis of the pigment porphyropsin, which is sensitive to longer wavelengths than is rhodopsin (see under vitamin A₁). In general, carotenoids can be precursors of vitamins A₁ or A₂ with equal facility. However, neither beta-carotene nor zeaxanthin from the diet seem to be converted to vitamin A₂ in *Saccobranchus fossilis*, although lutein is readily converted (Barua, Singh and Das, 1973). Dietary vitamin A₁ can be converted by fish to vitamin A₂, and if feeding ceases, stored A₁ can similarly change to A₂ (Braekkan, Ingebrigtsen and Myklestad, 1969; *Salmo gairdneri*). Dietary A₁ is converted to A₂ not only in the liver but also the pyloric caecae (Lambertsen and Braekkan, 1969: same species).

Alimentary tract 2137; Egg 1998; Eye 2137; "Gonad" 2137; Heart 2137; Hepatopancreas 2137; Kidney 2137; Liver 1500, 2137; Muscle 2137; Spleen 2137; Stomach 2137

VITAMIN B (*see under* Thiamine (B₁), Riboflavin (B₂), Pyridoxine (B₆), Cyanocobalamine (B₁₂), Niacin, Biotin, Para-amino benzoic acid, Pantothenic acid, Folic acid, Inositol and Choline). A syndrome characteristic of a general deficiency of vitamins B consists of nervous excitability, loss of equilibrium and bloodshot eyes, while in advanced stages the fin membranes fray and mucus sloughs from the body.

‡VITAMIN C (Ascorbic acid) *7, 64, 76, 237*
The concentration in various organs varies seasonally. There are relatively high concentrations in the brain, and the testis contains more than the ovary. Deficiency results in lordosis (see Fig. 15) which shows as a kink in the spine, originating in a breakdown of intervertebral collagen. It is the proline-to-hydroxyproline step which is inhibited in vitamin C deficiency, and much less hydroxyproline is formed. In the same way, the collagenous supports of the gill filaments collapse and wounds will not heal. Autoradiographs of fish injected with radioactive ascorbic acid show well-defined layers of collagen in the skin and fins, the gill supports, pituitary, kidney and liver.
Some species, for example *Cyprinus carpio*, can synthesise this vitamin.
The concentration in the adrenals has been found to decrease during stress.
In *Cyprinus carpio*, ascorbic acid has been shown to prevent the intake of copper from the environment, and its accumulation in the tissues.
Adrenal 3601; Blood 3288; Cerebellum 1799; Cerebrum 1799; Dark muscle 1475; Kidney 3600, 3603; Medulla oblongata 1799; Muscle 2475; Optic lobes 1799

PROVITAMIN D
Liver 3020

‡VITAMIN D (Ergocalciferol) *7, 8, 10, 146, 264*
Present in fish lipids mainly as fatty acid esters. Most of it occurs in the liver, very little in the flesh, but the flesh of *Clupea harengus* is an exception with up to 100 units of vitamin D per g lipid.
There is very little in cyclostomes or elasmobranchs, perhaps because the vitamin is unnecessary in the absence of true bony structures. In teleosts (the bony fish), vitamin D concentration appears to relate to ecological conditions rather than taxonomy; it is usually abundant in migrating fish and low in bottom fish. Wide variation in the content in different parts of a fish make it difficult to generalise; further, the distribution seems to change from part to part of the body as the fish grows older.
It is likely that the synthesis, metabolism and physiological function of vitamin D in fish differ from those in mammals. Bony fish which store it receive very little in the diet. Fish rarely exposed to sunlight accumulate substantial stores of the vitamin, while *Carassius auratus* in strong sunlight contain very little. Fish livers cannot convert provitamin D to vitamin D in significant quantities if at all. It is not yet established whether fish require vitamin D to regulate calcium concentration, or indeed whether it serves any function at all. It is not known whether fish can be made deficient in vitamin D.
The level in the eggs of fish does not reflect that in the parental diet.
Alimentary tract 3673; Bone 3673; Brain 3673; Egg 3673; Eye 2188, 3673; Heart 3673; Intestine 3673; Kidney 2188, 3673; Lipid from body cavity 3673; Liver 2188, 3057, 3673; Muscle 2188, 3673; Ovary 2188, 3673; Pyloric caecae 2188, 3673; Skin 2188, 3673; Spleen 3673; Stomach 3673; Swim bladder 3673; Testis 3673

‡VITAMIN E (Tocopherol) *7, 10, 76, 146*
The tocopherols present in fish originate in the phytoplankton, the principal type being α-tocopherol. Some interconversion occurs, *Cyprinus carpio*, for example, converting γ or δ tocopherols to α-tocopherol (Higashi, Terada *et al.*, 1972). Tocopherol may also be converted to ubiquinone (same authors).

Of internal organs, the heart is richest in tocopherol and the gonads are also rich, becoming depleted during spawning. The concentration in the muscle of *Gadus morhua* tends to increase during starvation. Differences in muscle tocopherol content, both within and between species, seem to be a function of the lipid content.

Increased levels of linoleic acid in the diet have been shown by Watanabe, Takeuchi *et al.* (1977) to increase the need for tocopherol, judging from the onset of muscular dystrophy.

The deficiency symptoms are "clubbed" gills, anaemia, ceroid substances deposited in the liver, spleen and kidney, exophthalmus, poor growth and increased fragility of the erythrocytes.

Bone 2186; Dark muscle 1883, 2185, 2186; Eye 2185; Gill 2185, 2186; Heart 2185, 2186; Hepatopancreas 3395; Kidney 2185, 2186; Liver 2185, 2186; Muscle 1883, 2185, 2186, 3395; Ovary 1883, 2185, 2186; Pyloric caecae 2185; Skin 2185, 2186; Spleen 2185, 2186; Stomach + intestine 2186; Testis 1883, 2185, 2186

‡Wax esters *53, 120, 121, 125, 126, 144, 207, 261*
Long chain fatty acids esterified to long chain fatty alcohols are termed wax esters (they contain no glycerol). They are found in large amounts in marine animals, especially copepods, that inhabit environments where food is available only for short and irregular periods. Animals which have wax esters as the major part of their lipid store nearly always have very large amounts of lipid in relation to their body mass (Sargent, 1976).

There are both saturated and monounsaturated alcohols present, with 16:0 and 18:1 as the usual major constituents. The fatty acids are more diverse, but 18:1 is most often the main component, and 16:1 and 20:1 are often important (Nevenzel, 1970).

Although wax esters are quantitatively one of the most abundant lipid classes in the marine environment, they are difficult to digest compared with triglycerides (Patton, Nevenzel and Benson, 1975). The efficiencies of wax digestion between species depends on the architecture of the alimentary tract, since there are no specific wax-degrading enzymes other than triglyceride lipases. It was earlier thought that the deep-water or near-surface cold-water fish which contain considerable quantities of wax esters simply ingested them unchanged from the nearest source in the food chain, but now it is known that fish can synthesise them, modifying ingested lipids to their own characteristic patterns. Muscle is probably a major site of biosynthesis, and hepatopancreas and gut are even more active. Wax esters are found in the lipids of *Mugil* sp. only after the ovaries have matured, presumably without a change in the diet (Nevenzel, 1970). *Trichogaster cosby* produces large quantities of wax esters in the roe, although triglycerides are the prominent lipid in other parts of the fish (Rahn, Sand and Schlenk, 1973). The physiological role in gonads is not fully understood, except as a possible energy source.

The main function of wax esters is to provide buoyancy for fish which do not possess swim bladders: they are therefore common in deep-water fish which exhibit a pattern of daily vertical migration which would be difficult with a gas-filled swim bladder. The specific gravity is about 0·86, giving an upthrust of 0·188 g per gram of wax ester. This specialised use probably accounts for their virtual absence in other species which in fact consume large quantities from a copepod diet. In the cases where they act as buoyancy aids, they are not subject to hormone-controlled mobilisation as triglycerides are (Nevenzel, 1970). Certain species possess swim bladders full of wax esters in place of gas. Wax esters laid down in the ovaries also increase the buoyancy of the eggs.

Blood 2845, 3179, 3180; Depot fat 2399; "Gonad" 2398; Heart 2399; Intestine 2399; Kidney 2399; Liver 2399, 2557, 3179, 3180; Muscle 2398, 2399, 3180; Ovary 2310, 2399, 3169; Slime 2559; Spleen 2399; Stomach 2399; Swim bladder (fat-filled) 2398

XANTHINE OXIDASE *161*, *386*

Hepatopancreas 3481; Intestine 2468; Kidney 2468; Liver 1711, 2468

‡XANTHOPHYLLS—Volume 1 only

A general term for carotenoids containing oxygen. They form the basis for much of the skin pigmentation of coloured fish, and many species require large quantities in the diet to retain their normal appearance.

‡XANTHOPTERIN—Volume 1 only

XYLOSE

Muscle 3685

α-ZEACAROTENE-3, 17'-DIOL

Skin + fins 2727

β-ZEACAROTENE

Skin + fins 2727

β-ZEACAROTENE-3-OL

Skin + fins 2727

β-ZEACAROTENE-3, 17'-DIOL

Skin + fins 2727

β-ZEACAROTENE TRIOL

Skin + fins 2727

‡ZEAXANTHIN *145*, *317*

Egg 2132; Fin 1782, 1783; Gill 1783; Intestine 1782, 1783; Liver 1782, 1783, 2132; Muscle 1782, 1783, 2136; Skin 1783, 2136, 2726; Skin + fins 2715–2725, 2727; Sperm 1782; Testis 1781

‡ZINC *9*, *10*, *35*, *45*, *46*, *56*, *57*, *63*, *76*, *133*, *147*, *148*, *172*, *248*, *354*, *385*

In some species, such as *Boreogadus saida*, the concentration of zinc increases with body length, but in others it decreases and the scatter of values makes any interpretation difficult. There is no evidence for changes in concentration in different organs with age in *Pleuronectes platessa*, and this has been general experience in the muscle of many other species. There is a big uncontrolled variation in the zinc content of both eggs and sperm, both within one age-group and from year-group to year-group (*Cyprinus carpio*), although it has also been observed to vary inversely in the eggs with the age of the parent fish (same species). There is said to be more in the organs of male *Salmo gairdneri* than in those of the female, but the ovary is richer than the testis. The concentration in the ovary of *Gadus morhua* declines during maturation. When zinc is taken up by eggs, about 70% of it becomes bound to the chorion and 26% enters the perivitelline fluid. Little reaches the yolk or embryo (*Oncorhynchus kisutch*). The zinc in hatched *Cyprinus carpio* is found in the yolk granules, and after resorption of the sac it is transferred to the future bony tissues at the onset of their mineralisation (Sabodash, 1971). High concentrations have been found in the bones of various freshwater species (64–95 mg% : Nazarenko and Shutov, 1973). Gills of freshwater species have been reported to contain 13–16 mg%, perhaps linked to the high carbohydrase activity in which zinc is involved. Kidneys are quite rich in zinc (350–420 mg% of ash) perhaps because of their haematopoietic function. Liver contains more than muscle, a range quoted for the latter tissue being 0·2–15 mg% (many species).

Zinc is essential to fish—deficiency causes retardation of growth—but there is little quantitative information on requirements or regulatory mechanisms. At least one fish (*Morone saxatilis*) possesses a homeostatic mechanism for regulating the concentration in tissues, because very different concentrations of zinc in two diets have been shown to produce no detectable difference in the concentration of the metal in the fish.

The blood of elasmobranchs contains less than the blood of teleosts.

A diet of molluscs, which accumulate zinc, has been thought to account for high concentrations in some fish. Oysters downstream from a zinc smelting factory in Tasmania become as much as *ten percent* of zinc (dry weight basis). Such freaks are presumably best collected and then sold to a scrap metal merchant.

Bile 1533; Blastula 3718; Blood 1933, 2390, 3001, 3003, 3717; Bone 1533, 1534, 2281, 2786, 2850, 3001, 3004, 3017, 3115; Brain 3638; Brain + nerve cord 3003; Cartilage 3003; Dark muscle 2390, 2571, 2613; Egg 2001, 2390, 2941, 3155, 3156, 3718; Embryo 3638; Erythrocytes 2636; Fin 2786; Fry 2941, 3718; Fry + yolk 3718; Gall bladder + bile 2941; Gill 1533, 1622, 2390, 2786, 2850, 2941, 3001, 3003, 3017, 3115, 3638; "Gonad" 1622, 3003, 3638; Gut 2390, 3001, 3003; Heart 1622, 1890, 2328, 2390, 3001, 3003; Hepatopancreas 2328; Intestine 1890, 2328; Islet tissue 1804, 1904, 2703; Kidney 1533, 1622, 1890, 2040, 2328, 2390, 2941, 3001, 3003, 3115, 3638; Larva 3718; Liver 1533, 1534, 1561, 1622, 1890, 1904, 2040, 2268, 2328, 2390, 2611, 2850, 2941, 3001, 3003, 3004, 3018, 3115, 3638; Lung 1890; Muscle 1533, 1561, 1622, 1707–1709, 1763, 1793, 1884, 1893, 1904, 1929, 2040, 2390, 2491, 2571, 2613, 2677, 2786, 2828, 2829, 2850, 2886, 2901, 2941, 3001, 3003, 3004, 3017, 3019, 3115, 3294, 3402, 3467, 3638; Oocytes 3718; Ovary 1533, 2040, 2328, 2364, 3638; Pancreas 1890, 1904, 1929, 3610; Pyloric caecae 2390; Rectal gland 3003; Scales 1533, 1534, 2281, 2440, 2786, 3017; Skin 2786, 2941, 3001, 3003; Sperm 3155; Spermatic sac 2390; Spiral valve 3638; Spleen 1534, 1622, 1890, 2328, 2390, 3001, 3003, 3638; Stomach 1890, 3638; Superoxide dismutase 1494; Testis 1534, 2328, 2941, 3001; Uterus 3638; Yolk sac 3638

ZIRCONIUM
Scales 2440

PART 3   Index of Fish Names

In Volume 1 it was found necessary to correct very many of the Latin names of fish which had been misspelled in chemical papers. It was also thought desirable to give very brief notes on the geographical distribution of the fish, whether they came from fresh or salt water (or both), and whether they were teleosts, clasmobranchs or cyclostomes, such categories differing widely in their body chemistry. Notes on their favoured habitats were also provided, together with any special peculiarities such as the ability to breathe atmospheric air.

The system has been extended in the present volume to the greater number of species described, and it is now easier to recognise elasmobranchs, freshwater teleosts and saltwater teleosts by the use of different type faces. The diets of a number of species are also summarised, since these influence not only the lipid composition of the fish but also the contents of certain vitamins and the distribution of digestive enzymes in the gut. Giving the temperature ranges favoured by the fish, where I have been able to find them, should help those wishing to keep the fish alive in aquaria.

In addition to the reference works listed in Volume 1, the following books have been used for supplementary facts about the fish. Surprisingly little of the information has been contradictory, but in the few instances of disagreement the authors of the reference books are quoted by name.

Adler H. E. (1975). "Fish Behaviour. Why Fishes do what they do". T.F.H. Publications, Hong Kong.

Bailey, R. M., Fitch, J. E., Herald, E. S., Lachner, E. A., Lindsey, C. C., Robins, C. R. and Scott, W. B. (1970). "A List of Common and Scientific Names of Fishes from the United States and Canada" (3rd edition). American Fisheries Society, Spec. Publ. no. 6, Washington D.C.

Bardach, J. E., Ryther, J. H. and McLarney, W. O. (1972). "Aquaculture. The farming and Husbandry of Freshwater and Marine Organisms". Wiley-Interscience, New York.

Blanc, M., Banarescu, P., Gaudet, J.-L. and Hureau, J.-C. (1971). European inland water fish. A multilingual catalogue. Published for FAO by Fishing News (Books) Ltd., London.

Coutant, C. C. (1977). "Compilation of temperature preference data". *J. Fish. Res. Bd Can.* **34,** 739–745.

Davidson, A. (1975). "Fish and Fish Dishes of Laos". Imprimerie Nationale Vientiane, Laos.

Davidson, A. (1976). "Seafood of South-East Asia". Limited Edition published by the author at World's End, Chelsea (London).

Ehira, S. and Uchiyama, H. (1973). Formation of inosine and hypoxanthine in fish muscle during ice storage. *Bull. Tokai Reg. Fish Res. Lab.* **75**, 63–73.

Fischer, W. (Ed.) (1973). "FAO Species Identification Sheets for Fishery Purposes. Mediterranean and Black Sea". Volumes 1 and 2. FAO, Rome.

Fischer, W. and Whitehead, P. J. P. (Eds) (1974). "FAO Species Identification Sheets for Fishery Purposes. Eastern Indian Ocean (Fishing Area 57) and Western Central Pacific (Fishing Area 71)". Volumes 1–4. FAO, Rome.

Grant, E. M. (1972). "Guide to Fishes". Department of Primary Industries, Brisbane.

Hart, J. L. (1973). "Pacific Fishes of Canada". Bulletin no. 180, Fisheries Research Board of Canada, Ottawa. (This book gives meanings of the Latin and Greek names.)

Jhingran, V. G. (1975). "Fish and Fisheries of India". Hindustan Publishing Corporation (India), Delhi.

Legendre, V., Hunter, J. G. and McAllister, D. E. (1975). "French, English and Scientific Names of Marine Fishes of Arctic Canada". *Syllogeus* (7), 15 pp. National Museum of Natural Sciences, Ottawa.

Lythgoe, J. and Lythgoe, G. (1971). "Fishes of the Sea. The Coastal Waters of the British Isles, Northern Europe and the Mediterranean". Blandford Press, London.

Maitland, P. S. (1972). "Key to British Freshwater Fishes". Freshwater Biological Association, Scientific Publication no. 27, Ambleside.

Miller, D. J. and Lea, R. N. (1972). "Guide to the Coastal Marine Fishes of California". State of California, Department of Fish and Game.

Neve, P. and Al-Aiidi, H. (1972). Red Sea fish: check list no. 1. *Bull. mar. Res. Centre*, (2), Saudi Arabia.

Muus, B. J. and Dahlstrom, P. (1974). "Collins Guide to the Sea Fishes of Britain and North-western Europe". Translated by G. Vevers. Collins, London.

Muus, B. J. and Dahlstrom, P. (1971). "Collins Guide to the Freshwater Fishes of Britain and Europe" (Ed. A. Wheeler). Collins, London.

Schiotz, A. and Dahlstrom, P. (1972). "Collins Guide to Aquarium Fishes and Plants". Collins, London.

Scott, W. B. and Crossman, E. J. (1973). "Freshwater Fishes of Canada". Bulletin 184, Fisheries Research Board of Canada, Ottawa.

Wheeler, A. (1975). "Fishes of the World: an Illustrated Dictionary". (American consultant Editor T. H. Fraser). MacMillan, New York.

Most of the figures for temperature preference are taken from Coutant (1977).

All of the above books were used to re-check the fish species listed in Volume 1 as well as the additional species found only in the present volume. They have revealed that a number of species of fish were entered more than once in Volume 1 under different synonyms. These are now listed and brought under one heading, and as before I ask any readers finding further replications to let me know for the sake of any following volumes.

Chemical references sought under the names in the left-hand column will be found under the corresponding names in the right-hand column, with which they have been pooled.

Despite the number of books consulted, a considerable number of fish names in this section were not found, and so are given as spelt in the original papers in the hopes that they are correct. The geographical location is then given according to the continents in which the authors' laboratories occur.

In Volume 1, Appendix A, the classes and orders of fish were listed according to Starr Jordan's classification, so that the relationships of the different genera to each other could be seen. A more recent scheme which can be consulted is that of J. S. Nelson ("Fishes of the World", John Wiley and Sons, New York, London, Sydney and Toronto, 1976), who states, "No classification to date can claim to present the final truth."

Pneumatophorus colias	Scomber japonicus
Polistotrema stoutii	Eptatretus stoutii
Pomolobus pseudoharengus	Alosa pseudoharengus
Roccus americanus	Morone americana
Roccus saxatilis	Morone saxatilis
Scyllium canicula	Scyliorhinus canicula
Squalius cephalus	Leuciscus cephalus
Trygon pastinaca	Dasyatis pastinaca
Zeus japonicus	Zeus faber

Fish living exclusively in fresh water are shown in Italic script, thus: *Cyprinus carpio*.

Elasmobranchs (cartilaginous fish, the "shark" family) are shown in bold, thus: **Raja erinacea.**

Fish marked * are euryhaline and may spend part of their lives in fresh water, part in the sea.

The names of all bony marine fish *and of fish of which I have been unable to discover the nature* are shown in ordinary type, thus: Gadus morhua. The symbol ‡ immediately before the name of a fish shows that information about this species can also be found in Volume 1.

Figures following the name of a chemical substance are the numbers of papers in the bibliography, enabling the reader to find the original source. Figures in italics are references to page numbers in this volume, showing where a species has been mentioned in the text. Such information is of little practical help in the three or four species mentioned on virtually every page, but it is hoped that extra information can be gathered about the chemical biology of other individual species from these page references. If an obsolescent form of a name has been cited by an author, the text-page number is given by that name *and also* by the name in current use.

100 metres = 55 fathoms.

Abramis ballerus (Zope)
Central and E. Europe, River Volga, Sweden. Lower reaches of rivers and some lakes. Does not occur in brackish water. Overwinters in deeper water when it does not feed. Diet: zooplankton.
Calcium, Magnesium, Potassium, Sodium: 2864

Abramis blicca (Bream, White bream) *251*
Chloride, Potassium, Sodium: 1836, 2264

‡*Abramis brama* (Bream, Bronze bream, Carp bream) *9, 10, 147, 150, 213, 248, 387, 436*
Central, N. and E. Europe (not Iceland, Spain or N. Norway). Lakes, slow streams and brackish environments. Can live for some time out of water. Some populations from deep water are semi-anadromous. Diet: bottom-living invertebrates.
Aluminium 2677; Amino acids 1485; Biotin 3295; Cadmium 1972; Calcium 2677, 2864; Cobalt 1540, 2677; Copper 1533, 2677, 2829, 3564; Cyanocobalamin 3295; DNA 3203; Glycogen phosphorylase 2810; Inositol 3295; Iron 1533, 2677, 3564; Lactic dehydrogenase 3203; Magnesium 2677, 2864; Manganese 1533, 2677;

Mercury 2829; Niacin 3295; Pantothenic acid 3295; PABA 3295; 6-Phospho-gluconate dehydrogenase 3203; Phosphoglucose isomerase 3203; Potassium 2677, 2864; Pyridoxine 3295; Riboflavin 1465; RNA 3203; Selenium 2749; Sodium 2864; "Sugar" 2993; Thiamine 3295; Tin 2677; Vanadium 2677; Zinc 1533, 2677, 2829

‡*Abramis farenus*
Europe.
Volume 1 only

Abramis sapa (Danube bream)
Hungary, Roumania, Russia. Bottom-living, shoaling, mainly in rivers. Migratory in the Black Sea area, feeding in brackish water, spawning in rivers. Diet: mussels, shrimps.
Calcium, Magnesium, Potassium, Sodium: 2864

‡*Abramis vimba*
Europe: Danube basin, E. Baltic and tributaries. Keeps near the bottom.
Volume 1 only

Abudefduf saxatilis (Sergeant major)
World-wide in warm water, inshore on coral reefs and piers. Active swimmer.
DNA 2195; Succinic dehydrogenase 2750

‡Acanthistius serratus (Wirrah)
Seas of the southern hemisphere, Australia, on weedy foreshores of coasts and estuaries.
Volume 1 only

Acanthocephola limbata
Japan.
Trimethylamine oxide 2111

‡Acanthocybium solandri (Bastard mackerel, Jack mackerel, Kingfish, Mongrel mackerel, Pike mackerel, Wahoo)
Warmer parts of the Pacific. Australian coastal and Barrier Reef waters. A fast-swimming ocean species. Diet: fish, squid, cuttlefish.
Volume 1 only

Acanthodoras spinosissimus (Talking catfish)
Amazon Basin. Emits sounds which are amplified by the swim bladder.
DNA 2195

‡Acanthogobius flavimanus* (Genuine goby, Yellowfin goby) *294*
Japan, California. Estuarine, shallow bays.
Thiaminase 3473

Acanthopagrus butcheri (Black bream)
Australia.
Zinc 1893

‡Acanthopagrus schlegeli (Black Sea bream) *17*
    Japan.
    α-cryptoxanthin 2716; Cynthiaxanthin 2716; Diatoxanthin 2716; Dimethylamine
    2110; Formaldehyde 2110; Lutein 2716; Trimethylamine oxide 2111; Zeaxanthin
    2716

Acanthophthalmus kuhlii (Coolie loach)
    Indonesia, Thailand. Streams, living close to the bottom under weeds.
    DNA 2195

Acanthostracion quadricornis (Scrawled cowfish)
    Bermuda. Shores. Inactive.
    Succinic dehydrogenase 2750

‡Acanthurus bleekeri (Bleeker's lined surgeon-fish)
    Red Sea, India, Philippines, Java. Swims in schools near the shore. Diet: algae.
    Folic acid 2582

‡Acanthurus hepatus (Common surgeon, Doctor fish, Lancet fish)
    N. America: West Indies to Woods Hole.
    Volume 1 only

Acanthurus triostegus (Convict tang, Five-banded surgeonfish) *152*
    Whole of tropical Indo-Pacific, Galapagos Is., Marshall Is., Mexican coast.
    Around reefs and rocky areas, calm waters of lagoons. Diet: filamentous algae,
    coral.
    Carbonic anhydrase 3309

Acanthurus xanthopterus (Ringtailed surgeonfish) *339*
    Tropical. Great Barrier reef.
    Cytochromes, Fatty acids, Succinic dehydrogenase: 2296

Acentrogobius viridipunctatus (Green-spotted goby)
    Seas of India, common Bombay and Madras, on coastal reefs.
    Volume 1 only

Acheilognathus lanceolata
    Japan.
    Thiaminase 2297

Acheilognathus limbata
    Japan.
    Thiaminase 2294

‡Achoerodus gouldii (Blue groper, Giant pigfish)
    Southern half of Australian coast, along shores and reefs, in caverns and under
    rocky overhangs. Diet: molluscs, crustaceans.
    Volume 1 only

Acipenser baeri stenorrhynchus natio baicalensis (Baikal sturgeon)
    Lake Baikal (Russia).
    Calcium 2864; Magnesium 2864; Potassium 2864; Sodium 2466, 2864

‡Acipenser güldenstadti* (Russian sturgeon) *313*
    Rivers in Russia, Azov, Caspian and Black Seas; absent from Mediterranean.
    Poorly developed system for excreting ions, so adapts with difficulty to sea water of
    high salinity.
    Amino acids 2002; *free* amino acids 3326; GABA 3326; Calcium 2465, 2864–2866;
    Cerebrosides 2471; Corticosteroids 3460; Insulin 3052; Magnesium 2465, 2864–
    2866; Potassium 2465, 2864–2866; Sodium 2465, 2864–2866; Sulphatides 2471

‡Acipenser huso* (*see* Huso huso*)

Acipenser oxyrhynchus* (*see* A. sturio*) *37*

‡Acipenser ruthenus* (Sterlet)
    Danube basin, Black and Caspian Seas.
    Calcium 2864, 2865; Cerebrosides 2471; Magnesium 2864, 2865; Potassium 2864,
    2865; Sodium 2864, 2865; Sulphatides 2471

Acipenser sp. *2, 28*
    Fatty acids 2492; Phospholipid 2474

‡Acipenser stellatus* (Caspian sturgeon, Sevruga, Starred sturgeon)
    Rivers in Russia, Black, Azov and Caspian seas, occasionally Adriatic. Lives on the
    bottom, coming to the surface at night to feed.
    Amino acids 2002; Calcium 2465, 2864–2866; Cerebrosides 2471; Magnesium
    2465, 2864–2866; Potassium 2465, 2864–2866; Sodium 2465, 2864–2866; Sulpha-
    tides 2471

‡Acipenser sturio* = A. oxyrhynchus* (American Atlantic sturgeon, Sea sturgeon)
    Labrador to Gulf of Mexico, Norway to Mediterranean, Baltic and Black seas.
    Rivers. Winters in deep water with muddy bottom. Spends greater part of life in
    sea. Males outnumber females and are smaller. Diet: small fish eat algae, insect
    larvae, amphipods; larger fish eat molluscs, annelid worms and small fish.
    Amino acids 1405, Cortisol 2275, 3172; Cortisone 2275, 3172; 11-deoxycortico-
    sterone 2275; 11-deoxycortisol 2275; Fatty acids 1657, 2748, 3117; Testosterone
    2275, 3172

Acipenser transmontanus* (Pacific Coast sturgeon, White sturgeon)
    Northern California to Alaska. Anadromous but may spend most or even all of
    their lives in fresh water. Females grow faster than males. Diet: young feed on
    insect larvae, amphipods, mysids; adults on fish, crayfish, molluscs.
    Acid phosphatase 3526; Albumin 3525, 3526; Alkaline phosphatase 3525, 3526;
    Bicarbonate 3525, 3526; Calcium 3525, 3526; Chloride 3525, 3526; Citrate 3525,
    3526; DNA 2194; Globulin 3525, 3526; Magnesium 3525, 3526; Potassium 3525,
    3526; Sodium 3525, 3526; Sulphate 3525, 3526; Urea 3525, 3526

Aequidens portalegrensis
    DNA 2195

Agonus acipenserinus (Sturgeon poacher)
    Oregon to Alaska and both sides of Bering Sea. Swimming carried out largely by
    means of pectoral fins. Diet includes crustaceans and marine worms.
    D-Amino acid oxidase 1923; Calcium 3090; Chloride 3090; Magnesium 3090;
    Potassium 3090; Sodium 3090

Agonus cataphractus (Hooknose, Pogge) *312, 313*
    Estuarine waters around the British Isles, White Sea, Norwegian coast to Denmark.
    S. Iceland, Faroe, Channel. Soft bottoms, 5–200 m. Diet: small crustaceans.
    Free amino acids, Ammonia, Potassium, Sodium, Taurine: 1720, 3331

‡*Aila coila*
    India.
    Vitamin A_1, Vitamin A_2: 1500

Albula vulpes *242*

Alburnus alborella
    Europe.
    Amino acids 1655; Calcium 1528; Hydroxyproline 1655

Alburnus alburnus (Bleak)
    Europe. Lowland rivers. A gregarious shoaling fish. Diet: planktonic crustaceans,
    flying insects, larvae.
    Cadmium 1972; Cobalt 2850; Copper 2850; Iron 2850; Manganese 2850; Zinc 2850

Aldrovandia macrochir
    Atlantic and Indian oceans, S. Africa, 1100–3200 m. Possesses luminous organs.
    Mercury 3601

Alepisaurus ferox (Longnose lancet fish)
    Russia, Japan. Both pelagic and found below 1000 m.
    Fatty acids 2469, 3568

Alepocephalus sp. (Deepsea eel)
    Pacific Ocean, 1800 m.
    Diphosphatidyl glycerol, Fatty acids, Lysophosphatidyl choline, Phosphatidic acid,
    Phosphatidyl choline, Phosphatidyl ethanolamine, Phosphatidyl serine: 2987

Aleutera schoepfii
    DNA 2195

Allocyttus verrucosus (Oxeye oreo, Ore, Warty dory)
    S. Australia, S. Africa, Japan. Moderate depths down to 1646 m.
    Fatty acids, Fatty alcohols: 2780

Allolepis hollandi
    Japan.
    Fatty acids, Neutral lipids: 2153

‡Allomycterus jaculiferus
    Australia.
    Volume 1 only

Allothunnus fallai (Slender tuna) *142*
    Australia. Diet: zooplankton.
    Fatty acids, Triglycerides: 1546

‡**Alopias pelagicus** (Dog shark, Fox shark, Thresher, Whiptail shark). Perhaps same as **A. vulpinus.**
Trimethylamine oxide 3151

‡**Alopias profundus** (Thresher shark)
Japan.
Volume 1 only

Alopias vulpinus (Sea fox, Swivel tail, Thresher). Perhaps same as **A. pelagicus.**
Equatorial. S. Norway to S. Africa, Central and S. America, Japan to New Zealand. Migrates extensively just below surface of sea. Viviparous. Diet: pelagic shoaling fish, especially mackerel and herring, also squid.
Aluminium 3018, 3019; Amino acids 3019; *Free* amino acids 3019; Barium 3018; Bismuth 3018; Cholesterol 2572, 2768, 3019, 3020; Chromium 3018; Copper 3018, 3019; 7-dehydrocholesterol 2768; *Free* fatty acids 2572; Iron 3019; Lead 3019; Lithium 3018; Manganese 3018, 3019; Molybdenum 3018; Nickel 3018; Phospholipids 2572; Provitamin D 3019, 3020; Silver 3018; Sterol esters 2572; Strontium 3018; Tin 3018; Titanium 3018; Triglycerides 2572; Zinc 3018

Alosa chrysochloris (Skipjack herring)
Rivers of America. Avoids temperatures above 29°C or below 22°C.
DNA 2195

Alosa fallax (Twaite shad)
Europe.
Lactic dehydrogenase 1789

Alosa ficta
Europe.
Calcium 1528

Alosa kessleri pontica* *73, 75*
Black and Caspian seas, River Volga.
Aluminium, Cholesterol, Chromium, Cobalt, Copper, Gadolinium, Iron, Manganese, Nickel, Provitamin D, Silver, Titanium, Zinc: 2571

‡Alosa pseudoharengus* = Pomolobus pseudoharengus* (Alewife, Bang, Bigeye herring, Branch herring, Glut herring, Sawbelly, Walleye herring) *199, 240, 291, 343*
N. America: Newfoundland to N. Carolina. Landlocked in Great Lakes and "Finger" lakes of New York. Found in shallow waters in summer and autumn, deeper waters in winter and spring. Females bigger than males. Diet: plankton and young fish. Preferred temperature 19°.
Amino acids 1812; Calcium 3342, 3343; Chloride 1860; DNA 2195; Haematocrit 3343; Lactate 1843; Mercury 1953; Potassium 3342, 3343; Sodium 1860, 3342, 3343

Alosa sapidissima* (American shad)
N. America: Gulf of St. Lawrence to Florida. Introduced to Pacific coast, California to Alaska and Kamchatka. Coastal waters to 180 m. Coastal rivers. Spawns in

both fresh and brackish waters. Diet: small copepods and other crustaceans, fish. Avoids temperatures above 30°C.
Calcium 2540; Chloride 2540; DNA 2195; Glucose 2540; Lactate 2540; Magnesium 2540; Mercury 1953; Potassium 2540; Sodium 2540; "Sugar" 2063

‡Alosa sardina
Europe.
Volume 1 only

Ambloplites rupestris (Northern rock bass) *437*
Europe. Preferred temperatures range from 20·5 to 28·8°C according to different reference books.
Allantoinase 1775; Arginase 1776; Mutarotase 1480

‡*Amblypharyngodon mola*
India, Sri Lanka, Burma.
Erythrocytes, Leucocytes: 3408

Ameiurus catus
N. America.
Volume 1 only

‡*Ameiurus melas* (*see Ictalurus melas*)

‡*Ameiurus nebulosus* (*see Ictalurus nebulosus*)

‡*Amia calva* (Bowfin, Lawyer, Mudfish) *161, 265, 349*
N. America: Great Lakes to Florida. Swampy vegetated bays of warm lakes and sluggish streams. Uses accessory air-breathing, more at higher temperatures or during increased activity. Capable of aestivation. Males smaller than females. Mean preferred temperature 30·5°C, but a circadian rhythm of preferred temperatures, higher during the day than at night, has been discovered by Reynolds, Casterlin and Millington (1978).
Ammonia 3303; Angiotensinogen 2890; Bicarbonate 2262; Calcium 2108, 2262, 2263; Carbamyl phosphate synthetase 1777; Chloride 1957, 2262; Cholesterol 1441; Corticosterone 2275; Cortisol 2275; Creatin 3303; Creatinine 3303; Glucose 2250, 2262; Glycogen 1958, 2250; Haematocrit 2262; Lactate 2262; Magnesium 2262, 2263; Potassium 1957, 1958, 2108, 2262, 2263; Renin 2890; Sodium 1957, 1958, 2108, 2262, 2263; Urea 3303; Uric acid 3303

Ammodytes personatus *137*

Ammodytes sp.
Lactic dehydrogenase 1789

‡Ammodytes tobianus (Arctic sandlance, Lesser sandeel)
N. America: Southern California to Bering Sea. Newfoundland. W. Europe, including Iceland, south to Gibraltar. Sandy shores from mid-tide level down to 30 m. Shoals. Often buried in sand during day, active at night. Diet: zooplankton, worms, crustaceans and small fish.
Volume 1 only

Amphipnops cuchia (Mud eel) *276*

India. Found in ponds with abundant growth of water hyacinth. Must breathe air at regular intervals.
Chloride 1800; Erythrocytes 3288, 3408; Glucose 3288; Haematocrit 3288; Haemoglobin 3288; Leucocytes 1800; Sodium 1800; Vitamin A₁ 1500; Vitamin A₂ 1500; Vitamin C 3288

Amphiprion sebae *336*
Indian Ocean at temperatures from 23 to 27°C.

‡*Anabas scandens* = *A. testudineus* (Climbing perch, Walking fish)
India, Burma, Malaya, Philippines, China. Estuaries and fresh waters, canals, ditches, lakes and ponds. Air-breathing necessary because gills reduced in size. Aestivates. Diet: insects, water fleas, vegetable debris, fish.
Erythrocytes 3408; Glucose 3407; Lactate 3407; Leucocytes 3408; Vitamin C 1799

‡*Anabas testudineus* (*see A. scandens*)

‡Anago anago (Silvery conger)
Japan.
Volume 1 only

‡Anarhichas latifrons = A. denticulatus = Lycichthys denticulatus (Arctic wolf fish, Broad-headed catfish, Bull-headed catfish, Jelly cat) *46, 129* (photograph), *130*
Both sides of N. Atlantic, mostly north of the Arctic Circle. Found on soft bottoms, 300–1000 m. Females larger than males. Flesh is extremely soft, consisting of up to 95% water (see p. 130 for photomicrographs). Diet: hard-shelled invertebrates, esp. sea-urchins, brittle stars, molluscs.
Volume 1 only

‡Anarhichas lupus (Atlantic wolf fish, Catfish, Striped wolf fish) *46, 112, 207*
Both sides of Atlantic: Greenland, Spitzbergen, Murman coast, W. France; Davis Strait to New Jersey. Shallow, cool waters 100 to 300 m. Solitary, bottom-living. Males grow faster and mature later than females. Worn teeth replaced before the spawning season by new ones growing up from behind. Diet: hard-shelled invertebrates such as crabs, echinoderms, molluscs.
Amino acids 3672; Calcium 1909; Chitinase 1910; Chloride 1860, 1909; Cobalt 2491; Copper 2491; Fatty acids 2504; Hydroxyproline 3672; Iron 2491; Lysozyme 1910; Magnesium 1909; Manganese 2491; Mercury 1953; Potassium 1909; Sodium 1860, 1909; "Sugar" 2643; Zinc 2491

‡Anarhichas minor (Leopard fish, Lesser catfish, Spotted catfish, Spotted wolf fish) *46*
Both sides of Atlantic (further north than A. lupus). Grand Bank, Greenland, Spitzbergen, White Sea. Down to 460 m on muddy or fine-sandy bottoms. Males grow faster and mature later than females. Diet: hard-shelled invertebrates— echinoderms, crabs, molluscs.
Arsenic 1560; Zinc 3610

Anarrhichthys ocellatus (Wolf-eel)
D-Amino acid oxidase 1923

Anchovia delicatissima
DNA 2195

Anchoviella sp.
Lysophosphatidyl choline, Phosphatidic acids, Phosphatidyl choline, Phosphatidyl ethanolamine, Phosphatidyl inositol, Phosphatidyl serine, Phospholipid, Sphingomyelin: 2042

‡Anguilla anguilla* = A. vulgaris* (Eel) *2, 4, 6, 22, 23, 25, 41, 69, 72–74, 78, 79, 85, 91, 104, 120, 122, 166, 182, 186, 188, 209, 212, 213, 251, 252, 266, 272–274, 277, 284, 285, 287–289, 291–293, 295, 297, 299, 300, 302–304, 307, 310, 312–314, 316, 328, 330, 339, 365*
All Europe including Iceland, along coasts ascending rivers. Electrophoretic data seemed to show that this fish is the same species as the American eel, Anguilla rostrata, but according to Pantelouris, Arnason and Bumpus (1976) who studied variations in the liver esterase, there is so much variation in phenotype frequency in the two populations that such studies are unlikely on their own to resolve the question of whether one or two gene pools are involved.

Possesses a branchial chamber for air-breathing. The white muscle has high concentrations of carnosine in comparison with other teleosts (Partmann and Schlaszus, 1973). Catadromous, spawning in the Sargasso Sea, after which the adults die. Diet: a variety of small animals. Larger eels eat fish, ducklings and small mammals.

This species possesses a unique sequence of changes in the visual pigment system during its life cycle. Many other species possess both rhodopsin and porphyropsin, but this species exhibits a third as well, which appears during metamorphosis from yellow to mature silver forms, a golden-coloured rhodopsin known as "chrysopsin", characteristic of deep-sea fish.

When kept in water deficient in oxygen, Anguilla anguilla increase the proportion of haemoglobin having higher oxygen affinity in their blood.

As leptocephali, the youngest stage, their ionic composition approximates that of the sea water. As they grow, their osmoregulatory ability increases. Metamorphosis from yellow to silver forms causes no obvious changes in blood constituents, but the muscles become more aerobic and the fish uses up energy reserves, particularly 18:0 and 20:4 fatty acids. Adaptation of yellow eels to sea water involves an increase in the numbers of chloride cells in the gills as well as an increased amount of ATPase in each chloride cell. Silver eels transferred to sea water do not increase the number of chloride cells, but the ATPase level increases somewhat. These fish tolerate low oxygen concentrations and high concentrations of excretory products, so are easy to maintain in aquaria.

n-acetyl neuraminic acid 2548, 2932, 2933; Mg-ATPase 1575, 3182; Na-K-ATPase 1575, 3182, 3424, 3725; ATP 3597; Amino acids 1620; *Free* amino acids 2255, 2977; Anserine 2977; Arginase 2256; Argininosuccinate lyase 2256; Argininosuccinate synthetase 2256; Astaxanthin 1783; Bicarbonate 1576, 1916; Calcium 1528, 1921, 2176, 2514, 2933, 2934, 3294, 3360; Canthaxanthin 1783; Carbamoyl phosphate synthetase 2256; Carbon dioxide 1576; Carnosine 2255, 2977; β-Carotene 1783; Chloride 1575, 1576, 1802, 1916, 2431, 2432, 2514, 2517, 2518.

N-acetyl galactosamine 1467; *N*-acetyl neuraminic acid 1467; ATPase 2369; Alkaline phosphatase 2923; Amino acids 1467, 2444, 3669; *Free* amino acids 2290; Amylase 2840; Arsenic 3402; Calcium 2922; Carnosine 2689, 3368; Chloride 2201, 2920; Cholesterol 2445; Copper 3402; Cortisol 2196, 2203; Dimethylamine 2110; Erythrocytes 2905; Fatty acids 3671; Fructose 1,6 diphosphatase 2292, 2293; Fucose 2444; Galactose 2444; β-galactosidase 2840; Glucosamine 2444; Glucose 2291–2293; Glucose dehydrogenase 2836, 2837; Glucose-6-phosphatase 2838, 2839; Glucose-6-phosphate dehydrogenase 2837–2839, 3258; α-glucosidase 2840; β-glucosidase 2840; GOT 2291–2293; GPT 2291–2293; Glycogen 2157, 2291–2293; Haematocrit 2905; Haemoglobin 2905; Hexokinase 2836, 2838, 2839; Hyaluronidase 2436; Lead 3402; Manganese 3402; Mannose 2444; Mercury 3402; Phosphofructokinase 2292, 2293; Phosphoglucomutase 2838, 2839; 6-phosphogluconate dehydrogenase 2838; Phosphoglucose isomerase 2838, 2839; Potassium 2201, 2922; Renin 3317; Sialic acid 2444; Sodium 2199, 2201, 2920, 2922; Trimethylamine oxide 2111; Ubiquinone 2186; Vitamin D 3673; Vitamin E 2186; Zinc 3402

Anguilla rostrata* (American eel, Silver eel) *3, 159, 188, 212, 266, 274, 284, 291, 302, 303, 315, 409, 430*
W. Greenland, N. America: Labrador to West Indies. Harbours, estuaries, coastal marshes. May be the same as A. anguilla, but has fewer vertebrae. A voracious carnivore.
Mg-ATPase 2321; Na-K-ATPase 1642, 2321; ATP 1995; Albumin 3063; Angiotensinogen 2891; Arsenic 3638; Cadmium 3638; Calcium 1641, 3063, 3205; Chloride 1641, 2805, 3205; Cholesterol 1886, 3063; Copper 3638; Cortisol 1942; DNA 2195; Glucose 1640, 1886, 2560, 3063; Glycogen 1640, 1886, 2560; Guanosine triphosphate 1995; Haematocrit 1886, 3063; Haemoglobin 3063; Magnesium 1641, 3205; Mercury 1557, 1952, 3529, 3638; Pantothenic acid 3211; Potassium 1641, 1642, 2805, 3205; Pyridoxine 3211; Renin 2891; Sodium 1641, 1642, 1942, 2805, 3205; Urea 1886; Zinc 3638

Anisarchus medius (Stout eelblenny)
Alaska.
Calcium, Chloride, Magnesium, Potassium, Sodium: 3090

Anisotremus davidsoni (Grunt) *261*

‡Anisotremus interruptus (Mojarron)
Pacific coast of America: Magdalena Bay to Panama and the Galapagos Is.
Volume 1 only

‡Anodontostoma chacunda (Gizzard shad)
India, Thailand, Philippines, Java, Borneo to N. tip of Australia. Coastal waters, pelagic. Diet: detritus.
Folic acid 2582

Anoplarchus purpurascens *348*
Those from Alaska produce "antifreeze" compounds in their blood; those from California cannot do so.

Anoplogaster cornuta
  Russia. Shallow waters.
  Fatty acids 2469; Phosphatidyl choline 3064; Phosphatidyl ethanolamine 3064;
  Phosphatidyl inositol 3064; Phosphatidyl serine 2064; Phospholipid 3064; Poly-
  glycerophosphatides 3064; Sphingomyelin 3064

Anoplopoma fimbria (Black cod, Coalfish, Sablefish, Skil) *72, 75, 76, 121, 126, 253*
  S. California to Bering Sea and Japan. 366–1463 m. There are several separate
  stocks, but the fish tend to migrate. Moves into very deep water in winter months.
  Early stages are pelagic, adults somewhat sedentary on bottoms of firm mud or
  clay. Lacks a swim bladder, but the bones are filled with oil.
  Cholesterol 2538; DNA 2195; Dimethylamine 3439; Diphosphatidyl glycerol 3420;
  Fatty acids 2538; L-Fucose dehydrogenase 2769; Lysophosphatidyl choline 3420;
  Mercury 1697, 2099; Phosphatidic acid 3420; Phosphatidyl choline 3420;
  Phosphatidyl ethanolamine 3420; Phosphatidyl inositol 3420; Phosphatidyl serine
  3420; Phospholipids 2538; Sphingomyelin 3420; Triglycerides 2538; Trimethyl-
  amine 3439; Trimethylamine oxide 3439

‡*Anoptichthys jordani* (Blind cave fish, Blind tetra, Mexican cave characin) *264*
  Probably evolved from Astyanax mexicanus, but now unable to interbreed.
  Lateral line well developed, so the fish is well orientated in the total darkness where
  it lives.

Anostomus anostomus (Striped anostomus, Headstander)
  Guyana and Amazon basin. Swims in small shoals, or lives among dense vegetation
  in streams. Diet: worms and other small animals.
  DNA 2195

Antennarius ocellatus (Longlure frogfish)
  Tropical W. Atlantic, throughout the Caribbean. Glides slowly over the seabed.
  Diet: small fish and occasional crustaceans.
  DNA 2195

Antimora rostrata (Blue hake, Blue antimora, Flatnose codling) *34, 35, 261, 263, 437*
  Uruguay, Guadelupe Is., Mexico, Galapagos Is., Denmark to Gibraltar but absent
  from Mediterranean. A wide-ranging codlike fish inhabiting abyssal depths over
  much of the world: also seen in the Red Sea, Sea of Japan and Caribbean. Found
  at depths from 550–1800 m., but sometimes as deep as 2660 m. Females predominate in catches; large males uncommon. Diet: probably crustaceans and
  squid.
  Cholesterol 2538, 2990; Copper 1763; Diphosphatidyl glycerol 2987; 3420; Fatty
  acids 2538, 2987; *Free* fatty acids 2990; Glycolipids 2990; Iron 1763; Lactic
  dehydrogenase 1487; Lysolecithin 2990; Lysophosphatidyl choline 2987, 3420;
  Manganese 1763; Mercury 1496, 1763; Neutral lipid 2990; Phosphatidic acid
  2987, 3420; Phosphatidyl choline 2987, 2990, 3420; Phosphatidyl ethanolamine
  2987, 2990, 3420; Phosphatidyl inositol 2990, 3420; Phosphatidyl serine 2987,
  2990, 3420; Phospholipids 2538, 2990; Sphingomyelin 2987, 2990, 3420; Triglycerides 2538; Zinc 1763

Apeltes quadracus* (Fourspine stickleback, Pinfish)
Coastal waters of eastern N. America, Gulf of St. Lawrence to Virginia. Sometimes enters fresh water, but principally marine. Males build nests in which eggs are guarded.
DNA 2195

Aphanius dispar* *284*

Aphyocharax rubropinnis (Bloodfin)
Argentina (Paraná River). Swims in large, active shoals.
DNA 2195

Aphyosemion coeruleum
DNA 2195

Aplocheilus panchax (Blue panchax, Panchax)
India, S. E. Asia, Indonesia. Rivers, brackish pools in coastal waters, drains, ditches and pools connected to rivers. Hardy. Diet: mosquito larvae.
DNA 2195

‡*Aplodinotus grunniens* (Bubbler, Croaker, Freshwater drum, Sheepshead, Thunderpumper, White perch)
N. America: Great Lakes to Texas; California. Lakes and large streams, clear or turbid. Drumming sounds made by muscles connected to the swim bladder. Diet: bottom-living invertebrates, mostly molluscs. Preferred temperature ranges from 19·6 to 31°C according to different workers.
Allantoinase 1775; Amino acids 1812; Calcium 2264; Chloride 2264; Magnesium 2264; Potassium 2264; Sodium 2264; Thyroxine 2190

‡Apocryptes lanceolatus (Pointed-tailed goby)
India to Malaya. Coastal waters.
Volume 1 only

Apogon lineatus
Japan.
Trimethylamine oxide 2111

‡Apogon semilineatus (Bottom perch, Cardinal fish, Indian little fish)
S. E. Asia.
Pyridine nucleotide transhydrogenase 3167

‡**Aprionodon isodon** (Fine-tooth shark, Smooth-tooth shark)
Gulf of Mexico, Cuba, New York.
Volume 1 only

Apristurus macrorhynchus
Atlantic, Pacific and Indian Oceans. Deep waters.
Pristane, Squalene: 2403

Apteronotus albifrons (Tovira cavallo)
The Guyanas, Amazon, Orinoco, Rio Paraguay, Rio Parana. Diet: fish, crustaceans, insect larvae.
DNA 2195

Aptocyclus ventricosus
   Japan.
   Fatty acids, Neutral lipid: 2153

‡**Aptychotrema vincentiana**
   Australia.
   Volume 1 only

Aracana aurita (Striped cow fish)
   Australia.
   Cadmium, Copper, Manganese, Zinc: 1893

Arapaima gigas (Arapaima)
   Tropical S. America. A nest-builder. Swim bladder used as accessory respiratory
   organ. The largest freshwater fish in the world.
   DNA 2195

‡Archosargus probatocephalus (Sheepshead, Sheepshead porgy)
   America: Gulf of Mexico to Cape Cod.
   Ammonia 3303; Creatin 3303; Creatinine 3303; Erythrocytes 1647; Haematocrit
   1647; Haemoglobin 1647; Mutarotase 1480; Urea 3303; Uric acid 3303

‡Arctoscopus japonicus (Sandfish)
   Kamchatka to Japan and E. Korea. Coastal, buried in sand or mud at depths down
   to 150 m.
   Fatty acids 2153, 3666, 3667; Neutral lipid 2153

Areliscus joyneri
   Japan.
   Cadmium 2901; Copper 2901; Iron 2901; Lead 2901; Potassium 2900; Sodium
   2900; Zinc 2901

‡Argentina silus (Argentine, Greater silver smelt, Herring smelt)
   Both sides of N. Atlantic, 150–1000 m. Lives as a pelagic, shoaling fish. Diet: fish,
   euphausids and other pelagic crustacea.
   Amino acids 2663; Calcium 1909; Chloride 1909; Cholesterol 2515; Diamine
   oxidase 2231; Fatty acids 2663; *Free* fatty acids 2515; Glucose 2516; Haematocrit
   2516; Haemoglobin 2516; Lactate 2516; Magnesium 1909; Phosphatidyl choline
   2663; Phosphatidyl ethanolamine 2663; Phosphatidyl inositol 2663; Potassium
   1909; Sodium 1909; Sphingomyelin 2663

‡Argyreiosus brevoorti
   Lower California to Peru.
   Volume 1 only

Argyropelecus olfersi
   From deep water (c. 1000 m.)
   Phosphatidyl choline, Phosphatidyl ethanolamine, Phosphatidyl inositol, Phos-
   phatidyl serine, Polyglycerophosphatide, Sphingomyelin: 3064

‡Argyrops spinifer (Bowen snapper, Frying pan snapper, Long spined snapper, Spiny bream)
   East Africa to Japan and Australia. Reefs of Queensland, Red Sea. Inhabits a variety of sea-bottoms, 5–100 m. Diet: bottom-living invertebrates.
   Amino acids, Calcium, Iron, Niacin, Retinol, Riboflavin, Thiamine: 3690

‡Argyrosomus argentatus (White croaker)
   Japan. Muddy bottom of shore.
   Cadmium 2901; Caesium 2269; Calcium 3486; Cobalt 2269; Copper 2901; Iron 2901; Lead 2901; Potassium 2900; Sodium 2900; Strontium 3486; Thiaminase 3473; Trimethylamine oxide 2111; Zinc 2269, 2901

‡Argyrosomus regius (see Johnius regius)

Ariomma regulus
   World-wide in deep water of tropical seas.
   Amino acids 1812

Aristichthys nobilis (Bighead carp, Spotted silver carp)
   S. E. Asia. Fast-growing. Herbivorous.
   Adenosine diphosphate 2428; Adenosine monophosphate 2428; Adenosine triphosphate 2428; Amino acids 3468; Astaxanthin 1779; Canthaxanthin 1779; β-carotene 1779; Cholesterol 2495; Free fatty acids 2495; Isozeaxanthin 1779; Lutein 1779; Phospholipid 2495; Polyoxyxanthophyll 1779; RNA 3097; Taraxanthin 1779; Triglycerides 2495

‡Arius arius*
   India to China. Seas, estuaries and rivers.
   Volume 1 only

Arius dussumieri 68

Arius leiotetocephalus*
   Philippines, Java, Singapore, Malacca. Seas and estuaries.
   Volume 1 only

‡Arius manillensis (Manila sea catfish)
   Philippines.
   Folic acid 2582

‡Arius serratus (Catfish, Sawedged catfish)
   India: Sind.
   Volume 1 only

‡Arius sona* (Dusky catfish)
   India, Singapore. Seas, entering estuaries and tidal rivers.
   Volume 1 only

Arius sp. (Catfish)
   Amino acids 3092

Arius venosus (*see* Tachysurus venosus)

Arnoglossus laterna (Scaldfish)
Norwegian coast to Mediterranean and Morocco; absent from Black Sea. Shallow waters inshore on sandy bottoms, 10–60 m., occasionally over 200 m. Diet: small invertebrates.
Cadmium, Copper, Lead, Mercury, Zinc: 1707

Arnoldichthys spilopterus (Redeye characin)
Tropical W. Africa, Lagos to the Niger estuary. Favours 24 to 27°C.
DNA 2195

Arothron meleagris
Hawaii. Coral reefs.
Fatty acids, Phospholipids, Sterols, Triglycerides: 3031

‡Arripis georgianus (Ruff, Sea herring, Tommy rough)
Seas of Australia, New Zealand and neighbouring islands. Shallow, inshore waters, sometimes offshore.
Volume 1 only

‡Arripis trutta (Australian salmon, Salmon trout)
S. Australian coast. Inshore, especially near river mouths. Diet: crustaceans and small fish.
Copper, Zinc: 1893

Aseraggodes kobensis
Japan.
Trimethylamine oxide 2111

‡*Aspius aspius* (Asp)
Sweden and E. Europe to Russia. Rivers, lakes and brackish water. Diet: fish, sometimes frogs, ducklings.
Calcium 2864; Copper 3564; Fatty acids 2942; Iron 3564; Magnesium 2864; Potassium 2864; Selenium 2749; Sodium 2064

‡Astroconger myriaster (Common Japanese conger)
Japan, coastal.
Cholesterol 2445; NAD 3259; NADH 3259; Vitamin D 3673

‡*Astyanax mexicanus* (Mexican tetra)
N. and central America: Rio Balsas to tributaries of the Mississippi. Hardy, schooling.
Volume 1 only

‡Atheresthes evermanni (Japanese arrowtooth flounder)
Japan.
Fatty acids 2154

‡Atheresthes stomias (Arrowtooth flounder, Longjaw flounder, Turbot)
N. America: N. California to Bering Sea. Coastal, 18–900 m. Diet: fish and small crustaceans.
Mercury 1697

Atherina boyeri
Mediterranean, Black Sea.
Cadmium, Copper, Lead, Mercury, Zinc: 1709

Atherina hepsetus
E. Spain, France, Black Sea.
Cyanocobalamin 1522

Atherinops affinis (Topsmelt)
California to British Columbia. Females grow faster than males.
DNA 2195; Mercury 2751

‡Atherinopsis californiensis (California blue smelt, Jacksmelt)
California coast, bays.
Volume 1 only

‡Athlennes hians
Red Sea, India, Pacific, Japan, Atlantic: N. Carolina to Brazil.
Volume 1 only

Atopomycterus nichthemerus (Porcupine fish)
Australia
Cadmium, Copper, Manganese, Zinc: 1893

Atractosteus tristoechus
Cuba. Uses swim bladder as accessory respiratory organ.
Haematocrit, Haemoglobin: 3293

Atule mate (Longfish, Scad)
S. E. Asia. Occurs in large schools.
Folic acid 2582

‡Aulostomus maculatus (Trumpet fish)
America. Inactive.
Haematocrit, Haemoglobin: 3377

‡Austroglossus pectoralis (Agulhas sole)
S. Africa.
Volume 1 only

‡Auxis hira
Japan.
Volume 1 only

‡Auxis maru (*see* A. thazard)

‡Auxis rochei (*see* A. thazard; Fischer and Whitehead keep this as a separate species with the common name Bullet mackerel)

Auxis tapeinocephalus (Frigate mackerel)
   Japan.
   Free amino acids, Anserine, Carnosine, Creatin + creatinine, Taurine: 3369

‡Auxis tapeinosoma (*see* A. thazard)

‡Auxis thazard = A. rochei = A. tapeinosoma (Bullet mackerel, Frigate mackerel, Plain bonito)
   Warm parts of Atlantic, Indian and Pacific Oceans, also Mediterranean and occasionally around Britain. A schooling pelagic species that sometimes comes close inshore during the summer. Diet: fish, squid, crustaceans.
   α-Cryptoxanthin, Cynthiaxanthin, Diatoxanthin, *Free* histidine, Lutein, Tunaxanthin, Zeaxanthin: 2716

Babylonia japonica
   Japan.
   Cadmium, Copper, Manganese, Zinc: 1884

Bagarius bagarius 80
   India.
   Erythrocytes 3408; Glucose 3407; Lactate 3407; Leucocytes 3408

‡Bagre marinus (Gafftopsail, Sea catfish)
   N. America: Cape Cod to Panama. Fertilised eggs carried in the mouth of the male until they hatch. Makes noises with its swim bladder. Diet: Crabs, shrimps and fish.
   Arsenic 3638; Cadmium 3638; Copper 3638; DNA 2195; Mercury 3638; Zinc 3638

Bagrus docmac
   Nigeria, Ghana, Nile Basin, Great Lakes of Africa. Diet: adults are predatory, feeding on fish; young fish feed on insect larvae and crustaceans
   DNA 2195

Bairdiella chrysura
   N. Atlantic.
   Arsenic 3638; Cadmium 3638; Copper 3638; DNA 2195; Mercury 3638; Zinc 3638

Balantiocheilus melanopterus
   Thailand, Borneo, Sumatra. A hardy species.
   DNA 2195

‡Balistes capriscus = B. carolinensis (File fish, Grey triggerfish)
   Tropical Atlantic, both sides, south of Ireland and S. W. England; Mediterranean. Rocky or weedy areas near coasts. A feeble swimmer.
   Volume 1 only

‡Balistes hippocrepis
   Australia.
   Volume 1 only

Balistes vetula (Old wife, Queen triggerfish)
Tropical Atlantic. Common on reefs, also over sandy or sea-grass-covered areas from surface down to 46 m. Inactive. Diet: sea urchins and other invertebrates. Haematocrit, Haemoglobin: 3377

Barbus barbus (Common barbel) *38*
Rivers of the Carpathians, S. E. England, France to Russia. Prefers clear, rapid water in the middle reaches of rivers. Shelters in holes in the bank, in deep water, under stones etc. in winter. The roe is slightly poisonous to man. Diet: snails, mussels, worms, insects, sometimes plant debris.
Amino acids 1410; *Free* amino acids 1410; γ-Amino butyric acid (GABA) 1410; Ammonia 1410; Carotenoids 3264; DNA 3203; Lactic dehydrogenase 3203; Ornithine 1410; 6-Phosphogluconate dehydrogenase 3203; Phosphoglucose isomerase 3203; RNA 3203; Taurine 1410; Urea 1410

‡*Barbus carnaticus* (Carnatic carp)
India. Rivers in Madras and west coast. Diet: algae, leaves of aquatic plants, detritus, insects.
Volume 1 only

‡*Barbus chrysopoma* = *B. sarana* (Olive barb)
India: coasts of Deccan, Madras and Darjeeling. Streams, rivers, ponds, lakes.
Acid phosphatase, Alkaline phosphatase: 3227

Barbus conchonius (Rosy barb)
N. India, Bengal, Assam. Hardy: survives low water temperatures.
DNA 2195

‡*Barbus dubius*
India: Bowany River in Madras. Diet: dipteran larvae, corixid bugs, crustaceans, detritus, mud.
Volume 1 only

Barbus everetti (Clown barb)
Borneo, Sarawak.
DNA 2195

‡*Barbus fluviatilis*
Europe.
Glycogen phosphorylase 2810

‡*Barbus hexagonolepis*
India. Lower reaches of foothill rivers. Diet: fallen leaves, fruits, plant matter with some animal matter.
Volume 1 only

Barbus holubi = *B. capensis* (Clanwilliam yellowfish, Smallmouth yellowfish, Yellow-fish) *44*
S. Africa. Diet: invertebrates such as insect larvae, crustaceans, molluscs. Larger specimens may eat fish.
Carbon dioxide 2144; Erythrocytes 2141, 3566; Haematocrit 2141, 3566; Haemoglobin 2141, 3566; Leucocytes 3566; Oxygen 2144

Barbus kimberleyensis
  S. Africa.
  Carbon dioxide, Oxygen: 2144

‡*Barbus kolus*
  India: Deccan, Kistna River.
  Volume 1 only

Barbus meridionalis petenyi (Black barbel, Mountain barbel)
  Russia.
  Cobalt, Copper, Iron, Manganese, Zinc: 2850

‡*Barbus puntius*
  Bengal, Burma.
  Volume 1 only

‡*Barbus putitora* (Putitor mahseer)
  India.
  Volume 1 only

Barbus sachsi
  DNA 2195

‡*Barbus sarana* (*see B. chrysopoma*)

Barbus schwanenfeldi (Schwanenfeld's barb)
  Sumatra, Borneo, Malay peninsula, Thailand. Omnivorous. Sluggish.
  DNA 2195

‡*Barbus stigma*
  India, Burma.
  Acid phosphatase 3226, 3227; Alkaline phosphatase 3226, 3227; Cholesterol 3267,
  3268; DNA 2315; RNA 2315

Barbus tetrazona (Sumatra barb, Tiger barb)
  Sumatra, Borneo. Hardy. Swims in schools. Rather aggressive.
  DNA 2195

Barbus titteya (Cherry barb)
  Sri Lanka. Shady streams, rills of foothill streams. Diet: algae.
  DNA 2195

‡*Barbus tor*
  India. Rapids, hill streams.
  Volume 1 only

Bathygadus vaillanti
  Europe. These specimens caught at 1000 m.
  Cardiolipid 2469; Fatty acids 2469; Phosphatidyl choline 2469, 3064; Phosphatidyl
  ethanolamine 2469, 3064; Phosphatidyl inositol 2469, 3064; Phosphatidyl serine
  2469, 3064; Polyglycerophosphatide 3064; Sphingomyelin 2469, 3064

Bathysaurus agazzizi
  America. Deep ocean waters.
  Mercury 1496

Bdellostoma cirrhatum (*see* Eptatretus cirrhatum)

‡Belone belone (Garfish, Garpike)
  All Europe, Mediterranean and Black Seas. Oceanic near surface, also inshore.
  Vertebral bones are green-coloured. Excellent swimmers: can leap into the air,
  Diet: crustaceans, herrings, sprats, sand-eels.
  Volume 1 only

‡*Belonesox belizanus* (Pike topminnow)
  S. Mexico, Honduras, Guatemala. Muddy waters, river backwaters, marshes and
  lakes. Predatory. Viviparous.
  Volume 1 only

Benthophilus macrocephalus
  Volga, Caspian Sea.
  Calcium, Magnesium, Potassium, Sodium: 2864

‡Beryx splendens (Alfoncino)
  Japan, American coast; probably worldwide. Lives among rocks, 183–732 m.
  Astaxanthin diester 3466; Creatin 2855; Creatinine 2855

Betta splendens (Siamese fighting fish) *58, 59*
  Malay peninsula, Thailand. Standing or slow-moving waters. Combative. Can
  breathe air at surface with accessory breathing organs. Diet: small crustaceans,
  mosquito larvae.
  DNA 2195

Blennius fluviatilis
  Glucose, Sodium: 2804

‡Blennius pavo (Peacock blenny)
  Mediterranean. Very shallow water, usually on mud and sand near rocks. Very
  tolerant of extremes of temperature and salinity.
  Glucose, Sodium: 2804

Blennius pholis (Shanny) *137, 162, 169, 326*
  Shetland and S. Norway to S. Spain. Rocky coasts, rock pools.

‡Blennius sanguinolentus (Redspeckled blenny)
  Mediterranean and N. E. Atlantic from Senegal to English Channel. Black Sea,
  Shallow water amongst rocks. Voracious carnivores.
  Cyanocobalamin 1522

Blennius sphinx
  Glucose, Sodium: 2804

‡Blepsias draciscus
Volume 1 only

Blicca bjoerkna (White bream)
All central Europe, Volga, E. England; not Italy, Spain or Norway. Shallow warm lowland lakes with dense vegetation; lower reaches of rivers. Prefers deeper water in winter. Females larger than males. Diet: insect larvae, small snails, worms.
Cadmium 1972; Calcium 2864; Copper 2829; Magnesium 2864; Mercury 2829; Potassium 2864; Sodium 2864; Zinc 2829

‡Boleophthalmus boddaertii* (Mud hopper)
India, coast of Burma to Malaya. Chiefly in brackish water, sometimes in fresh water; occasionally out of water altogether.
Volume 1 only

Boleophthalmus pectinirostris
Japan.
Fructose, Galactose, Glucose, Xylose: 3685

‡Boops boops — Box boops (Bogue) *152*
South from Sweden and S. Ireland to Mediterranean and Canary Islands. Shallow water amongst rocks, down to 100 m. Diet: seaweeds, sponges, small crustaceans.
Free amino acids 3140; Cadmium 1707, 1709; Copper 1707, 1709; Lead 1707, 1709; Mercury 1707, 1709; Zinc 1707, 1709

Boops salpa (Salema) *152*
Mediterranean, Black Sea, Biscay to S. Africa. Lives in schools over rocky bottoms covered with seaweed and in vegetated areas in the littoral zone. Diet: mainly seaweeds.
Cadmium 1709; Chitinase 1719; Copper 1708, 1709; Lead 1708, 1709; Mercury 1708, 1709; Zinc 1708, 1709

‡Boreogadus saida* (Arctic cod, Polar cod) *397, 400, 466*
Circumpolar, observed further north than any other species. Found down to 730 m. Pelagic, usually at temperatures below 5°C. Tolerates brackish water. Supercools at —1·7°C (not resistant to freezing). Diet: planktonic organisms.
Arsenic, Cadmium, Copper, Iron, Zinc: 1561

Bothrocara mollis
Japan.
Fatty acids, Neutral lipid: 2153

‡Box boops (*see* Boops boops)

Brachydanio rerio (Zebra fish) *73, 74, 77, 78*
India. Tolerates wide temperature range, but needs 24°C for spawning.
DNA 2195

Brama raii (Bream)
Cholesterol 1785

‡Branchiostegus japonicus (Red tilefish)
    S. Japan, Korea, in waters down to 146 m.
    Cadmium 2901; Cholesterol 2445; Copper 2901; Iron 2901; Lead 2901; Potassium
    2900; Sodium 2900; Vitamin D 3673; Zinc 2901

‡**Breviraja isotrachys**
    Japan.
    Volume 1 only

Breviraja semirnovi
    Japan.
    Trimethylamine oxide 2111

‡Brevoortia patronis (Gulf menhaden)
    Gulf of Mexico, coast of Texas. Avoids temperatures above 30°C.
    Volume 1 only

‡Brevoortia tyrannus (Menhaden, Mossbunker, Pogy) *108*
    N. America: Nova Scotia to Florida. Large shoals near the shore. Very oily flesh.
    Diet: microscopic organisms, especially diatoms in the plankton.
    Erythrocytes 1647; Haematocrit 1647; Haemoglobin 1647; Mercury 1715, 1953;
    "Sugar" 1818, 2062, 2063

‡Brosme brosme (Cusk, Torsk, Tusk)
    Both sides of Atlantic, Iceland and Greenland, N. Norway to Ireland. Found on
    hard bottoms, 70–1000 m. Solitary. Diet: fish and large crustaceans.
    Diamine oxidase 2231; FREE fatty acids 1671; Formaldehyde 1671; Mercury
    1953, 2482

Brotulides emmeles
    Caught at about 1000 m.
    Phosphatidyl choline, Phosphatidyl ethanolamine, Phosphatidyl inositol, Phos-
    phatidyl serine, Phospholipid, Polyglycerophosphatide, Sphingomyelin: 3064

Buglossidium luteum (Solenette)
    S. Norway, Denmark, British Isles, N. Africa, Mediterranean. Coastal on shallow,
    sandy bottoms, 5–37 m. Diet: small worms and crustaceans.
    Lactic dehydrogenase 1789

‡Caesio chrysozona (Golden-banded fusilier, Golden caesio, Yellow-striped caesio)
    Red Sea, Indian Ocean, Philippines, Japan, Formosa, Solomon Is. Shallow waters;
    rocky and coral reef areas. Diet: small invertebrates.
    Folic acid 2582

‡Caesio cuning
    India, Thailand, Sumatra, Philippines, Okinawa, N. Australia. Solomon Is.
    Volume 1 only

Calamoichthys calabaricus
    DNA 2194

‡Calamus calamus (Saucereye porgy)
   West Indies north to Florida keys.
   DNA 2195

Calamus penna
   Russia.
   Cardiolipid 2469; Cerebroside 2469; Fatty acids 2469; Ganglioside 2469; Phosphatidyl choline 2469; Phosphatidyl ethanolamine 2469; Phosphatidyl inositol
   2469; Phosphatidyl serine 2469; Sialic acid 2470; Sphingomyelin 2469; Sulphatides
   2469

Calamus pennatula
   America. Inactive.
   Haematocrit, Haemoglobin: 3377

Calamus proridens
   America. Inactive.
   Haematocrit, Haemoglobin: 3377

Calamus sp.
   Russia.
   Cardiolipid 2469; Cerebroside 2469, 2470; Fatty acids 2469; Phosphatidyl choline
   2469; Phosphatidyl ethanolamine 2469; Phosphatidyl inositol 2469; Phosphatidyl
   serine 2469; Sphingomyelin 2469; Sulphatides 2469, 2470

‡*Callichrous bimaculatus* (Butter catfish)
   India to Indonesia.
   Volume 1 only

Callichthys callichthys (Cascarudo)
   Tropical S. America: Guyanas to Paraguay and Uruguay. An armoured catfish
   which deposits eggs in a bubble-nest. The thin-walled stomach serves as an
   accessory respiratory organ.
   DNA 2195

Callionymus beniteguri
   Japan.
   Trimethylamine oxide 2111

‡Callionymus lyra (Dragonet)
   Mid-Norway and Iceland southwards to Mediterranean, W. Baltic. Found on
   grounds with a sandy bottom, shallow to 400 m or more. Skin slimy and scale-less.
   Diet: small crustaceans, worms and molluscs.
   Lactic dehydrogenase 1789

Callionymus punctatus
   Astacene, β-Carotene, Cynthiaxanthin, Diatoxanthin, Lutein, Tunaxanthin,
   Zeaxanthin: 2716

Callorhynchus callorhynchus (Ghost shark)
   Japan.
   Caesium, Cobalt, Zinc: 2269

Callorhynchus capensis—a holocephalan, not a true elasmobranch (Elephant shark, Joseph, Josup)
S. Africa. Shallow waters. Produces a large egg-case.
Chloride, Urea: 2165

Callorhynchus millii (Elephant shark, Ghost shark)
Australia, New Zealand. Down to 55 m.
Copper, Zinc: 1893

Callyodon ovifrons (Parrot fish)
Japan.
Amino acids (in biliverdin) 3669

‡Cambarus clarkii
Volume 1 only

Campostoma anomalum (Stoneroller)
N. America. Freshwater streams at high altitude. The intestine is wound around the swim bladder. Avoids temperatures above 24°C.
Mercury 2252

‡Cantherines unicornu
Japan.
Volume 1 only

Canthigaster rivulatus
Japan.
Pyridine nucleotide transhydrogenase 3167

‡*Caprinus aoratus*
Japan.
Volume 1 only

‡Carangoides ajax
Hawaii.
Volume 1 only

‡Caranx angolensis
Portugal.
Volume 1 only

‡Caranx crumenophthalmus (*see* Selar crumenophthalmus)

‡Caranx delicatissimus (Striped jack)
Japan, along shores.
Volume 1 only

‡Caranx djedaba
Tanzania, Red Sea, Madagascar, India, Thailand, Formosa, Philippines.
Volume 1 only

‡Caranx equula (Kingfish)
  Japan, Formosa. Shores.
  Trimethylamine oxide 2111

‡Caranx hippos (*see* C. sexfasciatus)

Caranx ignobilis *79, 242*

‡Caranx kalla (Golden scad)
  Red Sea, India, Malaya, Philippines, Java, N. Australia, Solomon Is. Coastal
  waters and trawling grounds.
  Volume 1 only

Caranx latus (*see* C. sexfasciatus)

‡Caranx leptolepis (Slender-scaled scad, Yellowstripe trevally)
  Seas of India to Malaya and Australia. Coastal waters, pearl banks, trawling
  grounds.
  Volume 1 only

‡Caranx mertensii
  Japan.
  Volume 1 only

Caranx ruber
  America. Inactive.
  Haematocrit, Haemoglobin: 3377

‡Caranx sexfasciatus* = C. hippos* = C. latus* (Banded cavalla, Crevalle Jack,
  Dusky Jack, Great trevally, Horseye jack, Horse mackerel, Jurel, Six-banded
  trevally, Turrum *79*
  Red Sea, India, China, Japan, Philippines, Australia, both coasts of the Americas.
  Warm seas, sandy bays, brackish waters, entering rivers. Coral and rocky reefs.
  Diet: crustaceans and fish.
  DNA 2195; Folic acid 2582; Succinic dehydrogenase 2750

Caranx stellatus *70*

†*Carassius auratus* (Crucian carp, Golden carp, Goldfish, Johnny carp) *11, 18, 29, 34,*
  35, 37, 41, 45, 79, 88, 89, 100, 102, 115, 140, 144, 145, 149, 157, 160, 166, 168, 171,
  191, 231–233, 235, 236, 238, 240, 242, 259, 264, 268, 272, 274, 280, 281, 284, 285,
  301, 302, 314, 320–324, 326–337, 340, 343, 383, 398, 403, 434, 435, 447, 456,
  459, 464
  China originally, but introduced widely elsewhere. Rich weedy lakes and canals.
  More active by day than by night. Hybridizes readily with *Cyprinus carpio*. Tolerates
  low oxygen concentrations and high temperatures. Preferred temperature ranges
  from 24°C to 30°C according to different workers.
  Acetate 3419; *N*-acetyl histidine 1504; Acid phosphatase 2532; Adenosine
  diphosphate 1951, 3419; Adenosine monophosphate 1951, 3419; Mg-ATPase 2343,
  2821; Na-K-ATPase 2821; Adenosine triphosphate 1951, 3419; Adrenocorticotropic hormone 3290, 3291; Alanine 3419; Aldehyde oxidase 2468; Aldosterone

1688; Alk-l-enylacylglycerophosphatidyl choline 1850; Alk-l-enylacylglycerophosphatidyl ethanolamine 1850; Alk-l-enyl ethers 1850; *Free* amino acids 2553; γ-Amino butyric acid 2553; Ammonia 2553, 3303; Androgens 3208; Arginase 2256; Argininosuccinate synthetase 2256; Arsenic 2611; Astaxanthin 2132; Bicarbonate 3419; Bromide 2611; Cadmium 1716, 2611; Calcium 1716, 2057, 2656; Canthaxanthin 2132; Carbamoyl phosphate synthetase 2256; Carbonic anhydrase 2764; β-Carotene 2132; Cerebrosides 3222; Chloride 1674, 2057, 2639, 2656, 3090, 3505, 3509, 3517, 3711; Cholesterol 2055, 2765, 3222; Choline phosphotransferase 2551; Choline plasmalogen 3222; Citrate 1951; Cobalt 2611; Copper 2611; Corticosteroids 1963; Corticosterone 1688; Cortisol 1688, 2122, 2742, 3068, 3289, 3290, 3334; Cortisone 1688; Creatin 3303, 3419; Creatin phosphate 3419; Creatinine 3303; 11-deoxycorticosterone 1688; DNA 2195, 2998; Diacylglycerophosphatidyl choline 1850; Diacylglycerophosphatidyl ethanolamine 1850; Ethanolamine plasmalogen 3222; *Free* fatty acids 2765–2767; Fructose 1,6 diphosphate 1951; Fructose-6-phosphate 1951; Glucose 1607, 1687, 1689, 1951, 2742, 2766, 3234, 3505, 3509, 3517, 3696; Glucose-6-phosphatase 1523; Glucose-6-phosphate 1951; Glutamate 3419; Glycogen 1523, 1607, 1792, 2966; Glycogen phosphorylase 1523; Gonadotropin 2020; Haematocrit 2057; Haemoglobin 2247; Histamine 3662; 17α-Hydroxyprogesterone 1688; Inosine monophosphate 3419; 4-Keto 4'-hydroxy β carotene 2132; Lactate 2742, 3419; Lutein 2132; Magnesium 1716, 1951, 2057; Oestrogens 3208; Ornithine 2553; Phosphatidic acid 2551, 3222; Phosphatidyl choline 2551, 3222; Phosphatidyl ethanolamine 2551, 3222; Phospholipid 2765, 3222; Phosphorylase 1524; Potassium 1674, 1716, 2057, 2639, 3090, 3505, 3584, 3711; Progesterone 1688; Prolactin 2532; Propionate 3419; Pyruvate 1951; Sodium 1674, 1716, 2057, 2500, 2639, 2656, 3090, 3505, 3509, 3517, 3584, 3711; Sperm (in semen) 2057; Sphingomyelin 2551; Succinic dehydrogenase 2166; "Sugar" 1686, 2916; Sulphatides 3222; Taurine 2553; Thiaminase 2297; Thorium 2611; Thyroxine 2266; Trimethylamine oxide 2111, 2129; Triose phosphate 1951; Uranium 2611; Urea 3303; Uric acid 3303; Vitamin A_1 2137; Vitamin A_2 2137; Vitamin D 3673; Xanthine oxidase 2468; Zeaxanthin 2132; Zinc 2611

‡*Carassius auratus braziliensis*
Brazil.
Volume 1 only

‡*Carassius auratus gibelio* (Gibel, Gibellian, Silver crucian carp) *273*
Japan. Has no anatomic stomach and no discrete pancreas.
Cobalt 2850; Copper 2850; Iron 2850; Manganese 2850; Protease 2325; Trypsin 2325; Zinc 2850

‡*Carassius carassius* (Crucian carp, Golden carp, Prussian carp) *27, 78, 79, 83, 84, 87, 89, 93–95, 101, 149, 266, 271, 280, 437, 449*
Japan and Far East, introduced elsewhere. Still waters, slowly-flowing rivers and marshes. Tolerates low oxygen concentrations and low temperatures. May be able to live completely anaerobically.
L-adenine 2342; Aluminium 2677; Amylase 2840; Calcium 2677; Cobalt 1540, 2677; Copper 2677; Creatin 2348; Fatty acids 3666, 3667; β-Galactosidase 2840; Glucose 2342, 2699; β-Glucosidase 2840; Glycogen 2342, 2348, 2699; Iron 2677; Lactate 2342, 2348; Magnesium 2677; Magnanese 2677; Potassium 2677; Pyruvate 2342; Succinate 2342; Tin 2677; Vanadium 2677; Zinc 2677

Carassius cuvieri (Crucian carp) *425*
Japan.
Glucose-6-phosphate dehydrogenase 3258

Carcharhinus acronatus
DNA 2194

‡**Carcharhinus albimarginatus** (Reef whitetip shark)
Tropical Indian and Pacific Oceans, Red Sea. Reefs, atolls. Diet: fish, squid.
Volume 1 only

‡**Carcharhinus brachyurus**
Volume 1 only

Carcharhinus carcharias
Trimethylamine oxide 3151

Carcharhinus falciformis (Silky shark)
N. Atlantic.
Arsenic 3638; Cadmium 3638; Copper 3638; Mercury 3638; Trimethylamine
oxide 3151; Zinc 3638

‡**Carcharhinus gangeticus*** (*see* **C. leucas**)

‡**Carcharhinus glaucus** (*see* **Prionace glauca**)

‡**Carcharhinus japonicus**
Japan.
Volume 1 only

‡**Carcharhinus leucas*** = **C. gangeticus*** (Bull shark, Cub shark, Ground shark)
20, 311
India, Japan, W. Atlantic from N. Carolina to Brazil. N. Peru to S. California,
including Lake Nicaragua which is a freshwater lake. In fresh water the concentration of serum urea is reduced (Thorson, Cowan and Watson, 1973). Slow-swimming,
viviparous. Diet: fish, squid. A scavenger.
Acid phosphatase 3525; Albumin 3523; Alkaline phosphatase 3523; 3525;
Ammonia 3431; Bicarbonate 3430, 3525; Calcium 3430, 3431, 3523, 3525;
Chloride 3430, 3431, 3525; Globulin 3523; Haematocrit 3430; Magnesium 3427,
3430, 3431, 3525; Potassium 3430, 3431, 3525; Sodium 3430, 3431, 3525; Sulphate
3525; Trimethylamine oxide 3430; Urea 3430, 3431, 3525.
Fish taken from Lake Nicaragua, when they have been called **Carcharhinus
leucas nicaraguensis,** have been submitted to chemical analysis as follows:
Acid phosphatase 3525; Albumin 3523; Alkaline phosphatase 3523, 3525;
Bicarbonate 3427, 3525; Calcium 3427, 3523, 3525; Chloride 3427, 3525; Globulin
3523; Magnesium 3427, 3525; Potassium 3427, 3525; Sodium 3427, 3525; Sulphate
3427, 3525; Urea 3427, 3525

‡**Carcharhinus limbatus** (Small black-tipped shark, Spotfin ground shark) *322*
Possibly world-wide in tropical and subtropical waters. In W. Atlantic found
from N. Carolina to Brazil near the shore. Active, fast-swimming, viviparous.
DNA 2194; Methyltransferase 1625

‡**Carcharhinus longimanus** (Long-winged shark, Whitetip shark)
All warm seas, usually offshore. Diet: tuna and other fish. Viviparous. Given as
Pterolamiops longimanus in reference 3018.
Aluminium 3018, 3019; Amino acids 3019; *Free* amino acids 3019; Anserine
3368; Balenine 3368; Barium 3018; Bismuth 3018; Carnosine 3368; Cerebroside
2469, 2470; Cholesterol 2572, 2768, 3019, 3020; Chromium 3018; Cobalt 3019;
Copper 3018, 3019; 7-Dehydrocholesterol 2768; Fatty acids 2469, 2904; *Free*
fatty acids 2572; Ganglioside 2469; Iron 3019; Lead 3018, 3019; Manganese 3018,
3019; Nickel 3018, 3019; 11-Oxycorticosteroid 2905; Phosphatidyl choline 2469;
Phosphatidyl ethanolamine 2469; Phosphatidyl inositol 2469; Phosphatidyl serine
2469; Phospholipids 2572; Provitamin D 3019, 3020; Sialic acid 2470; Silver 3018,
3019; Sterol esters 2572; Strontium 3018; Sulphatides 2469, 2470; Tin 3018, 3019;
Titanium 3018, 3019; Triglycerides 2572; Zinc 3018, 3019

‡**Carcharhinus mackiei**
Australia.
Volume 1 only

‡**Carcharhinus maculipinnis** (Black-tipped shark, Spinner shark)
N. America.
Creatin, Creatinine 2855

‡**Carcharhinus melanopterus** FRESHWATER ELASMOBRANCH.
Thailand, Malaya (Perak).
Fatty acids 1449

Carcharhinus menisorrah
Red Sea.
Fatty acids 1449

‡**Carcharhinus milberti** (Brown shark, Sandbar shark)
Both sides of Atlantic. Mediterranean. Inshore. Viviparous.
2'3' *cyclic* adenosine monophosphate 3' phosphoester hydrolase 3450; Arsenic 3638;
Cadmium 3638; Cholesterol 2572; Copper 3638; *Free* fatty acids 2572; Mercury
3638; Phospholipids 2575; Sterol esters 2572; Triglycerides 2572; Zinc 3638

‡**Carcharhinus obscurus** (Dusky shark) *322*
Pacific Ocean. Western Atlantic from George's Bank to Brazil. Eastern Atlantic
in warm waters, inshore and offshore. Active. Diet: fish.
Acid mucopolysaccharides 3344; Arginine 1653; Arsenic 3638; Cadmium 3638;
Chondroitin sulphate 3344; Copper 3638; Heparitin sulphate 3344; Hyaluronic
acid 3344; Mercury 3638; Zinc 3638

Carcharhinus plumbeus
S. Atlantic.
Cholesterol, 7-dehydrocholesterol: 2768

‡**Carcharias aethalorus**
  N. America.
  Volume 1 only

‡**Carcharias arenarius** (Grey nurse)
  Australia: S. Queensland to S. Australia and Tasmania. Viviparous.
  Volume 1 only

‡**Carcharias brachyurus**
  Japan.
  Volume 1 only

‡**Carcharias ellioti** (Elliot's grey shark)
  India.
  Volume 1 only

‡**Carcharias littoralis**
  Volume 1 only

‡**Carcharias menisaurah**
  India.
  Volume 1 only

Carcharias taurus (Sand shark)
  Both sides of Atlantic: Gulf of Maine to Florida and S. Brazil; Mediterranean,
  W. Africa. Sluggish, living close to sea bottom. Viviparous. Diet: a variety of fish,
  squid, crabs, lobsters.
  Mutarotase 1480

Careproctus segaliensis
  Japan.
  Fatty acids, Neutral lipids: 2153

Carnegiella strigata (Marbled hatchet fish)
  At surface of small forest pools in Amazon and Guyanas region.
  DNA 2195

Carpiodes carpio (River carpsucker)
  Central regions of United States, particularly large, silted rivers. Avoids temper-
  atures above 34·5°C or below 26°C.
  Allantoicase 1775; Allantoinase 1775; Arginase 1776; Mutarotase 1480

‡*Carpiodes meridionalis*
  S. Mexico, Guatemala.
  Volume 1 only

Caspialosa caspia
  Volga River.
  Calcium, Magnesium, Potassium, Sodium: 2864

Caspialosa kessleri
Volga river.
Calcium, Magnesium, Potassium, Sodium: 2864

‡Caspialosa kessleri pontica*
Black Sea. Diet: fish, crustaceans.
Volume 1 only

‡Catherines modestus
Volume 1 only

‡*Catla catla* (Indian carp) *27, 34, 72, 76*
India: Bengal, Punjab. Burma, Thailand. Introduced into fresh waters of Sri
Lanka. Diet: (young) water fleas, planktonic algae, vegetable debris; (adult)
crustaceans, algae, plants, rotifers, insects. Zooplankton is the main food.
Alkaline phosphatase 3093; *Free* amino acids 3277; Ascorbic acid 2475; Ascorbic
acid oxidase 2475; Diketogulonic acid 2475; "Sugar" 1798

‡*Catostomus catostomus* (Longnose sucker, Northern sucker, Red sucker, Sturgeon sucker)
Right across N. America except Newfoundland. Siberia. Prefers clear, cold water.
Generally fresh water lake bottoms and tributary streams, but tolerates brackish
water. Upper lethal temperature 27°C: preferred temperature 12°C. Diet: bottom-
living invertebrates.
Mercury 3649

Catostomus clarkii 110

‡*Catostomus commersonii* (Bay mare, Black mullet, Brook sucker, Common sucker, White
sucker) *49, 320, 325*
N. America: Great Lakes to Colorado, Missouri and Georgia. Not Alaska. Prefers
warm, shallow lakes and tributary rivers. Meristic characters vary from area to
area. Females grow faster than males and live longer. Distinct dwarf populations
occur. Best hatching rate at 15°C, best growth at 27°C (McCormick, Jones and
Hokanson, 1977). Preferred temperature 18–22°C. Bottom-living. Diet: midge
larvae, amphipods, molluscs.
Chloride 2182; Creatin phosphate 2690; Glycogen 2690, 2691; Haemoglobin
2247; Lactate 2690; Mercury 1557, 3214, 3649; Phosphorylase 2691; Potassium
2182; Sodium 2182

‡**Catulus torazame**
Japan.
Volume 1 only

‡Caulolatilus princeps (Ocean whitefish)
Cape San Lucas to Galapagos. Not common north of Point Conception, California.
DNA 2195; Diphosphatidyl glycerol 3420; Lysophosphatidyl choline 3420;
Phosphatidic acid 3420; Phosphatidyl choline 3420; Phosphatidyl ethanolamine
3420; Phosphatidyl inositol 3420; Phosphatidyl serine 3420; Sphingomyelin 3420

Cebedichthys violaceus
DNA 2195

‡Centrolophus japonicus
  Japan.
  Volume 1 only

Centrolophus niger (Blackfish, Black ruff)
  S. Africa, Mediterranean, N. Atlantic, Australia—probably world-wide. Mid-
  water. Diet: fish, crustaceans, jelly fish.
  Amino acids 1812

Centrolophus sp.
  Tasmania.
  Cholesterol, Fatty acids, Glyceryl ethers, Hydrocarbons: 2779

‡**Centrophorus atromarginatus** (Fin shark)
  Japan. Viviparous.
  Volume 1 only

Centrophorus sp.
  Pristane, Squalene: 2403

‡**Centrophorus squamosus**
  Iceland, Scottish coast to Madeira. Also S. Africa and New Zealand. 400–1500 m.
  Diet: fish and deep-water crustaceans.
  Volume 1 only

‡Centropomus armatus
  N. America.
  Volume 1 only

‡Centropomus robalito
  N. America.
  Volume 1 only

‡Centropristes striatus (Blackfish, Black sea bass, Black perch, Black Will, Tallywag)
  Atlantic coast of United States, Cape Ann to N. Florida. Common inshore on
  rocky bottom near wrecks and wharves, from shallow water to 130 m. Older females
  often change sex to become fertile males.
  Arsenic 3638; Cadmium 3638; Copper 3638; DNA 2195; Mercury 3638; "Sugar"
  1455; Zinc 3638

‡**Centroscyllium fabricii** (Black dogfish)
  Both sides of N. Atlantic. Japan. Surface to 1500 m. Viviparous. Diet: squid,
  crustaceans and jelly fish.
  Volume 1 only

Centroscyllium ritteri
  Pristane, Squalene 2403

‡**Centroscymnus coelolepis** (Portuguese shark) *266*
  Both sides of N. Atlantic, Azores, Mediterranean, Japan. 330–2700 m. Viviparous.
  Absorption maximum of visual pigment is at 472 nm, the lowest recorded in fish
  (Dartnall, 1972).
  Volume 1 only

‡**Centroscymnus owstoni**
Japan. Deep-sea.
Volume 1 only

Centroscymnus sp. *207*
Alkyl diacyl glycerols, Cholesterol, Hydrocarbons, Neutral lipids, Triglycerides,
Wax esters: 3180

‡Cephalopholis atromarginatus
Volume 1 only

‡Cephalopholis fulvus (Butter fish, Coney, Nigger fish, Yellow fish)
West Indies, Florida to Brazil. Shore line to 46 m or deeper. Diet: crustaceans.
DNA 2195; Haematocrit 3377; Haemoglobin 3377

‡**Cephaloscyllium umbratile**
Japan.
Volume 1 only

Cephaloscyllium uter
DNA 2194

Cepola rubescens (Red bandfish)
Mediterranean, N. Atlantic as far as W. Scotland. Usually buried in stiff mud.
Diet: planktonic crustaceans and other small invertebrates.
Cadmium, Copper, Lead, Mercury, Zinc: 1707

‡Ceratocottus namiyei (Ceratocottus, Elf sculpin)
Japan, Korea.
Volume 1 only

Ceratoscopelus maderensis (Horned lantern fish)
Newfoundland to Mediterranean in 2700 m.
Amino acids 1812; Guanine 3148

Ceratoscopelus warmingil
N. Atlantic.
Arsenic, Cadmium, Copper, Mercury, Zinc: 3638

‡**Cestracion zygaena**
Japan.
Volume 1 only

‡**Cetorhinus maximus** = **Selachus maximus** (Basking shark) *309*
N. and S. Atlantic and Pacific Oceans, Murman coast to Madeira and Mediterranean; California to Alaska. Not found in Tropics. May exceed 11 metres in
length; mature at about 7 m. Rather sluggish. Gregarious. Hibernates in winter.
Viviparous. Gill rakers reabsorbed in winter, re-formed in February. Liver may
be 25% of body weight. Diet: plankton.
Mercury 2482; Pristane 2403; Squalene 2403

‡Chaenocephalus aceratus (Icefish, White crocodile fish) *277, 278*
   Antarctic. 5–340 m. Blood contains no haemoglobin. Heart is 2 to 3 times larger
   than that of red-blooded fish from same area.
   Amino acids 3057; *Free* amino acids 3057; Carbohydrates 3311; Chloride 3311;
   Lactate 2170, 2171; Potassium 3311; Sodium 3311; Thyroxine 3477

Chaenogobius isaza (Freshwater goby)
   Japan: Lake Biwa.
   Astacene, β-carotene, Cryptoxanthin, Cynthiaxanthin, Diatoxanthin, β-doradecin,
   Lutein, Tunaxanthin, Zeaxanthin: 2715

‡Chaenomugil proboscideus
   N. America.
   Volume 1 only

‡Chaetodipterus faber (Angelfish, Moonfish, Spadefish, Three-banded sheepshead,
   Three-tailed porgy, Tripletail)
   Cape Cod to Rio de Janiero, W. Indies. Rocky bottoms and in wrecks. Diet:
   invertebrates, plant matter.
   DNA 2195

Chaetodon miliaris *242*

Chaetodon ocellatus (Spotfin butterfly fish)
   West Indies among coral reefs. New England to Brazil.
   DNA 2195

Chaetodon ornatissimus (Butterfly fish)
   Hawaii. Coral reefs. Bones filled with oil: 66–80% of lipid on dry weight basis.
   Fatty acids, Phospholipids, Sterols, Triglycerides: 3031

Chaeturichthys hexanema
   Japan.
   Trimethylamine oxide 2111

Chalcalburnus chalcoides (Danube bleak, Shemaia)
   Volga. Restricted areas of central Europe mostly around Black Sea. Iran, basins of
   Tigris and Euphrates. Shoaling. Diet: plankton, aquatic insects, molluscs, worms.
   Calcium 2864; Magnesium 2864; Potassium 2864; Selenium 2749; Sodium 2864

Chalceus macrolepidotus (Pink-tailed characin)
   S. America. A lively, shoaling fish.
   DNA 2195

Chalinura brevibarbis
   America. Deep ocean waters.
   Mercury 1496

Chalinura carapina
   America. Deep ocean waters.
   Mercury 1496

Champsocephalus gunnari *106*
  Antarctic. Blood lacks haemoglobin. Myoglobin is absent from the equivalent of
  'dark' muscle.

Chanda ranga *83*

‡*Channa argus* (Snake-head fish) *268*
  Japan.
  β-Carotene 2726; Cryptoxanthin 2726; Cynthiaxanthin 2726; Lutein 2726;
  Tunaxanthin 2726; Vitamin A_1 2137; Vitamin A_2 2137; Zeaxanthin 2726

Channa gachua (Brown snakehead)
  India. Active.
  Erythrocytes 3408; Fatty acids 3224; Glucose 3407; Lactate 3407; Leucocytes 3408

Channa marulius (Giant snakehead)
  India.
  Fatty acids 3224

Channa punctatus (*see Ophicephalus punctatus*) *80, 365, 418*

Channa striatus (Striped snakehead)
  India.
  Alkaline phosphatase 3404; Fatty acids 3224

‡Chanos chanos* (Giant herring, Milk fish, Moreton Bay salmon, Salmon herring,
  White mullet) *242*
  Red Sea, India, Indonesia, Philippines, Australia, W. United States. Coastal
  waters and lagoons. Freely enters rivers. Can tolerate high temperatures. Fast
  swimmer. Vegetarian, eating algae and larger plants, though Jhingran also lists
  lamellibranchs and fish eggs in its diet and the FAO list gives bottom invertebrates.
  Grows quickly.
  Folic acid 2582

Chauliodus sloanei (Sloane's viperfish)
  Mid-depths of Atlantic and Mediterranean; Grand Bank area. Most common
  between 1000 and 1800 m but at night rises to 50–800 m.
  Fatty acids 2469

Cheilinus rhodochrous (Wrasse)
  Kona coast of Hawaii. Shallow reefs. Possesses a swimbladder but also oil-filled
  bones. Omnivorous but possesses no stomach and no pyloric caccae.
  Cholesterol, Fatty acids, Phospholipid, Triglyceride: 3028

Cheilinus undulatus (Hump-headed maori, Giant wrasse)
  Widespread in tropical Indo-Pacific and Australian coastal waters. Also found in
  deep waters off reefs.
  Amino acids (in biliverdin) 3669

Cheilopogon exsiliens
  Russia.
  Cardiolipid 2469; Cerebroside 2469, 2470; Fatty acids 2469; Phosphatidyl choline 2469; Phosphatidyl ethanolamine 2469; Phosphatidyl inositol 2469; Phosphatidyl serine 2469; Sphingomyelin 2469; Sulphatide 2469, 2470

Cheilotrema saturnum
  DNA 2195

‡*Chela clupeoides*
  India: Assam. Burma. Rivers.
  Volume 1 only

Chela goru
  India.
  Erythrocytes, Leucocytes: 3408

Chela mouhoti
  Thailand. Streams and ponds.
  DNA 2195

‡*Chela phulo*
  India.
  Volume 1 only

‡Chelidonichthys capensis
  S. Africa,
  Volume 1 only

‡Chelidonichthys kumu (Gurnard, Red gurnard) *72, 75, 76*
  Japan, Australia, S. Africa. Deep or shallow water.
  Astaxanthin diester 3466; Cholesterol 2445; Dimethylamine 3439; Histidine 3166; Thiaminase 3473; Trimethylamine 3439; Trimethylamine oxide 3439

‡Chelidoperca hirundinacea (Prince's small porgy)
  Japan.
  Volume 1 only

Chelon labrosus* (*see* Crenimugil labrosus*)

Chilodus punctatus (Spotted headstander)
  Northern S. America. Shallow, marshy waters often low in dissolved oxygen.
  DNA 2195

‡**Chimaera monstrosa** (Rabbit fish, Rat-tail, Ratfish) *309*
  Europe: N. Norway and Iceland to southern tip of Africa. Mediterranean. Deep-water trawling grounds. Lives close to bottom, 200–500 m. but in shallower water in winter. This fish is a primitive relative of the elasmobranchs which retains urea in the body fluids. The liver is $\frac{1}{4}$ of the body weight. The plasma is isosmotic with sca water (Robertson, 1976), and has a remarkably high concentration of sodium

chloride, which may be correlated with the primitive state of the rectal gland (Fänge and Fugelli, 1963). Diet: crustaceans, molluscs, fish, echinoderms.

Alk-l-enyl diglycerides 2118; Alkyl diglycerides 2118; Amino acids 2118; *Free* amino acids 2118; Ammonia 3135; Betaine 3135; Bicarbonate 3135; Calcium 1908, 1909, 3135; Chitinase 1910; Chloride 1905, 1906, 1908, 1909, 3135; Cholesterol 2515; Creatin 3135; Creatinine 3135; Diglycerides 2118; Fatty acids 2118; *Free* fatty acids 2118, 2515; Glucose 1908, 2516; Haematocrit 2516; Haemoglobin 2516; Hydrocarbons 2118; Lactate 2516, 3135; Lysozyme 1910; Magnesium 1908, 1909, 3135; Monoglyceride 2118; Non-protein nitrogen 3135; Phospholipids 2118; Potassium 1905, 1906, 1908, 1909, 3135; Sodium 1905, 1906, 1908, 1909, 3135; Sterols 2118; Sterol esters 2118; Sulphate 3135; Triglycerides 2118; Trimethylamine oxide 3135; Urea 1905, 1906, 2118, 3135

‡**Chimaera phantasma** (Ghost shark, Silver shark)
Japan. Oviparous.
Volume 1 only

Chimaera sp.
Galactosamine, Hexuronic acid, Sulphate: 3098

‡Chionodraco kathleenae
Antarctic.
Volume 1 only

Chirocentrus dorab (Dorab, Knife-fish, Leaping silver-bar, Ribbon fish, Wolf herring)
Red Sea, E. Africa, India, Australia. Coastal waters down to 110 m. Powerful swimmer. Can leap out of the water. Predacious. Diet: crustaceans and fish.
Volume 1 only

Chitonotus pugetensis (Roughback sculpin)
D-amino acid oxidase 1923

‡Chlorophthalmus albatrossis
Japan.
Volume 1 only

Chloroscombrus chrysurus
DNA 2195

Chondrostoma soetta
N. Italy only. Lives in shoals in middle regions of rivers. Diet: bottom-living animals and plants.
Calcium 1528

‡Chorinemus tolooparah (Leather jacket)
Volume 1 only

Chromus agilis
Hawaii. Coral reefs. Possesses reserves of oil in the bones (12–49% dry matter).
Fatty acids, Phospholipids, Sterols, Triglycerides: 3031

‡Chrysophrys datnia = Mylio latus = Sparus latus (Japanese silver bream, Yellowfin
  seabream)
  Madagascar, Red Sea, India, Sri Lanka, Japan, China, Australia. Coastal waters
  down to 50 m. Enters river mouths and estuaries. Diet: echinoderms, worms,
  crustaceans and molluscs.
  Volume 1 only

‡Chrysophrys major = Pagrosomus major = Pagrus major (Genuine porgy, Red sea
  bream, Sea bream, Silver sea bream) *145, 398, 403*
  Japan, Hawaii. Shores. Bottom-living, 10–150 m on rough or soft grounds. Diet:
  echinoderms, worms, molluscs, crustaceans, fish.
  Adenosine diphosphate 2456; Adenosine monophosphate 1871, 2456; Adenosine
  triphosphate 2456; Amino acids 2456; *Free* amino acids 2455, 2456; α-Amino-
  n-butyric acid 2455; Ammonia 2455, 2456; Amylase 2393; Anserine 2455, 3368;
  Arsenic 3402; Caesium 2269; Calcium 3486; Carbohydrase 2393; Citrulline 2455;
  Cobalt 2269; Collagen 3462; Connective tissue 3462; Copper 3402; Creatin
  2455, 2456; Creatinine 2455, 2456; Elastin 3462; Ethanolamine 2455; Haematocrit
  2300; Haemoglobin 2300; Histidine 3166; Hyaluronidase 2436; *Free* hydroxyproline 2455; Inosine 2455; Inosine monophosphate 1871, 1873, 2455, 2456;
  Maltase 2393; Manganese 3402; Mercury 3402; Ornithine 2455; Strontium 3486;
  Taurine 2455, 2456; Thiaminase 3473; Trimethylamine 1873, 2388, 2456;
  Trimethylamine oxide 2111, 2455, 2456; Vitamin D 3673; Vitamin E 2185; Zinc
  2269, 3402

‡*Chrysostoma garua*
  India, Burma. Rivers.
  Volume 1 only

Chylomycterus schoepfi (Porcupine fish, Striped burr fish)
  Cape Cod to Florida and Brazil. Uses fin propulsion, but can use "jet" propulsion
  by forcing jets of water through the gill openings.
  2'3' cyclic adenosine monophosphate 3' phosphoester hydrolase 3450; DNA 2195

Cichlosoma biocellatum *295*
  DNA 2195

Cichlosoma meeki
  DNA 2195

‡*Cirrhina cirrhosa* (White carp)
  India: Godavery, Kistna and Cauvery rivers. Diet: detritus, algae, sand, mud.
  Volume 1 only

‡*Cirrhina mrigala* (Carp) *34, 73, 74, 92*
  India: Sind, Punjab. Burma. Rivers. Bottom feeder, omnivorous. Diet: decayed
  plant and animal matter, algae, mud.
  Alkaline phosphatase 2858, 3093; Amino acids 3177; *Free* amino acids 3277;
  Calcium 2858; Erythrocytes 3408; Glucose 3407; Iron 2858; Lactate 3407;
  Leucocytes 3408; "Sugar" 1798

‡*Cirrhina reba*
    India. Rivers. Diet: phytoplankton, detritus, mud, decaying leaves.
    Amino tripeptidase 3186; Vitamin A_1 1500; Vitamin A_2 1500

Cirrhites pinnulatus (Hawkfish)
    Kona coast of Hawaii. A shallow reef fish. Possesses oil-filled bones and no swim bladder.
    Cholesterol, Fatty acids, Phospholipid, Triglycerides: 3028

Citharichthys sordidus (Mottled sand dab; Pacific sand dab)
    California to Bering Sea down to 300 m. Common in shallow water. Diet: a wide range of small fish, squid and crustaceans. Possibly two spawnings in a season.
    DNA 2195

Citharus linguatula
    Mediterranean.
    Cadmium, Copper, Lead, Mercury, Zinc: 1707

‡*Clarias batrachus* = *C. magur* (Fresh water catfish, Teysmann's spotted catfish, Walking catfish) *27, 28, 34, 35, 49, 53, 56, 72, 76, 192, 213, 270, 365*
    India, Sri Lanka, Burma, Malaya, Philippines. Fresh and brackish waters. Amphibious, coming on land at night or during rain; may aestivate. Can tolerate low water oxygen levels stilll using aquatic respiration. Air-breathing commonest at night, reducing danger of predation. Diet: worms, prawns, insects, fish, decaying organic matter.
    Acetyl choline 2957; Acid phosphatase 2316, 3227, 3230; Alkaline phosphatase 2316, 3227, 3228, 3230; Amino tripeptidase 3186; Amylase 1425, 2800; Ascorbic acid 1799; Calcium 3278, 3279, 3406; Cellulase 2800; Cholesterol 3268, 3278, 3279, 3403; DNA 2195; Erythrocytes 3408; Folic acid 2582; Glucose 1539, 2361, 2416, 3278, 3279, 3406, 3407; Glycogen 1431, 2416; Histamine 2956; Iron 3278, 3279; Lactate 3407; Leucocytes 3408; Lipase 1425, 2800; Non-protein nitrogen 2361, 3278, 3279; 5'-nucleotidase 2316; Protease 2800; Sucrase 1425; Trypsin 1425

Clarias gariepinus (see *C. mossambicus*)

‡*Clarias lazera*
    Egypt, Israel, Syria.
    Carbohydrates 3686; DNA 2195; Glucose 3686; Glycogen 3686

‡*Clarias magur* (see *C. batrachus*) *72, 76*

Clarias mossambicus (Catfish, Mud barbel)
    E. Africa, Zambesi, Transvaal. Lakes, slow-moving parts of rivers. In dry season buries deep into the mud, using accessory breathing organs.
    DNA 2195; Erythrocytes 2141; Haematocrit 2139, 2141; Haemoglobin 2139, 2141; "Sugar" 2139

Cleisthenes herzensteini (Pacific Ocean flounder)
    Amino acids 3468

‡Clidoderma asperrimum (Roughscale sole, Sharkskin flounder)
Japan, S. British Columbia.
Fatty acids 2153, 2154; Neutral lipid 2153

Clinocottus analis
DNA 2195

Clinostomus funduloides (Rosyside dace)
N. America. High altitude freshwater streams.
Mercury 2252

‡Clupanodon pseudohispanicus
S. America.
Volume 1 only

‡Clupanodon punctatus
Japan.
β-Carotene, α-Cryptoxanthin, Cynthiaxanthin, Diatoxanthin, Lutein, Tunaxanthin, Zeaxanthin: 2718

‡Clupanodon thrissa (Gizzard shad)
Japan.
Volume 1 only

†Clupea alosa
Adriatic Sea.
Volume 1 only

‡*Clupea caspialosa*
Russia.
Volume 1 only

‡Clupea harengus (Atlantic herring) *33, 34, 76, 124, 128, 129, 150, 168, 169, 182, 199, 200, 207, 244, 251, 253, 257, 278, 407, 444, 459, 464*
Both sides of the Atlantic, Spitzbergen to Gibraltar. Pelagic, from surface to 200m. Different races spawn in spring and autumn. Fat reserves are under the skin, in the muscle and round the intestine. Swims continuously in order to breathe. Diet: zooplankton, crustaceans and sand-eel larvae.
Alanine aminotransferase 2793; Amino acids 1485, 3082, 3101; Arginase 2256; Argininosuccinate lyase 2256; Arsenic 1631; Aspartate aminotransferase 2793; Astaxanthin 1781; Cadmium 1631, 1972, 2148; Calcium 1909, 3294; Canthaxanthin 1781; Carbamoyl phosphate synthetase 2256; "Carbohydrate" 1486, 1874; Cephalins 3056; Chitinase 1910; Chloride 1909; Cholesterol 2515, 3056; Cobalt 2491; Copper 2491, 3294; DNA 3203; Fatty acids 1414, 2748; *Free* fatty acids 2515, 3056; Fluoride 2404, 3294; Glucose 2516; Glycerides 3056; Haematocrit 2516; Haemoglobin 2516; Iodide 3294; Iron 2491, 3294; Lactate 2516; Lactic dehydrogenase 1789; 3203; Lead 1631; Lutein epoxy 1781; Lysolecithin 3056; Lysozyme 1910; Magnesium 1909, 2462, 2643; Manganese 2491, 3294; Mercury 1631, 1953, 2148, 2482, 3529; Nickel 2491; Ornithine transcarbamoylase 2256;

Phosphatidyl choline 3056; 6-Phosphogluconate dehydrogenase 3203; Phospho-glucose isomerase 3203; Phospholipids 3056; Potassium 1909, 3294; RNA 3203; Sodium 1909, 3294; Sphingomyelin 3056; "Sugar" 2643; Triglycerides 1486, 1874; Urate oxidase 1711; Vitamin E 1883; Xanthine oxidase 1711; Zeaxanthin 1781; Zinc 2491

‡Clupea harengus membranus (Baltic herring) *339*
Baltic Sea. Probably the same species as the Atlantic herring, C. harengus, but is much smaller (23–24 per kilogramme, compared with 5–7 per kilo) and its average lipid content is only 4% compared with 15% in C. harengus (Linko and Kaitaranto, 1976).
Cathepsin (frozen tissue) 1924; Chloride 2489; Cholesterol 1581, 1785; Diphos-phatidyl glycerol 1581; Fatty acids 3238; *Free* fatty acids 1581; Hydrocarbons 2568; Hypoxanthine 2490; Magnesium 2489; Phosphatidyl choline 1581; Potassium 2489; Pristane 2568; Sodium 2489; Squalene 2568; Triglycerides 1581

‡Clupea ilisha* (*see* Hilsa ilisha)

‡Clupea nordmani
Europe.
Volume 1 only

‡Clupea pallasii (Pacific herring) *124, 250*
S. California to Bering Sea. Japan, Korea. Pacific and Atlantic herring are not different enough to warrant full species rank, so this fish is now considered only as a subspecies (Hart, 1973).
Amino acids 2854; *Free* amino acids 2854; Creatin 2855; Creatin phosphokinase 2696; Creatinine 2855; α-Cryptoxanthin 2718; Cynthiaxanthin 2718; DNA 2195; Diacyl glyceryl ethers 2399; Diatoxanthin 2718; Fatty acids 2449–2451, 3666, 3667; *Free* fatty acids 2399; *Free* fatty alcohols 2399; Glutamate-oxaloacetate transaminase 2696; α-Hydroxybutryate dehydrogenase 2696; Lactic dehydrogenase 2696; Lutein 2718; Ornithine aminotransferase 3611; Partial glycerides 2399; Phospholipids 2399; Sterol esters 2399; Sterols 2399; Thiaminase 3473; Tri-glycerides 2399; Trimethylamine oxide 3151; Tunaxanthin 2718; Vitamin D 3673; Wax esters 2399; Zeaxanthin 2718

‡Clupea pilchardus (Pilchard)
Europe.
Volume 1 only

‡Clupea sprattus = Sprattus sprattus (Sprat) *208*
All W. Europe except Iceland, Mediterranean and Black Seas. Shallow waters near coasts. Tolerates wide variations in salinity, also wide variations in temperature (found from 4°C to 36°C). Pelagic. 10–50 m (summer) down to 150 m in winter. Diet: zooplankton, particularly copepods.
Aluminium 2677; Amino acids 1485; Cadmium 1972; Calcium 2677; Cephalin 3056; Cholesterol 1785, 3056; Cobalt 2491, 2677; Copper 2491, 2677; Cytochrome oxidase 2011; DNA 3203; Fatty acids 1731; *Free* fatty acids 3056; Glycerides 3056; Iron 2491, 2677; Lactic dehydrogenase 1789, 2011, 3203; Lecithin 3056; Lysolecithin 3056; Magnesium 2677; Magnanese 2491, 2677; 6-phosphogluconate

dehydrogenase 3203; Phosphoglucose isomerase 3203; Phospholipids 3056; Potassium 2677; Pyruvate kinase 2011; RNA 3203; Sphingomyelin 3056; Tin 2677; Vanadium 2677; Zinc 2491, 2677

Clupisoma garua
India.
Vitamin A_1, Vitamin A_2: 1500

‡Cnidoglanis macrocephalus (Estuary catfish) *309*
Australia: Arafura Sea. Muddy bottoms in estuaries, sandy bays and inshore waters. Secretes salt by the "dendritic organ", an exterior organ posterior to the anus.
Sodium 2461

‡*Cobitis taenia* (Spined loach, Weatherfish)
Europe apart from Iceland, Ireland, Scotland or Norway. Asia, N. Africa. Still or running water with muddy or sandy bottom (burrows in mud). Mainly nocturnal. Swallows bubbles of air under conditions of oxygen lack. Intestine can serve as respiratory organ. Sedentary. Diet: small crustaceans and rotifers.
Volume 1 only

†Coelorhynchus coelorhynchus (Soldier fish)
Europe.
Volume 1 only

‡Coelorhynchus multispinulosus
Japan.
Volume 1 only

‡Coilia dussumieri (Gold-spotted grenadier)
India to Malaya, Java, Singapore. Coastal waters and estuaries.
Volume 1 only

Coilia mystus
β-Carotene, α-Cryptoxanthin, Cynthiaxanthin, Diatoxanthin, Lutein, Zeaxanthin: 2718

Colisa fasciata (Giant gourami) *239, 392*
Pakistan, E. coast of India, Burma. Muddy waters. Possesses accessory respiratory organs. Makes bubble nest. More aggressive than C. lalia.
Erythrocytes 1424, 2326, 3408; Glycogen 2851; Haemoglobin 2326; Lactate 2851; Leucocytes 1424, 2326, 3408; Lymphocytes 2326; Monocytes 2326; Neutrophils 2326; Thrombocytes 1424

Colisa lalia (Dwarf gourami)
India: Ganges, Jumna and Brahmaputra rivers. Densely weeded waterways, slow streams and backwaters. Possesses accessory respiratory organs. Makes bubble nest.
DNA 2195

‡Cololabis saira (Pacific saury, Skipper) *72, 75, 250*
Japan. S. California to Alaska, Hawaii. Cold waters. Common offshore, surface to 230 m. Diet: small surface-living crustaceans.

Arsenic 3402; Collagen 3462; Connective tissue 3462; Copper 3402; Creatin 2855; Creatinine 2855; Cynthiaxanthin 2717; Diatoxanthin 2717; Dimethylamine 3439; Elastin 3462; *Free* histidine 3166; Lutein 2717; Manganese 3402; Mercury 3402; Thiaminase 2297; Trimethylamine 3439; Trimethylamine oxide 3439; Tunaxanthin 2717; Vitamin D 3673; Zeaxanthin 2717; Zinc 3402

‡Colotomus japonicus
Japan.
Volume 1 only

‡Conger conger (Conger eel) *122, 152*
Sweden to W. Africa. Mediterranean, E. America. Rocky shores and deep waters. Active at night. Found down to at least 1000 m. Spawns only once. Never found in fresh water. Diet: fish, crustaceans (crabs and lobsters), cephalopods.
Calcium 2583; Carnosine 2689; Chitinase 1719; Lactic dehydrogenase 1789; Mercury 1891

Conger myriaster
Japan.
Trimethylamine oxide 2111

Conger sp.
Arsenic, Cadmium, Copper, Mercury, Zinc: 3638

Conger triporiceps
Russia.
Fatty acids 2469

‡Congriscus megastomus
Japan.
Volume 1 only

Coregonus albula (European cisco, Pollan, Vendace, White fish)
Mid-Norway to central Europe. England and Scotland, Russia. Usually in deep waters of lakes, but in autumn found in shallows on gravel. Diet: small planktonic crustaceans, insect larvae, molluscs and young fish.
Cadmium 1972; Cholesterol 1954, 2578, 3283; Cholesterol esters 2578, 3283; Glycerides 2578, 3283; Hydrocarbons 2578; Mercury 3617; Phospholipids 1954, 2577, 3283; Triglycerides 1954, 2577

‡*Coregonus artedii* (*see Leucichthys artedii*) *153, 397*

Coregonus autumnalis migratorius
Lake Baikal (Russia). Coastal areas of the lake, migrating to river mouths to spawn. Diet: small crustaceans and fry of fish.
Calcium, Magnesium, Potassium, Sodium: 2864

‡*Coregonus clupeaformis* (Humpback whitefish, Lake whitefish, Whitefish) *36, 39*
Northern N. America. Rivers and lakes. Diet: plankton (chiefly crustaceans), molluscs, insect larvae, shrimps, depending on the locality. Prefers temperatures of 12–17°C.
ATPase 2414; Arsenic 2611; Bromide 2611; Cadmium 2611; Cobalt 2611; Copper 2611; Mercury 1557, 3214, 3529; Thorium 2611; Uranium 2611; Zinc 2611

‡*Coregonus clupeoides* (Gwyniad, Powan)
European lakes, deep water.
Bicarbonate 3525; Calcium 3525; Chloride 3525; Furan fatty acids 2092; Magnesium 3525; Potassium 3525; Sodium 3525; Sulphate 3525

Coregonus hoyi (Bloater)
N. America: Lakes Superior and Michigan. Avoids temperatures above 10°C or below 6°C.
Arsenic, Bromide, Cadmium, Cobalt, Copper, Thorium, Uranium, Zinc: 2611

‡*Coregonus lavaretus* (Gwyniad, Houting, Lavaret, Pollan, Powan, Schelly)
Northern, Western and Central Europe (not Iceland). There are many local variations in body shape. Diet: (lake populations) planktonic crustaceans, some bottom-living organisms; (river populations) crustaceans, molluscs, insect larvae.
Aldosterone 1969; Astaxanthin 1781, 1782; Calcium 2864; Canthaxanthin 1781, 1782; Corticosterone 1969; Cortisol 1969, 1970; Deoxycorticosterone 1969; 11-Deoxycortisol 1969; 4-Hydroxy-α-carotene 1782; 18-Hydroxy-deoxycorticosterone 1969; 4-Hydroxy-4-keto-β-carotene 1781, 1782; Isozeaxanthin 1781, 1782; Lutein 1782; Lutein monoepoxide 1782; Magnesium 2864; Sodium 2864; "Sugar" 2993; Tunaxanthin 1782; Zeaxanthin 1781, 1782

Coregonus lavaretus lavaretoides (Shuisk whitefish)
Russia.
Phosphatidyl choline, Phosphatidyl ethanolamine, Phosphatidyl inositol, Phosphatidyl serine, Sphingomyelin: 2755

Coregonus lavaretus maraena
Cobalt 1540

‡*Coregonus muksun*
Baltic Sea to Siberia.
Volume 1 only

‡*Coregonus nasus* (Broad whitefish, Whitefish) *49, 52*
Northern central Europe apart from Norway; around Switzerland; Siberia to Canada. Fresh and brackish waters.
Glucose-6-phosphatase, Glycogen, Glycogen phosphorylase 3540

‡*Coregonus nasus sensu 56, 385*
Bay of Bothnia.
Calcium, Copper, Magnesium, Zinc: 2268

Coregonus peled
Cadmium 1972; Cobalt 1540

Coregonus sp. *266*
Lake Maggiore.
Calcium, Strontium 1528

Coreoperca kawamebari (Japanese perch) *434*
Japan.
β-carotene, Cryptoxanthin, Cynthiaxanthin, Diatoxanthin, Lutein, Tunaxanthin, Zeaxanthin: 2720

Correina umbra *112*

‡Corvina nigra (*see* Sciaena umbra)

Corydoras aeneus (Bronze corydoras)
Venezuela and Trinidad to La Plata system. Corydoras species have thin-walled stomachs which serve as additional respiratory organs.
DNA 2195

Corydoras elegans
DNA 2195

Corydoras julii (Leopard corydoras)
Lower Amazon.
DNA 2195

Corydoras melanistius (Black-spotted corydoras, Guyana catfish)
Northern S. America.
DNA 2195

Corydoras myersi
DNA 2195

Corydoras punctatus
Bolivia and Guyanas to Amazon Basin.
DNA 2195

Corydoras undulatus
DNA 2195

‡Coryphaena hippurus (Dolphin fish, Dolshin, Dorado)
Japan, Australia, E. Indies, Hawaii, W. Atlantic, Mediterranean (not Black Sea), Red Sea. Oceanic in warm water. Fast swimmer. Males grow larger than females. A fish-eating predator. Diet also includes squid and crustaceans.
Amino acids 1495; Cardiolipid 2469; Cerebroside 2470; α-Cryptoxanthin 2716; Fatty acids 2469; *Free* histidine 3166; Lutein 2716; Mercury 3127; Phosphatidyl choline 2469; Phosphatidyl ethanolamine 2469; Phosphatidyl inositol 2469; Phosphatidyl serine 2469; Sphingomyelin 2469; Sulphatide 2470; Thiaminase 2297; Trimethylamine oxide 3151; Tunaxanthin 2716; Zeaxanthin 2716

Coryphaenoides abyssorum *261*

Coryphaenoides acrolepis (Pacific rat tail, Roughscale, Rat tail) *261*
Guadelupe Is., Mexico, California, Alaska, Kamchatka, Japan. 155–2470 m.
Cholesterol 2538, 2990; Diphosphatidyl glycerol 3420; Fatty acids 2538, 3029;

Free fatty acids 2990; L-fucose dehydrogenase 2769; Glycolipid 2990; Lysolecithin 2990; Lysophosphatidyl choline 3420; Neutral lipids 2990; Phosphatidic acid 3420; Phosphatidyl choline 2990, 3420; Phosphatidyl ethanolamine 2990, 3420; Phosphatidyl inositol 2990, 3420; Phosphatidyl serine 2990, 3420; Phospholipids 2538, 2990; Sphingomyelin 2990, 3420; Triglycerides 2538

‡Coryphaenoides rupestris (Rat tail, Rock grenadier, Roundnose grenadier)
N. Norway to S. England. Iceland, S. Greenland, Newfoundland. 183–2200 m. Bottom-living. Diet: deep-sea prawns and other invertebrates.
Calcium 1908, 1909; Chloride 1908, 1909; Cholesterol 2515; Diamine oxidase 2231; *Free* fatty acids 2515; Glucose 1908, 2516; Haematocrit 2516; Haemoglobin 2516; Hypoxanthine 1583; Inosine 1583; Inosine monophosphate 1583; Lactate 2516; Magnesium 1908, 1909; Potassium 1908, 1909; Sodium 1908, 1909; Trimethylamine 1583

Coryphaenoides sp.
Peru-Chile trench (deep water).
Cholesterol, Fatty acids, Phosphatidyl choline, Phosphatidyl ethanolamine, Phosphatidyl serine, Phospholipid, Sphingomyelin: 3032

‡Cottunculus thompsoni (Pallid sculpin)
N. America, Atlantic coast.
Volume 1 only

Cottus aleuticus (Aleutian sculpin)
Ornithine aminotransferase 3611

Cottus bubalis (Longspined sea scorpion)
Europe.
Lactic dehydrogenase 1789

Cottus carolinae (Banded sculpin)
N. America.
Mercury 2252

‡*Cottus gobio* (Bull head, Miller's thumb)
Europe, apart from Iceland, N. Scandinavia, Scotland and Ireland. Present in Siberia and Near East, Baltic Sea. Prefers clean water with sandy or stony bottom. Solitary except in breeding season. Active at night. Diet: fish and invertebrates, most crustaceans.
Volume 1 only

‡Cottus kazika
Japan.
Volume 1 only

‡*Cottus pollux*
Japan. Rivers.
Cryptoxanthin, Cynthiaxanthin, Diatoxanthin, β-Doradecin, Lutein, Tunaxanthin, Zeaxanthin: 2715.

Cottus reinii
   Japan.
   Astacene, β-Carotene, Cryptoxanthin, Cynthiaxanthin, Diatoxanthin, β-Dora-
   decin, Lutein, Tunaxanthin, Zeaxanthin: 2715

‡Cottus scorpius (*see* Myoxocephalus scorpius)

Crenicichla saxatilis (Ringtailed pike cichlid)
   Venezuela to Paraguay and Uruguay.
   DNA 2195

‡Crenilabrus melops (Baillon's wrasse, Corkwing, Gilt-head)
   Europe south of Faroes and Shetland to Mediterranean and the Azores. Rocky
   shores below mid-tide level. Slightly deeper water in winter. Diet: crustaceans and
   molluscs.
   Volume 1 only

‡Crenilabrus pavo = C. tinca (Peacock wrasse) *152*
   Europe. Diet: mostly echinoderms.
   Cadmium 1707; Calcium 2864; Chitinase 1719; Copper 1707; Lead 1707;
   Mercury 1707; Sodium 2864; Zinc 1707.

‡Crenilabrus quinquemaculatus (Five-spotted wrasse)
   Russia, Mediterranean, on rocky bottoms, sometimes in water less than 1 m deep.
   Nest-building.
   Volume 1 only.

‡Crenilabrus tinca (*see* C. pavo)

Crenimugil labrosus* = Chelon labrosus* (thick-lipped mullet) *293, 306, 312, 313*
   England, S. Ireland, to N. Africa, Mediterranean, Black Sea. Sometimes migrates
   in small shoals to Faroes and Iceland. Inshore and estuarine; enters rivers. Cannot
   live long in completely fresh water. Mg-ATPase 1974; Na-K-ATPase 1974;
   Chloride 2520; Potassium 2519, 2520; Sodium 2519, 2520

‡*Cristivomer namaycush* (*see Salvelinus namaycush*)

Crossocheilus latius
   India.
   Vitamin A_1, Vitamin A_2: 1500

Cryptacanthodes maculatus (Ghostfish, Spotted wrymouth, Warmouth)
   Atlantic coast of N. America: Grand Bank to New Jersey. Burrows in mud on soft
   bottom down to 110 m. Diet: mud shrimps and amphipods.
   Mutarotase 1480

Ctenolabrus rupestris (Goldsinny) *126*
   Norway to N. Africa, Mediterranean and Black Seas, British Is. Seaweed zone
   0–20 m. Probably dies after spawning. Diet: small crustaceans, worms.
   Cytochrome oxidase, Lactic dehydrogenase: 2009

Ctenopharyngodon idellus (Grass carp, White amur) *12, 151*
Native to China and Amur River; introduced restricted areas of E. Europe. Herbivorous, but larva eats insect larvae and crustaceans. Much cultivated for human consumption because of its conversion of vegetable matter into animal protein.
Adenosine diphosphate 2428; Adenosine monophosphate 2428; Adenosine triphosphate 2428; Aluminium 3467; Amino acids 3468; Amylase 2840; Astaxanthin 1779; Biotin 3453, 3454; Calcium 2264, 2864, 3467; Canthaxanthin 1779; β-Carotene 1779; Chloride 2264; Cholesterol 2495; Copper 3467; DNA 2025; Erythrocytes 2626; *Free* fatty acids 2495; β-Galactosidase 2840; Glucose dehydrogenase 2836, 2837; Glucose-6-phosphatase 2838; Glucose-6-phosphate dehydrogenase 2837, 2838; α-Glucosidase 2840; β-Glucosidase 2840; Haemoglobin 2626; Hexokinase 2836, 2838; Inositol 3453; Iron 3467; Isozeaxanthin 1779; Lutein 1779; Magnesium 2264, 2864, 3467; Manganese 3467; Niacin 3453, 3454; Pantothenic acid 3453, 3454; Phosphoglucose isomerase 2838; Phosphoglucomutase 2838; 6-Phosphogluconate dehydrogenase 2838; Phospholipid 2495; Polyoxyxanthophyll 1779; Potassium 2264, 2864, 3467; Pyridoxine 3453, 3454; RNA 2025, 3097; Sodium 2264, 2864, 3467; Taraxanthin 1779; Thiamine 3453, 3454; Triglycerides 2495; Zinc 2328

Cubiceps gracilis
An open ocean fish of New Zealand, E. Atlantic, Mediterranean. Often lives in association with jelly fish.
Cholesterol, Fatty acids, Glyceryl ethers, Hydrocarbons: 2779

Cubiceps sp.
Amino acids 1812

Culaea inconstans (Brook stickleback)
N. America. Slow streams and shallow lakes among dense vegetation in large shoals. Good salt tolerance. Diet: insect larvae, crustaceans, molluscs, fish eggs.
Chloride 1428, 1429; Glucose 1428; Guanine 1867; Hypoxanthine 1867; Potassium 1428, 1429; Sodium 1428, 1429

‡Cybium commersonii (*see* Scomberomorus commersonii)

‡Cybium kuhli
India.
Volume 1 only

Cycleptus elongatus
Allantoicase, Allantoinase: 1775

‡Cyclopterus lumpus (Henfish, Lumpfish, Lumpsucker, Sea-hen)
Arctic, both sides of N. Atlantic, Davis Straits to New Jersey, Murman coast to France and Portugal. Bottom-living on stony ground from low water mark to 300 m. Young are pelagic. No scales or swim bladder. Eggs guarded by the male. These fish have watery, gelatinous flesh. Diet: crustaceans, small fish and comb-jellies.
Calcium 1909; Chloride 1860, 1909; Cholesterol 2515; Fatty acids 1657;

Free fatty acids 2515; Glucose 2516; Haematocrit 2516; Haemoglobin 2516; Lactate 2516; Magnesium 1909; Mercury 1953; Potassium 1909; Sodium 1860, 1909

Cyclothone atraria
Japan.
Diacyl glyceryl ethers 2398, 2400; *Free* fatty acids 2398, 2400; Fatty alcohols 2398; *Free* fatty alcohols 2400; Partial glycerides 2398, 2400; Phospholipids 2398, 2400; Sterols 2398, 2400; Triglycerides 2398, 2400; Wax esters 2398

Cyclothone sp.
Russia.
Fatty acids 2469

Cymatogaster aggregata (Shiner perch, Shiner seaperch, Yellow shiner) *29*
California to Alaska. Viviparous. Males are mature at birth but smaller than females. Larger females produce larger young at birth. Diet: (young) copepods; (adult) mussels, algae, barnacles.
DNA 2195; Ornithine aminotransferase 3611.

‡**Cynias manazo**
Japan.
Volume 1 only

‡Cynoglossus bengalensis (Bengal tongue sole)
India to Philippines and Indonesia. Muddy and sandy bottoms, often shallow areas, river estuaries and brackish waters. Diet: bottom-living invertebrates.
Volume 1 only

Cynoglossus interruptus
Japan.
Trimethylamine oxide 2111

Cynoglossus robustus
Arsenic, Copper, Manganese, Mercury, Zinc: 3402

Cynoglossus semifasciatus
India.
Volume 1 only

‡*Cynolebias adloffi* (Annual fish)
Volume 1 only

Cynolebias bellotti 47, 58, 59 (Photograph), *60*
S. America. Females live longer than males

‡Cynoscion arenarius (Sand trout)
N. America.
Fatty acids 2882

‡Cynoscion nebulosus = Eriscion nebulosus (Speckled trout, Spottedsea trout, Spotted squeteague, Spotted weakfish)
Gulf of Mexico, Texas to New York.
Arsenic 3638; Cadmium 3638; Copper 3638; Erythrocytes 1647; Haematocrit 1647; Haemoglobin 1647; Mercury 3638; Mutarotase 1480; Zinc 3638

Cynoscion petranus (Weakfish)
Choline, Cyanocobalamin, Folic acid: 3125

‡Cynoscion regalis (Grey trout, Sea trout, Shecutts, Squeteague, Weakfish)
E. coast of N. America: Nova Scotia to Florida. In summer in shallow water over sandy bottoms; in winter down to 100 m. Diet: crabs, shrimps and other small crustaceans from the sea bottom, molluscs and fish.
Volume 1 only

Cynoscion virescens (Sea trout)
Choline, Cyanocobalamin, Folic acid: 3125

‡Cyprinodon macularius (Desert pupfish) 322
N. America: springs and streams of the desert from S. Nevada to Sonora. Artesian and desert water holes in S.W. California. Prefers a temperature of about 36°C.
Volume 1 only

Cyprinodon rubrofluviatilis* (Red River pupfish)
Red River, Texas. A freshwater fish but able to tolerate sea water.
Potassium, Sodium: 3121

Cyprinodon variegatus (Sheepshead minnow, Variegated pupfish) 295, 298, 383
Cape Cod to Texas and Mexico, in brackish as well as salt water in shallow bays and inlets. Males fight each other fiercely during breeding season.
Mg-ATPase (magnesium-activated adenosine triphosphatase) 2378; Na-K-ATPase 2378; DNA 2195

‡Cyprinus carassius
Japan.
Volume 1 only

‡Cyprinus carpio* (Carp, Common carp) 3, 4, 7, 9–12, 17, 18, 30, 32, 34, 44, 51, 55, 63, 67–69, 72–76, 88, 90, 91, 100, 116, 132, 139, 140, 145–147, 149, 151, 152, 155, 157–162, 166–169, 171–182, 184, 187, 191–199, 201, 212, 213, 215, 217–220, 222, 223, 227–229, 232–235, 237, 238, 240–242, 259, 271, 280, 319, 326–330, 337, 338, 340, 342, 343, 345, 361, 364, 384–386
Universal, originally Asia. Slow-running rivers and lakes. Prefers warm and weedy waters. Can live and flourish in brackish water and has occasionally been caught in the sea (Barraclough and Robinson, 1971). Survives long periods out of water but does not possess accessory breathing organs and gills cannot use atmospheric air. Can live anaerobically in water for long periods. Larger fish become sexually mature before smaller. Has poor ability to utilise carbohydrates, relying largely on proteins as an energy source. Carbohydrates are not readily mobilised during starvation. Glycogen levels are high in carp tissues, especially the liver (Murat,

1976b). The liver lacks glycogen phosphorylase* — carp seem to be unique in this respect — and glycogen appears to be degraded by an amylase system. Omnivorous. Seems to have much higher contents of zinc in various organs than other fish species of the same family (Jeng and Lo, 1974). Carp cannot be used for nutritional studies on Vitamin C, since they synthesise it (M. Sato, personal communication 1977). Avoids temperatures above 35°C or below 27°C when given a choice. (*Note added in proof: This enzyme now found in carp liver.

Acetyl choline hydrolase 3362; Acid phosphatase 2874, 3010; Adenosine diphosphate 1584, 1852, 2918, 3219, 3721; ADP-ribose: see NADH; Adenosine monophosphate 1584, 1852, 1871, 2918, 3219, 3721; Adenosine monophosphate deaminase 2480; Adenosine triphosphatase (ATPase) 2344; Ca-ATPase (calcium-mediated ATPase) 1505; ATP 1584, 1852, 2001, 2918, 3721; ATP-ribose: see NADPH; Adrenaline 2736, 3091, 3340; Albumin 2845; Alkaline phosphatase 2464, 2874, 3373; Allantoicase 1775, 3547; Allantoinase 1775, 3547; Aluminium 2677, 3467; Amino acids 1485, 1749, 2013, 2019, 2484, 3433, 3468, 3561, Free amino acids 1749, 1851, 1852, 2013, 2679, 2977, 3164, 3433; Ammonia 1851, 1852, 3007, 3009, 3303; Amylase 1456, 2150, 2393, 2395, 2820, 2840, 2939, 2940, 3256, 3260; γ-Amylase 2810, 2811; Anserine 2977; Arginase 1776, 2256, 3544, 3547; Arginine 3544, 3547; Argininosuccinate lyase 2256; Argininosuccinate synthetase 2256; Bicarbonate 2262, 2264; Biotin 3453, 3454; Cadmium 1972; Calcium 2082, 2240, 2244, 2262–2264, 2288, 2464, 2677, 2698, 2864, 2892, 3021, 3386, 3467, 3503; Carbamoyl phosphate synthetase 2256; Carbohydrase 2393; Carbon dioxide 2142, 2144; Carnosine 2977; Cathepsins A, B and C 1756; Cathepsins A and B 1749; Chloride 1765, 2082, 2240, 2244, 2262, 2264, 2288, 3503; Cholesterol 1441, 1954, 2001, 2425, 2445; Chromium 3115; Citrate 1852; Citrate synthase 1505; Cobalt 1540, 2677, 3115; Copper 1793, 2001, 2677, 3467, 3677; Creatin 3303; Creatinine 1765, 3303; Creatin phosphokinase 2344; Cytidine monophosphate 1584, 3219; Cytidine diphosphate 1584; Cytidine triphosphate 1584; Cytochrome oxidase 2344; Dehydroascorbatase 3678; DNA 1584, 1589, 2001, 2098, 2195, 2282, 2616, 3190, 3203, 3481; Dimethylamine 2110; DOPA 3091; Dopamine 3091; Epimerase 3398; Erythrocytes 1749, 1949, 2626, 3371; Fatty acids (complete analysis) 1912, 2492, 3394; Fatty acids (a single figure for a total value) 2845; Free fatty acids 2734, 2816; UNSATURATED fatty acids 1954; Fatty alcohols (a single figure) 2845; Formaldehyde 2110; Fructose 2783; Fructose-1,6-diphosphatase 3256; Fructose-1,6-diphosphate 1852; Fructose-6-phosphate 1852; Fucose 3337; Galactose 3337; β-Galactosidase 2840; Glucose 1584, 2262, 2288, 2734, 2783, 2810, 2816, 3337, 3645; Glucose dehydrogenase 2836, 2837; Glucose-6-phosphatase 2810, 2834, 2838, 2839, 3010, 3256; Glucose-6-phosphate 1852; Glucose-6-phosphate dehydrogenase 2837–2839, 3256, 3258; β-glucosidase 2840; Glutamate dehydrogenase 3007, 3010; Glutamate oxaloacetate transaminase (GOT) 2834, 3373, 3648; Glutamate pyruvate transaminase (GPT) 2702, 2820, 2834, 3373, 3648; Glutamine 3007; Glutamine synthetase 3010, 3546; γ-Glutamyl transferase 3010; Glutathione 1748; Glycerol-3-phosphate dehydrogenase 1505; α-Glycerophosphate 1852; Glycine 2087; Glycogen 1510, 1589, 1749, 1752, 1753, 1792, 2001, 2344, 2543, 2783, 2810–2812, 2816, 2832, 3049, 3052, 3372, 3374, 3644, 3645, 3648; Glycogen phosphorylase 2810, 2815; Glycyl-L-leucine dipeptidase 1749, 1756; Guanosine diphosphate 1584, 3721; Guanosine monophosphate 1584, 3219, 3721; Guanosine triphosphate 1584, 3721; L-Gulonolactone oxidase 3677; Haematocrit 1505, 1749, 1949, 2139, 2262, 2845, 3371; Haemoglobin 1505, 1584, 1749, 1949, 2082, 2139, 2247, 2626, 3371; Hexokinase 1505, 2344, 2836, 2838, 2839; Hexos-

amines 2087, 3337; Hexose 2087; Hexuronic acid 3337; Histidine 3166; Hyaluronidase 2436; Hydroxyproline 1749, 2087, 2484, 3695; Inosine monophosphate
1852, 1871, 2918, 3219; Inositol 3453; Insulin 3052; Iron 1793, 2677, 3115, 3467;
Isomerase 3398; Lactate 1749, 1753, 1851, 1852, 2262, 2288, 2344, 2812, 3645;
Lactic dehydrogenase 1505, 2344, 3010, 3203, 3373; Lanthanum 3115; Leucine
amino peptidase 1749, 1756; Leucocytes 1949; Lysophosphatidyl choline 2845;
Magnesium 2082, 2240, 2244, 2262–2264, 2462, 2463, 2677, 2698, 2864, 302!,
3386, 3467, 3503; Malate 1852; Malate dehydrogenase 1505, 2344; Maltase
2395; Manganese 1793, 2001, 2677, 3467; Mannose 3337; Myoglobin 2344;
Niacin 3453, 3454; NAD (nicotinamide adenine dinucleotide, formerly called
diphosphopyridine nucleotide) 1584, 3219, 3259, 3721; NADH (reduced form of
NAD) 3219, 3259; NADP (nicotinamide adenine dinucleotide phosphate, formerly
called triphosphopyridine nucleotide) 1584, 3721; NADPH (reduced NADP)
3219; Noradrenaline 2736, 3091, 3340; Ornithine 2977; Ornithine transcarbamoylase 2256; Oxygen 2142, 2144; Pantothenic acid 3453, 3454; Partial glycerides
2845; "Pentose" 2087; Pepsin 2395, 3256; Phosphatidyl choline 2001, 2845;
Phosphatidyl ethanolamine 2845; Phosphofructokinase 3256; Phosphoglucomutase
2838, 2839; 6-Phosphogluconate dehydrogenase 2838, 3203, 3256; Phosphoglucose
isomerase 2838, 2839, 3203, 3256; Phospholipid 1954, 2425, 2474, 2845; Phosphorylase 2344; Potassium 1584, 1749, 1750, 1753, 1836, 2082, 2240, 2244, 2262–
2264, 2288, 2677, 2864, 2892, 3021, 3467, 3503; Proline 2087; Protease 2150, 2939,
2940, 3481; Pyridine nucleotide transhydrogenase 3167; Pyridoxine 3453, 3454;
Pyruvate 1749, 1753, 2344; Pyruvate kinase 2344; RNA 1584, 1589, 2001, 2098,
2282, 2616, 3190, 3203, 3481; Sarcosine 2977, 3433; Scandium 3115; Selenium
2749; Sialic acids 3337; Sodium 1584, 1749, 1750, 1753, 1836, 2082, 2240, 2244,
2262–2264, 2288, 2864, 2892, 3021, 3467, 3503; Sphingomyelin 2845; Sterols 2845;
Sterol esters 2845; Succinic dehydrogenase 2344; "Sugar" 1451, 1749, 2082, 2139,
2150, 2509, 2790, 2812, 2832, 3216, 3562; Taurine 2977; Thiaminase 2297, 2299
Thiamine 3453, 3454; Tin 2677; Transaldolase 3398; Transketolase 3398;
Triglycerides 1954, 2845; Triose phosphate dehydrogenase 1505; Trypsin 2395,
3256; Tyrosine 2087; Ubiquinone 2186; Urea 2288, 3303, 3544, 3546, 3547;
Uric acid 3303, 3544, 3547; Uricase 3544, 3547; Uridine diphosphate (UDP)
3219, 3721; UDP-N-acetyl glucosamine 3721, 3722; UDP-glucose 3722; UDP-
glucuronic acid 3722; UDP-hexoses 3219, 3721; UDP-uronic acids 3219; Uridine
monophosphate 1584, 3219, 3721; Uridine triphosphate 1584, 3721; Vanadium
2677; Vitamin A 3395; Vitamin D 3673; Vitamin E 2186, 3395; Wax esters 2845;
Xanthine oxidase 3481; Zinc 1793, 2001, 2328, 2677, 3115, 3155, 3156, 3467

‡*Cyprinus carpio communis*
   India.
   Volume 1 only

Cyprinus carpio haematopterus
   Lake Baikal (Russia).
   Magnesium, Potassium, Sodium: 2864

‡*Cyprinus carpio nudus*
   India.
   Volume 1 only

Cyprinus carpio specularis
   India.
   Volume 1 only

‡Cypselurus agoo
   Japan.
   Volume 1 only

‡Cypselurus oligolepis (Flying fish)
   Tanzania, Singapore, Sumatra, Java, Philippines, China.
   Volume 1 only

‡Cypselurus opisthopus (Flying fish)
   Java, Celebes, Japan.
   Volume 1 only

Cypselurus sp. *72, 75, 76*
   Japan.
   Dimethylamine, Trimethylamine, Trimethylamine oxide: 3439

Dactylopagrus carponemus (Sea carp)
   Australia.
   Copper, Zinc: 1893

‡Dactylopterus orientalis
   Japan.
   Volume 1 only

‡**Dalatias atromarginatus**
   Japan.
   Volume 1 only

‡**Dalatias licha** (Armour shark, Black shark, Dalatias, Kitefin shark, Seal shark)
   Atlantic, Mediterranean, Japan, Queensland (rare). 350–650 m.
   Viviparous. Diet: fish, squid.
   Free fatty acids, Pristane, Squalene, Triglycerides, Wax and sterol esters: 2557

Dalatias phillpsi
   Trimethylamine oxide 3151

Damalichthys vacca (Pile seaperch)
   Pacific.
   Ornithine aminotransferase 3611

‡*Danio aequipinnatus* = *D. malabaricus* (Giant danio)
   India, Sri Lanka. Small streams and ponds.
   DNA 2195

‡*Danio malabaricus* (*see D. aequipinnatus*)

‡**Dasyatis akajei** (Japanese sting ray, Red skate, Red sting ray)
S. Japan. Viviparous.
Anserine 3368

‡**Dasyatis americana** (Southern sting ray) *313, 314*
W. Atlantic: New Jersey to Brazil. Coastal waters, always shallow, usually buried
in sand. Diet: crustaceans, molluscs, worms and fish.
Amino acids (single figure); Potassium, Sodium, Trimethylamine oxide, Urea:
1945

Dasyatis brevicaudatus (Stingray)
Indo-Pacific, S. Africa to Australia and New Zealand. Shallow sandy areas and
in vicinity of reefs. Has been known to enter estuaries.
Copper, Zinc: 1893

‡**Dasyatis centroura** (Northern stingray, Roughtail stingray)
Both sides of Atlantic. Cape Cod to Cape Hatteras, north to Gascony. Grows to
large size.
Arginine 1653; Glucose 3664

‡**Dasyatis pastinaca = Trygon pastinaca** (Sting ray)
Norway and N. Scotland to Madeira. Mediterranean and Black Seas. Calm shallow
water above 60 m over sand, shingle or mud. Viviparous. Can tolerate low salinity.
Diet: bottom-living organisms.
Adrenaline 3340; Chloride 2280; Corticosterone plus cortisol 1704; Fatty acids
3088; Glycogen 2543, 3049; Noradrenaline 3340; Potassium 2280; Sodium 2280

Dasyatis sabina (Stingray) *310, 312*
Coast of Texas. Euryhaline but does not tolerate completely fresh water. 2'3'-*cyclic*
adenosine monophosphate-3'-phosphoester hydrolase; 3450 *Free* amino acids
1594; α-Amino adipate 1594; γ-Amino butyrate 1594; Ammonia 1594; Calcium
3558, 3559; Chloride 3558, 3559; Creatinine 1594; Ethanolamine 1594; Glutamine
1594; Haematocrit 3559; Ornithine 1594; Potassium 3558, 3559; Sarcosine 1594;
Sodium 3558, 3559; Taurine 1594; Urea 1594, 3558, 3559

Dasyatis sayi (Sting ray)
2'3'-*cyclic* adenosine monophosphate-3'-phosphoester hydrolase 3450
DNA 2194

‡**Dasyatis uarnak** FRESHWATER ELASMOBRANCH (Banded whip-tail
stingray)
Malaya: Perak River.
Volume 1 only

‡**Dasyatis zugei**
India.
Volume 1 only

Dasycottus setiger (Spinyhead sculpin)
D-amino acid oxidase 1923

‡**Deania eglantina** (Broad harbour shark).
Japan.
Volume 1 only.

Deania kaikauras
Trimethylamine oxide 3151

Deania sp. *207*
Alkyl diacyl glycerols, Cholesterol, Hydrocarbons, Neutral lipids, Triglycerides,
Wax esters: 3180

‡Decapterus lajang (*see* D. macrosoma)

‡Decapterus macrosoma = D. lejang (Layang scad, Sear)
Natal, Philippines, Formosa, S. Japan, Australia. Warm coastal waters. Diet:
small invertebrates.
Folic acid 2582

‡Decapterus maruadsi (Round scad)
Indo-Australian archipelago, Japan. Warm coastal waters down to 20 m. Diet:
pelagic and bottom-living animals.
Cadmium 2901; Copper 2901; Fatty acids 3446; Iron 2901; Lead 2901; Potassium
2900; Sodium 2900; Zinc 2901

‡Decapterus punctatus (Cigar fish, Dotted scad, Quiaquia, Round robin, Scad)
W. Atlantic: Cape Cod to Brazil.
Arsenic, Cadmium, Copper, Mercury, Zinc: 3638

‡Decapterus rhonchus
Portugal.
Volume 1 only

‡Dentex dentex = D. vulgaris (Common dentex)
British Is. to Senegal, Mediterranean. Various habitats down to 200 m. Rocky
ground. Diet: fish, squid.

‡Dentex filosus (*see* D. gibbosus)

‡Dentex gibbosus = D. filosus (Pink dentex)
Portugal to Angola. Mediterranean. Mud and gravel bottoms down to 150 m.
Volume 1 only

Dentex macrocanus (Yellow porgy)
Japan.
Caesium, Cobalt, Zinc: 2269

Dentex macrophthalmus (Large-eye dentex)
Spain to Angola. Mediterranean. Inshore and offshore down to 500 m. Carnivorous.
Mercury 1891

‡Dentex vulgaris (*see* D. dentex)

Dermatolepis inermis
  DNA 2195

Dermogenys pusillus (Halfbeak)
  S.E. Asia, Indonesia, Philippines, Surface of fresh and brackish waters in small streams and pools. Viviparous. Diet: mosquito larvae.
  DNA 2195

‡Diaphus coeruleus (Headlight fish)
  Red Sea, India.
  Volume 1 only

Diaphus mollis
  N. Atlantic.
  Arsenic, Cadmium, Copper, Mercury, Zinc: 3638

Diaphus theta *120*

‡Diapterus evermanni = Moharra evermanni
  S. America, Atlantic waters of Panama.
  Volume 1 only

‡Dicentrarchus labrax* (European bass, Sea bass) *93, 134, 154, 182, 184, 306, 320*
  Norway and Baltic Sea to Senegal, Mediterranean and Black Seas. Coasts of England and Ireland. Surface to below 100 m. Inshore around rocky outcrops; sometimes well up rivers. Voracious, predatory. Diet: small herring and other shoaling fish, crustaceans and squid. Slow-growing.
  Cadmium 1707; Carbohydrates 3357; Copper 1707; Lactic dehydrogenase 1789; Lead 1707; Mercury 1707; Non-protein nitrogen 3357; Potassium 2519; Sodium 2519; Zinc 1707

Dicologoglossa cuneata
  Gulf of Cadiz.
  Mercury 1891

Dinolestes lewini (Longfinned pike)
  Australia.
  Copper, Zinc: 1893

Diodon holacanthus (Balloonfish, Porcupine fish, Spiny puffer)
  Worldwide in tropical waters. Mangrove swamps, reefs, sandy bays. Rarely deeper than 6 m. Diet: hard-shelled invertebrates, especially crabs, sea urchins and gastropod molluscs.
  Astacene, β-Carotene, α-Cryptoxanthin, α-Doradecin, Lutein, Tunaxanthin, Zeaxanthin: 2725

Diodon hystrix (Porcupine fish)
  All warm seas. Favours shallow water over turtle grass and sandy flats. Flesh poisonous to man. Diet: sea urchins, gastropod molluscs, crabs, hermit crabs.
  Potassium, Sodium: 2392

Diplectrum formosum
  Russia.
  Fatty acid 2469

‡Diplectrum radiale
  Cuba to Brazil
  Volume 1 only

Diplodus annularis (*see* D. sargus) *152*

‡Diplodus argenteus
  West Indies to Argentina.
  DNA 2195

Diplodus bermudensis (Bream)
  Bermuda shores. Active swimmer.
  Succinic dehydrogenase 2750

Diplodus holbrooki
  DNA 2195

‡Diplodus sargus=D. annularis=D. vulgaris (Blacktail, Dassie, Marine sargus, Sargo,
  Sea carp, Two-banded bream, White seabream) *152*
  Bay of Biscay to Cape of Good Hope, African coasts of the Indian Ocean, Bermuda,
  Mediterranean, Black Sea. Sandy, muddy or vegetated bottoms close to shore down
  to 50 m. Often enters saline littoral lagoons. Ambisexual, probably protandric.
  Adrenaline 3340; Cadmium 1707; Chloride 2864, 3711; Copper 1707; Cortico-
  sterone+cortisol 1704; Cyanocobalamin 1522; 11β-Hydroxytestosterone 2273;
  Lead 1707; Mercury 1707; 1891; Noradrenaline 3340; Potassium 2864; 3711;
  Sodium 2864, 3711; Zinc 1707

Diplodus vulgaris (*see* D. sargus)

Dissostichus eleginoides (Toothfish)
  Atlantic.
  Aluminium 2040; Amino acids 3057; Bismuth 2040; Calcium 2040, 3057;
  Chromium 2040; Cobalt 2040; Copper 2040; Iron 2040, 3057; Magnesium 2040;
  Manganese 2040; Nickel 2040; Polyunsaturated fatty acids 3057; Potassium 2040,
  3057; Silver 2040; Tin 2040; Vanadium 2040; Vitamin E 3057; Zinc 2040

Dissostichus mawsoni (Giant Antarctic cod) *330, 333, 346*
  Antarctic. Blood contains glycoprotein "antifreeze". Aglomerular kidney (DeVries,
  1974). No swim bladder (Dobbs, 1974). Usually found from 20 to 220 m. Upper
  lethal temperature 7-8°C. Diet: fish, shellfish, zooplankton. High blood pH
  (8·2–8·3): Qvist, Weber *et al.* (1977).
  Amino acids 1917, 2064, 2448; Calcium 1840; Chloride 1840; Galactosamine
  1917; Galactose 1917; Haematocrit 3108; Magnesium 1840; Potassium 1840;
  Sodium 1840

‡Ditrema temmincki (Sea chub, Surf perch)
Japan, Shores. Viviparous.
Astacene 2716; Caesium 2269; Calcium 3486; β-Carotene 2716; Cobalt 2269;
α-Cryptoxanthin 2716; Cynthiaxanthin 2716; Diatoxanthin 2716; α-Doradecin
2716; Lutein 2716; Nicotinamide adenine dinucleotide 3259; Strontium 3486;
Tunaxanthin 2716; Zeaxanthin 2716; Zinc 2269

‡Döderleinia berycoides (Grouper)
Japan, Korea.
Adenosine monophosphate 1871; Cadmium 2901; Copper 2901; Inosine monophosphate 1871; Iron 2901; Lead 2901; Potassium 2900; Sodium 2900; Trimethylamine 1871; Zinc 2901

Dormitator latifrons
Eastern tropical Pacific. Brackish streams. A facultative air-breather possessing
one of the highest haemoglobin concentrations of any fish.
Haemoglobin 3437

Dormitator maculatus *288*

‡Dorosoma cepedianum* (Gizzard shad, Hickory shad)
S.E. coast of N. America: Cape Cod to Texas. Enters streams and is sometimes
landlocked. Herbivorous. Avoids temperatures above 30°C or below 24°C.
DNA, RNA 2125

‡Dorosoma petenense* (Threadfin shad)
Gulf of Mexico. Central America. Introduced into Californian freshwater lakes.
Volume 1 only

†Dorosoma thrissa
Japan.
Volume 1 only

Drepane africana
S. Atlantic.
Cholesterol 2768

‡Drepane punctata (Butterfish, Concertina fish, Sicklefish, Spotted batfish)
Red Sea, E. Africa, Persian Gulf, India, Burma, Malaya, China, Australia.
Shallow sea and brackish water of estuaries; shallow waters around reefs and
headlands. Sandy or muddy bottoms. Diet: bottom-living invertebrates and fish.
Amino acids, Calcium, Iron, Niacin, Riboflavin, Thiamine, Vitamin A: 3690

‡Drepanopsetta platessoides (*see* Hippoglossoides platessoides)

‡Duymaeria flagellifera (Wrasse)
Japan, Korea, Formosa. Sub-tropical.
Pyridine nucleotide transhydrogenase 3167

Echelus myrus
  Mediterranean.
  Cadmium, Copper, Lead, Mercury, Zinc: 1707

Echeneis naucrates (Pilot sucker, Shark sucker)
  Wide distribution in warm seas. Transported long distances by sucker attachment
  to sharks, ships or turtles. Also found free-living (inactive).
  DNA 2195; Haematocrit 3377; Haemoglobin 3377

Electrophorus electricus (Electric eel)
  Guyanas, Orinoco River, middle and lower Amazon Basin. Pools and shaded
  streams and creeks, often in very turbid water. The electric organs occupy 4/5
  of the sides of the body. Diet: fish. Air-breathing obligatory. Most of CO_2 elimination via vestigial gills and skin.
  Acetyl choline 3725; Ammonia 2686; Bicarbonate 2686; Calcium 2686; Chloride
  2686; Esterase 3725; Fumarase 3725; Glycogen 2121; Lactic dehydrogenase 3725;
  Magnesium 2686; Phosphatidyl choline 3451; Phosphatidyl inositol 3451; Potassium 1836, 2264, 2686; Sialic acid 3699; Sodium 1836, 2264, 2686; Sphingolipids
  3451; Steroid esters 3451; Urea 2686

‡Elegatis bipinnulatus (Rainbow runner)
  Tanzania, Red Sea, India, Philippines, Japan, Australia, Hawaii. Inshore coastal
  waters, coral and rocky reefs and open sea. Vigorous. Diet: crustaceans and fish.
  FREE amino acids, Anserine, Carnosine, Creatin+creatinine, Taurine: 3369

Eleginus gracilis (Saffron cod, Wachna cod) *348*
  Alaska.
  Amino acids 3109; Amino galactose 3109; Fatty acids 2152; Galactose 3109;
  Neutral lipids 2152

‡Eleginus navaga
  Russia.
  Cholesterol, Non-esterified fatty acids, Phospholipids: 3237

‡Eleutheronema tetradactylum*=Polynemus tetradactylus* (Blind tassel fish,
  Cooktown salmon, Fourfinger threadfin, Giant threadfin, Tassel fish)
  India, Malaya, Philippines, China to N. and W. Australia. Shallow coastal
  waters over muddy bottoms. Brackish waters, ascending rivers to spawn. Often
  found in muddy water. Not blind, but eyelid becomes opaque after death, hence
  the first trivial name above. Diet: prawns, crabs, fish, polychaets, amphipods
  Volume 1 only

‡Elops hawaiensis (Giant herring, Ten-pounder)
  Singapore, Java, Philippines, Formosa, Hawaii, Australia. Pelagic.
  Volume 1 only

‡Elops saurus* (Bigeye herring, Bonefish, Giant herring, John Mariggle, Ladyfish,
  Ten-pounder)
  W. Atlantic: Massachusetts, W. Indies to Brazil, India, Sri Lanka. Vigorous.

Common in mangrove swamps, sheltered bays and salt marshes. Diet: fish and crustaceans.
DNA 2195

‡Embiotoca jacksoni (Black surfperch)
Vancouver Is. to Todos Santos Bay (Pacific coast of N. America). Surface to 38 m.
DNA 2195

Embiotoca lateralis (Striped seaperch)
California to Alaska. Viviparous. Strongly hierarchical in captivity. Diet: crustaceans, worms, mussels, herring eggs.
Ornithine aminotransferase 3611

‡**Emissola antarctica**
Australia.
Volume 1 only

‡Enedrias nebulosus (Blenny)
Japan.
Volume 1 only

‡Engraulis encrasicholus (Anchovy) *137, 208*
Sweden, Britain to Mediterranean and Black Seas. Pelagic, down to 150 m in marine or estuarine waters. Eggs shed in batches over a long period. Diet: plantonic organisms.
Cadmium 1709; Copper 1708, 1709; Fatty acids 1731; Lead 1708, 1709; Mercury 1708, 1709, 1891; Zinc 1708, 1709

‡Engraulis encrasicholus ponticus *74–76*
Black Sea.
Aluminium 2571; Cholesterol 2571; Chromium 2571; Copper 2571; Cyanocobalamin 1522; Iron 2571; Manganese 2571; Provitamin D 2571; Silver 2571; Zinc 2571

‡Engraulis japonicus (Anchovy, Halfmouth sardine)
Japan.
β-Carotene 2718; Cryptoxanthin 2718; Cynthiaxanthin 2718; Diatoxanthin 2718; Lutein 2718; Thiaminase 2297; 2299; Vitamin D 3673; Zeaxanthin 2718

‡Engraulis mordax (Anchovy, Northern anchovy) *155, 374*
N. America: S. California to N. Vancouver Is. in dense shoals. Favours water from 14·5 to 18·5°C. Diet: planktonic organisms.
Free amino acids 3200; L-Amino *n*-butyric acid 3200; DNA 2195; Ornithine 3200; Taurine 3200

‡Entosphenus japonicus (*see* Lampetra japonicus)

‡Entosphenus lamottei* (*see* Lampetra lamottei*)

‡Entosphenus tridentatus CYCLOSTOME (Pacific lamprey)
Japan. S. California to Alaska. Penetrates all major rivers, often to headwaters.
Dies 1–14 days after spawning. Some landlocked populations occur, and these are
not parasitic as adults.
Vitamin D 3673

‡Eopsetta grigorjewi (Roundnose flounder, Shotted halibut)
Japan, Korea. Diet: crustaceans.
Connective tissue 3462; Fatty acids 2154

‡Eopsetta jordani (Brill, Petrale sole)
N. America: S. California to Alaska. 18–550 m. Diet: a wide range of fish, also
crustaceans and small bottom-living invertebrates.
Cathepsin 1993; DNA 2195; Mercury 1697

‡Epinephelus aeneus (White grouper)
Warmer parts of Mediterranean, S. Spain, coast of W. Africa. Sandy and muddy
bottoms of continental shelf down to 150 m.
Cholesterol, 7-dehydrocholesterol: 2768

‡Epinephelus akaara
Japan.
Volume 1 only

Epinephelus corallicola* (Grouper)
Madras, Singapore, Java, Philippines, New Guinea, N. Australia. In sea, entering
fresh water.
Folic acid 2582

‡Epinephelus fario (Garrupa, Rock-cod, Spotted grouper, Trout reef-cod)
Japan, China Sea, Java. Coastal waters and pearl banks.
Thiaminase 3473

‡Epinephelus fasciatus (Banded reef-cod, Black-tipped grouper, Black-tipped rock
cod, Red-banded grouper, Red hata)
Madagascar, Red Sea, India, Philippines, Japan, China, W. Australia. Shores,
coral reefs. Diet: bottom-living invertebrates and fish.
Vitamin D 3673

‡Epinephelus gigas (Dusky perch)
Portugal, Britain, Mediterranean. 100–400 m in rocks where holes and caves
abound. Solitary.
Cholesterol 1785

‡Epinephelus goreënsis
Portugal.
Volume 1 only

‡Epinephelus guttatus (Cabrilla, Red hind)
Florida to Brazil, Madagascar, Red Sea, India, Philippines, N. Australia. Shores.
Inactive.
DNA 2195; Haematocrit 3377; Haemoglobin 3377; Succinic dehydrogenase 2750

Epinephelus itajara (Jewfish)
Atlantic and Pacific coasts of N. America. Lives around sunken wrecks and piers, under coral ledges and in caves. Males appear to become functional females late in life. Diet: crustaceans, including large spiny lobsters, fish, turtles.
2'3'-*cyclic*-adenosine monophosphate-3'-phosphoester hydrolase 3450

‡Epinephelus morio (Red grouper)
Atlantic coast of N. and S. America from Virginia to Brazil.
Ammonia 3303; Creatin 3303; Creatinine 3303; DHA 2195; Urea 3303; Uric acid 3303

Epinephelus niveatus
Fatty acids 2469; Gangliosides 2469; Sialic acid 2470

‡Epinephelus septemfasciatus (Grouper, True bass)
Japan.
Pyridine nucleotide transhydrogenase 3167

‡Epinephelus striatus (Hamlet, Nassau grouper, Rockfish)
E. America: Florida to Brazil.
DNA 2195; Haematocrit 3377; Haemoglobin 3377

Eptatretus burgeri CYCLOSTOME (Hagfish)
Pacific coast of Japan, Sea of Japan to S. Korea. 5-7 m. Most active at night. Parasitic on other fish.
Hexosamine, Mucopolysaccharide, Sulphate, Uronic acid: 1434

Eptatretus cirrhatum=Bdellostoma cirratum CYCLOSTOME
Arginase 3113

‡Eptatretus stoutii=Polistotrema stoutii CYCLOSTOME (Hagfish, Pacific hagfish) *158, 285*
California to S.E. Alaska. 9–1450 m. Parasitic on larger fish. Virtually blind. Large subcutaneous blood sinuses result in a value for blood plasma of 13·8% of the total body weight compared with about 5% for lampreys (Robertson, 1974). Blood usually isosmotic with sea water. The concentration of *some* ions of the blood very similar to that in sea water. This fish is very permeable to the water of the sea but not to ions, particularly Ca and Mg. In sea water of different dilutions, the blood Na and Cl decline in proportion to their decrease in the medium, but Ca and Mg remain at a constant level (McFarland and Munz, 1965). The digestive tract is believed to be almost non-functional. The pituitary appears not to control either gametogenesis or thyroid function (Matty, Tsuneki *et al.*, 1976). Very oily flesh.
Albumin 3523; Alkaline phosphatase 3523; Amino acids 2561; Bicarbonate 3523, 3525; Calcium 2649, 2808, 3523, 3525; Chloride 2649, 2808, 3523, 3525; DNA 2194; L-fucose dehydrogenase 2769; Globulin 3523; Glucose 2649, 2808; Haematocrit 2649; Iodine (protein-bound) 2178; Magnesium 2649, 2808, 3523, 3525; Potassium 2649, 2808, 3523, 3525; Sodium 2649, 2655, 2808, 3523, 3525; Sulphate 2808, 3523, 3525; Thyroxine 2178

Equetus lanceolatus (Jack-knife fish)
W. Atlantic: Bermuda to Brazil. Rocky or coral habitats down to 18 m. Cardiolipid 2469; Cerebroside 2469, 2470; Fatty acids 2469; Ganglioside 2469; Phosphatidyl choline 2469; Phosphatidyl ethanolamine 2469; Phosphatidyl inositol
2469; Phosphatidyl serine 2469; Sialic acid 2470; Sphingomyelin 2469; Sulphatide
2469, 2470

‡Erilepis zonifer (Skilfish)
Japan, California, Alaska. Surface to 440 m. Very oily flesh.
Volume 1 only

Erimyzon sucetta (Lake chubsucker) *17, 18*

‡Eriscion nebulosus (*see* Cynoscion nebulosus)

‡Errex zachirus (Longfinned sole, Rex sole)
N. Pacific. Waters of moderate depth.
Volume 1 only

‡Erythrichthys schlegeli
Japan.
Volume 1 only

‡Erythrocles schlegeli
Japan, Korea.
Volume 1 only

Esomus danrica
India.
Erythrocytes, Leucocytes: 3408

Esox americanus vermicularis (Grass pickerel)
N. America: lower Great Lakes to Louisiana and central Texas. Sluggish streams,
ponds, ditches, always amongst dense vegetation. Diet: (young) insect larvae,
crustaceans; (adult) fish, crustaceans. Preferred temperature 26°C.
Esterase 2221

‡*Esox lucius* (Northern pike, Pickerel, Pike) *43, 49, 55, 69, 97, 121, 147, 155, 182, 183,*
189, 193, 194, 208, 210, 229, 233, 265, 342, 364
Europe (except Spain) in streams and lakes near the shore. Siberia. Baltic Sea
in brackish water. Not Iceland or coastal Norway. Decreases in growth rate north-
ward with increase in longevity. Females live longer and achieve greater maximum
size. A predator, hunting almost any fish, water birds, aquatic animals and amphibians. Relatively high capacity for concentrating zinc in tissues (Nazarenko
and Shutov, 1973).
Allantoicase 1775; Allantoinase 1775; Aluminium 2677, 3017; Amino acids 1485,
2447, 3433; *Free* amino acids 2977, 3433; Anserine 2977; Arginase˙ 1776, 2256;
Argininosuccinate lyase 2256; Argininosuccinate synthetase 2256; Barium 3017;
Bicarbonate 2262; Cadmium 1972, 2148; Calcium 1528, 2262–2264, 2677, 2864,
2924; Carbamoyl phosphate synthetase 2256; Carnosine 2977; Chloride 1765,

1836, 2182, 2262, 2924; Cholesterol 2284, 3426; Cobalt 1540, 2677; Copper 2677, 2829, 3017; Creatin phosphate 2690; Creatinine 1765; DNA 2447; Epimerase 3398; Erythrocytes 2801; Esterase 2221; Fatty acids 2026, 2441, 2492, 3088, 3117; *Free* fatty acids 2284; Furan fatty acids 2026; Glucose 2262, 2284, 3426; Glycogen 2284, 2690, 2691; Guanine 1867; Haematocrit 2262, 2284, 2801; Haemoglobin 2801; Hypoxanthine 1867; Iron 2677, 3017; Isomerase 3398; Lactate 2262, 2690; Leucocytes 2801; Lymphocytes 2801; Magnesium 2262–2264, 2677, 2864, 2924; Manganese 2677, 3017; Mercury 1557, 2148, 2371, 2829, 3214, 3529, 3617, 3649; Ornithine 2977; Ornithine transcarbamoylase 2256; Phosphorylase 2691; Polysaccharides 2447; Potassium 1836, 2182, 2262–2264, 2677, 2864, 2924; RNA 2447; Sarcosine 2977, 3433; Sodium 1836, 2182, 2262–2264, 2864, 2924; "Sugar" 2063, 2447, 2993; Taurine 2977; Tin 2677; Transaldolase 3398; Transketolase 3398; Urate oxidase 1711; Urea 3547; Vanadium 2677; Xanthine oxidase 1711; Zinc 2677, 2829, 3017

‡*Esox niger* (Chain pickerel, Eastern pickerel, Green pike, Jack)
Eastern N. America: Massachusetts to Florida. Lowland streams and swamps. Solitary. Predacious carnivore. Tolerates temperatures from 0 to 37°C, but preferred temperature 24°C; voluntarily avoids temperatures above 27°C or below 20°C. Never wholly fish-eating, but eats some crustaceans and insect larvae. Volume 1 only

Etelis carbunculus
Japan.
Mercury 2888; Selenium 2888

‡Etelis evurus (Cachucho)
Japan.
Volume 1 only

Etelis oculatus
DNA 2195

Etheostoma nigrum (Johnny darter)
N. America
Glucose 3284

‡**Etmopterus spinax**=**Spinax niger** (Latern shark: perhaps should be Lantern shark (?), Velvet belly)
All W. Europe, including Iceland and Mediterranean. 220–270 m. Viviparous. Bottom-dwelling. Possesses luminous organs, unusual in sharks. Diet: fish, squid, prawns.
Antimony 2534; Arsenic 2534; Calcium 1909; Chitinase 1910; Chloride 1906, 1909; Cholesterol 2515; *Free* fatty acids 2515; Glucose 2516; Haematocrit 2516; Haemoglobin 2516; Lactate 2516; Lysozyme 1910; Magnesium 1909; Mercury 2534; Potassium 1906, 1909; Sodium 1906, 1909; Urea 1906

Etroplus crossotus
DNA 2195

‡Etroplus maculatus* (*see* E. suratensis*) *30*

‡Etroplus suratensis*=E. maculatus* (Banded etroplus, Green chromide, Pearl spot, Spotted etroplus)
Sri Lanka, Indian continent. Tolerates fresh water for short periods but is in better condition in salt water. Fry feed in schools on mucus secreted by the parent. Diet: diatoms, algae, crustaceans, detritus, insects.
Volume 1 only

‡Etrumeus micropus (Bigeye sardine, Market sardine, Round herring)
Japan.
Caesium 2269; Cholesterol 2445; Cobalt 2269; α-Cryptoxanthin 2718; Lutein 2718; NAD (nicotinamide adenine dinucleotide) 3259; NADH (reduced form of NAD) 3259; Tunaxanthin 2718; Zeaxanthin 2718; Zinc 2269

Etrumeus terres (Round herring)
Atlantic.
Calcium, Iron: 3057

Eucalia inconstans
DNA 2195

Eucinostomus argenteus (Silver jenny)
W. Atlantic in shallow water over sandy or muddy bottom. Inactive.
Haemoglobin 3377

‡Eucinostomus gula (Shad, Silver jenny)
W. Atlantic: New England and Bermuda to Argentina. Mostly in mangrove-lined tidal creeks, occasionally in turtle-grass beds, at depths around 1 m down to 9 m on sandy or muddy bottoms.
DNA 2195

‡Eucitharus linguatula (Spotted flounder)
Adriatic Sea.
Volume 1 only

‡**Eugaleus galeus** (*see* **Galeorhinus galeus**)

Eugerres plumieri
Caribbean.
Glycogen, Monoamine oxidase, Phosphorylase A: 1855

‡Eumakaira nigra
Japan.
Volume 1 only

‡*Eupomotis gibbosus* (*see Lepomis gibbosus*)

Euthynnus affinis yaito (*see* E. alletteratus)

Euthynnus alletteratus=E. affinis (False albacore, Little tuna, Mackerel tuna)
E. and W. coasts of southern Atlantic, Mediterranean, New Zealand to Brazil, Biscay to S. Africa, S.E. Asia to Australia. A schooling fish which is found in inshore waters. Diet: clupeoid fish, squid, crustaceans.
Free amino acids 3369; Anserine 3369; Cadmium 3638; Carnosine 3369; Copper 2828, 3638; Creatin + creatinine 3369; Mercury 2828, 3638; Taurine 3369; Zinc 2828, 3638.

‡Euthynnus lineatus
Pacific coast of Mexico.
Volume 1 only

‡Euthynnus pelamys (*see* Katsuwonus pelamis)

‡Euthyopteroma virgatum
Japan.
Volume 1 only

‡Eutrigla gurnardus (*see* Trigla gurnardus)

Eutropiichthys vacha
India.
Vitamin A_1, Vitamin A_2: 1500

Eutropius grenfelli
DNA 2195

‡Evynnis cardinalis (Cardinal seabream)
Japan, S. China Sea, northern part of Philippines. Surface to 100 m. Lives over a variety of sea bottoms. Common close to reefs or on rough ground.
Volume 1 only

‡Evynnis japonica (Crimson sea bream) *398*
Japan.
Glucose-6-phosphate dehydrogenase 3258

Exallias brevis
Hawaii. Tropical marine reefs. Stores quantities of oil in its skull (27% lipid, dry weight basis).
Fatty acids, Phospholipids, Sterols, Triglycerides: 3031

Exocoetus volitans (Flying fish)
Astacene, α-Cryptoxanthin, α-Doradecin, Lutein, Tunaxanthin, Zeaxanthin: 2717

Exodon paradoxus
N.E. of S. America. Aggressive. Diet: mostly scales from other fish.
DNA 2195

‡Fistularia petimba (Flute mouth)
Indian Ocean, Japan, N. New Guinea, shores of New South Wales and Queensland, E. Africa to W. tropical America. Shores and estuaries. Active predator. Diet: fish.
Mercury 2888; Selenium 2888; Thiaminase 2297

Forsterygion robustum *30*

Forsterygion varium *30*

‡Fugu niphobles* (Globefish, Grass puffer) *149, 459*
Japan.
Trimethylamine oxide 2111, 2929

Fugu ocellatus obscurus
Japan.
Pyridine nucleotide transhydrogenase 3167

‡Fugu pardalis (Globefish, Puffer)
Japan.
Nicotinamide adenine dinucleotide (NAD), NADH (reduced NAD): 3259

‡Fugu rubripes (Tiger puffer)
Japan.
Cadmium 2901; Cholesterol 2445; Copper 2901; Fatty acids 3488; Galactosyl ceramide 3488; Glucosyl ceramide 3488; Iron 2901; Lead 2901; Potassium 2900; Sodium 2900; Sulphatide 3488; Zinc 2901

‡Fugu vermicularis porphyreus (Mafugu, Shosaifugu) *209*
Japan.
Adenosine diphosphate 2456; Adenosine monophosphate 2456; Amino acids 2456; FREE amino acids 2456; Ammonia 2456; Creatin 2456; Creatinine 2456; Hydroxy-proline 2456; Inosine monophosphate 2456; Taurine 2456; Trimethylamine 2456; Trimethylamine oxide 2111, 2456

Fundulus catenatus (Ozark studfish)
Missouri River.
Cortisol, Sodium 1856

Fundulus chrysotus (Golden ear killifish) *384, 404*
S. Carolina to Florida. Fresh or brackish water. Bottom-living. Thermotolerant.
Chloride 2745

‡*Fundulus diaphanus* (Banded killifish) *312, 313*
Eastern N. America, Quebec to Cape Hatteras. Not marine, but a freshwater fish that is salt tolerant. Tolerates 30‰ on immediate transfer, and 40‰ with acclimation. Prefers quiet waters of lakes and ponds. Forms small schools over sand, gravel or detritus.
FREE amino acids, Ammonia, Chloride, Potassium, Sodium, Taurine: 1430

Fundulus grandis (Gulf killifish) *48, 328, 330, 342, 383, 384, 404, 409, 451*
N. America.
Chloride 2745, 3502; Cortisol 1976; Glucose 1523, 3502; Glucose-6-phosphatase 1523; Glycogen phosphorylase 1523; 5-hydroxytryptamine 1927; potassium 3502; Sodium 3502

‡Fundulus heteroclitus* (Killifish, Mummichog, Saltwater minnow) *6, 34, 35, 37, 44, 49, 197, 235, 239, 252, 255, 264, 281, 284–286, 289, 291, 297, 301, 304, 312, 313, 324, 334, 338, 341–343, 345, 386, 409, 419, 454*
Coast of N. America (Labrador to Mexico) in estuaries and brackish tidal pools. Tolerant of very low oxygen levels, also of big variations in temperature and salinity. Buries in mud during winter. Schools in shallow waters. Omnivorous, also scavenging drifting refuse. The lipid composition of the brain conforms to that of the usual vertebrate brain, with low triglyceride, high cholesterol and high phospholipid contents. However, phosphatidyl choline rather than phosphatidyl ethanolamine is the major phospholipid, in contrast to the brains of birds and mammals. The amount of glycolipid is small (Bailey, 1973).
Mg-ATPase (magnesium-activated adenosine triphosphatase) 2321; Na-K-ATPase 2321, 2379; Bicarbonate 2371, 3039, 3492; Calcium 2971, 3039, 3339, 3492; Carbon dioxide 3339; Chloride 1860, 2971, 2972, 3039, 3339, 3492, 3497, 3503, 3506; Cholesterol 1479, 3039, 3339, 3492; Corticosterone 2576; Cortisol 2527, 2576; DNA 2195; Glucose 1525, 2527, 3039, 3339, 3492, 3499, 3503, 3506, 3507; Glucose-6-phosphatase 1525; Glucose-6-phosphate dehydrogenase 1955; Glycogen 3039, 3499, 3507; Glycogen phosphorylase 1525, 3515; Glycolipid 1479; Haematocrit 3339, 3507; Magnesium 3039, 3339, 3492; Neutral lipid 1479; Non-protein nitrogen 3039, 3492; Phosphatidyl choline 1479; Phosphatidyl ethanolamine 1479; 6-phosphogluconate dehydrogenase 1955; Phospholipid 1479, 3339; Phosphorylase 1524; Potassium 2972, 3039, 3339, 3492, 3503, 3506; Sodium 1860, 2972, 3039, 3339, 3492, 3494, 3497, 3503, 3506; Triglycerides 1479; Urea 3039, 3339, 3492

‡*Fundulus kansae* (Plains killifish) *286, 400, 401*
N. America.
Volume 1 only

Fundulus majalis
DNA 2195

Fundulus olivaceus (Blackspotted topminnow)
N. America.
Sodium 1857

‡Fundulus parvipinnis* (California killifish) *284*
N. America. Tolerates salinity from fresh water to salines greater than full-strength sea water.
Volume 1 only

Fundulus similis *383*

‡Furcina osimae
Japan.
Volume 1 only

Gadiculus argenteus (Silvery pout)
N. Norway and Iceland to Biscay, but not North Sea or Irish Sea. 60–1000 m over muddy ground. Diet: worms and small crustaceans.
Copper, Lead, Mercury, Zinc: 1708

‡Gadus aeglefinus (*see* Melanogrammus aeglefinus)

‡Gadus callarias (Baltic cod) *9, 28, 36, 39, 41, 42, 44, 46–48, 53, 61, 206*
 Baltic Sea and approaches.
 Amino acids 1812, 2705; *Free* amino acids 2704; Alanine 2704; Arsenic 1631;
 Aspartic acid 2704; Cadmium 1631; Calcium 2294; Cathepsin (in frozen tissue)
 1924; Cholesterol 1785; 3239; Cobalt 2491; Copper 2491; Fatty acids 3088;
 Free fatty acids 3239; Glutamic acid 2704; Glycogen 1559; Iron 2491; Lead
 1631; Manganese 2491; Mercury 1631; Mercury 3617 (this value may relate to
 G. morhua); Phospholipids 3239; Sterol esters 3239; Triglycerides 3239; Tri-
 methylamine 2380; Trimethylamine oxide 2380, Zinc 2491

Gadus luscus
 Fucose, Galactosamine, Galactose, Glucosamine, Glucose, Hexosamines, Hexoses,
 Hydroxyproline, Mannose, Uronic acid: 2770

‡Gadus macrocephalus (Grey cod, Pacific cod)
 Japan, Korea, Bering Sea, Alaska, California. 9–550 m.
 Adenosine diphosphate 1871; Adenosine monophosphate 1871; Adenosine tri-
 phosphate 1871; Calcium 3090, 3486; Chloride 3090; Fatty acids 2152, 3666,
 3667; Inosine monophosphate 1871, 1873; Magnesium 3090; Neutral lipids 2152;
 Potassium 3090; Sodium 3090; Strontium 3486; Trimethylamine 1873, 2388;
 Trimethylamine oxide 3151; Vitamin D 3673

Gadus minutus (Poor cod)
 Lactic dehydrogenase 1789

‡Gadus morhua (often given in the literature as G. callarias) (Atlantic cod, Cod.
 Immature form known as codling) *4, 6, 27–32, 39–41, 43–46, 49, 52, 54, 60, 61,
 63, 74, 75, 79, 87, 88, 93–97, 99, 103, 106–109, 112, 114, 117, 119, 122, 131, 137–
 139, 144, 146, 150, 162, 163, 167–169, 171–173, 183, 185, 186, 189, 195, 196, 201–
 203, 205–207, 209–211, 222–224, 226, 227, 229, 241, 245, 247, 248, 252, 254, 259,
 277, 278, 319–322, 337–339, 349, 351, 358–381, 384, 386, 387, 392, 400, 407, 408,
 411, 414, 415, 416, 428, 430, 435–437, 442, 444, 446, 452, 455, 458, 463, 465, 467*
 Both sides of Atlantic: Nova Zemlaya to Biscay, Greenland, Newfoundland and
 Labrador coasts. Usually bottom-living in shallow offshore waters down to 450 m
 or more at 2–10°C. Earlier it was thought that the osmoregulatory system broke
 down at temperatures below 4°C and eventually caused the death of the fish, but
 work by Harden Jones and Scholes (1974) has shown that they survive for at least 80
 days at 0°C, and other work is quoted by the same authors showing that 60 days
 at −1·4° still is not fatal. The muscle water content varies with the temperature
 (77·9% at −1·5°C up to 82·1% at 16°C—same authors), and at lower temperatures
 the blood shows increased osmolality. However, there is no evidence to suggest that
 this is the result of osmoregulatory failure. The upper temperature limit is around
 16–18°C, but there is evidence that younger fish survive the highest temperatures
 better than do older fish (Dando, personal communication). The intensity of haem
 pigmentation in the dark muscle of this species relates to the physical activity during
 recent weeks, so migratory stocks of cod have a darker dark muscle than have
 stationary stocks. Large specimens become more depleted at spawning time than

small specimens, since larger fish produce a larger proportion of their body weight as eggs. The water content of the muscle is usually close to 80%, but this value can be increased to as much as 95% after prolonged starvation in the laboratory. In fish from the wild, values of over 87% have been recorded. As in carp, older fish survive severe starvation better than do younger fish. Diet: carnivorous, feeding on a variety of marine creatures, but larger specimens prefer to eat fish. Crabs and shrimps are eaten at certain times of the year.

n-Acetyl histidine 2181; Acid phosphatase 2958; ATPase (Adenosine triphosphatase) 2345; Adrenaline 1409; Alanine amino transferase 2793; Aldolase 1789; Alkaline phosphatase 2958; n-Alkanes (series) 2119; Amino acids 1412, 1577, 1786, 2609, 2772, 3082, 3672; *Free* amino acids 2977, 3329; *Free* amino acids (a single figure) 2181; Ammonia 3303; Amylase 2958; Anserine 2977; Arginase 2256; Argininosuccinate lyase 2256; Argininosuccinate synthetase 2256; Arsenic 1631; Aspartate aminotransferase 2793; Astaxanthin 2507; Cadmium 1631, 1972, 2148, 2364; Calcium 1786, 1908, 1909, 2364, 3294; Carbamoyl phosphate synthetase 2256; Carboxypeptidase A 2958; Carboxypeptidase B 2958; Cardiolipid 3233; Carnosine 2977; Cephalin (*see* Phosphatidyl ethanolamine); Chitinase 1910; Chloride 1860, 1908, 1909, 2113, 3294; Cholesterol 1419, 1581, 1954, 2515, 3056, 3237; Chymotrypsin 2958; Cobalt 2364, 2491; Collagen 1577; Copper 2364, 2491, 2901, 3294; Creatin 2855, 3303; Creatin phosphate 2899; Creatinine 2855, 3303; Cytochrome oxidase 1579, 2009, 2011; Diamine oxidase 2231; Diphosphatidyl glycerol 1581; Fatty acids 2007, 3153; *Free* fatty acids 1419, 1581, 1671, 2515, 3056, 3237; Furan fatty acids 2092; Unsaturated fatty acids 1954; Fluoride 2404, 3294; Formaldehyde 1671; Fructose-1,6-diphosphate 1638; Fructose monophosphate 1638; Fumarase 1579; Glucose 1908, 2113, 2516; Glucose-1-phosphate 1638; Glucose-6-phosphate 1638; Glucose-6-phosphate dehydrogenase 1579; Glucose phosphate isomerase 1789; Glyceraldehyde phosphate dehydrogenase 1789; Glycerides 3056; Glycerol phosphate dehydrogenase 1579; Glycogen 2607, 2899; Haematocrit 2516; Haemoglobin 2516; Hexokinase 1579; Histidine 2181; Hydrocarbons 1419; Hydroxyproline 1577, 2772, 3672; Iodine 3294; Iron 1786, 2364, 2491, 2901, 3294; Lactate 1638, 1789, 2516, 2899; Lactic dehydrogenase 1579, 1789 (name given as G. callarias), 2009, 2011; Lead 1631, 2364, 2901; Leucine amino peptidase 2958; Lysolecithin 3056; Lysozyme 1910; Magnesium 1908, 1909, 2364, 2462, 2463, 3294; Malic dehydrogenase 1579; Malic enzyme 2794–2796; Manganese 2364, 2491, 3294; Mercury 1631, 1953, 2148, 2364, 2482; Niacin 1786; Nickel 2491; Nitrite 1864; Noradrenaline 1409; Ornithine 2977; Ornithine transcarbamoylase 2256; Pantothenic acid 3211; Phosphatidic acid 3233; Phosphatidyl choline 1419, 1581, 3056, 3233; Phosphatidyl ethanolamine 3056, 3233; Phosphatidyl inositol 3233; Phosphatidyl serine 3233; Phosphoenolpyruvate carboxykinase 2794, 2796; Phosphofructokinase 1579; Phosphoglucomutase 1789; 6-phosphogluconate dehydrogenase 1579; Phosphoglycerate kinase 1789; Phospholipids 1419, 1577, 1954, 2599, 3047, 3056, 3237; Phosphopyruvate hydratase 1789; Potassium 1908, 1909, 2364, 2900, 3294; Pristane 2007; Proline 2772; Propionyl-CoA 2796; Protease 2958; Pyridoxine 3211; Pyruvate 1789; Pyruvate kinase 1579, 1789, 2011; Retinol (*see* Vitamin A); Riboflavin 1786; Ribonuclease 2958; Sarcosine 2977; Serine ethanolamine phosphate 2181; Sodium 1786, 1860, 1908, 2364, 2900, 3294; Sphingomyelin 1419, 3056, 3233; Squalene 2007; Sterol esters 1419; "Sugar" 1577, 2643; Taurine 2977; Thiamine 1786; Threonine ethanolamine phosphate 2181; Triglycerides 1419, 1581, 1954, 3237; Trimethylamine 2380; Trimethylamine oxide 2380; Triose phosphate isomerase 1789; Trypsin

2958; Urate oxidase 1711; Urea 3303; Uric acid 3303; Vitamin A 3237; Vitamin A aldehyde (retinal) 3047; Xanthine oxidase 1711; Zinc 2364, 2491, 2901, 3610

‡Gadus navaga (Wachna cod) *49*
N. Russia.
Cholesterol 1954; Creatin 2855; Creatinine 2855; Unsaturated fatty acids 1954; Phospholipids 1954; Triglycerides 1954

‡Gadus ogac (Fjord cod, Greenland cod)
Arctic. W. Greenland to Point Barrow, Alaska.
Arsenic 1560

‡Gadus pollachius = Pollachius pollachius (Pollack), *410*
Norway to N. Africa, not Iceland. Mainly inshore, near rocks, down to 200 m. Diet: deep-sea prawns, sandeels, herring, sprats.
Chitinase, Lysozyme: 1910

‡Gadus poutassou (*see* Micromesistius poutassou)

‡Gadus virens (*see* Pollachius virens)

Gaidropsarus cimbrius
Europe.
Calcium 1909; Chloride 1909; Cholesterol 2515; *Free* fatty acids 2515; Glucose 2516; Haematocrit 2516; Lactate 2516; Magnesium 1909; Potassium 1909; Sodium 1909

Gaidropsarus mediterraneus
Calcium, Chloride, Magnesium, Potassium, Sodium: 2864

‡Galeichthys felis (Sea cat)
N. America: Cape Cod to Texas. Bays and harbours. Fertilised eggs carried in the mouth of the male until hatched.
DNA 2195

‡**Galeocerdo arcticus** (Leopard shark, Spotted shark, Tiger shark, Tigrone)
Tropical seas, occasionally Iceland.
Volume 1 only

‡**Galeocerdo cuvieri** (Tiger shark)
World-wide in tropical or sub-tropical waters. In W. Atlantic ranges from Cape Cod to Uruguay, in E. Pacific from Peru to S. California. Inshore and offshore, often enters river mouths. A scavenger. Viviparous. Very aggressive. Diet: a wide variety of marine life.
Volume 1 only

‡**Galeorhinus australis** (School shark, Snapper shark, Tope)
Australia. 4–180 m depth. Viviparous.
Copper, Zinc: 1893

‡**Galeorhinus galeus = Eugaleus galeus** (Sweet William, Tope)
Iceland, mid-Norway to Mediterranean, S. Africa. Also other temperate and tropical seas. 40–100 m. Viviparous. Solitary. Lives close to sea bottom. Diet: bottom-
living fish, especially flat fish.
Potassium, Sodium: 2562

‡**Galeorhinus zyopterus** (Oil shark, Soupfin shark)
S. California to N. British Columbia. Chile and Peru. 50–400 m, mlaes usually
living in the greater depths. Epipelagic. Viviparous. Males smaller than females.
Diet: a wide variety of fish and squid.
Trimethylamine oxide 3151

‡**Galeus glaucus**
Japan.
Volume 1 only

Gambusia affinis holbrooki* (Top minnow) *11, 324*
Atlantic coast of N. America, New Jersey to Florida. Feeds at the surface, especially
on insect larvae. Viviparous. Preferred temperature 27–31°C.
DNA 2195

‡*Gardonus rutilus*
Volume 1 only for bibliography: page reference this volume: *416*

‡Garra taeniata
DNA 2195

‡Garrupa nigrita (Black grouper, Black jewfish)
S. Atlantic, Gulf coast of America, Cuba, Brazil, perhaps Sicily.
Volume 1 only

Gasteropelecus laevis (Silver hatchetfish)
Lower Amazon in shaded pools. Diet: insects, insect larvae, crustaceans.
DNA 2195

‡Gasterosteus aculeatus* (Pinfish, Spantickle, Three-spined stickleback, Tiddler)
300, 301, 305
Northern hemisphere. A shore fish (in deeper water in winter), equally at home in
fresh or salt water, and can breed in either. Nest-building, eggs being guarded by
the male. Hardy and pugnacious. Marine form known as Gasterosteus aculeatus
trachurus, freshwater form G.a.leiurus. Great morphological variability within the
species. Voracious. Diet: fish eggs and fry, small crustaceans, worms.
DNA 2195; Magnesium 2864, Potassium 2864, Sodium 2864

Gasterosteus aculeatus microcephalus
Japan.
Astacene, β-Carotene, α-Cryptoxanthin, Cynthiaxanthin, Diatoxanthin, Lutein,
Tunaxanthin, Zeaxanthin: 2717

‡Genypterus capensis (Kingklip)
S. Africa. 54–465 m.
Volume 1 only

Geophagus jurupari
DNA 2195

Geotrea australis* CYCLOSTOME (Korokoro, Piharau, Pouched lamprey)
S. Australia, Tasmania, New Zealand. Rivers and coastal waters. As adult,
parasitic on other fish, sucking the blood.
DNA 3136

‡Gephyroberyx japonicus
Japan.
Volume 1 only

‡Germo alalunga (*see* Thunnus alalunga)

‡Germo germo (*see* Thunnus alalunga)

‡Germo macropterus (*see* Thunnus albacares)

‡Gerres filamentosus* (Longrayed silverbiddy, Spotted mojarras, Whipfin mojarra)
E. and S. Africa, India, Malaya, Philippines, New Guinea, Australia. Seas and
mouths of rivers, pearl banks, shallow waters down to 30 m in schools. Diet:
bottom-living animals.
Folic acid 2582

‡Gillichthys mirabilis (Long-jawed goby, Mudsucker) *162, 168, 300, 336*
Pacific coast of N. America, Japan. Shallow areas of bays; mudflats. Hardy and
eurythermal, but avoids temperatures above 23°C or below 9°C. Preferred temperature 22°C.
Sodium 2831

Ginglymostoma cirratum (Nurse shark) *459*
Both sides of tropical and subtropical Atlantic. Common in shallow water.
Viviparous. Inhabits water at 23–30°C. Can convert tertiary amines such as
choline and trimethylamine to trimethylamine oxide, a facility not possessed by all
elasmobranchs.
2′3′-*cyclic*-adenosine monophosphate-3′-phosphoester hydrolase 3450; Amine
oxidase 2030; Chloride 1666; DNA 2194; Methyl transferase 1625; Sodium 1666;
Trimethylamine oxidase 2030; Urea 1666

‡Girella elevata
Australia.
Volume 1 only

Girella melanichthys
Japan.
Trimethylamine oxide 2111

‡Girella nigricans (California bluefish, Greenfish, Opaleye, White spot)
Coast of S. California, intertidal to 30 m. Preferred temperature 26 to 31°C. Diet:
algae and eelgrass with associated animal food.
DNA 2195

‡Girella punctata
Japan.
Free histidine 3166

‡Girella tricuspidata* (Black bream, Blackfish, Darkie, Luderick)
Australia, especially New South Wales, Tasmania and New Zealand. Rivers and estuaries, sheltered coastal waters in weedy places. Diet: algae and associated animals.
Volume 1 only

‡Glossanodon semifasciatus (Deep sea smelt)
Japan.
Volume 1 only

‡Glossogobius giuris* (Bareyed goby, Flathead goby) *36*
E. Africa, India, China, Japan, Australia and all parts of the Indo-Australian archipelago. Seas, rivers, swamps and lakes. A fused ventral fin enables the fish to cling to rocks, etc.
Folic acid 2582; Vitamin A_1 1500; Vitamin A_2 1500

‡**Glyphis glaucus** (Great blue shark)
Japan, Europe, America. Viviparous.
Anserine 3368; Balenine 3368; Cholesterol 2768; 7-dehydrocholesterol 2768; Fatty acids 3666, 3667; Glycine 2087; Hexosamine 2087; Hexose 2087; Hydroxyproline 2087; Pentose 2087; Proline 2087; Tyrosine 2087

‡Glyptocephalus cynoglossus (Grey—or gray—sole, Pole flounder, Witch, Witch flounder) *129, 132, 173*
Both sides of N. Atlantic. 50–1700 m on soft bottoms. Bottom-living at 5–7°C. Diet: mainly worms, starfish, molluscs, crustaceans.
Calcium 1908, 1909; Chitinase 1910; Chloride 1860, 1908, 1909; Cholesterol 2515; Cobalt 2491; Copper 2491; *Free* fatty acids 2515; Diamine oxidase 2231; Glucose 1908, 2516; Haematocrit 2516; Haemoglobin 2516; Iron 2491; Lactate 2516; Lysozyme 1910; Magnesium 1908, 1909; Manganese 2491; Potassium 1908, 1909; Sodium 1860, 1908, 1909; "Sugar" 2643; Zinc 2491

Glyptocephalus stelleri (Japanese rex sole)
Japan.
Fatty acids 2154

‡Glyptocephalus zachirus (Rex sole)
S. California to Bering Sea. 20–720 m. Slow-growing; lives to at least 24 years. Delicate: does not survive handling well.
D-Amino acid oxidase 1923; Calcium 2090; Cathepsin 1993; Chloride 3090; DNA 2195; Magnesium 3090; Mercury 1697; Potassium 3090; Sodium 3090

‡Gnathagnus elongatus (Blue mishima puffer fish)
Japan.
Volume 1 only

Gnathonemus petersi
  W. Africa, Niger to Congo on soft bottoms. More active by night than by day,
  but sluggish.
  DNA 2195

‡*Gobio gobio* (Gudgeon)
  Europe except S. Italy, S. Spain, Iceland and Norway. A bottom-living fish of
  swift waters and clean gravel. Inshore in lakes. Diet: bottom-living insect larvae,
  crustaceans and molluscs.
  Volume 1 only

Gobius batrachocephalus (Flathead goby, Toad goby)
  Black Sea, Sea of Azov. Inhabits estuaries on sand or shell grounds, inshore down
  to 40 m. Diet: small fish.
  Corticosterone + cortisol 1704

‡Gobius giuris* (*see* Glossogobius giuris*)

‡*Gobius lota*
  Mediterranean and Black Seas. Brackish water in estuaries and lagoons on mud
  and eel-grass beds.
  Volume 1 only

‡Gobius melanostomus* = Neogobius melanostomus* (Blackspotted goby, Goby,
  Round goby) *13, 51, 53, 290*
  Russia: Borders of Black Sea, Azov Sea, Sea of Marmora. Bottom-living fish
  inhabiting brackish inshore waters over shell grounds. Penetrates far upstream.
  Females smaller than males. Diet: mostly molluscs, some crustaceans. Spawns
  several times in a season at diminishing intervals.
  Aluminium 2677; Calcium 2677; Cholesterol 1690, 1691; Cobalt 2677; Copper
  2677; *Free* fatty acids 1691; Iron 2677; Magnesium 2677; Manganese 2677;
  Phospholipids 1690, 1691; Potassium 2677; Sterol esters 1691; Tin 2677; Triglycerides 1690, 1691; Vanadium 2677; Zinc 2677

Gobius niger jozo (Black goby)
  Mediterranean and Black Seas. Trondheim fjord to Morocco. Tolerates brackish
  and estuarine waters, 30–40 m. Diet: small crustaceans, polychaete worms,
  molluscs, fish fry.
  Cadmium 1707, 1709; Chromium 2015; Copper 1707, 1709; Lead 1707, 1709,
  2015; Mercury 1707, 1709, 2015; Zinc 1707, 1709

Gobius ophiocephalus (Snakehead goby)
  Coast of N. Mediterranean, Adriatic and Black Seas, Sea of Azov. Mainly on
  muddy bottoms covered with eel grass. Does not enter fresh water. Diet: small
  crabs, shrimps, fish.
  Calcium, Chloride, Magnesium, Potassium, Sodium: 2864

Gobius paganellus (Rocky goby)
  English Channel to Mediterranean.
  Lactic dehydrogenase 1789

Gobius sadanundio
    DNA 2195

Gobius sp.
    Glycogen 2543

‡Goniistius zonatus (Striped morwong)
    Japan, China Sea. Rocky bottoms.
    Pyridine nucleotide transhydrogenase 3167

Gonostoma denudatum *126*
    Deep water. Possesses a swim bladder and well-ossified bones, unlike G. elongatum.

Gonostoma elongatum *126*
    Russia. A deep-water fish with a reduced quantity of swimming musculature which
    is watery. It has poorly-ossified bones in order to become almost neutrally buoyant
    without the aid of a swim bladder.
    Fatty acids 2469; Phosphatidyl choline 3064; Phosphatidyl ethanolamine 3064;
    Phosphatidyl inositol 3064; Phosphatidyl serine 3064; Polyglycerophosphatides
    3064; Sphingomyelin 3064

‡Gymnacanthus pistilliger
    Japan.
    Volume 1 only

‡Gymnacanthus tricuspis (Arctic staghorn sculpin)
    Arctic and N. Atlantic Oceans. In deep fjords of northern Labrador they live
    permanently at $-1\cdot7°C$ in the supercooled state.
    Volume 1 only

Gymnapastes marmoratus (Soldier fish)
    Australia.
    Copper, Manganese, Zinc: 1893

Gymnocorymbus ternetzi (Blackamoor, Black tetra)
    Rio Paraguary, S. America. Sluggish. Shoaling.
    DNA 2195

‡Gymnocranius griseus (Ginkgo fish, Grey large-eye bream, Large-eyed bream,
    Meichi porgy)
    India, Malaysia, Japan to East Indies and N. coast of Australia. Coastal waters
    down to 80 m. Diet: bottom-living crustaceans and fish.
    Volume 1 only

Gymnodraco acuticeps
    Antarctic. Aglomerular.
    Calcium 1840; Chloride 1804, 1860; Magnesium 1840; Potassium 1840; Sodium
    1840, 1860

Gymnogobius macrognathus
    Sakhalin.
    Calcium, Magnesium, Potassium, Sodium: 2864

‡Gymnothorax kidako (Moray eel)
   Japan.
   NAD (nicotinamide adenine dinucleotide), NADH (reduced NAD): 3259

Gymnothorax moringa (Spotted moray)
   Florida to Brazil, 3–15 m. Usually hides in rocky crevices.
   DNA 2195; Haematocrit 3377; Haemoglobin 3377

Gymnothorax nigromarginatus
   Russia.
   Cerebroside 2469, 2470; DNA 2195; Fatty acids 2469; Sulphatide 2469, 2470

Gymnothorax reticularis
   Japan.
   Trimethylamine oxide 2111

Gymnotus carapo (Banded knifefish, Electric eel)
   Guatemala to Argentina from coast to Andes. Shaded creeks in slow and still
   water, particularly peaty water. Fin-propelled. Forages in the dark. Diet: (young)
   crustaceans and insect larvae; (adult) shrimps. fish.
   DNA 2195

Gymnura macrura (Lesser butterfly ray)
   S. Africa. Warm temperate regions of W. Atlantic. Shallow waters with sandy
   bottom. Diet: a variety of invertebrates. Viviparous.
   Arginine 1653; DNA 2194

Gyrinocheilus aymonieri
   Cambodia, Thailand. Mostly mountain areas in swift-running or still waters. Very
   quick swimmer. Diet: algae.
   DNA 2195

Haemulon aurolineatus
   Russia.
   Cerebroside 2469; Fatty acids 2469; Ganglioside 2469; Sialic acid 2470; Sulphatide
   2469

‡Haemulon flavolineatum (French grunt, Openmouthed grunt, Yellow grunt)
   Florida, W. Indies to Brazil. Shore line to 15 m.
   DNA 2195

Haemulon melanurum
   America. Inactive.
   DNA 2195; Haematocrit 3377; Haemoglobin 3377

Haemulon parrai
   America. Inactive.
   Haematocrit 3377; Haemoglobin 3377

‡Haemulon plumieri (Boar grunt, Common grunt, Ronco ronco, Squirrel fish)
   W. Indies to Rio de Janeiro. Inactive.
   DNA 2195; Haematocrit 3377; Haemoglobin 3377

‡Haemulon sciurus (Bluestriped grunt, Boar grunt, Humpback grunt, Yellow grunt)
Florida, Bermuda to Brazil on reefs.
DNA 2195; Haematocrit 3377; Haemoglobin 3377; Succinic dehydrogenase 2750

Halichoeres bivittatus (Slippery Dick)
Bermuda, shores. Sluggish.
Succinic dehydrogenase 2750

Halichoeres poecilopterus (Pudding wife)
Japan.
NAD (nicotinamide adenine dinucleotide) 3259; NADH (reduced NAD) 3259;
Pyridine nucleotide transhydrogenase 3167

‡Halieutea stellata (Red batfish, Red rattlefish)
Japan, Korea, China. Medium-deep waters.
Cadmium 2901; Copper 2901; Iron 2901; Lead, 2901; Potassium 2900; Sodium
2900; Zinc 2901

Haplogenys mucronatus
Japan.
Cadmium 2901; Copper 2901; Iron 2901; Lead 2901; Potassium 2900; Sodium
2900; Zinc 2901

Haplochromis longirostris
DNA 2195

Haplochromis parvidens
DNA 2195

Haplochromis quiarti
DNA 2195

Haplochromis squamipinnis
DNA 2195

Haplochromis squamulatus
DNA 2195

Harengula humeralis (Redear sardine) 73, 74
Caribbean Sea, Florida to Venezuela. Enters estuaries. Shoaling. Diet: plankton.
Glycogen 3646

‡Harengula sardina (Sardina de Ley)
W. Indies.
Volume 1 only

Harengula zunasi (Shad)
Japan.
Caesium 2269; Cobalt 2269; α-Cryptoxanthin 2718; Diatoxanthin 2718; Lutein
2718; Thiaminase 2297; Tunaxanthin 2718; Zeaxanthin 2718; Zinc 2269

‡Harpadon nehereus (Bombay duck, Bummalo)
Tanzania, India, China, Java, Borneo. Coastal and in estuaries. Migratory, living
offshore for part of the year. Diet: small fish and crustaceans.
Volume 1 only

Hauliodus sloanei
Caught at about 1000 m.
Phosphatidyl choline, Phosphatidyl ethanolamine, Phosphatidyl inositol, Phos-
phatidyl serine, Polyglycerophosphatides, Sphingomyelin: 3064

Helicolenus dactylopterus (Blackbelly rosefish, Bluemouth, Rockfish)
Nova Scotia to Virginia, S. Norway to Madeira and Mediterranean. 200–800 m.
Predatory. Diet: fish, crustaceans, squid, sea urchins, brittle stars.
Mercury 1891

‡Helicolenus hilgendorfi (Hilgendorf saucord)
Mediterranean, Japan. Deep waters.
Astaxanthin diester 3466

Helicolenus papillosis (Red rock gurnard)
Australia.
Cadmium, Copper, Manganese, Zinc: 1893

Helostoma rudolfi
DNA 2195

‡*Helostoma temmincki* (Kissing gourami)

Thailand, Malaya, Sumatra, Borneo, Indonesia. Ponds, streams, swamps, in well-
vegetated areas which are often deficient in oxygen. Possesses accessory respiratory
organs above the gills. Diet: wide variety of plant and animal food.
Volume 1 only

‡Helotes sexlineatus (Sixlined perch, Striped perch)
India, Australia, Japan. Inshore. Diet: invertebrates, fish.
Volume 1 only

‡*Hemibarbus barbus* (Skin carp)
Japan. Rivers and lakes.
Volume 1 only

Hemigrammus caudovittatus (Buenos Aires tetra)
Argentina. Partly vegetarian.
DNA 2195

Hemigrammus ocellifer (Beacon fish, Head and tail light tetra)
Amazon Basin and Guyana.
DNA 2195

‡Hemilepidotus gilberti
Japan.
Volume 1 only

Hemilepidotus hemilepidotus (Red Irish lord)
    California to Alaska, Aleutian Is., Bering Sea, Kamchatka. Shallow waters. Diet:
    crabs, barnacles, mussels.
    Calcium, Chloride, Magnesium, Potassium, Sodium: 3090

Hemilepidotus jordani (Yellow sculpin)
    Alaska.
    Calcium, Chloride, Magnesium, Potassium, Sodium: 3090

Hemirhamphus balao
    Fatty acids 2469

‡Hemirhamphus georgii (Long-billed half-beak)
    India, Java, Philippines, New Guinea. Tropical and subtropical seas, near shore.
    Volume 1 only

‡Hemirhamphus sajori* (Half beak, Japanese needlefish)
    Japan. Coastal. Occasionally enters rivers. Diet: crustaceans.
    Thiaminase 2297

Hemiscyllium plagiosum (Lip shark)
    Calcium, Chloride, Magnesium, Potassium, Sodium, Urea: 1681, 3654

‡Hemitripterus americanus (Gurnet, Puffbelly, Sea raven, Whip sculpin) *297, 321*
    Atlantic coast of N. America: Newfoundland to Chesapeake Bay down to 182 m.
    Can inflate body cavity with water. Diet: bottom-living invertebrates, especially
    crustaceans and fish.
    Mg-ATPase (magnesium-activated adenosine triphosphatase) 2321; Na-K-ATPase
    2321; Chloride 1860; Cortisol 2961; Cortisone 2961; DNA 2195; Haematocrit
    2961; Mercury 1953; Sodium 1860; "Sugar" 2643

‡Heptatretus (? Eptatretus) okinoseanus CYCLOSTOME
    Japan.
    Volume 1 only

Hesperoleucus symmetricus (Western roach) *265*
    Acetylserotonin methyltransferase 2095

Heterodontus francisci (Horn shark) *327*
    Gulf of California to Monterey Bay. Shallow waters to 150 m. Sluggish. Eggs laid
    in horny case. Preferred temperature 24°C. Diet: hard-shelled animals.
    Alkaline phosphatase 3525; Bicarbonate 3525; Calcium 3525; Chloride 3525;
    Cholesterol 3525; Cyanocobalamin 2868; DNA 2194; Eosinophils 2868; Erythro-
    cytes 2868; Folic acid 2868; Haematocrit 2868; Haemoglobin 2868; Heterophils
    2868; Leucocytes 2868; Lymphocytes 2868; Magnesium 3525; Neutrophils 2868;
    Potassium 3525; Sodium 3525; Sulphate 3525; Testosterone 2868; Thrombocytes
    2868; Urea 3525

Heterodontus japonicus (Cat shark, Port Jackson shark)
    Japan. Warm waters.
    NAD (nicotinamide adenine dinucleotide), NADH (reduced form of NAD): 3259

‡**Heterodontus philippi** (*see* **H. portusjacksoni**)

Heterodontus portusjacksoni = **H. philippi** (Port Jackson shark)
S. Australia. Egg-laying.
Amino acids 2859, 2860

Heteromycteris japonicus
Japan.
Trimethylamine oxide 2111

‡*Heteropneustes fossilis* = *Saccobranchus fossilis* (Stinging catfish) *27, 72, 232, 237, 317, 385*
India, Burma, Vietnam, Thailand. Ponds in low country, swamps and marshes.
Has accessory respiratory organs. Very active and hardy. Diet: insects, molluscs,
small fish, ostracods, debris, algae. The fish has no regular food preference.
Acetyl choline 2957; Acid phosphatase 2316; Alkaline phosphatase 2316, 3404;
Ascorbic acid 1799; Basophils 2969; Calcium 3278; Cholesterol 3268, 3278;
Eosinophils 2969; Erythrocytes 2326, 2362, 2967, 2969, 3408; Glucose 2419, 3278,
3405, 3407; Glycogen 2419; Haematocrit 2362, 2967, 2969; Haemoglobin 2326,
2362, 2967, 2969; Histamine 2955; Iron 3278; Lactate 3405, 3407; Leucocytes 2326,
2362, 2967, 2969; Lymphocytes 2326, 2969; Monocytes 2969; Neutrophils 2326,
2969; Non-protein nitrogen 3278; 5′-nucleotidase 1468, 2316; Spindle cells 2969;
Succinic dehydrogenase 3363; Vitamin A_1 1500; Vitamin A_2 1500

‡**Heteroscymnus longus**
Japan.
Volume 1 only

Hexagrammos decagrammus (Kelp greenling)
S. California to S.E. Alaska, Aleutian Is. Abundant along rocky shores of British
Columbia. Shallows to 45 m. Diet: worms, crustaceans, and small fish.
DNA 2195

Hexagrammos lagocephalus (Rock greenling)
D-Amino acid oxidase 1923

‡Hexagrammos octogrammus (Alaska greenfish, Masked greenling) *265*
Aleutian Is. westward to Petropaulski and Robben Is. N. British Columbia, Gulf
of Alaska, Okhotsk Sea.
Volume 1 only

‡Hexagrammos otakii (Greenling)
Japan, Korea.
Calcium 3486; β-Carotene 2716; Connective tissue 3462; α-Cryptoxanthin 2716;
Diatoxanthin 2716; α-Doradecin 2716; Lutein 2716; NAD (nicotinamide adenine
dinucleotide) 3259; NADH (reduced NAD) 3259; Strontium 3486; Thiaminase
3473; Trimethylamine oxide 2111; Tunaxanthin 2716; Zeaxanthin 2716

‡Hexagrammos stelleri (White spotted greenling)
Japan, N. California to Bering Sea. Rocky shores, sandy beaches.
Ornithine aminotransferase 3611

‡**Hexanchus griseus** = **H. corinum** (Cow shark, Grey shark, Mud shark, Sixgill shark)
S. California to Alaska, Japan, Australia. Temperate areas of all oceans. Mediterranean. Atlantic: Iceland to English Channel. Not in Tropics. Deep water over mud bottoms. Sluggish. Viviparous. Diet: most large marine creatures; wide variety of fish, particularly hake and rays, marine mammals.
Arsenic 2535

‡Hilsa ilisha* (Hilsa River shad, Sable fish)
Persian Gulf ascending the Tigris, Seas of India, Burma, Malaya, ascending rivers to breed.
Volume 1 only

‡Hilsa toli* (Chinese herring, Shad, Sablefish, Toli shad)
India, Malaya, China, Taiwan. Coastal waters, estuaries, rivers.
Volume 1 only

Hiodon alosoides (Goldeye)
Widely distributed in N. America in turbid waters, large lakes and muddy rivers. Mainly nocturnal. Avoids temperatures above 28·5°C or below 22°C. Diet: insects, insect larvae, small fish.
Allantoicase 1775; Alltoinase 1775; Arginase 1776; Mercury 3649; Thyroxine 2190

Hiodon tergisus (Mooneye)
Calcium 2264; Chloride 2264; Magnesium 2264; Mercury 3649; Potassium 2264; Sodium 2264

Hippocampus erectus (Spotted seahorse)
Atlantic coast of N. America: Cape Cod to N. Carolina. Lives among eelgrass and seaweed. Diet: small copepods, amphipods and other crustacea.
DNA 2195

‡Hippoglossoides dubius (Flathead flounder, Flathead sole, Red halibut)
Japan, Kamchatka, Korea.
Adenosine monophosphate 2456; Adenosine triphosphate 2456; Amino acids 2456; Free amino acids 2456, 3166; Ammonia 2456; Creatin 2456; Creatinine 2456; Fatty acids 2154; Hydroxyproline 2456; Taurine 2456, 3166; Thiaminase 3473; Trimethylamine 2456; Trimethylamine oxide 2456

‡Hippoglossoides elassodon (Flathead sole, Paper sole; young known as Cigarette paper)
N. America: N. California to Bering Sea. Sea of Japan. Surface to 550 m.
D-Amino acid oxidase 1923; Ornithine aminotransferase 3611

‡Hippoglossoides platessoides = Drepanopsetta platessoides (American plaice, Blackback, Canadian plaice, Flounder, Long rough dab, Sand dab, Sole) *27, 34, 35*
Both sides of N. Atlantic: W. Greenland, Labrador to Rhode Is., Spitzbergen to English Channel. 4–700 m, rarely on the shore line on mud or fine sand. Tolerates wide ranges of temperature and salinity. Diet: small cod, sand eels, gobies, worms. small brittle stars, crustaceans, molluscs.

Arsenic 1560; Chloride 1860; Cobalt 2491; Copper 2491; Cytochrome oxidase 2011; Glucose-6-phosphatase 3305; Iron 2491; Lactic dehydrogenase 2011, 3305; Manganese 2491; Mercury 1956; Nickel 2491; Pyruvate kinase 2011, 3305; Sodium 1860; Zinc 2491

‡Hippoglossus hippoglossus (Atlantic halibut)
Cold waters of the Atlantic, south to Cape Cod (W) and France (E), on sand, gravel or clay bottoms, 50–2000 m, at temperatures of 3–9°C and high salinity. May reach 250 kg in weight. Moves into deep water to escape rising temperature. Females grow faster than males. Active predator. Diet: fish, cephalopods, large crustaceans.
Amino acids 3101; *Free* amino acids 2977; Anserine 2977; Arsenic 2613; Cadmium 2613; Calcium 3294; Carnosine 2977; Chloride 3294; Cholesterol 1785; Copper 2613; Cortisol 3609; Cortisone 3609; Creatin 2855; Creatinine 2855; Formaldehyde 1656; Iodide 3294; Iron 2613, 3294; Lead 2613; Magnesium 2462, 2463, 3294; Mercury 1953, 2482, 2613; Ornithine 2977; Potassium 3294; Sarcosine 2977; Selenium 2613; Sodium 3294; Taurine 2977; Trimethylamine oxide 3151; Zinc 2613, 3610

‡Hippoglossus stenolepis (Pacific halibut) *252*
Pacific coast of N. America, Sea of Japan. Shallow waters to 1100 m. Spawns in winter. Voracious and active predator. Diet: mostly fish, some squid, crabs and clams.
Amino acids 2484; Chloride 1582; Hydroxyproline 2484; Mercury 2100; Potassium 1582; Sodium 1582

Hirundichthys affinis *46*

‡Histiophorus orientalis (Swordfish)
Volume 1 only

Holocanthus isabelita (Angel fish)
Bermuda shores. Inactive.
Succinic dehydrogenase 2750

‡Holocentrus ascensionis (Longjaw squirrelfish, Squirrelfish)
Atlantic coast of N. America, Ascension Is., St. Helena. Shore line to 15 m. Rocky or coral areas. Active at night. Diet: mainly crustaceans.
DNA 2195; Haematocrit 3377; Haemoglobin 3377; Succinic dehydrogenase 2750

Holocentrus ensifer (Squirrelfish)
Kona coast of Hawaii. A shallow reef fish. Carnivorous-omnivorous. Possesses swim bladder.
Cholesterol, Fatty acids, Phospholipid, Triglycerides: 3028

Holocentrus rufus
Haematocrit, Haemoglobin: 3377

Holocentrus spinifer *152*
Marshall Is. Coral reefs. Predatory.
Carbonic anhydrase 3309

Hoplerthrinus unitaeniatus
   Amazon River.
   Ammonia, Bicarbonate, Calcium, Chloride, Magnesium, Potassium, Sodium: 2686

Hoplias malabaricus (Haimara, Tararira, Tigerfish)
   Widely distributed in northern and central S. America. Shallow, stagnant pools.
   Predatory. Can breathe air. Diet: fish, shrimps.
   Ammonia 2686; Bicarbonate 2686; Calcium 2686; Chloride 2686; DNA 2195;
   Magnesium 2686; Potassium 2686; Sodium 2686; Urea 2686

‡Hoplopagrus güntheri (Pargo)
   Pacific coast of tropical America
   Volume 1 only

‡*Huro salmoides* (*see Micropterus salmoides*)

‡Huso huso* = Acipenser huso* (Beluga, Giant sturgeon, Hausen)
   N. America, Mediterranean, Black Sea, Caspian Sea, basin of Amur River
   Normally pelagic and solitary.
   Calcium 2465, 2864; Cerebrosides 2471; Magnesium 2465, 2864; Potassium 2465,
   2864; Sodium 2465, 2864; Sulphatides 2471

Hydrocynus vittatus
   S. Africa.
   Carbon dioxide, Oxygen: 2144

‡**Hydrolagus affinis** (Deepwater chimaera)
   Both sides of N. Atlantic in fairly deep water.
   Volume 1 only

‡**Hydrolagus colliei** (Ratfish) *3, 235, 266*
   S. California to S.E. Alaska. Shallow water to 900 m. Males undergo striking colour
   change during courtship. Eggs shed in pairs.
   Alkaline phosphatase 3525; D-Amino acid oxidase 1923; Angiotensinogen 2890;
   Arsenic 2535; Bicarbonate 3525; Calcium 3111, 3525; Chloride 3111, 3525;
   Cholesterol 3525; DNA 2194; Fatty acids 3031; Glucose 3111; Glutamine synthetase
   3611; Glycogen 2980; Magnesium 3111, 3525; Ornithine aminotransferase 3611;
   Phospholipids 3031; Potassium 3111, 3525; Renin 2890; Sodium 3111, 3525;
   Sterols 3031; Sulphate 3111, 3525; Triglycerides 3031; Trimethylamine oxide
   3111; Urea 3111, 3525

‡Hynnis momsa
   Philippines.
   Volume 1 only

Hyperoglyphe bythites
   Amino acids 1812

Hypoatherina tsurugae
   Japan.
   NAD (nicotinamide adenine dinucleotide), NADH (reduced NAD): 3259

Hypodytes rubripinnis
Japan.
Trimethylamine oxide 2111

‡**Hypolophus sephen** FRESH WATER ELASMOBRANCH
Thailand.
Volume 1 only

Hypomesus japonicus (Sea smelt, Surf smelt)
Japan.
Astacene 2723; β-Carotene 2722; Cryptoxanthin 2722, 2723; Cynthiaxanthin
2722, 2723; Diatoxanthin 2722, 2723; Fatty acids 3666, 3667; Lutein 2722, 2723;
Zeaxanthin 2722, 2723

‡*Hypomesus olidus=H. transpacificus* (Pond smelt) *317, 434*
Japan, Korea, Alaska, Siberia. Can live in brackish water near river mouths but is
usually wholly a freshwater fish.
β-Carotene 2721–2723; Cryptoxanthin 2721–2723; Cynthiaxanthin 2721–2723;
Diatoxanthin 2721–2723; Fatty acids 3667; Lutein 2721–2723; Zeaxanthin 2721–
2723

‡*Hypophthalmichthys molitrix* (Silver carp, Tolstol) *12, 134, 135*
China and the Amur Basin of Russia; introduced elsewhere. Lowland parts of
rivers. Very long intestine because of its diet of phytoplankton. Young feed on
zooplankton.
Aluminium 3467; Amino acids 3468; Amylase 2840; Astaxanthin 1779; Calcium
2864, 3467; Canthaxanthin 1779; β-Carotene 1779; Cholesterol 2495; Copper
3467; Erythrocytes 2626; *Free* fatty acids 2495; β-Galactosidase 2840; Glucose
dehydrogenase 2836; β-Glucosidase 2840; Haemoglobin 2626; Hexokinase 2836;
Iron 3467; Isozeaxanthin 2779; Lutein 1779; Magnesium 2864, 3467; Manganese
3467; Phospholipid 2495; Polioxyxanthophyll 1779; Potassium 2864, 3467; RNA
3097; Silver 3467; Sodium 2864, 3467; Taraxanthin 1779; Thiaminase 1464;
Thiamine 1464; Triglycerides 2495; Zinc 2328, 3467

Hyporhamphus unifasciatus
DNA 2195

Hypostomus plecostomus
DNA 2195

‡*Hyriopsis velthuizeni*
Indonesia.
Volume 1 only

Hysoblennius hentz
DNA 2195

Icelinus filamentosus (Filamented sculpin, Threadfin sculpin)
S. California to British Columbia. 37–110 m. Diet: crustaceans.
DNA 2195

‡Icelus spatula (Spatulate sculpin)
    Arctic: Bering Sea, Kamchatka coast, Labrador. In deep fjords of northern
    Labrador it lives permanently at −1·7°C in the supercooled state.
    Volume 1 only

Ichthyomyzon bdellium CYCLOSTOME
    Southern United States.
    DNA 3136

Ichthyomyzon fossor CYCLOSTOME (Northern brook lamprey)
    Mississippi River drainage, Lakes Michigan and Ontario. Lives in creeks and
    small rivers buried in sand or mud. Diet: fine organic matter. Not parasitic.
    DNA 3136

Ichthyomyzon gagei CYCLOSTOME
    Southern United States.
    DNA 3136

‡*Ichthyomyzon unicuspis* CYCLOSTOME (Silver lamprey)
    N. America. Intolerant of salt water. Does not utilise smaller streams.
    Volume 1 only

Ictalurus furcatus (Blue catfish)
    Mississippi River system. Larger rivers and lakes of the Gulf States.
    Ammonia 3303; Chenodesoxycholic acid 2408; Cholic acid 2408; Creatin 3303;
    Creatinine 3303; Urea 3303; Uric acid 3303

‡*Ictalurus melas* = *Ameiurus melas* (American catfish, Black bullhead, Common bullhead,
    Horned pout, Small catfish) *6, 121, 244*
    N. America: Great Lakes southward. Shallow, silty lakes and rivers. Introduced
    to central and western Europe; not Iceland, Ireland or Spain. Can tolerate 35°C
    after acclimatisation. The adults are almost entirely nocturnal. Often incorrectly
    identified as *I. nebulosus* (Wheeler, 1978).
    Esterase 2221; L-Fucose dehydrogenase 2769; Thyroxine 2190

Ictalurus natalis (Yellow bullhead) *349*
    Mississippi River. Preferred temperature 28·4°C. Active at night.
    Bicarbonate 2262; Calcium 2262-2264; Chloride 2262; Esterase 2221; Glucose
    2262; Haematocrit 2262; Lactate 2262; Magnesium 2262-2264; Potassium 2262-
    2264; Sodium 2262-2264

‡*Ictalurus nebulosus* = *Ameiurus nebulosus* (Brown bullhead) *235, 270, 280, 323, 327, 330,*
    343, 344
    N. America, extensively introduced elsewhere. Still or slowly flowing waters, fresh
    and occasionally brackish. Prefers abundant vegetation on sandy or muddy bottoms.
    Nocturnal feeders. Wide temperature tolerance. Selects temperatures between 12 and
    31°C according to different workers. Diet: filamentous algae among other things.
    Calcium 2080; Chloride 1702, 3501, 3503; Copper 1627; DNA 1915, 2195;
    Fructose-6-phosphate kinase 1915; Glucose 1523, 1702, 3501, 3503; Glucose 6-
    phosphatase 1523; Glucose-6-phosphate dehydrogenase 1915; Glutamic oxaloacetic

transaminase 1702; Glycogen phosphorylase 1523, 3514; Haematocrit 1702; Haemoglobin 1702; Hexokinase 1915; Lactate 1639; Lactic dehydrogenase 1702; 6-Phosphogluconate dehydrogenase 1915; Potassium 2080, 3501, 3503; Pyruvate 1639; Pyruvate kinase 1915; Sodium 2080, 3501, 3503; "Sugar" 2791, 2823

‡*Ictalurus punctatus* (Channel catfish, Fiddler, White cat) *139, 142, 143, 146, 218, 232, 240, 241, 257, 319, 339, 384, 395, 421*
N. America: rivers of the Great Lakes region, Mississippi Valley, streams leading to Gulf of Mexico. Introduced into England. Sometimes found in brackish waters. Females spawn once a year, but males may spawn several times. Prefer cool, clear deeper water with sand, gravel or rubble bottom. Largely sedentary. Survives up to 33°C if acclimatised gradually. Avoids temperatures above 32–35°C and below 23–26°C. Omnivorous.
Alanine aminotransferase 3633; Aldehyde oxidase 2468; Allantoicase 1775; Allantoinase 1775; *Free* amino acids 3637; γ-Amino benzoic acid 3637; Ammonia 3637; Arginase 1776, 3634; Aspartate aminotransferase 3633; Calcium 2503, 3353; Carbamoyl phosphate synthetase 3634; Chenodesoxycholic acid 2408; Chloride 1805, 1806, 2264, 2429, 2896, 2897; Cholic acid 2408; Cortisol 2742; Desoxycholic acid 2408; Esterase 2221; Glucose 2742; Glutamic dehydrogenase 3633; Glutamine synthetase 3636; Guanine 1867; Haematocrit 2429, 2896; Hydroxyproline 3637; Hypoxanthine 1867; Lactate 2429, 2742; Magnesium 2503, 3353; Mutarotase 1480; Ornithine 3637; Ornithine transcarbamoylase 3634; Potassium 2429, 2503, 2896, 2897, 3353; Sodium 1806, 2429, 2503, 2896, 2897, 3353; "Sugar" 2503; Taurine 3637; Thiaminase 2190; Urea 3637; Xanthine oxidase 2468

Ictiobus bubalis = *I. cyprinellus* (Buffalo carp, Bigmouth buffalo, Smallmouth buffalo)
There is some confusion in the naming of this fish in the literature. Usually both names are described separately. Central Canada and United States in large rivers and lakes, close to the bottom. A large, powerful fish.
Allantoinase 1775; Arginase 1776; Calcium 3145; Erythrocytes 1698; Haematocrit 1698; Haemoglobin 1698; Leucocytes 1698; Strontium 3145

Ictiobus cyprinellus (*see I. bubalis*)

‡*Idus idus* = *Leuciscus idus* (Orfe) *169, 232, 237, 328, 329, 331*
Europe N. of the Alps, E. of the Rhine to Siberia. Running waters, lakes and lagoons, also in brackish parts of the Baltic Sea. In clear water which is not too shallow.
Arginase 2694; Calcium 2864; DNA 2085, 2195; Glucose 2085, 2086; Glucose-6-phosphate 2085, 2086; Isocitrate dehydrogenase 2979; Lactate 2085, 2086; Magnesium 2864; Potassium 2864; Pyruvate 2085, 2086; RNA 2085; Sodium 2864

‡*Idus melanotus*
Germany.
Volume 1 only

Ilisha elongata
Japan.
α-Cryptoxanthin, Cynthiaxanthin, Diatoxanthin, Lutein, Tunaxanthin, Zeaxanthin: 2718

Ilisha filigera (Bigeye ilisha)
  Coasts of India to New Guinea, S. China Sea.
  Amino acids, Calcium, Iron, Niacin, Riboflavin, Thiamine, Vitamin A: 3690

‡Inegocia meerdervoosti
  Japan.
  Volume 1 only

Ipnops sp.
  These specimens caught at 5800 m depth.
  Phospholipids 3064

Ischikauia steenackeri
  Japan.
  Cynthiaxanthin, Diatoxanthin, α-Doradecin, Lutein, Zeaxanthin: 2719

‡Isopsetta isolepis (Butter sole, Scalyfin flounder)
  N. America: S. California to S.E. Alsaka. Soft, silty bottoms, Shallow water to
  145 m. Migrates to shallows in summer, to deep water in winter.
  Volume 1 only

Istiophorus orientalis
  Mercury 2887

Istiophorus platypterus (Sailfish)
  Wide distribution in Atlantic, Pacific and Indian Oceans. Strongly migratory,
  living in surface waters. Diet: fish and squid.
  Aluminium 3019; Amino acids 3019; *Free* amino acids 3019; Barium 3019;
  Cholesterol 3019, 3020; Copper 3019; Iron 3019; Lead 3019; Manganese 3019;
  Provitamin D 3019; Strontium 3019; Titanium 3019

‡**Isuropsis glaucus**
  Japan.
  Anserine 3367, 3368; Balenine 3367, 3368; Trimethylamine oxide 3367; Urea 3367

‡**Isurus glaucus** (*see* **I. oxyrhynchus**)

Isurus oxyrhynchus = **I. glaucus** (Blue pointer, Blue shark, Grey-blue shark,
  Mako shark, Sharpnosed mackerel shark) *78, 322*
  Japan, George's Bank to Gulf of Mexico and Caribbean, Atlantic and Indian
  Oceans. Powerful swimmer. Body temperature can be higher than ambient. Diet:
  fish, squid.
  Cholesterol 3020; Corticosterone 3456; 1α-Hydroxycorticosterone 3456; Pro-
  vitamin D 3020

Jenkinsia stolifera *264*
  Cayman Is. A clupeid, pelagic, schooling fish.

Johnius coitor (*see* Sciaena coitor)

Johnius dussumieri (Bearded croaker, Dussumier's silver jewfish, Whiskered croaker) S.E. Asia westward to E. Africa. Collects in large shoals. Coastal waters down to 40 m. Diet: small fish, invertebrates.
Amino acids, Calcium, Iron, Niacin, Riboflavin, Thiamine, Vitamin A: 3690

‡Johnius regius = Argyrosomus regius (Meagre, Sciaena)
Mediterranean, Great Britain to Guinea, North Sea. Not Black Sea. Found in shallow water. Can withstand brackish waters. Can make drumming noise with the swim bladder. Pelagic. Diet: fish.
Volume 1 only

‡Johnius umbra (see Sciaena umbra)

‡Kareius bicoloratus (Stone flounder) 69, 73, 307
Japan, Korea, China.
Adenosine diphosphate 2456; Adenosine monophosphate 2456; Mg-ATPase (magnesium-activated adenosine triphosphatase) 3532; Na-K-ATPase 3532; Adenosine triphosphate 2456; Amino acids 2456; Free amino acids 2456; Ammonia 2456; Creatin 2456; Creatinine 2456; Esterase 2782; Fatty acids 2154, 3666, 3667; Hydroxyproline 2456; Inosine monophosphate 2456; Lipase 2782; Taurine 2456; Trimethylamine 2456; Trimethylamine oxide 2456; Ubiquinone 2186; Vitamin E 2186

‡Katsuwonus pelamis = Euthynnus pelamis (Bonita, Ocean bonito, Skipjack, Watermelon) 72, 73, 75, 256, 322, 459
All warm seas. Deep water from 18–20°C, sometimes inshore. Active feeder. Spawning takes place throughout the year. Migratory in schools. Diet: herring-like fish, shrimps, crustaceans, cephalopods.
Adenosine diphosphate 1871; Adenosine monophosphate 1871; Adenosine triphosphate 1871; Aluminium 3019; Amino acids 3019, 3369; Free amino acids 3019, 3369; Anserine 3369; Barium 3019; Cadmium 2390; Calcium 3386; Carnosine 3369; Cholesterol 2445, 3019, 3020; Chromium 2390; Cobalt 2390; Copper 2390, 3019; Creatin + Creatinine 3369; DNA 2195; Dimethylamine 3439; Fructose phosphate 1745; Glucose 1745; Glucose dehydrogenase 2836; Glucose phosphate 1745; Glycogen 1996; Haemoglobin 3370; Hexokinase 2836; Free histidine 3166; Inosine monophosphate 1871; Iron 3019, 3441; Lactate 1745, 1996; Lead 2390, 3019; Magnesium 3386; Manganese 2390, 3019; Mercury 2390, 3127, 3397, 3626; Myoglobin 3370; NAD (nicotinamide adenine dinucleotide) 1745, 3259; NADH (reduced NAD) 3259; Non-protein nitrogen 1996; Nucleosidase 1408; Phosphatase 1408; Provitamin D 3019, 3020; Purine nucleosidase 1408; Pyridine nucleotide transhydrogenase 3167; Pyrophosphatase 1408; Pyruvate 1745; Ribose 1996; Selenium 3397; Strontium 3019; "Sugar" 1745; Taurine 3369; Thiaminase 2297; Titanium 3019; Trimethylamine 3439; Trimethylamine oxide 3151, 3439; Ubiquinone 2186; Vitamin D 3673; Vitamin E 2186; Zinc 2390

‡Katsuwonus vagans (Skipjack)
Japan.
Collagen 3462; Connective tissue 3462; Elastin 3462; Vitamin E 2185

‡Konosirus punctatus (Gizzard shad, Japanese gizzard) *72, 75, 152*
 Japan, along shores.
 Cadmium 2901; Calcium 3486; Copper 2901; Dimethylamine 3439; Iron 2901;
 Lead 2901; Potassium 2900; Sodium 2900; Strontium 3486; Thiaminase 2297;
 Trimethylamine 2388, 3439; Trimethylamine oxide 2111, 3439; Zinc 2901

Kryptopterus bicirrhis (Glass catfish)
 S.E. Asia. Lives in schools in middle and upper water layers.
 DNA 2195

‡Kyphosus cinerascens (Rudderfish)
 Red Sea, Japan.
 Volume 1 only

Kyphosus lembus
 Japan.
 Trimethylamine oxide 2111

Labeo bata
 India. Sluggish. Diet: vegetable debris, algae, mud.
 Acid phosphatase 3227; Alkaline phosphatase 3227; Amino acids 2050; Cholesterol
 3267, 3268; Erythrocytes 3408; Glucose 3407; Hydroxyproline 2050; Lactate
 3407; Leucocytes 3408

Labeo bicolor (Redtailed shark)
 Thailand. Aggressive. Diet: algae.
 DNA 2195

‡*Labeo boga*
 India, Burma. Rivers.
 Volume 1 only

‡*Labeo calbasu* (Orangefin labeo)
 India, Bengal, Burma. Sluggish. Diet: vegetable debris, microscopic plants,
 detritus, mud.
 Erythrocytes 3408; Glucose 3407; Lactate 3407; Leucocytes 3408

Labeo capensis (Mudfish, Mudsucker, Orange River sandfish) *280*
 S. Africa. Rivers and lakes.
 Carbon dioxide 2144; Erythrocytes 2140; Haematocrit 2139; 2140; Haemoglobin
 2139, 2140; Oxygen 2144; "Sugar" 2139, 2143

Labeo diplostomus
 India.
 Glucose, Lactate: 3407

‡*Labeo fimbriatus* (Fringe-lipped carp) *73, 74*
 India: Sind, Punjab, Deccan; probably N.E. Bengal. Sluggish. Bottom feeder.
 Diet: algae, decayed organic matter.
 Erythrocytes 3408; Glucose 3407; Glycogen 1563; Lactate 3407; Leucocytes 3408

‡*Labeo gonius*
India, Bengal, Assam, Burma.
Acid phosphatase 3227; Alkaline phosphatase 3227; Cholesterol 3267, 3268

‡*Labeo kontius* (Cauvery carp)
India: rivers along base of Neilgherries, Cauvery and Coleroon down to coast.
Marginal and bottom feeder. Diet: decayed leaves, detritus, mud, algae.
Volume 1 only

Labeo niloticus
River Nile. Diet: algae, detritus.
Chloride, Haematocrit, Haemoglobin: 2678

‡*Labeo paral*
India.
Volume 1 only

‡*Labeo rohita* (Rohu carp) *34, 73, 74*
India, Assam, Burma. Sluggish. Diet: vegetable debris, microscopic plants,
decaying higher plants, detritus, mud.
Alkaline phosphatase 2858, 3093; *free* amino acids 3277; Amylase 1425;
Calcium 2858; Cholesterol 2858; Erythrocytes 1476, 3408; Glucose 3407; Glycogen
1563; Haemoglobin 1476; Iron 2858; Lactate 3407; Leucocytes 1476, 3408;
Lipase 1425, 1563; Lysophosphatidyl choline 3436; Phosphatidic acid 3436;
Phosphatidyl ethanolamine 3436; Phosphatidyl inositol 3436; Phosphatidyl serine
3436; Sphingomyelin 3436; Succinic dehydrogenase 1563; Sucrase 1425; "Sugar"
1798; Trypsin 1425

Labeo rosae (Mudfish)
S. Africa.
Carbon dioxide, Oxygen: 2144

Labeo umbratus (Moggel, Mudfish, Mud mullet, Mudsucker) *239*
Southern parts of the Cape province (S. Africa). Rivers and lakes.
Carbon dioxide 2144; Erythrocytes 2140, 2146; Haematocrit 2139, 2140; 2146;
Haemoglobin 2139, 2140, 2146; Oxygen 2144; "Sugar" 2139

‡Labracoglossa argentiventris
Japan to Philippines.
Volume 1 only

‡Labrax lupus* (*see* Dicentrarchus labrax*)

‡Labrus berggylta (Ballan wrasse, Bergylt) *207*
Mid-Norway south to Canary Is. (not Iceland). Rocky shores and steep under-
water cliffs down to 20 m. A nest-builder. Diet: molluscs, crustacea, barnacles.
Cytochrome oxidase 2009; Fatty acids 2504; Lactic dehydrogenase 2009

Labrus ossifragus
Europe.
Cytochrome oxidase 2009; 2011; Lactic dehydrogenase 2009, 2011; Pyruvate
kinase 2011

‡Labrus turdus (Green wrasse)
  Europe. Mediterranean. A coastal species living near rocks and sea grass.
  Cadmium, Copper, Lead, Mercury, Zinc: 1707, 1709

‡Lachnolaimus maximus (Capitaine, Hogfish)
  Puerta Rica, W. Indies.
  Volume 1 only

Lactophrys trigonus (Buffalo, Trunkfish)
  Massachusetts and Bermuda to Brazil. Sea grass beds, along reefs down to 37 m.
  Diet: bottom-living invertebrates and plants.
  Cerebroside 2470; DNA 2197; Fatty acids 2469; Haematocrit 3377; Haemoglobin
  3377; Sialic acid 2470; Sulphatide 2470

Lactophrys triqueter (Smooth trunkfish)
  Massachusetts and Bermuda to S. Brazil. Diet: worms, crabs, shrimps, tunicates.
  DNA 2195

‡Lagocephalus lunaris (Puffer)
  Japan.
  FREE histidine 3166; Trimethylamine oxide 2111

‡Lagodon rhomboides* (Bream, Pinfish, Sailor's choice) *276, 289, 327*
  Atlantic and Gulf coast of United States. Cape Cod to Cuba. Active swimmer.
  Marine, but will tolerate fresh water if some calcium is present.
  Erythrocytes 1647; Haematocrit 1647; Haemoglobin 1647; Succinic dehydrogenase
  2750

‡**Lamna cornubica** (Porbeagle)
  Japan. Europe.
  Adenosine diphosphate 3367; Adenosine monophosphate 3367; Adenosine
  triphosphate 3367; *free* amino acids 3367; Ammonia 3367; Anserine 3367;
  Balenine 3367; Carnosine 3367; Creatin 3367; Creatinine 3367; Inosine monophosphate 3367; Taurine 3367; Trimethylamine 3367; Trimethylamine oxide
  3151, 3367; Urea 3367

Lamna ditropis (*see* **L. nasus**)

‡**Lamna nasus** = **L. ditropis** (Mackerel shark, Porbeagle, Salmon shark) *78, 322*
  Newfoundland to S. Carolina; Murman coast to Mediterranean and N.W. Africa.
  Surface to 150 m or deeper. Strong swimmer. Viviparous. Newly-born young have
  been nourished by having eaten the unfertilised eggs in the mother's uterus. Often
  found in colder water than other sharks. Diet: a wide range of surface-living fish
  and squid; sometimes bottom-living animals.
  Amino acids 3441; Iron 3441; Mercury 2482

Lampanyctus pusillus
  N. Atlantic.
  Arsenic, Cadmium, Copper, Mercury, Zinc: 3638

‡Lampetra fluviatilis* (*see* Petromyzon fluviatilis*) *37, 111, 182, 232, 233, 240*

‡*Lampetra japonica* = *Entosphenus japonicus*, sometimes called *Entosphenus lamottei* (wrongly) in the literature. CYCLOSTOME. (Arctic lamprey, River eighteyes lamprey) Japan, N. Russia, N.W. Canada. Some populations parasitise fish in the sea, but other populations do not feed from time of metamorphosis until death from spawning. Both anadromous and dwarf freshwater forms found. Muscle exceptionally rich in Vitamin A.
Vitamin D 3673

‡*Lampetra lamottei* * CYCLOSTOME (American brook lamprey)
Restricted area of eastern N. America. Cold brooks and small rivers. Non-parasitic.
DNA 3136

‡Lampetra marinus* CYCLOSTOME (Lamprey)
N.W. coasts of Europe, Iceland, Atlantic coast of N. America, occasionally Baltic, Mediterranean.
Volume 1 only

‡*Lampetra planeri* CYCLOSTOME (Brook lamprey, Planer's lamprey)
Japan, Europe (not Iceland, Spain or Norway), N. Asia and western N. America. Upper reaches of rivers at spawning time. Non-parasitic and non-migratory, spending all of its life in streams and rivers.
Chloride 1633, 2114, 2115; DNA 3136; Glucose 2544; Glycogen 2543; Haematocrit 1633: Potassium 1633: Sodium 1633

‡Lateolabrax japonicus (Sea bass, Sea perch) *76, 459*
Japan, Korea, China Sea. Shores.
Adenosine diphosphate 3482; Adenosine monophosphate 3482; Adenosine triphosphate 3482; *Free* amino acids, a single value expressed as tyrosine 3482; Balenine 3368; Calcium 3486; Carnosine 3368; β-Carotene 2716; Collagen 3462; Connective tissue 3462; α-Cryptoxanthin 2716; Cynthiaxanthin 2716; Diatoxanthin 2716; Dimethylamine 3439; Elastin 3462; *Free* histidine 3166; Hypoxanthine 3482; Inosine 3482; Inosine monophosphate 3482; Lutein 2716; NAD (nicotinamide adenine dinucleotide) 3259; NADH (reduced form of NAD) 3259; Strontium 3486; Thiaminase 3473; Trimethylamine 3439; 3482; Trimethylamine oxide 3439; Tunaxanthin 2716; Zeaxanthin 2716

‡Lates calcarices
Philippines.
Volume 1 only

‡Lates calcarifer* (Barramundi, Cockup, Giant perch, Palmer, Sea perch, Silver sea perch)
Persian Gulf, E. Africa, Seas of India, China and Australia. Coastal waters, estuaries and lagoons 10–40 m, ascending rivers for food. Diet: fish, crustaceans, snails, worms.
Volume 1 only

Lates niloticus (Nile perch)
Widely distributed in Africa. Vigorous. Females larger than males at same age. Voracious carnivore. Diet: mostly fish.
Chloride, Haematocrit. Haemoglobin: 2678

‡Laticauda laticaudata
  Japan.
  Volume 1 only

‡Laticauda semifasciata
  Japan.
  Volume 1 only

‡Latimeria chalumnae (Coelacanth, Lantern fish) *155, 156, 161, 266, 461*
  Madagascar 150–400 m. The only living member of the order Crossopterygii, members of which are thought to have given rise to the amphibia. This is consistent with studies showing that nitrogen metabolism and ion regulation are more like those of elasmobranchs, dipnoi (lungfish) and amphibia than of teleosts ("modern" bony fish). The vertebral column is poorly developed, with only a few cartilaginous elements surrounding the nerve cord. Viviparous—Smith, Rand *et al.* (1975). Latimeria possesses the complete enzyme system for making urea from ammonia, a facility usually confined to elasmobranchs.
  Comparing the bile salts of this species with those of Protopterus, Lepidosiren or Neoceratodus (lungfishes), Amos, Anderson *et al.* (1977) found that that of Latimeria stands biochemically outside of the lungfish group. All four of these primitive osteichtheans have some amphibian affinities (from studies of bile salts). They contain alcohols found in amphibian bile, but only Latimeria contains latimerol, which has not been detected elsewhere.
  Latimeria was not discovered until 1938. From then until 1972 about 70 have been caught, but most of them were in very poor condition by the time they became available for study (Hamoir, Piront *et al.*, 1973). The wavelength of maximum absorption of the visual pigments is 473 nm, giving maximum sensitivity in deep water (Dartnall, 1972). The fish maintains high blood osmolarity by the accumulation of high levels of urea and trimethylamine oxide (Griffith, Umminger *et al.*, 1974). The ancestors of Latimeria are found in the upper Devonian, both in freshwater and saltwater deposits. Maetz (1974) suggests that the relatively low salt concentrations found in the body fluids may indicate a freshwater origin.
  Before it became "famous" by its recognition as a Crossopterygian by Smith in 1938, the coelacanth benefited the natives of Madagascar through a sort of industrial application. The horny skin was used to roughen the surface of punctured bicycle inner tubes, prior to sticking on the repair patch.
  Mg-ATPase (magnesium-activated adenosine triphosphatase) 2075; Na-K-ATPase 2075; Albumin 1717; Amino acids 1567, 1685, 3594; *Free* amino acids 2105, 2625; Amino acids (total: a single figure) 2076, 2078, 2079; Angiotensinogen 2890; Arginase 2035; Arginino-succinate synthetase 2035; Bicarbonate 2076, 2078, 2079; Calcium 1717, 2076, 2078, 2079; Carbamoyl phosphate synthetase 2035; Carbohydrates 2076, 2078, 2079; Carbon dioxide 2078; Chloride 1717, 2076, 2078, 2079, 2625; Citrulline 2105; Creatin 2076, 2078, 2625; Creatinine 2076, 2078, 2625; DNA 1706, 3425; Fatty acids 1832, 2762, 3469; Glucose 2076, 2078, 2079; Glucuronate 2078; Glycoprotein 2079; Haematocrit 2257, 3656; Haemoglobin 3656; Lactate 2076, 2078, 2079; Magnesium 1717, 2076, 2078, 2079; Non-protein nitrogen 2078, 2079; Ornithine 2105; Ornithine carbamoyl transferase 2035; Phospholipid 2079; 2762; Potassium 1717, 2076, 2078, 2079, 2625; Renin 2890; Sodium 1717, 2076, 2078, 2079, 2625; Sulphate 2076, 2078, 2079; Taurine 2105; Triglyceride 2762; Trimethylamine oxidase 2035; Trimethylamine oxide 2076, 2078, 2079, 2625; Urea 1717, 2076, 2078, 2079, 2105, 2625

Latridopsis forsteri (Bastard trumpeter)
Coasts of S. Australia, Tasmania. Mainly offshore.
Copper, Zinc: 1893

‡*Lebistes reticulatus (see Poecilia reticulata)*

Leiocassis poecilopterus
DNA 2195

‡Leiognathus argenteus
Japan.
Volume 1 only

‡Leiognathus bindus (Orangefinned pony fish)
E. Africa, India: Coromandel coast, China, Philippines, Java, Borneo. Shallow
waters down to 35 m near bottom in schools. Diet: small bottom-living animals.
Volume 1 only

‡Leiognathus daura (Golden-striped pony fish)
S. Arabia, India, Thailand, Philippines, Australia. Shallow waters down to 15 m
over muddy ground, in schools. Diet: small bottom-living anaimals.
Volume 1 only

‡Leiognathus equulus* (Common slipmouth, Greater pony fish, Slimy, Soapy)
Red Sea, Tanzania, Philippines, Japan, Australia. In sea down to 30 m, brackish
waters and rivers. Shoals in shallow, inshore water. Diet: small bottom-living
animals.
Folic acid 2582

‡Leiognathus nuchalis (Slimy)
Japan.
Trimethylamine oxide 2111

Leionura atun (Snoek)
S. Africa, Australia.
Copper, Zinc: 1893

‡Leiostomus xanthurus (Cape May goody, Goody, Lafayette, Norfolk spot, Oldwife,
Porgy, Postcroaker, Spot, Yellowtail)
S. Atlantic and Gulf coasts of United States. Cape Cod to Texas. Avoids temper-
atures above 37·5°C.
Aldehyde oxidase 2468; Arsenic 3638; Cadmium 3638; Copper 3638; Erythrocytes
1647; Haemoglobin 1647; Mercury 3638; Xanthine oxidase 2468; Zinc 3638

‡Lepidion inosimae
Japan.
Volume 1 only

Lepidion oidema
Japan.
Dimethylamine, Formaldehyde: 3665

‡Lepidocybium flavobrunneum (Castor oil fish, Escolar)
   Worldwide in warm seas. Mesopelagic. Body oil consists primarily of wax in place
   of glyceride.
   Fatty acids, Fatty alcohols: 2781

Lepidophanes indicus
   N. Atlantic.
   Arsenic, Cadmium, Copper, Mercury, Zinc: 3638

‡Lepidopsetta bilineata (Rock sole)
   Japan, S. California to Bering Sea. Coastal, 1–183 m, moving into deeper water in
   winter. Diet: bottom-living invertebrates.
   Calcium 3090; Chloride 3090; Magnesium 3090; Ornithine aminotransferase
   3611; Potassium 3090; Sodium 3090

‡Lepidopsetta mochigarei (Rock flatfish)
   Japan.
   Volume 1 only

Lepidorhombus whiffiagonis (Megrim, Sailfluke)
   Europe, including Iceland and Mediterranean. 10–600 m on soft bottoms. Diet:
   small bottom-living fish.
   Lactic dehydrogenase 1789; Urate oxidase 1711; Xanthine oxidase 1711

Lepidosiren paradoxa (South American lung fish)
   Central S. America. Paraná and Amazon River systems. Swamps of the Chaco.
   Structurally the most advanced of the air breathers. Dies if denied access to air.
   Aestivates in a cocoon of mucus. Young have external gills.
   Albumin 3524; Aldosterone 2274; Angiotensinogen 2890; Bicarbonate 3524;
   Calcium 3524; 3526; Chloride 3524; Cholesterol 3526; Corticosterone 2274;
   Cortisol 2274; 11-Deoxycortisol 2274; DNA 2998; Globulin 3524; Magnesium
   3524; Phospholipids 3526; Potassium 3524; Renin 2890; Sodium 3524; Sulphur
   3524; Triglycerides 3526; Urea 3524

‡Lepidotrigla güntheri
   Japan.
   Volume 1 only

‡Lepidotrigla microptera
   Japan.
   Trimethylamine oxide 2111

Lepisosteus ferox
   DNA 2194

‡Lepisosteus osseus* (Billfish, Billy Gar, Common garpike, Longnose gar, Needlenose,
   Ohio gar) 161
   N. America: Maryland to Florida in streams and brackish water; occasionally in
   the sea. Also Great Lakes and Mississippi Valley. Females grow faster than males,

become bigger and live longer. Prefer quiet weedy shallows of warm lakes and
large rivers. Can respire by gulping air at the surface, so can survive in stagnant
pools. Eggs are poisonous to mammals and birds. Avoids temperatures above
34·5°C or below 29°C. Preferred temperature reported as 25°C or 33°C by different
authors. Diet: fish, crustaceans.
Ammonia 3303; Angiotensinogen 2890; Cerebroside 2233; Cholesterol 2233;
Creatin 3303; Creatinine 3303; Diphosphatidyl glycerol 1680; Fatty acids 1680;
Phosphatidic acid 1680; Phosphatidyl choline 1680, 2233; Phosphatidyl ethanolamine 1680, 2233; Phosphatidyl inositol 1680, 2233; Phosphatidyl serine 1680, 2233;
Renin 2890; Sphingomyelin 1680, 2233; Sulphatide 2233; Urea 3303; Uric acid
3303

Lepisosteus platostomus (Shortnose gar)
E. central states of N. America; not on Atlantic coast. Lowland lakes, backwaters
of rivers usually in clear water. Avoids temperatures above 34·5°C or below 29°C.
Allantoicase 1775; Allantoinase 1775; Arginase 1776; Bicarbonate 2262; Calcium
2262–2264; Carbamoyl phosphate synthetase 1777; Cardiolipid 2407; Chloride
2262; Cholesterol 2407; Diglycerides 2407; *Free* fatty acids 2407; Glucose 2262;
Haematocrit 2262; Lactate 2262; Magnesium 2262–2264; Phosphatidyl choline
2407; Phosphatidyl ethanolamine 2407; Potassium 2262–2264; Sodium 2262–2264;
Sphingomyelin 2407; Triglycerides 2407

Lepisosteus platyrhynchus *265*

‡*Lepisosteus productus*
Mexico.
Volume 1 only

‡Lepisosteus spatula* (Alligator gar)
Lower Mississippi Valley (N. America), also in salt or brackish water from Florida
along the coast of the Gulf of Mexico. Voracious predator. Diet: fish, ducks,
waterfowl.
Riboflavin 2881

Lepomis cyanellus (Green sunfish) *331, 374*
Cytochrome C 3281

‡*Lepomis gibbosus* = *Eupomotis gibbosus* (Bream, Common sunfish, Harlequin roach,
Kiver, Northern Pomotis, Perch, Pond perch, Pumpkinseed, Quiver, Redbelly,
Roach, Robin, Robin perch, Ruff, Sand perch, Sun bass, Tobacco box, Yellowbelly,
Yellow perch) *270, 374*
Eastern N. America; introduced England, central W. Europe. Weedy lakes, lower
reaches of rivers. Prefers clear water and cover of submerged vegetation. Avoids
temperatures above 31°C or below 22°C. Diet: snails, aquatic insects, fish fry and
other small aquatic animals.
Aldehyde oxidase 2468; Calcium 1528; Haemoglobin 2247; Mutarotase 1480;
Xanthine oxidase 2468

‡*Lepomis macrochirus* (Bluegill, Bream, Chainsided perch, Gilded sunfish, Gold perch,
Perch, Sunfish) *28, 137, 138, 162, 218, 269, 270, 280, 320, 323, 382, 383, 425*

S.E. and central N. America: Ohio Valley, south-westward to Missouri and Kentucky. Introduced to Africa. Shallow, weedy warm water of lakes and ponds; slow rivers. Moves little. Avoids temperatures above 32–35°C or below 26–29°C. Diet: aquatic insects, small fish.
Adenosine triphosphatase 1772; Aldehyde oxidase 2468; Lactate 1639; Pyruvate 1639; Xanthine oxidase 2468

‡Lepophidium brevibarbe
  W. Indies to Brazil.
  Volume 1 only

Lepophidium profundorum
  Russia.
  Cardiolipid 2469; Cerebroside 2469, 2470; Fatty acids 2469; Ganglioside 2469; Phosphatidyl choline 2469, 3064; Phosphatidyl ethanolamine 2469, 3064; Phosphatidyl inositol 2469, 3064; Phosphatidyl serine 2469, 3064; Phospholipid 3064; Polyglycerophosphatides 3064; Sialic acid 2470; Sphingomyelin 2469, 3064; Sulphatide 2469, 2470

Leporinus striatus
  DNA 2195

Leptocephalus wilsoni (Conger eel)
  Australia.
  Cadmium, Copper, Zinc: 1893

‡Leptocottus armatus* (Cabezon, Staghorn sculpin)
  S. California to Gulf of Alaska. Coastal shallow water to 90 m. Often lies buried in bottom sand. Voracious feeder.
  Succinic dehydrogenase 1727

‡Leptoscarus japonicus (Japanese parrotfish)
  Japan.
  Volume 1 only

Lethrinus chrysostomus (Sweetlip emperor) *339*
  Tropical. Great Barrier Reef.
  Cytochromes, Fatty acids, Succinic dehydrogenase: 2296

‡Lethrinus opercularis (Starry pigface bream)
  Aden, India, Philippines, Formosa to Samoa. Coastal waters, entering harbours, pearl banks and trawling grounds.
  Volume 1 only

‡*Leucichthys artedi* = *Coregonus artedi* (Cisco, Greyback, Lake herring, Shallow-water cisco, Tullibee) *153*
  N. America: Lakes Erie, St. Clair, Superior and Huron. May occur in large rivers in shoals. Spawning date (autumn) depends on there being a low water temperature. Avoids temperatures above 20°C; prefers 7–10°C. Diet: plankton, crustaceans.

Although not strictly a carnivore, this species has an unusually high level of arginase in the liver.
Allantoinase 1775; Arginase 1776; Arsenic 2611; Bromide 2611; Cadmium 2611; Cobalt 2611; Copper 2611; Thorium 2611; Uranium 2611; Zinc 2611

Leucicorus sp. *262*
Russia. Abyssal: these specimens caught at 6000 m. Extremely low brain phospholipid.
Cardiolipid 2469; Phosphatidyl choline 2469; 3064; Phosphatidyl ethanolamine 2469, 3064; Phosphatidyl inositol 2469, 3064; Phosphatidyl serine 2469, 3064; Phospholipid 3064; Polyglycerophosphatide 3064

Leuciscus aula
Europe.
Calcium 1528

‡*Leuciscus cephalus* = *Squalius cephalus* (Chub) *38*
Europe and Asia Minor, except Iceland, Norway, Ireland and Sicily. Rivers and lakes. In the Baltic it can live in waters where the salinity is not too high. Diet: insect larvae, worms, molluscs, plant material.
Amino acids 1410; *Free* amino acids 1410; Ammonia 1410; Calcium 1528; Carotenoids 3264; Cobalt 2850; Copper 2850; DNA 3203; Iron 2850; Lactic dehydrogenase 3203; Manganese 2850; 6-phosphogluconate dehydrogenase 3203; Phosphoglucose isomerase 3203; RNA 3203; Taurine 1410; Zinc 2850

‡*Leuciscus erythrophthalmus*
Volume 1 only

‡*Leuciscus hakonensis*
Japan.
Volume 1 only

‡*Leuciscus idus* (*see Idus idus*)

‡*Leuciscus leuciscus* (Dace) *146*
Europe, except Iceland, Scotland and Norway. Rivers and streams near the surface, preferring cool, running water. Gregarious. Diet: a wide range of insect larvae, crustaceans, worms and plants. Takes flying insects.
Volume 1 only

Leuciscus leuciscus baikalensis
Lake Baikal (Russia).
Calcium, Magnesium, Potassium, Sodium: 2864

Leuciscus pigus
Europe.
Calcium 1528

‡*Leuciscus rutilus*
Glucose, Glycogen, Sodium: 2802, 2804

Leuciscus souffia agassizi
  Europe.
  Amino acids, Hydroxyproline: 1655 (Hydroxyproline is always listed separately)

Leucopsarion petersi (Ice goby) *64*

‡Leuresthes tenuis (Grunion)
  California. Sandy coasts. Spawns in large numbers on beaches at high tide. Avoids
  temperatures above 34°C or below 20°C. Preferred temperature 25°C.
  Volume 1 only

Lichia vadigo (Pampano)
  Cholesterol 1785

  (Note: The spelling Limanda is not universal. Limander is often used.)
‡Limanda angustirostris
  Japan.
  Volume 1 only

Limanda aspera *31, 51, 328, 329, 333*

‡Limanda ferruginea (Rusty dab, Yellowtail flounder)
  E. side of N. America (Labrador to Virginia). Confined to the continental shelf,
  37–73 m, on sandy or muddy bottoms. Diet: small crustaceans, molluscs, worms
  and occasional small fish.
  Chloride, Sodium: 1860

‡Limanda herzensteini (Flounder, Japanese dab, Sand dab, Smallmouthed sole)
  Japan.
  Cadmium 2901; Caesium 2269; Cobalt 2269; Copper 2901; Fatty acids 2154, 3666,
  3667; *Free* histidine 3166; Iron 2901; Lead 2901; Potassium 2900; Sodium 2900;
  Zinc 2269, 2901

Limanda irrdorum
  Japan.
  Calcium, Strontium: 3486

‡Limanda limanda (Dab)
  Europe: France to White Sea, W. Baltic, Iceland, 20–150 m often on sandy banks.
  Diet: echinoderms, hermit crabs, sand-hoppers, worms, molluscs, small fish.
  Lactic dehydrogenase 1789; Urate oxidase 1711; Xanthine oxidase 1711

‡Limanda yokohamae (Mud dab)
  Japan.
  Collagen 3462; Connective tissue 3462; Elastin 3462; Trimethylamine oxide 2111

Limandella yokohamae
  Japan.
  Thiaminase 3473

Liopsetta glacialis (Arctic flounder)
Russia, Canadian Arctic.
Cholesterol, *Free* fatty acids, Phospholipids, Triglycerides, Vitamin A: 3237

‡Liparis koefoedi (Gelatinous seasnail)
Circumpolar. In fjords of northern Labrador can live all year round at $-1 \cdot 7°C$ in the supercooled state.
Volume 1 only

Liparis tanakai
Japan.
Fatty acids, Neutral lipids: 2153

‡Lithognathus mormyrus = Pagellus mormyrus (Bontrok, Marmor bream, Striped seabream, Zee-basje)
Biscay to Senegal, Mediterranean. Absent from Black Sea. Muddy, sandy or vegetated bottoms down to 30 m. Sometimes enters saline littoral pools. Diet: crustaceans, fish.
Cadmium 1707; Copper 1707; Formaldehyde 1656; Lead 1707; Mercury 1707, 1891; Zinc 1707

‡Liza dussumieri* (*see* Mugil dussumieri*)

Liza ramada* (Grey mullet) *293, 306*
No change in plasma concentrations of ions over a wide range of external salinities.
Mg-ATPase (magnesium-activited adenosine triphosphatase) 1974; Na-K-ATPase 1974; Chloride 2520; Potassium 2520; Sodium 2520

Lobianchia dofleini
N. Atlantic.
Arsenic, Cadmium, Copper, Mercury, Zinc: 3638

‡Lophiomus setigerus (Angler)
Japan, Korea, China. Rocky or weedy bottoms.
Vitamin D 3673

‡Lophius americanus (*see* Lophius piscatorius) *156*

‡Lophius litulon (Angler, Goosefish)
Japan.
Adenosine diphosphate 2456; Adenosine monophosphate 2456; Amino acids 2456; *Free* amino acids 2456; Ammonia 2456; Arsenic 3402; Copper 3402; Creatin 2456; Creatinine 2456; Fatty acids 3666, 3667; Hydroxyproline 2456; Inosine monophosphate 2456; Lead 3402; Manganese 3402; Mercury 2887, 3402; Taurine 2456; Trimethylamine 2456; Trimethylamine oxide 2111, 2456; Zinc 3402

‡Lophius piscatorius = Lophius americanus (Allmouth, Angler, Bellowsfish, Fishing frog, Goosefish, Monk) *49, 156, 459*
Both sides of N. Atlantic, Gulf of St. Lawrence to Brazil, N. Europe to Mediterranean. Intertidal to 550 m or more on a variety of bottoms. Migrates down to

2000 m in spawning season. Possesses a few glomeruli in the kidney, but these seem to be non-functional (Oguri, Ogawa and Sokabe, 1972). Blood glucose has been known to average only 7·6 mg% (Wright, 1958). Diet: fish, occasional sea-birds. Mg-ATPase (magnesium-stimulated adenosine triphosphatase) 2321; Na-K-ATPase 2321; Amino acids 3447; Ammonia 2083, 3303; Cadmium 1707; Calcium 1909, 2083; Chitinase 1901; Chloride 1909, 1944, 2083, 2963; Cholesterol 2515; Copper 1707, 1708, 2963; Creatin 2083, 3303; Creatinine 2083, 3303; DNA 2195; *Free* fatty acids 2515; Glucose 2516, 3664; Haematocrit 2516; Haemoglobin 2516; Iron 2963; Lactate 2516; Lactic dehydrogenase 1789; Lead 1707, 1708; Lysozyme 1910; Magnesium 2083; Mercury 1707, 1708; Potassium 1909, 2963; Sodium 1909, 1944, 2963; "Sugar" 1455; Urea 2083, 3303; Uric acid 2083, 3303; Zinc 1707, 1708, 3610

‡Lophius setigerus
   Japan.
   Volume 1 only

‡Lophopsetta maculata (Sundial, Windowpane)
   Atlantic coast of United States: Gulf of St. Lawrence to S. Carolina. Bottom-living in shallow water.
   Volume 1 only

Loricaria parva (Vieja)
   S. America, rivers. Thin-walled stomach serves as respiratory organ. Diet: algae.
   DNA 2195

‡*Lota lota* (Burbot, Eel-pout) *213, 269*
   N. and central Europe (not Iceland, Ireland, Scotland or Spain). Asia and right across N. America southward to about 40°N. Lakes and streams. Prefers bottom of clear waters, under rocks or in holes. This is the only gadoid living entirely in fresh water. Spawns in mid-winter under the ice (Canada). Optimum temperature in other seasons 15–18°C (given as 11·4°C in Coutant's review). Upper limit 23°C. Voracious predator. Diet: crustaceans, insect larvae, fish.
   Amino acids 2447; Calcium 1528, 1908, 2864; Chloride 1908; DNA 2447; Fatty acids 3117; Galactose 3141; Glucose 3141; Guanine 1867; Hypoxanthine 1867; Magnesium 2864; Mannose 3141; Mercury 1557, 3649; Potassium 1908, 2864; "Proteinase" 3622; RNA 2447; Sodium 1908, 2864; Thyroxine 2190

‡*Lota lota maculosa* (Alekey trout, Burbot, Lake lawyer, Ling, Mud blower)
   N. America: New England northwards to Arctic. Rivers and lakes.
   Amino acids 1812

‡*Lota molva*
   Volume 1 only

‡Lotella maximowiczi
   Japan.
   Fatty acids, Neutral lipids: 2152

Lotella phycis
Japan.
Dimethylamine, Formaldehyde: 3665

‡*Lucioperca lucioperca* = *L. sandra* (Pike-perch, Sander)
Central Europe, Baltic. Warm, shallow water with hard bottom.
Aluminium 2677; *para*-Amino benzoic acid 3295; Biotin 3295; Cadmium 1972;
Calcium 2677, 2864; Cobalt 2677; Copper 2677; Cyanocobalamin 3295; Fatty
acids 2492, 3117; Inositol 3295; Iron 2677; Magnesium 2677, 2864; Manganese
2677; Niacin 3295; Pantothenic acid 3295; Potassium 2677, 2864; Pyridoxine 3295;
Sodium 2864; "Sugar" 2993; Thiamine 3295; Tin 2677; Vanadium 2677; Zinc
2677

Lumpenella nigricans
Japan.
Fatty acids, Neutral lipids: 2153

Lumpenus sagitta (Eel blenny, Pacific snake blenny, Snake prickleback)
California to Bering Sea, Aleutian Is. down to 207 m. Jumps out of aquarium.
Diet: (young) copepods; (adult) worms.
Calcium, Chloride, Magnesium, Potassium, Sodium: 3090

(*Note:* the name of the following genus is sometimes spelt Lutjanus)
‡Lutianus analis (Mutton fish, Mutton snapper, Pargo)
E. America: Woods Hole to Brazil. Tidal creeks with mangroves, shallow bays
with turtle grass and in more open water on sandy bottoms. Inactive. Diet: fish,
crustaceans.
Haematocrit, Haemoglobin: 3377

Lutianus apodus (Schoolmaster)
New England, Bermuda to Brazil. West Indian coral reefs. Shallow water. Inactive.
Haematocrit, Haemoglobin: 3377

‡Lutianus aya
United States to Brazil.
Volume 1 only

‡Lutianus blackfordii (Pensacola snapper, Red snapper)
N. America: Florida
Volume 1 only

‡Lutianus campechanus (Mexican snapper, Red snapper)
E. America: Long Island to Texas, Puerta Rica
DNA 2195

‡Lutianus griseus* (Cabelellerote, Grey snapper, Lawyer, Mangrove snapper)
Both sides of tropical Atlantic, especially West: New York to Brazil. Inshore in
creeks among mangrove, rocky areas, reefs and occasionally fresh water.
DNA 2195

‡Lutianus hastingsi (Bermuda silk snapper)
Volume 1 only

Lutianus johnii (John's snapper, Moses perch)
S.E. Asia. Shallow waters and mangrove. Diet: bottom-living invertebrates, fish.
Amino acids, Calcium, Iron, Niacin, Riboflavin, Thiamine, Vitamin A: 3690

‡Lutianus malabaricus (Largemouthed nannygai, Malabar snapper, Nannygai, Red
bream, Red emperor, Red jaw, Red snapper, Scarlet sea perch, Snapper)
India, Malaya, Philippines, Australia: reef waters of Queensland. Pearl banks and
trawling grounds. Down to at least 60 m. Diet: bottom-living invertebrates, fish.
Volume 1 only

‡Lutianus rivulatus (Flute porgy, Snapper)
India, Red Sea, Japan, China.
Volume 1 only

Lutianus sebae (Emperor snapper, Government bream, Red snapper)
Indo-Pacific, also S. Africa. Robust. Swims in schools on reefs and over sandy and
rocky grounds. Juveniles found in shallow mangrove and sea grass areas. Adults
down to 100 m. Diet: crustaceans, fish.
Trimethylamine oxide 3151

‡Lutianus synagris (Biajaiba, Lane snapper, Red tail snapper)
E. America: Florida to Brazil, Puerta Rica. Inactive.
Free fatty acids 2439; Haematocrit 3377; Haemoglobin 3377; Monoglycerides
+ diglycerides 2439; Phospholipids 2439; Sterol esters 2439; Triglycerides 2439;
Vitamin A 2439

Lycichthys denticulatus (*see* Anarhichas latifrons)

Lycodes brevipes (Shortfin eelpout)
Oregon, Bering Sea, Okhotsk Sea. 27–642 m.
Chloride, Magnesium, Potassium, Sodium: 3090

Lycodes diapterus (Black eelpout)
S. California to Alaska. Japan.
Calcium, Chloride, Magnesium, Potassium, Sodium: 3090

Lycodes nakamurai
Japan.
Fatty acids, Neutral lipids: 2153

Lycodes tanakai
Japan.
Fatty acids, Neutral lipids: 2153

‡Lycodes turneri (Polar eelpout)
Arctic Ocean, Labrador coast. In deep fjords of northern Labrador these fish live
at −1·7°C in supercooled state.
Volume 1 only

Lyopsetta exilis (Slender sole)
California to S.E. Alaska. Shallow water down to 513 m.
DNA 2195; Ornithine aminotransferase 3611

‡**Mabula japonica**
Japan.
Volume 1 only

‡*Macquaria australasica* (Macquarie perch, Mountain perch, Murray perch)
Australia. Fast-flowing rivers.
Volume 1 only

‡Macrodon ancylodon (Sea trout)
S. America.
Choline, Cyanocobalamin, Folic acid: 3125

Macrognathus aculeatum (Freshwater mudeel) *80*
India.
Erythrocytes, Leucocytes: 3408

‡*Macrones cavasius = M. aor = M. nigriceps* (Dwarf catfish)
India, Assam, Burma, Java, Borneo, Sumatra. Rivers and lakes.
Volume 1 only

‡*Macrones punctatus*
India: Bowany River.
Volume 1 only

‡*Macrones seenghala*
India. Rivers.
Volume 1 only

‡*Macrones vittatus = Mystus vittatus* (Striped dwarf catfish)
India, Burma. Ponds and streams up to 3000 feet.
Cholesterol 3267; DNA 2824; Erythrocytes 2326, 2362, 3408; Glucose 3407;
Haematocrit 2362; Haemoglobin 2326, 2362; Lactate 3407; Leucocytes 2326;
3408; Lymphocytes 2326; Neutrophils 2326; RNA 2824; Vitamin A_1 1500;
Vitamin A_2 1500

Macropodus cupanus dayi (Brown spiketailed paradise fish)
S. India, Burma, S. Vietnam. Hardy. Possesses accessory respiratory organs.
DNA 2195

Macropodus opercularis (Paradise fish) *30*
Korea, China, Vietnam, Formosa. Drainage ditches, paddy fields. Hardy. Possesses
accessory respiratory organs.
DNA 2195

‡Macrorhamphosus sagifue (Egret piper)
Japan. Deep sea.
Volume 1 only

Macrouronus novaezelandiae (New Zealand whiptail)
    Australia, New Zealand.
    Copper, Zinc: 1893

‡Macrourus berglax (Rough-head grenadier, Smooth-spined rat tail)
    United States to Greenland and Norway, Spitzbergen. 183–1240 m. A bottom
    feeder.
    Volume 1 only

‡Macrozoarces americanus (Eel-pout, Muttonfish, Ocean pout)
    Western N. Atlantic, Newfoundland to Delaware. A bottom species at depths of
    15–180 m on hard or semi-hard bottoms.
    Chloride 1860; Sodium 1860; "Sugar" 2643

Macrurus rupestris (North Atlantic grenadier) *206, 207*

Maena maena
    Mediterranean.
    Free amino acids 3140; Cadmium 1707; Copper 1707; Lead 1707; Mercury 1707;
    Zinc 1707

Maena smary
    Mediterranean.
    Cadmium, Copper, Lead, Mercury, Zinc: 1707

Makaira ampla (Pacific blue marlin)
    Mercury 3127

‡Makaira marlina (Giant black marlin)
    California to Cape San Lucas
    Volume 1 only

‡Makaira mazara = M. nigricans (Black marlin, Black spearfish, Blue marlin, Real
    swordfish)
    Worldwide in tropical and warm seas. Migratory. Diet: fish and (secondarily)
    squid.
    Free amino acids 3369; Anserine 3369; Arsenic 2886; Cadmium 2886; Carnosine
    3369; Chromium 2886; Copper 2886; Creatin + creatinine 3369; Lead 2886;
    Mercury 2888, 3274; Selenium 2888; Taurine 3369; Trimethylamine 2388;
    Vitamin D 3673; Zinc 2886

‡Makaira mitsukurii (Pacific marlin, Spear fish, Striped marlin, Swordfish) *321*
    Japan, Formosa, Hawaii, California. Surface, Oceanic.
    Free amino acids 3369; Anserine 3369; Arsenic 2888; Cadmium 2888; Carnosine
    3369; Chromium 2888; Copper 2888; Creatin + creatinine 3369; *Free* histidine
    3166; Lead 2888; Mercury 2887, 2888; Selenium 2888; Taurine 3369; Zinc 2888

‡Makaira nigricans (*see* M. mazara)

Malacanthus plumieri (Sand tilefish)
S. Carolina to Brazil, Caribbean, Ascension Is. Sandy bottoms in shallow water. Burrows in sand. Diet: small fish, crustaceans.
Cerebroside 2469, 2470; Fatty acids 2469; Haematocrit 3377; Haemoglobin 3377; Sulphatide 2469, 2470

Malacocottus gibber
Japan.
Fatty acids, Neutral fats: 2153

Malacosteus niger (Loosejaw)
Worldwide, tropical and temperate (not Mediterranean). 900–1800 m.
Fatty acids 2469

Malapterurus electricus (Electric catfish)
Central Africa, Nile Valley. Mostly in swamps, occasionally in river reed beds. Aggressive; administers a powerful shock. Scaleless.
DNA 2195

Mallotus villosus (Capelin) *52, 53, 67*
Circumpolar (North). Pelagic shoaling fish, depth 150 m by day, close to surface by night. Males die after spawning. The left ovary has been observed to be more fecund than the right. Fat reserves are under the skin and lining the body cavity. Diet: zooplankton, almost entirely copepods. Larger fish eat amphipods, shrimps, own eggs.
Fatty acids 1416; Fluoride 2404; Phospholipid 1416; Triglyceride 1416

Marcusenius longianalis
DNA 2195

Marcusenius nigricans
DNA 2195

‡Marlina marlina
Volume 1 only

‡*Mastacembalus armatus* (Spiny eel)
India, Sri Lanka, Burma, Malaya, China. Fresh and brackish waters of the plains and hills up to 4000 feet. In well-weeded swamps and also open waters in large rivers and lakes. Diet: a wide variety of bottom-living insects, crustaceans and small fish.
Acid phosphatase 3227; Alkaline phosphatase 3227, 3404; Erythrocytes 3408; Glucose 3407; Lactate 3407; Leucocytes 3408; Vitamin A_1 1500; Vitamin A_2 1500

Mastacembalus pancalus (Spiny eel)
E. India, Bangladesh. Large rivers and coastal plains. Tolerates estuarine conditions.
Vitamin A_1 1500; Vitamin A_2 1500

‡Masturus lanceolatus (Nippletailed ocean sunfish, Sharptail ocean sunfish)
Cosmopolitan in temperate and tropical waters.
Volume 1 only

Medialuna californiensis
DNA 2195

‡Megalaspis cordyla (Hardtail, Hardtail scad, Torpedo trevally)
Red Sea, Tanzania, S. Arabia, India, Malaya, Hong-Kong, Formosa, Philippines,
Queensland, Hawaii. Warm coastal waters down to 60 m. Diet: small crustaceans,
fish.
Volume 1 only

Megalops atlanticus (Tarpon)
Albumin, Alkaline phosphatase, Calcium, Globulin: 3523

‡Megalops cyprinoides* (Bony mullet, Indian tarpon, Oxeye herring, Tarpon)
E. Africa, India, China, Philippines, Australia, Hawaii. Seas and estuaries,
entering fresh water. Ponds. Pelagic. Very voracious. Uses a modified swim
bladder for breathing air. Diet: fish, crustaceans, mysids, insects.
Volume 1 only

‡Melanogrammus aeglefinus = Gadus aeglefinus (Haddock) *41, 51–54, 79, 138, 167,
232, 248, 338, 359, 367*
S. Norway to N. Africa, Gibralter to Sicily, W. Greenland to Virginia. Bottom-
living, 40–300 m. Not found inshore. Tires easily and tends to be delicate in
captivity. Diet: brittle stars, molluscs, worms, herring- and capelin eggs, young
fish. "Grazes" the bottom of the sea in the manner of a cow. Preferred temperature
5–6°C.
n-Acetyl histidine 2181; Alanine aminotransferase 2793; Amino acids 1812; *Free*
amino acids 2977; *Free* amino acids, a single combined figure 2181; Anserine
2977; Aspartate amino transferase 2793; Calcium 1149, 3294; Carnosine 2977;
Chitinase 1910; Chloride 1860, 1909; Cholesterol 2515; Copper 3294; Cytochrome
oxidase 2009; *Free* fatty acids 2515, 3243; Fluoride 2404, 3294; Glucose 2516,
3576; Haematocrit 2516; Haemoglobin 2516; Histidine 2181; Iodide 3294; Iron
3294; Lactate 2516; Lactic dehydrogenase 2009; Lysozyme 1910; Magnesium
1149, 3294; Manganese 3294; Mercury 1953, 2482; Nitrite 1864; Ornithine 2977;
Pantothenic acid 3211; Phospholipids 3243; Potassium 1909, 3294; Pyridoxine
3211; Sarcosine 2977; Serine ethanolamine phosphate 2181; Sodium 1860, 1909,
3294; Sterol esters 3243; Strontium 1478; "Sugar" 2643; Taurine 2977; Threonine
ethanolamine phosphate 2181; Triglycerides 3243; Urate oxidase 1711; Xanthine
oxidase 1711; Zinc 3610

Melanonus zugmayeri
Caught at 1000 m
Phospholipid 3064

Melanotaenia fluviatilis (Crimson-spotted rainbow fish, Pinkear)
E. Australia. Protracted spawning season.
DNA 2195

Melanotaenia nigrans (Australian red-tailed rainbow fish)
E. Australia. Fresh and brackish waters. Active and hardy.
DNA 2195

‡Menacanthus cirrhifer
   Japan.
   Volume 1 only

‡Mene maculata (Moonfish)
   Aden, Tanzania, Japan, East Indies, China, Philippines, Queensland, Hawaii.
   Deep coastal water off reefs but sometimes enters estuaries.
   Volume 1 only

‡Menidia menidia (Atlantic silverside, Sand smelt)
   W. Atlantic: Gulf of St. Lawrence and Nova Scotia to Chesapeake Bay. Shore
   waters and estuaries. Tolerates brackish water. Avoids temperatures above 32°C.
   Volume 1 only

Menticirrhus americanus
   DNA 2195

Menticirrhus littoralis (Gulf kingfish, King whiting)
   Atlantic coast of N. America.
   Volume 1 only

Menticirrhus saxatilis (Northern kingfish, Sea mullet, Whiting)
   W. Atlantic: Cape Cod to Florida. Found in schools close to hard or sandy sea
   bed. Diet: crustaceans, small fish. Lacks swimbladder.
   Aldehyde oxidase, Xanthine oxidase: 2468

‡Merlangius merlangus = Gadus merlangus (Whiting) *79, 138, 249, 339, 359, 437*
   Europe, including Iceland, often close inshore over muddy ground. In Mediter-
   ranean restricted to Aegean and Adriatic Seas. Diet: small fish, prawns, swimming
   crabs.
   Amino acids 3082; *Free* amino acids 2977; Anserine 2977; Arginase 2256;
   Argininosuccinate lyase 2256; Argininosuccinate synthetase 2256; Cadmium 2148;
   Calcium 1909; Carnosine 2977; Chloride 1909; Cholesterol 2515; *Free* fatty
   acids 2515; Fucose 2770; Galactosamine 2770; Galactose 2770; Glucosamine 2770;
   Glucose 2770; Haematocrit 2516; Haemoglobin 2516; Hexosamines 2770; Hexoses
   2770; Hydroxyproline 2770; Magnesium 1909; Mannose 2770; Mercury 2148;
   Potassium 1909; Sarcosine 2977; Sodium 1909; Taurine 2977; Urate oxidase 1711;
   Uronic acid 2770; Xanthine oxidase 1711

‡Merlangus carbonarius
   Europe.
   Volume 1 only

‡Merluccius bilinearis (American hake, New England hake, Old England hake,
   Silverfish, Silver hake, Stockfish, Whiting)
   Eastern N. America: Newfoundland to N. Carolina and in deeper water to the
   Bahamas. Found down to 122 m.
   Amino acids 1812; DNA 2195; *Free* fatty acids 1671; Formaldehyde 1671;
   Mercury 1953; "Sugar" 2063

‡Merluccius capensis (Stockfish) *209, 210*
  S. Africa to Angola, 37–914 m. Inshore in summer, deeper water in winter.
  Fatty acids 3616; Phosphatidyl choline 2454; Phosphatidyl ethanolamine 2454;
  Phosphatidyl inositol 2454; Phosphatidyl serine 2454; Phospholipids 2454, 3616;
  Sphingomyelin 2454; Triglycerides 3616

Merluccius gayi (Hake)
  Japan.
  Caesium, Cobalt, Zinc: 2269

‡Merluccius merluccius (Hake) *112*
  Coasts of Europe, Mediterranean and N. Africa, straying to Greenland. Black Sea.
  100–1000 m. Lives near bottom by day but moves up during the night to feed on
  other fish.
  Amino acids 3672; *Free* amino acids 3140; Cadmium 1707, 1709; 2786; Calcium
  1909; Cathepsin (in frozen tissue) 1924; Chloride 1909; Cholesterol 2515; Chromium
  2786; Cobalt 2786; Copper 1707–1709, 2786; *Free* fatty acids 2515; Formaldehyde 1656; Glucose 2516; Haematocrit 2516; Haemoglobin 2516; Hydroxyproline
  3672; Iron 2786; Lactate 2516; Lactic dehydrogenase 1789; Lead 1707–1709,
  2786; Magnesium 1909; Manganese 2786; Mercury 1707–1709, 1891; Nickel
  2786; Potassium 1909; Sodium 1909; Strontium 2786; Trimethylamine oxide
  3151; Zinc 1707–1709, 2786

Merluccius paradoxus *210*
  Fatty acids, Phospholipids, Triglycerides: 3616

‡Merluccius productus (Pacific hake) *251, 252*
  S. California to Gulf of Alaska. Coastal. Surface to 900 m. Soft-fleshed. Migrates
  vertically each day, feeding near the surface at nightfall. Migrates offshore in
  winter. Diet: fish, squid, crustaceans.
  DNA 2195; Mercury 1697; Ornithine aminotransferase 3611

‡Merluccius senegalensis
  Volume 1 only

Merluccius sp.
  Diacyl glyceryl ethers, *Free* fatty acids, *Free* fatty alcohols, Partial glycerides,
  Phospholipids, Sterol esters, Sterols, Triglycerides, Wax esters: 2399

Metynnis hypsauchen
  DNA 2195

Metynnis roosevelti
  DNA 2195

Microdonophis erabo
  Japan.
  Trimethylamine oxide 2111

‡Microgadus proximus (Pacific tomcod)
    N. California to Gulf of Alaska. Coastal. Surface to 260 m on sandy or muddy
    bottoms. Diet: crustaceans, fish.
    D-Amino acids oxidase 1923; DNA 2195; Ornithine aminotransferase 3611

‡Microgadus tomcod* (Atlantic tomcod, Frostfish, Snig)
    N. American coasts; Newfoundland to Virginia, inshore and in brackish water.
    Eggs laid in river mouths. Occasionally a permanent resident in fresh water.
    Midwinter spawner, usually under the ice. Voracious. Diet: usually shrimps,
    amphipods.
    Chloride 1860; Sodium 1860; "Sugar" 2643

‡Micromesistius poutassou = Gadus poutassou (Blue whiting, Couch's whiting)
    W. Europe including Iceland, Mediterranean. Oceanic in large shoals. 100 m to
    several thousand meters. Shoals and appears not to eat when spawning in March-
    April, migrates northwards after spawning and the shoals disperse while the fish
    feed. The liver varies enormously in size during the year, from a long fat-rich organ
    which takes up a fair proportion of the body cavity and extends its full length, to
    a stage where it can hardly be found: just a few strands of connective-tissue-like
    material remain. Diet: pelagic crustaceans, fish.
    Amino acids 1786; Cadmium 1707, 2786; Calcium 1786, 1909; Chloride 1909;
    Cholesterol 2515; Chromium 2786; Cobalt 2786; Copper 1707, 1708, 2786;
    Cytochrome oxidase 2009; Diamine oxidase 2231; *Free* fatty acids 2515; Glucose
    2516; Haematocrit 2516; Haemoglobin 2516; Iron 1786, 2786; Lactate 2516;
    Lactic dehydrogenase 1789, 2009; Lead 1707, 1708, 2786; Magnesium 1909;
    Manganese 2786; Mercury 1707, 1708; Niacin 1786; Nickel 2786; Potassium 1909;
    Riboflavin 1786; Sodium 1786, 1909; Strontium 2786; Thiamine 1786; Zinc 1707,
    1708, 2786

Micropogon furnieri (Croaker)
    Coasts of S. America.
    Carbohydrate 3311; Chloride 3311; Choline 3125; Cyanocobalamin 3125; Folic
    acid 3125; Potassium 3311; Sodium 3311

‡Micropogon undulatus (Corvina, Croaker, Hardhead, Roncodina)
    Atlantic coast of N. America: Cape Cod to Texas. Shallow, sandy shores in summer,
    deeper waters in winter offshore. Avoids temperatures above 38°C.
    DNA 2195; Erythrocytes 1647; Haematocrit 1647; Haemoglobin 1647; Mutarotase
    1480

‡*Micropterus dolomieui* = *M. dolomieu* (Bass, Bass hogfish, Black perch, Little bass,
    Small-mouthed black bass *and many other names*) *30*
    N. America, especially eastern central regions. Rocky and sandy areas of lakes and
    rivers. Introduced to Europe. Prefers deep waters in the heat of summer. Preferred
    temperature from 18 to 31°C according to various writers. Upper lethal temperature
    35°C. Diet: (young) crustaceans, insect larvae; (adult) fish, amphibians, inverte-
    brates.
    Mg-ATPase (magnesium-activated adenosine triphosphatase) 2321, 3023; Na-K-
    ATPase 2321, 3023; DNA 2098; RNA 2098

‡*Micropterus salmoides* = *Huro salmoides* (Black bass, Largemouth bass *and many other names*) *182, 218, 343*
S.E. and central N. America. Introduced to Europe and other parts of America. Weedy lakes and large slow rivers; occasionally brackish water. Growth rate and ultimate size greater in females, which mature later than males Preferred temperature around 27°C; upper lethal temperature 36°C only after acclimatisation; avoids temperatures above 30°C or below 21–27°C if given free choice. Poor tolerance for low oxygen concentrations. Fairly active predator. Diet: fish.
Aldehyde oxidase 2468; Calcium 1528, 2263, 2264; Magnesium 2263, 2264; Mutarotase 1480; Potassium 2263, 2264; Sodium 2263, 2264; Xanthine oxidase 2468

Microstomus achne (Japanese Dover sole, Slime flounder)
Japan.
Fatty acids 2154, 3666, 3667

‡Microstomus hireguro
Japan.
Volume 1 only

‡Microstomus kitaharae
Japan.
Volume 1 only

‡Microstomus kitt (*see* Pleuronectes microcephalus)

‡Microstomus pacificus (Dover sole, Slime sole, Slippery sole)
S. California to Bering Sea. Muddy bottoms, surface to 1100 m. Hardy. A prolonged period of its early life is pelagic. Diet: soft-bodied invertebrates, particularly worms.
DNA 2195; Mercury 1697; Ornithine aminotransferase 3611

‡Microstomus stelleri
Japan.
Connective tissue 3462

‡Miichthys imbricatus
Japan.
Volume 1 only

Minytrema melanops (Spotted sucker)
Mississippi River.
Bicarbonate 2262; Calcium 2262–2264; Chloride 2262; Glucose 2262; Haematocrit 2262; Lactate 2262; Magnesium 2262–2264; Potassium 2262–2264; Sodium 2262–2264

‡*Misgurnus anguillicaudatus* (Dojo fish, Loach) *149*
Japan, China.
DNA 2195; Galactose + sialic acid 3476; Glucosamine 3476; NAD (nicotinamide adenine dinucleotide) 3259; NADH (reduced NAD) 3259; Pyridine nucleotide transhydrogenase 3167; Trimethylamine oxide 2111

‡*Misgurnus fossilis* (Mudfish, Pond loach, Weatherfish) *10, 15, 16, 18, 19, 248, 329, 330*
Japan. Central and E. Europe and Baltic. Not Britain, France or Scandinavia.
Swallows bubbles of air under conditions of oxygen lack; intestinal breathing used.
Acid ribonuclease 2486; Adenosine diphosphate 3704; Adenosine monophosphate
3704; Adenosine triphosphate 3689, 3704; Adenylate kinase 3704; Aldolase 3703;
Alkaline ribonuclease 2486; α-Amylase 3708, 3709; γ-Amylase 3708, 3709; Amylo-
1,6-glucosidase 3708, 3709; "Branching" enzyme (glycogenolytic) 3708, 3709;
Citrate 3704; Citrate synthetase 3688; Dihydroxyacetone phosphate 3689;
Enolase 3703; Fructose diphosphatase 3703; Fructose-1,6-diphosphate 3704, 3707;
Glucose 3704, 3707; Glucose-6-phosphatase 3701; Glucose-6-phosphate 3707;
Glucose-6-phosphate dehydrogenase 1889, 3703; Glutamate dehydrogenase 3688;
Glutathione reductase 1889; Glyceraldehyde-3-phosphate 3689; α-Glycerophos-
phate dehydrogenase 3702; Glycogen 3705, 3706; Glycogen phosphorylase 3701,
3704; Glycogen synthetase 3704–3706, 3708, 3709; Hexokinase 3704; Hexose
monophosphates, including fructose-6-phosphate 3704, 3706, 3708; Lactate 3689;
Lactic dehydrogenase 3702; Malic dehydrogenase 3688; "Malic enzyme" 1889;
NAD (nicotinamide adenine dinucleotide) 3689; NADH (reduced NAD) 3689;
NADP (NAD phosphate) 1889; NADPH 1889; NADP-isocitrate dehydrogenase
1889; *Oligo*-1,4→1,4 glucantransferase 3708, 3709; Phosphoenol pyruvate 3704;
Phosphoenol pyruvate carboxykinase 3703; Phosphoglucomutase 3701; 6-Phos-
phogluconate dehydrogenase 1889, 3703; 3-Phosphoglycerate 3689; Phospho-
glycerate kinase 3702, 3703; Phosphohexose isomerase 3701; Phospholipid 2223;
Phosphorylase 2763, 3705, 3706, 3708, 3709; Potassium 1531; Pyruvate 3689, 3707;
Pyruvate carboxylase 3688; Pyruvate dehydrogenase 3688; Sodium 1531;
Transaldolase 3703; Transketolase 3703; Triose phosphate dehydrogenase 3702,
3703; Triose phosphate isomerase 3703; Uridine diphosphate-glucose pyrophosphorylase 3706, 3709; Uridine diphosphoglucose 3704

Mistichthys luzonensis *58*
Grows to only 14 mm in length.

Moenkhausia oligolepis (Glass tetra)
Amazon, Guyana. Standing or sluggish waters. Diet: varied.
DNA 2195

‡Mola mola (Common mola, Headfish, Ocean sunfish)
Wide distribution in tropical and temperate seas. Preferred depth unknown
(183–366 m according to Wheeler), but sometimes found drifting at surface. Can
swim entirely with the dorsal and ventral fins. Scaleless skin. Diet: zooplankton,
eel larvae, small deep-sea fish, jelly-fish.
Fatty acids, Phospholipids, Triglycerides: 2234

Mollienesia sp. *83*

‡Molva byrkelange = M. dypterygia (Blue ling, Lesser ling)
Both sides of Atlantic. N. Norway to Iceland and Ireland, 200–1500 m.
Mercury 2482; Zinc 3610

‡Molva molva (Ling)
  Iceland, Murman coast to France. Occasionally W. Atlantic. Commonest between
  100 and 600 m. Diet: fish, crustaceans, starfish.
  Calcium 1909; Chloride 1909; Cholesterol 2515; Haematocrit 2516; Haemoglobin
  2516; Lactic dehydrogenase 1789; Magnesium 1909; Mutarotase 1480; Potassium
  1909; Sodium 1909

‡Monacanthus cirrhifer (Filefish) *149, 459*
  Japan.
  Trimethylamine oxide 2929

 Monodactylus argenteus* (Diamond fish, Fingerfish, Kite fish, Mono, Moonfish)
  Knysna to Natal, Indian Seas to S. Pacific. Enters rivers.
  DNA 2195

‡*Monopterus albus* (Flute alba, Paddy eel, Rice eel, Swamp eel)
  Burma, Malaya, Indonesia, China, Formosa, Japan. Fresh or brackish waters,
  rivers, ponds, ditches, swamps, rice fields. Scale-less. Can live for long periods out
  of water, burrowing in mud in the dry season.
  Volume 1 only

‡Monotaxis grandoculis (Humpnose, Large-eye bream, Levovangan, Roundtoothed
  large-eyed bream)
  E. Africa, Red Sea, India, Sri Lanka, Pacific Islands eastwards to Hawaii,
  N. Australia. Coastal reefs and trawling grounds down to 60 m. Diet: bottom-living
  invertebrates and fish.
  Volume 1 only

Mordacia mordax CYCLOSTOME
  S.E. Australia.
  Acetoacetyl CoA deacylase 3026; DNA 3136; Glucose 3025; Glycogen 3025;
  Hydroxymethyl glutaryl CoA synthase 3026; 3-Oxoacid CoA transferase 3026;
  Phosphoenolpyruvate carboxykinase 3025; Pyruvate carboxylase 3025

Moroco steindachneri
  Japan.
  β-Carotene 2719; Cryptoxanthin 2719; Cynthiaxanthin 2719; Diatoxanthin 2719;
  α-Doradecin 2719; Lutein 2719; Thiaminase 2297; Zeaxanthin 2719

‡Morone americana* = Roccus americanus* (Sea perch, Silver perch, White perch)
  57, 305, 330
  Atlantic coast of N. America, Nova Scotia to S. Carolina. Brackish water, ascending
  streams. Frequently landlocked. Thrives in a variety of habitats, but seems to do
  best in water that reaches 24°C or more in summer. Moves onshore at night,
  offshore into deeper water at dawn. Preferred temperature 32°C. Avoids temperatures above 35°C.
  Cholinesterase 1869

Morone chrysops (White bass)
America.
Allantoicase 1775; Allantoinase 1775; Arginase 1776; Arsenic 2611; Bromide 2611; Cadmium 2611; Calcium 2264; Chloride 2264; Cobalt 2611; Copper 2611; Magnesium 2264; Potassium 2264; Sodium 2264; Thorium 2611; Uranium 2611; Zinc 2611

‡Morone labrax (*see* Dicentrarchus labrax)

‡Morone saxatilis*=Roccus saxatilis* (Striped bass) *407, 467*
Atlantic coast of N. America, Gulf of St. Lawrence to Gulf of Mexico. Pacific coast, Mexico to British Columbia. Introduced Pacific coast. Coastal or in brackish or fresh water. Spawns in fresh or slightly salty water. Voracious carnivore. Does not eat steadily, but gorges and then stops feeding until digestion is complete. Preferred temperature 22°C; avoids temperatures above 24°C or below 21°C. Diet: fish, crustaceans.
Arsenic 3638; Cadmium 3638; Calcium 1734; Cholesterol 1734; Copper 2941, 3638; Cynthiaxanthin 2716; DNA 2195; Diatoxanthin 2716; Glucose 1734; Haematocrit 1734, 1735; Haemoglobin 1734, 1735; Lutein 2716; Mercury 3638; Potassium 1734, 1735; Sodium 1734, 1735; Tunaxanthin 2716; Uric acid 1734; Zeaxanthin 2716

Morulius chrysophekadion (Black carp, Black shark)
Thailand, Borneo, Java, Cambodia, Sumatra. Diet: algae and higher plants.
DNA 2195

‡*Moxostoma aureolum* = *M. macrolepidotum* (Large-scaled sucker, Mullet, Northern redhorse, Shorthead redhorse, White sucker)
Eastern and central N. America. Shallow clear waters over bottoms of sand or gravel.
Allantoicase 1775; Allantoinase 1775; Arginase 1774, 1776; Calcium 2264; Chloride 2264; Magnesium 2264; Mercury 3649; Potassium 2264; Sodium 2264

‡*Moxostoma macrolepidotum* (*see M. aureolum*)

Moxostoma sp. (Redhorse sucker)
Canada.
Thyroxine 2190

‡Mugil auratus (Golden-grey mullet)
Britain and S. Norway south to Natal, Mediterranean, Black Sea; introduced Caspian Sea. Shallow waters of varying salinity.
Adrenaline 3340; Amino acids 2422, 3468; *Free* amino acids 2422; Cadmium 1707; Calcium 2862, 2864; Chloride 2862, 2864; Chromium 2015; Copper 1707, 1708; Cyanocobalamin 1522; Lead 1707, 1708, 2015; Magnesium 2862, 2864; Mercury 1707, 1708, 2015; Noradrenaline 3340; Potassium 2862, 2864; Sodium 2862, 2864; Sulphate 2862; Zinc 1707, 1708

Mugil capito* (Grey mullet, Harder, Thinlip grey mullet)
Europe, S. Africa. Shallow brackish waters. Enters estuaries and rivers to feed but spawns in the sea. A fast swimmer. Diet: minute organisms and suspended organic matter.
Cyclic-3'5'-adenosine monophosphate 1771

‡Mugil cephalus* = M. japonicus* = M. oeur* (Bully mullet, Flathead mullet, Grey mullet, Haader, Mangrove mullet, River mullet, Sea mullet, Springer, Striped mullet, True mullet) *83, 110, 152, 242, 247, 273, 276, 282, 283, 300, 305, 317, 327, 328, 334, 339, 383*
Widely distributed in tropical and temperate waters. Not anadromous, but found in fresh and salt waters. Spawns in sea water. Males only 2/3 size of females. Can adapt well to variations in temperature. A fast swimmer, leaping out of the water when disturbed. Diet: diatoms, algae and minute animal material in the bottom mud; organic detritus.
Amino acids 2422; *Free* amino acids 2422; Arsenic 3638; Astacene 2724; Cadmium 1709, 3638; Calcium 3015, 3160, 3486; β-Carotene 2724; Chloride 2894, 2895; Cholesterol 2310, 2559; Copper 1709, 1893, 3015, 3638; Corticosterone 1704; Cryptoxanthin 2724; Cynthiaxanthin 2724; Cytochromes 2296; DNA 2195; Diacyl glyceryl ethers 2399; Diatoxanthin 2724, 2725; Diglycerides 2559; Erythrocytes 1647; Fatty acids 1817, 2296, 2310, 2399, 3170, 3265, 3333; *Free* fatty acids 2310, 2399, 2559; Fatty alcohols 3170; *Free* fatty alcohols 2310, 2399; Formaldehyde 1656; Glucose-6-phosphate dehydrogenase 3258; Haematocrit 1647, 3015; Haemoglobin 1647; Hydrocarbons 2559; Isocryptoxanthin 2724; Lead 1709; Lutein 2724, 2725; Lysolecithin 3265; Mercury 1709, 3638; Mono-glycerides 2559; Partial glycerides 2399; Phosphatidyl choline 3265; Phosphatidyl ethanolamine 3265; Phosphatidyl serine 3265; Phospholipid 2399, 2559, 3265; Potassium 2894, 2895, 3160; Prolactin 3160; Sodium 2894, 2895, 3160; Sphingo-myelin 3265; Squalene 2559; Sterol esters 2399; Sterol and wax esters 2559; Sterols 2399; Strontium 3486; Succinic dehydrogenase 2296; Triglycerides 2310, 2399, 2559; Trimethylamine oxide 2111; Thiaminase 2297; Tunaxanthin 2724; 2725; Wax esters 2310, 2399; Zeaxanthin 2724, 2725; Zinc 1709, 1893, 3688

‡Mugil chelo* (Thick-lipped grey mullet)
Iceland and mid-Norway south to Mediterranean. Black Sea. Inshore and estuarine. Enters rivers for feeding but spawns in the sea.
Chromium, Lead, Mercury: 2015

Mugil corsula
India.
Acid phosphatase, Alkaline phosphatase: 3227

‡Mugil curema (Blue-black mullet, Lisa, White mullet)
Both coasts of N. America. Warm and temperate seas. Shallow waters in schools near the surface. Inshore waters, estuaries and low-salinity pools.
Erythrocytes, Haematocrit, Haemoglobin: 1647

‡Mugil dussumieri* = Liza dussumieri* = Liza subviridis* (Brown-banded mullet, Dussumier's mullet, Flat-tailed mullet, Greenback mullet, Grey mullet)
India, Sri Lanka, Singapore, Java, Sumatra, Philippines. Generally believed to

be migratory. Spawns in the sea, but schools from shallow coastal waters enter lagoons and estuaries to feed. Also found in rice fields and mangrove swamps. Diet: minute bottom-living organisms, organic matter from mud or sand. Perhaps floating algae.
Volume 1 only

‡Mugil japonicus* (see M. cephalus*)

‡Mugil melinopterus (Black-finned mullet)
Philippines, Vanicolo, Tonga, Samoa, Fiji.
Folic acid 2582

‡Mugil oeur* (see M. cephalus*)

‡Mugil parsia* (Gold-spot mullet)
Red Sea, E. Africa, India, China, Fiji, Samoa. Fresh and brackish waters (Weber and Beaufort); seas and estuaries (Day). Diet: algae, diatoms, copepods, polychaets, detritus.
Volume 1 only

Mugil saliens* (Leaping grey mullet)
Mediterranean, Black Sea, Atlantic: Coast of Spain to S. Africa. Fast swimmer, leaping out of the water when disturbed. Enters rivers and estuaries to feed but spawns in the sea. Diet: minute organisms, suspended organic matter.
Amino acids 2422; Free amino acids 2422; Chromium 2015; Cyanocobalamin 1522; Lead 2015; Mercury 2015

‡Mugil speigleri* = Valamugil speigleri* (Grey mullet, Speigler's grey mullet)
Seas of India, Malaya, Java, Borneo. Schools in shallow coastal waters and enters lagoons, estuaries and rivers to feed. Spawns in sea. Diet: minute bottom-living organisms and organic matter in mud and sand, perhaps also floating algae.
Volume 1 only

‡Mugil tade* = Liza tade* (Tade grey mullet)
Red Sea, India, Philippines, China, Australia (not Australia according to Fischer and Whitehead). Shallow coastal waters entering lagoons, estuaries and rivers, rice fields, mangrove.
Volume 1 only

‡Mugil vaigiensis* = Liza vaigiensis* (Diamondscale mullet, Long-finned mullet)
Red Sea, E. Africa, India, Malaya, China, Philippines, Australia. Seas, estuaries and fresh water. Diet: minute organisms, organic matter, perhaps floating algae.
Folic acid 2582

‡Mulloides flavolineatus (Goldenbanded goatfish)
Red Sea, India, Malaya, Philippines, Japan, China, Australia. Harbours.
Volume 1 only

‡Mullus barbatus (Red mullet, Striped mullet). May be same species as M. surmulletus.
Russia, British Is. to Senegal. Israel coast. Sand and mud bottoms down to 300 m.
Adrenaline 3340; Arginase 2256; Argininosuccinate lyase 2256; Argininosuccinate

synthetase 2256; Cadmium 1707, 1709; Carbamoyl phosphate synthetase 2256; Chromium 2015; Copper 1707–1709; Formaldehyde 1656; Lead 1707–1709, 2015; Mercury 1707–1709, 2015; Noradrenaline 3340; Ornithine transcarbamoylase 2256; Zinc 1707–1709

‡Mullus barbatus ponticus
Black Sea, Azov Sea.
Cyanocobalamin 1522

‡Mullus surmulletus = M. surmuletus (Red mullet)
S. Norway and Denmark, S.W. to Britain, France, Mediterranean and Canaries. Mostly on rough ground, down to 90 m. Diet: small bottom-living animals buried in mud.
Cadmium 1709; Copper 1708, 1709; Lead 1708, 1709; Mercury 1708, 1709; Zinc 1708, 1709

‡Muraena helena (Greek moray, Moray eel)
S. England, France, Mediterranean. Inshore amongst rocks. Vicious when captured. Diet: fish, squid, cuttlefish.
Volume 1 only

‡Muraena pardalis
Japan.
Volume 1 only

Muraena sp.
These specimens from India.
Amino acids 3092

‡Muraenesox cinereus (Daggertooth pike-conger, Pike eel, Sharptoothed eel, Silver conger eel)
India, Burma and Malaysia to Hong Kong. Brackish and salt waters of lagoons and shallow coastal inlets, rarely open sea. Active and pugnacious. Down to 100 m over soft bottoms. Diet: bottom-living fish.
Arsenic 3402; Cadmium 2901; Copper 2901, 3402; Iron 2901; Lead 2901; Manganese 3402; Mercury 3402; Potassium 2900; Sodium 2900; Zinc 2901, 3402

‡Muraenesox talabonoides* (Indian pike-conger)
Seas and estuaries of India and Malaya, Indonesia, Hong Kong. Down to 100 m over soft bottoms. Diet: bottom-living fish.
Volume 1 only

Muraenolepis microps
Antarctic.
Carbohydrates, Chloride, Potassium, Sodium: 3311

Mustelus antarcticus (Gummy shark)
New Zealand, S. Australia. 2–220 m.
Zinc 1893

Mustelus californicus
DNA 2194

‡**Mustelus canis** (*see* **Scyliorhinus canicula**)

‡**Mustelus griseus** (Dogshark)
Japan. Viviparous.
Anserine, Balenine, Trimethylamine oxide, Urea: 3367

‡**Mustelus kanekonis**
Japan.
Adenosine diphosphate, Adenosine monophosphate, Adenosine triphosphate,
Free amino acids, Ammonia, Anserine, Balenine, Carnosine, Creatin, Creatinine,
Inosine monophosphate, Taurine, Trimethylamine, Trimethylamine oxide, Urea:
3367

‡**Mustelus laevis** (*see* **Mustelus mustelus**)

‡**Mustelus manazo** (Gummy shark, Star-spotted shark)
Japan, in shallow bays. Viviparous.
Free amino acids 3166; Taurine 3166; Urea 3166; Vitamin D 3673

‡**Mustelus mustelus** = **M. laevis** (Smooth hound, Sweet William)
Britain, France, Mediterranean, occasionally America. 10–150 m on sandy and
muddy bottoms. Mainly nocturnal. Viviparous. Diet: mainly crustaceans, but also
molluscs, worms, fish.
Volume 1 only

Mustelus norris
DNA 2194

Mycteroperca interstitialis
DNA 2195

‡Mycteroperca tigris (Rockfish)
W. Indies north to Bermuda.
DNA 2195

‡Mylio australis* (Bream)
Australia. Creeks, estuaries, rivers, coastal waters.
Volume 1 only

‡Mylio butcheri
Australia.
Volume 1 only

Mylio latus (*see* Chrysophrys datnia)

‡Mylio macrocephalus (Black bream, Black porgy)
Japan.
Adenosine monophosphate 1871; Calcium 3486; Inosine monophosphate 1871, 1873; Strontium 3486; Trimethylamine 1873

‡Myliobatis aquila (Eagle ray)
Britain to Mediterranean. Active. Pelagic. Viviparous. Diet: molluscs, crustaceans.
Volume 1 only

Myliobatis californicus
DNA 2194

Myliobatis freminvillei
DNA 2194

‡Myliobatis maculata
Seas of India to Malaya.
Volume 1 only

Mylopharyngodon piceus (Black carp)
Japan. Herbivorous.
Glucose dehydrogenase 2836; Hexokinase 2836; RNA 3097

Myoxocephalus aeneus (Grubby, Little sculpin)
Coastal waters of N. America, Strait of Belle Is. to New Jersey. Estuaries, low tide to 27 m. Tolerates wide range of temperatures. Diet: marine worms, shrimps, crabs, molluscs, ascidians and the young of many fish species.
Chloride, Sodium: 1860

‡Myoxocephalus groenlandicus (Shorthorn sculpin)
Atlantic coast of N. America.
Volume 1 only

‡Myoxocephalus nivosus
Japan.
Volume 1 only

‡Myoxocephalus octodecimspinosus (Longhorn sculpin)
Western N. Atlantic: Newfoundland to Virginia. Coastal, down to 200 m.
Mg-ATPase (magnesium-activated adenosine triphosphatase) 2321; Na-K-ATPase 2321; Chloride 1860; DNA 2195; Sodium 1860

Myoxocephalus polyacanthocephalus (Great sculpin)
Washington, Alaska, Bering Sea, Aleutian Is., Kamchatka, Hokkaido. Moderate depths. Diet: small fish and "other items".
D-Amino acid oxidase 1923; Calcium 3090; Chloride 3090; Magnesium 3090; Potassium 3090; Sodium 3090

Myoxocephalus quadricornis *342*
Calcium 2924; Chloride 2924, 2925; Magnesium 2924, 2925; Potassium 2924; Sodium 2924, 2925

‡Myoxocephalus scorpius = Cottus scorpius (Bullhead, Bull rout, Daddy sculpin, Father lasher, Greenland sculpin, Shorthorn sculpin, Shortspined cottus) *342*
Both sides of N. Atlantic and the Arctic. Littoral on sandy or muddy grounds, also estuaries. Eggs guarded by the male. Descends to below 20 m in winter, probably to avoid freezing (DeVries, 1974). Voracious predator. Diet: crustaceans, eggs and larvae of other fish.
Arsenic 1560; Calcium 2862, 2864, 2924; Chloride 1860, 2862, 2864, 2924, 2925; Glucose 2924; Haematocrit 2924; Haemoglobin 2924; Magnesium 2861, 2862, 2864, 2924, 2925; Potassium 2862, 2864, 2924; Sodium 1860, 2861, 2862, 2864, 2924, 2925; "Sugar" 1903; Sulphate 2862

Myoxocephalus verrucosus (Sculpin) *348*
Alaska.
Amino acids, Amino galactose, Galactose: 3109

Myripristis arayomus (Squirrel fish)
Inshore.
Mercury 3127

‡*Mystus aor* (probably *Macrones cavasius*)
India.
Erythrocytes 3408; Glucose 3407; Lactate 3407; Leucocytes 3408; Vitamin A_1, Vitamin A_2: 1500

Mystus bleekeri
India.
Erythrocytes 3408; Glucose 3407; Lactate 3407; Leucocytes 3408

Mystus cavasius (*see M. aor*)

‡*Mystus seenghala 41*
India.
Alkaline phosphatase 3404; Cholesterol 3267; Erythrocytes 3408; Glucose 3407; Lactate 3407; Leucocytes 3408

‡*Mystus vittatus* (*see Macrones vittatus*)

‡Myxine glutinosa CYCLOSTOME (Atlantic hagfish, Borer, Hagfish, Northern hagfish) *24, 72, 75, 166, 302, 312, 313, 409, 429*
Wide distribution in Arctic seas and both coasts of N. Atlantic. 30–500 m on muddy bottoms in which they burrow. Parasitic on other fish. Prefers low temperatures (10–13°C) and low light intensity. Does not osmoregulate, and the blood is approximately isosmotic with the external medium; Myxine prefers high or medium salinity. Adults hermaphrodite, the sex organ being part testis, part ovary, but only one part functional in any individual. The haemoglobin of the hagfish has only one oxygen-binding site, unlike all known haemoglobins of other higher vertebrates. The blood-brain barrier is poorly developed or absent (Murray, Jones et al., 1975). Cortisol, corticosterone and aldosterone appear to be absent from this species. The bile contains a characteristic unique bile salt, myxinol, which is said to be a less efficient detergent than are the bile salts of species higher up the evolutionary scale.

Amino acids 2964, 2965; Ammonia 3135; Bicarbonate 3135; Calcium 1909, 3102, 3135; Chloride 1909, 2006, 3135; Cholesterol 2515, 2761; Cobalt 1904; Corticosterone 2275, 3608; Cortisol 2275, 3608; Cortisone 2275; 11-Deoxycorticosterone 2275; 11-Deoxycortisol 2275; *Free* fatty acids 2515; Galactosamine 3098; Glucose 2516; Haematocrit 2516; Haemoglobin 2516; Hexuronic acid 3098; 1-α-Hydroxycorticosterone 3608; Lactate 2516; Magnesium 1909, 3102, 3135; Manganese 1904; Non-protein nitrogen 3135; Phospholipid 2761; Potassium 1700, 1909, 3135; Sodium 1909, 3135; Sulphate 3098, 3135; Testosterone 2275; Thyroxine 2177; Triglyceride 2761; Trimethylamine oxide 1700; Urea 1906, 3135; Zinc 1904

Nandus nandus
India, Burma. Lowland fresh waters and brackish water. Predatory.
Erythrocytes 3408; Leucocytes 3408; Vitamin A_1 1500; Vitamin A_2 1500

‡**Narcacion nobilianus**
N. America.
Volume 1 only

Narcine brasiliensis
DNA 2194

‡**Narke japonica** (Electric ray, Torpedo)
Japan. Coastal. Viviparous.
Trimethylamine oxide 2111

Naso lituratus (Surgeonfish)
Hawaii. Shallow reefs, 1–10 m.
Diphosphatidyl glycerol, Fatty acids, Lysophosphatidyl choline, Phosphatidic acid, Phosphatidyl choline, Phosphatidyl ethanolamine, Phsophatidyl serine, Sphingomyelin: 2987

Navodon modestus (Black scraper, Filefish, Oval filefish)
Japan, Korea. Coastal. Diet: polychaets, crustaceans.
Astacene 2716; Caesium 2269; β-Carotene 2716; Cobalt 2269; α-Cryptoxanthin 2716; Cynthiaxanthin 2716; Diatoxanthin 2716; Lutein 2716; Pyridine nucleotide transhydrogenase 3167; Trimethylamine oxide 2111; Tunaxanthin 2716; Zeaxanthin 2716; Zinc 2269

Negaprion brevirostris* (Lemon shark) *310, 459*
W. Atlantic: New Jersey to Brazil. Inshore shallow waters, brackish waters and even fresh water. Can convert tertiary amines such as choline and trimethylamine to trimethylamine oxide, an ability not possessed by some elasmobranchs (various authors quoted by Goldstein and Palatt, 1974).
2′3′-*cyclic* adenosine monophosphate-3′-phosphoester hydrolase 3450; *Mixed function* amine oxidase 2030; DNA 2194; Trimethylamine oxidase 2030

Negogaleus sp.
Trimethylamine oxide 3151

‡*Nemacheilus barbatulus* (Loach, Stone loach)
Europe except extreme S. and N. Pure waters of brooks and shore regions of clear lakes.
Volume 1 only

‡Nemadactylus douglasii (Morwong)
Australia.
Volume 1 only

Nemadactylus macropterus (Perch)
Australia.
Copper, Zinc: 1893

Nematonurus pectoralis
Japan.
Fatty acids, Neutral lipids: 2152

‡Nemipterus japonicus = Synagris japonicus (Japanese threadfin bream)
Tanzania, Red Sea, Aden, India, Japan, China, Philippines, N. Australia. Bottom-living, shoreline to 60 m. Males grow quickly and are larger than the females at same age. Diet: a wide range of bottom-living animals, such as worms, crustaceans, mussels, cephalopods, fish.
Volume 1 only

Nemipterus sp.
Trimethylamine oxide 3151

‡Nemipterus taeniopterus (Ribbon-finned nemipterid)
Tanzania, India, Thailand, China, Philippines, Australia.
Folic acid 2582

‡Nemipterus virgatus (Golden threadfin bream)
Japan, Formosa, Philippines, Java, S. Vietnam. Muddy bottoms, 20–200 m. Males grow to a larger size than females. Diet: motile bottom-living animals, including crabs, prawns, squid, fish.
Volume 1 only

Neobythites fasciatus
Japan.
Trimethylamine oxide 2111

‡*Neoceratodus forsteri* (Burnett salmon, Lungfish) *154*
Australia: Mary and Burnett Rivers (S. Queensland). Introduced elsewhere. Cartilaginous skeleton. Unlike other lungfish species, does not burrow or aestivate. Carnivorous.
Bicarbonate 3526; Calcium 3526; Chloride 3526; DNA 2998; Magnesium 3526; Sodium 3526; Urea 3526

‡*Neogobius melanostomus* (*see Gobius melanostomus*)

Neomaenis blackfordi (Red snapper)
    Calcium, Strontium: 3145

‡Neoplatycephalus richardsoni (Tiger flathead)
    S. Australia.
    Volume 1 only

Neothunnus albacora (*see* Thunnus albacares)

Neothunnus macropterus (*see* Thunnus albacares)

‡*Neotropius kavalchor*
    India.
    Volume 1 only

‡Neptunus trituberculatus
    Volume 1 only

Netuma barbus
    S. America.
    Carbohydrate, Chloride, Potassium, Sodium: 3311

‡Nibea argentata
    Japan.
    Volume 1 only

‡Nibea schlegeli
    Japan.
    Volume 1 only

‡Niphon spinosus
    Japan, Philippines. Deep water.
    Cholesterol 2445

Nomeus gronowi (Bluebottle fish, Man-of-war fish)
    S. Africa, tropical Atlantic, Sargasso; Indo-Pacific Oceans. Often found associated
    with poisonous jelly fish, but is apparently unaffected by the sting.
    Amino acids 1812

Notacanthus fascidens
    Japan.
    Fatty acids, Neutral lipids: 2153

‡Notacanthus nasus (Largescale tapirfish, Spiny eel)
    Atlantic in deep water.
    Volume 1 only

‡*Notemigonus crysoleucas* (Bitterhead, Bream, Chub, Dace, Golden shiner, Gudgeon,
    Roach, Shiner, Sunfish, Windfish, Young shad) *214, 216, 268, 430*

Eastern and central N. America: Nova Scotia, Maryland, Dakota. Prefers clear, weedy quiet waters, lakes rather than rivers. Introduced to western N. America. Prolonged spawning period. Active swimmer. Preferred temperatures 17–24°C. Volume 1 only

‡*Notemigonus crysoleucas boscii* (Golden shiner)
N. America.
Fatty acids 2492

‡*Notopterus chitala* (Featherback)
India: fresh waters of Sind, Bengal, Assam. Burma, Thailand, Malaya, Java, Sumatra, Borneo. Rivers, swamps, canals. Can breathe air. Diet: insects, shrimps, small surface fish.
Erythrocytes 3408; Glucose 3407; Lactate 3407; Leucocytes 3408

‡*Notopterus notopterus* = *N. kapirat* (Featherback) *191, 192*
India, Burma, Thailand. Rivers, swamps, canals. The air bladder functions as an accessory respiratory organ.
Alkaline phosphatase 3404; Erythrocytes 3408; Glucose 2851, 2852, 3407; Glycogen 2851, 2852; Lactate 2851, 2852, 3407; Leucocytes 3408

Notorhynchus cepedianus (Sevengilled Shark)
Australia.
Zinc 1893

Notoscopelus caudispinus
N. Atlantic.
Arsenic, Cadmium, Copper, Mercury, Zinc: 3638

‡Notothenia gibberifrons (Atlantic marine goby, Green notothenia)
Antarctic: Scotia Sea off S. Georgia Is.
Carbohydrates, Potassium, Sodium: 3311

Notothenia kempi
Antarctic.
Carbohydrates, Chloride, Non-protein nitrogen: 1827

‡Notothenia larseni
Antarctic.
Carbohydrates, Chloride, Non-protein nitrogen: 1827

‡Notothenia neglecta *321, 348, 349, 385*
Antarctic.
Carbohydrates 3310, 3311; Chloride 3310, 3311; Potassium 3310, 3311; Reducing sugar 3310; Sodium 3310, 3311; Thyroxine 3477; Urea 3310

‡Notothenia rossii = N. marmorata *40, 53, 104* (photograph), *336, 348, 349*
Antarctic.
Amino acids 3057; *Free* amino acids 3057; Calcium 3057; Carbohydrates 3310, 3311; Chloride 3310, 3311; Cholesterol 3241; *Free* fatty acids 3241; Iron 3057; Phospholipid 3241; Potassium 3310, 3311; Reducing sugar 3310; Sodium 3310, 3311; Sterol esters 3241; Triglycerides 3241; Urea 3310; Vitamin E 3057

Notothenia sp. *74, 278*
Aluminium, Calcium, Copper, Iron, Magnesium, Manganese, Potassium, Silver, Tin, Vanadium, Zinc: 2040

Nototropis sp.
Mg-ATPase (magnesium-activated adenosine triphosphatase), Na-K-ATPase: 2321

Noturus flavus (Stonecat)
Canada.
Thyroxine 2190

Noturus gyrinus (Tadpole madtom) *121, 122*

Oblada melanura (Saddled bream)
Portugal to Canary Is., Mediterranean and Black Seas. Lives near vegetated bottoms in coastal waters, often near surface. Diet: small invertebrates.
Copper, Lead, Mercury, Zinc: 1708

‡Ocyurus chrysurus (Yellowtail snapper)
S. Florida to Brazil. Cape Verde Is. Close to reefs in open water. Inactive. Diet: animal plankton, small fish.
DNA 2195; Haematocrit 3377; Haemoglobin 3377

Ocyurus japonicus
Thiaminase 3473

Odontamblyops rubicundus
Fructose, Galactose, Glucose, Xylose: 3685

Odontaspis arenarius (Grey nurse shark)
Australia. Close to bottom in inshore waters as shallow as 2 m. Diet: fish.
Collagen, Elastin: 2508

‡Odontogadus merlangus euximus
Black Sea.
Cyanocobalamin 1522

Ogcocephalus nasutus (Redbellied batfish, Shortnose)
Caribbean Sea, Florida and Bahamas to Guyana. Shoreline to 90 m on flat sandy or muddy bottoms. Sluggish. Diet: molluscs, fish, crustaceans, worms.
DNA 2195

‡*Oligonus macquariensis*
Australia.
Volume 1 only

‡Oligoplites saurus (Leathercoat, Leatherjacket, Runner)
Both coasts of central America, Peru to S. California. Galapagos Is. Inshore, shallow. Common in turbid areas and estuaries. Leaps clear of the water at times.
Volume 1 only

Ompok bimaculatus
India.
Erythrocytes, Leucocytes: 3408

Ompok pabo
India.
Vitamin A_1, Vitamin A_2: 1500

‡Oncorhynchus gorbuscha* (Humpback salmon, Pink salmon) *42, 44, 48, 49, 57, 64, 65, 208, 238, 248, 257, 415, 416*
Pacific, N. California to Bering Sea. Korea, Japan, Siberian Arctic. Usually does not migrate far from salt water. Most commonly they live two years and spend little time in fresh water as juveniles. Preferred temperature 9–12°C. Oncorhynchus species of salmon all die soon after spawning, unlike Salmo salar, a proportion of the females of which survive, return to the sea and undertake a further spawning migration later. The cause of death is not really known, but since it is accompanied by very high levels of blood cortisol, this hormone may be responsible: slow-release pellets of cortisol implanted in Salmo gairdneri, which normally survives spawning, cause the death of the fish in a few weeks, with all the symptoms shown by the Oncorhynchus spp. The high level of cortisol promotes the gluconeogenesis needed to provide the migrating fish with carbohydrates for swimming, and may ultimately kill the fish because of impaired clearance which results in very high concentrations. Life can be prolonged if the spawned fish are given food, but the respite is always temporary. (*See* review of spawning death on p. 112 of Volume 1 and p. 64 of the present volume.)
Albumin 2267; Aluminium 2040, 2440; Amino acids 3472; *Free* amino acids 2857; Barium 2440; Bismuth 2040; Calcium 2040, 2864, 3455; Cholesterol 2267, 2992, 3137; Chromium 2040, 2440; Cobalt 2040; Copper 2040, 2440; Creatin 2855; Creatin phosphokinase 2696; Creatinine 2267, 2855; DNA 1527, 2856; Diglyceride 2992; Diphosphatidyl glycerol 3420; Fatty acids 3137, 3158; *Free* fatty acids 2992, 3137; Globulin 2267; Glucose 2267, 3455; Glucose dehydrogenase 3235; Glutamate oxaloacetate transaminase 2696; Gonadotrophin 1759; Haematocrit 3455; α-Hydroxybutyrate dehydrogenase 2696; Insulin 3052; Iron 2040; Lactic dehydrogenase 2696; Lanthanum 2440; Lead 2440; Lysophosphatidyl choline 3420; Magnesium 2040, 2440, 2864; Manganese 2040, 2440; Nickel 2040, 2440; Phosphatidic acid 3420; Phosphatidyl choline 3420; Phosphatidyl ethanolamine 3420; Phosphatidyl inositol 3420; Phosphatidyl serine 3420; Phospholipids 2267, 2992; Potassium 2040, 2864, 3455; RNA 1527, 2856; Silicon 2440; Silver 2040, 2440; Sodium 2440, 2864, 3455; Sphingomyelin 3420; Strontium 2440; Tin 2040, 2440; Titanium 2440; Triglycerides 2992, 3137; Trimethylamine oxide 3151; Urea 2267; Uric acid 2267; Vanadium 2040; Zinc 2040, 2440; Zirconium 2440

‡Oncorhynchus keta* (Chum salmon, Dog salmon) *13, 43, 51, 239, 315, 316, 318, 460*
Japan, Kamchatka, Alaska, Bering Sea, California. Frequently spawns near river outlets, having less ability than other salmon to surmount obstacles. Spends little time in fresh water as a juvenile. Preferred temperature of small specimens 14°C. *See* also under O. gorbuscha for account of spawning death.
Adenosine triphosphatase 2414; Amino acids 3472; *Free* amino acids 3691; Calcitonin 1729; Cholesterol 1437, 2445; DNA 2282, 3223, 3676; Fatty acids

3388; *Free* fatty acids 1437; Glucose dehydrogenase 3235; Glycerides 3388; Hydrocarbons 1437; Phosphatidyl choline 3388; Phosphatidyl ethanolamine 3388; Phospholipids 1437; RNA 2282, 3223, 3676; Sterols 3388; Triglycerides 1437; Ubiquinone 3188; Vitamin D 3673

‡Oncorhynchus kisutch* (Coho salmon, Silver salmon) *21, 23, 42, 115, 143, 231, 232, 236, 237, 240, 241, 274, 284, 291, 292, 306, 384, 414, 415, 467*
N. California to Bering Sea, Korea, Japan, Russia. Anadromous in rivers and streams, but progeny do not all return to the sea. Those that remain in fresh water mature but never spawn. Preferred temperature 11–17°C. *See* also under O. gorbuscha for account of spawning death.
Adenosine triphosphatase 3714; Amino acids 3472; Ascorbic acid 3600, 3601; Bicarbonate 2264, 3604; Calcium 2264; Carbonic anhydrase 2764; Chloride 2264, 3604; Cholesterol 3604; Cortisol 3600; DNA 2195; Diphosphatidyl glycerol 3420; Fatty acids 1597; Fucose 3094; Glucose 2665, 2667, 3604; Glucose dehydrogenase 3235; Glycogen 2665, 2667; Haematocrit 2665, 3604; Haemoglobin 3604; Hexosamine 3094; Lactate 2667; 2741; Leucocytes 2309; Lysophosphatidyl choline 3420; Magnesium 2264, 2861, 2864; Mercury 1557, 3529; Ornithine aminotransferase 3611; Phosphatidic acid 3420; Phosphatidyl choline 3420; Phosphatidyl ethanolamine 3420; Phosphatidyl inositol 3420; Phosphatidyl serine 3420; Potassium 2264, 2864; Sialic acid 3094; Sodium 2264, 2861, 2864; Sphingomyelin 3420; "Sugar" 3619; Thyroxine 1854; Urea 3604

Oncorhynchus macrostomus
Glucose-6-phosphate dehydrogenase 3258

‡Oncorhynchus masou* (Cherry salmon, Masu, Trout) *22, 172, 208, 209, 318*
Korea to Kamchatka. The most tolerant to heat of the Pacific salmon. Uses fatty acids 16:0 and 18:1 as main source of energy during metamorphosis. Diet: insects. Note: references to dimethylamine, DNA and RNA below relate to Oncorhynchus masou ishikawae.
Amylase 2936–2938; Arginase 2936, 2937; Calcium 2864; Cholesterol 3253; DNA 2282; Diglycerides 2948; Dimethylamine 2110; Fatty acids 2948, 2951; *Free* fatty acids 2948, 3253; Fructose-1,6-diphosphatase 2938; Glutamate dehydrogenase 2938; Glutamate-oxaloacetate transaminase 2936–2938; Glutamate-pyruvate transaminase 2936–2938; Guanine 1966, 2156; Hexokinase 2938; Hydrocarbons 2948; Hypoxanthine 1966, 2156; Inosine 1966, 2156; Inosine monophosphate 2156; Inosinic acid 1966; Magnesium 2864; Phosphofructokinase 2938; 6-phosphogluconate dehydrogenase 2938; Phospholipids 2948; Potassium 2864; Protease 2936–2938; Pyruvate kinase 2938; RNA 2282; Sodium 2864; Sterols 2948; Sterol esters 2948; Triglycerides 2948, 3253

‡Oncorhynchus nerka* (Blueback, Red salmon, Sockeye salmon) *7, 37, 38, 41, 48, 57, 61, 64, 65, 116, 163, 170, 171, 182, 187, 199, 211, 220, 236, 237, 248, 250, 253, 268, 293, 300, 301, 309, 315, 316, 324, 383, 400, 407, 409, 429*
S. Oregon to Bering Sea and Japan. Possesses fewer pyloric caecae than are found in other Pacific salmon. Some specimens never go to sea. Preferred temperatures 11–13°C, avoiding temperatures above 21°C. *See* also under O. gorbuscha for account of spawning death.

Amino Acids 3472; D-Amino acid oxidase 1923; Amylase 2936–2938; Arginase 2936, 2937; Calcitonin 3588; Calcium 1484, 2864, 3588; Carotenoids 1764; Cholesterol 1437, 3253; Choline 2910; Copper 1933; Corticosteroids (total) 1844; Cortisol 1844, 1846; Cortisone 1844, 1900; DNA 2282; Ethanolamine 2910; Fatty acids 2473, 2910, 3088, 3666, 3667; *Free* fatty acids 1437, 2533, 2660, 3253; Fructose-1,6-diphosphatase 2938; Fucose 3094; Glucose 2533, 2660; Glucose dehydrogenase 2936; Glutamate dehydrogenase 2938; Glutamate oxaloacetate transaminase, 2936–2938; Glutamate pyruvate transaminase 2936–2938; Glycogen 1725, 2660; Gonadotropin 1760; Growth hormone 2660; Guanine 1966; Haematocrit 2533, 2660; Hexokinase 2938; Hexosamine 3094; Hexose 3094; Hexuronic acid 3094; Hydrocarbons 1437; Hypoxanthine 1966; Lactate 1725, 2741; Magnesium 1484, 2861, 2863, 2864; Ornithine aminotransferase 3611; Phosphofructokinase 2938; 6-Phosphogluconate dehydrogenase 2938; Phospholipids 1437; Potassium 1484, 2863, 2864; Prolactin 2660; Protease 2936–2938; Pyruvate kinase 2938; RNA 2282; Seromucoid 3094; Sialic acid 3094; Sodium 1484, 2861, 2863, 2864; Triglycerides 1437, 3253; Zinc 1933

‡*Oncorhynchus nerka kennerlyi* (Kickaninny, Kokanee, Little redfish, Silver trout) *51, 65* N. America. A genetically landlocked race of O. nerka. Can and will migrate with the anadromous form. Generally die at four years of age but can live to eight. Adenosine diphosphate 3219, 3220; Adenosine monophosphate 3219, 3220; Adenosine triphosphatase (total) 2863; Na-K-ATPase 2863; Adenosine triphosphate 3219, 3220; DNA 2283; Fatty acids 2951; Guanosine monophosphate 3220; Inosine monophosphate 3219, 3220; Nicotinamide adenine dinucleotide (NAD) 3219, 3220; NADP 3219, 3220; NADPH (reduced form of the phosphate) 3219, 3220; RNA 2283; Succinic dehydrogenase 2863; Uridine diphosphate (UDP) 3219, 3220; UDP-*N*-acetylhexosamine 3220; UDP-hexoses 3219, 3220; UDP-uronic acids 3219, 3220; Uridine monophosphate 3219, 3220

Oncorhynchus sp. *220* Amylase 2936; Arginase 2936; Glutamate oxaloacetate transaminase 2936; Glutamate pyruvate transaminase 2936; Pantothenic acid 3211; Protease 2936; Pyridoxine 3211; Ubiquinone 2186; Vitamin E 2186

Oncorhynchus tschawytscha* (Chinook salmon, King salmon, Quinnat salmon, Spring salmon, Tyee) *5, 48, 143, 146, 221, 254, 284, 285, 292* S. California to Bering Sea and Japan, Aleutian Is. Introduced to New Zealand. Spawning runs are earlier as one moves north. *See* also under O. gorbuscha for account of spawning death. Preferred temperature 12–17°C. Diet in sea: anchovies, herring, squid, crustacea. (*Author's personal note:* it seems incredible that the clumsy and almost unspellable Oncorhynchus tschawytscha Walbaum should ever have been substituted for the more manageable Oncorhynchus chouicha Bean. I seriously considered using the latter spelling throughout this book (both names are based on an Indian name) but took fright at the probable consequences . . .) Adenosine triphosphatase 3714; Alkaline phosphatase 3525, 3526; Amino acids 3472; Bicarbonate 3525, 3526; Calcium 3313, 3525, 3526; Chloride 1582, 3525, 3526; Citrate 3525, 3526; DNA 2195; Fucose 3094, 3095; Glucose dehydrogenase 3235; Glutamine synthetase 3592; Glycogen 1725; "Hexose" 3095; Hexosamine

3094, 3095; Lactate 1725; Magnesium 3313, 3525, 3526; Ornithine aminotransferase (in parr) 3611; Potassium 1582, 3313, 3525, 3526; Sialic acid 3094, 3095;
Sodium 1582, 3313, 3525, 3526; Succinic dehydrogenase 1727; Sulphate 3525,
3526; Urea 3525, 3526; Vitamin D 3673

Onigocia spinosa
    Japan.
    Trimethylamine oxide 2111

‡*Ophicephalus argus*
    Japan.
    Volume 1 only
    (*Note:* the alternative spelling "Ophiocephalus" is frequently encountered. All
    species of this genus have accessory respiratory organs)

‡*Ophicephalus marulius* (Giant snakehead)
    India, Sri Lanka, Sumatra, Borneo, China. Rivers and inland fresh waters up to
    1500 feet.
    Cholesterol 3267, 3268

Ophicephalus obscurus
    India.
    DNA 2195

‡*Ophicephalus punctatus* = *Channa punctatus* (Green snakehead, Murrel) *56, 61, 62, 80,
162, 163, 239, 337, 339, 365, 405*
    India, Burma. Stagnant fresh or brackish waters in low country. Active, carni-
    vorous. Aestivates.
    Acid phosphatase 2317; Alkaline phosphatase 2317, 3404; *Free* amino acids
    3276; *Free* amino acids (a single figure) 3232; Amino tripeptidase 3186; Ascorbic
    acid 1799; Calcium 3278; Cholesterol 2318, 3267–3269, 3278; DNA 3105;
    Erythrocytes 2326, 3408; Fatty acids 3224; Glucose 2417, 2418, 3407, 3278;
    Haemoglobin 2326; 17-Hydroxycorticosteroid 3150; Iron 3278; Lactate 3407;
    Leucocytes 2326, 3408; Lymphocytes 2326; Monocytes 2326; Non-protein nitrogen
    3278; 5'-Nucleotidase 2314; RNA 3105; Vitamin A$_1$ 1500; Vitamin A$_2$ 1500

‡*Ophicephalus striatus* (Mudfish, Murrel, Striped snakehead) *68, 338*
    Plains of India, Sri Lanka, Burma, China, Philippines. Introduced to Hawaii.
    Fresh waters and swamps. Can exist for considerable periods out of water. Burrows
    into mud during droughts, subsisting on stored lipid.
    Amino acids 2051; Calcium 3278; Cholesterol 3267, 3268, 3278; Folic acid 2582;
    Glucose 3278; Hydroxyproline 2051; Iron 3278; Non-protein nitrogen 3278;
    5'-Nucleotidase 3229

‡*Ophicephalus tadianus*
    Japan.
    Volume 1 only

‡Ophichthys boro*
    India and Malaya. Seas and estuaries, ascending large rivers. A scale-less fish.
    Volume 1 only

Ophichthys gomesi
N. Atlantic.
Arsenic, Cadmium, Copper, Mercury, Zinc: 3638

Ophichthys ocellatus
N. Atlantic.
Arsenic, Cadmium, Copper, Mercury, Zinc: 3638

Ophichthys urolophus
Japan.
Trimethylamine oxide 2111

‡Ophiodon barbatum (Snake blenny)
Adriatic and North Seas. Biscay to Senegal. Sandy and muddy bottoms down to
150 m.
Volume 1 only

‡Ophiodon elongatus (Cultus cod, lingcod)
S. California to Kodiak Is., Alaska and Bering Sea. Surface to increasing depths
with increasing age. Cannibalistic. Voracious feeder. Diet: fish, squid.
Arsenic 2535; Glutamate oxaloacetate dehydrogenase 2696; α-Hydroxybutyrate
dehydrogenase 2696; Lactic dehydrogenase 2696; Mercury 1697; "Sugar" 3619

‡Ophioscion venezuelae
S. America.
Volume 1 only

‡Ophisurus macrorhynchus (Offshore snake, Sandsnake)
Japan.
Trimethylamine oxide 2111

‡Ophthalmolepis lineolatus (Maori)
S. Australia.
Volume 1 only

‡Opisthopterus tartoor = O. tardoore (Tardoore)
India, Malaya, Java, Sumatra, New Guinea, possibly Hong Kong. Coastal waters.
Pelagic.
Volume 1 only

‡Oplegnathus fasciatus (Japanese parrot bass, Japanese parrot fish)
Japan.
Adenosine monophosphate 1871; Inosine monophosphate 1871; Nicotinamide
adenine dinucleotide (NAD) 3259; NADH (reduced NAD) 3259; Trimethylamine
oxide 2111

Oplegnathus punctatus
Japan.
Trimethylamine oxide 2111

Opsanus beta
DNA 2195

‡Opsanus tau* (Oysterfish, Sapo, Scorpion, Slimer, Toadfish) *58, 211, 326, 343, 430*
  N. America: Massachusetts coast to W. Indies. Shallow water on sandy or muddy
  bottom. Possesses no glomeruli. Skin scale-less. Very sluggish. Can grunt loudly;
  swim bladder much bigger in male than female, probably because of the different
  sounds emitted by the two sexes (Fine, 1975). The toadfish is a marine fish which
  has been observed to enter fresh water, but does not migrate far into freshwater
  habitats (Nishimura, Sawyer and Nigrelli, 1976). Diet: invertebrates and small
  fish.
  Angiotensinogen 2891; Arginase 3112; Argininosuccinate lyase 3112; Argininosuccinate synthetase 3112; Carbamoyl phosphate synthetase 3112; Cortisol 2891;
  DNA 2195; Haematocrit 2891; Mutarotase 1480; Ornithine carbamoyl transferase
  3112; Renin 2891; Sodium 2891; "Sugar" 2791, 3411; Zinc 1804

Opsariichthys uncirostris
  Japan.
  Astacene, Cynthiaxanthin, Diatoxanthin, α-Doradecin, Lutein, Zeaxanthin: 2719

Orcynus thynnus
  Calcium, Iodide, Iron, Sodium: 3294

‡Orthagoriscus mola
  Europe.
  Volume 1 only

Orthopristis chrysoptera
  Bermuda. Shores.
  DNA 2195; Succinic dehydrogenase 2750

Orthopristis forbesi *261*
  Deep water.

‡*Oryzias latipes* (Highcyes, Japanese killifish, Medaka, Rice fish) *13, 148, 385*
  Japan, China. Lowland paddy fields. Wide temperature tolerance.
  Amino acids 2848; *Free* amino acids 2848; *Peptide* amino acids 2848; Calcium
  2236; β-Carotene 2717; α-Cryptoxanthin 2717; Cynthiaxanthin 2717; DNA 2195;
  Lutein 2717; Magnesium 2237; Manganese 2238; Trimethylamine oxide 2111;
  Tunaxanthin 2717; Zeaxanthin 2717

Osmerus dentex (Japanese smelt)
  Astacene, β-Carotene, Cryptoxanthin, Cynthiaxanthin, Diatoxanthin, Lutein,
  Zeaxanthin: 2722

‡Osmerus eperlanus* (*see* O. mordax*)

‡Osmerus mordax* = O. eperlanus* (American smelt, European smelt, Rainbow
  smelt, Sparling) *268, 437*
  Atlantic coast of N. America, E. Labrador to Virginia: introduced elsewhere for
  example the Great Lakes. Spitzbergen to France (not Iceland). Seas, rivers and
  lakes. Wide depth distribution but tends to prefer deeper waters. Some landlocked
  populations exist. A schooling, pelagic species with a tendency to die after spawning.

Preferred temperature 7–8°C, avoiding temperatures above 14°C or below 6°C. Diet: insect larvae, small crustaceans.

Amino acids 1812; *Para*-amino benzoic acid 3295; Arsenic 2611; Biotin 3295; Cadmium 2611; Chloride 1860; Cobalt 2611; Copper 2611; Cyanocobalamin 3295; DNA 3203; Inositol 3295; Lactic dehydrogenase 3203; Niacin 3295; Pantothenic acid 3295; 6-Phosphogluconate dehydrogenase 3203; Phosphoglucose isomerase 3203; Pyridoxine 3295; RNA 3203; Sodium 1860; Thiamine 3295; Thorium 2611; Uranium 2611

‡*Osphronemus gorami* (Gouramy)
Originally from E. Indian Is., Malaya, Sumatra, Java, China. Introduced to Australia, India, Sri Lanka. Rivers and brackish waters. Prefers shallow, weedy ponds. Possesses accessory respiratory organs. Diet: vegetation, but will rise to a fly or beetle.
Volume 1 only

‡*Osteocheilus hasselti* (Hasselt's bonylipped barb)
Indonesia, Malacca, Thailand, Sumatra, Java, Borneo. Rivers, less often in lakes. Diet: algae and other plants.
Volume 1 only

Osteoglossum bicirrhosum (Arawana)
Tropical S. America. Forms large shoals near the surface of shallow reedy backwaters and lakes. Probably a mouth-brooder.
DNA 2195

Otocinclus affinis
DNA 2195

‡Otolithes ruber (Longtooth salmon, Lesser tigertoothed croaker, Rosy jewfish, Snapper salmon, Silver jewfish, Tigertoothed croaker)
India to Malaya, Japan to Australia, down to 40 m. Coastal. Diet: fish, invertebrates.
Volume 1 only

Otophidium scrippsi
DNA 2195

Otophidium welshi
DNA 191

Oxygaster bacaila
India.
Vitamin A_1, Vitamin A_2: 1500

Pagellus acarne (Axillary seabream) *152*
British Is. to Senegal; Mediterranean. Omnivorous. Ambisexual: protandric. Mud or sandy mud, 5–100 m, sometimes 400 m. Diet: crustaceans, molluscs, fish.
11 β-Hydroxytestosterone 2273; Mercury 1891

‡Pagellus bellotti
 Europe.
 Volume 1 only

Pagellus bogarevo (Blackspot seabream, Red seabream
 Norway to Mediterranean, N. Africa, Canary Is. 150–300 m as adults; juveniles
 inshore on sandy and muddy bottoms. Diet: invertebrates, fish.
 Cadmium, Copper, Lead, Mercury, Zinc: 1707

Pagellus centrotodontus (Common Seabream)
 Europe.
 Lactic dehydrogenase 1789

‡Pagellus erythrinus (Pandora, Red seabream)
 Scandinavia to Angola, Mediterranean. Shallow water, sandy-mud or gravel
 bottoms down to 100 m. Ambisexual, probably protogynous. Diet: various invertebrates.
 Cadmium 1707, 1709; Copper 1707, 1709; 11 β-Hydroxytestosterone 2273; Lead
 1707, 1709; Mercury 1707, 1709; Zinc 1707, 1709

‡Pagellus mormyrus (*see* Lithognathus mormyrus)

Pagetopsis macropterus *278, 279* (Photograph)
 Antarctic. Illustrated in Fig. 109. Haemoglobinless. Dorsal fin is raised whenever
 oxygen concentration falls in the surrounding water, suggesting that it acts as a
 supplementary gas exchanger.

‡Pagrosomus auratus
 Australia.
 Volume 1 only

‡Pagrosomus major (*see* Chrysophrys major)

‡Pagrosomus unicolor
 Japan.
 Volume 1 only

‡Pagrus ehrenbergi
 S. Atlantic.
 Cholesterol 2768

Pagrus major (*see* Chrysophrys major)

‡Pagrus pagrus (Couch's seabream)
 Britain to Senegal, Mediterranean. Over 20 m on sand and sea-grass.
 Copper, Mercury, Zinc: 2828

‡Palinurichthys perciformis (American barrel fish, Barrel fish, Black rudder fish)
 Wide distribution in the Atlantic. Often found under floating wreckage or sea-
 weed.
 Volume 1 only

‡Palometa media
  N. America.
  Volume 1 only

Pampus argenteus (*see* Stromateus cinereus)

Pandaka pygmaea *58*
  The smallest known fish, maximum length 11 mm.

‡*Pangasius pangasius* (Pungas catfish)
  India, Burma, Java. Large rivers and estuaries. Nocturnally active. Old specimens
  may lose their teeth. Diet: refuse, bottom-living invertebrates.
  Volume 1 only

Pantodon buchholzi (Butterfly fish)
  Tropical W. Africa, Nigeria to Congo. Stagnant, weedy backwaters of rivers, ponds
  and ditches. Can leap from water and glide in air on pectoral fins. Diet: insects.
  DNA 2195

Parabassogigas sp.
  Peru-Chile trench (deep water).
  Cholesterol, Fatty acids, Lysophosphatidyl choline, Phosphatidyl choline, Phos-
  phatidyl ethanolamine, Phosphatidyl serine, Phospholipid, Sphingomyelin: 3032

‡Paracaesio caeruleus
  Japan.
  Volume 1 only

‡Parachaenichthys charcoti
  Antarctic.
  Potassium, Sodium: 3311

‡Parachaenichthys georgianus
  Antarctic.
  Carbohydrate, Chloride, Potassium, Sodium: 3311

Paracheilognathus rhombea
  Japan.
  Thiaminase 2297

Paracottus kessleri
  Russia: Lake Baikal.
  Magnesium, Sodium: 2864

Paracottus kneri
  Russia: Lake Baikal.
  Calcium, Magnesium, Potassium, Sodium: 2864

‡Paralabrax clathratus (Kelp bass)
Pacific coast of N. America.
Albumin 3523; Alkaline phosphatase 3523; Calcium 3523; Diphosphatidyl glycerol 3420; Globulin 3523; Lysophosphatidyl choline 3420; Mercury 2751; Phosphatidic acid 3420; Phosphatidyl choline 3420; Phosphatidyl ethanolamine 3420; Phosphatidyl inositol 3420; Phosphatidyl serine 3420; Sphingomyelin 3420

Paralabrax maculatofasciatus (Sand bass)
America.
Diphosphatidyl glycerol, Lysophosphatidyl choline, Phosphatidic acid, Phosphatidyl choline, Phosphatidyl ethanolamine, Phosphatidyl inositol, Phosphatidyl serine, Sphingomyelin: 3420

Paralabrax nebulifer
DNA 2195

Paralichthys californicus (California halibut)
California to Oregon. Sandy bottoms 18–90 m. Diet: fish, especially anchovies.
DNA 2195

Paralichthys dentatus (Summer flounder)
Maine to S. Carolina. 18–145 m offshore, coming into shallow or muddy bottoms in summer. Diet: small fish, squid, crabs, shrimps, marine worms, sand dollars.
Aldehyde oxidase, Xanthine oxidase: 2468

‡Paralichthys lethostigmus (Southern flounder) *313*
Gulf of Mexico to New York coast.
Arsenic 3638; Cadmium 3638; Copper 3638; Erythrocytes 1647; Haematocrit 1647; Haemoglobin 1647; Mercury 3638; Zinc 3638

‡Paralichthys olivaceus (Bastard halibut, Japanese flounder, Plaice)
Japan, Hong Kong. Moderately deep water in winter, moving inshore to about 20 m in summer to spawn.
Adenosine diphosphate 1871; Adenosine monophosphate 1871; Adenosine triphosphate 1871, 2456; Amino acids 2456; *Free* amino acids 2456; Ammonia 2456; Calcium 3486; Collagen 3462; Connective tissue 3462; Creatin 2456; Creatinine 2456; Elastin 3462; *Free* histidine 3166; Hypoxanthine 1872; Inosine monophosphate 1871, 2456; Strontium 3486; Taurine 2456; Trimethylamine oxide 2111, 2456; Ubiquinone 2186; Vitamin D 2188, 3673; Vitamin E 2186

‡Paramyxine atami CYCLOSTOME
Japan. Parasitic.
Hexosamine, Mucopolysaccharide, Sulphate, Uronic acid: 1434

‡Parapeneopsis stylifera
Volume 1 only

Parapeneus multifasciatus (Goatfish)
A shallow-reef fish from the Kona coast of Hawaii. No swimbladder.
Cholesterol, Fatty acids, Phospholipid, Triglyceride: 3028

Parapercis pulchella
Japan.
Pyridine nucleotide transhydrogenase 3167

Paraplagusia japonica
Japan.
Trimethylamine oxide 2111

‡Parapristipoma trilineatum (Grunt, Striped pigfish) *72, 75, 76*
Japan, China Sea. Warm waters near the shore.
Arsenic 3402; Cadmium 2901; Caesium 2269; Cholesterol 2445; Cobalt 2269;
Copper 2901, 3402; α-Cryptoxanthin 2716; Cynthiaxanthin 2716; Diatoxanthin
2716; Dimethylamine 3439; Iron 2901; Lead 2901; Lutein 2716; Manganese 3402;
Mercury 3402; Potassium 2900; Sodium 2900; Thiaminase 3473; Trimethylamine
3439; Trimethylamine oxide 3439; Tunaxanthin 2716; Zeaxanthin 2716; Zinc
2269, 2901, 3402

‡*Parasilurus asotus* (Catfish, Mudfish) *425*
Japan, Russia. Inland waters. Diet: crustaceans, fish.
Calcium 2864; β-Carotene 2727; Cryptoxanthin 2727; Cynthiaxanthin 2727;
Diatoxanthin 2727; 9′10′-Dihydro-β-zeacarotene-3, 17′diol 2727; Lutein 2727;
Magnesium 2864; Potassium 2864; Sodium 2864; Trimethylamine oxide 2111;
β-Zeacarotene 2727; β-Zeacarotene-3-ol 2727; β-Zeacarotene triol 2727; Zeaxan-
thin 2727

‡Parastromateus niger = Stromateus niger (Black batfish, Blue skate, Brown pomfret,
Butterfish, Halibut, Slade, Turbot) *68*
Natal, Tanzania, Persian Gulf, India, Malaya, China, Japan, Philippines, Australia
(not Australia according to Fischer and Whitehead, 1974) Midwaters down to 100m.
Diet: crustaceans, small fish.
Amino acids 3124

Parathunnus mebachi (*see* Thunnus obesus)

Parathunnus obesus (*see* Thunnus obesus)

Parathunnus sibi (*see* Thunnus obesus)

Parauchenoglanis guttatus
DNA 2195

‡Parophrys vetulus (English sole, Lemon sole) *221*
S. California to Gulf of Alaska. Sandy or muddy bottoms, surface to 550 m. Moves
into shallower water in spring, deeper water in winter. Diet: clams and their
siphons, other molluscs, marine worms, crustaceans.
D-Amino acid oxidase 1923; Cathepsins 1993; DNA 2195; Mercury 1697, 2751;
Ornithine aminotransferase 3611; Vitamin E 2185 (name may not be correct in
this entry)

‡Pelamys chilensis (Striped mackerel)
India to Japan.
Volume 1 only

Pelates quadrilineatus (Croaker, Fourlined therapon, Trumpeter perch) *307*
  E. Africa to N. Australia, China and S. Japan. Inshore waters and estuaries. Diet:
  invertebrates, fish.
  Calcium, Magnesium, Potassium, Sodium: 1788

Pelecus cultratus
  R. Volga.
  Calcium, Magnesium, Potassium, Sodium: 2864

Pelmatochromis kribensis
  DNA 2195

Peprilus paru (Harvest fish)
  W. Indies and central American coast to Brazil and sometimes Argentina. Diet:
  stinging jellyfish and other animals.
  Erythrocytes, Haematocrit, Haemoglobin: 1647

Peprilus simillimus (Butterfish, Pacific pompano) *121, 126*
  California, Vancouver. Inshore. Pelagic. Has poorly calcified bones which are
  filled with oil. Lacks swim bladder. Diet: small crustaceans.
  Cholesterol 2538; DNA 2195; Fatty acids 2538; Phospholipids 2538; Triglycerides
  2538

Peprilus triacanthus (Butterfish, Dollarfish, Harvest fish)
  Gulf of St. Lawrence to Florida. Inshore in bays and estuaries. Oily flesh. Diet:
  small fish, squid, crustaceans, sea-gooseberries.
  Amino acids 1812

‡*Perca flavescens* = *P. fluviatilis* = *P. perca* (American perch, Eurasian perch, Lake perch,
  Perch, Raccoon perch, Ringed perch, River perch, Yellow Ned, Yellow perch)
  38, 53, 146, 149, 155, 161, 208, 265, 314, 437
  Circumpolar in lakes or slow rivers, warm or cold. America, Europe apart from
  Iceland, Norway, Spain or Russia. Occasionally found in brackish waters. Females
  grow faster than males and achieve greater ultimate size. More northerly populations grow more slowly and live longer. Preferred temperature 20°C (reported
  variously as lying between 7 and 28°C); upper lethal limit up to 33°C. Gregarious
  and voracious. Diet: (juvenile) insect larvae, crustaceans; (adult) fish.
  Adenosine diphosphate 2550; Adenosine triphosphate 2550; Aldolase 1475;
  Allantoinase 1775; Aluminium 2677; Amino acids 1655; *para*-amino benzoicacid;
  3295; Arginase 1776, 2256; Argininosuccinate lyase 2256; Arsenic 2611; Botini
  3295; Cadmium 1972, 2611, 2148; Calcium 2622–2624, 2677, 2864; Carbamoyl
  phosphate synthetase 2256; Carotenoids 3264; Chloride 2622, 2623; Cobalt 1540,
  2611, 2677; Copper 2611, 2677, 2829; Cyanocobalamin 3295; DNA 2195;
  Dihydroxyacetone phosphate 2550; Furan fatty acids 2092; Fructose-6-phosphate
  2550; Glucose 2550; Glucose-6-phosphate 2550; Glucose-6-phosphate dehydrogenase 1475; Glucose phosphate isomerase 1475; Glutathione reductase 1475;
  Glyceraldehyde phosphate dehydrogenase 1475; Hexokinase 1475; Hydroxyproline
  1655; Inositol 3295; Iron 2677; Lactate 2550; Lactic dehydrogenase 1475;
  Magnesium 2622–2624, 2677, 2864; Manganese 2677; Mercury 1557, 2148, 2829,
  3617, 3649; Niacin 3295; NAD (nicotinamide adenine dinucleotide) 2550; NADH

(reduced NAD) 2550; NADP (NAD phosphate) 2550; Ornithine transcarbamoylase 2256; Pantothenic acid 3295; Phosphofructokinase 1475; Phosphoglucomutase
1475; 6-phosphogluconate dehydrogenase 1475; 2-phosphoglycerate 2550; 3-
phosphoglycerate 2550; Phosphoglycerate kinase 1475; Phosphoglyceric acid 2550;
Potassium 2550, 2622–2624, 2677, 2864; Pyridoxine 3295; Pyruvate 2550; Pyruvate
kinase 1475; Riboflavin 1465; Sodium 2550, 2622–2624, 2864; Strontium 1528;
"Sugar" 2993; Thiamin 3295; Thorium 2611; Tin 2677; Triose phosphate
isomerase 1475; Uranium 2611; Urate oxidase 1711; Urea 3547; Vanadium 2677;
Xanthine oxidase 1711; Zinc 2677, 2829

‡*Perca fluviatilis* (*see P. flavescens*) *146, 155, 265, 314*

‡*Perca perca* (*see P. flavescens*)

‡Periophthalmodon australis (Mud skipper)
   Volume 1 only

Periophthalmus expeditionium *154*
   Allantoicase, Allantoinase, Arginase, Ornithine carbamoyl transferase, Urate
   oxidase: 2071

Periophthalmus gracilis *154*
   Allantoicase, Allantoinase, Arginase, Ornithine carbamoyl transferase, Urate
   oxidase: 2071

Periophthalmus sobrinus* (Mudskipper) *154*
   Amphibious. Completely euryhaline. Distributed in intertidal environments of
   Old World tropics. Muddy, mangrove areas. Excretes both urea and ammonia,
   but mostly urea when out of water.
   Chloride, Sodium: 2047

Periophthalmus vulgaris *307*

Petrometopon cruentatus
   DNA 2195

‡Petromyzon fluviatilis* = Lampetra fluviatilis* CYCLOSTOME (Lampern,
   Lamprey, River lamprey) *37, 111, 182, 232, 233, 240*
   Coastal waters of Europe, Siberia and S. Greenland. Estuaries and easily accessible
   lakes, rivers and streams. Parasitic. Intestine degenerates during spawning
   migration. Proposed by Potter and Brown (1975) as ancestral species of Lampetra
   planeri: haemoglobins of the two species have identical electrophoretical mobility.
   Adenosine diphosphate 3196; Adenosine monophosphate 3196; Adenosine
   triphosphate 3196; Amino acids 2964; Calcium 3037, 3038; Chloride 3037; DNA
   3136; Fatty acids 3088, 3197; Galactosamine 3098, 3141; Galactose 3141;
   Glucosamine 3141; Glucose 3116, 2513, 2544, 3141; Glycerol kinase 3196;
   Glycerol-3-phosphate dehydrogenase 1249; Glycogen 2116, 2543, 3049, 3052,
   3196; Hexuronic acid 3098; Insulin 3052; Magnesium 3037, 3038; Malic dehydrogenase 3196; Mannose 3141; Phosphoenolpyruvate carboxykinase 2628; Potassium 3037, 3038; Pyruvate carboxylase 3196; Sodium 3037, 3038; Sulphate 3038,
   3098

‡Petromyzon marinus* CYCLOSTOME (Lamper eel, Sea lamprey) *25, 48, 52, 148, 187, 235, 302, 304, 318, 320, 409*
E. and W. Atlantic. Mediterranean. Landlocked in Great Lakes. The largest and most predacious of the lampreys. During spawning migration, the intestine degenerates to a hollow thread and the sight deteriorates to complete blindness. Death follows spawning. Cortisol, corticosterone and aldosterone are not found in this species. Diet: (larvae) microscopic plankton and detritus; adults are parasitic on fish.
Adenosine triphosphate 3149; Adrenaline 2737, 2738, 2740; Albumin 3523, 3525; Alkaline phosphatase 3523, 3525; Bicarbonate 3523, 3525; Calcium 3038, 3523, 3525; Chloride 2114, 2711, 3038, 3523, 3525; Citrate 3525; DNA 2194, 3136; Globulin 3523, 3525; Glucose 3149; Glucose-6-phosphate 3149; Glycogen 3149; Insulin 3051; Lactate 3149; Magnesium 3038, 3523, 3525; Noradrenaline 2737, 2738, 2740; Phenylethanolamine-N-methyl transferase 2740; Phosphocreatin 3149; Potassium 3038, 3523, 3525; Sodium 2711, 3038, 3523, 3525; Sulphate 3038, 3523, 3525

Petromyzon tridentata = Lampetra tridentata CYCLOSTOME
Albumin, Alkaline phosphatase, Bicarbonate, Calcium, Chloride, Globulin, Magnesium, Potassium, Sodium, Sulphate: 3523

‡Phanerodon furcatus (White seaperch, White surfperch)
S. California to Vancouver Is. down to 42 m. Most common in sheltered bays. DNA 2195

‡Phinoplagusia japonica (incorrect: *see* Rhinoplagusia japonica)

‡*Phoxinus phoxinus* (Minnow) *286*
All Europe except S. Spain, S. Italy, Norway and Iceland. Clear stony lakes' rivers and streams. Diet: small bottom-living insects, crustaceans, fish fry.
Volume 1 only

Phrynorhombus norvegicus (Norwegian topknot)
Coasts of Norway, S. Iceland, British Is., on stony ground. Diet: worms, crustaceans, fish eggs.
Lactic dehydrogenase 1789

Phrynorhombus regius (Eckstrom's topknot)
Europe.
Lactic dehydrogenase 1789

Phycis blennoides (Greater forkbeard)
Iceland and Norway to Morocco, Mediterranean. Absent from Black Sea. Bottom-dwelling on muddy grounds, usually 150–300 m, occasionally to 800 m. Diet: crustaceans, fish.
Cadmium, Copper, Lead, Mercury, Zinc: 1707

Phycis phycis
Mediterranean.
Cadmium, Copper, Lead, Mercury, Zinc: 1709

Phycis tenuis
  DNA 2195

Physiculus barbatus (Cod)
  Australia.
  Copper, Zinc: 1893

Pimelodella gracilis
  DNA 2195

Pimelodus clarias
  DNA 2195

Pimelodus maculatus *340*

Pimelometopon pulchrum (Sheepshead)
  America, Galapagos Is. in kelp beds in rocky areas among islands.
  Diphosphatidyl glycerol, Lysophosphatidyl choline, Phosphatidic acid, Phosphatidyl choline, Phosphatidyl ethanolamine, Phosphatidyl inositol, Phosphatidyl
  serine, Sphingomyelin: 3420

Pimephales notatus (Bluntnose minnow)
  Preferred temperature 29°C, avoiding temperatures above 31°C or below 21°C.
  DNA 2195

Pimephales promelas (Fathead minnow) *121, 320*

Planiprora fusca (Dusky flathead)
  Australia.
  Cholesterol, Diglycerides, *Free* fatty acids, Hydrocarbons, Monoglycerides,
  Phospholipids, Squalene, Sterol and Wax esters, Triglycerides: 2559

Platichthys dentatus (Flounder)
  Calcium, Strontium: 3145

‡Platichthys flesus* = Pleuronectes flesus* (Flounder) *46, 246, 274, 288, 289, 293, 312,
  313*
  Europe (excluding Iceland), Arctic Ocean to Gibraltar, Mediterranean and Black
  Seas. Migrates to fresh water for part of its early life. Common in inshore waters
  within the 55 m line. Sandy rivers and lakes near the sea. Overwinter out at sea
  and perhaps in a few lakes. Diet: a variety of small animals; (young) crustaceans;
  (older) molluscs and small fish.
  Aldolase 2880; *Free* amino acids 1965, 3329, 3552; γ-Amino butyric acid 1965,
  3710; Cadmium 1972; Calcium 1909, 2650; Carbonic anhydrase 1668, 2700;
  Chloride 1909, 1965, 2650, 3710; Cholesterol 3056, 3237; Cobalt 2491; Copper
  2491; Cyanocobalamin 1522; DNA 1881; *Free* fatty acids 3056, 3237; Fructose-
  1,6-*bis*-phosphatase 2880; Glucose-6-phosphatase 2880; Glucose-6-phosphate
  dehydrogenase 2880; Glutamate decarboxylase 1964; Glyceraldehyde-3-phosphate
  dehydrogenase 2880; Glycerides 3056; α-Glycerophosphate dehydrogenase 2880;
  Haematocrit 2650; Hexokinase 2880; Iron 2491; Lactic dehydrogenase 1789, 2880;

Lysophosphatidyl choline 3056; Magnesium 1909, 2650; Manganese 2491; Mercury 3617; Phosphatidyl choline 3056; Phosphatidyl ethanolamine 3056; Phosphofructokinase 2880; Phospholipids 3056, 3237; Potassium 1909, 1965, 2253, 2650, 3552, 3710; Pyruvate kinase 2880; RNA 1881; Sodium 1909, 1965, 2253, 2650, 3552, 3710; Sphingomyelin 3056; Taurine 1965, 3552, 3710; Triglycerides 3237; Urate oxidase 1711; Xanthine oxidase 1711; Zinc 2491, 3610

‡Platichthys flesus luscus
Black Sea.
Volume 1 only

‡Platichthys stellatus* (Emcrywheel, Grindstone, Starry flounder) *156, 253, 300, 307*
California to Bering Sea, Japan. Shallow water to 270 m on sandy bottoms. Occasionally in deep water. Tolerates low salinity, and young fish travel upstream for some distance. Females live longer than males.
Mg-ATPase (magnesium-activated adenosine triphosphatase) 3532; Na-K-ATPase 3532; D-Amino acid oxidase 1923; Calcium 1948; Carbonic anhydrase 2131; Chloride 1948; Glutamine synthetase 3592; Magnesium 1948; Mercury 1697; Ornithine aminotransferase 3611; Potassium 1948; Sodium 1948; "Sugar" 3619

‡Platophrys pantherinus (Leopard flounder)
Red Sea, E. Africa, India, Malaya, Philippines, Japan, N. Australia, Hawaii, Tahiti. Coastal waters.
Volume 1 only

Platycephalus bassensis (Sand flathead)
Australia.
Copper, Zinc: 1893

‡Platycephalus indicus (Bartailed flathead, Indian flathead, River gurnard, Sand gurnard)
E. Africa, Red Sea, India, Philippines, Japan, China, W. Australia. Sandy bottom near shore. Sea and brackish water. Can change colour to match surroundings. Lives on bottom, often buried in sand. Cannot swim far, but darts a short distance when disturbed.
Cadmium 1884; Copper 1884; Manganese 1884; Thiaminase 3473; Zinc 1884

Platypoecilus maculatus
Lactic dehydrogenase 3213

Platyrhina sinensis (Chinese guitar fish)
Japan, China.
Cadmium 2901; Copper 2901; Iron 2901; Lead 2901; Potassium 2900; Sodium 2900; Trimethylamine oxide 2111

‡**Platyrhinoidis triseriata** (Thornback)
California coast: Thurloe Head to San Francisco. Shallow water to 45 m.
DNA 2194

‡Plecoglossus altivelis* (Ayu, Sweet smelt) *26, 43, 51*
   Japan, China, Formosa. Migratory, breeding in fresh water, fry overwintering in
   the sea. Some spawn more than once, using gravel-bottomed small streams for the
   purpose. Landlocked populations are known, but are rather stunted. Quantities of
   gastric amylase and pepsin increase during metamorphosis, indicating a change of
   diet. Diet: (young) crustaceans; (adult) diatoms, blue-green algae.
   Adenosine monophosphate 3366; *Free* amino acids 3366; α-Amino butyric acid
   3366; γ-Amino butyric acid 3366; Ammonia 3366; Amylase 2393; Anserine
   3366; Arsenic 3402; Astacene 2723; Carbohydrase 2393; Carnosine 2689, 3366;
   β-Carotene 2722, 2723; Cholesterol 2445; Copper 3402; Cryptoxanthin 2722,
   2723; Cynthiaxanthin 2722, 2723; Ethanolamine 3366; Fatty acids 2951, 3666,
   3667; Inosine monophosphate 3366; Lead 3402; Lutein 2722, 2723; Maltase 2393;
   Manganese 3402; Mercury 3402; Ornithine 3366; Taurine 3366; Trimethylamine
   oxide 2111; Ubiquinone 2186; Vitamin D 3673; Vitamin E 2185, 2186; Zeaxanthin
   2722, 2723; Zinc 3402

Plectropoma maculatum (Coral trout) *339*
   Great Barrier Reef. Tropical.
   Cytochromes, Fatty acids. Succinic dehydrogenase: 2296

‡Pleurogrammus azonus (Atka mackerel)
   Japan.
   Vitamin D 3673

‡Pleurogrammus monopterygius (Atka fish)
   Japan.
   Volume 1 only

Pleuronectes americanus *232*

‡Pleuronectes cynoglossus (*see* Glyptocephalus cynoglossus)

‡Pleuronectes flesus* (*see* Platichthys flesus*) *51, 52, 288, 289, 312*

‡Pleuronectes flesus luscus (*see* Platichthys flesus luscus)

Pleuronectes herzensteini (Yellow-striped plaice) *42, 47*

‡Pleuronectes limanda (Mud dab)
   Europe.
   Volume 1 only

‡Pleuronectes microcephalus = Microstomus kitt (Lemon sole, Smear dab)
   Europe: N. Spain to White Sea and Iceland. Any type of bottom between 40 and
   200 m. Inactive. Diet: crustaceans, scale-worms, barnacles, chitons.
   Amino acids 3082; Calcium 1909; Chloride 1909; Haematocrit 2516; Haemoglobin
   2516; Magnesium 1909; Potassium 1909; Sodium 1909; Urate oxidase 1711;
   Xanthine oxidase 1711

Plotosus lineatus (Catfish) *309*
Possesses an external "dendritic organ" near the anus for salt excretion. The organ possesses chloride cells, which appear to be absent from the gills.
Chloride, Potassium, Sodium: 3521

‡Pneumatophorus colias (*see* Scomber japonicus)

‡Pneumatophorus diego (*see* Scomber japonicus)

‡Pneumatophorus japonicus (*see* Scomber japonicus)

Podonema longipes
Japan.
Fatty acids, Neutral lipids: 2152, 2155

Podothecus sachi
Japan.
Fatty acids, Neutral lipids: 2153

Poecilia formosa
Glucose-6-phosphate dehydrogenase, α-Glycerophosphate dehydrogenase: 1956

Poecilia latipinna (Green molly, Sailfin molly) *300*
E. America, Carolina to Yukatan in fresh and brackish pools and streams. Diet: algae, crustaceans, insect larvae.
DNA 2195; Sodium 1490

‡*Poecilia reticulata* = *Lebistes reticulatus* (Belly fish, Guppy, Millions, Rainbow fish) *20, 60, 245, 336*
Native to N. of Amazon region, Guyanas, Venezuela, Barbados, Trinidad. Introduced S. England. Fresh and brackish waters, ditches, even wells. Very fecund. Viviparous. Hardy. Omnivorous. Preferred temperature 27–29°C.
Free amino acids 1824; Chloride 1824; DNA 1705; Ornithine 1824; Potassium 1824; Sodium 1824; Taurine 1824; Urea 1824

Poeciliopsis—various hybrids under the specific names of latidens, monacha, lucida, occidentalis.
DNA 1705
(*Note:* some Poeciliopsis populations are found in nature only as females, producing all-female offspring by gynogenetic or hybridogenetic means.)

Poeciliopsis latidens
DNA 1705

Poeciliopsis lucida
DNA 1705

Poeciliopsis monacha
DNA 1705

Poeciliopsis occidentalis
  DNA 1705

Poeciliopsis viriosa
  DNA 1705

‡Pogonias cromis (Banded drum, Big drum, Black drum, Drumfish, Grey drum)
  E. America: Long Island to mouth of Rio Grande, rarely Bay of Fundy. Gulf of
  Mexico. Bottom feeder.
  DNA 2195

‡Polistotrema stoutii (see Eptatretus stoutii)

Polistotrema tridentata CYCLOSTOME
  Bicarbonate, Calcium, Chloride, Magnesium, Potassium, Sodium, Sulphate: 3525

‡Pollachius virens = Gadus virens (Blisterback, Boston bluefish, Coalfish, Coley,
  Pollock, Saithe) *13, 41, 73, 74, 76, 79, 83, 85, 88, 89, 93, 101–103, 105, 134, 251 253*
  Both sides of N. Atlantic: Chesapeake Bay to Hudson Strait, N. Norway, Greenland
  and Iceland to Biscay, surface to 200 m or more. The most active gadoid, occurring
  in large schools. Contains more dark muscle than other gadoids. Diet: (young)
  copepods, euphausids, fish fry; (adults) other fish. Strongly migratory.
  Adenosine triphosphatase 2345; *Free* amino acids 2977; Anserine 2977; Arsenic
  1631; Cadmium 1631, 2148; Calcium 1909, 3294; Carnosine 2977; Chloride 1909;
  Cholesterol 2515; Cytochrome oxidase 2009; *Free* fatty acids 1671, 2515; Total
  fatty acids (single figure) 2871; Formaldehyde 1671; Glucose 2516; Iodide 3294;
  Lactate 2347, 2516; Lactic dehydrogenase 2009; Lead 1631; Magnesium 1909;
  Mercury 1631, 1953, 2148, 2482; Ornithine 2977; Phospholipid 2871; Potassium
  1909, 3294; Sarcosine 2977; Sodium 1909, 3294; Sterol esters 2871; Sterols 2871;
  "Sugar" 1455; Taurine 2977; Triglycerides 2871; Trimethylamine oxide 3151;
  Urate oxidase 1711; Xanthine oxidase 1711; Zinc 3610

‡Polymixia japonica = P. nobilis (Barbudo, Japanese salmon de alto, Stout beardfish)
  Widely distributed in all tropical oceans, 183–640 m.
  Volume 1 only

‡Polynemus indicus* (Bastard mullet, Dara, Indian tasselfish, Threadfin)
  Madagascar, India to Australia and N. Tasmania. Seas and estuaries, inshore
  waters and rivers, usually at depths of less than 60 m. Muddy and sandy bottoms.
  Diet: (young) plankton; (adults) crustaceans and fish.
  Amino acids 3092

‡Polynemus microstoma
  Formosa, Philippines, Borneo, New Guinea.
  Volume 1 only

‡Polynemus paradiseus* (Paradise threadfin)
  Burma, Malaya, Pakistan, Bay of Bengal. Enters rivers to spawn. Shallow, sandy
  bottoms. Diet: crustaceans, especially shrimps; small fish, bottom-living organisms.
  Volume 1 only

‡Polynemus tetradactylus* (*see* Eleutheronema tetradactylum*)

Polyodon spathula (Paddlefish) *48–50, 53*
  Mississippi River system, N. Dakota to New York. Diet: plankton, small crustacea,
  filtered out by gill rakers.
  Acid phosphatase 3526; Albumin 3526; Alkaline phosphatase 3526; Arginase 1776;
  Bicarbonate 3526; Calcium 2056, 3526; Carbamoyl phosphate synthetase 1777;
  Chloride 2056, 3526; Cholesterol 2056; Citrate 3526; Cortisol 2056; Globulin
  3526; Glucose 2056; Lactate 2056; Magnesium 2056, 3526; Non-protein nitrogen
  2056; Potassium 2056, 3526; Sodium 2056, 3526; Sulphate 3526; Urea 3526

‡Polyprion americanus = Serranus guaza (Atlantic wreckfish, Cernier, Stone bass)
  Wide distribution: Atlantic, Mediterranean, Cape of Good Hope, Indian Ocean.
  Found around floating debris and down to 1000 m. Probably fish-eating predator.
  Volume 1 only

‡Polyprion oxygeneios
  Volume 1 only

Polypterus bichir
  DNA 2194

Polypterus senegalus (Nile bichir)
  African great lakes and their river systems, in weedy margins. Diet: small fish and
  frogs. Swim bladder acts as respiratory organ.
  Angiotensinogen, Renin: 2890

Pomacanthus arcuatus (given incorrectly as P. arentus) (French angelfish, Grey
  angelfish)
  New England to S.E. Brazil, W. Indies, Caribbean.
  Cerebroside 2470; Fatty acids 2469; Ganglioside 2469; Sialic acid 2470; Sulphatide
  2470

Pomacentrus jenkinsi
  Hawaii. Tropical reefs. Contains considerable lipid stores in the bones.
  Fatty acids, Phospholipids, Sterols, Triglycerides: 3031

Pomacentrus variabilis
  Tropical: Florida. Changes from bright blue and yellow as a juvenile to uniform
  dark as adult. Concentration of carotenoid in the skin declines steadily with growth,
  though the absolute amount per fish changes irregularly.
  Dihydroxy-α-carotene 1516

Pomadasys hasta (Head grunt, Javelin grunter, Lined silver grunt, Silver grunt)
  Natal and Indian seas to Australia. Coastal waters on reefs and sandy bottoms to
  60 m. Enters estuaries. Tolerates almost fresh water. Diet: crustaceans, fish.
  Amino acids, Calcium, Iron, Niacin, Riboflavin, Thiamine, Vitamin A: 3690

‡Pomadasys jubelina = Pristipoma jubellini
  Europe.
  Cholesterol 2768

‡Pomatomus pedica
  Australia.
  Volume 1 only

‡Pomatomus saltatrix = P. saltator (Bluefish, Elft, Greenfish, Skip mackerel, Snap
  mackerel, Tailor) *34, 35, 122, 473*
  Widespread in warm seas, for example off Bermuda, W. Africa, Malaya, Australia,
  Tasmania. Not E. Pacific. Inshore and offshore in large shoals. Enters estuaries and
  swims upstream to brackish water limit. Ferocious predator, killing more than it
  eats. Diet: small fish. Has the fastest known rate of gas secretion into the swim
  bladder (Wittenberg *et al.*, 1964, quoted by Ross, 1976)
  Aldehyde oxidase 2468; Amino acids 1812; Arsenic 3638; Cadmium 3638;
  Copper 1763, 3638; DNA 2195; Iron 1763; Manganese 1763; Mercury 1763, 1891,
  3638; Xanthine oxidase 2468; Zinc 1763, 3638

‡Pomolobus pseudoharengus* (*see* Alosa pseudoharengus*) *199*

‡*Pomoxis annularis* (Bachelor, Crappie, Shad, Silver perch, Speckled perch, Timber
  crappie, Tinmouth, Tin perch, White crappie, White perch)
  S.E. and central N. America in silted streams and lakes and in muddy, slow-moving
  areas of large rivers. Preferred temperature reported variously between 10 and
  20°C. Diet: (young) crustaceans; (adult) fish.
  Allantoinase 1775; Arginase 1776; DNA 2125; Mutarotase 1480; RNA 2125

‡*Pomoxis nigromaculatus* (Black crappie)
  E. and central N. America, introduced to other parts of N. America. Fresh and
  occasionally brackish waters; clear, quiet, warm waters of ponds, lakes and large
  rivers among abundant vegetation. Usually found in schools. Preferred temperature
  reported variously to lie between 20 and 30°C.
  Arginase 1774, 1776; Calcium 2264; Chloride 2264; Magnesium 2264; Potassium
  2264; Sodium 2264

Porichthys notatus (Plainfin midshipman, Singing fish)
  California to S.E. Alaska. Intertidal to 265 m. Tolerates exposure to air. Diet:
  crustaceans, fish.
  D-Amino acid oxidase 1923; DNA 2195; Ornithine aminotransferase 3611; "Sugar"
  3619

Porichthys porosissimus (Atlantic midshipman)
  Virginia to Argentina and Caribbean. Inshore on sand or mud. Grunts and
  whistles.
  DNA 2195

Poroderma africanum (Striped dogfish) *214, 215, 309, 310*
  Cape Peninsula (S. Africa).
  Chloride, Sodium: 2164

‡Poronotus triacanthus (Butterfish, Dollarfish, Harvestfish, Shiner)
  Atlantic coast of N. America: Nova Scotia to Florida, usually inshore.
  DNA 2195

Potamorrhaphis guianensis
DNA 2195

Potamotrygon circularis FRESHWATER ELASMOBRANCH *310*
Amazon River system.

Potamotrygon motoro FRESHWATER ELASMOBRANCH (Freshwater stingray, River ray) *310, 311*
Rivers of Paraguay over sand or mud. Viviparous. Poison spine in tail. This and the previous species occur in the Amazon River system as much as 5000 km from the sea, and never enter salt water. Their urea content is lower than that of many higher vertebrates (only 2–3 mg urea nitrogen per ml of body fluid, never more than 5 mg). This fact poses many questions, especially as they have been found unable to add urea to their body fluids when put into salt water (Thorson, 1967; Thorson, 1970). The limit of ambient salinity for P. motoro is 20·6‰ Thorson concluded that the genus was probably not derived from a marine ancestor. Watts and Watts (1974) say that one cannot tell if these fish are descended from forms that have NEVER conserved urea or from marine elasmobranchs secondarily adapted to fresh water. The activities of enzymes of the ornithine-urea cycle are much less than those in the marine rays.
Albumin 2077; Ammonia 2686; Bicarbonate 2077, 2686; Calcium 2077, 2686, 3428; Chloride 2077, 2686, 3428; Cholesterol 2077; Erythrocytes 2077; Glucose 2077; Leucocytes 2077; Magnesium 2077, 2686, 3428; Monocytes 2077; Potassium 2077, 2686, 3428; Sodium 2077, 2686; Thrombocytes 2077; Trimethylamine oxide 3428; Urea 2077, 2686, 3428

Potamotrygon sp. FRESHWATER ELASMOBRANCH
S. America: Tichito and Yavari Rivers.
Ammonia 2008; Calcium 3429; Chloride 2008, 3429; Haematocrit 2008; Magnesium 3429; Methyltransferase 1625; Potassium 3429; Sodium 2008, 3429; Trimethylamine oxide 3429; Urea 2008, 3429

Priacanthus arenatus (Bigeye, Catalufa) May be same as Pomacanthus arcuatus. Tropical Atlantic, W. Indies, S. Africa. Below 15 m in small schools over reefs. A nocturnal feeder.
DNA 2195

‡Priacanthus boops
Warm waters south of Japan.
Fatty acids, Neutral lipids: 2153

‡Priacanthus hamrur (Goggle eye, Scad)
Red Sea, tropical Indian Ocean, Pacific, E. Africa. Hides in crevices on reefs, becoming active at night. 9–24 m.
Volume 1 only

‡Priacanthus japonicus
Japan.
Volume 1 only

Priacanthus macracanthus (Red bigeye)
Indo-Australian archipelago, Japan to New South Wales, west to Bay of Bengal.
Bottom living down to 200 m. Diet: a wide range of bottom-living animals.
Cadmium 2901; Copper 2901; Iron 2901; Lead 2901; Potassium 2900; Sodium
2900; Zinc 2901

‡**Prionace glauca = Carcharhinus glaucus = Charcharias glaucus** (Blue dog,
Blue shark, Great blue shark, Whaler) *207*
World-wide in subtropical and temperate waters of all oceans. Usually offshore,
near surface. Viviparous. Sluggish except when feeding. Diet: squid, shoaling fish.
An occasional scavenger.
Alkyldiacyl glycerols 3180; Aluminium 3018, 3019; Amino acids 2426, 3019;
FREE amino acids 3019; Anserine 3367; Balenine 3367; Barium 3018; Bismuth
3018; Cholesterol 2572, 3019, 3020, 3180; Chromium 3018; Cobalt 3018; Copper
3018, 3019; Corticosterone 3456; 11-Dehydrocorticosterone 3456; 11-Deoxycorti-
costerone 3456; DNA 2194; *Free* fatty acids 2572; Haematocrit 2334; Haemo-
globin 2334; Hydrocarbons 3180; 1α-Hydroxycorticosterone 3456; Iron 3019;
Lead 3018, 3019; Lithium 3018; Manganese 3018, 3019; Neutral lipids 3180;
Nickel 3018, 3019; Phospholipids 2572; Provitamin D 3019, 3020; Silver 3018;
Sterol esters 2572; Strontium 3018, Tin 3018, 3019; Titanium 3018, 3019;
Triglycerides 2572, 3180; Trimethylamine oxide 3151, 3367; Urea 3367; Wax
esters 3180; Zinc 3018, 3019

‡Prionotus carolinus (Common gurnard, Common searobin, Northern searobin)
E. Coast of United States, Bay of Fundy to S. Carolina and Venezuela. Inshore
waters in summer, deeper offshore in winter. Bottom-living on smooth, hard
grounds, 9–73 m. Can emit loud drumming sound. Diet: wide range of crustaceans,
molluscs, worms and small fish.
DNA 2195

Prionotus evolans (Striped searobin)
Cape Cod to S. Carolina in shallow water.
Amino acids 1812; Mutarotase 1480

Prionotus roseus
Russia.
Cardiolipid 2469; Cerebroside 2469, 2470; Fatty acids 2469; Ganglioside 2469;
Phosphatidyl choline 2469; Phosphatidyl ethanolamine 2469; Phosphatidyl
inositol 2469; Phosphatidyl serine 2469; Sialic acid 2470; Sphingomyelin 2469;
Sulphatide 2469, 2470

Prionotus scitulus
DNA 2195

Prionotus strigatus
Glucose 3664

‡Prionurus microlepidotus (Surgeonfish)
Japan. Shores.
Volume 1 only

‡Prionurus microlepis
   Japan.
   Volume 1 only

Pristiophorus cirratus (Common saw shark)
   S. Indo-Pacific, S. Australia. Sluggish. Viviparous. Diet: mostly invertebrates,
   bottom-living fish.
   Copper, Zinc: 1893

‡Pristipoma commersonii
   E. Africa, Red Sea, India, China, Formosa, Philippines, Australia.
   Volume 1 only

Pristipoma jubellini (*see* Pomadasys jubellina)

‡Pristipoma olivaceum (Olive grunter)
   Madagascar, S. Arabia, India, Malay Straits. Trawling grounds.
   Volume 1 only

‡Pristipomoides amoenus
   Japan.
   Volume 1 only

Pristipomoides filamentosus
   Japan.
   Astacene, Tunaxanthin, Zeaxanthin: 2716

‡Pristipomoides sieboldii
   Japan.
   Volume 1 only

‡**Pristis microdon*** FRESHWATER ELASMOBRANCH (Sawfish, Smalltoothed
   sawfish)
   Thailand, Malaya (Perak). Atlantic and Indian Oceans, shallow inshore waters
   and estuaries. Lake Nicaragua has a permanently freshwater population. River
   Zambesi; perhaps also Walsh River (N. Queensland). Bottom-living. Diet: small
   benthic organisms, fish.
   Volume 1 only

Pristis pectinatus
   DNA 2194

Pristis perotteti FRESHWATER ELASMOBRANCH (Freshwater sawfish)
   Lake Nicaragua.
   Calcium, Chloride, Magnesium, Potassium, Sodium: 3427

‡**Pristiurus melanostomus** (Blackmouthed dogfish)
   Scandinavia to Madeira in deep muddy water, usually 180–900 m. Eggs laid in
   cases.
   Volume 1 only

‡Prochilodus laticeps
    S. America
    Volume 1 only

‡Prognichthys agoo (Flying fish)
    Japan, Formosa
    Caesium 2269; Cobalt 2269; Lutein 2717; Thiaminase 2297; Tunaxanthin 2717;
    Vitamin D 3673; Zeaxanthin 2717; Zinc 2269

‡Promethichthys prometheus (Black tuna, Snake mackerel)
    Japan, Hawaii, Australia.
    Volume 1 only

Prosopium cylindraceum (Round whitefish)
    N. America, E. Russia. American Great Lakes except L. Erie. Streams and rivers,
    inshore in lakes. Preferred temperature 17·5°C. Diet: insect larvae and pupae, fish
    eggs.
    Arsenic, Bromide, Cadmium, Cobalt, Copper, Thorium, Uranium, Zinc: 2611

‡*Prosopium williamsoni* (Grayling, Rocky Mountain whitefish)
    N. America: lakes and streams of western N. America. Prefers large streams to
    small. Seldom occurs deeper than 20 m.
    Volume 1 only

‡*Protopterus aethiopicus* (Lungfish) *170*
    Widely distributed in eastern and central Africa. Amphibious. Obligatory air-
    breather; the gill is the pathway for only 10% of the oxygen uptake compared
    with the lungs. Can aestivate, but in African lakes is rarely forced to do so. Young
    lose their external gills at about 15 cm length. Diet: molluscs, crabs, fish.
    Amino acids 1703; Ammonia 3304; Angiotensinogen 2890; Arginase 2256;
    Argininosuccinate lyase 2256; Argininosuccinate synthetase 2256; Basophils 1814;
    Bicarbonate 1813; Calcium 1813, 3304; Carbamoyl phosphate synthetase 2256;
    Chloride 1813, 3304; Creatin 3304; Creatinine 1813, 3304; DNA 2998; Eosinophils
    1814; Erythrocytes 1814; Glucose 1813; Glycogen 3304; Haemoglobin 1814;
    Lactate 1813; Leucocytes 1814; Lymphocytes 1814; Magnesium 1813, 3304;
    Neutrophils 1814; Ornithine transcarbamoylase 2256; Potassium 1813, 3304;
    Renin 2890; Sodium 1813; Sulphate 1813, 3304; Thrombocytes 1814; Urea 1813,
    3304; Uric acid 3304

Protopterus amphibius
    E. Kenya, particularly the drainage area of Tana River. All Protopterus species
    possess the complete mechanism for making urea from ammonia, a rare thing for
    a bony fish. The oxygen-binding characteristics and multiplicity of the isolated
    haemoglobin from active *P. amphibius* were shown by Weber, Johansen *et al.* (1977)
    to be the same as in specimens aestivating for 30 months. *Protopterus* species aestivate
    in hardened packed soil during drought, and can exist in this state for more than
    4 years, during which time the metabolic rate may decrease to 10% of the level of
    active, swimming lungfish. Nitrogen excretion switches from ammonia to urea,
    which can reach 3% of the body weight. The oxygen affinity of the blood increases

markedly, probably because of the big decrease in the concentration of guanosine triphosphate in the erythrocytes (same authors).
Adenosine triphosphate, Guanosine triphosphate, Haematocrit, Haemoglobin: 2331

‡*Protopterus annectens* (Lungfish, Mudfish)
Africa. Swamps, small creeks and the marginal vegetation of larger waters. Aestivates often, in cocoons at the ends of burrows.
Albumin 3526; Amino acids 1620; Bicarbonate 3526; Calcium 3526; Chloride 3526; Globulin 3526; Magnesium 3526; Potassium 3526; Sodium 3526; Sulphate 3526; Urea 3526

Protozygaena sp.
Trimethylamine oxide 3151

‡Psenopsis anomala (Butterfish, Wart perch)
Japan, Korea.
Fatty acids 3666, 3667

Psenopsis obscura
Amino acids 1812

‡Psetta maxima = Rhombus maximus = Scophthalmus maximus (Brill, Turbot)
139, 142, 143, 260
Europe, including Iceland, Mediterranean, Black Sea. Sandy or rocky bottoms. Inshore from 0–80 m. Tolerates brackish water. Scaleless on upper surface. Males smaller than females. Diet: fish, such as sand-eels and gobies, molluscs, crustaceans.
FREE amino acids 2977; Anserine 2977; Cadmium 1707; Calcium 1740; Carnosine 2977; Cathepsin (in frozen tissue) 1924; Copper 1707; Lactic dehydrogenase 1789; Lead 1707; Magnesium 1740; Mercury 1707; Ornithine 2977; Pantothenic acid 3211; Sarcosine 2977; Taurine 2977; Transketolase 1738; Zinc 1707, 3610

‡Psettichthys melanostictus (Sand flounder, Sand sole)
N. California to Bering Sea. Sandy bottoms. Less than 183 m in depth. Active forager. Diet: fish, small crustaceans, bottom-living invertebrates.
Mercury 1697; Ornithine aminotransferase 3611

‡Psettodes belcheri
S. Atlantic. 18–91 m.
Cholesterol 2768

Psettodes erumei (Adalah, Bigmouth flounder, Indian halibut, Indian turbot, Queensland halibut)
W. Africa, India, Malaya, China, Japan, Philippines, Australia. Coastal, down to 91 m. Muddy and sandy bottoms. Swims upright although it is a flat fish. Eyes may be on R or L. Diet: mainly bottom-living animals.
Folic acid 1865

‡*Pseudobagrus aurantiacus*
Japan. Rivers.
Volume 1 only

‡*Pseudoentropius garus*
India.
Volume 1 only

Pseudogobio esocinus
Japan.
Thiaminase 2297

Pseudolabrus celidotus *28*

‡Pseudolabrus japonicus (Spotted wrasse, Wrasse)
Japan.
Pyridine nucleotide transhydrogenase 3167

Pseudoperilampus typus
Dimethylamine, Formaldehyde: 2110

‡Pseudopleuronectes americanus (Blackback, George's Bank flounder, Winter flounder) *37, 43, 50, 63, 123, 156, 231, 240, 273, 348, 385*
Atlantic coast of N. America: Labrador to Georgia. Bottom-dwelling from shallow waters to 143 m on soft mud to harder bottoms, commonest 2–37 m. Tolerates low temperatures well: produces an "antifreeze" in the blood in winter. Diet: bottom-living crustaceans, molluscs and marine worms, also probably the siphons of clams.
Mg-ATPase (magnesium-activated adenosine triphosphatase) 2321; Na-K-ATPase 2321; Amino acids 1861; Chloride 1860, 1932, 3520; DNA 2195, 2998; 20β-Dihydro-17α-hydroxyprogesterone 1652; Erythrocytes 1932, 3520; Haematocrit 3520; Haemoglobin 1932, 3520; 17α-hydroxyprogesterone 1652; 11β-Hydroxytestosterone 2273; 11-Ketotestosterone 1652, 2273; Mercury 1953; Sodium 1860, 1932, 3520; "Sugar" 2643; Testosterone 1652

‡*Pseudorasbora parva* (Stone moroko)
Japan, Korea, China. Introduced central Europe and Israel.
Volume 1 only

‡Pseudorhombus oligodon (Roughscale flounder)
Bay of Bengal, Philippines, Formosa, Japan, China. Shallower muddy and sandy bottoms of the continental shelf. Diet: bottom-living animals.
Volume 1 only

Pseudorhombus pentophthalmus
Japan.
Trimethylamine oxide 2111

Pseudoscaphirhynchus kaufmanni (Great Amu-Dar'ya shovelnose)
Sodium, Urea: 2466

‡Pseudoscarus guacamaia (Green parrotfish)
E. America: Florida to Rio de Janeiro.
Volume 1 only

‡Pseudosciaena anea* (Croaker, Greyfin jewfish)
India, Philippines, S. China. Seas and mouths of rivers.
Volume 1 only

‡Pseudosciaena crocea = Collichthys crocea (Yellow croaker)
Japan, China. Coastal waters and estuaries. Spawns close to estuaries. Diet:
crustaceans, fish.
Volume 1 only

Pseudosciaena manchurica
Japan.
Trimethylamine oxide 2111

‡Psilocranium nigricans (Dusky morwong)
Australia, Tasmania. Rocky bottoms among dense algae.
Volume 1 only

‡Pterogobius elapoides (Stretched silk)
Japan, Korea.
Volume 1 only

Pterophyllum eimekei (Angel fish)
Amazon Basin. Well-weeded, slow-flowing water.

Pterophyllum scalare *235*

‡*Ptychocheilus oregonensis* (Northern squawfish, Squawfish, Whitefish)
Western N. America: Oregon, Washington, British Columbia. Prefers still waters
of lakes to swift streams, close to bottom. Diet: (young) insect larvae, plankton,
molluscs, small fish; (adult) mostly fish.
Volume 1 only

Pungitius sinensis
α-Cryptoxanthin, Cynthiaxanthin, Diatoxanthin, Lutein, Tunaxanthin, Zeaxan
thin: 2717

Pungtungia herzi
Japan.
Thiaminase 2297

Puntius gonionotus = *Barbus goniotus*
Malaysia. Herbivorous.
Calcium, Chloride, Magnesium, Potassium, Sodium: 3292

‡*Puntius javanicus* (Tawes)
Thailand, Sumatra, Java, Indonesia.
Volume 1 only

Puntius sarana = *Barbus sarana*
India.
Vitamin A_1, Vitamin A_2: 1500

Puntius sophore
India. Sluggish.
Erythrocytes, Leucocytes: 3408

Puntius stigma
India. Sluggish.
Erythrocytes, Leucocytes: 3408

Puntius ticto
India. Sluggish.
Erythrocytes, Leucocytes: 3408

Pyrrhulina rachoviana
DNA 2195

Rachycentron canadum (Cobia, Runner, Sergeant fish)
Tropical Atlantic, Pacific and Indian Oceans. Open sea, occasionally inshore and even estuaries. Swift and voracious. Diet: fish, crabs, squid, shrimps.
DNA 2195

‡**Raja asterias** (Starry ray)
Europe. Resting on or half buried in mud and sandy ground 7–40 m. Occasionally 120 m. Eggs laid in cases. Diet: mainly crustaceans.
Volume 1 only

‡**Raja batis** (Blue skate, Flapper skate, Grey skate)
Europe: N. Iceland to Madeira, Mediterranean. Sandy or muddy bottoms, 30–600 m. Eggs laid in capsules. Diet: fish, crustaceans, worms, crabs, lobsters, octopodes. Other elasmobranchs such as dogfish and rays are included in its diet.
Amino acids 3082; Cardiolipid 3233; Chloride 1909; Glycine 2087; Haematocrit 2516; Haemoglobin 2516; Hexosamine 2087; "Hexose" 2087; Hydroxyproline 2087; Lysophosphatidyl choline 3233; Magnesium 1909; "Pentose" 2087; Phosphatidic acid 3233; Phosphatidyl choline 3233; Phosphatidyl ethanolamine 3233; Phosphatidyl inositol 3233; Phosphatidyl serine 3233; Potassium 1909; Proline 2087; Sodium 1909; Sphingomyelin 3233; Tyrosine 2087

‡**Raja binoculata** (Big skate)
S. California to Gulf of Alaska, 5–110 m. Eggs shed in horny cases. Breeds throughout the year, more intensively during the summer.
Glutamine synthetase 3592; Trimethylamine oxide 3110; Urea 3110

‡**Raja brachyura** (Blonde ray)
Europe: Britain to Mediterranean and Madeira. Shallow waters. Eggs laid in capsules.
Volume 1 only

‡**Raja circularis** (Sandy ray)
W. Europe (except Iceland). Mediterranean. Deep waters on sandy bottom. Eggs laid in capsules.
Carbamoyl phosphate synthetase, Urea: 3587

‡**Raja clavata** (Roker, Sea fox, Thornback ray)
Europe: Iceland to Madiera and Mediterranean, W. Baltic and Black Seas. 2–500 m on mud, sand, gravel or rock. Eggs laid in capsules. Weakly electric. Diet: crabs, prawns, small fish.
Cadmium 1707; Calcium 2864; Chloride 1836, 2280, 2864; Copper 1707; Corticosterone + cortisol 1704; 1α-Hydroxycorticosterone 2276; Iron 3003; Lactic dehydrogenase 1789; Lead 1707; Magnesium 2864; Manganese 3003; Mercury 1707; Potassium 1836, 2280, 2864; Zinc 1707, 3003

‡**Raja diaphanes** (Clear ray)
E. coast of United States.
Glucose 3664

‡**Raja eglanteria** (Bobtailed skate, Brier ray, Clearnosed skate, Possum ray, Sea possum, Skate, Summer skate)
E. coast of N. America: Cape Cod to Florida. Shallow waters along beaches and down to 120 m.
Arsenic 3638; Cadmium 3638; Copper 3638; DNA 2194; Mercury 3638; Zinc 3638

‡**Raja erinacea** (Hedgehog skate, Little skate, Tobacco box) *164, 165, 186, 310, 312–314, 459*
Western N. Atlantic: Gulf of St. Lawrence, Massachusetts Bay to Florida, at depths down to 150 m, on sandy and gravelly bottoms, less often on mud and rocks. Breeds during whole year with peaks of activity in October to January and June-July. Eggs laid in cases. Diet: a wide range of crustaceans, worms, bivalves, squid, fish.
Mg-ATPase (magnesium-activated adenosine triphosphatase) 2075; Na-K-ATPase 2075; α-Amino butyrate 1594; Amino acids (a single figure) 1945; *Free* amino acids 1594; α-Amino adipate 1594; β-Amino butyrate 1954; γ-Amino butyrate 1594; Ammonia 1594; Arginine 1653; Bicarbonate 1596; Bile acids 1596; Calcium 1596; Chloride 1596; Citrulline 1594; Creatinine 1594; DNA 2194; Ethanolamine 1594; Glucose 2058; Glutamine 1594; 1α-Hydroxycorticosterone 2276; *Free* hydroxyproline 1594; Magnesium 1596; Ornithine 1594; Potassium 1596, 1945; Sarcosine 1594; Sodium 1596, 1945; Taurine 1594; Trimethylamine oxide 1945; Urea 1594, 1811, 1945, 2996

‡**Raja fullonica** (Fuller's ray, Shagreen ray)
Europe: Iceland to Mediterranean. 35–350 m on sandy bottom. Eggs laid in cases. Diet: fish, crustaceans, molluscs.
Volume 1 only

‡**Raja hollandi**
Japan.
Volume 1 only

‡**Raja inornata** (California skate, Common skate)
Californian coast, 18–655 m.
Volume 1 only

‡**Raja kenojei** (Flat back, Sea wall ray, Spiny rasp skate)
Japan.
Volume 1 only

Raja laevis (Barndoor skate)
Atlantic coast of N. America, Grand Bank to N. Carolina, shallow water to 182 m.
Tolerates wide temperature range. Eggs laid in cases. Diet: molluscs, squid, worms,
lobsters and a wide range of fish species.
Corticosterone 3456; 11-Dehydrocorticosterone 3456; 11-Deoxycorticosterone
3456; Glucose 2058; 1α-Hydroxycorticosterone 2276, 3456

‡**Raja lintea** (Pale ray)
S. Greenland, S. Iceland, S. Norway to W. Ireland, 150–200 m. Lays eggs. Diet:
bottom-living fish, cephalopods, crustaceans.
Calcium 1909; Chloride 1909; Cholesterol 2515; Haematocrit 2516; Haemoglobin
2516; Magnesium 1909; Potassium 1909; Sodium 1909

‡**Raja macrocorda**
Japan.
Volume 1 only

Raja macrorhynchus
Mediterranean.
Formaldehyde 1656

Raja miraletus (Brown ray)
Mediterranean. Biscay to Senegal. Absent from Black Sea. Muddy and sandy
bottoms, 30–300 m. Diet: mainly crustaceans.
Cadmium, Copper, Lead, Mercury, Zinc: 1707

‡**Raja montagui** (Homelyn ray, Spotted ray)
British and French coasts. Denmark to Mediterranean, 25–100 m. Eggs laid in
cases. Diet: mainly crustaceans but also fish, crabs, prawns, shrimps.
Potassium, Sodium: 1836

‡**Raja naevus** (Cuckoo ray)
Coasts of Britain and France, Mediterranean, 20–150 m. Eggs laid in cases.
Volume 1 only

‡**Raja ocellata** (Big skate, Eyed skate, Winter skate)
Atlantic coast of N. America, Grand Bank to N. Carolina. Shallow water to 100 m
on sandy or gravelly bottoms. Found in shallower waters in winter, deeper in
summer.
Adenosine triphosphatase 2272; Chloride 2232; Corticosterone 3456; 11-Dehydro-
corticosterone 3456; 11-Deoxycorticosterone 3456; Glucose 2058; 1α-Hydroxy-
corticosterone 2276, 3456; Potassium 2232; Sodium 2232

‡**Raja oxyrhynchus** (Longnosed skate)
W. Europe (not Iceland). Mediterranean. On or half-buried in sand or mud,
48–900 m. Eggs laid in cases. Diet: fish, prawns.
Volume 1 only

‡**Raja radiata** (Atlantic prickly skate, Starry skate, Thorny skate) *310*
Both sides of N. Atlantic, Iceland and Greenland, north to Spitzbergen. Offshore,
deep water (30–600 m) on mud, sand or stones. Eggs laid in capsules. Prefers
temperatures below 10°C. Diet: small fish, crabs, prawns.

Calcium 1909; Chitinase 1910; Chloride 1909; Cholesterol 2515; Corticosterone 3456; 11-Dehydrocorticosterone 3456; 11-Deoxycorticosterone 3456; *Free* fatty acids 2515; Glucose 2058, 2516; Haematocrit 2516; Haemoglobin 2516; 1α-Hydroxycorticosterone 2276, 3456; Lactate 2516; Lysozyme 1910; Magnesium 1909; Mercury 1953; Potassium 1909; Sodium 1909; Testosterone 1795

‡**Raja scabrata** (Atlantic prickly skate)
Volume 1 only

Raja sp.
Arsenic 2535; Bicarbonate 2692; Calcium 2692; Chloride 2692; Galactosamine 3141; Galactose 3141; Glucosamine 3141; Glucose 2692, 3141; Magnesium 2692; Mannose 3141; Potassium 2692; Sodium 2692; Sulphate 2692; Urate oxidase 1711; Urea 2692; Xanthine oxidase 1711

‡**Raja stabuliforis** (Barndoor skate, Peck-nosed skate, Winter skate)
N. America: Massachusetts to Florida.
Volume 1 only

Raja tengu
Cadmium 2901; Copper 2901; Iron 2901; Lead 2901; Potassium 2900; Sodium 2900; Zinc 2901

Raja trachura
DNA 2194

‡**Raja undulata** (Painted ray, Undulate ray)
S. England and Ireland to Mediterranean and N. Africa. Sandy bottoms offshore down to 200 m. Eggs laid in cases.
Volume 1 only

Raniceps raninus (Lesser forkbeard, Tadpole fish)
Mid-Norway, British Is., Channel. Lives on bottom on stony ground in the sea-weed belt down to 100 m. Solitary. Diet: sea-stars, crustaceans, worms, gobies.
Cytochrome oxidase, Lactic dehydrogenase: 2009

‡*Rasbora daniconius* (Common rasbora) *272*
India, Sri Lanka, Burma, Malaya, Tanzania. Rivers and ponds. Can live anaerobically.
Erythrocytes, Leucocytes: 3408

‡Rastrelliger brachysoma (Short-bodied mackerel)
Philippines, Java, Thailand to Fiji. In large schools in coastal waters between 10–50 m. Diet: minute plankton organisms.
Folic acid 2582

‡Rastrelliger kanagurta (Longjawed mackerel, Indian mackerel, Rake-gilled mackerel)
E. Africa, Red Sea, Mediterranean (*via* the Suez Canal), India to Queensland, China and Japan. Open sea. Pelagic, occurring in large schools. Diet: plankton organisms, mainly crustaceans.

Calcium 2313; Iron 2313; Lysophosphatidyl choline 2042; Niacin 2313; Phospha-
tidic acids 2042; Phosphatidyl choline 2042; Phosphatidyl ethanolamine 2042;
Phosphatidyl inositol 2042; Phosphatidyl serine 2042; Phospholipid 2042;
Riboflavin 2313; Sphingomyelin 2042; Thiamine 2313

Rastrelliger neglectus (Chub mackerel)
    Thailand.
    Amino acids, Fatty acids, Hypoxanthine: 2406

‡Reinhardtius hippoglossoides (Blue halibut, Greenland halibut, Greenland turbot,
    Little halibut, Newfoundland turbot, Turbot) 27, 196
    Arctic and N. Atlantic in deep, cold water, usually 250–1600 m. Northwards
    from Iceland, Faroe. Mexico to Bering Sea and Sea of Japan. Swims in upright
    position like a "round" fish. Active predator. Diet: deepsea prawns, fish, squid.
    Arsenic 1560; Cobalt 2491; Copper 2491; Fatty acids 2505; Iron 2491; Manganese
    2491; Mercury 2482; Zinc 2491

‡Reinhardtius matsuurae
    Japan.
    Volume 1 only

‡Reporhamphus melanochir
    Australia.
    Volume 1 only

‡Rhabdosargus sarba* = Sparus sarba* (Goldlined seabream, Silver bream, Tarwhine,
    Yellowfin bream)
    Madagascar, Tanzania, Red Sea, Mauritius, India, Japan, China, Australia.
    Shallow coastal waters, river mouths on sandy and rough grounds and in clear
    patches between reefs. Enters rivers.
    α-Cryptoxanthin, Cynthiaxanthin, Diatoxanthin, Lutein, Tunaxanthin, Zeaxan-
    thin: 2716

Rhacochilus vacca (Pile perch)
    California to Alaska. Rocky shores and old piers. Viviparous. Diet: mussels,
    including the shells.
    DNA 2195; Mercury 2751

Rhamphocottus richardsoni (Grunt sculpin)
    California to Bering Sea, coastal waters and shallow pools down to 165 m. Tolerates
    low salinity. Diet: copepods, amphipods, larvae of fish and other animals, crus-
    taceans.
    DNA 2195

‡Rhigophila dearborni
    Antarctic. Freezes at −1·5°C, so may freeze in physical contact with oceanic ice.
    Upper lethal temperature +6°C, not raised by acclimation (DeVries, 1974).
    Possesses glomeruli. Very sluggish.
    Calcium 1840; Carbohydrate 1827; Chloride 1827, 1840; Haematocrit 3108;
    Magnesium 1840; Non-protein nitrogen 1827; Potassium 1840; Sodium 1840

‡**Rhincodon typus** (Whale shark)
Worldwide in warm seas. The largest living fish, reaching 18 m (60 feet) in length.
Eggs laid in cases. Diet: small plankton animals, small fish.
Volume 1 only

Rhinichthys atratulus (Blacknose dace) *323*

Rhinobatus lentiginosus (Atlantic guitarfish, Spotted guitarfish)
W. Atlantic. Bottom-living, bays and estuaries. Diet: small crustaceans.
Arsenic, Cadmium, Copper, Mercury, Zinc: 3638

Rhinobatus percellens
Russia.
Cardiolipid, Fatty acids, Phosphatidyl choline, Phosphatidyl ethanolamine,
Phosphatidyl inositol, Phosphatidyl serine, Sphingomyelin: 2469

Rhinobatus productus
DNA 2194

Rhinomugil corsula*
India. Diet: algae, insects, molluscs.
Vitamin A_1, Vitamin A_2: 1500

Rhinoplagusia japonica (Black cow tongue)
Japan, Korea, Formosa.
Thiaminase 3473

Rhinoptera bonasus (Cownosed ray)
American Atlantic, New England to Brazil. Coastal, Migratory. Powerful swimmer.
Diet: hard-shelled invertebrates.
Arsenic, Cadmium, Copper, Mercury, Zinc: 3638

Rhinoptera quadriloba
DNA 2194

Rhodeus amarus *328, 329, 335*

Rhomboplites aurorubeus
Russia.
Cardiolipid 2469; Cerebroside 2469, 2470; Fatty acids 2469; Phosphatidyl
choline 2469; Phosphatidyl ethanolamine 2469; Phosphatidyl inositol 2469;
Phosphatidyl serine 2469; Sphingomyelin 2469; Sulphatide 2469, 2470

‡Rhombus maximus (*see* Psetta maxima)

‡Rhombus meoticus = Scophthalmus meoticus (Black Sea turbot)
Amino acids 3468

‡**Rhynchobatus djeddensis** (Fiddler, White-spotted shovelnose ray, Sand shark)
Red Sea, E. Africa, India, Malaya, Australia. Coastal (warm season) or deep

water in cooler weather. A sedentary, bottom-feeding fish. Diet: bottom-living crustaceans, squid, molluses.
Volume 1 only

‡Rhynchocymba nystromi
    Japan.
    Volume 1 only

Rita rita
    India: Indus, Jumna, Ganges and Irrawaddi rivers. Sluggish.
    Acid phosphatase 3227; Alkaline phosphatase 3227, 3404; Erythrocytes 3408; Glucose 3407; Lactate 3407; Leucocytes 3408

Rivulus urophthalmus (Green rivulus)
    Amazon Basin and the Guianas.
    DNA 2195

‡Roccus americanus* (*see* Morone americana*) *57, 330*

Roccus chrysops (*see Morone chrysops*)

Roccus lineatus
    Amino acids 1812

‡Roccus saxatilis (*see* Morone saxatilis)

‡*Rooseveltiella nattereri* (Natterer's piranha, Red piranha)
    Amazon Basin, Orinoco and Parana river systems. Predatory, eating fish and invertebrates, but known to attack man and other large animals with rapidly fatal results.
    Volume 1 only

‡Rutilus rutilus* (Roach) *45, 164, 436*
    Europe, except Scotland, Iceland, Norway, Spain, Italy. Introduced Ireland. Still or slowly-flowing water at heights up to 900 m; lagoons and weedy marshes. Migratory stocks also found in fresh and salt water. Tolerates low oxygen concentrations, warm temperatures and moderate polluton. Preferred temperature 27°C. Diet: crustaceans, molluscs, plants.
    Aluminium 2677; Amino acids 1485; *Para*-amino benzoic acid 3295; Arginase 2256; Argininosuccinate lyase 2256; Argininosuccinate synthetase 2256; Biotin 3295; Cadmium 1972; Calcium 2677; Carbamoyl phosphate synthetase 2256; Cobalt 1540, 2677; Copper 1533, 2281, 2677; Cyanocobalamin 3295; DNA 2872, 3203; Furan fatty acids 2092; Inositol 3295; Iron 1533, 2281, 2677; Lactic dehydrogenase 3203; Magnesium 2677; Manganese 1533, 2281, 2677; Niacin 3295; Ornithine transcarbamoylase 2256; Pantothenic acid 3295; 6-Phosphogluconate dehydrogenase 3203; Phosphoglucose isomerase 3203; Potassium 1836, 2264, 2677; Pyridoxine 3295; Riboflavin 1465; RNA 2872, 3203; Sodium 1836, 2264; Strontium 1478; Thiamine 3295; Tin 2677; Vanadium 2677; Zinc 1533, 2281, 2677

Rutilus rutilus caspicus
R. Volga, Caspian Sea.
Calcium 2864; Magnesium 2864; Potassium 2864; Selenium 2749; Sodium 2864

Rutilus rutilus lacustris
Lake Baical (Russia).
Magnesium, Potassium, Sodium 2864

Ruvettus pretiosus (Castor oil fish) *126, 266*
Pacific. Wax esters of cetyl and oleyl alcohols found all over the body, probably to buoy the fish (lacks a swimbladder). The dermis and bones of the skull are richest in these wax esters, so the fish at rest probably has the head elevated.
Fatty acids, fatty alcohols: 2781

‡*Saccobranchus fossilis* (*see Heteropneustes fossilis*)

‡Salangichthys microdon* (Common ice fish, Glassfish, Whitefish)
Japan, Korea to coast of Russia. Spawns in estuaries.
β-Carotene, Cryptoxanthin, Cynthiaxanthin, Lutein, Zeaxanthin: 2722, 2723

Salmo clarki* (Coastal cut-throat trout, Sea trout, Yellowstone cut-throat) *27, 34, 134*
N. California to S.E. Alaska. W. centre of N. America. Marine coastal to small streams and lakes. Some remain permanently in fresh water. Develops different colours or patterns in different rivers. Diet: a wide variety of crustaceans, insects (including flying insects).
Acetyl cholinesterase 2222; Calcium 1765, 2054; Chloride 1765, 2054; Creatinine 1765; Glycogen 2206; Haemoglobin 2206; Hexosamine 3094; Magnesium 1765, 2054; Potassium 1765, 2054; Sialic acid 3094; Sodium 1765, 2054; Urea 1765

Salmo fario* (*see* S. trutta*)

Salmo gairdneri* = S. irideus* (Donaldson trout, Rainbow trout. Called a steelhead trout if sea-run) *3, 7, 10, 11, 13–15, 17, 20–25, 31, 34–36, 38, 39, 43, 48, 49, 51, 55–57, 62, 63, 69, 73, 74, 76, 79–82, 85, 86, 96, 98, 100, 115, 116, 118–120, 134, 136, 137, 139–143, 145, 147, 148, 151, 153, 156, 158, 159, 168, 169, 187, 192–194, 206, 211, 213, 218, 222, 225, 227, 232, 236, 237, 240, 241, 243, 247, 249, 250, 255, 256, 258, 259, 261, 265, 268, 269, 272–277, 280–282, 284, 290–292, 294, 300, 301, 304, 308, 314, 317, 323, 324, 326–329, 333–335, 342, 345, 365, 379, 383–385, 392, 398, 399, 400, 403, 406, 407, 408, 415, 419, 425, 429, 435, 436, 439, 440, 448, 453, 463, 466*
N. America. Widely introduced elsewhere. The most extensively investigated species in this book. Usually remains in fresh water, but may go to sea. Atlantic and Pacific coasts of N. America are the marine localities. Now found in Europe, excluding Iceland and Black Sea but including Spain, Cyprus, Crete. The anadromous fish may return several times to spawn. Probably identical to Salmo mykiss on the Asiatic coast of the Pacific. Natural diet: insect larvae, molluscs, crustaceans. Large specimens eat fish. Preferred temperature 13–22°C.
Acetoacetate 3572; Acetoacetyl CoA deacylase 3026; Acetyl cholinesterase 1989, 3362; Acetyl serotonin methyltransferase 2095; Acid glucosidase 2757; Acid phosphatase 2757; Acid ribonuclease 2757; Actomyosin 2830; Adenine 3066; Adenosine diphosphate (ADP) 3219, 3721; ADP ribose (*see* NADH); Adenosine monophosphate (AMP) 3219, 3721; *Cyclic* 3′5′-AMP 3417; AMP deaminase 3572;

NADH (reduced NAD) 3219, 3572; NAD-malate dehydrogenase 1488; NAD nucleosidase 2621; NAD-pyrophosphatase 2621; NADP (—phosphate) 3219, 3572, 3721; NADP-isocitrate dehydrogenase 1488; NADP-malate dehydrogenase 1488; NADPH (reduced NADP) 3219, 3572; Mg-P-nitrophenyl phosphatase 2621; K-P-nitrophenylphosphatase 2621; Noradrenaline 2754; Nucleoside diphosphatase 2621; 5'nucleotidase 2621; *Cyclic* 3'5'-nucleotide phosphodiesterase 3674; Oestrogen 3210; Ornithine 2898, 2977, 3217; Ornithine aminotransferase 3611; Ornithine transcarbamoylase 2256; 3-Oxoacid CoA transferase 3026; Partial glycerides 2399; "Pentose" 2844; Phenylalanine 2743; Phenylethanolamine-N-methyl transferase 2740; Phosphatidyl choline 1454, 2847; Phosphatidyl ethanolamine 1454, 2847; Phosphoenolpyruvate carboxykinase 3025; Phosphofructokinase 1744, 2938; Phosphoglucomutase 2838, 2839; 6-phosphogluconate dehydrogenase 1488, 2838, 2938, 3203; Phosphoglucose isomerase 2838, 2839, 3203; Phospholipid 2330, 2399, 2847, 2849, 3138; Phosphorylase 1744; Plasmalogen 1454; Potassium 1960, 2055, 2260, 2261, 2264, 2640, 3187, 3314, 3717, 3718; Protease 2936–2938; Putrescine 3217; Pyruvate 1639, 2340, 3572; Pyruvate carboxylase 3025; Pyruvate kinase 2938; Reticulocytes 3570; RNA 2059, 2282, 2373, 2614, 2681, 3203, 3217, 3391, 3719; Sarcosine 2977; Sialic acid 2844, 3095; Sodium 1537, 1538, 1960, 2055, 2260, 2261, 2264, 2499, 2640, 3187, 3314, 3717, 3718; Spermidine 3217; Spermine 3217; Sphingomyelin 1454, 2847; Sphingosine 1454; Sterols 2399; Sterol esters 2399, 2847; Strontium 3438; Succinate 2340; Succinate-INT-dehydrogenase 2621; "Sugar" 1547; Taurine 2977; Thiaminase 2297; Thrombocytes 1669; Thyroxine 1445, 2190, 2529; Triglycerides 1454, 2399, 2847, 3138, 3252, 3253; Uracil 3066; Urea 1765, 3187, 3603; Uric acid 3187; Uricase 2621; Uridine diphosphate (UDP) 3219, 3721; UDP-N-acetyl galactosamine 3219; UDP-N-acetyl glucosamine 3219, 3721, 3722; UDP-hexoses 3219, 3721; UDP-uronic acids 3219; Uridine monophosphate 3219, 3721; Uridine triphosphate 3721; Vitamin A$_1$ 1998; Vitamin A$_2$ 1998; Vitamin C (*see* ascorbic acid); Vitamin E 3673; Wax esters 2399; Zeaxanthin 2136; Zinc 1534, 1622, 3717, 3718

‡*Salmo gairdneri kamloops* (Kamloops trout)
   N. America. A local variant of *S. gairdneri*.
   Cortisol 1847; Erythrocytes 2633; Glucose 2633; Granulocytes 2633; Haemoglobin 2633; Leucocytes 2633; Lymphocytes 2633; Thrombocytes 2633; Uridine diphosphate glucose 3722; Uridine diphosphate glucuronic acid 3722

Salmo gairdneri shasta
   Erythrocytes, Glucose, Granulocytes, Haemoglobin, Leucocytes, Lymphocytes: 2634

‡Salmo milktschitsch*
   Japan.
   Volume 1 only

Salmo mykiss (probably the same as *S. gairdneri*)
   Russia.
   Calcium, Magnesium, Potassium, Sodium: 1484

‡*Salmo salar** (Atlantic salmon, Black salmon) *21–25, 28, 38, 64, 110, 114, 115, 118, 121, 124, 136, 145, 148, 151, 156, 172, 194, 251, 254–257, 273, 290, 292, 294, 312, 322, 325, 337, 351, 397, 400, 423, 454, 457*

Both sides of N. Atlantic: N.E. Labrador to New York; Arctic Circle to Portugal; Baltic Sea. May spawn more than once, but fewer males than females succeed in doing this. The young fish grow more rapidly in the sea than in the river where they hatched, and their food in the sea consists of small fish and crustaceans. Male parr (juvenile form) can become sexually mature and join in the spawning act with sea-run adults. Preferred temperature 6–18°C.

Na-K-ATPase (adenosine triphosphatase which is activated by sodium and potassium ions) 2638; Adrenaline 1940; 2740; Alanine aminotransferase 2793; Aldosterone 1969; Amino acids 1620, 1938; *Free* amino acids 1938, 1939; Anserine 1766; Arginase 2256; Argininosuccinate lyase 2256; Argininosuccinate synthetase 2256; Aspartate aminotransferase 2793; Cadmium 1972; Calcium 2264, 3294; Carbamoyl phosphate synthetase 2256; Chloride 2264; Cholesterol 1712, 1954; Cobalt 2363, 2491; Copper 1769, 2491, 2829, 3294; Corticosterone 1969; Cortisol 1969; Deoxycorticosterone 1969; 11-Deoxycortisol 1969; Dihydroxyacetone phosphate 1572; Fatty acids 1657, 1712, 3117; *Unsaturated* fatty acids 1954; Furan fatty acids 2092; Fluoride 3294; Glucose 3614, 3615; Glycerides 1712; α-Glycerophosphate 1572; Glycogen 3613, 3615; Gonadotropin 1760; Haematocrit 1936, 3142, 3316; Haemoglobin 1936, 3142, 3316; Histidine 1766; 18-Hydroxydeoxycorticosterone 1969; 11β-Hydroxytestosterone 2273; Iodide 3294; Iron 2491; 11-Ketotestosterone 2273; Lactate 1572, 1573, 3613, 3615; Lactic dehydrogenase 2012; Magnesium 2264; Malate 1572; Manganese 2491, 3294; Mercury 1953, 2829; Nickel 2491; Noradrenaline 1940, 2740; Ornithine transcarbamoylase 2256; Phenylethanolamine-N-methyl transferase 2740; Phospholipid 1712, 1954; Potassium 2264, 3294; Pyruvate 1572; Sodium 2264, 3294; Strontium 1478; "Sugar" 2993; Triglycerides 1954; Zinc 2491, 2829, 3294

‡Salmo trutta* = S. fario* (Brown trout, Sea trout) *22, 38, 40, 43, 49, 53, 56, 63, 110, 112, 141, 146, 147, 161, 193, 249, 268, 279, 280, 289, 301, 314, 322, 338, 344, 345, 384, 306, 154*
N. coast of Europe. Introduced widely elsewhere: now present in all continents except Antarctica (for distribution map, see MacCrimmon, Marshall and Gots, 1970). Anadromous in unpolluted streams, estuaries, rivers and lakes. Some forms live permanently in fresh water. Most adults survive spawning and spawn again. Preferred temperature 12–18°C. Diet in fresh water: aquatic and flying insects; in sea water: crustacea, small fish.
Albumin 3242; Aldosterone 1969; Amino acids 1655; *Free* amino acids 3140; Amylase 1456, 2936; Arginase 2936; Bicarbonate 2262; Calcium 1528, 2262–2264, 2636, 2864, 3294; Carotenoids 3264; Chloride 2262; Cholesterol 1920, 2637, 3242; Cholesterol esters 1920; Cobalt 2491; Copper 1893, 2491, 2636, 3294; Corticosterone 1969; Cortisol 1969; Deoxycorticosterone 1969; 11-Deoxycortisol 1969; DNA 3203; Di- and tri-glycerides 3242; Erythrocytes 1550; Fatty acids 1565, 1657; *Free* fatty acids 2637, 3242; Furan fatty acids 2092; Globulin 3242; Glucose 2262, 2994; Glutamate-oxaloacetate transaminase 2936; Glutamate-pyruvate transaminase 2936; Glycogen 2994; Glycogen phosphorylase 2810; Gonadotropin 1760; Haematocrit 1550, 2262, 3316; Haemoglobin 1550, 2995, 3316; 18-Hydroxydeoxycorticosterone 1969; Hydroxyproline 1655; Iodide 3294; Iron 2491, 3294; Lactate 1639, 2262; Lactic dehydrogenase 3203; Leucocytes 1550; Lymphocytes 1550; Lyso-phosphatidyl choline 1565; Magnesium 2262–2264, 2636, 2864; Malic dehydrogenase 1920; Manganese 2491, 2636, 3294; Neutrophils 1550; Phosphatidyl choline 1565; Phosphatidyl ethanolamine 1565; Phosphatidyl

inositol 1565; Phosphatidyl serine 1565; 6-Phosphogluconate dehydrogenase 3203; Phosphoglucose isomerase 3203; Phospholipid 3242; Potassium 2262–2264, 2636, 2864, 3294; Protease 2936; Pyruvate 1639; RNA 3203; Sodium 2262–2264, 2636, 2864, 3294; Sphingomyelin 1565; Sterol esters 3242; "Sugar" 2062; Urate oxidase 1711; Xanthine oxidase 1711; Zinc 1893, 2491, 2636

‡Salvelinus alpinus* (Arctic char, Blueback trout, Greenland charr, Hudson Bay salmon, Sea trout) *113, 251, 253, 284, 285, 324*
Circumpolar. May be landlocked. Poor, stony lakes; prefers considerable depths. There are isolated groups in central Europe. Tends to migrate to fresh water in winter to avoid freezing (temperature of fresh water is never below 0°C). Diet: midge larvae, molluscs, small fish.
N-acetyl galactosamine 3652; *N*-acetyl glucosamine 3652; Amino acids 3652; Calcium 1484, 1528, 2864; Chloride 3130; Fucose 3652; Glucose 3652; Mannose 3652; Potassium 1484, 2864, 3130; Sialic acid 3652; Sodium 1484, 2864, 3130

‡Salvelinus fontinalis* (Coaster, Eastern brook trout, Sea trout, Speckled char, Speckled trout) *13, 34, 35, 116, 117, 134, 146, 153, 166, 169, 218, 221, 232, 239, 257, 268, 269, 274, 324, 327–329, 335, 340, 343, 383, 385, 399*
Originally N.E. America only, but introduced elsewhere. Essentially a freshwater fish, but may go to sea. Found in cold swift streams. When in lakes, prefers shallow water. Preferred temperature 11–16°C (MacCrimmon and Campbell, 1969) or variously reported in Coutant's review as lying between 8 and 20°C, avoiding temperatures above 20°C or below 14°C.
Alk-1-enylacylglycerophosphatidyl choline 1849; Alk-1-enylacylglycerophosphatidyl ethanolamine 1849; Amylase 2936, 2937; Arginase 2936, 2937; Bicarbonate 2262; Calcium 2262–2264, 2636; Chloride 2262, 2664; Cholesterol 2637; Copper 2636; DNA 3203; Diacylglycerophosphatidyl choline 1849; Diacylglycerophosphatidyl ethanolamine 1849; Fatty acids 1471, 1849; *Free* fatty acids 2637; Glucose 2262; Glucose-6-phosphate dehydrogenase 3684; Glutamate-oxaloacetate transaminase 2664, 2936, 2937; Glutamate-pyruvate transaminase 2936, 2937; Glycogen 3076; Gonadotropin 1760, 2906; Guanine 1867, 1966; Haematocrit 2262, 2664; Haemoglobin 2664; Hexose-6-phosphate dehydrogenase 3345, 3684; Hypoxanthine 1867, 1966; Inosine 1966; Inosinic acid 1966; Lactate 1950, 2262, 3076; Lactic dehydrogenase 3203; Magnesium 2262–2264, 2636; Manganese 2636; Mercury 2252; Ornithine aminotransferase 3611; 6-Phosphogluconate dehydrogenase 3203, 3684; Phosphoglucose isomerase 3203; Potassium 2262–2264, 2636; Protease 2936, 2937; RNA 3203; Sodium 2262–2264, 2636; Thyroxine 2190, 3618; Zinc 2636

Salvelinus leucomaenis
Sakhalin (Russia).
Calcium 2864; Fatty acids 2951; Magnesium 2864; Potassium 2864; Sodium 2864

‡Salvelinus malma* (Dolly Varden, Malma trout)
Waters of Kamchatka and Alaska, descending to the sea. Some populations remain in fresh water. Males mature earlier than females. Diet: mainly fish.
Magnesium 2864; Mercury 1557; Potassium 2864; Sodium 2864

‡Salvelinus namaycush namaycush* = Cristivomer namaycush* (Lake char, Lake trout, Mackinaw trout) *34, 35, 406, 438*

N. America: Lake Superior, Lake Michigan. Usually freshwater, but occasionally anadromous. Preferred temperature 11·7°C (McCauley and Tait, 1970), or lying between 10 and 15°C according to Coutant's review.
Amylase 2936; Arginase 2936; Arsenic 2611; Bicarbonate 2217; Bromide 2611; Cadmium 2611; Calcium 2264; Chloride 2217, 2264; Cobalt 2611; Copper 2611; Glutamate-oxaloacetate transaminase 2936; Glutamate-pyruvate transaminase 2936; Haematocrit 2217, 3316; Haemoglobin 2217, 3316; Hexose-6-phosphate dehydrogenase 3345; Magnesium 2264; Mercury 1557, 3529; Potassium 2264; Protease 2936; Sodium 2264; "Sugar" 1548, 2509; Thorium 2611; Uranium 2611; Zinc 2611

‡*Salvelinus namaycush siscowet* (Siscowet trout)
N. America. All intermediate stages between the two S. namaycush varieties are found. The main characteristic of this one is an extremely high lipid content.
Volume 1 only

Salvelinus pluvius
Amylase, Arginase, Glutamate-oxaloacetate transaminase, Glutamate-pyruvate transaminase, Protease: 2936

‡*Salvelinus willughbii* (Char, Windermere char) *267*
England: Lake Windermere. May not be genetically different from S. alpinus. Divided into spring- and autumn spawners.
Volume 1 only

Sander lucioperca 155, 158

‡Sarda sarda (Atlantic bonito, Cape Katonkel, Pelamid, Shortfinned tunny)
Atlantic: Shetland to S. Africa, Mediterranean, Black Sea, Newfoundland to Uruguay. Strongly migratory. Shoaling predators. Often jump clear of the water. Usually found in water of 15–24°C. Diet: pilchards, scad, grey mullet.
DNA 2195

Sarda velox
DNA 2195

‡Sardina pilchardus (Pilchard when large, Sardine when small) *208*
Norway to Britain and Canary Is. down to 55 m. Black and Mediterranean Seas. Pelagic, migratory; may enter brackish water. Diet: plankton, crustaceans, fish eggs. Cadmium 1707, 1709; Chromium 2015; Copper 1707–1709; Fatty acids 1731; Lactic dehydrogenase 1789; Lead 1707–1709, 2015; Mercury 1707–1709, 1891, 2015; Zinc 1707–1709

‡Sardinella albella (Short-bodied sardine, White sardinella)
Red Sea to India; Taiwan to N. Australia. Coastal waters, pelagic.
Volume 1 only

‡Sardinella aurita (Gilt sardine, Golden sardine)
Both sides of Atlantic. Portugal to S. Africa, Mediterranean. Surface waters.
Choline 3125; Cyanocobalamin 3125; Folic acid 3125; Phosphatidyl choline 3064;

Phosphatidyl ethanolamine 3064; Phosphatidyl inositol 3064; Phosphatidyl serine 3064; Polyglycerophosphatides 3064; Sphingomyelin 3064

‡Sardinella eba
   Portugal.
   Volume 1 only

‡Sardinella fimbriata (Fringe-scale sardine)
   Red Sea, India, Malaya, perhaps northern tip of Australia. Coastal waters.
   Volume 1 only

‡Sardinella longiceps (Indian sardine, Oil sardine)
   E. Africa, India, Malaya, Philippines, Java. Coastal waters, pelagic. Diet: plankton,
   especially diatoms.
   Lysophosphatidyl choline, Phosphatidic acids, Phosphatidyl choline, Phosphatidyl
   ethanolamine, Phosphatidyl inositol, Phosphatidyl serine, Phospholipid, Sphingomyelin: 2042

‡Sardinella perforata (Perforated scale sardine)
   S. Arabia, Malaya, Thailand, Sumatra, Java, Borneo, Philippines, China. Coastal
   waters.
   Volume 1 only

Sardinella sirm (Indian sardine, Spotted sardinella)
   E. Africa to Indo-Australian archipelago, north to Okinawa. Coastal waters.
   Pelagic.
   Folic acid 2582

Sardinia melanosticta (see Sardinops melanosticta)

‡Sardinops caeruleus (California sardine, Pacific sardine, Pilchard)
   S. California to S.E. Alaska. Filter-feeder, straining minute plants and animals
   through its gill-rakers.
   Pantothenic acid, Pyridoxine: 3211

Sardinops melanosticta = Sardinia melanosticta (True sardine) *72, 75, 442, 459*
   Japan, Korea. Pelagic. Diet: diatoms, crustaceans.
   Amino acids 3101; Anserine 3368; Arsenic 3402; Cadmium 2901; Copper 2901,
   3402; α-Cryptoxanthin 2718; Dimethylamine 3439; Fatty acids 2151; *Free*
   histidine 3166; Iron 2901; Lead 2901, 3402; Lutein 2718; Magnesium 2462, 2463;
   Manganese 3402; Mercury 3402; Potassium 2900; Sodium 2900; Thiaminase
   2297; Trimethylamine 2388, 3439; Trimethylamine oxide 2111, 3439; Tunaxanthin
   2718; Vitamin D 2188, 3673; Zeaxanthin 2718; Zinc 2901, 3402

‡Sardinops ocellata (South African pilchard)
   S. Africa. Shore line down to 183 m. Diet: plankton.
   Volume 1 only

Sargus sargus (White bream)
   Adriatic.
   Cadmium 1709; Cholesterol 1785; Copper 1708, 1709; Lead 1708, 1709; Mercury
   1708, 1709; Zinc 1708, 1709

‡Saurida tumbil (Greater lizardfish)
E. Africa, Red Sea, India, Malaya, China, Japan, Australia. A ferocious bottom fish, living on muddy grounds down to 100 m. Diet: bottom-living invertebrates, especially worms, fish.
Cadmium 2901; Copper 2901; Dimethylamine 2110; Formaldehyde 2110; Iron 2901; Lead 2901; Potassium 2900; Sodium 2900; Zinc 2901

‡Saurida undosquamis (Brushtooth lizardfish, Largescaled grinner, True lizardfish)
E. Africa, Japan, Philippines, China, Formosa, Australia; immigrated to E. Mediterranean. Coastal; muddy bottoms to 100 m. Diet: bottom-living invertebrates, fish.
Adenosine monophosphate 1871; Cholesterol 2445; Dimethylamine 2110; Formaldehyde 2110; Inosine monophosphate 1871; Trimethylamine 1871; Trimethylamine oxide 2111

‡Sawara niphonia (Japanese Spanish mackerel, Spotted mackerel)
Japan, Australia.
Volume 1 only

Scaphirhynchus platorynchus (Shovelnose sturgeon)
Mississippi River system. Found only in fresh water.
Arginase 1776; Calcium 2264, 2265; Carbamoyl phosphate synthetase 1777; Chloride 2264, 2265; Cholesterol 2265; DNA 2194; Magnesium 2264, 2265; Potassium 2264, 2265; Sodium 2264, 2265

‡Scardinius erythrophthalmus (Rudd) 63, 267–269, 344, 453
England, Ireland, Germany, Sweden. Europe to Asia Minor, except the Iberian peninsula and S. Italy. Not Iceland or Norway. Still and slowly-flowing waters, sometimes brackish. Hardy, but avoids temperatures above 28·5°C. Diet: aquatic insects, larvae, crustaceans and some plant matter.
Aluminium 2677, 3563; Amino acids 1655; Arginase 2256; Argininosuccinate lyase 2256; Argininosuccinate synthetase 2256; Calcium 1528, 2677, 2864; Carbamoyl phosphate synthetase 2256; Cobalt 2677; Copper 2677, 3563; DNA 3217; Glucose 1607; Glycogen 1607; Hydroxyproline 1655; Iron 2677, 3563; Magnesium 2677, 2864; Manganese 2677; Potassium 2677, 2864; Putrescine 3217; Riboflavin 1465; RNA 3217; Sodium 2864; Spermidine 3217; Spermine 3217; Strontium 1528; Tin 2677; Vanadium 2677; Zinc 2677

Scartelaos histophorus
Arginase, Ornithine carbamoyl transferase: 2071

‡Scarus croicensis (Mottlefin parrotfish, Striped parrotfish)
Florida and Bermuda to Brazil. Found in large shoals on or close to the reef.
Volume 1 only

Scarus cyawgnathus (Parrotfish)
Japan.
Amino acids in biliverdin 3669

Scarus gibbus (Parrot fish)
Japan. Poisonous to eat. The flesh contains mostly scaritoxin, while the gut contents and liver contain ciguatoxin (Yasumoto, Nakajima et al., 1977).
Amino acids in biliverdin 3669

‡Scarus guacamaia (Parrot fish, Rainbow parrotfish)
    Bermuda, throughout the Caribbean to N. Argentina on reefs. Sometimes reported
    to produce cocoons of mucus for sleeping in at night.
    Volume 1 only

Scarus jonesi *152*
    Marshall Is. A coral reef fish which feeds on coral.
    Carbonic anhydrase 3309

‡Scarus mechipunctatus
    Tanzania, Hong Kong, Sumatra, Java to New Guinea.
    Volume 1 only

Scarus vetula (Queen parrotfish)
    Bermuda, Bahamas, Florida to Caribbean Sea, on reefs. Secretes a mucus envelope
    in which it sleeps at night. Diet: coral growths, algae.
    DNA 2195

Scatophagus argus* (Mia mia, Scat, Spotted butterfish, Spotted scat)
    E. Africa, Indian Ocean to China and Australia, entering rivers. Readily adapts
    to fresh water. Diet: plant matter and bottom detritus.
    DNA 2195: Lysozyme 3173

Schedophilus medusophagus (Barrelfish, Cornish blackfish) *121, 126*
    Atlantic, Mediterranean. Lacks swim bladder. Bones filled with oil: the bones are
    poorly calcified. Pelagic. Diet: medusae, crustaceans.
    Cholesterol, Fatty acids, Phospholipids, Triglycerides: 2538

Schedophilus pemarco
    Amino acids 1812

Schilbe marmoratus
    Africa.
    DNA 2195

‡Sciaena antarctica* (Butterfish, Jewfish, Kingfish, Mulloway, River kingfish, Silver
    jew)
    Australia. Coastal, reefs, ascending rivers.
    Volume 1 only

‡Sciaena aquila (Meagre)
    Shetland and Kattegat southward to Mediterranean, W. coast of Africa to Gulf
    of Guinea. Shallow waters, sometimes entering estuaries.
    Volume 1 only

Sciaena cirrhosa
    E. Atlantic.
    Mercury 1891

‡Sciaena coitor* = Johnius coitor* (Coitor croaker)
India, Burma, Malaya, Sumatra, Java, Australia. Large rivers descending to
inshore and coastal waters of the sea at certain seasons, where it is found down to
40 m. Diet: small fish, invertebrates.
Volume 1 only

Sciaena deliciosa (False whiting)
Japan.
Caesium, Cobalt, Zinc: 2269

‡Sciaena diacanthus* — Protonibea diacanthus* (Spotted croaker, two-spined
jewfish)
E. Africa, India, Malaya and China, Hongkong, Philippines, Australia. Sea and
mouths of rivers. Coastal waters down to 60 m over muddy bottoms. Migratory.
Diet: crustaceans, particularly small crabs.
Volume 1 only

‡Sciaena dussumieri (*see* Johnius dussumieri)

‡Sciaena hololepidota
Volume 1 only

Sciaena ronchus
E. Atlantic.
Mercury 1891

‡Sciaena schlegeli
Japan.
Volume 1 only

Sciaena sp. (Jewfish)
India.
Amino acids 3092

‡Sciaena umbra = Johnius umbra = Corvina nigra (Brown meagre, Corb, Dark
drum)
Mediterranean and Black seas, Atlantic: S. Biscay to Senegal. Enters estuaries.
Coastal, 5–20 m on rocky bottoms. Nocturnally active. Diet: crustaceans, molluscs,
occasionally fish.
Adrenaline 3340; Corticosterone + Cortisol 1704; Noradrenaline 3340

‡Sciaenoides brunneus* = Otolithoides biauritus (Bronze croaker)
India, Malaya, Sumatra, China. Enters mouths of rivers from sea. Diet: fish,
invertebrates.
Volume 1 only

‡Sciaenops ocellata (Bass, Channel bass, Red bass, Red drum, Redfish, Sea bass,
Spot-tail, Spotted bass) *26, 459*
S. Atlantic and Gulf coasts of United States, Texas to New Jersey, on sandy shores.
Erythrocytes, Haematocrit, Haemoglobin: 1647

Scoliodon palasorrah
Red Sea.
Fatty acids 1449

‡**Scoliodon walbeehmii** (Milk shark, Sharpnosed shark)
Japan, Indian Ocean.
Volume 1 only

Scomber australasicus (*see* S. japonicus) *88, 433*

Scomber colias (*see* S. japonicus) *72–74, 79*

Scomber japonicus = Pneumatophorus colias = Pneumatophorus diego = Scomber australasicus = Scomber colias (Chub mackerel, Japanese mackerel, Matreel, Pacific mackerel, Slimy mackerel, Spanish mackerel) *69, 72–75, 79, 88, 459*
Japan, Formosa, Korea. Chile to Gulf of Alaska, Red Sea, Indian and Pacific Oceans, Mediterranean. Coastal, fairly shallow water down to 45 m. Migratory. Gluttonous feeder. Diet: small fish, crustaceans.
Adenosine diphosphate 2456; Adenosine monophosphate 2456; Adenosine triphosphate 1499, 2456; Amino acids 2456, 3441; *Free* amino acids 2456, 2687, 3166; Ammonia 2456; Arsenic 3402; Cadmium 2901; Caesium 2269; Calcium 3386, 3486; β-Carotene 2716; Cathepsin 1924; Cholesterol 1785, 2445; Cobalt 2269; Copper 2901, 3402; Creatin 2456; Creatinine 2456; Cynthiaxanthin 2716; Diacyl glyceryl ethers 2399; Dimethylamine 3439; Esterase 2782, 2843; Fatty acids 3389, 3485, 3667; *Free* fatty acids 2399, 3389; Saturated fatty acids 3389; *Free* fatty alcohols 2399; α-Glucosidase 2843; Partial glycerides 2399; *Free* histidine 3166; Hyaluronidase 2436; Inosine monophosphate 2456; Iron 2901, 3441; Lead 2901, 3402; Lipase 2872; Lutein 2716; Magnesium 3386; Manganese 3402; Mercury 2888, 3402; Monoenoic acids 3389; Neutral lipids 3389; NAD (nicotinamide adenine dinucleotide 3259; NADH (reduced NAD) 3259; Phosphatase 2843; Phospholipid 2399, 3389; Polyenoic acids 3389; Potassium 2900; Protease 2843; Selenium 2888; Sodium 2900; Sterols 2399; Sterol esters 2399; Strontium 3486; Taurine 2456, 3166; Threonine aldolase 2835; Triglycerides 2399; Trimethylamine 2456, 3439; Trimethylamine oxide 2111, 2456, 3151, 3439; Tunaxanthin 2716; Vitamin D 2188, 3673; Wax esters 2399; Zinc 2269, 2901, 3402

‡Scomber scombrus (Atlantic mackerel) *53, 68, 73, 74, 89, 91, 110, 150, 444*
Both sides of N. Atlantic, including Iceland; restricted to continental shelf. Mediterranean and Black seas. Avoids colder waters. Pelagic in large shoals. Relies on continuous swimming for its oxygen supply. Does not possess swim bladder, so can perform rapid changes of depth. Lipid reserves are in the muscle and under the skin. Diet: does not feed in winter; in spring feeds mainly on zooplankton; after spawning feeds on small herrings, sprats and sand eels.
Amino acids 1412, 3101; Cadmium 1707, 1709; Calcium 1909, 3294; Cardiolipid 3233; Chloride 1909, 3294; Cholesterol 2117, 2515; Chromium 2015; Cobalt 2491; Copper 1707–1709, 2491, 3294; Cytochrome oxidase 2011; DNA 2195; Diglycerides 2117; Fatty acids 1413, 2117; *Free* fatty acids 2117, 2515; Fluoride 3294; Formaldehyde 1656; Glucose 2516; Glycogen 3643; Haematocrit 2516; Haemoglobin 2516; Histamine 2120; Iodide 3294; Iron 2491; Lactate 1789, 2516; Lactic dehydrogenase 1789, 2011; Lead 1707–1709, 2015; Lyso-phosphatidyl

ethanolamine 3233; Magnesium 1909, 2462, 2463, 3294; Manganese 2491, 3294; Mercury 1707–1709, 1953, 2015, 2482; Monoglycerides 2117; Neutral lipids 2117; Nickel 2491; Pantothenic acid 3211; Phosphatidic acid 3233; Phosphatidyl choline 3233; Phosphatidyl inositol 3233; Phosphatidyl serine 3233; Phospholipid 2117; Pyruvate 1789; Pyruvate kinase 2011; Pyridoxine 3211; Sodium 1909, 3294; Sphingomyelin 3233; Triglycerides 2117; Urate oxidase 1711; Xanthine oxidase 1711; Zinc 1707–1709, 2491

‡Scomber tapeinocephalus (Spotted mackerel)
Japan, Korea, Formosa.
Volume 1 only

‡Scomberesox saurus (Atlantic saury, Billfish, Needlefish, Saurel, Saury pike, Skipjack, Skipper)
Temperate parts of Atlantic, Pacific and Indian Oceans. Mediterranean. Black Sea. Coast and open sea in shoals near surface. Can leap clear of the water if pursued. Diet: small fish and crustaceans.
Arsenic 2534; Antimony 2534; Cadmium 2534; Calcium 3057; Iron 3057; Mercury 2534

‡Scomberoides lysan
Red Sea, Tanzania, India, Thailand, Philippines, Formosa, N. Australia.
Volume 1 only

‡Scomberomorus cavalla (Kingfish, King mackerel)
Atlantic coast of N. America: Cape Cod to Brazil. Seaward side of reefs or offshore. Active swimmer, pursuing schools of smaller fish for food.
DNA 2195

‡Scomberomorus commersonii = Cybium commersonii (Barracuta, Barred Spanish mackerel, Doggie, Katonkel, Kingfish, Serra, Snook)
Madagascar, Tanzania, Red Sea, India, Philippines, China, Japan, Queensland, Tasmania, Fiji. Sea and brackish water. Migrates seasonally. Pelagic in schools, 15–200 m. Diet: small schooling fish such as sardines, anchovies.
Calcium 2313; Folic acid 2582; Iron 2313; Niacin 2313; Riboflavin 2313; Thiamine 2313

‡Scomberomorus guttatus* (Indo-Pacific Spanish mackerel, Spotted Spanish mackerel)
India, Malaya, Sumatra, Java, Borneo, China. Not New Guinea or Australia. Seas and coastal waters between 15 and 200 m, entering rivers. Diet: small schooling fish, squid, crustaceans.
Volume 1 only

‡Scomberomorus maculatus (Bay mackerel, Spanish mackerel, Spotted cybium, Spotted mackerel)
E. United States, Maine to Brazil. W. African coast, occasionally entering estuaries. Mainly prefers open water.
Aldehyde oxidase 2468; Arsenic 3638; Cadmium 3638; Copper 3638; Mercury 3638; Xanthine oxidase 2468; Zinc 3638

‡Scomberomorus niphonius (Spanish mackerel)
Japan, Korea, China.
Volume 1 only

‡Scomberomorus regalis (Black-spotted Spanish mackerel, Kingfish, Painted mackerel, Sierra, Spotted cero)
E. America: Cape Cod to Brazil, Cuba. Comes close inshore over reefs, active swimmer. Diet: small clupeoid fish.
DNA 2195; Haematocrit 3377; Haemoglobin 3377

‡Scombrops boops (Bigeye, Japanese bluefish)
Japan.
α-Cryptoxanthin 2716; α-Doradecin 2716; Lutein 2716; Pyridine nucleotide transhydrogenase 3167; Thiaminase 3473; Tunaxanthin 2716

Scophthalmus aquosus (Brill, Sand flounder, Spotted flounder, Window pane)
Eastern N. America: Gulf of St. Lawrence to S. Carolina. Shallow water on sandy bottom. Tolerates wide range of temperatures. Diet: mysids, shrimps, small fish.
Chloride, Sodium: 1860

‡Scophthalmus maeoticus (Black Sea turbot) *112*
Black Sea, Mediterranean. Down to 100 m. Diet: small fish.
Cyanocobalamin 1522

Scophthalmus maximus (*see* Psetta maxima) *139, 142, 143, 260*

Scophthalmus rhombus (Bass, Brill) *114*
Mid-Norway to Denmark, British Is., N. Africa, Mediterranean and Black seas. Sandy or mixed bottom, 5–50 m. Diet: bottom-living fish, crustaceans, molluscs.
Cadmium 1709; Copper 1709; Lactate 1789; Lactic dehydrogenase 1789; Lead 1709; Mercury 1709; Pyruvate 1789; Urate oxidase 1711; Xanthine oxidase 1711; Zinc 1709

Scorpaena braziliensis
DNA 191

Scorpaena guttata

‡Scorpaena porcus (Black scorpionfish, Rascasse, Rockfish, Sea ruff, Small-scaled scorpionfish) *27, 53, 69, 152, 156, 157, 208, 311*
Mediterranean, Black Sea, Canary Is. to Biscay. Lies among rocks in shallow water. Sedentary and solitary. Dorsal spines possess venom glands.
Adrenaline 3340; Cadmium 1707, 1709; Calcium 2862, 2864; Chitinase 1719; Chloride 2862, 2864; Cholesterol 3245, 3246, 3272; Copper 1707, 1709; Corticosterone + Cortisol 1704; Cyanocobalamin 1522; *Free* fatty acids 3246, 3272; Glycogen 2543, 3049, 3052; Insulin 3052; Lead 1707, 1709; Magnesium 2862, 2864; Mercury 1707, 1709; Noradrenaline 3340; Phospholipids 3245, 3246, 3272; Potassium 2862, 2864, 2875; Sodium 2862, 2864, 2875; Sulphate 2862; Triglycerides 3245, 3246, 3272; Zinc 1707, 1709

‡Scorpaena scrofa (Large-scaled scorpionfish, Rascasse, Red scorpionfish)
France south to Mediterranean and Madeira on sandy or stony ground. 20–200 m.
Rests on the bottom during daytime. Solitary. Preferred temperature 20°C,
avoiding above 26°C or below 8°C.
Cadmium, Copper, Lead, Mercury, Zinc: 1707, 1709

Scorpaena sp.
Cardiolipid 2469; Cerebroside 2469; Fatty acids 2469; Ganglioside 2469; Phos-
phatidyl choline 2469; Phosphatidyl ethanolamine 2469; Phosphatidyl inositol 2469;
Phosphatidyl serine 2469; Sialic acid 2470; Sphingomyelin 2469; Sulphatide 2469

‡Scorpaenichthys marmoratus (Cabezon, Giant marbled sculpin)
S. California to N. British Columbia and S.E. Alaska. Coastal on rocky, sandy or
muddy bottoms. Intertidal to 183 m. Eggs are toxic. Females grow faster than
males. Sluggish. Diet: large variety of crabs, molluscs, fish.
Volume 1 only

Scorpaenoides littoralis
Astacene, β-Carotene, α-Cryptoxanthin, Cynthiaxanthin, Diatoxanthin, α-
Doradecin, Lutein, Tunaxanthin, Zeaxanthin: 2716

‡**Scyliorhinus canicula = Scyllium canicula = Mustelus canis** (Lesser spotted
dogfish, Rough hound, Small spotted dogfish, Smooth dogfish) *155, 235, 246, 310,*
416, 425, 461
Norway to Senegal, Mediterranean. Mainly bottom-living, 3–110 m. Bays and
estuaries, ocean beaches on mud, sand or gravel. Nocturnal. Diet: small fish,
crustaceans, molluscs.
Acid mucopolysaccharides 3344; Mg-ATPase (magnesium-activated adenosine
triphosphatase) 2075; Na-K-ATPase 2075; Adrenaline 2739; Aldehyde oxidase
2468; Amino acids 1620, 3152; Amino butyric acid 2943; δ-Amino laevulinic
dehydratase 1907; Arginase 1653, 2256; Argininosuccinate lyase 2256; Argininosuccinate synthetase 2256; Bicarbonate 2692; Blast cells 1907; Calcium 2692;
Carbamoyl phosphate synthetase 1443, 3587; Cardiolipid 3233; Chloride
1438, 2692, 2997; Cholesterol 1987, 2761; Chondroitin sulphate 3344;
DNA 2194; *Free* fatty acids 1987; Formaldehyde 1656; Fructose-1,6-diphosphat-
ase 2685; Fucose 2770; Galactosamine 2770; Galactose 2770; Glucosamine 2770;
Glucose 2692, 2770, 3664; Glutamate 2944; Glutamate oxaloacetate transaminase
2685; Glycerol-3-phosphate dehydrogenase 1744; Glycine 2944; Granulocytes
1907; Haematocrit 1907; Haemoglobin 1907; Heparitin sulphate 3344; Hexokinase 1744; Hexosamines 1678, 2770; Hexoses 2770; Hyaluronic acid 3344;
Hydrocarbons 1987; Hydroxyproline 2770, 3152; Isocitrate dehydrogenase 2685;
Lactic dehydrogenase 1744, 1789, 2685, 3551; Leucocytes 1907; Lymphocytes
1907; Magnesium 2692; Malic dehydrogenase 2685; Mannose 2770; Noradrenaline 2739; Ornithine transcarbamoylase 2256; Phosphatidic acid 3233; Phosphatidyl choline 3233; Phosphatidyl ethanolamine 3233; Phosphatidyl inositol 3233;
Phosphatidyl serine 3233; Phosphofructokinase 1744, 2685, 3551; Phospholipids
2761; Phosphorylase 1744; Potassium 2562, 2692; Pyruvate kinase 3551; Sodium
2562, 2692, 2997; Sphingomyelin 3233; Sulphate 2692; Taurine 2943; Thrombocytes 1907; Triglycerides 1987, 2761; Tri-isophosphate dehydrogenase 3551;
Trimethylamine oxide 3151; Urate oxidase 1711; Urea 2692, 2997, 3587; Uronic
acid 1678, 2770; Xanthine oxidase 1711, 2468

‡**Scyliorhinus stellaris** = **Scyllium catulus** (Bounce, Bull huss, Greater spotted
   dogfish, Huss, Nursehound) *4, 114, 310*
   Britain to Biscay, Mediterranean. Inshore to 60 m on rough ground. Nocturnal,
   scavenging. Eggs laid in cases. Diet: crabs, squid, fish.
   Carbamoyl phosphate synthetase 3587; Carbon dioxide 3041; Chloride 3041;
   Lactate 3040, 3041; Potassium 2562; Sodium 2562, 3041; Urea 3587

‡**Scyliorhinus torazame** (Tiger shark)
   Japan, Korea. Cold waters.
   Volume 1 only

‡**Scyllium canicula** (*see* **Scyliorhinus canicula**)

‡**Scyllium catulus** (*see* **Scyliorhinus stellaris**)

‡**Scyllium stellare** (*see* **Scyliorhinus stellaris**)

‡**Scymnodon jonsonii**
   Europe.
   Volume 1 only

‡**Scymnodon squamulosus**
   Japan.
   Volume 1 only

‡**Scymnorhinus licha**
   Japan.
   Volume 1 only

Sebastes aleutianus (Rougheye rockfish)
   California to Aleutian Is., 92–732 m. Common offshore, rare inshore.
   Mercury 1697

Sebastes auriculatus (Brown rockfish)
   California to Alaska. Viviparous.
   Cytochrome oxidase, Lactic dehydrogenase, Pyruvate kinase: 3630

‡Sebastes baramenuke
   Japan.
   Fatty acids, Neutral lipids: 2153

Sebastes caurinus
   D-Amino acid oxidase 1923; Glutamine synthetase 3592

‡Sebastes dactylopterus = Helicolenus dactylopterus (Rockfish)
   British Is. to Cape Verde. Bottom-living, 200–800 m.
   Volume 1 only

Sebastes diploproa (Splitnose rockfish)
   D-Amino acid oxidase 1923

‡Sebastes flammeus (Rockfish)
  Japan.
  Volume 1 only

Sebastes flavidus (Yellowtail rockfish)
  California to Alaska, Kodiak and Admiralty Is. Viviparous. Diet: lanternfish,
  crustaceans, squid.
  Mercury 1697

‡Sebastes inermis (Black rockfish, Japanese broun, Stingfish) Probably the same as
  Sebastodes inermis, but data given under the latter name are listed separately. *72,
  75, 76*
  Japan.
  FREE amino acids 3166; Arsenic 1703; Astacene 2716; β-Carotene 2716; Copper
  1703; α-Cryptoxanthin 2716; Cynthiaxanthin 2716; Diatoxanthin 2716; Dime-
  thylamine 3439; α-Doradecin 2716; Lead 1703; Lutein 2716; Manganese 1703;
  Mercury 1703; Taurine 3166; Trimethylamine 3439; Trimethylamine oxide 3439;
  Tunaxanthin 2716; Zeaxanthin 2716; Zinc 1703

Sebastes maliger (Quillback rockfish)
  D-Amino acid oxidase 1923; "Sugar" 3619

‡Sebastes marinus (Norway haddock, Ocean perch, Redfish, Rosefish, Soldier) *122,
  207*
  Both sides of N. Atlantic, in cold waters of gullies and deep water slopes, 100–640 m.
  During daylight close to sea bottom on muddy or rocky ground, pelagic at night.
  Virtually always dead on landing because expanded swim bladder forces stomach
  out of mouth. Diet: pelagic crustaceans, arrow worms, cod spawn, herrings,
  capelin.
  FREE amino acids 2977; Anserine 2977; Arsenic 1631; Cadmium 1631; Calcium
  3294; Carnosine 2977; Cholesterol 1785; Cobalt 2491; Copper 2491; Fatty acids
  2504; Iron 2491, 3294; Lead 1631; Manganese 2491; Mercury 1631, 1953, 2482;
  Ornithine 2977; Potassium 3294; Sarcosine 2977; Sodium 3294; Taurine 2977;
  Trimethylamine oxide 3151; Zinc 2491, 3610

‡Sebastes matsubarae
  Japan.
  Vitamin D 3673

Sebastes mentella
  Europe.
  Mercury 2482

Sebastes miniatus (Vermilion rockfish) Probably the same as Sebastodes miniatus, but
  data given under the latter name are listed separately.
  California to Vancouver Is., 183–274 m.
  Cytochrome oxidase, Lactic dehydrogenase, Pyruvate kinase: 3630

Sebastes pinniger (Canary rockfish)
  California to Alaska, 91–364 m on hard bottoms.
  Mercury 1697

Sebastes ruberrimus *121*
  Canada. Possesses 12–49% of lipid in bones (dry weight).
  Fatty acids, Phospholipids, Sterols, Triglycerides: 3031

Sebastes rubrivinctus (Flag rockfish)
  Oregon.
  Mercury 1697

Sebastes saxicola (Stripetail rockfish)
  D-Amino acid oxidase 1923

Sebastes sp.
  Arsenic 2535

‡Sebastes thompsoni (Black rockfish)
  Astaxanthin diester 3466

Sebastes viviparus (Norway haddock)
  Norway, S. Iceland to Oslo and S. Ireland. Coastal and bottom-living, 50–300 m.
  Chloride 1909; Fatty acids 3118; Magnesium 1909; Potassium 1909; Sodium 1909

‡Sebastes vulpes (Sometimes given as Sebastichthys vulpes)
  Japan.
  Collagen 3462; Connective tissue 3462; DNA 2282; Elastin 3462; RNA 2282

‡Sebastichthys capensis (Jacopever)
  Atlantic coast of S. Africa, 37–274 m.
  Volume 1 only

‡Sebastiscus albofasciatus
  Japan.
  Volume 1 only

Sebastiscus marmoratus (Rockfish, Scorpionfish) *49, 50, 57, 239, 286*
  Japan, Korea, China. Shores, rocky bottoms. Viviparous.
  Astaxanthin 2716, 3466; Cadmium 2901; β-Carotene 2716; Copper 2901;
  α-Cryptoxanthin 2716; Cynthiaxanthin 2716; Diatoxanthin 2716; α-Doradecin
  2716; Iron 2901; Lead 2901; Lutein 2716; Potassium 2900; Pyridine nucleotide
  transhydrogenase 3167; Sodium 2900; Trimethylamine oxide 2111; Tunaxanthin
  2716; Zeaxanthin 2716; Zinc 2901

‡Sebastodes alaskanus
  N. America.
  Volume 1 only

‡Sebastodes alutus (Longjaw rockfish, Pacific Ocean perch)
  S. California to Bering Sea.
  Volume 1 only

‡Sebastodes baramenuke (*see* Sebastes baramenuke)

‡Sebastodes caurinus (Copper rockfish)
   S. California to S.E. Alaska.
   Volume 1 only

Sebastodes dalli
   DNA 2195

‡Sebastodes elongatus (Greenstriped rockfish)
   S. California to Strait of Georgia. Fairly deep waters.
   Volume 1 only

‡Sebastodes flammeus
   Japan.
   Volume 1 only

‡Sebastodes flavidus (Yellowtail rockfish)
   S. California to Vancouver Is.
   Volume 1 only

‡Sebastodes goodei (Chili-pepper)
   Coast of California.
   Volume 1 only

Sebastodes güntherii
   Japan.
   Calcium, Strontium: 3406

‡Sebastodes inermis (Japanese stingfish) See also Sebastes inermis
   Japan.
   Caesium, Cobalt, Zinc: 2269

‡Sebastodes iracundus
   Japan.
   Volume 1 only

‡Sebastodes maliger (Orange-spotted rockfish, Quillback rockfish)
   S. California to Gulf of Alaska, down to 273 m.
   Volume 1 only

‡Sebastodes matsubarae (Matsubara stingfish) Probably the same as Sebastes
   matsubarae.
   Japan. Deep waters.
   Volume 1 only

‡Sebastodes melanops (Black rockfish)
   N. California to Gulf of Alaska. Shores, among rocks.
   D-Amino acid oxidase 1923; Ornithine aminotransferase 3611

Sebastodes miniatus (Vermilion rockfish) Probably the same as Sebastes miniatus,
   which is listed separately.
   California to Vancouver, 183–274 m.
   Carbon dioxide (gas), Carbonic anhydrase, Chloride, Glucose, Glycogen, Haematocrit, Lactate, Nitrogen gas, Oxygen gas, Potassium, Sodium: 1794

‡Sebastodes paucispinis (Bocaccio)
   S. California to Queen Charlotte Sound, below 364 m.
   DNA 2195

‡Sebastodes pinniger (Canary rockfish, Orange rockfish)
   California to Alaska, 91–364 m on hard bottoms.
   DNA 2195

‡Sebastodes ruberrimus (Rasphead rockfish, Red cod, Red snapper, Turkey rockfish)
   Probably the same as Sebastes ruberrimus, which is listed separately.
   S. California to Gulf of Alaska.
   Glutamate-oxaloacetate transaminase, α-Hydroxybutyrate dehydrogenase, Lactic
   dehydrogenase: 2696

  Sebastodes schlegeli (Black rockfish)
   Japan.
   Calcium, Strontium: 3486

‡Sebastolobus macrochir (Channel rockfish, Spinycheek)
   Japan.
   Astaxanthin diester 3466; Calcium 3486; Fatty acids 3666, 3667; Strontium 3486;
   Trimethylamine 2388

‡Sebastopyr ruberrimus (Red rockfish, Tambor)
   Pacific coast of N. America.
   Volume 1 only

‡**Selachus maximus** (*see* **Cetorhinus maximus**) *309*

‡Selar crumenophthalmus = Caranx crumenophthalmus (Bigeye scad, Goggle-eye
   Jack).
   S.E. Asia, W. Indies, Pacific coast of Mexico, Portugal, usually over shallow reefs
   and inshore where the water is cloudy, down to 80 m. An active, schooling fish.
   Diet: crustaceans, fish.
   Volume 1 only

‡Selene vomer (Atlantic lookdown, Horsehead, Moonfish)
   Warm waters of the Atlantic and Pacific coasts of the Americas, in shallow water
   over soft, sandy or muddy bottoms.
   Volume 1 only

‡*Semotilus atromaculatus* (Creek chub, Horned dace, Mud chub, Silver chub) *334*
   N. America: Maine, New Jersey, Kansas, Wyoming. Small clear brooks, shore
   waters of small lakes. Omnivorous, hardy.

‡Seriola aureovittata (Yellowtail)
   Japan, Korea, warm waters.
   Free amino acids, Anserine, Carnosine, Creatin + Creatinine, Taurine: 3369

‡Seriola dorsalis (White salmon, Yellowtail)
　　Pacific coast of N. America, Santa Barbara Is. Surface to 24 m. Active predator.
　　Diet: squid, sardine, mackerel, swimming crabs and other animals.
　　Volume 1 only

‡Seriola dumerili (Amberjack, Rudderfish, Yellowtail)
　　Mediterranean to W. Indies, Massachusetts to Brazil. Found in small fast-swimming
　　groups, usually around rocks, inshore and in deep water. Migratory. A roving
　　predator feeding extensively on fish.
　　Volume 1 only

‡Seriola purpurascens (Allied kingfish, Amberjack, Rudderfish)
　　Japan, Korea, Australia. Fast-swimming.
　　　Free amino acids 3369; Anserine 3369; Carnosine 3369; Creatin + Creatinine
　　3369; Taurine 3369; Thiaminase 3473

‡Seriola quinqueradiata (Amberfish, Yellowtail) *69, 72, 73, 75, 140, 184, 221, 232,
239, 258, 286, 312, 459*
　　Japan, Formosa. Osmotic pressure of the serum changes according to that of the
　　environment.
　　Adenosine diphosphate 1871, 2918; Adenosine monophosphate 1871, 2918;
　　Adenosine triphosphate 1871, 2918; Amino acids 3393; *Free* amino acids 1882,
　　3369; Amylase 2480, 3256; Anserine 3369; Arsenic 3402; Caesium 2269; Calcium
　　2278, 3406; Carnosine 3369; Chloride 2278; Cholesterol 2445, 3162; Cobalt 2269;
　　Copper 3402; Creatin 1882; Creatin + Creatinine 3369; DNA 2282; Dimethyl-
　　amine 3439; Esterase 2782; Fatty acids 3389; *Free* fatty acids 2278, 3389;
　　Saturated fatty acids 3389; Fructose-1,6-diphosphatase 3256; β-Galactosidase
　　2480; Glucose 2278; Glucose dehydrogenase 2836, 2837; Glucose-6-phosphatase
　　3256; Glucose-6-phosphate dehydrogenase 2837, 3256, 3258; β-Glucosidase 3480;
　　Glutamate oxaloacetate transaminase 3162; Glutamate pyruvate transaminase
　　3162; Glycogen 3162; Haematocrit 2846; Hexokinase 2836; *Free* histidine 1882,
　　3166; Hyaluronidase 2436; Inosine monophosphate 1871, 2918; Lead 3402;
　　Lipase 2782; β-Lipoprotein 3162; Magnesium 2278; Manganese 3402; Mercury
　　3402; Monoenoic acids 3389; Neutral lipids 3389; NAD (nicotinamide adenine
　　dinucleotide) 3259; NADH (reduced NAD) 3259; Pepsin 3256; Phosphatase 1408;
　　Phosphofructokinase 3256; Phosphogluconate dehydrogenase 3256; Phospho-
　　glucose isomerase 3256; Phospholipid 3389; Polyenoic acids 3389; Potassium 2278;
　　Purine nucleosidase 1408; Pyridine nucleotide transhydrogenase 3167; Pyrophos-
　　phatase 1408; Pyruvate 2298; DNA 2282; Sodium 2278; Strontium 3486; Taurine
　　1882, 3369; Thiaminase 3473; Thiamine 2298; Triglycerides 3162; Trimethyl-
　　amine 3439; Trimethylamine oxide 1882, 3439; Trypsin 3256; Ubiquinone 2186;
　　Vitamin D 2188, 3637; Vitamin E 2186; Zinc 2269, 3402

Seriolella violacea
　　Amino acids 1812

‡Serranus aeneus
　　Europe.
　　Volume 1 only

Serranus atrarius
    Glucose 3664

Serranus cabrilla (Cabrilla seabass)
    Mediterranean, English Channel to Angola, rarely Black Sea. Sedentary. Found in
    shallow coastal waters over rocky uneven grounds, also deeper waters down to
    500 m over mud and coral. A simultaneous hermaphrodite. Diet: cephalopods,
    fish, crustaceans.
    Cadmium 1707; Copper 1707; 11 β-Hydroxytestosterone 2273; Lead 1707;
    Mercury 1707; Zinc 1707

Serranus gigas
    Mediterranean.
    Formaldehyde 1656

‡Serranus scriba (Banded seaperch, Painted comber) *383*, *423*
    Mediterranean, Black Sea, E. Atlantic north to Biscay. Above 30 m amongst rocks,
    sand or sea-grass. Hermaphrodite. Aggressive and hardy.
    Adrenaline + Noradrenaline 3474; Cholinesterase 3474; Glucose kinase 3551;
    Glucose-6-phosphate dehydrogenase 3551; Glycogen 2797; Isocitrate dehydro-
    genase 3551; Lactic dehydrogenase 3551; Phosphofructokinase 3551; Phosphory-
    lase 3551; Pyruvate kinase 3551; Tri-isophosphate dehydrogenase 3551

Serrivomer sector (Snipe eel)
    America.
    Mercury 3626

Sicyases sanguineus (Chilean clingfish) *154*
    Amphibious.
    Ammonia, Urea: 2049 *Note:* the same data are given in reference 2044

‡Siganus fuscescens
    Japan.
    Volume 1 only

‡Sillaginoides punctatus (King George's whiting, Spotted whiting)
    S. coasts of Australia, in moderate depths on sandy bottoms. An omnivorous
    predator, eating a wide range of invertebrates and fish.
    Volume 1 only

‡Sillago bostockii
    Australia.
    Volume 1 only

‡Sillago japonica (Sand borer)
    Japan.
    Trimethylamine 2388

‡Sillago maculata (Diver whiting, Trumpeter whiting, Winter whiting)
    Australia, New Guinea. Weedy flats or sandy or gravelly sea bottoms. Estuaries.
    Diet: small invertebrates.
    Volume 1 only

Sillago punctata (Spotted whiting)
Australia.
Copper, Zinc: 1893

‡Sillago sihama (Indian whiting, Northern whiting, Sand smelt, Smelt)
Red Sea, Japan, Indo-Pacific. Small bays and estuaries on shallow, sandy bottoms. Often buries itself in the sand, but can skip along surface of the water. Diet: small crustaceans, worms, sand hoppers.
Caesium 2269; Cobalt 2269; *Free* histidine 3166; NAD (Nicotinamide adenine dinucleotide) 3259; NADH (reduced NAD) 3259; Trimethylamine oxide 2111; Vitamin D 3673; Zinc 2269

‡*Silonia silondia* (Silond catfish)
India: lower Ganges. Perhaps Burma. Diet: mainly invertebrates, large specimens eating fish.
Volume 1 only

‡*Silure clarias*
Katanga.
Volume 1 only

‡*Silurus glanis* (Catfish, Sheatfish, Wels) *172, 194*
Central and E. Europe in lakes and large rivers. Quiet, weedy waters with soft bottoms. Solitary. Tolerates brackish water. Chiefly nocturnal, hiding close to bottom by day. Diet: fish, also frogs, crayfish, water voles, ducklings.
Alkaline phosphatase 2773; Aluminium 2677; Amino acids 3433; *Free* amino acids 1507, 3433; Arginase 2256; Argininosuccinate lyase 2256; Argininosuccinate synthetase 2256; Calcium 2677, 2864; Cobalt 2677; Copper 1793, 2677; Fatty acids 2492; Glutamate-oxaloacetate transaminase 2773; Glutamate-pyruvate transaminase 2773; Iron 1793, 2677; Magnesium 2677, 2864; Manganese 1793, 2677; Potassium 2677, 2864; Sarcosine 3433; Sodium 2864; Tin 2677; Vanadium 2677; Zinc 1793, 2677

‡Simenchelys parasiticus (Slime eel, Snubnose eel)
Western N. Atlantic, Long Is. to Newfoundland, on slopes of offshore banks. Azores, S. Africa, W. Pacific off Japan. 700–2640 m. Partially parasitic. Probably also scavenges for food. Very slimy, like hagfish.
Volume 1 only

Solea nascaris nasuta = Pegusa lascaris (Sand sole)
British Isles to Cape of Good Hope, Mediterranean. On muddy ground and sandy bottoms, 6–100 m. Diet: small molluscs, worms, crustaceans.
Cadmium 1707; Calcium 2864; Chloride 2864; Copper 1707; Lead 1707; Mercury 1707; Potassium 2864; Sodium 2864; Zinc 1707

‡Solea solea = S. vulgaris (Dover sole, Sole) *46, 258* (photograph)
Europe: south of Faroe and Bergen to Mediterranean, both inshore and offshore down to 180 m on a soft bottom. Often found in estuaries and littoral ponds. May be killed by winter cold in the North Sea. Males somewhat smaller than females at same age. Lies buried in sand during the day and hunts at night. Diet: thin-shelled bivalves, bristle worms, crustaceans, small fish.

Arginase 2256; Argininosuccinate lyase 2256; Argininosuccinate synthetase 2256; Cadmium 1707, 1709; Chromium 2015; Copper 1707–1709; Formaldehyde 1656; Lactic dehydrogenase 1789; Lead 1707–1709, 2015; Mercury 1707–1709, 1891, 2015; Ornithine transcarbamoylase 2256; Urate oxidase 1711; Xanthine oxidase 1711; Zinc 1707–1709

Solea variegata (Thickback sole)
Europe.
Lactic dehydrogenase 1789

‡**Somniosus microcephalus** = **S. pacificus** (Greenland shark, Ground shark, Gurry shark, Sleeper shark)
S. California to Gulf of Alaska. Japan. Both sides of N. Atlantic and Arctic Oceans. Coastal in winter, deeper waters in summer. Very sluggish. Usually 200–600 m over muddy ground at 0–7°C. Viviparous, voracious, omnivorous. The fresh flesh is poisonous to man, but safe if dried. Diet: prefers cod and halibut, but also eats seals, porpoises, squid, seabirds.
Calcium 1908, 1909; Chloride 1908, 1909; Haematocrit 2516; Haemoglobin 2516; Magnesium 1908, 1909; Potassium 1908, 1909; Sodium 1908, 1909

‡**Somniosus pacificus** (*see* **S. microcephalus**)

Spaliodon sp.
Trimethylamine 3151

‡Sparisoma brachiale
Caribbean.
Volume 1 only

Sparisoma chrysopterum (Red-tailed parrotfish)
Bermuda, shores, inactive.
Succinic dehydrogenase 2750

‡Sparisoma squalidum
S. America.
Volume 1 only

Sparisoma viride
DNA 2195

‡Sparus aries
Japan.
Volume 1 only

Sparus auratus (Gilthead seabream)
British Is. to Senegal; Mediterranean and Black seas. Coastal waters down to 60 m. Diet: molluscs, crustaceans, worms.
Mercury 1891

‡Sparus berda* = Mylio berda* (Black bream, Picnic seabream)
    E. Africa, Red Sea, India, Philippines, China, Japan, Australia, Solomon Is.
    Bottom-living on rough and muddy-sand grounds in coastal waters, especially
    around river mouths. Down to 50 m. Diet: molluscs, crustaceans, worms, echino-
    derms.
    Volume 1 only

‡Sparus latus (*see* Chrysophrys datnia)

‡Sparus macrocephalus
    Japan.
    Volume 1 only

‡Sparus sarba (*see* Rhabdosargus sarba)

‡Sphaeroides maculatus (Balloonfish, Blowfish, Northern puffer, Swellfish)
    Atlantic coast of United States from Florida to Cape Cod. Shallow water on sandy
    bottom, in which it often burrows.
    Ammonia 3303; Creatin 3303; Creatinine 3303; DNA 2195; Mutarotase 1480;
    Potassium 2392; Sodium 2392; "Sugar" 2062; Urea 3303; Uric acid 3303

Sphaeroides nephelus
    DNA 2195

Sphaeroides niphobles (Swellfish)
    Cryptoxanthin, α-Cryptoxanthin, Cynthiaxanthin, Diatoxanthin, α-Doradecin,
    Lutein, Tunaxanthin, Zeaxanthin: 2725

‡Sphaeroides pardalis
    Japan.
    Volume 1 only

‡Sphaeroides spadiceus
    Japan.
    Volume 1 only

‡Sphaeroides spengleri (Southern puffer, Swelltoad, Tambor)
    Portugal, W. Indies, Madeiras, Canaries.
    Fatty acids 2469; Gangliosides 2469; Potassium 2392; Sialic acid 2470; Sodium
    2392

‡Sphaeroides vermicularis
    Japan.
    Volume 1 only

‡Sphyraena argentea (California barracuda, Pacific barracuda)
    S. California to Gulf of Alaska. Coastal. Female spawns several times during the
    season. Surface to 18 m, close to shore. Voracious feeder.
    DNA 2195; *Free* histidine 3166

‡Sphyraena barracuda (Great barracuda)
All tropical seas except E. Pacific. Common on Atlantic coast of S. America, W. Indies. Usually solitary, but may shoal. Ferocious. Inactive for much of the time. Diet: fish, some of which are toxic to man; the flesh of this fish is accordingly sometimes toxic also.
Cholesterol 1785; Haematocrit 3377; Haemoglobin 3377

Sphyraena borealis
DNA 2195

‡Sphyraena guachancho (Guachanche)
Portugal, W. Indies, New England to Brazil. Usually found in small shoals in turbid water along silty shores.
Volume 1 only

‡Sphyraena japonica (Japanese barracuda, Seapike, Snook)
Japan.
Calcium 3386; Magnesium 3386; NAD (nicotinamide adenine dinucleotide) 3259; NADH (reduced NAD) 3259; Trimethylamine 2388

‡Sphyraena jello (Banded barracuda, Dingo fish, Giant seapike, Pickhandle barracuda, Slender seapike)
Natal, Seychelles, Madagascar, Red Sea, India, Malaya, China, Philippines, Australia. Sea and brackish water. Savage. Often swims near the surface. Diet: fish.
Volume 1 only

‡Sphyraena obtusata (Blunt-jawed seapike, Obtuse barracuda, Striped barracuda)
E. Africa, Red Sea, India, Thailand, China, Philippines, Australia, New Zealand, Fiji. A coastal species which enters estuaries. Diet: fish.
Folic acid 2582

Sphyraena picuda
Japan.
Fatty acids 3568

Sphyraena picudilla
Cardiolipid 2469; Cerebroside 2469, 2470; Fatty acids 2469; Ganglioside 2469; Phosphatidyl choline 2469; Phosphatidyl ethanolamine 2469; Phosphatidyl inositol 2469; Phosphatidyl serine 2469; Sialic acid 2469; Sphingomyelin 2469; Sulphatide 2469, 2470

‡Sphyraena pinguis (Good salmon, Japanese dwarf barracuda, Red barracuda)
Japan.
Glucose-6-phosphate dehydrogenase 3258; *Free* histidine 3166

‡Sphyraena schlegeli
Japan.
Cadmium 2901; Copper 2901; Iron 2901; Lead 2901; Potassium 2900; Sodium 2900; Zinc 2901

Sphyrna lewini
  N. Atlantic.
  Arsenic 3638; Cadmium 3638; Copper 3638; DNA 2194; Mercury 3538; Zinc
  3638

‡**Sphyrna malleus** (*see* **S. zygaena**)

‡**Sphyrna tiburo** (Bonnetnose shark, Shovelhead)
  Both sides of Atlantic; central American Pacific coast. Shallow coastal waters.
  Sluggish. Viviparous.
  Arsenic 3638; Cadmium 3638; Copper 3638; DNA 2194; Mercury 3638; Zinc 3638

‡**Sphyrna zygaena** = **S. malleus** (Cross-staff shark, Hammerhead shark, Smooth
  hammerhead)
  Warm parts of Atlantic and Pacific. India. Often seen near the surface, inshore and
  offshore. Found from surface down to 400 m.
  Volume 1 only

Spicara smaris (Picarel, Sea bass, Sea perch, Smarid) *27, 111, 116, 163, 325*
  Mediterranean, Black Sea. Diet: various invertebrates.
  Adrenaline 3340; Amino acids 3527; Corticosterone + Cortisol 1704; Cyanocobalamin 1522; Glycogen 2543, 3049; Insulin 3052; Mercury 1891; Noradrenaline
  3340

‡Spinax niger (*see* Etmopterus spinax)

Spirinchus lanceolatus (Largemouth smelt, Longfin smelt)
  Japan.
  Astacene 2722; β-Carotene 2722; Cryptoxanthin 2722; Cynthiaxanthin 2722;
  Diatoxanthin 2722; Fatty acids 3666, 3667; Lutein 2722; Vitamin E 2185;
  Zeaxanthin 2722

‡Spondyliosoma cantharus = Salpa salpa (Black bream, Black sea bream, Old wife)
  Mid-Norway south to Canaries, Mediterranean and Black seas. Deep water in
  winter, inshore in summer, near rocks. Lives in rather large shoals over seaweed
  or mud.
  Cadmium 1707; Copper 1707; Lactic dehydrogenase 1789; Lead 1707; Mercury
  1707; Zinc 1707

Spratelloides japonicus
  Japan.
  NAD (nicotinamide adenine dinucleotide) 3259; NADH (reduced NAD) 3259;
  Thiaminase 2297

‡Sprattus sprattus (*see* Clupea sprattus)

‡Sprattus sprattus phalericus
  Russia.
  Volume 1 only

‡*Squalius cephalus* (*see Leuciscus cephalus*)

‡**Squalus acanthias** = **Squalus suckleyi** (Atlantic spiny dogfish, Grayfish, Pacific spiny dogfish, Piked dogfish, Spined dogfish, Spur dog) *3, 6, 20, 21, 44, 57, 125, 155, 164, 165, 207, 221, 225, 232, 235, 309, 310, 400, 412, 453*
Wide distribution in cold waters, anywhere between the surface and 950 m, close to bottom on mud. Rather sluggish, but may migrate considerably. Spines slightly poisonous. Vitamin A more concentrated in the livers of older fish. Cannot synthesise trimethylamine oxide from precursors, unlike some other elasmobranchs (Goldstein and Palatt, 1974). Almost all of the salt excretion is done through the rectal gland. Diet: cod, herrings, invertebrates such as squid, jelly fish, crabs.
Adenosine deaminase 2873; Adenosine diphosphate 3219; Adenosine monophosphate 3219; Mg-ATPase (magnesium-activated adenosine triphosphatase) 2321; Na-K-ATPase 2224, 2321, 2377; Adenosine triphosphate 3134, 3219; Adrenaline 3340; Alkyldiacyl glycerol 3180; *Mixed function* amine oxidase 2030; D-Amino acid oxidase 1923; *Free* amino acids 3567; Ammonia 3134, 3567; Arsenic 2535, 3638; Betaine 3134, 3567; Bicarbonate 1595, 1596, 1636, 1637, 2692, 2693; Bile acids 1595, 1596; Bile salts 2988; Cadmium 1707, 2901, 3638; Calcium 1595, 1596, 1636, 1637, 1909, 2024, 2161, 2692, 2864, 3134; Calcitonin 1729; Cerebroside 2376; Chloride 1595, 1596, 1636, 1637, 1906, 1909, 2024, 2359, 2692, 2693, 3134, 3418; Cholesterol 1530, 2377, 2988, 3179, 3180; Choline 3567; Connective tissue 3462; Copper 1707, 2901, 3638; Corticosterone 3456; Corticosterone + Cortisol 1704; Creatin 2855, 3134, 3567; Creatin phosphate 3134; Creatin phosphokinase 2696; Creatinine 2855, 3134, 3567; Cyanocobalamin 1522; Cytochrome oxidase 2011; 11-Dehydrocorticosterone 3456; DNA 2194, 2998; Diacyl glyceryl ethers 3179; Diglycosylceramides 2376, 2377; Diphosphatidyl glycerol 1530, 2377; Fatty acids 1530, 2007, 2748, 3088, 3180; Furan fatty acids 2092; Fatty aldehydes 1530; Galactosamine 3087; Galactosyl ceramide 1530, 2377; Ganglioside 1530, 2377; Glucosamine 3087; Glucose 2692; Glucosyl ceramide 1530; Glutamate-oxaloacetate transaminase 2696; Glutamine synthetase 3592; Glycogen 2980; Guanine deaminase 2873; Guanosine monophosphate 3219; Haematocrit 1636, 2516; Haemoglobin 2516; Hydrocarbons 3180; α-Hydroxybutyrate dehydrogenase 2696; 1α-hydroxycorticosterone 3456; Hypoxanthine 3446; Hypoxanthine-guanine phosphoribosyl transferase 2873; Inosine monophosphate 3219; Iron 2901; Lactic dehydrogenase 2011, 2696; Lead 1707; 2901; Magnesium 1595, 1596, 1636, 1637, 1909, 2692, 2864, 3134; Mercury 1697, 1707, 2482, 3638; Neutral lipid 3180; NAD (nicotinamide adenine dinucleotide, formerly diphosphopyridine nucleotide) 3219; NADH (reduced NAD) 3219; NADP (NAD phosphate, formerly triphosphopyridine nucleotide) 3219; NADPH (reduced NADP) 3219; Noradrenaline 3340; Ornithine aminotransferase 3611; Phosphatidyl choline 1530, 2377; Phosphatidyl ethanolamine 1530, 2377; Phosphatidyl inositol 1530, 2377; Phosphatidyl serine 1530, 2377; Phosphorylase 3054; Phosphorylase kinase 3054; Potassium 1595, 1596, 1636, 1637, 1767, 1906, 1909, 2024, 2562, 2692, 2864, 2900, 3134, 3418; Pristane 2007, 2403; Purine nucleoside orthophosphate ribosyl transferase 2873; Pyruvate kinase 2011; Sarcosine 3567; Sodium 1595, 1596, 1636, 1637, 1906, 1909, 2024, 2562, 2692, 2693, 2864, 2900, 3134, 3148; Sphingomyelin 1530, 2376, 2377; Squalene 2007, 2403; Sulphate 1636, 2692, 3134; Sulphatides 1530, 2376, 2377; Taurine 3567; Thymidine phosphorylase 2873; Triglycerides 2377, 2805, 3179, 3180; Trimethylamine oxidase 2030; Trimethylamine oxide 1636, 3134, 3567; Urate oxidase 2873; Urea 1636, 1637, 1906, 2024, 2359, 2692,

3134, 3567; UDP (uridine diphosphate) 3219; UDP-N-acetyl galactosamine 3219; UDP-N-acetyl glucosamine 3219; UDP-hexoses 3219; Uridine monophosphate 3219; Wax esters 3179, 3180; Zinc 1707, 2901, 3638

‡Squalus brevirostris
Japan.
Volume 1 only

‡Squalus mitsukurii
Japan.
Anserine 3367, 3368; Balenine 3367, 3368; Carnosine 3368; Trimethylamine oxide 3367; Urea 3367

‡Squalus suckleyi (*see* S. acanthias)

‡Squatina angelus (*see* S. squatina)

Squatina californica
DNA 2194

‡Squatina japonica (Canopy shark, Japanese angel-fish, Japanese monkfish)
Japan. Buried in sand for most of the time.
Volume 1 only

‡Squatina squatina = S. angelus (Angel fish, Angel ray, Monkfish)
W. Europe: Shetland to Canary Is., Mediterranean. Cape Cod to N. Carolina. 5–100 m on sand or gravel. Viviparous. Buried by day, active at night. Active swimmer. Diet: small fish, molluscs, crustaceans.
DNA 2194

Stenobrachius leucopsarus *120*

Stenotomus chrysops
DNA 2195; "Sugar" 2062, 2063

‡Stenotomus versicolor (Bream, Common scup, Fair maid, Porgy, Scuppang)
Atlantic coast of United States.
Amino acids 1812

‡Stephanolepis cirrhifer (File fish, Leatherfish, Porky)
Japan, Korea, E. China Sea. 10–30 m.
Arsenic 3402; Caesium 2269; β-Carotene 2716; Cobalt 2269; Copper 3402; α-Cryptoxanthin 2716; Cynthiaxanthin 2716; Diatoxanthin 2716; *Free* histidine 3166; Lutein 2716; Manganese 3402; Mercury 3402; NAD (nicotinamide adenine dinucleotide) 3259; NADH (reduced NAD) 3259; Pyridine nucleotide transhydrogenase 3167; Tunaxanthin 2716; Zeaxanthin 2716; Zinc 2269, 3402

Stephanolepis hispidus
DNA 2195

‡Stereolepis gigas (California jewfish, Giant seabass)
Californian coast, W. Pacific 30–46 m on rocky bottoms. Grows to a great size.
Diet: fish, crustaceans.
Volume 1 only

Sternoptix diaphana (Transparent hatchet fish)
Atlantic: Newfoundland to Santa Cruz Is., Indian and Pacific Oceans. 182–1829 m
or deeper.
Fatty acids 2469; Phosphatidyl choline 3064; Phosphatidyl ethanolamine 3064;
Phosphatidyl inositol 3064; Phosphatidyl serine 3064; Polyglycerophosphatides
3064; Sphingomyelin 3064

Sternopygus macrurus (Cuchilla, Electric eel, Sabre)
Northeast part of S. America, Guyanas, Amazon, Orinoco basins in streams,
trenches, ditches, backwaters of rivers. Active at night. Diet: insects, shrimps, fish.
DNA 2195

Stichaeus grigorjewi (Arctic shanny, Japanese prickleback, Northern blenny)
Contains a toxic lipoprotein, dinogunellin, which induces severe gastrointestinal
disorders in warm-blooded animals (Hatano and Hashimoto, 1974).
Amino acids 2138; Fatty acids 2138, 3389; *Free* fatty acids 3389; Saturated fatty
acids 3389; Monoenoic acids 3389; Polyenoic acids 3389; Neutral lipid 3389;
Phospholipids 3389

Stizostedion canadense (Sauger)
Canada. Preferred temperature 19°C, avoiding temperatures above about 28°C.
Allantoicase 1775; Allantoinase 1775; Arginase 1776; Mercury 1557, 3649;
Thyroxine 2190

Stizostedion lucioperca (Pike-perch, Zander)
Central and N. Europe. Introduced W. Europe. Thrives in large lakes or slow
rivers in murky water. Diet: fish.
Cobalt 1540, 2850; Copper 2850; Iron 2850; Manganese 2850; Zinc 2850

‡*Stizostedion vitreum* (Blue pike, Dory, Glasseye, Jack salmon, Pike-perch, Spike,
Walleye, Walleyed pike, White-eye, Yellow pike) *35, 36, 58*
N. America: fresh and occasionally brackish waters. Tolerates a wide variety of
environmental conditions but prefers large, shallow, turbid lakes or hard-bottomed
lakes and rivers, 5–10 m. Preferred temperature 21–23°C. Diet: fish, also some
insects and crustaceans.
Allantoicase 1775; Allantoinase 1775; Arginase 1776; Arsenic 2611; Bicarbonate
2262; Bromide 2611; Cadmium 2611; Calcium 2072, 2073, 2262–2264, 3145;
Chloride 2072, 2073, 2262; Cobalt 2611; Copper 2611; Glucose 2262; Guanine
1867; Haematocrit 2262; Hypoxanthine 1867; Lactate 2262; Magnesium 2072,
2073, 2262–2264; Mercury 1557, 3214; Potassium 2072, 2073, 2262–2264; Sodium
2072, 2073, 2262–2264; Strontium 3145; Thorium 2611; Uranium 2611; Urea
2072, 2073; Uric acid 2072, 2073; Zinc 2611, 3649

‡Stolephorus commersonii (Commerson's anchovy, Longjawed anchovy)
Madagascar to India and Philippines, N. Australia. Coastal, pelagic. Diet: zooplankton.
Folic acid 2582

Stolephorus japonicus
Japan.
α-Cryptoxanthin, Cynthiaxanthin, Lutein, Tunaxanthin, Zeaxanthin: 2718

Stromateoides sinensis
Japan.
Cadmium 2901; Copper 2901; Iron 2910; Lead 2901; Potassium 2900; Sodium 2900; Zinc 2901

‡Stromateus cinereus* = Pampus argenteus* (Grey pomfret, Harvest fish, Silver pomfret, White pomfret)
India, Malaya, China, Japan, Philippines; introduced to Hawaii. Not New Guinea or Australia. In schools over muddy bottoms down to 100 m. Enters brackish waters. Diet: planktonic and bottom-living invertebrates.
Amino acids 1812; Arsenic 3402; Calcium 2313; Copper 3402; Iron 2313; Lead 3402; Lysophosphatidyl choline 2042; Manganese 3402; Mercury 3402; Niacin 2313; Phosphatidic acid 2042; Phosphatidyl choline 2042; Phosphatidyl ethanolamine 2042; Phosphatidyl inositol 2042; Phosphatidyl serine 2042; Phospholipid 2042; Riboflavin 2313; Sphingomyelin 2042; Thiamine 2313; Zinc 3402

Stromateus maculatus
Chile, New Zealand.
Cholesterol, Fatty acids, Glyceryl ethers, Hydrocarbons: 2779

‡Stromateus niger (see Parastromateus niger)

‡Stromateus sinensis (White pomfret)
India, Malaya, China.
Amino acids 3124

Stromateus stellatus
Amino acids 1812

Strongylura exilis
DNA 2195

Strongylura gigantea (Needlefish)
Hawaii. Shallow reefs, 1–10 m.
Diphosphatidyl glycerol, Fatty acids, Lysophosphatidyl choline, Phosphatidic acid, Phosphatidyl choline, Phosphatidyl ethanolamine, Phosphatidyl serine, Sphingomyelin: 2987

Strongylura marina* (Atlantic needlefish, Silver gar)
W. Atlantic, Maine to Texas. Can enter river mouths. Voracious predator. Diet: squid and other invertebrates, fish.
DNA 2195

Strongylura notata
  Inactive.
  Haematocrit, Haemoglobin: 3377

Suggrundus meerdervoorti
  Japan.
  Trimethylamine oxide 2111

Symbranchus marmoratus
  Amazon River.
  Ammonia, Bicarbonate, Calcium, Chloride, Magnesium, Potassium, Sodium,
  Urea: 2686

Symphurus atricauda
  DNA 2195

‡Synaphobranchus affinis
  Japan.
  Volume 1 only

Synaphobranchus branchistomas (Slickhead)
  Pacific, deep sea (1800 m).
  Diphosphatidyl glycerol, Fatty acids, Lysophosphatidyl choline, Phosphatidic
  acid, Phosphatidyl choline, Phosphatidyl ethanolamine, Phosphatidyl serine,
  Sphingomyelin: 2987

‡Synaphobranchus kaupi = S. pinnatus (Gray's cut-throat eel, Kaup's deepsea eel,
  Longnose eel)
  Wide distribution in deep waters of the Atlantic (Greenland to Brazil and
  S. Africa). 800 to below 3000 m.
  Fatty acids, Neutral lipids: 2153

‡Synaphobranchus pinnatus (*see* S. kaupi)

Syngnathus floridae
  DNA 2195

Syngnathus fuscus (Northern pipefish)
  Gulf of St. Lawrence to N. Carolina. Coastal waters, sometimes in brackish inlets
  among seaweed and eelgrass. Diet: minute copepods, amphipods, fish eggs.
  DNA 2195

Synodontis nigriventris (Upside-down catfish)
  Central Congo. Hardy. Diet: algae.
  DNA 2195

Synodontis schall (Upside-down catfish)
  Africa: wide distribution, Nile to Senegal and Nigeria. Diet: molluscs, insect larvae,
  fish.
  DNA 2195

Synodus foetens
  DNA 2195

Synodus hoshinonis
  Japan.
  Dimethylamine 2110; Formaldehyde 2110; Trimethylamine oxide 2111

Synodus intermedius (Sand diver)
  Bermuda shores. Inactive.
  Succinic dehydrogenase 2750

Synodus lucioceps (California lizardfish)
  California 18–46 m. Diet: fish, squid.
  DNA 2195

‡Tachysurus venosus = Arius venosus (Veined catfish)
  Madagascar, Malaya, Java, Borneo. Not Philippines or Australia. Coastal waters
  down to about 10 m. Diet: invertebrates, small fish.
  Volume 1 only

‡Taeniotoca lateralis (Striped surf-fish)
  W. America: Vancouver to Todos Santos Bay.
  Volume 1 only

‡Taius tumifrons (Yellowback seabream, Yellow porgy, Yellow seabream)
  Japan, Korea, northern coasts of Phillippines. Muddy and muddy-sandy grounds,
  50–250 m. Diet: a wide range of bottom-living invertebrates, fish.
  Arsenic 3402; Cadmium 2901; Cholesterol 2445; Copper 2901, 3402; Iron 2901;
  Lead 2901; Manganese 3402; Mercury 2888, 3402; Potassium 2900; Selenium
  2888; Sodium 2900; Trimethylamine 2388; Vitamin D 3673; Zinc 2901, 3402

‡Tanakius kitaharae (Flounder)
  Japan.
  Volume 1 only

‡Tarpon atlanticus (Silverfish, Tarpon)
  Both sides of Atlantic: Long Island to Brazil; range not given for E. Atlantic.
  Coastal. A very large fish. Larvae live in salt marshes, swamps and estuaries,
  surviving poor oxygenation by means of an accessory breathing organ.
  Volume 1 only

Taurulus bubalis *349*

‡Tautoga onitis (Blackfish, Tautog)
  Atlantic coast of N. America: Nova Scotia to S. Carolina. Coastal. Can enter
  brackish water.
  DNA 2195; Glucose 3664

‡Tautogolabrus adspersus (Bergall, Blue perch, Cunner, Nipper, Perch, Sea perch)
Atlantic coast of N. America within a few miles of shore, on sea bottom, also
around rocks and wrecks.
DNA 2195

‡Teathis javus
Philippines.
Volume 1 only

Temnodon saltator (Tasergal)
Cholesterol 1785

‡Tetranarce occidentalis = Torpedo occidentalis (Atlantic torpedo, Crampfish,
Electric fish, Numbfish)
Atlantic coast of United States: Cape Cod to Cuba.
Volume 1 only

Tetraodon fluviatilis (Green pufferfish)
India, Philippines. Fresh and brackish waters. Uses fin propulsion.
DNA 2195

Tetraodon palembangensis
Thailand, Sumatra, Borneo.
DNA 2195

‡Tetrapturus angustirostris (Shortbill spearfish)
Tropical Pacific. Epipelagic.
Volume 1 only

‡Tetrapturus audax (Striped marlin)
Throughout warmer waters of Pacific and Indian oceans. Diet: fish, squid.
Volume 1 only

‡Tetrapturus mitsukurii
Japan.
Volume 1 only

Thalassoma bifasciatum (Bluehead wrasse)
Caribbean Sea to S. America coast. Diet: zooplankton, parasites from other fish.
DNA 2195

Thalassoma duperreyi (Saddleback wrasse)
Hawaii. A shallow tropical reef fish. No stomach or pyloric caecae; however,
omnivorous.
Diphosphatidyl glycerol, Fatty acids, Lysophosphatidyl choline, Phosphatidic acid,
Phosphatidyl choline, Phosphatidyl ethanolamine, Phosphatidyl serine, Sphingo-
myelin: 2987

‡Thaleichthys pacificus* (Candlefish, Eulachon, Oolakan) *454*
N. California to Bering Sea and Pribilof Is. Spawns in rivers from Mad River
northwards. Young move out to sea soon after hatching. Dried fish may be lit

like a candle. Oil unique among fish oils in being solid at room temperature. 10% of the lipid is squalene: this is unique outside the elasmobranchs.
Volume 1 only

‡Theragra chalcogramma (Alaska pollack, Walleye pollock) *72, 75, 76, 190–192, 338, 459*
W. America, Carmel to Bering Sea; Japan. Surface to 386 m, mainly in mid-water. Diet: wide variety of invertebrates, especially crustaceans, and small fish including young salmon.
Adenosine monophosphate 1871; Amino acids 3271; Collagen 3462; Connective tissue 3462; α-Cryptoxanthin 2716; Diacylglyceryl ethers 2399; Dimethylamine 3439; Elastin 3462; Fatty acids 2152, 3389, 3666, 3667; *Free* fatty acids 2399, 3389; Saturated fatty acids 3389; *Free* fatty alcohols 2399; Inosine monophosphate 1871, 1873; Lutein 2716; Mercury 2888; Monoenoic (fatty) acids 3389; Neutral lipids 2152, 3389; Partial glycerides 2399; Phospholipids 2399, 3389; Polyenoic (fatty) acids 3389; Selenium 2888; Sterols 2399; Sterol esters 2399; Thiaminase 3473; Triglycerides 2399; Trimethylamine 1873, 3439; Trimethylamine oxide 3439; Tunaxanthin 2716; Wax esters 2399; Zeaxanthin 2716

‡ *Therapon bidyana* (Bidyan grunter, Black bream, Grunter, Silver perch, Sooty grunter)
Australia. Inland streams, water holes.
Volume 1 only

‡Therapon jarbua* (Crescent perch, Jarbua therapon, Spiky trumpeter, Striped grunt, Tigerfish, Zebrafish)
E. Africa, Red Sea, India, Philippines, Japan, N. Australia. Coastal waters and estuaries, extending into *almost* fresh water. Very active. Produces loud noises with its swim bladder. Diet: invertebrates, fish.
Volume 1 only

‡Therapon oxyrhynchus* = Pelates oxyrhynchus* (Blotched therapon)
India, Japan, Formosa, Philippines. Inshore, sometimes in brackish waters. The young enter fresh water. Diet: invertebrates, fish.
Volume 1 only

Therapon plumbeus (Silver grunt)
Philippines.
Folic acid 2582

Therapon puta (Target perch)
India.
Lysozyme 3173

‡Therapon theraps (Large-scaled banded grunter)
E. Africa, India, Malaya, Philippines, China, Australia.
Volume 1 only

Thrissocles mystax (Anchovy, Moustached anchovy)
India, Burma, Malaya; Amoy to Queensland. Coastal, pelagic. Diet: plankton organisms.
Lysophosphatidyl choline, Phosphatidic acids, Phosphatidyl choline, Phosphatidyl ethanolamine, Phosphatidyl inositol, Phosphatidyl serine, Phospholipid, Sphingomyelin: 2042

‡Thunnus alalunga = Germo alalunga = Germo germo = Thunnus germo (Albacore, Longfinned albacore, Longfinned tuna) *400, 433, 450, 454*
All warm seas: Japan, Hawaii, Australia, California, Atlantic, parts of Mediterranean. Surface waters down to 185 m at temperatures above 14°C (prefers 17 to 21°C) and salinity of 35·5 ‰. Body temperature may be considerably warmer than that of the environment. Feeds night and day near surface. Diet: small shoaling fish, euphausids, squid.
Aluminium 3019; Amino acids 1412, 3019; *Free* amino acids 3019; Anserine 3368; Barium 2981, 3019; Caesium 2981; Calcium 2981; Carnosine 3368; Cholesterol 2445, 3019, 3020; Copper 3019; Iron 3019; Lead 2981, 3019; Manganese 3019; Mercury 3397; Potassium 2981; Provitamin D 3019, 3020; Rubidium 2981; Selenium 3397; Strontium 2981, 3019; Titanium 3019

‡Thunnus albacares = Germo macropterus = Neothunnus albacora = Neothunnus macropterus = Thunnus albacora (Allison's tuna, Autumn albacore, Yellowfin tuna) *34, 68, 72, 73, 75, 76, 106, 322*
Circumtropical. Pelagic. Prefers 22–28°C, but tolerates temperatures down to 14°C. Migratory. Comes close inshore. Diet: surface fish, including flying fish, squid, pelagic crustaceans.
Aluminium 3018, 3019; Amino acids 1946, 3019; *Free* amino acids 3019, 3166, 3369; Anserine 3368, 3369; Arsenic 2886; Balenine 3368; Barium 3018, 3019; Bismuth 3018; Cadmium 2886; Carnosine 3368; 3369; Cholesterol 2572, 2768, 3019, 3020; Chromium 2886, 3018; Cobalt 3018; Copper 2886, 3018, 3019; Creatin + Creatinine 3369; 7-Dehydrocholesterol 2768; Dimethylamine 3439; *Free* fatty acids 2572; Iron 3019; Lead 2886, 3018, 3019; Lithium 3018; Manganese 3018, 3019; Mercury 2887, 2888, 3127, 3397, 3487; Molybdenum 3018; Nickel 3018; Phospholipids 2572; Provitamin D 3019, 3020; Selenium 2888, 3397; Silver 3018; Sterol esters 2572; Strontium 3018, 3019; Taurine 3166, 3369; Tin 3018; Titanium 3018, 3019; Triglycerides 2572; Trimethylamine 3439; Trimethylamine oxide 3439, 3668; Vitamin D 3673; Zinc 2886, 3018

‡Thunnus albacora (*see* T. albacares)

‡Thunnus germo (*see* T. alalunga)

‡Thunnus maccoyii (Southern bluefin tuna)
Southern oceans: Indonesia to S. Australia, Tasmania, New Zealand, Chile, S. Africa. A powerful migratory fish. Diet: cephalopods, crustaceans, fish.
Free amino acids 3369; Anserine 3368, 3369; Carnosine 3369; Creatine + Creatinine 3369; Taurine 3369

‡Thunnus obesus = Parathunnus mebachi = Parathunnus obesus = Parathunnus sibi (Bigeye tuna) *72, 75, 322, 437*
Both sides of Atlantic, Pacific, Azores, Canary Is., Indian Ocean, Japan, Australia. Absent from Mediterranean. Pelagic. Coastal, but avoids low salinity near river mouths. Enters deep water during the day, surfacing at night. Tolerates 13–27°C. Strongly migratory, swimming perhaps thousands of miles to seasonal feeding grounds. Diet: crustaceans (mainly prawns), squid, fish.
Aluminium 3018, 3019; Amino acids 2484, 3019, 3441; *Free* amino acids 3019, 3369; Anserine 3368, 3369; Arsenic 2886; Barium 3018; Bismuth 3018; Cadmium

‡Thynnus thunnina (Little tunny)
   Tropical Atlantic, Mediterranean, India, Malaya.
   Volume 1 only

‡Thyrsites atun (Barracouta, Snoek)
   S. Africa, S. Australia, New Zealand, S. America. Migratory in large shoals.
   Sometimes enters estuaries. Rapacious predator. Diet: a large range of smaller fish
   species, also krill.
   Volume 1 only

Tilapia alcalica
   Africa. Lakes.
   Potassium, Sodium: 2530

Tilapia aurea 37
   Palestine.
   Deoxycorticosterone, 11 β-Hydroxytestosterone, 11-Ketotestosterone, Testosterone:
   2391

Tilapia grahami
   Potassium, Sodium: 2530

Tilapia leucosticta
   DNA 2195; Potassium 2530; Sodium 2530

‡ Tilapia macrochir 172
   Congo, Zambesi, Kafue and Okavango river systems (Africa).
   Laminarinase 3034

‡ Tilapia melanopleura
   Upper Congo to S. Africa. Strict herbivore.
   Volume 1 only

Tilapia melanotheron 384

‡Tilapia mossambica* = T. natalensis* (Bream, Java tilapia, Leatherjacket, Mozambique mouthbrooder, Mudfish, St. Peter's fish, Tilapia) 115, 188, 240, 271, 290,
   313, 318, 342, 374
   Originally from S. Africa, introduced to India and Sri Lanka. Brackish and fresh
   water. May even breed in sea water. Preferred temperature 28·5°C, avoiding
   temperatures above 33·5°C.
   Adenosine diphosphate 2428; Adenosine monophosphate 2428; Adenosine
   triphosphate 2428; Amino acids 1914, 3390; Free amino acids 3250; total Free
   amino acids (a single figure) 3548; Chloride 1444; Folic acid 2582; Glycogen 2523;
   Haematocrit 2139; Haemoglobin 2139; Lysozyme 3173; Sodium 1444; "Sugar"
   2139; Thiaminase 2297; Zinc 2328

‡Tilapia natalensis* (see T. mossambica*)

Tilapia nigra (Black cichlid)
   Athi river system in Kenya; African lakes.
   Potassium, Sodium: 2530

Tilapia nilotica (St. Peter's fish) *114, 257, 290*
Egypt, Palestine, Thailand, Vietnam. Herbivorous. Female tends the fertilised eggs in her mouth. Preferred temperature 28–30°C.
Amylase 2840; Chloride 2678; DNA 2195; β-Galactosidase 2840; Glucose 2219; β-Glucosidase 2840; Glycogen 2219; Haematocrit 2678; Haemoglobin 2678

Tilapia zillii* *55, 56, 311, 327*
An estuarine fish which is found in fresh water. Shows increases in total serum protein with increase in the external salinity.
Agranulocytes 1898; Albumin 1911, 3154; Basophils 1898; Creatinine 1911, 3154; DNA 2195; Eosinophils 1898; Erythrocytes 1898, 1911, 3154; Globulins 3154; Granulocytes 3154; Haematocrit 1911, 3154; Haemoglobin 1911, 3154; Leucocytes 1898, 1911, 3154; Lymphocytes 1898, 1911; Monocytes 1898, 3154; Neutrophils 1898, 3154; Potassium 2530; Sodium 2530; "Sugar" 1911, 3154

‡*Tinca tinca* = *T. vulgaris* (Tench) *68, 149, 155, 172, 194, 212, 213, 277, 279, 299, 311, 343*
Europe except Scotland and central and N. Scandinavia. Arctic Ocean drainage area. Introduced N. America. Weedy still waters with soft bottom near shore. Tolerates low oxygen concentrations and salinity up to 10 parts per thousand. Slow-moving, sluggish; inactive in winter especially. Skin gives off copious mucus. Avoids temperatures above 26°C. Diet: bottom-living insect larvae, small crustaceans, molluscs.
Adrenaline 1815; Aluminium 2677; Amino acids 3433; FREE amino acids 1507, 2977, 3433; Anserine 2977; Arginase 2256; Argininosuccinate lyase 2256; Argininosuccinate synthetase 2256; Biotin 3453, 3454; Cadmium 1972; Calcium 1528, 2677, 2864; Carbamoyl phosphate synthetase 2256; Carnosine 2977; Cobalt 1540, 2677, 2850; Copper 1793, 2677, 2829, 2850; DNA 3203; Free fatty acids 1816; Gluocse 1815, 1816; Glycogen 1815, 1816; Glycogen phosphorylase 2810, 2815; Inositol 3453; Insulin 1815, 1816; Iron 1793, 1838, 2677, 2850; Lactate 1815, 1816; Lactic dehydrogenase 3203; Magnesium 2677, 2864; Manganese 1793, 2677, 2850; Mercury 2829, 3617; Niacin 3453, 3454; Ornithine 2977; Ornithine transcarbamoylase 2256; Pantothenic acid 3453, 3454; 6-Phosphogluconate dehydrogenase 3203; Phosphoglucose isomerase 3203; Phosphorylase 1815; Potassium 2677, 2864; Pyridoxine 3453, 3454; RNA 3203; Sarcosine 2977; Sodium 2804, 2864; "Sugar" 1492, 3562; Taurine 2977; Thiamine 3453, 3454; Tin 2677; Urea 3547; Vanadium 2677; Zinc 1793, 2677, 2829, 2850

‡*Tinca vulgaris* (*see T. tinca*)

Todarodes sagittatus
Mediterranean.
Formaldehyde 1656

Torpedo californica
DNA 2194

‡**Torpedo marmorata** (Marbled electric ray) *35*
S. England and S. Ireland to Mediterranean. Shallow waters, on or half buried in sand or mud. Solitary, Nocturnal, Viviparous. Electric discharge 45–220 volts. Diet: small fish, molluscs, crustaceans.

Acetyl choline 1556, 1862, 1863, 2303; N-acetyl neuraminic acid 2472; Adenosine triphosphate 1556, 2303; Adrenaline + Noradrenaline 3474; Amino acids 2946; *Free* amino acids 3565; γ-Amino butyric acid 2946; Cerebroside 2472; Choline acetyl transferase 2302; Cholinesterase 1556, 2302, 3474; Diphosphoinositide 2474; Ethanolamine 2946; Fatty acids 1603, 2472, 2474; Gangliosides 2472; Glucose kinase 3551; Glucose-6-phosphate dehydrogenase 3551; 1α-Hydroxycorticosterone 3456; Isocitrate dehydrogenase 3551; Lactic dehydrogenase 2302, 3551; Lysophosphatidyl choline 1556; Lysophosphatidyl ethanolamine 1556; Monophosphoinositide 2474; NADH-cytochrome c oxoreductase 1556; 5'-nucleotidase 2302; Ornithine 2946; Phosphatidyl choline 1556, 2474; Phosphatidyl ethanolamine 1556, 2474; Phosphatidyl serine 2474; Phosphofructokinase 3551; Phospholipid 2474; Phosphorylase 3551; Polyglycerophosphatides 2474; Pyruvate kinase 3551; Serotonin 3474; Sphingomyelin 1556, 2474; Sulphatide 2472; Taurine 2946; Tri-isophosphate dehydrogenase 3551; Triphosphoinositide 2474; Zinc 1929

‡**Torpedo nobiliana** (Atlantic torpedo, Electric ray, Numbfish, Torpedo)
Both sides of Atlantic, Mediterranean, tropical W. Africa. Grows to considerable size. Lives partly buried in sand or mud in fairly deep water. Viviparous. Electric discharge 170–220 volts. Diet: fish, which are killed by the electric shock.
Arginine 1653

‡**Torpedo occidentalis** (*see* **Tetranarce occidentalis**)

‡**Torpedo ocellata** = **T. torpedo** (Eyed electric ray)
Biscay to Angola. Mediterranean. Half buried in sand or sea grass beds. Shallow to 200 m. Viviparous. Voltages up to 220 volts produced.
Cardiolipid 2457; Chloride 2280; Phosphatidic acid 2457; Phosphatidyl choline 2457; Phosphatidyl ethanolamine 2457; Phosphatidyl inositol 2457; Phosphatidyl serine 2457; Phospholipids 2457; Potassium 2280; Sialogangliosides 2458; Sodium 2280; Sphingomyelin 2457; Zinc 1929

Torpedo torpedo (*see* **T. ocellata**)

‡Trachichthodes affinis
Australia.
Volume 1 only

‡Trachinocephalus myops (Bluntnose lizardfish, Offshore lizard fish, Painted grinner, Painted saury, Snakefish)
Pacific, Indian and Atlantic Oceans. Japan to Australia. Bays and inshore, partly buried in sand. Shallow to 387 m on sand, shell, rock or mud bottom. Diet: small bottom-living invertebrates, fish.
Dimethylamine 2110; Formaldehyde 2110; Pyridine nucleotide transhydrogenase 3167; Trimethylamine oxide 2111

‡Trachinotus carolinus* (Butterfish, Carolina pompano, Cobbler fish, Common pampano)
Cape Cod, Gulf of Mexico, W. Indies, Brazil, India. Diet: molluscs, young fish, vegetable debris, crab larvae, isopods, invertebrate eggs.
Aldehyde oxidase, Xanthine oxidase: 2468

Trachurus symmetricus (Jack mackerel) *89, 114*
   Tropical mid-Pacific to Alaska down to 400 m. Good night vision. Diet: variable,
   often macroplankton, sometimes lantern fish, squid.
   Glycogen 3089

‡Trachurus trachurus (Horse mackerel, Maasbanker, Rough scad, Scad) *116*
   Mid-Norway to southern tip of Africa, Mediterranean, Florida, Japan. Large
   shoals in coastal waters during summer, deeper waters down to 500 m during winter.
   Migratory, pelagic. Very young specimens often found swimming among the
   tentacles of large jellyfish. Diflcult to estimate fecundity because sex products
   develop over a period and are released in batches, giving a prolonged spawning
   period (Macer, 1974).
   Cadmium 1707, 1709, 2786; Cathepsin 1924; Chloride 1909; Cholesterol 1785;
   Chromium 2786; Cobalt 2786; Copper 1707, 1709, 2786, 2828; Creatin 2855;
   Creatinine 2855; Fatty acids 3667; Haematocrit 2516; Haemoglobin 2516; Iron
   2786; Lactic dehydrogenase 1789; Lead 1707, 1709, 2786; Manganese 2786;
   Mercury 1707, 1709, 1891, 2828; Nickel 2786; Potassium 1909; Sodium 1909;
   Strontium 2786; Trimethylamine oxide 3151; Vitamin D 2188; Zinc 1707, 1709,
   2786, 2828

‡Trematomus bernacchii *47, 264, 327, 333, 346, 349*
   Antarctic, down to 700 m. Sluggish benthic. Not frozen in contact with ice at
   sub-zero temperatures. Aglomerular kidney (DeVries, 1974). Relatively high
   blood pH (8·2–8·3)—Qvist, Weber *et al.* (1977). Diet: polychaete worms, molluscs,
   crustaceans.
   Calcium 1840, 3079; Carbohydrates 1827, 1831; Chloride 1827, 1831, 1840, 3079;
   Magnesium 1840, 3079; Non-protein nitrogen 1827, 1831; Potassium 1840, 3079,
   3311; Sodium 1840, 3079, 3311; Urea 1831

‡Trematomus borchgrevinki *47, 327, 346, 347* (photograph)
   Antarctic. Resistant to freezing as in T. bernacchii. Optimal temperature −1·9
   to −1·7°C. Swimming activity declines at −0·8°C and ceases at +2°C. Dies at
   +5 or 6°C, this limit not being raised by acclimation (DeVries, 1974). High blood
   pH (8·2–8·3)—Qvist, Weber *et al.* (1977). A photograph of this fish is given in
   Fig. 124. Aglomerular, pelagic.
   Amino acids 1917, 2448; Calcium 1840; Carbohydrates 1827, 1831; Chloride 1827,
   1831, 1840; Galactosamine 1917; Galactose 1917; Haematocrit 3108; Magnesium
   1840; Non-protein nitrogen 1827, 1831; Potassium 1840; Sodium 1840; Urea 1827,
   1831

Trematomus centronotus
   Antarctic. Aglomerular.
   Calcium 1840; Chloride 1840, 1860; Magnesium 1840; Potassium 1840; Sodium
   1840, 1860

‡Trematomus hansoni *346*
   Antarctic. Resistant to freezing as in T. bernacchii. Aglomerular.
   Calcium 1840; Carbohydrates 1827, 1831; Chloride 1827, 1831, 1840; Magnesium
   1840; Non-protein nitrogen 1827, 1831; Potassium 1840; Sodium 1840

Trematomus lepidorhinus
  Antarctic. Aglomerular.
  Calcium 1840; Chloride 1840, 1860; Magnesium 1840; Potassium 1840; Sodium
  1840, 1860

‡Trematomus loennbergii
  Antarctic. Aglomerular. Bottom-dwelling. Resistant to freezing, but serum does
  freeze at −1·8°C; the fish itself therefore freezes occasionally in contact with ice
  (Wohlschlag, 1964).
  Calcium 1840; Chloride 1827, 1840, 1860; Haematocrit 3108; Magnesium 1840;
  Non-protein nitrogen 1827; Potassium 1840; Sodium 1840, 1860

Trematomus newnesi *348*
  Antarctic. Aglomerular.
  Calcium 1840; Carbohydrates 3311; Chloride 1840, 1860, 3311; Magnesium 1840;
  Potassium 1840; Sodium 1840, 1860, 3311

Trematomus nicolai
  Antarctic. Aglomerular.
  Calcium 1840; Chloride 1840, 1860; Magnesium 1840; Potassium 1840; Sodium
  1840, 1860

Trematomus sp.
  Fatty acids 2987

‡**Triakis scyllia** (Brown smooth dogfish, Incense burner, Leopard shark)
  India, Japan. Weedy shore-bottoms.
  NAD (nicotinamide adenine dinucleotide, formerly diphosphopyridine nucleotide)
  3259; NADH (reduced NAD) 3259; Pristane 2403; Squalene 2403; Vitamin D
  3673

‡**Triakis semifasciata** (Cat shark, Leopard shark)
  California, Mexico to Oregon. In bays along beaches. Active. Tolerant of un-
  favourable conditions in aquaria.
  Bile salts 2988; DNA 2194

‡Tribolodon hakonensis* (Dace) *425*
  Japan. The only Cyprinoid that can inhabit salt water. Diet: vegetable and animal
  matter.
  Astacene 2719; Cryptoxanthin 2719; Cynthiaxanthin 2719; Diatoxanthin 2719;
  α-Doradecin 2719; Lutein 2719; Vitamin D 3673; Zeaxanthin 2719

‡Trichiurus haumela* (*see* T. lepturus*)

‡Trichiurus japonicus* (*see* T. lepturus*)

‡Trichiurus lepturus* = T. haumela* = T. japonicus* (Bandfish, Cutlass fish,
  Hairtail, Largehead hairtail, Ribbonfish, Scabbardfish, Snakefish)
  Britain, Portugal, W. Atlantic (N. Carolina to W. Indies), Africa, India to Japan
  and Australia. Surface to 350 m. Scaleless. May enter rivers. Sometimes found in
  extremely shallow water. Diet: crustaceans, cephalopods, fish.

Arsenic 3402; Cadmium 2901; Cholesterol 1785; Copper 2901, 3402; Folic acid 2582; Iron 2901; Lead 2901, 3402; Manganese 3402; Mercury 3402; Potassium 2900; Sodium 2900; Thiaminase 3473; Trimethylamine oxide 2111; Zinc 2901, 3402

‡Trichiurus savala = Lepturacanthus savala (Smallhead hairtail, Smallhead ribbon-fish)
India, Malaya, China, Australia. Bottom-living as well as pelagic. Diet: crustaceans, cephalopods, fish.
Amino acids, Calcium, Iron, Niacin, Riboflavin, Thiamine, Vitamin A: 3690

‡Trichodon stelleri
Japan.
Volume 1 only

Trichogaster cosby (Opaline gouramy) *53, 465*
Tropical. Unusual in that wax esters are the major lipids of the eggs although triacylglycerol is the major lipid in the fish body (Sargent, 1976). Female eats unfertilised eggs.
Fatty acids 3170; Fatty alcohols 3170; Phosphatidyl choline 3169; Phosdhatidyl ethanolamine 3169; Triglycerides 3169; Wax esters 3169

Trichogaster fasciatus
India.
Acid phosphatase 3227; Alkaline phosphatase 3227; Vitamin A_1 1500; Vitamin A_2 1500

Trichogaster leeri (Pearl gourami)
Malay peninsula, Thailand, Sumatra, Borneo. Well-weeded swamps, often in water poor in oxygen. Diet: vegetable matter and insect larvae.
DNA 2195

‡ *Trichodon stelleri*
Volume 1 only

‡ *Trichogaster pectoralis* (Siamese goramy, Snakeskin gourami)
Native to Thailand, Malaya, Indonesia. Introduced Sri Lanka. Lakes, ponds and still or sluggish waters generally. Diet: aquatic plants.
Folic acid 2582

‡ *Trichogaster trichopterus* (Three-spot gourami)
Indo-Australian archipelago, S.E. Asia generally. Weedy streams, canals. Possesses accessory breathing organ. Bubble-nest builder.
DNA 2195

‡Trigla corax (*see* T. lucerna)

‡Trigla cuculus = T. pini = Aspitrigla cuculus (Elleck, Piper, Red gurnard)
Norway to Mauritania, Mediterranean. 5–250 m, various localities.
Volume 1 only

‡Trigla gurnardus = Eutrigla gurnardus = Trigla milvus (Grey gurnard)
Norway and Iceland to Senegal, Mediterranean, Black Sea, W. Baltic. Muddy or
sandy bottom to 200 m. May enter estuaries. Emits noises. Diet: small fish, prawns,
crabs.
Calcium 1909; Chloride 1909; Cholesterol 2516; *Free* fatty acids 2515; Haematocrit 2516; Haemoglobin 2516; Magnesium 1909; Potassium 1909; Sodium 1909

Trigla lineata (*see* Trigloporus lastoviza)

‡Trigla lucerna* = T. corax* = T. hirundo* (Saphirine gurnard, Tubfish, Yellow
gurnard) *76, 81*
W. Europe (except Iceland), Mediterranean, Black Sea. Common close inshore on
sand, mud or gravel. A bottom-living marine fish which can tolerate fresh water.
Can emit noises. An excellent swimmer which can jump out of the water. Diet:
sprats, pilchards, sand smelts, fish eggs.
Adenosine triphosphatase 2353; Cadmium 1707; Copper 1707; Lactic dehydrogenase 1789; Lead 1707; Mercury 1707; Zinc 1707

Trigla lyra (Piper gurnard)
British Is. to Senegal, Mediterranean. Not Black Sea. Muddy bottoms 300–700 m
usually, sometimes as shallow as 50 m. Diet: crustaceans, echinoderms, worms, fish,
molluscs.
Cadmium, Copper, Lead, Mercury, Zinc: 1707

‡Trigla milvus (*see* T. gurnardus)

‡Trigla pini (*see* T. cuculus)

Trigla sp.
Urate oxidase, Xanthine oxidase: 1711

Trigloporus lastoviza = Trigla lineata (Streaked gurnard)
E. Atlantic, Mediterranean. Bottom-living on sand or mud, 20–100 m. Diet:
crustaceans.
Cadmium 1707, 1709; Copper 1707, 1709; Lactic dehydrogenase 1789; Lead 1707,
1709; Mercury 1707, 1709; Zinc 1707, 1709

Trinectes maculatus (Dwarf flounder, Hogchoker)
Massachusetts Bay to Panama. Coastal, common in bays and estuaries. Juveniles
tolerate almost fresh water. Diet: marine worms, small crustaceans.
DNA 2195

‡Trisotropis venenosus (Rockfish, Yellowfinned grouper)
Florida, Bahamas.
Volume 1 only

‡Trudis bassensis westraliae (Cliff flathead)
Australia.
Volume 1 only

‡**Trygon imbricata** (Scaly stingray)
India: Coromandel coast.
Volume 1 only

‡**Trygon microps**
India.
Volume 1 only

‡**Trygon pastinaca** (*see* **Dasyatis pastinaca**)

‡**Trygon uarnak** (*see* **Dasyatis uarnak**)

‡**Trygon violacea** (Blue stingray)
Europe. Warm, shallow water. A more active swimmer than other rays.
Volume 1 only

‡Trypauchen wakae
Japan.
Volume 1 only

‡Tylosurus acus (Agujon, Houndfish)
W. Indies.
Volume 1 only

‡Tylosurus giganteus
Seychelles, India, Philippines, Japan, N. Australia, Sandwich Is.
Volume 1 only

Tylosurus melanotus
Japan.
Thiaminase 2297

Typhlogobius californiensis (Blind goby)
Coast of California. Lives its entire life in burrows dug by the ghost shrimp
Callianassa. The eyes degenerate as the fish grows until it is blind.
DNA 2195

Ulua mandibularis (Cale-cale trevally)
Burma. Indo-Australian archipelago. Shallow coastal areas. Diet: crustaceans, fish.
Amino acids, Calcium, Iron, Niacin, Riboflavin, Thiamine, Vitamin A: 3690

Umbra limi (Central mudminnow)
Central N. America in silt-bottomed lakes and ponds. Burrows into mud and silt.
Tolerates low temperatures and low oxygen conditions.
DNA 2195

Umbrina cirrhosa
Mediterranean.
Cadmium, Copper, Lead, Mercury, Zinc: 1707

‡Umbrina sinuta
India: Sind
Volume 1 only

‡Upeneoides bensasi (Goatfish, Salmonet, Surmullet)
Japan. Shores, on muddy bottom.
Volume 1 only

Upeneoides sulphureus (Yellow goatfish)
Madagascar, India, Thailand, Philippines, S. China, S. Japan, Fiji, New Hebrides.
On trawling grounds.
Folic acid 2582

Upeneus bensasi. Perhaps same as Upeneoides bensasi. (Yellowfin goatfish)
E. Africa, Japan, Malaya, Philippines. Coastal waters in schools down to 40 m.
Diet: bottom-living animals.
Trimethylamine oxide 2111

‡Uranoscopus japonicus (Japanese stargazer, Mishima puffer fish)
Japan, Korea.
Cadmium 2901; Copper 2901; Iron 2901; Lead 2901; Potassium 2900; Sodium
2900; Zinc 2901

‡Uranoscopus scaber (Sea ladybird, Stargazer)
Spain to Senegal, Mediterranean and Black seas, 3–100 m. Spends much time
partly buried in sand or mud. Possesses poisonous spines. Capable of generating
electric shocks. Diet: fish.
Adrenaline 3340; Amino acids 3527; Cadmium 1707, 1709; Chloride 2864;
Copper 1707–1709; Corticosterone + Cortisol 1704; Lead 1707–1709; Mercury
1707–1709; Noradrenaline 3340; Potassium 2864; Sodium 2864; Zinc 1707–1709

Urolophus halleri
DNA 2194

‡**Urolophus mucosus**
Australia.
Volume 1 only

‡Urophycis blennoides (Forkbeard hake)
Volume 1 only

‡Urophycis chesteri (Longfin hake)
Eastern N. America on the continental slope.
Volume 1 only

‡Urophycis chuss (Forkbeard, Ling, Mud hake, Red hake, Squirrel hake, Thimble-
eyed ling, White hake)
N.W. Atlantic (Newfoundland to Virginia) from shallow water to over 900 m, on
soft bottom, gravel or shells. Tolerates wide temperature range. Diet: (young)
crustaceans, copepods, amphipods; (adult) prawns, shrimps, fish and occasionally
worms, molluscs.
Mercury 1953

‡Urophycis tenuis (Codling, Hake, Ling, Old English hake, Squirrel hake, White hake)
Distribution as for U. chuss (often caught together). Low tide to 1000 m.
Volume 1 only

‡Usacaranx georgianus (Silver bream, Silver trevally, Skipjack, White trevally)
Australia. Coastal.
Volume 1 only

‡Verasper moseri
Japan.
Fatty acids 2154

‡*Vimba vimba* (Vimba, Zahrte) *43*
Sweden, Austria, Black and Caspian Seas, lower reaches of rivers and lakes. Spawns
on stones in streams and rivers. Enters low-salinity regions of estuaries and the sea.
Diet: bottom-living insects over mud.
Albumin 2023; Copper 2829; Globulin 2023; Mercury 2829; Sodium 2023; Zinc
2829

‡*Wallago attu* = *Wallagonia attu* (Boal, Freshwater shark, Mulley) *41*
India, Sri Lanka, Burma, Java, Sumatra. Deep waters of rivers. Predatory. A large,
voracious catfish. Diet: fish.
Acid phosphatase 3227; Alkaline phosphatase 3227, 3404; Amylase 1425; Calcium
3176; Cholesterol 3267, 3268; Erythrocytes 3408; Fatty acids 2014; Glucose 3407;
Lactate 3407; Leucocytes 3408; Lipase 1425; Magnesium 3176; Sodium 3176;
Sucrase 1425; Trypsin 1425

Xenentodon canciloides (Garfish)
India, Sri Lanka, Burma, Malay Peninsula, Thailand. Lives near surface. Diet: fish,
amphibians.
Erythrocytes 3408; Leucocytes 3408; Vitamin A_1 1500; Vitamin A_2 1500

Xenocara dolichoptera (Bluechin xenocara)
Amazon and the Guianas.
DNA 2195

Xenodermichthys copei *126*
A deepwater fish which maintains nearly neutral buoyancy by having watery
musculature and poorly-ossified bones. There is no swim bladder.

Xenomystus nigri (False featherback)
Central and W. Africa. Overgrown waters and pools. Hardy in captivity. Can
breathe air.
DNA 2195

‡Xesurus scalprum
Japan.
Volume 1 only

‡Xiphias gladius (Broadbill swordfish, Swordfish) *73, 437*
  Wide range over Atlantic: Iceland and N. Norway to S. Africa. Pacific: Chile to
  Oregon. Red Sea, Mediterranean, Black and Azov Seas. Japan to Australia. An
  oceanic traveller, voracious and fast-swimming in surface waters to below 600 m.
  Solitary. The flesh can contain appreciable quantities of mercury, apparently a
  natural phenomenon since comparable concentrations have been found in old
  museum specimens caught long before the advent of industrial pollution on the
  modern scale. Diet: mackerel, garfish, herring, squid.
  Aluminium 3018, 3019; Amino acids 1494, 3019; *Free* amino acids 3019;
  Ammonia 1494; Barium 3018; Bismuth 3018; Cholesterol 2572, 3019, 3020;
  Chromium 3018; Cobalt 3018; Copper 1494, 3018, 3019; DNA 2195; *Free* fatty
  acids 2572; Formaldehyde 1656; Hypoxanthine 1865; Iron 3019; Lead 3018, 3019;
  Manganese 3018, 3019; Mercury 1463, 1891, 1928, 2371; Molybdenum 3018;
  Nickel 3018, 3019; Phospholipids 2572; Provitamin D 3019, 3020; Silver 3018,
  3019; Sterol esters 2572; Strontium 3018; Thiaminase 3473; Tin 3018, 3019;
  Titanium 3018, 3019; Triglycerides 2572; Trimethylamine oxide 3151; Zinc 1494,
  3018, 3019

Xiphophorus helleri (Swordtail)
  S. Mexico, Guatemala. Females can change to males, but not the other way round.
  DNA 1705, 2195; Glucose-6-phosphate dehydrogenase 1956; α-Glycerophosphate
  dehydrogenase 1956; Lactic dehydrogenase 1956, 3213

Xiphophorus maculatus (Platy)
  Mexico to N. British Honduras. Swamp pools, ponds and lakes. Viviparous.
  DNA 2195; Glucose-6-phosphate dehydrogenase 1955, 1956; α-Glycerophosphate
  dehydrogenase 1956; Lactic dehydrogenase 1955, 1956; 6-phosphogluconate
  dehydrogenase 1955

Xiphophorus milleri
  Glucose-6-phosphate dehydrogenase, α-Glycerophosphate dehydrogenase, Lactic
  dehydrogenase: 1956

Xiphophorus montezumae
  Glucose-6-phosphate dehydrogenase, α-Glycerophosphate dehydrogenase: 1956

Xystreurys liolepis
  DNA 2195

‡*Zacco platypus* (Common minnow)
  Japan, China, Korea.
  Astacene 2719; Cryptoxanthin 2719; Cynthiaxanthin 2719; Diatoxanthin 2719;
  α-Doradecin 2719; Fatty acids 1466; Lutein 2719; Trimethylamine oxide 2111;
  Vitamin D 3673; Zeaxanthin 2719

Zacco temmincki
  Japan.
  Cynthiaxanthin 2719; Diatoxanthin 2719; α-Doradecin 2719; Lutein 2719;
  Thiaminase 2297; Zeaxanthin 2719

Zalembius rosaceus
  DNA 2195

Zaniolepis latipinnis (Longspine combfish, Longspined greenling)
  S. California to Vancouver, down to 110 m.
  DNA 2195

‡Zebrias zebra (Striped sole, Zebra sole)
  India, Japan, Formosa, Malaya. Shallow coastal waters on sandy or muddy
  bottoms. Diet: small bottom-living invertebrates.
  Volume 1 only

‡Zeus australis (John Dory)
  Australia.
  Volume 1 only

‡Zeus faber = Z. japonicus (John Dory, St. Peter's fish)
  S. Norway to S. Africa, Mediterranean, Japan, Australia. From close inshore to
  200 m. Solitary or in small shoals. A somewhat feeble swimmer. Diet: pilchards,
  sprats, sand-smelts.
  Cadmium 1707; Cholesterol 1785; Copper 1707, 2828; Dimethylamine 2110;
  Formaldehyde 2110; Lead 1707; Mercury 1707, 1891, 2828; Trimethylamine
  oxide 2111; Urate oxidase 1711; Xanthine oxidase 1711; Zinc 1707, 2828

Zeus japonicus (*see* Z. faber)

‡Zoarces viviparus (Eel pout, Viviparous blenny) *41, 44, 285, 385*
  S. and E. Britain northwards to White Sea and Baltic. 4–28 m usually. On sand
  or mud or amongst weed, also in brackish water. Viviparous. Diet: sandhoppers,
  worms, molluscs, small fish.
  Total *Free* amino acids (a single value) 2476; Ammonia 2476; Calcium 2476;
  Chloride 2476; *Free* fatty acids 3000; Haematocrit 2476; Magnesium 2476;
  Neutral lipids 3000; Potassium 2476; Sodium 2476

‡Zonichthys falcatus (Madregal, Rock Salmon)
  W. Indies, Florida.
  Volume 1 only

‡**Zygaena blochii** (Arrow-headed hammerhead shark)
  India, Malaya and beyond.
  Volume 1 only

APPENDIX Common Names of Fish and their Latin Equivalents

This list comprises all the discoverable names of all the fish mentioned or listed in both the present and the earlier volume. Preferred synonyms have been substituted for those given in Volume 1. Sometimes more than one Latin name is appended to a single common name, and in such cases the reader should be aware of possible pitfalls. If there are two or more specific names under one genus, the list is probably correct as far as it goes, though it may be incomplete. It is reasonable that two or more related species of similar appearance should have been given the same common name. Where, however, there are two generic names each with the same specific name (and the same common name, of course), then it is likely that only one actual fish is involved, one of the names being obsolete. As an example, the genera Sebastes *and* Sebastodes *seem to have been used more or less interchangeably in the literature, and lacking authentic ruling I have had to put either name as it was recorded. The reader will probably find other examples.*

ADALAH   *Psettodes erumei*
AFRICAN LUNGFISH   *Protopterus aethiopicus, Protopterus annectens*
AGUJON   *Tylosurus acus*
AGULHAS SOLE   *Austroglossus pectoralis*
ALASKA GREENFISH   *Hexagrammos octogrammus*
ALBACORE   *Thunnus thynnus thynnus, Thunnus alalunga*
ALBACORE, AUTUMN   *Thunnus albacares*
ALBACORE, FALSE   *Euthynnus alletteratus*
ALBACORE, LONGFINNED   *Thunnus alalunga*
ALEKEY TROUT   *Lota lota*
ALEUTIAN SCULPIN   *Cottus aleuticus*
ALEWIFE   *Alosa pseudoharengus*
ALFONCINO   *Beryx splendens*
ALLMOUTH   *Lophius piscatorius*
ALLIED KINGFISH   *Seriola purpurascens*
ALLIGATOR GAR   *Lepisosteus spatula*
ALLISON'S TUNA   *Thunnus albacares*
AMBERFISH   *Seriola quinqueradiata*
AMBERJACK   *Seriola dumerili, Seriola purpurascens*
AMERICAN ATLANTIC STURGEON   *Acipenser oxyrhynchus, Acipenser sturio*
AMERICAN BARRELFISH   *Palinurichthys perciformis*

AMERICAN BROOK LAMPREY   *Lampetra lamottei*
AMERICAN CATFISH   *Ictalurus melas*
AMERICAN EEL   *Anguilla bostoniensis, Anguilla rostrata*
AMERICAN HAKE   *Merluccius bilinearis*
AMERICAN PERCH   *Perca flavescens*
AMERICAN PLAICE   *Hippoglossoides platessoides*
AMERICAN SHAD   *Alosa sapidissima*
AMERICAN SMELT   *Osmerus mordax*
AMUR, WHITE   *Ctenopharyngodon idella*
ANCHOVY   *Engraulis encrasicholus, Engraulis japonicus, Engraulis mordax, Thrissocles mystax*
ANCHOVY, COMMERSON'S   *Stolephorus commersonii*
ANCHOVY, GOLD-SPOTTED GRENADIER   *Coilia dussumieri*
ANCHOVY, LONGJAWED   *Stolephorus commersonii*
ANCHOVY, MOUSTACHED   *Thrissocles mystax*
ANCHOVY, NORTHERN   *Engraulis mordax*
ANGEL FISH   *Angelichthys isabelita, Chaetodipterus faber, Holocanthus isabelita, Pterophyllum eimekei*
ANGELFISH, FRENCH   *Pomacanthus arcuatus*
ANGELFISH, GREY   *Pomacanthus arcuatus*
ANGEL RAY   *Squatina squatina*
ANGLEMOUTH, LONGTOOTH   *Gonostoma elongatum*
ANGLER   *Lophiomus setigerus, Lophius litulon, Lophius piscatorius*
ANNUAL FISH   *Cynolebias adloffi*
ANOSTOMUS, STRIPED   *Anostomus anostomus*
ANTARCTIC COD, GIANT   *Dissostichus mawsoni*
ANTIMORA, BLUE   *Antimora rostrata*
ARAPAIMA   *Arapaima gigas*
ARAWANA   *Osteoglossum bicirrhosum*
ARCTIC CHAR   *Salvelinus alpinus*
ARCTIC COD   *Boreogadus saida*
ARCTIC FLOUNDER   *Liopsetta glacialis*
ARCTIC GRAYLING   *Thymallus thymallus*
ARCTIC LAMPREY   *Lampetra japonica*
ARCTIC SANDLANCE   *Ammodytes tobianus*
ARCTIC SHANNY   *Stichaeus grigorjewi*
ARCTIC STAGHORN SCULPIN   *Gymnocanthus tricuspis*
ARCTIC WOLF-FISH   *Anarhichas latifrons*
ARGENTINE   *Argentina silus*
ARGENTINE, JAPANESE   *Argentina semifasciata*
ARMOUR SHARK   *Dalatias licha*
ARROWHEADED HAMMERHEAD SHARK   *Zygaena blochii*
ARROWTOOTH FLOUNDER   *Atheresthes stomias*
ASP   *Aspius aspius*
ATKA FISH   *Pleurogrammus monopterygius*
ATKA MACKEREL   *Pleurogrammus asotus*
ATLANTIC BONITO   *Sarda sarda*
ATLANTIC COD   *Gadus morhua*
ATLANTIC GUITARFISH   *Rhinobatus lentiginosus*
ATLANTIC HAGFISH   *Myxine glutinosa*

ATLANTIC HALIBUT   *Hippoglossus hippoglossus*
ATLANTIC HERRING   *Clupea harengus*
ATLANTIC LOOKDOWN   *Selene vomer*
ATLANTIC MACKEREL   *Scomber scombrus*
ATLANTIC MARINE GOBY   *Notothenia gibberifrons*
ATLANTIC MIDSHIPMAN   *Porichthys porosissimus*
ATLANTIC NEEDLEFISH   *Strongylura marina*
ATLANTIC PRICKLY SKATE   *Raja radiata, Raja scabrata*
ATLANTIC SAURY   *Scomberesox saurus*
ATLANTIC SILVERSIDE   *Menidia menidia notata*
ATLANTIC SPINY DOGFISH   *Squalus acanthias*
ATLANTIC TOMCOD   *Microgadus tomcod*
ATLANTIC TORPEDO   *Tetranarce occidentalis, Torpedo nobiliana*
ATLANTIC WOLF FISH   *Anarhichas lupus*
ATLANTIC WRECKFISH   *Polyprion americanus*
AUSTRALIAN RED-TAILED RAINBOW FISH   *Melanotaenia nigrans*
AUSTRALIAN SALMON   *Arripis trutta*
AUTUMN ALBACORE   *Thunnus albacares*
AXILLARY SEABREAM   *Pagellus acarne*
AYU   *Plecoglossus altivelis*

BACHELOR   *Pomoxis annularis*
BAILLON'S WRASSE   *Crenilabrus melops*
BALLAN WRASSE   *Labrus bergylta*
BALLOON FISH   *Diodon holocanthus, Sphaeroides maculatus*
BALTIC COD   *Gadus callarias*
BALTIC HERRING   *Clupea harengus membranus*
BANDED BARRACUDA   *Sphyraena jello*
BANDED CAVALLA   *Caranx sexfasciatus*
BANDED DRUM   *Pogonias cromis*
BANDED ETROPLUS   *Etroplus suratensis*
BANDED KILLIFISH   *Fundulus diaphanus*
BANDED KNIFEFISH   *Gymnotus carapo*
BANDED REEFCOD   *Epinephelus fasciatus*
BANDED SCULPIN   *Cottus carolinae*
BANDED SEAPERCH   *Serranus scriba*
BANDED TUNA   *Scomberomorus commersonii*
BANDED WHIPTAIL STINGRAY   *Dasyatis uarnak*
BANDFISH   *Trichiurus lepturus*
BANDFISH, RED   *Cepola rubescens*
BANG   *Alosa pseudoharengus*
BARB, CHERRY   *Barbus titteya*
BARB, CLOWN   *Barbus everetti*
BARB, HASSELT'S BONY-LIPPED   *Osteocheilus hasselti*
BARB, OLIVE   *Barbus chrysopoma*
BARB, ROSY   *Barbus conchonius*
BARB, SCHWANENFELD'S   *Barbus schwanenfeldi*
BARB, SUMATRA   *Barbus tetrazona*
BARB, TIGER   *Barbus tetrazona*

BARBEL, BLACK   *Barbus meridionalis petenyi*
BARBEL, COMMON   *Barbus barbus*
BARBEL, MOUNTAIN   *Barbus meridionalis petenyi*
BARBEL, MUD   *Clarias mossambicus*
BARBER EEL   *Plotosus anguillaris*
BARBUDO   *Polymixia japonica*
BAR-EYED GOBY   *Glossogobius giuris*
BARNDOOR SKATE   *Raja laevis*
BARRACOUTA   *Thrysites atun*
BARRACUDA   *Sphyraena picuda*
BARRACUDA, BANDED   *Sphyraena jello*
BARRACUDA, CALIFORNIA   *Sphyraena argentea*
BARRACUDA, GREAT   *Sphyraena barracuda*
BARRACUDA, JAPANESE   *Sphyraena japonica*
BARRACUDA, JAPANESE DWARF   *Sphyraena pinguis*
BARRACUDA, OBTUSE   *Sphyraena obtusata*
BARRACUDA, PACIFIC   *Sphyraena argentea*
BARRACUDA, PICKHANDLE   *Sphyraena jello*
BARRACUDA, RED   *Sphyraena pinguis*
BARRACUDA, STRIPED   *Sphyraena obtusata*
BARRACUTA   *Scomberomorus commersonii*
BARRAMUNDI   *Lates calcarifer*
BARRED SPANISH MACKEREL   *Scomberomorus commersonii*
BARREL FISH   *Palinurichthys perciformis, Schedophilus medusophagus*
BARREL FISH, AMERICAN   *Palinurichthys perciformis*
BASKING SHARK   *Cetorhinus maximus*
BASS   *Dicentrarchus labrax, Micropterus dolomieui, Sciaenops ocellata, Scophthalmus rhombus*
BASS, BLACK   *Micropterus salmoides*
BASS, BLACK SEA   *Centropristes striatus*
BASS, BLACK, SMALL-MOUTHED   *Micropterus dolomieui*
BASS, CHANNEL   *Sciaenops ocellata*
BASS, EUROPEAN   *Dicentrarchus labrax*
BASS, GIANT SEA   *Stereolepis gigas*
BASS HOGFISH   *Micropterus dolomieui*
BASS, KELP   *Paralabrax clathratus*
BASS, LARGEMOUTH   *Micropterus salmoides*
BASS, LITTLE   *Micropterus dolomieui*
BASS, NORTHERN ROCK   *Amblioplites rupestris*
BASS, RED   *Sciaenops ocellata*
BASS, SAND   *Paralabrax maculatofasciatus*
BASS, SEA   *Dicentrarchus labrax, Lateolabrax japonicus, Sciaenops ocellata, Spicara smaris*
BASS, SPOTTED   *Sciaenops ocellata*
BASS, STONE   *Polyprion americanus*
BASS, STRIPED   *Morone saxatilis*
BASS, SUN   *Lepomis gibbosus*
BASS, TRUE   *Epinephelus septemfasciatus*
BASS, WHITE   *Morone chrysops*
BASTARD HALIBUT   *Paralichthys olivaceus*
BASTARD MACKEREL   *Acanthocybium solandri*
BASTARD MULLET   *Polynemus indicus*

BASTARD TRUMPETER   *Latridopsis forsteri*
BATFISH, BLACK   *Parastromateus niger*
BATFISH, RED   *Halieutea stellata*
BATFISH, REDBELLIED   *Ogcocephalus nasutus*
BATFISH, SPOTTED   *Drepane punctata*
BAY MACKEREL   *Scomberomorus maculatus*
BAY MARE   *Catostomus commersonii*
BEACONFISH   *Hemigrammus ocellifer*
BEARDFISH, STOUT   *Polymixia japonica*
BELLOWS FISH   *Lophius piscatorius*
BELLY FISH   *Poecilia reticulata*
BELLY, PUFF   *Hemitripterus americanus*
BELLY, VELVET   *Etmopterus spinax*
BELUGA   *Huso huso*
BENGAL TONGUE SOLE   *Cynoglossus bengalensis*
BERGALL   *Tautogolabrus adspersus*
BERGYLT   *Labrus bergylta*
BERMUDA SILK SNAPPER   *Lutianus hastingsi*
BIAJAIBA   *Lutianus synagris*
BICHIR   *Polypterus senegalus*
BIDYAN GRUNTER   *Therapon bidyana*
BIG DRUM   *Pogonias cromis*
BIGEYE   *Priacanthus arenatus, Scombrops boops*
BIGEYE ILISHA   *Ilisha filigera*
BIGEYE, RED   *Priacanthus macracanthus*
BIGEYE SARDINE   *Etrumeus micropus*
BIGEYE SCAD   *Selar crumenophthalmus, Trachurops crumenophthalmus*
BIGEYE TUNA   *Thunnus obesus*
BIGEYE HERRING   *Alosa pseudoharengus, Elops saurus*
BIGHEAD   *Aristichthys nobilis*
BIGHEAD CARP   *Aristichthys nobilis*
BIGMOUTH BUFFALO   *Ictiobus bubalis*
BIGMOUTH FLOUNDER   *Psettodes erumei*
BIG SKATE   *Raja binoculata, Raja ocellata*
BILLFISH   *Lepisosteus osseus, Scomberesox saurus*
BILLY GAR   *Lepisosteus osseus*
BITTERHEAD   *Notemigonus crysoleucas*
BIWA SALMON   *Oncorhynchus rhodurus*
BLACKAMOOR   *Gymnocorymbus ternetzi*
BLACKBACK   *Hippoglossoides platessoides, Pseudopleuronectes americanus*
BLACK BARBEL   *Barbus meridionalis petenyi*
BLACK BASS   *Micropterus salmoides*
BLACK BASS, SMALL-MOUTHED   *Micropterus dolomieui*
BLACK BATFISH   *Parastromateus niger*
BLACKBELLY ROSEFISH   *Helicolenus dactylopterus*
BLACK BREAM   *Acanthopagrus butcheri, Girella tricuspidata, Mylio macrocephalus, Sparus berda, Spondyliosoma cantharus, Therapon bidyana*
BLACK BULLHEAD   *Ictalurus melas*
BLACK CARP   *Morulius chrysoplekadion, Mylopharyngodon piceus*
BLACK CICHLID   *Tilapia nigra*

BLACK COD   *Anoplopoma fimbria*
BLACK COW TONGUE   *Rhinoplagusia japonica*
BLACK CRAPPIE   *Pomoxis nigromaculatus*
BLACK DOGFISH   *Centroscyllium fabricii*
BLACK DRUM   *Pogonias cromis*
BLACK EELPOUT   *Lycodes diapterus*
BLACKFINNED MULLET   *Mugil melinopterus*
BLACKFISH   *Centrolophus niger, Centropristes striatus, Girella tricuspidata, Tautoga onitis*
BLACKFISH, CORNISH   *Schedophilus medusophagus*
BLACK GOBY   *Gobius niger*
BLACK GROUPER   *Garrupa nigrita*
BLACK JEWFISH   *Garrupa nigrita*
BLACK MARLIN   *Makaira mazara*
BLACK MOLLIE   *Mollienesia* sp.
BLACKMOUTH DOGFISH   *Pristiurus melanostomus*
BLACK MULLET   *Catostomus commersonii*
BLACKNOSE DACE   *Rhinichthys atratulus*
BLACK PERCH   *Centropristes striatus, Micropterus dolomieui*
BLACK POMFRET   *Parastromateus niger*
BLACK PORGY   *Mylio macrocephalus*
BLACK ROCKFISH   *Sebastes inermis, Sebastes thompsoni, Sebastodes melanops, Sebastodes schlegeli*
BLACK RUDDERFISH   *Palinurichthys perciformis*
BLACK RUFF   *Centrolophus niger*
BLACK SCORPIONFISH   *Scorpaena porcus*
BLACK SCRAPER   *Navodon modestus*
BLACK SEA BASS   *Centropristes striatus*
BLACK SEA BREAM   *Acanthopagrus schlegeli, Spondyliosoma cantharus*
BLACK SEA ROUND GOBY   *Neogobius melanostomus*
BLACK SEA HARDTAIL   *Trachurus mediterraneus ponticus*
BLACK SEA PICKEREL   *Spicara smaris*
BLACK SEA SCAD   *Trachurus mediterraneus ponticus*
BLACK SEA TURBOT   *Scophthalmus maeoticus*
BLACK SHARK   *Dalatias licha, Morulius chrysophekadion*
BLACK SPEARFISH   *Makaira mazara*
BLACKSPOT SEABREAM   *Pagellus bogaraveo*
BLACK-SPOTTED CORYDORAS   *Corydoras melanistius*
BLACK-SPOTTED GOBY   *Gobius melanostomus*
BLACK-SPOTTED SPANISH MACKEREL   *Scomberomorus regalis*
BLACK-SPOTTED TOP MINNOW   *Fundulus olivaceus*
BLACK SURFPERCH   *Embiotoca jacksoni*
BLACKTAIL   *Diplodus annularis*
BLACK TETRA   *Gymnocorymbus ternetzi*
BLACK-TIPPED GROPER   *Epinephelus fasciatus*
BLACK-TIPPED ROCK COD   *Epinephelus fasciatus*
BLACK-TIPPED SHARK   *Carcharhinus maculipinnis*
BLACK-TIPPED SHARK, SMALL   *Carcharhinus limbatus*
BLACK TUNA   *Promethichthys prometheus*
BLACK WILL   *Centropristes striatus*
BLEAK   *Alburnus alburnus, Alburnus lucidus*

BLEAK, DANUBE *Chalcalburnus chalcoides*
BLEEKER'S LINED SURGEONFISH *Acanthurus bleekeri*
BLENNY *Enedrias nebulosus*
BLENNY, EEL *Lumpenus sagitta*
BLENNY, NORTHERN *Stichaeus grigorjewi*
BLENNY, PEACOCK *Blennius pavo*
BLENNY, PACIFIC SNAKE *Lumpenus sagitta*
BLENNY, RED-SPECKLED *Blennius sanguinolentus*
BLENNY, SNAKE *Ophiodon barbatum*
BLENNY, VIVIPAROUS *Zoarces viviparus*
BLIND CAVE-FISH *Anoptichthys jordani*
BLIND GOBY *Typhlogobius californiensis*
BLIND TASSEL FISH *Eleutheronema tetradactylon*
BLIND TETRA *Anoptichthys jordani*
BLISTER-BACK *Pollachius virens*
BLOATER *Coregonus hoyi*
BLONDE RAY *Raja brachyura*
BLOODFIN *Aphyocharax rubropinnis*
BLOTCHED THERAPON *Therapon oxyrhynchus*
BLOWER, MUD *Lota lota*
BLOWFISH *Sphaeroides maculatus*
BLUE ANTIMORA *Antimora rostrata*
BLUEBACK *Oncorhynchus nerka*
BLUEBACK TROUT *Salvelinus alpinus*
BLUE-BLACK MULLET *Mugil curema*
BLUEBOTTLE FISH *Nomeus gronowi*
BLUE CATFISH *Ictalurus furcatus*
BLUECHIN XENOCARA *Xenocara dolichoptera*
BLUE DOG *Prionace glauca*
BLUEFIN *Thunus thynnus thynnus*
BLUEFIN, SOUTHERN *Thunnus maccoyii*
BLUEFIN TUNA *Thunnus thynnus thynnus*
BLUEFIN TUNA, PACIFIC *Thunnus thynnus orientalis*
BLUEFIN TUNA, SOUTHERN *Thunnus maccoyii*
BLUEFISH *Pomatomus saltatrix*
BLUEFISH, BOSTON *Pollachius virens*
BLUEFISH, CALIFORNIA *Girella nigricans*
BLUEFISH, JAPANESE *Scombrops boops*
BLUEGILL *Lepomis macrochirus*
BLUEGILL SUNFISH *Lepomis macrochirus*
BLUE GROPER *Achoerodus gouldii*
BLUE HAKE *Antimora rostrata*
BLUE HALIBUT *Reinhardtius hippoglossoides*
BLUEHEAD WRASSE *Thalassoma bifasciatum*
BLUE LING *Molva byrkelange*
BLUE MARLIN *Makaira mazara*
BLUE MARLIN, PACIFIC *Makaira ampla*
BLUE MISHIMA PUFFER FISH *Gnathagnus elongatus*
BLUEMOUTH *Helicolenus dactylopterus*
BLUE PANCHAX *Aplocheilus panchax*

BLUE PERCH   *Tautogolabrus adspersus*
BLUE PIKE   *Stizostedion vitreum*
BLUE POINTER   *Isurus glaucus*
BLUE SHARK   *Isurus oxyrinchus, Prionace glauca*
BLUE SHARK, GREAT   *Glyphis glaucus*
BLUE SKATE   *Parastromateus niger, Raja batis*
BLUE SMELT, CALIFORNIA   *Atherinops californiensis*
BLUE STING-RAY   *Trygon violacea*
BLUE STRIPED GRUNT   *Haemulon sciurus*
BLUE WHITING   *Micromesistius poutassou*
BLUNTJAWED SEA PIKE   *Sphyraena obtusata*
BLUNTNOSE LIZARDFISH   *Trachinocephalus myops*
BLUNTNOSE MINNOW   *Pimephales notatus*
BOAL   *Wallago attu*
BOAR GRUNT   *Haemulon plumieri, Haemulon sciurus*
BOBTAILED SKATE   *Raja eglantaria*
BOCACCIO   *Sebastodes paucispinis*
BOGUE   *Boops boops*
BOMBAY DUCK   *Harpadon nehereus*
BONITA   *Katsuwonus pelamis*
BONITO, ATLANTIC   *Sarda sarda*
BONITO, OCEAN   *Katsuwonus pelamis*
BONITO, PACIFIC   *Sarda chiliensis*
BONITO, PLAIN   *Auxis thazard*
BONNETNOSE SHARK   *Sphyrna tiburo*
BONTROK   *Lithognathus mormyrus*
BONY MULLET   *Megalops cyprinoides*
BORER, SAND   *Sillago japonica*
BOSTON BLUEFISH   *Pollachius virens*
BOTTOM PERCH   *Apogon semilineatus*
BOWEN SNAPPER   *Argyrops spinifer*
BOUNCE   *Scylliorhinus stellaris*
BOWFIN   *Amia calva*
BRANCH HERRING   *Alosa pseudoharengus*
BREAM   *Abramis blicca, Abramis brama, Brama raii, Diplodus bermudensis, Lagodon rhomboides, Lepomis gibbosus, Mylio australis, Notemigonus crysoleucas, Stenotomus versicolor, Tilapia mossambica*
BREAM, BLACK   *Acanthopagrus butcheri, Girella tricuspidata, Mylio macrocephalus, Sparus berda, Spondyliosoma cantharus, Therapon bidyana*
BREAM, BLACK SEA   *Acanthopagrus schlegeli*
BREAM, BLACK SEA   *Spondyliosoma cantharus*
BREAM, BRIDLED PIG-FACE   *Lethrinus cinereus*
BREAM, BRONZE   *Abramis brama*
BREAM, CARDINAL SEA   *Evynnis cardinalis*
BREAM, COMMON SEA   *Pagellus centrotodontus*
BREAM, COUCH'S SEA   *Pagrus pagrus*
BREAM, CRIMSON SEA   *Evynnis japonica*
BREAM, DANUBE   *Abramis sapa*
BREAM, GOLDEN THREADFIN   *Nemipterus virgatus*
BREAM, GREY LARGE-EYE   *Gymnocranius griseus*

BREAM, HUMPNOSE LARGE-EYE   *Monotaxis grandoculis*
BREAM, JAPANESE RED   *Chrysophrys major*
BREAM, JAPANESE SILVER   *Chrysophrys datnia*
BREAM, JAPANESE THREADFIN   *Nemipterus japonicus*
BREAM, LARGE-EYED   *Gymnocranius griseus*
BREAM, MARMOR   *Lithognathus mormyrus*
BREAM, RED   *Lutianus malabaricus*
BREAM, RED SEA   *Chrysophrys major, Pagellus erythrinus*
BREAM, ROUND-TOOTHED LARGE-EYED   *Monotaxis grandoculis*
BREAM, SADDLED   *Oblada melanura*
BREAM, SEA   *Chrysophrys major*
BREAM, SILVER   *Rhabdosargus sarba, Usacaranx georgianus*
BREAM, SPINY   *Argyrops spinifer*
BREAM, STARRY PIGFACE   *Lethrinus opercularis*
BREAM, TWO-BANDED   *Diplodus sargus*
BREAM, WHITE   *Abramis blicca, Blicca bjoerkna, Sargus sargus*
BREAM, YELLOWFIN   *Rhabdosargus sarba*
BREAM, YELLOW SEA   *Taius tumifrons*
BRIDLED PIGFACE BREAM   *Lethrinus cinereus*
BRIER RAY   *Raja eglantaria*
BRILL   *Eopsetta jordani, Scophthalmus aquosus, Scophthalmus maximus, Scophthalmus rhombus*
BROADBILL SWORDFISH   *Xiphias gladius*
BROAD HARBOUR SHARK   *Deania eglantina*
BROADHEADED CATFISH   *Anarhichas latifrons*
BROAD WHITEFISH   *Coregonus nasus*
BRONZE BREAM   *Abramis brama*
BRONZE CORYDORAS   *Corydoras aeneus*
BRONZE CROAKER   *Sciaenoides brunneus*
BROOK CHAR   *Salvelinus fontinalis*
BROOK LAMPREY   *Lampetra planeri*
BROOK LAMPREY, AMERICAN   *Lampetra lamottei*
BROOK LAMPREY, NORTHERN   *Ichthyomyzon fossor*
BROOK STICKLEBACK   *Culaea inconstans*
BROOK SUCKER   *Catostomus commersonii*
BROOK TROUT, EASTERN   *Salvelinus fontinalis*
BROUN, JAPANESE   *Sebastes inermis*
BROWN-BANDED MULLET   *Mugil dussumieri*
BROWN BULLHEAD   *Ictalurus melas*
BROWN MEAGRE   *Sciaena umbra*
BROWN POMFRET   *Parastromateus niger*
BROWN RAY   *Raja miraletus*
BROWN ROCKFISH   *Sebastes auriculatus*
BROWN SHARK   *Carcharhinus milberti*
BROWN SMOOTH DOGFISH   *Triakis scyllia*
BROWN SNAKEHEAD   *Channa gachua*
BROWN SPIKETAILED PARADISE FISH   *Macropodus cupanus dayi*
BROWN TROUT   *Salmo trutta*
BRUSHTOOTH LIZARDFISH   *Saurida undosquamis*
BUBBLER   *Aplodinotus grunniens*

BUENOS AIRES TETRA   *Hemigrammus caudovittatus*
BUFFALO   *Lactophrys trigonus*
BUFFALO, BIGMOUTH   *Ictiobus bubalis*
BUFFALO CARP   *Ictiobus bubalis*
BUFFALO, SMALLMOUTH   *Ictiobus bubalis*
BULLET MACKEREL   *Auxis thazard*
BULLHEAD   *Cottus gobio, Myoxocephalus scorpius*
BULLHEAD, BLACK   *Ictalurus melas*
BULLHEAD, BROWN   *Ictalurus melas*
BULLHEAD, COMMON   *Ictalurus melas*
BULLHEADED CATFISH   *Anarhichas latifrons*
BULLHEAD, YELLOW   *Ictalurus natalis*
BULL HUSS   *Scylliorhinus stellaris*
BULL ROUT   *Myoxocephalus scorpius*
BULL SHARK   *Carcharhinus leucas*
BULLY MULLET   *Mugil cephalus*
BUMMALO   *Harpadon nehereus*
BURBOT   *Lota lota*
BURNETT SALMON   *Neoceratodus forsteri*
BURRFISH, STRIPED   *Chilomycterus schoepfi*
BUTTER CATFISH   *Callichrous bimaculatus*
BUTTERFISH   *Cephalopholis fulvus, Drepane punctata, Parastromateus niger, Peprilus simillimus, Peprilus triacanthus, Poronotus triacanthus, Psenopsis anomala, Sciaena antarctica, Trachinotus carolinus*
BUTTERFLY FISH   *Pantodon buchholzi*
BUTTERFLY FISH, SPOTFIN   *Chaetodon ocellatus*
BUTTERFLY RAY, LESSER   *Gymnura macrura*
BUTTER SOLE   *Isopsetta isolepis*

CABELELLEROTE   *Lutianus griseus*
CABEZON   *Leptocottus armatus, Scorpaenichthys marmoratus*
CABRILLA   *Epinephelus guttatus*
CABRILLA SEABASS   *Serranus cabrilla*
CACHUCHO   *Etelis evurus*
CAESIO, GOLDEN   *Caesio chrysozona*
CALE-CALE TREVALLY   *Ulua mandibularis*
CALIFORNIA BARRACUDA   *Sphyraena argentea*
CALIFORNIA BLUEFISH   *Girella nigricans*
CALIFORNIA BLUE SMELT   *Atherinopsis californiensis*
CALIFORNIA HALIBUT   *Paralichthys californicus*
CALIFORNIA KILLIFISH   *Fundulus parvipinnis*
CALIFORNIA JEWFISH   *Stereolepis gigas*
CALIFORNIA LIZARD FISH   *Synodus lucioceps*
CALIFORNIA SARDINE   *Sardinops caerula*
CALIFORNIA SKATE   *Raja inornata*
CANADIAN PLAICE   *Hippoglossoides platessoides*
CANARY ROCKFISH   *Sebastodes pinniger*
CANDLEFISH   *Thaleichthys pacificus*
CANOPY SHARK   *Squatina japonica*

CAPE KATONKEL   *Sarda sarda*
CAPELIN   *Mallotus villosus*
CAPE MAY GOODY   *Leiostomus xanthurus*
CAPITAINE   *Lachnolaimus maximus*
CARDINAL FISH   *Apogon semilineatus*
CARDINAL SEABREAM   *Evynnis cardinalis*
CARNATIC CARP   *Barbus carnaticus*
CAROLINA POMPANO   *Trachinotus carolinus*
CARP   *Cirrhina mrigala, Cyprinus carpio*
CARP, BIGHEAD   *Aristichthys nobilis*
CARP, BLACK   *Morulius chrysophekadion, Mylopharyngodon piceus*
CARP BREAM   *Abramis brama*
CARP, BUFFALO   *Ictiobus bubalis*
CARP, CARNATIC   *Barbus carnaticus*
CARP, CAUVERY   *Labeo kontius*
CARP, CRUCIAN   *Carassius carassius, Carassius cuvieri*
CARP, FRINGE-LIPPED   *Labeo fimbriatus*
CARP, GOLDEN   *Carassius auratus, Carassius carassius*
CARP, GRASS   *Ctenopharyngodon idella*
CARP, INDIAN   *Catla catla*
CARP, JOHNNY   *Carassius auratus*
CARP, PRUSSIAN   *Carassius carassius*
CARP, ROHU   *Labeo rohita*
CARP, SEA   *Dactylopagrus carponemus, Diplodus annularis, Diplodus sargus*
CARP, SILVER   *Hypophthalmichthys molitrix*
CARP, SILVER CRUCIAN   *Carassius auratus gibelio*
CARP, SKIN   *Hemibarbus barbus*
CARP, SPOTTED SILVER   *Aristichthys nobilis*
CARPSUCKER, RIVER   *Carpiodes carpio*
CARP, WHITE   *Cirrhina cirrhosa*
CASCARUDO   *Callichthys callichthys*
CASPIAN STURGEON   *Acipenser stellatus*
CASTOR OIL FISH   *Lepidocybium flavobrunneum, Ruvettus pretiosus*
CATALUFA   *Priacanthus arenatus*
CATFISH   *Anarhichas lupus, Arius serratus, Clarias gariepinus, Parasilurus asotus, Silurus glanis*
CATFISH, AMERICAN   *Ictalurus melas*
CATFISH, BLUE   *Ictalurus furcatus*
CATFISH, BROADHEADED   *Anarhichas latifrons*
CATFISH, BULLHEADED   *Anarhichas latifrons*
CATFISH, BUTTER   *Callichrous bimaculatus*
CATFISH, CHANNEL   *Ictalurus punctatus*
CATFISH, DUSKY   *Arius sona*
CATFISH, DWARF   *Macrones cavasius*
CATFISH, DWARF, STRIPED   *Macrones vittatus*
CATFISH EEL, STRIPED   *Plotosus anguillaris*
CATFISH, ELECTRIC   *Malapterus electricus*
CATFISH, ESTUARY   *Cnidoglanis macrocephalus*
CATFISH, FRESHWATER   *Clarias batrachus*
CATFISH, GLASS   *Kryptopterus bicirrhis*

CATFISH, GUYANA   *Corydoras melanistius*
CATFISH, LESSER   *Anarhichas minor*
CATFISH, MANILA SEA   *Arius manillensis*
CATFISH, PUNGAS   *Pangasius pangasius*
CATFISH, SAW-EDGED   *Arius serratus*
CATFISH, SEA   *Bagre morina, Plotosus anguillaris*
CATFISH, SILOND   *Silonia silondia*
CATFISH, SMALL   *Ictalurus melas*
CATFISH, SPOTTED   *Anarhichas minor*
CATFISH, STINGING   *Heteropneustes fossilis*
CATFISH, TALKING   *Acanthodoras spinosissimus*
CATFISH, TEYSMANN'S SPOTTED   *Clarias batrachus*
CATFISH, UPSIDE-DOWN   *Synodontis nigriventris, Synodontis schall*
CATFISH, VEINED   *Tachysurus venosus*
CAT, JELLY   *Anarhichas latifrons*
CAT, SEA   *Galeichthys felis*
CAT SHARK   *Heterodontus japonicus, Triakis semifasciatum*
CAT, WHITE   *Ictalurus punctatus*
CAUVERY CARP   *Labeo kontius*
CAVALLA, BANDED   *Caranx sexfasciatus*
CAVALLO, TOVIRA   *Apteronotus albifrons*
CAVE FISH, BLIND   *Anoptichthys jordani*
CENTRAL MUDMINNOW   *Umbra limi*
CERO, SPOTTED   *Scomberomorus regalis*
CHAIN PICKEREL   *Esox niger*
CHAINSIDED PERCH   *Lepomis macrochirus*
CHANNEL BASS   *Sciaenops ocellata*
CHANNEL CATFISH   *Ictalurus punctatus*
CHANNEL ROCKFISH   *Sebastolobus macrochir*
CHAR   *Salvelinus willughbii*
CHARACIN, MEXICAN CAVE   *Anoptichthys jordani*
CHARACIN, PINK-TAILED   *Chalceus macrolepidotus*
CHARACIN, REDEYED   *Arnoldichthys spilopterus*
CHAR, ARCTIC   *Salvelinus alpinus*
CHARLIE, DARKIE   *Dalatias licha*
CHARR, BROOK   *Salvelinus fontinalis*
CHARR, GREENLAND   *Salvelinus alpinus*
CHARR, LAKE   *Salvelinus namaycush*
CHAR, SPECKLED   *Salvelinus fontinalis*
CHAR, WINDERMERE   *Salvelinus willughbii*
CHERRY BARB   *Barbus titteya*
CHERRY SALMON   *Oncorhynchus masou, Oncorhynchus rhodurus*
CHICKWICK   *Cynoscion regalis*
CHILEAN CLINGFISH   *Sicyases sanguineus*
CHILI-PEPPER   *Sebastodes goodei*
CHIMAERA, DEEPWATER   *Hydrolagus affinis*
CHINESE GUITAR FISH   *Platyrhina sinensis*
CHINESE HERRING   *Hilsa toli*
CHINESE SNAKEHEAD   *Channa argus*
CHINOOK SALMON   *Oncorhynchus tschawytscha*

CHOICE, SAILOR'S   *Lagodon rhomboides*
CHROMIDE, GREEN   *Etroplus suratensis*
CHUB   *Leuciscus cephalus, Notemigonus crysoleucas*
CHUB, CREEK   *Semotilus atromaculatus*
CHUB MACKEREL   *Rastrelliger neglectus, Scomber japonicus*
CHUB, MUD   *Semotilus atromaculatus*
CHUB, SEA   *Ditrema temmincki*
CHUB, SILVER   *Semotilus atromaculatus*
CHUBSUCKER, LAKE   *Erimyzon sucetta*
CHUM SALMON   *Oncorhynchus keta*
CICHLID, BLACK   *Tilapia nigra*
CICHLID, FIREMOUTH   *Cichlasoma meeki*
CICHLID, RINGTAILED PIKE   *Crenicichla saxatilis*
CIGARETTE PAPER   *Hippoglossoides elassodon*
CIGARFISH   *Decapterus punctatus*
CISCO   *Leucichthys artedii*
CISCO, LAKE   *Leucichthys artedii*
CISCO, SHALLOW WATER   *Leucichthys artedii*
CLANWILLIAM YELLOWFISH   *Barbus holubi*
CLEARNOSED SKATE   *Raja eglantaria*
CLEAR RAY   *Raja diaphenes*
CLIFF FLATHEAD   *Trudis bassensis westraliae*
CLIMBING PERCH   *Anabas scandens*
CLINGFISH, CHILEAN   *Sicyases sanguineus*
CLOWN BARB   *Barbus everetti*
COALFISH   *Anoplopoma fimbria, Pollachius virens*
COASTAL CUTTHROAT TROUT   *Salmo clarkii*
COASTER   *Salvelinus fontinalis*
COBBLERFISH   *Trachinotus carolinus*
COBIA   *Rachycentron canadum*
COCKUP   *Lates calcarifer*
COD   *Gadus morhua, Physiculus barbatus*
COD, ARCTIC   *Boreogadus saida*
COD, ATLANTIC   *Gadus morhua*
COD, BALTIC   *Gadus callarias*
COD, BANDED REEF   *Epinephelus fasciatus*
COD, CULTUS   *Ophiodon elongatus*
COD, FJORD   *Gadus ogac*
COD, GIANT ANTARCTIC   *Dissostichus mawsoni*
COD, GREENLAND   *Gadus ogac*
COD, GREY   *Gadus macrocephalus*
CODLING   *Urophycis tenuis*: also immature *Gadus morhua*
CODLING, FLATNOSE   *Antimora rostrata*
COD, PACIFIC   *Gadus macrocephalus*
COD, POLAR   *Boreogadus saida*
COD, POOR   *Gadus minutus*
COD, RED   *Sebastodes ruberrimus*
COD, ROCK   *Epinephelus fario*
COD, SAFFRON   *Eleginus gracilis*
COD, TROUT REEF   *Epinephelus fario*

COD, WACHNA *Gadus nevaga, Eleginus gracilis*
COELACANTH *Latimeria chalumnae*
COHO SALMON *Oncorhynchus kisutch*
COITOR CROAKER *Sciaena coitor*
COLEY *Pollachius virens*
COMBFISH, LONGSPINE *Zaniolepis latipinnis*
COMBER, PAINTED *Serranus scriba*
COMMERSON'S ANCHOVY *Stolephorus commersonii*
COMMON BARBEL *Barbus barbus*
COMMON BULLHEAD *Ictalurus melas*
COMMON CARP *Cyprinus carpio*
COMMON DENTEX *Dentex dentex*
COMMON EEL *Anguilla anguilla*
COMMON GAR PIKE *Lepisosteus osseus*
COMMON GRUNT *Haemulon plumieri*
COMMON GURNARD *Prionotus carolinus*
COMMON ICE FISH *Salangichthys microdon*
COMMON JAPANESE CONGER *Astroconger myriaster*
COMMON MINNOW *Zacco platypus*
COMMON MOLA *Mola mola*
COMMON PAMPANO *Trachinotus carolinus*
COMMON RASBORA *Rasbora daniconius*
COMMON SAW SHARK *Pristiophorus cirratus*
COMMON SCUP *Stenotomus versicolor*
COMMON SEA BREAM *Pagellus centrotodontus*
COMMON SEA ROBIN *Prionotus carolinus*
COMMON SHAD *Alosa sapidissima*
COMMON SKATE *Raja inornata*
COMMON SLIPMOUTH *Leiognathus equulus*
COMMON SUCKER *Catostomus commersonii*
COMMON SUNFISH *Lepomis gibbosus*
COMMON SURGEON *Acanthurus hepatus*
CONCERTINA FISH *Drepane punctata*
CONEY *Cephalopholis fulvus*
CONGER, COMMON JAPANESE *Astroconger myriaster*
CONGER EEL *Conger conger, Leptocephalus wilsoni*
CONGER EEL, SILVER *Muraenesox cinereus*
CONGER, SILVERY *Anago anago*
CONVICT TANG *Acanthurus triostegus*
COOKTOWN SALMON *Eleutheronema tetradactylon*
COOLIE LOACH *Acanthophthalmus kuhlii*
COPPER ROCKFISH *Sebastodes caurinus*
CORALFISH *Abudefduf saxatilis*
CORAL TROUT *Plectropoma maculatum*
CORB *Sciaena umbra*
CORKWING *Crenilabrus melops*
CORNISH BLACKFISH *Schedophilus medusophagus*
CORVINA *Micropogon undulatus*
CORYDORAS, BLACK SPOTTED *Corydoras melanistius*
CORYDORAS, BRONZE *Corydoras aeneus*

CORYDORAS, LEOPARD   *Corydoras julii*
C-O SOLE   *Pleuronichthys coenosus*
COUCH'S SEA BREAM   *Pagrus pagrus*
COUCH'S WHITING   *Micromesistius poutassou*
COWFISH, SCRAWLED   *Acanthostracion quadricornis*
COWFISH, STRIPED   *Aracana aurita*
COW-NOSED RAY   *Rhinoptera bonasus*
COW SHARK   *Hexanchus griseus*
CRAMPFISH   *Tetranarce occidentalis*
CRAPPIE   *Pomoxis annularis*
CRAPPIE, BLACK   *Pomoxis nigromaculatus*
CRAPPIE, TIMBER   *Pomoxis annularis*
CRAPPIE, WHITE   *Pomoxis annularis*
CREEK CHUB   *Semotilus atromaculatus*
CRESCENT PERCH   *Therapon jarbua*
CREVALLE JACK   *Caranx sexfasciatus*
CRIMSON SEA BREAM   *Evynnis japonica*
CRIMSON-SPOTTED RAINBOW FISH   *Melanotaenia fluviatilis*
CROAKER   *Aplodinotus grunniens, Micropogon furnieri, Micropogon undulatus, Pelates quadrilineatus, Pseudosciaena anea*
CROAKER, BRONZE   *Sciaenoides brunneus*
CROAKER, COITOR   *Sciaena coitor*
CROAKER, LESSER TIGER-TOOTHED   *Otolithes ruber*
CROAKER, SPOTTED   *Sciaena diacanthus*
CROAKER, TIGER-TOOTHED   *Otolithes ruber*
CROAKER, WHISKERED   *Johnius dussumieri*
CROAKER, WHITE   *Argyrosomus argentatus*
CROAKER, YELLOW   *Pseudosciaena crocea*
CROCODILE FISH, WHITE   *Chaenocephalus aceratus*
CROCODILE GLASSFISH   *Chaenocephalus aceratus*
CROSS-STAFF SHARK   *Sphyrna zygaena*
CRUCIAN CARP   *Carassius carassius, Carassius cuvieri*
CRUCIAN CARP, SILVER   *Carassius auratus gibelio*
CUB SHARK   *Carcharhinus leucas*
CUCHILLA   *Sternopygus macrurus*
CUCKOO RAY   *Raja naevus*
CULTUS COD   *Ophiodon elongatus*
CUNNER   *Tautogolabrus adspersus*
CUSK   *Brosme brosme*
CUTLASS FISH   *Trichiurus lepturus*
CUTTHROAT EEL, GRAY'S   *Synaphobranchus kaupi*
CUTTHROAT TROUT, COASTAL   *Salmo clarkii*
CYBIUM, SPOTTED   *Scomberomorus maculatus*

DAB   *Limanda limanda*
DAB, JAPANESE   *Limanda herzensteini*
DAB, LONG ROUGH   *Hippoglossoides platessoides*
DAB, MUD   *Limanda yokohamae, Pleuronectes limanda*
DAB, RUSTY   *Limanda ferruginea*

DAB, SAND   *Hippoglossoides platessoides, Limanda herzensteini*
DAB, SMEAR   *Pleuronectes microcephalus*
DACE   *Leuciscus leuciscus, Notemigonus crysoleucas, Tribolodon hakonensis*
DACE, BLACKNOSE   *Rhinichthys atratulus*
DACE, HORNED   *Semotilus atromaculatus*
DACE, ROSYSIDE   *Clinostomus funduloides*
DADDY SCULPIN   *Myoxocephalus scorpius*
DAGGERTOOTH PIKE-CONGER   *Muraenesox cinereus*
DALATIAS   *Dalatias licha*
DANIO, GIANT   *Danio aequipinnatus*
DANUBE BLEAK   *Chalcalburnus chalcoides*
DANUBE BREAM   *Abramis sapa*
DARA   *Polynemus indicus*
DARK DRUM   *Sciaena umbra*
DARKIE   *Girella tricuspidata*
DARKIE CHARLIE   *Dalatias licha*
DARTER, JOHNNY   *Etheostoma nigrum*
DASSIE   *Diplodus annularis*
DEEP SEA EEL   *Alepocephalus* sp.
DEEP SEA SMELT   *Glossanodon semifasciatus*
DEEPWATER CHIMAERA   *Hydrolagus affinis*
DEMPSEY, JACK   *Cichlasoma biocellatum*
DENTEX, COMMON   *Dentex dentex*
DENTEX, LARGE-EYE   *Dentex macrophthalmus*
DENTEX, PINK   *Dentex gibbosus*
DESERT PUPFISH   *Cyprinodon macularius*
DIAMOND FISH   *Monodactylus argenteus*
DIAMOND-SCALE MULLET   *Mugil vaigiensis*
DICK, SLIPPERY   *Halichoeres bivittatus*
DINGO FISH   *Sphyraena jello*
DIVER, SAND   *Synodus intermedius*
DIVER WHITING   *Sillago maculata*
DOCTOR FISH   *Acanthurus hepatus*
DOG, BLUE   *Prionace glauca*
DOGFISH, ATLANTIC SPINY   *Squalus acanthias*
DOGFISH, BLACK   *Centroscyllium fabricii*
DOGFISH, BLACKMOUTHED   *Pristiurus melanostomus*
DOGFISH, BROWN SMOOTH   *Triakis scyllia*
DOGFISH, GREATER SPOTTED   *Scylliorhinus stellaris*
DOGFISH, LARGE SPOTTED   *Scyllium stellaris*
DOGFISH, LESSER SPOTTED   *Scyliorhinus canicula*
DOGFISH, PACIFIC SPINY   *Squalus acanthias*
DOGFISH, PIKED   *Squalus acanthias*
DOGFISH, SMALL SPOTTED   *Scyliorhinus canicula*
DOGFISH, SPINED   *Squalus acanthias*
DOGFISH, SMOOTH   *Scyliorhinus canicula*
DOGFISH, STRIPED   *Poroderma africanum*
DOGGIE   *Scomberomorus commersonii*
DOG SALMON   *Oncorhynchus keta*
DOG SHARK   *Alopias pelagicus, Mustelus griseus*

DOG SHARK, YELLOW   *Scoliodon sorrakowah*
DOG, SPUR   *Squalus acanthias*
DOJO FISH   *Misgurnus anguillicaudatus*
DOLLARFISH   *Peprilus triacanthus, Poronotus triacanthus*
DOLLY VARDEN   *Salvelinus malma*
DOLSHIN   *Coryphaena hippurus*
DONALDSON TROUT   *Salmo gairdneri*
DORAB   *Chirocentrus dorab*
DORADO   *Coryphaena hippurus*
DORY   *Stizostedion vitreum*
DORY, JOHN   *Zeus australis, Zeus faber, Zeus japonicus*
DORY, WARTY   *Allocyttus verrucosus*
DOTTED SCAD   *Decapterus punctatus*
DOVER SOLE   *Microstomus pacificus, Solea solea*
DOVER SOLE, JAPANESE   *Microstomus achne*
DRAGONET   *Callionymus lyra*
DRUM, BANDED   *Pogonias cromis*
DRUM, BIG   *Pogonias cromis*
DRUM, BLACK   *Pogonias cromis*
DRUM, DARK   *Sciaena umbra*
DRUMFISH   *Pogonias cromis*
DRUM, FRESHWATER   *Aplodinotus grunniens*
DRUM, GREY   *Pogonias cromis*
DRUM, RED   *Sciaenops ocellata*
DUCK, BOMBAY   *Harpadon nehereus*
DUSKY CATFISH   *Arius sona*
DUSKY FLATHEAD   *Planiplora fusca*
DUSKY JACK   *Caranx sexfasciatus*
DUSKY MORWONG   *Psilocranium nigricans*
DUSKY PERCH   *Epinephelus gigas*
DUSKY SHARK   *Carcharhinus obscurus*
DUSSUMIER'S MULLET   *Mugil dussumierii*
DUSSUMIER'S SILVER JEWFISH   *Johnius dussumierii*
DWARF BARRACUDA, JAPANESE   *Sphyraena pinguis*
DWARF CATFISH   *Macrones cavasius*
DWARF CATFISH, STRIPED   *Macrones vittatus*
DWARF FLOUNDER   *Trinectes maculatus*
DWARF GOURAMI   *Colisa lalia*

EAGLE RAY   *Myliobatis aquila*
EASTERN BROOK TROUT   *Salvelinus fontinalis*
EASTERN PICKEREL   *Esox niger*
ECKSTROM'S TOPKNOT   *Phrynorhombus regius*
EEL, AMERICAN   *Anguilla bostoniensis, Anguilla rostrata*
EEL, BARBER   *Plotosus anguillaris*
EEL BLENNY   *Lumpenus sagitta*
EELBLENNY, STOUT   *Anisarchus medius*
EEL, COMMON   *Anguilla anguilla*
EEL, CONGER   *Conger conger (Leptocephalus wilsoni)*

EEL, Deepsea   *Alepocephalus* sp.
EEL, Electric   *Gymnotus carapo, Electrophorus electricus, Sternopygus macrurus*
EEL, Freshwater   *Anguilla japonica*
EEL, Gray's cutthroat   *Synaphobranchus kaupi*
EEL, Japanese   *Anguilla japonica*
EEL, Kaup's deepsea   *Synaphobranchus kaupi*
EEL, Lamper   *Petromyzon marinus*
EEL, Longfin   *Anguilla dieffenbachii*
EEL, Longnose   *Synaphobranchus kaupi*
EEL, Moray   *Muraena helena*
EEL, Mud   *Amphipnus cuchia*
EEL, Paddy   *Monopterus albus*
EEL, Pike   *Muraenesox cinereus*
Eelpout   *Lota lota, Macrozoarces americanus, Zoarces viviparus*
EELPOUT, Black   *Lycodes diapterus*
EELPOUT, Shortfin   *Lycodes brevipes*
EEL, Rice   *Monopterus alba*
EEL, Saud   *Ammodytes* sp.
EEL, Sharptoothed   *Muraenesox cinereus*
EEL, Shortfinned   *Anguilla dieffenbachii*
EEL, Silver *Anguilla rostrata*
EEL, Silver conger   *Muraenesox cinereus*
EEL, Slime   *Simenchelys parasiticus*
EEL, Snipe   *Serrivomer sector*
EEL, Snubnose   *Simenchelys parasiticus*
EEL, Spiny   *Mastacembelus armatus, Mastacembelus pancalus, Notacanthus nasus*
EEL, Striped catfish   *Plotosus anguillaris*
EEL, Swamp   *Monopterus albus*
Egret piper   *Macrorhamphosus sagifue*
eighteyes lamprey, River   *Lampetra japonica*
Electric catfish   *Malapterurus electricus*
Electric eel   *Gymnotus carapo, Electrophorus electricus, Sternopygus macrurus*
Electric fish   *Tetranarce occidentalis*
Electric ray   *Narke japonica, Torpedo nobiliana*
electric ray, Eyed   *Torpedo torpedo*
electric ray, Marbled   *Torpedo marmorata*
Elephant shark   *Callorhynchus millii*
Elephant-snout fish   *Mormyrus kannume*
Elf sculpin   *Ceratocottus namiyei*
Elft   *Pomatomus saltatrix*
Elleck   *Trigla cuculus*
Elliot's grey shark   *Carcharias ellioti*
Emerywheel   *Platichthys stellatus*
emperor, Red   *Lutianus malabaricus*
Emperor snapper   *Lutianus sebae*
emperor, Sweetlip   *Lethrinus chrysostomus*
English sole   *Parophrys vetulus*
Escolar   *Lepidocybium flavobrunneum, Ruvettus pretiosus*
Estuary catfish   *Cnidoglanis macrocephalus*
etroplus, Banded   *Etroplus suratensis*

ETROPLUS, SPOTTED   *Etroplus suratensis*
EULACHON   *Thaleichthys pacificus*
EURASIAN PERCH   *Perca flavescens*
EUROPEAN BASS   *Dicentrarchus labrax*
EUROPEAN SMELT   *Osmerus mordax*
EYED ELECTRIC RAY   *Torpedo torpedo*
EYED SKATE   *Raja ocellata*

FAIR MAID   *Stenotomus versicolor*
FALSE ALBACORE   *Euthynnus alletteratus*
FALSE FEATHERBACK   *Xenomystus nigri*
FALSE WHITING   *Sciaena deliciosa*
FATBACK   *Pomatomus saltatrix*
FATHEAD MINNOW   *Pimephales promelas*
FATHER LASHER   *Myoxocephalus scorpius*
FEATHERBACK   *Notopterus chitala, Notopterus notopterus*
FEATHERBACK, FALSE   *Xenomystus nigri*
FIDDLER   *Ictalurus punctatus, Rhyncobatus djiddensis*
FIGHTING FISH, SIAMESE   *Betta splendens*
FILAMENTED SCULPIN   *Icelinus filamentosus*
FILEFISH   *Balistes capriscus, Monacanthus cirrhifer, Navodon modestus, Stephanolepis cirrhifer*
FILEFISH, OVAL   *Navodon modestus*
FINETOOTH SHARK   *Aprionodon isodon*
FINGERFISH   *Monodactylus argenteus*
FIN SHARK   *Centrophorus atromarginatus*
FIREMOUTH CICHLID   *Cichlasoma meeki*
FISHING FROG   *Lophius piscatorius*
FIVE-BANDED SURGEON FISH   *Acanthurus triostegus*
FIVE-SPOTTED WRASSE   *Crenilabrus quinquemaculatus*
FJORD COD   *Gadus ogac*
FLAG ROCKFISH   *Sebastes rubrivinctus*
FLAPPER SKATE   *Raja batis*
FLAT BACK   *Raja kenoji*
FLATFISH, ROCK   *Lepidopsetta mochigarei*
FLATHEAD, BAR-TAILED   *Platycephalus indicus*
FLATHEAD, CLIFF   *Trudis bassensis westraliae*
FLATHEAD, DUSKY   *Planiplora fusca*
FLATHEAD FLOUNDER   *Hippoglossoides dubius*
FLATHEAD GOBY   *Glossogobius giuris, Gobius batrachocephalus, Gobius giuris*
FLATHEAD, INDIAN   *Platycephalus indicus*
FLATHEAD MULLET   *Mugil cephalus*
FLATHEAD, SAND   *Platycephalus bassensis*
FLATHEAD SOLE   *Hippoglossoides dubius, Hippoglossoides elassodon*
FLATHEAD, TIGER   *Neoplatycephalus richardsoni*
FLATNOSE CODLING   *Antimora rostrata*
FLAT-TAILED MULLET   *Mugil dussumieri*
FLOUNDER   *Hippoglossoides platessoides, Limanda herzensteini, Platichthys dentalus, Platichthys flesus, Tanakius kitaharae*

FLOUNDER, ARCTIC *Liopsetta glacialis*
FLOUNDER, ARROWTOOTH *Atheresthes stomias*
FLOUNDER, BIGMOUTH *Psettodes erumei*
FLOUNDER, DWARF *Trinectes maculatus*
FLOUNDER, FLATHEAD *Hippoglossoides dubius*
FLOUNDER, FROG *Pleuronichthys cornutus*
FLOUNDER, GEORGE'S BANK *Pseudopleuronectes americanus*
FLOUNDER, JAPANESE *Paralichthys olivaceus*
FLOUNDER, JAPANESE ARROWTOOTH *Atheresthes evermanni*
FLOUNDER, LEOPARD *Platophrys pantherinus*
FLOUNDER, LONGJAW *Atheresthes stomias*
FLOUNDER, PACIFIC OCEAN *Cleisthenes herzensteini*
FLOUNDER, POLE *Glyptocephalus cynoglossus*
FLOUNDER, ROUGHSCALE *Pseudorhombus oligodon*
FLOUNDER, ROUNDNOSE *Eopsetta grigorjewi*
FLOUNDER, SAND *Psettichthys melanostictus, Scophthalmus aquosus*
FLOUNDER, SCALYFIN *Isopsetta isolepis*
FLOUNDER, SLIME *Microstomus achne*
FLOUNDER, SOUTHERN *Paralichthys lethostigmus*
FLOUNDER, SPOTTED *Eucitharus linguatula, Scophthalmus aquosus*
FLOUNDER, STARRY *Platichthys stellatus*
FLOUNDER, STONE *Kareius bicoloratus*
FLOUNDER, SUMMER *Paralichthys dentatus*
FLOUNDER, WINTER *Pseudopleuronectes americanus*
FLOUNDER, WITCH *Glyptocephalus cynoglossus*
FLOUNDER, YELLOWTAIL *Limanda ferruginea*
FLUKE, SAIL *Lepidorhombus whiffiagonis*
FLUTE-MOUTH *Fistularia petimba*
FLUTE PORGY *Lutianus rivulatus*
FLYING FISH *Cypselurus oligolepis, Cypselurus opisthopus, Exocoetus volitans, Prognichthys
agoo*
FORKBEARD *Urophycis chuss*
FORKBEARD, GREATER *Phycis blennoides*
FORKBEARD, LESSER *Raniceps raninus*
FORKED-BEARD HAKE *Urophycis blennoides*
FOURFINGER THREADFIN *Eleutheronema tetradactylum*
FOURLINED THERAPON *Pelates quadrilineatus*
FOURSPINE STICKLEBACK *Apeltes quadracus*
FOX, SEA *Alopias caudatus, Alopias greyi, Alopias vulpinus, Raja clavata*
FOX SHARK *Alopias pelagicus*
FRENCH ANGELFISH *Pomacanthus arcuatus*
FRENCH GRUNT *Haemulon flavolineatum*
FRESHWATER CATFISH *Clarias batrachus*
FRESHWATER EEL *Anguilla japonica*
FRESHWATER DRUM *Aplodinotus grunniens*
FRESHWATER GOBY *Chaenogobius isaza*
FRESHWATER MUD EEL *Macrognathus aculeatum*
FRESHWATER SAWFISH *Pristis perotteti*
FRESHWATER SHARK *Wallago attu*
FRESHWATER STINGRAY *Potamotrygon motoro*

FRIGATE MACKEREL   *Auxis tapeinocephalus, Auxis thazard*
FRINGELIPPED CARP   *Labeo fimbriatus*
FRINGE-SCALE SARDINE   *Sardinella fimbriata*
FROG, FISHING   *Lophius piscatorius*
FROGFISH, LONGLURE   *Antennarius ocellatus*
FROG FLOUNDER   *Pleuronichthys cornutus*
FROSTFISH   *Microgadus tomcod*
FRYING PAN SNAPPER   *Argyrops spinifer*
FULLER'S RAY   *Raja fullonica*
FUSILIER, GOLDEN-BANDED   *Caesio chrysozona*

GAFFTOPSAIL   *Bagre morina*
GAR, BILLY   *Lepisosteus osseus*
GARFISH   *Belone belone, Xenentodon canciloides*
GAR, LONGNOSE   *Lepisosteus osseus*
GAR, MISSISSIPPI ALLIGATOR   *Lepisosteus spatula*
GAR, OHIO   *Lepisosteus osseus*
GAR PIKE, COMMON   *Lepisosteus osseus*
GARRUPA   *Epinephelus fario*
GAR, SHORTNOSE   *Lepisosteus platostomus*
GAR, SILVER   *Strongylura marina*
GELATINOUS SEASNAIL   *Liparis koefoedi*
GENUINE GOBY   *Acanthogobius flavimanus*
GENUINE PORGY   *Chrysophrys major*
GEORGE'S BANK FLOUNDER   *Pseudopleuronectes americanus*
GHOSTFISH   *Cryptacanthodes maculatus*
GHOST SHARK   *Callorhynchus callorhynchus, Callorhynchus millii, Chimaera phantasma*
GIANT ANTARCTIC COD   *Dissostichus mawsoni*
GIANT BLACK MARLIN   *Makaira marlina*
GIANT DANIO   *Danio aequipinnatus*
GIANT GOURAMI   *Colisa fasciata*
GIANT HERRING   *Chanos chanos, Elops hawaiensis, Elops saurus*
GIANT MARBLED SCULPIN   *Scorpaenichthys marmoratus*
GIANT PERCH   *Lates calcarifer*
GIANT PIGFISH   *Achoerodus gouldii*
GIANT SEA BASS   *Stereolepis gigas*
GIANT SNAKEHEAD   *Ophicephalus marulius*
GIANT THREADFIN   *Eleutheronema tetradactylum*
GIANT WRASSE   *Cheilinus undulatus*
GIBEL   *Carassius auratus gibelio*
GIBELLIAN   *Carassius auratus gibelio*
GILDED SUNFISH   *Lepomis macrochirus*
GILTHEAD   *Crenilabrus melops*
GILTHEAD SEABREAM   *Sparus auratus*
GILT SARDINE   *Sardinella aurita*
GINKGO FISH   *Gymnocranius griseus*
GIZZARD, JAPANESE   *Konosirus punctatus*
GIZZARD SHAD   *Anodontostoma chacunda, Clupanodon thrissa, Dorosoma cepedianum, Konosirus punctatus*

GLASS CATFISH   *Kryptopterus bicirrhis*
GLASSEYE   *Stizostedion vitreum*
GLASSFISH   *Salangichthys microdon*
GLASSFISH, CROCODILE   *Chaenocephalus aceratus*
GLASS TETRA   *Moenkhausia oligolepis*
GLOBEFISH   several species of the genus *Fugu*
GLUT HERRING   *Alosa pseudoharengus*
GOATFISH   *Parapeneus multifasciatus, Upeneoides bensasi*
GOATFISH, GOLDEN-BANDED   *Mulloides flavolineatus*
GOATFISH, YELLOW   *Upeneoides sulphureus*
GOATFISH, YELLOWFIN   *Upeneus bensasi*
GOBY   *Gobius melanostomus*
GOBY, ATLANTIC MARINE   *Notothenia gibberifrons*
GOBY, BAR-EYED   *Glossogobius giuris*
GOBY, BLACK   *Gobius niger*
GOBY, BLACK SEA ROUND   *Neogobius melanostomus*
GOBY, BLACK SPOTTED   *Gobius melanostomus*
GOBY, BLIND   *Typhlogobius californiensis*
GOBY, FLATHEAD   *Glossogobius giuris, Gobius batrachocephalus*
GOBY, FRESHWATER   *Chaenogobius isaza*
GOBY, GENUINE   *Acanthogobius flavimanus*
GOBY, GREEN-SPOTTED   *Acentrogobius viridipunctatus*
GOBY, ICE   *Leucopsarion petersi*
GOBY, LONG-JAWED   *Gillichthys mirabilis*
GOBY, POINTED-TAILED   *Apocryptes lanceolatus*
GOBY, ROCK   *Gobius paganellus*
GOBY, ROUND   *Gobius melanostomus*
GOBY, SMALL-SCALED   *Oxyurichthys microlepis*
GOBY, SNAKEHEAD   *Gobius ophiocephalus*
GOBY, TOAD   *Gobius batrachocephalus*
GOBY, YELLOWFIN   *Acanthogobius flavimanus*
GOGGLE-EYE   *Priacanthus hamrur*
GOGGLE-EYE JACK   *Selar crumenophthalmus*
GOLDEN-BAND FUSILIER   *Caesio chrysozona*
GOLDEN-BANDED GOAT FISH   *Mulloides flavolineatus*
GOLDEN CAESIO   *Caesio chrysozona*
GOLDEN CARP   *Carassius auratus, Carassius carassius*
GOLDEN EAR KILLIFISH   *Fundulus chrysotus*
GOLDEN-GREY MULLET   *Mugil auratus*
GOLDEN SARDINE   *Sardinella aurita*
GOLDEN SCAD   *Caranx kalla*
GOLDEN SHINER   *Notemigonus crysoleucas*
GOLDEN-STRIPED PONY FISH   *Leiognathus daura*
GOLDEN THREADFIN BREAM   *Nemipterus virgatus*
GOLDEYE   *Hiodon alosoides*
GOLDFISH   *Carassius auratus*
GOLDLINED SEABREAM   *Rhabdosargus sarba*
GOLD PERCH   *Lepomis macrochirus*
GOLDSINNY   *Ctenolabrus rupestris*
GOLDSPOT MULLET   *Mugil parsia*

GOLD-SPOTTED GRENADIER ANCHOVY *Coilia dussumieri*
GOOD SALMON *Sphyraena pinguis*
GOODY, CAPE MAY *Leiostomus xanthurus*
GOOSEFISH *Lophius litulon, Lophius piscatorius*
GORAMY, SIAMESE *Trichogaster pectoralis*
GOURAMI, DWARF *Colisa lalia*
GOURAMI, GIANT *Colisa fasciata*
GOURAMI, KISSING *Helostoma temmincki*
GOURAMI, PEARL *Trichogaster leeri*
GOURAMI, SNAKESKIN *Trichogaster pectoralis*
GOURAMI, THREE-SPOT *Trichogaster trichopterus*
GOURAMY *Trichogaster cosby*
GOURAMY, OPALINE *Trichogaster cosby*
GRASS CARP *Ctenopharyngodon idella*
GRASS PICKEREL *Esox americanus vermicularis*
GRASS PUFFER *Fugu niphobles*
GRAYFISH *Squalus acanthias*
GRAYLING *Prosopium williamsoni, Thymallus thymallus*
GRAYLING, ARCTIC *Thymallus thymallus*
GRAY'S CUTTHROAT EEL *Synaphobranchus kaupi*
GREAT BARRACUDA *Sphyraena barracuda*
GREAT BLUE SHARK *Glyphis glaucus*
GREATER FORKBEARD *Phycis blennoides*
GREATER LIZARD FISH *Saurida tumbil*
GREATER PONY FISH *Leiognathus equulus*
GREATER SILVER SMELT *Argentina silus*
GREATER SPOTTED DOGFISH *Scylliorhinus stellaris*
GREATER WEEVER *Trachinus draco*
GREAT LAKES TROUT *Salvelinus namaycush*
GREAT SCULPIN *Myoxocephalus polyacanthocephalus*
GREAT TREVALLY *Caranx sexfasciatus*
GREEK MORAY *Muraena helena*
GREEN CHROMIDE *Etroplus suratensis*
GREENFISH, ALASKA *Hexagrammos octogrammus*
GREENLAND CHARR *Salveninus alpinus*
GREENLAND COD *Gadus ogac*
GREENLAND HALIBUT *Reinhardtius hippoglossoides*
GREENLAND SCULPIN *Myoxocephalus scorpius*
GREENLAND SHARK *Somniosus microcephalus*
GREENLING *Hexagrammos otakii*
GREENLING, KELP *Hexagrammos decagrammus*
GREENLING, LONGSPINED *Zaniolepis latipinnis*
GREENLING, MASKED *Hexagrammos octogrammus*
GREENLING, ROCK *Hexagrammos lagocephalus*
GREENLING, WHITE SPOTTED *Hexagrammos stelleri*
GREEN MOLLY *Poecilia latipinna*
GREEN NOTOTHENIA *Notothenia gibberifrons*
GREEN PARROTFISH *Pseudoscarus guacamaia*
GREEN PIKE *Esox niger*
GREEN PUFFERFISH *Tetraodon fluviatilis*

GREEN SNAKEHEAD   *Ophicephalus punctatus*
GREEN-SPOTTED GOBY   *Acentrogobius viridipunctatus*
GREENSTRIPED ROCKFISH   *Sebastodes elongatus*
GREEN SUNFISH   *Lepomis cyanellus*
GREEN WRASSE   *Labrus turdus*
GRENADIER, NORTH ATLANTIC   *Macrurus rupestris*
GRENADIER, ROCK   *Coryphaenoides rupestris*
GRENADIER, ROUGH-HEAD   *Macrourus berglax*
GRENADIER, ROUNDNOSE   *Coryphaenoides rupestris*
GREY ANGELFISH   *Pomacanthus arcuatus*
GREYBACK   *Leucichthys artedi*
GREY-BLUE SHARK   *Isurus glaucus*
GREY COD   *Gadus macrocephalus*
GREY DRUM   *Pogonias cromis*
GREYFIN JEWFISH   *Pseudosciaena anea*
GREY GURNARD   *Trigla gurnardus*
GREY LARGE-EYE BREAM   *Gymnocranius griseus*
GREY MULLET   *Liza ramada, Mugil capito, Mugil cephalus, Mugil dussumieri, Mugil speigleri*
GREY MULLET, THICK-LIPPED   *Mugil chelo*
GREY NURSE   *Carcharias arenarius*
GREY POMFRET   *Stromateus cinereus*
GREY SHARK   *Hexanchus griseus*
GREY SHARK, ELLIOT'S   *Carcharias ellioti*
GREY SKATE   *Raja batis*
GREY SNAPPER   *Lutianus griseus*
GREY SOLE   *Glyptocephalus cynoglossus*
GREY TRIGGER FISH   *Balistes capriscus*
GRINDSTONE   *Platichthys stellatus*
GRINNER, LARGE-SCALE   *Saurida undosquamis*
GRINNER, PAINTED   *Trachinocephalus myops*
GROPER, BLACK-TIPPED   *Epinephelus fasciatus*
GROPER, BLUE   *Achoerodus gouldii*
GROUND SHARK   *Carcharhinus leucas*
GROUPER, *Döderleinia berycoides, Epinephelus corallicola, Epinephelus gigas, Epinephelus septemfasciatus*
GROUPER, BLACK   *Garrupa nigrita*
GROUPER, NASSAU   *Epinephelus striatus*
GROUPER, RED   *Epinephelus morio*
GROUPER, RED-BANDED   *Epinephelus fasciatus*
GROUPER, SPOTTED   *Epinephelus fario*
GROUPER, WHITE   *Epinephelus aeneus*
GROUPER, YELLOW-FINNED   *Trisotropis venenosus*
GRUBBY   *Myoxocephalus aeneus*
GRUNION   *Leuresthes tenuis*
GRUNT   *Anisotremus davidsoni, Parapristipoma trilineatum*
GRUNT, BLUE-STRIPED   *Haemulon sciurus*
GRUNT, BOAR   *Haemulon plumieri, Haemulon sciurus*
GRUNT, COMMON   *Haemulon plumieri*
GRUNTER, BIDYAN   *Therapon bidyana*

GRUNTER, JAVELIN   *Pomadasys hasta*
GRUNTER, LARGE-SCALE BANDED   *Therapon theraps*
GRUNTER, OLIVE   *Pristipoma olivaceum*
GRUNTER, SILVER   *Pomadasys hasta*
GRUNTER, SOOTY   *Therapon bidyana*
GRUNT, FRENCH   *Haemulon flavolineatum*
GRUNT, HEAD   *Pomadasys hasta*
GRUNT, HUMPBACK   *Haemulon sciurus*
GRUNT, JAPANESE   *Parapristipoma trilineatum*
GRUNT, LINED SILVER   *Pomadasys hasta*
GRUNT, OPEN-MOUTHED   *Haemulon flavolineatum*
GRUNT SCULPIN   *Rhamphocottus richardsoni*
GRUNT, SILVER   *Pomadasys hasta, Therapon plumbeus*
GRUNT, STRIPED   *Therapon jarbua*
GRUNT, YELLOW   *Haemulon flavolineatum, Haemulon sciurus*
GUAGUANCHE   *Sphyraena guachancho*
GUDGEON   *Gobio gobio, Notemigonus crysoleucas*
GUITAR FISH, ATLANTIC   *Rhinobatus lentiginosus*
GUITAR FISH, CHINESE   *Platyrhina sinensis*
GUITAR FISH, SPOTTED   *Rhinobatus lentiginosus*
GULF KILLIFISH   *Fundulus grandis*
GULF KINGFISH   *Menticirrhus littoralis*
GULF MENHADEN   *Brevoortia patronus*
GUMMY SHARK   *Mustelus antarcticus, Mustelus manazo*
GUPPY   *Poecilia reticulata*
GURNARD, COMMON   *Prionotus carolinus*
GURNARD, GREY   *Trigla gurnardus*
GURNARD, PIPER   *Trigla lyra*
GURNARD, RED   *Chelidonichthys kumu, Trigla cuculus*
GURNARD, RED ROCK   *Helicolenus papillosis*
GURNARD, RIVER   *Platycephalus indicus*
GURNARD, SAND   *Platycephalus indicus*
GURNARD, SAPHIRINE   *Trigla lucerna*
GURNARD, STREAKED   *Trigla lastoviza, Trigla lineata*
GURNARD, YELLOW   *Trigla lucerna*
GURNET   *Hemitripterus americanus*
GURRY SHARK   *Somniosus microcephalus*
GUYANA CATFISH   *Corydoras melanistius*
GWYNIAD   *Coregonus clupeoides, Coregonus lavaretus*

HAADER   *Mugil cephalus*
HADDOCK   *Melanogrammus aeglefinus*
HADDOCK, NORWAY   *Sebastes marinus, Sebastes viviparus*
HAGFISH   *Eptatretus burgeri, Eptatretus stoutii, Myxine glutinosa*
HAGFISH, ATLANTIC   *Myxine glutinosa*
HAGFISH, NORTHERN   *Myxine glutinosa*
HAGFISH, PACIFIC   *Eptatretus stoutii*
HAIMARA   *Hoplias malabaricus*
HAIRTAIL   *Trichiurus haumela, Trichiurus lepturus*

HAIRTAIL, LARGEHEAD   *Trichiurus lepturus*
HAIRTAIL, SMALLHEAD   *Trichiurus savala*
HAKE   *Merluccius merluccius, Urophycis tenuis*
HAKE, AMERICAN   *Merluccius bilinearis*
HAKE, BLUE   *Antimora rostrata*
HAKE, FORKED-BEARD   *Urophycis blennoides*
HAKE, LONGFIN   *Urophycis chesteri*
HAKE, MUD   *Urophycis chuss*
HAKE, NEW ENGLAND   *Merluccius bilinearis*
HAKE, OLD ENGLAND   *Merluccius bilinearis*
HAKE, OLD ENGLISH   *Urophycis tenuis*
HAKE, PACIFIC   *Merluccius productus*
HAKE, RED   *Urophycis chuss*
HAKE, SILVER   *Merluccius bilinearis*
HAKE, SQUIRREL   *Urophycis chuss, Urophycis tenuis*
HAKE, WHITE   *Urophycis chuss, Urophycis tenuis*
HALFBEAK   *Dermogenys pusillus*
HALFBEAK FISH   *Hemirhamphus sajori*
HALFBEAK, LONGBILLED   *Hemirhamphus georgii*
HALFMOUTHED SARDINE   *Engraulis japonicus*
HALIBUT   *Hippoglossus hippoglossus, Parastromateus niger*
HALIBUT, ATLANTIC   *Hippoglossus hippoglossus*
HALIBUT, BLUE   *Reinhardtius hippoglossoides*
HALIBUT, CALIFORNIA   *Paralichthys californicus*
HALIBUT, GREENLAND   *Reinhardtius hippoglossoides*
HALIBUT, INDIAN   *Psettodes erumei*
HALIBUT, LITTLE   *Reinhardtius hippoglossoides*
HALIBUT, PACIFIC   *Hippoglossus stenolepis*
HALIBUT, QUEENSLAND   *Psettodes erumei*
HALIBUT, RED   *Hippoglossoides dubius*
HALIBUT, SHOTTED   *Eopsetta grigorjewi*
HAM   *Epinephelus striatus*
HAMLET   *Epinephelus striatus*
HAMMERHEAD SHARK   *Sphyrna zygaena*
HAMMERHEAD SHARK, ARROW-HEADED   *Zygaena blochii*
HAMMERHEAD, SMOOTH   *Sphyrna zygaena*
HARBOUR SHARK, BROAD   *Deania eglantina*
HARDER   *Mugil capito*
HARDHEAD   *Micropogon undulatus*
HARDTAIL   *Megalaspis cordyla*
HARDTAIL SCAD   *Megalaspis cordyla*
HARLEQUIN ROACH   *Lepomis gibbosus*
HARVEST FISH   *Peprilus paru, Peprilus triacanthus, Poronotus triacanthus, Stromateus cinereus*
HASSELT'S BONY-LIPPED BARB   *Osteocheilus hasselti*
HATA, RED   *Epinephelus fasciatus*
HATCHET FISH, MARBLED   *Carnegiella strigata*
HATCHET FISH, SILVER   *Gasteropelecus galeus*
HATCHET FISH, TRANSPARENT   *Sternoptyx diaphana*
HAUSEN   *Huso huso*

HAWKFISH *Cirrhites pinnulatus*
HEAD AND TAIL LIGHT TETRA *Hemigrammus ocellifer*
HEADFISH *Mola mola*
HEAD, GILT *Crenilabrus melops*
HEAD GRUNT *Pomadasys hasta*
HEADLIGHT FISH *Diaphus coeruleus*
HEADSTANDER *Anostomus anostomus*
HEADSTANDER, SPOTTED *Chilodus punctatus*
HEDGEHOG SKATE *Raja erinacea*
HENFISH *Cyclopterus lumpus*
HERRING, ATLANTIC *Clupea harengus*
HERRING, BALTIC *Clupea harengus membranus*
HERRING, BIGEYED *Alosa pseudoharengus, Elops saurus*
HERRING, BRANCH *Alosa pseudoharengus*
HERRING, CHINESE *Hilsa toli*
HERRING, GIANT *Chanos chanos, Elops hawaiensis, Elops saurus*
HERRING, GLUT *Alosa pseudoharengus*
HERRING, LAKE *Leucichthys artedi*
HERRING, OXEYE *Megalops cyprinoides*
HERRING, PACIFIC *Clupea pallasii*
HERRING, ROUND *Etrumeus micropus, Etrumeus terres*
HERRING, SALMON *Chanos chanos*
HERRING, SEA *Arripis georgianus*
HERRING SMELT *Argentina silus*
HERRING, WALLEYED *Alosa pseudoharengus*
HERRING, WOLF *Chirocentrus dorab*
HICKORY SHAD *Dorosoma cepedianum*
HIGHEYES *Oryzias latipes*
HILGENDORF SAUCORD *Helicolenus hilgendorfi*
HILSA *Hilsa ilisha*
HIME SALMON *Oncorhynchus nerka*
HIND, RED *Epinephelus guttatus*
HOGCHOKER *Trinectes maculatus*
HOGFISH *Lachnolaimus maximus*
HOGFISH, BASS *Micropterus dolomieui*
HOGSNAPPER *Lachnolaimus maximus*
HOMELYN RAY *Raja montagui*
HOOKNOSE *Agonus cataphractus*
HOPPER, MUD *Boleophthalmus boddaerti*
HORNED LANTERN FISH *Ceratoscopelus maderensis*
HORNED DACE *Semotilus atromaculatus*
HORNED POUT *Ictalurus nebulosus*
HORN SHARK *Heterodontus francisci*
HORSEHEAD *Selene vomer*
HORSE MACKEREL *Caranx sexfasciatus, Thunnus thynnus thynnus, Trachurus mediterraneus ponticus, Trachurus trachurus*
HORSE MACKEREL, JAPANESE *Trachurus japonicus*
HOUNDFISH *Tylosurus acus*
HOUND, ROUGH *Scyliorhinus caniculus*
HOUND, SMOOTH *Mustelus mustelus*

HOUTING   *Coregonus lavaretus*
HUDSON BAY SALMON   *Salvelinus alpinus*
HUMPBACK GRUNT   *Haemulon sciurus*
HUMPBACK SALMON   *Oncorhynchus gorbuscha*
HUMPBACK WHITEFISH   *Coregonus clupeaformis*
HUMP HEADED MAORI   *Cheilinus undulatus*
HUMPNOSE LARGE-EYE BREAM   *Monotaxis grandoculis*
HUSS   *Scyliorhinus stellaris*

ICEFISH   *Chaenocephalus aceratus*
ICE FISH, COMMON   *Salangichthys microdon*
ICE GOBY   *Leucopsarion petersi*
IDE   *Idus idus*
ILISHA, BIGEYE   *Ilisha filigera*
INCENSE BURNER   *Triakis scyllia*
INDIAN CARP   *Catla catla*
INDIAN FLATHEAD   *Platycephalus indicus*
INDIAN HALIBUT   *Psettodes erumei*
INDIAN LITTLE FISH   *Apogon semilineatus*
INDIAN MACKEREL   *Rastrelliger kanagurta*
INDIAN PIKE-CONGER   *Muraenesox talabonoides*
INDIAN SARDINE   *Sardinella longiceps, Sardinella sirm*
INDIAN TARPON   *Megalops cyprinoides*
INDIAN TASSEL FISH   *Polynemus indicus*
INDIAN TURBOT   *Psettodes erumei*
INDIAN WHITING   *Sillago sihama*

JACK   *Esox niger*
JACK, CREVALLE   *Caranx sexfasciatus*
JACK DEMPSEY   *Cichlasoma biocellatum*
JACK, DUSKY   *Caranx sexfasciatus*
JACK, GOGGLE-EYE   *Selar crumenophthalmus*
JACK, HORSE-EYE   *Caranx sexfasciatus*
JACK-KNIFE FISH   *Equetus lanceolatus*
JACK MACKEREL   *Acanthocybium solandri, Trachurus japonicus, Trachurus symmetricus*
JACK SALMON   *Stizostedion vitreum*
JACKSMELT   *Atherinopsis californiensis*
JACK, STRIPED   *Caranx delicatissimus*
JACKET, LEATHER   *Chroinemeus tolooparah*
JACOPEVER   *Sebastichthys capensis*
JAPANESE ANGEL SHARK   *Squatina japonica*
JAPANESE ARGENTINE   *Argentina semifasciata*
JAPANESE ARROWTOOTH FLOUNDER   *Atheresthes evermanni*
JAPANESE BARRACUDA   *Sphyraena japonica*
JAPANESE BLUEFISH   *Scombrops boops*
JAPANESE BROUN   *Sebastes inermis*
JAPANESE CONGER, COMMON   *Astroconger myriaster*
JAPANESE DAB   *Limanda herzensteini*
JAPANESE DOVER SOLE   *Microstomus achne*

JAPANESE DWARF BARRACUDA   *Sphyraena pinguis*
JAPANESE EEL   *Anguilla japonica*
JAPANESE FLOUNDER   *Paralichthys olivaceus*
JAPANESE GIZZARD   *Konosirus punctatus*
JAPANESE GRUNT   *Parapristipoma trilineatum*
JAPANESE HORSE MACKEREL   *Trachurus japonicus*
JAPANESE KILLIFISH   *Oryzias latipes*
JAPANESE MACKEREL   *Scomber japonicus*
JAPANESE MONKFISH   *Squatina japonica*
JAPANESE NEEDLEFISH   *Hemirhamphus sajori*
JAPANESE PARROT BASS   *Oplegnathus fasciatus*
JAPANESE PARROTFISH   *Leptoscarus japonicus, Oplegnathus fasciatus*
JAPANESE PERCH   *Coreoperca kawamebari*
JAPANESE PRICKLEBACK   *Stichaeus grigorjewi*
JAPANESE RED BREAM   *Chrysophrys major*
JAPANESE REX SOLE   *Glyptocephalus stelleri*
JAPANESE SALMON DE ALTO   *Polymixia japonica*
JAPANESE SILVER BREAM   *Chrysophrys datnia*
JAPANESE SMELT   *Osmerus dentex*
JAPANESE SPANISH MACKEREL   *Sawara niphonia*
JAPANESE SPOTTED MACKEREL   *Pneumatophorus japonicus tapeinocephalus*
JAPANESE STARGAZER   *Uranoscopus japonicus*
JAPANESE STINGFISH   *Sebastodes inermis*
JAPANESE STING RAY   *Dasyatis akajei*
JAPANESE THREADFIN BREAM   *Nemipterus japonicus*
JARBUA THERAPON   *Therapon jarbua*
JAVA TILAPIA   *Tilapia mossambica*
JAVELIN GRUNTER   *Pomadasys hasta*
JELLY CAT   *Anarhichas latifrons*
JENNY, SILVER   *Eucinostomus argenteus, Eucinostomus gula*
JEWFISH   *Epinephelus itajara, Sciaena antarctica*
JEWFISH, BLACK   *Garrupa nigrita*
JEWFISH, CALIFORNIA   *Stereolepis gigas*
JEWFISH, DUSSUMIER'S SILVER   *Johnius dussumieri*
JEWFISH, GREYFIN   *Pseudosciaena anea*
JEWFISH, ROSY   *Otolithes ruber*
JEWFISH, SILVER   *Otolithes ruber*
JEWFISH, TWOSPINED   *Sciaena diacanthus*
JEW, RED   *Lutianus malabaricus*
JEW, SILVER   *Sciaena antarctica*
JOHN DORY   *Zeus australis, Zeus faber, Zeus japonicus*
JOHN MARIGGLE   *Elops saurus*
JOHNNY CARP   *Carassius auratus*
JOHNNY DARTER   *Etheostoma nigrum*
JOHN'S SNAPPER   *Lutianus johnii*
JUREL   *Caranx sexfasciatus*

KAMLOOPS TROUT   *Salmo gairdneri kamloops*
KATONKEL   *Scomberomorus commersonii*

KATONKEL, CAPE   *Sarda sarda*
KAUP'S DEEPSEA EEL   *Synaphobranchus kaupi*
KELP BASS   *Paralabrax clathratus*
KELP GREENLING   *Hexagrammos decagrammus*
KICKANINNY   *Oncorhynchus nerka kennerlyi*
KILLIFISH   *Fundulus heteroclitus*
KILLIFISH, BANDED   *Fundulus diaphanus*
KILLIFISH, CALIFORNIA   *Fundulus parvipinnis*
KILLIFISH, GOLDEN EAR   *Fundulus chrysotus*
KILLIFISH, GULF   *Fundulus grandis*
KILLIFISH, JAPANESE   *Oryzias latipes*
KILLIFISH, PLAINS   *Fundulus kansae*
KINGFISH   *Acanthocybium solandri, Caranx equula, Sciaena antarctica, Scomberomorus cavalla, Scomberomorus commersonii, Scomberomorus regalis*
KINGFISH, ALLIED   *Seriola purpurascens*
KINGFISH, GULF   *Menticirrhus littoralis*
KINGFISH, NORTHERN   *Menticirrhus saxatilis*
KINGFISH, RIVER   *Sciaena antarctica*
KING GEORGE WHITING   *Sillaginodes punctatus*
KINGKLIP   *Genypterus capensis*
KING MACKEREL   *Scomberomorus cavalla*
KING SALMON   *Oncorhynchus tschawytscha*
KING WHITING   *Menticirrhus littoralis*
KISSING GOURAMI   *Helostoma temmincki*
KITEFIN SHARK   *Dalatias licha*
KITE FISH   *Monodactylus argenteus*
KIVER   *Lepomis gibbosus*
KNIFEFISH   *Chirocentrus dorab*
KNIFEFISH, BANDED   *Gymnotus carapo*
KOKANEE   *Oncorhynchus nerka kennerlyi*
KOROKORO   *Geotrea australis*

LABEO, ORANGEFIN   *Labeo calbasu*
LADYBIRD, SEA   *Uranoscopus scaber*
LADYFISH   *Elops saurus*
LAFAYETTE   *Leiostomus xanthurus*
LAKE CHARR   *Salvelinus namaycush*
LAKE CHUBSUCKER   *Erimyzon sucetta*
LAKE CISCO   *Leucichthys artedii*
LAKE HERRING   *Leucichthys artedii*
LAKE LAWYER   *Lota lota*
LAKE PERCH   *Perca flavescens*
LAKE TROUT   *Salvelinus namaycush*
LAKE WHITEFISH   *Coregonus clupeaformis*
LAMPER EEL   *Petromyzon marinus*
LAMPREY   *Petromyzon marinus*
LAMPREY, AMERICAN BROOK   *Lampetra lamottei*
LAMPREY, ARCTIC   *Lampetra japonica*
LAMPREY, BROOK   *Lampetra planeri*

LAMPREY, NORTHERN BROOK *Ichthyomyzon fossor*
LAMPREY, PACIFIC *Entosphenus tridentatus*
LAMPREY, PLANER'S *Lampetra planeri*
LAMPREY, POUCHED *Geotrea australis*
LAMPREY, RIVER EIGHTEYES *Lampetra japonica*
LAMPREY, SEA *Petromyzon marinus*
LAMPREY, SILVER *Ichthyomyzon unicuspis*
LANCET FISH *Acanthurus hepatus*
LANCET FISH, LONGNOSE *Alepisaurus ferox*
LANE SNAPPER *Lutianus synagris*
LANTERN FISH *Latimeria chalumnae*
LANTERN FISH, HORNED *Ceratoscopelus maderensis*
LANTERN SHARK *Etmopterus spinax*
LARGE-EYED BREAM *Gymnocranius griseus*
LARGE-EYED BREAM, ROUNDTOOTHED *Monotaxis grandoculis*
LARGE-EYE DENTEX *Dentex macrophthalmus*
LARGE-HEADED RIBBONFISH *Trichiurus haumela*
LARGE-HEAD HAIRTAIL *Trichiurus lepturus*
LARGEMOUTH BASS *Micropterus salmoides*
LARGEMOUTHED NANNYGAI *Lutianus malabaricus*
LARGEMOUTH SMELT *Spirinchus lanceolatus*
LARGESCALED BANDED GRUNTER *Therapon theraps*
LARGESCALED GRINNER *Saurida undosquamis*
LARGESCALED SCORPION FISH *Scorpaena scrofa*
LARGESCALED SUCKER *Moxostoma aureolum*
LARGESCALE TAPIRFISH *Notacanthus nasus*
LARGE SPOTTED DOGFISH *Scyllium stellare*
LASHER, FATHER *Myoxocephalus scorpius*
LAVARET *Coregonus lavaretus*
LAWYER *Amia calva, Lutianus griseus*
LAWYER, LAKE *Lota lota*
LAYANG SCAD *Decapterus macrosoma*
LEAPING GREY MULLET *Mugil saliens*
LEAPING SILVER BAR *Chirocentrus dorab*
LEATHERCOAT *Oligoplites saurus*
LEATHERFISH *Stephanolepis cirrhifer*
LEATHER JACKET *Chorinemus tolooparah, Oligoplites saurus, Tilapia mossambica*
LEMON SHARK *Negaprion brevirostris*
LEMON SOLE *Parophrys vetulus, Pleuronectes microcephalus*
LEOPARD CORYDORAS *Corydoras julii*
LEOPARD FISH *Anarhichas minor*
LEOPARD FLOUNDER *Platophrys pantherinus*
LEOPARD SHARK *Galeocerdo arcticus, Triakis scyllia, Triakis semifasciatum*
LESSER BUTTERFLY RAY *Gymnura macrura*
LESSER CATFISH *Anarhichas minor*
LESSER FORKBEARD *Raniceps raninus*
LESSER LING *Molva byrkelange*
LESSER SANDEEL *Ammodytes tobianus*
LESSER SPOTTED DOGFISH *Scyliorhinus canicula*
LESSER TIGER-TOOTHED CROAKER *Otolithes ruber*

LEVOVANGAN *Monotaxis grandoculis*
LINED SILVER GRUNT *Pomadasys hasta*
LING *Lota lota, Molva molva, Urophycis chuss, Urophycis tenuis*
LING, BLUE *Molva byrkelange*
LINGCOD *Ophiodon elongatus*
LING, LESSER *Molva byrkelange*
LING, THIMBLE-EYED *Urophycis chuss*
LIP SHARK *Hemiscyllium plagiosum*
LISA *Mugil curema*
LITTLE BASS *Micropterus dolomieui*
LITTLE FISH, INDIAN *Apogon semilineatus*
LITTLE HALIBUT *Reinhardtius hippoglossoides*
LITTLE REDFISH *Oncorhynchus nerka kennerlyi*
LITTLE SCULPIN *Myoxocephalus aeneus*
LITTLE SKATE *Raja erinacea*
LITTLE TUNA *Euthynnus affinis yaito, Euthynnus alletteratus*
LITTLE TUNNY *Thynnus thunnina*
LIZARDFISH, BLUNTNOSE *Trachinocephalus myops*
LIZARDFISH, BRUSHTOOTH *Saurida undosquamis*
LIZARDFISH, CALIFORNIA *Synodus lucioceps*
LIZARDFISH, GREATER *Saurida tumbil*
LIZARDFISH, TRUE *Saurida undosquamis*
LIZZARDFISH, OFFSHORE *Trachinocephalus myops*
LOACH *Misgurnus anguillicaudatus, Nemacheilus barbatulus*
LOACH, COOLIE *Acanthophthalmus kuhlii*
LOACH, POND *Misgurnus fossilis*
LOACH, SPINED *Cobitis taenia*
LOACH, STONE *Nemacheilus barbatulus*
LONGBILLED HALFBEAK *Hemirhamphus georgii*
LONGFIN EEL *Anguilla dieffenbachii*
LONGFIN HAKE *Urophycis chesteri*
LONGFINNED ALBACORE *Thunnus alalunga*
LONGFINNED MULLET *Mugil vaigiensis*
LONGFINNED PIKE *Dinolestes lewini*
LONGFINNED SOLE *Errex zachirus*
LONGFINNED TUNA *Thunnus alalunga*
LONGFIN SMELT *Spirinchus lanceolatus*
LONGFISH *Atule mate*
LONGHORN SCULPIN *Myoxocephalus octodecimspinosus*
LONGJAW ANCHOVY *Stolephorus commersonii*
LONGJAW FLOUNDER *Atheresthes stomias*
LONGJAW GOBY *Gillichthys mirabilis*
LONGJAW MACKEREL *Rastrelliger kanagurta*
LONGJAW ROCKFISH *Sebastodes alutus*
LONGJAW SQUIRRELFISH *Holocentrus ascensionis*
LONGLURE FROGFISH *Antennarius ocellatus*
LONGNOSE EEL *Synaphobranchus kaupi*
LONGNOSE GAR *Lepisosteus osseus*
LONGNOSE LANCET FISH *Aleposaurus ferox*
LONGNOSE SKATE *Raja oxyrhynchus*

Longnose sucker   *Catostomus catostomus*
Longrayed silver biddy   *Gerres filamentosus*
Long rough dab   *Hippoglossoides platessoides*
Longspine combfish   *Zaniolepis latipinnis*
Longspine greenling   *Zaniolepis latipinnis*
Longspine sea scorpion   *Cottus bubalis*
Longspine snapper   *Argyrops spinifer*
Longtooth anglemouth   *Gonostoma elongatum*
Longtooth salmon   *Otolithes ruber*
Longwinged shark   *Carcharhinus longimanus*
Lookdown, Atlantic   *Selene vomer*
Loosejaw   *Malacosteus niger*
Lord, Red Irish   *Hemilepidotus hemilepidotus*
Luderick   *Girella tricuspidata*
Lumpfish   *Cyclopterus lumpus*
Lump sucker   *Cyclopterus lumpus*
Lungfish, African   *Protopterus aethiopicus, Protopterus annectens*
Lungfish, Australian   *Neoceratodus forsteri*
Lungfish, South American   *Lepidosiren paradoxa*

Maasbanker   *Trachurus trachurus*
Mackerel, Atka   *Pleurogrammus azonus*
Mackerel, Atlantic   *Scomber scombrus*
Mackerel, Barred Spanish   *Scomberomorus commersonii*
Mackerel, Bastard   *Acanthocybium solandri*
Mackerel, Bay   *Scomberomorus maculatus*
Mackerel, Black-spotted Spanish   *Scomberomorus regalis*
Mackerel, Bullet   *Auxis thazard*
Mackerel, Chub   *Rastrelliger neglectus, Scomber japonicus*
Mackerel, Frigate   *Auxis tapeinocephalus, Auxis thazard*
Mackerel, Horse   *Caranx sexfasciatus, Thunnus thynnus thynnus, Trachurus mediter-*
   raneus ponticus, Trachurus trachurus
Mackerel, Indian   *Rastrelliger kanagurta*
Mackerel, Jack   *Acanthocybium solandri, Trachurus japonicus, Trachurus symmetricus*
Mackerel, Japanese   *Scomber japonicus*
Mackerel, Japanese Spanish   *Sawara niphonia*
Mackerel, Japanese spotted   *Pneumatophorus japonicus tapeinocephalus*
Mackerel, King   *Scomberomorus cavalla*
Mackerel, Longjaw   *Rastrelliger kanagurta*
Mackerel, Mongrel   *Acanthocybium solandri*
Mackerel, Pacific   *Pneumatophorus japonicus, Scomber japonicus*
Mackerel, Painted   *Scomberomorus regalis*
Mackerel, Pike   *Acanthocybium solandri*
Mackerel, Rake-gilled   *Rastrelliger kanagurta*
Mackerel, Short-bodied   *Rastrelliger brachysoma*
Mackerel shark   *Lamna nasus*
Mackerel, Skip   *Pomatomus saltatrix*
Mackerel, Slimy   *Scomber japonicus*
Mackerel, Snake   *Promethichthys prometheus*

MACKEREL, SNAP   *Pomatomus saltatrix*
MACKEREL, SPANISH   *Scomber japonicus, Scomberomorus commersonii, Scomberomorus niphonius*
MACKEREL, SPOTTED   *Sawara niphonia, Scomber tapeinocephalus, Scomberomorus maculatus*
MACKEREL, SPOTTED SPANISH   *Scomberomorus guttatum*
MACKEREL, STRIPED   *Pelamys chilensis*
MACKEREL TUNA   *Euthynnus alletteratus*
MACKINAW TROUT   *Salvelinus namaycush*
MACQUARIE PERCH   *Macquaria australasica*
MADREGAL   *Zonichthys falcatus*
MADTOM, TADPOLE   *Noturus gyrinus*
MAHSEER, PUTITOR   *Barbus putitora*
MAID, FAIR   *Stenotomus versicolor*
MAKO SHARK   *Isurus glaucus, Isurus oxyrhynchus*
MALABAR SNAPPER   *Lutianus malabaricus*
MALMA TROUT   *Salvelinus malma*
MANGROVE MULLET   *Mugil cephalus*
MANGROVE SNAPPER   *Lutianus griseus*
MANILA SEA CATFISH   *Arius manillensis*
MAN-OF-WAR FISH   *Nomeus gronowi*
MAORI   *Ophthalmolepis lineolatus*
MAORI, HUMP-HEADED   *Cheilinus undulatus*
MARBLED ELECTRIC RAY   *Torpedo marmorata*
MARBLED HATCHET FISH   *Carnegiella strigata*
MARBLED SCULPIN, GIANT   *Scorpaenichthys marmoratus*
MARE, BAY   *Catostomus commersonii*
MARIGGLE, JOHN   *Elops saurus*
MARINE SARGUS   *Diplodus sargus*
MARKET SARDINE   *Etrumeus micropus*
MARLIN, BLACK   *Makaira mazara*
MARLIN, BLUE   *Makaira mazara*
MARLIN, GIANT BLACK   *Makaira marlina*
MARLIN, PACIFIC   *Makaira mitsukurii*
MARLIN, PACIFIC BLUE   *Makaira ampla*
MARLIN, STRIPED   *Makaira mitsukurii, Tetrapturus audax*
MARMOR BREAM   *Lithognathus mormyrus*
MASKED GREENLING   *Hexagrammos octogrammus*
MASU   *Oncorhynchus masou*
MATREEL   *Scomber japonicus*
MATSUBARA STINGFISH   *Sebastodes matsubarae*
MEAGRE   *Johnius regius, Sciaena aquila*
MEAGRE, BROWN   *Sciaena umbra*
MEDAKA   *Oryzias latipes*
MEGRIM   *Lepidorhombus whiffiagonis*
MEICHI PORGY   *Gymnocranius griseus*
MENHADEN   *Brevoortia tyrannus*
MENHADEN, GULF   *Brevoortia patronus*
MEXICAN CAVE CHARACIN   *Anoptichthys jordani*
MEXICAN SNAPPER   *Lutianus campechanus*
MEXICAN TETRA   *Astyanax mexicanus*

MIA MIA   *Scatophagus argus*
MIDSHIPMAN, ATLANTIC   *Porichthys porosissimus*
MIDSHIPMAN, PLAINFIN   *Porichthys notatus*
MILK FISH   *Chanos chanos*
MILK SHARK   *Scoliodon walbeehmii*
MILLER'S THUMB   *Cottus gobio*
MILLIONS FISH   *Poecilia reticulata*
MINNOW   *Phoxinus phoxinus*
MINNOW, BLACK-SPOTTED TOP   *Fundulus olivaceus*
MINNOW, BLUNTNOSE   *Pimephales notatus*
MINNOW, COMMON   *Zacco platypus*
MINNOW, FATHEAD   *Pimephales promelas*
MINNOW, SALTWATER   *Fundulus heteroclitus*
MINNOW, SHEEPSHEAD   *Cyprinodon variegatus*
MINNOW, TOP   *Gambusia holbrooki*
MISHIMA PUFFER FISH   *Uranoscopus japonicus*
MISHIMA PUFFER FISH, BLUE   *Gnathagnus elongatus*
MOGGEL   *Labeo umbratus*
MOJARRAS, SPOTTED   *Gerres filamentosus*
MOJARRON   *Anisotremus interruptus*
MOLA, COMMON   *Mola mola*
MOLLY, BLACK   *Mollienesia* sp.
MOLLY, GREEN   *Poecilia latipinna*
MOLLY, SAILFIN   *Poecilia latipinna*
MONGREL MACKEREL   *Acanthocybium solandri*
MONKFISH   *Lophius piscatorius, Squatina squatina*
MONKFISH, JAPANESE   *Squatina japonica*
MONO   *Monodactylus argenteus*
MOONEYE   *Hiodon tergisus*
MOONFISH   *Chaetodipterus faber, Mene maculata, Monodactylus argenteus, Selene vomer*
MORAY EEL   *Gymnothorax kidako, Muraena helena*
MORAY, GREEK   *Muraena helena*
MORAY, SPOTTED   *Gymnothorax moringa*
MORETON BAY SALMON   *Chanos chanos*
MOROKO, STONE   *Pseudorasbora parva*
MORWONG   *Nemadactylus douglasii*
MORWONG, DUSKY   *Psilocranium nigricans*
MORWONG, STRIPED   *Goniistius zonatus*
MOSES PERCH   *Lutianus johnii*
MOSSBUNKER   *Brevoortia tyrannus*
MOTTLED SAND DAB   *Citharichthys sordidus*
MOTTLEFIN PARROTFISH   *Scarus croicensis*
MOUNTAIN BARBEL   *Barbus meridionalis petenyi*
MOUNTAIN PERCH   *Macquaria australasica*
MOUSTACHED ANCHOVY   *Thrissocles mystax*
MOUTHBROODER, MOZAMBIQUE   *Tilapia mossambica*
MOUTH, FLUTE-   *Fistularia petimba*
MOZAMBIQUE MOUTHBROODER   *Tilapia mossambica*
MUD BARBEL   *Clarias mossambicus*
MUD BLOWER   *Lota lota*

MUD CHUB   *Semotilus atromaculatus*
MUD DAB   *Limanda yokohamae, Pleuronectes limanda*
MUD EEL   *Amphipnus cuchia*
MUD EEL, FRESHWATER   *Macrognathus aculeatum*
MUDFISH   *Amia calva, Labeo capensis, Labeo rosae, Labeo umbratus, Misgurnus fossilis,*
   Ophicephalus striatus, Parasilurus asotus, Protopterus annectens
MUD HAKE   *Urophycis chuss*
MUD HOPPER   *Boleophthalmus boddaerti*
MUD MINNOW, CENTRAL   *Umbra limi*
MUD MULLET   *Labeo umbratus*
MUD SHARK   *Hexanchus griseus*
MUD SKIPPER   *Periophthalmodon australis, Periophthalmus sobrinus*
MUDSUCKER   *Gillichthys mirabilis, Labeo capensis, Labeo umbratus*
MULLET   *Moxostoma aureolum, Mugil cephalus*
MULLET, BASTARD   *Polynemus indicus*
MULLET, BLACK   *Catostomus commersonii*
MULLET, BLACK-FINNED   *Mugil melanopterus*
MULLET, BLUE-BLACK   *Mugil curema*
MULLET, BONY   *Megalops cyprinoides*
MULLET, BROWN-BANDED   *Mugil dussumieri*
MULLET, BULLY   *Mugil cephalus*
MULLET, DIAMOND-SCALE   *Mugil vaigiensis*
MULLET, DUSSUMIER'S   *Mugil dussumierii*
MULLET, FLATHEAD   *Mugil cephalus*
MULLET, FLAT-TAILED   *Mugil dussumieri*
MULLET, GOLDEN-GREY   *Mugil auratus*
MULLET, GOLDSPOT   *Mugil parsia*
MULLET, GREENBACK   *Mugil dussumieri*
MULLET, GREY   *Liza ramada, Mugil capito, Mugil cephalus, Mugil dussumieri, Mugil*
   speigleri
MULLET, GREY, THICK-LIPPED   *Mugil chelo*
MULLET, LEAPING GREY   *Mugil saliens*
MULLET, LONGFINNED   *Mugil vaigiensis*
MULLET, MANGROVE   *Mugil cephalus*
MULLET, MUD   *Labeo umbratus*
MULLET, RED   *Mullus barbatus, Mullus surmulletus*
MULLET, RIVER   *Mugil cephalus*
MULLET, SEA   *Menticirrhus saxatilis*
MULLET, SPEIGLER'S GREY   *Mugil speigleri*
MULLET, STRIPED   *Mugil cephalus, Mullus barbatus*
MULLET, TADE GREY   *Mugil tade*
MULLET, THICK LIPPED   *Crenimugil labrosus*
MULLET, THICK LIPPED GREY   *Chelon labrosus*
MULLET, THIN LIP GREY   *Mugil capito*
MULLET, TRUE   *Mugil cephalus*
MULLET, WHITE   *Chanos chanos, Mugil curema*
MULLEY   *Wallago attu*
MULLOWAY   *Sciaena antarctica*
MUMMICHOG   *Fundulus heteroclitus*
MURRAY PERCH   *Macquaria australasica*

MURREL   *Ophicephalus punctatus, Ophicephalus striatus*
MUTTONFISH   *Lutianus analis, Macrozoarces americanus*
MUTTON SNAPPER   *Lutianus analis*

NANNYGAI   *Lutianus malabaricus*
NANNYGAI, LARGEMOUTHED   *Lutianus malabaricus*
NARROW BARRED SPANISH MACKEREL   *Cybium commersonii*
NASSAU GROUPER   *Epinephelus striatus*
NEEDLEFISH   *Scomberesox saurus, Strongylura gigantea*
NEEDLEFISH, ATLANTIC   *Strongylura marina*
NEEDLEFISH, JAPANESE   *Hemirhamphus sajori*
NEEDLENOSE   *Lepisosteus osseus*
NED, YELLOW   *Perca flavescens*
NEMIPTERID, RIBBON-FINNED   *Nemipterus taeniopterus*
NEW ENGLAND HAKE   *Merluccius bilinearis*
NEWFOUNDLAND TURBOT   *Reinhardtius hippoglossoides*
NEW ZEALAND WHIPTAIL   *Macrouronus novaezelandae*
NIGGERFISH   *Cephalopholis fulvus*
NILE PERCH   *Lates niloticus*
NIPPER   *Tautogolabrus adspersus*
NIPPLE-TAILED OCEAN SUNFISH   *Masturus lanceolatus*
NORFOLK SPOT   *Leiostomus xanthurus*
NORTH ATLANTIC GRENADIER   *Macrurus rupestris*
NORTHERN ANCHOVY   *Engraulis mordax*
NORTHERN BLENNY   *Stichaeus grigorjewi*
NORTHERN BROOK LAMPREY   *Ichthyomyzon fossor*
NORTHERN HAGFISH   *Myxine glutinosa*
NORTHERN KINGFISH   *Menticirrhus saxatilis*
NORTHERN PIKE   *Esox lucius*
NORTHERN PIPEFISH   *Syngnathus fuscus*
NORTHERN POMOTIS   *Lepomis gibbosus*
NORTHERN PUFFER   *Sphaeroides maculatus*
NORTHERN REDHORSE   *Moxostoma aureolum, Moxostoma macrolepidotum*
NORTHERN ROCK BASS   *Ambloplites rupestris*
NORTHERN SEAROBIN   *Prionotus carolinus*
NORTHERN SQUAWFISH   *Ptychocheilus oregonensis*
NORTHERN STINGRAY   *Dasyatis centroura*
NORTHERN SUCKER   *Catostomus catostomus*
NORTHERN WHITING   *Sillago sihama*
NORWAY HADDOCK   *Sebastes marinus, Sebastes viviparus*
NORWEGIAN TOPKNOT   *Phrynorhombus norvegicus*
NOTOTHENIA, GREEN   *Notothenia gibberifrons*
NUMBFISH   *Tetranarce occidentalis, Torpedo nobiliana*
NURSE, GREY   *Carcharias arenarius, Odontaspis arenarius*
NURSEHOUND   *Scyliorhinus stellaris*
NURSE SHARK   *Ginglymostoma cirratum*

OBTUSE BARRACUDA   *Sphyraena obtusata*
OCEAN PERCH   *Sebastes marinus*

OCEAN PERCH, PACIFIC   *Sebastodes alutus*
OCEAN POUT   *Macrozoarces americanus*
OCEAN SUNFISH   *Mola mola*
OCEAN SUNFISH, NIPPLETAILED   *Masturus lanceolatus*
OCEAN SUNFISH, SHARP TAIL   *Masturus lanceolatus*
OCEAN WHITEFISH   *Caulolatilus princeps*
OFFSHORE LIZZARD FISH   *Trachinocephalus myops*
OFFSHORE SNAKE   *Ophisurus macrorhynchus*
OHIO GAR   *Lepisosteus osseus*
OILFISH   *Ruvettus pretiosus*
OIL SARDINE   *Sardinella longiceps*
OIL SHARK   *Galeorhinus zyopterus*
OLD ENGLAND HAKE   *Merluccius bilinearis*
OLD ENGLISH HAKE   *Urophycis tenuis*
OLD WIFE   *Balistes vetula, Leiostomus xanthurus, Spondyliosoma cantharus*
OLIVE BARB   *Barbus chrysopoma*
OLIVE GRUNTER   *Pristipoma olivaceum*
OOLAKAN   *Thaleichthys pacificus*
OPALEYE   *Girella nigricans*
OPALINE GOURAMY   *Trichogaster cosby*
OPENMOUTHED GRUNT   *Haemulon flavolineatum*
ORANGE-FIN LABEO   *Labeo calbasu*
ORANGE-FINNED PONY FISH   *Leiognathus bindus*
ORANGE RIVER SANDFISH   *Labeo capensis*
ORANGE ROCKFISH   *Sebastodes pinniger*
ORANGE-SPOTTED ROCKFISH   *Sebastodes maliger*
ORE   *Allocyttus verrucosus*
OREO, OX-EYE   *Allocyttus verrucosus*
OVAL FILEFISH   *Navodon modestus*
OX-EYE HERRING   *Megalops cyprinoides*
OX-EYE OREO   *Allocyttus verrucosus*
OYSTERFISH   *Opsanus tau*
OZARK STUDFISH   *Fundulus catenatus*

PACIFIC BARRACUDA   *Sphyraena argentea*
PACIFIC BLUEFIN TUNA   *Thunnus thynnus orientalis*
PACIFIC BLUE MARLIN   *Makaira ampla*
PACIFIC BONITO   *Sarda chiliensis*
PACIFIC COAST STURGEON   *Acipenser transmontanus*
PACIFIC COD   *Gadus macrocephalus*
PACIFIC HAGFISH   *Eptatretus stoutii*
PACIFIC HAKE   *Merluccius productus*
PACIFIC HALIBUT   *Hippoglossus stenolepis*
PACIFIC HERRING   *Clupea pallasii*
PACIFIC LAMPREY   *Entosphenus tridentatus*
PACIFIC MACKEREL   *Pneumatophorus japonicus, Scomber japonicus*
PACIFIC MARLIN   *Makaira mitsukurii*
PACIFIC OCEAN FLOUNDER   *Cleisthenes herzensteini*
PACIFIC OCEAN PERCH   *Sebastodes alutus*

PACIFIC POMPANO   *Peprilus simillimus*
PACIFIC RAT-TAIL   *Coryphaenoides acrolepis*
PACIFIC SAND DAB   *Citharichthys sordidus*
PACIFIC SARDINE   *Sardinops caerula*
PACIFIC SAURY   *Cololabis saira*
PACIFIC SNAKE BLENNY   *Lumpenus sagitta*
PACIFIC SPINY DOGFISH   *Squalus acanthias*
PACIFIC TOMCOD   *Microgadus proximus*
PADDLEFISH   *Polyodon spathula*
PADDY EEL   *Monopterus albus*
PAINTED COMBER   *Serranus scriba*
PAINTED GRINNER   *Trachinocephalus myops*
PAINTED MACKEREL   *Scomberomorus regalis*
PAINTED RAY   *Raja undulata*
PAINTED SAURY   *Trachinocephalus myops*
PALE RAY   *Raja lintea*
PALLID SCULPIN   *Cottunculus thompsoni*
PALMER   *Lates calcarifer*
PAMPANO   *Citula dorsalis, Lichia vadigo*
PAMPANO, COMMON   *Trachinotus carolinus*
PANCHAX   *Aplocheilus panchax*
PANCHAX, BLUE   *Aplocheilus panchax*
PANDORA   *Pagellus erythrinus*
PAPER SOLE   *Hippoglossoides elassodon*
PARADISE FISH   *Macropodus opercularis*
PARADISE FISH, BROWN SPIKETAILED   *Macropodus cupanus dayi*
PARADISE THREADFIN   *Polynemus paradiseus*
PARGO   *Hoplopagrus güntheri, Lutianus analis*
PARROT BASS, JAPANESE   *Oplegnathus fasciatus*
PARROT FISH   *Callyodon ovifrons, Scarus cyawgnuthus, Scarus gibbus, Scarus guacamaia*
PARROT FISH, GREEN   *Pseudoscarus guacamaia*
PARROT FISH, JAPANESE   *Leptoscarus japonicus, Oplegnathus fasciatus*
PARROT FISH, MOTTLEFIN   *Scarus croicensis*
PARROT FISH, QUEEN   *Scarus vetula*
PARROT FISH, RAINBOW   *Scarus guacamaia*
PARROT FISH, REDTAILED   *Sparisoma chrysopterum*
PARROT FISH, STRIPED   *Scarus croicensis*
PEACOCK BLENNY   *Blennius pavo*
PEACOCK WRASSE   *Crenilabrus pavo*
PEARL GOURAMI   *Trichogaster leeri*
PEARL SPOT   *Etroplus suratensis*
PECK-NOSED SKATE   *Raja stabuliforis*
PELAMID   *Sarda sarda*
PENSACOLA SNAPPER   *Lutianus blackfordii*
PERCH   *Lepomis gibbosus, Lepomis macrochirus, Nemadactylus macropterus, Perca flavescens, Tautogolabrus adspersus*
PERCH, AMERICAN   *Perca flavescens*
PERCH, BLACK   *Micropterus dolomieui*
PERCH, BLUE   *Tautogolabrus adspersus*
PERCH, BOTTOM   *Apogon semilineatus*

PERCH, CLIMBING *Anabas scandens*
PERCH, CRESCENT *Therapon jarbua*
PERCH, DUSKY *Epinephelus gigas*
PERCH, EURASIAN *Perca flavescens*
PERCH, GIANT *Lates calcarifer*
PERCH, GOLD *Lepomis macrochirus*
PERCH, JAPANESE *Coreoperca kawamebari*
PERCH, LAKE *Perca flavescens*
PERCH, MACQUARIE *Macquaria australasica*
PERCH, MOSES *Lutianus johnii*
PERCH, MOUNTAIN *Macquaria australasica*
PERCH, MURRAY *Macquaria australasica*
PERCH, NILE *Lates niloticus*
PERCH, OCEAN *Sebastes marinus*
PERCH, PACIFIC OCEAN *Sebastodes alutus*
PERCH, PIKE *Lucioperca lucioperca*
PERCH, PILE *Rhacochilus vacca*
PERCH, POND *Lepomis gibbosus*
PERCH, RINGED *Perca flavescens*
PERCH, RIVER *Perca flavescens*
PERCH, SAND *Lepomis gibbosus*
PERCH, SCARLET SEA *Lutianus malabaricus*
PERCH, SEA *Lateolabrax japonicus, Lates calcarifer, Morone americana, Spicara smaris, Tautogolabrus adspersus*
PERCH, SHINER *Cymatogaster aggregata*
PERCH, SILVER *Morone americana, Pomoxis annularis, Therapon bidyana*
PERCH, SILVER SEA *Lates calcarifer*
PERCH, SIX-LINED *Helotes sexlineatus*
PERCH, SPECKLED *Pomoxis annularis*
PERCH, STRIPED *Helotes sexlineatus*
PERCH, SURF *Ditrema temmincki*
PERCH, TARGET *Therapon puta*
PERCH, TIN *Pomoxis annularis*
PERCH, TRUMPETER *Pelates quadrilineatus*
PERCH, WART *Psenopsis anomala*
PERCH, WHITE *Aplodinotus grunniens, Morone americana, Pomoxis annularis*
PERCH, YELLOW *Lepomis gibbosus, Perca flavescens*
PERFORATED SCALE SARDINE *Sardinella perforata*
PERMIT *Trachinotus falcatus*
PESCADINHA *Sillago sihama*
PETRALE SOLE *Eopsetta jordani*
PICKEREL *Esox lucius, Spicara smaris*
PICKEREL, BLACK SEA *Spicara smaris*
PICKEREL, CHAIN *Esox niger*
PICKEREL, EASTERN *Esox niger*
PICKEREL, GRASS *Esox americanus vermicularis*
PICKHANDLE BARRACUDA *Sphyraena jello*
PICNIC SEABREAM *Sparus berda*
PIGFACE BREAM, BRIDLED *Lethrinus cinereus*
PIGFACE BREAM, STARRY *Lethrinus opercularis*

PIGFISH, GIANT   *Achoerodus gouldii*
PIGFISH, STRIPED   *Parapristipoma trilineatum*
PIHARAU   *Geotrea australis*
PIKE   *Esox lucius*
PIKE, BLUE   *Stizostedion vitreum*
PIKE, BLUNT-JAWED SEA   *Sphyraena obtusata*
PIKE CICHLID, RINGTAILED   *Crenicichla saxatilis*
PIKE CONGER, DAGGERTOOTH   *Muraenesox cinereus*
PIKE CONGER, INDIAN   *Muraenesox talabonoides*
PIKE EEL   *Muraenesox cinereus*
PIKE, GIANT SEA   *Sphyraena jello*
PIKE, GREEN   *Esox niger*
PIKE, LONGFINNED   *Dinolestes lewini*
PIKE MACKEREL   *Acanthocybium solandri*
PIKE, NORTHERN   *Esox lucius*
PIKE-PERCH   *Lucioperca lucioperca, Stizostedion lucioperca*
PIKE, SAURY   *Scomberesox saurus*
PIKE, SEA   *Sphyraena japonica*
PIKE TOPMINNOW   *Belonesox belizanus*
PIKE, WALLEYED   *Stizostedion vitreum*
PIKE, YELLOW   *Stizostedion vitreum*
PIKED DOGFISH   *Squalus acanthias*
PILCHARD   *Clupea pilchardus, Sardina pilchardus, Sardinops caerula, Sardinops ocellata*
PILCHARD, SOUTH AFRICAN   *Sardinops ocellata*
PILE PERCH   *Rhacochilus vacca*
PILE SEAPERCH   *Damalichthys vacca*
PILOT SUCKER   *Echeneis naucrates*
PINFISH   *Apeltes quadracus, Gasterosteus aculeatus, Lagodon rhomboides*
PINKEAR   *Melanotaenia fluviatilis*
PINK DENTEX   *Dentex gibbosus*
PINK SALMON   *Oncorhynchus gorbuscha*
PINKTAILED CHARACIN   *Chalceus macrolepidotus*
PIPEFISH, NORTHERN   *Syngnathus fuscus*
PIPER   *Trigla cuculus*
PIPER, EGRET   *Macrorhamphosus sagifue*
PIPER GURNARD   *Trigla lyra*
PIRANHA, NATTERER'S   *Rooseveltiella nattereri*
PIRANHA, RED   *Rooseveltiella nattereri*
PLAICE   *Paralichthys olivaceus, Pleuronectes platessa*
PLAICE, AMERICAN   *Hippoglossoides platessoides*
PLAICE, CANADIAN   *Hippoglossoides platessoides*
PLAICE, YELLOW-STRIPED   *Pleuronectes herzensteini*
PLAIN BONITO   *Auxis thazard*
PLAINFIN MIDSHIPMAN   *Porichthys notatus*
PLAINS KILLIFISH   *Fundulus kansae*
PLANER'S LAMPREY   *Lampetra planeri*
PLATY   *Xiphophorus maculatus*
POACHER, STURGEON   *Agonus acipenserinus*
POGGE   *Agonus cataphractus*
POGY   *Brevoortia tyrannus*

POINTED-TAILED GOBY   *Apocryptes lanceolatus*
POINTER, BLUE   *Isurus glaucus*
POLAR COD   *Boreogadus saida*
POLAR EEL-POUT   *Lycodes turneri*
POLE FLOUNDER   *Glyptocephalus cynoglossus*
POLLACK   *Gadus pollachius, Gadus virens*
POLLAN   *Coregonus albula, Coregonus lavaretus*
POLLOCK, WALLEYE   *Theragra chalcogramma*
POMFRET, BLACK   *Parastromateus niger*
POMFRET, BROWN   *Parastromateus niger*
POMFRET, GREY   *Stromateus cinereus*
POMFRET, SILVER   *Stromateus cinereus*
POMFRET, WHITE   *Stromateus cinereus, Stromateus sinensis*
POMOTIS, NORTHERN   *Lepomis gibbosus*
POMPANO, CAROLINA   *Trachinotus carolinus*
POMPANO, PACIFIC   *Peprilus simillimus*
POMPANO, SNUBNOSE   *Trachinotus falcatus*
POND LOACH   *Misgurnus fossilis*
POND PERCH   *Lepomis gibbosus*
POND SMELT   *Hypomesus olidus*
PONY FISH, GOLDEN STRIPED   *Leiognathus daura*
PONY FISH, GREATER   *Leiognathus equulus*
PONY FISH, ORANGE-FINNED   *Leiognathus bindus*
POOR COD   *Gadus minutus*
PORBEAGLE   *Lamna cornubica, Lamna nasus*
PORCUPINE FISH   *Atopomycterus nichthemerus, Chilomycterus schoepfi, Diodon holocanthus, Diodon hystrix*
PORGY   *Leiostomus xanthurus, Stenotomus chrysops, Stenotomus versicolor*
PORGY, BLACK   *Mylio macrocephalus*
PORGY, FLUTE   *Lutianus rivulatus*
PORGY, GENUINE   *Chrysophrys major*
PORGY, MEICHI   *Gymnocranius griseus*
PORGY, PRINCE'S SMALL   *Chelidoperca hirundinacea*
PORGY, SAUCEREYE   *Calamus calamus*
PORGY, SHEEPSHEAD   *Archosargus probatocephalus*
PORGY, THREETAILED   *Chaetodipterus faber*
PORGY, YELLOW   *Dentex macrocanus, Taius tumifrons*
PORKY   *Stephanolepis cirrhifer*
PORT JACKSON SHARK   *Heterodontus japonicus, Heterodontus philippi*
PORTUGUESE SHARK   *Centroscymnus coelolepis*
POSSUM RAY   *Raja eglantaria*
POSSUM, SEA   *Raja eglantaria*
POSTCROAKER   *Leiostomus xanthurus*
POUT, HORNED   *Ictalurus melas*
POUT, OCEAN   *Macrozoarces americanus*
POUTASSOU   *Micromesistius poutassou*
POWAN   *Coregonus clupeoides, Coregonus lavaretus*
PRICKLEBACK, JAPANESE   *Stichaeus grigorjewi*
PRICKLEBACK, SNAKE   *Lumpenus sagitta*
PRICKLY SKATE, ATLANTIC   *Raja radiata, Raja scabrata*

PRINCE'S SMALL PORGY *Chelidoperca hirundinacea*
PRUSSIAN CARP *Carassius carassius*
PUDDING WIFE *Halichoeres poecilopterus*
PUFFER *Fugu ocellatus obscurus, Fugu pardalis, Lagocephalus lunaris*
PUFFER FISH, BLUE MISHIMA *Gnathagnus elongatus*
PUFFER FISH, MISHIMA *Uranoscopus japonicus*
PUFFER, GRASS *Fugu niphobles*
PUFFER, NORTHERN *Sphaeroides maculatus*
PUFFER, SOUTHERN *Sphaeroides spengleri*
PUFFER, TIGER *Fugu rubripes*
PUMPKINSEED *Lepomis gibbosus*
PUNCTATUS *Konosirus punctatus*
PUNGAS CATFISH *Pangasius pangasius*
PUPFISH, DESERT *Cyprinodon macularius*
PUPFISH, RED RIVER *Cyprinodon rubrofluviatilis*
PUPFISH, VARIEGATED *Cyprinodon variegatus*
PUTITOR MAHSEER *Barbus putitora*

QUEEN PARROTFISH *Scarus vetula*
QUEENSLAND HALIBUT *Psettodes erumei*
QUEEN TRIGGERFISH *Balistes vetula*
QUIAQUIA *Decapterus punctatus*
QUILLBACK ROCKFISH *Sebastodes maliger*
QUINNAT SALMON *Oncorhynchus tschawytscha*
QUIVER *Lepomis gibbosus*

RABBIT FISH *Chimaera monstrosa*
RACCOON PERCH *Perca flavescens*
RAINBOW FISH *Poecilia reticulata*
RAINBOW FISH, AUSTRALIAN RED-TAILED *Melanotaenia nigrans*
RAINBOW FISH, CRIMSON SPOTTED *Melanotaenia fluviatilis*
RAINBOW PARROTFISH *Scarus guacamaia*
RAINBOW RUNNER *Elegatis bipinnulatus*
RAINBOW SMELT *Osmerus mordax*
RAINBOW TROUT *Salmo gairdneri*
RAKE-GILLED MACKEREL *Rastrelliger kanagurta*
RASBORA, COMMON *Rasbora daniconius*
RASCASSE *Scorpaena porcus, Scorpaena scrofa*
RASPHEAD ROCKFISH *Sebastodes ruberrimus*
RATFISH *Chimaera monstrosa, Hydrolagus colliei*
RAT-TAIL *Coryphaenoides rupestris*
RAT-TAIL, PACIFIC *Coryphaenoides acrolepis*
RAT-TAIL, ROUGHSCALE *Coryphaenoides acrolepis*
RAT-TAIL, SMOOTH SPINED *Macrourus berglax*
RATTLEFISH, RED *Halieutea stellata*
RAVEN, SEA *Hemitripterus americanus*
RAY, ANGEL *Squatina squatina*
RAY, BANDED WHIPTAIL STING- *Dasyatis uarnak*

RAY, BLONDE   *Raja brachyura*
RAY, BRIER   *Raja eglantaria*
RAY, BROWN   *Raja miraletus*
RAY, CLEAR   *Raja diaphenes*
RAY, COW-NOSED   *Rhinoptera bonasus*
RAY, CUCKOO   *Raja naevus*
RAY, EAGLE   *Myliobatis aquila*
RAY, ELECTRIC   *Narke japonica, Torpedo nobiliana*
RAY, ELECTRIC, EYED   *Torpedo torpedo*
RAY, FULLER'S   *Raja fullonica*
RAY, HOMELYN   *Raja montagui*
RAY, JAPANESE STING   *Dasyatis akajei*
RAY, LESSER BUTTERFLY   *Gymnura macrura*
RAY, MARBLED ELECTRIC   *Torpedo marmorata*
RAY, PAINTED   *Raja undulata*
RAY, PALE   *Raja lintea*
RAY, POSSUM   *Raja eglantaria*
RAY, RED STING   *Dasyatis akajei*
RAY, RIVER   *Potamotrygon motoro*
RAY, ROUGHTAIL STING   *Dasyatis centroura*
RAY, SANDY   *Raja circularis*
RAY, SEA WALL   *Raja kenoji*
RAY, SHAGREEN   *Raja fullonica*
RAY, SPOTTED   *Raja montagui*
RAY, STARRY   *Raja asterias*
RAY, STING   *Dasyatis pastinaca*
RAY, THORNBACK   *Raja clavata*
RAY, UNDULATE   *Raja undulata*
RAY, WHITE-SPOTTED SHOVELNOSE   *Rhynchobatus djiddensis*
REAL SWORDFISH   *Makaira mazara*
RED-BANDED GROUPER   *Epinephelus fasciatus*
RED BANDFISH   *Cepola rubescens*
RED BARRACUDA   *Sphyraena pinguis*
RED BASS   *Sciaenops ocellata*
RED BATFISH   *Halieutea stellata*
REDBELLIED BATFISH   *Ogcocephalus nasutus*
REDBELLY   *Lepomis gibbosus*
RED BIGEYE   *Priacanthus macracanthus*
RED BREAM   *Lutianus malabaricus*
RED COD   *Sebastodes ruberrimus*
RED DRUM   *Sciaenops ocellata*
REDEAR SARDINE   *Harengula humeralis*
RED EMPEROR   *Lutianus malabaricus*
REDEYED CHARACIN   *Arnoldichthys spilopterus*
REDFISH   *Sciaenops ocellata, Sebastes marinus*
REDFISH, LITTLE   *Oncorhynchus nerka kennerlyi*
RED GROUPER   *Epinephelus morio*
RED GURNARD   *Chelidonichthys kumu, Trigla cuculus*
RED HAKE   *Urophycis chuss*
RED HALIBUT   *Hippoglossoides dubius*

RED HATA   *Epinephelus fasciatus*
RED HIND   *Epinephelus guttatus*
REDHORSE, NORTHERN   *Moxostoma aureolum, Moxostoma macrolepidotum*
REDHORSE, SHORTHEAD   *Moxostoma macrolepidotum*
RED IRISH LORD   *Hemilepidotus hemilepidotus*
RED JEW   *Lutianus malabaricus*
RED MULLET   *Mullus barbatus, Mullus surmulletus*
RED PIRANHA   *Rooseveltiella nattereri*
RED RATTLEFISH   *Halieutea stellata*
RED RIVER PUPFISH   *Cyprinodon rubrofluviatilis*
RED ROCKFISH   *Sebastopyr ruberrimus*
RED ROCK GURNARD   *Helicolenus papillosis*
RED SALMON   *Oncorhynchus nerka*
RED SCORPIONFISH   *Scorpaena scrofa*
RED SEABREAM   *Chrysophrys major, Pagellus bogaraveo, Pagellus erythrinus*
RED SKATE   *Dasyatis akajei*
RED SNAPPER   *Lutianus blackfordii, Lutianus campechanus, Lutianus malabaricus, Neomaenis
    blackfordi, Sebastodes ruberrimus*
RED-SPECKLED BLENNY   *Blennius sanguinolentus*
RED STING RAY   *Dasyatis akajei*
RED SUCKER   *Catostomus catostomus*
REDTAILED PARROTFISH   *Sparisoma chrysopterum*
REDTAILED SHARK   *Labeo bicolor*
RED TAIL SNAPPER   *Lutianus synagris*
RED TILEFISH   *Branchiostegus japonicus*
REEF-COD, BANDED   *Epinephelus fasciatus*
REEF-COD, TROUT   *Epinephelus fario*
REEF WHITETIP SHARK   *Carcharhinus albimarginatus*
REX SOLE   *Errex zachirus, Glyptocephalus zachirus*
REX SOLE, JAPANESE   *Glyptocephalus stelleri*
RIBBON-FINNED NEMIPTERID   *Nemipterus taeniopterus*
RIBBONFISH   *Chirocentrus dorab, Trichiurus lepturus*
RIBBONFISH, LARGE-HEADED   *Trichiurus haumela*
RIBBONFISH, SMALL-HEADED   *Trichiurus savala*
RICE EEL   *Monopterus alba*
RICEFISH   *Oryzias latipes*
RINGED PERCH   *Perca flavescens*
RINGTAILED PIKE CICHLID   *Crenicichla saxatilis*
RINGTAILED SURGEONFISH   *Acanthurus xanthopterus*
RIVER CARPSUCKER   *Carpiodes carpio*
RIVER EIGHT-EYES LAMPREY   *Lampretra japonica*
RIVER GURNARD   *Platycephalus indicus*
RIVER KINGFISH   *Sciaena antarctica*
RIVER MULLET   *Mugil cephalus*
RIVER PERCH   *Perca flavescens*
RIVER RAY   *Potamotrygon motoro*
RIVER SHAD   *Hilsa ilisha*
ROACH   *Lepomis gibbosus, Notemigonus crysoleucas, **Rutilus rutilus***
ROACH, HARLEQUIN   *Lepomis gibbosus*
ROACH, WESTERN   *Hesperoleucus symmetricus*

ROBIN   *Lepomis gibbosus*
ROBIN, ROUND   *Decapterus punctatus*
ROBIN PERCH   *Lepomis gibbosus*
ROCK   *Morone saxatilis*
ROCK COD   *Epinephelus fario*
ROCK COD, BLACK-TIPPED   *Epinephelus fasciatus*
ROCKFISH   *Epinephelus striatus, Helicolenus dactylopterus, Morone saxatilis, Mycteroperca tigris, Scorpaena porcus, Sebastes dactylopterus, Sebastes flammeus, Sebastiscus marmoratus, Trisotropis venenosus*
ROCKFISH, BLACK   *Sebastes inermis, Sebastes thompsoni, Sebastodes melanops, Sebastodes schlegeli*
ROCKFISH, BROWN   *Sebastes auriculatus*
ROCKFISH, CANARY   *Sebastodes pinniger*
ROCKFISH, CHANNEL   *Sebastolobus macrochir*
ROCKFISH, COPPER   *Sebastodes caurinus*
ROCKFISH, FLAG   *Sebastodes rubrivinctus*
ROCKFISH, GREEN STRIPED   *Sebastodes elongatus*
ROCKFISH, LONGJAW   *Sebastodes alutus*
ROCKFISH, ORANGE-SPOTTED   *Sebastodes maliger*
ROCKFISH, QUILLBACK   *Sebastodes maliger*
ROCKFISH, RASPHEAD   *Sebastodes ruberrimus*
ROCKFISH, RED   *Sebastopyr ruberrimus*
ROCKFISH, ROUGHEYE   *Sebastes aleutianus*
ROCKFISH, SPLITNOSE   *Sebastes diploproa*
ROCKFISH, STRIPETAIL   *Sebastes saxicola*
ROCKFISH, TURKEY   *Sebastodes ruberrimus*
ROCKFISH, VERMILION   *Sebastes miniatus*
ROCKFISH, YELLOWTAIL   *Sebastes flavidus*
ROCK FLATFISH   *Lepidopsetta mochigarei*
ROCK GOBY   *Gobius paganellus*
ROCK GREENLING   *Hexagrammos lagocephalus*
ROCK GRENADIER   *Coryphaenoides rupestris*
ROCK GURNARD, RED   *Helicolenus papillosis*
ROCK SALMON   *Zonichthys falcatus* (a trivial name also given by the British fish trade to *Squalus acanthias* to make it sound more appetising than "dogfish")
ROCK SOLE   *Lepidopsetta bilineata*
ROCKY MOUNTAIN WHITEFISH   *Prosopium williamsoni*
ROHU CARP   *Labeo rohita*
ROKER   *Raja clavata*
RONCODINA   *Micropogon undulatus*
RONCO RONCO   *Haemulon plumieri*
ROSEFISH   *Sebastes marinus*
ROSEFISH, BLACKBELLY   *Helicolenus dactylopterus*
ROSY BARB   *Barbus conchonius*
ROSY JEWFISH   *Otolithes ruber*
ROSYSIDE DACE   *Clinostomus funduloides*
ROUGHBACK SCULPIN   *Chitonotus pugetensis*
ROUGH DAB, LONG   *Hippoglossoides platessoides*
ROUGHEYE ROCKFISH   *Sebastes aleutianus*
ROUGH-HEAD GRENADIER   *Macrourus berglax*

Rough hound   *Scyliorhinus canicula*
Rough scad   *Trachurus trachurus*
Roughscale flounder   *Pseudorhombus oligodon*
Roughscale rat tail   *Coryphaenoides acrolepis*
rough, Tommy   *Arripis georgianus*
Roughtail stingray   *Dasyatis centroura*
Round goby   *Gobius melanostomus*
round goby, Black sea   *Neogobius melanostomus*
Round herring   *Etrumeus micropus, Etrumeus terres*
Roundnose flounder   *Eopsetta grigorjewi*
Roundnose grenadier   *Coryphaenoides rupestris*
Round Robin   *Decapterus punctatus*
Round scad   *Decapterus maruadsi*
Roundtoothed large-eyed bream   *Monotaxis grandoculis*
Round whitefish   *Prosopium cylindraceum*
Rudd   *Scardinius erythrophthalmus*
Rudderfish   *Kyphosus cinerascens, Seriola dumerilii, Seriola purpurascens*
rudderfish, Black   *Palinurichthys perciformis*
Ruff   *Arripis georgianus, Lepomis gibbosus*
ruff, Black   *Centrolophus niger*
ruff, Sea   *Scorpaena porcus*
Rungh scad   *Trachurus japonicus*
Runner   *Oligoplites saurus, Rachycentron canadum*
runner, Rainbow   *Elegatis bipinnulatus*
Russian sturgeon   *Acipenser güldenstadti*
Rusty dab   *Limanda ferruginea*

Sablefish   *Anoplopoma fimbria, Hilsa ilisha, Hilsa toli*
Sabre   *Sternopygus macrurus*
Saddleback wrasse   *Thalassoma duperreyi*
Saddled bream   *Oblada melanura*
Saffron cod   *Eleginus gracilis*
Sailfin Molly   *Poecilia latipinna*
Sailfish   *Istiophorus platypterus*
Sailor's choice   *Lagodon rhomboides, Orthopristis chrysoptera*
Saint Peter's fish   *Tilapia mossambica, Tilapia nilotica, Tilapia zillii, Zeus faber*
    (The melanin pigmentation on the flank of *Melanogrammus aeglefinus* is known
    among some fishermen as "St. Peter's thumbprint")
Saithe   *Pollachius virens*
Salema   *Boops salpa*
salmon, Australian   *Arripis trutta*
salmon, Biwa   *Oncorhynchus rhodurus*
salmon, Burnett   *Neoceratodus forsteri*
salmon, Cherry   *Oncorhynchus masou*
salmon, Chinook   *Oncorhynchus tschawytscha*
salmon, Chum   *Oncorhynchus keta*
salmon, Coho   *Oncorhynchus kisutch*
salmon, Cooktown   *Eleutheronema tetradactylon*
salmon de alto, Japanese   *Polymixia japonica*

SALMON, DOG   *Oncorhynchus keta*
SALMON, GOOD   *Sphyraena pinguis*
SALMON HERRING   *Chanos chanos*
SALMON, HIME   *Oncorhynchus nerka*
SALMON, HUDSON BAY   *Salvelinus alpinus*
SALMON, HUMPBACK   *Oncorhynchus gorbuscha*
SALMON, JACK   *Stizostedion vitreum*
SALMON, LONGTOOTH   *Otolithes ruber*
SALMON, MORETON BAY   *Chanos chanos*
SALMON, PINK   *Oncorhynchus gorbuscha*
SALMON, QUINNAT   *Oncorhynchus tschawytscha*
SALMON, RED   *Oncorhynchus nerka*
SALMON, ROCK   *Zonichthys falcatus*
SALMON SHARK   *Lamna ditropis, Lamna nasus*
SALMON, SILVER   *Oncorhynchus kisutch*
SALMON, SNAPPER   *Otolithes ruber*
SALMON, SOCKEYE   *Oncorhynchus nerka*
SALMON, SPRING   *Oncorhynchus tschawytscha*
SALMON TROUT   *Arripis trutta*
SALMON, WHITE   *Seriola dorsalis*
SALMONET   *Upeneoides bensasi*
SALT WATER MINNOW   *Fundulus heteroclitus*
SANDBAR SHARK   *Carcharhinus milberti*
SAND BASS   *Paralabrax maculatofasciatus*
SAND BORER   *Sillago japonica, Sillago sihama*
SAND DAB   *Hippoglossoides platessoides, Limanda herzensteini*
SAND DAB, MOTTLED   *Citharichthys sordidus*
SAND DAB, PACIFIC   *Citharichthys sordidus*
SAND DIVER   *Synodus intermedius*
SAND EEL   *Ammodytes* spp.
SAND EEL, LESSER   *Ammodytes tobianus*
SANDER   *Lucioperca lucioperca*
SANDFISH   *Arctoscopus japonicus*
SANDFISH, ORANGE RIVER   *Labeo capensis*
SAND FLATHEAD   *Platycephalus bassensis*
SAND FLOUNDER   *Psettichthys melanostictus, Scophthalmus aquosus*
SAND GURNARD   *Platycephalus indicus*
SANDLANCE, ARCTIC   *Ammodytes tobianus*
SAND PERCH   *Lepomis gibbosus*
SAND SHARK   *Carcharias taurus, Rhynchobatus djeddensis*
SAND SMELT   *Menidia menidia notata, Sillago sihama*
SAND SNAKE   *Ophisurus macrorhynchus*
SAND SOLE   *Psettichthys melanostictus, Solea lascaris*
SAND TILEFISH   *Malacanthus plumieri*
SAND TROUT   *Cynoscion arenarius*
SANDY RAY   *Raja circularis*
SAPHIRINE GURNARD   *Trigla lucerna*
SAPO   *Opsanus tau*
SARDINA DE LEY   *Harengula sardina*
SARDINE   *Sardina pilchardus*

SARDINE, CALIFORNIA   *Sardinops caerula*
SARDINE, FRINGE-SCALE   *Sardinella fimbriata*
SARDINE, GILT   *Sardinella aurita*
SARDINE, GOLDEN   *Sardinella aurita*
SARDINE, HALF-MOUTHED   *Engraulis japonicus*
SARDINE, INDIAN   *Sardinella longiceps, Sardinella sirm*
SARDINE, MARKET   *Etrumeus micropus*
SARDINE, OIL   *Sardinella longiceps*
SARDINE, PACIFIC   *Sardinops caerula*
SARDINE, PERFORATED SCALE   *Sardinella perforata*
SARDINE, REDEAR   *Harengula humeralis*
SARDINE, SHORT-BODIED   *Sardinella albella*
SARDINE, TRUE   *Sardinops melanosticta*
SARDINELLA, SPOTTED   *Sardinella sirm*
SARDINELLA, WHITE   *Sardinella albella*
SARGO   *Diplodus sargus*
SARGUS, MARINE   *Diplodus sargus*
SAUCEREYE PORGY   *Calamus calamus*
SAUCORD, HILGENDORF   *Helicolenus hilgendorfi*
SAUGER   *Stizostedion canadense*
SAUREL   *Scomberesox saurus*
SAURY   *Cololabis saira*
SAURY, ATLANTIC   *Scomberesox saurus*
SAURY, PACIFIC   *Cololabis saira*
SAURY, PAINTED   *Trachinocephalus myops*
SAURY PIKE   *Scomberesox saurus*
SAW-BELLY   *Alosa pseudoharengus*
SAW-EDGED CATFISH   *Arius serratus*
SAWFISH   *Pristis microdon*
SAWFISH, FRESHWATER   *Pristis perotteti*
SAWFISH, SMALL-TOOTHED   *Pristis microdon*
SCABBARD FISH   *Trichiurus lepturus*
SCAD   *Atule mate, Priacanthus hamrur, Trachurus trachurus*
SCAD, BIGEYE   *Selar crumenophthalmus*
SCAD, BLACK SEA   *Trachurus mediterraneus ponticus*
SCAD, GOLDEN   *Caranx kalla*
SCAD, HARDTAIL   *Megalaspis cordyla*
SCAD, LAYANG   *Decapterus macrosoma*
SCAD, ROUGH   *Trachurus trachurus*
SCAD, ROUND   *Decapterus maruadsi*
SCAD, RUNGH   *Trachurus japonicus*
SCAD, SLENDER-SCALED   *Caranx leptolepis*
SCALDFISH   *Arnoglossus laterna*
SCALYFIN FLOUNDER   *Isopsetta isolepis*
SCALY STINGRAY   *Trygon imbricata*
SCARLET SEA PERCH   *Lutianus malabaricus*
SCAT, SPOTTED   *Scatophagus argus*
SCHELLY   *Coregonus lavaretus*
SCHOOLMASTER   *Lutianus apodus*
SCHOOL SHARK   *Galeorhinus australis*

SCHWANENFELD'S BARB   *Barbus schwanenfeldi*
SCIAENA   *Johnius regius*
SCORPION   *Opsanus tau*
SCORPIONFISH   *Sebastiscus marmoratus, Sebastodes baramenuke*
SCORPIONFISH, BLACK   *Scorpaena porcus*
SCORPIONFISH, LARGE-SCALED   *Scorpaena scrofa*
SCORPIONFISH, RED   *Scorpaena scrofa*
SCORPIONFISH, SMALL-SCALED   *Scorpaena porcus*
SCRAPER, BLACK   *Navodon modestus*
SCRAWLED COWFISH   *Acanthostracion quadricornu*
SCULPIN, ALEUTIAN   *Cottus aleuticus*
SCULPIN, ARCTIC STAGHORN   *Gymnacanthus tricuspis*
SCULPIN, BANDED   *Cottus carolinae*
SCULPIN, DADDY   *Myoxocephalus scorpius*
SCULPIN, ELF   *Ceratocottus namiyei*
SCULPIN, FILAMENTED   *Icelinus filamentosus*
SCULPIN, GIANT MARBLED   *Scorpaenichthys marmoratus*
SCULPIN, GREAT   *Myoxocephalus polyacanthocephalus*
SCULPIN, GREENLAND   *Myoxocephalus scorpius*
SCULPIN, GRUNT   *Rhamphocottus richardsoni*
SCULPIN, LITTLE   *Myoxocephalus aeneus*
SCULPIN, LONGHORN   *Myoxocephalus octodecimspinosus*
SCULPIN, PALLID   *Cottunculus thompsoni*
SCULPIN, ROUGHBACK   *Chitonotus pugetensis*
SCULPIN, SHORTHORN   *Myoxocephalus groenlandicus, Myoxocephalus scorpius*
SCULPIN, SPATULATE   *Icelus spatula*
SCULPIN, SPINYHEAD   *Dasycottus setiger*
SCULPIN, STAGHORN   *Leptocottus armatus*
SCULPIN, THREADFIN   *Icelinus filamentosus*
SCULPIN, WHIP   *Nemitripterus americanus*
SCULPIN, YELLOW   *Hemilepidotus jordani*
SCUP   *Stenotomus chrysops*
SCUP, COMMON   *Stenotomus versicolor*
SCUPPANG   *Stenotomus versicolor*
SEA BASS   *Dicentrarchus labrax, Lateolabrax japonicus, Sciaenops ocellata, Spicara smaris*
SEA BASS, BLACK   *Centropristes striatus*
SEA BASS, CABRILLA   *Serranus cabrilla*
SEA BASS, GIANT   *Stereolepis gigas*
SEA BREAM   *Chrysophrys major*
SEA BREAM, AXILLARY   *Pagellus acarne*
SEA BREAM, BLACK   *Acanthopagrus schlegeli*
SEA BREAM, BLACKSPOT   *Pagellus bogaraveo*
SEA BREAM, CARDINAL   *Evynnis cardinalis*
SEA BREAM, COMMON   *Pagellus centrotodontus*
SEA BREAM, COUCH'S   *Pagrus pagrus*
SEA BREAM, CRIMSON   *Evynnis japonica*
SEA BREAM, GILTHEAD   *Sparus auratus*
SEA BREAM, GOLDLINED   *Rhabdosargus sarba*
SEA BREAM, PICNIC   *Sparus berda*
SEA BREAM, RED   *Chrysophrys major, Pagellus bogaraveo, Pagellus erythrinus*

SEA BREAM, SILVER *Chrysophrys major*
SEA BREAM, STRIPED *Lithognathus mormyrus*
SEA BREAM, WHITE *Diplodus sargus*
SEA BREAM, YELLOW *Taius tumifrons*
SEA BREAM, YELLOWBACK *Taius tumifrons*
SEA BREAM, YELLOWFIN *Chrysophrys datnia*
SEA CARP *Dactylopagrus carponemus, Diplodus annularis, Diplodus sargus*
SEA CAT *Galeichthys felis*
SEA CHUB *Ditrema temmincki*
SEA FOX *Alopias caudatus, Alopias greyi, Alopias vulpinus, Raja clavata*
SEA HEN *Cyclopterus lumpus*
SEA HERRING *Arripis georgianus*
SEAHORSE, SPOTTED *Hippocampus erectus*
SEA LADYBIRD *Uranoscopus scaber*
SEA LAMPREY *Petromyzon marinus*
SEA MULLET *Menticirrhus saxatilis, Mugil cephalus*
SEA PERCH *Lateolabrax japonicus, Lates calcarifer, Morone americana, Spicara smaris,
Tautogolabrus adspersus*
SEA PERCH, BANDED *Serranus scriba*
SEA PERCH, PILE *Damalichthys vacca*
SEA PERCH, SCARLET *Lutianus malabaricus*
SEA PERCH, SHINER *Cymatogaster aggregata*
SEA PERCH, SILVER *Lates calcarifer*
SEA PERCH, STRIPED *Embiotoca lateralis*
SEA PERCH, WHITE *Phanerodon furcatus*
SEA PIKE *Sphyraena japonica*
SEA PIKE, BLUNT-JAWED *Sphyraena obtusata*
SEA PIKE, GIANT *Sphyraena jello*
SEA PIKE, SLENDER *Sphyraena jello*
SEA POSSUM *Raja eglantaria*
SEA RAVEN *Hemitripterus americanus*
SEA ROBIN, COMMON *Prionotus carolinus*
SEA ROBIN, NORTHERN *Prionotus carolinus*
SEA ROBIN, STRIPED *Prionotus evolans*
SEA RUFF *Scorpaena porcus*
SEA SCORPION, LONGSPINED *Cottus bubalis*
SEA SMELT *Hypomesus japonicus*
SEA SNAIL, GELATINOUS *Liparis koefoedi*
SEA STURGEON *Acipenser oxyrhynchus, Acipenser sturio*
SEA TROUT *Cynoscion regalis, Cynoscion virescens, Macrodon ancylodon, Salmo trutta,
Salvelinus alpinus, Salvelinus fontinalis*
SEA TROUT, SPOTTED *Eriscion nebulosus*
SEA WALL RAY *Raja kenoji*
SEAL SHARK *Dalatias licha*
SEAR *Decapterus macrosoma*
SERGEANT FISH *Rachycentron canadum*
SERGEANT MAJOR *Abudefduf saxatilis*
SERRA *Scomberomorus commersonii*
SEVENGILLED SHARK *Notorhynchus cepedianus*
SEVRUGA *Acipenser stellatus*

SHAD   *Eucinostomus gula, Harengula zunasi, Hilsa toli, Pomoxis annularis*
SHAD, AMERICAN   *Alosa sapidissima*
SHAD, COMMON   *Alosa sapidissima*
SHAD, GIZZARD   *Anodontostoma chacunda, Dorosoma cepedianum*
SHAD, HICKORY   *Dorosoma cepedianum*
SHAD, RIVER   *Hilsa ilisha*
SHAD, THREADFIN   *Dorosoma petenense*
SHAD, TOLI   *Hilsa toli*
SHAD, TWAITE   *Alosa fallax*
SHAD, YOUNG   *Notemigonus crysoleucas*
SHAGREEN RAY   *Raja fullonica*
SHALLOW-WATER CISCO   *Leucichthys artedi*
SHANNY, ARCTIC   *Stichaeus grigorjewi*
SHARK, ARMOUR   *Dalatias licha*
SHARK, ARROW-HEADED HAMMERHEAD   *Zygaena blochii*
SHARK, BASKING   *Cetorhinus maximus*
SHARK, BLACK   *Dalatias licha, Morulius chrysophekadion*
SHARK, BLACK-TIPPED   *Carcharhinus maculipinnis*
SHARK, BLUE   *Isurus oxyrhynchus, Prionace glauca*
SHARK, BONNETNOSE   *Sphyrna tiburo*
SHARK, BROAD HARBOUR   *Deania eglantina*
SHARK, BROWN   *Carcharhinus milbertei*
SHARK, BULL   *Carcharhinus leucas*
SHARK, CANOPY   *Squatina japonica*
SHARK, CAT   *Heterodontus japonicus, Triakis semifasciatum*
SHARK, COMMON SAW-   *Pristiophorus cirratus*
SHARK, COW   *Hexanchus griseus*
SHARK, CROSS-STAFF   *Sphyrna zygaena*
SHARK, CUB   *Carcharhinis leucas*
SHARK, DOG   *Alopias pelagicus, Mustelus griseus*
SHARK, DUSKY   *Carcharhinus obscurus*
SHARK, ELEPHANT   *Callorhynchus millii*
SHARK, ELLIOT'S GREY   *Carcharias ellioti*
SHARK, FIN   *Centrophorus atromarginatus*
SHARK, FINETOOTH   *Aprionodon isodon*
SHARK, FOX   *Alopias pelagicus*
SHARK, FRESHWATER   *Wallago attu*
SHARK, GHOST   *Callorhynchus callorhynchus, Callorhynchus millii, Chimaera phantasma*
SHARK, GREAT BLUE   *Glyphis glaucus*
SHARK, GREENLAND   *Somniosus microcephalus*
SHARK, GREY   *Hexanchus griseus*
SHARK, GREY-BLUE   *Isurus glaucus*
SHARK, GROUND   *Carcharhinus leucas, Somniosus microcephalus*
SHARK, GUMMY   *Mustelus antarcticus, Mustelus manazo*
SHARK, GURRY   *Somniosus microcephalus*
SHARK, HAMMERHEAD   *Sphyrna zygaena*
SHARK, HORN   *Heterodontus francisci*
SHARK, KITEFIN   *Dalatias licha*
SHARK, LANTERN   *Etmopterus spinax*
SHARK, LEMON   *Negaprion brevirostris*

SHARK, LEOPARD   *Galeocerdo arcticus, Triakis scyllia, Triakis semifasciatus*
SHARK, LIP   *Hemiscyllium plagiosum*
SHARK, LONGWINGED   *Carcharhinus longimanus*
SHARK, MACKEREL   *Lamna nasus*
SHARK, MAKO   *Isurus glaucus*
SHARK, MILK   *Scoliodon walbeehmii*
SHARK, MUD   *Hexanchus griseus*
SHARK, NURSE   *Ginglymostoma cirrhatum*
SHARK, OIL   *Galeorhinus zyopterus*
SHARK, PORT JACKSON   *Heterodontus japonicus, Heterodontus philippi*
SHARK, PORTUGUESE   *Centroscymnus coelolepis*
SHARK, REDTAILED   *Labeo bicolor*
SHARK, REEF WHITETIP   *Carcharhinus albimarginatus*
SHARK, SALMON   *Lamna ditropis, Lamna nasus*
SHARK, SAND   *Carcharias taurus, Rhynchobatus djeddensis*
SHARK, SANDBAR   *Carcharhinus milberti*
SHARK, SCHOOL   *Galeorhinus australis*
SHARK, SEVENGILLED   *Notorhynchus cepedianus*
SHARK, SHARPNOSED   *Scoliodon walbeehmii*
SHARK, SHARPNOSED MACKEREL   *Isurus oxyrhynchus*
SHARK, SILKY   *Carcharhinus falciformis*
SHARK, SILVER   *Chimaera phantasma*
SHARK, SIXGILL   *Hexanchus griseus*
SHARKSKIN FLOUNDER   *Clidoderma asperrimum*
SHARK, SEAL   *Dalatias licha*
SHARK, SLEEPER   *Somniosus microcephalus*
SHARK, SMALL BLACK-TIPPED   *Carcharhinus limbatus*
SHARK, SMOOTH-TOOTH   *Aprionodon isodon*
SHARK, SNAPPER   *Galeorhinus australis*
SHARK, SOUPFIN   *Galeorhinus zyopterus*
SHARK, SPINNER   *Carcharhinus maculipinnis*
SHARK, SPOTFIN GROUND   *Carcharhinus limbatus*
SHARK, SPOTTED   *Galeocerdo arcticus*
SHARK, STAR-SPOTTED   *Mustelus manazo*
SHARKSUCKER   *Echeneis naucrates*
SHARK, THRESHER   *Alopias profundus*
SHARK, TIGER   *Galeocerdo arcticus, Galeocerdo cuvier, Scylliorhinus torazame*
SHARK, WHALE   *Rhincodon typus*
SHARK, WHIPTAIL   *Alopias pelagicus*
SHARK, WHITE-TIP   *Carcharhinus longimanus*
SHARK, YELLOW DOG   *Scoliodon sorrakowah*
SHARPNOSED MACKEREL SHARK   *Isurus oxyrhynchus*
SHARPNOSED SHARK   *Scoliodon walbeehmii*
SHARPTAIL OCEAN SUNFISH   *Masturus lanceolatus*
SHARPTOOTHED EEL   *Muraenesox cinereus*
SHEATFISH   *Silurus glanis*
SHECUTTS   *Cynoscion regalis*
SHEEPSHEAD   *Aplodinotus grunniens, Archosargus probatocephalus, Pimelometopon pulchrum*
SHEEPSHEAD MINNOW   *Cyprinodon variegatus*
SHEEPSHEAD, THREEBANDED   *Chaetodipterus faber*

Sheepshead porgy   *Archosargus probatocephalus*
Shemaia   *Chalcalburnus chalcoides*
Shiner   *Notemigonus crysoleucas, Poronotus triacanthus*
Shiner, Golden   *Notemigonus crysoleucas boscii*
Shiner perch   *Cymatogaster aggregata*
Shiner seaperch   *Cymatogaster aggregata*
Shiner, Yellow   *Cymatogaster aggregata*
Shortbill spearfish   *Tetrapturus angustirostris*
Shortbodied mackerel   *Rastrelliger brachysomus*
Shortbodied sardine   *Sardinella albella*
Shortfin eelpout   *Lycodes brevipes*
Shortfinned eel   *Anguilla dieffenbachii*
Shortfinned tunny   *Sarda sarda*
Shorthead redhorse   *Moxostoma aureolum, Moxostoma macrolepidotum*
Shorthorn sculpin   *Myoxocephalus groenlandicus, Myoxocephalus scorpius*
Shortnose   *Ogcocephalus nasutus*
Shortnose gar   *Lepisosteus platostomus*
Shortspine cottus   *Myoxocephalus scorpius*
Shotted halibut   *Eopsetta grigorjewi*
Shovelhead   *Sphyrna tibura*
Shovelnose sturgeon   *Scaphirhynchus platorynchus*
Shuisk whitefish   *Coregonus lavaretus lavaretoides*
Siamese fighting fish   *Betta splendens*
Siamese goramy   *Trichogaster pectoralis*
Sicklefish   *Drepane punctata*
Sierra   *Scomberomorus regalis*
silk snapper, Bermuda   *Lutianus hastingsi*
silk, Stretched   *Pterogobius elapoides*
Silky shark   *Carcharhinus falciformis*
Sillago   *Sillago japonica*
sillago, Silver   *Sillago sihama*
sillago, Trumpeter   *Sillago maculata*
Silond catfish   *Silonia silondia*
silver bar, Leaping   *Chirocentrus dorab*
silver-biddy, Longrayed   *Gerres filamentosus*
Silver bream   *Rhabdosargus sarba, Usacaranx georgianus*
silver bream, Japanese   *Chrysophrys datnia*
Silver carp   *Hypophthalmichthys molitrix*
silver carp, Spotted   *Aristichthys nobilis*
Silver chub   *Semotilus atromaculatus*
Silver conger eel   *Muraenesox cinereus*
Silver crucian carp   *Carassius auratus gibelio*
Silver eel   *Anguilla rostrata*
Silverfish   *Merluccius bilinearis, Tarpon atlanticus*
Silver gar   *Strongylura marina*
Silver grunt   *Pomadasys hasta, Therapon plumbeus*
Silver grunter   *Pomadasys hasta*
Silver hake   *Merluccius bilinearis*
Silver hatchetfish   *Gasteropelecus levis*
Silver jenny   *Eucinostomus argenteus, Eucinostomus gula*

SILVER JEW   *Sciaena antarctica*
SILVER JEWFISH   *Otolithes ruber*
SILVER JEWFISH, DUSSUMIER'S   *Johnius dussumieri*
SILVER LAMPREY   *Ichthyomyzon unicuspis*
SILVER PERCH   *Morone americana, Pomoxis annularis, Therapon bidyana*
SILVER POMFRET   *Stromateus cinereus*
SILVER SALMON   *Oncorhynchus kisutch*
SILVER SEABREAM   *Chrysophrys major*
SILVER SEAPERCH   *Lates calcarifer*
SILVER SHARK   *Chimaera phantasma*
SILVERSIDE, ATLANTIC   *Menidia menidia notata*
SILVER SILLAGO   *Sillago sihama*
SILVER SMELT, GREATER   *Argentina silus*
SILVER TREVALLY   *Usacaranx georgianus*
SILVER TROUT   *Oncorhynchus nerka kennerlyi*
SILVER WHITING   *Sillago sihama*
SILVERY CONGER   *Anago anago*
SILVERY POUT   *Gadiculus argenteus*
SINGING FISH   *Porichthys notatus*
SISCOWET TROUT   *Salvelinus namaycush siscowet*
SIX-BANDED TREVALLY   *Caranx sexfasciatus*
SIX-GILL SHARK   *Hexanchus griseus*
SIX-LINED PERCH   *Helotes sexlineatus*
SKATE   *Raja batis, Raja eglantaria*
SKATE, ATLANTIC PRICKLY   *Raja radiata, Raja scabrata*
SKATE, BARN-DOOR   *Raja laevis, Raja stabuliforis*
SKATE, BIG   *Raja binoculata, Raja ocellata*
SKATE, BLUE   *Parastromateus niger, Raja batis*
SKATE, BOB-TAILED   *Raja eglantaria*
SKATE, CALIFORNIA   *Raja inornata*
SKATE, CLEAR-NOSED   *Raja eglantaria*
SKATE, COMMON   *Raja inornata*
SKATE, EYED   *Raja ocellata*
SKATE, FLAPPER   *Raja batis*
SKATE, GREY   *Raja batis*
SKATE, HEDGEHOG   *Raja erinacea*
SKATE, LITTLE   *Raja erinacea*
SKATE, LONG-NOSED   *Raja oxyrhynchus*
SKATE, PECK-NOSED   *Raja stabuliforis*
SKATE, RED   *Dasyatis akajei*
SKATE, SPINY RASP   *Raja kenoji*
SKATE, STARRY   *Raja radiata*
SKATE, SUMMER   *Raja eglantaria*
SKATE, THORNY   *Raja radiata*
SKATE, WINTER   *Raja ocellata, Raja stabuliforis*
SKIL   *Anoplopoma fimbria*
SKILFISH   *Erilepis zonifer*
SKIN CARP   *Hemibarbus barbus*
SKIPJACK   *Katsuwonus pelamis, Katsuwonus vagans, Scomberesox saurus, Usacaranx georgianus*

SKIP MACKEREL   *Pomatomus saltatrix*
SKIPPER   *Cololabis saira, Scomberesox saurus*
SLADE   *Parastromateus niger*
SLEEPER SHARK   *Somniosus microcephalus*
SLENDER-SCALED SCAD   *Caranx leptolepis*
SLENDER SEAPIKE   *Sphyraena jello*
SLENDER SOLE   *Lyopsetta exilis*
SLENDER TUNA   *Allothunnus fallai*
SLICKHEAD   *Synaphobranchus branchistomas*
SLIME EEL   *Simenchelys parasiticus*
SLIME FLOUNDER   *Microstomus achne*
SLIMER *Opsanus tau*
SLIME SOLE   *Microstomus pacificus*
SLIMY   *Leiognathus equulus*
SLIMY MACKEREL   *Scomber japonicus*
SLIPMOUTH, COMMON   *Leiognathus equulus*
SLIPPERY DICK   *Halichoeres bivittatus*
SLIPPERY SOLE   *Microstomus pacificus*
SLOANE'S VIPERFISH   *Chauliodus sloanei*
SMALL BLACK-TIPPED SHARK   *Carcharhinus limbatus*
SMALL CATFISH   *Ictalurus melas*
SMALL-HEADED RIBBONFISH   *Trichiurus savala*
SMALLHEAD HAIRTAIL   *Trichiurus savala*
SMALLMOUTH BUFFALO   *Ictiobus bubalis*
SMALL-MOUTHED BLACK BASS   *Micropterus dolomieui*
SMALL-MOUTHED SOLE   *Limanda herzensteini*
SMALLMOUTH YELLOWFISH   *Barbus holubi*
SMALL PORGY, PRINCE'S   *Chelidoperca hirundinacea*
SMALL-SCALED GOBY   *Oxyurichthys microlepis*
SMALL-SCALED SCORPIONFISH   *Scorpaena porcus*
SMALL SPOTTED DOGFISH   *Scyliorhinus canicula*
SMALL-TOOTHED SAWFISH   *Pristis microdon*
SMARID   *Spicara smaris*
SMEAR DAB   *Pleuronectes microcephalus*
SMELT   *Osmerus mordax, Sillago sihama*
SMELT, AMERICAN   *Osmerus mordax*
SMELT, CALIFORNIA BLUE   *Atherinopsis californiensis*
SMELT, DEEP SEA   *Glossanodon semifasciatus*
SMELT, EUROPEAN   *Osmerus mordax*
SMELT, GREATER SILVER   *Argentina silus*
SMELT, HERRING   *Argentina silus*
SMELT, JAPANESE   *Osmerus dentex*
SMELT, LARGEMOUTH   *Spirinchus lanceolatus*
SMELT, LONGFIN   *Spirinchus lanceolatus*
SMELT, POND   *Hypomesus olidus*
SMELT, RAINBOW   *Osmerus mordax*
SMELT, SAND   *Menidia menidia notata, Sillago sihama*
SMELT, SEA   *Hypomesus japonicus*
SMELT, SURF   *Hypomesus japonicus*
SMELT, SWEET   *Plecoglossus altivelis*

SMELT, TOP   *Atherinops affinis*
SMOOTH DOGFISH   *Scyliorhinus canicula*
SMOOTH HAMMERHEAD   *Sphyrna zygaena*
SMOOTH HOUND   *Mustelus mustelus*
SMOOTH-SPINED RAT-TAIL   *Macrourus berglax*
SMOOTH-TOOTH SHARK   *Aprionodon isodon*
SMOOTH TRUNKFISH   *Lactophrys triqueter*
SNAKE BLENNY   *Ophiodon barbatum*
SNAKEFISH   *Trachinocephalus myops, Trichiurus lepturus*
SNAKEHEAD, BROWN   *Channa gachua*
SNAKEHEAD, CHINESE   *Channa argus*
SNAKEHEAD FISH   *Channa argus*
SNAKEHEAD, GIANT   *Channa marulius, Ophicephalus marulius*
SNAKEHEAD GOBY   *Gobius ophiocephalus*
SNAKEHEAD, GREEN   *Channa punctatus*
SNAKESHEAD, STRIPED   *Channa striatus*
SNAKE MACKEREL   *Promethichthys prometheus*
SNAKE, OFFSHORE   *Ophisurus macrorhynchus*
SNAKE PRICKLEBACK   *Lumpenus sagitta*
SNAKE, SAND   *Ophisurus macrorhynchus*
SNAKESKIN GOURAMI   *Trichogaster pectoralis*
SNAP MACKEREL   *Pomatomus saltatrix*
SNAPPER   *Lutianus malabaricus, Lutianus rivulatus* (Note: all these *"Lutianus"* species
    can be spelt *"Lutjanus"*)
SNAPPER, BERMUDA SILK   *Lutianus hastingsi*
SNAPPER, BOWEN   *Argyrops spinifer*
SNAPPER, EMPEROR   *Lutianus sebae*
SNAPPER, FRYING PAN   *Argyrops spinifer*
SNAPPER, GREY   *Lutianus synagris*
SNAPPER, JOHN'S   *Lutianus johnii*
SNAPPER, LANE   *Lutianus synagris*
SNAPPER, LONG-SPINED   *Argyrops spinifer*
SNAPPER, MALABAR   *Lutianus malabaricus*
SNAPPER, MANGROVE   *Lutianus griseus*
SNAPPER, MEXICAN   *Lutianus campechanus*
SNAPPER, MUTTON   *Lutianus analis*
SNAPPER, PENSACOLA   *Lutianus blackfordii*
SNAPPER, RED   *Lutianus blackfordii, Lutianus campechanus, Lutianus malabaricus, Neo-
    maenis blackfordi, Sebastodes ruberrimus*
SNAPPER, RED TAIL   *Lutianus synagris*
SNAPPER SALMON   *Otolithes ruber*
SNAPPER SHARK   *Galeorhinus australis*
SNAPPER, YELLOWTAIL   *Ocyurus chrysurus*
SNIG   *Microgadus tomcod*
SNIPE EEL   *Serrivomer sector*
SNOCK   *Sphyraena japonica*
SNOEK   *Thyrsites atun*
SNOOK   *Scomberomorus commersonii*
SNUBNOSE EEL   *Simenchelys parasiticus*
SNUBNOSE POMPANO   *Trachinotus falcatus*

SOAPY   *Leiognathus equulus*
SOCKEYE SALMON   *Oncorhynchus nerka*
SOLDIER   *Sebastes marinus*
SOLDIERFISH   *Coelorhynchus coelorhynchus, Gymnapastes marmoratus*
SOLE   *Hippoglossoides platessoides, Solea solea*
SOLE, AGULHAS   *Austroglossus pectoralis*
SOLE, BENGAL TONGUE   *Cynoglossus bengalensis*
SOLE, BUTTER   *Isopsetta isolepis*
SOLE, C-O   *Pleuronichthys coenosus*
SOLE, DOVER   *Microstomus pacificus, Solea solea*
SOLE, ENGLISH   *Parophrys vetulus*
SOLE, FLATHEAD   *Hippoglossoides dubius, Hippoglossoides elassodon*
SOLE, GREY   *Glyptocephalus cynoglossus*
SOLE, JAPANESE DOVER   *Microstomus achne*
SOLE, JAPANESE REX   *Glyptocephalus stelleri*
SOLE, LEMON   *Parophrys vetulus, Pleuronectes microcephalus*
SOLE, LONG-FINNED   *Errex zachirus*
SOLENETTE   *Buglossidium luteum*
SOLE, PAPER   *Hippoglossoides elassodon*
SOLE, PETRALE   *Eopsetta jordani*
SOLE, REX   *Errex zachirus, Glyptocephalus zachirus*
SOLE, ROCK   *Lepidopsetta bilineata*
SOLE, ROUGHSCALE   *Clidoderma asperrimum*
SOLE, SAND   *Psettichthys melanostictus, Solea lascaris*
SOLE, SLENDER   *Lyopsetta exilis*
SOLE, SLIME   *Microstomus pacificus*
SOLE, SLIPPERY   *Microstomus pacificus*
SOLE, SMALL-MOUTHED   *Limanda herzensteini*
SOLE, STRIPED   *Zebrias zebra*
SOLE, THICKBACK   *Solea variegata*
SOLE, ZEBRA   *Zebrias zebra*
SOOTY GRUNTER   *Therapon bidyana*
SOUPFIN SHARK   *Galeorhinus zyopterus*
SOUTH AFRICAN PILCHARD   *Sardinops ocellata*
SOUTH AMERICAN LUNGFISH   *Lepidosiren paradoxa*
SOUTHERN BLUEFIN   *Thunnus maccoyii*
SOUTHERN BLUEFIN TUNA   *Thunnus maccoyii*
SOUTHERN FLOUNDER   *Paralichthys lethostigmus*
SOUTHERN PUFFER   *Sphaeroides spengleri*
SOUTHERN STINGRAY   *Dasyatis americana*
SPADEFISH   *Chaetodipterus faber*
SPANISH MACKEREL   *Scomber japonicus, Scomberomorus commersonii, Scomberomorus maculatus, Scomberomorus niphonius*
SPANISH MACKEREL, BARRED   *Scomberomorus commersonii*
SPANISH MACKEREL, BLACK-SPOTTED   *Scomberomorus regalis*
SPANISH MACKEREL, NARROW BARRED   *Cybium commersoni*
SPANISH MACKEREL, SPOTTED   *Scomberomorus guttatum*
SPANTICKLE   *Gasterosteus aculeatus*
SPARLING   *Osmerus mordax*
SPATULATE SCULPIN   *Icelus spatula*

SPEARFISH   *Makaira mitsukurii*
SPEARFISH, BLACK   *Makaira mazara*
SPEARFISH, SHORTBILL   *Tetrapturus angustirostris*
SPECKLED CHAR   *Salvelinus fontinalis*
SPECKLED PERCH   *Pomoxis annularis*
SPECKLED TROUT   *Cynoscion nebulosus, Salvelinus fontinalis*
SPEIGLER'S GREY MULLET   *Mugil speigleri*
SPIKE   *Stizostedion vitreum*
SPIKY TRUMPETER   *Therapon jarbua*
SPINED DOGFISH   *Squalus acanthias*
SPINED LOACH   *Cobitis taenia*
SPINNER SHARK   *Carcharhinus maculipinnis*
SPINY BREAM   *Argyrops spinifer*
SPINYCHEEK   *Sebastolobus macrochir*
SPINY DOGFISH, ATLANTIC   *Squalus acanthias*
SPINY DOGFISH, PACIFIC   *Squalus acanthias*
SPINY EEL   *Mastacembelus armatus, Mastacembelus pancalus, Notacanthus nasus*
SPINYHEAD SCULPIN   *Dasycottus setiger*
SPINY RASP SKATE   *Raja kenoji*
SPLITNOSE ROCKFISH   *Sebastes diploproa*
SPOT   *Leiostomus xanthurus*
SPOTFIN BUTTERFLY FISH   *Chaetodon ocellatus*
SPOTFIN GROUND SHARK   *Carcharhinus limbatus*
SPOT, NORFOLK   *Leiostomus xanthurus*
SPOT, PEARL   *Etroplus suratensis*
SPOT-TAIL   *Sciaenops ocellata*
SPOTTED BASS   *Sciaenops ocellata*
SPOTTED BATFISH   *Drepane punctata*
SPOTTED BUTTERFISH   *Scatophagus argus*
SPOTTED CATFISH   *Anarhichas minor*
SPOTTED CATFISH, TEYSMANN'S   *Clarias batrachus*
SPOTTED CERO   *Scomberomorus regalis*
SPOTTED CROAKER   *Sciaena diacanthus*
SPOTTED CYBIUM   *Scomberomorus maculatus*
SPOTTED DOGFISH, GREATER   *Scyliorhinus stellaris*
SPOTTED DOGFISH, LESSER   *Scyliorhinus canicula*
SPOTTED ETROPLUS   *Etroplus suratensis*
SPOTTED FLOUNDER   *Scophthalmus aquosus*
SPOTTED GREENLING, WHITE   *Hexagrammos stelleri*
SPOTTED GROUPER   *Epinephelus fario*
SPOTTED GUITAR FISH   *Rhinobatus lentiginosus*
SPOTTED HEADSTANDER   *Chilodus punctatus*
SPOTTED MACKEREL   *Sawara niphonia, Scomber tapeinocephalus, Scomberomorus maculatus*
SPOTTED MACKEREL, JAPANESE   *Pneumatophorus japonicus tapeinocephalus*
SPOTTED MOJARRAS   *Gerres filamentosus*
SPOTTED MORAY   *Gymnothorax moringa*
SPOTTED RAY   *Raja montagui*
SPOTTED SARDINELLA   *Sardinella sirm*
SPOTTED SCAT   *Scatophagus argus*
SPOTTED SEAHORSE   *Hippocampus erectus*

SPOTTED SEA TROUT   *Eriscion nebulosus*
SPOTTED SHARK   *Galeocerdo arcticus*
SPOTTED SILVER CARP   *Aristichthys nobilis*
SPOTTED SPANISH MACKEREL   *Scomberomorus guttatum*
SPOTTED SQUETEAGUE   *Eriscion nebulosus*
SPOTTED SUCKER   *Minytrema melanops*
SPOTTED WEAKFISH   *Eriscion nebulosus*
SPOTTED WHITING   *Sillago punctata*
SPOTTED WOLF-FISH   *Anarhichas minor*
SPOTTED WRASSE   *Pseudolabrus japonicus*
SPOTTED WRYMOUTH   *Cryptacanthodes maculatus*
SPOT, WHITE   *Girella nigricans*
SPRAT   *Clupea sprattus*
SPRING SALMON   *Oncorhynchus tschawytscha*
SPRINGER   *Mugil cephalus*
SPUR DOG   *Squalus acanthias*
SQUAWFISH   *Ptychocheilus oregonensis*
SQUAWFISH, NORTHERN   *Ptychocheilus oregonensis*
SQUETEAGUE   *Cynoscion regalis*
SQUIRRELFISH   *Haemulon plumieri, Holocentrus ascensionis, Holocentrus ensifer, Myripristis arayomus*
SQUIRRELFISH, LONGJAW   *Holocentrus ascensionis*
SQUIRREL HAKE   *Urophycis chuss, Urophycis tenuis*
STAGHORN SCULPIN   *Leptocottus armatus*
STAGHORN SCULPIN, ARCTIC   *Gymnocanthus tricuspis*
STARGAZER   *Uranoscopus scaber*
STARRED STURGEON   *Acipenser stellatus*
STAR-SPOTTED SHARK   *Mustelus manazo*
STARRY FLOUNDER   *Platichthys stellatus*
STARRY PIGFACE BREAM   *Lethrinus opercularis*
STARRY RAY   *Raja asterias*
STARRY SKATE   *Raja radiata*
STEELHEAD   *Salmo gairdneri*
STERLET   *Acipenser ruthenus*
STICKLEBACK, BROOK   *Culaea inconstans*
STICKLEBACK, FOURSPINE   *Apeltes quadracus*
STICKLEBACK, THREESPINE   *Gasterosteus aculeatus*
STINGFISH, JAPANESE   *Sebastodes inermis*
STINGFISH, MATSUBARA   *Sebastodes matsubarae*
STINGING CATFISH   *Heteropneustes fossilis*
STINGRAY   *Dasyatis brevicaudatus, Dasyatis pastinaca, Dasyatis sabina, Dasyatis sayi*
STINGRAY, BLUE   *Trygon violacea*
STINGRAY, BANDED WHIPTAIL   *Dasyatis uarnak*
STINGRAY, FRESHWATER   *Potamotrygon motoro*
STINGRAY, JAPANESE   *Dasyatis akajei*
STINGRAY, NORTHERN   *Dasyatis centroura*
STINGRAY, RED   *Dasyatis akajei*
STINGRAY, ROUGHTAIL   *Dasyatis centroura*
STINGRAY, SCALY   *Trygon imbricata*
STINGRAY, SOUTHERN   *Dasyatis americana*

STOCKFISH   *Merluccius bilinearis, Merluccius capensis*
STONE BASS   *Polyprion americanus*
STONE CAT   *Noturus flavus*
STONE FLOUNDER   *Kareius bicoloratus*
STONE LOACH   *Nemacheilus barbatulus*
STONE MOROKO   *Pseudorasbora parva*
STONEROLLER   *Campostoma anomalum*
STOUT BEARDFISH   *Polymixia japonica*
STOUT EELBLENNY   *Anisarchus medius*
STREAKED GURNARD   *Trigla lastoviza, Trigla lineata*
STRETCHED SILK   *Pterogobius elapoides*
STRIPED ANOSTOMUS   *Anostomus anostomus*
STRIPED BASS   *Morone saxatilis*
STRIPED BURRFISH   *Chilomycterus schoepfi*
STRIPED CATFISH EEL   *Plotosus anguillaris*
STRIPED COW FISH   *Aracana aurita*
STRIPED DOGFISH   *Poroderma africanum*
STRIPED DWARF CATFISH   *Macrones vittatus*
STRIPED-FACE UNICORN FISH   *Naso literatus*
STRIPED GRUNT   *Therapon jarbua*
STRIPED JACK   *Caranx delicatissimus*
STRIPED MACKEREL   *Polamys chilensis*
STRIPED MARLIN   *Makaira mitsukurii, Tetrapturus audax*
STRIPED MORWONG   *Goniistius zonatus*
STRIPED MULLET   *Mugil cephalus, Mullus barbatus*
STRIPED PARROTFISH   *Scarus croicensis*
STRIPED PERCH   *Helotes sexlineatus*
STRIPED PIGFISH   *Parapristipoma trilineatum*
STRIPED SEABREAM   *Lithognathus mormyrus*
STRIPED SEAPERCH   *Embiotoca lateralis*
STRIPED SEAROBIN   *Prionotus evolans*
STRIPED SNAKEHEAD   *Ophicephalus striatus*
STRIPED SOLE   *Zebrias zebra*
STRIPED SURF-FISH   *Taeniotoca lateralis*
STRIPED WOLF-FISH   *Anarhichas lupus*
STRIPER   *Morone saxatilis*
STRIPETAIL ROCKFISH   *Sebastes saxicola*
STUDFISH, OZARK   *Fundulus catenatus*
STURGEON   *Acipenser sturio, Huso huso*
STURGEON, AMERICAN ATLANTIC   *Acipenser oxyrhynchus*
STURGEON, CASPIAN   *Acipenser stellatus*
STURGEON, GIANT   *Huso huso*
STURGEON, PACIFIC COAST   *Acipenser transmontanus*
STURGEON POACHER   *Agonus acipenserinus*
STURGEON, RUSSIAN   *Acipenser güldenstadti*
STURGEON, SEA   *Acipenser oxyrhynchus*
STURGEON, SHOVELNOSE   *Scaphirhynchus platorynchus*
STURGEON SUCKER   *Catostomus catostomus*
STURGEON, WHITE   *Acipenser transmontanus*
SUCKER, BROOK   *Catostomus commersonii*

SUCKER, COMMON   *Catostomus commersonii*
SUCKER, LARGE-SCALED   *Moxostoma aureolum*
SUCKER, LONG-NOSED   *Catostomus catostomus*
SUCKER, NORTHERN   *Catostomus catostomus*
SUCKER, PILOT   *Echeneis naucrates*
SUCKER, RED   *Catostomus catostomus*
SUCKER, SPOTTED   *Minytrema melanops*
SUCKER, STURGEON   *Catostomus catostomus*
SUCKER, WHITE   *Catostomus commersonii, Moxostoma aureolum*
SUMATRA BARB   *Barbus tetrazona*
SUMMER FLOUNDER   *Paralichthys dentatus*
SUMMER SKATE   *Raja eglantaria*
SUN BASS   *Lepomis gibbosus*
SUNDIAL   *Lophopsetta maculata*
SUNFISH   *Lepomis macrochirus, Notemigonus crysoleucas*
SUNFISH, BLUEGILL   *Lepomis macrochirus*
SUNFISH, COMMON   *Lepomis gibbosus*
SUNFISH, GILDED   *Lepomis macrochirus*
SUNFISH, GREEN   *Lepomis cyanellus*
SUNFISH, NIPPLE-TAILED OCEAN   *Masturus lanceolatus*
SUNFISH, OCEAN   *Mola mola*
SUNFISH, SHARP-TAIL OCEAN   *Masturus lanceolatus*
SURF FISH, STRIPED   *Taeniotoca lateralis*
SURF PERCH   *Ditrema temmincki*
SURF PERCH, BLACK   *Embiotoca jacksoni*
SURF PERCH, WHITE   *Phanerodon furcatus*
SURF SMELT   *Hypomesus japonicus*
SURGEON, COMMON   *Acanthurus hepatus*
SURGEONFISH   *Naso literatus, Prionurus microlepidotus*
SURGEONFISH, BLEEKER'S LINED   *Acanthurus bleekeri*
SURGEONFISH, FIVE-BANDED   *Acanthurus triostegus*
SURGEONFISH, RINGTAILED   *Acanthurus xanthopterus*
SURMULLET   *Upeneoides bensasi*
SWAMP EEL   *Monopterus albus*
SWEETLIP EMPEROR   *Lethrinus chrysostomus*
SWEET SMELT   *Plecoglossus altivelis*
SWEET WILLIAM   *Galeorhinus galeus, Mustelus mustelus*
SWELLFISH   *Sphaeroides niphobles*
SWELLTOAD   *Sphaeroides spengleri*
SWIVEL TAIL   *Alopias caudatus, Alopias greyi, Alopias vulpinus*
SWORDFISH   *Histiophorus orientalis, Makaira mitsukurii, Xiphias gladius*
SWORDFISH, BROADBILL   *Xiphias gladius*
SWORDFISH, REAL   *Makaira mazara*
SWORDTAIL   *Xiphophorus helleri*

TADE GREY MULLET   *Mugil tade*
TADPOLE FISH   *Raniceps raninus*
TADPOLE MADTOM   *Noturus gyrinus*
TAILOR   *Pomatomus saltatrix*

TAIL, SWIVEL *Alopias caudatus, Alopias greyi, Alopias vulpinus*
TALKING CATFISH *Acanthodoras spinosissimus*
TALLYWAG *Centropristes striatus*
TAMBOR *Sebastopyr ruberrimus, Sphaeroides spengleri*
TANG, CONVICT *Acanthurus triostegus*
TAPIRFISH, LARGESCALE *Notacanthus nasus*
TARARIRA *Hoplias malabaricus*
TARDOORE *Opisthopterus tartoor*
TARGET PERCH *Therapon puta*
TARPON *Megalops atlanticus, Megalops cyprinoides, Tarpon atlanticus*
TARPON, INDIAN *Megalops cyprinoides*
TARWHINE *Rhabdosargus sarba*
TASERGAL *Temnodon saltator*
TASSEL FISH *Eleutheronema tetradactylon*
TASSEL FISH, BLIND *Eleutheronema tetradactylon*
TASSEL FISH, INDIAN *Polynemus indicus*
TAUTOG *Tautoga onitis*
TAWES *Puntius javanicus*
TENCH *Tinca tinca*
TENPOUNDER *Elops hawaiensis, Elops saurus*
TETRA, BLACK *Gymnocorymbus ternetzi*
TETRA, BLIND *Anoptichthys jordani*
TETRA, BUENOS AIRES *Hemigrammus caudovittata*
TETRA, GLASS *Moenkhausia oligolepis*
TETRA, HEAD AND TAIL LIGHT *Hemigrammus ocellifer*
TETRA, MEXICAN *Astyanax mexicanus*
TEYSMANN'S SPOTTED CATFISH *Clarias batrachus*
THERAPON, BLOTCHED *Therapon oxyrhynchus*
THERAPON, FOURLINED *Pelates quadrilineatus*
THERAPON, JARBUA *Therapon jarbua* (sic)
THICKBACK SOLE *Solea variegata*
THICK LIPPED GREY MULLET *Mugil chelo*
THICK LIPPED MULLET *Crenimugil labrosus*
THIMBLE-EYED LING *Urophycis chuss*
THINLIP GREY MULLET *Mugil capito*
THORNBACK *Platyrhinoidis triseriata*
THORNBACK RAY *Raja clavata*
THORNY SKATE *Raja radiata*
THREADFIN *Polynemus indicus*
THREADFIN BREAM, JAPANESE *Nemipterus japonicus*
THREADFIN, FOURFINGER *Eleutheronema tetradactylum*
THREADFIN, GIANT *Eleutheronema tetradactylum*
THREADFIN, PARADISE *Polynemus paradiseus*
THREADFIN SCULPIN *Icelinus filamentosus*
THREADFIN SHAD *Dorosoma patenense*
THREE-BANDED SHEEPSHEAD *Chaetodipterus faber*
THREE-SPINED STICKLEBACK *Gasterosteus aculeatus*
THREE-SPOT GOURAMI *Trichogaster trichopterus*
THREE-TAILED PORGY *Chaetodipterus faber*
THRESHER: SEVERAL SPECIES OF *Alopias*

THRESHER SHARK   *Alopias profundus*
THUMB, MILLER'S   *Cottus gobio*
THUNDERPUMPER   *Aplodinotus grunniens*
TIDDLER   *Gasterosteus aculeatus*
TIGER BARB   *Barbus tetrazona*
TIGERFISH   *Hoplias malabaricus, Therapon jarbua*
TIGER FLATHEAD   *Neoplatycephalus richardsoni*
TIGER PUFFER   *Fugu rubripes*
TIGER SHARK   *Galeocerdo arcticus, Galeocerdo cuvier, Scylliorhinus torazame*
TIGER-TOOTHED CROAKER   *Otolithes ruber*
TIGRONE   *Galeocerdo arcticus*
TILAPIA   *Tilapia mossambica*
TILAPIA, JAVA   *Tilapia mossambica*
TILEFISH, RED   *Branchiostegus japonicus*
TILEFISH, SAND   *Malacanthus plumieri*
TIMBER CRAPPIE   *Pomoxis annularis*
TINMOUTH   *Pomoxis annularis*
TIN PERCH   *Pomoxis annularis*
TOADFISH   *Opsanus tau*
TOAD GOBY   *Gobius batrachocephalus*
TOBACCO BOX   *Lepomis gibbosus, Raja erinacea*
TOLI SHAD   *Hilsa toli*
TOLSTOL   *Hypophthalmichthys molitrix*
TOMCOD, ATLANTIC   *Microgadus tomcod*
TOMCOD, PACIFIC   *Microgadus proximus*
TOMMY ROUGH   *Arripis georgianus*
TONGUE, BLACK COW   *Rhinoplagusia japonica*
TONGUE SOLE, BENGAL   *Cynoglossus bengalensis*
TOOTHFISH   *Dissostichus eleginoides*
TOPE   *Galeorhinus zyopterus* (and other species)
TOPKNOT, ECKSTOM'S   *Phrynorhombus regius*
TOPKNOT, NORWEGIAN   *Phrynorhombus norvegicus*
TOP MINNOW   *Gambusia holbrooki*
TOP MINNOW, PIKE   *Belonesox belizanus*
TOP SMELT   *Atherinops affinis*
TORPEDO   *Narke japonica, Torpedo nobiliana*
TORPEDO, ATLANTIC   *Tetranarce occidentalis, Torpedo nobiliana*
TORPEDO TREVALLY   *Megalaspis cordyla*
TORSK   *Brosme brosme* ("Torsk" is also the Norwegian name for *Gadus morhua*)
TOVIRA CAVALLO   *Apteronotus albifrons*
TRANSPARENT HATCHET FISH   *Sternoptyx diaphana*
TREVALLY, CALE-CALE   *Ulua mandibularis*
TREVALLY, GREAT   *Caranx sexfasciatus*
TREVALLY, SILVER   *Usacaranx georgianus*
TREVALLY, SIX-BANDED   *Caranx sexfasciatus*
TREVALLY, TORPEDO   *Megalaspis cordyla*
TREVALLY, WHITE   *Usacaranx georgianus*
TREVALLY, YELLOWSTRIPE   *Caranx leptolepis*
TRIGGER FISH, GREY   *Balistes capriscus*
TRIGGERFISH, QUEEN   *Balistes vetula*

Triple tail   *Chaetodipterus faber*
trout, Alekey   *Lota lota maculosa*
trout, Blueback   *Salvelinus alpinus*
trout, Brown   *Salmo trutta*
trout, Coastal cut-throat   *Salmo clarkii*
trout, Coral   *Plectropoma maculatum*
trout, Donaldson   *Salmo gairdneri*
trout, Eastern brook   *Salvelinus fontinalis*
trout, Great Lakes   *Salvelinus namaycush*
trout, Grey   *Cynoscion regalis*
trout, Kamloops   *Salmo gairdneri kamloops*
trout, Lake   *Salvelinus namaycush*
trout, Mackinaw   *Salvelinus namaycush*
trout, Malma   *Salvelinus malma*
trout, Rainbow   *Salmo gairdneri*
Trout reef-cod   *Epinephelus fario*
trout, Salmon   *Arripis trutta*
trout, Sand   *Cynoscion arenarius*
trout, Sea   *Cynoscion regalis, Cynoscion virescens, Macrodon ancylodon, Salvelinus alpinus,
    Salvelinus fontinalis, Salmo trutta*
trout, Silver   *Oncorhynchus nerka kennerlyi*
trout, Siscowet   *Salvelinus namaycush siscowet*
trout, Speckled   *Cynoscion nebulosus, Salvelinus fontinalis*
trout, Spotted sea-   *Eriscion nebulosus*
True bass   *Epinephelus septemfasciatus*
True lizard fish   *Saurida undosquamis*
True mullet   *Mugil cephalus*
True sardine   *Sardinops melanosticta*
trumpeter, Bastard   *Latridopsis forsteri*
Trumpeter perch   *Pelates quadrileatus*
Trumpeter sillago   *Sillago maculata*
trumpeter, Spiky   *Therapon jarbua*
Trumpeter whiting   *Sillago maculata*
Trunkfish   *Lactophrys trigonus*
trunkfish, Smooth   *Lactophrys triqueter*
Tubfish   *Trigla lucerna*
Tullibee   *Leucichthys artedii*
Tuna   *Thunnus thynnus thynnus*
tuna, Allison's   *Thunnus albacares*
tuna, Banded   *Scomberomorus commersonii*
tuna, Bigeye   *Thunnus obesus*
tuna, Black   *Promethichthys prometheus*
tuna, Bluefin   *Thunnus thynnus thynnus*
tuna, Little   *Euthynnus affinis yaito, Euthynnus alletteratus*
tuna, Longfinned   *Thunnus alalunga*
tuna, Mackerel   *Euthynnus alletteratus*
tuna, Pacific bluefin   *Thunnus thynnus orientalis*
tuna, Slender   *Allothunnus fallai*
tuna, Yellowfin   *Thunnus albacares*
Tunny   *Thunnus thynnus thynnus*

TURBOT   *Atheresthes stomias, Parastromateus niger, Psetta maxima*
TURBOT, BLACK SEA   *Scophthalmus maeoticus*
TURBOT, INDIAN   *Psettodes erumei*
TURBOT, NEWFOUNDLAND   *Reinhardtius hippoglossoides*
TURKEY ROCKFISH   *Sebastodes ruberrimus*
TURRUM   *Caranx sexfasciatus*
TUSK   *Brosme brosme*
TWAITE SHAD   *Alosa fallax*
TWO-BANDED BREAM   *Diplodus sargus*
TWO-SPINED JEWFISH   *Sciaena diacanthus*
TYEE   *Oncorhynchus tschawytscha*

UNDULATE RAY   *Raja undulata*
UNICORN FISH, STRIPED-FACE   *Naso literatus*
UPSIDE-DOWN CATFISH   *Synodontis nigriventris, Synodontis schall*

VARIEGATED PUPFISH   *Cyprinodon variegatus*
VEINED CATFISH   *Tachysurus venosus*
VELVET BELLY   *Etmopterus spinax*
VENDACE   *Coregonus albula*
VERMILION ROCKFISH   *Sebastes miniatus*
VIEJA   *Loricaria parva*
VIMBA   *Vimba vimba*
VIPERFISH, SLOANE'S   *Chauliodus sloanei*
VIVIPAROUS BLENNY   *Zoarces viviparus*

WACHNA COD   *Eleginus gracilis, Gadus nevaga*
WAHOO   *Acanthocybium solandri*
WALKING FISH   *Anabas testudineus*
WALLEYE   *Stizostedion vitreum*
WALLEYED HERRING   *Alosa pseudoharengus*
WALLEYED PIKE   *Stizostedion vitreum*
WALLEYE POLLOCK   *Theragra chalcogramma*
WARMOUTH   *Cryptacanthodes maculatus*
WART PERCH   *Psenopsis anomala*
WARTY DORY   *Allocyttus verrucosus*
WATERMELON   *Katsuwonus pelamis*
WEAKFISH   *Cynoscion petranus, Cynoscion regalis*
WEATHERFISH   *Cobitis taenia, Misgurnus fossilis*
WEEVER, GREATER   *Trachinus draco*
WELS   *Silurus glanis*
WESTERN ROACH   *Hesperoleucus symmetricus*
WHALER   *Prionace glauca*
WHALE SHARK   *Rhincodon typus*
WHIPFIN MOJARRA   *Gerres filamentosus*
WHIP SCULPIN   *Hemitripterus americanus*

WHIPTAIL, NEW ZEALAND *Macrouronus novaezelandae*
WHIPTAIL SHARK *Alopias pelagicus*
WHIPTAIL STINGRAY, BANDED *Dasyatis uarnak*
WHISKERED CROAKER *Johnius dussumieri*
WHITE AMUR *Ctenopharyngodon idella*
WHITE BASS *Morone chrysops*
WHITE BREAM *Abramis blicca, Blicca bjoerkna, Sargus sargus*
WHITE CARP *Cirrhina cirrhosa*
WHITE CAT *Ictalurus punctatus*
WHITE CRAPPIE *Pomoxis annularis*
WHITE CROAKER *Argyrosomus argentatus*
WHITE CROCODILE FISH *Chaenocephalus aceratus*
WHITE EYE *Stizostedion vitreum*
WHITEFISH *Coregonus albula, Coregonus clupeaformis, Coregonus nasus, Ptychocheilus oregonensis, Salangichthys microdon*
WHITEFISH, BROAD *Coregonus nasus*
WHITEFISH, HUMPBACK *Coregonus clupeaformis*
WHITEFISH, LAKE *Coregonus clupeaformis*
WHITEFISH, OCEAN *Caulolatilus princeps*
WHITEFISH, ROCKY MOUNTAIN *Prosopium williamsoni*
WHITEFISH, ROUND *Prosopium cylindraceum*
WHITEFISH, SHUISK *Coregonus lavaretus lavaretoides*
WHITE GROUPER *Epinephelus aeneus*
WHITE HAKE *Urophycis chuss, Urophysis tenuis*
WHITE MULLET *Chanos chanos, Mugil curema*
WHITE PERCH *Aplodinotus grunniens, Morone americana, Pomoxis annularis*
WHITE POMFRET *Stromateus cinereus, Stromateus sinensis*
WHITE SALMON *Seriola dorsalis*
WHITE SARDINELLA *Sardinella albella*
WHITE SEABREAM *Diplodus sargus*
WHITE SEAPERCH *Phanerodon furcatus*
WHITE SPOT *Girella nigricans*
WHITE SPOTTED GREENLING *Hexagrammos stelleri*
WHITE SPOTTED SHOVELNOSE RAY *Rhynchobatus djeddensis*
WHITE STURGEON *Acipenser transmontanus*
WHITE SUCKER *Catostomus commersonii, Moxostoma aureolum*
WHITE SURFPERCH *Phanerodon furcatus*
WHITE TIP SHARK *Carcharhinus longimanus*
WHITE TREVALLY *Usacaranx georgianus*
WHITING *Menticirrhus saxatilis, Merlangius merlangus, Merluccius bilinearis*
WHITING, BLUE *Micromesistius poutassou*
WHITING, COUCH'S *Micromesistius poutassou*
WHITING, DIVER *Sillago maculata*
WHITING, FALSE *Sciaena deliciosa*
WHITING, INDIAN *Sillago sihama*
WHITING, KING *Menticirrhus littoralis*
WHITING, KING GEORGE *Sillaginoides punctatus*
WHITING, NORTHERN *Sillago sihama*
WHITING, SILVER *Sillago sihama*
WHITING, SPOTTED *Sillaginoides punctatus*

WHITING, TRUMPETER   *Sillago maculata*
WHITING, WINTER   *Sillago maculata*
WIFE, OLD   *Spondyliosoma cantharus*
WIFE, PUDDING   *Halichoeres poecilopterus*
WILL, BLACK   *Centropristes striatus*
WILLIAM, SWEET   *Galeorhinus galeus, Mustelus mustelus*
WINDERMERE CHAR   *Salvelinus willughbii*
WINDFISH   *Notemigonus crysoleucas*
WINDOWPANE   *Lophopsetta maculata, Scophthalmus aquosus*
WINTER FLOUNDER   *Pseudopleuronectes americanus*
WINTER SKATE   *Raja ocellata, Raja stabuliforis*
WINTER WHITING   *Sillago maculata*
WIRRAH   *Acanthistius serratus*
WITCH   *Glyptocephalus cynoglossus*
WITCH FLOUNDER   *Glyptocephalus cynoglossus*
WOLF EEL   *Anarrhichthys ocellatus*
WOLF-FISH, ARCTIC   *Anarhichas latifrons*
WOLF-FISH, ATLANTIC   *Anarhichas lupus*
WOLF-FISH, SPOTTED   *Anarhichas minor*
WOLF-FISH, STRIPED   *Anarhichas lupus*
WOLF HERRING   *Chirocentrus dorab*
WRASSE   *Cheilinus rhodochrous, Duymaeria flagellifera, Pseudolabrus japonicus*
WRASSE, BAILLON'S   *Crenilabrus melops*
WRASSE, BALLAN   *Labrus berggylta*
WRASSE, BLUEHEAD   *Thalassoma bifasciatum*
WRASSE, FIVE-SPOTTED   *Crenilabrus quinquemaculatus*
WRASSE, GIANT   *Cheilinus undulatus*
WRASSE, GREEN   *Labrus turdus*
WRASSE, PEACOCK   *Crenilabrus pavo*
WRASSE, SADDLEBACK   *Thalassoma duperreyi*
WRASSE, SPOTTED   *Pseudolabrus japonicus*
WRECKFISH, ATLANTIC   *Polyprion americanus*
WRYMOUTH, SPOTTED   *Cryptacanthodes maculatus*

XENOCARA, BLUECHIN   *Xenocara dolichoptera*

YELLOWBELLY   *Lepomis gibbosus*
YELLOWBACK SEABREAM   *Taius tumifrons*
YELLOW BULLHEAD   *Ictalurus natalis*
YELLOW CROAKER   *Pseudosciaena crocea*
YELLOW DOG SHARK   *Scoliodon sorrakowah*
YELLOWFIN BREAM   *Rhabdosargus sarba*
YELLOWFIN GOATFISH   *Upeneus bensasi*
YELLOWFIN GOBY   *Acanthogobius flavimanus*
YELLOWFIN SEABREAM   *Chrysophrys datnia*
YELLOWFIN TUNA   *Thunnus albacares*
YELLOWFINNED GROUPER   *Trisotropis venenosus*
YELLOWFISH   *Barbus holubi, Cephalopholis fulvus*

YELLOWFISH, CLANWILLIAM   *Barbus holubi*
YELLOWFISH, SMALLMOUTH   *Barbus holubi*
YELLOW GOATFISH   *Upeneoides sulphureus*
YELLOW GRUNT   *Haemulon flavolineatum, Haemulon sciurus*
YELLOW GURNARD   *Trigla lucerna*
YELLOW NED   *Perca flavescens*
YELLOW PERCH   *Lepomis gibbosus, Perca flavescens*
YELLOW PIKE   *Stizostedion vitreum*
YELLOW PORGY   *Dentex macrocanus, Taius tumifrons*
YELLOW SCULPIN   *Hemilepidotus jordani*
YELLOW SEABREAM   *Taius tumifrons*
YELLOW SHINER   *Cymatogaster aggregata*
YELLOW STRIPED CAESIO   *Caesio chrysozonus*
YELLOW STRIPED PLAICE   *Pleuronectes herzensteini*
YELLOWSTRIPE TREVALLY   *Caranx leptolepis*
YELLOWSTONE CUT-THROAT   *Salmo clarkii*
YELLOWTAIL   *Leiostomus xanthurus, Seriola aureovittata, Seriola dorsalis, Seriola dumerilii, Seriola quinqueradiata*
YELLOWTAIL FLOUNDER   *Limanda ferruginea*
YELLOWTAIL ROCKFISH   *Sebastodes flavidus*
YELLOWTAIL SNAPPER   *Ocyurus chrysurus*
YOUNG SHAD   *Notemigonus crysoleucas*

ZAHRTE   *Vimba vimba*
ZANDER   *Stizostedion lucioperca*
ZEBRA FISH   *Brachydanio rerio, Therapon jarbua*
ZEBRA SOLE   *Zebrias zebra*
ZEE-BASJE   *Lithognathus mormyrus*
ZIEGE   *Pelecus cultratus*
ZOPE   *Abramis ballerus*

Bibliography and Author Index

None of these references was quoted in the earlier book, so the sequential numbering continues from that of the last reference of Volume 1. A very few have a suffix a or b as well as a number: these were added at a late stage in the preparation of the book. The abbreviations of journal titles follow the World List of Scientific Periodicals (Butterworth, London). All of the papers quoted in the book have been read in the original (or a translation thereof) unless it is specifically stated that an abstract only was seen.

A number of Russian journals now appear in English translation, and where possible I have tried to use these rather than the originals. The journal name given shows which version was seen: Hydrobiol. J (Eng.) or Gidrobiol. Zh. (Russ.); J. Evol. Biochem. Physiol. or Zh. Evol. Biokhim. Fiziol. and some others. The subject matter is of course the same in either case, but the page numbers are different.

As stated at the beginning, this volume is dedicated to Professor Serfaty of Toulouse University. The great contribution made by this scholar to fisheries science can be gauged from the fact that papers by Bouche, Créac'h, Gas, Labat, Murat, Parent, Pequignot, Pequin and Vellas, all distinguished in their respective fields, have originated in his laboratory.

References marked with an asterisk (*) have yielded chemical data for Parts 2 and 3, where they are identified by their sequential number. Figures in italics following a reference indicate the pages in the text where it has been quoted.

Latin names of fish, where mentioned, are exactly as spelled by the authors and not necessarily those in vogue, but I have corrected a number of printing errors in the titles of papers.

*1408. Abe, H., Shimizu, C. and Matsuura, F. (1976). Occurrence and distribution of NAD(P) splitting enzymes in fish tissues. *Bull. Jap. Soc. scient. Fish.* **42,** 703–711.

*1409. Abrahamsson, T. and Nilsson, S. (1975). Effects of nerve sectioning and drugs on the catecholamine content in the spleen of the cod, *Gadus morhua. Comp. Biochem. Physiol.* **51C,** 231–233.

*1410. Accardi, N. and Macri, A. (1973). Amino acids—free and total—in the edible parts of mammals, birds, fish and molluscs. *Archo. Vet. ital.* **24,** 11–17.

1411. Acher, R., Chauvet, J. and Chauvet, M.-T. (1972). Phylogeny of the neurohypophysial hormones. Two new active peptides isolated from a cartilaginous fish, *Squalus acanthias. Eur. J. Biochem.* **29,** 12–19. *6*

*1412. Acher, R., Chauvet, J., Chauvet, M.-T. and Crepy, D. (1968). Molecular evolution of neurohypophysial hormones: comparison of the active principles of three bony fishes. *Gen. comp. Endocr.* **11,** 535–538.

*1413. Ackman, R. G. and Eaton, C. A. (1971). Mackerel lipids and fatty acids. *J. Can. Inst. Food Technol.* **4,** 169–174. *53, 68, 74*

*1414. Ackman, R. G., Eaton, C. A. and Hingley, J. (1975). *J. Can. Inst. Food Sci. Technol.* **8,** 155–159.

 1415. Ackman, R. G., Hingley, J. and MacKay, K. T. (1972). Dimethyl sulphide as an odour component in Nova Scotia fall mackerel. *J. Fish. Res. Bd Can.* **29,** 1085–1088. *150*

*1416. Ackman, R. G., Ke, P. J., MacCallum, W. A. and Adams, D. R. (1969). Newfoundland capelin lipids: fatty acid composition and alterations during frozen storage. *J. Fish. Res. Bd Can.* **26,** 2037–2060. *52, 53*

 1417. Adamova, L. G. and Novikov, G. G. (1973). Serum protein composition in herbivorous fishes. *Biol. Nauki* **16** (5), 44–49. From *Chem. Abstr.* **79,** 50894w (1973). *62*

 1418. Adams, B. L., Zaugg, W. S. and McLain, L. R. (1973). Temperature effect on parr-smolt transformation in steelhead trout (*Salmo gairdneri*) as measured by gill sodium-potassium stimulated adenosine triphosphatase. *Comp. Biochem. Physiol.* **44A,** 1333–1339. *24*

*1419. Addison, R. F. and Ackman, R. G. (1971). Erythrocyte lipids of Atlantic cod, *Gadus morhua. Can. J. Biochem.* **49,** 873–876.

 1420. Adibi, S. A. (1971). Interrelationships between level of amino acids in plasma and tissues during starvation. *Am. J. Physiol.* **221,** 829–838. *194*

 1421. Adler, H. E. (1975). "Fish behaviour: why fishes do what they do." TFH Publications Ltd., Hong Kong. *235*

 1422. Adron, J. W., Blair, A., Cowey, C. B. and Shanks, A. M. (1976). Effects of dietary energy level and dietary energy source on growth, feed conversion and body composition of turbot (*Scophthalmus maximus* L.). *Aquaculture*, **7,** 125–132. *139, 142*

 1423. Agarwal, S. and John, P. A. (1975). Functional morphology of the urinary bladder in some teleostean fishes. *Forma et Functio*, **8,** 19–26. *307*

*1424. Agrawal, U. and Srivastava, A. K. (1976). Catecholamines and the abundance of blood cells in a fresh water tropical teleost (*Colisa fasciatus*) in relation to cold-shock. *Archs Anat. microsc. Morph. exp.* **65,** 231–240. *239*

*1425. Agrawal, V. P., Sastry, K. V. and Kaushab, S. K. S. (1975). Digestive enzymes of three teleost fishes. *Acta Physiol. hung.* **46,** 93–98.

*1426. Ahmad, M. M. and Matty, A. J. (1975). Insulin secretion in response to high and low protein ingestion in rainbow trout (*Salmo gairdneri*). *Pak. J. Zool.* **7,** 1–6. *365*

1427. Ahmad, R. U. (1972). Quantitative ("morphological") colour changes on prolonged black and white background adaptations of the minnow *Phoxinus phoxinus* (L.) and the effects of chromatic spinal section on these colour changes. *J. comp. Physiol.* **77,** 170–189. *245*

*1428. Ahokas, R. A. and Duerr, F. G. (1975a). Salinity tolerance and extracellular osmoregulation in two species of euryhaline teleosts, *Culaea inconstans* and *Fundulus diaphanus. Comp. Biochem. Physiol.* **52A,** 445–448.

*1429. Ahokas, R. A. and Duerr, F. G. (1975b). Tissue water and intracellular osmoregulation in two species of euryhaline teleosts, *Culaea inconstans* and *Fundulus diaphanus. Comp. Biochem. Physiol.* **52A,** 449–454.

*1430. Ahokas, R. A. and Sorg, G. (1977). The effect of salinity and temperature on intracellular osmoregulation and muscle free amino acids in *Fundulus diaphanus. Comp. Biochem. Physiol.* **56A,** 101–105. *313*

*1431. Ahsan, S. N. and Ahsan, J. (1975). Changes in liver glycogen in starved and normally fed, growth hormone treated *Clarias batrachus* (Linn). *Ann. Zool.* **11,** 53–58. *192*

1432. Aida, K., Hirose, K., Yokote, M. and Hibiya, T. (1973). Physiological studies on gonadal maturation of fishes—II. Histological changes in the liver cells of ayu following gonadal maturation and oestrogen administration. *Bull. Jap. Soc. scient. Fish.* **39,** 1107–1115. *43, 50*

1433. Aida, K., Ngan, P.-V. and Hibiya, T. (1973). Physiological studies on gonadal maturation of fishes—I. Sexual difference in composition of plasma protein of ayu in relation to gonadal maturation. *Bull. Jap. Soc. scient. Fish.* **39,** 1091–1096. *43, 50*

*1434. Akiyama, F. and Seno, N. (1973). Studies on the mucopolysaccharides from hagfish skin. *Nat. Sci. Rep. Ochanomizu Univ.* **23,** 79–100.

1435. Akulin, V. N. (1969). Fatty acid composition of muscle phospholipids of sockeye salmon, *Oncorhynchus nerka*, at various stages of its life cycle. *Zh. Evol. Biokhim. Fiziol.* **5,** 411–414. From *Chem Abstr.* **72,** 1122q (1970). *316*

1436. Akulin, V. N., Chebotareva, M. A. and Kreps, E. M. (1969). Fatty acids of brain, and muscle and liver phospholipids, of the anadromous salmon, *Oncorhynchus nerka*, from freshwater and marine habitats. *Zh. Evol. Biokhim. Fiziol.* **5,** 446–456. From *Chem Abstr.* **72,** 52275z (1970). *316*

*1437. Akulin, V. N., Svetashev, V. I. and Salmenkova, E. A. (1975). Intraspecific genetic variation of phospholipids in the blood serum of the salmon *Oncorhynchus nerka* and *O. keta. Zh. Evol. Biokhim. Fiziol.* **11,** 306–308. From *Chem. Abstr.* **83** 40484f (1975).

*1438. Albers, C., Pleschka, K. and Spaich, P. (1969). Chloride distribution between red blood cells and plasma in the dogfish (*Scyliorhinus canicula*). *Resp. Physiol.* **7**, 295–299.

1439. Aldrin, J. F. and Grandgirard, A. (1971). Quality of *Thunnus albacares*. Chemical evaluation. *Recl. Méd. vét.* **147**, 583–606. *34, 68*

1440. Aler, G. M. (1971). The study of prolactin in the pituitary gland of the Atlantic eel (*Anguilla anguilla*) and the Atlantic salmon (*Salmo salar*) by immuno-fluorescence technique. *Acta Zool., Stockh.* **52**, 145–156. *300*

*1441. Alexander, C. and Day, C. E. (1973). Distribution of serum lipoproteins of selected vertebrates. *Comp. Biochem. Physiol.* **46B**, 295–312.

1442. Alexander, K. M. (1970). A study on the lipid distribution pattern in muscles of two teleosts *Arius dussumieri* and *Ophiocephalus striatus*. *Fish. Technol.* **7**, 81–85. *68*

*1443. Alexander, M. D., Haslewood, E. S., Haslewood, G. A. D., Watts, D. C. and Watts, R. L. (1968). Osmotic control and urea biosynthesis in selachians. *Comp. Biochem. Physiol.* **26**, 971–978.

*1444. Allanson, B. R., Bok, A. and van Wyk, N. I. (1971). The influence of exposure to low temperature on *Tilapia mossambica* Peters (Cichlidae). II. Changes in serum osmolarity, sodium and chloride ion concentrations. *J. Fish. Biol.* **3**, 181–185. *342*

*1445. Allen, D. M. (1977). Measurements of serum thyroxine and the proportions of rhodopsin and porphyropsin in rainbow trout. *Can. J. Zool.* **55**, 836–842. *269*

1446. Allen, D. M. and McFarland, W. N. (1973). The effect of temperature on rhodopsin-porphyropsin ratios in a fish. *Vision Res.* **13**, 1303–1309. *268*

1447. Allen, D. M., McFarland, W. N., Munz, F. W. and Poston, H. A. (1973). Changes in the visual pigments of trout. *Can. J. Zool.* **51**, 901–914. *268*

1448. Allen, K. O. and Strawn, K. (1971). Rate of acclimation of juvenile channel catfish, *Ictalurus punctatus*, to high temperatures. *Trans. Am. Fish Soc.* **100**, 665–671. *323*

*1449. Amer, M. M., Ahmad, A. K. S. and El-Zeany, B. A. (1972). Analysis of some red sea-fish liver oils. *Oléagineux*, **27**, 153–155.

1450. Ameyaw-Akumfi, C. (1975). II. The functional morphology of the body and tail muscles of the tuna *Katsuwonus pelamis* Linnaeus. *Zool. Anz. Jena*, **194**, 367–375. (*Note*: this title is as given in the paper). *80, 81*

*1451. Amlacher, E. (1957). Blood sugar in normal carp and in pathological water-bloating of the belly. *Arch. FischWiss.* **8**, 12–32. From Chavin and Young (1970).

1452. Amos, B., Anderson, I. G., Haslewood, G. A. D. and Tökes, L. (1977). Bile salts of the lungfishes *Lepidosiren, Neoceratodus* and *Protopterus* and those of the coelacanth *Latimeria chalumnae* Smith. *Biochem J.* **161**, 201–204. *565*

1453. Ananthanarayanan, V. S. and Hew, C. L. (1977). Structural studies on the freezing-point-depressing protein of the winter flounder *Pseudopleuronectes americanus. Biochem. biophys. Res. Commun.* **74**, 685–689. *349*

*1454. Ando, K. (1968). Biochemical studies on the lipids of cultured fishes. *J. Tokyo Univ. Fish.* **54**, 61–96. *14, 15*

*1455. Andreen-Svedberg (1933). On the distribution of sugar between plasma and corpuscles in animal and human blood. *Skand. Arch. Physiol.* **66**, 113–190. From Chavin and Young (1970).

*1456. Andreev, A. K. (1958). Muscle amylase of fishes. *Biochemistry, N.Y.* **23**, 851–854.

1457. Andrejeva, A. P. (1971). The collagen thermostability of some species and subspecies of the gadoid fish. *Tsitologiya,* **13**, 1004–1008. *29, 339*

1458. Andrews, J. W. and Stickney, R. R. (1972). Interactions of feeding rates and environmental temperature on growth, food conversion, and body composition of channel catfish. *Trans. Am. Fish. Soc.* **101**, 94–99. *339*

1459. Andriashev, A. P. (1970). Cryopelagic fishes of the Arctic and Antarctic and their significance in polar ecosystems. *In* "Antarctic Ecology" (Ed. Holdgate, M. W.), vol. 1, pp. 297–304. Academic Press, New York and London. *322*

1460. Anon. (1969). Geochemical ecology of freshwater fish. *Vop. Biol., Mater. Konf.* 159–164. Ed. H. Maurina. Izd. "Zinatne". Riga, USSR. From *Chem. Abstr.* **72**, 52385k (1970). *147*

1461. Arai, K., Kawamura, K. and Hayashi, C. (1973). The relative thermo-stabilities of the actomyosin-ATPase from the dorsal muscles of various fish species. *Bull. Jap. Soc. scient. Fish.* **39**, 1077–1085. *336*

1462. Arai, S., Nose, T. and Hashimoto, Y. (1972). *Bull. Freshwat. Fish. Res. Lab., Tokyo* **22**, 69–83, *146*

*1463. Arima, S. and Umemoto, S. (1976). Mercury in aquatic organisms—II. Mercury distribution in muscles of tunas and swordfish. *Bull. Jap. Soc. scient. Fish.* **42**, 931–937.

*1464. Arsan, O. M. and Malyarevskaya, A. Ya. (1969). The effect of food on thiaminase activity and the content of thiamine in the liver and intestine of silver carp. *Hydrobiol. J.* **5**, (6), 79–81. *134, 135*

*1465. Arsan, O. M. and Malyarevskaya, A. Ya. (1974). Total riboflavin content in the organs and tissues of some freshwater fishes. *Hydrobiol. J.* **10**, 64–66. *146*

*1466. Asakawa, M. (1973). Fatty acids in muscle lipids of *Zacco platypus*. (Temminck et Schlegel). *Rep. Educ. Dep., Kumamoto Univ., part 1, Nat. Sci.* **22,** 93–99.

*1467. Asakawa, M. (1974). Sialic acid-containing glycoprotein in the external mucus of eel, *Anguilla japonica* Temminck et Schlegel—II. Carbohydrate and amino acid composition. *Bull. Jap. Soc. scient. Fish.* **40,** 303–308.

*1468. Asghar, S. S., Khawaja, D. K. and Jafri, A. K. (1972). 5′-Nucleotidase activity in the tissues of the cat-fish, *Heteropneustes fossilis* Bloch. *Broteria,* **41,** 3–7.

 1469. Ashley, L. M. (1972). Nutritional pathology. *In* "Fish Nutrition" (Ed Halver, J. E.), Chapter 10, pp. 439–537. Academic Press, New York and London. *4, 7, 146, 389*

*1470. Astakhova, L. P. (1976). The effect of muscle work and fatigue on glycogen content of the brain in the teleost fish *Trachurus mediterraneus ponticus*. *J. Evol. Biochem. Physiol.* **12,** 82–84. *114*

*1471. Atchison, G. J. (1975). Fatty acid levels in developing brook trout (*Salvelinus fontinalis*) eggs and fry. *J. Fish. Res. Bd Can.* **32,** 2513–2515. *13*

 1472. Atherton, W. D. and Aitken, A. (1970). Growth, nitrogen metabolism and fat metabolism in *Salmo gairdneri*, Rich. *Comp. Biochem. Physiol.* 719–747. *141, 142, 324*

 1473. Austreng, E. (1976). Fat and protein in diets for salmonoid fish. III. Different types of fat in dry diets for rainbow trout (*Salmo gairdneri*, Richardson). *Meld. Norg. Landbr.* **55** (7), 18 pp. From *Chem. Abstr.* **85,** 175975d (1976). *142*

 1474. Azam, F. and Hodson, R. E. (1977). Dissolved ATP in the sea and its utilisation by marine bacteria. *Nature, Lond.* **267,** 696–697. *148*

*1475. Bachand, L. and Leray, C. (1975). Erythrocyte metabolism in the yellow perch (*Perca flavescens* Mitchill)—I. Glycolytic enzymes. *Comp. Biochem. Physiol.* **50B,** 567–570.

*1476. Bagchi, M. M. and Ibrahim, K. H. (1974). A note on the haemotological study of Rohu, *Labeo rohita* (Ham.). *J. Inland Fish. Soc. India* **6,** 93–94.

 1477. Bagenal, T. B. (1971). The interrelation of the size of fish eggs, the date of spawning and the production cycle. *J. Fish Biol.* **3,** 207–219. *9*

*1478. Bagenal, T. B., Mackereth, F. J. H. and Heron, J. (1973). The distinction between brown trout and sea trout by the strontium content of their scales. *J. Fish Biol.* **5,** 555–557. *147*

*1479. Bailey, C. F. (1973). Lipids of the fertilised egg and adult brain of *Fundulus heteroclitus*. *J. exp. Zool.* **185,** 265–275. *539*

*1480. Bailey, J. M., Fishman, P. H. and Mulhern, S. (1969). Studies on mutarotases. IV. Mutarotase in kidneys of saltwater versus freshwater fish. *Proc. Soc. exp. Biol. Med.* **131,** 861–863. *317*

1481. Bailey, R. M., Fitch, J. E., Herald, E. S., Lachner, E. A., Lindsey, C. C., Robins, C. R. and Scott, W. B. (1970). "A List of Common and Scientific Names of Fishes from the United States and Canada" (3rd Edn). American Fisheries Society, Special Publication no. 6, Washington D.C. *ix*

1482. Baines, G. W. (1975). Blood pH effects in eight fishes from the teleostean family Scorpaenidae. *Comp. Biochem. Physiol.* **51A,** 833–843. *123, 262*

1483. Bakerman, S. (1962). Quantitative extraction of acid soluble human skin collagen with age. *Nature, Lond.* **196,** 375–376. *205*

*1484. Bakhteyeva, V. T. (1975). Cation concentration in the blood serum of the sockeye, *Oncorhynchus nerka,* of different intraspecific groups. *Journal of Ichthyology* **15,** 980–984. *248*

*1485. Bal', V. V. and Mel'kova, L. A. (1970). Characteristics of the amino acid composition of muscle proteins of fish in the Volga-Caspian basin. *Izv. vyssh. ucheb. Zaved. Pishch. Tekhn.* (6), 38–40 (no volume number given).

*1486. Balbontin, F., de Silva, S. S. and Ehrlich, K. F. (1973). A comparative study of anatomical and chemical characteristics of reared and wild herring. *Aquaculture,* **2,** 217–240. *257*

*1487. Baldwin, J. (1975). Selection for catalytic efficiency of lactate dehydrogenase M_4: correlation with body temperature and levels of anaerobic glycolysis. *Comp. Biochem. Physiol.* Special issue, Ed. Hochachka, P. W. "Biochemistry at Depth". **52B,** 33 37.

*1488. Baldwin, J. and Reed, K. C. (1976). Cytoplasmic sources of NADPH for fat synthesis in rainbow trout liver: effect of thermal acclimation on enzyme activities. *Comp. Biochem. Physiol.* **54B,** 527–529.

1489. Baldwin, J., Storey, K. B. and Hochachka, P. W. (1974). Lactate dehydrogenase M_4 of an abyssal fish: strategies for function at low temperature and high pressure. *Comp. Biochem. Physiol.* Special issue, Ed. Hochachka, P. W. "Biochemistry at Depth". **52B,** 19–23. *263*

*1490. Ball, J. N. and Ingleton, P. M. (1973). Adaptive variations in prolactin secretion in relation to external salinity in the teleost *Poecilia latipinna. Gen. comp. Endocrinol.* **20,** 312–325. *300*

1491. Bamford, O. S. (1974). Oxygen reception in the rainbow trout (*Salmo gairdneri*). *Comp. Biochem. Physiol.* **48A,** 69–76. *273*

*1492. Bange-Barnoud, R. (1965). Evolution of lactic acid and of plasma glucose in tench during asphyxia by confinement. *C. r. Séanc. Soc. Biol.* **159,** 400–403. From Chavin and Young (1970).

1493. Bange-Barnoud, R., Bange, C., Vanel, H. and Pottu, J. (1971). Influence of starvation on blood proteids and the free α-amine compounds in the blood of the tench (*Tinca tinca* L.). *Annales de l'Institut Michel Pacha, Laboratoire Maritime de Physiologie* **4,** 77–101. *213*

*1494. Bannister, J. V., Anastasi, A. and Bannister, W. H. (1977). Cytosol superoxide dismutase from swordfish (*Xiphias gladius* L.) liver. *Comp. Biochem. Physiol.* **56B,** 235–238.

*1495. Bannister, J. V. and Bannister, W. H. (1976). Isolation and general characterisation of myoglobin from the dolphin fish *Coryphaena hippurus* (L.). *Comp. Biochem. Physiol.* **53B,** 57–60.

*1496. Barber, R. T., Vijayakumar, A. and Cross, F. A. (1972). Mercury concentrations in recent and ninety-year-old benthopelagic fish. *Science, N.Y.* **178,** 636–639. *33, 35*

1497. Barraclough, W. E. and Robinson, D. G. (1971). Anomalous occurrence of carp (*Cyprinus carpio*) in the marine environment. *J. Fish. Res. Bd Can.* **28,** 1345–1347. *521*

1498. Barroso, L. M. (1967). Biology and fishery of the 'peixe-voador' (*Hirundichthys affinis* Gunther) in the northern Rio Grande. *Bol. Estud. Pesca. (Braz.)* **7,** 9–37. *46*

*1499. Bartlett, G. R. (1976). Phosphate compounds in red cells of reptiles, amphibians and fish. *Comp. Biochem. Physiol.* **55A,** 211–214.

*1500. Barua, A. B. and Singh, H. T. (1972). Vitamin A_2 in liver oils of fresh water fishes. *Indian J. Biochem. Biophys.* **9,** 128–130.

1501. Barua, A. B., Tombi Singh, H. and Das, R. C. (1973). Conversion of lutein into dehydroretinol by the freshwater fish, *Saccobranchus fossilis*. *Br. J. Nutr.* **30,** 1–12. *463*

1502. Bashamohideen, M. and Parvatheswararao (1972). Adaptations to osmotic stress in the fresh-water euryhaline teleost *Tilapia mossambica*. IV. Changes in blood glucose, liver glycogen and muscle glycogen levels. *Mar. Biol.* **16,** 68–74. *290*

*1503. Basile, C., Goldspink, G., Modigh, M. and Tota, B. (1976). Morphological and biochemical characterisation of the inner and outer ventricular myocardial layers of adult tuna fish (*Thunnus thynnus* L.) *Comp. Biochem. Physiol.* **54B,** 279–283. *89*

*1504. Baslow, M. H., Turlapaty, P. and Lenney, J. F. (1969). N-Acetyl histidine metabolism in the brain, heart and lens of the goldfish, *Carassius auratus*, in vivo: evidence of rapid turnover and a possible intermediate. *Life Sci.* **8,** 535–541.

*1505. Bass, A., Ošťádal, B., Pelouch, V. and Vítek, V. (1973). Differences in weight parameters, myosin-ATPase activity and the enzyme pattern of energy supplying metabolism between the compact and spongious cardiac musculature of carp (*Cyprinus carpio*) and turtle *Testudo horsfieldi*). *Pflügers Arch. ges. Physiol.* **343,** 65–77.

1506. Bass, R. J. and Avault, J. W. (1975). Food habits, length-weight relationship, condition factor, and growth of juvenile red drum, *Sciaenops ocellata*, in Louisiana. *Trans. Am. Fish. Soc.* **104,** 35–45. *26*

*1507. Bassiouni, S. S. (1968). Changes of free amino acids during cold storage of fish in superchilled state. *Proc. Congr. Refrig., Ostend* (Ed. Doucet, M.). Hoger Technisch Instituut, Zeedijk 101, Oostende.

1508. Basulto, S. (1976). Induced saltwater tolerance in connection with inorganic salts in the feeding of Atlantic salmon (*Salmo salar* L.). *Aquaculture* **8,** 45–55. *318*

1509. Bauernfeind, J. C. (1976). Canthaxanthin: a pigmenter for salmonids. *Progve Fish Cult.* **38,** 180–183.

*1510. Bazhenova, K. Ya. and Shcherbina, M. A. (1975). Chemical composition of carp fingerling muscles during winter starvation. *J. Hydrobiol.* **11,** 60–62.

1511. Beamish. F. W. H. (1964). Influence of starvation on standard and routine oxygen consumption. *Trans. Am. Fish. Soc.* **93,** 103–107. *169*

1512. Beatty, D. D. (1969a). Vistal pigments of three species of cartilaginous fish. *Nature, Lond.* **222,** 285 only. *266*

1513. Beatty, D. D. (1969b). Visual pigment changes in juvenile kokanee salmon in response to thyroid hormones. *Vision Res.* **9,** 855–864. *7, 268*

1514. Beatty, D. D. (1969c). Visual pigments of the burbot, *Lota lota*, and seasonal changes in their relative proportions. *Vision Res.* **9,** 1173–1183. *269*

1515. Beatty, D. D. (1975). Visual pigments of the American eel *Anguilla rostrata*. *Vision Res.* **15,** 771–776. *266*

*1516. Beecher, H. A. (1975). Carotenoids in colour change of *Pomacentrus variabilis* *Q. Jl Fla Acad. Sci.* **38,** 106–113.

1517. Beese, G. and Kändler, R. (1969). Contributions to the biology of three North Atlantic catfish species, *Anarhichas lupus* L., *A. minor* Olafs and *A. denticulatus* Kr. *Ber. dt. wiss. Kommn. Meeresforsch.* **20,** 21–59. *46*

1518. Behrisch, H. W. (1972). Molecular mechanisms of adaptations to low temperature in marine poikilotherms. Some regulatory properties of dehydrogenases from two arctic species. *Mar. Biol.* **13,** 267–275. *328, 329, 333*

1519. Beitinger, T. L. (1975). Diel activity rhythms and thermoregulatory behaviour of bluegill in response to unnatural photoperiods. *Biol. Bull.* **149,** 96–108. *383*

1520. Beitinger, T. L. and Magnuson, J. J. (1976). Low thermal responsiveness in the bluegill, *Lepomis macrochirus*. *J. Fish. Res. Bd Can.* **33,** 293–295. *323*

1521. Benedetti, I. (1974). The glycogen in the central nervous system during the development of a teleost. I. *Gambusia affinis. Atti Accad. naz. Lincei Rc., Classe de Scienze fisiche, matematiche e naturali* **57,** 713–717. *11*

*1522. Benzhitskii, A. G. (1973). Vitamin B_{12} in the internal organs of Black Sea fish. *Biol. Morya* **30,** 101–112.

*1523. Benziger, D. and Umminger, B. L. (1971). Glycogenolytic enzymes in the livers of thermally-acclimated teleosts. *Am. Zool.* **11,** 670 only. *328, 330*

*1524. Benziger, D. and Umminger, B. L. (1972). Hepatic phosphorylase activity in thermally-acclimated fish. *Am. Zool.* **12,** xxviii–xxix.

*1525. Benziger, D. and Umminger, B. L. (1973). Role of hepatic glycogenolytic enzymes in the cold-induced hyperglycaemia of the killifish, *Fundulus heteroclitus. Comp. Biochem. Physiol.* **45A,** 767–772. *344*

1526. Benziger, D. and Umminger, G. L. (1974). The effect of pH and cold acclimation upon glucose-6-phosphatase activity in the goldfish, *Carassius auratus. Comp. Biochem. Physiol.* **47B,** 243–254. *344*

*1527. Berdyshev, G. D. (1968). Causes and mechanisms of the death of far-eastern salmon following spawning. *Izv. tikhookean. nauchno-issled. Inst. ryb. Khoz. Okeanogr.* **65,** 145–156.

*1528. Berg, A. (1972). Studies on the metabolism of calcium and strontium in freshwater fish. IV. Calcium and strontium relationships in fishes of two northern Italian lakes and their general radioecological implications. *Memorie Ist. ital. Idrobiol.* **29,** 145–167. *147*

1529. Berger, T. S. and Panasenko, L. D. (1974). Relationship between beginning of spawning migrations and fatness of mature cod. *ICES Demersal Fish (Northern) Committee, paper CM 1974/F.23* published by International Council for the Exploration of the Sea, Charlottenlund, Denmark. *41, 167*

*1530. Bergh, C.-H., Larson, G. and Samuelsson, B. E. (1975) Fatty acid and aldehyde composition of major phospholipids in salt gland of marine birds and spiny dogfish. *Lipids,* **10,** 299–302.

*1531. Beritashvili, D. R., Kvavilashvili, I. S. and Kafiani, C. A. (1969). Redistribution of K^+ in cleaving eggs of a fish *Misgurnus fossilis. Expl Cell Res.* **56,** 113–116. *15*

1532. Berman, S. A. (1969). Some patterns in the accumulation of microelements from the environment in the organs and tissues of freshwater fish. *Uch. Zap., Latv. Gos. Univ.* **100,** 3–11. *147*

*1533. Berman, S. A. and Ilzin', A. E. (1968). Distribution of the trace elements manganese, iron, copper and zinc in the organs and tissues of freshwater edible fish. *Mikroelem. Organizme Ryb Ptits* (Ed. Bermane, S.) 5–18. Izd. "Zinatne": Riga, USSR. *248*

*1534. Berman, S. A. and Vitin', I. V. (1968). The quantitative characteristics and physiological action of certain trace elements in the organs of the rainbow trout during early ontogenesis. *Mikroelem. Organizme Ryb Ptits*, 19–35. Riga USSR. *34, 35, 45, 46, 56, 57, 148, 385*

1535. Bern, H. A. (1975). Prolactin and osmoregulation. *Am. Zool.* **15,** 937–948. *301, 305*

1536. Best, A. C. G. and Bone, Q. (1973). The terminal neuromuscular junctions of lower chordates. *Z. Zellforsch. mikrosk. Anat.* **143,** 495–504. *87*

1537. Beyenbach, K. W. (1974). Magnesium excretion by the rainbow trout, *Salmo gairdneri*. Ph.D. Thesis, Washington State Univ. University Microfilms no. 74–28,866.

*1538. Beyenbach, K. W. and Kirschner, L. B. (1975). Kidney and urinary bladder functions of the rainbow trout in Mg and Na excretion. *Am. J. Physiol.* **229,** 389–393. *156*

*1539. Bhatt, S. D. (1974). Effect of glucose loading on blood sugar and on the histology of the pancreatic islets in *Clarias batrachus* (Linn.) *Acta anat.* **88,** 76–83. *365*

*1540. Bican, J. (1976). Cobalt content in some fresh-water fishes and their tissues. *Zivocisna Vyroba* **21,** 917–923.

1541. Bilinski, E. (1974). Biochemical aspects of fish swimming. *In* "Biochemical and Biophysical Perspectives in Marine Biology" (Eds Malins, D. C. and Sargent, J. R.), pp. 239–288. Academic Press, London and New York. *92, 123, 211*

*1542. Billard, R., Richard, M. and Breton, B. (1976). Stimulation of gonadotropic secretion by the hypophysis after castration of rainbow trout; variation in the response during the reproductive cycle. *C.r. hebd. Séanc. Acad. Sci. Paris,* **283,** 171–174.

1543. Bilton, H. T. and Robins, G. L. (1971a). Effects of starvation, feeding, and light period on circulus formation on scales of young sockeye salmon (*Oncorhynchus nerka*). *J. Fish. Res. Bd Can.* **28,** 1749–1755. *171*

1544. Bilton, H. T. and Robins, G. L. (1971b). Response of young sockeye salmon (*Oncorhynchus nerka*) to prolonged periods of starvation. *J. Fish. Res. Bd Can.* **28,** 1757–1761. *171*

1545. Bilton, H. T. and Robins, G. L. (1973). The effects of starvation and subsequent feeding on survival and growth of Fulton Channel sockeye salmon fry (*Oncorhynchus nerka*). *J. Fish. Res. Bd Can.* **30,** 1–5. *182*

*1546. Bishop, D. G., James, D. G. and Olley, J. (1976). Lipid composition of slender tuna (*Allothunnus fallai*) as related to lipid composition of their feed (*Nyctiphanes australis*). *J. Fish. Res. Bd Can.* **33,** 1156–1161. *142*

*1547. Black, E. C. (1957a). Alterations in the blood level of lactic acid in certain salmonoid fishes following muscular activity—1. Kamloops trout *Salmo gairdneri*. *J. Fish. Res. Bd Can.* **14,** 117–134.

*1548. Black, E. C. (1957b). Alterations in the blood level of lactic acid in certain salmonoid fishes following muscular activity—II. Lake trout, *Salvelinus namaycush*. *J. Fish. Res. Bd Can.* **14,** 645–649.

1549. Black, V. S. (1951). Changes in body chloride, density, and water content of chum (*Oncorhynchus keta*) and coho (*O. kisutch*) salmon fry when transferred from fresh water to sea water. *J. Fish. Res. Bd Can.* **8,** 164–177. *284*

*1550. Blaxhall, P. C. and Daisley, K. W. (1973). Routine haematological methods for use with fish blood. *J. Fish Biol.* **5,** 771–781.

1551. Blaxter, J. H. S. (1975). Reared and wild fish—how do they compare? *10th European Symp. on Mar. Biol., Ostend*, Sept. 17–23 1975, **1,** 11–26. *260*

1552. Blaxter, J. H. S. and Ehrlich, K. F. (1973). Changes in behaviour during starvation of herring and plaice larvae. *In* "The Early Life History of Fish" (Ed. Blaxter, J. H. S.), pp. 575–588. Spinger-Verlag, Berlin. *128, 129, 171, 182*

1553. Blaxter, J. H. S. and Tytler, P. (1972). Pressure discrimination in teleost fish. *Symp. Soc. exp. Biol.* **26,** 417–443. *242*

1554. Blaxter, J. H. S., Wardle, C. S. and Roberts, B. L. (1971). Aspects of the circulatory physiology and muscle systems of deep-sea fish. *J. mar. biol. Ass. U.K.* **51,** 991–1006. *127*

1555. Blažka, P. (1958). The anaerobic metabolism of fish. *Physiol. Zoöl.* **31,** 117–128. *271, 280*

*1556. Bleasdale, J. E., Hawthorne, J. N., Widlund, L. and Heilbronn, E. (1976). Phospholipid turnover in *Torpedo marmorata* electric organ during discharge in vivo. *Biochem. J.* **158,** 557–565.

*1557. Bligh, E. G. (1972). Mercury in Canadian fish. *J. Can. Inst. Food Sci. Technol.* **5,** A6–A14. *35*

1558. Block, R. M. (1974). Effects of acute cold shock on the Channel catfish. *AEC Symp. Series* **32,** 109–118. *232, 241*

*1559. Bogoyavlenskaya, M. P. and Vel'tishcheva, I. F. (1972). Some data on the age changes in the fat and carbohydrate metabolism of Baltic Sea cod. *Trudy vses. nauchno-issled. Inst. morsk, ryb. Khoz. Okeanogr.* **85,** 56–62. *47, 48, 53, 61*

*1560. Bohn, A. (1975). Arsenic in marine organisms from West Greenland. *Mar. Pollut. Bull.* **6,** 87–89.

*1561. Bohn, A. and McElroy, R. O. (1976). Trace metals (As, Cd, Cu, Fe, and Zn) in arctic cod, *Boreogadus saida*, and selected zooplankton from Strathcona sound, northern Baffin Island. *J. Fish. Res. Bd Can.* **33,** 2836–2840.

1562. Bokdawala, F. D. and George, J. C. (1967a). A histochemical study of the red and white muscles of the carp, *Cirrhina mrigala*. *J. Anim. Morph. Physiol.* **14,** 60–68. *73, 74, 92*

*1563. Bokdawala, F. D. and George, J. C. (1967b). A quantitative study of fat, glycogen, lipase and succinic dehydrogenase in fish muscle. *J. Anim. Morph. Physiol.* **14,** 223–230. *73, 74, 101*

1564. Bolaffi, J. L. and Booke, H. E. (1974). Temperature effects on lactate dehydrogenase isozyme distribution in skeletal muscle of *Fundulus heteroclitus* (pisces: cyprinidontiformes). *Comp. Biochem. Physiol.* **48B,** 557–564. *334*

*1565. Bolis, L. and Luly, P. (1972). Membrane lipid pattern and non-electrolytes permeability in *Salmo trutta* L. red blood cells. *Biomembranes,* **3,** 357–362.

1566. Bonaventura, J., Bonaventura, C. and Sullivan, B. (1974). Urea tolerance as a molecular adaptation of elasmobranch haemoglobins. *Science, N.Y.* **186,** 57–59.

*1567. Bonaventura, J., Gillen, R. G. and Riggs, A. (1974). The haemoglobins of the crossopterygian fish, *Latimeria chalumnae* (Smith). *Archs. Biochem. Biophys.* **163,** 728–734.

1568. Bone, Q. (1972). Buoyancy and hydrodynamic functions of integument in the castor oil fish, *Ruvettus pretiosus* (Pisces: Gempylidae). *Copeia* (1), 78–87 (no volume number given). *126*

1569. Bone, Q. and Roberts, B. L. (1969). The density of elasmobranchs. *J. mar. biol. Ass. U.K.* **49,** 913–937. *112, 127*

1570. Booke, H. E. (1968). Cytotaxonomic studies of the coregonine fishes of the great lakes, USA: DNA and karyotype analysis. *J. Fish. Res. Bd Can.* **25,** 1667–1687. *57*

1571. Booth, F. W. and Kelso, J. R. (1973). Cytochrome oxidase of skeletal muscle: adaptive response to chronic disuse. *Can. J. Physiol. Pharmacol.* **51,** 679–681. *119*

*1572. Börjeson, H. and Fellenius, E. (1976). Towards a valid technique of sampling fish muscle to determine redox substrates. *Acta physiol. scand.* **96,** 202–206.

*1573. Börjeson, H. and Höglund, L. B. (1975). Muscle and blood lactate in juvenile *Salmo salar* exposed to high pCO₂. *Rep. Inst. Freshwat. Res. Drottningholm* **54,** 5–7. *114*

1574. Börjeson, H. and Höglund, L. B. (1976). Swimbladder gas and Root effect in young salmon during hypercapnia. *Comp. Biochem. Physiol.* **54A,** 335–339. *273*

*1575. Bornancin, M. and de Renzis, G. (1972). Evolution of the branchial sodium outflux and its components, especially the Na/K exchange and the Na-K dependent ATPase activity during adaptation to sea water in *Anguilla anguilla*. *Comp. Biochem. Physiol.* **43A,** 577–591.

*1576. Bornancin, M., de Renzis, G. and Maetz, J. (1977). Branchial Cl transport, anion-stimulated ATPase and acid-base balance in *Anguilla anguilla* adapted to fresh water: effects of hyperoxia. *J. comp. Physiol.* **117B**, 313–322. *272*

*1577. Börresen, T. (1976). Isolation and characterisation of cell walls of cod muscle cells. Thesis for "Licentiatus technicae", Institute for Technical Biochemistry, Technical University, Trondheim, Norway.

*1578. Borriraja, V., Henderson, I. W. and Chester Jones, I. (1973). Renal fractions affecting the concentration of plasma cortisol in the eel. *J. Endocr.* **57**, xiii–xiv.

*1579. Boström, S.-L., Fänge, R. and Johansson, R. G. (1972). Enzyme activity patterns in gas gland tissue of the swimbladder of the cod (*Gadus morrhua*). *Comp. Biochem. Physiol.* **43B**, 473–478.

*1580. Boström, S.-L. and Johansson, R. G. (1972). Enzyme activity patterns in white and red muscle of the eel (*Anguilla anguilla*) at different developmental stages. *Comp. Biochem. Physiol.* **42B**, 533–542. *23, 72–74*

*1581. Bosund, I. and Ganrot, B. (1969). Lipid hydrolysis in frozen Baltic herring. *J. Food Sci.* **34**, 13–18.

*1582. Botta, J. R., Richards, J. F. and Tomlinson, N. (1973). Flesh pH, colour, thaw drip, and mineral concentration of Pacific halibut (*Hippoglossus stenolepis*) and chinook salmon (*Oncorhynchus tshawytscha*) frozen at sea. *J. Fish. Res. Bd Can.* **30**, 71–77.

*1583. Botta, J. R. and Shaw, D. H. (1976). Chemical and sensory analysis of roundnose grenadier (*Coryphaenoides rupestris*) stored in ice. *J. Food Sci.* **41**, 1285–1288.

*1584. Bouche, G. (1975). Researches on the nucleic acids and protein synthesis during prolonged starvation and refeeding in carp. Thesis Docteur D'Etat, mention sciences, Université Paul Sabatier de Toulouse. *197, 215, 337, 384*

1585. Bouche, G., Créac'h, Y., Lacombe, C. and Narbonne, J.-F. (1973). Starvation and refeeding in the carp (*Cyprinus carpio* L.) VI. Influence of four methods of refeeding on the nitrogen metabolism. *Archs Sci. physiol.* **27**, 25–35. *215*

1586. Bouche, G., Gas, N. and Créac'h, Y. (1969). Influence of prolonged starvation on the nucleic acids of carp (*Cyprinus carpio* L.) liver. *J. Physiol., Paris*, **61**, Suppl. 2, 230 only. *215*

1587. Bouche, G., Murat, J. C. and Parent, J. P. (1971). Study of the influence of synthetic (dietary) regimes on protein synthesis and the carbohydrate and lipid reserves in the liver of starving carp. *C. r. Séanc. Soc. Biol.* **165**, 2202–2205. *227*

1588. Bouche, G., Narbonne, J. F. and Créac'h, Y. (1972). Starvation and refeeding in carp (*Cyprinus carpio* L.). IV. Influence on the polysomes of the hepatocyte. *Archs Sci. physiol.* **26**, 111–120. *216*

1588a. Bouche, G., Narbonne, J. F. and Serfaty, A. (1972). Starvation and refeeding in carp (*Cyprinus carpio* L.). III. Influence on polysomal and ribosomal RNA and on the soluble RNA. *Archs Sci. physiol.* **26**, 101–109. *217*

1589. Bouche, G., Parent, J.-P. and Serfaty, A. (1975). Influence of two methods of rearing on the growth and body composition of the common carp (*Cyprinus carpio* L.). *J. physiol., Paris*, **70**, 659–668.

1590. Bouche, G. and Vellas, F. (1975). The speeds of renewal of the proteins of liver, muscle and plasma in carp (*Cyprinus carpio*) submitted to total and prolonged starvation. *Comp. Biochem. Physiol.* **51A**, 185–193. *196, 197*

1591. Bouche, G., Vellas, F. and Serfaty, A. (1973). Influence of total prolonged starvation followed by a period of realimentation on the nucleic acids and the proteins of the white muscle of the common carp. *C.r. Séanc. Soc. Biol.* **167**, 148–149. *168, 169, 228*

*1592. Boucher-Firly, S. (1934). Sugar, free and protein-bound, in the eel. Influence of asphyxia. *C.r. Séanc. Soc. Biol.* **116**, 6–8. From Chavin and Young 1970.

1593. Boulekbache, H., Rosenberg, A.-J. and Joly, C. (1970). Isoenzymes of lactic dehydrogenase in the course of early stages of development of the egg of trout (*Salmo irideus*, Gibb). *C.r. hebd. Séanc. Acad. Sci., Paris*, **271**, 2414–2417. *17*

*1594. Boyd, T. A., Cha, C.-J., Forster, R. P. and Goldstein, L. (1977). Free amino acids in tissues of the skate *Raja erinacea* and the stingray *Dasyatis sabina*: effects of environmental dilution. *J. exp. Zool.* **199**, 435–442. *312*

*1595. Boyer, J. L. (1971). A comparative study of the composition of hepatic and gallbladder bile in *Squalus acanthias*. *Bull. Mt. Desert Isl. biol. Lab.* **11**, 4–5. *164, 225*

*1596. Boyer, J. L., Schwartz, J. and Smith, N. (1976). Biliary secretion in elasmobranchs. I. Bile collection and composition. *Am. J. Physiol.* **230**, 970–973. *164, 165*

*1597. Braddock, R. J. and Dugan, L. R. (1969). Fatty acids of Lake Michigan coho salmon. *J. Am. Oil Chem. Soc.* **46**, 428 only.

1598. Braekkan, O. R., Ingebrigtsen, O. and Myklestad, H. (1969). Uptake and storage of vitamin A in rainbow trout. *Int. Z. VitamForsch.* **39**, 123–130. *463*

1599. Bratland, P., Krishnan, S. and Sundnes, G. (1976). Studies on the long term storage of living saithe, *Pollachius virens* Linnaeus, 1758. *FiskDir. Skr. Serie Havundersøkelser*, **16**, 279–300. *93*

1600. Braune, H. J. and Gronow, G. (1975). Temperature as a stressor in *Idus idus* L. (Teleostei). *Zool. Anz.* **194**, 22–34. *237*

1601. Brawn, V. M. (1969a). Buoyancy of Atlantic and Pacific herring. *J. Fish. Res. Bd Can.* **26**, 2077–2091. *124*

1602. Brawn, V. M. (1969b). Feeding behaviour of cod (*Gadus morhua*). *J. Fish. Res. Bd Can.* **26,** 583–596. *134*

*1603. Breckenridge, W. C. and Vincendon, G. (1971). Docosahexaenoic acid in the electric organ of the torpedo. *C. r. hebd. Séanc. Acad. Sci., Paris*, **273,** 1337–1339.

1604. Breder, C. M. and Bird, P. M. (1975). Cave entry by schools and associated pigmentary changes of the marine clupeid, *Jenkinsia. Bull. mar. Sci.* **25,** 377–386. *264*

1605. Breer, H. (1974). Possible correlations between body temperature and brain ganglioside pattern. *IRCS: Library Compendium*, **2,** 1619 only. *340*

1606. Breer, H. (1975). Ganglioside pattern and thermal tolerance of fish species. *Life Sci.* **16,** 1459–1464. *340*

*1607. Breer, H. and Rahmann, H. (1974). Temperature effect on brain glycogen of fish. *Brain Res.* **74,** 360–365. *344*

1608. Breer, H. and Rahmann, H. (1976). Involvement of brain gangliosides in temperature adaptation of fish. *J. therm. Biol.* **1,** 233–235. *340*

1609. Brehe, J. E. (1974). A study of calcium metabolism in *Fundulus kansae*, a teleost with acellular bone. Ph.D. Thesis, University of Missouri. University Microfilm no. 75–15,971.

*1610. Breton, B. and Billard, R. (1977). Effects of photoperiod and temperature on plasma gonadotropin and spermatogenesis in the rainbow trout *Salmo gairdnerii* Richardson. *Annls Biol. anim. Biochem. Biophys.* **17,** 331–340. *36, 249*

1611. Brett, J. R. (1972). The metabolic demand for oxygen in fish, particularly salmonids, and a comparison with other vetebrates. *Resp. Physiol.* **14,** 151–170. *2, 383*

1612. Brett, J. R., Shelbourn, J. E. and Shoop, C. T. (1969). Growth rate and body composition of fingerling sockeye salmon, *Oncorhynchus nerka*, in relation to temperature and ration size. *J. Fish. Res. Bd Can.* **26,** 2363–2394. *325*

1613. Brett, J. R. and Zala, C. A. (1975). Daily pattern of nitrogen excretion and oxygen consumption of sockeye salmon (*Oncorhynchus nerka*) under controlled conditions. *J. Fish. Res. Bd Can.* **32,** 2479–2486. *163, 170*

1614. Bridges, C. D. B. (1967a). Photopigments in the char of Lake Windermere (*Salvelinus willughbii* Günther), forma autumnalis and forma vernalis. *Nature, Lond.* **214,** 205–206. *267*

1615. Bridges, C. D. B. (1967b). Spectroscopic properties of porphyropsins. *Vision Res.* **7,** 349–369. *266*

1616. Bridges, C. D. B. (1969). Yellow corneas in fishes. *Vision Res.* **9,** 435–436. *265*

1617. Bridges, C. D. B. and Delisle, C. E. (1974). Postglacial evolution of the visual pigments of the smelt, *Osmerus eperlanus mordax*. *Vision Res.* **14**, 345–356. *268*

1618. Bridges, C. D. B. and Yoshikami, S. (1970a). The rhodopsin-porphyropsin system in freshwater fishes—I. Effects of age and photic environment. *Vision Res.* **10**, 1315–1332. *63, 267–269*

1619. Bridges, C. D. B. and Yoshikami, S. (1970b). The rhodopsin-porphyropsin system in freshwater fishes—2. Turnover and interconversion of visual pigment prosthetic groups in light and darkness: role of the pigment epithelium. *Vision Res.* **10**, 1333–1345. *268*

*1620. Brisson, A., Marchelidon, J. and Lachiver, F. (1974). Comparative studies on the amino acid composition of thyroglobulins from various lower and higher vertebrates: phylogenetic aspects. *Comp. Biochem. Physiol.* **49B**, 51–63.

1621. Brizinova, P. N. and Strel'tsova, S. V. (1969). Intensity of digestion of the protein component of food by *Salmo irideus*. *Izv. gos. nauchno-issled. Inst. ozern. rechn. ryb. Khoz.* **68**, 46–59. From *Chem. Abstr.* **73**, 117837b (1970). *151*

*1622. Brooks, R. R., Lewis, J. R. and Reeves, R. D. (1976). Mercury and other heavy metals in trout of central North Island, New Zealand. *N.Z. J. Mar. Freshwat. Res.* **10**, 233–244.

1623. Brotchi, J. (1968). Histo-enzymological identification of slow and rapid fibres of skeletal vertebrate muscles. *Archs int. Physiol. Biochim.* **76**, 299–310. *75*

1624. Brothers, E. B., Mathews, C. P. and Lasker, R. (1976). Daily growth increments in otoliths from larval and adult fishes. *Fishery Bull. Natl. Oceanic Atmos. Adm. (US).* **74**, 1–8. *373*

*1625. Brown, E. A. B. and Trams, E. G. (1968). Catecholamine metabolism in elasmobranch interrenal body. *Comp. Biochem. Physiol.* **25**, 1099–1105.

1626. Brown, G. W. and Cohen, P. P. (1960). Comparative biochemistry of urea synthesis. 3. Activities of urea-cycle enzymes in various higher and lower vertebrates. *Biochem. J.* **75**, 82–91. *161*

*1627. Brungs, W. A., Leonard, E. N. and McKim, J. M. (1973). Acute and long-term accumulation of copper by the brown bullhead, *Ictalurus nebulosus*. *J. Fish. Res. Bd Can.* **30**, 583–586.

1628. Brunori, M. (1975). Molecular adaptation to physiological requirements: the haemoglobin system of trout. *Curr. Top. cell. Regul.* **9**, 1–39. *122, 123*

1629. Bryan, J. E. and Larkin, P. A. (1972). Food specialisation by individual trout. *J. Fish. Res. Bd Can.* **29**, 1615–1624. *134*

1630. Buell, J. W. (1973). Argon-nitrogen ratios in the swimbladder gas of physostomous fishes with particular reference to the rainbow trout, *Salmo gairdnerii*. Ph.D. Thesis, Oregon University. *261*

*1631. Bugdahl, V. and von Jan, E. (1975). Quantitative determination of trace metals in frozen fish, fish oil and fish meal. *Z. lebensmittelunters. u. Forsch.* **157,** 133–140.

*1632. Buhler, D. R., Stokes, R. M. and Caldwell, R. S. (1977). Tissue accumulation and enzymatic effects of hexavalent chromium in rainbow trout (*Salmo gairdneri*). *J. Fish. Res. Bd Can.* **34,** 9–18.

*1633. Bull, J. M. and Morris, R. (1967). Studies on freshwater osmoregulation in the ammocoete larva of *Lampetra planeri* (Bloch). I. Ionic constituents, fluid compartments, ionic compartments and water balance. *J. exp. Biol.* **47,** 485–494.

 1634. Bulow, F. J. (1969). Biochemical indicators of recent growth of fishes: RNA and DNA. Ph.D. Thesis, Iowa State University, University Microfilm no. 69–15,600. *216*

 1635. Bulow, F. J. (1970). RNA-DNA ratios as indicators of recent growth rates of a fish. *J. Fish. Res. Bd Can.* **27,** 2343–2349.

*1636. Burger, J. W. (1967). Problems in the electrolyte economy of the spiny dogfish, *Squalus acanthias*. *In* "Sharks, Skates and Rays" (Eds Gilbert, P. W., Mathewson, R. F. and Rall, D. P.), pp. 177–185. The Johns Hopkins Press, Baltimore.

*1637. Burger, J. W. and Hess, W. N. (1960). Function of the rectal gland in the spiny dogfish. *Science, N.Y.* **131,** 670–671. *309*

*1638. Burt, J. R. (1971). Changes in sugar phosphate and lactate concentration in trawled cod (*Gadus callarias*) muscle during frozen storage. *J. Sci. Fd Agric.* **22,** 536–539.

*1639. Burton, D. T. and Spehar, A. M. (1971). A re-evaluation of the anaerobic endproducts of fresh-water fish exposed to environmental hypoxia. *Comp. Biochem. Physiol.* **40A,** 945–954. *280*

*1640. Butler, D. G. (1968). Hormonal control of gluconeogenesis in the North American eel (*Anguilla rostrata*). *Gen. Comp. Endocr.* **10,** 85–91. *3, 37, 188*

*1641. Butler, D. G. (1969). Corpuscles of Stannius and renal physiology in the eel (*Anguilla rostrata*). *J. Fish. Res. Bd Can.* **26,** 639–654.

*1642. Butler, D. G. and Carmichael, F. J. (1972). (Na$^+$-K$^+$)-ATPase activity in the eel (*Anguilla rostrata*) gills in relation to changes in environmental salinity: role of adrenocortical steroids. *Gen. comp. Endocr.* **19,** 421–427. *291, 302*

 1643. Butler, J. L. and Pearcy, W. G. (1972). Swimbladder morphology and specific gravity of myctophids off Oregon. *J. Fish. Res. Bd Can.* **29,** 1145–1150. *120*

 1644. Bykov, V. P. (1969). Dependence of certain physico-chemical properties of raw fish upon the condition of the fish when alive. *Ryb. Khoz.* **45,** 70–71. *68*

1645. Cahill, G. F., Owen, O. E., Felig, P. and Morgan, A. P. (1969). The endocrine control of metabolism during fasting. *In* "Progress in Endocrinology" (Eds Gual, C. and Ebling, F. J. G.), pp. 148–151. Excerpta Medica Foundation, Amsterdam. 148–151. *188*

1646. Caldwell, R. S. (1969). Thermal compensation of respiratory enzymes in tissues of the goldfish. *Comp. Biochem. Physiol.* **31,** 79–93. *328, 329*

*1647. Cameron, J. N. (1970a). Blood characteristics of some marine fishes of the Texas Gulf coast. *Tex. J. Sci.* **21,** 275–283. *110*

1648. Cameron, J. N. (1970b). The influence of environmental variables on the haematology of pinfish (*Lagodon rhomboides*) and striped mullet (*Mugil cephalus*). *Comp. Biochem. Physiol.* **32,** 175–192. *276, 327*

1649. Cameron, J. N. (1971). Methaemoglobin in erythrocytes of rainbow trout. *Comp. Biochem. Physiol.* **40A,** 743–749. *259*

1650. Cameron, J. N. (1975). Blood flow distribution as indicated by tracer microspheres in resting and hypoxic arctic Grayling (*Thymallus arcticus*). *Comp. Biochem. Physiol.* **52A,** 441–444. *77, 78*

1651. Campbell, C. M. and Davies, P. S. (1975). Thermal acclimation in the teleost, *Blennius pholis* (L). *Comp. Biochem. Physiol.* **52A,** 147–151. *169*

*1652. Campbell, C. M., Walsh, J. M. and Idler, D. R. (1976). Steroids in the plasma of the winter flounder (*Pseudopleuronectes americanus* Walbaum). A seasonal study and investigation of steroid involvement in oocyte maturation. *Gen. comp. Endocr.* **29,** 14–20. *37*

*1653. Campbell, J. W. (1961). Studies on tissue arginase and ureogenesis in the elasmobranch, *Mustelus canis*. *Archs Biochem. Biophys.* **93,** 448–455.

1654. Campbell, S. and Love, R. M. (1978). Energy reserves of male and female haddock (*Melanogrammus aeglefinus* L.) from the Moray Firth. *J. Cons. int. Explor. Mer* **38,** 120–121. *52*

*1655. Cantoni, C., Beretta, G. and Calcinardi, C. (1975). Observations on the amino acids of flesh and skin of freshwater fishes. *Archo vet. ital.* **26,** 87–91.

*1656. Cantoni, C., Bianchi, M. A. and Beretta, G. (1976). Formaldehyde contents in fishes, molluscs and crustacea caught in the Mediterranean Sea. *Archo vet. ital.* **27,** 145–148.

*1657. Cantoni, C., Bianchi, M. A., Renon, P. and Beretta, G. (1975). Caviar, substitute products and gonads of salmonid fishes. *Archo vet. ital.* **26,** 181–187.

1658. Carbery, J. T. (1970). Correlation between total serum protein and albumin/globulin ratio in malnourished brown trout. *Vet. Rec.* **87,** 175 only. *193*

1659. Carey, F. G. and Lawson, K. D. (1973). Temperature regulation in free-swimming bluefin tuna. *Comp. Biochem. Physiol.* **44A,** 375–392. *322*

1660. Carey, F. G. and Teal, J. M. (1969a). Mako and porbeagle: warm-bodied sharks. *Comp. Biochem. Physiol.* **28,** 199–204. *78, 321, 322*

1661. Carey, F. G. and Teal, J. M. (1969b). Regulation of body temperature by the bluefin tuna. *Comp. Biochem. Physiol.* **28,** 205–213. *322*

1662. Carey, F. G., Teal, J. M., Kanwisher, J. W., Lawson, K. D. and Beckett, J. S. (1971). Warm-bodied fish. *Am. Zool.* **11,** 135–143. *322*

1663. Carey, F. G., Teal, J. M. and Kleijn, K. (1972). Body temperatures of black-tip sharks *Carcharhinus limbatus*. *Deep Sea Res.* **19,** 179–181. *322*

1664. Carlisky, N. J. and Barrio, A. (1972). Nitrogen metabolism of the South American lungfish *Lepidosiren paradoxa*. *Comp. Biochem. Physiol.* **41B,** 857–873. *154*

1665. Carmichael, D. J. and Lawrie, R. A. (1967). Bovine collagen. I. Changes in collagen solubility with animal age. *J. Food Technol.* **2,** 299–311. *205*

*1666. Carrier, J. C. and Evans, D. H. (1972). Ion, water and urea turnover rates in the nurse shark, *Ginglymostoma cirrhatum*. *Comp. Biochem. Physiol.* **41A,** 761–764.

1667. Carrier, J. C. and Evans, D. H. (1976). The role of environmental calcium in freshwater survival of the marine teleost, *Lagodon rhomboides*. *J. exp. Biol.* **65,** 529–538. *289*

*1668. Carter, N., Auton, J. and Dando, P. (1976). Red cell carbonic anhydrase levels in flounders, *Platichthys flesus* L., from salt water and fresh water. *Comp. Biochem. Physiol.* **55B,** 399–401.

*1669. Casillas, E. and Smith, L. S. (1977). Effect of stress on blood coagulation and haematology in rainbow trout (*Salmo gairdneri*). *J. Fish Biol.* **10,** 481–491.

1670. Castell, C. H. and Bishop, D. M. (1973). Effect of season on salt-extractable protein in muscle from trawler-caught cod and on its stability during frozen storage. *J. Fish. Res. Bd Can.* **30,** 157–160. *97*

*1671. Castell, C. H., Smith, B. and Dyer, W. J. (1973). Effects of formaldehyde on salt extractable proteins of gadoid muscle. *J. Fish. Res. Bd Can.* **30,** 1205–1213

1672. Castell, J. D., Lee, D. J. and Sinnhuber, R. O. (1972). Essential fatty acids in the diet of rainbow trout (*Salmo gairdneri*): lipid metabolism and fatty acid composition. *J. Nutr.* **102,** 93–100. *142*

1673. Castilla, C. and Murat, J.-C. (1975). Effects of insulin on protein in carp liver. *C.r. Séanc. Soc. biol. Toulouse,* **169,** 1605–1608. *430*

*1674. Catlett, R. H. and Millich, D. R. (1976). Intracellular and extracellular osmoregulation of temperature acclimated goldfish: *Carassius auratus* L. *Comp. Biochem. Physiol.* **55A**, 261–269. *343*

1675. Cattell, S. A. (1973). The seasonal cycle of vitamin B_{12} in the Strait of Georgia, British Columbia. *J. Fish. Res. Bd Can.* **30**, 215–222. *149*

1676. Cech, J. J., Rowell, D. M. and Glasgow, J. S. (1977). Cardiovascular responses of the winter flounder *Pseudopleuronectes americanus* to hypoxia. *Comp. Biochem. Physiol.* **57A**, 123–125. *273*

1677. Cech, J. J. and Wohlschlag, D. E. (1973). Respiratory responses of the striped mullet, *Mugil cephalus* (L.) to hypoxic conditions. *J. Fish. Biol.* **5**, 421–428. *273*

*1678. Čejková, J., and Bolková, A. (1973). Acid mucopolysaccharides in non-swelling dogfish corneas. *Ophthalmic Res.* **5**, 362–370.

1679. Chaikovskaya, A. V. (1974). On the amino acid composition of mucous matter of some species of Black Sea fishes. *Bionika Resp. Mezlved Sb.* (8), 145–148 (no volume number given). *112*

*1680. Chako, G. K., Goldman, D. E. and Pennock, B. E. (1972). Composition and characterisation of the lipids of garfish (*Lepisosteus osseus*) olfactory nerve, a tissue rich in axonal membrane. *Biochim. biophys. Acta*, **280**, 1–16.

*1681. Chan, D. K. O. and Wong, T. M. (1977). Physiological adjustments to dilution of the external medium in the lip-shark, *Hemiscyllium plagiosum* (Bennett). 1. Size of body compartments and osmolyte composition. *J. exp. Zool.* **200**, 71–84.

1682. Chapman, C. J. and Hawkins, A. D. (1973). A field study of hearing in the cod, *Gadus morhua* L. *J. comp. Physiol.* **85**, 147–167. *242*

1683. Charlon, N. (1969). Relation between respiratory metabolism in fish, oxygen level and temperature. *Bull. Soc. Hist. nat. Toulouse* **105**, 136–156. *320*

1684. Charlon, N., Barbier, B. and Bonnet, L. (1970). Resistance of rainbow trout (*Salmo gairdneri* Richardson) to sudden variations in temperature. *Ann. Hydrobiol.* **1**, 73–89. *323*

*1685. Chauvet, J.-P. and Acher, R. (1972). Isolation of coelacanth (*Latimeria chalumnae*) myoglobin. *FEBS Lett.* **28**, 16–18.

*1686. Chavin, W. (1964). Sensitivity of fish to environmental alterations. *Publs gt. Lakes Res. Div.* **11**, 54–67. *232, 236*

*1687. Chavin, W. (1973). Teleostean endocrine and paraendocrine alterations of utility in environmental studies. *In* "Responses of Fish to Environmental Changes" (Ed. Chavin, W.), Chapter 6, pp. 199–239. Charles C. Thomas, Springfield, Illinois. *231, 232, 238, 302, 383*

*1688. Chavin, W. and Singley, J. A. (1972). Adrenocorticoids of the goldfish, *Carassius auratus* L. *Comp. Biochem. Physiol.* **42B,** 547–562.

*1689. Chavin, W. and Young, J. E. (1970). Factors in the determination of normal serum glucose levels of goldfish, *Carassius auratus* L. *Comp. Biochem. Physiol.* **33,** 629–653. *34, 191, 232*

*1690. Chepurnov, A. V. and Tkachenko, N. K. (1973). Changes in the lipid composition of females and males of the Black Sea round goby (*Neogobius melanostomus*) in the spawning period and in early ontogenesis. *Communications of the all-Union symposium on the study of the Black and Mediterranean Seas and the utilisation and preservation of their resources. Part 1. Biological and ecological-physiological studies of fishes and invertebrates.* pp. 212–216. Sevastopol. *Izdat. Naukova Dumka, Kiev.* *13, 51, 53*

*1691. Chepurnov, A. V. and Tkachenko, N. K. (1974). Quantitative and qualitative characteristics of lipids in spawning females and progeny during embryonic development of *Gobius melanostomus* from the Sea of Azov. *Akad. Nauk Ukrain SSR Ordena Trudovogo Krasnogo Znameni Inti. Biol. Yuzhnykh Morei (Biol. Prod. Yuzn. Morei)*, 200–206.

1692. Chernyshov, V. I., Yakubov, S. M., Kozlov, Yu. P. and Tarusov, B. N. (1972). The role of lipid antioxidants in the appearance of various physiological characteristics of fish organs. *Nauch. Dokl. vyssh. Shk. Biologisheskie Nauki*, (2), 40–45. *34, 317*

1693. Cherry, D. S., Dickson, K. L. and Cairns, J. (1975). Temperatures selected and avoided by fish at various acclimation temperatures. *J. Fish. Res. Bd Can.* **32,** 485–491. *323*

1694. Chester Jones, I., Ball, J. N., Henderson, I. W., Sandor, T. and Baker, B. I. (1974). Endocrinology of fishes. *In* "Chemical Zoology" (Eds Florkin, M. and Schaer, B. T.), vol. 8, Chapter 14, pp. 523–593. Academic Press, London and New York. *188*

1695. Chidambaram, S., Meyer, R. K. and Hasler A. D. (1972). Effects of hypophysectomy, pituitary autografts, prolactin, temperature and salinity of the medium on survival and natraemia in the bullhead, *Ictalurus melas*. *Comp. Biochem. Physiol.* **43A,** 443–457. *299*

1696. Childress, J. J. and Nygaard, M. H. (1973). The chemical composition of midwater fishes as a function of depth of occurrence off southern California. *Deep Sea Res.* **20,** 1093–1109. *127*

*1697. Childs, E. A. and Gaffke, J. N. (1973). Mercury content of Oregon groundfish. *Fish. Bull. Natl. Oceanic Atmos. Adm. (US)*, **71,** 713–717. *35*

*1698. Chlebeck, A. and Phillips, G. L. (1969). Haematological study of two buffalofishes, *Ictiobus cyprinellus* and *I. bubalus* (Catostomidae). *J. Fish. Res. Bd Can.* **26,** 2881–2886.

1699. Cho, C.Y., Slinger, S. J. and Bayley, H. S. (1976). Influence of level and type of dietary protein, and of level of feeding on feed utilisation by rainbow trout. *J. Nutr.* **106,** 1547–1556. *258*

*1700. Cholette, C. and Gagnon, A. (1973). Isosmotic adaptation in *Myxine glutinosa* L.—II. Variations of the free amino acids, trimethylamine oxide and potassium of the blood and muscle cells. *Comp. Biochem. Physiol.* **45A,** 1009–1021. *313*

1701. Cholette, C., Gagnon, A. and Germain, P. (1970). Isosmotic adaptation in *Myxine glutinosa* L.—1. Variations of some parameters and role of the amino acid pool of the muscle cells. *Comp. Biochem. Physiol.* **33,** 333–346. *312*

*1702. Christensen, G. M., McKim, J. M., Brungs, W. A. and Hunt, E. P. (1972). Changes in the blood of the brown bullhead (*Ictalurus nebulosus* (Lesueur)) following the short and long term exposure to copper (II). *Toxic. appl. Pharmac.* **23,** 417–427.

*1703. Christomanos, A. and Reinhard, F. (1973). Amino acid composition of the haemoglobin of the lungfish, *Protopterus aethiopicus.* *Folia Biochim. Biol. Graeca* **10,** 29–30. From *Chem. Abstr.* **80,** 129517e (1974).

*1704. Chuiko, V. A. (1968). The content of glucocorticoids in plasma of fishes from the Black Sea. *Zh. Evol. Biokhim. Fiziol.* **4,** 384–386. *112*

*1705. Cimino, M. C. (1974). The nuclear DNA content of diploid and triploid *Poeciliopsis* and other Poeciliid fishes with reference to the evolution of unisexual forms. *Chromosoma,* **47,** 297–307.

*1706. Cimino, M. C. and Bahr, G. F. (1973). The nuclear DNA content and chromatin ultrastructure of the coelacanth *Latimeria chalumnae.* *J. Cell Biol.* **59,** 55A only. (*Note:* the same values for chemical composition were quoted again in *Expl Cell Res.* **88,** 263–272 (1974)).

*1707. Ciusa, W., D'Arrigo, V. and Giaccio, M. (1976). Research on the content of trace elements of several species of fish caught in the Adriatic from Termoli to Split. *Quad. Merceol.* **15,** 155–172.

*1708. Ciusa, W. and Giaccio, M. (1972). The content of trace elements of some fish species from the Adriatic in relation to the presence of industrial wastes. *Boll. Laboratori chim. prov.* **23,** 137–145.

*1709. Ciusa, W., Giaccio, M., di Donato, F. and Lucianetti, L. (1973). II. Content of copper, zinc, cadmium, mercury and lead in some species of fish from the Tyrrhenian Sea. *Quad. Merceol.* **12,** 33–48.

1710. Clayden, A. D. (1972). Simulation of the changes in abundance of the cod (*Gadus morhua* L.) and the distribution of fishing in the North Atlantic. *Fishery Invest., Lond. Ser. 2,* **27** (1), 58 pp. *247*

*1711. Cleere, W. F., Bree, S. and Coughlan, M. P. (1976). Urate oxidase and xanthine dehydrogenase activities in liver extracts from fish caught in Irish waters. *Comp. Biochem. Physiol.* **54B,** 117–119.

*1712. Clément, J., Lecerf, J. and Fontaine, M. (1970). Lipid constituents of the Corpuscles of Stannius in *Anguilla anguilla* L. and *Salmo salar* L. *Annls Biol. anim. Biochim. Biophys.* **10,** 631–642.

*1713. de Clerck, R., Vanderstappen, R. and Vyncke, W. (1974). Mercury content of fish and shrimps caught off the Belgian coast. *Ocean Manage.* **2,** 117–126. *437*

*1714. Cobb, J. L. S., Fox, N. C. and Santer, R. M. (1973). A specific ringer solution for the plaice (*Pleuronectes platessa* L.). *J. Fish Biol.* **5,** 587–591.

*1715. Cocoros, G., Cahn, P. H. and Siler, W. (1973). Mercury concentrations in fish, plankton and water from three western Atlantic estuaries. *J. Fish Biol.* **5,** 641–647.

*1716. van Coillie, R. and Rousseau, A. (1974). Distribution of minerals in the scales of freshwater fish and its relations with the surrounding water. *Verh. int. Verein. theor. angew. Limnol.* **19,** 2440–2447.

*1717. Cole, D. F. (1973). Intraocular fluid composition in the coelacanth, *Latimeria chalumnae*. *Expl Eye Res.* **16,** 389–395.

 1718. Coleman, R. (1973). Phospholipids and the hepato-portal system. *In* "Form and Function of Phospholipids" (Eds Ansell, G. B. Hawthorne, J. N. and Dawson, R. M. C.), Chapter 13, pp. 345–375. Elsevier, Amsterdam. *208*

*1719. Colin, D. A. (1972). Relationship between the nature of the food and the importance of chitinolytic activity of the alimentary canal in several marine teleosts. *C. r. Séanc. Soc. Biol.* **166,** 95–98. *152*

*1720. Colley, L., Fox, F. R. and Huggins, A. K. (1974). The effect of changes in external salinity on the non-protein nitrogenous constituents of parietal muscle from *Agonus cataphractus*. *Comp. Biochem. Physiol.* **48A,** 757–763. *313*

 1721. Colley, L. and Huggins, A. K. (1970). The non-protein nitrogenous constituents in the parietal muscle of the eel *Anguilla anguilla* and their possible role in adaptation to changes in salinity. *Biochem. J.* **117,** 41p–42p. *313*

 1722. Conant, E. B. (1973). Regeneration in the African lungfish, *Protopterus*. III. Regeneration during fasting and aestivation. *Biol. Bull.* **144,** 248–261. *169*

 1723. Connell, D. W. (1974). A kerosene-like taint in the sea mullet, *Mugil cephalus* (Linnaeus). 1. Composition and environmental occurrence of the tainting substance. *Aust. J. Mar. Freshwat. Res.* **25,** 7–24. *247*

 1724. Connell, J. J. and Howgate, P. F. (1969). Sensory and objective measurement of the quality of frozen stored haddock of different initial freshnesses. *J. Sci. Fd Agric.* **20,** 469–476. *367*

*1725. Connor, A. R., Elling, C. H., Black, E. C., Collins, G. B., Gauley, J. R. and Trevor-Smith, E. (1964). Changes in glycogen and lactate levels in migrating salmonid fishes ascending experimental "endless" fishways. *J. Fish. Res. Bd Can.* **21,** 255–290. *48*

1726. Conte, F. P. (1969). Salt secretion. *In* "Fish Physiology" (Eds Hoar, W. S. and Randall, D. J.), vol. 1, Chapter 3, 241–292. Academic Press, London and New York. This reference was quoted in my Volume 1 as being "in the press". *287*

*1727. Conte, F. P. and Tripp, M. J. (1970). Succinic acid dehydrogenase activity in the gill epithelium of euryhaline fishes. *Int. J. Biochem.* **1,** 129–138.

1728. Conte, F. P., Wagner, H. H. and Harris, T. O. (1963). Measurement of blood volume in the fish (*Salmo gairdneri gairdneri*). *Am. J. Physiol.* **205,** 533–540. *2*

*1729. Copp, D. H. (1976). Comparative endocrinology of calcitonin. *In* "Handbook of Physiology; Section 7: Endocrinology" (Eds Greep, R. O. and Astwood, E. B.), pp. 431–442. American Physiological Society, Washington DC. *286*

1730. Corner, E. D. S., Denton, E. J. and Forster, G. R. (1969). On the buoyancy of some deep-sea sharks. *Proc. R. Soc.* **B171,** 415–429. *125*

*1731. Cortesi, P., Borgatti, A. R., Crisetig, G. and Mancini, L. (1969). Free fatty acids in fresh muscles of clupeiformes of the Adriatic Sea and their significance in relation to frozen storage. *Atti Soc. ital. Sci. vet.* **23,** 853–857.

1732. Couillault, J. (1967). Variations in the concentration of total chloride in the minnow, (*Phoxinus phoxinus* L.). *C. r. Séanc. Soc. Biol.* **161,** 2251–2254. *286*

1733. Coulter, G. W. (1967). Low apparent oxygen requirements of deep-water fishes in Lake Tanganyika. *Nature, Lond.* **215,** 317–318. *270*

*1734. Courtois, L. A. (1975). Blood and serum analysis of adult striped bass, *Morone saxatilis*, captured in the Sacramento River. *Calif. Fish Game* **61,** 245–246.

*1735. Courtois, L. A. (1976). Haematology of juvenile striped bass, *Morone saxatilis* (Walbaum), acclimated to different environmental conditions. *Comp. Biochem. Physiol.* **54A,** 221–223.

1736. Coutant, C. C. (1977). Compilation of temperature preference data. *J. Fish. Res. Bd Can.* **34,** 739–745. *322, 470*

1737. Covert, J. B. and Reynolds, W. W. (1977). Survival value of fever in fish. *Nature, Lond.* **267,** 43–45. *324*

*1738. Cowey, C. B. (1976). Use of synthetic diets and biochemical criteria in the assessment of nutrient requirements of fish. *J. Fish. Res. Bd Can.* **33,** 1040–1045.

*1739. Cowey, C. B., Brown, D. A., Adron, J. W. and Shanks, A. M. (1974). Studies on the nutrition of marine flatfish. The effect of dietary protein content on certain cell components and enzymes in the liver of *Pleuronectes platessa. Mar. Biol.* **28,** 207–213. *137 257*

*1740. Cowey, C. B., Coombs, T. L. and Adron, J. W. (1976). The renal and serum concentrations of calcium, magnesium and phosphorus in captive and wild turbot (*Scophthalmus maximus*). *Mar. Biol.* **38,** 111–115. *260*

1741. Cowey, C. B., Lush, I. E. and Knox, D. (1969). Studies on crystalline lactate dehydrogenase from cardiac and skeletal muscle of plaice (*Pleuronectes platessa*) with particular reference to temperature. *Biochim. Biophys. Acta*, **191**, 205–213. *111*

1742. Cowey, C. B. and Sargent, J. R. (1972). Fish nutrition. *Adv. Mar. Biol.* **10**, 383–492. *140, 146*

1743. Cowie, W. P. and Little, W. T. (1966). The relationship between the toughness of cod stored at −29°C and its muscle protein solubility and pH. *J. Food Technol.* **1**, 335–343. *360*

*1744. Crabtree, B. and Newsholme, E. A. (1972). The activities of phosphorylase, hexokinase, phosphofructokinase, lactate dehydrogenase and the glycerol-3-phosphate dehydrogenases in muscles from vertebrates and invertebrates. *Biochem. J.* **126**, 49–58. *92*

*1745. Crawford, L., Irwin, E. J., Spinelli, J. and Brown, W. D. (1970). Premortem stress and postmortem biochemical changes in skipjack tuna and their relation to quality of the canned product. *J. Food Sci.* **35**, 849–851.

1746. Crawshaw, L. I. (1977). Physiological and behavioural reactions of fishes to temperature change. *J. Fish. Res. Bd Can.* **34**, 730–734. *326*

1747. Crawshaw, L. I. and Hammel, H. T. (1974). Behavioural regulation of internal temperature in the brown bullhead, *Ictalurus nebulosus*. *Comp. Biochem. Physiol.* **47A**, 51–60. *323*

*1748. Créac'h, Y. (1963). Soluble thiols and thiol proteins in the mirror carp (*Cyprinus carpio* L.). *C. r. Séanc. Soc. Biol.* **157**, 2093–2096.

*1749. Créac'h, Y. (1972). Experimental starvation in carp: nitrogen metabolism and hydromineral equilibrium. Thesis Docteur ès-sciences naturelles, University Paul Sabatier de Toulouse. *167, 168, 171, 172, 194, 196, 200, 201, 222, 227, 229, 364*

*1750. Créac'h, Y. and Bouche, G. (1969). Influence of prolonged starvation on the composition of the blood of the carp (*Cyprinus carpio* L.). *Rech. Hydrobiol. Continentale* 51–60 (no volume number). *213*

1751. Créac'h, Y. and Gas, N. (1971). Some biochemical and structural changes in the muscle of carp undergoing starvation. *J. Physiol., Paris*, **63**, 33 only. *189, 199*

*1752. Créac'h, Y. and Murat, J. C. (1974). Starvation and refeeding in carp (*Cyprinus carpio* L.): VII. Metabolism of glucose-1-^{14}C and of glucose-6-^{14}C. *Archs Sci. physiol.* **28**, 157–172. *3, 141, 182, 228*

*1753. Créac'h, Y., Murat, J.-C. and Bouche, G. (1970). Starvation and refeeding in the carp (*Cyprinus carpio*). II. Importance of electrolytic factors. *Archs Sci. physiol.* **24**, 253–266. *172, 189*

1754. Créac'h, Y., Nopoly, L. and Serfaty, A. (1969). Variations in the proteolytic activity of tissues of the common carp (*Cyprinus carpio*) during a prolonged fast. *Archs Sci. physiol.* **23,** 351–364. *195*

1755. Créac'h, Y. and Serfaty, A. (1974). Starvation and refeeding in the carp (*Cyprinus carpio* L.). *J. Physiol., Paris,* **68,** 245–260. *189*

*1756. Créac'h, Y., Serfaty, A. and Vellas, F. (1969). Peptidase activities in the carp (*Cyprinus carpio*). Tissue localisation and effect of fasting. *C. r. Séanc. Soc. Biol.* **163,** 1217–1220. *195*

1757. Créac'h, Y., Vellas, F., Bouche, G. and Serfaty, A. (1971). Loss of nitrogen in carp (*Cyprinus carpio* L.) during prolonged starvation. *J. Physiol., Paris,* **63,** 683–688. *218*

1758. Crescitelli, F. (1969). The visual pigment of a chimaeroid fish. *Vision Res.* **9,** 1407–1414. *266*

*1759. Crim, L. W., Meyer, R. K. and Donaldson, E. M. (1973). Radioimmunoassay estimates of plasma gonadotrophin levels in the spawning pink salmon. *Gen. comp. Endocr.* **21,** 69 76. *18*

*1760. Crim, L. W., Watts, E. G. and Evans, D. M. (1975). The plasma gonadotrophin profile during sexual maturation in a variety of salmonoid fishes. *Gen. comp. Endocr.* **27,** 62–70. *37*

1761. Cristy, M. (1974). Effects of prolactin and thyroxine on the visual pigments of trout, *Salmo gairdneri. Gen. comp. Endocr.* **23,** 58–62. *7, 269*

1762. Cristy, M. (1976). Effects of temperature and light intensity on the visual pigments of rainbow trout. *Vision Res.* **16,** 1225–1228. *268*

*1763. Cross, F. A., Hardy, L. H., Jones, N. Y. and Barber, R. T. (1973). Relation between total body weight and concentration of manganese, iron, copper, zinc, and mercury in white muscle of bluefish (*Pomatomus saltatrix*) and a bathyl-demersal fish *Antimora rostrata. J. Fish. Res. Bd Can.* **30,** 1287–1291. *34, 35*

*1764. Crozier, G. F. (1970). Tissue carotenoids in prespawning and spawning sockeye salmon (*Oncorhynchus nerka*). *J. Fish. Res. Bd Can.* **27,** 973–975. *38, 57*

*1765. Cruea, D. D. (1969). Some chemical and physical characteristics of fish sperm. *Trans. Am. Fish. Soc.* **98,** 785–788.

*1766. Crush, K. G. (1970). Carnosine and related substances in animal tissues. *Comp. Biochem. Physiol.* **34,** 3–30.

*1767. Cserr, H. F., Fenstermacher, J. D. and Rall, D. P. (1972). Brain-barrier systems in sharks. *Comp. Biochem. Physiol.* **42A,** 73–78. *136*

1768. Cuendet, G. S., Loten, E. G., Cameron, D. P., Renold, A. E. and Marliss, E. B. (1975). Hormone-substrate responses to total fasting in lean and obese mice. *Am. J. Physiol.* **228,** 276–283. *189*

*1769. Cuill, T. O., Hamilton, A. F. and Egan, D. A. (1970). Copper distribution in the liver. *Ir. vet. J.* **24,** 21–25.

1770. Cuong, N. K. and Vinogradova, Z. A. (1968). Amino acid composition of grey Black Sea mullet. *Gidrobiol. Zh. Akad. Nauk Ukr. SSR* **4** (4), 58–61. From *Chem. Abstr.* **69,** 94014g (1969). *313*

*1771. Cuthbert, A. W. and Pic, P. (1973). Adrenoceptors and adenyl cyclase in gills. *Br. J. Pharmacol.* **49,** 134–137.

*1772. Cutcomp, L. K., Yap, H. H., Cheng, E. Y. and Koch, R. B. (1971). ATPase activity in fish tissue homogenates and inhibitory effects of DDT and related compounds. *Chemico-Biol. Interactions,* **3,** 439–447.

1773. Cuzon, G. and Ceccaldi, H. J. (1972). Evolution of lymph proteins of *Penaeus kerathurus* during starvation. *Tethys,* **3,** 247–250. *196*

*1774. Cvancara, V. A. (1968). Liver arginase activity in Missouri River freshwater fishes. *Am. Zool.* **8,** 764 only.

*1775. Cvancara, V. A. (1969a). Distribution of liver allantoinase and allantoicase activity in fresh-water teleosts. *Comp. Biochem. Physiol.* **29,** 631–638.

*1776. Cvancara, V. A. (1969b). Studies on tissue arginase and ureogenesis in freshwater teleosts. *Comp. Biochem. Physiol.* **30,** 489–496. *153*

*1777. Cvancara, V. A. (1974). Liver carbamyl phosphate synthetase in the primitive freshwater bony fishes (Chondrostei, Holostei). *Comp. Biochem. Physiol.* **49B,** 785–787.

1778. Cvancara, V. A. and Conte, F. P. (1970). Gill alkaline phosphatase activity during salt water adaptation of sockeye salmon (*Oncorhynchus nerka*) Walbaum. *Int. J. Biochem.* **1,** 597–604. *309*

*1779. Czeczuga, B. (1971). Carotenoids in fish. III. Carotenoids and vitamin A in phytophagous fish from heated waters. *Verh. int. Verein. Limnol.* **18,** 1198–1203.

1780. Czeczuga, B. (1973). Carotenoids in fish. II. Carotenoids and vitamin A in some fishes from the coastal region of the Black Sea. *Hydrobiologia,* **41,** 113–125. *135*

*1781. Czeczuga, B. (1974). Carotenoids in the fish milt. *Bull. Acad. pol. Sci. Sér. Sci. Biol.* **22,** 211–214.

*1782. Czeczuga, B. (1975a). Carotenoids in fish. IV. Salmonidae and thymallidae from Polish waters. *Hydrobiologia,* **46,** 223–239.

*1783. Czeczuga, B. (1975b). Carotenoids in fish. V. Anguilla anguilla (L.). *Acta Hydrobiol.* **17,** 311–317.

1784. Daan, N. (1973). A quantitative analysis of the food intake of North Sea cod, *Gadus morhua*. *Neth. J. Sea Res.* **6**, 479–517. *134*

*1785. Dabrowski, T., Stodilnik, L. and Tillak, S. (1973). Investigating cholesterol content in the tissues of selected marine fish. *Acta Ichthylogica et Piscatoria*, **3**, 77–85.

*1786. Dagbjartsson, B. (1975). Utilisation of blue whiting, *Micromesistius poutassou*, for human consumption. *J. Fish. Res. Bd Can.* **32**, 747–751.

1787. Dahl, H. A. and Nicolaysen, K. (1971). Actomyosin ATPase activity in Atlantic hagfish muscles. *Histochemie*, **28**, 205–210. *72, 75*

*1788. Dall, W. and Milward, N. E. (1969). Water intake, gut absorption and sodium fluxes in amphibious and aquatic fishes. *Comp. Biochem. Physiol.* **30**, 247–260. *307*

*1789. Dando, P. R. (1969a). Lactate metabolism in fish. *J. mar. biol. Ass. U.K.* **49**, 209–223. *4, 114, 361*

1790. Dando, P. R. (1969b). A glucosephosphate isomerase inhibitor of seasonal occurrence in cod (*Gadus morhua*) and other fish. *J. mar. biol. Ass. U.K.* **49**, 447–453. *443*

1791. Danilenko, T. P. (1970). Dynamics of glycogen in the early stages of the embryogeny of *Carassius auratus*. *Gidrobiol. Zh.* **6** (4), 84–90. From *Chem. Abstr.* **74**, 61980u (1971). *11*

*1792. Danilenko, T. P. (1971). Glycogen dynamics in carp and Chinese carp oocytes during the process of maturation. *Tsitologiya i Genetiki*, **5**, 164–168. *18*

*1793. Danilov, M. M. and Shevchenko, V. V. (1973). Dynamics of change in the mineral substance content in fish muscles under conditions of prolonged fasting. *Vop. Pitan.* (4), 55–56 (no volume number given). *172*

*1794. D'Aoust, B. G. (1970). The role of lactic acid in gas secretion in the teleost swimbladder. *Comp. Biochem. Physiol.* **32**, 637–668.

*1795. Darrow, D. C. and Fletcher, G. L. (1972). Quantification of testosterone and testosterone glucuronide in testicular and peripheral plasma of mature thorny skate (*Raja radiata*). *Gen. comp. Endocrinol.* **19**, 373–375.

1796. Dartnall, H. J. A. (1972). Visual pigment of the coelacanth. *Nature, Lond.* **239**, 341–342. *266, 503, 565*

1797. Das, A. B. and Krishnamoorthy, R. V. (1969). Biochemical changes of muscle proteins in goldfish (*Carassius auratus*) during thermal acclimatisation. *Experientia*, **25**, 594–595. *337*

*1798. Das, B. S. (1961). Comparative study of the blood biochemistry of three species of Indian carp. *Trans. Am. Fish. Soc.* **90**, 1–5.

*1799. Das, M. and Patnaik, B. K. (1977). Distribution of ascorbic acid in brain regions of some airbreathing teleosts. *Comp. Physiol. Ecol.* **2,** 29–32.

*1800. Das, S. and Das, V. K. (1976). Sodium chloride regulation in the freshwater burrowing mud eel *Amphipnous cuchia* (Ham.). *Z. angew. Zool.* **63,** 291–297.

*1801. Dave, G., Johansson, M.-L., Larsson, Å., Lewander, K. and Lidman, U. (1974). Metabolic and haematological studies on the yellow and silver phases of the European eel, *Anguilla anguilla* L.—II. Fatty acid composition. *Comp. Biochem. Physiol.* **47B,** 583–591. *25*

*1802. Dave, G., Johansson-Sjöbeck, M.-L., Larsson, Å., Lewander, K. and Lidman, U. (1975). Metabolic and haematological effects of starvation in the European eel, *Anguilla anguilla* L.—I. Carbohydrate, lipid, protein and inorganic ion metabolism. *Comp. Biochem. Physiol.* **52A,** 423–430. *4, 182, 186, 188, 213*

*1803. Dave, G., Johansson-Sjöbeck, M.-L., Larsson, Å., Lewander, K. and Lidman, U. (1976). Metabolic and haematological effects of starvation in the European eel, *Anguilla anguilla* L.—III. Fatty acid composition. *Comp. Biochem. Physiol.* **53B,** 509–515. *209*

*1804. Davidson, J. (1958). Zinc content of toadfish (*Opsanus tau*) islet tissue. *Anat. Rec.* **130,** 403 only.

*1805. Davis, K. B. and Simco, W. A. (1976a). Diurnal measurements of plasma chloride in catfish. *Copeia* 608–609 (no volume number given). *384*

*1806. Davis, K. B. and Simco, B. A. (1976b). Salinity effects on plasma electrolytes of channel catfish, *Ictalurus punctatus*. *J. Fish. Res. Bd Can.* **33,** 741–746.

 1807. Davis, R. M. and Fenderson, O. C. (1971). Histological comparisons of the adrenal-cortical cells of hatchery and wild landlocked Atlantic salmon (*Salmo salar*). *J. Fish. Res. Bd Can.* **28,** 505–508. *257*

*1808. Dean, J. M. (1969). The metabolism of tissues of thermally acclimated trout (*Salmo gairdneri*). *Comp. Biochem. Physiol.* **29,** 185–196. *73, 74, 88, 329, 345*

 1809. Dean, J. M. (1973). The response of fish to a modified thermal environment. *In* "Responses of Fish to Environmental Changes" (Ed. Chavin, W.), Chapter 2, pp. 33–63. Charles C. Thomas, Springfield, Illinois. *329*

 1810. Declerck, D. and Vyncke, W. (1973). Determination of the condition of Greenland halibut (*Rheinhardtius hippoglossoides* Walb). *Fourth meeting of research workers from European fish technology institutes*, Hamburg, 10–13 September 1973. *196*

*1811. Deetjen, P., Antkowiak, D. E. and Boylan, J. W. (1972). Urea reabsorption by the skate nephron: micropuncture of collecting ducts in *Raja erinacea*. *Bull. Mt Desert Isl. biol. Lab.* **12,** 28–29.

*1812. Degens, E. T., Deuser, W. G. and Haedrich, R. L. (1969). Molecular structure and composition of fish otoliths. *Mar. Biol.* **2**, 105–113.

1812a. Degnan, K. J., Karnaky, K. J. and Zadunaisky, J. A. (1977). Active chloride transport in the *in vitro* opercular skin of a teleost (*Fundulus heteroclitus*), a gill-like epithelium rich in chloride cells. *J. Physiol., Lond.* **271**, 155–191. *297*

1812b. Dejours, P., Toulmond, A. and Truchot, J. P. (1977). The effect of hyperoxia on the breathing of marine fishes. *Comp. Biochem. Physiol.* **58A**, 409–411. *273*

*1813. DeLaney, R. G., Lahiri, S., Hamilton, R. and Fishman, A. P. (1977). Acid-base balance and plasma composition in the aestivating lungfish (*Protopterus*). *Am. J. Physiol.* **232**, R10–R17. *154*

*1814. DeLaney, R. G., Shub, C. and Fishman, A. P. (1976). Haematological observations on the aquatic and aestivating African lungfish, *Protopterus aethiopicus*. *Copeia*, 423–434 (no volume number given). *277*

*1815. Demaël-Suard, A. (1972). Influence of severe anoxia on the endocrinal regulation of glucose metabolism in the cyprinoid fish, *Tinca vulgaris* L. *C. r. Séanc. Soc. Biol.* **166**, 394–398. *279*

*1816. Demaël-Suard, A., Garin, D., Brichon, G., More, M. and Peres, G. (1974). Glyconeogenesis on the part of glycine ^{14}C in the tench (*Tinca vulgaris* L.) during asphyxia. *Comp. Biochem. Physiol.* **47A**, 1023–1033. *279*

*1817. Deng, J. C., Orthoefer, F. T., Dennison, R. A. and Watson, M. (1976). Lipids and fatty acids in mullet (*Mugil cephalus*): Seasonal and locational variations. *J. Food Sci.* **41**, 1479–1483.

*1818. Denis, W. (1922). The non-protein organic constituents in the blood of marine fish. *J. biol. Chem.* **54**, 693–700. From Chavin and Young (1970).

1819. Denton, E. J., Liddicoat, J. D. and Taylor, D. W. (1972). The permeability of gases of the swim bladder of the conger eel (*Conger conger*). *J. mar. biol. Assoc. U.K.* **52**, 727–746. *122*

1820. Denton, E. J. and Marshall, N. B. (1958). The buoyancy of bathypelagic fishes without a gas-filled swimbladder. *J. mar. biol. Ass. U.K.* **37**, 753–767. *126, 127*

1821. Denton, E. J., Muntz, W. R. A. and Northmore, D. P. M. (1971). The distribution of visual pigment within the retina in two teleosts. *J. mar. biol. Ass. U.K.* **51**, 905–915. *269*

*1822. Denton, J. E. and Yousef, M. K. (1975). Seasonal changes in haematology of rainbow trout, *Salmo gairdneri*. *Comp. Biochem. Physiol.* **51A**, 151–153. *385*

*1823. Denton, J. E., Yousef, M. K., Yousef, I. M. and Kuksis, A. (1974). Bile acid composition of rainbow trout, *Salmo gairdneri*. *Lipids*, **9**, 945–951. *34, 225*

*1824. Dépêche, J. and Schoffeniels, E. (1975). Changes in electrolytes, urea and free amino acids of *Poecillia reticulata* embryos following high salinity adaptation of the viviparous female. *Biochem. Syst. Ecol.* **3,** 111–119. *20*

1825. Desai, I. D. (1969). Regulation of lysosomal enzymes. 1. Adaptive changes in enzyme activities during starvation and refeeding. *Can. J. Biochem.* **47,** 785–790. *221*

1826. Deufel, J. (1975). Physiological effect of carotenoids on Salmonidae. *Hydrologie,* **37,** 244–248. *39*

*1827. DeVries, A. L. (1970). Freezing resistance in Antarctic fishes. *In* "Antarctic Ecology" (Ed. Holdgate, M. W.), vol. 1, pp. 320–328. Academic Press, London and New York. *346*

1828. DeVries, A. L. (1971). Glycoproteins as biological antifreeze agents in Antarctic fishes. *Science N.Y.* **172,** 1152–1155. *346*

1829. DeVries, A. L. (1974). Survival at freezing temperatures. *In* "Biochemical and biophysical perspectives in marine biology" (Eds Malins, D. C. and Sargent, J. R.), pp. 289–330. Academic Press, London and New York. *324, 343, 345, 348, 528, 592, 631, 674*

1830. DeVries, A. L., DeVries, Y. L., Dobbs, G. H. and Raymond, J. A. (1974). Studies of the Antarctic cod, *Dissostichus mawsoni. Antarct. J., U.S.* **9,** 107–108. *346, 348*

*1831. DeVries, A. L. and Wohlschlag, D. E. (1969). Freezing resistance in some Antarctic fishes. *Science, N.Y.* **163,** 1073–1075. *262, 346*

*1832. Devys, M., Thierry, A., Barbier, M. and Janot, M.-M. (1972). Preliminary observations on the lipids of the oocyte of the coelacanth (*Latimeria chalumnae*). *C.r. hebd. Séanc. Acad. Sci., Paris,* **275,** 2085–2087.

1833. Deyl, Z. (1972). Role of connective tissue changes in an organism aging. *Int.rn. Congr. Gerontol., Kiev USSR,* **2,** 110–112. *136*

1834. Deyoe, C. W., Tiemeier, O. W. and Suppes, C. (1968). Effects of protein, amino acid levels, and feeding methods on growth of fingerling channel catfish. *Progve Fish Cult.* **30,** 187–195. *146*

1835. Dharmamba, M. and Maetz, J. (1972). Effects of hypophysectomy and prolactin on the sodium balance of *Tilapia mossambica* in fresh water. *Gen. comp. Endocrinol.* **19,** 175–183. *299*

*1836. Diamond, J. M. (1962a). The reabsorptive function of the gall-bladder. *J. Physiol., Lond.* **161,** 442–473. *164*

1837. Diamond, J. M. (1962b). The mechanism of water transport by the gall-bladder. *J. Physiol., Lond.* **161,** 503–527. *164*

*1838. van Dijk, J. P., Lagerwerf, A. J., van Eijk, H. G. and Leijnse, B. (1975). Iron metabolism in the tench (*Tinca tinca* L.). I. Studies by means of intravascular administration of ^{59}Fe (III) bound to plasma. *J. comp. Physiol.* **99,** 321–330.

1839. Dobbs, G. H. (1974). Aglomerulism in antarctic teleost fishes. Ph.D. Thesis, University of California. University Microfilm number 75–9480. *158, 528*

*1840. Dobbs, G. H. and DeVries, A. L. (1975). Renal function in antarctic teleost fishes: serum and urine composition. *Mar. Biol.* **29,** 59–70. *349*

1841. Dobbs, G. H., Lin, Y. and DeVries, A. L. (1974). Aglomerulism in antarctic fish. *Science N.Y.* **185,** 793–794. *346, 348*

1842. Dockray, G. J. and Pickering, A. D. (1972). The influence of the gonad on the degeneration of the intestine in migrating river lampreys: *Lampetra fluviatilis* L. (Cyclostomata). *Comp. Biochem. Physiol.* **43A,** 279–286. *37*

*1843. Dominy, C. L. (1971). Changes in blood lactic acid concentrations in alewives (*Alosa pseudoharengus*) during passage through a pool and weir fishway. *J. Fish. Res. Bd Can.* **28,** 1215–1217.

*1844. Donaldson, E. M. and Dye, H. M. (1975). Corticosteroid concentrations in sockeye salmon (*Oncorhynchus nerka*) exposed to low concentrations of copper. *J. Fish. Res. Bd Can.* **32,** 533–539.

1845. Donaldson, E. M. and Fagerlund, U. H. M. (1969). Cortisol secretion rate in gonadectomised female sockeye salmon (*Oncorhynchus nerka*): effects of oestrogen and cortisol treatment. *J. Fish. Res. Bd Can.* **26,** 1789–1799. *38*

*1846. Donaldson, E. M. and Fagerlund, U. H. M. (1970). Effect of sexual maturation and gonadectomy at sexual maturity on cortisol secretion rate in sockeye salmon (*Oncorhynchus nerka*). *J. Fish. Res. Bd Can.* **27,** 2287–2296. *37, 38, 48*

*1847. Donaldson, E. M. and McBride, J. R. (1967). The effects of hypophysectomy in the rainbow trout *Salmo gairdnerii* (Rich.) with special reference to the pituitary-interrenal axis. *Gen. comp. Endocrinol.* **9,** 93–101. *236*

1848. Doneen, B. A. and Bern, H. A. (1974). *In vitro* effects of prolactin and cortisol on water permeability of the urinary bladder of the teleost *Gillichthys mirabilis* (L.). *J. exp. Zool.* **187,** 173–179. *409, 448*

*1849. Driedzic, W. and Roots, B. I. (1975). Glycerophosphatide content and composition of trout (*Salvelinus fontinalis* M.) brain. *J. therm. Biol.* **1,** 7–10. *340*

*1850. Driedzic, W., Selivonchick, D. P. and Roots, B. I. (1976). Alk-l-enyl ether-containing lipids of goldfish (*Carassius auratus* L.) brain and temperature acclimation. *Comp. Biochem. Physiol.* **53B,** 311–314. *29, 340*

*1851. Driedzic, W. R. and Hochachka, P. W. (1975). The unanswered question of high anaerobic capabilities of carp white muscle. *Can. J. Zool.* **53,** 706–712. *280*

*1852. Driedzic, W. R. and Hochachka, P. W. (1976). Control of energy metabolism in fish white muscle. *Am. J. Physiol.* **230**, 579–582. *116*

1853. Drilhon, A., Fine, J. M., Boffa, G. A., Amouch, P. and Drouhet, J. (1966) Groups of transferrins in the eel. Phenotypic differences between Atlantic. and Mediterranean eels. *C. r. hebd. Séanc. Acad. Sci., Paris*, **262**, 1315–1318. *252*

*1854. Drongowski, R. A., Wood, J. S. and Bouck, G. R. (1975). Thyroid activity in coho salmon from Oregon and Lake Michigan. *Trans. Am. Fish. Soc.* **104**, 349–352.

*1855. Drujan, B. D. and Díaz Borges, J. M. (1972). Adrenaline induced changes in the metabolism of glycogen in the teleost retina. *J. Fish. Biol.* **4**, 79–85.

*1856. Duff, D. W. and Fleming, W. R. (1972a). Sodium metabolism of the freshwater cyprinodont, *Fundulus catenatus*. *J. comp. Physiol.* **80**, 179–189.

*1857. Duff, D. W. and Fleming, W. R. (1972b). Some aspects of sodium balance in the freshwater cyprinodont *Fundulus olivaceus*. *J. comp. Physiol.* **80**, 191–199.

1858. Duman, J. G. and DeVries, A. L. (1972). Freezing behaviour of aqueous solutions of glycoproteins from the blood of an antarctic fish. *Cryobiology*, **9**, 469–472. *346*

1859. Duman, J. G. and DeVries (1974). The effects of temperature and photoperiod on antifreeze production in cold water fishes. *J. exp. Zool.* **190**, 89–98. *348*

*1860. Duman, J. G. and DeVries, A. L. (1975). The role of macromolecular anti-freezes in cold water fishes. *Comp. Biochem. Physiol.* **52A**, 193–199. *348*

*1861. Duman, J. G. and DeVries, A. L. (1976). Isolation, characterisation, and physical properties of protein antifreezes from the winter flounder, *Pseudopleuronectes americanus*. *Comp. Biochem. Physiol.* **54B**, 375–380. *349*

*1862. Dunant, Y., Israël, M., Lesbats, B. and Manaranche, R. (1976). Loss of vesicular acetylcholine in the *Torpedo* electric organ on discharge against high external resistance. *J. Neurochem.* **27**, 975–977.

*1863. Dunant, Y., Israël, M., Lesbats, B., Manaranche, R. and Mastour, P. (1975). Periodic variations in the level of acetyl choline during the stimulation of the electric organ of the torpedo. *C. r. hebd. Séanc. Acad. Sci., Paris*, **280**, 641–643.

*1864. Dyer, W. J. (1946). Colorimetric nitrite determination. *J. Fish. Res. Bd Can.* **6**, 414–418.

*1865. Dyer, W. J. and Hiltz, D. I. (1969). Nucleotide degradation in frozen swordfish muscle. *J. Fish. Res. Bd Can.* **26**, 1597–1603. *73*

1866. Døving, K. B., Nordeng, H. and Oakley, B. (1974). Single unit discrimination of fish odours released by char (*Salmo alpinus* L.) populations. *Comp. Biochem. Physiol.* **47A**, 1051–1063. *113*

*1867. Eales, J. G. (1969). A comparative study of purines responsible for silvering in several freshwater fishes. *J. Fish. Res. Bd Can.* **26,** 1927–1931.

1868. Eales, J. G. and Sinclair, D. A. R. (1974). Enterohepatic cycling of thyroxine in starved and fed brook trout, *Salvelinus fontinalis* (Mitchill). *Comp. Biochem. Physiol.* **49A,** 661–672. *166*

*1869. Edwards, G. D. (1971). Normal brain cholinesterase activity in the white perch. *U.S. Nat. tech. inform. Serv. Rep.* **AD726361.** Edgewood Arsenal, Maryland. *57, 330*

1870. Edwards, R. R. C., Finlayson, D. M. and Steele, J. H. (1972). An experimental study of the oxygen consumption, growth, and metabolism of the cod (*Gadus morhua* L.). *J. exp. mar. Biol. Ecol.* **8,** 299–309. *138, 139*

*1871. Ehira, S. (1976). A biochemical study on the freshness of fish. *Bull. Tokai reg. Fish. Res. Lab.* **88,** 132 pp.

*1872. Ehira, S. and Uchiyama, H. (1973). Formation of inosine and hypoxanthine in fish muscle during ice storage. *Bull. Tokai reg. Fish. Res. Lab.* **75,** 63–73.

*1873. Ehira, S. and Uchiyama, H. (1974). Freshness-lowering rates of cod and sea bream viewed from changes in bacterial count, total volatile base- and tri-methylamine-nitrogen, and ATP related compounds. *Bull Jap. Soc. scient. Fish.* **40,** 479–487.

*1874. Ehrlich, K. F. (1973). Chemical changes during growth and starvation of herring larvae. *In* "The Early Life History of Fish" (Ed. Blaxter, J. H. S.), pp. 301–323. Springer-Verlag, Berlin.

*1875. Ehrlich, K. F. (1974). Chemical changes during growth and starvation of larval *Pleuronectes platessa. Mar. Biol.* **24,** 39–48. *15, 16*

1876. Ehrlich, K. F. (1975). A preliminary study of the chemical composition of sea-caught larval herring and plaice. *Comp. Biochem. Physiol.* **51B,** 25–28. *257*

1876a. Ehrlich, K. F., Blaxter, J. H. S. and Pemberton, R. (1976). Morphological and histological changes during the growth and starvation of herring and plaice larvae. *Mar. Biol.* **35,** 105–118. *199, 200*

1877. Eichhorn, G. L. and Butzow, J. J. (1966). Physical chemical studies on the crosslinking of collagen with age. *Int. Congr. Geront. Proc.* 7th, **2,** 5–6. *205*

1878. Eisler, R. and LaRoche, G. (1972). Elemental composition of the estuarine teleost *Fundulus heteroclitus* (L.). *J. exp. mar. Biol. Ecol.* **9,** 29–42. *33, 35*

1879. Ekberg, D. R. (1958). Respiration in tissues of goldfish adapted to high and low temperatures. *Biol. Bull. mar. biol. Lab., Woods Hole,* **114,** 308–316. *326*

1880. Emery, A. R. (1973). Preliminary comparisons of day and night habits of freshwater fish in Ontario lakes. *J. Fish. Res. Bd Can.* **30,** 761–774. *267*

*1881. Emmersen, B. K. and Emmersen, J. (1976). Protein, RNA and DNA metabolism in relation to ovarian vitellogenic growth in the flounder, *Platichthys flesus* (L.). *Comp. Biochem. Physiol.* **55B**, 315–321.

*1882. Endo, K., Kishimoto, R., Yamamoto, Y. and Shimizu, Y. (1974). Seasonal variations in chemical constituents of yellowtail muscle—II. Nitrogenous extractives. *Bull. Jap. Soc. scient. Fish.* **40**, 67–72.

*1883. Engelhardt, F. R., Geraci, J. R. and Walker, B. L. (1975). Tocopherol composition of frozen Atlantic herring (*Clupea harengus harengus*) tissues and oil. *J. Fish. Res. Bd Can.* **32**, 807–809. *76*

*1884. Enomoto, N. and Uchida, Y. (1973). Cadmium and other heavy metal contents in marine products from Ariake Sea and in canned goods on the market. *Agric. Bull. Saga Univ.* **35**, 69–75.

1885. Ensor, D. M. and Ball, J. N. (1972). Prolactin and osmoregulation in fishes. *Fedn Proc. Fedn Am. Socs exp. Biol.* **31**, 1615–1623. *300*

*1886. Epple, A. and Lewis, T. L. (1977). Metabolic effects of pancreatectomy and hypophysectomy in the yellow American eel, *Anguilla rostrata* LeSueur. *Gen. comp. Endocrinol.* **32**, 294–315.

1887. Epstein, F. H., Katz, A. I. and Pickford, G. E. (1967). Sodium- and potassium-activated adenosine triphosphatase of gills: role in adaptation of teleosts to salt water. *Science, N.Y.* **156**, 1245–1247. *291*

1888. Erman, Ye. Z. (1969). The nitrogen-saving effect of carbohydrates in the carp. *Vop. Ikhtiol.* **9**, 615–617. From *Aq. Biol. Abstr.* **3** (1), Aq629 (1971). *139*

*1889. Ermolaeva, L. P. and Mil'man, L. S. (1973). Characteristics of NADPH generation in oocytes and embryos of the loach *Misgurnus fossilis*. *J. evol. Biochem. Physiol.* **9**, 490–494.

*1890. Establier, R. (1970). Content of copper, iron, manganese and zinc in various organs of the tuna, *Thunnus thynnus* (L.) from the gulf of Cadiz. *Investigación pesq.* **34**, 399–408.

*1891. Establier, R. (1972). The concentration of mercury in tissues of fish, shell-fish and crustaceans of N.W. Africa coast and Gulf of Cádiz. *Investigación pesq.* **36**, 355–364.

1892. Esteller, A., de la Higuera, M., Lopez, M. A., Zamora, S. and Murillo, A. (1975). Concentrating ability of the gall bladder. Comparative study in some vertebrate species. *Revta. esp. Fisiol.* **31**, 91–94. From *Chem. Abstr.* **83**, 92707a (1975). *166*

*1893. Eustace, I. J. (1974). Zinc, cadmium, copper and manganese in species of finfish and shellfish caught in the Derwent Estuary, Tasmania. *Aust. J. mar. freshwat. Res.* **25**, 209–220.

1894. Evans, D. H. (1969). Studies on the permeability to water of selected marine, freshwater and euryhaline teleosts. *J. exp. Biol.* **50,** 689–703. *289*

1895. Evans, D. H. (1975). Ionic exchange mechanisms in fish gills. *Comp. Biochem. Physiol.* **51A,** 491–495. *287, 289*

1896. Evans, D. H., Mallery, C. H. and Kravitz, L. (1973). Sodium extrusion by a fish acclimated to sea water: physiological and biochemical description of a Na-for-K exchange system. *J. exp. Biol.* **58,** 627–636. *288*

1897. Everson, I. and Ralph, R. (1970). Respiratory mechanisms of *Chaenocephalus aceratus. In* "Antarctic Ecology" (Ed. Holdgate, M. W.), vol. 1, pp. 315–319. Academic Press, London and New York. *277*

*1898. Ezzat, A. A., Shabana, M. B. and Farghaly, A. M. (1974). Studies on the blood characteristics of *Tilapia zilli* (Gervais) I. Blood cells. *J. Fish Biol.* **6,** 1–12. *55, 56*

1899. Fagade, S. O. (1974). Age determination in *Tilapia melanotheron* (Ruppell) in the Lagos Lagoon, Lagos, Nigeria. *In* "Ageing of Fish" (Ed. Bagenal, T. B.), pp. 71–77. Unwin Bros., Old Woking, England. *384*

*1900. Fagerlund, U. H. M. and Donaldson, E. M. (1970). Dynamics of cortisone secretion in sockeye salmon (*Oncorhynchus nerka*) during sexual maturation and after gonadectomy. *J. Fish. Res. Bd Can.* **27,** 2323–2331. *48, 236, 237*

1901. Fahy, W. E. and O'Hara, R. K. (1977). Does salinity influence the number of vertebrae developing in fishes? *J. Cons. perm. int. Explor. Mer* **37,** 156–161. *318*

1902. Falkina, E. A. and Davydova, Z. M. (1970). Effect of growing conditions on the fat and glycogen content in the hepatic tissue of carp hatched during the current year. *Doklady T.S.Kh.A.* (*Rep. Timiryasev Agric. Acad.*), **164,** 355–358. *67, 259*

*1903. Falkmer, S. (1961). Experimental diabetes research in fish. *Acta Endocr.* **37,** Suppl. 59, 1–122.

*1904. Falkmer, S., Emdin, S., Havu, N., Lundgren, G., Marques, M., Östberg, Y., Steiner, D. F. and Thomas, N. W. (1973). Insulin in invertebrates and cyclostomes. *Am. Zool.* **13,** 625–638.

*1905. Fänge, R. and Fugelli, K. (1962). Osmoregulation in chimaeroid fishes. *Nature, Lond.* **196,** 689 only.

*1906. Fänge, R. and Fugelli, K. (1963). The rectal salt gland of elasmobranchs, and osmoregulation in chimaeroid fishes. *Sarsia,* **10,** 27–34. *309, 508*

*1907. Fänge, R. and Johansson-Sjöbeck, M.-L. (1975). The effect of splenectomy on the haematology and on the activity of δ-amino laevulinic acid dehydratase (Ala-D) in haemopoietic tissues of the dogfish, *Scyliorhinus canicula* (elasmobranchii). *Comp. Biochem. Physiol.* **52A,** 577–580.

*1908. Fänge, R., Larsson, Å. and Lidman, U. (1972). Fluids and jellies of the acousticolateralis system in relation to body fluids in *Coryphaenoides rupestris* and other fishes. *Mar. Biol.* **17,** 180–185.

*1909. Fänge, R., Lidman, U. and Larsson, Å. (1976). Comparative studies of inorganic substances in the blood of fishes from the Skagerrak Sea. *J. Fish Biol.* **8,** 441–448.

*1910. Fänge, R., Lundblad, G. and Lind, J. (1976). Lysozyme and chitinase in blood and lymphomyeloid tissues of marine fish. *Mar. Biol.* **36,** 277–282.

*1911. Farghaly, A. M., Ezzat, A. A. and Shabana, M. B. (1973). Effect of temperature and salinity changes on the blood characteristics of *Tilapia zilli* G. in Egyptian littoral lakes. *Comp. Biochem. Physiol.* **46A,** 183–193. *311, 327*

*1912. Farkas, T. and Csengeri, I. (1976). Biosynthesis of fatty acids by the carp, *Cyprinus carpio* L., in relation to environmental temperature. *Lipids,* **11,** 401–407. *340*

1913. Farmer, G. J. and Beamish, F. W. H. (1969). Oxygen consumption of *Tilapia nilotica* in relation to swimming speed and salinity. *J. Fish. Res. Bd Can.* **26,** 2807–2821. *290*

*1914. Farmer, S. W., Papkoff, H., Bewley, T. A., Hayashida, T., Nishioka, R. S., Bern, H. A. and Li, C. H. (1977). Isolation and properties of teleost prolactin. *Gen. comp. Endocrinol.* **31,** 60–71.

*1915. Farnararo, M., Bruni, P., Vincenzini, M. T., Favilli, F. and Vanni, P. (1977). An enzyme levels profile drawn from the study of the main metabolic pathways of the brain in different animals. *Comp. Biochem. Physiol.* **57B,** 219–222.

*1916. Farrell, A. P. and Lutz, P. L. (1975). Apparent anion imbalance in the fresh water adapted eel. *J. comp. Physiol.* **102,** 159–166. *285*

*1917. Feeney, R. E. (1974). A biological antifreeze. A glycoprotein in the blood of polar fishes lowers the freezing temperature. *Am. Scient.* **62,** 712–719. *349*

1918. Feeney, R. E. and Osuga, D. T. (1971). Blood proteins and muscle enzymes of cold-adapted antarctic fishes. *In* "Research in the Antarctic" (Ed. Quam, L. O.), pp. 227–257. American Association for the Advancement of Science, Washington. *330, 333*

1919. Feldmeth, C. R. and Waggoner, J. P. (1972). Field measurements of tolerance to extreme hypersalinity in the California killifish, *Fundulus parvipinnis. Copeia,* 592–594 (no volume number given). *284*

*1920. Felinska, S. (1972). Seasonal changes in blood serum of trout females *Salmo trutta* L. *Acta Ichthyologica et Piscatoria,* **2** (2), 15–19. *40*

*1921. Fenwick, J. C. and Forster, M. E. (1972). Effects of stanniectomy and hypophysectomy on total plasma cortisol levels in the eel (*Anguilla anguilla* L.). *Gen. comp. Endocrinol.* **19,** 184–191.

1922. Fessler, J. L. and Wagner, H. H. (1969). Some morphological and biochemical changes in steelhead trout during the parr-smolt transformation. *J. Fish. Res. Bd Can.* **26**, 2823–2841. *22, 25*

*1923. Fickeisen, D. H. and Brown, G. W. (1977). D-amino acid oxidase in various fishes. *J. Fish Biol.* **10**, 457–465.

*1924. Fik, M. (1972). Activity of muscular cathepsins of some marine fishes. *Acta lehthyologica et Piscatoria*, **2** (2), 105–111.

1925. Fine, M. L. (1975). Sexual dimorphism of the growth rate of the swim bladder of the toadfish, *Opsanus tau*. *Copeia*, (3), 483–490 (no volume number given). *58, 603*

1926. Fingerman, M. (1974). Comparative endocrinology. *In* "Experimental Marine Biology" (Ed. Mariscal, R. N.), Chapter 5, pp. 165–223. Academic Press, London and New York. *365, 418*

*1927. Fingerman, S. W. (1976). Circadian rhythms of brain 5-hydroxytryptamine and swimming activity in the teleost, *Fundulus grandis*. *Comp. Biochem. Physiol.* **54C**, 49–53. *383, 451*

*1928. Fiorenzi, G., Russo, G. M. and Milazzo, A. (1973). Research on the amount of mercury present in swordfish. *Quad. Merceol.* **12**, 1–32.

*1929. Fischer, W. and Güthert, H. (1968). On the zinc content of the endocrine pancreatic tissue and in the musculature of the zitterochen *Torpedo marmorata* and *Torpedo ocellata*. *Hoppe-Zeyler's Z. physiol. Chem.* **349**, 573–574. *35*

1930. Fleming, W. R. (1974). Electrolyte metabolism of teleosts—including calcified tissues. *In* "Chemical Zoology" (Eds Florkin, M. and Scheer, B. T.), vol. 8, Chapter 12, pp. 471–508. Academic Press, London and New York. *286–288*

1931. Fleming, W. R., Brehe, J. and Hanson, R. (1973). Some complicating factors in the study of the calcium metabolism of teleosts. *Am. Zool.* **13**, 793–797. *286*

*1932. Fletcher, G. L. (1975). The effects of capture, "stress", and storage of whole blood on the red blood cells, plasma proteins, glucose, and electrolytes of the winter flounder (*Pseudopleuronectes americanus*). *Can. J. Zool.* **53**, 197–206. *231, 232*

*1933. Fletcher, G. L., Watts, E. G. and King, M. J. (1975). Copper, zinc, and total protein levels in the plasma of sockeye salmon (*Oncorhynchus nerka*) during their spawning migration. *J. Fish. Res. Bd Can.* **32**, 78–82.

*1934. Fletcher, T. C. and White, A. (1973). Lysozyme activity in the plaice (*Pleuronectes platessa* L.). *Experientia*, **29**, 283 285.

*1935. Fletcher, T. C. and White, A. (1976). The lysozyme of the plaice *Pleuronectes platessa* L. *Comp. Biochem. Physiol.* **55B**, 207–210.

*1936. Foda, A. (1973). Changes in haematocrit and haemoglobin in Atlantic salmon (*Salmo salar*) as a result of furunculosis disease. *J. Fish. Res. Bd Can.* **30,** 467–468.

1937. Fontaine, M., Delerue, N., Martelly, E., Marchelidon, J. and Milet, C. (1972). Role of the Corpuscles of Stannius in calcium exchange with the external medium in a teleost fish, the eel (*Anguilla anguilla*), *C. r. hebd. Séanc. Acad. Sci., Paris,* **275,** 1523–1528. *304*

*1938. Fontaine, M. and Marchelidon, J. (1971a). Amino acid contents of the brain and the muscle of young salmon (*Salmo salar* L.) at parr and smolt stages. *Comp. Biochem. Physiol.* **40A,** 127–134. *22, 194*

*1939. Fontaine, M. and Marchelidon, J. (1971b). Modification in the concentrations of certain free amino acids in the brain and muscle of young *Salmo salar* L. during smoltification. *C. r. hebd. Séanc. Acad. Sci., Paris,* **272,** 94–97. *22*

*1940. Fontaine, M., Mazeaud, M. and Mazeaud, F. (1963). Blood adrenaline in *Salmo salar* L. at several stages of its life cycle and migrations. *C. r. hebd. Séanc. Acad. Sci., Paris,* **256,** 4562–4565. *22, 64*

1941. Forrest, J. N., Cohen, A. D., Schon, D. A. and Epstein, F. H. (1973). Na transport and Na-K-ATPase in gills during adaptation to seawater: effects of cortisol. *Am. J. Physiol.* **224,** 709–713. *291, 302*

*1942. Forrest, J. N., MacKay, W. C., Gallagher, B. and Epstein, F. H. (1973). Plasma cortisol response to saltwater adaptation in the American eel *Anguilla rostrata*. *Am. J. Physiol.* **224,** 714–717. *302, 303*

1943. Forster, M. E. (1970). Ph.D. Thesis, University of Sheffield. From Chester Jones, Ball, Henderson, Sandor and Baker (1974). *120*

*1944. Forster, R. P. and Danforth, J. W. (1972). Osmoregulatory role of the urinary bladder in the stenohaline marine teleosts. *Bull. Mt Desert Isl. biol. Lab.* **12,** 35–37. *156*

*1945. Forster, R. P. and Goldstein, L. (1976). Intracellular osmoregulatory role of amino acids and urea in marine elasmobranchs. *Am. J. Physiol.* **230,** 925–931. *313, 314*

*1946. Fosmire, G. J. and Brown, W. D. (1976). Yellow fin tuna (*Thunnus albacares*) myoglobin: characterisation and comparative stability. *Comp. Biochem. Physiol.* **55B,** 293–299.

*1947. Fossatt, B., Lahlou, B. and Bornancin, M. (1974). Involvement of a Na-K-ATPase in sodium transport by fish urinary bladder. *Experientia,* **30,** 376–377.

*1948. Foster, R. C. (1976). Renal hydromineral metabolism in starry flounder, *Platichthys stellatus*. *Comp. Biochem. Physiol.* **55A,** 135–140. *156, 307*

*1949. Fourie, F. le R. and Hattingh, J. (1976). A seasonal study of the haematology of carp (*Cyprinus carpio*) from a locality in the Transvaal, South Africa. *Zool. Afr.* **11,** 75–80. *44*

*1950. Fraser, J. M. and Beamish, F. W. H. (1969). Blood lactic acid concentrations in brook trout, *Salvelinus fontinalis*, planted by air drop. *Trans. Am. Fish. Soc.* **98,** 263–267.

*1951. Freed, J. M. (1971). Properties of muscle phosphofructokinase of cold- and warm-acclimated *Carassius auratus*. *Comp. Biochem. Physiol.* **39B,** 747–764. *320*

*1952. Freeman, H. C. and Horne, D. A. (1973). Total mercury and methylmercury content of the American eel (*Anguilla rostrata*). *J. Fish. Res. Bd Can.* **30,** 454–456.

*1953. Freeman, H. C., Horne, D. A., McTague, B. and McMenemy, M. (1974). Mercury in some Canadian Atlantic coast fish and shellfish. *J. Fish. Res. Bd Can.* **31,** 369–372.

*1954. Frejmane, T. Kh. and Grundule, M. V. (1975). Chromatographic distribution of lipids in different tissues of carp (*Cyprinus carpio* L.). *Trans Latvian Acad. Sci.* no. 3, **332,** 106–110.

*1955. Fried, G. H. and Schreibman, M. P. (1972). Alterations of pentose shunt activity in tissues of teleosts. *Comp. Biochem. Physiol.* **42B,** 517–522.

*1956. Fried, G. H., Schreibman, M. P. and Kallman, K. D. (1969). Enzymatic activities in tissues of teleosts. *Comp. Biochem. Physiol.* **28,** 771–776.

*1957. Friede, R. L. and Hu, K. H. (1971). Hydrogen ion transfer and pH control in bowfin brain in vitro. *Brain Res.* **25,** 161–169.

*1958. Friede, R. L., Hu, K. H. and Johnstone, M. (1969). Glial footplates in the bowfin. I. Fine structure and chemistry. *J. Neuropath. exp. Neurol.* **28,** 513–539.

1959. Friedman, L. and Shibko, S. I. (1973). Nonnutrient components of the diet. *In* "Fish Nutrition" (Ed. Halver, J. E.), Chapter 5, pp. 181–254. Academic Press, London and New York. *395*

*1960. Fromm, P. O. (1963). Studies on renal and extra-renal excretion in a fresh-water teleost, *Salmo gairdneri*. *Comp. Biochem. Physiol.* **10,** 121–128. *217, 218*

1961. Frontier-Abou, D. (1969). Variation in the total composition of the muscle in three species of Carangidae. *Ann. Nutr. Aliment.* **23,** 313–334. *68, 79*

1962. Fry, F. E. J. and Hochachka, P. W. (1970). Fish. *In* "Comparative Physiology of Thermoregulation" (Ed. Whittow, G. C.), vol. 1, Chapter 3, pp. 79–134. Academic Press, London and New York. *249, 330, 334*

*1963. Fryer, J. N. (1975). Stress and adrenocorticosteroid dynamics in the goldfish, *Carassius auratus*. *Can. J. Zool.* **53,** 1012–1020. *236*

*1964. Fugelli, K., Storm-Mathisen, J. and Fonnum, F. (1970). Synthesis of γ-aminobutyric acid in fish erythrocytes. *Nature, Lond.* **228,** 1001 only.

*1965. Fugelli, K. and Zachariassen, K. E. (1976). The distribution of taurine, gamma-aminobutyric acid and inorganic ions between plasma and erythrocytes in flounder (*Platichthys flesus*) at different plasma osmolalities. *Comp. Biochem. Physiol.* **55A,** 173–177. *313*

*1966. Fujii, Y., Yamada, J. and Onishi, T. (1971). Studies on silvering of fish skin—I. Purines in the skin of cultured salmon and trout. *Bull. Jap. Soc. scient. Fish.* **37** 55–62. *22*

1967. Fujino, K. (1970). Immunological and biochemical genetics of tunas. *Trans. Am. Fish. Soc.* **99,** 152–178. *249*

1968. Fukuda, H. (1958b: 1958a is in Volume 1 of this work). Studies on the succinic dehydrogenase of fish—V. Difference of succinic dehydrogenase activity between various fishes and fish-organs. *Bull. Jap. Soc. scient. Fish.* **24,** 24–28. *75, 111*

*1969. Fuller, J. D., Mason, P. A. and Fraser, R. (1976). Gas-liquid chromatography of corticosteroids in plasma of salmonidae. *J. Endocr.* **71,** 163–164.

*1970. Fuller, J. D., Scott, D. B. C. and Fraser, R. (1976). The reproductive cycle of *Coregonus lavaretus* (L.) in Loch Lomond, Scotland, in relation to seasonal changes in plasma cortisol concentration. *J. Fish Biol.* **9,** 105–117.

1971. Funkhouser, D., Goldstein, L. and Forster, R. P. (1972). Urea biosynthesis in the South American lungfish, *Lepidosiren paradoxa:* relation to its ecology. *Comp. Biochem. Physiol.* **41A,** 439–443. *154*

*1972. Gajewska, R. (1977). Cadmium content in salt- and fresh-water fish. *Bromatologia Chemia Toksykologiczna* **10,** 137–140.

1973. Galasun, P. T. and Shemchuk, V. R. (1971). Composition of rainbow trout serum proteins dependent on ecological and other factors. *Ryb. Khoz.* (13), 74–79. From *Chem. Abstr.* **77,** 2973h (1972). *35, 49*

*1974. Gallis, J.-L. and Bourdichon, M. (1976). Changes of (Na⁺-K⁺) dependent ATPase activity in gills and kidneys of two mullets *Chelon labrosus* (Risso) and *Liza ramada* (Risso) during fresh water adaptation. *Biochimie,* **58,** 625–627. *293, 306*

1975. Gantayat, S. C. and Patnaik, B. K. (1975). Studies on collagen in some species of Indian fishes: I. Influence of sex and temperature on the collagen content of the skin and muscle of *Ophiocephalus punctatus*. *Sci. Cult.* (*India*) **41,** 404–406. *56, 338, 339*

*1976. Garcia, L. E. and Meier, A. H. (1973). Daily rhythms in concentration of plasma cortisol in male and female gulf killifish, *Fundulus grandis*. *Biol. Bull. mar. biol. Lab., Woods Hole,* **144,** 471–479. *48, 383*

1977. Garling, D. L. and Wilson, R. P. (1977). Effects of dietary carbohydrate-to-lipid ratios on growth and body composition of fingerling channel catfish. *Progve Fish Cult.* **39,** 43–47. *139*

1978. Garside, E. T. and Jordan, C. M. (1968). Upper lethal temperatures at various levels of salinity in the euryhaline cyprinodonts *Fundulus heteroclitus* and *F. diaphanus* after isosmotic acclimation. *J. Fish. Res. Bd Can.* **25,** 2717–2720. *323*

1979. Gas, N. (1972). Structural alterations in the white muscle of carp (*Cyprinus carpio* L.) during prolonged starvation. *C. r. hebd. Séanc. Acad. Sci., Paris,* **275,** Ser. D, 1403 1406. *173, 175, 176, 200*

1980. Gas, N. (1973). Cytophysiology of the liver of carp (*Cyprinus carpio* L.). II. Modes of alteration of the ultrastructures during prolonged experimental starvation. *J. Physiol., Paris,* **66,** 283–302. *177, 179, 201*

1981. Gas, N. (1975). Influence of prolonged starvation and refeeding on the somatotropic cells of the hypophysis of carp. An ultrastructural study. *J. Microsc. Biol. cell.* **23,** 289–300. *219, 220*

1982. Gas, N. (1976). Cytophysiology of the digestive apparatus and of muscular tissue of the carp. Structural and functional modifications induced by starvation and refeeding. Thesis, Docteur d'Etat, University Paul Sabatier de Toulouse. *178, 179*

1983. Gas, N., Bouche, G. and Serfaty, A. (1971). Cytophotometric study of the evolution of nucleic acids in the liver of carp (*Cyprinus carpio* L.) during starvation and refeeding. *J. Physiol., Paris,* **63,** 625–633.

1984. Gas, N. and Noaillac-Depeyre, J. (1976). Studies on intestinal epithelium involution during prolonged fasting. *J. Ultrastruct. Res.* **56,** 137–151. *171, 181*

1985. Gas, N. and Pequignot, J. (1972). Restoration of the structures of the liver cell of carps re-nourished by two synthetic regimes after a prolonged starvation. *C. r. Séanc. Soc. Biol.* **166,** 446–453. *179*

1986. Gas, N. and Serfaty, A. (1972). Cytophysiology of the liver of the carp (*Cyprinus carpio* L.). Consecutive modifications to the ultrastructure during maintenance of conditions of winter starvation. *J. Physiol., Paris,* **64,** 57–67. *178, 179*

*1987. Gastaud, J. M. (1973). Variations in neutral lipids during development of the eggs of *Scyllium canicula* (L.). *Revue int. Océanogr. Méd.* **31–32,** 221–232.

1988. Gatz, A. J. (1973). Speed, stamina, and muscles in fishes. *J. Fish. Res. Bd Can.* **30,** 325–328. *79*

*1989. Gaudet, M., Racicot, J.-G. and Leray, C. (1975). Enzyme activities of plasma and selected tissues in rainbow trout *Salmo gairdneri* Richardson. *J. Fish Biol.* **7,** 505–512.

1990. Gee, J. H. (1977). Effects of size of fish, water temperature and water velocity on buoyancy alteration by fathead minnows, *Pimephales promelas. Comp. Biochem. Physiol.* **56A**, 503–508. *121, 320*

1991. Gee, J. H. and Gee, P. A. (1976). Alteration of buoyancy by some Central American stream fishes, and a comparison with North American species. *Can. J. Zool.* **54**, 386–391. *121*

1992. Gee, J. H., Machniak, K. and Chalanchuk, S. M. (1974). Adjustment of buoyancy and excess internal pressure of swimbladder gases in some North American freshwater fishes. *J. Fish Res. Bd Can.* **31**, 1139–1141. *121*

*1993. Geist, G. M. and Crawford, D. L. (1974). Muscle cathepsins in three species of Pacific sole. *J. Food Sci.* **39**, 548–551.

1994. Gelineo, S. (1969). Haemoglobin concentration in blood of fish. *Bull. Acad. serbe Sci. Cl. Sci. math. nat., Sci. nat.* **12**, 25–67. From *Chem. Abstr.* **73**, 22593e (1970). *44, 55, 110, 262*

*1995. Geoghegan, W. D. and Poluhowich, J. J. (1974). The major erythrocytic organic phosphates of the American eel, *Anguilla rostrata. Comp. Biochem. Physiol.* **49B**, 281–290.

*1996. George, C. (1975). Biochemical differences between the red and white meat of tuna and changes in quality during freezing and storage. *Fish. Technol.* **12**, 70–74. *73*

*1997. Georgiev, G. (1970). Carotenoid and carotene levels in the liver of American trout (*Salmo irideus*) from natural and artificial pools. *Nauchni Trud. vissh. vet.-med. Inst. Sofia*, **22**, 153–159. From *Chem. Abstr.* **80**, 12684r (1974).

*1998. Georgiev, G. S. (1971). Carotenoids and vitamin A content in *Salmo irideus* eggs and their significance in the initial periods of the embryogenesis. *Folia Balcanica*, **2** (9), 11pp. *10, 258*

1999. Georgiev, G. S. (1972a). Content of vitamins A_1 and A_2 in certain tissues of sexually mature rainbow trouts. *C. r. Acad. bulg. Sci.* **25**, 271–274. *57, 146*

2000. Georgiev, G. (1972b). Studies on the blood of rainbow trout, *Salmo irideus. Arch. exp. Vet. Med.* **26**, 733–739. From *Chem. Abstr.* **78**, 82213u (1973). *55, 276*

*2001. Gerasimova, T. D. and Privezentsev, Yu. A. (1972). Biochemical characteristics of the spawn of females of a scaled variety of carp. *Prudovoc Ryb. Dokl. T.S.Kh.A.* **190**, 117–120.

*2002. Geraskin, P. P., Logunov, A. I. and Luk'yanenko, V. I. (1972). On the amino acid composition of haemoglobins from cartilaginous ganoids. *Zh. evol. Biokhim. Fiziol.* **8**, 26–30. *2*

2003. Gerking, S. D. (1955a). Influence of rate of feeding on body composition and protein metabolism of bluegill sunfish. *Physiol. Zoöl.* **28**, 267–282. *137, 138*

2004. Gerking, S. D. (1955b). Endogenous nitrogen excretion of bluegill sunfish. *Physiol. Zoöl* **28,** 283–289. *28*

2005. Gerking, S. D. (1971). Influence of rate of feeding and body weight on protein metabolism of bluegill sunfish. *Physiol. Zoöl.* **44,** 9–19. *138*

*2006. Germain, P. and Gagnon, A. Unpublished, quoted by Robertson, 1974.

*2007. Gershbein, L. L. and Singh, E. J. (1969). Hydrocarbons of dogfish and cod livers and herring oil. *J. Am. Oil Chem. Soc.* **46,** 554–557.

*2008. Gerst, J. W. and Thorson, T. B. (1977). Effects of saline acclimation on plasma electrolytes, urea excretion, and hepatic urea biosynthesis in a freshwater stingray, *Potamotrygon* sp. Garman, 1877. *Comp. Biochem. Physiol.* **56A,** 87–93.

*2009. Gesser, H. and Fänge, R. (1971). Lactate dehydrogenase and cytochrome oxidase in the swimbladder of fish. *Int. J. Biochem.* **2,** 163–166.

2010. Gesser, H. and Poupa, O. (1973). The lactate dehydrogenase system in the heart and skeletal muscle of fish: a comparative study. *Comp. Biochem. Physiol.* **46B,** 683–690. *78, 111*

*2011. Gesser, H. and Poupa, O. (1974). Relations between heart muscle enzyme pattern and directly measured tolerance to acute anoxia. *Comp. Biochem. Physiol.* **48A,** 97–103. *280*

*2012. Gesser, H. and Sundell, L.-E. (1971). Functional aspects of lactate dehydrogenase isoenzymes of Atlantic salmon (*Salmo salar* L.). *Int. J. Biochem.* **2,** 462–472.

*2013. Gheracopol, O. (1972). The dynamics of the amino acids of the pond carp. *Bul. Inst. Cerc. pisc.* **31,** 55–78.

*2014. Ghosh, A., Ghosh, A., Hoque, M. and Dutta, J. (1976). Fatty acids of Boal fish oil by urea fractionation and gas-liquid chromatography. *J. Sci. Fd Agric.* **27,** 159–164.

*2015. Giaccio, M. (1970). Research on the content of trace metals of some fish species in the Adriatic Sea. *Quad. Merceol.* **9,** 29–39.

2016. Giles, M. A. and Vanstone, W. E. (1976a). Changes in ouabain-sensitive adenosine triphosphatase activity in gills of coho salmon (*Oncorhynchus kisutch*) during parr-smolt transformation. *J. Fish. Res. Bd Can.* **33,** 54–62. *24*

2017. Giles, M. A. and Vanstone, W. E. (1976b). Ontogenetic variation in the multiple haemoglobins of coho salmon (*Onocrhynchus kisutch*) and effect of environmental factors on their expression. *J. Fish. Res. Bd Can.* **33,** 1144–1149. *274*

2018. Gill, T. S. and Khanna, S. S. (1976). Effect of glucagon on the principal islets of a fresh-water fish, *Channa punctata* (Bloch). *Acta anat.* **95,** 93–100. *418*

*2019. Gillen, R. G. and Riggs, A. (1972). Structure and function of the haemoglobins of the carp, *Cyprinus carpio. J. biol. Chem.* **247,** 6039–6046.

*2020. Gillet, C., Billard, R. and Breton, B. (1977). Effects of the temperature on the level of plasma gonadotrophin and on spermatogenesis in goldfish, *Carassius auratus. Can. J. Zool.* **55,** 242–245.

2021. Girard, J.-P. (1976). Salt excretion by the perfused head of trout adapted to sea water and its inhibition by adrenaline. *J. comp. Physiol.* **111,** 77–91. *304*

2022. Girard, J. P. and Istin, M. (1975). Isoenzymes of carbonic anhydrase of a euryhaline fish. Variations related to the osmoregulation. *Biochim. biophys. Acta,* **381,** 221–232. *287–289*

*2023. Girzadaite, Z. L. and Lesauskiene, L. B. (1972). Certain biochemical changes in the body of migrating female vimba. *Liet. TSR Mokslv Acad. Darb.* **57,** 69–78. *43*

*2024. Gitlin, D., Perricelli, A. and Gitlin, J. D. (1973). Immunoglobulin synthesis in foetal sharks. *Comp. Biochem. Physiol.* **45A,** 247–256. *20, 21*

*2025. Giurca, R. (1972). Contributions to the comparative study of the seasonal biorhythm of gonads and pituitary nucleic acids in *Ctenopharyngodon idella,* reared in ponds or living in natural waters. *Bul. Inst Cerc. pisc.* **31,** 45–54.

*2026. Glass, R. L., Krick, T. P. and Eckhardt, A. E. (1974). New series of fatty acids in northern pike (*Esox lucius*). *Lipids,* **9,** 1004–1008, *210*

2026a. Glass, R. L., Krick, T. P., Olson, D. L. and Thorson, R. L. (1977). The occurrence and distribution of furan fatty acids in spawning male freshwater fish. *Lipids,* **12,** 828–836. *416*

2027. Glass, R. L., Krick, T. P., Sand, D. M., Rahn, C. H. and Schlenk, H. (1975). Furanoid fatty acids from fish lipids. *Lipids,* **10,** 695–702.

2028. Godin, J.-G., Dill, P. A. and Drury, D. E. (1974). Effects of thyroid hormones on behaviour of yearling Atlantic salmon (*Salmo salar*). *J. Fish. Res. Bd Can.* **31,** 1787–1790. *22*

2029. Goedmakers, A. and Verboom, B. L. (1974). Studies on the maturation and fecundity of the pike, *Esox lucius* Linnaeus, 1758. *Aquaculture,* **4,** 3–12. *43*

*2030. Goldstein, L. and Dewitt-Harley, S. (1973). Trimethylamine oxidase of nurse shark liver and its relation to mammalian mixed function amine oxidase. *Comp. Biochem. Physiol.* **45B,** 895–903.

2031. Goldstein, L. and Forster, R. P. (1970). Nitrogen metabolism in fishes. *In* "Comparative Biochemistry of Nitrogen Metabolism. 2. The Vertebrates" (Ed. Campbell, J. W.), pp. 495–518. Academic Press, London and New York. *159*

2032. Goldstein, L. and Forster, R. P. (1971a). Urea biosynthesis and excretion in freshwater and marine elasmobranchs. *Comp. Biochem. Physiol.* **39B,** 415–421. *311*

2033. Goldstein, L. and Forster, R. P. (1971b). Osmoregulation and urea metabolism in the little skate *Raja erinacea. Am. J. Physiol.* **220,** 742–746. *310*

2034. Goldstein, L. and Funkhouser, D. (1972). Biosynthesis of trimethylamine oxide in the nurse shark, *Ginglymostoma cirratum. Comp. Biochem. Physiol.* **42A,** 51–57. *459*

*2035. Goldstein, L., Harley-DeWitt, S. and Forster, R. P. (1973). Activities of ornithine-urea cycle enzymes and of trimethylamine oxidase in the coelacanth, *Latimeria chalumnae. Comp. Biochem. Physiol.* **44B,** 357–362.

2036. Goldstein, L., Oppelt, W. and Maren, T. H. (1968). Osmotic regulation and urea metabolism in the lemon shark *Negaprion brevirostris. Am. J. Physiol.* **215,** 1493–1497. *310*

2037. Goldstein, L. and Palatt, P. J. (1974). Trimethylamine oxide excretion rates in elasmobranchs. *Am. J. Physiol.* **227,** 1268–1272. *593, 660*

2038. Goll, D. E., Hoekstra, W. G. and Bray, R. W. (1964). Age-associated changes in bovine muscle connective tissue. 1. Rate of hydrolysis by collagenase. *J. Food Sci.* **29,** 608–613. *204*

2039. Gollnick, P. D., Armstrong, R. B., Saltin, B., Saubert, C. W., Sembrowich, W. L. and Shepherd, R. E. (1973). Effect of training on enzyme activity and fibre composition of human skeletal muscle. *J. appl. Physiol.* **34,** 107–111. *119*

*2040. Golovkin, N. A., Krainova, L. S., Uvarova, N. A., Vorob'eva, V. V. and Nosko, V. A. (1973). Macro and microelement composition of various kinds of food-fish from the oceans of the world. *Ryb. Khoz.* (8), 66–71 (no volume number given). *72, 73, 76*

2041. Gomez-Jarabo, G., Mataix, F. J., Illera, M. and Varela, G. (1976). The influence of age on the nutritive utilisation of protein in trout (*Salmo gairdneri*). *Investigación pesq.* **40,** 561–569. *62*

*2042. Gopakumar, K. and Nair, M. R. (1971). Phospholipids of five Indian food fishes. *Fish. Technol.* **8,** 171 173.

2043. Gopakumar, K. and Nair, M. R. (1972). Fatty acid composition of eight species of Indian marine fish. *J. Sci. Fd Agric.* **23,** 493–496. *339*

*2044. Gordon, M. S. (1970). Patterns of nitrogen excretion in amphibious fishes. *In* "Urea and the Kidney" (Eds Schmidt-Nielsen, B. and Kerr, D. W. S.), pp. 238–242. Excerpta Medica Foundation, Amsterdam.

2045. Gordon, M. S. (1972a). Comparative studies on the metabolism of shallow-water and deep-sea marine fishes. I. White-muscle metabolism in shallow-water fishes. *Mar. Biol.* **13,** 222–237. *27, 110, 262, 326*

2046. Gordon, M. S. (1972b). Comparative studies on the metabolism of shallow-water and deep-sea marine fishes. II. Red-muscle metabolism in shallow-water fishes. *Mar. Biol.* **15,** 246–250. *71*

*2047. Gordon, M. S., Boëtius, J., Boëtius, I., Evans, D. H., McCarthy, R. and Oglesby, L. C. (1965). Salinity adaptation in the mudskipper fish *Periophthalmus sobrinus*. *Hvalråd. Skr.* **48,** 85–93.

2048. Gordon, M. S., Boëtius, I., Evans, D. H., McCarthy, R. and Oglesby, L. C. (1969). Aspects of the physiology of terrestrial life in amphibious fishes. I. The mudskipper, *Periophthalmus sobrinus*. *J. exp. Biol.* **50,** 141–149. *154*

*2049. Gordon, M. S., Fischer, S. and Tarifeño, E. (1970). Aspects of the physiology of terrestrial life in amphibious fishes. II. The Chilean clingfish, *Sicyases sanguineus*, *J. exp. Biol.* **53,** 559–572. *154*

*2050. Goswami, A. K. (1975). Amino acid composition of eye lens of the fish *Labeo bata* at different stages of growth. *Curr. Sci.* **44,** 309–310.

*2051. Gowri, C. and Joseph, K. T. (1968). Characterisation of acid soluble collagen from a "live fish" or air breathing fish of India group. *Leath. Sci.* **15,** 300–305. *338*

*2052. Grabowski, S. J. (1973). Effects of fluctuating and constant temperatures on some haematological characteristics, tissue glycogen levels, and growth of steelhead trout (*Salmo gairdneri*). Ph.D. Thesis, University of Idaho.

2053. Granroth, B. and Hattula, T. (1976). Formation of dimethyl sulphide by brackish water algae and its possible implication for the flavour of Baltic herring. *Finnish Chemical Letters,* 148–150 (no volume number given). *150*

*2054. Grant, B. F. Unpublished, quoted by Grant, Mehrle and Russell (1970).

*2055. Grant, B. F. and Mehrle, P. M. Unpublished, quoted by Grant, Mehrle and Russell (1970).

*2056. Grant, B. F., Mehrle, P. M. and Russell, T. R. (1970). Serum characteristics of spawning paddlefish (*Polyodon spathula*). *Comp. Biochem. Physiol.* **37,** 321–330. *48–50, 53*

*2057. Grant, B. F. (given in the paper as Grant, F. B.), Pang, P. K. T. and Griffith, R. W. (1969). The twenty-four-hour seminal hydration response in goldfish (*Carassius auratus*)—1. Sodium, potassium, calcium, magnesium, chloride and osmolality of serum and seminal fluid. *Comp. Biochem. Physiol.* **30,** 273–280.

*2058. Grant, W. C., Hendler, F. J. and Banks, P. M. (1969). Studies on blood-sugar regulation in the little skate *Raja erinacea*. *Physiol. Zoöl.* **42,** 231–247. *186*

*2059. Gras, J., Bannier, Y. and Gudefin, Y. (1975). The content of nucleic acids in the muscle of the rainbow trout (*Salmo gairdneri* Richardson): variations related to gonad maturation. *Experientia,* **31,** 283–284.

2060. Gras, J., Perrier, H., Perrier, C. and Gautheron, D. (1969). Study of extra-cellular space in the muscle tissue of rainbow trout (*Salmo gairdnerii* Rich.): effect of acetylcholine and adrenaline. *C. r. Séanc. Soc. Biol.* **163,** 189-192. From *Aq. Biol. Abstr.* **1** (9) Aq4505. *314*

2061. Grauman, G. R. (1972). Changes in the biochemical composition of eggs depending on the morphobiological peculiarities in Baltic cod females. *Trudy vses. nauchno-issled. Inst. morsk. ryb. Khoz. Okeanogr.* **85,** 63–67. *9, 28*

*2062. Gray, I. E. (1928). The effect of insulin on the blood sugar of fishes. *Am. J. Physiol.* **84,** 566–573. From Chavin and Young (1970).

*2063. Gray, I. E. and Hall, F. G. (1929). The distribution of sugar in the blood of fishes. *J. Elisha Mitchell scient. Soc.* **45,** 142–146. From Chavin and Young (1970).

*2064. Greene, F. C. and Feeney, R. E. (1970). Properties of muscle glyceraldehyde-3-phosphate dehydrogenase from the cold-adapted antarctic fish *Dissostichus mawsoni*. *Biochim. Biophys. Acta* **220,** 430–442. *330*

2065. Greer-Walker, M. (1966). The effect of exercise on skeletal muscle fibres. *Comp. Biochem. Physiol.* **19,** 791–797. *118*

2066. Greer-Walker, M. (1968). Muscle physiology of cod. *Ann. Rep. Lowestoft Fish. Lab. MAFF* 44 only. *87, 103, 321*

2067. Greer-Walker, M. (1970). Growth and development of the skeletal muscle fibres of the cod (*Gadus morhua* L.). *J. Cons. perm. int. Explor. Mer* **33,** 228–244. *30–32, 61, 79*

2068. Greer-Walker, M., Burd, A. C. and Pull, G. A. (1972). The total numbers of white skeletal muscle fibres in cross section as a character for stock separation in North Sea herring (*Clupea harengus* L.). *J. Cons. perm. int. Explor. Mer* **34,** 238–243. *244*

2069. Greer-Walker, M. and Pull, G. (1973). Skeletal muscle function and sustained swimming speeds in the coalfish *Gadus virens* L. *Comp. Biochem. Physiol.,* **44A,** 495–501. *105*

2070. Greer-Walker, M. and Pull, G. A. (1975). A survey of red and white muscle in marine fish. *J. Fish Biol.* **7,** 295–300. *79*

*2071. Gregory, R. B. (1977). Synthesis and total excretion of waste nitrogen by fish of the periophthalmus (mudskipper) and scartelaos families. *Comp. Biochem. Physiol.* **57A,** 33–36. *154*

*2072. Gregory, R. W. (1969). Physical and chemical properties of walleye pike, *Stizostedion vitreum* (Mitchill), sperm and seminal plasma. Ph.D. Thesis, Colorado State University. *35, 58*

*2073. Gregory, R. W. (1970). Physical and chemical properties of Walleye sperm and seminal plasma. *Trans. Am. Fish. Soc.,* **99,** 518–525.

2074. Griffith, R. W. (1974). Pituitary control of adaptation to fresh water in the teleost genus *Fundulus. Biol. Bull. mar. biol. Lab., Woods Hole,* **146,** 357–376. *299*

*2075. Griffith, R. W. and Burdick, C. J. (1976). Sodium-potassium activated adenosine triphosphatase in coelacanth tissues: high activity in rectal gland, *Comp. Biochem. Physiol.* **54B,** 557–559.

*2076. Griffith, R. W., Mathews, M. B., Umminger, B. L., Grant, B. F., Pang, P. K. T., Thomson, K. S. and Pickford, G. E. (1975). Composition of fluid from the notochordal canal of the coelacanth, *Latimeria chalumnae. J. exp. Zool.* **192,** 165–172.

*2077. Griffith, R. W., Pang, P. K. T., Srivastava, A. K. and Pickford, G. E. (1973). Serum composition of freshwater stingrays (Potamotrygonidae) adapted to fresh and dilute sea water. *Biol. Bull. mar. biol. Lab., Woods Hole,* **144,** 304–320. *311*

*2078. Griffith, R. W., Umminger, B. L., Grant, B. F., Pang, P. K. T., Goldstein, L. and Pickford, G. E. (1976). Composition of bladder urine of the coelacanth, *Latimeria chalumnae. J. exp. Zool.* **196,** 371–380. *156*

*2079. Griffith, R. W., Umminger, B. L., Grant, B. F., Pang, P. K. T. and Pickford, G. E. (1974). Serum composition of the coelacanth, *Latimeria chalumnae* Smith. *J. exp. Zool.* **187,** 87–102. *565*

*2080. Grigg, G. C. (1969). Temperature-induced changes in the oxygen equilibrium curve of the blood of the brown bullhead, *Ictalurus nebulosus. Comp. Biochem. Physiol.* **28,** 1203–1223. *327*

2081. Grigg, G. C. (1974). Respiratory function of blood in fishes. *In* "Chemical Zoology. Volume 8. Deuterostomians, Cyclostomes and Fishes" (Eds Florkin, M. and Scheer, B. T.), Chapter 9, pp. 331–368. Academic Press, London and New York. *327*

*2082. Grigo, F. (1975). How much is carp (*Cyprinus carpio*) stressed by temperature? 1. Blood composition, with a special look at the serum electrolytes. *Zool. Anz., Jena* **8,** 215–233. *232, 241, 327, 329, 330*

*2083. Grollman, A. (1929). The urine of the goosefish (*Lophius piscatorius*): its nitrogenous constituents with special reference to the presence in it of trimethylamine oxide. *J. biol. Chem.* **81,** 267–278. *459*

2084. Groninger, H. S. (1959). The occurrence and significance of trimethylamine oxide in marine animals. *Spec. scient. Rep. U.S. Fish Wildl. Serv.,* **333,** 22 pp. *459*

*2085. Gronow, G. (1974a). Nucleic acid and substrate contents of the dorsal epaxial muscle of teleosts during "biological stress". *Mar. Biol.* **24,** 313–327.

*2086. Gronow, G. (1974b). Stress in *Idus idus* L. (Teleostei) due to capture, anaesthesia and experimental environment. *Zool. Anz., Jena* **193,** 17–34. *232, 237*

*2087. Gross, J., Dumsha, B. and Glazer, N. (1958). Comparative biochemistry of collagen. Some amino acids and carbohydrates. *Biochem. Biophys. Acta,* **30,** 293–297.

*2088. Grove, D. J., Starr, C. R., Allard, D. R. and Davies, W. (1972). Adrenaline storage in the pronephros of the plaice, *Pleuronectes platessa* L. *Comp. gen. Pharmacol.* **3,** 205–212.

2089. Groves, T. D. D. (1970). Body composition changes during growth in young sockeye (*Oncorhynchus nerka*) in fresh water. *J. Fish. Res. Bd Can.* **27,** 929–942. *41*

2090. Guerin-Ancey, O. (1976a). Experimental study on the excretion of nitrogen by bass (*Dicentrarchus labrax*) during growth. I. Effects of the temperature and of the weight of the body on the excretion of ammonia and urea. *Aquaculture,* **9,** 71–80. *320*

2091. Guerin-Ancey, O. (1976b). Experimental study on the nitrogenous excretion of bass (*Dicentrarchus labrax*) during growth. III. Effects of water volume and initial ammonia concentration on the excretion of ammonia and urea. *Aquaculture,* **9,** 253–258. *154*

*2092. Gunstone, F. D., Wijesundera, R. C., Love, R. M. and Ross, D. (1976). Relative enrichment of furan-containing fatty acids in the liver of starving cod. *Chem. Commun.,* 630–631 (no volume number given). *211*

2093. Haen, P. J. and O'Rourke, F. J. (1969a). Comparative electrophoretic studies of soluble eyelens proteins of some Irish freshwater fishes. *Proc. R. Ir. Acad.* **68,** Sect. B, 67–75. *62*

2094. Haen, P. J. and O'Rourke, F. J. (1969b). Comparative electrophoretic studies of the water-soluble proteins of some Irish freshwater fishes. *Proc. R. Ir. Acad.* **68,** 101–108. *63, 68*

*2095. Hafeez, M. A. and Quay, W. B. (1970). Pineal acetylserotonin methyltransferase activity in the teleost fishes, *Hesperoleucus symmetricus* and *Salmo gairdneri*, with evidence for lack of effect of constant light and darkness. *Comp. gen. Pharmacol.* **1,** 257–262. *265*

2096. Hagenmaier, H. E. (1972). Hatching process in fish. II. Purification and characterisation of hatching secretion in rainbow trout (*Salmo gairdneri*). *Experientia* **28**, 1214–1215. From *Chem. Abstr.* **77**, 162134p (1972). *13*

2097. Haider, G. (1972). Haematological observations on rainbow trout (*Salmo gairdneri* Rich.). VI. Leucocyte count. *Zool. Anz., Jena* **188**, 304–316. From *Aq. Sci. fish. Abstr.* **3** (1), 3Q285B (1973). *213*

*2098. Haines, T. A. (1973). An evaluation of RNA-DNA ratio as a measure of long-term growth in fish populations. *J. Fish. Res. Bd Can.* **30**, 195–199. *30, 217*

*2099. Hall, A. S., Teeny, F. M. and Gauglitz, E. J. (1976). Mercury in fish and shellfish of the Northeast Pacific. II. Sablefish, *Anoplopoma fimbria*. *Fish. Bull. Natl. Oceanic and Atmos. Adm.* (*US*), **74**, 791–797.

*2100. Hall, A. S., Teeny, F. M., Lewis, L. G., Hardman, W. H. and Gauglitz, E. J. (1976). Mercury in fish and shellfish of the Northeast Pacific. I. Pacific halibut, *Hippoglossus stenolepis*. *Fish. Bull. Natl. Oceanic Atmos. Adm.* (*US*), **74**, 783–789.

2101. Halver, J. E. (1972) (Editor). "Fish Nutrition." Academic Press, London and New York. 713 pp. This book was mentioned in Volume 1 as "in press".

2102. Halver, J. E. (1972). The vitamins. *In* "Fish Nutrition" (Ed. Halver, J. E.), Chapter 2, pp. 29–103. Academic Press, New York and London. *146*

2103. Hamoir, G., Focant, B. and Distèche, M. (1972). Proteinic criteria of differentiation of white, cardiac and various red muscles in carp. *Comp. Biochem. Physiol.* **41B**, 665–674. *73, 74, 76, 88*

2104. Hamoir, G., Marechal, R. and Bassleer, R. (1973). Electron spin resonance spectra of white, cardiac and various red skeletal muscles of the carp. *Cyprinus carpio* L. *Experientia*, **29**, 25–26. *74*

*2105. Hamoir, G., Piront, A., Gerday, Ch. and Dando, P. R. (1973). Muscle proteins of the coelacanth *Latimeria chalumnae* Smith. *J. mar. biol. Ass. U.K.* **53**, 763–784. *565*

2106. Hampson, B. L. (1976). Ammonia concentration in relation to ammonia toxicity during a rainbow trout rearing experiment in a closed freshwater-seawater system. *Aquaculture*, **9**, 61–70. *154*

2107. Hanson, A. (1966). Differences in the value of N-acetylhistidine in freshwater and marine teleosts. *C. r. Séanc. Soc. Biol.* **160**, 265–268.

*2108. Hanson, R. C., Duff, D., Brehe, J. and Fleming, W. R. (1976). The effect of various salinities, hypophysectomy, and hormone treatments on the survival and sodium and potassium content of juvenile bowfin, *Amia calva*. *Physiol. Zoöl.* **49**, 376–385.

2109. Hara, T. J. (1977). Further studies on the structure–activity relationships of amino acids in fish olfaction. *Comp. Biochem. Physiol.* **56A**, 559–565.

*2110. Harada, K. and Yamada, K. (1972). Studies on the production of formaldehyde and dimethylamine in fishes. *J. Shimonoseki Univ. Fish*. **21**, 239–248.

*2111. Harada, K. and Yamada, K. (1973). Distribution of trimethylamine oxide in fishes and other aquatic animals—V. Teleosts and elasmobranchs. *J. Shimonoseki Univ. Fish*. **22**, 77–94.

2112. Harden Jones, F. R. and Marshall, N. B. (1953). The structure and functions of the teleostean swimbladder. *Biol. Rev*. **28**, 16–83. *122*

*2113. Harden Jones, F. R. and Scholes, P. (1974). The effect of low temperature on cod, *Gadus morhua*. *J. Cons. perm. int. Explor. Mer* **35**, 258–271. *xii, 349, 540*

*2114. Hardisty, M. W. (1956). Some aspects of osmotic regulation in lampreys. *J. exp. Biol*., **33**, 431–447.

*2115. Hardisty, M. W. (1957). Osmotic conditions during the embryonic and early larval life of the brook lamprey (*Lampetra planeri*). *J. exp. Biol*. **34**, 237–252.

*2116. Hardisty, M. W., Zelnik, P. R. and Moore, I. A. (1975). The effects of subtotal and total isletectomy in the river lamprey, *Lampetra fluviatilis*. *Gen. comp. Endocrinol*. **27**, 179–192. *6*

*2117. Hardy, R. and Keay, J. N. (1972). Seasonal variations in the chemical composition of Cornish mackerel, *Scomber scombrus* (L), with detailed reference to the lipids. *J. Food Technol*. **7**, 125–137.

*2118. Hardy, R. and Mackie, P. R. (1971). Observations on the chemical composition and toxicity of ratfish (*Chimaera monstrosa*). *J. Sci. Fd Agric*. **22**, 382–388.

*2119. Hardy, R., Mackie, P. R., Whittle, K. J. and McIntyre, A. D. (1974). Discrimination in the assimilation of *n*-alkanes in fish. *Nature, Lond*. **252**, 577–578. *xii*

*2120. Hardy, R. and Smith, J. G. M. (1976). The storage of mackerel (*Scomber scombrus*). Development of histamine and rancidity. *J. Sci. Fd Agric*. **27**, 595–599.

*2121. Hargreaves, A. B. and Wanderley, A. G. (1969). Studies on the intermediary metabolism of the electric organ of the *Electrophorus electricus* (L.). *Anais Acad. bras. Cienc*. **41**, 277–283.

*2122. Hargreaves, G. and Porthé-Nibelle, J. (1974). Plasma cortisol concentrations in two teleost fishes, *Anguilla anguilla* L. and *Carassius aruatus* L.: a comparison of two assay systems. *Steroids*, **24**, 251–260.

2123. Harkness, R. D., Marko, A. M., Muir, H. M. and Neuberger, A. (1954). The metabolism of collagen and other proteins of the skin of rabbits. *Biochem. J*. **56**, 558–569. *205*

*2124. Harms, U. and Kunze, J. (1977). Determination of cobalt in small samples of tissues and organs of the rainbow trout (*Salmo gairdneri*) by flameless atomic absorption spectroscopy. *Z. Lebensmittelunters. u. -Forsch.* **164,** 204–207.

*2125. Harves, M. T. (1972). RNA to DNA ratios as indicators of metabolic activity in fish affected by temperature. M.A. Thesis, Zool. Dept., DePauw University. 21 pp.

2126. Haschemeyer, A. E. V. (1973). Control of protein synthesis in the acclimation of fish to environmental temperature changes. *In* "Responses of Fish to Environmental Changes" (Ed. Chavin, W.), Chapter 1, pp. 3–32. Charles C. Thomas, Springfield, Illinois. *326, 328, 329*

2127. Hashimoto, K. (1972). Kinetics of haemoglobin. IV. Respiratory function of fish haemoglobin. *Respiration and Circulation (Kokkyo to Junkan).* **20,** 749–758. *23*

2128. Hashimoto, R. (1974). Investigation of feeding habits and variation of inhabiting depths with cod (*Gadus macrocephalus*) distributed on the north-eastern fishing ground in Japan. *Bull. Tohoku reg. Fish. Res. Lab.* **33,** 51–67. *167*

*2129. Hashimoto, Y. and Okaichi, T. (1958a). Trimethylamine oxide in fish muscle. I. The origin of trimethylamine oxide in goldfish muscle. *Bull. Jap. Soc. scient. Fish.* **24,** 640–644. *149, 150*

2130. Hashimoto, Y. and Okaichi, T. (1958b). Trimethylamine oxide in fish muscle. II. Trimethylamine oxide in the muscle of eels kept in fresh and brackish water. *Bull. Jap. Soc. scient. Fish.* **24,** 645–647. *149, 312*

*2131. Haswell, M. S. (1977). Carbonic anhydrase in flounder erythrocytes. *Comp. Biochem. Physiol.* **56A,** 281–282.

*2132. Hata, M. and Hata, M. (1971). Carotenoid pigments in goldfish (*Carassius auratus*) I. Composition and distribution of carotenoids. *Int. J. Biochem.* **2,** 11–19.

2133. Hata, M. and Hata. M. (1972a). Carotenoid pigments in goldfish—IV. Carotenoid metabolism. *Bull. Jap. Soc. scient. Fish.* **38,** 331–338. *144, 145*

2134. Hata, M. and Hata, M. (1972b). Carotenoid pigments in goldfish—V. Conversion of zeaxanthin to astaxanthin. *Bull. Jap. Soc. scient. Fish.* **38,** 339–343.

2135. Hata, M. and Hata, M. (1973). Studies on astaxanthin formation in some fresh-water fishes. *Tohoku J. agric. Res.* **24,** 192–196. *398*

*2136. Hata, M. and Hata, M. (1975). Carotenoid pigments in rainbow trout, *Salmo gairdneri irideus. Tohoku J. agric. Res.* **26,** 35–40.

*2137. Hata, M., Hata, M. and Onishi, T. (1973). Conversion of β-carotene and retinol$_1$ to retinol$_2$ in freshwater fish. *Tohoku J. agric. Res.* **24,** 197–204. *268*

*2138. Hatano, M. and Hashimoto, Y. (1974). Properties of a toxic phospholipid in the northern blenny roe. *Toxicon*, **12**, 231–236. *662*

*2139. Hattingh, J. (1972). Observations on the blood physiology of five South African freshwater fish. *J. Fish Biol.* **4**, 555–563.

*2140. Hattingh, J. (1973a). A study of some blood constituents of two species of mudfish. *Comp. Biochem. Physiol.* **46A**, 613–617.

*2141. Hattingh, J. (1973b). Some blood parameters of the yellowfish (*Barbus holubi*) and the barbel (*Clarias gariepinus*). *Zool. Afr.* **8**, 35–39.

*2142. Hattingh, J. (1975). The survival of carp (*Cyprinus carpio*) outside water. *S. Afr. J. med. Sci.* **41**, 11–15.

*2143. Hattingh, J. (1976a). The influence of carbon dioxide on the blood sugar concentration in the fresh-water fish, *Labeo capensis* (Smith). *Comp. Biochem. Physiol.* **53A**, 235–236. *280*

*2144. Hattingh, J. (1976b). Effects of transportation on swimbladder gases. *S. Afr. J. Sci.* **72**, 61–62.

2145. Hattingh, J. (1977). The effect of tricaine methanesulphonate (MS-222) on the microhaematocrit of fish blood. *J. Fish Biol.* **10**, 453–455.

*2146. Hattingh, J. and van Pletzen, A. J. J. (1974). The influence of capture and transportation on some blood parameters of fresh water fish. *Comp. Biochem. Physiol.* **49A**, 607–609. *239*

2147. Hauss, R. (1975). Effects of temperature on proteins, enzymes and isoenzymes out of organs of the fish *Rhodeus amarus* Bloch. II. Influence of the adaptation temperature on brain. *Zool. Anz., Jena*, **194**, 262–278. *328, 329, 335*

*2148. Havre, G. N., Underdal, B. and Christiansen, C. (1973). Cadmium concentrations in some fish species from a coastal area in southern Norway. *Oikos*, **24**, 155–157.

2149. Hay, J. B., Hodgins, M. B. and Roberts, R. J. (1976). Androgen metabolism in skin and skeletal muscle of the rainbow trout (*Salmo gairdnerii*) and in accessory sexual organs of the spur dogfish (*Squalus acanthias*). *Gen. comp. Endocrinol.* **29**, 402–413. *199*

*2150. Hayama, K. and Ikeda, S. (1972). Studies on the metabolic changes of fish caused by diet variations—I. Effect of dietary composition on the metabolic changes of carp. *Bull. Jap. Soc. scient. Fish.* **38**, 639–643. *140*

*2151. Hayashi, K. and Takagi, T. (1977). On the fatty acid composition of fish affected by excessive stress. *Bull. Jap. Soc. scient. Fish.* **43**, 1189–1194.

*2152. Hayashi, K. and Yamada, M. (1975a). The lipids of marine animals from various habitat depths—II. On the fatty acid composition of the neutral lipids in six species of gadiformes. *Bull. Jap. Soc. scent. Fish.* **41,** 1153–1160.

*2153. Hayashi, K. and Yamada, M. (1975b). The lipids of marine animals from various habitat depths—III. On the characteristics of the component fatty acids in the neutral lipids of deep-sea fishes. *Bull. Jap. Soc. scient. Fish.* **41,** 1161–1175.

*2154. Hayashi, K. and Yamada, M. (1975c). The lipids of marine animals from various habitat depths—IV. On the fatty acid composition of the neutral lipids in nine species of flatfishes. *Bull. Fac. Fish. Hokkaido Univ.* **26,** 265–276. *209*

*2155. Hayashi, K. and Yamada, M. (1976). The lipids of marine animals from various habitat depths. V. Composition of wax esters and triglycerides of the gadoid fish, *Podonema longipes*. *Bull. Fac. Fish. Hokkaido Univ.* **26,** 356–366.

*2156. Hayashi, S. (1971). Biochemical studies on the skin of fish—II. Seasonal change of purine content of masu salmon from parr to smolt. *Bull. Jap. Soc. scient. Fish.* **37,** 508–512. *22*

*2157. Hayashi, S. and Ooshiro, Z. (1975a). Gluconeogenesis and glycolysis in isolated perfused liver of the eel. *Bull. Jap. Soc. scient. Fish.* **41,** 201–208.

2158. Hayashi, S. and Ooshiro, Z. (1975b). Glycogenolysis and glyconeogenesis by eel liver slices. *Mem. Fac. Fish. Kagoshima Univ.* **24,** 119–122. *233*

2159. Hayden, J. B., Cech, J. J. and Bridges, D. W. (1975). Blood oxygen dissociation characteristics of the winter flounder, *Pseudopleuronectes americanus*. *J. Fish. Res. Bd Can.* **32,** 1539–1544. *123*

*2160. Hayes, L. W., Tinsley, I. J. and Lowry, R. R. (1973). Utilisation of fatty acids by the developing steelhead sac-fry, *Salmo gairdneri*. *Comp. Biochem. Physiol.* **45B,** 695–707. *13, 14*

*2161. Hayslett, J. P., Epstein, M., Spector, D., Myers, J. D. and Murdaugh, H. V. (1972). Lack of effect of calcitonin on renal function in the elasmobranch. *Squalus acanthias*. *Comp. Biochem. Physiol.* **43A,** 223–226. *6*

2162. Haywood, G. P. (1973a). Hypo-osmotic regulation coupled with reduced metabolic urea in the dogfish *Poroderma africanum*: an analysis of serum osmolarity, chloride, and urea. *Mar. Biol.* **23,** 121–127. *214*

2163. Haywood, G. P. (1973b). The effect of food shortage upon osmoregulation in the dogfish *Poroderma africanum* under laboratory conditions. *S. Afr. J. Sci.* **69,** 154 only. *214, 310*

*2164. Haywood, G. P. (1975). A preliminary investigation into the roles played by the rectal gland and kidneys in the osmoregulation of the striped dogfish *Poroderma africanum*. *J. exp. Zool.* **193,** 167–176. *309*

*2165. Haywood, G. P., Brown, A. C. and Cook, P. A. (1974). Composition of the blood of *Callorhynchus capensis* Dumeril (Holocephali). *S. Afr. J. Sci.* **70,** 74 only.

*2166. Hazel, J. R. (1972). The effect of temperature acclimation upon succinic dehydrogenase activity from the epaxial muscle of the common goldfish (*Carassius auratus* L.)—I. Properties of the enzyme and the effect of lipid extraction. *Comp. Biochem. Physiol.* **43B,** 837–861. *329*

2167. Hazel, J. R. and Prosser, C. L. (1974). Molecular mechanisms of temperature compensation in poikilotherms. *Physiol. Rev.* **54,** 620–677. *330, 331, 340*

2168. Hazel, J. R. and Schuster, V. L. (1976). The effects of temperature and thermal acclimation upon the osmotic properties and nonelectrolyte permeability of liver and gill mitochondria from rainbow trout (*Salmo gairdneri*). *J. exp. Zool.* **195,** 425–438. *329*

2169. Hebb, C., Morris, D. and Smith, M. W. (1969). Choline acetyltransferase activity in the brain of goldfish acclimated to different temperatures. *Comp. Biochem. Physiol.* **28,** 29–36. *330*

*2170. Hemmingsen, E. A. and Douglas, E. L. (1970). Respiratory characteristics of the haemoglobin-free fish *Chaenocephalus aceratus*. *Comp. Biochem. Physiol.* **33,** 733–744. *237, 278*

*2171. Hemmingsen, E. A. and Douglas, E. L. (1972). Respiratory and circulatory responses in a haemoglobin-free fish, *Chaenocephalus aceratus*, to changes in temperature and oxygen tension. *Comp. Biochem. Physiol.* **43A,** 1031–1043. *278*

2172. Hemmingsen, E. A., Douglas, E. L. and Grigg, G. C. (1969). Oxygen consumption in an antarctic haemoglobin-free fish, *Pagetopsis macropterus*, and in three species of *Notothenia*. *Comp. Biochem. Physiol.* **29,** 467–470. *278*

2173. Hemmingsen, E. A., Douglas, E. L., Johansen, K. and Millard, R. W. (1972). Aortic blood flow and cardiac output in the haemoglobin-free fish *Chaenocephalus aceratus*. *Comp. Biochem. Physiol.* **43A,** 1045–1051. *277*

2174. Henderson, I. W. and Chester Jones, I. (1972). Hormones and osmoregulation in fish. *Annales de l'Institut Michel Pacha Laboratoire maritime de Physiologie*, **5,** part 2, 69–235. *305*

2175. Henderson, I. W. and Chester Jones, I. (1974). Actions of hormones on osmoregulatory systems of fish. *Fortschr. Zool.* **22** (2): Comparative Endocrinology: (Proc. Internat. Symp., 1973). 391–418. *304, 305*

*2176. Henderson, I. W., Sa'di, M. N. and Hargreaves, G. (1974). Studies on the production and metabolic clearance rates of cortisol in the European eel, *Anguilla anguilla* (L.). *J. Steroid Biochem.* **5,** 701–707. *303*

*2177. Henderson, N. E. (1976). Thyroxine concentrations in plasma of normal and hypophysectomised hagfish, *Myxine glutinosa* (Cyclostomata). *Can. J. Zool.* **54,** 180–184.

*2178. Henderson, N. E. and Lorscheider, F. L. (1975). Thyroxine and protein-bound iodine concentrations in plasma of the Pacific hagfish, *Eptatretus stouti* (cyclostomata). *Comp. Biochem. Physiol.* **51A,** 723–726.

2179. Herwig, H. J. (1976). Comparative ultrastructural investigations of the pineal organ of the blind cave fish, *Anoptichthys jordani*, and its ancestor, the eyed river fish, *Astyanax mexicanus. Cell Tissue Res.* **167,** 297–324. *264*

2180. Hettler, W. F. (1976). Influence of temperature and salinity on routine metabolic rate and growth of young Atlantic menhaden. *J. Fish Biol.* **8,** 55–65. *108*

*2181. van Heyningen, R. and Linklater, J. (1976). Serine and threonine ethanolamine phosphate diesters, and some other unusual compounds in the lens of the cod fish (*Gadus morhua*) and haddock (*Gadus aeglefinus*). *Exp. Eye Res.* **23,** 29–34.

*2182. Hickman, C. P. (1965). Studies on renal function in freshwater teleost fish. *Trans. R. Soc. Can.* **3,** Ser. IV, 213–236.

2183. Higashi, H., Kaneko, T., Ishii, S., Ushiyama, M. and Sugihashi, T. (1966). Effect of ethyl linoleate, ethyl linolenate and ethyl esters of highly unsaturated fatty acids on essential fatty acid deficiency in rainbow trout. *J. Vitam.* **12,** 74–79. *143*

2184. Higashi, H., Terada, K., Morinaga, K. and Nakahira, T. (1972). Studies on roles of tocopherols in fish. (IV). Mutal conversion of tocopherol-homologues in carps, when α, γ or δ tocopherol was given to them (preliminary report). *Vitamins (Japan),* **45** (3), 121–125.

*2185. Higashi, H., Terada, K. and Nakahira, T. (1970). Studies on the roles of tocopherols in fish. (1). Tocopherol contents and ratio of each nember of tocopherol-homologues in marine animals. *Vitamins (Japan),* **42,** 1–7.

*2186. Higashi, H., Terada, K. and Nakahira, T. (1972). Studies on roles of tocopherols in fish. (III). Ubiquinone and tocopherol content in fish (part 1). *Vitamins (Japan),* **45,** 113–120. *75, 464*

2187. Higashi, H., Terada, K., Takada, S. and Koyama, T. (1976). Effect of starvation on vitamin A, E and other lipid components of eels. *Vitamins (Japan),* **50,** 265–273. From *Chem. Abstr.* **85,** 90621k (1976). *171*

*2188. Higashi, H., Yamakawa, T., Kinumaki, T., Sugii, K. and Iwasaki, K. (1961), Determination of vitamin D in fish and fish products by chromatography with Japanese acid clay. *J. Vitam.* **7,** 215–230.

2189. Higgs, D. A. and Eales, J. G. (1971). Iodide and thyroxine metabolism in the brook trout. *Salvelinus fontinalis* (Mitchill), during sustained exercise. *Can. J. Zool.* **49,** 1255–1269. *116*

*2190. Higgs, D. A. and Eales, J. G. (1973). Measurement of circulating thyroxine in several freshwater teleosts by competitive binding analysis. *Can. J. Zool.* **51,** 49–53. *218*

2191. de la Higuera, M., Murillo, A., Varela, G. and Zamora, S. (1976). Diet effect on fatty acids composition in trout (*Salmo gairdneri*). *Revta esp. Fisiol.* **32,** 317–322. *142*

2192. de la Higuera, M., Murillo, A., Varela, G. and Zamora, S. (1977). The influence of high dietary fat levels on protein utilisation by the trout (*Salmo gairdnerii*). *Comp. Biochem. Physiol.* **56A,** 37–41. *142*

2193. Hillman, H. H. (1972). "Certainty and Uncertainty in Biochemical Techniques". Sussex University Press, Brighton, England. *viii*

*2194. Hinegardner, R. (1976). The cellular DNA content of sharks, rays and some other fishes. *Comp. Biochem. Physiol.* **55B,** 367–370.

*2195. Hinegardner, R. and Rosen, D. E. (1972). Cellular DNA content and the evolution of teleostean fishes. *Am. Nat.* **106,** 621–644.

*2196. Hirano, T. (1969). Effects of hypophysectomy and salinity change on plasma cortisol concentration in the Japanese eel, *Anguilla japonica. Endocr. jap.* **16,** 557–560.

2197. Hirano, T. and Bern, H. A. (1972). The teleost gall bladder as an osmoregulatory organ. *Endocr. jap.* **19,** 41–46. *225*

2198. Hirano, T., Johnson, D. W., Bern, H. A. and Utida, S. (1973). Studies on water and ion movements in the isolated urinary bladder of selected freshwater, marine and euryhaline teleosts. *Comp. Biochem. Physiol.* **45A,** 529–540. *301*

*2199. Hirano, T., Kamiya, M., Saishu, S. and Utida, S. (1967). Effects of hypophysectomy and urophysectomy on water and sodium transport in isolated intestine and gills of Japanese eel (*Anguilla japonica*). *Endocr. jap.* **14,** 182–186. *308*

2200. Hirano, T. and Mayer-Gostan, N. (1976). Eel oesophagus as an osmoregulatory organ. *Proc. natn. Acad. Sci. U.S.A.* **73,** 1348–1350. *308*

*2201. Hirano, T., Satou, M. and Utida, S. (1972). Central nervous system control of osmoregulation in the eel (*Anguilla japonica*). *Comp. Biochem. Physiol.* **43A,** 537–544.

2202. Hirano, T. and Utida, S. (1968). Effects of ACTH and cortisol on water movement in isolated intestine of the eel, *Anguilla japonica. Gen. comp. Endocrinol.* **11,** 373–380. *308*

*2203. Hirano, T. and Utida, S. (1971). Plasma cortisol concentrations and the rate of intestinal water absorption in the eel, *Anguilla japonica. Endocr. jap.* **18,** 47–52. *302, 308*

2204. Hislop, J. R. G. and Hall, W. B. (1974). The fecundity of whiting, *Merlangius merlangus* (L.) in the North Sea, the Minch and at Iceland. *J. Cons. perm. int. Explor. Mer.* **36,** 42–49. *249*

2205. Hoar, W. S. (1939). The weight-length relationship of the Atlantic salmon. *J. Fish. Res. Bd Can.* **4,** 441–460. *351*

*2206. Hochachka, P. W. (1961). The effect of physical training on oxygen debt and glycogen reserves in trout. *Can. J. Zool.* **39,** 767–776. *118, 119, 256*

2207. Hochachka, P. W. (1965). Isoenzymes in metabolic adaptation of a poikilotherm: subunit relationships in lactic dehydrogenases of goldfish. *Archs Biochem. Biophys.* **111,** 96–103. *334*

2208. Hochachka, P. W. (1972). Enzymatic adaptations to deep sea life. *In* "The Biology of the Oceanic Pacific" (Ed. Miller, C. B.), pp. 107–136. Oregon State University Press, Corvallis. *263, 278*

2209. Hochachka, P. W. (1975a). How abyssal organisms maintain enzymes of the "right" size. *Comp. Biochem. Physiol.* **52B;** Special Issue (Ed. Hochachka, P. W). "Biochemistry at Depth". 39–41. *263*

2210. Hochachka, P. W. (1975b). An exploration of metabolic and enzyme mechanisms underlying animal life without oxygen. *In* "Biochemical and Biophysical Perspectives in Marine Biology" (Eds Malins, D. C. and Sargent, J. R.), vol. 2, pp. 107–137. Academic Press, London and New York. *281*

2211. Hochachka, P. W. and Clayton-Hochachka, B. (1973). Glucose-6-phosphate dehydrogenase and thermal acclimation in the mullet fish. *Mar. Biol.* **18,** 251–259. *328, 333, 334*

2212. Hochachka, P. W. and Hayes, F. R. (1962). The effect of temperature acclimation on pathways of glucose metabolism in the trout. *Can. J. Zool.* **40,** 261–270. *335*

2213. Hochachka, P. W., Moon, T. W. and Mustafa, T. (1972). The adaptation of enzymes to pressure in abyssal and midwater fishes. *Symp. Soc. exp. Biol.* **26,** 175–195. *263*

2214. Hochachka, P. W., Storey, K. B. and Baldwin, J. (1975). Design of acetylcholinesterase for its physical environment. *Comp. Biochem. Physiol.* **52B;** Special Issue (Ed. Hochachka, P. W.) "Biochemistry at Depth". 13–18. *263*

2215. Hodgins, H. O., Ames, W. E. and Utter, F. M. (1969). Variants of lactate dehydrogenase isozymes in sera of sockeye salmon (*Oncorhynchus nerka*). *J. Fish. Res. Bd Can.* **26,** 15–19. *253*

*2216. Hodson, P. V. (1976). δ-amino laevulinic acid dehydratase activity of fish blood as an indicator of a harmful exposure to lead. *J. Fish. Res. Bd Can.* **33,** 268–271.

*2217. Hoffert, J. R. and Fromm, P. O. (1966). Effect of carbonic anhydrase inhibition on aqueous humour and blood bicarbonate ion in the teleost (*Salvelinus namaycush*). *Comp. Biochem. Physiol.* **18,** 333–340.

*2218. Hoffert, J. R. and Fromm, P. O. (1973). Effect of acetazolamide on some haematological parameters and ocular oxygen concentration in rainbow trout. *Comp. Biochem. Physiol.* **45A,** 371–378.

*2219. Hoffman, A., Disney, J. G., Grimwood, B. E. and Jones, N. R. (1970). Glucose levels in fresh *Tilapia* muscle. *J. Fish. Res. Bd Can.* **27,** 801–803. *114, 257*

2220. Hofmann, K. (1973). Is averaging of pH values permissable? *Die Fleischwirtschaft* **2,** 258–259. *363*

*2221. Hogan, J. W. (1971a). Some enzymatic properties of plasma esterases from channel catfish (*Ictalurus punctatus*). *J. Fish. Res. Bd Can.* **28,** 613–616.

*2222. Hogan, J. W. (1971b). Brain acetylcholinesterase from cutthroat trout. *Trans. Am. Fish. Soc.* **100,** 672–675.

*2223. Hoida, E. A., Kusen', S. J. and Mukalov, I. O. (1975). Study of phospholipids during embryogenesis of *Misgurnus fossilis*. *Ukr. biokhim. Zh.* **47,** 370–373.

*2224. Hokin, L. E., Dahl, J. L., Deupree, J. D., Dixon, J. F., Hackney, J. F. and Perdue, J. F. (1973). Studies on the characterisation of the sodium-potassium transport adenosine triphosphatase. *J. biol. Chem.* **248,** 2593–2605.

2225. Holeton, G. F. (1970). Oxygen uptake and circulation by a haemoglobinless antarctic fish (*Chaenocephalus aceratus* Lonnberg) compared with three red-blooded antarctic fish. *Comp. Biochem. Physiol.* **34,** 457–471. *277*

2226. Holeton, G. F. (1974). Metabolic cold adaptation of polar fish: fact or artefact? *Physiol. Zoöl.* **47,** 137–152. *326*

2227. Holeton, G. F. (1975). Respiration and morphometrics of haemoglobinless antarctic icefish. *In* "Respiration of Marine Organisms" (Eds Cech, J. J., Bridges, D. W. and Horton, D. B.), pp. 198–211. Research Institute of the Gulf of Maine (TRIGOM), P.O. Box 2320, South Portland, Maine. *277*

2228. Holeton, G. F. (1976). Respiratory morphometrics of white and red blooded antarctic fish. *Comp. Biochem. Physiol.* **54A,** 215–220. *277, 278*

2229. Holliday, F. G. T. (1969). The effects of salinity on the eggs and larvae of teleosts. *In* "Fish Physiology" (Eds Hoar, W. S. and Randall, D. J.), vol. 1, Chapter 4, pp. 293–311. Academic Press, London and New York. *270, 290*

2230. Holloway, J. R. (1974). The morphology and hydroxysteroid dehydrogenase activity of the interrenal tissue and Corpuscles of Stannius of *Morone americana*: a comparison between estuarine and land-locked populations. Ph.D. Thesis, Lehigh University. University Microfilms no. 74–21,427. *305*

*2231. Holstein, B. (1975). Intestinal diamine oxidase of some teleostean fishes. *Comp. Biochem. Physiol.* **50B,** 291–297.

*2232. Holt, W. F. and Idler, D. R. (1975). Influence of the interrenal gland on the rectal gland of a skate. *Comp. Biochem. Physiol.* **50C,** 111–119. *309*

*2233. Holton, J. B. and Easton, D. M. (1971). Major lipids of non-myelinated (olfactory) and myelinated (trigeminal) nerve of garfish, *Lepisosteus osseus*. *Biochim. biophys. Acta,* **239,** 61–70.

*2234. Hooper, S. N., Paradis, M. and Ackman, R. G. (1973). Distribution of trans-6-hexadecenoic acid, 7-methyl-7-hexadecenoic acid and common fatty acids in lipids of the ocean sunfish *Mola mola*. *Lipids,* **8,** 509–516.

*2235. Hopkirk, G., Wills, R. B. H., Sumner, J. L. and Davis, S. R. (1976). The New Zealand eel industry. I. Raw material quality. *Food Technol. N.Z.* **11,** March issue, pp. 25, 27 and 29.

*2236. Hori, R. (1973). On the relationship between water-soluble protein and calcium in the egg of *Oryzias latipes*. *Protoplasma,* **78,** 285–290. *13*

*2237. Hori, R. (1975). On the magnesium content of the egg of the Medaka, *Oryzias latipes*, and its changes accompanying fertilisation. *Protoplasma,* **84,** 71–73.

*2238. Hori, R. and Iwasaki, S. (1976). On the manganese content of the egg of *Oryzias latipes* and its changes during the early development. *Protoplasma,* **87,** 403–407. *148*

2239. Horoszewicz, L. (1973). Lethal and "disturbing" temperatures in some fish species from lakes with normal and artificially elevated temperature. *J. Fish Biol.* **5,** 165–181. *323*

*2240. Houston, A. H. (1973). Environmental temperature and the body fluid system of the teleost. *In* "Responses of Fish to Environmental Changes" (Ed. Chavin, W.), Chapter 4, pp. 87–162. Charles C. Thomas, Springfield, Illinois. *274, 318, 341*

*2241. Houston, A. H. and Cyr, D. (1974). Thermoacclimatory variation in the haemoglobin systems of goldfish (*Carassius auratus*) and rainbow trout (*Salmo gairdneri*). *J. exp. Biol.* **61,** 455–461. *327*

2242. Houston, A. H. and DeWilde, M. A. (1969). Environmental temperature and the body fluid system of the fresh-water teleost—III. Haematology and blood volume of thermally acclimated brook trout, *Salvelinus fontinalis*. *Comp. Biochem. Physiol.* **28,** 877–885. *327*

2243. Houston, A. H., DeWilde, M. A. and Madden, J. A. (1969). Some physiological consequences of aortic catheterisation in the brook trout (*Salvelinus fontinalis*). *J. Fish. Res. Bd Can.* **26,** 1847–1856. *239*

*2244. Houston, A. H., Madden, J. A. and DeWilde, M. A. (1970). Environmental temperature and the body fluid system of the fresh-water teleost—IV. Water-electrolyte regulation in thermally acclimated carp, *Cyprinus carpio*. *Comp. Biochem. Physiol.* **34,** 805–818. *341, 342, 385*

2245. Houston, A. H., Madden, J. A., Woods, R. J. and Miles, H. M. (1971a). Some physiological effects of handling and tricaine methane-sulphonate anaesthetisation upon the brook trout, *Salvelinus fontinalis*. *J. Fish. Res. Bd Can.* **28,** 625–633. *232, 239*

2246. Houston, A. H., Madden, J. A., Woods, R. J. and Miles, H. M. (1971b). Variations in the blood and tissue chemistry of brook trout, *Salvelinus fontinalis*, subsequent to handling, anaesthesia, and surgery. *J. Fish. Res. Bd Can.* **28,** 635–642. *232*

*2247. Houston, A. H., Mearow, K. M. and Smeda, J. S. (1976). Further observations upon the haemoglobin systems of thermally-acclimated freshwater teleosts: pumpkinseed (*Lepomis gibbosus*), white sucker (*Catostomus commersoni*), carp (*Cyprinus carpio*), goldfish (*Carassius auratus*) and carp-goldfish hybrids. *Comp. Biochem. Physiol.* **54A,** 267–273.

2248. Howells, K. F. and Goldspink, G. (1974). The effects of age and exercise on the succinic dehydrogenase content of individual muscle fibres from fast, slow and mixed hamster muscles. *Histochemistry*, **38,** 195–201. *119*

2249. Hsu, W.-J., Rodriguez, D. B. and Chichester, C. O. (1972). The biosynthesis of astaxanthin. VI. The conversion of (^{14}C) lutein and (^{14}C) β-carotene in goldfish. *Int. J. Biochem.* **3,** 333–338. *144, 145*

*2250. Hu, K. H. and Friede, R. L. (1971). Factors affecting glucose and glycogen content of bowfin brain *in vitro*. *Brain Res.* **25,** 143–151.

2251. Huang, C. T. and Hickman, C. P. (1968). Binding of inorganic iodide to the plasma proteins of teleost fishes. *J. Fish. Res. Bd Can.* **25,** 1651–1656. *50*

*2252. Huckabee, J. W., Feldman, C. and Talmi, Y. (1974). Mercury concentrations in fish from the Great Smoky Mountains national park. *Analytica chim. Acta,* **70,** 41–47.

*2253. Huddart, H. (1971). The subcellular distribution of potassium and sodium in some skeletal muscles. *Comp. Biochem. Physiol.* **38A,** 715–721.

2254. Hudson, R. C. L. (1973). On the function of the white muscles in teleosts at intermediate swimming speeds. *J. exp. Biol.* **58,** 509–522. *100, 102*

*2255. Huggins, A. K. and Colley, L. (1971). The changes in the non-protein nitrogenous constituents of muscle during the adaptation of the eel *Anguilla anguilla* L. from fresh water to sea water. *Comp. Biochem. Physiol.* **38B,** 537–541. *313*

*2256. Huggins, A. K., Skutsch, G. and Baldwin, E. (1969). Ornithine-urea cycle enzymes in teleostean fish. *Comp. Biochem. Physiol.* **28,** 587–602.

*2257. Hughes, G. M. and Itazawa, Y. (1972). The effect of temperature on the respiratory function of coelacanth blood. *Experientia*, **28**, 1247 only.

2258. Hulet, W. H., Fischer, J. and Reitberg, B. J. (1972). Electrolyte composition of anguilliform leptocephali from the straits of Florida. *Bull. mar. Sci. Gulf Caribb.* **22**, 432–448. *24*

2259. Hume, A., Farmer, J. W. and Burt, J. R. (1972). A comparison of the flavours of farmed and trawled plaice. *J. Food Technol.* **7**, 27–33. *260*

*2260. Hunn, J. B. (1969a). Chemical composition of rainbow trout urine following acute hypoxic stress. *Trans. Am. Fish. Soc.* **98**, 20–22. *282*

*2261. Hunn, J. B. (1969b). Inorganic composition of gallbladder bile from fasted rainbow trout. *Progve Fish Cult.* **31**, 221–222.

*2262. Hunn, J. B. (1972a). Blood chemistry values for some fishes of the upper Mississippi River. *J. Minn. Acad. Sci.* **38**, 19–21.

*2263. Hunn, J. B. (1972b). Concentrations of some inorganic constituents in gall-bladder bile from some freshwater fishes. *Copeia*, (4), 860–861 (no volume number given). *225*

*2264. Hunn, J. B. (1976). Inorganic composition of gallbladder bile from freshwater fishes. *Copeia*, (3), 602–605 (no volume number given).

*2265. Hunn, J. B. and Christenson, L. M. (1977). Chemical composition of blood and bile of the shovelnose sturgeon. *Progve Fish Cult.* **39**, 59–61.

*2266. Hurlburt, M. E. (1977). Effects of thyroxine administration on plasma thyroxine levels in the goldfish, *Carassius auratus* L. *Can. J. Zool.* **55**, 255–258.

*2267. Hutton, K. E. (1968). Characteristics of the blood of adult pink salmon at three stages of maturity. *Fishery Bull. Fish Wildl. Serv. U.S.* **66**, 195–202. *44, 49*

*2268. Hyvärinen, H. and Valtonen, T. (1973). Seasonal changes in the liver mineral content of *Coregonus nasus* (Pallas) *sensu* (Svärdson) in the Bay of Bothnia. *Comp. Biochem. Physiol.* **45B**, 875–881. *56, 385*

*2269. Ichikawa, R. and Ohno, S. (1974). Levels of cobalt, caesium and zinc in some marine organisms in Japan. *Bull. Jap. Soc. scient. Fish.* **40**, 501–508.

2270. Idler, D. R. (1973). Comments on "Structure and function of the adrenal gland of fishes" by David Gordon Butler. *Am. Zool.* **13**, 881–884. *112*

2271. Idler, D. R., Bitners, I. I. and Schmidt, P. J. (1961). 11-ketotestosterone: an androgen for sockeye salmon. *Can. J. Biochem. Physiol.* **39**, 1737–1742. *38, 199*

*2272. Idler, D. R. and Kane, K. M. (1976). Interrenalectomy and Na-K-ATPase activity in the rectal gland of the skate *Raja ocellata*. *Gen. comp. Endocrinol.* **28**, 100–102.

*2273. Idler, D. R., Reinboth, R., Walsh, J. M. and Truscott, B. (1976). A comparison of 11-hydroxytestosterone and 11-ketotestosterone in blood of ambisexual and gonochoristic teleosts. *Gen comp. Endocrinol.* **30,** 517–521.

*2274. Idler, D. R., Sangalang, G. B. and Truscott, B. (1972). Corticosteroids in the South American lungfish. *Gen. comp. Endocrinol.* Suppl. 3, 238–244.

*2275. Idler, D. R., Sangalang, G. B. and Weisbart, M. (1971). Are corticosteroids present in the blood of all fish? *Horm. Steroids, Proc. Int. Congr., 3rd, 1970.* (Ed. James, V. H. T.), pp. 983–989. Excerpta Medica, Amsterdam.

*2276. Idler, D. R. and Truscott, B. (1969). Production of 1α-hydroxycorticosterone *in vivo* and *in vitro* by elasmobranchs. *Gen. comp. Endocrinol.* Suppl. 2, 325–330.

2277. Idler, D. R., Truscott, B. and Stewart, H. C. (1969). Some distinct aspects of steroidogenesis in fish. *In* "Progress in Endocrinology" (Eds Gaul, C. and Ebling, F. J. G.), pp. 724–729. Excerpta Medica Foundation, Amsterdam. *6*

*2278. Ikeda, Y., Ozaki, H. and Uemitsu, K. (1975). Effect of handling on serum level of chemical constituents in yellow tail. *Bull. Jap. Soc. scient. Fish.* **41,** 803–811. *232, 239*

2279. Ikeda, Y., Ozaki, H. and Yasuda, H. (1974). The effect of starvation and reduced diet on the growth of scales in goldfish. *Bull. Jap. Soc. scient. Fish.* **40,** 859–868. *171*

*2280. Il'inskii, O. B. and Krasnikova, T. L. (1974). Ionic composition of jelly of Lorenzini ampullae of Mediterranean electric rays. *Zh. evol. Biokhim. Fiziol.* **10,** 417–419.

*2281. Ilzina, A. (1968). Influence of spawning on the levels of manganese, iron, copper and zinc in the viscera and tissues of roaches (*Rutilus rutilus*) and on the accumulation of these trace elements in the ovaries in different phases of sexual maturity. *Mikroelem. Organizyme Ryb. Ptits* (Ed. Bermane, S.), Izd. "Zinatne", Riga, USSR. 53–62. *45*

*2282. Imura, K. and Saito, T. (1968). Nucleic acid contents in various tissues of some fishes. *Bull. Fac. Fish. Hokkaido Univ.* **19,** 132–139. *43, 51*

*2283. Imura, K. and Saito, T. (1969). Seasonal variations in the metabolic activities of tissue constituents of some fishes—1. Changes in nucleic acid contents of some tissues of kokanee salmon, *Oncorhynchus nerka f. kenerlyi. Bull. Fac. Fish. Hokkaido Univ.* **20,** 202–210. *51, 65*

*2284. Ince, B. W. and Thorpe, A. (1976). The effects of starvation and force-feeding on the metabolism of the northern pike, *Esox lucius* L. *J. Fish Biol.* **8,** 79–88. *97, 182, 183, 193, 229, 364*

2285. Ince, B. W. and Thorpe, A. (1977). Glucose and amino acid-stimulated insulin release *in vivo* in the European silver eel (*Anguilla anguilla* L.) *Gen. comp. Endocrinol.* **31,** 249–256. *365*

2286. Infante, O. (1974). The excretion of nitrogen by fed and starved carps. *Arch. Hydrobiol.* Suppl. **47**, 239–281. *386*

*2287. Ingram, P. (1970). Uridine diphosphate glucose-glycogen glucosyl transferase from trout liver. *Int. J. Biochem.* **1**, 263–273.

*2288. Inokuchi, M., Kato, A., Sasahara, M., Aoshima, Y. and Watanabe, K. (1975). Chemical properties of the vitreous humour and serum of the carp. *J. Tokyo Women's Med. Coll.* **45**, 687–691.

2289. Inui, Y. (1969). Hepatectomy in eels. Its operation technique and effects on blood glucose. *Bull. Jap. Soc. scient. Fish.* **35**, 975–978. *232–234*

*2290. Inui, Y., Arai, S. and Yokote, M. (1975). Gluconeogenesis in the eel—IV. Effects of hepatectomy, alloxan, and mammalian insulin on the behaviour of plasma amino acids. *Bull. Jap. Soc. scient. Fish.* **41**, 1105–1111.

*2291. Inui, Y. and Yokote, M. (1974). Gluconeogenesis in the eel—I. Gluconeogenesis in the fasted eel. *Bull. Freshwat. Fish. Res. Lab.*, Tokyo, **24**, 33–45. *187–189, 203, 204*

*2292. Inui, Y. and Yokote, M. (1975a). Gluconeogenesis in the eel—III. Effects of mammalian insulin on the carbohydrate metabolism of the eel. *Bull. Jap. Soc. scient. Fish.* **41**, 965–972.

*2293. Inui, Y. and Yokote, M. (1975b). Gluconeogenesis in the eel—IV. Gluconeogenesis in the hydrocortisone-administered eel. *Bull. Jap. Soc. scient. Fish.* **41**, 973–981.

*2294. Ipatov, V. V. and Shaldaeva, R. E. (1974). Some data on the dynamics of total calcium in the blood serum of Baltic cod. *Ryb. Issled. v Basseine Baltiiskogo Morya*, (10), 87–93 (no volume number). *44*

2295. Iredale, D. G. and York, R. K. (1976). Purging a muddy-earthy flavour taint from rainbow trout (*Salmo gairdneri*) by transferring to artificial and natural holding environments. *J. Fish. Res. Bd Can.* **33**, 160–166. *248*

*2296. Irving, D. O. and Watson, K. (1976). Mitochondrial enzymes of tropical fish: a comparison with fish from cold-waters. *Comp. Biochem. Physiol.* **54B**, 81–92. *339*

*2297. Ishihara, T., Kinari, H. and Yasuda, M. (1973). Studies on thiaminase I in marine fish—II. Distribution of thiaminase in marine fish. *Bull. Jap. Soc. scient. Fish.* **39**, 55–59.

*2298. Ishihara, T., Yasuda, M., Kashiwagi, S., Akiyama, M. and Yagi, M. (1974). Studies on thiaminase I in marine fish—VI. Preventive effect of thiamine on nutritional disease of yellowtail fed anchovy (2). *Bull. Jap. Soc. scient. Fish.* **40**, 775–781.

*2299. Ishihara, T., Yasuda, M. and Morooka, H. (1972). Studies on thiaminase I in marine fish—I. Thiaminase in anchovy. *Bull. Jap. Soc. scient. Fish.* **38**, 1281–1287.

*2300. Ishioka, H. and Fushimi, T. (1975). Some haematological properties of matured red sea bream, *Chrysophrys major* Temminck et Schlegel. *Nansei Kaiku Suisan Kenkyujo Kenkyu Hōkoku (Bull. Nansei Reg. Fish. Lab.*), **8**, 11–20.

2301. Ishiwata, N. (1968). Ecological studies on the feeding of fishes—V. Size of fish and satiation amount. *Bull. Jap. Soc. scient. Fish.* **34**, 781–784. *28*

*2302. Israël, M., Gautron, J. and Lesbats, B. (1970). Subcellular fractionation of the electric organ of *Torpedo marmorata. J. Neurochem.* **17**, 1441–1450.

*2303. Israël, M., Lesbats, B., Marsal, J. and Meunier, F.-M. (1975). Fluctuations of the level of tissue acetylcholine and adenosine triphosphate during the stimulation of the electric organ of the torpedo. *C. r. hebd. Séanc. Acad. Sci., Paris,* **280**, Ser. D, 905–908.

2304. Ito, T. (1976). Uptake of dissolved ammonium and nitrate ion by the fry of common carp, crucian carp and loach from surrounding water. *Bull. Freshwat. Fish. Res. Lab., Tokyo,* **26**, 27–33. *149*

*2305. Iuchi, I. (1973). Chemical and physiological properties of the larval and the adult haemoglobins in rainbow trout, *Salmo gairdneri irideus. Comp. Biochem. Physiol.* **44B**, 1087–1101. *2, 22*

2306. Iuchi, I. and Yamagami, K. (1969). Electrophoretic pattern of larval haemoglobins of the salmoniod fish, *Salmo gairdneri irideus. Comp. Biochem. Physiol.* **28**, 977–979. *13*

2307. Iverson, J. L. (1972). Per cent fatty acid composition and quality differences of chinook and coho salmon. *Jnl Ass. off. analyt. Chem.* **55**, 1187–1190. *209*

2308. Iwahashi, M. and Wakui, H. (1976). Intesification of colour of fancy carp with diet. *Bull. Jap. Soc. scient. Fish.* **42**, 1339–1344.

*2309. Iwama, G. K., Greer, G. L. and Larkin, P. A. (1976). Changes in some haematological characteristics of coho salmon (*Oncorhynchus kisutch*) in response to acute exposure to dehydroabietic acid (DHAA) at different exercise levels. *J. Fish. Res. Bd Can.* **33**, 285–289.

*2310. Iyengar, R. and Schlenk, H. (1967). Wax esters of mullet (*Mugil cephalus*) roe oil. *Biochemistry,* **6**, 396–402.

2311. Jackim, E. and LaRoche, G. (1973). Protein synthesis in *Fundulus heteroclitus* muscle. *Comp. Biochem. Physiol.* **44A**, 851–866. *197, 281, 324*

2312. Jacquest, W. L. and Beatty, D. D. (1972). Visual pigment changes in the rainbow trout, *Salmo gairdneri. Can. J. Zool.* **50**, 1117–1126. *7, 49, 268*

*2313. Jadhav, M. G. and Magar, N. G. (1970). Preservation of fish by freezing and glazing: III. Effect of freezing, glazing and frozen storage on the B-vitamins and essential minerals present in the fish flesh. *Fish. Technol.* **7**, 158–163.

*2314. Jafri, A. K., Asghar, S. S. and Khawaja, D. K. (1970). 5'nucleotidase activity in the tissues of the freshwater murrel, *Ophicephalus punctatus* Bloch. *Enzymologia*, **39**, 205–210.

*2315. Jafri, A. K. and Mustafa, S. (1976a). Nucleic acids in the dark and white muscles of a freshwater carp, *Barbus stigma* (Cuv. and Val.). *Curr. Sci.* **45**, 415–416.

*2316. Jafri, A. K. and Mustafa, S. (1976b). Phosphatases & 5'-nucleotidase in the dark & white muscles of two freshwater cat-fishes *Clarias magur* (Linn.) *Heteropneustes fossilis* (Bloch). *Indian J. exp. Biol.* **14**, 292–294. *72, 76*

*2317. Jafri, A. K. and Shaffi, S. A. (1975). Distribution of acid and alkaline phosphatase activity in the normal organs of freshwater teleost. I.—*Ophicephalus punctatus* Bloch. *Broteria*, **44**, 93–100.

*2318. Jafri, A. K. and Shreni, K. D. (1975). Influence of age on the total liver cholesterol of the freshwater murrel, *Ophicephalus punctatus* Bloch. *Indian J. exp. Biol.* **13**, 86–87. *61, 62*

2319. Jamieson, A. and Jones, B. W. (1967). Two races of cod at Faroe. *Heredity*, **22**, 610–612. *107, 252, 382*

2320. Jamieson, A. and Thompson, D. (1972). Blood proteins in North Sea cod (*Gadus morhua* L.). *XII Europ. Conf. Anim. blood Groups Biochem. Polymorph.*, Budapest, 585–591. *252*

*2321. Jampol, L. M. and Epstein, F. H. (1970). Sodium- potassium-activated adenosine triphosphatase and osmotic regulation by fishes. *Am. J. Physiol.* **218**, 607–611. *306*

2322. Janicki, R. and Lingis, J. (1970). Mechanism of ammonia production from aspartate in teleost liver. *Comp. Biochem. Physiol.* **37**, 101–105. *160*

2323. Jankowsky, H.-D. (1968a). On structure and metabolic rate of the skeletal muscle of the eel (*Anguilla vulgaris* L.). *In* "Quantitative Biology of Metabolism" (Ed. Locker, A.) (*3rd int. Symp., Biol. Anstalt Helgoland;* Sept. 26–29, 1967, pp. 91–94. Springer-Verlag, Berlin. *69, 74, 85, 87, 331*

2324. Jankowsky, H. D. (1968b). Adaptation of fish within the normal range of temperature. *Helgoländer wiss. Meeresunters.* **18**, 317–362. From *Chem. Abstr.* **70**, 35501m (1969). *328, 329*

*2325. Jany, K.-D. (1976). Studies on the digestive enzymes of the stomachless bonefish *Carassius auratus gibelio* (Bloch); endopeptidases. *Comp. Biochem. Physiol.* **53B**, 31–38.

*2326. Javaid, M. Y. and Lone, K. P. (1973). Haematology of fishes of Pakistan. *Acta physiol. latinoam.* **23**, 396–402.

2327. Jeng, S. S. and Chiang, H. L. (1974). Lactate dehydrogenase in muscle of spotted mackerel. *Bull. Inst. Zool., Acad. Sin. (Taiwan)* **13,** 61–67. *88*

*2328. Jeng, S. S. and Lo, H. W. (1974). High zinc concentration in common carp viscera. *Bull. Jap. Soc. scient. Fish.* **40,** 509 only. *522*

2329. Jirge, S. K. (1970). Changes in the distribution of glycogen in the liver at various stages of development of *Tilapian* larvae. *Annls Histochim.* **15,** 283–287. *11*

*2330. Jitariu, M., Chera, E., Duca, E., Linck, G., Rotimberg, P. and Szilagyi, I. (1975). Lipido-carotenoid metabolism in *Salmo gairdneri* during embryogenesis. *Revue Roum. Biol.* **20,** 269–274. *14*

*2331. Johansen, K., Lykkeboe, G., Weber, R. E. and Maloiy, G. M. O. (1976). Respiratory properties of blood in awake and aestivating lungfish, *Protopterus amphibius. Resp. Physiol.* **27,** 335–345. *277*

*2332. Johansson, M.-L., Dave, G., Larsson, Å., Lewander, K. and Lidman, U. (1974). Metabolic and haematological studies on the yellow and silver phases of the European eel, *Anguilla anguilla* L.—III. Haematology. *Comp. Biochem. Physiol.* **47B,** 593–599. *22*

*2333. Johansson-Sjöbeck, M.-L., Dave, G., Larsson, Å., Lewander, K. and Lidman, U. (1975). Metabolic and haematological effects of starvation in the European eel, *Anguilla anguilla* L.—II. Haematology. *Comp. Biochem. Physiol.* **52A,** 431–434. *213*

*2334. Johansson-Sjöbeck, M.-L. and Stevens, J. D. (1936). Haematological studies on the blue shark, *Prionace glauca* L. *J. mar. biol. Ass. U.K.* **56,** 237–240.

2335. Johnson, A. G. and Beardsley, A. J. (1975). Biochemical polymorphism of starry flounder, *Platichthys stellatus*, from the northwestern and northeastern Pacific Ocean. *Anim. Blood Groups Biochem. Genet.* **6,** 9–18. *253*

2336. Johnson, A. G., Utter, F. M. and Hodgins, H. O. (1971). Phosphoglucomutase polymorphism on Pacific Ocean perch, *Sebastodes alutus. Comp. Biochem. Physiol.* **39B,** 285–290.

2337. Johnson, C. R. (1976). Diet variations in the thermal tolerance of *Gambusia affinis affinis* (Pisces: poeciliidae). *Comp. Biochem. Physiol.* **55A,** 337–340. *324*

2338. Johnson, D. W. (1973). Endocrine control of hydromineral balance in teleosts. *Am. Zool.* **13,** 799–818. *301*

2339. Johnston, G. E. and Eales, J. G. (1970). Influence of body size on silvering of Atlantic salmon (Salmo salar) at parr-smolt transformation. *J. Fish. Res. Bd Can.* **27,** 983–987. *21*

*2340. Johnston, I. A. (1975a). Studies on the swimming musculature of the rain bow trout. II. Muscle metabolism during severe hypoxia. *J. Fish Biol.* **7** 459–467. *3, 73, 76, 281*

2341. Johnston, I. A. (1975b). Pyruvate kinase from the red skeletal musculature of the carp (*Carassius carassuis* L.). *Biochem. biophys. Res. Commun.* **63,** 115–120. *280*

*2342. Johnston, I. A. (1975c). Anaerobic metabolism in the carp (*Carassius carassius* L.). *Comp. Biochem. Physiol.* **51B,** 235–241. *271*

*2343. Johnston, I. A., Davison, W. and Goldspink, G. (1975). Adaptations in Mg^{2+}-activated myofibrillar ATPase activity induced by temperature acclimation. *FEBS Lett.* **50,** 293–295. *328, 333, 336, 337*

*2344. Johnston, I. A., Davison, W. and Goldspink, G. (1977). Energy metabolism of carp swimming muscles. *J. comp. Physiol.* **114,** 203–216. *101*

2345. Johnston, I. A., Frearson, N. and Goldspink, G. (1972). Myofibrillar ATPase activities of red and white myotomal muscles of marine fish. *Experientia,* **28,** 713–714. *71, 75, 92*

2346. Johnston, I. A., Frearson, N. and Goldspink, G. (1973). The effects of environmental temperature on the properties of myofibrillar adenosine triphosphatase from various species of fish. *Biochem. J.* **133,** 735–738. *336*

*2347. Johnston, I. A. and Goldspink, G. (1973a). A study of glycogen and lactate in the myotomal muscles and liver of the coalfish (*Gadus virens* L.) during sustained swimming. *J. mar. biol. Ass. U.K.* **53,** 17–26. *73, 101, 103*

*2348. Johnston, I. A. and Goldspink, G. (1973b). A study of the swimming performance of the crucian carp *Carassius carassius* (L.) in relation to the effects of exercise and recovery on biochemical changes in the myotomal muscles and liver. *J. Fish Biol.* **5,** 249–260. *78, 89*

*2349. Johnston, I. A. and Goldspink, G. (1973c). Some effects of prolonged starvation on the metabolism of the red and white myotomal muscles of the plaice *Pleuronectes platessa*. *Mar. Biol.* **19,** 348–353. *93, 95–97*

2350. Johnston, I. A. and Goldspink, G. (1973d). Quantitative studies of muscle glycogen utilisation during sustained swimming in crucian carp (*Carrasius carassius* L.). *J. exp. Biol.* **59,** 607–615. *79, 102*

2351. Johnston, I. A. and Goldspink, G. (1975). Thermodynamic activation parameters of fish myofibrillar ATPase enzyme and evolutionary adaptations to temperature. *Nature, Lond.* **257,** 620–622. *331*

2352. Johnston, I. A., Patterson, S., Ward, P. and Goldspink, G. (1974). The histochemical demonstration of myofibrillar adenosine triphosphatase activity in fish muscle. *Can. J. Zool.* **52,** 871–877. *83, 84*

*2353. Johnston, I. A. and Tota, B. (1974). Myofibrillar ATPase in the various red and white trunk muscles of the tunny (*Thunnus thynnus* L.) and the tub gurnard (*Trigla lucerna* L.). *Comp. Biochem. Physiol.* **49B,** 367–373. *76, 81, 82*

2354. Johnston, I. A., Walesby, N. J., Davison, W. and Goldspink, G. (1975). Temperature adaptation in myosin of antarctic fish. *Nature, Lond.* **254,** 74–75. *336*

2355. Johnston, I. A., Ward, P. S. and Goldspink, G. (1975). Studies on the swimming musculature of the rainbow trout. I. Fibre types. *J. Fish Biol.* **7,** 451–458. *80, 82–84*

2356. Jones, B. J. and Pearson, W. D. (1976). Variations in haematocrit values of successive blood samples from bluegill. *Trans. Am. Fish. Soc.* **105,** 291–293. *425*

2357. Jones, B. W. (1966). The cod and the cod fishery at Faroe. *Fishery Invest., Lond. Ser.* 2, **24** (5), 32 pp. *382*

2358. Jones, R. and Hislop, J. R. G. (1972). Investigations into the growth of haddock, *Melanogrammus aeglefinus* (L.) and whiting, *Merlangius merlangus* (L.) in aquaria. *J. Cons. perm. int. Explor. Mer.* **34,** 174–189. *137, 138*

*2359. Jones, R. T. and Price, K. S. (1974). Osmotic responses of spiny dogfish (*Squalus acanthias* L.) embryos to temperature and salinity stress. *Comp. Biochem. Physiol.* **47A,** 971–979.

2360. Jordan, J. (1976). The influence of body weight on gas exchange in the air-breathing fish, *Clarias batrachus. Comp. Biochem. Physiol.* **53A,** 305–310. *28, 270*

*2361. Joshi, B. D. (1974). Effect of starvation on blood glucose and nonprotein nitrogen levels of the fish *Clarias batrachus. Experientia,* **30,** 772–773. *192*

*2362. Joshi, B. D. and Tandon, R. S. (1977). Seasonal variations in haematologic values of freshwater fishes. I. *Heteropneustes fossilis* and *Mystus vittatus. Comp. Physiol. Ecol.* **2,** 22–26.

*2363. Julshamn, K. and Braekkan, O. R. (1975). The relation between total cobalt and cobalt in vitamin B_{12} during the maturation of ovaries in salmon (*Salmo salar*). *Comp. Biochem. Physiol.* **52B,** 381–382.

*2364. Julshamn, K. and Braekkan, O. R. (1976). The relation between the concentration of some main elements and the stages of maturation of ovaries in cod (*Gadus morrhua*). *FiskDir. Skr. Ser. Ernaer.* **1,** 1–15. *46*

2365. Jurcă, V., Cazacu, G. and Cazacu, C. (1973). Polyacrilamide gel electrophoresis of proteins during embryogenesis of *Cyprinus carpio, Hypophthalmichthys molitrix* and *Ctenopharyngodon idella. Studii Cerc. Biochim.* **16,** 29–34. *12*

*2366. Jürss, K. and Nicolai, B. (1976). Biochemical changes in liver and muscle of the rainbow trout (*Salmo gairdneri*) during starvation. *Zool. Jb. Abt. allg. Zool. Physiol. Tiere,* **80,** 101–109. *187, 227*

2367. Kallner, A. (1968). Bile acids in bile of cod, *Gadus callarias.* Hydroxylation of deoxycholic acid and chenodeoxycholic acid in homogenates of cod liver. Bile acids and steroids. *Acta chem. scand.* **22,** 2361–2370.

2368. Kaloustian, K. V. and Poluhowich, J. J. (1976). The role of organic phosphates in modulating the oxygenation behaviour of eel haemoglobin. *Comp. Biochem. Physiol.* **53A,** 245–248. *274, 315*

*2369. Kamiya, M. (1972). Sodium-potassium-activated adenosinetriphosphatase in isolated chloride cells from eel gills. *Comp. Biochem. Physiol.* **43B,** 611–617.

2370. Kamiya, M. and Utida, S. (1968). Changes in activity of sodium-potassium-activated adenosinetriphosphatase in gills during adaptation of the Japanese eel to sea water. *Comp. Biochem. Physiol.* **26,** 675–685. *291*

*2371. Kamps, L. R., Carr, R. and Miller, H. (1972). Total mercury-monomethyl-mercury content of several species of fish. *Bull. Environ. Contam. Toxicol.* **8,** 273–279.

2372. Kamyshnaya, M. S. and Shatunovsky, M. I. (1969). Lipid composition in the humpback salmon in their natural habitat rivers and in acclimatised regions. *Vest. mosk. gos. Univ.* **24** (2), 33–37. *257*

*2373. Karamucheva, L., Georgiev, G., Sotirov, N. and Emanuilova, E. (1972). The influence of vitamin B_{12} on growth and some haematological and bio-chemical characteristics of the rainbow trout (*Salmo irideus*). *Izv. Inst. Obsh. srav. Patol. (Sofia),* **14,** 275–283. *172*

2374. Karlsson, J. and Bengt, S. (1971). Diet, muscle glygogen, and endurance performance. *J. appl. Physiol.* **31,** 203–206. *141*

2375. Karlsson, J., Sjödin, B., Thorstensson, A., Hultén, B. and Frith, K. (1975). LDH isozymes in skeletal muscles of endurance and strength trained athletes. *Acta physiol. scand.* **93,** 150–156. *118*

*2376. Karlsson, K. A., Samuelsson, B. E. and Steen, G. O. (1968). Sulphatides and sodium ion transport, sphingolipid composition of the rectal gland of spiny dogfish. *FEBS Lett.* **2,** 4–6.

*2377. Karlsson, K. A., Samuelsson, B. E. and Steen, G. O. (1974). The lipid composition of the salt (rectal) gland of spiny dogfish. *Biochim. biophys Acta,* **337,** 356–376.

2377a. Karnaky, K. J., Degnan, K. J. and Zadunaisky, J. A. (1977). Chloride transport across isolated opercular epithelium of killifish: a membrane rich in chloride cells. *Science, N.Y.* **195,** 203–205. *297*

*2378. Karnaky, K. J., Ernst, S. A. and Philpott, C. W. (1976). Teleost chloride cell. I. Response of pupfish *Cyprinodon variegatus* gill Na, K-ATPase and chloride cell fine structure to various high salinity environments. *J. cell Biol.* **70,** 144–156. *295, 298*

2378a. Karnaky, K. J. and Kinter, W. B. (1977). Killifish opercular skin: a flat epithelium with a high density of chloride cells. *J. exp. Zool.* **199,** 355–364. *297*

*2379. Karnaky, K. J., Kinter, L. B., Kinter, W. B. and Stirling, C. E. (1976). Teleost chloride cell. II. Autoradiographic localisation of gill Na, K-ATPase in killifish *Fundulus heteroclitus* adapted to low and high salinity environments. *J. cell Biol.* **70**, 157–177.

*2380. Karnicka, B. and Jurewicz, I. (1971). Changes in the content of trimethylamine oxide, trimethylamine and total volatile basic nitrogen in fresh and frozen fish. *Pr. morsk. Inst. ryb. Gdyni*, **16B**, 193–203.

2381. Kashiwada, K., Teshima, S. and Kanazawa, A. (1970). Studies on the production of B vitamins by intestinal bacteria of fish—V. Evidence of the production of vitamin B_{12} by microorganisms in the intestinal canal of carp, *Cyprinus carpio*. *Bull. Jap. Soc. scient. Fish.* **36**, 421–424. *146*

2382. Kashiwagi, M. and Sato, R. (1968). A comparison of some blood properties between two groups of chum salmon, *Oncorhynchus keta* (Walbaum), reared in a salt water pond and in a fresh water pond. *Tohoku J. agric. Res.* **19**, 56–61. *315*

2383. Kashiwagi, M. and Sato, R. (1969). Studies on the osmoregulation of the chum salmon, *Ocorhynchus keta* (Walbaum). 1. The tolerance of the eyed period eggs, alevins and fry of the chum salmon to sea water. *Tohoku J. agric. Res.* **20**, 41–47. *315*

2384. Katayama, T., Miyahara, T., Kunisaki, Y., Tanaka, Y. and Imai, S. (1973). Carotenoids in the sea bream, *Chrysophrys major* Temminck and Schlegel—II. Carotenoids in the sea bream, *Chrysophrys major* Temminck and Schlegel, the red sea bream *Evynnis japonica* Tanaka, marine red colour fish, and the metabolism to astaxanthin. *Mem. Fac. Fish. Kagoshima Univ.* **22**, 63–72. *398*

2385. Katayama, T., Miyahara, T., Shimaya, M. and Chichester, C. O. (1972). The biosynthesis of astaxanthin. X. The carotenoids in the red carp, *Cyprinus carpio* Linne, and the interconversion of β-[15, 15'-³H₂] carotene into their body astaxanthin. *Int. J. Biochem.* **3**, 569–572. *145*

2386. Katayama, T., Shintani, K., Shimaya, M., Imai, S. and Chichester, C. O. (1972). The biosynthesis of astaxanthin—IX. The transformation of labelled astaxanthin from the diet of sea bream, *Chrysophrys major* Temminck and Schlegel, to their body astaxanthin. *Bull. Jap. Soc. scient. Fish.* **38**, 1399–1403. *145*

2387. Katayama, T., Tsuchiya, H. and Chichester, C. O. (1971). The biosynthesis of astaxanthin—V. Interconversion of the algal carotenoids, *Stigeoclonium* sp. into fish carotenoids, fancy red carps. *Mem. Fac. Fish. Kagoshima Univ.* **20**, 173–184. *145*

*2388. Kato, N. and Uchiyama, H. (1973). An automation analysis of trimethylamine in fish muscle. *Bull. Jap. Soc. scient. Fish.* **39**, 899–903.

2389. Kato, T. (1972). Artificial silvering of rainbow trout reared in blue tank. *Bull. Freshwat. Fish. Res. Lab.*, Tokyo, **22**, 39–45. *26*

*2390. Katsuki, Y., Yasuda, K., Ueda, K. and Kimura, Y. (1975). Study on amounts of trace elements in marine fishes (II). Distribution of heavy metals in bonito tissue. *Ann. Rep. Tokyo Metrop. Res. Lab. Publ. Health*, **26**, 196–199.

*2391. Katz, Y. and Eckstein, B. (1974). Changes in steroid concentration in blood of female *Tilapia aurea* (Teleostei, Cichlidae) during initiation of spawning. *Endocrinology*, **95**, 963–967. *36*

*2392. Katzman, R., Lehrer, G. M. and Wilson, C. E. (1969). Sodium and potassium distribution in puffer fish supramedullary nerve cell bodies. *J. gen. Physiol.* **54**, 232–249.

*2393. Kawai, S. and Ikeda, S. (1971). Studies on digestive enzymes of fishes—I. Carbohydrases in digestive organs of several fishes. *Bull. Jap. Soc. scient. Fish.* **37**, 333–337.

 2394. Kawai, S. and Ikeda, S. (1972). Studies on digestive enzymes of fishes—II. Effect of dietary change on the activities of digestive enzymes in carp intestine. *Bull. Jap. Soc. scient. Fish.* **38**, 265–270. *151*

*2395. Kawai, S. and Ikeda, S. (1973a). Studies on digestive enzymes of fishes—III. Development of the digestive enzymes of rainbow trout after hatching and the effect of dietary change on the activities of digestive enzymes in the juvenile stage. *Bull. Jap. Soc. scient. Fish.* **39**, 819–823. *17, 151*

 2396. Kawai, S. and Ikeda, S. (1973b). Studies on digestive enzymes of fishes—IV. Development of the digestive enzymes of carp and black sea bream after hatching. *Bull. Jap. Soc. scient. Fish.* **39**, 877–881. *17*

 2397. Kawatsu, H. (1974). Studies on the anaemia of fish—IV. Further note on the anaemia caused by starvation in rainbow trout. *Bull. Freshwat. Fish. Res. Lab., Tokyo*, **24**, 89–94. *213*

*2398. Kayama, M. (1975). Studies on the lipids of micronektonic fishes caught in Sagami and Suruga Bays, with special reference to their wax esters. *J. Japan Oil Chem. Soc. (Yukagaku)*, **24**, 435–440.

*2399. Kayama, M., Horii, I. and Ikeda, Y. (1974). Studies on fish roe lipids, especially on mullet roe wax esters. *J. Japan Oil Chem. Soc. (Yukagaku)*, **23**, 290–295.

*2400. Kayama, M. and Ikeda, Y. (1975). Studies on the lipids of micronectonic fishes caught in Sagami and Suruga Bays, with special reference to their wax esters. *J. Japan Oil Chem. Soc. (Yukagaku)*, **24**, 435–440.

 2401. Kayama, Mand Nevenzel, J. C.2 (1974). Wax ester biosynthesis by midwater marine animals.*Mar. Biol.* **24**, 79–285. *53, 144*

 2402. Kayama, M. and Shimada, H. (1972). Biosynthesis of squalene and cholesterol in the fish—II. Mevalonate as a key precursor *in vitro*. *Bull. Jap. Soc. scient. Fish.* **38**, 741–751.

*2403. Kayama, M., Tsuchiya, Y. and Nevenzel, J. C. (1969). The hydrocarbons of shark liver oils. *Bull. Jap. Soc. scient. Fish.* **35,** 653–664.

*2404. Ke, P. J., Power, H. E. and Regier, L. W. (1970). Fluoride content of fish protein concentrate and raw fish. *J. Sci. Fd Agric.* **21,** 108–109.

 2405. Keast, A. (1970). Food specialisations and bioenergetic interrelations in the fish of some small Ontario waterways. *In* "Marine Food Chains" (Ed. Steel, J. H.), pp. 377–411. Oliver and Boyd, Edinburgh. *365*

*2406. Keay, J. N., Rattagool, P. and Hardy, R. (1972). Chub mackerel of Thailand (*Rastrelliger neglectus*, Van Kampen): a short study of its chemical composition, cold storage and canning properties. *J. Sci. Fd Agric.* **23,** 1359–1368.

*2407. Keesey, J. C., Sallee, T. L. and Adams, G. M. (1972). Neutral lipids and phospholipids of unmyelinated nerve trunks from lobster and garfish. *J. Neurochem.* **19,** 2225–2228.

*2408. Kellogg, T. F. (1975). The biliary bile acids of the channel catfish, *Ictalurus punctatus*, and the blue catfish, *Ictalurus furcatus*. *Comp. Biochem. Physiol.* **50B,** 109–111.

 2409. Kelly, K. O. (1969). Factors affecting the texture of frozen fish. *In* "Freezing and Irradiation of Fish" (Ed. Kreuzer, R.), pp. 339–342. Fishing News (Books) Ltd., London. *360*

 2410. Kelly, K. O., Jones. N. R., Love, R. M. and Olley, J. (1966). Texture and pH in fish muscle related to "cell fragility" measurements. *J. Food Technol.* **1,** 9–15. *360*

 2411. Kelly, T. R. (1969). Quality in frozen cod and limiting factors on its shelf life. *J. Food Technol.* **4,** 95–103. *360*

 2412. Kemp, P. and Smith, M. W. (1970). Effect of temperature acclimatisation on the fatty acid composition of goldfish intestinal lipids. *Biochem. J.* **117,** 9–15. *340*

 2413. Kent, J. D. and Hart, R. G. (1976). The effect of temperature and photoperiod on isozyme induction in selected tissues of the Creek Chub, *Semotilus atromaculatus*. *Comp. Biochem. Physiol.* **54B,** 77–80. *334*

*2414. Khalyapin, B. D., Ashmarin, I. P. and Nusenbaum, L. M. (1972). Some biochemical characteristics of fish muscle tissue under different conditions of muscle activity. *Vest. leningr. gos. Univ.* (21), Ser. Biol. (4), 90–97.

 2415. Khan, S. H. and Siddiqui, A. Q. (1970). Effect of asphyxiation on the blood constituents of the murrel, *Ophicephalus punctatus* Bloch. *Broteria (Cienc. nat.)* **39,** 187–195. *239*

*2416. Khanna, S. S. and Bhatt, S. D. (1972). Studies on the blood glucose level and glycogen content in some organs of a fresh-water teleost, *Clarias batrachus* (Linn.). *Proc. natn. Acad. Sci. India* **42B,** 415–422. *192*

*2417. Khanna, S. S. and Gill, T. S. (1972). Further observations on the blood glucose level in *Channa punctatus* (Bloch.). *Acta Zool.* **53,** 127–133.

*2418. Khanna, S. S. and Gill, T. S. (1973). Effect of glucose loading on the blood glucose level and histology of the principal islets in *Channa punctatus. Endocr. jap.* **20,** 375–384. *365*

*2419. Khanna, S. S. and Rekhari, K. (1972). Changes in the blood glucose and histology of the pancreatic islets of *Heteropneustes fossilis* (Bl.) after treatment with alloxan. *Acta anat.* **82,** 619–632.

 2420. Khawaja, D. K. and Jafri, A. K. (1968). Changes in the biochemical composition of two common cat-fishes (*Wallagonia attu* Block and *Mystus seenghala* Sykes) in relation to length. *Hydrobiologia,* **32,** 245–255. *41*

 2421. Khokhar, R. (1971). The chromatic physiology of the catfish *Ictalurus melas* (Rafinesque)—I. The melanophore responses of intact and eyeless fish. *Comp. Biochem. Physiol.* **39A,** 531–543. *245*

*2422. Khung, I. K. (1971). Amino acid composition of the muscles of the mullet found in the Black Sea and in the harbour of Shabolat. *Biol. Morya* **22,** 193–210.

 2423. Kida, K. and Tamoto, K. (1969). Studies on the muscle of aquatic animals. IV. On the relation between various pH values and organic acids of Nagazuka muscle (*Stichaeus grigorjewi* Herzenstein). *Sci. Rep. Hokkaido Fish. Exp. Sta.* **11,** 41–51. *361*

 2424. Kim, E. D. (1974a). Age-related and yearly changes in the amino acid content in eggs and sperm of carp. *Raznokachestvennost Rannego Ontog. Ryb.* 65–93. (Ed. V. I. Vladimirov) "Naukova Dumka" Kiev, USSR. From *Chem. Abstr.* **84,** 133070d (1976). *10*

*2425. Kim, E. D. (1974b). Age-related changes in the content of cholesterol and phospholipids in carp eggs and sperm. *Raznokachestvennost Rannego Ontog. Ryb.* 114–126. (Ed. V. I. Vladimirov) "Naukova Dumka" Keiv, USSR. From *Chem. Abstr.* **84,** 133072f (1976). *11, 63*

*2426. Kimura, S. and Kubota, M. (1966). Studies on elastoidin. 1. Some chemical and physical properties of elastoidin and its components. *J. Biochem. Tokyo* **60,** 615–621.

 2427. Kinumaki, T., Sugii, K., Iida, H. and Takahashi, T. (1972). Addition of fat soluble vitamins to the feeding stuffs for parent rainbow trout with particular reference to the effect on the vitamin levels of eggs and fry. *Bull. Tokai reg. Fish. Res. Lab.* **71,** 133–160. *10*

*2428. Kirilenko, N. S. and Ermolaev, K. K. (1976). Comparative characteristics of high-energy compounds in the muscles of fish raised under various conditions. *Gidrobiol. Zh.* **12**, 77–81. From *Chem. Abstr.* **85**, 90487w (1976).

*2429. Kirk, W. L. (1973). The Influence of sodium chloride upon certain blood and tissue electrolytes of channel catfish, *Ictalurus punctatus*, during recovery from hypoxic stress. Ph.D. Thesis, University of Southern Illinois, University Microfilm no. 74–6268. Later published as: Kirk, W. L. (1974). The effect of hypoxia on certain blood and tissue electrolytes of channel catfish, *Ictalurus punctatus* (Rafinesque). *Trans. Am. Fish. Soc.* **103**, 593–600. *240*

2430. Kirsch, R. (1972a). Plasma chloride and sodium, and chloride space in the European eel, *Anguilla anguilla* L. *J. exp. Biol.* **57**, 113–131. *284, 285, 314, 315*

*2431. Kirsch, R. (1972b). The kinetics of peripheral exchanges of water and electrolytes in the silver eel (*Anguilla anguilla* L.) in fresh and in sea water. *J. exp. Biol.* **57**, 489–512.

*2432. Kirsch, R. and Mayer-Gostan, N. (1973). Kinetics of water and chloride exchanges during adaptation of the European eel to sea water. *J. exp. Biol.* **58**, 105–121.

2433. Kirsch, R. and Nonnotte, G. (1977). Cutaneous respiration in three freshwater teleosts. *Resp. Physiol.* **29**, 339–354. *277*

2434. Kirschner, L. B. (1969). ATPase activity in gills of euryhaline fish. *Comp. Biochem. Physiol.* **29**, 871–874. *293*

2435. Kirsipuu, A. (1975). Blood serum lipo- and glycoproteids in the pike (*Esox lucius*): results of a paper-electrophoretic investigation. *Eesti NSV Tead. Akad. Toim. Boil. seer*, **24**, 68–71. *43*

*2436. Kitamikado, M. and Yamamoto, H. (1969). Distribution of hyaluronidase in fish tissues. *Bull. Jap. Soc. scient. Fish.* **35**, 466–470.

2437. Kizevetter, I. V. (1968). Chemical properties of fats from Pacific Ocean fish. *Maslob.-zhirov. Prom.* **34**, 38–39. From *Chem. Abstr.* **70**, 36511b (1969). *463*

*2438. Klar, G. T. (1973). Effects of exercise on serum lactate dehydrogenase activity of catchable-size hatchery rainbow trout, *Salmo gairdneri*. M.Sc. Thesis, Utah State University. *120*

*2439. Klaro, R. and Lapin, V. I. (1971). Alteration of some biochemical characteristics of organs and tissues of the lane snapper (*Lutjanus synagris* L..) in the Gulf of Batabano during maturation. *J. Ichthyol.* **11**, 759–773.

*2440. Klokov, V. K. and Frolenko, L. A. (1970). Elemental chemical composition of scales of humpback salmon. *Izv. tikhookean. nauchno-issled. Inst. ryb. Khoz. Okeanogr.* **71**, 159–167. *248*

*2441. Kluytmans, J. H. F. M. and Zandee, D. I. (1973). Lipid metabolism in the northern pike (*Esox lucuis* L.)—II. The composition of the total lipids and of the fatty acids isolated from lipid classes and some tissues of the northern pike. *Comp. Biochem. Physiol.* **44B,** 459–466.

2442. Kluytmans, J. H. F. M. and Zandee, D. I. (1974). Lipid metabolism in the northern pike (*Esox Lucius* L.)—3. In vivo incorporation of 1–^{14}C-acetate in the lipids. *Comp. Biochem. Physiol.* **48B,** 641–649. *208*

2443. Knight, H. T. and Olson, L. J. (1974). Mercury distribution in American smelt from Lake Michigan. *Am. Midl. Nat.* **91,** 451–452. *437*

*2444. Kodama, M., Hashimoto, K. and Matsuura, F. (1975). Studies on the haptoglobin of eel—II. Physico-chemical properties. *Bull. Jap. Soc. scient. Fish.* **41,** 1021–1025.

*2445. Koga, Y. (1970). Studies on cholesterol in foods. Part 1. On fish. *Eiyo to Shokuryo,* **23,** 260–268.

2446. Kohler, A. C. and Fitzgerald, D. N. (1969). Comparisons of food of cod and haddock in the Gulf of St. Lawrence and on the Nova Scotia Banks. *J. Fish. Res. Bd Can.* **26,** 1273–1287. *134*

*2447. Komarova, M. L. (1969). Chemical composition of the mucous substance of the pike and burbot. *Bionika* (3), 84–90.

*2448. Komatsu, S. K. and Feeney, R. E. (1970). A heat labile fructosediphosphate aldolase from cold-adapted antarctic fishes. *Biochim. biophys. Acta,* **206,** 305–315.

*2449. Kondo, H. (1974). Studies on the lipids of herring. I. The lipids of the northeastern Kamchatka herring. *Bull. Fac. Fish. Hokkaido Univ.* **25,** 68–77.

*2450. Kondo, H. (1975). Studies on the lipids of herring. II. The lipids of the northern Okhotsk herring. *Bull. Fac. Fish. Hokkaido Univ.* **26,** 289–301.

*2451. Kondo, H. (1976). Studies on the lipids of the herring. IV. The lipids of the Bristol herring and the Unimak herring. *Bull. Fac. Fish. Hokkaido Univ.* **27,** 96–105.

2452. Kondrat'eva, T. P. (1975). Effect of muscular load on total protein content and fractional composition of blood serum of the horse mackerel. *Samoochishchenie Bioprod. Okhr. Vodoemov Vodotokov Ukr. Mater. Resp. Konf. Ukr. Fil. Vses. Gidrobiol. O-va.,* 3rd, p. 181 only. (Ed. Topachevskii, A. V.), "Naukova Dumka": Kiev, USSR. From *Chem. Abstr.* **83,** 190634u (1975). *116*

2453. Kondratovics, E. (1969). Level of trace elements in rainbow trout (*Salmo irideus*). *Latv. Lopkopibas Vet. Zinat. Petnieciska Inst. Raksti* **22,** 29–38. From *Chem. Abstr.* **73,** 22627u (1970). *35, 56, 57, 147*

*2454. de Koning, A. J. (1968). A study of phospholipids: in particular those of marine origin. *S. Afr. J. Sci.* **64**, 345–349.

*2455. Konosu, S. and Watanabe, K. (1976). Comparison of nitrogenous extractives of cultured and wild red sea breams. *Bull. Jap. Soc. scient. Fish.* **42**, 1263–1266.

*2456. Konosu, S., Watanabe, K. and Shimizu, T. (1974). Distribution of nitrogenous constituents in the muscle extracts of eight species of fish. *Bull. Jap. Soc. scient. Fish.* **40**, 909–915.

*2457. Kostić, D., Rakić, L. and Vraneešvić, A. (1972). Phospholipid composition of different parts of the brain and electric organ of the electric ray *Torpedo ocellata*. *Zh. Evol. Biokhim. Fiziol.* **8**, 494–498.

*2458. Kostić, D., Vranešević, A., Vrbaški, S. and Rakić, L. (1975). Ganglioside in various brain structures of the electric fish *Torpedo ocellata*. *Acta med. iugosl.* **29**, 289–295.

2459. Kott, E. (1970). Differences between the livers of spawning male and female sea lamprey (*Petromyzon marinus*). *Can. J. Zool.* **48**, 745–750. *52*

2460. Kott, E. (1971). Liver and muscle composition of mature lampreys. *Can. J. Zool.* **49**, 801–805. *52, 187*

*2461. Kowarsky, J. (1973). Extra-branchial pathways of salt exchange in a teleost fish. *Comp. Biochem. Physiol.* **46A**, 477–486. *309*

*2462. Kownacki, E. and Doboszyńska, B. (1976a). The content of magnesium in fish meat and fish products. II. The content of magnesium in the meat of selected fish species and in the fish products. *Bromat. Chem. Toksykol.* **9**, 205–212.

*2463. Kownacki, E. and Doboszyńska, B. (1976b). The content of magnesium in fish meat and in fish products. *Bromatol. Chem. Toksykol.* **9**, 349–356.

*2464. Koyama, J. and Itazawa, Y. (1977). Effects of oral administration of cadmium on fish—I. Analytical results of the blood and bones. *Bull. Jap. Soc. scient. Fish.* **43**, 523–526.

*2465. Krayushkina, D. S., Dyubin, V. P., Moiseenko, S. N. and Khristoforov, O. L. (1973). Composition of blood serum cations of sturgeons in various periods of their life cycle. *Dokl. Akad. Nauk., SSSR Biochem.* **212**, 1007–1010.

*2466. Krayushkina, L. S. and Moiseenko, S. N. (1977). Reactions of the freshwater sturgeons, the Baykal sturgeon and the great Amu-Dar'ya shovelnose, to change in salinity of the environment. *Dokl. (Proc.) Acad. Sci. USSR Biological Sciences*, **232**, 15–18.

2467. Krebs, F. (1975). The influence of oxygen tension on the temperature adaptation in Gibel carp, *Carassius auratus gibelio* Bloch. *Arch. Hydrobiol.* **76**, 1–4. *273*

*2468. Krenitsky, T. A., Tuttle, J. V., Cattau, E. L. and Wang, P. (1974). A comparison of the distribution and electron acceptor specificities of xanthine oxidase and aldehyde oxidase. *Comp. Biochem. Physiol.* **49B,** 687–703.

*2469. Kreps, E. M., Avrova, N. F., Chebotarëva, M. A., Chirkovskaya, E. V., Krasilnikova, V. I., Kruglova, E. E., Levitina, M. V., Obukhova, E. L., Pomazanskaya, L. F., Pravdina, N. I. and Zabelinskii, S. A. (1975). Phospholipids and glycolipids in the brain of marine fish. *Comp. Biochem. Physiol.* **52B,** 283–292.

*2470. Kreps, E. M., Avrova, N. F., Chebotarëva, M. A., Chirkovskaya, E. V., Levitina, M. V., Pomazanskaya, L. F. and Pravdina, N. I. (1975). Some aspects of comparative biochemistry of brain lipids in teleost and elasmobranch fish. *Comp. Biochem. Physiol.* **52B,** 293–299.

*2471. Kreps, E. M., Avrova, N. F., Krasil'nikova, V. I., Kruglova, E. E., Levitina, M. V., Obukhova, E. L., Pomazanskaya, L. F., Pravdina, N. N., Chebotarëva, M. A. and Chirkovskaya, E. V. (1975). The biochemistry of the brain lipids of Acipenseridae. *J. Evol. Biochem. Physiol.* **11,** 196–203.

*2472. Kreps, E. M., Avrova, N. F., Krasil'nikova, V. I., Levitina, M. V. and Obukhova, E. L. (1973). Cerebrosides, sulphatides, and gangliosides of brain and electric organ of ray *Torpedo marmorata. J. Evol. Biochem. Physiol.* **9,** 24–31.

*2473. Kreps, E. M., Chebotarëva, M. A. and Akulin, V. N. (1969). Fatty acid composition of brain and body phospholipids of the anadromous salmon, *Oncorhynchus nerka*, from fresh-water and marine habitat. *Comp. Biochem. Physiol.* **31,** 419–430. *316*

*2474. Kreps, E. M., Krasil'nikova, V. I., Pomazanskaya, L. F., Pravdina, N. I., Smirnov, A. A. and Chirkovskaya, E. V. (1973). Phospholipids and their fatty acids in the brain and electric organ of the ray *Torpedo marmorata. J. Evol. Biochem. Physiol.* **9,** 15–23.

*2475. Krishnamoorthy, R. V. and Narasimhan, T. (1972). Ascorbic acid and fat content in the red and white muscles of carp, *Catla catla. Comp. Biochem. Physiol.* **43B,** 991–997. *72, 76*

*2476. Kristoffersson, R., Broberg, S. and Oikari, A. (1974). Annual changes in some blood constituents of female brackish water *Zoarces viviparus* (L.), Teleostei, with special reference to the reproductive cycle and the embryotrophe. *Hydrobiol. Bull.* **8,** 117–123. *44, 385*

2477. Krivobok, M. N. and Storozhuk, A. Ya. (1970). The effect of the size and age of Volga sturgeon on the weight and chemical composition of mature eggs. *J. Ichthyol.* **10,** 761–765. *28, 29*

2478. Krivobok, M. N. and Tokareva, G. I. (1972). Dynamics of weight variations of the body and separate organs of Baltic cod during the maturation of gonads. *Trudy vses. nauchno-issled. Inst. morsk. ryb. Khoz. Okeanogr.* **85,** 46–55. *39, 46*

2479. Krompecher, I., Laczko, J., Ladanyi, P., Laszlo, M. B. and Levai, G. (1970). Comparative morphology, electron microscopy, enzymology and biochemistry of cardiac, red, and white muscles of the hen (*Gallus domesticus*). *Acta biol. hung.* **21**, 43–54. From *Chem. Abstr.* **73**, 22645y (1970). *71*

*2480. Kruckeberg, W. C. and Chilson, O. P. (1973). Red blood cell AMP-deaminase: levels of activity in haemolysates from twenty different vertebrate species. *Comp. Biochem. Physiol.* **46B**, 653–660.

2481. Krueger, H. M., Saddler, J. B., Champan, G. A., Tinsley, I. J. and Lowry, R. R. (1968). Bioenergetics, exercise, and fatty acids of fish. *Am. Zool.* **8**, 119–129. *115*

*2482. Krüger, K. E., Nieper, L. and Auslitz, H.-J. (1975). Determination of the mercury content of sea fish in the fishing grounds of the German deep-sea and inshore fisheries. *Archiv. Lebensmittelhyg.* **26**, 201–207.
(*Note:* These authors also give the mercury content of four freshwater species, but as they were said to be "heavily contaminated" they have not been quoted in parts II and III of this volume.)

2483. Kruggel, W. G., Field, R. A. and Miller, G. J. (1970). Physical and chemical properties of epimysial acid-soluble collagen from meats of varying tenderness. *J. Food Sci.* **35**, 106–110. *360*

*2484. Kubota, M. and Kimura, S. (1975). The distribution of collagen and some properties of intramuscular collagen in fish. *Hikaku kagaku* (*Leather Chemistry*), **21**, 80–85.

2485. Kurogi, A. (1969). Studies on lactate dehydrogenase from tissues of fishes. *Miyazaki Daigaku Nogakubu, Kenkyu Jiho* (*Rep. Fac. Agric. Miyazaki Univ.*), **16**, 1–60. *111, 317*

*2486. Kusen, S. I. and Oleshko, P. S. (1974). Changes in acid and alkaline ribonuclease activity during early embryogenesis in *Misgurnus fossilis. Ukr. Biochim. Zh.* **46**, 168–172. From *Chem. Abstr.* **81**, 75216f (1974).

2487. Kutty, M. N. (1968). Influence of ambient oxygen on the swimming performance of goldfish and rainbow trout. *Can. J. Zool.* **46**, 647–653. *115, 272*

2488. Kutty, M. N. (1972). Respiratory quotient and ammonia excretion in *Tilapia mossambica. Mar. Biol.* **16**, 126–133. *115, 271, 280*

*2489. Kuusi, T. and Kytökangas, R. (1970). On the changes in the main mineral constituents of Baltic herring fillets while standing in saline solutions. *Maatalovst. Aikakaurk.* (*J. Sci. Agric. Soc. Finland*), **42**, 30–44.

*2490. Kuusi, T. and Löytömäki, M. (1972). On the effectiveness of EDTA in prolonging the shelf life of fresh fish. *Z. Lebensmittelunters. u.-Forsch.* **149**, 196–204.

*2491. Kuzma, W. (1971). Determination of the contents of iron, copper, zinc, manganese, cobalt and nickel in the flesh of some marine fishes. *Pr. morsk. Inst. ryb. Gdyni*, **16,** Ser. B, 205–219.

*2492. Kuznetsov, D. I., Grishina, N. I., Nekrasova, L. V. and Semienova, L. I. (1975). Fatty-acid composition of fat in sea and fresh-water fishes, of sea invertebrates and mammals. *Vop. Pitan.* (6), 62–70 (no volume number given).

2493. Kuznetsov, V. A. (1973). The fecundity and the quality of eggs of bream *Abramis brama* L. *Vop. Ikhtiol.* **13,** 805–815. From *Aq. Sci. Fish. Abstr.* **4** (5), 4Q4564F (1974). *9*

2494. Kwain, W.-H. (1975). Embryonic development, early growth, and meristic variation in rainbow trout (*Salmo gairdneri*) exposed to combinations of light intensity and temperature. *J. Fish. Res. Bd Can.* **32,** 397–402. *243*

*2495. Kyrylenko, N. S. and Skrodska, I. E. (1974). Age pecularities in lipid fractions of tissues and blood in fishes of Amur complex. *Ukr. biokhem. Zh.* 745–748 (no volume number given).

2496. Laarman, P. W., Willford, W. A. and Olson, J. R. (1976). Retention of mercury in the muscle of yellow perch (*Perca flavescens*) and rock bass (*Ambloplites rupestris*). *Trans. Am. Fish. Soc.* **105,** 296–300. *437*

2497. Labat, R., Kugler-Laffont, J., Cadastraing, A. and Bonnet, L. (1969). The pH of the surroundings and its effects on the electrocardiograph of several freshwater teleosts. *Bull. Soc. Hist. nat. Toulouse*, **105,** 455–463. *149*

2498. Lachner, A. (1972). Ammonia as metabolic product in fish, with special reference to ammonia excretion under stress conditions. *Münchner Beiträge zur Abwässer-, Fischerei- und Fluss-Biologie*, **23,** 32–41. *162*

*2499. Lahlou, B., Crenesse, D., Bensahla-Talet, A. and Porthe-Nibelle, J. (1975). Adaptation of the trout *Salmo irideus* to sea water: effects of plasma electrolytes, gill fluxes and intestinal transport of sodium. *J. Physiol., Paris*, **70,** 593–603. *291*

*2500. Lahlou, B., Henderson, I. W. and Sawyer, W. H. (1969). Sodium exchanges in goldfish (*Carassius auratus* L.) adapted to a hypertonic saline solution. *Comp. Biochem. Physiol.* **28,** 1427–1433. *284*

2501. Lajtha, A. and Sershen, H. (1975). Changes in the rates of protein synthesis in the brain of goldfish at various temperatures. *Life Sci.* **17,** 1861–1868. *320*

2502. Lam, T. J. and Leatherland, J. F. (1970). Effect of hormones on survival of the marine form (*Trachurus*) of the threespine stickleback (*Gasterosteus aculeatus* L.) in deionised water. *Comp. Biochem. Physiol.* **33,** 295–302. *301*

*2503. Lambert, M. A. (1970). Variation in the level of certain blood constituents of channel catfish, *Ictalurus punctatus*. Ph.D. Thesis, Kansas State University.

*2504. Lambertsen, G. (1972). Lipids in fish fillet and liver—a comparison of fatty acid compositions. *FiskDir. Skr. Ser. Teknol. Undersøk.* **5** (6), 15 pp. *207*

*2505. Lambertsen, G. (1973). Lipids in marine fish. *Wissenschaftliche Veröffentlichungen Deutschen Gesellschaft für Ernahrung*, **24**, 25–31.

2506. Lambertsen, G. and Braekkan, O. R. (1969). In vivo conversion of vitamin A_1 to vitamin A_2. *Acta chem. scand.* **23**, 1063–1064. *463*

*2507. Lambertsen, G. and Braekkan, O. R. (1971). Method of analysis of astaxanthin and its occurrence in some marine products. *J. Sci. Fd Agric.* **22**, 99–101.

*2508. Lander, J. (1964). Title unknown. B.Sc. Med. Dissertation, University of Sydney. Quoted by Satchell, G. H. "Circulation in Fishes" (1971). Cambridge monographs in experimental biology no. 18, p. 23. Cambridge University Press. *67*

*2509. Lang, F. G. and Macleod, I. I. R. (1920). Observations on the reducing substances in the circulating fluid of certain invertebrates and fishes. *Q. Jl exp. Physiol.* **12**, 331 337. From Chavin and Young (1970).

2510. Lapennas, G. N. and Schmidt-Nielsen, K. (1977). Swimbladder permeability to oxygen. *J. exp. Biol.* **67**, 175–196. *122*

2511. Lapi, L. A. and Mulligan, T. J. (1976). Salmon population identification using energy dispersive X-ray microanalysis. *Scanning Electron Microscopy*, **9**, 591–596. *248*

2512. Lapin, V. I. (1973). Comparative study of the fat content and qualitative lipid composition of the river flounder (*Platichthys flesus* L.) from White and Black seas. *Nauch. Dokl. vyssh. Shk. Biol. Nauk.* (3), 41–48 (no volume number given). *46, 246*

*2513. Larsen, L. O. (1976). Blood glucose levels in intact and hypophysectomised river lampreys (*Lampetra fluviatilis* L.) treated with insulin, "stress", or glucose, before and during the period of sexual maturation. *Gen. comp. Endocrinol.* **29**, 1–13.

*2514. Larsson, Å. and Fänge, R. (1969). Chemical differences in the blood of yellow and silver phases of the European eel ("*Anguilla anguilla*" L.). *Archs int. Physiol. Biochim.* **77**, 701–709. *25*

*2515. Larsson, Å. and Fänge, R. (1977). Cholesterol and free fatty acids (FFA) in the blood of marine fish. *Comp. Biochem. Physiol.* **57B**, 191–196.

*2516. Larsson, Å., Johansson, M.-L. and Fänge, R. (1976). Comparative study of some haematological and biochemical blood parameters in fishes from the Skagerrak. *J. Fish Biol.* **9**, 425–440.

*2517. Larsson, Å. and Lewander, K. (1972). Effects of glucagon administration to eels (*Anguilla anguilla* L.). *Comp. Biochem. Physiol.* **43A,** 831–836.

*2518. Larsson, Å. and Lewander, K. (1973). Metabolic effects of starvation in the eel, *Anguilla anguilla* L. *Comp. Biochem. Physiol.* **44A,** 367–374. *182, 186, 212*

*2519. Lasserre, P. (1971). Increase of $(Na^+ + K^+)$-dependent ATPase activity in gills and kidneys of two euryhaline marine teleosts, *Crenimugil labrosus* (Risso, 1826) and *Dicentrarchus labrax* (Linnaeus, 1758) during adaptation to fresh water. *Life Sci.* **10,** 113–119. *293, 306*

*2520. Lasserre, P. and Gallis, J.-L. (1975). Osmoregulation and differential penetration of two grey mullets, *Chelon labrosus* (Risso) and *Liza ramada* (Risso) in estuarine fish ponds. *Aquaculture,* **5,** 323–344.

2521. Lasserre, P. and Gilles, R. (1971). Modification of the amino acid pool in the parietal muscle of two euryhaline teleosts during osmotic adjustment. *Experientia,* **27,** 1434–1435. *313*

2522. Laugaste, K. (1969). Seasonal dynamics of the relative weight, glycogen, and fat levels of bream liver. *Eesti NSV Tead. Akad. Toim., Biol.* **18,** 379–386. From *Chem. Abstr.* **72,** 40197n (1970). *387*

*2523. Laul, R. T., Pradhan, P. V. and Bhagwat, A. M. (1974). Effect of muscular exercise on glycogen content in *Tilapia mossambica*, Peters (in captivity). *J. biol. Sci.* **17,** 72–77.

2524. Lavéty, J. and Love, R. M. (1972). The strengthening of cod connective tissue during starvation. *Comp. Biochem. Physiol.* **41A,** 39–42. *33, 201, 202*

2525. Lawrie, R. A. (1950). Some observations on factors affecting myoglobin concentrations in muscle. *J. agric. Sci., Camb.* **40,** 356–366. *106*

2526. Lawrie, R. A. (1953). The activity of the cytochrome system in muscle and its relation to myoglobin. *Biochem. J.* **55,** 298–305. *106*

*2527. Leach, G. J. and Taylor, M. H. (1977). Seasonal measurements of serum glucose and serum cortisol in a natural population of *Fundulus heteroclitus*. *Comp. Biochem. Physiol.* **56A,** 217–223. *386*

2528. Lear, W. H. (1970). Fecundity of Greenland halibut (*Reinhardtius hippoglossoides*) in the Newfoundland–Labrador area. *J. Fish. Res. Bd Can.* **27,** 1880–1882. *27*

*2529. Leatherland, J. F., Cho, C. Y. and Slinger, S. J. (1977). Effects of diet, ambient temperature, and holding conditions on plasma thyroxine levels in rainbow trout (*Salmo gairdneri*). *J. Fish. Res. Bd Can.* **34,** 677–682. *169, 326*

*2530. Leatherland, J. F., Hyder, M. and Ensor, D. M. (1974). Regulation of plasma Na^+ and K^+ concentrations in five African species of *Tilapia* fishes. *Comp. Biochem. Physiol.* **48A,** 699–710.

2531. Leatherland, J. F. and Lam, T. J. (1969). Prolactin and survival in deionised water of the marine form (trachurus) of the threespine stickleback, *Gasterosteus aculeatus* L. *Can. J. Zool.* **47,** 989–995. *301*

*2532. Leatherland, J. F. and McKeown, B. A. (1973). Circadian rhythm in the plasma levels of prolactin in goldfish, *Carassius auratus* L. *J. Interdiscip. Cycle Res.* **4,** 137–143.

*2533. Leatherland, J. F., McKeown, B. A. and John, T. M. (1974) Circadian rhythm of plasma prolactin, growth hormone, glucose and freey fatty acid in juvenile kokanee salmon, *Oncorhynchus nerka. Comp. Biochem. Physiol.* **47A,** 821–828. *383*

*2534. Leatherland, T. M., Burton, J. D., Culkin, F., McCartney, M. J. and Morris, R. J. (1973). Concentrations of some trace metals in pelagic organisms and of mercury in northeast Atlantic Ocean water. *Deep Sea Res.* **20,** 679–685.

*2535. LeBlanc, P. J. and Jackson, A. L. (1973). Arsenic in marine fish and invertebrates. *Mar. Pollut. Bull. NS,* **4,** 88–90.

*2536. Lech, J. J. (1970). Glycerol kinase and glycerol utilisation in trout (*Salmo gairdneri*) liver. *Comp. Biochem. Physiol.* **34,** 117–124.

2537. Lee, D. J. and Sinnhuber, R. O. (1973). Lipid requirements. In "Fish Nutrition" (Ed. Halver, J. E.), Chapter 4, pp. 145–180. Academic Press, London and New York. *5, 143*

*2538. Lee, R. F., Phleger, C. F. and Horn, M. H. (1975). Composition of oil in fish bones: possible function in neutral buoyancy. *Comp. Biochem. Physiol.* **50B,** 13–16. *121, 126*

2539. Léger, C., Luquet, P. and Boudon, M. (1976). Effects of a sucrose-free diet on the rainbow trout reared at a temperature of 16°C. 11. Evolution of the body compartments particularly according to the fatty acids ω9, ω6, ω3. Action of a change in temperature. *Ann. Hydrobiol.* **7,** 185–201. *139*

*2540. Leggett, W. C. and O'Boyle, R. N. (1976). Osmotic stress and mortality in adult American shad during transfer from saltwater to freshwater. *J. Fish Biol.* **8,** 459–469.

2541. Leggett, W. C. and Power, G. (1969). Differences between two populations of landlocked Atlantic salmon (*Salmo salar*) in Newfoundland. *J. Fish. Res. Bd Can.* **26,** 1585–1596. *136*

2542. Leibson, L. G. (1972). Metabolism and its endocrine regulation in fishes of different motor activity. *Zh. Evol. Biokhim. Fiziol.* **8,** 280–288. From *Chem. Abstr.* **77,** 85944y. *112*

*2543. Leibson, L. and Plisetskaya, E. M. (1968). Effect of insulin on blood sugar level and glycogen content in organs of some cyclostomes and fish. *Gen. comp. Endocrinol.* **11,** 381–392. *110, 111*

*2544. Leibson, L. G. and Plisetskaya, E. M. (1969). Hormonal control of blood sugar level in cyclostomes. *Gen. comp. Endocrinol.* Suppl 2, 528–534. *232, 233*

2545. Leibson, L., Plisetskaya, E. and Leibush, B. (1976). The comparative study of mechanism of insulin action on muscle carbohydrate metabolism. *In* "The Evolution of Pancreatic Islets" (Eds Grillo, T. A. I., Leibson, L. and Epple, A.), pp. 345–362. Pergamon Press, Oxford. *365*

2546. Leloup, J. and Fontaine, M. (1960). Iodine metabolism in lower vertebrates. *Ann. N.Y. Acad. Sci.* **86** art. 2, 316–353. *110, 116*

*2547. Leloup-Hatey, J. (1976). Method for measuring the speed of metabolic clearance and of secretion of cortisol in the eel (*Anguilla anguilla* L.). *Can. J. Physiol. Pharmacol.* **54,** 262–276.

*2548. Lemoine, A. M. (1974). Action of prolactin from hypophysectomised eels in sea water. Effect on the N-acetyl-neuraminic acid of the gills. *C. r. Séanc. Soc. Biol.* **168,** 398–402. *299*

2549. Lemoine, A.-M. and Olivereau, M. (1973). Action of prolactin on intact and hypophysectomised eels. IX. Effect on the concentration of N-acetyl-neuraminic acid in the skin in sea-water. *Acta zool.* **54,** 223–228. *299*

*2550. Leray, C. and Bachand, L. (1975). Erythrocyte metabolism in the yellow perch (*Perca flavescens* Mitchill). Intermediates, nucleotides and free energy changes in glycolytic reactions. *Comp. Biochem. Physiol.* **51B,** 349–353.

*2551. Leslie, J. M. and Buckley, J. T. (1976). Phospholipid composition of goldfish (*Carassius auratus* L.) liver and brain and temperature-dependence of phosphatidyl choline synthesis. *Comp. Biochem. Physiol.* **53B,** 335–337. *340*

2552. LeTendre, G. C. (1968). Blood pH of channel catfish. *Iowa. St. J. Sci.* **43,** 223–228. *257*

*2553. Levi, G., Morisi, G., Coletti, A. and Catanzaro, R. (1974). Free amino acids in fish brain: normal levels and changes upon exposure to high ammonia concentrations in vivo, and upon incubation of brain slices. *Comp. Biochem. Physiol.* **49A,** 623–636. *259*

2554. Lewander, K. (1976). Insulin in fish. *Zool. Revy,* **37,** 44–46. *365*

*2555. Lewander, K., Dave, G., Johansson, M.-L., Larsson, Å. and Lidman, U. (1974). Metabolic and haematological studies on the yellow and silver phases of the European eel, *Anguilla anguilla* L.—1. Carbohydrate, lipid, protein and inorganic ion metabolism. *Comp. Biochem. Physiol.* **47B,** 571–581. *22, 25, 104*

*2556. Lewander, K., Dave, G., Johansson-Sjöbeck, M.-L., Larsson, Å. and Lidman, U. (1976). Metabolic effects of insulin in the European eel, *Anguilla anguilla* L. *Gen. comp. Endocrinol.* **29,** 455–467.

*2557. Lewis, R. W. (1969). Studies on the stomach oils of marine animals—1. Oils of the black shark *Dalatias licha* (Bonnaterre). *Comp. Biochem. Physiol.* **31,** 715–724.

2558. Lewis, R. W. (1970a). The densities of three classes of marine lipids in relation to their possible role as hydrostatic agents. *Lipids,* **5,** 151–153. *125*

*2559. Lewis, R. W. (1970b). Fish cutaneous mucus: a new source of skin surface lipid. *Lipids,* **5,** 947–949.

2559a. Lewis, R. W. (1971). Squalene distribution in fish with normal and pathologically fatty livers. *Int. J. Biochem.* **2,** 609–614. *74, 92, 454*

*2560. Lewis, T. L., Parke, W. W. and Epple, A. (1977). Pancreatectomy in a teleost fish, *Anguilla rostrata* (American eel). *Lab. anim. Sci.* **27,** 102–109.

*2561. Li, S.-L., Tomita, S. and Riggs, A. (1972). The haemoglobins of the Pacific hagfish, *Eptatretus stoutii*. 1. Isolation, characterisation, and oxygen equilibria. *Biochim. biophys. Acta,* **278,** 344–354.

*2562. Liddicoat, J. D. and Roberts, B. L. (1972). The ionic composition of the lateral-line canal fluid of dogfish. *J. mar. biol. Ass. U.K.* **52,** 653–659.

2563. Lientz, J. C. and Smith, C. E. (1974). Some haematological parameters for hatchery-reared cutthroat trout. *Progve Fish Cult.* **36,** 49–50. *27, 34*

2564. de Ligny, W. (1969). Serological and biochemical studies on fish populations. *Oceanogr. mar. Biol.* **7,** 411–513. *249*

2565. Lin, H., Romsos, D. R., Tack, P. I. and Leveille, G. A. (1977). Influence of dietary lipid on lipogenic enzyme activities in coho salmon, *Oncorhynchus kisutch* (Walbaum). *J. Nutr.* **107,** 846–854. *143*

2566. Lin, Y., Dobbs, G. H. and DeVries, A. L. (1974). Oxygen consumption and lipid content in red and white muscles of antarctic fishes. *J. exp. Zool.* **189,** 379–382. *74, 80*

2567. Lindsey, C. C. (1968). Temperatures of red and white muscle in recently caught marlin and other large tropical fish. *J. Fish. Res. Bd Can.* **25,** 1987–1992. *78*

*2568. Linko, R. R. and Kaitaranta, J. (1976). Hydrocarbons of Baltic herring lipids. *Riv. Ital. Sostanze Grasse,* **53,** 37–39. *512*

2569. Linthicum, D. S. and Carey, F. G. (1972). Regulation of brain and eye temperatures by the bluefin tuna. *Comp. Biochem. Physiol.* **43A,** 425–433. *322*

2570. Lisovskaya, V. I. (1973). Composition of lipids of red and white muscles of mackerel (*Trachurus mediterraneus ponticus*) and anchovy (*Engraulis encrasicholus ponticus*) in the northwestern part of the Black Sea. *Mater. Vses. Simp. Izuch. Chern. Sredizemnogo Morei, Ispol'z. Okhr. Ikh Resur.* **2,** 142–145. From *Chem. Abstr.* **81,** 148747s. *74–76*

*2571. Lisovskaya, V. I. and Petkevich, T. A. (1968). The biochemical composition of muscle tissue in certain Black Sea fish. *Ryb. Khoz.* **44** (9), 65–66. *73–75*

*2572. Lisovskaya, V. I. and Rudenko, A. G. (1973). The lipid content of the liver of certain epipelagic game fish. *Biol. Morya*, **30**, 119–124.

2573. Little, G. H., Atkinson, B. G. and Frieden, E. (1973). Changes in the rates of protein synthesis and degradation in the tail of *Rana catesbiana* tadpoles during normal metamorphosis. *Devl Biol.* **30**, 366–373. *198*

2574. Liu, R. K. and Walford, R. L. (1969). Laboratory studies on life-span, growth, aging, and pathology of the annual fish, *Cynolebias bellottii* Steindachner. *Zoologica*, **54**, 1–16. *47, 58–60*

2575. Liu, R. K. and Walford, R. L. (1970). Observations on the lifespans of several species of annual fishes and of the world's smallest fishes. *Exp. Gerontol.* **5**, 241–246. *58, 320*

*2576. Liversage, R. A., Price, B. W., Clarke, W. C. and Butler, D. G. (1971). Plasma adrenocorticosteroid levels in adult *Fundulus heteroclitus* (killifish) following hypophysectomy and pectoral fin amputation. *J. exp. Zool.* **178,** 23–27.

*2577. Lizenko, E. I., Siderov, V. S. and Potapova, O. I. (1972). Fish lipids. II. Seasonal dynamics of phosphatides and triglycerides in the large vendace *Coregonus albula* L. *In* "Salmonidae of Karelia. Issue 1, Ecology, Parasites, Biochemistry" (Eds Potapova, O. I. and Smirnov, Y. A.), pp. 164–169. Petrozavodsk.

*2578. Lizenko, E. I., Siderov, V. S., Potapova, O. I. and Nefedova, Z. A. (1972). Fish lipids. III. Contents of glycerides and phosphatides in different organs of the vendace in relation to its habitat conditions. *In* "Salmonidae of Karelia. Issue 1. Ecology, Parasites, Biochemistry" (Eds Potapova, O. I. and Smirnov, Y. A.), pp. 170–177. Petrozavodsk.

*2579. Lloyd, R. and White, W. R. (1967). Effect of high concentration of carbon dioxide on the ionic composition of rainbow trout blood. *Nature, Lond.* **216,** 1341–1342. *282*

2580. Lockwood, S. J. (1974). The use of the von Bertalanffy growth equation to describe the seasonal growth of fish. *J. Cons. perm int. Explor. Mer.* **35**, 175–179. *384*

*2581. Loginova, T. A. (1969). Carotenoid metabolism during the ovogenesis of rainbow trout. *Izv. Gos. Nauch.-issled. Inst. Ozern. rech. ryb. Khoz.* **65,** 193–196. *38*

*2582. Lontoc, A. V., Gonzalez, O. N. and Dimaunahan, L. B. (1966). Folic acid content of some Philippine foods. *Philipp. J. Sci.* **95,** 311–320.

*2583. Lopez, E. and Deville-Peignoux, J. (1974). Endocrine regulation of bone metabolism in several species of teleost fish. *In* "Comparative Physiology of Calcium Exchange" (Proceedings of a seminar at Lyons in March 1973 under the direction of D. Pansu). SIMEP edition. Pp. 23–32. Villeurbanne. *6*

2584. Lotan, R. (1973). Osmoregulation during adaptation to fresh water in the euryhaline teleost *Aphanius dispar* Rüppell (Cyprinodontidae, Pisces). *J. comp. Physiol.* **87**, 339–349. *284*

2585. Love, R. M. (1969). Condition of fish and its influence on the quality of the frozen product. *In* "Freezing and Irrradiation of Fish" (Ed. Keuzer, R.), pp. 40–45. Fishing News (Books) Ltd., London. *94, 185, 186*

2586. Love, R. M. (1970). "The Chemical Biology of Fishes". Academic Press, London and New York. Referred to as Volume 1 in the text of this present book.

2587. Love, R. M. (1973). Gaping of fillets. Ministry of Agriculture, Fisheries and Food, Torry Research Station, Aberdeen, Scotland. Advisory Note no. 61. 6 pp. *358*

2588. Love, R. M. (1974). Colour stability in cod (*Gadus morhua* L.) from different grounds. *J. Cons. perm. int. Explor. Mer* **35**, 207–209. *245, 246, 353*

2589. Love, R. M. (1975). Variability in Atlantic cod (*Gadus morhua*) from the northeast Atlantic: a review of seasonal and environmental influences on various attributes of the flesh. *J. Fish. Res. Bd Can.* **32**, 2333–2342. *ix, 225, 229, 358, 368, 377*

2590. Love, R. M. (1976). Processing cod: the influence of season and fishing ground. Ministry of Agriculture, Fisheries and Food, Torry Research Station, Aberdeen, Scotland. Advisory Note no. 71. 8 pp.

2591. Love, R. M. (1978). Dark colour in white fish flesh. Ministry of Agriculture, Fisheries and Food, Torry Research Station, Aberdeen, Scotland. Advisory Note no. 76. 6 pp. *369*

2592. Love, R. M. (1979). The post-mortem pH of cod and haddock muscle and its seasonal variation. *J. Sci. Fd Agric.* **30**, 433–438. *363, 364, 366, 367*

2593. Love, R. M. and Elerian, M. K. (1964). Protein denaturation in frozen fish. VIII. The temperature of maximum denaturation in cod. *J. Sci. Fd Agric.* **15**, 805–809. *105*

2594. Love, R. M. and Haq, M. A. (1970a). The connective tissues of fish. III. The effect of pH on gaping in cod entering rigor mortis at different temperatures. *J. Food Technol.* **5**, 241–248. *359*

2595. Love, R. M. and Haq, M. A. (1970b). The connective tissues of fish. IV. Gaping of cod muscle under various conditions of freezing, cold-storage and thawing. *J. Food Technol.* **5**, 249–260. *359*

2596. Love, R. M., Haq, M. A. and Smith, G. L. (1972). The connective tissues of fish. V. Gaping in cod of different sizes as influenced by a seasonal variation in the ultimate pH. *J. Food Technol.* **7,** 281–290. *359*

2597. Love, R. M. and Haraldsson, S. B. (1958). Thaw rigor and cell rupture. *Nature, Lond.* **181,** 1334 only. *189*

2598. Love, R. M. and Haraldsson, S. B. (1961). The expressible fluid of fish fillets. XI. Ice crystal formation and cell damage in cod muscle frozen before rigor mortis. *J. Sci. Fd Agric.* **12,** 442–449. *190*

*2599. Love, R. M., Hardy, R. and Nishimoto, J. (1975). Lipids in the flesh of cod (*Gadus morhua* L.) from Faroe Bank and Aberdeen Bank in early summer and autumn. *Mem. Fac. Fish., Kagoshima Univ.* **24,** 123–126. *74, 97, 206, 368*

2600. Love, R. M. and Hume, A. H. (1975). The quality of farmed products. *Fish Farm. Int.* **2,** 36–37. *260*

2601. Love, R. M. and Lavéty, J. (1972). The connective tissues of fish. VII. Postmortem hydration and ice crystal formation in myocommata, and their influence on gaping. *J. Food Technol.* **7,** 431–441. *360*

2602. Love, R. M. and Lavéty, J. (1977). Wateriness of white muscle: a comparison between cod (*Gadus morhua*) and jelly cat (*Lycichthys denticulatus*). *Mar. Biol.* **43,** 117–121. *129–131*

2603. Love, R. M., Lavéty, J. and Garcia, N. G. (1972). The connective tissues of fish. VI. Mechanical studies on isolated myocommata. *J. Food Technol.* **7,** 291–301. *359*

2604. Love, R. M., Munro, L. J. and Robertson, I. (1977). Adaptation of the dark muscle of cod to swimming activity. *J. Fish Biol.* **11,** 431–436. *107–109, 120, 369*

2605. Love, R. M. and Muslemuddin, M. (1972). Protein denaturation in frozen fish. XII. The pH effect and cell fragility determinations. *J. Sci. Fd Agric.* **23,** 1229–1238. *361*

2606. Love, R. M., Muslemuddin, M., Ong, L. K. and Smith, G. L. (1974). Protein denaturation in frozen fish. XIV. Cell fragility measurements on frozen and thawed cod caught on different fishing grounds. *J. Sci. Fd Agric.* **25,** 1563–1569.

2607. Love, R. M., Robertson, I., Lavéty, J. and Smith, G. L. (1974a). Some biochemical characteristics of cod (*Gadus morhua* L.) from the Faroe Bank compared with those from other fishing grounds. *Comp. Biochem. Physiol.* **47B,** 149–161. *27, 79, 80, 106, 107, 137, 163, 247, 361, 364*

2608. Love, R. M., Robertson, I., Smith, G. L. and Whittle, K. J. (1974b). The texture of cod muscle. *J. Texture Stud.* **5,** 201–212. *247, 360, 365–367*

*2609. Love, R. M., Yamaguchi, K., Créac'h, Y. and Lavéty, J. (1976). The connective tissues and collagens of cod during starvation. *Comp. Biochem. Physiol.* **55B**, 487–492. *33, 63, 201*

2610. Low, P. S. and Somero, G. N. (1976). Adaptation of muscle pyruvate kinases to environmental temperatures and pressures. *J. exp. Zool.* **198**, 1–11. *333*

*2611. Lucas, H. F. and Edgington, D. N. (1970). Concentrations of trace elements in Great Lakes fishes. *J. Fish. Res. Bd Can.* **27**, 677–684.

2612. Lunde, G. (1972). The absorption and metabolism of arsenic in fish. *FiskDir. Skr. Serie Teknol. Undersøk.* **5** (12). 16 pp. *397*

*2613. Lunde, G. (1973). Analysis of trace elements, phosphorus and sulphur, in the lipid and the non-lipid phase of halibut (*Hippoglossus hippoglossus*) and tunny (*Thunnus thynnus*). *J. Sci. Fd Agric.* **24**, 1029–1038.

*2614. Luquet, P. and Durand, G. (1970). Development of the concentration of nucleic acids in the epaxial musculature during growth of rainbow trout (*Salmo gairdnerii*); respective roles of multiplication and of enlargement of the cells. *Annls Biol. anim. Biochim. Biophys.* **10**, 481–492. *31*

2615. Luquet, P. and Hannequart, G. (1971). Development in the trout. Changes in nucleic acid contents of different body fractions. *Annls Biol. anim. Biochim. Biophys.* **11**, 657–668. *32*

*2616. Luquet, P. and Hannequart, M.-H. (1974). Relations between the length of the fish, the weight of the brain and its contents of nucleic acids in royal carp. *C. r. hebd. Séanc. Acad. Sci., Paris* **278**, 3371–3374. *32*

2617. Luquet, P., Léger, C. and Bergot, F. (1975). Effects of carbohydrate suppression in diets of rainbow trout kept at a temperature of 10°C. 1.—Growth in relation to level of protein ingestion. *Ann. Hydrobiol.* **6**, 61–70. *3, 141*

2618. Lush, I. E. (1969). Polymorphism of a phosphoglucomutase isoenzyme in herring (*Clupea harengus*). *Comp. Biochem. Physiol.* **30**, 391–395. *253*

2619. Lush, I. E. (1970). Lactate dehydrogenase isoenzymes and their genetic variation in coalfish (*Gadus virens*) and cod (*Gadus morhua*). *Comp. Biochem. Physiol.* **32**, 23–32. *88, 253*

2620. Lush, I. E. and Cowey, C. B. (1968). Genetic variation of cod and coalfish lactate dehydrogenase. *Biochem. J.* **110**, 33p–34p. *252*

*2621. Lutz, F. (1973). Isolation and some characteristics of liver plasma membranes from rainbow trout. *Comp. Biochem. Physiol.* **45B**, 805–811.

*2622. Lutz, P. L. (1972a). Extracellular spaces and composition of various tissues of perch. *Comp. Biochem. Physiol.* **41A**, 77–88. *314, 315*

*2623. Lutz, P. L. (1972b). Body compartmentalisation and ion distribution in the teleost (*Perca fluviatilis*). *Comp. Biochem. Physiol.* **41A,** 181–193.

*2624. Lutz, P. L. (1972c.). Ionic patterns in the teleost. *Comp. Biochem. Physiol.* **42A,** 719–733.

*2625. Lutz, P. L. and Robertson, J. D. (1971). Osmotic constituents of the coelacanth *Latimeria chalumnae* Smith. *Biol. Bull. mar. biol. Lab., Woods Hole,* **141,** 553–560. *155*

*2626. Lyakhnovich, V. P. and Leonenko, Ye. N. (1971). Age-related changes in some of the characteristics of the blood of the silver carp [*Hypophthalmichthys molitrix* (Val.)], the grass carp [*Ctenopharyngodon idella* (Val.)] and the pond carp [*Cyprinus carpio* (L.)]. *J. Ichthyol.* **11,** 743–750.

2627. Lyman, C. P. (1968). Body temperature of exhausted salmon. *Copeia* 631–633 (no volume number given). *322*

*2628. Lyzlova, E. M. and Verzhbinskaya, N. A. (1976). Phosphoenolpyruvate carboxykinase in tissues of the lamprey *Lampetra fluviatilis*. *J. Evol. Biochem. Physiol.* **12,** 65–67. *182*

(Note: Names beginning with either Mac or Mc are both listed under Mac.)

2629. McBride, J. R. and van Overbeeke, A. P. (1971). Effects of androgens, oestrogens and cortisol on the skin, stomach, liver, pancreas, and kidney in gonadectomised adult sockeye salmon (*Oncorhynchus nerka*). *J. Fish. Res. Bd Can.* **28,** 485–490. *199*

2630. McBride, J. R. and van Overbeeke, A. P. (1975). Effects of thiourea treatment on sexually maturing and gonadectomised male sockeye salmon (*Oncorhynchus nerka*). *J. Fish. Res. Bd Can.* **32,** 11–19. *199*

2631. MacCallum, W. A., Jaffray, J. I., Churchill, D. N. and Idler, D. R. (1968). Condition of Newfoundland trap-caught cod and its influence on quality after single and double freezing. *J. Fish. Res. Bd Can.* **25,** 733–755. *361*

2632. MacCallum, W. A., Jaffray, J. I., Churchill, D. N., Idler, D. R. and Odense, P. H. (1967). Postmortem physicochemical changes in unfrozen Newfoundland trap-caught cod. *J. Fish. Res. Bd Can.* **24,** 651–676. *359, 362*

*2633. McCarthy, D. H., Stevenson, J. P. and Roberts, M. S. (1973). Some blood parameters of the rainbow trout (*Salmo gairdneri* Richardson). 1. The Kamloops variety. *J. Fish Biol.* **5,** 1–8.

*2634. McCarthy, D. H., Stevenson, J. P. and Roberts, M. S. (1975). Some blood parameters of the rainbow trout (*Salmo gairdneri* Richardson). II. The Shasta variety. *J. Fish Biol.* **7,** 215–219.

2635. McCarthy, J. J. and Whitledge, T. E. (1972). Nitrogen excretion by the anchovy (*Engraulis mordax* and *E. ringens*) and jack mackerel (*Trachurus symmetricus*). *Fish. Bull. Natl. Oceanic Atmos. Adm.* (*US*), **70**, 395–401. *155, 161*

*2636. McCartney, T. H. (1969). The chemical composition of the trout erythrocyte. *Fish. Res. Bull. N.Y.* **32**, 32–33. (This journal is otherwise known as the Annual Report of the Cortland Hatchery).

*2637. McCartney, T. H. (1971). Phosphorus, total cholesterol, and total free fatty acid distribution in erythrocytes of three species of trout. *Fish. Res. Bull. N.Y.* **33**, 5–8.

*2638. McCartney, T. H. (1976). Sodium-potassium dependent adenosine triphosphatase activity in gills and kidneys of Atlantic salmon (*Salmo salar*). *Comp. Biochem. Physiol.* **53A**, 351–353. *24, 156*

*2639. McCarty, L. S. and Houston, A. H. (1976). Effects of exposure to sublethal levels of cadmium upon water-electrolyte status in the goldfish (*Carassius auratus*). *J. Fish Biol.* **9**, 11–19.

*2640. McCarty, L. S. and Houston, A. H. (1977). $Na^+ : K^+-$ and HCO_3^-- stimulated ATPase activities in the gills and kidneys of thermally acclimated rainbow trout, *Salmo gairdneri*. *Can. J. Zool.* **55**, 704–712.

2641. McCauley, R. W. and Tait, J. S. (1970). Preferred temperature of yearling lake trout, *Salvelinus namaycush*. *J. Fish. Res. Bd Can.* **27**, 1729–1733.

2642. McCormick, J. H., Jones, B. R. and Hokanson, K. E. F. (1977). White sucker (*Catostomus commersoni*) embryo development, and early growth and survival at different temperatures. *J. Fish. Res. Bd Can.* **34**, 1019–1025. *325, 502*

*2643. McCormick, N. A. and Macleod, J. J. R. (1925). The effect on the blood sugar of fish of various conditions including removal of the principal islets (isletectomy). *Proc. R. Soc.* **B98**, 1–29. From Chavin and Young (1970).

2644. MacCrimmon, H. R. and Campbell, J. S. (1969). World distribution of brook trout, *Salvelinus fontinalis*. *J. Fish. Res. Bd Can.* **26**, 1699–1725. *638*

2645. MacCrimmon, H. R. and Kwain, W.-H. (1969). Influence of light on early development and meristic characters in the rainbow trout, *Salmo gairdnerii* Richardson. *Can. J. Zool.* **47**, 631–637. *243, 244*

2646. MacCrimmon, H. R., Marshall, L. and Gots, B. L. (1970). World distribution of brown trout, *Salmo trutta*: further observations. *J. Fish. Res. Bd Can.* **27**, 811–818. *637*

2647. MacDonald, J. R. (1970). An occurrence of male predominance among repeat spawning Atlantic salmon (*Salmo salar*). *J. Fish. Res. Bd Can.* **27**, 1491–1492. *64*

2648. Macer, C. T. (1974). The reproductive biology of the horse mackerel *Trachurus trachurus* (L.) in the North Sea and the English Channel. *J. Fish Biol.* **6,** 415–438.

*2649. McFarland, W. N. and Munz, F. W. (1965). Regulation of body weight and serum composition by hagfish in various media. *Comp. Biochem. Physiol.* **14,** 383–398. *285, 533*

*2650. Macfarlane, N. A. A. (1974). Effects of hypophysectomy on osmoregulation in the euryhaline flounder, *Platichthys flessus* (L.), in sea water and in fresh water. *Comp. Biochem. Physiol.* **47A,** 201–217.

2651. MacFarlane, N. A. A. and Maetz, J. (1974). Effects of hypophysectomy on sodium and water exchanges in the euryhaline flounder, *Platichthys flesus* (L.). *Gen. comp. Endocrinol.* **22,** 77–89. *299*

2652. McGill, A. S. (1974). An investigation into the chemical composition of the cold storage flavour components of cod. *IFST mini-symposium on freezing,* Institute of Food Science and Technology, U.K. 24–26. *368*

2653. McGill, A. S., Hardy, R., Burt, J. R. and Gunstone, F. D. (1974). Hept-*cis*-4-enal and its contribution to the off-flavour in cold-stored cod. *J. Sci. Fd Agric.* **25,** 1477–1489. *368*

2654. Machniak, K. and Gee, J. H. (1975). Adjustment of buoyancy by tadpole madtom, *Noturus gyrinus*, and black bullhead, *Ictalurus melas*, in response to a change in water velocity. *J. Fish. Res. Bd Can.* **32,** 303–307. *121, 122*

*2655. McInerny, J. E. (1974). Renal sodium reabsorption in the hagfish, *Eptatretus stouti*. *Comp. Biochem. Physiol.* **49A,** 273–280.

*2656. Mackay, W. C. (1975). Effect of temperature on fluid absorption by teleost gall bladder. *Comp. Biochem. Physiol.* **50A,** 383–385. *166*

2657. Mackay, W. C. and Beatty, D. D. (1968a). The effect of temperature on renal function in the white sucker fish, *Catostomus commersonii*. *Comp. Biochem. Physiol.* **26,** 235–245. *320*

2658. Mackay, W. C. and Beatty, D. D. (1968b). Plasma glucose levels of the white sucker, *Catostomus commersoni*, and the northern pike, *Esox lucius*. *Can. J. Zool.* **46,** 797–803. *49*

2659. McKeown, B. A. and Hazlett, C. A. (1975). The effect of salinity on pituitary, thyroid and interrenal cells in immature adults of the landlocked sea lamprey, *Petromyzon marinus*. *Comp. Biochem. Physiol.* **50A,** 379–381. *304*

*2660. McKeown, B. A., Leatherland, J. F. and John, T. M. (1975). The effect of growth hormone and prolactin on the mobilisation of free fatty acids and glucose in the Kokanee salmon, *Oncorhynchus nerka*. *Comp. Biochem. Physiol.* **50B,** 425–430. *116, 187, 211, 220*

2661. McKeown, B. A. and van Overbeeke, A. P. (1972). Prolactin and growth hormone concentrations in the serum and pituitary gland of adult migratory sockeye salmon. *J. Fish. Res. Bd Can.* **29,** 303–309. *300*

2662. McKeown, B. A. and Peter, R. E. (1976). The effects of photoperiod and temperature on the release of prolactin from the pituitary gland of the goldfish, *Carassius auratus* L. *Can. J. Zool.* **54,** 1960–1968. *383*

*2663. Mackie, P. R. and Hardy, R. (1969). A lipid analysis of the greater silver smelt (*Argentina silus* (Ascanius) and) an evaluation of its potential for food and fish meal production. *J. Food Technol.* **4,** 241–254.

*2664. McKim, J. M., Christensen, G. M. and Hunt, E. P. (1970). Changes in the blood of brook trout (*Salvelinus fontinalis*) after short-term and long-term exposure to copper. *J. Fish. Res. Bd Can.* **27,** 1883–1889.

*2665. McLeay, D. J. (1973). Effects of a 12-hr and 25-day exposure to kraft pulp mill effluent on the blood and tissues of juvenile coho salmon. *J. Fish. Res. Bd Can.* **30,** 395–400.

2666. McLeay, D. J. (1977). Development of a blood sugar bioassay for rapidly measuring stressful levels of pulpmill effluent to salmonid fish. *J. Fish. Res. Bd Can.* **34,** 477–485. *231*

*2667. McLeay, D. J. and Brown, D. A. (1975). Effects of acute exposure to bleached kraft pulpmill effluent on carbohydrate metabolism of juvenile coho salmon (*Oncorhynchus kisutch*) during rest and exercise. *J. Fish. Res. Bd Can.* **32,** 753–760.

*2668. McMillan, P. J., Hooker, W. M., Roos, B. A. and Deftos, L. J. (1976). Ultimobranchial gland of the trout (*Salmo gairdneri*). 1. Immunohistology and radioimmunoassay of calcitonin. *Gen. comp. Endocrinol.* **28,** 313–319.

2669. McNabb, R. A. and Mecham, J. A. (1971). The effects of different acclimation temperatures on gas secretion in the swimbladder of the bluegill sunfish, *Lepomis macrochirus*. *Comp. Biochem. Physiol.* **40A,** 609–616. *320*

2670. McNabb, R. A. and Pickford, G. E. (1970). Thyroid function in male killifish, *Fundulus heteroclitus*, adapted to high and low temperatures and to fresh water and sea water. *Comp. Biochem. Physiol.* **33,** 783–792. *304, 326*

2671. Madden, J. A. and Houston, A. H. (1976). Use of electroanaesthesia with freshwater teleosts: some physiological consequences in the rainbow trout, *Salmo gairdneri* Richardson. *J. Fish Biol.* **9,** 457–462. *291*

2672. Maetz, J. (1971). Fish gills: mechanisms of salt transfer in fresh water and sea water. *Phil. Trans. R. Soc.* **B262,** 209–249. *287, 288*

2673. Maetz, J. (1973). Transport mechanisms in sea-water adapted fish gills. *Alfred Benzon Symp.* **5,** 427–444. *287–289*

2674. Maetz, J. (1974). Aspects of adaptation to hypo-osmotic and hyper-osmotic environments. *In* "Biochemical and Biophysical Perspectives in Marine Biology" (Eds Malins, D. C. and Sargent, J. R.), pp. 1–167. Academic Press, London and New York. *287–289, 293–295, 299, 300, 305, 565*

2675. Maetz, J. and Bornancin, M. (1975). Biochemical and biophysical aspects of salt excretion by chloride cells in teleosts. *Fortschr. Zool.* **23**, "Excretion" Ed Wessing, A. (Proc. Int. Symp., Mainz, 1974), pp. 322–362. *287, 295*

2676. Maetz, J. and Skadhauge, E. (1968). Drinking rates and gill ionic turnover to external salinities in the eel. *Nature, Lond.* **217**, 371–373. *307*

*2677. Magomaev, A. (1972). The mineral composition of flesh of commercial fish in the Caspian Basin. *Ryb. Khoz.* (7), 75–76 (no volume number given). *147*

*2678. Mahdi, M. A. (1972). Haematological studies on some Nile fishes, *Tilapia nilotica, Lates niloticus*, and *Labeo niloticus*. *Mar. Biol.* **15**, 359–360.

*2679. Maksimov, V. Ya. (1969). The free amino acids contents of the gonads, liver and muscular tissue of silver carp after hibernation. *Sb. Prudovomu Rybovodstvu*, 163–167. *10*

2680. Malessa, P. (1969). Temperature adaptation of the eel (*Anguilla vulgaris*). III. Intensity and distribution of the activity of succinate dehydrogenase and cytochrome oxidase in the lateral muscle of juvenile and adult animals. *Mar. Biol.* **3**, 143–158. *72, 74, 78, 79, 105, 328*

*2681. Malikova, E. M. and Loyanich, A. A. (1974). Effect of the age and sex of rainbow trout on the concentration of nucleic acids in the liver. *Rybokhoz. Issled. v Basseine Baltiiskogo Morya*, **10**, 82–86. *31*

2682. Malins, D. C. and Barone, A. (1970). Glyceryl ether metabolism: regulation of buoyancy in dogfish *Squalus acanthias*. *Science, N.Y.* **167**, 79–80. *viii, 125*

2683. Malins, D. C. and Sargent, J. R. (1974). *The preface to* "Biochemical and Biophysical Perspectives in Marine Biology" (Eds Malins, D. C. and Sargent, J. R.), p. vii. Academic Press, London and New York. *xi*

2684. Malvin, R. L., Carlson, E., Legan, S. and Churchill, P. (1970). Creatinine reabsorption and renal function in the freshwater lamprey. *Am. J. Physiol.* **218**, 1506–1509. *320*

*2685. Mályusz, M. and Thiemann, V. (1976). The effect of urea, thiourea and acetamide on the renal and branchial enzyme-pattern of the dogfish *Scyliorhinus canicula*. *Comp. Biochem. Physiol.* **54B**, 177–179. *155*

*2686. Mangum, C. P., Haswell, M. S. and Johansen, K. (1977). Low salt and high pH in the blood of Amazon fishes (1). *J. exp. Zool.* **200**, 163–168.

*2687. Manita, H., Koizumi, C. and Nonaka, J. (1970). Changes in free amino acids during aseptic autolysis of the muscle of mackerel. *Bull. Jap. Soc. scient. Fish.* **36,** 963–971.

2688. Mann, H. (1969). Factors affecting the taste of fish. *Fette Seifen Anstr-Mittel,* **71,** 1021–1024. *150*

*2689. Mano, T. and Senju, T. (1969). Distribution of carnosine in several species of fishes and shell fishes. *J. Jap. Soc. Fd Nutr. (Eiyo to Shokuryo),* **22,** 164–167.

*2690. Manohar, S. V. (1970). Postmortem glycolytic and other biochemical changes in white muscle of white sucker (*Catostomus commersoni*) and northern pike (*Esox lucius*) at 0C. *J. Fish. Res. Bd Can.* **27,** 1997–2002. *69*

*2691. Manohar, S. V. and Boese, H. (1971). Postmortem changes in the glycogen phosphorylase activity of the muscle of white sucker (*Catostomus commersoni*) and northern pike (*Esox lucius*). *J. Fish. Res. Bd Can.* **28,** 1325–1326.

*2692. Maren, T. H. (1967). Special body fluids of the elasmobranch. *In* "Sharks, Skates and Rays" (Eds Gilbert, P. W., Mathewson, R. F. and Rall, D. P.). Chapter 19, pp. 287–292. The Johns Hopkins Press, Baltimore.

*2693. Maren. T. H., Wistrand, P., Swenson, E. R. and Talalay, A. B. C. (1975). The rates of ion movement from plasma to aqueous humour in the dogfish, *Squalus acanthius. Invest. Ophthalmol.* **14,** 662–673.

*2694. Marinescu, A. G. (1973). Variation of the arginase activity related to the nutrition factor in the process of fish adaptation to temperature. *Rev. Roum. Biol.-Zool.* **18,** 289–294. *218*

2695. Marinescu, A. G. (1975). Oxygen consumption and some metabolites in dorsal muscle of *Idus idus* during starvation. *Zool. Anz.* **194,** 210–214. *169*

*2696. Márquez, E. D. (1976). A comparison of glutamic-oxalacetate transaminase, lactate dehydrogenase, α-hydroxybutyrate dehydrogenase, and creatine phosphokinase activities in non-spawning, pre-spawning, and spawning pink salmon. *Comp. Biochem. Physiol.* **54B,** 121–123. *65, 111*

2697. Marquez, J. R. S. (1960). Age and size at sexual maturity of white goby (*Glossogobius giurus*), a common species of fish of Laguna de Bay, with notes on its food habits. *Philipp. J. Fish.* **8,** 71–79. *36*

*2698. Martyshev, F. G., Maslova, N. I. and Kudryashova, Yu. V. (1973). The physiological and biochemical evaluation of the sperm of male carp reared at different feeding densities. *Izvestiya Timiryazevkoi Sel Skokhozyaistvennoi Akademii,* **5,** 187–191.

*2699. Mar'yanovskaya, M. V. (1972). Some indices of the carbohydrate metabolism of one-year and two-year crucian carp during the growing season and over-wintering. *Doklady TSKhA,* **185,** 117–121. *27*

*2700. Mashiter, K. E. and Morgan, M. R. J. (1975). Carbonic anhydrase levels in the tissues of flounders adapted to sea water and fresh water. *Comp. Biochem. Physiol.* **52A,** 713–717. *288*

2701. Masic, D. and Hamm, R. (1971a). Isozymes of aspartate aminotransferase in the skeletal muscle of carp. *Arch. FischWiss.* **22,** 110–120. From *Chem. Abstr.* **76,** 124431e (1972). *72*

2702. Masic, D. and Hamm, R. (1971b). Alanine-amino transferase in the skeletal muscle of carp. *Arch. FischWiss.* **22,** 256–262.

*2703. Maske, H. and Munk, K. (1956). On the distribution of insulin and zinc in different cell components of the giant islets in flounders and plaice (*Pleuronectidae*). *Z. Naturf.* **11B,** 407–415. *365*

*2704. Maslennikova, N. V. (1970). Content of free amino acids in the muscles, liver and gonads of the maturing Baltic cod. *J. Ichthyology,* **10,** 566–571. *42*

*2705. Maslennikova, N. V. and Korzhenko, V. P. (1972). Amino acid composition of total protein in the liver and testes of Baltic cod during spermatogenesis. *Nauch. Dokl. vyssh. Shk. Biol. Nauk.* **105** (9), 44–48. *42*

2706. Maslova, N. I. (1973). The amino acids composition of the total proteins in the body of two year old carp reared under intensive conditions. *Izvestiya Timiryazevskoi Sel Skokhozyaistvennoi Akademii,* **3,** 185–191. *195*

2707. Mason, J. C. (1975). Seaward movement of juvenile fishes, including lunar periodicity in the movement of coho salmon (*Oncorhynchus kisutch*) fry. *J. Fish. Res. Bd Can.* **32,** 2542–2547. *384*

2708. Masoni, A. and Payan, P. (1974). Urea, insulin and para-amino-hippuric acid (PAH) excretion by the gills of the eel, *Anguilla anguilla* L. *Comp. Biochem. Physiol.* **47A,** 1241–1244. *310*

2709. Massaro, E. J. and Booke, H. E. (1971). Photoregulation of the expression of lactate dehydrogenase isozymes in *Fundulus heteroclitus* (Linnaeus). *Comp. Biochem. Physiol.* **38B,** 327–332. *252, 255*

2710. Mataix, F. J., Gómez-Jarabo, G., Illera, M. and de la Higuera, M. (1976). Influence of the age and dietary protein levels on protein productive value in trout ("*Salmo gairdnerii*"). *Rev. Nutr. anim. (Sp.)* **14,** 95–102. *61*

*2711. Mathers, J. S. and Beamish, F. W. H. (1974). Changes in serum osmotic and ionic concentrations in landlocked *Petromyzon marinus*. *Comp. Biochem. Physiol.* **49A,** 677–688. *318*

2712. Mathur, G. B. (1967). Aenerobic respiration in a cyprinoid fish *Rasbora daniconius* (Ham). *Nature, Lond.* **214,** 318–319. *272*

2713. Matsunga, K. (1975). Concentration of mercury by three species of fish from Japanese rivers. *Nature, Lond.* **257,** 49–50. *437*

2714. Matsuno, T., Higashi, E. and Akita, T. (1973). Carotenoid pigments in gobies and five related fishes. *Bull. Jap. Soc. scient. Fish.* **39,** 159–163. *317*

*2715. Matsuno, T. and Katsuyama, M. (1975). Comparative biochemical studies of carotenoids in fishes—VI. Carotenoids of Japanese sculpins and white gobies. *Bull. Jap. Soc. scient. Fish.* **41,** 675–679.

*2716. Matsuno, T. and Katsuyama, M. (1976a.). Comparative biochemical studies of carotenoids in fishes—IX. On the nineteen species of fishes in the division percichthyes. *Bull. Jap. Soc. scient. Fish.* **42,** 645–649.

*2717. Matsuno, T. and Katsuyama, M. (1976b). Comparative biochemical studies of carotenoids in fishes—IX. Carotenoids of two species of flying fish, mackerel pike, killifish, three-spined stickleback and Chinese eight-spined stickleback. *Bull. Jap. Soc. scient. Fish.* **42,** 761–763.

*2718. Matsuno, T. and Katsuyama, M. (1976c.) Comparative biochemical studies of carotenoids in fishes—XII. On the nine species of fishes in the order clupeida. *Bull. Jap. Soc. scient. Fish.* **42,** 765–768.

*2719. Matsuno, T. and Katsuyama, M. (1976d). Comparative biochemical studies of carotenoids in fishes—XIII. Carotenoids in six species of leuciscinaeous fishes. *Bull. Jap. Soc. scient. Fish.* **42,** 847–850.

*2720. Matsuno, T., Katsuyama, M. and Ishida, T. (1976). Comparative biochemical studies of carotenoids in fishes—X. Carotenoids of Japanese perch. *Bull. Jap. Soc. scient. Fish.* **42,** 651–654.

*2721. Matsuno, T., Katsuyama, M., Iwasaki, N. and Isshihara, Y. (1974). Carotenoid pigments in pond smelt. *Bull. Jap. Soc. scient. Fish.* **40,** 409–412. *317*

*2722. Matsuno, T., Katsuyama, M. and Kashizaki, M. (1976). Comparative biochemical studies of carotenoids in fishes—VIII. Carotenoids of large-mouth smelt and Japanese smelt. *Bull. Jap. Soc. scient. Fish.* **42,** 465–467.

*2723. Matsuno, T., Katsuyama, M. and Uemura, M. (1975). Comparative biochemical studies of carotenoids in fishes—VII. Carotenoids of common ice-fish and sea smelt. *Bull. Jap. Soc. scient. Fish.* **41,** 681–684.

*2724. Matsuno, T., Nagata, S. and Chiba, K. (1975). Comparative biochemical studies of carotenoids in fishes—V. Comparative studies of carotenoids between fresh water origin and sea water origin striped mullets. *Bull. Jap. Soc. scient. Fish.* **41,** 459–464. *317*

*2725. Matsuno, T., Nagata, S., Sato, Y. and Watanabe, T. (1974). Comparative biochemical studies of carotenoids in fishes—II. Carotenoids of horse mackerel, swell fishes, porcupine fishes and striped mullet. *Bull. Jap. Soc. scient. Fish.* **40,** 579–584.

*2726. Matsuno, T., Nagata, S. and Uemura, M. (1974). Comparative biochemical studies of carotenoids in fishes—I. Carotenoids of Chinese snakehead. *Bull. Jap. Soc. scient. Fish.* **40,** 489–492.

*2727. Matsuno, T., Nagata, S. and Uemura, M. (1975). Comparative biochemical studies of carotenoids in fishes—III. Carotenoids of Japanese common catfish. *Bull. Jap. Soc. scient. Fish.* **41,** 343–349.

2728. Matta, J. T., Hassón-Voloch, A. and Hargreaves, A. B. (1975). Lactate dehydrogenase from the electric organ of *Electrophorus electricus* (L.)—isozyme analysis. *Comp. Biochem. Physiol.* **52B,** 351–354. *433*

2729. Matty, A. J., Tsuneki, K., Dickhoff, W. W. and Gorbman, A. (1976). Thyroid and gonadal function in hypophysectomised hagfish. *Eptatretus stouti. Gen. comp. Endocrinol.* **30,** 500–516. *533*

2730. Matyukhin, V. A., Neshumova, T. V. and Dement'yev, Ya. V. (1975). Temperature changes of the red and white muscles of the Baikal grayling (*Thymallus arcticus baicalensis*) at different swimming speeds. *J. Ichthyol.* **15,** 794–798. *102*

*2731. Mayer, N. and Nibelle, J. (1969). Sodium space in fresh-water and sea-water eels. *Comp. Biochem. Physiol.* **31,** 589–597. *314*

2732. Mayerle, J. A. and Butler, D. G. (1971). Effects of temperature and feeding on intermediary metabolism in North American eels (*Anguilla rostrata* LeSueur). *Comp. Biochem. Physiol.* **40A,** 1087–1095. *212*

2733. Mazeaud, F. (1965). Action of noradrenaline on the blood glucose of the carp. *C. r. Séanc. Soc. Biol.* **159,** 2159–2161. *232, 233*

*2734. Mazeaud, F. (1969). Free fatty acids and glucose in the plasma of the carp (*Cyprinus carpio* L.) after asphyxia or agitation "musculaire épuisante". *C. r. Séanc. Soc. Biol.* **163,** 558–561. *232, 238*

2735. Mazeaud, F. (1973). Research on the regulation of free fatty acids in plasma and on blood sugar in fish. Thesis Docteur Ès-Sciences Naturelles, University of Paris. *6, 39, 45, 212, 232, 237*

*2736. Mazeaud, M. (1964). Influence of several factors in the adrenalin and noradrenalin in the blood of carp. *C. r. Séanc. Soc. Biol.* **158,** 2018–2021. *235*

*2737. Mazeaud, M. (1969a). Adrenaline and noradrenaline in the blood of the marine lamprey (*Petromyzon marinus* L.). *C. r. Séanc. Soc. Biol.* **163,** 349–352. *48, 235*

*2738. Mazeaud, M. (1969b). Biosynthesis of adrenaline in the heart of the marine lamprey (*Petromyzon marinus* L.). *C. r. Séanc. Soc. Biol.* **163,** 2051–2055.

*2739. Mazeaud, M. (1969c). Influence of stress on the content of catecholamines in the plasma and the "corps axillaires" of an elasmobranch, la rousette (*Scyliorhinus canicula* L.). *C. r. Séanc. Soc. Biol.* **163,** 2262–2266. *235*

*2740. Mazeaud, M. M. (1972). Epinephrine biosynthesis in *Petromyzon marinus* (cyclostoma) and *Salmo gairdneri* (teleost). *Comp. gen. Pharmacol.* **3,** 457–468.

*2741. Mearns, A. J. (1971). Lactic acid regulation in salmonoid fishes. Ph.D. Thesis, University of Washington. *4, 272*

*2742. Mehrle, P. M. Unpublished, quoted by Grant, Mehrle and Russell (1970).

*2743. Mehrle, P. M. and DeClue, M. E. (1973). Phenylalanine determination in fish serum: adaptation of a mammalian method to fish. *Analyt. Biochem.* **52,** 660–661.

*2744. Mehrle, P. M., Stalling, D. L. and Bloomfield, R. A. (1971). Serum amino acids in rainbow trout (*Salmo gairdneri*) as affected by DDT and Dieldrin. *Comp. Biochem. Physiol.* **38B,** 373–377. *116*

*2745. Meier, A. H., Lynch, G. R. and Garcia, L. E. (1973). Daily rhythms of plasma chloride in two teleosts, *Fundulus grandis* and *Fundulus chrysotus*. *Copeia* (1), 90–92 (no volume number given). *384*

*2746. Meister, R., Zwinglestein, G. and Brichon, G. (1976). Influence of the acclimation temperature on the metabolism of phospholipids of the eel (*Anguilla anguilla*) in fresh water. *J. Physiol., Paris,* **72,** 79–103.

*2747. Meister, R., Zwinglestein, G. and Jouanneteau, J. (1973). Salinity and fatty acid composition of tissular phosphoglycerides in the eel (*Anguilla anguilla*). *Annales de l'Institut Michel Pacha Laboratoire maritime de Physiologie,* **6,** 58–71. *316*

*2748. Meizies, A. and Reichwald, I. (1973). The lipids in flesh and roe of fresh and smoked fish. *J. Nutr. Sci.* (*Z. ErnährWiss.*) **12,** 248–251.

*2749. Melikova, P. K., Dzhafarov, A. I. and Guseinov, T. M. (1976). Selenium content in tissues of fish inhabiting the Mingechaur and Varvarinsk reservoirs. *Selen Biol., Mater. Nauchn. Konf., 2nd 1975* **2,** 145–147, 159–173. Ed Gasanov, G. G. "Elm", Baku, USSR. From *Chem. Abstr.* **86,** 52860a (1977).

*2750. Mengebier, W. L. (1976). A comparison of succinic dehydrogenase activity in brain homogenates of Bermuda shore fishes relative to body weight and activity. *Comp. Biochem. Physiol.* **55B,** 387–389. *111*

*2751. Merliss, M. (1973). The mercury hazard of pier and surf caught fish. *J. Fla med. Ass.* **60,** 31–32.

2752. Mertz, E. T. (1972). The protein and amino acid needs. *In* "Fish Nutrition" (Ed. Halver, J. E.), Chapter 3, pp. 105–143. Academic Press, London and New York. *5, 139*

*2753. Meşter, R., Scripcariu, D. and Niculescu, S. (1973). Effect of temperature on the isozymic pattern of pond loach (*Misgurnus fossilis* L.). II. Malate dehydrogenase and succinate dehydrogenase. *Rev. Roum. Biol. (Zool.),* **18,** 153–161. *329, 330*

*2754. Meyer, W. and Sauerbier, I. (1977). The development of catecholamines in embryos and larvae of the rainbow trout (*Salmo gairdneri* Rich.). *J. Fish Biol.* **10**, 431–435. *20*

*2755. Mikhkieva, V. S., Siderov, V. S., Titova, V. F. and Lizenko, E. I. (1972). Fish Lipids. IV. Phospholipids of the Shuisk whitefish *Coregonus lavaretus lavaretoides N. Schuensis* Pravdin. *In* "Salmonidae of Karelia, Issue 1. Ecology, Parasites, Biochemistry" (Eds Potapova. O. I. and Smirnov, Y. A.), pp. 178–183. Petrozavodsk.

2756. Mikulin, A. Ye. and Soin, S. G. (1975). The functional significance of carotenoids in the embryonic development of teleosts. *J. Ichthyol.* **15**, 749–759.

*2757. Milanesi, A. A. and Bird, J. W. C. (1972). Lysosomal enzymes in aquatic species—II. Distribution and particle properties of thermally acclimated muscle lysosomes of rainbow trout, *Salmo gairdneri. Comp. Biochem. Physiol.* **41B**, 573–591. *328*

2758. Miles, H. M. (1971). Renal function in migrating adult coho salmon. *Comp. Biochem. Physiol.* **38A**, 787–826. *306*

2759. Miles, H. M. and Smith, L. S. (1968). Ionic regulation in migrating juvenile coho salmon, *Oncorhynchus kisutch. Comp. Biochem. Physiol.* **26**, 381–398. *292*

2760. Miller, G. E., Grant, P. M., Kishore, R., Steinkruger, F. J., Rowland, F. S. and Guinn, V. P. (1972). Mercury concentrations in museum specimens of tuna and swordfish. *Science, N.Y.*, **175**, 1121–1122. *437*

*2761. Mills, G. L. and Taylaur, C. E. (1971). The distribution and composition of serum lipoproteins in eighteen animals. *Comp. Biochem. Physiol.* **40B**, 489–501.

*2762. Mills, G. L. and Taylaur, C. E. (1973). The distribution and composition of serum lipoproteins in the coelacanth (*Latimeria*). *Comp. Biochem. Physiol.* **44B**, 1235–1241.

*2763. Mil'man, L. S. and Yurovitskii, Yu. G. (1969). Phosphorylase in the developing embryo of the loach, *Misgurnus fossilis*, and the control of its activity. *Fermenty Evol. Zhivotn.* 126–132. From *Chem. Abstr.* **74**, 29357k (1971).

*2764. Milne, R. S. and Randall, D. J. (1976). Regulation of arterial pH during fresh water to sea water transfer in the rainbow trout, *Salmo gairdneri. Comp. Biochem. Physiol.* **53A**, 157–160.

*2765. Minick, M. C. and Chavin, W. (1972a). Effects of vertebrate insulins upon serum FFA and phospholipid levels in the goldfish, *Carassius auratus* Linnaeus. *Comp. Biochem. Physiol.* **41A**, 791–804. *41*

*2766. Minick, M. C. and Chavin, W. (1972b). Effects of alloxan, streptozotocin or D-Mannoheptulose upon serum free fatty acid and serum glucose levels in goldfish, *Carassius auratus* L. *Comp. Biochem. Physiol.* **42B**, 367–376.

*2767. Minick, M. C. and Chavin, W. (1973). Effects of catecholamines upon serum FFA levels in normal and diabetic goldfish, *Carassius auratus* L. *Comp. Biochem. Physiol.* **44A,** 1003–1008.

*2768. Mironova, V. N., Kandyuk, R. P. and Klimashevskii, V. M. (1973). Sterol content of liver of south Atlantic fishes. *Biol. Morya*, **30,** 137–140.

*2769. Mobley, P. W., Metzger, R. P. and Wick, A. N. (1972). The occurrence of D-Fucose (D-Arabinose) dehydrogenase in selected vertebrate species. *Comp. Biochem. Physiol.* **43B,** 509–516.

*2770. Moczar, E., Payrau, P. and Robert, L. (1969). Distribution of the carbo-hydrates in the soluble and insoluble fractions of the stroma of fish corneas. *Comp. Biochem. Physiol.* **30,** 73–82.

2771. Modigh, M. and Tota, B. (1975). Mitochondrial respiration in the ventricular myocardium and in the white and deep red myotomal muscles of juvenile tuna fish (*Thunnus thynnus* L.). *Acta Physiol. scand.* **93,** 289–294. *86, 88*

*2772. Mohr, V. (1971). On the constitution and physical-chemical properties of the connective tissues of mammalian and fish skeletal muscle. Ph.D. Thesis, University of Aberdeen, Scotland. *122*

*2773. Molnar, G. (1973). Seasonal variation of alkaline phosphatase and trans-aminase content in the blood of healthy silurids (*Silurus glanis*). *Agrartud. Egyet. Közl.* 3–14 (no volume number given). From *Chem. Abstr.* **82,** 14306j (1975).

2774. Moon, T. W. (1975). Temperature adaptation: isozymic function and the maintenance of heterogeneity. *In* "Isozymes. II. Physiological Function" (Ed. Markert, C. L.), pp. 207–220. Academic Press, London and New York. *333*

2775. Moon, T. W. and Hochachka, P. W. (1971a). Effects of thermal acclimatiom on multiple forms of the liver-soluble NADP$^+$-linked isocitrate dehydrogenase in the family salmonidae. *Comp. Biochem. Physiol.* **40B,** 207–213. *333*

*2776. Moon, T. W. and Hochachka, P. W. (1971b). Temperature and enzyme activity in poikilotherms. Isocitrate dehydrogenase in rainbow-trout liver. *Biochem. J.* **123,** 695–705. *333*

2777. Moon, T. W. and Idler, D. R. (1974). The binding of 1 α-hydroxycortico-sterone to tissue soluble proteins in the skate *Raja ocellata*. *Comp. Biochem. Physiol.* **48B,** 499–506. *409*

2778. Moore, R. H. (1970). Changes in the composition of the swimbladder gas of the striped mullet, *Mugil cephalus*, during hypoxia. *Comp. Biochem. Physiol.* **34,** 895–899. *283*

*2779. Mori, M., Hikichi, S., Kamiya, H. and Hashimoto, Y. (1972). Three species
        of teleost fish having diacyl glyceryl ethers in the muscle as a major lipid. *Bull.
        Jap. Soc. scient. Fish.* **38,** 56–63.

*2780. Mori, M., Saito, T. and Nakanishi. Y. (1966). Occurrence and chemical
        properties of wax in the muscle of an African fish, *Allocyttus verrucosus. Bull.
        Jap. Soc. scient. Fish.* **32,** 668–672.

*2781. Mori, M., Saito, T., Nakanishi, Y., Miyazawa, K. and Hashimoto, Y. (1966).
        The composition and toxicity of wax in the flesh of castor oil fishes. *Bull. Jap.
        Soc. scient. Fish.* **32,** 135–145.

*2782. Morishita, T. and Takahashi, T. (1969). Studies on the esterase and lipase
        of fish—III. On the esterase and lipase in the fish muscle. *J. Fac. Fish. pref.
        Univ. Mie-Tsu,* **8,** 41—51. *69, 72, 73*

*2783. Moroz, I. Ye. (1971). Dynamics of metabolism in the carp [*Cyprinus carpio* (L.)]
        during overwintering. *J. Ichthyol.* **11,** 592–596.

*2784. Morozova, A. L. (1973). Some pecularities of the carbohydrate-phosphorus
        metabolism in muscles of fishes of different ecology. *Trudy vses. gidrobiol.
        Obshch.* **18,** 128–135. *69*

*2785. Morozova, A. L. and Trusevich, V. V. (1971). Carbohydrate content in the
        tissues of the scad *Trachurus mediterraneus ponticus* Aleev during intense muscle
        activity. *Evolyutsiya vegetat. Funktsii* (Ed. Kreps, M.), pp. 56–63. Leningrad.
        232, 237, 386

*2786. Morozova, N. P., Tikhomirova, A. A. and Tkachenko, V. N. (1974). Transient
        and heavy metals in commercial fish from the southern Atlantic. *Trudy vses.
        nauchno-issled. Inst. mork. ryb. Khoz. Okeanogr.* **100,** 45–50.

 2787. Morris, R. W. (1965). Seasonal changes in metabolism of four south tem-
        perate marine fishes. *Trans. R. Soc. N.Z.* **6,** 141–152. *28, 30*

 2788. Morris, R. W. (1970). Thermogenesis and its possible survival value in fishes.
        In "Antarctic Ecology" (Ed. Holdgate, M. W.), vol. 1, pp. 337–343. Academic
        Press, London and New York. *321*

 2789. Morrow, J. E. and Mauro, A. (1950). Body temperature of some marine
        fishes. *Copeia,* (2), 108–116 (no volume number given). *321*

*2790. Motelică, I. (1965). Observations regarding the influence of temperature on
        "normal" glycaemia in the carp (*Cyprinus carpio* L.). *Rev. roum. Biol. Ser. Zool.*
        10, 159–164. From Chavin and Young (1970).

*2791. Moule, M. L. and Nace, P. F. (1963). Reducing substances in the blood of
        normal and alloxan-treated fish. *Can. J. Biochem. Physiol.* **41,** 2397–2407.
        From Chavin and Young (1970).

2792. Moule, M. L. and Yip, C. C. (1973). Insulin biosynthesis in the bullhead, *Ictalurus nebulosus*, and the effect of temperature. *Biochem. J.* **134,** 753–761. *344*

*2793. Mounib, M. S. and Eisen, J. S. (1969). Alanine and aspartate aminotransferase in eggs and sperm of fish. *Life Sci.* **8,** 531–534.

*2794. Mounib, M. S. and Eisan, J. S. (1972a). Fixation of carbon dioxide by the testes of rabbit and fish. *Comp. Biochem. Physiol.* **43B,** 393–401.

*2795. Mounib, M. S. and Eisan, J. S. (1972b). Mitochondrial and cytosol malic enzymes in the testicular tissue of cod and rabbit. *Endocrinology,* **91,** 1375–1379.

*2796. Mounib, M. S. and Eisan, J. S. (1973). Fixation of carbon dioxide and some of the enzymes involved in cod eggs. *Int. J. Biochem.* **4,** 207–212.

*2797. Mršulja, B. B. and Rakić, L. M. (1974). Circadian rhythm of glycogen content in various brain structures of *Serranus scriba* Cuv. *J. exp. mar. Biol. Ecol.* **15,** 43–48. *383*

2798. Mugiya, Y. (1974). Calcium-45 behaviour at the level of the otolithic organs of rainbow trout. *Bull .Jap. Soc. scient. Fish.* **40,** 457–463. *222, 223*

2799. Mugiya, Y. and Watabe, N. (1977). Studies on fish scale formation and resorption—II. Effect of oestradiol on calcium homeostasis and skeletal tissue resorption in the goldfish, *Carassius auratus,* and the killifish, *Fundulus heteroclitus. Comp. Biochem. Physiol.* **57A,** 197–202. *37*

*2800. Mukhopadhyay, P. K. (1977). Studies on the enzymatic activities related to varied patterns of diets in the air-breathing catfish, *Clarias batrachus* (Linn.). *Hydrobiologia* **52,** 235–237.

*2801. Mulcahy, M. F. (1970). Blood values in the pike *Esox lucius* L. *J. Fish Biol.* **2,** 203–209. *55*

*2802. Müller, R. (1974). Carbohydrate metabolism and osmomineral balance of *Leuciscus rutilus* L. *Zool. Jb. Abt. allg. Zool. Physiol. Tiere* **78,** 85–107.

2803. Müller, R. (1977). Temperature selection of goldfish (*Carassius auratus* L.) and brook trout (*Salvelinus fontinalis* Mitch.) after heterogeneous temperature acclimation. *J. therm. Biol.* **2,** 5–7. *323*

*2804. Müller, R., Böke, K., Martin-Neumann, U. and Hanke, W. (1974). Salt water adaptation and metabolism in teleosts. *Fortschr. Zool.* **22,** 465–467. *301*

*2805. Munroe, V. R. and Poluhowich, J. J. (1974). Ionic composition of the plasma and whole blood of marine and fresh water eels, *Anguilla rostrata. Comp. Biochem. Physiol.* **49A,** 541–544. *315*

2806. Munshi, J. S. D., Ojha, J. and Mittal, A. K. (1975). Succinic dehydrogenase activity of the respiratory muscles of a fresh-water teleost, *Bagarius bagarius* (Ham.) (Sisoridae, Pisces). *Acta anat.* **92**, 543–559. *80*

2807. Muntz, W. R. A. (1976). Visual pigments of cichlid fishes from Malawi. *Vision Res.* **16**, 897–903. *267*

*2808. Munz, F. W. and McFarland, W. N. (1964). Regulatory function of a primitive vertebrate kidney. *Comp. Biochem. Physiol.* **13**, 381–400. *158*

2809. Munz, F. W. and McFarland, W. N. (1973). The significance of spectral position in the rhodopsins of tropical marine fishes. *Vision Res.* **13**, 1829–1874. *266*

*2810. Murat, J. C. (1976a). Studies on the mobilisation of tissular carbohydrates in the carp. Thesis, Docteur d'Etat, University of Toulouse. *3, 171, 191, 228, 232–234, 237, 271, 280, 345, 386*

*2811. Murat, J. C. (1976b). Studies on glycogenolysis in carp liver: evidence for an amylase pathway for glygogen breakdown. *Comp. Biochem. Physiol.* **55B**, 461–465. *4, 521, 522*

*2812. Murat, J. C. and Parent, J. P. (1975). Effect of temperature acclimation on growth and carbohydrate metabolism in carp. Preliminary data. *Cahiers Lab. Montereau*, **2**, 23–34. *319, 386*

2813. Murat, J. C., Parent, J. P. and Balas, D. (1972). Data on the activity of glycogen phosphorylase of teleosts. *J. Physiol., Paris*, **65**, 458–459. *73*

2814. Murat, J. C., Parent, J. P. and Serfaty, A. (1972). Starvation and refeeding in carp (*Cyprinus carpio* L.). V. Influence of four methods of refeeding on carbohydrate metabolism. *Archs Sci. physiol.* **26**, 349–357. *228*

*2815. Murat, J. C., Parent, J. P. and Serfaty, A. (1973). Study of the activity in vitro of the glycogen phosphorylase of the carp (*Cyprinus carpio* L.). *Experientia*, **29**, 36–37.

*2816. Murat, J. C. and Serfaty, A. (1970). On the subject of a hypoglycaemic effect of thyroxine in the carp (*Cyprinus carpio* L.). *C. r. Séanc. Soc. Biol.* **164**, 1842–1843. *7, 238*

2817. Murat, J. C. and Serfaty, A. (1971). Seasonal variations in the effect of thyroxine on the glucose metabolism of the carp. *J. Physiol., Paris*, **63**, 80 only. *7, 386*

2818. Muravskaya, Z. A. (1972). Rate of nitrogen excretion and oxygen consumption in some Black Sea fish with different ecology. *Nauch. Dokl. vyssh. Shk. Biol. Nauk.* (4), 39–42 (no volume number given). *27, 28, 116*

2819. Muravskaya, Z. A. and Belokopytin, Yu. S. (1975). Effect of the activity of moving on nitrogen excretion and oxygen consumption in the sea bass. *Biol. Morya*, (5), 39–44 (no volume number given). *112, 116, 163, 325*

*2820. Murayama, S., Onishi, T., Tominaga, M. and Sasaki, H. (1971). Biochemical studies on wintering of culture carp—VIII. Effect of water temperature on hepatopancreatic enzyme activity and result of rearing experiment. *Bull. Tokai reg. Fish. Res. Lab.* **66,** 167–172.

*2821. Murphy, P. G. and Houston, A. H. (1974). Environmental temperature and the body fluid system of the fresh-water teleost—V. Plasma electrolyte levels and branchial microsomal (Na⁺–K⁺) ATPase activity in thermally acclimated goldfish (*Carassius auratus*). *Comp. Biochem. Physiol.* **47B,** 563–570. *27, 34, 35*

2822. Murray, M., Jones, H., Cserr, H. F. and Rall, D. P. (1975). The blood-brain barrier and ventricular system of *Myxine glutinosa*. *Brain Res.* **99,** 17–33. *592*

*2823. Murrell, L. R. and Nace, P. F. (1959). Experimental diabetes in the catfish: normal and alloxan-diabetic blood glucose and pancreatic histology. *Endocrinology*, **64,** 542–550. From Chavin and Young (1971).

*2824. Mustafa, S. and Jafri, A. K. (1976). Dynamics of nucleic acid turnover in the dark and white muscles of cat-fish, *Mystus vittatus* (Bloch) during growth in the pre-maturity phase. *Zool. Anz., Jena,* **196,** 237 240.

2825. Mysliwski, A., Zawistowski, S. and Dabrowski, T. (1969). Histochemistry of the red and white muscle fibres in mackerel (*Scomber colias*). *Folia morph.* **28,** 389–396. *72–74*

2826. Møller, D. (1968). Genetic diversity in spawning cod along the Norwegian coast. *Hereditas*, **60,** 1–32. *252*

2827. Møller, D. and Nævdal, G. (1973). Comparison of blood proteins of coalfish from Norwegian and Icelandic waters. *FiskDir. Skr. Ser. HavUnders.* **16,** 177–181. *251, 252*

*2828. Nabrzyski, M. (1975a). Assay of mercury, copper and zinc contents in meat tissue of tunny and some other Atlantic fishes, as well as of *Illex illecembrosus* and *Peneus*. *Bromatologia i Chemia Toksykologiczno*, **8,** 171–177.

*2829. Nabrzyski, M. (1975b). Mercury, copper, and zinc content in the meat tissue of some fresh-water fish. *Bromatologia i Chemia Toksykologiczno*, **8,** 313–319.

*2830. Nag, A. C. (1972). Ultrastructure and adenosine triphosphatase activity of red and white muscle fibres of the caudal region of a fish, *Salmo gairdneri*. *J. Cell Biol.* **55,** 42–57. *73, 74, 76, 79, 85*

*2831. Nagahama, Y., Nishioka, R. S. and Bern, H. A. (1973). Responses of prolactin cells of two euryhaline marine fishes, *Gillichthys mirabilis* and *Platichthys stellatus*, to environmental salinity. *Z. Zellforsch. mikrosk. Anat.* **136,** 153–167. *300*

*2832. Nagai, M. and Ikeda, S. (1971). Carbohydrate metabolism in fish—I. Effects
        of starvation and dietary composition on the blood glucose level and the
        hepatopancreatic glycogen and lipid contents in carp. *Bull. Jap. Soc. scient.
        Fish.* **37,** 404–409. *182, 192*

 2833. Nagai, M. and Ikeda, S. (1972). Carbohydrate metabolism in fish—III.
        Effect of dietary composition on metabolism of glucose-U-^{14}C and glutamate-
        U-^{14}C in carp. *Bull. Jap. Soc. scient. Fish.* **38,** 137–143. *3, 139, 140*

*2834. Nagai, M. and Ikeda, S. (1973). Carbohydrate metabolism in fish— IV.
        Effect of dietary composition on metabolism of acetate-U-^{14}C and L-alanine-
        U-^{14}C in carp. *Bull. Jap. Soc. scient. Fish.* **39,** 633–643. *3, 140, 185*

*2835. Nagayama, F. and Kawamura, M. (1973). Threonine aldolase of mackerel.
        Bull. Jap. Soc. scient. Fish. **39,** 683–687.

*2836. Nagayama, F., Ohshima, H. and Takeuchi, T. (1973). Activities of hexo-
        kinase and glucose dehydrogenase in fish liver. *Bull. Jap. Soc. scient. Fish.* **39,**
        1349 only.

*2837. Nagayama, F., Oshima, H. and Takeuchi, T. (1975). Studies on the enzyme
        system of carbohydrate metabolism in fish—II. Purification of glucose-6-
        phosphate dehydrogenase and glucose dehydrogenase. *Bull. Jap. Soc. scient.
        Fish.* **41,** 1063–1067.

*2838. Nagayama, F., Ohshima, H. and Umezawa, K. (1972). Distribution of
        glucose-6-phosphate metabolising enzymes in fish. *Bull. Jap. Soc. scient. Fish.*
        38, 589–593. *3*

*2839. Nagayama, F., Ohshima, H., Umezawa, K. and Kaiho, M. (1972). Effect
        of starvation on the activities of glucose-6-phosphate metabolising enzymes
        in fish. *Bull. Jap. Soc. scient. Fish.* **38,** 595–598.

*2840. Nagayama, F. and Saito, Y. (1968). Distribution of amylase, α- and β-
        glucosidase and β-galactosidase in fish. *Bull. Jap. Soc. scient. Fish.* **34,** 944–949.

 2841. Nagayama, F. and Saito, Y. (1969). Studies of β-galactosidase of the rainbow
        trout liver   III. Enzyme activity and the isozyme pattern of the yearling fed
        with high carbohydrate feeds. *Bull. Jap. Soc. scient. Fish.* **35,** 1017–1020. *153*

 2842. Nagayama, F., Yamada, T. and Tauti, M. (1968). Activities of UDPglucose
        dehydrogenase, UDPglucuronyl transferase, and some glycosidases of fresh-
        water fish during the adaptation to salt water. *Bull. Jap. Soc. scient. Fish.* **34,**
        950–954. *317*

*2843. Nagayama, F., Yasumura, S., Sakuma, S. and Hikosaka, M. (1971). Effect
        of temperature on hydrolase activity in mackerel tissue. *Bull. Jap. Soc. scient.
        Fish.* **37,** 634–637.

*2844. Nakagawa, H. (1970). Studies on rainbow trout egg (*Salmo gairdnerii irideus*). II. Carbohydrate in the egg protein. *J. Fac. Fish. Anim. Husb. Hiroshima Univ.* **9,** 57–63.

*2845. Nakagawa, H., Kayama, M. and Asakawa, S. (1976). Biochemical studies on carp plasma protein—I. Isolation and nature of an albumin. *Bull. Jap. Soc. scient. Fish.* **42,** 677–685.

*2846. Nakagawa, H., Nanba, K., Kayama, M. and Murachi, S. (1977). Electrophoretic properties of plasma protein relating to some blood properties in cultured yellow tail. *Bull. Jap. Soc. scient. Fish.* **43,** 75-81

*2847. Nakagawa, H. and Tsuchiya, Y. (1976). Studies on rainbow trout egg (*Salmo gairdnerii irideus*). VI. Changes of lipid composition in yolk during development. *J. Fac. Fish. Anim. Husb. Hiroshima Univ.* **15,** 35–46.

*2848. Nakano, E. and Yamamoto, S. (1972). Amino acid component in the fish egg. *Devl Biol.* **28,** 528–530.

*2849. Nambu, Z., Yamagami, K. and Terayama, H. (1975). Studies on some compound lipids in larval and adult erythrocytes of the rainbow trout. *Annotnes zool. jap.* **48,** 65–74. *23*

*2850. Naplatarova, M., Todorov, M. and Săjikova, M. (1975). Content of certain trace elements in the organs and tissues of freshwater fish. *Agrophysical studies (Agrofiz. Issled.)*, **2,** 137–140.

*2851. Narasimhan, P. V. and Sundararaj, B. I. (1971a). Circadian variations in carbohydrate parameters in two teleosts, *Notopterus notopterus* (Pallas) and *Colisa fasciata* (Bloch and Schneider). *Comp. Biochem. Physiol.* **39B,** 89–99.

*2852. Narasimhan, P. V. and Sundararaj, B. I. (1971b). Effects of stress on carbohydrate metabolism in the teleost *Notopterus notopterus* (Pallas). *J. Fish Biol.* 441–451. *192*

2853. Narayansingh, T. and Eales, J. G. (1975). The influence of physiological doses of thyroxine on the lipid reserves of starved and fed brook trout, *Salvelinus fontinalis* (Mitchill). *Comp. Biochem. Physiol.* **52B,** 407–412. *169*

*2854. Nasedkina, E. A. and Belova, T. V. (1971). The change of composition of the free amino acids during the curing of salt herrings. *Issled. Tekhnol. Ryb. Prod.* (no. 5), 30–36.

*2855. Nasedkina, E. A. and Krasnitskaya, A. L. (1972). A method of measuring the amount of creatine and creatinine in the tissue of fish and fish products. *Issled. Inst. Ryb. Khoz. Okeanogr.* **83,** 39–43.

*2856. Nasedkina, E. A. and Pushkareva, N. F. (1974). Some biochemical indicators of the marine hunchback salmon (*Oncorhynchus gorbuscha* W.) at various stages in its development. *Izv. tikhookean, nauchno-issled. Inst. ryb. Khoz. Okeanogr.* 94–99 (no volume number given).

*2857. Nasedkina, E. A. and Puskareva, H. F. (1969). Amino acid composition of the roe and body fibres of the maritime pink salmon. *Ryb. Khoz.* (12), 53–56 (no volume number given). *42*

*2858. Naseem, S. M. and Siddiqui, A. Q. (1970). Seasonal variations in the biochemical composition of blood serum of *Cirrhina mrigal* (Ham.) and *Labeo rohita* (Ham.). *Broteria Cienc. nat.* **39,** 197–204.

*2859. Nash, A. R., Fisher, W. K. and Thompson, E. O. P. (1976). Haemoglobins of the shark, *Heterodontus portusjacksoni.* II. Amino acid sequence of the α-chain. *Aust. J. Biol. Sci.* **29,** 73–97.

*2860. Nash, A. R. and Thompson, E. O. P. (1974). Haemoglobins of the shark, *Heterodontus portusjacksoni. Aust. J. Biol. Sci.* **27,** 607–615.

*2861. Natochin, Yu. V. and Gusev, G. P. (1970). The coupling of magnesium secretion and sodium reabsorption in the kidney of teleost. *Comp. Biochem. Physiol.* **37,** 107–111. *156, 157*

*2862. Natochin, Yu. V., Gusev. G. P., Goncharevskaya, O. A., Lavrova, E. A. and Shakhmatova, E. I. (1972). Effect of diuretics on the secretion and reabsorption of ions in the kidney of marine teleosts. *Comp. Biochem. Physiol.* **43A,** 253–258.

*2863. Natochin, Yu. V., Krayushkina, L. S., Maslova, M. N., Sokolova, M. M., Bakhteeva, V. T. and Lavrova, E. A. (1975). Activity of enzymes in the gills and kidney and endocrine factors in the regulation of ionic exchange in downstream-migrating and spawning sockeye *Oncorhynchus nerka* (Walb.). *Vop. Ikhtiol.* **15,** 131–140. *293*

*2864. Natochin, Yu. V. and Lavrova, E. A. (1974). The influence of water salinity and stage in life history on ion concentration of fish blood serum. *J. Fish Biol.* **6,** 545–555. *56, 64, 285*

*2865. Natochin, Yu. V., Luk'yanenko, V. I., Lavrova, Ye. A. and Metallov, G. F. (1975). Cation content of the blood serum during the marine and river periods of the life of sturgeons. *J. Ichthyol.* **15,** 799–804.

*2866. Natochin, Yu. V., Luk'yanenko, V. I., Lavrova, E. A., Metallov, G. F. and Sabinin, G. V. (1975). Iso-osmotic regulation in the Russian sturgeon *Acipenser güldenstadti* during the marine phase. *Zh. Evol. Biokhim. Fiziol.* **11,** 583–587.

2867. Nazarenko, L. D. and Shutov, I. S. (1973). Content of copper and zinc in fish of Kubyshev reservoir. *Mater. Pavolzh. Konf. Fiziol. Uchastiem. Biokhim. Farmakol. Morfol. 6th,* **2,** 16 only. *467, 534*

*2868. Neale, N. L., Honn, K. V. and Chavin, W. (1977). Haematological responses to thermal acclimation in a cold water squaliform (*Heterodontus francisci* Girard). *J. comp. Physiol.* **115B,** 215–222. *327*

*2869. Nebeker, A. V., Bouck, G. R. and Stevens, D. G. (1976). Carbon dioxide and oxygen-nitrogen ratios as factors affecting salmon survival in air-supersaturated water. *Trans. Am. Fish. Soc.* **105**, 425–429. *272*

2870. Nebeker, A. V. and Brett, J. R. (1976). Effects of air-supersaturated water on survival of Pacific salmon and steelhead smolts. *Trans. Am. Fish. Soc.* **105**, 338–342. *272*

*2871. Nechaev, A. P., Eremenko, T. V., Radostina, T. A., Storozhuk, A. Ya. and Shatunovski, M. I. (1975). Study of the seasonal dynamics of the practical composition of the lipids in the organs and tissues of *Pollachius virens* (L.) from the North Sea. *Trudy vses. nauchno-issled. Inst. mork. ryb. Khoz. Okeanogr.* **96**, 121–126. *13*

*2872. Nedovesova, Z. P. and Zhukins'kii, V. M. (1975). The nucleic acid content in the spermatozoa of males of the sea-roach of different ages. *Dopov. Akad. Nauk ukr. SSR*, Ser. B, 457–459 (no volume number given). *11*

*2873. Nelson, J. A. and Cseri, II. F. (1976). Transport and metabolism of purines by isolated choroid plexus, liver and brain in the spiny dogfish, *Squalus acanthias. Comp. Biochem. Physiol.* **53B**, 371–377.

*2874. Nesen, E. N. (1974). Activities of alkaline and acid phosphatases in the early developmental stages of carp. *Raznokachestvennost Rannego Ontog. Ryb* 180–190. Ed. Vladimirov, V. I. "Naukova Dumka", Kiev, USSR. From *Chem. Abstr.* **84**, 133073g (1976).

*2875. Nesterov, V. P. (1972). Functional specificity of the distribution of Na$^+$ and K$^+$ in the muscles of cyclostomates and marine bony fish. *Dokl. Akad. Nauk SSSR*, **206**, 1022–1024.

2876. Nevenzel, J. C. (1970). Occurrence, function and biosynthesis of wax esters in marine organisms. *Lipids*, **5**, 308–319. *465*

2877. Nevenzel, J. C., Rodegker, W., Robinson, J. S. and Kayama, M. (1969). The lipids of some lantern fishes (Family myctophidae). *Comp. Biochem. Physiol.* **31**, 25–36. *121, 125, 261*

2878. Newsome, G. E. and Leduc, G. (1975). Seasonal changes of fat content in the yellow perch (*Perca flavescens*) of two Laurentian lakes. *J. Fish. Res. Bd Can.* **32**, 2214–2221. *53, 208*

2879. Neyfakh, A. A. and Abramova, N. B. (1974). Biochemical embryology of fishes. *In* "Chemical Zoology. Volume 8. Deuterostomians, Cyclostomes and Fishes" (Eds Florkin, M. and Scheer, B. T.), Chapter 6, pp. 261–286. Academic Press, London and New York. *17*

*2880. Nicholls, F., Nicholls, P. and Sand, O. (1976). Phosphofructokinase and related glycolytic enzyme activities in flounder (*Platichythys flesus*, L.) liver. *Comp. Biochem. Physiol.* **54B**, 461–466.

*2881. Nicol, J. A. C. and Arnott, H. J. (1972). Riboflavin in the eyes of gars (Lepisosteidae). *Can. J. Zool.* **50,** 1211–1214.

*2882. Nicol, J. A. C., Arnott, H. J., Mizuno, G. R., Ellison, E. C. and Chipault, J. R. (1972). Occurrence of glyceryl tridocosahexaenoate in the eye of the sand trout *Cynoscion arenarius. Lipids,* **7,** 171–177.

2883. Nieto, M. and Johnson, H. A. (1972). Temperature and DNA turnover in the goldfish. *Cell Tiss. Kinet.* **5,** 115–119. *337*

2884. Niimi, A. J. (1972a). Changes in the proximate body composition of largemouth bass (*Micropterus salmoides*) with starvation. *Can. J. Zool.* **50,** 815–819. *182, 183*

2885. Niimi, A. J. (1972b). Total nitrogen, nonprotein nitrogen, and protein content in largemouth bass (*Micropterus salmoides*) with reference to quantitative protein estimates. *Can. J. Zool.* **50,** 1607–1610. *218*

*2886. Nishigaki, S., Tamura, Y., Maki, T., Yamada, H., Shimamura, Y. and Kimura, Y. (1974a). Studies on the behaviour of accumulation of trace elements in fishes (II). Relation between body weight and concentration of copper and zinc in muscle of seafishes. *Ann. Rep. Tokyo metropolitan Res. Lab. public Health,* **25,** 241–244.

*2887. Nishigaki, S., Tamura, Y., Maki, T., Yamada, H., Shimamura, Y. and Kimura, Y. (given incorrectly as Kimuma). (1974b). Investigation on mercury levels in tuna, marlin and marine products (II). Relation between body weight and concentration of mercury in muscle tissues. *Ann. Rep. Tokyo metropolitan Res. Lab. public Health,* **25,** 245–249.

*2888. Nishigaki, S., Tamura Y., Maki, T., Yamada, H., Shimamura, Y., Ochiai, S. and Kimura, Y. (1974). Studies on the behaviour of accumulation of trace elements in fishes. I. Mercury-selenium correlations in connection with body weight in muscle of seafish. *Ann. Rep. Tokyo metropolitan Res. Lab. public Health,* **25,** 235–239.

2889. Nishikawa, K. (1975). Seasonal changes in the histological activity of the thyroid gland of the medaka, *Oryzias latipes. Bull. Fac. Fish. Hokkaido Univ.* **26,** 23–33. *385*

*2890. Nishimura, H., Ogawa, M. and Sawyer, W. H. (1973). Renin-angiotensin system in primitive bony fishes and a holocephalian. *Am. J. Physiol.* **224,** 950–956.

*2891. Nishimura, H., Sawyer, W. H. and Nigrelli, R. F. (1976). Renin, cortisol and plasma volume in marine teleost fishes adapted to dilute media. *J. Endocr.* **70,** 47–59. *306, 307, 603*

*2892. Noaillac-Depeyre, J. (1974). Cytophysiology of the intestine of the common carp (*Cyprinus carpio* L.). Modifications during the course of prolonged experimental starvation. Thesis Docteur de Specialité, University of Toulouse, *172, 179, 180*

2893. Noble, R. W., Pennelly, R. R. and Riggs, A. (1975). Studies of the functional properties of the haemoglobin from the benthic fish, *Antimora rostrata. Comp. Biochem. Physiol.* **52B,** 75–81. Special Issue, Ed. Hochachka, P. W. "Biochemistry at Depth". *123*

*2894. Nordlie, F. G. (1976). Influence of environmental temperature on plasma ionic and osmotic concentrations in *Mugil cephalus* Lin. *Comp. Biochem. Physiol.* **55A,** 379–381.

*2895. Nordlie, F. G. and Leffler, C. W. (1975). Ionic regulation and the energetics of osmoregulation in *Mugil cephalus* Lin. *Comp. Biochem. Physiol.* **51A,** 125–131. *290*

*2896. Norton, V. A. M. (1975). Osmoregulation in the channel catfish, *Ictalurus punctatus* (Rafinesque). Ph. D.Thesis, Memphis University. University Microfilms no. 76–10, 872. *240*

*2897. Norton, V. M. and Davis, K. B. (1977). Effect of abrupt change in the salinity of the environment on plasma electrolytes, urine volume and electrolyte excretion in channel catfish, *Ictalurus punctatus. Comp. Biochem. Physiol.* **56A,** 425–431.

*2898. Nose, T. (1972). Changes in pattern of free plasma amino acid in rainbow trout after feeding. *Bull. Freshwat. Fish Res. Lab. Tokyo,* **22,** 137–144.

*2899. Nowlan, S. S. and Dyer, W. J. (1969). Glycolytic and nucleotide changes in the critical freezing zone, -0.8 to $-5°C$, in prerigor cod muscle frozen at various rates. *J. Fish. Res. Bd Can.* **26,** 2621–2632.

*2900. Nozaki, Y. and Miyahara, S. (1974a). Studies on the inorganic components of marine animals—II. On the contents and forms of sodium and potassium in tissues of marine fishes. *Bull. Fac. Fish. Nagasaki Univ.* **37,** 23–28.

*2901. Nozaki, Y. and Miyahara, S. (1974b). Studies on the inorganic components of marine animals—III. On the contents of cadmium, zinc, copper, lead and iron in muscle and viscera of marine animals captured in the west sea area of Kyushu. *Bull. Fac. Fish. Nagasaki Univ.* **38,** 117–120.

2902. Nyman, O. L. (1969). Polymorphic serum esterases in two species of freshwater fishes. *J. Fish. Res. Bd Can.* **26,** 2532–2534. *251*

2903. Nyman, O. L. and Pippy, J. H. C. (1972). Differences in Atlantic salmon, *Salmo salar,* from North America and Europe. *J. Fish. Res. Bd Can.* **29,** 179–185. *251, 254*

*2904. Obukhova, E. L. and Avrova, N. F. (1976). Composition of the carbohydrate component and fatty acids in the chief gangliosides of the elasmobranch brain. *J. Evol. Biochem. Physiol.* **12,** 11–16.

*2905. Ochiai, A., Ogawa, M., Umeda, S. and Taniguchi, N. (1975). Changes in blood properties of maturing Japanese eel, *Anguilla japonica,* with hormone injection. *Bull. Jap. Soc. scient. Fish.* **41,** 609–614. *43*

*2906. O'Connor, J. M. (1972). Pituitary gonadotropin release patterns in pre-spawning brook trout, *Salvelinus fontinalis*, rainbow trout, *Salmo gairdneri*, and leopard frogs, *Rana pipiens*. *Comp. Biochem. Physiol.* **43A,** 739–746. *383*

2907. Odiorne, J. M. (1957). Colour changes. *In* "The Physiology of Fishes" (Ed. Brown, M. E.), vol. 2, pp. 387–401. Academic Press, London and New York. *245*

2908. Oduleye, S. O. (1975). The effects of calcium on water balance of the brown trout *Salmo trutta*. *J. exp. Biol.* **63,** 343–356. *289, 301*

2909. Oduleye, S. O. (1976). The effects of hypophysectomy, prolactin therapy and environmental calcium on freshwater survival and salinity tolerance in the brown trout *Salmo trutta* L. *J. Fish Biol.* **9,** 463–470. *301*

*2910. Ogawa, A., Zama, K. and Igarashi, H. (1971). Conjugated lipids of the red salmon kidney (Lipids of salmonoid fishes XI). *Bull. Fac. Fish. Hokkaido Univ.* **22,** 159–167.

2911. Ogawa, M. (1974). The effects of bovine prolactin, sea water and environ-mental calcium on water influx in isolated gills of the euryhaline teleosts, *Anguilla japonica* and *Salmo gairdneri*. *Comp. Biochem. Physiol.* **49A,** 545–553. *300, 301*

2912. Ogawa, M. (1975). The effects of prolactin, cortisol and calcium-free environ-ment on water influx in isolated gills of Japanese eel, *Anguilla japonica*. *Comp. Biochem. Physiol.* **52A,** 539–543. *301, 304*

2913. Ogino, C. and Chiou, J. Y. (1976). Mineral requirements in fish—II. Magnesium requirements of carp. *Bull. Jap. Soc. scient. Fish.* **42,** 71–75. *147*

2914. Ogino, C., Kakino, J. and Chen, M.-S. (1973). Protein nutrition in fish—II. Determination of metabolic faecal nitrogen and endogenous nitrogen excre-tions of carp. *Bull. Jap. Soc. scient. Fish.* **39,** 519–523. *162*

2915. Ogino, C. and Kamizono, M. (1975). Mineral requirements in fish—I. Effects of dietary salt-mixture levels on growth, mortality, and body com-position in rainbow trout and carp. *Bull. Jap. Soc. scient. Fish.* **41,** 429–434. *147*

*2916. Oguri, M. and Nace, P. F. (1966). Blood sugar and adrenal histology of the goldfish after treatment with mammalian adrenocorticotrophic hormone. *Chesapeake Sci.* **7,** 198–202. From Chavin and Young, 1970.

2917. Oguri, M., Ogawa, M. and Sokabe, H. (1972). Juxtaglomerular cells in aglomerular teleosts. *Bull. Jap. Soc. scient. Fish.* **38,** 195–200.

*2918. Ohta, F. (1972). Analysis of degradation-rate of nucleotides in fish-flesh system. *Mem. Fac. Fish. Kagoshima Univ.* **21,** 119–124.

2919. Ohwada, K., Otsuhata, M. and Taga, N. (1972). Seasonal cycles of vitamin B_{12}, thiamine and biotin in the surface water of Lake Tsukui. *Bull. Jap. Soc. scient. Fish.* **38,** 817–823. *149*

*2920. Oide, H. and Utida, S. (1968). Changes in intestinal absorption and renal excretion of water during adaptation to sea-water in the Japanese eel. *Mar. Biol.* **1,** 172–177.

2921. Oide, M. (1970). Purification and some properties of alkaline phosphatase from intestinal mucosa of the eel adapted to fresh water or sea water. *Comp. Biochem. Physiol.* **36,** 241–252. *308*

*2922. Oide, M. (1973a). Role of alkaline phosphatase in intestinal water absorption by eels adapted to sea water. *Comp. Biochem. Physiol.* **46A,** 639–645. *308*

*2923. Oide, M. (1973b). Effects of hypophysectomy and environmental salts on intestinal alkaline phosphatase of the eel in relation to sea water adaptation. *Comp. Biochem. Physiol.* **46A,** 647–651. *308*

*2924. Oikari, A. (1975a). Hydromineral balance in some brackish-water teleosts after thermal acclimation, particularly at temperatures near zero. *Ann. Zool. Fenn.* **12,** 215–229. *342*

*2925. Oikari, A. (1975b). Seasonal changes in plasma and muscle hydromineral balance in three Baltic teleosts, with special reference to the thermal response. *Ann. Zool. Fenn.* **12,** 230–236.

2926. Oizumi, K. and Monder, C. (1972). Localisation and metabolism of 1,2-^{3}H-25-hydroxycholecalciferol in goldfish (*Carassius auratus* L.). *Comp. Biochem. Physiol.* **42B,** 523–532. *7, 8, 264*

2927. Ojha, J. (1975). Cytochemical differentiation of red and white fibres in the respiratory muscles of a fresh-water mud-eel, *Macrognathus aculeatum* (Bloch). *Z. mikrosk.-anat. Forsch., Leipzig* **89,** 143–160. *80*

2928. Ojha, J. and Munshi, J. S. D. (1975). Cytochemical differentiation of muscle fibres by succinic dehydrogenase (SDH) activity in the respiratory muscles of an air-breathing fish, *Channa punctatus* (Bloch). *Anat. Anz.* **138,** 62–68. *80*

*2929. Okaichi, T., Manabe, M. and Hashimoto, Y. (1959). Trimethylamine oxide in fish muscle. III. The origin of trimethylamine oxide in marine fish muscle. *Bull. Jap. Soc. scient. Fish.* **25,** 136–140. *76, 149*

2930. Olivereau, M. (1970). Stimulation of the somatotropic cells of the hypophysis of the carp after an extended period of starvation. *C. r. hebd. Séanc. Acad. Sci., Paris,* **270,** 2343–2346. *218*

2931. Olivereau, M. (1971). Effect of an adaptation to an electrolyte-deficient medium on the chloride cells of eel gills. *C. r. Séanc. Soc. Biol.* **165,** 1009–1013. *295*

*2932. Olivereau, M. (1975). Dopamine, prolactin control, and osmoregulation in eels. *Gen. comp. Endocrinol.* **26,** 550–561.

*2933. Olivereau, M. and Lemoine, A.-M. (1972). Effects of variations in the external salinity on the level of N-acetyl-neuraminic acid (ANAN) in the skin of the eel. Simultaneous modifications of the prolactin cells of the hypophysis. *J. comp. Physiol.* **79,** 411–422. *299*

*2934. Olivereau, M. and Lemoine, A.-M. (1973). Action of prolactin in the intact and hypophysectomised eel. VIII. Effects of the plasma electrolytes in sea water. *J. comp. Physiol.* **86,** 65–75.

 2935. Onishi, T. (1970). Studies on the mechanism of decrease in the ribonucleic acid content in liver cells of fasted rats. 1. Effect of starvation on ribonucleic acid degradating and synthesising systems. *J. Biochem., Tokyo* **67,** 577–585. *214*

*2936. Onishi, T. and Murayama, S. (1969). Studies on enzymes of cultivated salmonoid fishes—I. Activities of protease, amylase, arginase, GPT (glutamic-pyruvic transaminase) and GOT (glutamic-oxaloacetic transaminase). *Bull. Tokai reg. Fish. Res. Lab.* **59,** 111–119. *57*

*2937. Onishi, T. and Murayama, S. (1970). Studies on enzymes of cultivated salmonoid fishes—II. Activities of protease, amylase, arginase, GPT (glutamic-pyruvic transaminase) and GOT (glutamic-oxaloacetic transaminase) in various growth stages. *Bull. Tokai reg. Fish. Res. Lab.* **63,** 123–132. *57. 151*

*2938. Onishi, T., Murayama, S. and Shibata, N. (1974). Studies on enzymes of cultivated salmonoid fishes—III. The change of the activities of several hepatic enzymes during their maturation process. *Bull. Tokai reg. Fish. Res. Lab.* **78,** 47–57.

*2939. Onishi, T., Murayama, S. and Takeuchi, M. (1973). Sequence of digestive enzyme levels in carp after feeding—I. Amylase and protease of intestinal content, hepatopancreas and gall-bladder. *Bull. Tokai reg. Fish. Res. Lab.* **75,** 23–31.

*2940. Onishi, T., Murayama, S. and Takeuchi, M. (1976). Changes in digestive enzyme levels in carp after feeding—III. Response of protease and amylase to twice-a-day feeding. *Bull. Jap. Soc. scient. Fish.* **42,** 921–929. *152*

*2941. O'Rear, C. W. (1971). Some environmental influences on the zinc and copper content of striped bass, *Morone saxatilis* (Walbaum). Ph.D. Thesis, Virginia Polytechnic Institute and State University. University microfilm number 72-16, 294.

 2942. Orlov, O. Y. and Gamburtzeva, A. G. (1976). Changeable coloration of cornea in the fish *Hexagrammos octogrammus*. *Nature, Lond.* **263,** 405–407. *265*

*2943. Osborne, N. N. (1971). Occurrence of GABA and taurine in the nervous systems of the dogfish and some invertebrates. *Comp. gen. Pharmacol.* **2,** 433–438.

*2944. Osborne, N. N. (1972). Occurrence of glycine and glutamic acid in the nervous system of two fish species and some invertebrates. *Comp. Biochem. Physiol.* **43B,** 579–585.

*2945. Osborne, N. N. and Simpson, T. H., unpublished, quoted by Wardle (1972a).

*2946. Osborne, N. N. (printed incorrectly as Osborn), Zimmermann, H., Dowdall, M. J. and Seiler, N. (1975). GABA and amino acids in the electric organ of torpedo. *Brain Res.* **88,** 115–119.

2947. Ose, Y., Funasaka, R. and Sato, T. (1975). Offensive odour of fish from the Nagara River. II. Volatile fatty acids as one of the offensive odour substances. *Eisei Kagaku* **21,** 28–34. From *Chem. Abstr.* **83,** 75698f (1975). *149*

*2948. Ota, T. (1976). Lipids of masu salmon—IV. Changes of lipid composition and fatty acid composition in flesh lipids of juvenile masu salmon in the early stage of sea water life. *Bull. Fac. Fish. Hokkaido Univ.* **27,** 30–36.

2949. Ota, T. and Yamada, M. (1971). Lipids of masu salmon *Oncorhynchus masou.* I. Variations of the lipid content and the fatty acid composition of juvenile masu salmon during the period of smolt-transformation, and on the influence of light upon those variations. *Bull. Fac. Fish. Hokkaido Univ.* **22,** 151–158. *25*

2950. Ota, T. and Yamada, M. (1974). Lipids of *Masu* salmon—III. Differences in the lipids of residual type and seaward migration type of *Masu* salmon parr during the period of seaward migration. *Bull. Jap. Soc. scient. Fish.* **40,** 707–713. *208, 209*

*2951. Ota, T. and Yamada, M. (1975). Fatty acids of four fresh-water fish lipids. *Bull. Fac. Fish. Hokkaido Univ.* **26,** 277–288.

2952. Otis, L. S., Cerf, J. A. and Thomas, G. J. (1957). Conditional inhibition of respiration and heart rate in the goldfish. *Science, N.Y.* **126,** 263–264. *242*

2953. Otto, R. G. and McInerney, J. E. (1970). Development of salinity preference in pre-smolt coho salmon, *Oncorhynchus kisutch. J. Fish. Res. Bd Can.* **27,** 793–800. *23*

2954. Ouchi, K. (1969). Effects of water temperature on the scale growth and width of the ridge distance in goldfish. *Bull. Jap. Soc. scient. Fish.* **35,** 25–31. *321*

*2955. Ovais, M. and Gupta, S. S. (1973). Histamine content of the digestive tract in a teleostean fish *Heteropneustes fossilis* in relation to spawning. *Curr. Sci.* **42,** 404 only.

*2956. Ovais, M. and Gupta, S. S. (1975). Histamine content of the digestive tract of a catfish *Clarias batrachus* (Linn.) in relation to spawning, sex and seasonal variation. *Indian J. Physiol. Pharmacol.* **19,** 90–93.

*2957. Ovais, M., Gupta, S. S. and Bhagwat, A. W. (1976). Acetylcholine content of the brain and visceral organs of the teleostean fish; *Heteropneustes fossilis* and *Clarias batrachus. Indian J. Physiol. Pharmacol.* **20,** 177–179.

*2958. Overnell, J. (1973). Digestive enzymes of the pyloric caeca and of their associated mesentery in the cod (*Gadus morhua*). *Comp. Biochem. Physiol.* **46B,** 519–531.

2959. Owen, J. M., Adron, J. W., Middleton, C. and Cowey, C. B. (1975). Elongation and desaturation of dietary fatty acids in turbot *Scophthalmus maximus* L., and rainbow trout, *Salmo gairdnerii* Rich. *Lipids* **10,** 528–531. *143*

2960. Owen, T. G. and Wiggs, A. J. (1971). Thermal compensation in the stomach of the brook trout (*Salvelinus fontinalis* Mitchill). *Comp. Biochem. Physiol.* **40B,** 465–473. *329*

2961. Owen, W. H. and Idler, D. R. (1972). Identification and metabolic clearance of cortisol and cortisone in a marine teleost, the sea raven *Hemitripterus americanus* Gmelin (family scorpaenidae). *J. Endocr.* **53,** 101–112.

2962. Packer, R. K. and Dunson, W. A. (1972). Anoxia and sodium loss associated with the death of brook trout at low pH. *Comp. Biochem. Physiol.* **41A,** 17–26. *269*

*2963. Palacios, L., Rubió, M. and Planas, J. (1972). Plasma chemical composition in the goosefish (*Lophius piscatorius*,L.). *J. Fish Biol.* **4,** 99–102. *Note:* the same chemical data are published in *Invest. pesq.* **36,** 283–292 (1972). *49*

*2964. Paléus, S. and Liljeqvist, G. (1972). The haemoglobins of *Myxine glutinosa* L. —II. Amino acid analysis, end group determinations and further investigations. *Comp. Biochem. Physiol.* **42B,** 611–617.

*2965. Paléus, S., Tota, B. and Liljeqvist, G. (1969). Crystalline hagfish cytochrome c. *Comp. Biochem. Physiol.* **31,** 813–817.

*2966. Palmer, T. N. and Ryman, B. E. (1972). Studies on oral glucose intolerance in fish. *J. Fish Biol.* **4,** 311–319. *140*

*2967. Pandey, B. N. (1977). Haematological studies in relation to environmental temperature and different periods of breeding cycle in an air breathing fish, *Heteropneustes fossilis*. *Folia haemat., Lpz.* **104,** 69–74.

2968. Pandey, B. N. and Munshi, J. S. D. (1976). Role of the thyroid gland in regulation of metabolic rate in an air-breathing siluroid fish, *Heteropneustes fossilis* (Bloch). *J. Endocr.* **69,** 421–425. *385*

*2969. Pandey, B. N., Pandey, P. K., Choubey, B. J. and Munshi, J. S. D. (1976). Studies on blood components of an air-breathing siluroid fish, *Heteropneustes fossilis* Bloch) in relation to body weight. *Folia haemat., Lpz.* **103,** 101–116. *27*

2970. Pandian, T. J. (1975). Mechanisms of heterotrophy. *In* "Marine Ecology" (Ed. Kinne, O.), vol. 2, Physiological Mechanisms Part 1. Chapter 3, pp. 61–249. John Wiley, London, New York, Sydney and Toronto. *156, 158–160*

*2971. Pang, P. K. T. (1971). The effects of complete darkness and vitamin C supplement on the killifish, *Fundulus heteroclitus*, adapted to sea water. *J. exp. Zool.* **178**, 15–22. *264*

*2972. Pang, P. K. T., Pang, R. K. and Griffith, R. W. (1975). Corpuscles of Stannius: lack of direct involvement in regulation of serum sodium, potassium and chloride in the teleost, *Fundulus heteroclitus*. *Gen. comp. Endocrinol.* **26**, 179–185.

2973. Pang, P. K. T., Pang, R. K. and Sawyer, W. H. (1974). Environmental calcium and the sensitivity of killifish (*Fundulus heteroclitus*) in bioassays for the hypocalcaemic response to stannius corpuscles from killifish and cod (*Gadus morhua*). *Endocrinology* **94**, 548–555. *401*

2974. Pannella, G. (1971). Fish otoliths: daily growth layers and periodical patterns. *Science, N.Y.* **173**, 1124–1127. *374*

2975. Pantelouris, E. M., Arnason, A. and Bumpus, R. (1976). New observations on esterase variation in the Atlantic eel. *J. exp. mar. Biol. Ecol.* **22**, 113–121. *251, 480*

2976. Pardo, R. J. and de Vlaming, V. L. (1976). In vivo and in vitro effects of prolactin on lipid metabolism in the cyprinid teleost *Notemigonus crysoleucas*. *Copeia*, 563–573 (no volume number given). *447*

*2977. Partmann, W. and Schlaszus, H. (1973). Investigations on the patterns of ninhydrin reactive substances in the muscle tissue of teleosts. *Z. Lebensmittelunters. u.-Forsch.* **152**, 8–17. *75, 76, 480*

2978. Parvatheswararao, V. (1972). Metabolic compensation during thermal acclimation in the tissues of a tropical freshwater fish, *Etroplus maculatus* (Teleostei). *Biol. Zbl.* **91**, 681–693. *30*

*2979. Passia, D. (1973). NADP+-isocitrate dehydrogenase from *Idus idus* (Pisces: Cyprinidae). I. Activity as function of adaptation temperature. *Mar. Biol.* **23**, 197–204. *329*

*2980. Patent, G. J. (1970). Comparison of some hormonal effects on carbohydrate metabolism in an elasmobranch (*Squalus acanthias*) and a holocephalan (*Hydrolagus colliei*). *Gen. comp. Endocrinol.* **14**, 215–242. *3, 110, 232, 235*

*2981. Patterson, C. and Settle, D. (1977). Comparative distributions of alkalies, alkaline earths and lead among major tissues of the tuna *Thunnus alalunga*. *Mar. Biol.* **39**, 289–295.

2982. Patterson, S. and Goldspink, G. (1972). The fine structure of red and white myotomal muscle fibres of the coalfish (*Gadus virens*). *Z. Zellforsch. mikrosk. Anat.* **133**, 463–474. *74, 85, 89*

2983. Patterson, S. and Goldspink, G. (1973a). The effect of starvation on the ultra-structure of the red and white myotomal muscles of the crucian carp (*Carassius carassius*). *Z. Zellforsch.mikrosk. Anat.* **146**, 375–384. *87, 93–95*

2984. Patterson, S. and Goldspink, G. (1973b). Oxidation of pyruvate and octonoate by red and white myotomal muscles of the crucian carp (*Carassius carassius*). *Experientia*, **29**, 629–630. *101*

*2985. Patterson, S., Johnston, I. A. and Goldspink, G. (1974). The effect of starvation on the chemical composition of red and white muscles in the plaice (*Pleuronectes platessa*). *Experientia*, **30**, 892–894. *93–96*

2986. Patterson, S., Johnston, I. A. and Goldspink, G. (1975). A histochemical study of the lateral muscles of five teleost species. *J. Fish Biol.* **7**, 159–166. *84*

*2987. Patton, J. S. (1975). The effect of pressure and temperature on phospholipid and triglyceride fatty acids of fish white muscle: a comparison of deepwater and surface marine species. *Comp. Biochem. Physiol.* **52B**, 105–110. Spec. Issue (Ed. Hochachka, P. W.) "Biochemistry at Depth". *339*

*2988. Patton, J. S. (1976). Comparative studies of triglyceride and wax ester digestion in fish and the characterisation of a novel nonspecific triglyceride lipase. Ph.D. Thesis, University of California. University Microfilm number 76-22,018.

2989. Patton, J. S., Nevenzel, J. C. and Benson, A. A. (1975). Specificity of digestive lipases in hydrolysis of wax esters and triglycerides studied in anchovy and other selected fish. *Lipids*, **10**, 575–583. *465*

*2990. Patton, S. and Thomas, A. J. (1971). Composition of lipid foams from swim bladders of two deep ocean fish species. *J. Lipid Res.* **12**, 331–335.

2991. Patton, S. and Trams, E. G. (1973). Salmon heart triglycerides during spawning migration. *Comp. Biochem. Physiol.* **46B**, 851–855. *65*

*2992. Patton, S., Zulak, I. M. and Trams, E. G. (1975). Fatty acid metabolism via triglyceride in the salmon heart. *J. mol. cell. Cardiol.* **7**, 857–865. *65, 66*

*2993. Pavlov, V. A. (1939). Haemoglobin and sugar content in the blood of some fresh water fishes (a comparative study). *Izv. vses. Inst. ozern. rechn. ryb. Khoz.* **21**, 120–142. From Chavin and Young (1970).

*2994. Pavlović, V. (1968). Seasonal dynamic of carbohydrate metabolism at two kinds of freshwater fish. *Z. vergl. Physiol.* **59**, 72–77. *344, 345, 386*

*2995. Pavlović, V., Mladenović-Gvozdenović, O. and Kekić, H. (1972). Sexual dimorphism and seasonal oscillations of an average haemoglobin content in the erythrocytes (MCH) of *Salmo trutta m Fario* L. and *Thymallus thymallus* L. near the spring of the river Bosna. *Bull. Sci. Cons. Acads RSF Youg., Sect. A,* **17**, 301–302. *56*

*2996. Payan, P., Goldstein, O. and Forster, R. P. (1973). Gills and kidneys in ureosmotic regulation in euryhaline skates. *Am. J. Physiol.* **224,** 367–372. *310*

*2997. Payan, P. and Maetz, J. (1970). Aqueous and mineral balance in elasmobranchs: arguments in favour of endocrine regulation. *Bull. Infs scient. tech. Saclay,* **146.** 77–96.

*2998. Pedersen, R. A. (1971). DNA content, ribosomal gene multiplicity and cell size in fish. *J. exp. Zool.* **177,** 65–78.

2999. Pegg, W. J., Kellar, E. C. and Harner, E. J. (1976). The influence of acid on the cyclic nature of oxygen consumption in various fishes. *Proc. W. Va Acad. Sci.* **48,** 1–67. From *Aq. Sci. Fish. Abstr.* **6** (11), 102, 6Q11798 (1976). *270*

*3000. Pekkarinen, M. and Kristoffersson, R. (1975). Seasonal changes in concentrations of plasma lipids in the brackish-water eel-pout, *Zoarces viviparus* (L.). *Ann. Zool. Fenn.* **12,** 260–262. *41*

*3001. Pentreath, R. J. (1973a). The accumulation and retention of ^{65}Zn and ^{54}Mn by the plaice, *Pleuronectes platessa* L. *J. exp. mar. Biol. Ecol.* **12,** 1–18.

*3002. Pentreath, R. J. (1973b). The accumulation and retention of ^{59}Fe and ^{58}Co by the plaice, *Pleuronectes platessa* L. *J. exp. mar. Biol. Ecol.* **12,** 315–326.

*3003. Pentreath, R. J. (1973c). The accumulation from sea water of ^{65}Zn, ^{54}Mn, ^{58}Co and ^{59}Fe by the thornback ray, *Raja clavata* L. *J. exp. mar. Biol. Ecol.* **12,** 327–334.

*3004. Pentreath, R. J. (1976). Some further studies on the accumulation and retention of ^{65}Zn and ^{54}Mn by the plaice, *Pleuronectes platessa.* *J. exp. mar. Biol. Ecol.* **21,** 179–189.

3005. Pequignot, J. and Gas, N. (1971). Histological modifications to the branchial epithelium under the influence of vagotomy in tench. *C. r. Séanc. Soc. Biol.* **165,** 1172–1175. *299*

3006. Pequin, L. (1967). Degradation and synthesis of glutamine in the carp (*Cyprinus carpio* L.). *Archs Sci. physiol.* **21,** 193–203. *159*

*3007. Pequin, L., Parent, J.-P. and Vellas, F. (1970). Glutamate dehydrogenase in the carp (*Cyprinus carpio* L.). Distribution and role in ammoniagenesis. *Archs Sci. physiol.* **24,** 315–322. *218*

3008. Pequin, L. and Serfaty, A. (1962). Blood ammonia in fresh water teleosts removed from water and in sudden anoxia. *C. r. Séanc. Soc. Biol.* **156,** 1167–1171. *242*

*3009. Pequin, L. and Serfaty, A. (1963). The excretion of ammonia in a fresh water teleost: *Cyprinus carpio. Comp. Biochem. Physiol.* **10,** 315–324.

*3010. Pequin, L., Vellas, F. and Bouche, G. (1969). Glutamine synthetase in the carp. *Archs Sci. physiol.* **23,** 469–480.

*3011. Perrier, H., Perrier, C., Gudefin, Y. and Gras, J. (1972). Adrenaline-induced hypercholesterolaemia in the rainbow trout (*Salmo gairdnerii* Richardson): a separate study in male and female trout and the effect of adrenergic blocking agents. *Comp. Biochem. Physiol.* **43A,** 341–347.

3012. Persson, P.-E. (1977a). Muddy/earthy off-flavours in fish. *Ympäristö ja terveys,* **8,** 515–521. *150*

3013. Persson, P.-E. (1977b). Muddy odour in bream from the Porvoo area. *Ympäristö ja terveys,* **8,** 522–526. *150*

3014. Pesch, G. (1970). Plasma protein variation in a winter flounder (*Pseudopleuronectes americanus*) population. *J. Fish. Res. Bd Can.* **27,** 951–954. *43, 50, 63*

*3015. Peterson, G. L. and Shehadeh, Z. H. (1971). Changes in blood components of the mullet, *Mugil cephalus* L., following treatment with salmon gonadotrophin and methyltestosterone. *Comp. Biochem. Physiol.* **38B,** 451–457.

3016. Peterson, R. H. and Anderson, J. M. (1969). Influence of temperature change on spontaneous locomotor activity and oxygen consumption of Atlantic salmon, *Salmo salar,* acclimated to two temperatures. *J. Fish. Res. Bd Can.* **26,** 93–109. *325*

*3017. Petkevich, A. N., Viller, G. E. and Arnantov, N. V. (1967). Effect of environment on the mineral composition of some organs and tissues of fish in a Novosibirsk reservoir. *Mikroelem. Biosfere Ikh. Primen. Sel. Khoz. Med. Sib. Dal'nego Vostoka, Dokl. Sib. Konf., 2nd 1964,* 220–222 (Ed. Makeev, O. V.).

*3018. Petkevich, T. A. (1973). Microelements in the livers of certain game fish and *Illex illecebrosus* in equatorial Atlantic waters. *Biol. Morya,* **30,** 132–134.

*3019. Petkevich, T. A., Kandyuk, R. P., Stepanyuk, I. A., Kostylev, E. F., Liskovskaya, V. I., Antsupova, L. V. and Poludina, V. P. (1974a). The food value of the flesh of some fish found in the Atlantic. *Ryb. Khoz.* 59–62 (no volume number given).

*3020. Petkevich, T. A., Kandyuk, R. P., Stepanyuk, I. A., Kostylev, E. F., Lisovskaya, V. I., Antsupova, L. V. and Poludina, V. P. (1974b). Characteristics of the liver of certain Atlantic game fish. *Ryb. Khoz.* (7), 71–72 (no volume number given).

*3021. Pfeffer, E., Pieper, A., Matthiesen, J. and Meske, C. (1977). Research on the metabolism of carp during starvation. *Fortschr. Tierphysiol. Tierernähr.* **8,** 7–18.

*3022. Pfeiler, E. J. (1973). Adenosine triphosphatase activity in gill tissue of rainbow trout (*Salmo gairdneri* Richardson) adapted to fresh water and salt water. Ph.D. Thesis, Washington State University.

*3023. Pfeiler, E. (1976). Gill ATPase activities in the smallmouth bass (*Micropterus dolomieui*). *Comp. Biochem. Physiol.* **53B,** 119–121.

*3024. Pfeiler, E. and Kirschner, L. B. (1972). Studies on gill ATPase of rainbow trout (*Salmo gairdneri*). *Biochim. biophys. Acta*, **282,** 301–310. *291*

*3025. Phillips, J. W. and Hird, F. J. R. (1977a). Gluconeogenesis in vertebrate livers. *Comp. Biochem. Physiol.* **57B.** 127–131.

*3026. Phillips, J. W. and Hird, F. J. R. (1977b). Ketogenesis in vertebrate livers. *Comp. Biochem. Physiol.* **57B,** 133–138.

3027. Phleger, C. F. (1971). Liver triglyceride synthesis failure in post-spawned salmon. *Lipids*, **6,** 347–349. *65*

*3028. Phleger, C. F. (1975). Bone lipids of Kona coast reef fish: skull buoyancy in the hawkfish, *Cirrhites pinnulatus*. *Comp. Biochem. Physiol.* **52B,** 101–104. Spec. Issue (Ed Hochachka, P. W.) "Biochemistry at Depth".

*3029. Phleger, C. F. and Benson, A. A. (1971). Cholesterol and hyperbaric oxygen in swimbladders of deep sea fishes. *Nature, Lond.* **230,** 122 only. *123, 261*

3030. Phleger, C. F., Benson, A. A. and Yayanos, A. A. (1973). Pressure effect on squalene-2,3-oxide cyclisation in fish. *Comp. Biochem. Physiol.* **45B,** 241–247. *123, 261*

*3031. Phleger, C. F. and Grimes, P. W. (1976). Bone lipids of marine fishes. *Physiol. Chem. Phys.* **8,** 447–456. *121*

*3032. Phleger, C. F. and Holtz, R. B. (1973). The membranous lining of the swimbladder in deep sea fishes—1. Morphology and chemical composition. *Comp. Biochem. Physiol.* **45B,** 867–873. *123*

3033. Piatek, M. (1970). Age, growth and changes of weight proportions and of chemical composition of eel during its life in Polish waters. *Acta Ichthyologica et Piscatoria*, **1,** 73–96. *41*

*3034. Piavaux, A. (1973). Non-bacterial origin of intestinal laminarinase in *Tilapia macrochir* Boulenger. *Archs int. Physiol. Biochim.* **81,** 737–743. *172*

3035. Pickering, A. D. (1973). The measurement of unidirectional sodium fluxes in the non-stressed ammocoete river lamprey, *Lampetra fluviatilis* L. *Comp. Biochem. Physiol.* **44A,** 613–623. *240*

3036. Pickering, A. D. (1976). Stimulation of intestinal degeneration by oestradiol and testosterone implantation in the migrating river lamprey, *Lampetra fluviatilis* L. *Gen. comp. Endocrinol.* **30,** 340–346. *37*

*3037. Pickering, A. D. and Dockray, G. J. (1972). The effects of gonadectomy on osmoregulation in the migrating river lamprey: *Lampetra fluviatilis* L. *Comp. Biochem. Physiol.* **41A,** 139–147.

*3038. Pickering, A. D. and Morris, R. (1970). Osmoregulation of *Lampetra fluviatilis* L. and *Petromyzon marinus* (Cyclostomata) in hyperosmotic solutions. *J. exp. Biol.* **53,** 231–243.

*3039. Pickford, G. E., Grant, F. B. and Umminger, B. L. (1969). Studies on the blood serum of the euryhaline cyprinodont fish, *Fundulus heteroclitus*, adapted to fresh or to salt water. *Trans. Conn. Acad. Arts Sci.* **43,** 25–70. *44, 284–286, 312, 313*

*3040. Piiper, J. and Baumgarten, D. (1969). Blood lactate and acid-base balance in the elasmobranch *Scyliorhinus stellaris* after exhausting activity. *Pubbl. Staz. zool. Napoli,* **37,** 84–94. *114*

*3041. Piiper, J., Meyer, M. and Drees, F. (1972). Hydrogen ion balance in the elasmobranch *Scyliorhinus stellaris* after exhausting activity. *Resp. Physiol.* **16,** 290–303. *4*

3042. Pinder, L. J. and Eales, J. G. (1969). Seasonal buoyancy changes in Atlantic salmon *(Salmo salar)* parr and smolt. *J. Fish. Res. Bd Can.* **26,** 2039–2100. *22, 25, 121, 125*

3043. Pinhorn, A. T. (1969). Fishery and biology of Atlantic cod *(Gadus morhua)* off the southwest coast of Newfoundland. *J. Fish Res. Bd Can.* **26,** 3133–3164. *46, 248*

3044. Pirskii, L. I., Morozova, T. I. and Berdyshev, G. D. (1969). Age changes in the quantity and composition of nucleic acids in plaice liver. *Gidrobiol. Zh.* **5** (5), 118–120. From *Chem. Abstr.* **72,** 97800h (1970). *31*

3045. Piskarev, A., Krylov, G. and Luk'yanitsa, L. (1958). Characteristics of the histological changes in fish on freezing. *Kholod. Tekh.* **4,** 48–52. *189*

3046. Plack, P. A. and Fraser, N. W. (1970). Effect of oestradiol 3-benzoate on the biosynthesis of egg proteins by cod. *Biochem. J.* **118,** (2), 13p–14p. *43*

*3047. Plack, P. A. and Pritchard, D. J. (1968). Effect of oestradiol 3-benzoate on the concentrations of retinal and lipids in cod plasma. *Biochem. J.* **106,** 257–262. *45*

3048. Planquette, P. (1975). Sexual dimorphism in *Lates niloticus. Cah. ORSTOM, Hydrobiol.* **9,** 9–12. From *Aq. Sci. Fish. Abstr.* **6** (1), 6Q280 (1976). *46*

*3049. Plisetskaya, E. (1968). Brain and heart glycogen content in some vertebrates and effect of insulin. *Endocrinol. exp.* **2,** 251–262.

3050. Plisetskaya, E. M. and Kus'mina, V. V. (1972). Glycogen content in organs of agnatha (Cyclostomata) and fish (Pisces). *J. Ichthyol.* **12,** 297–306. *68*

*3051. Plisetskaya, E. M. and Leibson, L. G. (1975). Functional characteristics of the pancreatic islets of cyclostomes and fish. *S'ezd vses. Fiziol. O-va. im. I.P.Pavlova, 12th* **2,** 164 (Ed. Bakuradze, A. N.) "Nauka", Leningrad. From *Chem. Abstr.* **85,** 90656a (1976).

*3052. Plisetskaya, E., Leibush, B. N. and Bondareva, V. (1976). The secretion of insulin and its role in cyclostomes and fishes. In "The Evolution of Pancreatic Islets" (Eds Grillo, T. A. I., Leibson, L. and Epple, A.). 251–269. Pergamon Press, Oxford.

3053. Plorina, A. (1970). Amino acid composition of various age herring meat protein. *Rybkhozyaistvennye Issledovaniya Basseine Baltiskogo Morya* (5), 189–194 (no volume number given). From *Chem. Abstr.* **74,** 123807d (1971). *33, 34, 199*

*3054. Pocinwong, S. (1975). Regulation of glycogen breakdown in relation to muscle contraction in the Pacific dogfish. Ph.D. Thesis, University of Washington.

3055. Pocklington, R. (1971). Free amino acids dissolved in north Atlantic Ocean waters. *Nature, Lond.* **230,** 374–375. *148*

*3056. Podeszewski, Z., Otto, B. and Partianowics, H. (1972). The lipids of Baltic industrial fish. Part 1. Lipid fractions of muscle tissue. *Bromatol. Chem. Toksykol.* **5,** 287–293.

3056a. Podrazhanskaya, S. G. and Iarzhombek, A. A. (1970). The weight of the liver of Baltic cod and Atlantic grenadier as an index of their fat content. *Trudy molodykh uchenykh VNIRO,* **4,** 88–91. *207*

*3057. Podsevalov, V. N. and Perova, L. I. (1973). Technochemical characteristics of some Atlantic species of fish. *Trudy Atl. nauchno-issled. Inst. ryb. Khoz. Okeanogr.* **52,** 146–164.

3058. Pokrovskii, A. A. and Korovnikov, K. A. (1970). Changes in the isoenzyme spectra of organs during starvation. *Biokhimiya,* **35,** 159–166. *221*

3059. Pokrovskii, A. A., Levachev, M. M. and Gapparov, M. M. (1973). Fatty acid composition of mitochondria membrane lipids as an indicator of the biological value of fat. *Vop. Pitan.* (4), 3–11 (no volume number given). *142*

3060. Pokrovskii, A. A. and Pyatnitskaya, G. K. (1969). Change in activity of some blood and liver enzymes in rats during experimental fasting. *Trudy gos. nauchno-issled. Inst. Psikhiat.* **57,** 554–561. *221*

3061. Poluhowich, J. J. (1970). An electrophoretic comparison of haemoglobins from American and European eels. *Comp. Biochem. Physiol.* **34,** 739–743. *252*

3062. Poluhowich, J. J. (1972). Adaptive significance of eel multiple haemoglobins. *Physiol. Zool.* **45,** 215–222. *315*

*3063. Poluhowich, J. J. and Parks, R. P. (1972). A comparative study of blood chemistry and respiration in marine and freshwater eels. *Progve Fish Cult.* **34,** 33–38. *284*

*3064. Pomazanskaya, L. F., Pravdina, N. I. and Chirkovskaya, E. V. (1975). Certain features of brain phospholipids in deep sea fishes. *J. evol. Biochem. Physiol.* **11,** 455–459. *261, 262*

3065. Ponomarenko, V. P. (1971). Particular features of the growth of cod at different periods in their life cycle. *Trudy polyar. nauchno-issled. Inst. morsk. ryb. Khoz. Okeanogr.* **17,** 181–187. *337, 338*

*3066. Popov, V. D. and Georgiov, G. (1971). Quantitative measurements of nucleic acids in certain tissues of the rainbow trout (*Salmo irideus* Gibb). *Dokl. bulg. Akad. Nauk.* **24,** 141–144. *51*

3067. Pora, E. A. and Precup, O. (1971). Nitrogen excretion of Black Sea *Gobius melanostomus* during several (4–7) days' adaptation to variation in salinity. *Studii Cerc. Biol. Ser. zool.* **23,** 35–46. From *Chem. Abstr.* **75,** 31964v (1971). *290*

*3068. Porthé-Nibelle, J. and Lahlou, B. (1974). Plasma concentrations of cortisol in hypophysectomised and sodium chloride-adapted goldfish (*Carassius auratus* L.). *J. Endocr.* **63,** 377–387. *236, 302*

3069. Poston, H. A. (1969a). The effect of excess levels of niacin on the lipid metabolism of fingerling brook trout. *Fish. Res. Bull. N.Y.* **31,** 9–12. *146*

3070. Poston, H. A. (1969b). The conversion of beta-carotene to vitamin A by fingerling brook trout. *Fish. Res. Bull. N.Y.* **32,** 41–43. *146*

3071. Poston, H. A. (1969c). Effects of massive doses of vitamin D_3 on fingerling brook trout. *Fish. Res. Bull. N.Y.* **32,** 48–50. *146*

3072. Poston, H. A. (1975). Influence of dietary protein and energy on swimming stamina, growth, and body composition of brown trout. *Progve Fish Cult.* **37,** 257–261. *141*

3073. Poston, H. A. and Livingston, D. L. (1971a). Effects of massive doses of dietary vitamin E on fingerling brook trout. *Fish. Res. Bull. N.Y.* **33,** 9–12. *146*

3074. Poston, H. A. and Livingston, D. L. (1971b). The effect of continuous darkness and continuous light on the functional sexual maturity of brook trout during their second reproductive cycle. *Fish. Res. Bull. N.Y.* **33,** 25–29. *249*

3075. Poston, H. A. and McCartney, T. H. (1974). Effect of dietary biotin and lipid on growth, stamina, lipid metabolism and biotin-containing enzymes in brook trout (*Salvelinus fontinalis*). *J. Nutr.* **104,** 315–322. *399*

*3076. Poston, H. A., McCartney, T. H. and Pyle, E. A. (1969). The effect of physical conditioning upon the growth, stamina and carbohydrate metabolism of brook trout. *Fish. Res. Bull. N.Y.* **31,** 25–31. *117, 118*

3077. Potapova, O. I. and Titova, V. F. (1969). Change in the oiliness of large whitefish in connection with the maturing of the gonads. *Vop. Ekol. Zhivotn.* 61–68 (no volume number given). From *Chem. Abstr.* **74,** 121884c (1971). *39*

3078. Potter, I. C. and Brown, I. D. (1975). Changes in haemoglobin electropherograms during the life cycle of two closely related lampreys. *Comp. Biochem. Physiol.* **51B,** 517–519. *610*

*3079. Potts, D. C. and Morris, R. W. (1968). Some body fluid characteristics of
        the antarctic fish, *Trematomus bernacchii*. *Mar. Biol.* **1,** 269–276. *349*

3080.   Potts, W. T. W. (1976). Ion transport and osmoregulation in marine fish.
        In "Perspectives in Experimental Zoology", vol. 1, Zoology (Ed. Davies, P. S.),
        pp. 65–75. Pergamon Press, Oxford. *294, 305*

3081.   Potts, W. T. W., Foster, M. A. and Stather, J. W. (1970). Salt and water
        balance in salmon smolts. *J. exp. Biol.* **52,** 553–564. *294*

*3082. Poulter, R. G. (1976). Fish muscle proteins in freezing and processing.
        Ph.D. Thesis, University of Nottingham.

*3083. Poupa, O., Gesser, H., Jonsson, S. and Sullivan, L. (1974). Coronary-supplied
        compact shell of ventricular myocardium in salmonids: growth and enzyme
        pattern. *Comp. Biochem. Physiol.* **48A,** 85–95. *22*

3084.   Powers, D. A. (1972). Haemoglobin adaptation for fast and slow water
        habitats in sympatric catostomid fishes. *Science, N.Y.* **177,** 360–362. *110*

3085.   Powers, D. A. (1974). Structure, function, and molecular ecology of fish
        haemoglobins. *Ann. N.Y. Acad. Sci.* **241,** 472–490. *271, 275, 276*

3086.   Pozefsky, T., Tancredi, R. G., Moxley, R. T., Dupre, J. and Tobin, J. D.
        (1976). Effects of brief starvation on muscle amino acid metabolism in
        nonobese man. *J. clin. Invest.* **57,** 444–449. *186, 189*

*3087. Praus, R. and Goldman, J. N. (1970). Glycosaminoglycans in the nonswelling
        corneal stroma of dogfish shark. *Invest. Ophthalmol.* **9,** 131–135.

*3088. Pravdina, N. I. and Chebotareva, M. A. (1973). Fatty acids of the brain
        phospholipids of the eel *Anguilla anguilla* and the ray *Dasiatis pastinaca*. *J. evol.
        Biochem. Physiol.* **9,** 540–542.

*3089. Pritchard, A. W., Hunter, J. R. and Lasker, R. (1971). The relation between
        exercise and biochemical changes in red and white muscle and liver in the
        jack mackerel, *Trachurus symmetricus*. *Fish. Bull. Natl. Oceanic Atmos. Adm.
        (US)* **69,** 379–386. *89, 114*

*3090. Prosser, C. L., Mackay, W. and Kato, K. (1970). Osmotic and ionic con-
        centrations in some Alaskan fish and goldfish from different temperatures.
        Physiol. Zool. **43,** 81–89. *342, 343*

*3091. Pustovoitova-Vosilene, M. E. (1972). Seasonal changes in the content of
        catecholamines and dopa in tissues of the carp *Cyprinus carpio*. *Zh. evol. Biokhim.
        Fiziol.* **8,** 93–94. *385*

*3092. Qadri, R. B., Riaz, M. and Khan, A. H. (1969). Studies on the isinglas of
        marine fish swim bladder. *Sci. Res. E. reg. Labs Pakistan Coun. Sci. Ind. Res.*
        6, 167–171.

*3093. Qayyum, A. and Naseem, S. M. (1968). Alkaline phosphatase activity in
        the blood serum of three species of carps. *J. Sci. Technol.* **6B,** 258–260.

*3094. Qureshi, M. D., Hledin, R. V., Vanstone, W. E. and Anastassiadis, P. A.
        (1971). Levels of constituents of glycoproteins in the sera of Pacific salmon.
        J. Fish. Res. Bd Can. **28,** 1173–1179.

*3095. Qureshi, M. D., Vanstone, W. E. and Anastassiadis, P. A. (1976). Resolution
        of glycoproteins of Pacific salmon's blood by electrophoresis and by fractional
        precipitation and chromatography. *Comp. Biochem. Physiol.* **55B,** 245–248.

 3096. Qvist, J., Weber, R. E., DeVries, A. L. and Zapol, W. M. (1977). pH and
        haemoglobin oxygen affinity in blood from the antarctic cod *Dissostichus
        mawsoni. J. exp. Biol.* **67,** 77–88. *528, 674*

*3097. Rabega, C., Nicolau, G., Rabega, M., Lungu, A. and Giurcă, R. (1973).
        Variations of the RNA level in hypophysis and gonad of some phytophagous
        fish species during sexual maturation and artificial reproduction. *An. Univ.
        Bucaresti, Biol. Anim.* **22,** 121–124.

*3098. Rahemtulla, F., Höglund, N.-G. and Løvtrup, S. (1976). Acid mucopoly-
        saccharides in the skin of some lower vertebrates (hagfish, lamprey and
        Chimaera). Comp. Biochem. Physiol. **53B,** 295–298.

*3099. Rahmann, H. and Breer, H. (1976). Neuraminic acid content of fish eggs
        during early ontogenesis. *Wilhelm Roux Arch. EntwMech. Org.* **180,** 253–256.

 3100. Rahn, C. H., Sand, D. M. and Schlenk, H. (1973). Wax esters in fish.
        Metabolism of dietary palmityl palmitate in the gourami (*Trichogaster cosby*).
        J. Nutr. **103,** 1441–1447. *465*

*3101. Rajniaková, A., Buchtová, V. and Smirnov, V. (1976). Amino acids and
        proteins in sea fish and fish products. *Prum. Potravin* **27,** 192–195.

*3102. Rall, D. P. and Burger, J. W. (1967). Some aspects of hepatic and renal
        excretion in *Myxine. Am. J. Physiol.* **212,** 354–356.

 3103. Rao, G. M. M. (1969). Effect of activity, salinity and temperature on plasma
        concentrations of rainbow trout. *Can. J. Zool.* **47,** 131–134. *116, 284, 290, 342*

 3104. Raschack, M. (1969). Research on osmo- and electrolyte regulation in
        teleosts from the Baltic Sea. *Int. Rev. ges. Hydrobiol.* **54,** 423–462. *285, 349*

*3105. Ray, A. K. and Medda, A. K. (1975). Effect of variations of temperature
        on the protein and RNA contents of liver and muscle of Lata fish (*Ophicephalus
        punctatus*). *Sci. Cult.* **41,** 532–534. *337*

 3106. Ray, A. K. and Medda, A. K. (1976). Effect of thyroid hormones and
        analogues on ammonia and urea excretion in Lata fish (*Ophicephalus punctatus*).
        Gen. comp. Endocrinol. **29,** 190–197. *162, 163*

3107. Raymond, J. A. and DeVries, A. L. (1972). Freezing behaviour of fish blood glycoproteins with antifreeze properties. *Cryobiology*, **9**, 541–547. *346*

*3108. Raymond, J. A. and DeVries, A. L. (1976). Some respiratory characteristics of the blood of four antarctic fishes (1). *J. exp. Zool.* **196**, 393–396.

*3109. Raymond, J. A., Lin, Y. and DeVries, A. L. (1975). Glycoprotein and protein antifreezes in two Alaskan fishes (1). *J. exp. Zool.* **193**, 125–130. *348*

*3110. Read, L. J. (1968). Urea and trimethylamine oxide levels in elasmobranch embryos. *Biol. Bull. mar. biol. Lab., Woods Hole*, **135**, 537–547.

*3111. Read, L. J. (1971a). Chemical constituents of body fluids and urine of the holocephalan *Hydrolagus colliei*. *Comp. Biochem. Physiol.* **39A**, 185–192.

*3112. Read, L. J. (1971b). The presence of high ornithine-urea cycle enzyme activity in the teleost *Opsanus tau*. *Comp. Biochem. Physiol.* **39B**, 409–413.

*3113. Read, L. J. (1975). Absence of ureogenic pathways in liver of the hagfish *Bdellostoma cirrhatum*. *Comp. Biochem. Physiol.* **51B**, 139–141.

3114. Reaves, R. S., Houston, A. H. and Madden, J. A. (1968). Environmental temperature and the body fluid system of the fresh-water teleost—II. Ionic regulation in rainbow trout, *Salmo gairdneri*, following abrupt thermal shock. *Comp. Biochem. Physiol.* **25**, 849–860. *241*

*3115. Rehwoldt, R., Karimian-Teherani, D. and Altmann, H. (1974). Distribution of selected metals throughout tissue samples of carp, *Cyprinus carpio*. *Ber. Österreichischen Studiengesellschaft für Atomenergie GMBH (SGAE Ber.)* no. 2283.

3116. Reichenbach-Klinke, H. H. (1972). Basic principles of digestion in fish. *Münchner Beiträge zur Abwasser-, Fischerei- und Flussbiologie* **23**, 13–19. *151*

*3117. Reichwald, I. and Meizies, A. (1973). Fatty acids in the lipids of the flesh of freshwater and marine fish. *Z. ErnährWiss.* **12**, 86–91.

*3118. Reimold, W. V. and Lang, K. (1972). The fatty acid content of tissue lipids of redfish (*Sebastes viviparus*). *Z. ErnährWiss.* **11**, 69–79.

3119. Reisenbichler, R. R. and McIntyre, J. D. (1977). Genetic differences in growth and survival of juvenile hatchery and wild steelhead trout, *Salmo gairdneri*. *J. Fish. Res. Bd Can.* **34**, 123–128. *255*

3120. Reitman, J., Baldwin, K. M. and Holloszy, J. O. (1973). Intramuscular triglyceride utilisation by red, white, and intermediate skeletal muscle and heart during exhausting exercise. *Proc. Soc. exp. Biol. Med.* **142**, 628–631. *71*

*3121. Renfro, J. L. and Hill, L. G. (1973). Sodium balance of the redriver pupfish *Cyprinodon rubrofluviatilis*. *Comp. Biochem. Physiol.* **44A**, 1353–1367.

3122. Renfro, J. L., Miller, D. S., Karnaky, K. J. and Kinter, W. B. (1976). Na-K-ATPase localisation in teleost urinary bladder by [^{3}H] ouabain auto-radiography. *Am. J. Physiol.* **231**, 1735–1743. *156*

3123. Reshetnikov, Yu. S., Paranyushkina, L. P. and Kiyashko, V. I. (1970). Seasonal changes of blood serum protein composition and fat content in whitefishes. *J. Ichthyol.* **10**, 804–813. *36*

*3124. Riaz, M., Fatima, R., Khan, A. H., Ali, S. M. and Ishaque, R. (1972). Evaluation of proteins of some marine edible fish found around Karachi coast. *Pakist. J. scient. ind. Res.* **15**, 272–274.

*3125. Ribiero, S. and Roitman, I. (1972). Microbiological assays of vitamins in fishes and crustaceans. 1. Folic acid, choline and vitamin B$_{12}$. *Rev. Microbiol.* **3**, 79–83.

3126. Riley, J. P. and Segar, D. A. (1970). The seasonal variation of the free and combined dissolved amino acids in the Irish Sea. *J. mar. biol. Ass. U.K.* **50**, 713–720. *148*

*3127. Rivers, J. B., Pearson, J. E. and Shultz, C. D. (1972). Total and organic mercury in marine fish. *Bull. environ. Contam. Toxicol.* **8**, 257–266.

3128. Roberts, J. L. (1971). (Book Review). *Q. Rev. Biol.* **46**, 89–90. *xii*

3129. Roberts, J. L. (1973). Effects of thermal stress on gill ventilation and heart rate in fishes. *In* "Responses of Fish to Environmental Changes" (Ed, Chavin, W.), Chapter 3, pp. 64–86. Charles C. Thomas, Springfield, Illinois. *241, 324*

*3130. Roberts, R. A. (1971). Preliminary observations on the ionic regulation of the arctic char *Salvelinus alpinus. J. exp. Biol.* **55**, 213–222. *284, 285*

3131. Roberts, R. J. (1970). Lateral lipidosis in intensively-farmed plaice. *Vet. Rec.* 402–404 (no volume number given). *143*

3132. Roberts, R. J. (1974). Melanin-containing cells of teleost fish and their relation to disease. *In* "Anatomic Pathology of Fishes" (Eds Migaki, G. W. and Ribelin, R. W.), pp. 129–135. University of Wisconsin Press, Madison, Wisconsin. *257*

3133. Robertson, J. D. (1974). Osmotic and ionic regulation in cyclostomes. *In* "Chemical Zoology, Volume 8, Deuterostomians, Cyclostomes and Fishes" (Eds Florkin, M. and Scheer, B. T.), Chapter 4, pp. 149–193. Academic Press, London and New York. *302, 533*

*3134. Robertson, J. D. (1975). Osmotic constituents of the blood plasma and parietal muscle of *Squalus acanthias* L. *Biol. Bull. mar. biol. Lab., Woods Hole*, **148**, 303–319.

*3135. Robertson, J. D. (1976). Chemical composition of the body fluids and muscle of the hagfish *Myxine glutinosa* and the rabbit-fish *Chimaera monstrosa*. *J. Zool., Lond.* **178**, 261–277. *166, 507*

*3136. Robinson, E. S., Potter, I. C. and Atkin, N. B. (1975). The nuclear DNA content of lampreys. *Experientia*, **31**, 912–913.

*3137. Robinson, J. S. and Mead, J. F. (1970). A potentially unique type of lipid storage in the migrating pink salmon. *Can. J. Biochem.* **48**, 837–840. *57, 208*

*3138. Robinson, J. S. and Mead, J. F. (1973). Lipid absorption and deposition in rainbow trout (*Salmo gairdnerii*). *Can. J. Biochem.* **51**, 1050–1058. *98, 206, 212*

3139. Roche, J., Fontaine, M. and Leloup, J. (1963). Halides. *In* "Comparative Biochemistry" (Eds Florkin, M. and Mason, H. S.), vol. 5, Chapter 6, pp. 493–547. Academic Press, London and New York. *399*

*3140. Romestand, B., Voss-Foucart, M.-F., Jeuniaux, C. and Trillès, J.-P. (1976). The free amino acids of the serum of the Cimothoidae (crustacea, isopods, parasites of fish) and of several teleosts. *Archs int. Physiol. Biochim.* **84**, 981–988.

*3141. Rönnemaa, T., Pikkarainen, J. and Kulonen, E. (1971). Carbohydrates associated with collagen preparations from various species. *Acta chem. fenn.* **B44**, 115–117.

*3142. Rooney, S. C., Roberts, F. L. and Dexter, R. P. (1972). Haematological parameters of immature Atlantic salmon. *Progve Fish Cult.* **34**, 152–155.

3143. deRoos, R. and deRoos, C. C. (1972). Comparative effects of the pituitary-adrenocortical axis and catecholamines on carbohydrate metabolism in elasmobranch fish. *Gen. comp. Endocrinol. Suppl.* **3**, 192–197. *235*

3144. Rosen, F., Roberts, N. R., Budnick, L. E. and Nichol, C. A. (1958). An enzymic basis for the gluconeogenic action of hydrocortisone. *Science N.Y.* **127**, 287–288. *188*

*3145. Rosenthal, H. L., Eves, M. M. and Cochran, O. A. (1970). Common strontium concentration of mineralised tissues from marine and sweet water animals. *Comp. Biochem. Physiol.* **32**, 445–450.

3146. Ross, D. A. (1978). Lipid metabolism of the cod, *Gadus morhua*. Ph.D. Thesis, University of Aberdeen. *97, 99, 100, 144, 183, 206, 211, 369, 379*

3147. Ross, D. A. and Love, R. M. (1979). Decrease in the cold store flavour developed by frozen fillets of starved cod (*Gadus morhua* (L.). *J. Food Technol.* **14**, 115–122. *209, 210, 368*

*3148. Ross, L. G. (1976). The permeability to oxygen of the swimbladder of the mesopelagic fish *Ceratoscopelus maderensis*. *Mar. Biol.* **37**, 83–87. *122, 619*

*3149. Rovainen, C. M., Lowry, O. H. and Passonneau, J. V. (1969). Levels of metabolites and production of glucose in the lamprey brain. *J. Neurochem.* **16,** 1451–1458.

*3150. Roy, B. B. (1964). Production of corticosteroids in vitro in some Indian fishes with experimental, histological and biochemical studies of adrenal cortex, together with general observations on gonads after hypophysectomy in *O.punctatus. Calcutta med. J.* **61,** 223–244.

*3151. Rublevskaya, N. A. (1971). The trimethylamine oxide nitrogen content in various objects of marine industry. *Ryb. Khoz.* **47,** 70–71.

*3152. Rusaouën, M., Pujol, J.-P., Bocquet, J., Veillard, A. and Borel, J.-P. (1976). Evidence of collagen in the egg capsule of the dogfish, *Scyliorhinus canicula. Comp. Biochem. Physiol.* **53B,** 539–543.

*3153. Rzhavskaya, F. M., Dubrovskaya, T. A. and Pravdina, L. V. (1975). Seasonal variations in the composition of cod-liver oil. *Vopr. Pitan.* (1), 76–80 (no volume number given).

*3154. Saad, M. A. H., Ezzat, A. and Shabana, M. B. (1973). Effect of pollution on the blood characteristics of *Tilapia zillii* G. *Water, Air Soil Pollut.* **2,** 171–179.

*3155. Sabodash, V. M. (1969). Zinc content in ripe sex products of the carp. *Hydrobiol. J.* **5,** 65–69. *63*

*3156. Sabodash, V. M. (1970). Dynamics of zinc contents in carp at early stages of its development. *Gidrobiol. Zh.* **6** (3), 74–80. From *Chem. Abstr.* **73,** 128276u (1970). *9, 63*

3157. Sabodash, V. M. (1971). Localisation of zinc in carp spawn, embryos and larvae. *Hydrobiol. J.* **7,** 36–41. *467*

*3158. Saddler, J. B. and Cardwell, R. (1971). The effect of tagging upon the fatty acid metabolism of juvenile pink salmon. *Comp. Biochem. Physiol.* **39A,** 709–721. *238*

3159. Saddler, J. B., Koski, K. V. and Cardwell, R. D. (1972). Fatty acid alterations during migration and early sea water growth of chum salmon (*Oncorhynchus keta*). *Lipids,* **7,** 90–95. *239, 316*

*3160. Sage, M. (1973). The relationship between the pituitary content of prolactin and blood sodium levels in mullet (*Mugil cephalus*) transferred from sea water to fresh water. *Contrib. Mar. Sci.* **17,** 163–167. *300*

3161. Sage, M. and de Vlaming, V. L. (1975). Seasonal changes in prolactin physiology. *Am. Zool.* **15,** 917–922. *417*

*3162. Sakaguchi, H. (1976). Changes in biochemical components in serum, hepatopancreas and muscle of yellowtail starvation. *Bull. Jap. Soc. scient. Fish.* **42,** 1267–1272.

3163. Sakaguchi, H. and Hamaguchi, A. (1969). Influence of oxidised oil and vitamin E on the culture of yellowtail. *Bull. Jap. Soc. scient. Fish.* **35,** 1207–1214. *258*

*3164. Sakaguchi, M. and Kawai, A. (1970a). The change in the composition of free amino acids in carp muscle with the growth of the fish. *Mem. Res. Inst. Fd Sci. Kyoto Univ.* **31,** 19–21. *12*

3165. Sakaguchi, M. and Kawai, A. (1970b). Histidine metabolism in fish—V. The effect of protein-deficiency and fasting on the activities of histidine deaminase and urocanase in carp liver. *Bull. Jap. Soc. scient. Fish.* **36,** 783–787. *153, 198*

*3166. Sakaguchi, M. and Kawai, A. (1971). Occurrence of histidine in the muscle extractives and its metabolism in fish. *Bull. Res. Inst. Fd Sci. Kyoto Univ.* **34,** 28–51.

*3167. Sakai, T., Shimizu, C. and Matsuura, F. (1975). Studies on pyridine nucleotide transhydrogenase in fish muscle—I. Distribution of the enzyme activity in fish. *Bull. Jap. Soc. scient. Fish.* **41,** 747–751.

3168. Sand, D. M., Hehl, J. L. and Schlenk, H. (1971a). Wax esters in fish: turnover of oleic acid in wax esters and triglycerides of gouramis. *Lipids* **6,** 562–566. *53*

*3169. Sand, D. M., Hehl, J. L. and Schlenk, H. (1971b). Biosynthesis of wax esters in fish. Metabolism of dietary alcohols. *Biochemistry,* **10,** 2536–2541.

*3170. Sand, D. M. and Schlenk, H. (1969). The polyunsaturated alcohols in wax esters of fish roe. *Lipids* **4,** 303–304.

3171. Sandor, T., Vinson, G. P., Chester Jones, I., Henderson, I. W. and Whitehouse, B. J. (1966). Biogenesis of corticosteroids in the European eel *Anguilla anguilla* L. *J. Endocr.* **34,** 105–115. *409*

*3172. Sangalang, G. B., Weisbart, M. and Idler, D. R. (1971). Steroids of a chondrostean: corticosteroids and testosterone in the plasma of the American Atlantic sturgeon, *Acipenser oxyrhynchus* Mitchill. *J. Endocr.* **50,** 413–421. *37*

*3173. Sankaran, K. and Gurnani, S. (1972). On the variation in the catalytic activity of lysozyme in fishes. *Indian J. Biochem. Biophys.* **9,** 162–165.

3174. Santa, N. and Motilica-Heino, I. (1972). Researches concerning the activation of the glucose utilisation systems in the carp (*Cyprinus carpio* L.). *Rev. Roum. Biol.-Zool.* **17,** 199–204. *139*

3175. Santer, R. M. (1976). The distribution of collagen bundles and an epicardial coronary vasculature in the plaice (*Pleuronectes platessa* L.) heart ventricle at different ages. *J. mar. biol. Ass. U.K.* **56,** 241–246. *60*

*3176. Saraswat, R. C. and Garg, R. K. (1974). Studies on the mineral constituents of fins of *Wallago attu* (Bloch and Schneider) at different stages of growth. *Indian J. Anim. Res.* **8**, 36–38.

*3177. Saraswat, R. C. and Ram, N. (1970). Amino acid composition of some skeletal elements of the carp *Cirrhina mrigala* (Ham.). *Indian J. Fish.* **17**, 21–25.

3178. Sargent, J. R. (1976). The structure, metabolism and function of lipids in marine organisms. *In* "Biochemical and Biophysical Perspectives in Marine Biology" (Eds Malins, D. C. and Sargent, J. R.), vol. 3, pp. 149–212. Academic Press, London and New York. *465, 676*

*3179. Sargent, J. R., Gatten, R. R. and McIntosh, R. (1971). Metabolic relationships between fatty alcohol and fatty acid in the liver of *Squalus acanthias*. *Mar. Biol.* **10**, 346–355.

*3180. Sargent, J. R., Gatten, R. R. and McIntosh, R. (1973). The distribution of neutral lipids in shark tissues. *J. mar. biol. Ass. U.K.* **53**, 649–656. *207*

3181. Sargent, J. R., Lee, R. F. and Nevenzel, J. C. (1976). Marine waxes. *In* "Chemistry and Biochemistry of Natural Waxes" (Ed. Kolattukudy, P. E.), Chapter 3, pp. 49–91. Elsevier, Amsterdam.

*3182. Sargent, J. R. and Thomson, A. J. (1974). The nature and properties of the inducible sodium-plus-potassium ion-dependent adenosine triphosphatase in the gills of eels (*Anguilla*) adapted to fresh water and sea water. *Biochem. J.* **144**, 69–75. *291*

3183. Sargent, J. R., Thomson, A. J. and Bornancin, M. (1975). Activities and localisation of succinic dehydrogenase and Na^+/K^+-activated adenosine triphosphatase in the gills of fresh water and sea water eels (*Anguilla anguilla*). *Comp. Biochem. Physiol.* **51B**, 75–79. *297*

3184. Sargent, J. R., Williamson, I. P. and Towse, J. B. (1970). Metabolism of mevalonic acid in the liver of the dogfish *Scyliorhinus caniculus*. *Biochem. J.* **117**, 26p only. *453*

3185. Sasayama, Y. and Takahashi, H. (1972). Effect of starvation and unilateral castration in male goldfish, *Carassius auratus*, and a design of bioassay for fish gonadotropin using starved goldfish. *Bull. Fac. Fish. Hokkaido Univ.* **22**, 267–279. *168*

*3186. Sastry, K. V. (1972). Amino tripeptidase activity in three teleost fishes. *Proc. India Acad. Sci. section B*, **76**, 251–257.

*3187. Satia, B. P., Donaldson, L. R., Smith, L. S. and Nightingale, J. N. (1974). Composition of ovarian fluid and eggs of the University of Washington strain of rainbow trout (*Salmo gairdneri*). *J. Fish. Res. Bd Can.* **31**, 1796–1799. *10, 11*

*3188. Sato, R., Sato, M. and Koizumi, S. (1972). A comparison of the ubiquinone contents between two groups of adult chum salmon, *Oncorhynchus keta*, caught both in the bay and the river. *Bull. Jap. Soc. scient. Fish.* **38**, 1079–1082. *318*

3189. Satomi, Y. (1969). Changes in the chemical composition (nucleic acid, phospholipid, Kjeldahl nitrogen, total phosphorus and water content) of carp fry under conditions of feeding, starving and of renewed feeding. *Bull. Freshwat. Fish. Res. Lab. Tokyo*, **19**, 47–72. *171*

*3190. Satomi, Y. (1972). Change in nucleic acid and phospholipid contents of carp tissues (white and red muscles, liver, intestine) during the growth phase. *Bull. Freshwat. Fish. Res. Lab. Tokyo*, **22**, 127–128.

3191. Satomi, Y. and Nose, T. (1971). Nucleic acid and phospholipid content of rainbow trout tissue (white muscle, red muscle, liver, digestive tract, bred using foodstuffs with different protein contents). *Bull. Freshwat. Fish. Res. Lab. Tokyo*, **21**, 99–105. *137*

3192. Saunders, L. H. and McKenzie, J. A. (1971). Comparative electrophoresis of arctic char. *Comp. Biochem. Physiol.* **38B**, 487–492. *251, 253*

3193. Saunders, R. L. (1963). Respiration of the Atlantic cod. *J. Fish. Res. Bd Can.* **20**, 373–386. *27, 169, 259*

3194. Saunders, R. L. and Henderson, E. B. (1969a). Survival and growth of Atlantic salmon fry in relation to salinity and diet. *Tech. Rep. Fish. Res. Bd Can.* **148**, 7 pp. + appendices. *292*

3195. Saunders, R. L. and Henderson, E. B. (1969b). Growth of Atlantic salmon smolts and post-smolts in relation to salinity, temperature and diet. *Tech. Rep. Fish. Res. Bd Can.* **149**, 20 pp. + appendices. *22*

*3196. Savina, M. V. and Wojtczak, A. B. (1977). Enzymes of gluconeogenesis and the synthesis of glycogen from glycerol in various organs of the lamprey (*Lampetra fluviatilis*). *Comp. Biochem. Physiol.* **57B**, 185–190.

*3197. Savina, M. V., Wroniszewska, A. and Wojtczak, L. (1975). Mitochondria from the lamprey (*Lampetra fluviatilis*). Oxidative phosphorylation and related processes. *Acta biochim. pol.* **22**, 229–238.

3198. Savitz, J. (1969). Effect of temperature and body weight on endogenous nitrogen excretion in the bluegill sunfish (*Lepomis macrochirus*). *J. Fish. Res. Bd Can.* **26**, 1813–1821. *162, 320*

3199. Savolainen, J. E. T. and Gyllenberg, H. G. (1970). Feeding of rainbow trouts with *Rhodotorula sanneii* preparations. III. Amounts and qualities of carotenoids. *Lebensm.-wiss. Technol.* **3**, 18–20. From *Food Sci. Technol. Abstr.* **2** (7), 7R276 (1970). *145*

*3200. Schafer, R. D. and Swann, E. (1974). Free amino acid variations in the anchovy, *Engraulis mordax* (Girard) from the Los Angeles coastal area. *Rev. Intern. Océanogr. Méd.* **33,** 103–110.

3201. Schattenberg, P.-J. (1973). Research on the growth in length of the skeletal muscle of fish. *Z. Zellforsch.* **143,** 587–596. *30*

*3202. Scheer, B. T. and Langford, R. W. (1976). Endocrine effects on the cation-dependent ATPases of the gills of European eels (*Anguilla anguilla* L.) and efflux of Na. *Gen. comp. Endocrinol.* **30,** 313–326. *291, 293, 302*

*3203. Schmidtke, J., Schulte, B., Kuhl, P. and Engel, W. (1976). Gene action in fish of tetraploid origin. V. Cellular RNA and protein content and enzyme activities in cyprinid, clupeoid, and salmonoid species. *Biochem. Genet.* **14,** 975–980.

3204. Schmidt-Nielson, B. (1973). Renal transport of urea in elasmobranchs. *Alfred Benzon Symp.* **5,** 608–621. *155, 310*

*3205. Schmidt-Nielsen, B. and Renfro, J. L. (1975). Kidney function of the American eel *Anguilla rostrata*. *Am. J. Physiol.* **228,** 420–431.

3206. Scholander, P. F. and Maggert, J. E. (1971). Supercooling and ice propagation in blood from arctic fishes. *Cryobiology*, **8,** 371–374. *345*

*3207. Schreck, C. B., Flickinger, S. A. and Hopwood, M. L. (1972). Plasma androgen levels in intact and castrate rainbow trout, *Salmo gairdneri*. *Proc. Soc. exp. Biol. Med.* **140,** 1009–1011.

3208. Schreck, C. B. and Hopwood, M. L. (1974). Seasonal and rogenand oestrogen patterns in the goldfish, *Carassius auratus*. *Trans. Am. Fish. Soc.* **103,** 375–378. *37*

*3209. Schreck, C. B., Lackey, R. T. and Hopwood, M. L. (1972). Evaluation of diet variation in androgen levels of rainbow trout, *Salmo gairnderi*. *Copeia* (4), 865–868 (no volume number given). *48, 384*

*3210. Schreck, C. B., Lackey, R. T. and Hopwood, M. L. (1973). Plasma oestrogen levels in rainbow trout *Salmo gairdneri* Richardson. *J. Fish Biol.* **5,** 227–230. *48*

*3211. Schroeder, H. A. (1971). Losses of vitamins and trace minerals resulting from processing and preservation of foods. *Am. J. clin. Nutr.* **24,** 562–573.

3212. Schultz, D. M. and Quinn, J. G. (1972). Fatty acids in surface particulate matter from the North Atlantic. *J. Fish. Res. Bd Can.* **29,** 1482–1486. *148*

*3213. Schwab, M., Ahuja, M. R. and Anders, F. (1976). Elevated levels of lactate dehydrogenase in genetically controlled melanoma of xiphophorin fish. *Comp. Biochem. Physiol.* **54B,** 197–199.

*3214. Scott, D. P. (1974). Mercury concentration of white muscle in relation to age, growth, and condition in four species of fishes from Clay Lake, Ontario. *J. Fish. Res. Bd Can.* **31,** 1723–1729.

3215. Seaburg, K. G. and Moyle, J. B. (1964). Feeding habits, digestive rates and
       growth of some Minnesota warmwater fishes. *Trans. Am. Fish. Soc.* **93,** 269–
       285. *365*

*3216. Secondat, M. (1950). Influence of muscular exercise on the value of blood
       sugar in carp, *Cyprinus carpio* L. *C. r. Séanc. Soc. Biol.* **231,** 796–797.

*3217. Seiler, N. and Lamberty, U. (1973). Interrelationships between polyamines
       and nucleic acids. Changes of polyamine and nucleic acid concentrations in
       the growing fish brain (*Salmo irideus* Gibb.). *J. Neurochem.* **20,** 709–717. *453*

3218. Seki, N. (1968). Studies on the organic phosphates in viscera of aquatic
       animals—III. Acid-soluble nucleotides in the liver of salmon. *Bull. Fac. Fish.
       Hokkaido Univ.* **19,** 46–51.

*3219. Seki, N. (1971). Nucleotides in fishery products. *Bull. Jap. Soc. scient. Fish.*
       37, 777–783.

*3220. Seki, N., Kanaya, T. and Saito, T. (1969). Seasonal variations in the metabolic
       activities of tissue constituents of some fishes— II. Acid-soluble nucleotides
       and related compounds in the liver of kokanee salmon. *Bull. Fac. Fish. Hokkaido
       Univ.* **20,** 211–216.

3221. Sekiguchi, H., Nagoshi, M., Horiuchi, K. and Nakanishi, N. (1976). Feeding,
       fat deposits and growth of sand-eels in Ise Bay, central Japan. *Bull. Jap. Soc.
       scient. Fish.* **42,** 831–835. *137*

*3222. Selivonchick, D. P. and Roots, B. I. (1976). Variation in myelin lipid com-
       position induced by change in environmental temperature of goldfish
       (*Carassius auratus* L.). *J. therm. Biol.* **1,** 131–135. *340*

*3223. Semenova, A. E. (1974). Nucleic acid content in the body of juvenile autumn
       chum salmon. *Izv. tikhookean, nauchno-issled. Inst. ryb. Khoz. Okeanogr.* **93,** 31–34.

*3224. Sen, P. C., Ghosh, A. and Dutta, J. (1976). Fatty acids of the lipids of
       murrels. *J. Sci. Fd Agric.* **27,** 811–818.

3225. Serebryakov, V. P. (1967). Cod reproduction in the northwest Atlantic.
       Trudy polyar. nauchno-issled. Inst. morsk. ryb. Khoz. Okeanogr. **20,** 205–242. *248*

*3226. Shaffi, S. A. and Jafri, A. K. (1974a). Distribution of acid and alkaline
       phosphatase activity in the gastrointestinal tract of common freshwater carp,
       Barbus stigma (Cuv. and Val.). *Broteria, Ser. Cienc. nat.* **43,** 45–47.

*3227. Shaffi, S. A. and Jafri, A. K. (1974b). The activity of acid and alkaline
       phosphatases in the eggs of some freshwater teleosts. *Indian J. Fish.* **21,** 296–298.

*3228. Shaffi, S. A., Jafri, A. K. and Khawaja, D. K. (1974a). Alkaline phosphatase
       activity in the ovary of the cat-fish, *Clarias batrachus* (Linn.) during maturation.
       Curr. Sci. **43,** 51 only.

*3229. Shaffi, S. A., Jafri, A. K. and Khawaja, D. K. (1974b). Distribution of
5′-nucleotidase activity in the tissues of a freshwater teleost, *Ophicephalus
striatus* Bloch. *Fish. Technol.* **11**, 156–157.

*3230. Shaffi, S. A., Jafri, A. K. and Khawaja, D. K. (1974c). Distribution of acid
and alkaline phosphatase activity in the gastro-intestinal tract of the freshwater
cat-fish, *Clarias batrachus* (Linn.). *Broteria*, **43**, 39–44.

 3231. Shaklee, J. B., Champion, M. J. and Whitt, G. S. (1974). Developmental
genetics of teleosts: a biochemical analysis of Lake Chubsucker ontogeny.
Devl Biol. **38**, 356–382. *17, 18*

*3232. Shakoori, A. R., Zaheer, S. A. and Ahmad, M. S. (1976). Response of blood
serum proteins and free amino acids pool to starvation in freshwater teleost
Channa punctatus (Bloch). *Pak. J. Zool.* **8**, 25–34.

*3233. Shapiro, I. M. (1970). The phospholipids of mineralised tissues. II. Elasmo-
branch and teleost skeletal tissues. *Calcif. Tissue Res.* **5**, 30–38.

*3234. Shapiro, S. A. and Hoffman, D. L. (1975). Effects of photoperiodicity on
serum glucose in goldfish (*Carassius auratus*). *Comp. Biochem. Physiol.* **52A,** 253–
254. *383*

*3235. Shatton, J. B., Halver, J. E. and Weinhouse, S. (1971). Glucose (hexose-6-
phosphate) dehydrogenase in liver of rainbow trout. *J. biol. Chem.* **246,**
4878–4885.

 3236. Shatunovskii, M. I. (1967). Changes in the biochemical composition of the
liver and blood of flounder from the White Sea during maturation of its
genital products in the summer-autumn period. *Vest. mosk. gos. Univ. Biol.
Pochvoved.* **22** (2), 22–30. *39*

*3237. Shatunovsky, M. I. (1969). Comparative study of blood serum lipids of cod,
navaga, fluke and arctic flounder of the White Sea. *Dokl. (Proc.) Acad. Sci.
USSR, Biological Sciences Sections*, **184,** 12–14.

*3238. Shatunovskii, M. I. (1970). Fatty-acid composition of neutral lipids in roe
and young and adult individuals of spring and autumn Baltic herring (*Clupea
harengus membras*) in the Riga gulf of the Baltic Sea. *Dokl. Akad. Nauk. SSSR*
195, 962–965. *339*

*3239. Shatunovskii, M. I., Bogoyavlenskaya, M. P., Vel'tishcheva, I. F. and
Maslennikova, N. V. (1975). Studies of generative metabolism in Baltic
cod (*Gadus Morhua* L.). *Trudy vses. nauchno-issled. Inst. morsk. ryb. Khoz. Okeanogr.*
96, 57–62. *39, 41*

 3240. Shatunovskii, M. I. and Denisova, L. I. (1968). Variation of lipids and glucose
in blood serum and glycogen in liver of navaga and cod of the White Sea.
Biol. Nauki (11), 46–51 (no volume number given). *49*

*3241. Shatunovskii, M. I. and Kozlov, A. N. (1973). Some characteristics of the qualitative composition of the fats of *Notothenia rossi marmorata* Fisher. *Nauch. Dokl. vyssh. Shk., Biol. Nauki*, **112**, 59–63. *40, 53*

*3242. Shatunovskii, M. I. and Novikov, G. G. (1971). Changes in some biochemical indices of the muscles and blood of the sea trout during ripening of the sex products. *In* "Zakonomernosti Rosta i Sozrevaniya Ryb" (Ed. Nikol'skii, G. V.), pp. 78–89. Moscow. *40, 43, 49, 52, 53*

*3243. Shatunovskii, M. I. and Shevchenko, V. V. (1973). Seasonal changes in some physiological and biochemical indices in North Sea haddock. *Trudy vses. nauchno-issled. Inst. morsk. ryb. Khoz. Okeanogr.* **93**, 322–327. *41, 52–54*

3244. Shaw, H. M. and Heath, T. J. (1974). The gallbladder of the guinea pig: its concentrating and contractile abilities. *Comp. Biochem. Physiol.* **49A**, 231–240. *225*

*3245. Shchepkin, V. Ya. (1971). Dynamics of lipid composition of the scorpionfish (*Scorpaena porcus* L.) in connection with maturation and spawning. *J. Ichthyol.* **11**, 262–267. *53, 208*

*3246. Shchepkin, V. Ya., Shul'man, G. E. and Goncharova, L. I. (1974). Lipid composition of muscles of different types in the teleosts *Trachurus mediterraneus ponticus* and *Scorpaena porcus*. *In* "Fiziol. Biochim. Nizshikh Pozronochnykn" (Ed. Kreps, E. M.), pp. 62–66. Nauka, Leningrad.

3247. Shcherbina, M. A. and Kazlauskene, O. P. (1974). Influence of oxygen concentration in water on the digestibility of nutrients by carp. *Hydrobiol. J.* **10**, 74–76. *280*

3248. Shelbourne, J. E. (1974). Population effects on the survival, growth and pigment of tank-reared plaice larvae. *In* "Sea Fisheries Research" (Ed. Harden Jones, F. R.), Chapter 18, pp. 357–377. Elek Science, London. *9*

3249. Shelbourne, J. E. (1975). Marine fish cultivation: pioneering studies on the culture of the larvae of the plaice (*Pleuronectes platessa* L.) and the sole (*Solea solea* L.). *Fishery Invest., Lond. Ser 2* **27**, no. 9, 29 pp. *9*

*3250. Shenoy, A. V. and James, M. A. (1972). Freezing characteristics of tropical fishes. II. Tilapia (*Tilapia mosambica*). *Fish. Technol.* **9**, 34–41. *318*

3251. Shevchenko, V. V. (1972). Dynamics of the content of dry fat-free residue and of lipid content in the body and organs of the North Sea haddock [*Melanogrammus aeglefinus* (L.)] in the course of growth and gonad maturation. *J. Ichthyol.* **12**, 830–837. *41, 46, 51, 167*

*3252. Shibata, N., Kinumaki, T. and Ichimura, H. (1974a). Triglyceride, cholesterol, free fatty acid, glucose and protein contents in plasma of cultured rainbow trout. *Bull. Tokai reg. Fish. Res. Lab.* **77**, 77–87. *211, 212*

*3253. Shibata, N., Kinumaki, T. and Ichimura, H. (1974b). Lipid contents of plasma and liver of cultured salmonoid fish. *Bull. Tokai reg. Fish. Res. Lab.* **78,** 17–21.

3254. Shier, W. T., Lin, Y. and DeVries, A. L. (1972). Structure and mode of action of glycoproteins from an antarctic fish. *Biochim. biophys. Acta* **263,** 406–413. *346*

3255. Shimeno, S. and Hosokawa, H. (1975). How much carbohydrate can fish utilise? Their metabolic characteristics and adaptability. *Kagaku to Seibutsu* (*Chemistry and living things*), **13,** 365–367. *140, 184, 221*

*3256. Shimeno, S., Hosokawa, H., Hirata, H. and Takeda, M. (1977). Comparative studies on carbohydrate metabolism of yellowtail and carp. *Bull. Jap. Soc. scient. Fish.* **43,** 213–217.

3257. Shimeno, S. and Takeda, M. (1972). Studies on hexose monophosphate shunt of fishes—I. Properties of hepatic glucose-6-phosphate dehydrogenase of barracuda. *Bull. Jap. Soc. scient. Fish.* **38,** 645–650. *1*

*3258. Shimeno, S. and Takeda, M. (1973). Studies on hexose monophosphate shunt of fishes—II. Distribution of glucose-6-phosphate dehydrogenase. *Bull. Jap. Soc. scient. Fish.* **39,** 461–466.

*3259. Shimizu, C., Abe, K. and Matsuura, F. (1969). Levels of oxidised and reduced nicotinamide-adenine dinucleotides in fish tissues. *Bull. Jap. Soc. scient. Fish.* **35,** 1034–1040.

*3260. Shimizu, Y., Onishi, T. and Murayama, S. (1969). Biochemical studies on wintering of culture carp—VI. Changes of vitamins B_2 content, amylase activity and GPT (glutamic-pyruvic transaminase) activity in hepatopancreas. *Bull. Tokai reg. Fish. Res. Lab.* **59,** 65–73.

3261. Shimma, Y., Ichimura, H. and Shibata, N. (1976). Effects of starvation on body weight, lipid contents and plasma constituents of maturing rainbow trout. *Bull. Jap. Soc. scient. Fish.* **42,** 83–89. *168*

3262. Shirai, N. and Utida, S. (1970). Development and degeneration of the chloride cell during seawater and freshwater adaptation of the Japanese eel, *Anguilla japonica*. *Z. Zellforsch.* **103,** 247–264.

3263. Shkorbatov, G. L., Gurevich, Zh. A., Kudryavtseva, G. S. and Trifonova, I. A. (1970). Experimental changes of general and protein heat-resistance during temperature adaptation of *Lebistes reticulatus* (guppy). *Biol. Nauki* (9), 27–29 (no volume number given). From *Chem. Abstr.* **74,** 1603p (1971). *336*

*3264. Shnarevich, I. D. and Sakhnenko, Ye. G. (1971). Dynamics of carotenoids in fish tissues and organs in relation to the sexual cycle. *Hydrobiol. J.* **7,** 77–80. *38*

*3265. Shoeb, Z. E., Salama, F. M. and El-Nockrashy, A. S. (1973). Investigations on fish oils—V. Phospholipid composition of *Anguilla vulgaris* and *Mugil cephalus*. *Die Nährung*, **17,** 31–40.

3266. Shrable, J. B., Tiemeier, O. W. and Deyoe, C. W. (1969). Effects of temperature on rate of digestion by channel catfish. *Progve Fish Cult.* **31,** 131–138. *319*

*3267. Shreni, K. D. and Jafri, A. K. (1974). Cholesterol content in the eggs of some freshwater teleosts. *Fish. Technol.* **11,** 158–160. *9*

*3268. Shreni, K. D. and Jafri, A. K. (1975a). Total cholesterol content of the brain and spinal cord of some freshwater fishes. *Indian J. med. Res.* **63,** 733–735.

*3269. Shreni, K. D. and Jafri, A. K. (1975b). Distribution of total cholesterol in the normal organs of the freshwater pond murrel, *Ophicephalus punctatus* Bloch. *Broteria Ser. Ciencia nat.* **44,** 3–7.

3270. Shterman, Ya. L. (1969). Variation of alkaline phosphatase activity in *Salmo irideus* and *Salmo salar* fed rations containing different amounts of phosphatides. *Izv. Gos. Nauch.-Issled. Inst. Ozer. Rechn. Ryb. Khoz.* **68,** 217–223. From *Chem. Abstr.* **74,** 29326z (1971). *151*

*3271. Shukolyukov, S. A., Korchagin, V. P., Fedosov, Yu. V., Chizhevich, E. P. and Tyurin, V. A. (1976). Extraction, amino acid composition and molecular weight of fish (*Theragra chalcogramma*) rhodopsin. *Biol. Morya*, 68–77 (no volume number given).

*3272. Shul'man, G. E. (1972). "Life Cycles of Fish. Physiology and Biochemistry." Moscow. Translated from Russian by N. Kaner. John Wiley and Sons, New York and Toronto (1974). *46, 137, 209, 246, 351, 352, 364, 370*

3273. Shul'man, G. E., Sigaeva, T. G. and Shchepkin, V. Ya. (1973). Fat loss in hardtails while swimming as a metabolic index. *Dokl. (Proc.) Acad. Sci. USSR, Biological Sciences Sections* (in English). **211,** 356–358. *92, 115*

*3274. Shultz, C. D. and Crear, D. (1976). The distribution of total and organic mercury in seven tissues of the Pacific blue marlin, *Makaira nigricans*. *Pacif. Sci.* **30,** 101–107.

*3275. Shuttleworth, T. J. and Freeman, R. F. H. (1973). The role of the gills in seawater adaptation in *Anguilla dieffenbachii*. I. Osmotic and ionic composition of the blood and gill tissue. *J. comp. Physiol.* **86,** 293–313.

*3276. Siddiqui, A. Q. and Siddiqui, A. H. (1977). Variation in the free amino acid content of skeletal muscle of *Ophicephalus punctatus* (Bloch). *J. Fish Biol.* **10,** 185–189.

*3277. Siddiqui, A. Q., Siddiqui, A. H. and Ahmad, K. (1973). Free amino acid contents of the skeletal muscle of carp at juvenile and adult stages. *Comp. Biochem. Physiol.* **44B,** 725–728. *34*

*3278. Siddiqui, N. (1974). Some chemical constituents in the blood plasma of four species of freshwater air-breathing fishes. *Curr. Sci.* **43,** 385 only.

*3279. Siddiqui, N. (1975a). Effect of feeding, spawning and size on chemical constituents of the blood plasma of *Clarias batrachus* (Linn.). *Indian J. exp. Biol.* **13,** 203–205. *26, 27, 34, 35, 49, 53, 56*

 3280. Siddiqui, N. (1975b). Variations in chemical constituents of blood plasma of *Clarias batrachus* (L.) during starvation. *Curr. Sci.* **44,** 126–127. *27, 213*

*3281. Sidell, B. D. (1977). Turnover of cytochrome c in skeletal muscle of green sunfish (*Lepomis cyanellus*, R.) during thermal acclimation. *J. exp. Zool.* **199,** 233–250. *331*

 3282. Sidell, B. D., Wilson, F. R., Hazel, J. and Prosser, C. L. (1973). Time course of thermal acclimation in goldfish. *J. comp. Physiol.* **84,** 119–127. *30, 331, 332*

*3283. Sidorov, V. S., Lizenko, E. I., Bolgova, O. M. and Nefedova, Z. A. (1972). Fish lipids—I. Methods of analysis. Tissue specificity of lipids of the vendace *Coregonus albula* L. *In* "Salmonidae of Karelia, Issue 1: Ecology, Parasites, Biochemistry" (Eds Potapova, O. I. and Smirnov, Y. A.), pp. 152–163. Petrozavodsk.

*3284. Silbergeld, E. K. (1974). Blood glucose: a sensitive indicator of environmental stress in fish. *Bull. environ. Contam. Toxicol.* **11,** 20–25.

 3285. Simkiss, K. (1974). Calcium metabolism of fish in relation to ageing. *In* "Ageing of Fish" (Ed. Bagenal, T. B.), pp. 1–12. Unwin Bros. Ltd., Gresham Press, Old Woking, Surrey. *374*

 3286. Simmons, D. J. (1971). Calcium and skeletal physiology in teleost fishes. *Clin. Orthopaedics and Related Research* **76,** 244–280. *401*

*3287. Simonarson, B. and Watts, D. C. (1969). Some fish muscle esterases and their variation in stocks of the herring (*Clupea harengus* L.). The nature of esterase variation. *Comp. Biochem. Physiol.* **31,** 309–318. *251*

*3288. Singh, B. R., Thakur, R. N. and Yadav, A. N. (1976). Changes in the blood parameters of an air-breathing fish during different respiratory conditions. *Folia haemat. Lpz.* **103,** 216–225. *276*

*3289. Singley, J. A. and Chavin, W. (1975a). Serum cortisol in normal goldfish (*Carassius auratus* L.). *Comp. Biochem. Physiol.* **50A,** 77–82. *34, 235, 383*

*3290. Singley, J. A. and Chavin, W. (1975b). The adrenocortical-hypophysial response to saline stress in the goldfish, *Carassius auratus* L. *Comp. Biochem. Physiol.* **51A,** 749–756. *236, 240*

*3291. Singley, J. A. and Chavin, W. (1976). The diel rhythm of circulating ACTH titre in the goldfish (*Carassius auratus* L.) *Comp. Biochem. Physiol.* **53A,** 291–293. *383*

*3292. Sinha, V. R. P. (1972). Gonadal hydration response and major electrolyte levels in serum and seminal fluid of *Puntius gonionotus* (Teleostei) injected with the fractionated fish pituitary extract. *J. Fish Biol.* **4,** 585–592.

*3293. Siret, J. R., Carmena, A. O. and Callejas, J. (1976). Erythrokinetic study in the fish manjuari (*Atractosteus tristoechus*). *Comp. Biochem. Physiol.* **55A,** 127–128.

*3294. Skramstad, K. H. (1969). Mineral substances in fish. *Tidsskr. HermetInd.* **55,** 14–20. *248*

*3295. Slapkauskaite, G. and Odintsova, E. N. (1974). Group B vitamins in fish. *Deposited Doc. VINITI* 7 pp. Available from BLLD. From *Chem. Abstr.* **86,** 152887h (1977).

3296. Slicher, A. M., Pickford, G. E. and Pang, P. K. T. (1966). Effects of "training" and of volume and composition of the injection fluid on stress-induced leukopenia in the mummichog. *Progve Fish Cult.* **28,** 216–219. *239*

3297. Smirnova, L. I. (1967). Effect of starvation on the possible life span of burbot erythrocytes. *In* "Metabolism and Biochemistry of Fishes" (Ed. Karzinkin, G. S.), pp. 176–178. Moscow. *213*

3298. Smit, H., Amelink-Koutstaal, J. M., Vijverberg, J. and von Vaupel-Klein, J. C. (1971). Oxygen consumption and efficiency of swimming goldfish. *Comp. Biochem. Physiol.* **39A,** 1–28. *100*

3299. Smith, A. C. (1969). Protein variation in the eye lens nucleus of the mackerel scad (*Decapterus pinnulatus*). *Comp. Biochem. Physiol.* **28,** 1161–1168. *251*

3300. Smith, A. C. and Ramos, F. (1976). Occult haemoglobin in fish skin mucus as an indicator of early stress. *J. Fish Biol.* **9,** 537–541. *242*

3301. Smith, C. L. (1973). Thermostability of some mitochondrial enzymes of lower vertebrates—II. Freshwater teleosts. *Comp. Biochem. Physiol.* **44B,** 789–801. *330, 331*

3302. Smith, C. L., Rand, C. S., Schaeffer, R. and Atz, J. W. (1975). *Latimeria,* the living coelacanth, is ovoviviparous. *Science, N.Y.* **190,** 1105–1106. *565*

*3303. Smith, H. W. (1929b: 1929a is in Volume 1). The excretion of ammonia and urea by the gills of fish. *J. biol. Chem.* **81,** 727–742. *157*

*3304. Smith, H. W. (1930). Metabolism of the lung-fish, *Protopterus aethiopicus*. *J. biol. Chem.* **88,** 97–130. *154, 170*

*3305. Smith, J. C. (1976). Body weight and the activities of pyruvate kinase, glucose-6-phosphatase and lactate dehydrogenase in the liver of the American plaice, *Hippoglossoides platessoides*. *Comp. Biochem. Physiol.* **53B,** 277–282. *34, 35*

3306. Smith, J. C. (1977). Body weight and the haematology of the American plaice, *Hippoglossoides platessoides*. *J. exp. Biol.* **67,** 17–28. *27*

3307. Smith, J. R. and Weber, L. J. (1976). The regulation of day-night changes in hydroxyindole-0-methyltransferase activity in the pineal gland of steelhead trout (*Salmo gairdneri*). *Can. J. Zool.* **54,** 1530–1534. *265*

3308. Smith, M. W. and Kemp, P. (1971). Parallel temperature-induced changes in membrane fatty acids and in the transport of amino acids by the intestine of goldfish (*Carassius auratus* L.). *Comp. Biochem. Physiol.* **39B,** 357–365. *340*

*3309. Smith, R. L. and Paulson, A. C. (1975). Carbonic anhydrase in some coral reef fishes: adaptation to carbonate ingestion? *Comp. Biochem. Physiol.* **50A,** 131–134. *152*

*3310. Smith, R. N. (1970). The biochemistry of freezing resistance of some antarctic fish. *In* "Antarctic Ecology" (Ed. Holdgate, M. W.), vol. 1, pp. 329–336. Academic Press, London and New York. *321, 348*

*3311. Smith, R. N. (1972). The freezing resistance of antarctic fish: 1. Serum composition and its relation to freezing resistance. *Bull. Br. Antarct. Surv.* **28,** 1–10. *349*

3312. Snieszko, S. F. (1972). Nutritional fish diseases. *In* "Fish Nutrition" (Ed. Halver, J. E.), Chapter 9, pp. 403–437. Academic Press, London and New York. *146, 193*

*3313. Snodgrass, P. J. and Halver, J. E. (1971). Potasium, sodium, magnesium and calcium contents of chinook salmon tissues during various stages of the life cycle. *Comp. Biochem. Physiol.* **38A,** 99–119. *284, 285*

*3314. Soivo, A., Nyholm, K. and Huhti, M. (1975). Concentrations of K^+, Na^+ and Mg^{++} in blood plasma of *Salmo gairdneri* Richardson in relation to the increase of haematocrit value in vitro. *Ann. Zool. Fenn.* **12,** 141–142.

*3315. Soivo, A., Westman, K. and Nyholm, K. (1974a). The influence of changes in oxygen tension on the haematocrit value of blood samples from asphyxic rainbow trout (*Salmo gairdneri*). *Aquaculture,* **3,** 395–401. *275*

*3316. Soivo, A., Westman, K. and Nyholm, K. (1974b). Changes in haematocrit values in blood samples treated with and without oxygen: a comparative study with four salmonid species. *J. Fish Biol.* **6,** 763–769. *275*

*3317. Sokabe, H., Oide, H., Ogawa, M. and Utida, S. (1973). Plasma renin activity in Japanese eels (*Anguilla japonica*) adapted to seawater or in dehydration. *Gen. comp. Endocrinol.* **21,** 160–167. *307*

3318. Somero, G. N. (1973). Thermal modulation of pyruvate metabolism in the fish *Gillichthys mirabilis:* the role of lactate dehydrogenase. *Comp. Biochem. Physiol.* **44B,** 205–209. *336*

3319. Somero, G. N. (1975a). Temperature: a "shaping force" in enzyme evolution. *Biochem. Soc. Ann. Symp.*, July 16th, Liverpool. "Biochemical Adaptation to Environmental Change". Item 1 (no pagination).

3320. Somero, G. N. (1975b). The roles of isozymes in adaptation to varying temperatures. *In* "Isozymes II. Physiological Functions" (Ed. Markert, C. L.), pp. 221–234. Academic Press, London and New York. *335*

3321. Somero, G. N. (1975c). Enzymic mechanisms of eurythermality in desert and estuarine fishes: genetics and kinetics. *In* "Environmental Physiology of Desert Organisms" (Ed. Hadley, N. F.), pp. 168–187. Dowden, Hutchinson & Ross, Stroudsberg, Pa. *335*

3322. Somero, G. N. and Doyle, D. (1973). Temperature and rates of protein degradation in the fish *Gillichthys mirabilis*. *Comp. Biochem. Physiol.* **46B**, 463–474. *162*

3323. Somero, G. N., Giese, A. C. and Wohlschlag, D. E. (1968). Cold adaptation of the antarctic fish *Trematomus bernacchii*. *Comp. Biochem. Physiol.* **26**, 223–233. *333*

3324. Somero, G. N. and Hochachka, P. W. (1971). Biochemical adaptation to the environment. *Am. Zool.* **11**, 159–167. *vii, 334*

3325. Somero, G. N. and Soulé, M. (1974). Genetic variation in marine fishes as a test of the niche-variation hypothesis. *Nature, Lond.* **249**, 670–672. *333*

*3326. Somkina, N. V. (1975). Metabolism in the brain of *Acipenser güldenstadti* in early ontogenesis and under the influence of salinity. *Vop. Ikhtiol.* **15**, 761–763. From *Chem. Abstr.* **84**, 56770c (1976). 313

3327. Somkina, N. V. and Krichevskaya, A. A. (1968). Brain amino acids of fishes. *Zh. Evol. Biokhim. Fiziol.* **4**, 489–493. From *Chem. Abstr.* **70**, 75491q (1969). *62, 313*

3328. Sorvachev, K. F. and Novikov, G. G. (1968). Free amino acid content of the muscles of various forms of sea trout. *Nauch. Dokl. vyssh. Shk. Biol. nauki* **2**, 54–58. *112*

*3329. Sorvachev, K. F. and Shatunovskii, M. I. (1968). Some information on the content of free amino acids in the tissues of the White Sea cod and flounder. *Po. Ekol. Treski Severnoi Atlantiki*, 133–143. *42, 62*

3330. Sousa, R. J. and Meade, T. L. (1977). The influence of ammonia on the oxygen delivery system of coho salmon haemoglobin. *Comp. Biochem. Physiol.* **58A**, 23–28. *154*

*3331. Soutter, A. M. and Huggins, A. K. (1977). The effects of starvation on the sodium, potassium, water and free amino acid content of parietal muscle from *Agonus cataphractus*. *Comp. Biochem. Physiol.* **58B**, 57–61.

3332. Speck, U. and Urich, K. (1969). Consumption of body constituents during starvation in the crayfish, *Orconectes limosus*. *Z. vergl. Physiol.* **63,** 410–414. From *Chem. Abstr.* **76,** 110582t (1972). *182*

*3333. Spener, F. and Sand, D. M. (1970). Neutral alkoxylipids and wax esters of Mullet (*Mugil cephalus*) roe. *Comp. Biochem. Physiol.* **34,** 715–719.

*3334. Spieler, R. E. (1974). Short-term serum cortisol concentrations in goldfish (*Carassius auratus*) subjected to serial sampling and restraint. *J. Fish. Res. Bd Can.* **31,** 1240–1242. *235*

3335. Spieler, R. E. and Meier, A. H. (1976). Short-term serum prolactin concentrations in goldfish (*Carassius auratus*) subjected to serial sampling and restraint. *J. Fish. Res. Bd Can.* **33,** 183–186. *447*

3336. Spieler, R. E., Meier, A. H. and Loesch, H. C. (1976). Seasonal variations in circadian levels of serum prolactin in striped mullet, *Mugil cephalus*. *Gen. comp. Endocrinol.* **29,** 156–160. *383, 447*

*3337. Spiro, R. G. (1970). The carbohydrate of collagens. *In* "Chemistry and Molecular Biology of the Intercellular Matrix" (Ed. Balazs, E. A.), vol. 1, pp. 195–215. Academic Press, London and New York.

3338. Srivastava, A. K. and Meier, A. H. (1972). Daily variation in concentration of cortisol in plasma in intact and hypophysectomised gulf killifish. *Science, N.Y.* **177,** 185–187. *383*

*3339. Srivastava, A. K. and Pickford, G. E. (1972). Effects of hypophysectomy on the blood serum of male killifish, *Fundulus heteroclitus*, in salt water. *Gen. comp. Endocrinol.* **19,** 290–303.

*3340. Stabrovskii, E. M. (1969). Adrenaline and noradrenaline in the organs of elasmobranch and teleost fishes from the Black Sea. *J. evol. Biochem. Physiol.* **5,** 127–142.

3341. Stanek, E. (1973). Observations on food and feeding of cod (*Gadus morhua* L.) in Labrador, Newfoundland and Nova Scotia waters. *Pr. morsk. Inst. ryb. Gdyni,* **17** Ser. A, 7–26. *167*

*3342. Stanley, J. G. (1969). Seasonal changes in the electrolyte metabolism in the alewife, *Alosa pseudoharengus*, in Lake Michigan. *Proc. 12th Conf. Great Lakes Res.* 91–97. Internat. Assoc. Great Lakes Res.

*3343. Stanley, J. G. and Colby, P. J. (1971). Effects of temperature on electrolyte balance and osmoregulation in the alewife (*Alosa pseudoharengus*) in fresh and sea water. *Trans. Am. Fish. Soc.* **100,** 624–638. *240, 291, 343*

*3344. Stefanovich, V. and Akiyama, K. (1970). Comparative studies of aortic acid mucopolysaccharides in fifteen species. *Comp. Biochem. Physiol.* **34,** 125–130.

*3345. Stegeman, J. J. and Goldberg, E. (1972). Properties of hepatic hexose-6-phosphate dehydrogenase purified from brook trout and lake trout. *Comp. Biochem. Physiol.* **43B.** 241–256.

3346. Stepanova, V. A. (1971). Fatty acid composition of total lipids in the plaice *Pleuronectes herzensteini* of various age groups. *In* "Evolutsiya Vegetativnykh Funktsii" (Ed. Kreps, E. M.), pp. 38–43. "Nauka" Leningrad. *42, 17*

3347. Sterne, J., Hirsch, C. and Pele, M. F. (1968b: 1968a is in Volume 1). Effects of exclusive glucose diet in the goldfish. *Diabete,* **16,** 113–117. From *Chem. Abstr.* **73,** 85191t (1969). *140*

3348. Stevens, E. D. (1972). Change in body weight caused by handling and exercise in fish. *J. Fish. Res. Bd Can.* **29,** 202–203. *240*

3349. Stevens, E. D. (1973). The evolution of endothermy. *J. theor. Biol.* **38,** 597–611. *116*

3350. Stevens, E. D. and Fry, F. E. J. (1971). Brain and muscle temperatures in ocean caught and captive skipjack tuna. *Comp. Biochem. Physiol.* **38A,** 203–211. *256*

3351. Stevens, E. D., Lam, H. M. and Kendall, J. (1974). Vascular anatomy of the counter-current heat exchanger of skipjack tuna. *J. exp. Biol.* **61,** 145–153. *xii, 321*

3352. Stevens, E. D. and Sutterlin, A. M. (1976). Heat transfer between fish and ambient water. *J. exp. Biol.* **65,** 131–145. *321*

*3353. Stickney, R. R. (1971). Determination of sodium, calcium, magnesium and potassium in channel catfish blood plasma. *Bull. Ga Acad. Sci.* **29,** 163–168.

3354. Stickney, R. R. and Andrews, J. W. (1971). Combined effects of dietary lipids and environmental temperature on growth, metabolism and body composition of channel catfish (*Ictalurus punctatus*). *J. Nutr.* **101,** 1703–1710. *339*

3355. Stickney, R. R. and Andrews, J. W. (1972). Effects of dietary lipids on growth, food conversion, lipid and fatty acid composition of channel catfish. *J. Nutr.* **102,** 249–258. *142, 143*

3356. Stickney, R. R. and Shumway, S. E. (1974). Occurrence of cellulase activity in the stomachs of fishes. *J. Fish Biol.* **6,** 779–790. *152*

*3357. Stirling, H. P. (1972). The proximate composition of the European bass, *Dicentrarchus labrax* (L.) from the Bay of Naples. *J. Cons. perm. int. Explor. Mer.* **34,** 357–364.

3358. Stirling, H. P. (1976). Effects of experimental feeding and starvation on the proximate composition of the European bass *Dicentrarchus labrax. Mar. Biol.* **34,** 85–91. *93, 134, 182, 184*

3359. Storoshuk, A. Ya. (1975). Seasonal dynamics of the physiological-biochemical condition of the pollack *Pollachius virens* (L.) from the North Sea. *Trudy vses. nauchno-issled. Inst. morsk. ryb. Khoz. Okeanogr.* **96,** 114–120. *41*

*3360. Stray-Pedersen, S. and Nicolaysen, A. (1975). Qualitative and quantitative studies of the capillary structure in the rete mirabile of the eel, *Anguilla vulgaris* L. *Acta physiol. scand.* **94,** 339–357.

3361. Stroganov, N. S. and Buzinova, N. S. (1969). Enzymes of the digestive tract in the grass carp. I. Amylase and lipase. *Vest. mosk. gos. Univ., Biol. Pochvoved.* **24** (3), 27–31. From *Chem. Abstr.* **71,** 110209y (1969). *151*

*3362. Studnicka, M. and Svobodova, Z. (1973). *Bul. Vysk. Ust. Rybarsky Hydrobiol. Vod.* **9** (4), 3–6. From *Aq. Sci. Fish. Abstr.* **4** (6), 4Q5823F (1974).

*3363. Subramanyam, O. V. (1974). Effect of salinity acclimation on the succinic dehydrogenase activity in a freshwater fish, *Heteropneustes fossilis* (Teleostei: siluroidea). *Proc. Indian Acad. Sci.* **80B,** 26–30. *317*

3364. Sumner, F. B. and Wells, N. A. (1933). The effects of optic stimuli upon the formation and destruction of melanin pigment in fishes. *J. exp. Zool.* **64,** 377–403. *245*

*3365. Sumner, J. L. and Hopkirk, G. (1976). Lipid composition of New Zealand eels. *J. Sci. Fd Agric.* **27,** 933–938.

*3366. Suyama, M., Hirano, T., Okada, N. and Shibuya, T. (1977). Quality of wild and cultured ayu—I. On the proximate composition, free amino acids and related compounds. *Bull. Jap. Soc. scient. Fish.* **43,** 535–540.

*3367. Suyama, M. and Suzuki, H. (1975). Nitrogenous constituents in the muscle extracts of marine elasmobranchs. *Bull. Jap. Soc. scient. Fish.* **41,** 787–790.

*3368. Suyama, M., Suzuki, T., Maruyama. M. and Saito, K. (1970). Determination of carnosine, anserine, and balenine in the muscle of animal, *Bull. Jap. Soc. scient. Fish.* **36,** 1048–1053.

*3369. Suyama, M. and Yoshizawa, Y. (1973). Free amino acid composition of the skeletal muscle of migratory fish. *Bull. Jap. Soc. scient. Fish.* **39,** 1339–1343.

*3370. Suzuki, N., Hashimoto, K. and Matsuura, F. (1973). Studies on the colour of skipjack meat. *Bull. Jap. Soc. scient. Fish.* **39,** 35–41.

*3371. Svobodová, Z. (1973). Influence of sex upon certain haematological indexes of the carp (*Cyprinus carpio* L.) during the third vegetative period. *Acta vet., Brno* **42,** 257–263. *55*

*3372. Svobodová, Z., Baranyiova, E. and Vavruska, A. (1972). Glycogen determination in hepatopancreas and musculature of the carp (*Cyprinus carpio* L.). *Bul. Vysk. Ust. Rybarsky Hydrobiol. Vod.* **8,** (4), 3–7. *68, 69*

*3373. Svobodová, Z. and Kulhǎnek, V. (1971). Activity of some enzymes in the organs and tissues of carp (*Cyprinus carpio*). *Pr. Vysk. Ust. Rybarsky Hydriobol. Vod.* **9,** 133–156.

*3374. Svobodová, Z. and Vavruška, A. (1975). Glycogen distribution in the striated muscles of the carp (*Cyprinus carpio* L.). *Bul. Vysk. Ust. Rybarsky Hydrobiol. Vod.* **11,** 23–26.

3375. Swallow, R. L. and Fleming, W. R. (1969). The effect of starvation, feeding, glucose and ACTH on the liver glycogen levels of *Tilapia mossambica. Comp. Biochem. Physiol.* **28,** 95–106. *188*

3376. Swaner, J. C. and Connor, W. E. (1975). Hypercholesterolaemia of total starvation: its mechanism via tissue mobilisation of cholesterol. *Am. J. Physiol.* **229,** 365–369. *208*

*3377. Swarts, W. (1969). Blood studies of some marine telcosts. *Trans. Am. Fish. Soc.* **98,** 328–331. *110*

3378. Swift, D. J. and Lloyd, R. (1974). Changes in urine flow rate and haematocrit value of rainbow trout *Salmo gairdneri* (Richardson) exposed to hypoxia. *J. Fish Biol.* **6,** 379–387. *275, 276*

3379. Symons, P. E. K. (1968). Increase in aggression and in strength of the social hierarchy among juvenile Atlantic salmon deprived of food. *J. Fish. Res. Bd Can.* **25,** 2387–2401. *172*

3380. Symons, P. E. K. (1969). Greater dispersal of wild compared with hatchery-reared juvenile Atlantic salmon released in streams. *J. Fish. Res. Bd Can.* **26,** 1867–1876. *256*

3381. Symons, P. E. K. (1970). The possible role of social and territorial behaviour of Atlantic salmon parr in the production of smolts. *Tech. Rep. Fish. Res. Bd Can.* **206,** 25 pp. *28*

3382. Syrovy, I., Gaspar-Godfroid, A. and Hamoir, G. (1970). Comparative study of the myosins from red and white muscles of the carp. *Archs int. Physiol. Biochim.* **78,** 919–934. *71, 72, 75*

3383. Szakolczai, J. (1969). Reaction of the intestine of the carp (*Cyprinus carpio* L.) to environmental stress. *Acta vet. hung.* **19,** 153–159. From *Aq. Biol. Abstr.* 2 (9), Aq6461 (1970). *240*

3384. Szepesi, B. (1976). Effect of starvation and food restriction on carbohydrate metabolism. *In* "Carbohydrate Metabolism" (Ed. Berdanier, C. D.), Chapter 7, pp. 151–210. Hemisphere Publishing Corporation, Washington DC. *136*

3385. Szeredy, I. (1970). Hydroxyproline contents and solubility conditions in various connective tissues. II. Examination of solubility in Ringer solution. *Fleischwirtschaft,* **50,** 481–482. *205*

*3386. Taguchi, T., Susuki, K. and Osakabe, I. (1969). Magnesium and calcium
        contents of fish and squid tissues. *Bull. Jap. Soc. scient. Fish.* **35,** 405–409.

*3387. Takama, K., Zama, K. and Igarashi, H. (1967). Changes in the flesh lipids
        of fish during frozen storage. Part I. Flesh lipids of bluefin tuna, *Thunnus
        orientalis. Bull. Fac. Fish. Hokkaido Univ.* **18,** 240–247.

*3388. Takama, K., Zama, K. and Igarashi, H. (1969). Changes in the lipids
        during the development of salmon eggs. *Bull. Fac. Fish. Hokkaido Univ.* **20,**
        118–126. *13*

*3389. Takama, K., Zama, K. and Igarashi, H. (1972). Changes in the flesh lipids
        of fish during frozen storage. Part II. Flesh lipids of several species of fish.
        Bull. Fac. Fish. Hokkaido Univ. **22,** 290–300.

*3390. Takashi, R., Morozuka, T. and Arai, K. (1974). Purification and properties
        of *Tilapia* myosin from dorsal muscle. *Bull. Jap. Soc. scient. Fish.* **40,** 1155–1161.

*3391. Takashima, F., Hibiya, T., Ngan, P.-V. and Aida, K. (1972). Endocrino-
        logical studies on lipid metabolism in rainbow trout—II. Effects of sex steroids,
        thyroid powder and adrenocorticotropin on plasma lipid content. *Bull. Jap.
        Soc. scient. Fish.* **38,** 43–49. *40*

 3392. Takashima, F., Hibiya, T., Watanabe, T. and Hara, T. (1971). Endocrino-
        logical studies on lipid metabolism in rainbow trout—I. Differences in lipid
        content of plasma, liver and visceral adipose tissue between sexually immature
        and mature females. *Bull. Jap. Soc. scient. Fish.* **37,** 307–311. *39, 40, 206*

*3393. Takeda, M. and Totsui, N. (1975). The amino acid composition in yellowtail
        larvae. *Kochi Univ. Scientific Res. Rep., Agric. Sci. 1974* **23,** 173–178. From *Chem.
        Abstr.* **86,** 2624f (1977).

*3394. Takeuchi, M. and Ishii, S. (1969). Biochemical studies on wintering of
        culture carp—II. Changes of the oil content, fatty acid composition and
        glycogen content in the muscle and hepatopancreas. *Bull. Tokai reg. Fish. Res.
        Lab.* **59,** 19–27. *361, 386*

*3395. Takeuchi, M. and Ishii, S. (1971). Biochemical studies on wintering of
        culture carp—IX. Changes in contents of vitamin A and E in various parts.
        Bull. Tokai reg. Fish. Res. Lab. **68,** 45–49.

 3396. Tamura, E. and Honma, Y. (1970). Histological changes in the organs and
        tissues of the gobiid fishes throughout the life-span—III. Haemopoietic organs
        in the ice-goby, *Leucopsarion petersi* Hilgendorf. *Bull. Jap. Soc. scient. Fish.* **36,**
        661–666. *64*

*3397. Tamura, Y., Maki, T., Yamada, H., Shimamura, Y., Ochiai, S., Nishigaki, S.
        and Kimura, Y. (1975). Studies on the behaviour of accumulation of trace
        elements in fishes (III). Accumulation of selenium and mercury in various
        tissues of tuna. *Ann. Rep. Tokyo metropolitan Res. Lab. public Health,* **26,** 200–204.

*3398. Tan, E. L. and Wood, T. (1969). Enzymes of the pentose phosphate cycle in muscles of rat, ox, frog, lobster, chicken, northern pike and carp, and Ehrlich ascites cells. *Comp. Biochem. Physiol.* **31**, 635–643.

3399. Tanaka, M., Kawai, S.-I. and Yamamoto, S. (1972). On the development of the digestive system and changes in activities of digestive enzymes during larval and juvenile stage of ayu. *Bull. Jap. Soc. scient. Fish.* **38**, 1143–1152. *26*

3400. Tanaka, T. (1969a). Biochemical studies on wintering of culture carp—III. Changes in moisture content and water holding capacity of carp muscle. *Bull. Tokai reg. Fish. Res. Lab.* **59**, 29–47. *184, 185, 361*

3401. Tanaka, T. (1969b). Relationship between freshness before freezing and cold storage deterioration in the north Pacific Alaska pollack—I. Histological studies on the muscle. *Bull. Tokai reg. Fish. Res. Lab.* **60**, 143–168. *190–192*

*3402. Tanaka, Y., Ikabe, K., Tanaka, R. and Kunita, N. (1974). Contents of heavy metals in foods (III). Contents of heavy metals in fishes and shellfishes. *J. Food Hyg. Soc. Jap.* **15**, 390–393.

*3403. Tandon, R. S. and Chandra, S. (1976a). Cyclic changes in serum cholesterol levels of fresh water cat fish *Clarias batrachus*. *Z. Tierphysiol. Tierernähr. Futtermittelk.* **36**, 179–183.

*3404. Tandon, R. S. and Chandra, S. (1976b). Serum alkaline phosphatase levels of some fresh water teleosts. *Z. Tierphysiol. Tierernähr. Futtermittelk.* **37**, 330–333.

*3405. Tandon, R. S. and Joshi, B. D. (1973). Blood glucose and lactic acid levels in the fresh water fish, *Heteropneustes fossilis*, following stress. *Z. Tierphysiol. Tierernähr. Futtermittelk.* **31**, 210–216. *232, 237*

*3406. Tandon, R. S. and Joshi, B. D. (1974). Seasonal variations in blood glucose and serum calcium levels of fresh water fishes. *Z. Tierphysiol. Tierernähr. Futtermittelk.* **33**, 108–112.

*3407. Tandon, R. S. and Joshi, B. D. (1975). Studies on the physiology of blood of some fresh water fishes of India. I. Normal blood glucose and lactic acid levels. *J. inland Fish. Soc. India* **7**, 1–6.

*3408. Tandon, R. S. and Joshi, B. D. (1976). Total red and white blood cell count of 33 species of fresh water teleosts. *Z. Tierphysiol. Tierernähr. Futtermittelk.* **37**, 293–297.

3409. Tano, S. and Shirahata, S. (1975). Effects of age and growth on macromolecular biosynthesis in salmon brain. *Radioisotopes*, **24**, 93–96. *61*

3410. Tarr, H. L. A. (1973). Enzymes and systems of intermediary metabolism. *In* "Fish Nutrition" (Ed. Halver, J. E.), Chapter 6, pp. 255–326. Academic Press, London and New York. *1, 361*

*3411. Tashima, L. and Cahill, G. F. (1968). Effects of insulin in the toadfish, *Opsanus tau. Gen. comp. Endocrinol.* **11,** 262–271. From Chavin and Young (1970).

3412. Taubert, B. D. and Coble, D. W. (1977). Daily rings in otoliths of three species of *Lepomis* and *Tilapia mossambica. J. Fish. Res. Bd Can.* **34,** 332–340. *374*

3413. Tauchi, H., Yoshioka, T. and Kobayashi, H. (1971). Age change of skeletal muscles of rats. *Gerontologia (Basel)* **17,** 219–227. From *Musc. Dyst. Abstr.* **16,** no. 821 (1972). *31, 61*

3414. Tepperman, H. M., Fabry, P. and Tepperman, J. (1970). Effect of periodic fasting and refeeding on rat kidney cortex enzymes, gluconeogenesis and water intake pattern. *J. Nutr.* **100,** 837–846. *186*

3415. Terjung, R. L., Winder, W. W., Baldwin, K. M. and Holloszy, J. O. (1973). Effects of exercise on the turnover of cytochrome *c* in skeletal muscle. *J. biol. Chem.* **248,** 7404–7406. *119*

3416. Terpin, K. M., Spotila, J. R. and Koons, R. R. (1976). Effect of photoperiod on the temperature tolerance of the blacknose dace, *Rhinichthys atratulus. Comp. Biochem. Physiol.* **53A,** 241–244. *323*

*3417. Terrier, M. and Perrier, H. (1975). Cyclic 3′, 5′-adenosine monophosphate level in the plasma of the rainbow trout (*Salmo gairdnerii* Richardson) following adrenaline administration and constrained exercise. *Experientia,* **31,** 196 only *232, 235*

*3418. Theodore, J., Robin, E. D., Murdaugh, H. V. and Cross, C. E. (1972). Cation transport and energy metabolism in the nucleated erythrocyte of the dogfish shark, *Squalus acanthias. Comp. Biochem. Physiol.* **42A,** 639–654.

*3419. van den Thillart, G., Kesbeke, F. and van Waarde, A. (1976). Influence of anoxia on the energy metabolism of goldfish *Carassius auratus* (L.). *Comp. Biochem. Physiol.* **55A,** 329–336. *281*

*3420. Thomas, A. J. and Patton, S. (1972). Phospholipids of fish gills. *Lipids,* **7,** 76–77.

3421. Thomas, N. W. (1971). The effect of streptozotocin on the fine structure of the beta cell of the cod pancreas. *Hormone metab. Res.* **3,** 21–23. *6, 430*

3422. Thomson, A. J. and Sargent, J. R. (1977). Changes in the levels of chloride cells and ($Na^+ + K^+$)-dependent ATPase in the gills of yellow and silver eels adapting to seawater. *J. exp. Zool.* **200,** 33–40. *292*

3423. Thomson, A. J., Sargent, J. R. and Owen, J. M. (1975). Effect of environmental changes on the lipid composition and ($Na^+ + K^+$)-dependent adenosine triphosphatase in the gills of the eel, *Anguilla anguilla. Biochem. Soc. Trans. 557th Meetg, Liverpool.* **3,** 668 only. *339*

*3424. Thomson, A. J., Sargent, J. R. and Owen, J. M. (1977). Influence of acclimation temperature and salinity on $(Na^+ + K^+)$-dependent adenosine triphosphatase and fatty acid composition in the gills of the eel (*Anguilla anguilla*). *Comp. Biochem. Physiol.* **56B**, 223–228. *339*

*3425. Thomson, K. S., Gall, J. G. and Coggins, L. W. (1973). Nuclear DNA contents of coelacanth erythrocytes. *Nature, Lond.* **241**, 126 only.

*3426. Thorpe, A. and Ince, B. W. (1974). The effects of pancreatic hormones, catecholamines, and glucose loading on blood metabolites in the northern pike (*Esox lucius* L.). *Gen. comp. Endocrinol.* **23**, 29–44. *233*

3426a. Thorpe, A. and Ince, B. W. (1976). Plasma insulin levels in teleosts determined by a charcoal-separation radioimmunoassay technique. *Gen. comp. Endocrinol.* **30**, 332–339. *379*

*3427. Thorson, T. B. (1967). Osmoregulation in fresh-water elasmobranchs. *In* "Sharks, Skates and Rays" (Eds Gilbert, P. W., Mathewson, R. F. and Rall, D. P.), Chapter 17, pp. 265–270. The Johns Hopkins Press, Baltimore. *620*

*3428. Thorson, T. B. (1970). Freshwater stingrays, *Potamotrygon* spp.: failure to concentrate urea when exposed to saline medium. *Life Sci.* **9**, 893–900. *310, 620*

*3429. Thorson, T. B., Cowan, C. M. and Watson, D. E. (1967). *Potamotrygon* spp.: elasmobranchs with low urea content. *Science, N.Y.* **158**, 375–377. *310*

*3430. Thorson, T. B., Cowan, C. M. and Watson, D. E. (1973). Body fluid solutes of juveniles and adults of the euryhaline bull shark *Carcharhinus leucas* from fresh water and saline environments. *Physiol. Zoöl.* **46**, 29–42. *155, 311, 499*

*3431. Thorson, T. B. and Gerst, J. W. (1972). Comparison of some parameters of serum and uterine fluid of pregnant, viviparous sharks (*Carcharhinus leucas*) and serum of their near-term young. *Comp. Biochem. Physiol.* **42A**, 33–40. *20*

3432. Thurow, F. (1970). On the reproduction of cod *Gadus morhua* (L.) in the Kiel bight. *Ber. dt. wiss. Kommn Meeresforsch.* **21**, 170–192. *36, 46*

*3433. Timoshina, L. A. (1970). Changes brought about in the amino acid composition of fish muscles and blood by starvation. *J. Ichthyol.* **10**, 342–347. *193, 194*

*3434. Timoshina, L. A. and Shabalina, A. A. (1972). Effect of starvation on the dynamics of concentration of amino acid and free fatty acid in rainbow trout. *Hydrobiol. J.* **8**, 36–41. *192–194*

3435. Tinsley, I. J., Krueger, H. M. and Saddler, J. B. (1973). Fatty acid content of coho salmon, *Oncorhynchus kisutch*—a statistical approach to changes produced by diet. *J. Fish. Res. Bd Can.* **30**, 1661–1666. *43, 143*

*3436. Tiwari, R. D., Srivastava, K. C. and Rastogi, S. C. (1970). Distribution of phospholipids in the various organs of *Labeo rohita*. *Indian J. Biochem.* **7,** 134–135.

*3437. Todd, E. S. (1972). Haemoglobin concentration in a new air-breathing fish. *Comp. Biochem. Physiol.* **42A,** 569–573.

*3438. Todorov, M., Naplatarova, M. and Suikova, M. (1971). Dynamics of trace elements in the fish body. II. Dynamics of the trace elements Cu, Mn, Sr and Ba during hatching of the rainbow trout (*Salmo irideus* Gibb) from eggs. *Nauchni Trud. vissh. selskostop Inst. Georgi Dimitrov. Zootekh. Fak.* **21,** 413–423. *148*

*3439. Tokunaga, T. (1970a). Trimethylamine oxide and its decomposition in the bloody muscle of fish—I. TMAO, TMA and DMA contents in ordinary and bloody muscles. *Bull. Jap. Soc. scient. Fish.* **36,** 502–510. *70, 72, 75, 76, 106* (*Note:* "Bloody muscle" (chi-ai) is the same as "dark muscle").

3440. Tokunaga, T. (1970b). Trimethylamine oxide and its decomposition in the bloody muscle of fish—II. Formation of DMA and TMA during storage. *Bull. Jap. Soc. scient. Fish.* **36,** 510–515. *459*

*3441. Tomita, H. and Tsuchiya, Y. (1971). Comparative studies on myoglobins. I. Spectral properties and amino acid compositions of myoglobins from shark, bony fishes, turtle and mammalia. *Tohoku J. agric. Res.* **22,** 228–238.

3442. Tomiyama, T., Kobayashi, K. and Ishio, S. (no date given). Absorption of ^{90}Sr (^{90}Y) by carp. In "Research in the Effects and Influences of the Nuclear Bomb Test Explosions II", pp. 1181–1187. Japanese Society for the Promotion of Science, Tokyo. *454*

3443. Tong, S. S. C., Young, W. D., Gutenmann, W. H. and Lisk, D. J. (1974). Trace metals in Lake Cayuga trout (*Salvelinus namaycush*) in relation to age. *J. Fish. Res. Bd Can.* **31,** 238–239. *34, 35*

3444. Torracca, A. M. V., Raschetti, R., Salvioli, R., Ricciardi, G. and Winterhalter, K. H. (1977). Modulation of the Root effect in goldfish by ATP and GTP. *Biochim. biophys. Acta.* **496,** 367–373. *214*

3445. de Torrengo, M. P. and Brenner, R. R. (1976). Influence of environmental temperature on the fatty acid desaturation and elongation activity of fish (*Pimelodus maculatus*) liver microsomes. *Biochim. biophys. Acts.* **424,** 36–44. *340*

*3446. Toyomizu, M., Nakamura, T. and Shono, T. (1976). Fatty acid composition of lipid from horse mackerel muscle—discussion of fatty acid composition of fish lipid. *Bull. Jap. Soc. scient. Fish.* **42,** 101–108.

*3447. Trakatellis, A. C., Tada, K., Yamaji, K. and Gardiki-Kouidou, P. (1975). Isolation and partial characterisation of anglerfish proglucagon. *Biochemistry, N.Y.* **14,** 1508–1512.

3448. Trams, E. G. (1969a). Hepatic insufficiency in spawning Pacific salmon. *Mar. Biol.* **4,** 1–3. *65*

3449. Trams, E. G. (1969b). Neurochemical observations on spawning Pacific salmon. *Nature, Lond.* **222,** 492–493. *65*

*3450. Trams. E. G. and Brown, E. A. B. (1974). The activity of 2′, 3′-cyclic adenosine monophosphate 3′-phosphoesterhydrolase in elasmobranch and teleost brain. *Comp. Biochem. Physiol.* **48B,** 185–189.

*3451. Trams, E. G. and Hoiberg, C. P. (1970). Lipid composition of tissues from *Electrophorus electricus. Proc. Soc. exp. Biol. Med.* **135,** 193–196.

3452. Treguer, P., le Corre, P. and Courtot, P. (1972). A method for determination of the total dissolved free fatty acid-content of sea water. *J. mar. biol. Ass. U.K.* **52,** 1045–1055. *148*

*3453. Trepšienė, O., Jankevičius, K. (1974). B vitamin complex in the nutriment and separate organs of the carp, white amur and tench which were under natural feeding conditions (3. Vitamin content in the tissues and organs of the third-year fish). *Trudy Akad. Nauk. Litovskoi SSR.* Ser. B, **4** (68), 93–100.

*3454. Trepšienė, O., Jankevičius, K. and Pečiukėnas, A. (1974). B vitamin complex in the nutriment and separate organs of the carp, white amur and tench which were under natural feeding conditions. (1. Vitamin content in the tissues of second-year fish). *Trudy Akad. Nauk. Litovskoi SSR,* Ser. B, **2** (66), 137–143.

*3455. Triplett, E. and Calaprice, J. R. (1974). Changes in plasma constituents during spawning migration of Pacific salmons. *J. Fish. Res. Bd Can.* **31,** 11–14. *64*

*3456. Truscott, B. and Idler, D. R. (1972). Corticosteroids in plasma of elasmobranchs. *Comp. Biochem. Physiol.* **42A,** 41–50.

*3457. Trusevich, V. A. (1974). Utilisation of energy-rich phosphates by white skeletal muscles of *Trachurus mediterraneous ponticus* during muscle exercise and fatigue. *In* "Fiziol. Biokhim. Nizshikh Posvonochnykh" (Ed. Kreps, E. M.), pp. 55–61. "Nauka", Leningrad. *325*

*3458. Trusevich, V. V. (1976). Phosphate metabolism in the red lateral muscles of scad *Trachurus mediterraneus* during muscle stress. *J. Evol. Biochem. Physiol.* **12,** 129 132.

3459. Tsai, S.-C., Boush, G. M. and Matsumura, F. (1975). Importance of water pH in accumulation of inorganic mercury in fish. *Bull. environ. Contam. Toxicol.* **13,** 188–193. *437*

*3460. Tsepelovan, P. G. and Rusakov, Yu. I. (1976). Corticosteroid content in blood of the Russian sturgeon *Acipenser güldenstadti* at various stages in the life cycle. *J. evol. Biochem. Physiol.* **12,** 68–70.

3461. Tsin, A. T. C. and Beatty, D. D. (1977). Visual pigment changes in rainbow trout in response to temperature. *Science, N.Y.* **195,** 1358–1360. *268*

*3462. Tsuchiya, Y. and Takahashi, I. (1950). The contents of connective tissue in fish muscles. *Tohoku J. agric. Res.* **1,** 209–213. *112*

3463. Tsukuda, H. (1975). Temperature dependency of the relative activities of liver lactate dehydrogenase isozymes in goldfish acclimated to different temperatures. *Comp. Biochem. Physiol.* **52B,** 343–345. *334*

3464. Tsukuda, H. and Ohsawa, W. (1971). Effects of acclimation temperature on the composition and thermostability of tissue proteins in the goldfish, *Carassius auratus* L. *Annotnes zool. jap.* **44,** 90–98. *336*

3465. Tsukuda, H. and Ohsawa, W. (1974). Effects of temperature acclimation on the isozyme pattern of liver lactate dehydrogenase in the goldfish, *Carassius auratus* (L.). *Annotnes zool. jap.* **47,** 206–214. *334*

*3466. Tsukuda, N. and Kitahara, T. (1974). Composition of the esterified fatty acids of astaxanthin diester in the skin of seven red fishes. *Bull. Tokai reg. Fish. Res. Lab.* **77,** 89–95.

*3467. Tsuladze, E. A. (1973). Mineral composition of the flesh of herbivorous and some other fish of Georgia. *Ryb. Khoz.* (9), 63–64 (no volume number given).

3468. Tsuladze, E. A. (1976). Amino acid composition of the muscle tissue of phytophagous fish. *Ryb. Khoz.* (9), 56–58 (no volume number given).

*3469. Tsuyuki, H. and Itoh, S. (1970). Composition of fatty acids in coelacanth oil. *Bull. Jap. Soc. scient. Fish.* **36,** 788–790.

3470. Tsuyuki, H. and Roberts, E. (1969). Muscle protein polymorphism of sablefish from the eastern Pacific Ocean. *J. Fish. Res. Bd Can.* **26,** 2633–2641. *253*

3471. Tsuyuki, H., Roberts, E. and Best, E. A. (1969). Serum transferrin systems and the haemoglobins of the Pacific halibut (*Hippoglossus stenolepis*). *J. Fish. Res. Bd Can.* **26,** 2351–2362. *252*

*3472. Tsuyuki, H. and Ronald, A. P. (1971). Molecular basis for multiplicity of Pacific salmon haemoglobins: evidence for in vivo existence of molecular species with up to four different polypeptides. *Comp. Biochem. Physiol.* **39B,** 503–522.

*3473. Tsuzimura, M., Michinaka, K. and Watanabe, S. (1972). Distribution of thiaminase in the edible part of sea water fish. *J. Jap. Soc. Fd Nutr.* **25,** 533–537.

*3474. Turpaev, T. M., Rakich, L., Manukhin, B. N., Volina, E. V. and Buznikov, G. A. (1973). Monoamines in the electric organ and central nervous system of the ray *Torpedo marmorata. J. evol. Biochem. Physiol.* **9,** 178–179.

3475. Turuk, T. N. (1972). Variations in the relative weight of the liver of Atlantic cod. *Trudy polyar. nauchno-issled. Inst. mosrk. rvh. Khoz. Okeanogr.* **28,** 88–95. *39, 41, 52*

*3476. Turumi, K. and Saito, J. (1953). A chemical study on the loach mucin. *Tohoku J. exp. Med.* **58,** 247–249.

*3477. Twelves, E. L., Everson, I. and Leith, I. (1975). Thyroid structure and function in two antarctic fishes. *Brit. Antarct. Surv. Bull.* **40,** 7–14. *385*

3478. Tyler, A. V. (1970). Rates of gastric emptying in young cod. *J. Fish. Res. Bd Can.* **27,** 1177–1189. *162, 319*

3479. Tytler, P. and Blaxter, J. H. S. (1973). Adaptation by cod and saithe to pressure changes. *Netherlands J. Sea Res.* **7,** 31–45. 7th European Symp. mar. Biol. *122*

3480. Ubels, J. L., Hoffert, J. R. and Fromm, P. O. (1977). Ocular oxygen toxicity: the effect of hyperbaric oxygen on the in vitro electroretinogram. *Comp. Biochem. Physiol.* **57A,** 29–32. *272*

*3481. Uchiyama, H., Ehira, S., Takeuchi, M. and Kobayashi, H. (1969). Biochemical studies on wintering of culture carp—VII. Seasonal changes in nucleic levels and activities of xanthine oxidase and protease in hepatopancreas of carp. *Bull. Tokai reg. Fish. Res. Lab.* **59,** 75–80. *386*

*3482. Uchiyama, H. and Kato, N. (1974). Partial freezing as a means of preserving fish freshness—I. Changes in free amino acids, TMA-N, ATP and its related compounds, and nucleic acids during storage. *Bull. Jap. Soc. scient. Fish.* **40,** 1145–1154.

*3483. Ueda, T. (1972a). Fatty acid composition of fish oils—II. The fatty acid compositions of Jack mackerel oil, in consideration of the dependency of the polar and the nonpolar lipids on the total one. *J. Shimonoseki Univ. Fish.* **20,** 279–295.

*3484. Ueda, T. (1972b). Fatty acid composition of fish oils—III. Fatty acid composition of oils from dorsal and ventral flesh in Jack mackerel. *J. Shimonoseki Univ. Fish.* **21,** 163–170.

*3485. Ueda, T. (1976). Changes in the fatty acid composition of mackerel lipid and probably related factors—I. Influence of the season, body length and lipid content. *Bull. Jap. Soc. scient. Fish.* **42,** 479–484.

*3486. Ueda, T., Suzuki, Y. and Nakamura, R. (1973). Accumulation of Sr in marine organisms—I. Strontium and calcium contents, CF and OR values in marine organisms. *Bull. Jap. Soc. scient. Fish.* **39,** 1253–1262.

*3487. Ueda, T. and Takeda, M. (1977). On mercury and selenium contained in tuna fish tissues—IV. Methyl mercury level in muscles and liver of yellowfin tuna. *Bull. Jap. Soc. scient. Fish.* **43,** 1115–1121.

*3488. Ueno, K., Ishizuka, I. and Yamakawa, T. (1975). Glycolipids of the fish testis. *J. Biochem., Tokyo*, **77**, 1223–1232.

3489. Ullrich, H. (1968). Second communication on blood-serum electrolytes of cod from the north-west Atlantic. *Fisch-Forsch.* **6**, 37–39. *254*

3490. Umminger, B. L. (1967). Sub-zero temperatures and supercooling in *Fundulus heteroclitus. Am. Zool.* **7**, 731 only. *343*

3491. Umminger, B. L. (1969a). Physiological studies on supercooled killifish (*Fundulus heteroclitus*). I. Serum inorganic constituents in relation to osmotic and ionic regulation at subzero temperatures. *J. exp. Zool.* **172**, 283–302. *342*

*3492. Umminger, B. L. (1969b). Physiological studies on supercooled killifish (*Fundulus heteroclitus*). II. Serum organic constituents and the problem of supercooling. *J. exp. Zool.* **172**, 409–423. *343*

3493. Umminger, B. L. (1969c). Physiological studies on supercooled killifish (*Fundulus heteroclitus*). III. Carbohydrate metabolism and survival at subzero temperatures. *J. exp. Zool.* **173**, 159–174. *343*

*3494. Umminger, B. L. (1969d). Osmotic and ionic regulation in the killifish, *Fundulus heteroclitus*, at subzero temperatures. *Am. Zool.* **9**, 588–589. *342*

3495. Umminger, B. L. (1969e). Serum chemistry of fresh-water-adapted *Fundulus heteroclitus* at temperatures near freezing. *Am. Zool.* **9**, 1092 only. *341, 344*

3496. Umminger, B. L. (1969f). Survival value of hyperglycaemia for supercooled killifish. *Bull. ecol. Soc. Am.* **50**, 69 only. *343*

*3497. Umminger, B. L. (1970a). Osmoregulation by the killifish, *Fundulus heteroclitus*, in fresh water at temperatures near freezing. *Nature, Lond.* **225**, 294–295. *343*

3498. Umminger, B. L. (1970b). Effects of temperature on serum protein components in the killifish, *Fundulus heteroclitus. J. Fish. Res. Bd Can.* **27**, 404–409. *338*

3499. Umminger, B. L. (1970c). Carbohydrate metabolism in hypophysectomised killifish at subzero temperatures. *Am. Zool.* **10**, 299 only. *343*

3500. Umminger, B. L. (1970d). Effects of subzero temperatures and trawling stress on serum osmolality in the winter flounder *Pseudopleuronectes americanus. Biol. Bull. mar. biol. Lab., Woods Hole*, **139**, 574–579. *240*

*3501. Umminger, B. L. (1970e). Serum chemistry of the brown bullhead, *Ictalurus nebulosus*, at temperatures near freezing. *Am. Zool.* **10**, 520 only.

*3502. Umminger, B. L. (1971a). Chemical studies of cold death in the gulf killifish, *Fundulus grandis. Comp. Biochem. Physiol.* **39A**, 625–632. *342*

*3503. Umminger, B. L. (1971b). Patterns of osmoregulation in freshwater fishes at temperatures near freezing. *Physiol. Zool.* **44,** 20–27. *343*

3504. Umminger, B. L. (1971c). Lack of pituitary involvement in the cold-induced hyperglycaemia of the killifish, *Fundulus heteroclitus. Experientia,* **27,** 701–702. *343*

*3505. Umminger, B. L. (1971d). Osmoregulatory overcompensation in the goldfish, *Carassius auratus,* at temperatures near freezing. *Copeia,* (4), 686–691 (no volume number given).

*3506. Umminger, B. L. (1971e). Osmoregulatory role of serum glucose in freshwater-adapted killifish (*Fundulus heteroclitus*) at temperatures near freezing. *Comp. Biochem. Physiol.* **38A,** 141–145. *343*

*3507. Umminger, B. L. (1972a). Physiological studies on supercooled killifish (*Fundulus heteroclitus*). IV. Carbohydrate metabolism in hypophysectomised killifish at subzero temperatures. *J. exp. Zool.* **181,** 217–222. *313*

3508. Umminger, B. L. (1972b). Homeostasis. *In* "McGraw-Hill Yearbook of Science & Technology", pp. 246–248. *343*

*3509. Umminger, B. L. (1973a). Death induced by injection stress in cold-acclimated goldfish, *Carassius auratus. Comp. Biochem. Physiol.* **45A,** 883–887. *232, 240*

3510. Umminger, B. L. (1973b). Exposure of the salt-water-adapted killifish, *Fundulus heteroclitus,* to subzero temperatures. *In* "Interact Symposium Proceedings" (Eds Laushey, L. M., Rieveschal, G., Berg, G. and Greenstreet, W. E.), pp. 11–12. National Environmental Research Centre, Cincinnati, Ohio. *344*

3511. Umminger, B. L. (1974). Mechanisms of cold adaptation in polar marine animals. *Volume of Abstracts, 3rd Symp. Antarct. Biol., Adaptations within Antarct. Ecosyst.* 26–30 Aug. 1974. Nat. Acad. Sci., Washington DC. *331*

3512. Umminger, B. L. and Bair, R. D. (1972). Hormonal regulation of the cold-induced hyperglycaemia of the killifish. *Am. Zool.* **12** (3), xxxiv only. *343, 344*

3513. Umminger, B. L. and Bair, R. D. (1973). Role of islet tissue in the cold-induced hyperglycaemia of the killifish, *Fundulus heteroclitus. J. exp. Zool.* **183,** 65–70. *343*

*3514. Umminger, B. L. and Benziger, D. (1975). In vitro stimulation of hepatic glycogen phosphorylase activity by epinephrine and glucagon in the brown bullhead, *Ictalurus nebulosus. Gen. comp. Endocrinol.* **25,** 96–104. *235*

*3515. Umminger, B. L., Benziger, D. and Levy, S. (1975). In vitro stimulation of hepatic glycogen phosphorylase activity by epinephrine and glucagon in the killifish, *Fundulus heteroclitus. Comp. Biochem. Physiol.* **51C,** 111–115. *235*

3516. Umminger, B. L. and Gist, D. H. (1971). Thermal optima in the responses of goldfish to injection stress and cortisol. *Am. Zool.* **11,** 652–653. *232, 233, 322*

*3517. Umminger, B. L. and Gist, D. H. (1973). Effects of thermal acclimation on physiological responses to handling stress, cortisol and aldosterone injections in the goldfish, *Carassius auratus. Comp. Biochem. Physiol.* **44A,** 967–977. *232, 240, 322*

3518. Umminger, B. L. and Kenkel, H. (1975). Ionoregulatory role of prolactin in salt-water-adapted killifish at subzero temperatures. *Am. Zool.* **15,** 796 only. *342*

3519. Umminger, B. L. and Kenkel, H. (1976). Salinity-temperature interactions and prolactin release in the killifish. *Am. Zool.* **16,** 217 only. *301*

*3520. Umminger, B. L. and Mahoney, J. B. (1972). Seasonal changes in the serum chemistry of the winter flounder, *Pseudopleuronectes americanus. Trans. Am. Fish. Soc.* **101,** 746–748. *385*

*3521. Umminger, B. L., Pucke, J. and Levy, S. J. (1976). Histophysiological studies of ionoregulation in the marine catfish, *Plotosus lineatus. Physiologist, Wash.* **19,** 396 only. *309*

3522. Unsicker, K., Polonius, T., Lindmar, R., Löffelholz, K. and Wolf, U. (1977). Catecholamines and 5-hydroxytryptamine in corpuscles of Stannius of the salmonid, *Salmo irideus* L. A study correlating electron microscopical, histochemical and chemical findings. *Gen. comp. Endocrinol.* **31,** 121–132. *304, 440*

*3523. Urist, M. R. (1963). The regulation of calcium and other ions in the serums of hagfish and lampreys. *Ann. N.Y. Acad. Sci.* **109,** Art. 1, 294–311.

*3524. Urist, M. R. (1973). Testosterone-induced development of limb gills of the lungfish, *Lepidosiren paradoxa. Comp. Biochem. Physiol.* **44A,** 131–135.

*3525. Urist, M. R. and van de Putte, K. A. (1967). Comparative biochemistry of the blood of fishes: identification of fishes by the chemical composition of serum. *In* "Sharks, Skates and Rays" (Eds Gilbert, P. W., Mathewson, R. F. and Rall, D. P.), Chapter 18, pp. 271–285. The Johns Hopkins Press, Baltimore. *25, 284*

*3526. Urist, M. R., Uyeno, S., King, E., Okada, M. and Applegate, S. (1972). Calcium and phosphorus in the skeleton and blood of the lungfish, *Lepidosiren paradoxa*, with comment on humoral factors in calcium homeostasis in the osteichthyes. *Comp. Biochem. Physiol.* **42A,** 393–408.

*3527. Uskova, E. T. and Chaikovskaya, A. V. (1975). Heterogeneity and chemical nature of protein components in sea fish mucous coats. *Gidrobiol. Zh.* **11,** 38–42.

3528. Uskova, E. T., Chaikovskaya, A. V., Ustimovich, D. A. and Davidenko, S. I. (1970). Chemical composition of the mucous substance of the skin of some species of Black Sea fish. *Gidrobiol. Zh.* **6**, 91–95. *112*

*3529. Uthe, J. F. (1971). Determination of total and organic mercury levels in fish tissue. *Int. Symp. Identification Meas. Environ. Pollut. (Proc.)* 207–212.

3530. Utida (Uchida), S. and Hirano, T. (1973). Effects of changes in environmental salinity on salt and water movement in the intestine and gills of the eel, *Anguilla japonica*. *In* "Responses of Fish to Environmental Changes" (Ed. Chavin, W.), Chapter 7, pp. 240–267. Charles C. Thomas, Springfield, Illinois. *295, 297*

3531. Utida, S. and Isono, N. (1967). Alkaline phosphatase activity in intestinal mucosa of the eel adapted to fresh water or sea water. *Proc. Japan Acad.* **43**, 789–792. *308*

*3532. Utida, S., Kamiya, M., Johnson, D. W. and Bern, H. A. (1974). Effects of freshwater adaptation and of prolactin on sodium-potassium-activated adenosine triphosphatase activity in the urinary bladder of two flounder species. *J. Endocr.* **62**, 11–14. *307*

3533. Utida, S., Kamiya, M. and Shirai, N. (1971). Relationship between the activity of Na^+-K^+-activated adenosinetriphosphatase and the number of chloride cells in eel gills with special reference to sea-water adaptation. *Comp. Biochem. Physiol.* **38A**, 443–447. *292*

3534. Utter, F. M. (1969). Biochemical polymorphisms in the Pacific hake (*Merluccius productus*): a. Esterase polymorphism in vitreous fluids; b. Lactate dehydrogenase isozymes; c. Transferrin variants. Ph.D. Thesis, University of California. *251, 252*

3535. Utter, F. M. (1971). Tetrazolium oxidase phenotypes of rainbow trout (*Salmo gairdneri*) and Pacific salmon (*Oncorhynchus* spp.). *Comp. Biochem. Physiol.* **39B**, 891–895. *254*

3536. Utter, F. M. and Hodgins, H. O. (1970). Phosphoglucomutase polymorphism in sockeye salmon. *Comp. Biochem. Physiol.* **36**, 195–199. *253*

3537. Utter, F. M., Hodgins, H. O. and Allendorf, F. W. (1974). Biochemical genetic studies of fishes: potentialities and limitations. *In* "Biochemical and Biophysical Perspectives in Marine Biology" (Eds Malins, D. C. and Sargent, J. R.), pp. 213–238. Academic Press, London and New York. *43, 250*

3538. Vaccaro, A. M., Raschetti, R., Ricciardi, G. and Morpurgo, G. (1975). Temperature adaptation at the haemoglobin level in *Carassius auratus*. *Comp. Biochem. Physiol.* **52A**, 627–634. *327*

3539. Vallyathan, N. V., Grinyer, I. and George, J. C. (1970). Effect of fasting and exercise on lipid levels in muscle. A cytological and biochemical study. *Can. J. Zool.* **48**, 377–383. *71*

*3540. Valtonen, T. (1974). Seasonal and sex-bound variation in the carbohydrate metabolism of the liver of the whitefish. *Comp. Biochem. Physiol.* **47A**, 713–727. *49, 52*

3541. Vanstone, W. E. and Markert, J. R. (1968). Some morphological and biochemical changes in coho salmon, *Oncorhynchus kisutch*, during parr-smolt transformation. *J. Fish. Res. Bd Can.* **25**, 2403–2418. *21*

3542. Varesmaa, E., Laine, J. J. and Niinivaara, F. P. (1968). The influence of food on the fatty acid composition of the rainbow trout (*Salmo gairdnerii*). *Z. Lebensmittelunters. u.-Forsch.* **138**, 150–154. *142*

3543. Vegas-Velez, M. (1973). The digestive enzymes of the teleosts and their relationship with the type of diet. *An. Cient. Lima*, **11**, 111–126. *152*

*3544. Vellas, F. and Créac'h, Y. (1971). Ureogenesis in starving carp. *Archs Sci. physiol.* **25**, 353–359. *218*

3545. Vellas, F. and Créac'h, Y. (1972). Importance of purine metabolism in the biosynthesis of urea in the common carp (*Cyprinus carpio* L.). *Archs Sci. physiol.* **26**, 207–218. *161*

*3546. Vellas, F. and Serfaty, A. (1974). Ammonia and urea in a freshwater teleost: the carp (*Cyprinus carpio* L.). *J. Physiol., Paris*, **68**, 591–614. *92, 158–162, 386*

*3547. Vellas-Clos, F. (1973). Research on ureogenesis in freshwater teleosts. Thesis Docteur es-sciences naturelles, University Paul Sabatier de Toulouse. *155, 158, 160–162, 217*

*3548. Venkatachari, S. A. T. (1974). Effect of salinity adaptation on nitrogen metabolism in the freshwater fish *Tilapia mossambica*. I. Tissue protein and amino acid levels. *Mar. Biol.* **24**, 57–63. *313*

3549. Venkataraman, R., Solanki, K. K. and Kandoran, M. K. (1968). Seasonal variation in the chemical composition of pomfrets—I. Black pomfret (*Parastromateus niger*). *Fish. Technol.* **5**, 113–122. *68*

*3550. Vernier, J.-M. and Sire, M.-F. (1976). Evolution of the glycogen content and of glucose-6-phosphatase activity in the liver of *Salmo gairdneri* during development. *Tissue and Cell*, **8**, 531–546.

*3551. Verzhbinskaya, N. A. (1973). Functional organisation of the glycolysis enzyme system in the muscle and nerve tissue of cephalopod molluscs and lower fishes. *J. Evol. Biochem. Physiol.* **8**, 230–237.

*3552. Vislie, T. and Fugelli, K. (1975). Cell volume regulation in flounder (*Platichthys flesus*) heart muscle accompanying an alteration in plasma osmolality. *Comp. Biochem. Physiol.* **52A**. 415–418.

3553. Viviani, R., Cortesi, P., Borgatti, A. R., Crisetig, G., Poletti, R. and Mancini, L. (1968). Seasonal variations in the muscular lipids of some clupeiforms of the Adriatic Sea. *Nuova Vet.* **44**, 340–346. *208*

3554. Vladimirov, V. I. (1974). Relation of the quality of carp embryos and larvae to the age of their mothers, the amino acid content in their eggs, and amino acid additives to water at the beginning of development. *Raznokachestvennost Rannego Ontog. Ryb.* 94–113. Ed. Vladimirov, V. I. "Naukova Dumka", Kiev, USSR. From *Chem. Abstr.* **84,** 133071e (1976). *10*

3555. de Vlaming, V. L. (1971). The effects of food deprivation and salinity changes on reproductive function in the estuarine gobiid fish, *Gillichthys mirabilis. Biol. Bull. mar. biol. Lab., Woods Hole,* **141,** 458–471. *168*

3556. de Vlaming, V. L. and Pardo, R. J. (1975). *In vitro* effects of insulin on liver lipid and carbohydrate metabolism in the teleost, *Notemigonus crysoleucas. Comp. Biochem. Physiol.* **51B,** 489–497. *430*

3557. de Vlaming, V. L. and Sage, M. (1972). Diurnal variation in fattening response to prolactin treatment in two cyprinodontid fishes, *Cyprinodon variegatus* and *Fundulus similis. Contrib. Mar. Sci.* **16,** 59–63. *383*

*3558. de Vlaming, V. L. and Sage, M. (1973). Osmoregulation in the euryhaline elasmobranch, *Dasyatis sabina. Comp. Biochem. Physiol.* **45A,** 31–44. *310*

*3559. de Vlaming, V. L., Sage, M. and Beitz, B. (1975). Pituitary, adrenal and thyroid influences on osmoregulation in the euryhaline elasmobranch, *Dasyatis sabina. Comp. Biochem. Physiol.* **52A,** 505–513.

3560. de Vlaming, V. L., Sage, M. and Tiegs, R. (1975). A diurnal rhythm of pituitary prolactin activity with diurnal effects of mammalian and teleostean prolactin on total body lipid deposition and liver lipid metabolism in teleost fishes. *J. Fish Biol.* **7,** 717–726. *447*

*3561. Vlasov, V. A. (1975). The amino acid composition of the muscles and body of this present summer's young carp, reared on different rations. *Doklady T S KH A,* **205,** 175–179.

*3562. Vorhauer, H. (1938). Research on blood sugar in carp (Cyprinidae). *Biochem. Z.* **296,** 90–98. From Chavin and Young (1970).

*3563. Vorob'yev, V. I. and Zaytsev, V. F. (1975). Dynamics of some trace elements in organs and tissues of the rudd. *Hydrobiol. J.* **11,** 57–60.

*3564. Vorob'yev, V. I., Zaytsev, V. F., Karpenko, V. L., Samilkin, N. S. and Shkodin, N. V. (1972). Time changes in concentrations of trace elements in the organs and tissues of some commercial fishes of the Volga delta. *Hydrobiol. J.* **8,** 41–45.

*3565. Vukadinović, V., Rakić, Lj. and Mićić, D. (1971). Free amino acids in brain regions of electric fish (*Torpedo marmorata*). *Jugoslav Physiol. Pharmacol.* **7,** 223–228.

*3566. van Vuren, J. H. J. and Hattingh, J. (1976). The seasonal haematology of the small-mouth yellowfish (*Barbus holubi*). *Zool. Afr.* **11,** 81–86. *44*

*3567. Vyncke, W. (1970). Influence of biological and environmental factors on nitrogenous extractives of the spurdog *Squalus acanthias*. *Mar. Biol.* **6,** 248–255. *44, 57*

*3568. Wada, S., Koizumi, C. and Nonaka, J. (1976). Lipids analysis of barracuda and longnose lancetfish. *Bull. Jap. Soc. scient. Fish.* **42,** 1145–1151.

3569. Wagner, H. H. (1974). Seawater adaptation independent of photoperiod in steelhead trout (*Salmo gairdneri*). *Can. J. Zool.* **52,** 805–812. *292*

*3570. Walker, R. L. and Fromm, P. O. (1976). Metabolism of iron by normal and iron deficient rainbow trout. *Comp. Biochem. Physiol.* **55A,** 311–318.

3571. Wallace, J. C. (1973). Observations on the relationship between the food consumption and metabolic rate of *Blennius pholis* L. *Comp. Biochem. Physiol.* **45A,** 293–306. *137, 162, 326*

*3572. Walton, M. J. and Cowey, C. B. (1977). Aspects of ammoniogenesis in rainbow trout, *Salmo gairdneri*. *Comp. Biochem. Physiol.* **57B,** 143–149. *159*

*3573. Ward, J. V. (1973). Molybdenum concentrations in tissues of rainbow trout (*Salmo gairdneri*) and kokanee salmon (*Oncorhynchus nerka*) from waters differing widely in molybdenum content. *J. Fish. Res. Bd Can.* **30,** 841–842.

3574. Ward, The Reverend S. (1776). The Natural History of Fishes, Volume I. London. Printed for F. Newbery.

3575. Wardle, C. S. (1971). New observations on the lymph system of the plaice *Pleuronectes platessa* and other teleosts. *J. mar. biol. Ass. U.K.* **51,** 977–990. *2*

*3576. Wardle, C. S. (1972a). The changes in blood glucose in *Pleuronectes platessa* following capture from the wild: a stress reaction. *J. mar. biol. Ass. U.K.* **52,** 635–651. *140, 231, 232*

3577. Wardle, C. S. (1972b). Some aspects of the physiology of the stress reaction of the marine teleost following capture from the wild. Ph.D. Thesis, University of Aberdeen. *114, 237*

3578. Wardle, C. S. (1975). Limit of fish swimming speed. *Nature, Lond.* **255,** 725–727. *87*

3579. Wardle, C. S. (1977). Effects of size on the swimming speeds of fish. *In* "Scale Effects in Animal Locomotion" (Ed. Pedley, T. J.), Chapter 19, pp. 299–313. Academic Press, London and New York. *87*

3580. Wardle, C. S. and Kanwisher, J. W. (1974). The significance of heart rate in free swimming cod, *Gadus morhua*: some observations with ultra-sonic tags. *Mar. Behav. Physiol.* **2,** 311–324. *242*

*3581. Watanabe, E. and Ando, K. (1972). Changes in cholesterol in developing rainbow trout eggs. *Bull. Jap. Soc. scient. Fish.* **38,** 711–715. *13*

3582. Watanabe, T., Takashima, F., Ogino, C. and Hibiya, T. (1970). Effects of α-tocopherol deficiency on carp. *Bull. Jap. Soc. scient. Fish.* **36,** 623–630. *146*

3583. Watanabe, T., Takeuchi, T., Matsui, M., Ogino, C. and Kawabata, T. (1977). Effect of α-tocopherol deficiency on carp—VII. The relationship between dietary levels of linoleate and α-tocopherol requirement. *Bull. Jap. Soc. scient. Fish.* **43,** 935–946. *465*

*3584. Watanabe, Y. and Miyamoto, H. (1973). Biochemical study of labyrinthine fluids (of the fish). *Med. J. Osaka Univ.* **23,** 273–282. *223, 224*

3585. Waterman, J. J. (1964). Measures, stowage rates and yields of fishery products. Ministry of Agriculture, Fisheries and Food, Torry Research Station, Aberdeen. Advisory note **17,** 12 pp. *278*

3586. Waterman, R. E. (1969). Development of the lateral musculature in the teleost, *Brachydanio rerio:* a fine structural study. *Am. J. Anat.* **125,** 457–494. *73, 74, 77*

*3587. Watts, D. C. and Watts, R. L. (1966). Carbamoyl phosphate synthetase in the elasmobranchii: osmoregulatory function and evolutionary implications. *Comp. Biochem. Physiol.* **17,** 785–798.

*3588. Watts, E. G., Copp, D. H. and Deftos, L. J. (1975). Changes in plasma calcitonin and calcium during the migration of salmon. *Endocrinology,* **96,** 214–218.

3589. Watts, R. L. and Watts, D. C. (1974). Nitrogen metabolism in fishes. *In* "Chemical Zoology, **8.** Deuterostomians, Cyclostomes and Fishes" (Eds Florkin, M. and Scheer, B. T.), Chapter 10, pp. 369–446. Academic Press, London and New York. *5, 116, 155, 156, 310, 620*

3590. Weatherley, A. H. (1970). Effects of superabundant oxygen on thermal tolerance of goldfish. *Biol. Bull. mar. biol. Lab., Woods Hole,* **139,** 229–238. *323*

3591. Weatherley, A. H. (1973). Effects of constant illumination and hyperoxia on thermal tolerance of goldfish. *Comp. Biochem. Physiol.* **45A,** 891–894. *323*

*3592. Webb, J. T. and Brown, G. W. (1976). Some properties and occurrence of glutamine synthetase in fish. *Comp. Biochem. Physiol.* **54B,** 171–175.

3593. Webb, P. W. (1971). The swimming energetics of trout. 1. Thrust and power output at cruising speeds. *J. exp. Biol.* **55,** 489–520. *80, 256*

*3594. Weber, R. E., Bol, J. F., Johansen, K. and Wood, S. C. (1973). Physicochemical properties of the haemoglobins of the coelacanth *Latimeria chalumnae.* *Arch. Biochem. Biophys.* **154,** 96–105.

3595. Weber, R. E., Johansen, K., Lykkeboe, G. and Maloiy, G. M. O. (1977). Oxygen-binding properties of haemoglobins from aestivating and active African lungfish. *J. exp. Zool.* **199,** 85–96. *623*

3596.   Weber, R. E., Lykkeboe, G. and Johansen, K. (1975). Biochemical aspects
        of the adaptation of haemoglobin-oxygen affinity of eels to hypoxia. *Life Sci.*
        17, 1345–1349. *274*

*3597. Weber, R. E., Lykkeboe, G. and Johansen, K. (1976). Physiological properties
        of eel haemoglobin: hypoxic acclimation, phosphate effects and multiplicity.
        J. exp. Biol. **64**, 75–88. *274*

*3598. Weber, R. E. and de Wilde, J. A. M. (1975). Oxygenation properties of
        haemoglobins from the flatfish plaice (*Pleuronectes platessa*) and flounder
        (*Platichthys flesus*). *J. comp. Physiol.* **101**, 99–110. *274*

3599.   Weber, R. E., Wood, S. C. and Lomholt, J. P. (1976). Temperature acclima-
        tion and oxygen-binding properties of blood and multiple haemoglobins of
        rainbow trout. *J. exp. Biol.* **65**, 333–345. *327*

*3600. Wedemeyer, G. (1969). Stress-induced ascorbic acid depletion and cortisol
        production in two salmonid fishes. *Comp. Biochem. Physiol.* **29**, 1247–1251.
        236, 237

*3601. Wedemeyer, G. (1972). Some physiological consequences of handling stress
        in the juvenile coho salmon (*Oncorhynchus kisutch*) and steelhead trout (*Salmo
        gairdneri*). *J. Fish. Res. Bd Can.* **29**, 1780–1783. *232, 240, 291*

3602.   Wedemeyer, G. (1973). Some physiological aspects of sublethal heat stress
        in the juvenile steelhead trout (*Salmo gairdneri*) and coho salmon (*Oncorhynchus
        kisutch*). *J. Fish. Res. Bd Can.* **30**, 831–834. *232, 241*

*3603. Wedemeyer, G. and Chatterton, K. (1970). Some blood chemistry values
        for the rainbow trout (*Salmo gairdneri*). *J. Fish. Res. Bd Can.* **27**, 1162–1164.

*3604. Wedemeyer, G. and Chatterton, K. (1971). Some blood chemistry values for
        the juvenile coho salmon (*Oncorhynchus kisutch*). *J. Fish. Res. Bd Can.* **28**, 606–
        608.

3605.   Wedemeyer, G. A., Meyer, F. P. and Smith, L. (1976). "Diseases of Fishes.
        Book 5: Environmental Stress and Fish Diseases" (Series edited by Snieszko,
        S. F. and Axelrod, H. R.). TFH Publications, Neptune, New Jersey. *272, 456*

*3606. Wedemeyer, G. A. and Nelson, N. C. (1975). Statistical methods for estimating
        normal blood chemistry ranges and variance in rainbow trout (*Salmo gairdneri*),
        Shasta strain. *J. Fish. Res. Bd Can.* **32**, 551–554.

3607.   Weihs, D. (1974). Energetic advantages of burst swimming of fish. *J. theor.
        Biol.* **48**, 215–229. *100*

*3608. Weisbart, M. and Idler, D. R. (1970). Re-examination of the presence of
        corticosteroids in two cyclostomes, the atlantic hagfish (*Myxine glutinosa* L.)
        and the sea lamprey (*Petromyzon marinus* L.). *J. Endocr.* **46**, 29–43.

*3609. Weisbart, M. and Idler, D. R. (1971). Identification and quantification of corticosteroids in the atlantic halibut, *Hippoglossus hippoglossus* L. *Gen. comp Endocrinol.* **17,** 416–423.

*3610. Weitzel, G., Strecker, F.-J., Roester, U., Fretzdorff, A.-M. and Buddecke, E. (1953). Zinc and insulin in the pancreas of bony fishes. *Hoppe-Seyler's Z. physiol. Chem.* **295,** 83–106.

*3611. Wekell, M. M. B. and Brown, G. W. (1973). Ornithine aminotransferase of fishes. *Comp. Biochem. Physiol.* **46B,** 779–795. *221*

 3612. Wendelaar Bonga, S. E., Greven, J. A. A. and Veenhuis, M. (1976). The relationship between the ionic composition of the environment and the secretory activity of the endocrine cell types of Stannius corpuscles in the teleost *Gasterosteus aculeatus. Cell Tiss. Res.* **175,** 297–312. *305*

*3613. Wendt, C. (1965). Liver and muscle glycogen and blood lactate in hatchery-reared *Salmo salar* L. following exercise in winter and summer. *Rep. Inst. Freshwat. Res. Drottningholm,* **46,** 167–184. *114*

*3614. Wendt, C. and Ericson, C. (1972). Blood glucose in hatchery-reared atlantic salmon (*Salmo salar* L.) following exercise. *Rep. Inst. Freshwat. Res. Drottningholm,* **52,** 204–215. *115*

*3615. Wendt, C. A. G. and Saunders, R. L. (1973). Changes in carbohydrate metabolism in young atlantic salmon in response to various forms of stress. *In* "International Atlantic Salmon Symposium 1972" (Eds Smith, M. W. and Carter, W. M.). International Atlantic Salmon Foundation, Spec. Publ. Ser., vol. 4, pp. 55–82. New York and St. Andrews, New Brunswick. *117, 118*

*3616. Wessels, J. P. H. and Spark, A. A. (1973). The fatty acid composition of the lipids from two species of hake. *J. Sci. Fd Agric.* **24,** 1359–1370. *209, 210*

*3617. Westöö, G. and Rydälv, M. (1969). Mercury and methylmercury in fish and crabs. *Vår Föda,* 19–111 (no volume number given).

 3617a. Wheeler, A. (1978). *Ictalurus melas* (Rafinesque, 1820) and *I. nebulosus* (Lesueur, 1819): the North American catfishes in Europe. *J. Fish Biol.* **12,** 435–439.

*3618. White, B. A. and Henderson, N. E. (1977). Annual variations in the circulating levels of thyroid hormones in the brook trout, *Salvelinus fontinalis*, as measured by radioimmunoassay. *Can. J. Zool.* **55,** 475–481. *385*

*3619 White, F. D. (1928). Reducing substances in the blood of the dogfish, *Squalus sucklii* and certain other fishes. *J. biol. Chem.* **77,** 655–669. From Chavin and Young (1970).

 3620. Whitelaw, D. A. (1973). Sodium uptake and ammonium excretion in the gill of the goldfish *C. auratus. S. Afr. J. Sci.* **69,** 217–219. *293*

3621. Whitt, G. S., Miller, E. T. and Shaklee, J. B. (1973). Developmental and biochemical genetics of lactate dehydrogenase isozymes in fishes. *In* "Genetics and Mutagenesis of Fish" (Ed. Schröder, J. H.), pp. 243–276. Springer-Verlag, Berlin. *432*

*3622. Wiggs, A. J. (1974). Seasonal changes in the thyroid proteinase of a teleost fish, the burbot, *Lota lota* L. *Can. J. Zool.* **52**, 1071–1078. *385*

3623. Wiles, M. (1969). Fibrous and cystic lesions in the ovaries of aged Atlantic cod (*Gadus morhua*): a preliminary report. *J. Fish. Res. Bd Can.* **26**, 3242–3246. *60, 61*

3624. Wilkins, N. P. (1972). Biochemical genetics of the Atlantic salmon *Salmo salar* L. 1. A review of recent studies. *J. Fish Biol.* **4**, 487–504. *254*

3625. Williams, P. E. and Goldspink, G. (1971). Muscle fibre growth. *J. Cell Sci.* **9**, 751–767. *31*

*3626. Williams, P. M. and Weiss, H. V. (1973). Mercury in the marine environment: concentration in sea water and in a pelagic food chain. *J. Fish. Res. Bd Can.* **30**, 293–295.

*3627. Wills, R. B. H. and Hopkirk, G. (1976). Distribution and fatty acid composition of lipids of eels (*Anguilla australis*). *Comp. Biochem. Physiol.* **53B**, 525–527. *68*

3628. Wilson, D. C. and Milleman, R. E. (1969). Relationship of female age and size to embryo number and size in the shiner perch, *Cymatogaster aggregata*. *J. Fish. Res. Bd Can.* **26**, 2339–2344. *29*

3629. Wilson, F. R. (1973). Enzyme changes of the goldfish (*Carassius auratus* L.) in response to temperature acclimation: I. An immunological approach. II. Isozymes. Ph.D. Thesis, University of Illinois. University Microfilm number 74–5737. *328, 335*

*3630. Wilson, F. R., Somero, G. and Prosser, C. L. (1974). Temperature-metabolism relations of two species of *Sebastes* from different thermal environments. *Comp. Biochem. Physiol.* **47B**, 485–491. *326, 336*

3631. Wilson, F. R., Whitt, G. S. and Prosser, C. L. (1973). Lactate dehydrogenase and malate dehydrogenase isozyme patterns in tissues of temperature-acclimated goldfish (*Carassius auratus* L.). *Comp. Biochem. Physiol.* **46B**, 105–116. *88, 335*

3632. Wilson, J. F. and Dodd, J. M. (1973). The role of melanophore-stimulating hormone in melanogenesis in the dogfish, *Scyliorhinus canicula* L. *J. Endocr.* **58**, 685–686. *246*

*3633. Wilson, R. P. (1973a). Nitrogen metabolism in channel catfish, *Ictalurus punctatus*—I. Tissue distribution of aspartate and alanine amino transferases and glutamic dehydrogenase. *Comp. Biochem. Physiol.* **46B**, 617–624. *257*

*3634. Wilson, R. P. (1973b). Nitrogen metabolism in channel catfish, *Ictalurus punctatus*—II. Evidence for an apparent incomplete ornithine-urea cycle. *Comp. Biochem. Physiol.* **46B,** 625–634.

3635. Wilson, R. P., Anderson, R. O. and Bloomfield, R. A. (1969). Ammonia toxicity in selected fishes. *Comp. Biochem. Physiol.* **28,** 107–118. *154*

*3636. Wilson, R. P. and Fowlkes, P. L. (1976). Activity of glutamine synthetase in channel catfish tissues determined by an improved tissue assay method. *Comp. Biochem. Physiol.* **54B,** 365–368.

3637. Wilson, R. P. and Poe, W. E. (1974). Nitrogen metabolism in channel catfish, *Ictalurus punctatus*—III. Relative pool sizes of free amino acids and related compounds in various tissues of the catfish. *Comp. Biochem. Physiol.* **48B,** 545–556.

*3638. Windom, H., Stickney, R., Smith, R., White, D. and Taylor, F. (1973). Arsenic, cadmium, copper, mercury, and zinc in some species of north Atlantic finfish. *J. Fish. Res. Bd Can.* **30,** 275–279.

*3639. Wingfield, J. C. and Grimm, A. S. (1977). Seasonal changes in plasma cortisol, testosterone and oestradiol-17βin the plaice, *Pleuronectes platessa* L. *Gen. comp. Endocrinol.* **31,** 1–11. *220*

3640. Winters, G. H. (1971). Fecundity of the left and right ovaries of Grand Bank capelin (*Mallotus villosus*). *J. Fish. Res. Bd Can.* **28,** 1029–1033. *67*

3641. Wittenberg, B. A., Wittenberg, J. B. and Caldwell, P. R. B. (1975). Role of myoglobin in the oxygen supply to red skeletal muscle. *J. biol. Chem.* **250,** 9038–9043. *106*

3642. Wittenberger, C. (1968b: 1968a is in Volume 1). Biology of the Black Sea scad (*Trachurus mediterraneus ponticus*). XV. Studies on the effort metabolism in *Trachurus* and *Gobius*. *Mar. Biol.* **2,** 1–4. *90*

*3643. Wittenberger, C. (1972). The glycogen turnover rate in mackerel muscles. *Mar. Biol.* **16,** 279–280. *89, 91*

*3644. Wittenberger, C. and Coprean, D. (1977). Some effects of denervation upon white and red muscles in carp. *Comp. Biochem. Physiol.* **56A,** 307–312.

*3645. Wittenberger, C., Coprean, D. and Morar, L. (1975). Studies on the carbohydrate metabolism of the lateral muscles in carp (influence of phloridzin, insulin and adrenaline). *J. comp. Physiol.* **101,** 161–172. *72–74, 90*

*3646. Wittenberger, C., Coro, A., Suárez, G. and Portilla, N. (1969). Composition and bioelectrical activity of the lateral muscles in *Harengula humeralis*. *Mar. Biol.* **3,** 24–27. *73, 74, 92*

3647. Wittenberger, C. and Deaciuc, I. V. (1970). Studies on the metabolism of glucose and acetate in fish muscle. *Regional Congr. IUPS, Brasov, Romania, Abstr.* 299 only. *91*

*3648. Wittenberger, C. and Giurgea, R. (1973). Transaminase activities in muscles and liver of the carp. *Rev. Roum. Biol. (Zool.)* **18**, 441–444. *187, 188*

*3649. Wobeser, G., Nielsen, N. O. and Dunlop, R. H. (1970). Mercury concentrations in tissues of fish from the Saskatchewan river. *J. Fish. Res. Bd Can.* **27**, 830–834.

3650. Wodtke, E. (1974). Effects of acclimation temperature on the oxidative metabolism of the eel (*Anguilla anguilla*). I. Liver and red muscle. Changes in the mitochondrial content and in the oxidative capacity of isolated coupled mitochondria. *J. comp. Physiol.* **91**, 309–332. *79, 91, 105, 330*

3651. Wohlschlag, D. E. (1964). Respiratory metabolism and ecological characteristics of some fishes in McMurdo Sound, Antarctica. *In* "Biology of the Antarctic Seas" (Ed. Lee, M. O.), pp. 33–62. American Geophysical Union, National Academy of Science, National Research Council Publication no. 1190. Washington DC. *46, 264, 326, 675*

*3652. Wold, J. K. and Selset, R. (1977). Glycoproteins in the skin mucus of the char (*Salmo alpinus* L.). *Comp. Biochem. Physiol.* **56B**, 215–218.

3653. Wolfert, D. R. (1969). Maturity and fecundity of walleyes from the eastern and western basins of Lake Erie. *J. Fish. Res. Bd Can.* **26**, 1877–1888. *36*

*3654. Wong, T. M. and Chan, D. K. O. (1977). Physiological adjustments to dilution of the external medium in the lip-shark *Hemiscyllium plagiosum* (Bennett). II. Branchial, renal and rectal gland function. *J. exp. Zool.* **200**, 85–96.

3655. Wood, S. C. and Johansen, K. (1973). Blood oxygen transport and acid-base balance in eels during hypoxia. *Am. J. Physiol.* **225**, 849–851. *2, 273*

*3656. Wood, S. C., Johansen, K. and Weber, R. E. (1972). Haemoglobin of the coelacanth. *Nature, Lond.* **239**, 283–285.

*3657. Wood, S. C., Johansen, K. and Weber, R. E. (1975). Effects of ambient Po_2 on haemoglobin-oxygen affinity and red cell ATP concentrations in a benthic fish, *Pleuronectes platessa*. *Resp. Physiol.* **25**, 259–267. *274*

3658. Woodhead, A. D. (1974a). Ageing changes in the Siamese fighting fish, *Betta splendens*—I. The testis. *Exp. Gerontol.* **9**, 75–81. *58*

3659. Woodhead, A. D. (1974b). Ageing changes in the Siamese fighting fish, *Betta splendens*—II. The ovary. *Exp. Gerontol.* **9**, 131–139. *58, 59*

3660. Woodhead, A. D. (1975). Endocrine physiology of fish migration. *Oceanogr. mar. Biol. Ann. Rev.* **13**, 287–382. *64, 116*

3661. Woodhead, P. M. J. (1969). Influence of oestradiol 3-benzoate upon the plasma content of calcium and vitamin A aldehyde in the cod, *Gadus morhua*. *J. mar. biol. Ass. U.K.* **49**, 939–944. *40, 44*

*3662. Woodruff, G. N., Oniwinde, A. B. and Kerkut G. A. (1969) Histamine in tissues of the snail, crab, goldfish, frog and mouse. *Comp. Biochem. Physiol.* **31,** 599–603.

3663. Worthington, R. E. and Lovell, R. T. (1973). Fatty acids of channel catfish (*Ictalurus punctatus*): variance components related to diet, replications within diets, and variability among fish. *J. Fish. Res. Bd Can.* **30,** 1604–1608. *142*

*3664. Wright, P. A. (1958). Glucagon and blood glucose in *Lophius piscatorius.* *Biol. Bull. mar. biol. Lab., Woods Hole,* **115,** 371 only.

*3665. Yamada, K. and Amano, K. (1965). Studies on the biological formation of formaldehyde and dimethylamine in fish and shellfish—VI. A note on the content of formaldehyde and dimethylamine in two species of gadoid fishes and two species of marine crabs. *Bull. Tokai reg. Fish. Res. Lab.* **41,** 89–96.

*3666. Yamada, M. (1972). New observations on the lipids of aquatic origin. *Mem. Fac. Fish. Hokkaido Univ.* **19,** 35–136.

*3667. Yamada, M. and Hayashi, K. (1975). Fatty acid composition of lipids from 22 species of fish and mollusk. *Bull. Jap. Soc. scient. Fish.* **41,** 1143–1152. *415*

*3668. Yamagata, M., Horimoto, K. and Nagaoka, C. (1969). Assessment of green tuna: determining trimethylamine oxide and its distribution in tuna muscles. *J. Food Sci.* **34,** 156–159. *68, 75, 106*

*3669. Yamaguchi, K. (1971). Biliproteins of marine animals. *Bull. Jap. Soc. scient. Fish.* **37,** 339–354.

3670. Yamaguchi, K., Hashimoto, K. and Matsuura, F. (1968). Studies on a blue-green serum pigment of eel—IV. Seasonal variation of concentration of pigment in serum. *Bull. Jap. Soc. scient. Fish.* **34,** 826–835. *144*

*3671. Yamaguchi, K., Hashimoto, K. and Matsuura, F. (1970). Studies on a blue-green serum pigment of eel—V. Lipid moiety. *Bull. Jap. Soc. scient. Fish.* **36,** 955–962.

*3672. Yamaguchi, K., Lavéty, J. and Love, R. M. (1976). The connective tissues of fish—VIII. Comparative studies on hake, cod and catfish collagens. *J. Food Technol.* **11,** 389–399. *12, 112*

*3673. Yamakawa, T., Kinumaki, T., Sugii, K. and Higashi, H. (1965). A method for the chemical determination of vitamin D in fish. *Bull. Tokai reg. Fish. Res. Lab.* **41,** 33–70. *34*

*3674. Yamamoto, M. and Massey, K. L. (1969). Cyclic 3',5'-nucleotide phosphodiesterase of fish (*Salmo gairdnerii*) brain. *Comp. Biochem. Physiol.* **30,** 941–954.

3675. Yamamoto, T. (1972). Electrical and mechanical properties of the red and white muscles in the silver carp. *J. exp. Biol.* **57,** 551–567. *89*

*3676. Yamamoto, T. S. (1974). DNA and RNA content of the dog salmon egg during early embryonic development. *J. Fac. Sci. Hokkaido Univ. Ser. VI, Zool.* **19,** 489–502.

*3677. Yamamoto, Y., Ishii, T., Sato, M. and Ikeda, S. (1977). Effect of dietary ascorbic acid on the accumulation of copper in carp. *Bull. Jap. Soc. scient. Fish.* **43,** 989–993.

*3678. Yamamoto, Y., Sato, M. and Ikeda, S. (1977). Biochemical studies on L-ascorbic acid in aquatic animals—IX. Existence of dehydroascorbatase in carp hepatopancreas. *Bull. Jap. Soc. scient. Fish.* **43,** 449–453.

3678a. Yamamoto, Y., Sato, M. and Ikeda, S. (1978). Existence of L-gulonolactone oxidase in some teleosts. *Bull. Jap. Soc. scient. Fish.* **44,** 775–779. *425*

3679. Yamashita, H. (1968a). Electrophoretic patterns of serum proteins in the blood of four species of puff-fish, genus *Fugu*, and their F_1 hybrids. *Mar. Biol.* **1,** 277–281. *50*

3680. Yamashita, H. (1968b). Haematological study of a species of rockfish, *Sebastiscus marmoratus*—IV. Change of the amount of blood elements and the electrophoretic pattern of serum protein under the influence of stress. *Bull. Jap. Soc. scient. Fish.* **34,** 1066–1071. *49, 57, 239*

3681. Yamashita, H. (1969). Haematological study of a species of rockfish, *Sebastiscus marmoratus*—V. Seasonal changes of blood elements, electrophoretic pattern of serum proteins and their percentage fractions. *Bull. Jap. Soc. scient. Fish.* **35,** 379–385. *50*

3682. Yamashita, H. (1970a). Blood characteristics of marine fish in relation to the change of osmotic pressure of sea water—I. Changes of osmotic pressure of serum and the electrophoretic pattern of the serum protein of rockfish. *Bull. Jap. Soc. scient. Fish.* **36,** 439–449. *286*

3683. Yamashita, H. (1970b). Blood characteristics of marine fish in relation to the change of osmotic pressure of sea water—II. Change of osmotic pressure of serum and the electrophoretic pattern of the serum protein of young yellowtail. *Bull. Jap. Soc. scient. Fish.* **36,** 450–454. *286, 312*

*3684. Yamauchi, T., Stegeman, J. J. and Goldberg, E. (1975). The effects of starvation and temperature acclimation on pentose phosphate pathway dehydrogenases in brook trout liver. *Archs Biochem. Biophys.* **167,** 13–20. *153, 221, 257, 328, 329, 335*

*3685. Yamazoe, Y. (1970). On the free sugars in the muscle of mutugoro (*Boleophthalmus pectinirostris*) and warasubo (*Odontamblyops rubicundus*). *J. Jap. Soc. Fd Nutr. (Eiyo to Shokuryo)*, **23,** 603–605.

*3686. Yanni, M. (1967). Effect of insulin on carbohydrate, water and fat contents of the tissues of *Clarias lazera. Proc. zool. Soc. UAR*, **2,** 129–140.

3687. Yasumoto, T., Nakajima, I., Chungue, E. and Bagnis, R. (1977). Toxins in the gut contents of parrotfish. *Bull. Jap. Soc. scient. Fish.* **43**, 69–74. *641*

3688. Yermolaeva, L. P. (1977). The role of enzymes of pyruvate and citrate metabolism in control of gluconeogenesis in oocytes and embryos of the loach, *Misgurnus fossilis* L. *Wilhelm Roux's Arch. Dev. Biol.* **181**, 321–331.

*3689. Yermolaeva, L. P. and Milman, L. S. (1974). Dependence between the ratio NAD+/NAD = H and the adenylic system in the cytoplasm of cells the loach oocytes and embryos. *Ontogenez.* **5**, 505–507. *20*

*3690. Yin-Yin, Aung-Tun-Myint and Khin-Nwe-Aung (1973). Nutritive values of some Burmese sea-fish. *Union Burma J. Life Sci.* **6**, 93–96.

3690a. Yoneda, T. (1977). On amino acids in the developing eggs of chum salmon, *Oncorhynchus keta. Bull. Fac. Fish. Hokkaido Univ.* **28**, 29–30.

*3691. Yoneda, T. and Ishihara, Y. (1975). On serum free amino acids of chum salmon, *Oncorhynchus keta*, changes of amino acid contents of the salmon sera before and after fresh water migration for spawning. *Bull. Fac. Fish. Hokkaido Univ.* **26**, 192–200.

3692. Yoshida, Y. and Sera, H. (1970). On chitinolytic activities in the digestive tracts of several species of fishes and the mastication and digestion of foods by them. *Bull. Jap. Soc. scient. Fish.* **36**, 751–754. *152*

3693. Yoshimizu, M., Kimura, T. and Sakai, M. (1976a). Studies on the intestinal microflora of salmonids—I. The intestinal microflora of fish reared in fresh water and sea water. *Bull. Jap. Soc. scient. Fish.* **42**, 91–99. *318*

3694. Yoshimizu, M., Kimura, T. and Sakai, M. (1976b). Studies on the intestinal microflora of salmonids—II. Effects of artificial transplanting from fresh water into sea water on the intestinal microflora of feeding and non-feeding fish. *Bull. Jap. Soc. scient. Fish.* **42**, 863–873. *172*

*3695. Yoshinaka, R., Sato, M. and Ikeda, S. (1973). Studies on collagenase of fish—I. Existence of collagenolytic enzyme in pyloric caeca of *Seriola quinqueradiata. Bull. Jap. Soc. scient. Fish.* **39**, 275–281.

*3696. Young, J. E. and Chavin, W. (1963). Serum glucose levels and pancreatic islet cytology in the normal and alloxan diabetic goldfish, *Carassius auratus* L. *Am. Zool.* **3**, 510 only.

3697. Young, J. Z. (1935). The photoreceptors of lampreys. II. The functions of the pineal complex. *J. exp. Biol.* **12**, 254–270. *264*

3698. Youson, J. H. (1975). Absorption and transport of exogenous protein in the archinephric duct of the opisthonephric kidney of the sea lamprey, *Petromyzon marinus* L. *Comp. Biochem. Physiol.* **52A**, 639–643. *148*

*3699. Yu, R. K. (1972). Isolation of gangliosides from the electric organ of *Electrophorus electricus*. *J. Neurochem.* **19**, 2467–2469.

3700. Yurkowski, M. and Tabachek, J.-A. L. (1974). Identification, analysis and removal of geosmin from muddy-flavoured trout. *J. Fish. Res. Bd Can.* **31**, 1851–1858. *150*

3701. Yurovitskii (sometimes spelt Yurowitzky), Yu. G. and Mil'man, L. S.) (1969a). Enzymes of hexose monophosphate metabolism in the developing embryo of the loach, *Misgurnus fossilis. Fermenty Evol. Zhivotn.* 136–139 (no volume number given). From *Chem. Abstr.* **74**, 29358m (1971).

*3702. Yurovitskii, Yu. G. and Mil'man, L. S. (1969b). Peculiarities of the triose metabolism in the developing loach embryo. *Dokl. (Proc.) Acad. Sci. USSR Biological Sciences Sections,* **184**, 15–18.

*3703. Yurowitzky (= Yurovitskii), Yu. G. and Milman, L. S. (1971). Coordinative changes in the activities of enzymes in carbohydrate metabolism during oogenesis in *Mysgurnus (Misgurnus) fossilis. FEBS Lett.* **14**, 105–106. *18, 19*

*3704. Yurowitzky, Yu. G. and Milman, L. S. (1972). Changes in enzyme activity of glycogen and hexose metabolism during oocyte maturation in a teleost, *Misgurnus fossilis* L. *Wilhelm Roux Arch. EntwMech. Org.* **171**, 48–54. *18*

*3705. Yurowitzky, Yu. G. and Milman, L. S. (1973a). Interconversion of active and inactive forms of phosphorylase and glycogen synthetase in oocytes and embryos of the loach (*Misgurnus fossilis*). *Wilhelm Roux Arch. EntwMech. Org.* **173**, 1–8.

*3706. Yurowitzky, Yu. G. and Milman, L. S. (1973b). Factors responsible for glycogenolysis acceleration in early embryogenesis of teleosts. *Wilhelm Roux Arch. EntwMech. Org.* **173**, 9–21. *18*

*3707. Yurovitskii, Yu. G. and Mil'man, L. S. (1973c). Gluconeogenesis in the oocytes of bony fishes. *Sov. J. dev. Biol.* **4**, 182–185.

*3708. Yurowitzky, Yu. G. and Milman, L. S. (1975a). Enzymes of glycogen metabolism in developing embryos of a teleost. *Wilhelm Roux Arch. Entw.Mech. Org.* **177**, 81–88. *19*

*3709. Yurowitskii, Yu. G. and Mil'man, L. S. (1975b). Changes in activity of enzymes of glycogen metabolism in loach oocytes and embryos. *Biochemistry, N.Y.* **40**, 821–825. *20*

*3710. Zachariassen, K. E. (1972). Concentrations of free amino acids and inorganic ions in red blood cells of flounder (*Pleuronectes flesus* L.) during adaptation to fresh water. *Acta physiol. scand.* **84**, 31A–32A. *313*

*3711. Zadunaisky, J. A. (1972). The electrolyte content, osmolarity and site of secretion of the aqueous humour in two teleost fishes (*Carassius auratus* and *Diplodus sargus*). *Exp. Eye Res.* **14,** 99–110. *285*

3712. Zakhar'in, Y. (1969). Influence of fasting on enzyme activity of the pentose phosphate pathway of liver and brain in rats. *Trudy gos. nauchno-issled. Inst. Psikhiat.* **57,** 574–582. *221*

3713. Zaugg, W. S. and McLain, L. R. (1970). Adenosinetriphosphatase activity in gills of salmonids: seasonal variations and salt water influence in coho salmon, *Oncorhynchus kisutch. Comp. Biochem. Physiol.* **35,** 587–596. *291, 292*

*3714. Zaugg, W. S. and McLain, L. R. (1972). Changes in gill adenosinetriphosphatase activity associated with parr-smolt transformation in steelhead trout, coho, and spring chinook salmon. *J. Fish. Res. Bd Can.* **29,** 167–171. *24, 292*

3715. Zaugg, W. S. and McLain, L. R. (1976). Influence of water temperature on gill sodium, potassium-stimulated ATPase activity in juvenile coho salmon (*Oncorhynchus kisutch*). *Comp. Biochem. Physiol.* **54A,** 419–421. *21*

*3716. Zaugg, W. S. and Wagner, H. H. (1973). Gill ATPase activity related to parr-smolt transformation and migration in steelhead trout (*Salmo gairdneri*): influence of photoperiod and temperature. *Comp. Biochem. Physiol.* **45B,** 955–965. *24, 292*

*3717. Zeitoun, I. H., Hughes, L. D. and Ullrey, D. E. (1977). Effect of shock exposures of chlorine on the plasma electrolyte concentrations of adult rainbow trout (*Salmo gairdneri*). *J. Fish. Res. Bd Can.* **34,** 1034–1039.

*3718. Zeitoun, I. H., Ullrey, D. E., Bergen, W. G. and Magee, W. T. (1976). Mineral metabolism during the ontogenesis of rainbow trout (*Salmo gairdneri*). *J. Fish. Res. Bd Can.* **33,** 2587–2591. *148*

*3719. Zeitoun, I. H., Ullrey, D. E., Bergen, W. G. and Magee, W. T. (1977). DNA, RNA, protein, and free amino acids during ontogenesis of rainbow trout (*Salmo gairdneri*). *J. Fish Res. Bd Can.* **34,** 83–88.

3720. Zeitoun, I. H., Ullrey, D. E. and Tack, P. I. (1974). Effects of water salinity and dietary protein levels on total serum protein and haematocrit of rainbow trout (*Salmo gairdnerii*) fingerlings. *J. Fish. Res. Bd Can.* **31,** 1133–1134. *136*

*3721. Zhivkov, V. (1971). Concentrations and synthesis of the acid-soluble nucleotides in the liver of various species of vertebrates. *Comp. Biochem. Physiol.* **39B,** 701–708.

*3722. Zhivkov, V., Tosheva, R. and Shivkova, Y. (1975). Concentration of uridine diphosphate sugars in various tissues of vertebrates. *Comp. Biochem. Physiol.* **51B,** 421–424.

3723. Zhukinskii, V. N. and Gosh, R. I. (1973). Viability of embryos in relation
       to the intensity of oxidative phosphorylation and activity of ATPase in
       ovulatory ovocytes of roach and bream. *Dopov. Akad. Nauk ukr. RSR.*, Ser. B,
       35, 1044–1047. From *Chem. Abstr.* **80,** 130785x (1973). *10*

3724. Ziecik, M. and Nodzynski, J. (1964). Chemical and weight composition of
       the comestible parts, waste and gonads of flounder (*Pleuronectes flesus*) during
       an annual cycle. *Zesz. nauk. wyzsz. Szk. roln. Olsztyn.* **18,** 263–280. From
       Chem. Abstr. **63,** 6056b (1965). *51, 52*

*3725. Zimmerman, H. and Denston, C. R. (1976). Adenosine triphosphate in
       cholinergic vesicles isolated from the electric organ of *Electrophorus electricus.*
       Brain Res. **111,** 365–376.

3726. Zwingelstein, G., Meister, R. and Brichon, G. (1975). Comparative metabol-
       ism of the phospholipids of organs concerned with osmoregulation in the
       European eel (*Anguilla anguilla*). *Biochimie,* **57,** 609–622.

3727. Zwinglestein, G., Meister, R. and Jouanneteau, J. (1973). Metabolism of
       phospholipids in the gill and liver of the eel. *Biochimie,* **55,** 1495–1497.

Subject Index